DIANE ATKINSON is the author of two illustrated history books, *Suffragettes in Pictures* and *Funny Girls: Cartooning for Equality*, and three biographies, *Love & Dirt, Elsie and Mairi Go to War* and *The Criminal Conversation of Mrs Norton*. A regular lecturer on the suffragettes at conferences and literary festivals, Diane Atkinson has also appeared on radio programmes including Woman's Hour, and has consulted on numerous television documentaries, as well as the film *Suffragette*, starring Meryl Streep and Helena Bonham-Carter. She lives in London.

dianeatkinson.co.uk
@DitheDauntless

RISE UP, WOMEN!

The Remarkable Lives of the Suffragettes

Diane Atkinson

BLOOMSBURY PUBLISHING
LONDON · OXFORD · NEW YORK · NEW DELHI · SYDNEY

BLOOMSBURY PUBLISHING
Bloomsbury Publishing Plc
50 Bedford Square, London, WC1B 3DP, UK

BLOOMSBURY, BLOOMSBURY PUBLISHING and the Diana logo are
trademarks of Bloomsbury Publishing Plc

First published in Great Britain 2018
This edition published 2019

A catalogue record for this book is available from the British Library.

ISBN: HB: 978-1-4088-4404-5; eBook: 978-1-4088-4406-9; PB: 978-1-4088-4405-2

2 4 6 8 10 9 7 5 3 1

Typeset by Newgen KnowledgeWorks Pvt. Ltd., Chennai, India.
Printed and bound in Great Britain by CPI Group (UK) Ltd, Croydon CR0 4YY

To find out more about our authors and books visit
www.bloomsbury.com and sign up for our newsletters.

For Patrick Hughes

We hand the key to the coming generations to unlock the door to Freedom and Equal Opportunity. It is for them to campaign for and bring to glorious fruition the great reforms we dreamed of, but being voteless women, were unable to negotiate.

Jessie Stephenson typescript, 'No Other Way' (1932)

Contents

Preface

Rise Up, Women! is a collective biography of the suffragette movement, illuminating the lives of more than a hundred women who took part in the militant campaign for votes for women in Great Britain between 1903 and 1914. It explores who the suffragettes were and what they brought to the most daring political campaign of the twentieth century.

For a long time the campaign of the Women's Social and Political Union (WSPU) has been dismissed as a hobby for self-interested middle-class women, but here we read what a large part working-class women played in the struggle for the right of women to vote. Despite danger, considerable suffering and public opprobrium, these women persisted unwaveringly in their aims.

Among them we meet, of course, the well-known Pankhurst family, Emmeline, Christabel, Sylvia and Adela; mill girl Annie Kenney, the WSPU's poster girl from Oldham; Emily Davison, whose deathly dash at the Derby in 1913 was captured on film; and Lady Constance Lytton, who adopted the alias 'Jane Warton' to experience how ordinary suffragettes were treated when they were sent to prison. But we also meet many lesser known figures such as Edith Rigby, a Preston doctor's wife whose unique dress sense declared her unconventional views and earned the enmity of her neighbours who tried to drive Mrs Rigby and her family out of town; or Dora Thewlis, a weaver, who was sixteen when she came from Huddersfield to be arrested in Westminster; bootmakers Alice Hawkins and her husband Alfred, who kept the WSPU's tricolour flying in Leicester during the militant campaign; Minnie Baldock, a shirt machinist, who founded the first

WSPU branch in Canning Town, east London, in 1906, and recruited many women from Poplar, Custom House and East and West Ham; Charlotte Drake, a mother of four from Custom House, who went to work with Sylvia Pankhurst in the East End; Ethel Moorhead, an artist from Dundee, who threw herself into the Scottish struggle on the death of her father; Grace Marcon, a clergyman's daughter from Norfolk, who was a masseuse and gymnastics teacher and joined the WSPU in 1910; music-hall artiste Kitty Marion, who started on stage in panto in Glasgow in 1890 and whose career and health were both undermined by her activism (in prison in 1913 she was force-fed more than 200 times); Mary Gawthorpe from Leeds who was apprenticed as a pupil teacher at thirteen; 'Tough Annie' Cappuccio, who lived in Stepney, where her father owned a sweet shop; Hannah Mitchell, a dressmaker from a poor farming family in Derbyshire, who escaped from her violent mother and joined the WSPU when disillusioned with the Independent Labour Party; Elizabeth Wolstenholme Elmy, and England's first woman doctor, Elizabeth Garrett Anderson, who were both in their seventies when they walked with the suffragettes to Parliament and were roughly handled by the police; sisters Annie, Florence, Minnie, Irene and Dora Spong, tunic-wearing, sandalled, vegetarian suffragettes, who were artists in music, dance, painting and weaving (Dora was also a midwife in the slums of Battersea and Tottenham); the 'Murphy' sisters (Leila and Rosalind Cadiz), who came to London from Dublin in 1911 to join suffragette protests and in 1912 smashed windows in their home city; bank manager's daughter May Billinghurst, who pushed herself around in an invalid tricycle; Ethel Smyth, who composed the suffragette battle anthem 'The March of the Women'; debutante and drug addict Lavender Guthrie, who committed suicide in 1914; the noble Fred and Emmeline Pethick-Lawrence, who gave the modern equivalent of hundreds of thousands of pounds of their own money to bankroll the campaign, only to be purged from the organisation in 1912, and yet who refused to reproach Mrs Pankhurst and her daughter Christabel for their callous behaviour; and from the USA, Alice Paul and Lucy Burns, who were studying in London when they became suffragettes, and left the United Kingdom with prison records, and who transplanted WSPU tactics to invigorate the American women's suffrage campaign. The lives of all these remarkable women, and a great many more who feature in this book, together make up the extraordinary story of the militant campaign for Votes for Women.

*

Sylvia Pankhurst's *The Suffragette Movement*, published in 1931, is a detailed account of the suffragette campaign and about the Pankhurst family's role. Underlying family tensions – of which there is no mention in Mrs Pankhurst's *My Own Story*, published in 1914, and Christabel's autobiography, *Unshackled: The Story of How We Won the Vote* (1959) – boiled over in the early days of 1914 when Sylvia was summoned to Paris to be admonished about her relationship with the Labour Party. Sylvia Pankhurst suffered much for the campaign – weeks of hunger- and sleep-striking, which gave her mother immense pride. Christabel disliked all politicians, not just Labour men: she was of the view that no politician could be trusted, and disapproved of Sylvia's close ties to her intimate friend Keir Hardie. In 1907 Christabel had said that Liberal politicians – many of whom professed to support women's suffrage – were 'as wily as serpents'; her opinion would harden as the lies piled up.

The militant campaign for the female vote was like a drama that ran for more than ten years: it had constant stars, scores of supporting actors, hundreds of walk-on parts and a vast chorus who created successful spectacles. These performances were written, directed and played out by a fluid group of politically motivated women, sometimes helped by men, who sacrificed and made friendships, reputations and employment in the struggle.

Mrs Pankhurst discovered, from hearing about 'the Battle of Peterloo' in Manchester in 1819, that you need a huge performance in front of a big audience to effect large political change. She knew the value of events that would later be broadcast via the newspapers to politicians, the voters and supporters.

The suffragette campaign was a defiant panorama of first nights, long runs, tragedies, comedies and *coups de théâtre*. The suffragettes, unlike the quieter, more staid suffragists of the National Union of Women's Suffrage Societies (NUWSS), practised street theatre, chalking pavements, mass demonstrations, arson and fire-bombing pillar boxes. Their pageants and interruptions of meetings all too often ended in the prison cells.

One hundred years after the historic moment when the vote was granted to some women it is time to take a fresh look at the daring and painful struggle that eventually achieved political representation for all British women, to reflect on what we would have done in their situation and, above all, to salute them.

Diane Atkinson,
London, May 2017

Branches of the Women's Social and Political Union, 1903–1914

1 Aberdeen
2 Dundee
3 Glasgow
4 Edinburgh
5 Newcastle
6 Belfast
7 Dublin
8 Cork
9 Scarborough
10 Barrow-in-Furness
11 Harrogate
12 York
13 Blackpool
14 Preston
15 Bradford
16 Leeds
17 Hull
18 Halifax
19 Southport
20 Rochdale
21 Huddersfield
22 Manchester
23 Doncaster
24 Rotherham
25 Sheffield
26 Liverpool
27 Birkenhead
28 Derby
29 Nottingham
30 Loughborough
31 Norwich
32 Shrewsbury
33 Wolverhampton
34 Birmingham
35 Leicester
36 Coventry
37 Northampton
38 Cambridge
39 Ipswich

40 Worcester
41 Bedford
42 Felixstowe
43 Hereford
44 Hitchin
45 Gloucester
46 Luton
47 Hertford
48 Carmarthen
49 Oxford
50 Pontypool
51 Newport
52 Cardiff
53 Barry
54 Bristol
55 Bath
56 Trowbridge
57 Newbury
58 Reading
59 Greater London*
60 Canterbury
61 Guildford
62 Redhill/Reigate
63 Royal Tunbridge Wells
64 Ilfracombe
65 Newquay
66 Truro
67 St Austell
68 Plymouth
69 Paignton
70 Torquay
71 Exeter
72 Lyme Regis
73 Bournemouth
74 Southampton
75 Gosport
76 Portsmouth
77 Worthing
78 Brighton
79 Hastings

SCOTLAND

IRELAND

ENGLAND

WALES

* Greater London had 35 societies

This map is a combination of research by Diane Atkinson and Elizabeth Crawford

Introduction

This illustration in the WSPU's Votes for Women *newspaper shows that by 1913 nineteen countries and states had given women the vote.*

In 1832 the Great Reform Act extended the franchise to give the vote to 'male persons' over the age of twenty-one who lived in the counties, and for the first time included small landowners, tenant farmers and shopkeepers, and householders living in the boroughs who paid a yearly rental of £10 or more.[1] It enlarged the existing electorate of half a million men by 300,000 new voters. The insertion of the word 'male' was the first statutory bar to women having the vote, and was the catalyst for the founding of the women's suffrage movement.[2] Mary Smith, a Yorkshire 'lady of rank and fortune', was dismayed by the terms of the Act, which enfranchised many men and no women. She asked Henry 'Orator' Hunt, the radical MP for Preston, to present a petition to Parliament, the first from a woman asking for the vote. Henry Hunt had opposed the Great Reform Bill on behalf of working men who were disenfranchised by its property qualifications. In the House of Commons on 3 August 1832, Hunt cited 'several excellent reasons why every unmarried female possessing the necessary pecuniary qualification' should be entitled to elect a Member of Parliament. Hansard reported that Hunt introduced the petition 'which might be a subject of mirth to some Hon. Gentlemen, but which was deserving of consideration'. The female petitioner stated that:

> she paid taxes and therefore did not see why she should not have a share in the election of a Representative; she also stated that women were liable to all punishments of the law, not excepting death, and ought to have a voice in the making of them … She expressed her indignation against those vile wretches who would not marry,

and yet would exclude females from a share in the legislation. The prayer of the petition was that every unmarried female, possessing the necessary pecuniary qualification, should be entitled to vote for Members of Parliament.[3]

After the briefest of discussions the petition was rejected. The MP for Oldham, William Johnston Fox, pointed out the 'egregious anomaly' that women were not enfranchised and yet a woman was likely to inherit the throne in the near future.[4]

Chartism, a working-class movement for political reform, was founded in 1838 and demanded manhood suffrage; annual parliaments; equal electoral districts; the abolition of property qualifications for MPs; the payment of MPs and the secret ballot.[5] Women played a significant role in Chartism and wished for legislation to reflect the needs of women and children.[6] A draft of the Charter had included a demand for female suffrage, but this was reduced to more votes for men.[7]

In 1851, Chartists Mrs Abiah Higginbotham and her husband, and Miss Anne Knight, a Quaker with pro-Chartist views, founded the Sheffield Female Political Association. An anonymous leaflet published in England in 1847, the year before the first women's rights convention at Seneca Falls in the United States, is thought to have been written by Anne Knight. It declared: 'Never will the nations of the Earth be well-governed, until both sexes ... have an influence and voice in the enactment and administration of the laws.'[8]

The Sheffield Female Political Association, the first organisation for women's suffrage in Britain, petitioned the House of Lords to 'take into consideration the propriety of enacting a law to include adult females within its provisions'. The SFPA was Higginbotham and Knight's response to being prevented – because of their gender – from speaking at an Abolition of Slavery meeting in London. Mrs Higginbotham chaired the Society's first public meeting at the Democratic Temperance Hotel in Queen Street, Sheffield, and signed a petition on behalf of the female inhabitants of Sheffield asking 'that the Houses of Parliament take into serious consideration the propriety of enacting a law which should include females within its provisions'.[9] The *Sheffield Independent* reported:

Women arise in their might and say: 'Seeing that the Queen is in the enjoyment of her prerogative as a woman, this meeting is of the opinion that until the enfranchisement of women is conceded, justice will not be done … and resolves to petition both the Houses of Parliament for the enactment of a bill which will enfranchise the whole female adult population of this empire.'[10]

A year after the SFPA was formed, it was agreed that a National Woman's Rights Association be established. However, it collapsed with the demise of Chartism in the late 1850s.

The Langham Place Group, which was active between 1858 and 1866, was made up of a number of determined middle-class women who campaigned on a variety of liberal and feminist issues to improve women's lives. Moderate and respectable, the group was led by childhood friends Barbara Leigh Smith Bodichon, born in 1827, and Elizabeth 'Bessie' Rayner Parkes, who was two years younger. The group named itself after the address of the *English Woman's Journal*, at 19 Langham Place, London, which had been launched in 1858.

At first, Bessie Parkes was nervous of confronting such a contentious issue as women's suffrage, but by 1864 opinions within the Group shifted and the *English Woman's Journal* printed extracts from 'The Enfranchisement of Women', an article by Harriet Taylor. Miss Taylor was the stepdaughter of John Stuart Mill, the newly elected Liberal MP for the City and Westminster, the first politician to mention women's suffrage in his election campaign of 1865.[11] In November 1865 Emily Davies, secretary of the Kensington Society, a ladies' discussion group of sixty-eight members founded earlier in the year, wrote to a friend that 'some people are inclined to begin a subdued agitation for the franchise'.

The Kensington Society included leading campaigners of the day: Miss Beale and Miss Buss; Elizabeth Wolstenholme Elmy; Frances Power Cobbe; Elizabeth Garrett Anderson and Barbara Leigh Bodichon. They debated topics of common interest of which women's suffrage was a strand, and many members shared a history of working for women's property rights in marriage and female education. Practice in formal debating in private drawing rooms gave women confidence in public speaking.[12]

The Kensington Society established the women's suffrage movement. On 7 June 1866 the Society delivered a petition of 1,500 signatures, entitled the 'Ladies' Petition of Barbara Leigh Bodichon and Others', asking for women's suffrage when Parliament was debating the 1866 Reform Bill: 'Your Petitioners humbly pray your honourable House to consider the expediency of providing for the representation of householders, without the distinction of sex, who possess such property or rental qualifications as your honourable House may determine.' A cross-section of women signed the petition, including schoolteachers, butchers' and blacksmiths' wives, dressmakers, shopkeepers, and women of means and leisure. Emily Davies and Elizabeth Garrett Anderson took the petition and, to avoid attention, hid it under the cart of a woman selling apples in Westminster Hall, from whence John Stuart Mill retrieved it. On 17 July 1866 he presented the large petition to the House of Commons, arguing that its value was that it had been organised and signed exclusively by women, and demonstrated clearly for the first time that women wanted the vote.[13] It was rejected.

On 20 May 1867 John Stuart Mill proposed an amendment to the Second Reform Bill, 'to strike out the words which were understood to limit the electoral franchise to males'. His central argument that 'taxation and representation go hand in hand' continued for the next fifty years of women's suffrage campaigning.[14] The 1867 Reform Act doubled the electorate of one million male householders to two million out of a total population in England and Wales of twenty-two million.[15]

John Stuart Mill was pleasantly surprised at the seventy-three votes cast in favour of his amendment; 196 voted against it in the brief debate. One of the votes in favour was that of a professor of political economy, Henry Fawcett, Liberal MP for Brighton since 1865. Fawcett had recently married Millicent Garrett, who went on to play a prominent part in the efforts of the moderate law-abiding suffragist campaign, and, indeed, lived to see all women over twenty-one get the vote in 1928. Mill helped found the London National Society of Women's Suffrage in August 1867; Lydia Becker had already founded the Manchester Committee for Women's Suffrage in January 1867; the Bristol Women's Suffrage Committee started in January 1868.[16] Their campaigning style was to collect signatures for petitions, hold drawing-room meetings and lobby MPs, mostly in private, but some-times daring to hold meetings in large venues, such as the Great Meeting in favour of women's suffrage in Edinburgh's Music Hall, in January 1871.

Despite being ridiculed in the House of Commons, Mill persisted and in 1868 asked the science and mathematics writer Mary Somerville to be the first name on a new petition which eventually secured 21,000 signatures.

The barrister Richard Pankhurst had been working for women's suf-frage with Elizabeth Wolstenholme and Lydia Becker in Manchester for a decade when he married Emmeline Goulden in 1879. He had spoken at the first public meeting calling for women to have the vote in Manchester in 1868. Shortly after their wedding Emmeline Pankhurst joined the executive committee of the Manchester National Society for Women's Suffrage. Before becoming the militant suffrage leader, Emmeline had been a moderate suffragist.[17]

Following John Stuart Mill's intervention, private members' bills or resolutions in favour of women's suffrage were presented to the House of Commons almost every year between 1870 and 1914. And 12,000 similar petitions were taken to the Commons between 1866 and 1914, and hundreds more to the House of Lords. Fearing that enfranchised women would vote for the opposition, no Conservative or Liberal government in office during those years was prepared to introduce its own bill, or allow the necessary time for a private members' bill to pass. Although women were excluded from the par-liamentary franchise, those who paid rates on their property could vote in local municipal elections, and stand for election as Poor Law Guardians and on School Boards.[18]

Supported by her husband, Mrs Millicent Fawcett began campaign-ing for women's suffrage in the 1870s, and in 1897 became the leader of the National Union of Women's Suffrage Societies (NUWSS), a federation of seventeen local suffrage societies in London, south-west England, Scotland, Kent, the Midlands, Lancashire and East Anglia, whose policies were decided by the members. In 1870 the women who demanded the vote were dubbed 'the shrieking sisterhood' by the novelist Eliza Lynn Linton.

The insistent campaigning of the suffragist and feminist agitation of the 1880s intensified after the 1884 Reform Act enfranchised a

further three and a half million men who were householders paying an annual rent of £10 or more for unfurnished lodgings. The
best-selling novelist Mrs Humphry Ward organised a petition
in 1889 signed by the 'great and the good' women of Victorian
society against female suffrage, to be presented to Parliament 'to
appeal to the common sense and the educated thought of the men
and women of England against the proposed extension of the
Parliamentary suffrage to women'.

By this time women in other parts of the world had already
begun to be enfranchised: in the United States in Wyoming in 1869
and Colorado in 1893; in New Zealand also in 1893. In 1902, South
Australia, Utah, Western Australia and New South Wales would
follow.

By the turn of the century within the NUWSS there was a group of
radical suffragists, mill workers from the cotton towns of Lancashire,
who held meetings at factory gates and street corners demanding
the vote. The best-known radical suffragist was Selina Cooper who
had gone to work in a mill at the age of ten.[19] In 1902 Christabel
Pankhurst's first contact with the struggle for the vote was with radical suffragists in Manchester, to whom she was introduced by the poet
and radical suffragist Eva Gore-Booth, and her intimate companion,
Esther Roper.

The Conservative Party had been in office since 1895 and in 1902
Prime Minister Lord Salisbury was succeeded by his nephew Arthur
Balfour.[20] In 1884, when in opposition, Lord Salisbury had expressed
pro-women's suffrage views, but when he became prime minister in
1895 his sentiments were lukewarm. Arthur Balfour was privately
and publicly supportive of the demand, but the strength of backbench
opposition gave him the excuse to do nothing to make it happen.[21]

Imperial politics had other matters on its mind: the growing threat
posed by Germany as an industrial and naval rival; awareness of the
widespread poverty of the nation and concerns about social and industrial unrest; the persistent demand for Home Rule in Ireland; and the
shocking revelation that at least a quarter of the young men who volunteered to serve in the Boer War were unfit to fight. This resulted in
the Interdepartmental Committee Report on Physical Deterioration,
published in 1904. Politicians and newspapers worried about the
quality of working-class motherhood and its impact on Britain and

the Empire, and found expression in the insistence that working-class mothers who did sweated work at home had undermined the health of the nation's sons and put the Empire at risk.[22]

During the 1890s British trade unionism expanded and joined forces with the Independent Labour Party. In 1901 there were two million trade union members, and four million by 1913. Forty per cent of the adult male population were still unenfranchised,[23] and neither the trade unions nor the burgeoning Labour Party had any intention of helping women get the vote, whom they assumed would be well off and would vote Conservative or Liberal.[24] The growing power of trade unionism, best demonstrated by the dock strike of 1911 and the first general rail strike in 1911, which Lloyd George managed to defuse, and then the London Dockers' strike in 1912, were grave concerns which the Liberal government was happy to be distracted by, instead of doing anything which might enfranchise women.

The struggle for Home Rule, an ambition of Liberalism and Irish Nationalism, suffered a setback during the years the Conservatives were in office in the 1890s leading up to the Liberal landslide of 1906. From 1910 the Liberals would increasingly rely on the Irish Nationalists to govern with their slim working majority and this arrangement would prove disruptive to the women's suffrage bills during Asquith's government in the years leading up to the outbreak of the First World War.[25] The Irish Nationalists were susceptible to the Liberals' argument that if women's suffrage succeeded the Home Rule Bill would fail.

The demand for votes for women continued to be easily brushed aside during the seven years from 1895 that a Conservative government was in power under Lord Salisbury. But then, in 1903, the foundation of the Women's Social and Political Union ensured that women's political campaigning would never be the same again. This is where our story begins.

I

62 Nelson Street, Manchester

The Launch of the Women's Social and Political Union 1903–5

Sylvia Pankhurst's loyalties to the Independent Labour Party are clear in the membership card she designed for the WSPU in 1906.

'It was in October, 1903, that I invited a number of women to my house in Nelson Street for purposes of organisation. We voted to call our new society the Women's Social and Political Union, partly to emphasise its democracy, and partly to define its object as political rather than propagandist. We resolved to limit our membership exclusively to women, to keep ourselves absolutely free from any party affiliation, and to be satisfied with nothing but action on our question. Deeds, not words, was to be our motto.'[1]

Mrs Emmeline Pankhurst, a forty-five-year-old widow, was the Registrar of Births and Deaths in Chorlton, and had a shop, Emerson's and Co., at 30 King Street, Manchester, which sold Liberty-style Arts and Crafts furniture and soft furnishings. Much of the stock had come from an earlier endeavour when she had opened the same kind of shop in various parts of London where the Pankhurst family had lived from 1886 to 1893,[2] but Mrs Pankhurst had no head for business and the ill-starred venture eventually closed in 1906. She had three daughters, Christabel, aged twenty-three in 1903, Sylvia, twenty-one, Adela, eighteen, and a son, Harry, then fourteen.

Emmeline Pankhurst often said she was born on the same date as the fall of the Bastille; in fact, she was born the day after, but it was too good a story to let a day spoil it. Her grandfather told Emmeline about the Battle of Peterloo, the great franchise demonstration on St Peter's Fields in 1819, when the Manchester justices had called out the troops to attack the people, and how he had 'barely escaped alive'.[3]

When she was five Emmeline was taken to her first political meeting by her mother, who was active in the abolition of slavery movement.

Emmeline tottered round the room with a 'lucky bag' collecting pennies for the newly emancipated slaves. In 1872, when Emmeline was fourteen, her mother took her to a woman's suffrage meeting to hear Miss Lydia Ernestine Becker speak. Lydia Becker was the secretary of the recently founded Manchester Society for Women's Suffrage and friends with leading radicals, including Dr Richard Pankhurst, whom Emmeline married in 1879 when she was twenty-one.[4]

Red-haired and bearded, Richard Pankhurst, known as 'the Red Doctor', was twenty-three years older than his wife. He was the son of an auctioneer, and in 1867 he became a founder member of the Manchester Society for Women's Suffrage. He stood for Parliament three times: in Manchester in 1883 as an independent radical Liberal; in Rotherhithe in 1885 as a radical; and in Gorton, Manchester, in 1895 as a candidate for the Independent Labour Party. He failed each time. Lydia Becker described him as 'a very clever little man with some extraordinary sentiments about life in general and women in particular'.[5]

In 1886 the Pankhursts left Manchester with their four children and moved to London where they hoped Richard's earnings as a barrister would support them, and that he might get elected to the House of Commons. The Pankhursts moved in Fabian and free-thinking circles, their Liberal views turning pink and then red.

Richard and Emmeline were present at the 'Bloody Sunday' riot on 13 November 1887 in Trafalgar Square, a protest against high unemployment and the draconian enforcement of law and order in Ireland. After his experience of being in a peaceful protest policed by 2,000 police constables and 400 troops, Richard Pankhurst joined the Law and Liberty League to defend the right to free speech and demonstration. The couple also joined the Women's Franchise League when it was founded in 1889. Trade union leaders Ben Tillett, Tom Mann and Keir Hardie (the first working man to become a Member of Parliament) were regular visitors to the Pankhursts'. Their visitors' book included some of the leading thinkers and activists of the day: the Italian anarchist Errico Malatesta; the Russian political refugee Peter Kropotkin; William Lloyd Garrison, an advocate of women's suffrage whose father had been a leading American slavery abolitionist; Dadabhai Naoroji, later the first Indian member of the House of Commons; the visionary socialist William Morris; and Annie Besant and Herbert Burrows, organisers of the Match Girls' Strike of 1888.[6]

The Pankhursts returned to Manchester in 1893, where Richard joined the Independent Labour Party and by 1895 he was on the national executive. In 1894 he began the legal battle to prevent the Duke of Devonshire, landowner of the Kinder Scout footpath in the Peak District, from closing public access. The campaign partly succeeded in 1897, but was only completely successful – despite a mass trespass in 1932 – as late as the 1960s. When he died in 1898 from a ruptured stomach ulcer, Richard left more debts than money.[7]

After his death, Mrs Pankhurst resigned as a Poor Law Guardian and looked for a salaried position. The family left their house in the suburb of Victoria Park, and moved to Nelson Street, a more modest address.[8] She got the job as the local Registrar of Births and Deaths, where infant mortality rates were twice the national average. 'It was touching to see how glad the women were to have a woman registrar to go to ... I was shocked to be reminded over and over again of the little respect there was in the world for women and children. I have had little girls of thirteen come to my office to register the births of their babies. In many cases I found that the child's own father or some male relative was responsible for her state.'[9] The Independent Labour Party offered to raise a subscription for Richard Pankhurst's widow, but Mrs Pankhurst rejected the idea and suggested instead that they build a hall in her husband's memory. The Pankhurst Hall was opened in Salford in October 1900 with murals painted by eighteen-year-old Sylvia Pankhurst. On 10 October 1900 Keir Hardie delivered the inaugural lecture.[10]

When the Pankhurst Hall opened Emmeline and her daughters were appalled to learn that women were prohibited from joining the local branch of the Independent Labour Party which would use the Hall as its headquarters,[11] so Mrs Pankhurst invited the wives of ILP members, after the leadership had denied them access to the Pankhurst Hall, to meet at her house in Nelson Street.

*

Christabel Pankhurst, born in 1880, was by 1900 in the family business of politics. She was taking classes in logic at Owen's College (now Manchester University) and had gone to a meeting of the Women's Debating Society. Christabel met the radical suffragists Esther Roper, a clergyman's daughter from a working-class background who was secretary of the North of England Society of Women's Suffrage

(NESWS), and her companion, Eva Gore-Booth, daughter of the Arctic explorer Sir Henry Gore-Booth. Esther was impressed by Christabel's contribution to the debate. Esther, Christabel and Eva became friends and for several summers holidayed together. Miss Roper and Miss Gore-Booth easily persuaded Christabel that the working woman needed the vote, as a weapon of self-defence, just as much as the working man. Christabel Pankhurst wrote: 'It was the sharp contrast between practical suffragism in our home circle and the inequality I saw meted out to women in general in the outer world that made me see in the suffrage cause one, not of merely academic interest, but of stern practical importance.'[12]

Christabel and her sister Sylvia had always been allowed to attend political meetings. 'The big double drawing-room housed a considerable company, and meetings and conferences would be held on industrial and social questions and women's suffrage.'[13] In her autobiography, Christabel describes how, when she was eleven, she recorded that 'Dr Pankhurst, as Chairman, said in his speech that if the suffrage was not given to women, the result would be terrible. If a body was half of it bound, how was it to be expected that it would grow and develop properly?'[14] One day Christabel startled her mother with the remark: 'How long you women have been trying for the vote. For my part, I mean to get it.'[15]

Esther Roper suggested Christabel read for a law degree at Owen's College and also join her and Eva in their campaigning work among factory women. A few days after her mother founded the WSPU, Christabel enrolled at Owen's College. Christabel's choice was pragmatic: 'it seemed that a knowledge of the law might prove useful in work for woman suffrage, and useful it was indeed to prove'.[16]

In 1903 Sylvia Pankhurst completed her studies at Manchester Art School, but she was tasked with running the struggling shop while her mother kept her day job and Christabel started her law degree. Then, in 1904, she took up her scholarship to study at the Royal College of Art in Kensington and, soon after, started a love affair with Keir Hardie, the MP for Merthyr Tydfil, which would last until his death in 1915. Hardie was thirty years older, estranged from his wife, and a family friend. Sylvia designed the WSPU membership card which showed working women, aproned and shawled, with a rippling banner demanding 'Votes', and a mother carrying a child. The image of working-class women walking shoulder to shoulder sent out a clear signal.[17]

An early member of the new organisation was Elizabeth Wolstenholme, a pioneer of all the feminist struggles of the previous forty years. Born in Manchester in 1833, the daughter of a Methodist minister, Elizabeth resembled a character from the pages of Mrs Gaskell's *Cranford*, her severe parting and old-fashioned dress looking quaint among the swept-up hairstyles of the new century. She and her lover, Benjamin Elmy, a silk manufacturer, were keen Secularists and they believed in 'free love': that couples should be able to live together without stigma and not have to marry. They grudgingly married in 1874 when Elizabeth was forty-two years old and six months pregnant. When Ben Elmy's business collapsed in the late 1880s, Mr and Mrs Elmy were forced to rely on handouts from 'the grateful fund' which her friends collected.

Mrs Elmy was seventy when she joined the Pankhursts' campaign. She pushed for the Cambridge Higher Examinations for women and for a programme of advanced lectures for women, which eventually led to the establishment of Newnham College, Cambridge. In the 1860s she was honorary secretary of the Married Women's Property Committee and campaigned for the right of married women to retain their own property, which otherwise passed to their husbands on the day they married. Her work had some success in the 1870 and 1882 Married Women's Property Acts.

In 1869 Elizabeth Wolstenholme urged Josephine Butler to join the campaign to repeal the Contagious Diseases Acts which allowed women suspected of working as prostitutes to be arrested, imprisoned and forcibly treated for venereal diseases. This notorious legislation was repealed in 1886. She was also the paid secretary of the Women's Franchise League founded in 1889.[18]

By the turn of the century only a tiny minority of the British population wanted women to have the vote. Conservative MPs believed in maintaining the status quo. They feared that if women were enfranchised many would vote for the Liberals or for the new Independent Labour Party. Some Liberals believed that women should have the vote, but in turn were afraid that their opponents might benefit. While some Liberal MPs supported women's suffrage, the prime ministers Henry Campbell-Bannerman and his successor Herbert Asquith opposed it. Asquith was a diehard critic and many of his Cabinet colleagues would follow suit. The Independent Labour Party, founded in 1892 to represent the interests of working men, believed that if property-owning women and not working-class women got the vote, the Conservative and Liberal parties would gain an important advantage. Many in the ILP were committed to votes for everyone, but most believed that men should have the vote first, and women afterwards.[19]

With the arrival of Mrs Elmy in the group Mrs Pankhurst turned to London, the capital of the Empire and the home of the mother of parliaments. In the autumn of 1903 Mrs Pankhurst joined a small deputation of members of the NUWSS to interview Sir Charles McLaren, Liberal Member of Parliament for Bosworth, Leicestershire, and other colleagues in the House of Commons, about their intentions.[20] As the meeting drew to a close, Emmeline Pankhurst, who had not been asked to speak, blurted out the question that hung in the air. 'Will Sir Charles McLaren tell us if any member is preparing to introduce a bill for women's suffrage? Will he tell us what he and the other members will pledge themselves to *do* for the reform they so warmly endorse?' When she seized the moment it did not go down well. McLaren was livid to have been put on the spot and the women left 'in confusion and wrath'. Mrs Pankhurst was reminded that she was an 'impertinent intruder' who had not been asked to speak and had no right to 'ruin the good impression they had made'.[21]

In February 1905 Emmeline and Sylvia Pankhurst lobbied for eight days leading up to 13 February, when the result of the private members' ballot would be announced. The successful member was permitted to introduce a bill of his choice. The Pankhursts spent their time in the Strangers' Lobby trying to persuade members who had pledged to support women's suffrage in the past to agree to give their slot to a women's suffrage bill, if their names were drawn in the ballot. It was Sylvia's first experience of lobbying: 'it would be an uphill task but I had no conception of how hard and discouraging it was to be. Members of Parliament gave all sorts of excuses for refusing to help, that they had some other measure in which they were interested, or said they preferred to wait until they had more experience before balloting for any kind of a bill.'[22] When the results of the ballot were announced Sylvia and her mother were the only women in the Lobby. 'We sat there on the shiny black leather seats and at last we saw with relief Mr Keir Hardie come hurrying towards us. He was so kind and helpful, the only kind and helpful person in the whole of Parliament it seemed.'[23] Emmeline and Sylvia tracked down the fourteen men whose names had been drawn. They all said 'No', except the recently elected Liberal Member of Parliament for St Albans, John Bamford Slack, a Methodist lay preacher whose wife Alice was a suffragist. John Slack had drawn the last of the fourteen places in the ballot. They put the date of Friday 12 May, when private members' bills were to be debated, in their diary and set to work again.[24]

John Slack's women's suffrage bill was the first to be debated in eight years. Mrs Pankhurst noticed 'a thrill of excitement animated not only our ranks but all the old suffrage societies'.[25] For the first time the established women's suffrage societies, which traced their lineage back to the 1860s, and the WSPU, the cheeky newcomers, worked together to get a big female presence inside and outside Parliament on 12 May. Mrs Nellie Martel, who had arrived in England from Australia where she already had the vote as well as political experience, was a new member of the WSPU and brought working women from the East End of London to the demonstration.[26]

Large numbers of suffragists and 400 working women entered the Lobby of the House of Commons and milled about on the terrace and in the passages leading off the Lobby. Mrs Pankhurst, Mrs Elmy and Mrs Martel were not hopeful and their fears were well-founded. The bill was deliberately 'talked out': parliamentary time was eaten up by a debate about carts travelling along public roads at night needing to carry a light at the rear as well as at the front. MPs laughed and applauded when the debate ended with only half an hour of business remaining.

Mrs Pankhurst seized her moment – something at which she excelled – and asked her companions to follow her outside. The police rushed to disperse them but the women headed for the statue of Richard the Lionheart, and Mrs Pankhurst helped hoist the tiny Mrs Elmy on to the plinth where she addressed them. Keir Hardie persuaded the police to let the women gather at the gates of Westminster Abbey; speeches were made and a resolution condemning the Conservative government was passed. The police took the womens' names but none were arrested.[27]

In 1903, when the WSPU was born, Annie Kenney was a 'card-room hand' in an Oldham cotton mill. It was poorly paid and dangerous work which employed thousands of young women in the north-west of England. Mill girls might suffer from a persistent cough and byssinosis caused by inhaling the cotton dust that thickened the air in the poorly ventilated mills. Her sisters Alice and Jane were also card-room hands, while Jessie was a 'reeler' who wound thread on to bobbins. Annie sang with the Clarion Vocal Union founded by Montagu Blatchford, co-founder of *The Clarion*, a socialist weekly. His brother Robert was the most influential man in Annie Kenney's life and political education.[28]

In her 1924 memoir *Memories of a Militant*, Annie Kenney remembered the impact Robert Blatchford's articles on socialism, philosophy and poetry had on her. Thousands of men and women in the Lancashire factories owed their education to him.

'He introduced us to Walt Whitman, William Morris, Edward Carpenter, John Ruskin, Omar Khayyam, the English poets, Emerson and Charles Lamb ... the reading of books made me more serious and at last I decided to join the Oldham Clarion. I could not sing, but I thought the practice would be good for me, and I felt I should like to meet others whose ideas were very much like my own ... On Sundays if a celebrated Labour man was speaking we were invited to sing at the meeting.'[29]

Annie's mother Ann Kenney imbued in her children a love of learning. She read stories which 'all seemed to be about London life among the poor ... on Sundays we would be allowed to invite any friends we liked to tea, I remember we had an urn; teapots were no good there were so many of us. When we assembled round the large table discussion would begin.'[30] Her parents and the older children read Ernst Haeckel, Herbert Spencer and Charles Darwin. 'Mother would be as interested as we were until the arguments got so heated that she felt it was wise to close the discussions because of the younger children.'[31] These discussions 'made me unwilling in later life to accept statements without proof'.

The Kenney family were materially poor, but rich in their upbringing. Annie was adamant that her kindly father and strong mother had made her who she was: 'to my mother I owe all that I have ever been, or done that has called upon courage or loyalty for its support'.[32] Three of the daughters became teachers, one son was a respected businessman, and in 1912 Rowland Kenney became the first editor of the *Daily Herald*.[33]

In 1889, aged ten, Annie Kenney ended her full-time schooling to work as a half-timer in Henry Atherton and Son's textile mill in Lancashire. She worked from six in the morning until half past noon and then went to school until five o'clock in the afternoon. Annie was proud to be earning money to help the family finances. 'I wore a shawl and bright clean clogs. When I arrived at the factory I was met by a group of girls, half-timers and full-timers, who all stood round the door and stared at me ... Your clogs were examined; thick or thin leather made a difference; your petticoat, your pinafore, the quality, the colour, stamped you accordingly.'[34]

When Annie was thirteen she became a full-timer, working until half past five in the evening, her formal education ended. 'My school knowledge was nil. I could not do arithmetic, I was a bad writer; geography was Greek to me; the only thing I liked was poetry.'[35] The Kenney children were exposed to a richer curriculum at home than at the village school.

Annie Kenney's journey to women's suffrage began when her mother died in January 1905 at their back-to-back house at 71 Redgrave Street, Oldham. Ann Kenney was fifty-three, had been a wife for twenty-two years and had borne eleven children. Annie and six of her siblings were still living at home. Their father was 'a born nurse, no hand was more tender than his in illness'.[36]

Annie found a new family when she met Christabel Pankhurst. Annie and Jessie and Jennie went to a meeting where they heard Christabel Pankhurst and Teresa Billington speak about women's suffrage.

I had never heard about votes for women ... I had never read any newspaper but *The Clarion* ... Miss Billington used a sledge-hammer of logic and cold reason – she gave me the impression that she was a good debater. I liked Christabel Pankhurst: I was afraid of Teresa Billington ... It was like a table where two courses were being served, one hot, the other cold. I found myself plate in hand, where the hot course was being served.[37]

Annie found herself promising to work up a meeting among the women factory workers of Oldham. Annie and Christabel walked together to the railway station and Annie was invited to the Pankhursts' house the following Saturday, after her half-day's work at the mill. 'The following week I lived on air; I simply could not eat ... It was as though half of me was present; where the other half was I never asked ... I instinctively felt a great change had come.'[38] On Saturday Annie finished her shift, changed her working clothes and went to the station. She was shown into the 'very artistically furnished' drawing room, where Christabel introduced Annie to her mother. Miss Kenney was a pale, blue-eyed woman of twenty-five, five feet four inches tall. One finger was missing on her left hand, severed by a whirling bobbin.[39] They arranged a WSPU meeting in Oldham. Christabel wrote the copy for a hand-bill and Annie and Jessie handed them out in the town. Very few turned up, only one of Annie's sisters, her school pal Alice Hurst and one more woman. But Annie was dauntless and every Saturday afternoon she returned to the Pankhursts to be trained for her first public speaking engagement, off Market Square in Manchester. Annie was terrified at the prospect but her new friends waved her concerns aside. 'I found myself at seven o'clock at night addressing a crowd. What I said I do not remember. I suppose I touched on labour, the unemployed, children, and finally summed the whole thing up by saying something about votes for women.'[40]

Annie became friends with Nellie Ellis, a twenty-five-year-old schoolteacher, and her younger sister Alice, a machinist, from Preston, and they visited mill towns all over Lancashire helping Annie hold street-corner meetings, and getting women to join the WSPU. Nellie remembered, 'Annie Kenney would do the speaking and my sister and I would stand there gazing at her and that attracted a few people. Annie had a very good speaking voice and people could hear it ... the streets in Lancashire are packed and the houses were packed close together ... We got imbued with a sense of duty, something that's got to be done.'[41]

Annie Kenney had the idea to take her WSPU comrades to follow the 'Wakes', travelling fairs, all over Lancashire during the summer weekends of 1905. Alongside the Salvation Army, the quack doctors, the tooth-drawers and the 'bearded lady' booths, they made suffrage speeches and some valuable new friends.[42]

Teresa Mary Billington was an early member of the Women's Social and Political Union. Her parents' unhappy marriage meant she had an unhappy childhood. When she was seventeen she clashed with her parents over their determination to stop her becoming a writer 'campaigning for great causes', and she ran away to live with her maternal grandfather, John Wilson, in Preston. Teresa studied at night school for her teaching certificate, hoping to earn a living from her pen in her spare time. She qualified and began a course which eventually gained her a B.Sc. from the University of London. By the time she joined the Ancoats University Settlement in Manchester in 1903 she was a twenty-seven-year-old elementary schoolteacher and a member of the Independent Labour Party.

In 1903 she refused to teach a religious education class, but was helped by Emmeline Pankhurst, a member of the Manchester School Board, who got her a transfer from a Catholic to a Jewish school. When Teresa met Mrs Pankhurst she found she lived up to her reputation: 'she was gracious, lovely and dominant … and a force, vital and resourceful. She had a beauty and graciousness, moving and speaking with a dignity, but with no uncertainty of mind or movement.' Teresa spent many hours at 62 Nelson Street in those early heady months, organising and booking speakers.[43]

When her school day ended, Teresa juggled her suffrage work with her role as the secretary of the Manchester branch of the Equal Pay League. Christabel remembered Miss Billington as 'a power in debate who could make short work of any platform opponent'. At the beginning of 1905 Emmeline Pankhurst and Keir Hardie asked her to become the first full-time woman organiser for the ILP.[44]

Mrs Edith Rigby was making her mark in Preston with her unconventional ideas and dress. She was tall, had 'wheat-gold hair' and 'speedwell blue eyes'. In 1893, a month before her twenty-first birthday, Edith Rayner married Charles Rigby, a doctor who was twenty years older than her.[45] Charlie allowed Edith the physical comfort and emotional space to create her own life at their home at 28 Winckley Square, a well-to-do address. She soon blossomed into a campaigner, developing her own sartorial style, wearing 'extraordinary dresses that looked as if they were made of blue sacking, and heavy amber coloured beads on chains.' Edith 'never raised her voice and was utterly different from everyone else'. Dr Rigby was 'tolerant, gentle in voice and manner and was like her in many ways, sharing her compassions if not all her passions.'[46] Charles Rigby indulged Edith's wish to have her own place; she rented a bungalow in Broughton and grew fruit and vegetables, travelling the eight-mile round trip by bicycle.

Preston, which by 1900 had a population of 100,000, had been the inspiration for Coketown in Dickens's *Hard Times*. Conditions in the heavily industrialised town had barely changed since Charles Dickens's visit:

> It was a town of red brick, or of brick that would have been red if the smoke and ashes had allowed it; but as matters stood, it was a town of unnatural red and black like the painted face of a savage. It was a town of machinery and tall chimneys out of which interminable serpents of smoke trailed themselves for ever and ever ... It had a black canal and a river that ran purple with ill-smelling dye ...[47]

Edith Rigby learned about the lives of mill girls and garment workers and in 1899 she opened St Peter's Club, a night school for working women in a room on the first floor of St Peter's School. Twice a week there were 'get-togethers', with singing, there were two sewing tables, lessons on hygiene and sports, and Edith's aerobics class with her sister Alice playing the piano.

Mrs Rigby's behaviour was an affront to many residents of Winckley Square. She treated her servants as equals, allowing them to eat their meals in the dining room, and did not insist they wore a uniform. She tried to persuade her neighbours that menial tasks should be shared by all members of the household, upsetting ladies and servants alike when she scrubbed her own front-door step. Edith's fondness for sandals and Turkish cigarettes offended many. Two ladies called on her and told her that her appearance and the way she treated her servants as equals was a disgrace, and that if she could not alter her ways perhaps she had better leave the area. Edith's response was to whitewash the front doors of her impertinent callers.[48] A niece remembered: 'When Edith became involved in suffrage her neighbours cut her in the street, tarred the stone work of her house and as far as it was possible for ladies to spit, they spat at her as she went by.'[49]

In 1904 Edith Rigby joined the Women's Social and Political Union and went to meetings at Mrs Pankhurst's house where she became friendly with Christabel and Adela Pankhurst and Annie Kenney. Edith's family believed that Christabel was 'responsible for her metamorphosis ... into a decidedly fiery angel'.[50]

The Rigbys' childlessness after more than a decade of marriage would have caused gossip over the tea cups in Winckley Square. When Edith was ready to have a child she had one: in December 1905, immersed in socialist and suffrage activities, she persuaded Charles that they should adopt a two-year-old boy whom they named Arthur, a freckle-faced redhead whom Edith dressed in kilts and tunics and velvet caps. Arthur, known as Sandy, was brought up to share her values and was seen helping Edith scrub the front step. Edith inspired a band of women in Preston to join the branch of the WSPU she founded in 1907.[51]

Mrs Flora Drummond joined the Women's Social and Political Union in the summer of 1905. Flora Gibson was born in Manchester in 1879 to Scottish parents. By 1881 her father Francis, a tailor, had moved the family to Scotland and her childhood years were spent on the Isle of Arran. Flora left school when she was fourteen and became a telegraphist, then studied to be a postmistress in Glasgow. Her obvious source of employment was the post office, but a bizarre new rule denied her this: she was an inch shorter than the regulation height of five feet two inches.[52]

On 26 September 1898 Flora Gibson married Joseph Drummond in Glasgow. Joe was an upholsterer born in Manchester and a local hero on Arran, having fallen overboard on the steamer taking him there on a holiday trip.[53] Flora and Joe's son Percival was born in July 1899 in Manchester but died aged twenty-two months, of gastroenteritis.[54] After the death of their child the couple became members of the Independent Labour Party, the Fabian Society and the Clarion Cycling Club. Joe Drummond was in and out of work and Flora had to supplement his wages. Hearing from comrades of the conditions that working women endured she went to find out for herself by taking a job in a garment factory. One of the factors that took her to 62 Nelson Street was the low wages that were one of the causes of prostitution. She became the main breadwinner and found better paid work as the manager of the Oliver Typewriter Company in Manchester.

In the summer of 1905 Flora Drummond travelled round the Lancashire cotton towns encouraging women to join the WSPU. She was remembered by Sylvia Pankhurst as 'brimful of self-assurance and audacity, she was always able to draw a laugh from her audience by jocular stories ... good at organizing and directing in a rough-and-ready way'.[55] Flora quickly earned a new name: 'the General'.

Hannah Mitchell, née Webster, made her way to women's suffrage via the Independent Labour Party of which she and her husband Gibbon were early members. Hannah recalled her parents Benjamin, a farmer, and Ann, a reluctant farmer's wife, as being opposite in character: Ann resented her last three children, Hannah, Sarah and Benjamin, often lashing out at them in wild rages. Benjamin, a hill farmer whose sheep nibbled a living from the harsh terrain, was a gentle man who taught all his children to read and write.[56]

Ann Webster decided her daughters should train to be dressmakers, so she sent Hannah to Glossop to learn dressmaking with Miss Brown, an 'elderly crippled lady' who ran a small business. Hannah was happy at Miss Brown's. 'Even a very strict mistress would have seemed kind after my mother's harshness, but Miss Brown was so kind and gentle she soon roused my interest, and for the first time I realized that work could also be a pleasure.'[57]

The antagonism between mother and daughter grew worse: 'she was determined to mould me to her pattern ... by nagging, ravings and beatings. But I was stronger now, and had no mind to allow myself to be thrashed.'[58] In 1888, Hannah walked the ten miles to Glossop to lodge with her eldest brother William, and his wife and baby son. 'Somewhere on the moorland road I left my childhood behind for ever.'[59] By 1891 she was nineteen years old and working in Bolton as a dressmaker, earning ten shillings a week.[60] Hannah learned the harsh conditions of the garment industry: low pay, long hours, seasonal unemployment, strict rules which included silence at all times, and a system of fines 'enforced by a thin-lipped shrew of a woman'.[61]

Hannah was caught up in the agitation for shorter working hours for shop assistants. At a meeting to ask for a weekly half-day holiday for shop workers, she was captivated and a lifelong support of trade unionism began: 'It was a wonderful experience, this slim young woman of the leisured classes, pleading for her working-class sisters, the clergyman bravely denouncing the grasping employer, the organizer appealing to the workers to join the union and demand their rights.'[62]

In September 1895, wearing a simple grey frock and a grey velvet hat, Hannah married a fellow lodger, Gibbon Mitchell, in the parish church at Hayfield, Derbyshire. The man who brought the couple together was Richard Pankhurst. During their courtship Gibbon and Hannah were keenly following 'the Red Doctor's' work to keep public access to the Kinder Scout footpath.[63] Their heads were full of the socialist idea that marriage should be a comradeship, and that birth control was 'the simplest way for the poor to help themselves and by far the surest way for women to obtain some measure of freedom'. Their only child, Frank Gibbon Mitchell, was born in 1896.[64]

The Mitchells moved to Newhall, a coal-mining village in Derbyshire. Local socialists pooled their savings to build a hall where they held their meetings, inviting well-known speakers, to whom the Mitchells often gave a bed for the night. In 1900 they moved to Ashton-under-Lyne, ten miles from Manchester, where Gibbon worked in the tailoring department at the Cooperative store. They joined the Independent Labour Party, and Gibbon became the lecture secretary, helping to set up a Labour church.[65]

In May 1904 Hannah was nominated by the Independent Labour Party as a Poor Law Guardian for Ashton-under-Lyne and duly appointed. She spoke on 'The Women's Cause' at Labour churches around Ashton: 'I found to my surprise that in a small way I was regarded as a popular speaker ... I already had a quick wit and a pretty good vocabulary and I had no difficulty in answering questions, or dealing with hecklers.'[66]

In 1904 Hannah met Emmeline Pankhurst, the widow of the man whom she and Gibbon revered, and heard Christabel speak about 'Votes for Women'. 'I was not very keen at first. My socialist friends harped so persistently on the evils of the "property qualification" that I had often said I would not help get votes for women on the "same terms as it is, or will be granted to men" little thinking how soon I would be in the thick of the militant fight.'[67] When Hannah heard Annie Kenney speak at Stalybridge Market she noticed how 'the audience, most of whom had come to scoff, were held spellbound by the charm and intensity of her appeal for the rights of her sex'.[68] Hannah realised that if 'women did not bestir themselves ... in spite of all their talk about equality they would be quite content to accept Manhood Suffrage, votes for all men, and that women's suffrage would take even longer'.[69]

Hannah threw herself into the WSPU's recruitment drive, gathering many women members of the ILP into their ranks. In the summer of 1905 she went round the Lancashire towns holding outdoor meetings, 'on a chair, or a soap box from the nearest shop, often lent only in the hope of seeing some fun'.[70] Though many of her male colleagues were against women's suffrage, Hannah and other WSPU speakers canvassed for votes for women under the auspices of the Independent Labour Party. 'With one or other of the small band of speakers I must have worked the Colne Valley from end to end ... going from door to door to ask the women to come out and listen.'[71] Meetings could be rowdy and her husband and his friends were often needed as stewards and bodyguards. 'They did not all approve of us, but as socialists they had some experience of the hooligan, and came to see the women got a fair hearing and keep the worst elements in good order.'[72]

When it was announced that Sir Edward Grey and Winston Spencer-Churchill were to speak at a Liberal rally at the Free Trade Hall in Manchester on Friday 13 October 1905, Christabel Pankhurst and Annie Kenney decided that they would put a question to Churchill: 'If you are elected will you do your best to make Woman Suffrage a government measure?' Winston Churchill, a careerist, who had the previous year defected from the Conservative Party to join the Liberals, was hoping to be elected for Manchester North-West. Sir Edward Grey had been the Liberal Member of Parliament for Berwick-upon-Tweed since 1885; his great-uncle, the 2nd Earl Grey, was prime minister when the 1832 Great Reform Act became law, and started the process of male suffrage.

Hopes were high among women's suffrage campaigners that the Liberal Party led by Sir Henry Campbell-Bannerman would win the forthcoming election and grant women the vote. Christabel's strategy was to challenge the Liberals 'on the fundamental principles of Liberalism – government of the people by the people, even such of the people who happened to be women. If the new Liberal Government were willing to enfranchise women, the Liberal leaders would say so, if not then militancy would begin. A straight question must be put to them and a straight answer obtained.'[73] But Christabel was astute enough to know that Churchill and Grey would not become hostages to fortune by answering the question. As Christabel and Annie set off from Nelson Street, Christabel told her mother: 'We shall sleep in prison tonight.' Her mother's face was 'drawn and cold' as they said goodbye. Emmeline Pankhurst had been preparing for this moment for two years. The WSPU's time had come.

Annie had made a banner with 'Will You Give Votes for Women?' painted on it, and had concealed it in her clothing. The women choreographed their protest. 'We decided that if we were not answered, to stand up and unfurl the banner so that all could see that the question that had been put was on Votes for Women.'[74] At question time some Labour men asked about the unemployed and were duly answered. Annie rose and asked her question, but was ignored. 'She stood there, a slender fragile figure. She had taken off her hat and her loosely-flowing hair gave her a childish look; her cheeks were flushed, her blue eyes blazing with earnestness.'[75] When the chairman asked for other questions Annie rose again and was 'pulled down by two enthusiastic Liberals'. Annie and Christabel then unfurled their banner and were 'dragged from the meeting and flung out of doors'.[76] The meeting broke up and some of the audience followed the women into the street. Annie tried to address them, 'but I found myself in custody and being marched off between two policemen. The strange thing was I had not the least fear. I did not feel ashamed at the crowds seeing me marched off. I had indeed started a new life. My admiration for Christabel and my belief in what I was doing kept me calm and determined.'[77]

Christabel wanted to go to prison but knew that she would not be locked up merely for disrupting a meeting. Assaulting a policeman was, however, a different matter:

> The police seemed to be skilled to frustrate my purpose. I could not strike them, my arms were being held. I could not even stamp on their toes – they seemed able to prevent that. Yet I must bring myself under arrest … Lectures on the law flashed to my mind. I could, even with all limbs helpless, commit a technical assault and so I found myself arrested and charged with 'spitting at a policeman'. It was not a real spit but only, how shall we call it, a 'pout', a perfectly dry purse of the mouth. I could not have *really* have done it, even to get the vote. Anyhow, there was no need, my technical assault was enough.

She felt it a 'great comfort "to be written of as a 'spitfire'"'.[78]

The press were shocked into writing about the women's protest, the first militant act of the WSPU. A packed Manchester City Police Court appearance got them 500 words in *The Times*. Christabel and Annie were summonsed for obstruction and Christabel for assaulting the police. The prosecuting solicitor said 'the conduct of the defendants, instead of being what one expected from educated ladies, was like that of women from the slums'.[79] Neither woman rejected the charges and said that, as they were denied votes, making a disturbance was the only way they could put forward their claim for political justice. Christabel was only sorry that one of the men on the receiving end had not been Sir Edward Grey, and was fined ten shillings and sixpence and costs or seven days for the assault; both were fined five shillings and costs or three days for obstruction. Christabel's sentences would run concurrently. The women refused to pay and were taken to Strangeways Prison. When Annie Kenney heard her sentence she felt 'a strange quivering sensation'. Rumour had it that Churchill tried to pay their fines, to minimise the publicity.[80]

Later that evening, in pouring rain, the WSPU organised an open-air meeting in Stevenson Square to protest against the prison sentences and Sir Edward Grey's refusal to answer the question. Mrs Pankhurst and Teresa Billington spoke from the back of a lorry, Mrs Pankhurst telling the crowd that she was proud of her daughter's 'courageous stand' and that 'these noble girls had undeceived the Liberal women as to the intentions of the Liberal party'.[81] There would be a rally to welcome the prisoners at the Free Trade Hall. Annie was first to be freed and was met by two sisters, the members of her choir and friends from the mill. Mrs Pankhurst said to Annie: 'As long as I have a home you must look upon it as yours. You will never have to return to factory life';[82] which was just as well as Annie Kenney had lost her job. When Christabel was released early in the morning she was greeted by a large crowd at the prison gates, including her mother, Annie Kenney, Keir Hardie, Teresa Billington, Hannah Mitchell and Mrs Elmy. That night the protesters returned to the Free Trade Hall. Annie and Christabel spoke of the future struggle for the vote for women, not of their time in prison. Mrs Elmy reported Annie Kenney confidently saying there was no shortage of women she knew who would go to prison 'to win freedom for their sisters'.

Annie Kenney had an epiphany which would inform the next dozen years of her life: 'I delivered my speech, and I trembled as I made it. I felt nervous when I saw the great hall full of earnest, excited faces. I knew *the* change had come in my life. The old life had gone, a new life had come ... The past seemed blotted out. I had started on a new cycle ... Christabel's speech was truth to me. She it was who lit the fire which consumed the past.'[83]

The protest and rally announced to the wider world that deeds not words was their way. Their organisation was militant, distinct from the moderate National Union of Women's Suffrage Societies (NUWSS).

At the beginning of December the Conservative government resigned ahead of the general election in January 1906. The Liberals announced a meeting at the Royal Albert Hall on 21 December. Mindful of events at the Free Trade Hall, the Liberals let it be known that they would not sell tickets to any woman they suspected might ask awkward questions. Annie Kenney wrote to Sir Henry Campbell-Bannerman asking him to state his policy on votes for women and warning him that she would be in the audience on the night; if he did not answer the question she would 'feel bound to rise in her place and make a protest'.[84] Annie received no reply. Keir Hardie managed to get tickets and Annie went dressed as a lady wearing a fur coat; Minnie Baldock, a new member of the WSPU from Canning Town in the East End of London, went dressed as her maid. Sylvia Pankhurst dressed Annie: 'We understood that most of the ladies would be in evening gowns, but it was essential to show as little of her face, neck and hair as possible, so after dressing her up in a light cream-colour we added a fur coat and thick dark veil.'[85] With Minnie Baldock, her 'maid', walking behind her, the women were allowed to take their seats in a private box. Teresa Billington sat above the speakers' platform.

Campbell-Bannerman did not respond to Annie's written question. She had hidden a small banner with the words 'Votes for Women' under her coat and she hung it over the edge of the box and called out, 'Will the Liberal Government give women the vote?' At the same time Teresa Billington unfurled a nine-foot-long banner painted with the words 'Will the Liberal Government give justice to working women?' There was a hush, but Campbell-Bannerman and his colleagues remained silent. The audience broke into a tumultuous uproar and the chairman vainly called for order. The organ played to drown the women's questions and Annie and Teresa were thrown out of the hall, but not arrested.[86] The next day Annie Kenney, Teresa Billington and Minnie Baldock called on Campbell-Bannerman at his residence at 39 Belgrave Square asking to speak to him. He told them he would deal with the question of women's suffrage 'soon'. Later that day when news of the visit to Belgrave Square reached Dora Montefiore, who had been at the protest in the Royal Albert Hall, she sent a postcard to Minnie Baldock: 'Warmest congratulations on your noble stand. You deserve the gratitude of all freedom-loving women.'[87]

Dora Montefiore had known Mrs Elmy for fifteen years and considered her 'one of the most wonderful women who devoted her life and her intellectual powers to the emancipation of women'.[88] Dora Fuller was born in 1851 and married George Barrow Montefiore, a prosperous merchant, in Australia in 1881. Their two children were born in 1883 and 1887, then in July 1889 George Montefiore died at sea, aged thirty-two. Dora became a campaigner for women's rights in Australia when she learned that she did not have the right to be her children's guardian since her husband had not written it into his will. In 1891 she held the first meeting of the Womanhood Suffrage League of New South Wales, of which she was the secretary. Dora Montefiore came to London in 1893. During the 1890s she campaigned on the executive committee of the Union of Practical Suffragists who devised the strategy of asking Liberal candidates directly if they would give women the vote, a tactic the WSPU now deployed. In 1898 Mrs Montefiore fell for George Belt, a married bricklayer's labourer, who was on the National Administration Committee of the ILP. It caused a scandal.[89]

Minnie Baldock was born Lucy Minnie Rogers in 1864 in Bromley-by-Bow. She worked in a shirt factory where 'sweated' conditions – long hours, low pay and poor sanitation – were the norm. Minnie Rogers married Henry Baldock in 1888. That year the country's attention was focused on the East End, a byword for poverty, disease, crime and sweatshops where women worked long hours for 'starvation wages' in vile conditions.

In 1892 Keir Hardie was elected MP for West Ham South and during the 1890s Henry and Minnie Baldock joined the Independent Labour Party and Henry became a councillor in West Ham. Minnie took part in the administration of the West Ham Unemployed Fund, a distress committee that helped the worst poverty. In 1903 she held a public meeting to protest at the low wages West Ham Council paid women who worked in their tramways department. West Ham Independent Labour Party asked Minnie to stand for election to the West Ham Board of Guardians in April 1905 and she was elected. Her children were now fourteen and eight years old.[90]

Minnie Baldock was the ideal woman to take the WSPU's message to the East End and build a branch where women's living and working conditions were some of the worst in the country. Canning Town, named after Lord Canning, the governor-general and first viceroy of India, was a tough riverside community. While the Baldocks were bringing up their children in Poplar the population had grown from 32,000 in 1841 to 169,000 in 1901, and by the turn of the century the population of Canning Town had grown from 1,000 in 1841 to 71,000.[91] In 1857 Charles Dickens described Canning Town:

> Rows of small houses, which may have cost eighty pounds a piece are built with their backs to the marsh ditches ... two to three yards of clay pipe 'drain' each house into an open cesspool under its back windows ... In winter time every block becomes now and then an island, and you may hear a sick man in an upper room complain of water trickling down over his bed ... the stench of the marsh in Canning Town is horrible.[92]

In 1905 the Baldocks were living at 10 Eclipse Road, Canning Town. It was still one of the most deprived and unhealthy parts of London. Before playing the role of Annie Kenney's maid, Minnie Baldock had been recruiting members to join an ILP Club for the 'Unemployed Women of South West Ham'. The first meeting was held on 29 January 1906, with Minnie in the chair and her friend Rosina Fennell the secretary. Rosina was thirty-seven, the mother of six children; her husband was a packer in a varnish works. The Fennells' eldest child, a girl of sixteen, was a pupil teacher at an elementary school; their youngest was five years old. At the meeting Minnie Baldock urged the women to combine together and Louisa Weight, a mother of five, suggested that the meeting send a letter to West Ham's distress committee asking for a meeting to discuss the plight of local women who were important contributors to their family budget. On 5 February 1906 a deputation of ten Canning Town women was received by the distress committee.[93]

The night after the visit to the distress committee forty women met again and heard Annie Kenney talk about the importance of women's suffrage. Annie had been introduced to Minnie Baldock by Dora Montefiore in December 1905 and when Annie came to 'rouse London' in January 1906 she stayed with Minnie and her family. During the winter of 1905–6 the unemployed women of West Ham evolved into Canning Town WSPU, the first of the organisation's branches in London.[94]

The Pankhurst family spent Christmas 1905 planning the next move, and appointed Annie Kenney as a paid organiser on £2 a week, far more than she earned in the mill. Her first task was to 'rouse London' in the new year.

On 19 February 1906 unemployed women travelled from Plaistow station to St James's Park for the state opening of Parliament to 'demonstrate the cause of women's suffrage'. Minnie Baldock and the Canning Town women were joined by other working women, and middle-class supporters including Dora Montefiore, and eventually three to four hundred women gathered in Parliament Square. Mrs Pankhurst confessed to being moved: 'My eyes were misty with tears as I saw them, standing in line, holding the simple white banners Sylvia had decorated, waiting for the word of command.'[95] The women walked to Caxton Hall in Caxton Street, which was to become the WSPU's headquarters for many subsequent deputations. When they arrived at the Hall they found a large audience had gathered. Sylvia later learned that there were 'many ladies of wealth and position who, inspired with curiosity by the newspaper accounts of the disturbances in December had disguised themselves in their maid's clothes in order that they might attend the meeting unrecognized'.[96] Emmeline Pankhurst, Dora Montefiore and Annie Kenney addressed the meeting during which a message was sent from the Commons that the King's Speech, which announced the government's legislative programme for the session, had not included women's suffrage. Mrs Pankhurst urged everyone to go to the House of Commons and lobby the members to introduce a suffrage bill. They left Caxton Hall and walked in the rain to the Strangers' Entrance but found that the House, which was normally open to women, was closed on the government's orders. Eventually permission was given for twenty women at a time to be admitted. Mrs Pankhurst recalled:

Through all the rain and cold those hundreds of women waited for hours for their turn to enter. Some never got in and for those of us who did there was small satisfaction. Not a member could be persuaded to take up our cause ... Out of the disappointment and dejection of that meeting I reaped a rich harvest of happiness ... those women had followed me to the House of Commons. They had defied the police and were awake at last ... Now they were ready to fight for their own human rights. Our militant movement was established.[97]

2

'Deeds Not Words'

The WSPU Moves to London 1906

Twenty-seven-year-old Mary Phillips selling Votes for Women *stands in the gutter to avoid being arrested for obstruction.*

A *Daily Mail* journalist, Charles Hands, was the first to use the word 'suffragette' on 10 January 1906.[1] Turning the word suffrage into suffragette, he made it feminine and small, like maisonette and brunette. But though it was coined as a term of abuse, the WSPU proudly made 'suffragette' their own, pronouncing it with a hard 'g' to emphasise that they would 'gette' the vote.[2] A week after 'suffragette' came into the language *Punch*'s cartoonist Bernard Partridge drew an ugly 'shrieking sister' being admonished by 'The Sensible Woman' suffragist: 'You Help Our Cause? Why, You're Its Worst Enemy.'[3] Now they owned the word, the time was ripe for the WSPU to become a national movement. *Punch*, the humorous and satirical magazine for the educated middle-class reader, had been around since 1841. Appearing so soon after the WSPU's first militant act, Partridge's drawing was a gift for a fledgling organisation intent on exploiting every media opportunity. Whatever way its message and methods were portrayed made little difference to the leadership: all publicity was good publicity.

Two people played a vital role in changing the WSPU from a small protest group into a nationwide organisation: Emmeline and Frederick Pethick-Lawrence. Keir Hardie had introduced his friends to Mrs Pankhurst. Mrs Pankhurst and Annie Kenney were invited to lunch at the couple's flat at 4 Clement's Inn off the Strand. The Pethick-Lawrences had an impressive record of supporting social reform and a tremendous capacity for friendship: with no children of their own they adopted many people into their lives. Annie was touched by their affection: 'From the first moment there sprang up a deep friendship between us that has never really been broken ... I was more like an adopted daughter than a friend, and many comforts and a few luxuries were very soon mine that had not been mine before meeting the two new friends who were to play such a leading part in the militant movement.'[4] Emmeline Pethick-Lawrence was equally impressed by Annie, moved by her conviction: 'She burst in on me in her rather breathless way and threw all my barriers down. I might have been a life-long friend by the complete trust in me that she showed.'[5] Annie asked Mrs Pethick-Lawrence to become the WSPU's treasurer, admitting to her that they had no money, and begged her to come to a committee meeting the next day at Sylvia Pankhurst's lodgings, 45 Park Walk, Chelsea. Emmeline Pethick-Lawrence agreed to go 'because I could not repulse her wistful eagerness'. When Annie left, Emmeline Pethick-Lawrence had second thoughts, realising that she was being drawn into something bigger than she had foreseen: 'I did not feel quite happy about my promise ... to tell the truth I had no fancy to be drawn into a small group of brave and reckless and quite helpless people who were prepared to dash themselves ... against one of the strongest governments of modern times.' Emmeline asked Mary Neal, a close friend, to accompany her, 'as I wanted to have the reinforcement of her extremely shrewd judgment and common sense'.[6]

Frederick William Lawrence was born in Paddington, London, in 1871 into a prosperous, self-made family. He was the grandson of a carpenter who came to London from Cornwall in 1809 with two guineas in his pocket. William Lawrence made the family's fortune in the building trade and shrewdly bought land in the City. He was to have become Lord Mayor of London in 1857, but he died in 1855.[7]

Fred studied at Cambridge and took a double first in mathematics and natural sciences, was President of the Union and trained as a barrister.[8] Fred's friend Percy Alden, who had studied at Oxford, was a Baptist minister in Canning Town. In 1899 Alden persuaded Fred to work with him. Fred Lawrence had considered standing as a Liberal Unionist candidate but his political views changed during his time in the East End. By 1901 he was the 'Poor Man's Lawyer' giving free legal advice. In 1900 Fred Lawrence inherited a large fortune when his elder brother died, and he bought the radical halfpenny newspaper *The Echo*, which Percy Alden edited, promoting the Independent Labour

Party.⁹ In 1899 Fred arranged a theatrical evening performed by the Esperance Working Girls' Club in Mansfield Hall in the East End. The girls were brought by Mary Neal and Emmeline Pethick. Mary and Emmeline also ran Maison Esperance, a co-operative dressmaking business in Wigmore Street, which paid its employees double the usual hourly rates of pay and operated an eight-hour day. Emmeline Pethick was in born Bristol in 1867. Her father, Henry, was a farmer who employed thirty men.¹⁰ For young women of her age and class, marriage was the next step but Emmeline dreaded the rigmarole of looking for a husband, wanting instead an independent life. In 1890 she applied to become a volunteer with the Sisterhood of the West London Mission.¹¹

Fred asked Emmeline to join *The Echo*'s editorial team and gradually 'mental sympathy and accord ripened into friendship and friendship into love'.¹² Emmeline Pethick married Fred Lawrence in Canning Town Hall in 1901, and they combined their surnames as a declaration of their feminist views.

In 1905 Fred and Emmeline visited South Africa, and became friends with the feminist writer Olive Schreiner. They read 'a startling account' of Christabel Pankhurst and Annie Kenney's protest at the Free Trade Hall in Manchester. 'It seemed that a revolting scene had taken place ... and many of our friends considered that the cause of woman suffrage had been given its death-blow for generations – and were surprised when I pleaded for a stay of judgment.'¹³

On the journey home the Pethick-Lawrences met Mabel Tuke who shared their interest in folk-singing and dancing. The Pethick-Lawrences later encouraged Mabel Tuke, whom Fred called 'Pansy' (for her large dark eyes), to join the WSPU. By the summer of 1906 she was in charge at 4 Clement's Inn. Their battle headquarters were paid for by a donation from Fred, and £100 was given by Keir Hardie and his friends.¹⁴ Annie Kenney remembered 'Pansy' as one of the 'big characters' of the movement, with plenty of 'plain common sense'. 'Parents who came to see whether their daughters could be entrusted to us always found in Mrs Tuke the born hostess.'¹⁵

Emmeline Pethick-Lawrence and Mary Neal went to Sylvia's lodgings to meet her landlady, Mrs Florence Roe, who was then the WSPU's honorary secretary, her aunt Mary Clarke, Annie Kenney, Miss Irene Fenwick Miller and Nellie Martel. The aim of the Central

London Committee of the Women's Social and Political Union was: 'To secure for women the Parliamentary Vote as it is or may be granted to men; to use the power thus obtained to establish equality of rights and opportunities between the sexes, and to promote the social and industrial well-being of the community.'[16]

Still with reservations about such a tiny group's ability 'to rouse London', Emmeline Pethick-Lawrence found herself agreeing to join the committee and take over from the WSPU's overworked treasurer, Margaret Travers Symons, who was also Keir Hardie's secretary. The Committee wrote to the prime minister, Sir Henry Campbell-Bannerman, requesting a meeting which he declined, telling them to put their thoughts in writing. As suffragists had been writing to politicians since the 1860s to no avail, the WSPU paid a surprise call on him at 10 Downing Street on the morning of 9 March 1906. Campbell-Bannerman's wife was then very ill, and would die later that year. He admitted to King Edward VII's private secretary that caring for his wife caused him to neglect his duties as prime minister.[17]

That day thirty women were outside 10 Downing Street, informing the doorkeeper that they wished to see the prime minister. After forty-five minutes two minions appeared and told them: 'You had better be off; you must not stand on this doorstep any longer' and slammed the door. Irene Fenwick Miller rapped at the door with the door knocker, a policeman arrested her and took her to Canon Row police station, the first suffragette to be arrested in London.

At this point, Flora Drummond, five months pregnant, pushed the brass knob and the door opened. She headed straight for the Cabinet Room but was caught and in turn taken to the police station. Annie Kenney started to address the women and one of the two doorkeepers, who were now locked outside, called for the police to arrest Annie. After an hour in custody Irene Fenwick Miller, Flora Drummond and Annie Kenney were released without charge. Henry Campbell-Bannerman agreed that he would see a deputation of pro-women's suffrage MPs, and the WSPU, and any other societies who wanted votes for women later, on 19 May.[18] The convention that ladies who were 'confined' should stay well out of sight was ignored by Flora Drummond. On 6 July her son was born and named Keir Hardie Drummond.[19]

James Keir Hardie himself was born in Lanarkshire in 1856, the illegitimate son of a farm servant. From the age of eleven he worked as a collier. He went to night school, taught himself short-hand and was active in the temperance movement. Keir Hardie married in 1878 and had four children. In the late 1880s he launched the *Labour Leader*, and moved to London in 1891. He was elected the Independent Labour MP for West Ham South a year later, but lost the seat in 1895. In 1900 Hardie was elected as the Independent Labour Party MP for Merthyr Tydfil and in 1906 became chairman of the party. Some of his party colleagues grumbled that due to Sylvia Pankhurst's influence their chairman's socialism was being diluted by feminism.[20]

On the evening of 25 April 1906 Keir Hardie secured a reading of a women's suffrage resolution in the House of Commons and women congregated in the Ladies' Gallery. At ten o'clock that night he introduced the motion that sex should not be a bar to having the vote, but hostile MPs started to talk the resolution out. The women in the Ladies' Gallery shouted 'Shame' and 'Justice', and the Speaker threatened to have them removed. William Randal Cremer, Liberal MP for Haggerston, Shoreditch, then proceeded to bait the women: 'Are we prepared to hand over the government of this country to women who are not breadwinners and have not to bear the burdens and responsibilities of life? I have been described as a woman-hater, well I have had two wives – and I think that is the best answer I can give.'[21] Sylvia Pankhurst had the measure of him, writing: 'Although one was angry with him, he was an object for pity as he stood there, undersized and poorly-made, obviously in bad health and with that narrow, grovelling and unimaginative point of view, flaunting his masculine superiority.'[22]

In the Ladies' Gallery Teresa Billington pushed a 'Votes for Women' banner through the grille and waved it over the MPs' heads, at which point the debate collapsed in jeers and shouts and Inspector Scantlebury, who was in charge of policing at the House of Commons, arrived to remove the women. Annie Kenney and Teresa Billington were identified as the 'principal offenders' and soon they were engaged in 'hand to hand fighting'. The protesters were dragged out, their hats and coats were pulled off and their belongings dumped in a heap in Palace Yard. 'Suffragettes Who Rioted in the House of

Commons Were Expelled' read a headline the next day. A reporter
from the *Daily Mirror* visited Sylvia Pankhurst and saw 'striking
proofs of the vigour of the leaders of the movement', with banners
being made in her studio.[23]

On 19 May a thousand women gathered on the Embankment, from
where a deputation set off for Whitehall to meet the prime minister. It included Mrs Elmy, Mrs Pankhurst, Mrs Pethick-Lawrence and
Keir Hardie, with Annie Kenney dressed as a mill worker, clogged
and shawled. Marching alongside the deputation were fifty textile
workers carrying banners. The WSPU banner, 'We demand Votes for
Women this Session' was lashed to a lorry which carried mill workers
who were too frail to walk. The lorry was followed by WSPU members and other women's suffrage societies, including 125 women from
Canning Town.[24]

Sir Charles McLaren MP introduced the deputation of eight women
to the prime minister. Mrs Pankhurst warned Campbell-Bannerman
that her members were adamant that 'no business could be more
pressing than this' and that 'they felt the question of votes for women
so deeply that they were prepared', if necessary, to sacrifice 'life itself,
or the means by which they lived'. She appealed to the government to
make such sacrifices unnecessary by 'doing this long-delayed act of
justice to women without delay'.[25]

Dispensing a few platitudes, and appearing to declare his personal
support for women's suffrage, Sir Henry Campbell-Bannerman then
dropped a bombshell: he could not help them as members of the
Cabinet were opposed to the idea. 'It would never do for me to make
any statement or pledge under these circumstances.' Keir Hardie
formally thanked the prime minister for receiving the deputation
and asked him again if 'ways and means' could not be found to give
women the vote during the current parliamentary session. Sir Henry
shook his head. Mrs Elmy told him that during the past forty years
she had seen the male electorate grow from 700,000 to seven million
and yet women were still being denied justice. The prime minister's
response was to tell them to 'go on converting the country', at which
Annie Kenney jumped up and said, 'Sir, we are not satisfied, and the
agitation will go on.'

At three o'clock the women who had waited on the Embankment
were joined in Trafalgar Square by 6,000 people, some supportive,

some curious bystanders and many hostile. Mrs Pankhurst chaired the meeting, Teresa Billington wore a red sash with 'Votes for Women' blazoned across her chest and Annie Kenney held Mrs Elmy's hand as the tiny old lady listened to her speech being read out. The *Daily Mirror* reported: 'It was a touching scene when the old lady came to the front ... As the eloquent words were delivered the old lady burst into tears and continually wiped her eyes with her handkerchief.'[26] She told the reporter, 'I have been fighting this cause half my life ... I shall go on fighting. Even an old woman can do something when she is in earnest.'[27]

Christabel Pankhurst identified Herbert Asquith, chancellor of the exchequer, as the leading enemy of women's suffrage in the Cabinet. Teresa Billington, Mrs Pankhurst, Annie Kenney and Mrs Roe travelled to Northampton to protest at a Liberal Party meeting Asquith was due to address at the Corn Exchange on 14 June. They held open-air meetings and gave out handbills saying that although Mr Asquith was a Liberal he was 'no lover of liberty'.

As soon as Asquith tried to speak 'wild scenes – the most exciting yet of the campaign of the "suffragettes" occurred'.[28] One WSPU supporter seated on the balcony waved a banner, shouting 'votes for women', and the 'wildest confusion followed during which there were personal encounters between men and women'.[29] A woman wrestled a banner out of a suffragette's hands. Teresa Billington 'drew a whip from under her cloak and lashed out wildly on the heads and shoulders of the men'.[30] She fought the three men who grabbed her and bundled her down the steps.

Mrs Pankhurst stood up and shouted: 'Will Mr Asquith give justice to women of this country?' and was ejected. Teresa Billington, whose dress was torn, urged the crowd to attack Asquith when he left the meeting. When Asquith emerged he was hurried through a cordon of policemen to his motor car and Annie Kenney darted forward but was grabbed by a policeman.[31]

When the suffragettes left Northampton by train that evening, happy with their week's work, they shouted from the carriage windows, 'You will soon hear of us again.' The next day Teresa Billington and Annie Kenney held a meeting in Plashet Park, East Ham, and explained how they had attended the Northampton meeting in disguise: Annie Kenney dressed 'like a newly-bereaved widow' and Teresa Billington dressed 'like a duchess in a long flowing gown with a train, long white coat, a big picture-hat, a feather boa and a cape'. Sylvia Pankhurst said that on the same day the women had been harrying Herbert Asquith, women in Finland were given the vote.[32]

Herbert Henry Asquith, born in 1853, was from a modest background. His father was a small-scale wool-stapler in Morley, Yorkshire (he bought fleeces from farmers and sold them directly to manufacturers). Asquith was academically gifted and won a Classics scholarship to Balliol College, Oxford, becoming President of the Union in 1874. Asquith's earnings were supplemented by the father of his first wife who died of typhoid in 1891 leaving five children. In 1894 Asquith married Margot Tennant whose wealth helped finance their extravagant lifestyle. Margot Asquith was intelligent, spoilt, opinionated, mischief-making and an outspoken opponent of women's suffrage. She had recently written to a friend: 'women have no reason, very little humour, hardly any sense of honour … and no sense of proportion.'[33] Herbert Asquith refused to see a WSPU deputation at his home on 19 June 1906, but a group of eight women, including Teresa Billington, Annie Kenney, Irene Fenwick Miller and Clara Mordan, besieged him for two hours. He eventually managed to slip away by the stable door, hidden in a motor car.[34] Two days later, on 21 June, the suffragettes returned. Adelaide Knight and thirty Canning Town comrades joined 150 other women who created 'a tremendous commotion' at Asquith's house when they were told that he would not receive them. When Annie Kenney pressed on she was arrested. Jane Sbarborough noticed servants in the upper rooms and women on the balconies of his house cheering Annie Kenney's arrest. Mrs Sbarborough called out that they should be ashamed of themselves and was bundled away by a policeman who asked why she was 'mixing yourself up with this lot?', insisting, 'I know they want half a pint of gin before breakfast in the morning.' When she was asked by the magistrate why a lady 'of her years [she was sixty-four] was interfering in an agitation of this sort' she replied: 'We want the vote. We see the misery that you men have done for years and we want to alter it. You would have sympathy if you lived down at Bow … and saw the misery there.'[35] Jane Sbarborough was a needlewoman, born in Quebec in 1842. She and her husband Fortunato Sbarborough, a shipping merchant from Genoa, lived in Bow.[36]

Mrs Adelaide Knight was one of the first members of Canning Town WSPU. A disease of the hip kept her in hospital where she immersed herself in books. In 1899 she married Donald Adolphus Brown, a black merchant seaman who adopted her surname.[37] Donald's father had murdered his wife in 1883 and his incarceration in Broadmoor Criminal Lunatic Asylum effectively left his children orphaned.[38] Donald Brown did well at the Greenwich Royal Hospital School for the Orphans of Seamen and Marines, joining the merchant navy in 1889.[39]

Alice Toyne, married to a barrister, was a passer-by:

> I saw ten police and three inspectors waiting about ... I walked along quietly and a policeman caught me by the arm and asked me what I wanted and what I was doing. I said, 'What is that to you' – and he gave me a fairly hefty push. As I did not want to be mauled ... I walked on and saw a line of policemen and a lady speaking to them – I did not know it was Miss Billington at the time – nor did I hear what was said but I distinctly saw a policeman hit her in the face when she took a step forward and the lady then either pushed or slapped him. I couldn't see which. Then the policeman took her by the throat, she turned purple and it looked as if she was being choked: a fat woman in the crowd intervened and had her wrist torn by the policeman's nails.[40]

Mrs Toyne emphasised that she was not a member of the WSPU, not part of the deputation, 'though I sympathise with it, after Miss Billington was taken off'.

Teresa Billington was charged with assault and sentenced to two months in prison or given the option of paying a fine of £10. The sentence was severe and when Keir Hardie raised the matter in Parliament it was reduced to one month. To Teresa Billington's intense irritation an anonymous reader of the *Daily Mirror* paid the fine and she served no time in Holloway. Her comrades, 'the Canning Town Three', Annie Kenney, Adelaide Knight and Jane Sbarborough, were charged with 'using behaviour whereby a breach of the peace might have been caused' and sentenced to six weeks in Holloway.

Teresa Billington gave details of her life to the *Daily Mirror*. She had been engaged for several years but 'refuses to be led to the altar until her war cry of "Votes for Women" passes into law'.[41] (She relented and married Frederick Lewis Greig, a socialist and the manager of a billiard-table factory in Glasgow, on 8 February 1907. They joined their names together.)

Minnie Baldock visited Mrs Sbarborough in Holloway and found the elderly lady 'happy under the circumstances'. She was eating and sleeping well, 'perhaps because my conscience is clear I feel so happy'. Jane was comfortable with a 'dear little cell' to herself, and saw her time in prison as the retreat she had always craved, 'somewhere I could be quiet, be still and that is what I am doing'. Minnie also saw Adelaide and Annie but heard that they were not allowed to talk to each other. Jane Sbarborough whispered to Minnie, '*we do* throw kisses at each other and Miss Kenney holds up her fingers one less each week'.[42]

On 14 August 1906 many WSPU members went to Hyde Park to welcome 'the Canning Town Three' on their release from Holloway that morning. Christabel Pankhurst denounced Herbert Asquith as 'the principal enemy of women's franchise and beyond conversion, and the only thing to do was to make him appear ridiculous'. Adelaide Knight told the crowd she had been in prison for six weeks and was 'willing to go for six months or years if doing so could knock some sense into men's brains'.[43]

Charlotte Despard and Edith How-Martyn were two new members with impressive campaigning credentials. Charlotte's white hair was swept high and covered with a black mantilla and she wore leather sandals instead of button boots. She was sixty-two and paid for a health clinic in Battersea and organised a soup kitchen for the unemployed. She campaigned for free school meals and medical inspections for school children and in 1894 was elected a Poor Law Guardian in Lambeth. Mrs Despard was impressed by the commitment of WSPU members: 'I had sought comradeship with men. I had marched with great processions of the unemployed … I had listened with sympathy to the fiery denunciations of governments and capitalist systems to which they belong. Amongst all these experiences I had not found what I met on the threshold of this young, vigorous Union of Hearts.'[44]

Edith How-Martyn, born in 1875, gave up her job as a science tutor to become joint honorary secretary with Charlotte Despard at Clement's Inn. Her father John was a grocer and her mother was in service before her marriage. In 1899 Edith married a science lecturer, George Martyn, and joined their surnames together. It was not possible for a woman to continue a teaching career after marriage, so Edith taught pupils at home. When she joined the WSPU, she was swept up by the spirit of the meeting: 'For the first time I felt I had met women who were strong and self-reliant. My inspiration was fired.'[45]

In June 1906 Christabel Pankhurst graduated with a first-class degree in law and moved to London to become the chief strategist of the WSPU on a salary of £2 10s a week. Annie's sister Jessie, nineteen, became Emmeline Pethick-Lawrence's secretary.[46] Annie Kenney admired Mrs Pethick-Lawrence: 'She must see where she is going, where the road will lead, and what the obstacles may be to block the path.' Strategy and fundraising were her strengths: Annie felt that in Emmeline Pethick-Lawrence, 'Providence sent the right woman at the right time to help in turning the little vessel into a great liner.'[47]

By the end of 1906 Mrs Pethick-Lawrence had the WSPU on a firm financial footing. The weekly running costs were the equivalent of £10,000 a week today, and included salaries for eight organisers: Annie Kenney, Minnie Baldock, Nellie Martel, Flora Drummond, Adela Pankhurst, Mary Gawthorpe, Helen Fraser and Christabel Pankhurst, who was the boss. Cash came from subscriptions from the fifty-eight branches which had sprung up throughout the country during the year, and donations from wealthy individuals like Clara Evelyn Mordan. Clara was at the WSPU's first meeting at Caxton Hall on 19 February and had given £17,000 by the end of the year. Elderly and ill with tuberculosis, Miss Mordan was unable to play an active part in the campaign; her wealth came from her family's manufacture of propelling pencils.[48]

Sales of tickets to meetings, and of books, postcards and pamphlets, helped pay running costs, but Mrs Pethick-Lawrence forecast that annual costs would rise to £20,000 if the WSPU continued to grow. She put her car at the disposal of the WSPU, plastered it with posters and named it 'La Suffragette'.[49] Emmeline was ingenious at making money work: fifteen years of charity work had taught her the virtues of thrift and had built a repertoire of fundraising ideas. Early on the suffragettes did not spend money on advertising, but chalked notices of meetings and slogans on pavements and produced their own posters. To save on the cost of hiring halls they held street meetings standing on chairs or orange boxes, and gathered in public parks.[50]

Mrs Pethick-Lawrence's understudy was Harriet Kerr, appointed in September as the general manager at Clement's Inn. An architect's daughter, she had been persuaded by the Pethick-Lawrences to give up her secretarial business and work for the WSPU.[51] Mrs Beatrice Sanders was the financial secretary at Clement's Inn. Annie Kenney remembered: 'If we were out in our petty cash book, it had to be made up out of our own pocket ... if there was a mistake, who could be expected to rectify it save ourselves.'[52] Beatrice Sanders was thirty-two years old when she went to work at Clement's Inn. Her father was a hairdresser and her mother a tobacconist. Her husband was a member of the Independent Labour Party, a lecturer for the Fabian Society and an alderman for the Progressive Party on the London County Council in 1904.[53]

Aeta Adelaide Lamb was twenty years old, thin, clever and shy. Sylvia Pankhurst remembered her 'flitting about like a disembodied spirit'. Aeta wrote some of Christabel Pankhurst's speeches. She 'found her niche in the militant suffrage movement, she was a tremendously strong feminist and ... bore all their sorrows and sufferings'.[54]

In July, Christabel Pankhurst travelled to Cockermouth in what is today Cumbria to campaign against the Liberal candidate, Frederick Edward Guest, at the by-election following the death of the sitting MP. This is when she announced the WSPU's by-election policy to 'keep the Liberals out' in reaction to their 'obdurate' refusal to give women the vote.[55]

The WSPU's friends in the Liberal Party were incensed by her 'ruthless logic' and Keir Hardie was 'grieved' by her decision to abandon all political allegiances. The Pankhurst family was divided: Christabel and her mother wanted to keep the WSPU independent of any political party, whereas Sylvia and Adela wanted closer ties with the Independent Labour Party. Christabel hired a stall in the marketplace and sold 'Votes for Women' pamphlets, held meetings every day for a week and hired a lorry to use as a platform. The crowd was bemused at being harangued by a pretty woman who looked so different from the expected 'shrieking sisterhood'. When the results of the election were announced on 6 August Christabel claimed a victory for the WSPU: the Liberals lost the seat to the Conservatives. The vote had been split three ways, since the Labour Party were contesting the seat for the first time.

The Pethick-Lawrences were impressed when Christabel went to live with them at Clement's Inn: 'We became aware of her "flair" for political affairs which was her special and unique gift ... her instinctive insight into the heart of a political problem ... It was astonishing to come into contact with a mind politically mature in a girl so simple and unpretentious.'[56]

Hannah Mitchell travelled from Ashton-under-Lyne for the suffragettes' planned visit to the House of Commons for the opening of Parliament on Tuesday 23 October. She stayed with Louise Cullen, known as Louie, the caretaker of a house in Kensington. Hannah remembered the luxury of staying in a big house and Louie bringing her a cup of tea in the morning. She felt shabby 'in her old brown costume' when she was invited to a reception by the Pethick-Lawrences.[57] A hundred and fifty WSPU women gathered at the Strangers' Entrance, each asking to see a Member of Parliament. Only twenty were admitted to the Lobby, and poorly dressed working women were not allowed to enter. Mrs Pankhurst asked the Liberal chief whip, George Whiteley, if the prime minister would consider their demand for the vote in the forthcoming session.[58] Hannah Mitchell and Louie Cullen each smuggled a 'Votes for Women' banner in with them. When Mrs Pankhurst and Mrs Pethick-Lawrence returned to the Lobby they brought the news that Henry Campbell-Bannerman refused to make women's suffrage a government measure. Mary Gawthorpe started to make a speech but was pulled off the chair by policemen, at which Hannah Mitchell and Louie Cullen unfurled their banners and Hannah draped hers over the base of a statue. A policeman snatched it and 'tore it to shreds'. Hannah was shocked to see Mrs Pankhurst knocked to the ground. 'We gathered round her, refusing to leave, and Members came rushing out of the House to watch the conflict, most of them guffawing loudly.'[59] Hannah and Louie broke through the cordon and walked out of the building.

Annie Kenney and Teresa Billington, who had not been allowed inside Parliament, were caught up in angry scenes outside. In the mêlée Inspector Scantlebury was pushed to the ground. Ten women were charged with using 'threatening and abusive language and behaviour with the intent of provoking a breach of the peace' and sentenced to two months in the second division of Holloway Gaol.[60] Annie Cobden-Sanderson, Irene Fenwick Miller, Mary Gawthorpe,

Minnie Baldock, Emmeline Pethick-Lawrence, Adela Pankhurst, Dora Montefiore, Teresa Billington, Edith How-Martyn and Annie Kenney were bailed by Fred Pethick-Lawrence. They appeared at Rochester Row police station the next morning.

Returning to Kensington, Hannah Mitchell and Louie Cullen noticed the charged atmosphere on the streets. Groups of people were 'discussing the astounding audacity of the voteless women, declaring loudly what they would do to them if they were the Government'. Hannah caught the midnight train home to Manchester.[61]

When Inspector Scantlebury tried to give evidence in court, several defendants interrupted him and the magistrate threatened to remand them. Scantlebury's colleague Inspector Jarvis described the 'pande-monium' he saw outside Parliament, women with their arms linked, trying to force their way into the House in a 'very disorderly and dis-graceful scene'. He mentioned that some of the women were in 'poor circumstances and had journeyed from the East End'.[62]

The rowdiness of the protest continued in court the next day: the women refused to acknowledge the authority of the magistrate, Mr Horace Smith, and there were complaints of 'rough usage' by the police, and cries of 'Shameful'. One woman produced a banner and waved it. Several defendants were dragged out of the dock by police constables. The magistrate ordered the ten accused to find £10 surety for six months' good behaviour, but all refused and were sentenced to two months in the second division at Holloway.[63]

Being placed in the second division cells meant that the suffragettes were treated as common criminals rather than political prisoners. During the nineteenth century men imprisoned for acts relating to political struggles won the right to be sent to the first division, which entitled them to wear their own clothes, enjoy freedom of association, receive books and write as many letters as they wished. Being placed in the sec-ond division meant the women were stripped of their own clothes, forced to wear prison clothing, to scrub floors and serve their time in solitary confinement. The dispute over political status in prison would later erupt and take the campaign in a new and harrowing direction.

Mary Gawthorpe was a schoolmistress in Leeds when she joined the WSPU at the beginning of the year 1906. She was soon appointed as a paid organiser. Pretty and petite, Mary Gawthorpe's photograph was one of the most popular postcards sold by the suffragettes; only the Pankhursts and Annie Kenney were more celebrated. Mary wrote to Christabel in Strangeways Prison: 'if it is necessary to go to prison in order to get the vote I am ready.' She was a charismatic orator: 'She is all fire and quick response, a flash of energy of sympathy and comprehensions.' One elderly man kept shouting at her, 'If you were my wife I'd give you poison.' Weary of the constant interruption, Mary replied, 'Yes, and if I were your wife I'd take it.' One heckler who was frustrated by her repartee threw a cabbage at her which she caught. She told the meeting: 'I was afraid that man might lose his head before the meeting was over.'[64]

Emmeline Pethick-Lawrence's father, Henry Pethick, was proud of her arrest. He travelled to London and remonstrated with the MPs of his acquaintance. 'Do you think we men who have supported the Liberal Party are going to tolerate having our daughters treated as criminals, because they have demanded the liberty we ourselves enjoy, while a blackguard obtained first-class treatment in prison?'[65] One of the men he berated was the home secretary, Herbert Gladstone, and Emmeline and her fellow suffragettes were moved to first division cells at Holloway Gaol.[66] Emmeline's time in prison was brief: she had a nervous collapse and was released after two days. With Mrs Pankhurst's approval she agreed not to take part in any militant action for the next six months. Fred took her to Italy to convalesce and he returned to take over as treasurer. On the third day of her sentence Dora Montefiore was released due to illness and Edith How-Martyn and Minnie Baldock were transferred to the hospital wing.[67]

Dora Montefiore's cell window was high and the glass was corrugated, making it impossible to see anything of the outside world. 'The only sign of outside life was the occasional flicker of the shadow of a bird as it flew across the window.' The bed was a wooden plank, and the mattress was rolled up in a corner, inside which were 'rather soiled-looking sheets'. Breakfast was a chunk of brown bread and cocoa; they went to chapel, and exercised in the yard. Dora's prison uniform was 'awful': her skirt barely reached her knees and her stockings were far too small. No garters were allowed and the women struggled when they 'marched in single file round and round the prison yard. I used to make continual vicious grabs at these detestable stockings.'[68]

The WSPU's campaign against the severity of the sentences worked, and the remaining prisoners were released a month early on 24 November. They were welcomed at a dinner organised by Mrs Millicent Fawcett of the NUWSS at the Savoy Hotel. A by-election in Huddersfield was imminent and the WSPU's new policy to canvass against the Liberals was deployed. When the results were published on 30 November the Liberal MP, Arthur Sherwell, kept his seat but with a reduced majority, due in part to the suffragettes' relentless campaign. The constituency, held by the Liberals since 1892, was 'worked up' by Mrs Pankhurst, Annie Kenney and Teresa Billington. Hannah Mitchell recalled her time in the town: 'It was a wonderful experience, like putting a match to a ready-built fire. The Yorkshire women rose to the call and followed us in hundreds.'[69]

Six weeks later Emmeline Pankhurst and Nellie Martel opened a WSPU branch in Huddersfield. The *Daily Mirror* saluted the women's efforts: 'when the suffragettes began their campaign they were mistaken for notoriety hunters, featherheads, flibbertigibbets. Their proceedings were not taken seriously. Now they have proved that they are in dead earnest, they have frightened the Government, they have broken the law, they have made votes for women practical politics.'[70]

Soon after Minnie Baldock's release from prison on 24 November, forty of the Canning Town members expressed their feelings in a signed petition: 'to show their appreciation of the loyal, brave and noble manner in which you bore imprisonment, faced slander and criticism. We present you with the names of those who are in entire sympathy with you ... so that you may have a lasting record of their love and admiration.'[71]

In November 1906 the WSPU enrolled Emily Davison. She was thirty-four years old and employed as a governess to the four children of Sir Francis Layland-Barratt, the Liberal MP for Torquay and High Sheriff for Cornwall. Emily went to work for the Layland-Barratts in 1902. While her involvement with the WSPU remained low-key she continued working for the family until, eighteen months later, her urge to 'come out' as a militant would lead her to resign and join the campaign.[72]

In December 1906 there were three more suffragette 'raids' to enter the House of Commons which resulted in twenty women and a young man being sent to prison. On the second 'raid' on 13 December,

Thomas Simmons, a clerk who worked for Fred Pethick-Lawrence, became the first man to be imprisoned for the suffragette cause. Near the public entrance of the House he 'ran backwards and forwards shouting "Votes for Women"'. When a policeman ordered him to go away Simmons pushed him and said he was 'going into the House'.[73] A group of suffragettes saw Simmons being arrested and dragged him away from the policeman, and one woman put her hands round the policeman's throat and tried to pull him down. Simmons said in court that he had acted deliberately to protest at the House of Commons denying women the vote. He chose to go to Brixton Prison for fourteen days rather than pay the twenty shillings fine.

Flora Drummond left her five-month-old son in Manchester with his father, and at 8 p.m. on 20 December 1906 she was one of five women arrested in an attempt to force their way into Parliament. Ivy Heppell came from Bristol, Mrs Jones and Mrs Hill from Manchester and Cardiff, and Helen Fraser from Glasgow. The police failed to stop Ivy Heppell and Mrs Jones from getting into the Strangers' Lobby where 'Miss Heppell sprang on to a form and tried to make a speech, while her companion shouted'. Both women were bundled out. At the other end of Palace Yard a suffragette waiting in a cab blew a police whistle and a group of police charged towards her. Then Flora Drummond and a handful of suffragettes who were waiting in two other cabs made a dash through the gates and reached the Members' Entrance. Flora got into the lobby and six policemen were needed to remove her. Outside she had a 'severe encounter with a policeman three times her size' and he had to call for help to carry her to the station. Flora Drummond was sentenced to two weeks in Holloway Gaol, where she spent Christmas that year.[74]

3

'Rise Up, Women!'

'These men are as wily as serpents' 1907

Mother-of-six Alice Hawkins was a bootmaker in Leicester whose husband Alfred supported women's suffrage.

In January 1907 Edith Rigby established a branch of the WSPU in Preston, a town she described as 'unprogressive and self-sufficient'. Her most fertile recruiting ground was the town's Independent Labour Party where she met Mrs Elizabeth Hesmondhalgh, a cotton winder who was married to a railway signalman. So keen was Edith to have Beth Hesmondhalgh join the suffragettes – she saw her as 'promising material' – that she asked Annie Kenney to help coax her into joining the militant movement: in turn, Beth wrote that Edith 'was so determined she even tried to get round my husband to persuade me. Well, I joined half against my will and the next thing I knew I was asked to face imprisonment!'[1]

On Sunday evenings Mrs Rigby would invite members to her house where they would discuss social and personal problems. Unconventional in so many ways, Edith refused to allow discussions about suffrage on the Sabbath; she provided tea and cakes and sat cross-legged on the floor chain-smoking Turkish cigarettes and listened sympathetically to women who had 'husband trouble'. Some of the better-off ladies of Preston supported the NUWSS which also had a presence in the town, but Edith's members, who were all working-class women, preferred the militant route.

When Flora Drummond and her comrades were released from Holloway on the morning of 3 January 1907, Joe Drummond, Christabel Pankhurst and Minnie Baldock were at the prison gates to take them to a 'Martyr's Breakfast' at a London hotel. Within twenty-four hours Flora was creating 'disorderly scenes' at Baldock, Hertfordshire, disrupting a meeting held by Mr Julius Bertram, the

Liberal MP for Hitchin, who had blocked Keir Hardie's women's suffrage Bill. Mrs Drummond stood up and announced: 'I have been in Holloway Gaol for fourteen days. I protest against Mr Bertram.' There was chaos as the locals tried to throw Flora out of the hall, but she and her supporters carried on yelling until she was carried out 'amid boisterous cheering'. Then Minnie Baldock stood up and spoke and was removed by stewards. Mr Bertram remarked that there was no desire for the franchise by most women in the country.[2]

On 7 January the *Daily Mirror* reported that the Pethick-Lawrences had adopted Annie Kenney and henceforth she was to be 'recognised as their daughter', although her father was alive and living in Oldham. Annie was known as 'the little militant', and her new 'parents', Emmeline and Fred, acknowledged her as one of the 'leading lights of the movement'.[3]

On Saturday 9 February 4,000 women braved the rain to walk in procession to Hyde Park, followed by a meeting at Exeter Hall in the Strand calling on the government to give women the vote during the current parliamentary session. The procession, which stretched for half a mile, was organised by the NUWSS. Millicent Fawcett's suffragists were joined by many suffragettes, including Mrs Despard, Mrs Cobden-Sanderson and Gertrude Ansell. Belonging to both organisations, going to each others' events and wearing both badges was quite usual. The weather was so beastly that their walk became known as 'the Mud March'. Some travelled in cars and carriages but most 'ploughed their way through Piccadilly where the gutters were sometimes inches deep in mud'.[4] Mrs Fawcett acknowledged the contribution the WSPU had made to revitalising the women's suffrage movement, but the Liberal women in the NUWSS interrupted and hissed when Keir Hardie spoke. In the presence of several hundred moderates, he saluted the work of the WSPU, saying that if women did get the vote it would be due to the militant tactics of the 'suffragettes' fighting brigade'.[5]

At dawn on 13 February Edith Rigby travelled by train to the WSPU's first ever 'Women's Parliament' in Caxton Hall which was a conveniently short walk from the Houses of Parliament. The meetings, held every year to coincide with the opening of the parliamentary session, were no mere talking shops. Caxton Hall would be decorated with banners, inspirational speeches would be made by the leadership and then women would 'take action' – the focus of the gathering – by walking to the House of Commons, thus exemplifying the suffragettes' motto 'Deeds Not Words'. Edith was one of fifty-seven women arrested that day and sent to Holloway for two weeks. Edith's husband Charlie responded to his local paper, the *Lancashire Daily Post*, about the day's events. The editor had hoped that the prisoners 'would undergo the full rigours of prison discipline ... and be allowed to serve their full term without any amelioration of their conditions'. Charles Rigby was proud of his wife: 'For at least ten years she has given every day and all the day to the tasks of visiting, organising, studying the cause of distress among her sisters ... her singleness of purpose undaunted by opposition, contempt, loss of friends, or anything else ... Because she thinks the mothers of this country ought to have a voice in its management ... prison is her reward.'[6]

When Parliament had opened on 12 February there was no mention of women's suffrage in the King's Speech. At Caxton Hall Annie Kenney moved the resolution:

> This meeting expresses its profound indignation at the omission from the King's Speech of any declaration that the Government intends to enfranchise the women of the country during the present session of Parliament, and calls upon the House of Commons to insist that precedence shall be given to a measure to remove from women the degrading disability of sex.[7]

Annie warned that if their demand was ignored she would take a thousand women cotton workers from the north of England to the House of Commons to 'voice their opinion there'. Mrs Pankhurst urged the audience to 'Rise up!' and 200 women stood and chorused, 'Now!' They left the building led by Charlotte Despard, and were escorted by police. As soon as they arrived at Abbey Green, opposite the Houses of Parliament, they faced a police cordon which would not let them pass. When the women refused to budge, mounted police charged but many of the women slipped through the cordon and some reached the door of St Stephen's Hall.

The *Daily Mirror* gave accounts of the suffragettes' encounter with the police over successive days. On 14 February it described the scene of 'desperate suffragette rioting'; 'screaming women belabour constables with umbrellas' and 'repeated assaults by hundreds of excited women on police'. At the doors of St Stephen's Hall mounted police prevented the women from entering the building: 'no sooner had the horses backed into the crowd than the women who had been scattered re-formed, and again and again charged the massive door ... Something like pandemonium ensued. The women began to fight like tigers, and they received and inflicted many bruises.' But the following day, after hearing evidence in Westminster Police Court, the tone changed and the *Daily Mirror* wrote of 'police brutality to women'; 'women were kicked and struck and even trampled under the horses' hooves'. The reporters suggested that 'the suffragettes are winning', and it emerged that the authorities were so nervous of suffragette incursions that women were to be banned from all areas of the Houses of Parliament unless they were accompanied by a Member of Parliament responsible for their good conduct.[8]

Charlotte Despard was one of fifty women and two men to be arrested that day. Most of the women were sentenced to two weeks in prison for 'disorderly conduct and interfering with the police in the execution of their duty'. Mrs Despard and Sylvia Pankhurst served three weeks in Holloway. (There was such pressure on the only women's prison in London that numerous suffragettes were sent to serve their time in Aylesbury Gaol.) Mrs Despard had not worn her mantilla, hoping not to be recognised as one of the 'ringleaders' of the WSPU. She led women from Caxton Hall to the House of Commons and the ensuing battle with the police lasted three hours, during which time thirty-four women were arrested. Mrs Despard was badly shaken when she was pushed by a horse. The time she served in prison left her with a burning desire, once they had the vote, to 'try to get our prison system reformed, which makes criminals of so many women'.[9]

Mrs Despard's brother, Sir John French, Inspector-General of the British Army, was asked by the *Daily Mirror* what he thought of his sister's behaviour. When asked if he intended to resign, Sir John said the idea was absurd: 'We have tried all we could to keep Mrs Despard from mixing up with these people ... if she will join in this foolish agitation she must expect to suffer.' He declared that her suffragette colleagues were 'all vain and some of them are a little mad. They get together and work themselves up into a state of bogus hunger for martyrdom ... It is only because they are women that the freaks of the suffragettes have been tolerated so long.' In his opinion the police had been 'far too lenient, this business ought not to have been allowed to go on as long'.[10]

Later that evening the women who had been released on the bail provided by Fred Pethick-Lawrence, and others who had not been arrested, attended a meeting in Caxton Hall. Moved by the accounts of the violent tussles, the women set off again to enter the House of Commons. Christabel urged the women not to be afraid of the police and to link arms. If they lost sight of their leaders they should become leaders themselves. When the suffragettes approached Parliament the police presence was even greater and they failed to get as close as they had that afternoon. The mounted police galloped into the procession which scattered, re-formed into groups of about a dozen, and tried to break through. This mini-riot lasted for an hour and twenty more women were arrested.[11]

Mrs Emma Sproson was arrested at Westminster Abbey and chose to go to prison rather than pay the fine of twenty shillings. She was thirty-nine years old, from Staffordshire and married to Frank Sproson, a postman. Emma's political education and public-speaking skills were honed at Sunday School and the church's debating society. When she attended a political meeting where Lord Curzon was speaking she asked him a question which he ignored because she was a woman: this was her political awakening.

Frank Sproson, the secretary of the Wolverhampton ILP, invited Emmeline Pankhurst to speak at a meeting in October 1906 and to stay at their home in Tettenhall. Emma chaired the meeting in October 1906 and joined the WSPU; she was captivated by Mrs Pankhurst's personality.

Frank wrote a proud letter to his wife in gaol: 'I was not surprised at your arrest and looked at the first morning paper I could lay my hands on and as I expected "Emma Sproson" amongst the arrested ... the children are all well, baby takes his food like a man, and with the exception of a slight irritation through cutting teeth is very well.'[12] After her release Emma was back in London in another suffragette demonstration in Westminster, arrested on 20 March and sentenced to a month in Holloway, where she was visited by Christabel Pankhurst.[13]

Christabel and Sylvia Pankhurst were among the arrested women and next day in court they found themselves the centre of attention – their favourite place. Christabel blamed the government for the women's injuries and warned the magistrate, Mr Curtis Bennett, that 'more will happen if we do not get justice'. Most of the fifty women who were sent to prison served two weeks in the first division, recognition at last that they were regarded as political prisoners rather than common criminals. Some women had their fines paid by their relatives, against their wishes, and were released after a few days. Suffragette prisoners managed to communicate with each other, including tapping Morse code on the water pipes that ran through their cells. To keep their spirits up they broke into song and 'the chorus ran through the cells'.[14]

The suffragists' 'Mud March' and the suffragettes' Women's Parliament yielded results: Mr W. H. Dickinson, Liberal MP for St Pancras North since 1906, and a supporter of Mrs Fawcett, put forward a Women's Enfranchisement Bill which would be debated on 8 March. In Mr Dickinson's opinion when women had the vote 'you open the political paths to women, and this will conduce many social reforms which men have been backward in carrying'.[15]

When they were released there was a 'Welcome Breakfast' at Eustace Miles' vegetarian restaurant in the Charing Cross Road. First, two brass bands played at Holloway Gaol. Three hundred women at the breakfast heard 'burning speeches' and the defiant promise of 'more trouble to come'. Christabel called the WSPU's Women's Parliament and the ensuing protest the 'twentieth century Peterloo'.[16] Christabel summed up the Liberal Cabinet: 'These men are as wily as serpents, and we must be wilier.'[17]

Edith Rigby spoke next, said she was pleased she had been to prison, and had told the prison chaplain how 'proud and glad' she was to be there. 'Prison is a grimy, serious institution, a new experience for many of us who have never known cold and hunger. It's good for us all to experience conditions which are quite beyond many people's social horizon.' Before returning to Preston, Edith spent a few days in Reading where she met by chance nineteen-year-old Charlotte Marsh, known as Charlie, who was training to become a sanitary inspector. Meeting Edith inspired Charlie to join the WSPU. As soon as she finished her course in 1909 she became a suffragette poster girl, dressing in armour as Joan of Arc and leading processions on a white horse.

Annie Kenney went to Preston a week later, in March, where she and Edith Rigby held a WSPU meeting at the Assembly Rooms to raise awareness of Mr Dickinson's Bill. One of the women present remembered Edith as 'almost shy and yet she was firm and sincere'.[18] Annie was a more seasoned performer; her Lancashire accent went down well, she was 'full of punch and pith' and her 'salty sense of humour' soon had the audience laughing. Annie said that if something was not done soon 'we'll see lads of twenty-one making laws for their own mothers!'[19]

While the suffragettes were serving their time in Holloway, the WSPU had dispatched English suffragettes to bolster the efforts of Scottish members to lobby against the Liberals at the South Aberdeen by-election on 20 February. By 1902 the women's suffrage movement was active in the West of Scotland, and in 1906 a branch of the WSPU was opened in Glasgow. Helen Fraser and Adela Pankhurst were sent to Aberdeen. Helen, the WSPU's first Scottish salaried organiser, rented office space in Union Street. Their propaganda told Aberdonians what women had recently endured in London. 'The doings outside the Houses of Parliament last night make painful reading ... the demonstrators WERE CRUSHED BY THE MOUNTED POLICE AGAINST THE RAILINGS OF THE ABBEY, AND TRAMPLED UNDER THEIR HORSES' HOOFS ... Electors of South Aberdeen – force this matter to an issue, and end this women's struggle for freedom by refusing to support the nominee of the Liberal Party.'[20]

An unpopular Liberal candidate, and the participation of the Independent Labour Party, combined with suffragette publicity to slash the Liberal majority from 4,000 to 400, a serious blow to the Scottish Liberals who regarded Aberdeen as their heartland. The local press were quite well disposed to the suffragette activity. The *Aberdeen Free Press* reported that the campaign 'showed that the movement is led by women of culture, high character, and intense moral earnestness'.[21] Buoyed by the success of their campaign, a WSPU branch was opened in Aberdeen by Caroline Phillips, a journalist on the *Aberdeen Daily Journal*. Caroline was delighted with her new members: 'Votes and politics are lively interesting subjects – not the dry dreary affairs that some of the older women ... make them.' The calibre of the new members was high: they were 'bright young accomplished people'.[22]

Annie Fraser, and a friend, Maggie Moffat, both actresses, were the first Scottish women to be arrested on a suffragette demonstration. They had travelled to London from Glasgow for the recent Women's Parliament and served two weeks in Holloway. Maggie's husband, Graham Moffat, the Scottish actor and playwright best known for his play *Bunty Pulls the Strings*, was a keen supporter of women's suffrage and responded to his wife's protest by founding the Glasgow Men's League for Women's Suffrage. A friend with whom Maggie and Annie stayed in London wrote to her husband, 'your wife went off to court this morning as smiling and as happy as if she had been going for a summer holiday. You have every reason to be proud of her.' When the magistrate told Annie Fraser she had been obstructing the police she replied, 'On the contrary they were obstructing me.'[23]

Mr Dickinson's Bill was read for the second time on 8 March 1907. Emmeline and Christabel Pankhurst went to the offices of the *Daily Mirror* to read the tickertape as the news came in. The bill was 'talked out' by the Liberal MP for Montgomery, John David Rees. If they had been allowed in the Ladies' Gallery they would have heard 'an extraordinary hurricane of cheers and counter cheers greeting the Speaker's decision'.[24] Despite writing to suffragists in Dunfermline promising to support the Bill, Henry Campbell-Bannerman told the House he was not 'very warmly enamoured of the bill because it would only enfranchise a small number of well-to-do women'.[25]

Two days before the second Women's Parliament of 1907 Annie Kenney and Emmeline Pankhurst made a flying visit to Hexham to support WSPU members canvassing against the election of Liberal Richard Holt. He won the by-election but his majority was slim, just over a thousand votes.[26]

At the Women's Parliament in Caxton Hall on 20 March, Lady Harberton, the pioneer of the divided skirt known as 'the Harberton', and President of the Rational Dress Society, offered to lead the WSPU procession to present a petition to Parliament. Christabel urged the women to 'rush the house and if possible seize the Mace and you will be the Cromwells of the twentieth century'.[27]

Florence Pomeroy, Viscountess Harberton, was in her sixties and a supporter of many forward-thinking causes. Campaigning for women's suffrage was a logical step for an individual who believed that womens' clothing was an instrument of their oppression.[28] Lady

Harberton and her deputation were forced back by the police and blocked by more than 500 policemen in Parliament Square. Despite hours of pushing and shoving they got nowhere near the entrance of the House of Commons. Wave after wave of women streamed out of Caxton Hall and many were arrested after 'a series of exciting scrimmages'[29] with the police.

Annie Kenney and Adela Pankhurst's contingent of 300 mill girls wearing clogs and shawls, initially mistaken for sightseers, managed to reach the Strangers' Entrance but failed to get any further. The 'Mill Girl Amazons' were most 'obstreperous' when they were arrested, 'struggling almost manfully with the police' even though they were hindered by their clogs slipping on the pavement.[30] By the end of the day seventy-four women and Alfred Orage, a friend of Mary Gawthorpe, had been arrested. Charged with disorderly conduct the protesters were sentenced to between two and four weeks in prison.

Dora Thewlis's arrest by two burly policemen, each grabbing one of her arms, made the front page of the *Daily Mirror* on the morning of 21 March. Known as 'the Baby Suffragette', Dora told the arresting officers that she would 'not go back to her mother until she had been in Holloway'.[31] Dora was sixteen, lived in Huddersfield and earned less than a pound a week as a weaver in a woollen mill. She had been encouraged to come to London by her mother Eliza, a socialist with suffragette sympathies. Eliza was proud that Dora had been sent to prison for two weeks for the Cause. When she was interviewed by the *Huddersfield Weekly Examiner* she claimed credit for her daughter's political journey: 'We have brought her up in Socialistic and progressive beliefs.' Eliza told the reporter that from the age of seven Dora had read the newspapers avidly and could 'hold her own' in political debates. They had been the first people in Huddersfield to help Mrs Pankhurst at the by-election. Dora served only half her sentence.[32]

On being released, Dora was smuggled into a taxi by a prison wardress and taken to King's Cross station, where Edith How-Martyn was able to snatch a few words with her while the wardress was buying the tickets. When the train began to move off, she pushed her guard to one side and, reaching the window, snatched a kiss from Mrs How-Martyn and waved goodbye.

Magistrate Horace Smith wrote to the Thewlises admonishing them for allowing their daughter to come to London. This prompted the following reply from James and Eliza Thewlis in the *Daily Mirror* and the *Huddersfield Weekly Examiner*: 'Dora journeyed to London with our consent and approval ... it is not our intention to bring a discredit to our daughter's actions by accepting the advice you tendered in your communication.'[33]

Ada Wright served two weeks in Holloway for her involvement. In the earliest days of the WSPU she drew out her savings of £12 and sent the money to Mrs Pankhurst at 62 Nelson Street. Bowled over by Annie Kenney and Christabel Pankhurst's protest at the Free Trade Hall, she gave up her long involvement with the NUWSS, for being 'ineffective for making the question of justice to women a living force', and threw herself into supporting the new militants. Ada was born in 1861 into a middle-class family and from a young age she had noticed the injustice of society towards women and 'for that reason I wished I had been born a boy'. While in Holloway she made up her mind to devote all her time to the WSPU, and volunteered for pavement chalking, unpaid clerical work at Clement's Inn and campaigning at by-elections.[34]

Patricia Woodlock came from Liverpool to take part with Lancashire women in the second Women's Parliament, and was sent to prison for a month for her protest in Parliament Square. A founder member of the Liverpool WSPU in 1906, this was Woodlock's third offence. When released she was described as a diehard, along with Emma Sproson and Aeta Lamb, who had been 'the most unruly and turbulent of spirits'.[35] Patricia Woodlock's father was a socialist and supported her suffragette escapades.[36]

Marguerite Sidley was sentenced to twelve days in prison. Marguerite was twenty years old when she started to take an interest in the militant movement; she was a shorthand typist for a firm of electrical engineers in London. The office of thirteen girls had buzzed with talk of the arrest of the eleven women in the Lobby of the House of Commons in October 1906. 'Much of the discussion – great condemnation by the other girls made me at once defend the suffragettes although admitting I knew nothing about the movement.'[37] In January Marguerite and her mother Lilian heard Emmeline and Christabel Pankhurst, Annie Kenney and Mary Gawthorpe speak at the Philharmonic Hall in Great Portland Street and joined the WSPU on the spot. Marguerite was not well enough to go to the second

Women's Parliament but worked unpaid at Clement's Inn. Her courage on 20 March and her refusal to pay the fine, electing to go to prison instead, and the fact that she had used up all her savings, were rewarded with the offer of a salaried position as a shorthand typist and chief clerk.

Years later Marguerite remembered: 'The prison doctor tried to frighten me into being bound over by saying I was going into consumption (which my own doctor feared). I replied, "If I'm ill you can put me in the infirmary – if I'm not you can leave me where I am."' The lack of air in her cell caused her to faint several times. When she was released her mother took her to Eastbourne to recover. Marguerite grew up in a home with progressive views, among them vegetarianism and theosophy.[38]

*

At the end of March 1907 the Pethick-Lawrences took Christabel Pankhurst, Annie Kenney and Mary Gawthorpe on holiday to Bordighera in Italy. They found themselves travelling on the same train from Paris as Henry Campbell-Bannerman. Annie spotted him in the dining-car: 'My heart bumped and I wondered what Christabel would expect of me. A look was enough: it meant "Do nothing".'[39] They sat at the table next to him and waited for him to finish his tea before telling him how glad they were to see him, and that although he did not know them they had been to his meetings. He invited them to join him. When he learned their names he told them he was very tired and was going away for a rest and hoped 'we would make no fuss'. Annie and Mary agreed not to but said they were troubled by his 'placid attitude' to women's suffrage. He replied, blaming his Cabinet colleagues for being against women having the vote.[40]

A by-election in Stepney announced for 10 May was the ideal opportunity for the Canning Town members to canvass against the Liberal-Labour candidate, Ben Cooper, a working-class Progressive member of the London County Council for Bow and Bromley who was hoping to win the seat from the Conservative and Unionist candidate.

Three weeks before polling day Flora Drummond spoke to Canning Town women and reminded them how much they all had in common. Flora herself had been poor and had worked long hours as a mantle maker. She spoke from the heart, condemning the 'terrible strain women had to endure through being crushed by man-made laws'. The events of this and other meetings are reported in the minute book of the WSPU's Canning Town branch, a precious record of the working-class suffragettes who campaigned for the vote. The book notes the resolutions they debated, gives the tiny sums the seamstresses, factory workers and charladies could afford to give – sometimes as little as a shilling from forty members present – and the words of women like Flora Drummond who urged them to do more.[41]

The WSPU's handbills for the Stepney by-election reported that more than 150 women had been to prison and that recently the Liberal government had sent out the mounted police 'to ride down the women who came to the House of Commons to demand their rights'.[42]

When Christabel addressed a meeting at Stepney Green on 2 May 1907, the mood was hostile: she and the other speakers were 'subjected to a running fire of interruption and at the end of the meeting the lorry on which they stood was seized by a number of young men'. The police intervened to end the 'disorderly scenes'.[43] The WSPU arranged dinner-hour meetings outside factory gates, and nightly gatherings drew large crowds. Enthusiasm for the militant women's message was now growing in Stepney.[44] Five suffragettes with 'Votes for Women' notices pinned on their dresses barged into Ben Cooper's campaign headquarters and 'flung down a bundle of suffragette literature'. The WSPU was delighted with the result: Ben Cooper lost by a thousand votes. Minnie Baldock and the Canning Town women recruited sixty women from Stepney and a new branch was started there.[45]

Jessie Stephenson, whose father was a gentleman farmer in Lincolnshire, worked with Mrs Pankhurst, Nellie Martel and Mary Gawthorpe at the Jarrow by-election at the end of June 1907, during her annual holiday. Her parents were at first distressed when their thirty-four-year-old daughter joined the WSPU, and then shocked when she became an active suffragette. She was torn: 'their discomfiture in the matter was the one abiding sore to me in all these proceedings.'[46] When Jessie explained this to Mrs Pethick-Lawrence, Emmeline explained that the price of sticking to her own ambitions was part of the sacrifice women were making to get the vote and promised to keep Jessie's name out of the press.

Jessie cycled around Jarrow and the outlying villages with a sign across her handlebars that read 'Keep the Liberal Out' and tried to engage people in conversation with an almost missionary zeal, but with dispiriting results. A clergyman's sister threw Jessie out of the rectory when she saw her 'Votes for Women' sign, and when she barged into a classroom to announce where Mrs Pankhurst was speaking that evening, the schoolmaster escorted her off the premises. She tried to ignore 'some extremely abusive and unpleasant things the master was pouring forth upon my innocent head'.[47]

Jessie worked closely with Mary Gawthorpe and 'loved her the first moment I looked into her laughing brown eyes ... she was very understanding'.[48] Mary gave the young recruit a masterclass in how to get up a meeting outside factory gates. Sending Jessie to borrow a chair from a local pub, Mary would start talking and Jessie would watch, encouraging people to listen. The men would stop at the 'unusual sight of a very nice woman' and Mary would urge them to vote against the Liberal candidate in Jarrow, Spencer Hughes, an engineer and journalist. There was also a desire to see the Labour candidate Peter Curran defeated: in January the Labour Party had rejected the women's suffrage Bill, which had almost pushed Keir Hardie into resigning from the very party he had created.[49] When Jessie returned to work in London before polling day she was greeted with disdain by her barrister boss: 'So you're one of the shrieking sisterhood.'[50] Jarrow was narrowly won by Peter Curran by less than 800 votes.[51],[52]

Jessie did not have a high opinion of the women's suffrage campaign led by Mrs Fawcett: 'It seemed to me a mushy old institution, dry as bones which held an annual meeting attended by a number of faint-hearted, very proper "Rights of Women" members.'[53]

She joined the WSPU in the autumn of 1906 after hearing Annie Kenney, Emmeline Pethick-Lawrence and Mrs Pankhurst and Christabel speak in London. The Pankhursts 'both looked so young and fresh, I could not tell which was the elder ... I was sitting in a crowded room of women, with feeling running high and it was as if one big heart was beating. My own was simply bursting.' Kenney, the Pankhursts and Gawthorpe 'stood there as firm as rocks, fearless as heroes'. Volunteers and donations were called for and Jessie sent her name up to the platform and pledged her

£50. When her name and donation were read out she felt she had 'severed a limb and sent it up to the platform'. The meeting collected £700 and Mrs Pethick-Lawrence doubled that amount with a personal donation. When the meeting ended Jessie was personally thanked by Christabel who asked her to 'go round and talk to them. I was a militant suffragette.'[54]

In June 1907 Mrs Louise Eates asked Minnie Baldock to speak at a drawing-room meeting in Knightsbridge, explaining that the hostess was 'anxious to put before her friends the case for women's suffrage as it is seen by Working Women ... She is anxious to have a *real* working woman to speak so I thought you could bring Mrs Sbarborough with you.' Minnie made an impression and was paid one shilling and sixpence for her expenses, and received 'many nice compliments'. In August Minnie spoke in Kensington with Mrs Pankhurst, 'to make the rich and idle women realise the difficulties that drive poor women to demand the vote'.[55]

An appeal to raise £20,000 by an annual subscription scheme of a pound a year was set in motion in July by Christabel Pankhurst, who wrote to the secretaries and treasurers of seventy branches: 'Apart from the means it will put into our hands of extending and developing this movement upon national lines, the raising of such a sum as this would be the greatest argument ... that women want the vote and are absolutely in earnest about it. It is an argument that politicians and the businessman will understand better than any other.'[56]

Rachel Barrett, a maths and science teacher at Penarth in Wales, got into trouble with her headmistress because of her suffragette activities. Rachel had been flour-bombed while helping Adela Pankhurst address a meeting at Cardiff docks. Reading the newspaper accounts of the suffragettes in 1906 Rachel, thirty-two years old, felt 'that they were doing the right and only thing. I had always been a suffragist – since I first began to think of the position of women at all, but with no hope of ever seeing women win the vote.' Rachel heard Nellie Martel speak in Cardiff and joined the WSPU at the end of the meeting.[57]

Rachel had abandoned her teaching career and was studying at the London School of Economics near the WSPU offices in Clement's Inn. She helped Adela Pankhurst at Bradford and Bury St Edmunds in August with Mrs Pankhurst, Nellie Martel and Aeta Lamb. During the college Christmas vacation Rachel worked to keep the Liberal candidate out at the Mid-Devon by-election and Christabel offered her a position as a paid organiser. Plans for an academic career were shelved: 'I was sorry to give up my work at the LSE, and all that it meant, but it was a definite call and I obeyed.'[58]

Within a year of the Pankhursts moving the WSPU to London, personal differences were starting to emerge. In September 1907 the way decisions were made caused the WSPU to divide into two different camps, in what became known as 'the Split'. Potential flash points had always been there: Teresa Billington-Greig (she married Frederick Greig in February 1907), Charlotte Despard and Edith How-Martyn preferred a democratic approach to policy-making, where decisions were agreed in committee as in the Independent Labour Party, but this was not Emmeline and Christabel Pankhurst's way.

Despard, Billington-Greig and How-Martyn suggested to the Pankhursts and the Pethick-Lawrences, and the committee of Annie Kenney, Mabel Tuke, Nellie Martel and Mary Gawthorpe, that WSPU policy should be decided by delegates at an annual conference and that the executive committee should be elected by the membership. Emmeline Pankhurst was astonished by the suggestion. The notion of diverting attention from the Cause to debates on a constitution, a conference and committees struck her as 'incongruous'. She was furious and cancelled the proposed annual meeting and threatened to tear up the constitution they had been using since 1903.[59]

Emmeline and Christabel's behaviour was undemocratic, and at odds with their roots, but bitter experience of the 'wiliness' of the 'serpents' – politicians – had hardened Christabel, who was impatient with the wide-eyed trust of some of the new members. Emmeline Pethick-Lawrence remembered: 'Newcomers were pouring into the Union. Many of them madly enthusiastic but ill-informed about the realities of the current state of affairs.' Christabel reasoned that the WSPU must not be sidetracked by a procedural debate and needed to respond very swiftly to political developments. She dreaded the time that committees would take to make decisions, and would not 'trust her mental offspring [the campaign for the vote] to the mercies of politically untrained minds'.[60]

Emmeline and Christabel Pankhurst believed that as leaders they had a responsibility to the women who would make sacrifices in

taking up militancy. They argued that the members had the right to
expect 'complete unity within the ranks'. The harsh price to be paid
for discipline would be a parting of the ways: some of those who had
been a part of the struggle from the earliest days would have to leave
if they disagreed with Mrs Pankhurst and Christabel.

Charlotte Despard dared to suggest that ignoring their constitution would 'outrage democratic principles', to which Mrs Pankhurst
replied that she was in sole control of the Union. Emmeline Pethick-
Lawrence summed up the dispute: 'these two notable women presented a great contrast, the one (Emmeline Pankhurst) aflame with
a single idea that had taken complete possession of her, the other
(Charlotte Despard) upheld by a principle that had actuated a long life
spent in the service of the people.'[61] The executive committee agreed
with Mrs Pankhurst and Christabel and there was nothing else for
Despard, Billington-Greig and How-Martyn to do but to resign.[62]

On 14 September 'the Split' was front-page news in the *Daily
Mirror*, with a photograph of Mrs Despard who had 'just seceded'
from the WSPU. A letter, probably written by Christabel and Fred
Pethick-Lawrence, was sent from Clement's Inn to the network of
organisers and members all over the country:

> We are not playing with experiments with representative Govern-
> ment ... We are a militant movement and we have to get the vote
> next session. The leaders of this movement are practical politicians;
> they have set out to do the almost impossible task – of creating an
> independent political party of women. They are fighting the strong-
> est Government of modern times and the strongest prejudice in
> human nature ... It is after all a voluntary militant movement; those
> who cannot follow the general must drop out of the ranks.[63]

Teresa Billington-Greig had long been a thorn in the Pankhursts' side.
Christabel was referring to Billington-Greig when she wrote, 'We have
against us others whose motives are less pure. They are disappointed
place-seekers and those who have thought that they were more capable of filling certain posts than those who have been selected.' Mrs
Pankhurst would not respond to any statements in the press made by
'the seceders' and reasoned that 'the sooner the incident is closed the
better it will be for the women's cause'.[64]

Despard, Billington-Greig and How-Martyn went on to found the militant Women's Freedom League (WFL), but this was not as militant as the suffragettes and was democratically run. (In 1912 Mrs Despard would be removed as president by members tired of her increasingly autocratic ways.) The three of them took the WFL's most senior positions of secretary, treasurer and organising secretary. The headquarters were off the Strand, and the WFL devised their own eye-catching publicity stunts, some of which landed them in prison. In the same way that NUWSS members supported some of the WSPU's less confrontational events, some members of the WFL also joined the WSPU in actions in the following years.

Annie Kenney had an unshakeable trust in the direction that Mrs Pankhurst and Christabel were taking. She remembered Christabel being irritated by decisions being made by committee: 'It was a stumbling block to her swift brain, so like all autocrats she swept it away. It was keeping her back from swift action. No general on a battlefield would have tolerated interference with sweeping tactics, and why should she?'[65] Altogether about seventy women left the WSPU to join the new WFL.

In the first week of October 1907 the WSPU took the bold step of publishing their own newspaper. The editorial of the first issue of *Votes for Women* was titled 'The Battle Cry'. Suffragettes were crusaders for women's freedom, and religious and military rhetoric would be a constant thread in their propaganda. Joan of Arc, who was beatified in 1909 and canonised in 1920, was their patron saint and suffragettes often led processions dressed in medieval-style armour and riding a white horse. Christabel's leading article created the militant template:

To women, far and wide the trumpet call goes forth. Come fight with us in our battle for freedom ... This is a battle in which all must take part; they must come ready for active endeavour and for strenuous service ... Do not leave any of your womanliness behind when you come into this movement. It is womanliness that we look for in those that fight in our ranks ... This is no anti-man crusade ... If you have any class feeling you must leave that behind for the women in our movement know no barriers of class or distinction. If you are tied to any man's political party you must break that tie for in this movement women are pledged to independence of all political parties till the vote is won ... The founder and leaders of the movement must lead, the non-commissioned officers must carry out their instructions, the rank and file must loyally share the burden of the fight. For there is no compulsion to come into our ranks, but those who come must come as soldiers ready to march onwards in battle array.[66]

Votes for Women was published first as a monthly, and then, from April 1908, as a weekly. On the first cover was 'The Haunted House', an image showing a seated woman hovering over the Houses of Parliament like a predatory spectre. Edited and funded by Fred and Emmeline Pethick-Lawrence, it was dedicated to 'the brave women who today are fighting for freedoms ... to all women all over the world, of whatever race, or creed or calling, whether they be with us or against us in this fight, we dedicate this paper'.[67] The militant campaign was organised in the pages of the newspaper, there was discussion of parliamentary legislation that adversely affected women and a sense of international sisterly solidarity was encouraged by their regular feature 'Women In Other Lands', reporting on feminism and women's suffrage around the world.

Fred Pethick-Lawrence remembered his wife working flat out at fundraising, writing articles and pamphleteering: 'I had to make an appointment even with my own wife if I wished to discuss anything of the movement with her.'[68]

Despite declaring that the WSPU was a non-political party organisation, behind the scenes Christabel Pankhurst was trying to outmanoeuvre the Liberal and Labour parties by wooing Arthur Balfour, the leader of the Conservative Party. Correspondence between the two might support the view that she was always of the conservative persuasion (she was not) and that she was turning her back on working-class women, but this would be to underestimate her shrewd political mind. Christabel was keener to inflict damage on the Liberals than to seriously believe that Mr Balfour would overturn his party's attachment to maintaining the status quo, and to give women the vote. She hoped that following recent by-elections in which Liberals were not re-elected, and in others where their majorities were greatly reduced, there was a possibility that the Conservatives would return to power, and that might force the Liberals into action.

On 6 October Christabel wrote to Arthur Balfour asking him to receive a WSPU deputation when he visited Birmingham the following month. 'They want to ask you whether, when you are next in office, you will extend the parliamentary franchise to women ... the time must come for you as leader of the party to declare your intention in regard to this matter.'[69] Christabel confided in Balfour that a large number of Mrs Fawcett's suffragists intended supporting Labour candidates at by-elections. She said that the women who had recently left the WSPU (Despard et al.) were also likely to support the Labour Party. Christabel suggested she was not anti-Labour but that she had no confidence that they would 'take effective action' with regard to votes for women.

On 23 October Mr Balfour replied courteously and at length, but he set out his familiar objections. He preferred to maintain the status quo as 'the existing electoral arrangements seem to work fairly well'; he was not convinced that the majority of women actually wanted the vote; if it had to happen then women's suffrage should be part of a bigger Reform Bill that granted the vote to men who were still unenfranchised, rather than making a special case for female suffrage. Balfour would not receive a WSPU deputation, using the excuse that 'they have filled up every available moment' in his itinerary. Determined to have the last word Christabel pleaded, 'If only you would say what you would regard as proof that demand exists! I know that we can fulfil any condition that you may lay down, but at present we are working in the dark.' Christabel's attempted seduction of Balfour had failed.[70]

In October 1907, Annie Kenney was dispatched to Bristol to organise the suffragette campaign in the West of England. She had been given precise instructions: 'I was expected to hold meetings, to canvass and to hold small "At Homes", raise the money, book the halls, draw up and distribute handbills, cut the bread and butter on the "At Home" day, make the tea, and pray that a few people would at least eat up what I had bought.' She would make the speech, appeal for new members, take the names of sympathisers and go round with a collecting plate. There were stalking duties: the suffragettes kept an eye on the press to see if a cabinet minister was due to visit, and were told to

> go and meet him at the station, follow him to his hotel, break up his meeting and see him off at his departure ... In the early days

I thought nothing of having a hard morning's work sending out
handbills, and chalking pavements, of speaking at a factory at twelve
o'clock, of speaking at the docks at half past one, of holding a woman's meeting at three o'clock and a large open-air one at seven, and
when it was over I would address envelopes for letters which I sent
out to the sympathisers or members in the district.

Annie Kenney described herself as a 'fanatic'.[71]

Hospitality was afforded by the Blathwayt family of Eagle House,
Batheaston, on the outskirts of Bath. Colonel and Mrs Blathwayt
opened their home to Annie and many suffragette speakers who
came to stay for rest and recuperation after prison, including hunger strikers. Colonel Linley Blathwayt, aged sixty-seven, a lifelong
Liberal who had served in the Indian Army, had become a supporter
of women's suffrage when his daughter Mary asked if her new suffragette friends could come to stay.

Bespectacled and earnest, Mary Blathwayt lived at home looking
after her chickens and studying insects, a passion she shared with
her father. She joined a local rifle club, but otherwise it was a dull
life until she joined the WSPU in July 1906, and then the NUWSS
in May 1907. In November Mary went with her friends Grace and
Aethel Tollemache, and the Blathwayts' parlourmaid, Ellen Morgan,
to Annie Kenney's meeting at the Victoria Rooms in Clifton, where
they met Emmeline Pethick-Lawrence and Christabel Pankhurst.
'The meeting began at 8 and lasted till about 10pm ... The room was
well-filled. But not overcrowded. After Annie [who was the last to
speak] had done speaking some young men at the back of the room
began to fight, and some other men turned them out.'[72]

Starstruck by the three eloquent women, Mary Blathwayt's life
took on a new direction. She handed out WSPU leaflets and posted
pamphlets through letter boxes and gave them out at factory gates to
women as they left work, but she did not abandon the NUWSS and
was elected onto Bath's executive committee. Suffragism, both moderate and militant, had taken over her life. Colonel Blathwayt even
designed an arboretum which was planted with trees by suffragette
ex-prisoners who came to stay. In 1904 the Blathwayts were the first
people in their village to own a motor car which they loaned to Annie
Kenney and her colleagues.[73]

At the end of November Minnie Baldock and her friends from Canning Town interrupted a meeting at Millwall School, on the Isle of Dogs. The speaker was Sydney Buxton, the local Liberal MP, who was the Postmaster General. Any likely looking suffragettes were banned from the meeting but Minnie managed to get a ticket for a front-row seat. As soon as she rose to speak, she was grabbed by stewards and hustled outside. Undeterred, she found a chair and stood on it under an open window of the meeting room, shouting 'Votes for women.'[74]

Some of the Canning Town WSPU women felt that Teresa Billington-Greig, who had spoken to the branch on many occasions, had been forced out of the WSPU, and were upset at Christabel's apparent abandonment of the democratic constitution – most of them had been members of the Independent Labour Party before they became suffragettes and Canning Town meetings ended with a rendition of 'The Red Flag'. On 3 December only fifteen women attended and the smallest collection in the history of the WSPU was recorded – threepence ha'penny. The women voiced their 'dissatisfaction' at how few speakers had visited the branch, and 'proposed to send a letter to Mrs Baldock to know why the Canning Town branch was neglected'. The minute-book entries end on 10 December 1907 and no other information about this pioneering branch survives.[75]

During December Emmeline Pankhurst and Nellie Martel were a provocative presence at the by-election for the Mid-Devon seat at Newton Abbot. The constituency had been Liberal since 1885 and the suffragettes had been warned it could be 'rough and boisterous ... its devotion, blind and unreasoning to the Liberal party'.[76] Emmeline, Nellie, Rachel Barrett, Aeta Lamb and Nellie Crocker found some of their meetings were 'turbulent'. Both Emmeline and Nellie were used to 'lively' meetings, but one night 'some young roughs dragged our lorry round and round until it seemed that we must be upset, and ... the language hurled at us was quite unfit for me to repeat'.[77] When the result of the by-election was announced and the Liberal seat was lost to the Conservatives, the suffragettes were blamed for splitting the vote.

On the way back to their lodgings Emmeline and Nellie were confronted by a gang of clay workers armed with clay cutters who were 'mad with rage and humiliation'. The women were attacked with 'showers of clay and rotten eggs'. Mrs Pankhurst says they

were not frightened, but 'the eggs were unbearable' and they escaped
into a grocer's shop. The windows were smashed and the grocer,
terrified his shop might be destroyed, ushered the suffragettes out
the back, but when they emerged 'the rowdies were waiting for us'.
They grabbed Nellie and 'beat her over the head with their fists'
and Emmeline and the grocer's wife tried to get Nellie back into the
shop, but Emmeline was hit on the back of the head and thrown to
the ground. Emmeline noticed a rain barrel nearby and feared she
would get a dunking, but the police arrived and 'the mob turned
tail and fled'. Her ankle was badly hurt and she hobbled for weeks.
The police stood guard until a motor car could be found to take the
women to Teignmouth.[78]

Christmas 1907 saw the first example of suffragette merchandise, a card game costing a shilling called 'Suffragette' which had
been devised by the Kensington branch of the WSPU. 'It is a novel
form of propaganda, but let it not be thought there is no fun in it.'
The names of the four sets are very suggestive: Piecrust Principles,
The Career of the Suffragettes, Broken Promises, The Sensational
Press.[79]

Clement's Inn closed for a short Christmas break and the Pethick-
Lawrences took Annie Kenney on holiday to Switzerland. The mill
girl who had never been abroad before made her third visit to Europe
in a year.

4

Purple, White and Green

Suffragette Spectacle 1908

Patricia Woodlock (left), thirty, of Liverpool, and Mabel Capper, twenty, of Manchester, advertise a 'monster meeting' in Heaton Park, Manchester, in 1908.

On the morning of 17 January 1908, Edith New, a schoolteacher, and Olivia Smith, a nurse, arrived in Downing Street. Under their coats they were wearing steel chains round their waists. They padlocked themselves to the railings outside Number 10, shouting 'Votes for women!' loud enough for the cabinet ministers inside to hear them. Sylvia Pankhurst said: 'Chains symbolically express the political bondage of womanhood, and for the practical reason that this device would prevent the women being dragged away'.[1] Policemen tried to destroy the padlocks. 'Considerable force was used before the chains could be broken.'[2] When Herbert Asquith, chancellor of the exchequer, arrived, more suffragettes tried to surround him but he was protected by a circle of policemen.

Two taxi cabs then pulled up, one of them carrying Flora Drummond and Elizabeth McArthur, and during the ensuing chaos the two women slipped into Number 10. Mrs Drummond knew 'the secret of the little knob' in the door, and pushed it. Miss Mary Garth, 'a frail, pale-complexioned girl', followed them. The women nearly reached the Cabinet Room where they intended to ask Sir Henry Campbell-Bannerman and the Cabinet if women's suffrage was to be included in the King's Speech at the opening of Parliament, but all three were grabbed by the porter and policemen and thrown out of the building. One of the suffragettes outside was knocked down in the mêlée. Flora Drummond was 'very violent' and 'tripped up a gentleman and he would have fallen had he not seized the rails'.[3] The suffragettes refused to leave Downing Street and five were arrested and taken to Canon Row police station. That afternoon their cases were heard by the chief magistrate, Sir Albert de Rutzen. Flora Drummond, Elizabeth McArthur, Edith New, Olivia Smith and Frances Thompson were sentenced to three weeks in the second division in Holloway Gaol. The next day a photograph of Flora Drummond, dwarfed by five burly policemen, appeared on the front page of the *Daily Mirror.* Olivia Smith told the court she had refused to unchain herself from the railings because 'I do not see why I should not chain myself up on a man's fence if I like. I did not hurt the fence, I did not hurt anybody ... it is my right to exert my individuality and accept my three weeks' imprisonment.'⁴ Edith New had already served two weeks in Holloway for her part in the protest at the House of Commons on 8 March 1907. Born in Swindon in 1877 and a member of the WSPU since 1906, Edith was a paid organiser. Before her suffragette days she had been a schoolteacher in Greenwich.⁵

In January 1908 the Leicester branch of the WSPU was set up by Mrs Alice Hawkins who spent two weeks in Holloway after being arrested in skirmishes with the police in Westminster in February 1907. Alice Riley, who worked in the boot and shoe industry before and after her marriage to Alfred Hawkins, was born in Stafford in 1863. In 1886 Alice went to work at Equity Shoes, a cooperative, where workers were encouraged to participate in political organisations.

Alice's husband, Alfred Hawkins, a shoe clicker – he cut the uppers from the leather – was born in 1857. The couple married in 1884, had six children and were long-standing political activists; they joined the Independent Labour Party in 1892, and met the Pankhursts in the mid-1890s. In 1896 Alice joined Equity Shoes' branch of the Women's Cooperative Guild, and was active in the Boot and Shoe Trade Union. In 1906, because of its failure to promote women's suffrage, Alice fell out with the ILP. Her husband looked after the children when Alice went to London to attend the Women's Parliament on 14 February 1907. One day in the exercise yard at Holloway Alice saw women with babies: 'The thought that a young life born into the world should have to spend its first months of life in prison. It was one more injustice to add to our cry for the right to stop some of these horrible things being allowed.'⁶ The Hawkinses invited Sylvia Pankhurst to Leicester and introduced her to the workers at the Equity Shoes factory. Sylvia spent the summer of 1907 with the Hawkins family, drawing and painting and writing about the women in the town's boot and shoe trade as they worked.⁷

In the January issue of *Votes for Women* the Pethick-Lawrences launched the campaign for 1908. They presented readers with stark choices:

> Are you going to play the woman or are you going to play the coward? Are you going to stand by and let others bear the brunt of battle? Are you going to say to yourself, 'I will be sympathetic; I will occasionally talk about it to my friends, perhaps I will give a little money, but I do not mean to risk my reputation or friendships or personal esteem by too prominently identifying myself with the cause of my sex' ... or are you made of sterner stuff than this? Are you going to come forward and say, I will be a battle comrade in the great fight; I will share the difficulties and the hardships; I will make the sacrifices that are required of me.

Fred and Emmeline urged: 'stand with us so that this year shall see the fulfilment of the promise for which women have worked so long.'[8]

During the first six weeks of 1908 Clement's Inn – which now employed twenty workers and had dozens of volunteers – made preparations for the three-day Women's Parliament at Caxton Hall, on 11–13 February. The WSPU's plan was to present a petition to the House of Commons on the first day by smuggling themselves into the building in two pantechnicons. The Trojan horse raid was the brainchild of Mrs Pankhurst's son, nineteen-year-old Harry, and twenty-one women almost succeeded.[9]

Clement's Inn hired two vans from a furniture remover. Inside each van were twenty-one suffragettes waiting to get out as soon as the vehicle reached its destination, St Stephen's Entrance, at four o'clock. Two artists, Marie and Georgina Brackenbury, were travelling in one van. Marie remembered: 'A great clattering of horses and a sense of jolting and rumbling which lasted for what seemed to us like an age. Suddenly the van stopped, and our hearts beat fast, and the doors swung open, and we saw the House of Commons before us and out we all flew.'[10] The suffragettes found themselves face to face with startled policemen: 'they had been warned to be ready for a suffragette attack ... but they had never suspected a ruse such as this.' The police stood to one side for the Members of Parliament who were approaching the building and the suffragettes darted forward and tried to get into

the House by joining the Members as they entered. The police seized
the women by 'the neck and threw us in the road. We picked ourselves up, and as smilingly as we could, came back to the doors [of the
House] only to be flung down again.'[11]

Next, hearing what had happened to the women in the pantechnicons, about fifty suffragettes, fired up by indignant speeches in
Caxton Hall, set off to the House of Commons, but found the roads
blocked by the police. Annie Kenney arrived in a cab looking distinctive in 'bright electric blue',[12] wisely having left her hat behind in
case she lost it. Christabel Pankhurst came too but was turned back as
the police recognised her. All the women arrested that day were bailed
by Fred Pethick-Lawrence and returned to Caxton Hall in the evening to report their experiences to a crowded, indignant meeting. The
meeting spilled out and 300 women set off to try to enter Parliament,
rebuffed by an enormous show of police strength. By the end of
the first day of the 1907 Women's Parliament fifty women had been
arrested and taken to Canon Row police station, forty-seven electing
to go to prison, with sentences of between four and eight weeks.

Edith Rigby, Beth Hesmondhalgh, Rose Towler and Grace
Alderman had travelled to London from Preston for the occasion.
Before they left Mrs Towler spent the week preparing enough food
to last her husband and four sons for two weeks in case she was sent
to prison. The four Preston women were in one of the furniture vans.
Edith Rigby led the charge towards St Stephen's Entrance, with Mrs
Towler, a schoolmistress, not far behind, 'brandishing their petitions
like a torch'.[13] Edith urged the women to push their way in but 'the
police rushed at them, driving them back into the crowd which pressed
towards them like an oncoming tide'.[14] They were 'tossed about as
though by the breakers of a stormy sea'.[15] Edith Rigby's wrists were
sprained and her thumbs bent back as she tried to fight past the police;
she was arrested and gaoled. Grace, Rose and Beth were also sentenced to a month in Holloway. Mrs Rigby wrote from prison: 'Do
not these things repay one thousandfold for the painful publicity and
personal suffering?'[16]

Twenty-three-year-old Grace Alderman, a machinist before her
marriage to a solicitor, was the chairwoman of Preston WSPU. She
found Edith Rigby to be 'dependable, straightforward and always
kind'.[17] When the meetings were held at the Rigbys' home at Winckley

Square, however, Edith was inflexible when it came to her husband Charlie's supper: 'At five minutes past nine promptly, no matter what stage the meeting might have progressed, Mrs Rigby would stand up and say, "Well, ladies, it's the doctor's supper time. I must go. You must stay on and finish what's to be done. Don't forget to close the door behind you! Good night and thank you." '[18]

The Brackenbury sisters, Marie and Georgina, and their widowed mother, Hilda, joined the WSPU in 1907. Roughed up as they tumbled out of a van on 11 February, the sisters were arrested and sent to Holloway Prison for six weeks. They were both members of the NUWSS and the WSPU, but chose to throw themselves into the militant organisation at the start of 1908. Their mother's upbringing and marriage to a general made her fearful of an organisation that challenged her notions of womanliness, but her daughters persuaded the seventy-six-year-old to put her anxieties to one side and she became an enthusiastic suffragette. Marie Brackenbury remembered: 'Night after night we wrestled over the new ideas and her soul was troubled. But she had always been a brave seeker after the truth, and one by one she gave up the old ways of thinking, and became fired with the just and true ideals of women.'[19]

Twenty-seven-year-old Elsa Gye, who had studied at the Guildhall School of Music, was in one of the pantechnicons and got six weeks in Holloway. In the summer of 1908 she returned to Nottingham with Minnie Baldock to build that town's branch of the WSPU. Elsa Gye got to know 'Daisy' Bullock from Long Eaton, Derbyshire, who worked in a lace factory. Elsa and Daisy met in December 1907 when Elsa was in Nottingham with Aeta Lamb to disrupt Herbert Asquith's meeting at the Mechanics' Institute. Despite the efforts of the Liberal stewards to keep any suffragettes out of the building, five women heckled the chancellor and were thrown out, only to convene a meeting outside.[20] Daisy introduced Elsa to her elder brother, Will, who had a B.Sc. in chemistry from University College, Nottingham, and was hoping to become a doctor. Their father, Charles Bullock, was a signalman on the Midland Railway. When William Bullock married Elsa Gye in Edinburgh in 1911 he was a medical student, able to pursue his studies because of the 'kindness of two friends', one of whom was Elsa. Before getting his degree Will had been a pupil-teacher, worked in a bicycle factory and as a clerk on the railways.[21]

A young woman of eighteen who called herself 'Vera Wentworth' also fell out of one of the vans. Like many of her comrades she was sentenced to six weeks in prison, but she had to serve an extra day for scratching 'Votes for Women' on the wall of her cell with hairpins. 'Vera' was born Jessie Spinks in Westminster in 1889, and was working in a shop when she joined the WSPU in 1906. In 1907 she formally changed her name to Vera Wentworth and became a full-time suffragette.[22] It was through her brother Wilfred that Jessie became friends with Fenner Brockway. Brockway, who called 'Wilfie Spinks' his 'explosive friend', had led an unsuccessful strike of women workers in the East End of London. He was eighteen years old, a socialist journalist and ardent admirer of Keir Hardie. Through Hardie's influence he volunteered to help out at Clement's Inn. 'Their faces dropped when they saw my youthfulness – and gave me envelopes to address.'[23]

Vera Wentworth was one of several young women who showed their devotion to Christabel Pankhurst by wearing a badge with her portrait on their chests. When Vera was released from Holloway in March 1908 she went to help at the Peckham by-election that month; the Liberals lost the seat after having won it in 1906, a result which delighted the suffragettes. According to Sylvia Pankhurst the Conservative voters who had gathered to hear the results were so happy that they hoisted Flora Drummond shoulder high.[24]

In the press the *Daily Chronicle* was appreciative: 'the Suffragettes are essentially heroic. First they lash themselves to the Premier's railings; now borrowing the idea from the Trojan horse, they burst forth from a pantechnicon van … A high standard of artifice has been set and it should be maintained.'

The second day of the Women's Parliament was devoted to deploring the prison sentences. Annie Kenney said she was prepared to go to prison for three months. Mary Blathwayt remembered Mrs Pethick-Lawrence being moved by Annie's commitment: 'She is generally all smiles but nearly broke down. She had to lean forward and cover her eyes with her handkerchief.'[25]

On the last day of the Women's Parliament Mrs Pankhurst led the deputation from Caxton Hall to the House of Commons, carrying a petition and a bunch of lilies. When Flora Drummond saw Mrs Pankhurst was struggling – her ankle was still painful from her recent by-electioneering in Newton Abbot – Flora asked a man with a dog-cart to take her to the House of Commons, but the police ordered Emmeline out of the cart. She was helped along by two women, but they were stopped by the police who told the three women they could only walk in single file. Mrs Pankhurst became 'faint from the pain' and could not walk unaided, and she asked two members to hold her arms as they walked towards Parliament Square. 'We walked with difficulty for the crowd was of incredible size. All around, as far as the eye could see, was the great moving, swaying, excited multitude, and surrounding us on all sides were regiments of uniformed police, foot and mounted.' As soon as they entered the Square Mrs Pankhurst was arrested. The women holding her refused to leave and they too were arrested. Thirteen women, including Minnie Baldock and Annie Kenney, were charged with obstructing the police and sentenced to four to six weeks in Holloway in the second division.

Their cases were heard at Westminster Police Court the next day. Mrs Pankhurst 'listened with a suspicion that my ears were playing tricks on my reason, to the most astonishing perjuries put forth by the prosecution'. The women were accused of leaving Caxton Hall singing and shouting, of 'the most riotous and vulgar behaviour', of knocking off policemen's helmets and 'assaulting officers left and right as we marched. Our testimony and that of our witnesses was ignored.' The government's ambition to revive the Tumultuous Petitioning to the Crown or Parliament Act, passed by King Charles II in 1661, which forbade any procession of more than thirteen persons, in order to ban suffragette protests in the environs of the House of Commons, was shelved.

Mrs Pankhurst was sent to Holloway for six weeks: it was her first time in prison. Within three days she was so run-down that she was transferred to the hospital wing, from where she sent a message to WSPU members which appeared in *Votes for Women* titled 'Work, Work, Work', telling them, 'not to be anxious about me ... and to be of good courage and work, work, work' for the success of the next meeting at the Royal Albert Hall. 'Whatever happens, I shall stay in Holloway till my six weeks are up!'[26]

Minnie Baldock smuggled out of gaol a defiant message to her comrades, saying she had 'gone to prison to help to free those who are bound by unjust laws and tyranny. I love freedom so dearly that I want all women to have it, and I will fight for it until they get it.'[27] The publicity surrounding the WSPU's third Women's Parliament lasted five days as their court appearances kept the story running. Annie Kenney noted that arrest and imprisonment 'worked miracles for the Cause'.[28] The 7,000 people – mostly women – present at the WSPU's meeting at the Albert Hall on 19 March raised £7,000 for campaign funds. Mrs Pankhurst, who had been released that morning, was in the chair. *Votes for Women* proudly announced it had been 'the largest gathering of women inside a hall which has ever taken place'.[29] Kate Parry Frye, by inclination a suffragist rather than a suffragette, was taken along by a friend and found the occasion thrilling: 'It was an exciting meeting … like magic the way it [the money] flowed in. It was all just a little too theatrical but very wonderful. Miss Annie Kenney interested me the most – she seems so "inspired" quite a second Joan of Arc.'[30] Annie said that 'gaol-birds created gaol-birds. Halls were overcrowded with would-be activists, donors and unpaid volunteers' and that 'pockets were emptied and prisons were filled'.[31]

For many women who had not yet joined the WSPU, newspaper reports of Mrs Pankhurst's activities would be a catalyst. On 21 March photographs of Emmeline Pankhurst's stage-managed arrival in Peckham, at a by-election, were on the front page of the *Daily Mirror*. A garlanded wagon carried her, festooned with 'Welcome Mrs Pankhurst' banners. Following behind were a dozen horse-drawn brakes for the suffragettes who were canvassing against the Liberals. The Liberal candidate, Thomas Gautrey, a former teacher, was the sort of man with whom other suffragettes would have had an affinity in the past. Tom Gautrey supported women's suffrage but because of the WSPU by-election policy he faced relentless opposition from the suffragettes. Christabel and her team kept up the pressure until every vote was counted: 'while the men in the crowd sheltered under umbrellas, the suffragette speakers boldly faced the tempest, and standing on the drays, which were used as platforms, appealed to voters "to keep the Liberal out", caring not one whit for the rain which drenched their clothes.'[32] Hecklers met their match: Christabel would point at one 'with a merry smile and play ever so gently with him, as a cat with a mouse'.[33] Tom Gautrey and the Liberals, who had won the seat in 1906, were heavily defeated by the Conservatives. Although issues such as free trade, temperance and licensing had been at stake, the WSPU were delighted with the result and took the credit for Gautrey's defeat.[34]

Mrs Pankhurst received considerable fanmail, including a letter from Beatrice Parlby of Hereford. Beatrice was typical of many educated middle-class women who felt their lives were unfulfilled or had stalled. In her reply Mrs Pankhurst told her new admirer 'how good it is to be back again amongst our women workers and to know that by going to prison great good has been done in the cause for which we are working'. Mrs Pankhurst hoped Miss Parlby would come to London on 21 June for 'Women's Sunday'.

Beatrice Parlby, the eldest of four daughters – all of whom were interested in women's suffrage – was born in Aylesbury in 1872. She studied at Royal Holloway College reading for the Oxford English Tripos but was disappointed with her results. Although women were not awarded degrees from Oxbridge they could sit the men's examinations and have their papers classified without being given a degree (this did not change until 1920 in Oxford and 1947 in Cambridge). Beatrice wrote an apologetic letter to her parents: 'I know I am worth more than a third ... I hope you won't all think me a dreadful fraud.'[35]

In 1901 Beatrice was teaching English at Burnley Grammar School where girls were admitted for the first time, although classes were segregated. At the age of twenty-eight her career unravelled when she fell madly in love with the headmaster, Henry Lincoln Joseland. Her feelings for him were unrequited: he knew nothing about her passion. Needing to leave her unhappy situation, Beatrice threw herself wholeheartedly into looking for another job; Henry Joseland gave her an excellent testimonial but she did not secure the post she wanted. Beatrice had a breakdown, and recovered, but her teaching career was over. She became a valuable foot soldier for the women's suffrage cause, helping to 'rouse the town' of Hereford. Sympathisers hosted drawing-room meetings, shopkeepers displayed suffragette handbills in their windows and Beatrice canvassed pluckily from door to door. Some time before 1914 she had another nervous breakdown and was again admitted to the County Asylum.[36]

Even though women's suffrage was not mentioned in the King's Speech on 29 January, time was given for the reading of a private members' bill, Henry Yorke Stanger's Women's Enfranchisement Bill, to be debated on 28 February. It proposed wide reform, enfranchising single and married women. Mr Stanger was the Liberal MP for North Kensington, where the suffragettes were a lively presence. Stanger had more liberal views on women's suffrage than many of his colleagues, but he worried about militancy and 'any incidents which might cause a feeling of disgust in the minds of the people. Their aim must be to convert their opponents to win recruits and for their army to strengthen the weak hands and confirm the feeble knees.'[37] Mr Stanger's bill easily passed its second reading in the House of Commons with a majority of 179 votes, but without government help it could not proceed.

On 1 April 1908, Sir Henry Campbell-Bannerman's failing health caused him to resign as prime minister. The death of his wife in August 1906 had precipitated his decline. Friends believed he should have resigned after her death but the bereft seventy-one-year-old soldiered on though 'his position was exacting in the extreme'.[38] Campbell-Bannermann was succeeded by his chancellor of the exchequer, Henry Herbert Asquith, who was summoned by King Edward VII from a holiday in Biarritz, and David Lloyd George replaced Asquith at the Treasury. Asquith and Lloyd George had revealed themselves to be no friends of women's suffrage. In fact, their attitude was an inversion of the WSPU's motto: words not deeds. At a suffragette meeting in the Portman Rooms about what the changes in government might mean, Christabel issued a broadside: 'If Mr Asquith won't bend to us he must break, and we believe we shall break him', adding, 'Mr Winston Churchill was our first victim, and if he seeks re-election I hope he will be our last'.[39] This was fighting talk: Christabel cannot have been confident that the vote would be granted in the current session of parliament, but controversy was one of her special strengths. On 22 April 1908 Henry Campbell-Bannerman died at 10 Downing Street.[40]

Politicians who were promoted had to stand for re-election to their seats. Before the late prime minister's funeral in Westminster Abbey, two constituencies were due to go to the polls: North-West Manchester, on 24 April 1908, and Kincardineshire, near Aberdeen, north-east Scotland, on the 25th. North-West Manchester was of special interest to the WSPU who were determined to frustrate their enemy, Winston Churchill, in his attempt to get re-elected.

One evening the suffragettes held a meeting 'in the moonlight' at the tramway depot where the socialists had a platform nearby for their candidate, who was fifteen minutes late. By this time the suffragettes' lorry was surrounded by a crowd of 500. Every time the socialists tried to interrupt the women they were howled down. The Pankhursts' long association with Manchester and the Independent Labour Party clearly counted for something when it came to audience behaviour: having a meeting at night for hundreds of women was potentially dangerous. After two hours the women drove off in their 'triumphal' lorry to loud cheers.[41]

Helen Craggs joined the WSPU in 1908 at the age of twenty, had campaigned at the Peckham by-election and was back in action in Manchester with 'General' Flora Drummond, who was on her home turf where her husband and toddler son, Keir Hardie Drummond, lived. Helen used the name 'Miss Millar' to spare the embarrassment of her father, Sir John Craggs. She chalked pavements and sold picture postcards of the stars of the movement. Helen was educated at Roedean but her father would not allow her to study medicine, a disappointing decision for a man who donated money to the study of tropical medicine. Helen Craggs was one of many suffragettes who had faced paternal hostility to their wish to pursue a career. In Helen's case becoming a suffragette was an extreme act of rebellion and one her parents would neither condone nor forgive.[42]

When the votes were counted on 24 April, Winston Churchill was shocked to find he had lost his seat to the Conservative candidate, William Joynson-Hicks, from whom he had taken it in 1906. The suffragettes were cock-a-hoop. Churchill's majority of 1,241 in 1906 had been wiped out. A number of issues lost the Liberals valuable votes, including the argument over free trade versus tariff reform, and Manchester's Jewish community were unhappy with the workings of the Aliens Act of 1905 which had introduced immigration controls for the first time. The well-organised WSPU, on home ground, had proved a formidable force, and claimed the Liberal defeat as their victory. Christabel Pankhurst and Annie Kenney had their revenge for being thrown out of the Free Trade Hall in 1905. The Liberal Party looked for another seat for Churchill: polling day in Dundee was announced for 9 May.[43]

As Winston Churchill tried to woo the voters of Dundee, where large numbers of women worked in the jam factories and jute mills, he was hounded by the suffragettes. Dundee had had a WSPU branch since 1906. Very experienced organisers including Mary Gawthorpe,

Helen Fraser from the Glasgow office, Rachel Barrett and Elsa Gye 'worked up' the constituency. They spoke at factory gates, hired the Gaiety Theatre twice for 'monster meetings', and held 200 meetings in the final week of campaigning, popping up anywhere to tell voters of the new prime minister's machinations. In the early hours on the morning of polling day Mary Gawthorpe took a group of local WSPU members and 'invaded' the office of the Dundee *Courier* and addressed a meeting of the night staff which went down well. Before Mary and her team left there 'were three cheers for the ladies'.[44]

Miss Molony, a member of the Women's Freedom League campaigning in Dundee, rang a bell so persistently throughout Churchill's speech at a dinner-hour meeting at a foundry that he had to give up and she addressed his audience instead. News of his retreat was reported as far afield as Newfoundland and New Zealand. Churchill told a local women's suffrage campaigner that he was 'not prepared' to exert himself 'to extract a Government pledge'.[45] Despite the suffragettes' best efforts Churchill retained the seat for the Liberals – the incumbent had been elevated to the House of Lords – although the Liberal majority was now 2,000 votes less than it had been in the 1906 general election. Issues such as free trade, temperance and Irish Home Rule, rather than votes for women, had been the big subjects of debate, but the suffragettes were pleased to think they had played a role in reducing Winston Churchill's majority.[46]

On 28 April Minnie Baldock received a letter from a new WSPU member, Emily Cobb, who was keen to support the Cause, offering to help Minnie with her activities in the build-up to the meeting in Hyde Park on 21 June. Not wanting the Baldock family to be neglected, Emily offered to pay a pound a week 'for someone to do your home [house] work and so set you free to do work which you *can* do and many of us can not'. She sent Minnie a cheque for £2 and promised to send another one if 'dear Mrs Baldock agreed to the plan'.[47]

On 20 May Prime Minister Asquith was asked by Liberal MPs who were in favour of women's suffrage about the fate of Mr Stanger's bill which had passed its second reading three months earlier. They were told that he would not oppose any amendment with regard to votes for women in a general Electoral Reform Bill, which had not been sought. A significant change, such as giving women the vote, could not be contemplated unless it was demonstrated that it had the

support of women of the country. When asked by a Liberal opponent of women's suffrage what would happen if a women's suffrage
amendment to a proposed Reform Bill was carried in the House of
Commons, he replied evasively: 'My honourable friend has asked
me a contingent question with regard to a remote and speculative
future.'[48] Asquith's obfuscation would earn him the WSPU sobriquet
'the right dishonourable double-faced Asquith'.[49]

Asquith had thrown down the gauntlet and the WSPU were happy
to seize it. A 'Women's Sunday' demonstration on 21 June, already
well advanced in the planning, would prove the extent of the demand
for women's suffrage. The leadership intended it 'would out-rival any
of the great franchise demonstrations held by the men' in the 1830s,
1860s and 1880s. Mrs Pankhurst said that the greatest number of
people ever to gather in Hyde Park had been 72,000 and the WSPU
was determined to fill the park with at least a quarter of a million.

Sunday had been chosen so that as many working women as possible could attend. Women who could not afford the train fares had
their expenses paid by better-off members in their local branch. Fred
Pethick-Lawrence was in charge of the arrangements for the 'monster meeting' that was to be 'the greatest franchise demonstration ever
known'. It was funded by his wife's idea of holding a 'Self-Denial
Week' in February, and the collection taken at the meeting at the
Royal Albert Hall on 19 March which had raised £7,000. Members
were asked to deny themselves something during that week, such as
a pair of stockings, or a tea and buns with friends, and donate the
money to WSPU funds. The idea was so effective that self-denial
weeks became an annual event.[50]

In the weeks leading up to 21 June, Emmeline Pethick-Lawrence
launched the tricolour combination she had devised. Black and white
photographs only tell half the suffragette story: if colour photographs
had been available, our impression of the militant movement would
be a riot of colour. The imaginative merchandising of the colour
scheme of purple, white and green announced the modernity of the
WSPU. Emmeline Pethick-Lawrence explained: 'Purple is the royal
colour. It stands for the royal blood that flows in the veins of every
suffragette, the instinct for freedom and dignity ... white stands for
purity in private and public life ... green is the colour of hope and the
emblem of spring.'[51] Working closely with Mrs Pethick-Lawrence,

Annie Kenney could see 'her love for pageantry. Her passion for colour and music introduced into the movement a lighter, freer, gayer side. Pageantry played a big part in popularising the movement.'[52]

Not only was the huge demonstration choreographed with precision, but the suffragettes' appearance was also closely directed. Mrs Pethick-Lawrence told them to 'be guided by the colours in your choice of dress'. She had arranged that 700 banners, which were being made by suffragettes all over the country, would be walked from the seven mainline railway stations in London to converge on Hyde Park. She was concerned that 'the effect will be very much lost unless the colours are carried out in the dress of every woman in the ranks. White or cream tussore [silk] should if possible be the dominant colour: the purple and green should be introduced where other colour is necessary.'[53]

Not to be outdone by the WSPU, Mrs Fawcett's NUWSS organised their own 'Great Procession' from Victoria Embankment to the Albert Hall eight days earlier, on 13 June. Some WSPU members went along to express to their support for an organisation working for the same goal, albeit in a different way. On that day 13,000 women walked in a two-mile-long procession through London carrying banners designed and made by the Artists' Suffrage League, founded in 1907, to further the cause of women's suffrage by the work and professional help of artists. Women from the Independent Labour Party, the Women's Cooperative Guild, the Women's Freedom League and the National Union of Women Workers took part.[54]

Clement's Inn was the battle headquarters. Thirty thousand women were expected to come to London to take part in the march and the fifteen rooms they rented at Number 4 bustled with women. Parcels of handbills, postcards and pamphlets were sent to suffragette activists all round the country, and bundles of *Votes for Women* newspapers were ready for sale on the street. The goal was to attract a quarter of a million people to hear the message in Hyde Park. Thirty trains brought women from seventy towns and cities. There were nine chief marshals, thirty group captains, seven group marshals, banner captains, forty banner marshals and captains, dozens of colour distributors and hundreds of railway station stewards and captains.[55]

A thousand pounds was spent on hiring hoardings in London and major cities and towns to carry the posters, measuring thirteen feet by ten feet, displaying photographs of the women who presided over each of the twenty platforms. Pavements were chalked, flyposting took place, suffragettes canvassed door-to-door and sandwich boards were carried up and down the streets in order to get the maximum turnout.[56] Ten silk and wool banners were unfurled for the first time at the Queen's Hall on 17 June. Mrs Pethick-Lawrence, in charge of the unfurling ceremony, first gave Clara Mordan the honour of unveiling the banner she had given. Miss Mordan's kindness to Annie Kenney when she first came 'to arouse' London in 1906, and her generosity ever since, was remembered. Miss Mordan, who was in poor health, expressed her regret that Mr and Mrs Asquith had declined to help them unfurl the banners, the prime minister's wife pleading that her husband's health forbade it. Clara Mordan scoffed, 'It was singular how exceedingly feeble the health of the poor gentlemen who legislated for us was. They were always compelled to go to the Riviera after they had passed through an election contest, yet the ladies of this Union were able to go through any number of contested elections, and worked hard from morning to night, and even from night until morning without appearing in any degree the worse for it.'[57] With that Clara Mordan tugged the white sheet that revealed a banner of two eagles carrying a shield on which had been embroidered the motto 'Hope Is Strong! Awake! Arise!' This banner, to be carried by the women of Bradford, was one of five designed by Sylvia Pankhurst, all of which were on WSPU propaganda. At the end of the ceremony of blessing the banners, Emmeline Pethick-Lawrence unveiled her own gift: a stunning banner which she had commissioned from the Artists' Suffrage League, a portrait of Mrs Pankhurst above the words: 'Founder of the Women's Social and Political Union, 1903, Champion of Womanhood, Famed for Deeds of Daring Rectitude'. Thirty brass and silver bands were hired to play all the way.[58]

Flora Drummond was put in charge of events in Hyde Park and this is where she acquired her nickname 'General' Drummond, by which she was known thereafter. Toye and Co., manufacturers of regalia, presented her with a purple, white and green peaked cap, a gold velvet sash embroidered in purple and green silk and a pair of epaulettes trimmed with gold braid and tassels. On horseback she looked every inch the general leading her troops into battle.[59]

On 18 June, the WSPU launched an 'attack' on the Houses of Parliament. Members enjoying tea on the terrace overlooking the river were startled to be invited to Women's Sunday by Mrs Drummond – who did not need a megaphone – standing on the roof of the cabin of a Thames steam launch. Accompanied by a posse of eight suffragettes in purple, white and green, a brass band struck up in the stern of the boat. As two police barges hove into view, Mrs Drummond's parting shot was, 'I am glad to see you have lady waiters, are you not afraid that some of them may be suffragettes?'[60]

Madame Tussaud's waxwork museum included a timely display. The day before the suffragettes' big day, John Tussaud, great-grandson of the founder, unveiled his new waxwork tableau. Emmeline Pankhurst, Mrs Pethick-Lawrence and Annie Kenney were seated at a table, and Christabel Pankhurst stood at her mother's shoulder, discussing business. WSPU leaflets decorated the set. The likenesses were good for the women had sat several times for John Tussaud.[61]

On the morning of the great day itself, Lancashire and Yorkshire cotton and woollen mill girls, Nottingham lace workers and Leicestershire boot and shoemakers arrived at King's Cross, St Pancras, Euston and Paddington stations. Factory and homeworkers from Canning Town, Poplar and Bethnal Green gathered in Trafalgar Square. Emmeline Pethick-Lawrence and Christabel Pankhurst led the procession from Victoria Embankment of 'women from many classes'.[62] The office staff at Clement's Inn marched with professional women, artists, teachers, florists and music and drama students in the Chelsea and Kensington procession.[63]

Jessie Stephenson lived at the Twentieth Century Club in Notting Hill which offered furnished rooms and board for educated women workers 'engaged in education, literary, secretarial or other similar work'. A few days before Women's Sunday Fred Pethick-Lawrence – whose male critics called him 'Mr Pathetic Lawrence' – took Jessie and the other chief marshals on a reconnaissance of Hyde Park. Jessie told him, 'This is the first time I've been on a battlefield before a battle.' Jessie woke at four o'clock on 21 June. She wore a new white lacy muslin dress, white shoes, stockings and gloves, a 'Votes for Women' sash, a white shady hat trimmed with sprigs of white may, and her chief marshal and speaker badges pinned to her chest. Walking to her platform Jessie noticed 'a whole lot of roughs had already installed themselves' and as she spoke 'they kept catching my eye and showing me queer missiles to be thrown at us – hidden under their coats or in pockets. Three men opened their coats and showed me three bells which signified they intended to ring to drown our voices.'[64]

The two grande dames of women's suffragism and feminism, seventy-five-year-old Mrs Elmy and seventy-eight-year-old Emily Davies, were taken to the park in a four-in-hand coach. The playwright George Bernard Shaw, the novelists H. G. Wells, Thomas Hardy and Israel Zangwill also attended. In Hyde Park there were twenty platforms each with a chair and several speakers. When Emmeline Pankhurst and Mrs Elmy climbed onto platform five, Emmeline saw 'crowds pouring in from all directions ... I was filled with amazement ... It was a gay and beautiful as well as an awe-inspiring spectacle, for the white gowns and flower-trimmed hats of the women, against the background of the ancient trees, gave the park the appearance of a vast garden in full bloom.'[65]

The press reacted well to Women's Sunday. The *Standard* reported: 'From first to last it was a great meeting, daringly conceived, splendidly stage-managed, and successfully carried out. Hyde Park has probably never seen a greater crowd of people.' The *Daily Mail* positively quivered: 'I am sure a great many people never realised until yesterday how young and dainty and charming most leaders of the movement are. And how well they spoke – with what free and graceful gestures; never at a loss for a word or an apt reply to an interruption; calm and collected, forcible, yet so far as I heard, not violent, earnest, but happily humorous as well.' The *Daily Express* also approved: 'The women suffragists provided London with the most astonishing and wonderful sights ... Wonderful and impressive were the processions of women, still more wonderful was the way in which London gathered to see them. The crowds in the streets fell in and marched behind.'

Furthermore, the reporter from the *Daily News* noted: 'Gleaming in the sunlight the seven hundred banners told their own story ... the massed spectators read the mottoes aloud as they went by, "Who would be free themselves must strike the blow", "Not chivalry but justice", "The only hope for the unemployed," "237 women were imprisoned for the vote" and "54 weeks of Holloway".'[66]

Mrs Broom was a professional photographer who took some of the best pictures we have of Women's Sunday. Helped by her eighteen-year-old daughter, Winnie, Christina Broom, less than five feet tall, managed to manoeuvre a tripod and a half-plate box camera through the packed park within six feet of the platforms. Mrs Broom's images of platform six – Mrs Rosamund Massy was in the chair and Katherine Douglas Smith and Elsie Howey were speakers – showed about forty women hugger-mugger with each other, and two youthful constables surrounded by a sea of smiling suffragette faces. Above the smile of every woman is a hat, mortar boards worn by the university women, or heavily decorated millinery, galleon-shaped confections with ribbons, feathers and artificial flowers, some with veils.

The Times's 'special correspondent' put the boorish behaviour of a minority down to boisterous high spirits and 'horse-play'. At times the mood was ugly. When Christabel Pankhurst took up her position a gaggle of young men rushed at her shouting 'We Want Chrissie! We Want Chrissie!' She was well-practised at repartee but when the pushing and shoving started, fights broke out and small children had to be put up on the platform for safety. Mounted police patrolling the park were kept busy breaking up knots of troublesome males. The spectacle of the banners and colour schemes, and the music of the thirty brass bands impressed *The Times*: 'the organisers of the demonstration had counted on an attendance of 250,000 … Probably it was doubled, and it would be difficult to contradict anyone who asserted confidently that it was trebled …' The normally peaceful Sunday streets of the West End 'resounded to the beat of the drum, the call of the bugle, and the tramp of marching feet'.[67]

Women's Sunday ended at five o'clock with the blowing of bugles, and with a 'Great Shout' of 'votes for women' the 'monster meeting' was over. Mrs Pankhurst glossed over some ugly scenes, the worst directed against Nellie Martel and herself. Nellie Martel's platform was nearly overturned by a gang of men, and Mrs Pankhurst was interrupted throughout by two sailors, one sitting on the other's shoulders, and in a stunt a bell rang and two men started a wrestling match, scattering her audience. Helen Fraser's letter to Isabel Seymour expressed disappointment: 'It was successful although not entirely satisfactory – the crowd was about half a million – the day was lovely … and at three platforms there was much rowdyism ... it seemed to me that the mass of people were simply curious – not opposed – simply indifferent.'[68]

On the evening of 21 June, euphoric with the success of the day, Christabel Pankhurst returned to Clement's Inn and sent a message to the prime minister, telling him that the WSPU had filled the park as no other franchise meeting had managed to do, and called on the government 'to grant votes to women without delay'. She asked what he intended to do about their demand and demanded that the franchise be extended to women 'who possess the same qualifications which now entitle men to vote'. She also called for a 'separate and distinct measure' before the introduction of the proposed Reform Bill; the WSPU did not want women's suffrage to get bogged down in the 'constitutional matters which will certainly arise when the Reform Bill is introduced'.[69]

Christabel Pankhurst told Asquith that the WSPU was holding a National Convention of Women at Caxton Hall on 30 June, to be followed by an evening demonstration in Parliament Square, and asked for his reply before then. The next morning Vaughan Robinson Nash, Asquith's private secretary, replied that the prime minister 'has nothing to add to the statement made to a deputation of members of Parliament on May 20th'.[70]

Christabel Pankhurst replied: 'it is evident that public meetings will have no effect in inducing the Government to grant votes to women' and informed Asquith that 'militant methods must once more be resorted to'.[71] The Women's Sunday demonstration had been a propaganda success: the WSPU's message had been heard by thousands of people whether the government liked it or not; the suffragettes had attracted hundreds of column inches of good press; the Union had launched the militants' colour scheme; but politically they had not achieved their goal.

5

Window-smashing and 'Rushing' Parliament

Suffragette Action 1908

Schoolteachers Mary Leigh and Edith New hold up bread smuggled out of Holloway after serving two months for breaking windows at 10 Downing Street on 29 June 1908.

The Women's Social and Political Union asked the public to gather in Parliament Square on the evening of 30 June to show their support for Mrs Pankhurst's deputation to the Houses of Parliament. In the afternoon, sashed, ribboned and badged, twelve women who had written to the prime minister requesting a meeting with him, including Emmeline Pethick-Lawrence, Jessie Stephenson, Florence Haig, Maud Joachim and Mary Phillips, left Caxton Hall with Mrs Pankhurst. The police cleared a way for the deputation to the doors of the Strangers' Entrance where Inspector Scantlebury waited. He told Mrs Pankhurst that the prime minister would not see her, at which she turned around and led the women back to Caxton Hall. In the early evening suffragettes arrived in hansom cabs in their best evening clothes, and more stood with megaphones on the tops of horse-drawn omnibuses, all calling on the crowd to help the women get through to Parliament. *The Times* underlined the derision of the 'mob': 'To suppose that these crowds had assembled to show sympathy ... would be the wildest absurdity. They had come merely for a cheap evening's entertainment and they had about as much sympathy with the women whom they came to see as the people who flocked to the Roman amphitheatres to see the wretches who were thrown to the lions.'[1] The police had been ordered to keep the women away from the House of Commons, and to disperse the crowd from Parliament Square – which was still open to traffic – but so many people had arrived in the Square and the roads leading to it that even with mounted policemen there was no possibility of the growing crowd being dispersed in an orderly manner. As the women tried to slip between the police cordons to enter the House of Commons they were arrested and taken to Canon Row police station. *The Times* reported that the 'fiercest scrimmage' happened just after nine o'clock that evening when three suffragettes got through the first line of policemen: 'The surging mob of supporters, mostly youths whom it would not be unfair to describe as "hooligans", drove the girls further into the forbidden area.' The police in the cordon and plain-clothes policemen who mingled in the crowd 'put in some very vigorous work and sent the intruders spinning in various directions'.[2]

In all twenty-seven women were arrested in Parliament Square that night and charged at Westminster Police Court with obstructing the police in the course of their duty, and sentenced to between one and three months in prison.

Portrait painter Florence Haig, a cousin of Douglas Haig (who would become Field Marshal Haig in 1915), was arrested and sent to Holloway for three months, her second stint in prison. In February and March she had served six weeks for her part in the pantechnicon raid. When Florence came out of Holloway she wrote to *Votes for Women:* 'It is wonderful how each woman who acts influences her own circle. Friends who before may have been but mildly in favour, are converted into active and eager workers for the cause. Coming out is so delightful that the stupidity of the time in Holloway is forgotten.'[3] Florence Haig's involvement with the WSPU began in 1907 when she hosted a meeting in her studio at which Mrs Pankhurst spoke.[4]

Maud Joachim was arrested later that evening. She was born in 1869, and Maud's family was affluent, intellectual and musical. Her father, Heinrich, was a wool merchant related to the Wittgensteins and her uncle Joseph was a renowned violinist of the nineteenth century and a protégé of Mendelssohn.[5] Maud's memory of prison was that it was like 'a fantastic dream, only one knows one could never dream anything so nonsensical: from the moment one goes into court and hears the topsy-turvy evidence of the police and sees the queer faces of the magistrate and his colleagues gazing at one, to the moment one leaves Holloway after having served one's time'.[6]

Mary Phillips, a member of Mrs Pankhurst's deputation, was sentenced to three months. She had no qualms about going to prison again: 'I thought prison was rather a joke … First you were undressed and weighed and measured; then you were given these awful clothes.' Prisoners were allowed a bath once a week: 'it was a queer sort of bath with walls coming right up, so that you could only get in over the end, and you didn't know how many people had bathed in it before'. However, it was better than nothing. Mary's parents and 'the Scots Team' of suffragettes gave her a Highland welcome when she was released on 18 September. Mary was piped out of Holloway by four bagpipers. She was taken in a 'wagon full of purple heather and immense Scotch thistles', drawn by a team of twelve suffragettes in Highland dress, to a WSPU reception at the Queen's Hall in central London. Vera Wentworth took the reins and banner-carrying suffragettes followed behind; copies of *Votes for Women* were sold from a press cart along the route. Mary was freed two days later than four of her comrades, punished by the prison authorities for trying to smuggle a note out of prison telling her mother, who was 'frail of health', that she was 'quite well and quite jolly' and that she must not worry.[7]

Mary Phillips was born in 1880. In 1904 she was the organising secretary for the Glasgow and West of Scotland Association for Women's Suffrage but had an epiphany when she joined the WSPU in 1907: 'I didn't enjoy anything until militancy began; when I was just a suffragist it was boring. When militancy began … my father said of course they are quite right to be militant, so presently I was converted too.'[8]

Mary Leigh and Edith New were the first suffragettes to smash windows. Incensed by the 'violence and indecency' inflicted on their comrades, they slipped away from the mêlée in Parliament Square on 30 June 1908, took a taxi to the prime minister's residence and broke two window panes. When they were arrested, Edith told the policeman, 'Freedom for the women of England! We are martyrs.'[9] At Canon Row police station both women stated they would do the same again, and Leigh told the police next time it would be a bomb.

In court the next day both Leigh and New were charged with wilful damage and sentenced to two months in Holloway in the third division with hard labour. Edith New told the Crown solicitor, Mr Herbert George Muskett, that they had had no option but to take the course they had and that the suffragettes had used every means possible to attain their object. All responsibility for the outcome rested on the shoulders of 'the autocrat of England', Herbert Asquith, who had 'made them outlaws by the laws of the land'.[10] Mary Leigh said that the only choice the suffragettes had was to rebel against the pressure of one man who should 'give in or pay the penalty. This fight is going on.'[11]

It was now that several Spong sisters started to play their part. Dora Spong was arrested and charged with obstruction on 30 June, and sent to prison for one month. When she became ill she was released early. Dora was born in Balham in 1871 and joined the WSPU in 1908, the first of five sisters to go to prison for the militant movement. The Spong women were encouraged in their suffragette careers by their mother, Frances, who took part in WSPU processions and demonstrations to Parliament. James Osborn Spong, the paterfamilias, raised no objection to their involvement in the militant campaign. The family business, Spong and Co., made labour-saving gadgets, many of them invented by James Spong, including knife cleaners, animal traps, burglar alarms and an 'apparatus for sounding an alarm in case of fire'. One of Spong's inventions, the meat mincer, was at odds with the vegetarian ethos of his wife and daughters. Spong and his cook were both carnivores, while the women of the family lived on vegetables, nuts and berries which they cultivated themselves. Minnie, the eldest of the five sisters, announced that she preferred to be known as Frances after her father named one of his mincers 'The Minnie' after her.

Dora Spong, a nurse, midwife and sanitary inspector, worked in the slums of Tottenham and Battersea. She was in the Finsbury branch of the Independent Labour Party, whose members wrote to her in Holloway, sending their 'hearty greetings across the prison wall', and expressed 'their admiration of the courage and determination displayed in submitting to the onus of the prison cell in the women's cause'.[12] Minnie, the eldest at forty, was a schoolteacher who went to work in Africa, returning to England in 1911. Annie Spong was an artist, known for her portraits of several Lord Mayors of London. She met Joseph Syddall at art school and lived with him for the rest of her life although they never married. When Annie's suffragette career was burgeoning she took up dancing, studying with Raymond Duncan, the brother of the celebrated Isadora Duncan. Performing in mime, leaping, skipping and jumping, Annie would dance as her sister Irene sang. Annie explained in *Votes for Women*: 'Through the systems of practising rhythmical gymnastics or dancing, we obtain a natural physical culture and mental culture at the same time, which is of real practical use in our everyday lives. Our awkwardness drops away, and we become more evenly balanced in body and mind, and instinctively become more human.'[13]

Florence Spong was a weaver and artistic dressmaker. She studied lace-making and wood-carving. Irene, at twenty-five the youngest Spong sister, had a light soprano voice and gave concerts to raise money for the WSPU, and also lessons in voice production to suffragette speakers. Irene served time in Holloway; she married in 1910 but continued to use her maiden name.[14]

Charlotte 'Charlie' Marsh was one of several suffragettes who jumped up on the railings of the House of Commons on 30 June. 'The crowd shouted and jeered and backed us up.' The police pulled them down but as soon as they left the women climbed up again and were arrested. The next day they were sentenced to a month in Holloway in the second division. Having completed her training as a sanitary inspector, Charlie Marsh joined the WSPU and travelled to London to help 'work up' the Women's Sunday demonstration. She was put under Mary Phillips's wing to learn the art of pavement chalking, and Mary remembered how 'gamely she stood the jeering and the rough handling we got down Lambeth Way'.[15]

Charlie Marsh was chosen to be the standard-bearer for many suffragette processions. Grace Roe recalled that Miss Marsh was 'a *born* suffragette. Even in the nursery she would line up her sisters and "lead the procession". No one who had once seen Charlie could ever forget her – a beautiful young girl with a great wealth of golden hair, her initials C.A.L.M., described her perfectly.'[16]

The death of the Liberal MP Sir Randal Cremer in July 1908 brought about a by-election in Haggerston,[17] a poor neighbourhood on the edge of the City of London. The Conservative women were led by Lady Gwendolen Guinness, the wife of their candidate, the Honourable Rupert Guinness. The socialist candidate Herbert Burrows, a retired civil servant, was supported by local working women. 'General' Drummond and other suffragettes campaigning against Walter Warren, the Liberal candidate, cycled round Haggerston on a tandem bicycle with purple, white and green ribbons streaming behind them. May Billinghurst, known as 'the cripple suffragette', joined Lewisham WSPU in 1907 and helped out in Haggerston, whizzing about the streets using her hands to power her invalid tricycle, canvassing door-to-door and holding street meetings. May Billinghurst was born in 1875, and an illness at the age of five left her paralysed from the waist down. She was a 'rescue' worker helping abandoned children on London's streets and eventually became superintendent of a children's home.[18]

Polling day was 1 August, which coincided with the release of twenty-four suffragettes from Holloway who were driven round the constituency urging everyone 'to keep the Liberals out'. The Conservatives won the seat, pushing the Liberals into second place.[19]

That summer a music-hall song was bawled raucously whenever suffragettes held open-air meetings. 'Put Me Upon an Island Where the Girls Are Few' was promoted as *the* anti-suffragette song. The chorus went:

Put me upon an island where the girls are few;
Put me amongst the most ferocious lions in the zoo;
You can put me upon a treadmill and I'll never, never fret,
But for pity's sake don't put me near a Suf-fra-gette.

In July 1908, the National Women's Anti-Suffrage League (NWASL) was founded at the Westminster Palace Hotel, London, by thirty peeresses and peers, half a dozen bishops, a clutch of anti-suffrage MPs and a number of well-known women from various walks of life in response to the growing ability of the WSPU to muster its members in Westminster, and wherever a by-election was contested, to express its demand for women's suffrage. The National Women's Anti-Suffrage League's aim was to 'organise the opposition which is manifest throughout the country on the part of women themselves to the extension of the franchise to women'.[20] Their objection to women having the franchise, and becoming Members of Parliament, did not include the exclusion of women from any policy-making – they believed that women's representation was more appropriate on municipal and other local bodies for their expertise in 'domestic and social affairs of the community'.

Mrs Humphry Ward, a best-selling novelist, was the best-known female 'anti'. Mrs Ward told the meeting that their opponents had presented their arguments with 'ability and earnestness in season and out of season, and enforced by methods legitimate and illegitimate'. She urged that if those who believed that women's suffrage would 'bring disaster upon England' did not act, 'the country would drift towards a momentous revolution, both social and political, before it has realised the dangers involved'. Mrs Ward stressed the 'danger' of giving women the vote: 'the admission to full political power of a number of voters debarred by nature and circumstance from the average political knowledge and experience open to men' would weaken the country and 'would be fraught with peril'.[21]

She described how the militant campaign was well-funded and 'served by women who seemed to give their whole time to its promotion' and that it was time for members of the League 'to bestir themselves'.[22]

Gertrude Bell's father was Thomas Hugh Bell, a wealthy ironmaster in Yorkshire. She was born in 1868 and enjoyed a privileged life and an excellent education. Even in 1908 Gertrude Bell's enthusiastic support for the anti-suffragists seemed bizarre when set against her own free life and ambition. Miss Bell was a noted Alpinist: in 1902 she and her two guides were caught in a storm on the north-east face of the Finsteraarhorn in the Bernese Alps in Switzerland, the most difficult route to the summit which had been opened that year for the first time. For two days they dangled off the side of the mountain and were lucky to survive. Gertrude Bell returned to the Swiss–Italian border in 1904 and climbed the Matterhorn.[23]

Another anti-suffragist was Violet Markham whose work in social reform led her to stridently oppose women's suffrage, believing that giving votes to women would fill the electorate with inexperienced and ignorant voters. (Emmeline Pethick-Lawrence's work with young working-class women in London had led her to draw the opposite conclusion.) Markham's autobiography reveals how her mother's influence had worked on her: 'She disliked all she knew about the suffrage pioneers, and was strongly opposed to votes for women.' Looking back forty years later, Violet Markham changed her mind: 'I came slowly but surely to change my mind and change it so fundamentally that I find it difficult now in retrospect to give a very coherent account of what took me into the other camp.'[24]

When Mary Leigh and Edith New were released from Holloway on 22 August they were greeted by Christabel and Mrs Pethick-Lawrence and by a brass band playing 'The Marseillaise'. The women who met them wore white dresses with belts, sashes and hats in the suffragette colours, and the wagon that trundled to the breakfast party at the Queen's Hall in Langham Place was hauled by twelve suffragettes. Mary and Edith were photographed holding up two inedible loaves of bread they had smuggled out of Holloway.

At this time Annie Kenney, her team of organisers and dozens of unpaid volunteers were in Bristol, the headquarters of the WSPU's West of England campaign which covered a vast area including South Wales. Bristol was fertile ground: the city had been used to women's suffrage and feminist campaigning since the late 1860s. By now the suffragettes were part of popular culture. During August there was a 'Suffragette Race' at a gymkhana at an agricultural show in Bristol. The riders had to ride to a point, ring a bell, release the 'dummy suffragettes' chained to the railings and carry them to the police station. The first rider to place his suffragette in prison was the winner.[25]

Clara Margaret Codd lived in Bath and was an active member of her local branch of the WSPU. A theosophist and socialist, she was working as a governess when she heard Christabel Pankhurst and Annie Kenney speak in 1907, and was moved by the latter's speech. 'The little Lancashire mill girl, small and slight, with a wealth of goldenish hair piled on her head, was truly, as Shelley would have phrased it, "a spirit of fire and dew".'[26] Clara noted that Annie's eyes were 'large and blue, so blazing that when she spoke with an inner mystic light they dominated her whole being'.[27] (Clara Codd and Annie remained friends until Annie's death in 1953.) At the end of the meeting Clara asked if she could be useful and then spent her summer holiday working for the WSPU in Bristol. Annie explained that she could not pay her 'but could put me up, if I did not mind sharing a large double bed with her'.[28]

Clara Codd became expert at chalking a notice on the pavement before a policeman or indignant local could stop her. She was attacked by more women than men, 'sometimes chased away by a shrieking woman, much to the embarrassment of her accompanying male relatives'.[29] At the end of the summer holidays she resigned her post as a governess. Annie asked a well-off supporter to give Clara ten shillings a week for her 'passing needs' and she continued to share Annie's big bed. 'Occasionally I awoke to find Annie trying to throttle me! In her dreams she was still fighting battles.'³⁰

Suffragette meetings turned boisterous when students from Bristol University took up positions in the gallery to heckle. Miss Codd remembered the women speakers always getting the better of the hecklers – 'young men are often not very quick on the uptake' – and the audience cheered when the suffragettes upstaged the students. Outdoor meetings were more unpredictable: Annie Kenney was keen to address the working men at the docks in Bristol, and some-times Clara and another woman would be sent as decoys to start a meeting, often drawing a rough crowd, while Annie would begin the real meeting nearby. When a gang of men and boys realised they had been tricked they hemmed her and her friend in against 'some railings which I clung to lest they trample me underfoot, and tried to tear my clothes off me'. Clara asked the only policeman in sight to help her but he gave her 'a frightened, sardonic smile and never stirred. Suddenly I felt a blunt instrument bruise on my back. Someone had tried to stab me through the railings.' Clara fought her way past her tormen-tors and ran off, chased by the crowd and pelted with 'mud and offal' all the way until she found a tram stop and was hauled aboard by a kind man.³¹

On 12 September 1908 Winston Churchill married Clementine Hozier at St Margaret's, Westminster. When their engagement was announced a month earlier an anonymous Manchester suffragette sent Churchill a sarcastic telegram at his office at the Board of Trade in Whitehall: 'Have great hopes of your speedy conversion but you said you would not be henpecked.' Churchill's bride was actually in favour of women's suffrage but against militancy.³²

By the end of September Mr Stanger's Women's Enfranchisement Bill had passed its second reading by a large majority in the House of Commons. Overjoyed at the spate of Liberal by-election defeats and reduced majorities, Mrs Pankhurst asked the prime minister to provide the necessary time to allow the bill to become law when Parliament reassembled. Mr Asquith's reply was that he would not. On Sunday 11 October, the WSPU held a meeting in Trafalgar Square at which Mrs Pankhurst, Christabel and Flora Drummond paced up and down the plinth between Landseer's lions at the foot of Nelson's Column, urging the crowd to 'Come and rush the House of Commons' at half past seven on the evening of 13 October, the third anniversary of the first militant protest at the Free Trade Hall. Fifty thousand hand-bills were printed to attract the maximum crowd; there were 'poster parades' of WSPU supporters wearing the posters as aprons were in London's streets in the days leading up to the 'Rush', and Flora Drummond was appointed 'general'.[33]

The next day Mrs Pankhurst, Christabel and Flora Drummond were summoned to appear at Bow Street to be charged with 'incit-ing the public to do a wrongful and illegal act', but instead the three women attended the WSPU's weekly Monday meeting at the Queen's Hall. The police waited outside Queen's Hall to arrest them and there was a stand-off: Mrs Pethick-Lawrence arranged that the women would go to court the next day. When they failed to turn up at the court on 13 October, Superintendent Wells and Inspector Jarvis went to Clement's Inn but the women were not there, hav-ing left a note to say that they would not be at headquarters until six o'clock that evening. The police searched the building but did not find them – Emmeline and Christabel were making plans on the roof terrace of the Pethick-Lawrences' flat at the top of the building. Inspector Jarvis and a couple of constables waited outside Clement's Inn to see who turned up, and warrants were issued for the arrest of the three women. At six o'clock, Flora Drummond and her husband Joe arrived, and when Mrs Pankhurst and Christabel came down from the roof all three were duly arrested by Inspector Jarvis and taken to Bow Street Court, accompanied by Minnie Baldock and Sylvia Pankhurst.[34]

Emmeline Pethick-Lawrence presided over the Women's Parliament at Caxton Hall before the 'Rush' that evening. When she arrived at the hall, suffragettes who had tickets were waiting outside. They were livid because a gang of about a hundred medical students had marched into the hall, from where they refused to move. When Mrs Pethick-Lawrence was greeted by whistles and catcalls, she reminded 'those young fellows that they were English men and believed in fair play. Was it fair play, was it sporting to interfere with women who were struggling to win the freedom which they already enjoyed and which had been won for them in the past?' She asked the man sitting nearest to the exit: 'Will you get up now and *go out of that door*!' He stood up and left and, row by row, was followed by the rest of the men. The suffragettes trooped in and the Women's Parliament could begin. The meeting passed a resolution expressing 'deep indignation at the persistent refusal of the Liberal Government to give political freedom to women' and demanded the opportunity for 'Mr Stanger's Women's Enfranchisement Bill to become law during the present session of Parliament'.[35]

Mrs Pethick-Lawrence sent eleven women, led by the artist Marion Wallace-Dunlop, to the House of Commons. They included Ada Flatman, Ada Wright (who had served time in Holloway in 1907) and Katherine Douglas Smith. Mrs Pethick-Lawrence stayed behind, firing up the audience with her rhetoric. Katherine Douglas Smith reported: 'Our women stood splendidly. Miss Wallace-Dunlop made a brave fight and broke through. She fought every inch of the way.'[36] Mrs Pethick-Lawrence dispatched more suffragettes to help their comrades, but they were met by a 'huge wall of policemen and barricades' and a cordon five men deep encircled every route to Parliament. The suffragettes pushed and shoved trying to get to the House of Commons through Parliament Square which was 'bristling with police and huge crowds'. When Una Dugdale and her comrades arrived she 'somehow managed to evade a policeman and ran to the door of Westminster Hall but alas! two plain clothes police caught me and dragged me like a sack of potatoes and flung me outside the gates again. One of them bent down and struck my head and face with both fists.'[37]

When the police tried to persuade the women to turn back, Ada Flatman said it was her 'duty as an English woman to go forward to see the Prime Minister'.[38] She was arrested, taken to Rochester Row police station and charged with 'wilful obstruction of the police in the execution of their duty'. At eight o'clock Mrs Margaret Symons, known as Maggie, got into the Chamber of the House of Commons and became the first suffragette to reach the floor of the House, able to do so because she was well known to the officials of Parliament. She asked Mr Howell Idris, the Liberal MP for Flint Boroughs, to take her to look through a window, known as the 'peep hole', into the Chamber. Before Idris could stop her she scampered through the nearby door: 'Suddenly, like an apparition, a lady in a picture hat and long cream serge coat dashed in ... and shouted "Leave off discussing the Children's Bill and turn your attention to the women's question!"'

Reporting her 'sensational dash' the next day the *Daily Mirror* said Mrs Symons' voice was 'half articulate and the lady seemed bordering on collapse'. An attendant picked her up in his arms and carried her out of the Chamber. Outside the battle raged on.[39]

Maggie Symons' involvement with the WSPU dated back to the suffragettes' earliest days. Her marriage to William Symons was over by 1906 – when she joined the WSPU. In 1909 she petitioned her husband for divorce citing his adulterous relationship with a music teacher. It was unusual for women to have the means to divorce husbands, but she succeeded and was divorced in 1911.[40]

During the 'Rush' of 13 October twenty-four women and twelve men were arrested and given prison sentences from three weeks to two months. Aeta Lamb, Lettice Floyd and Ada Wright were put in one cell at Cannon Street police station and sang songs until midnight when Frederick Pethick-Lawrence came to bail them all. On 14 October Mrs Pankhurst, Christabel and Mrs Drummond appeared before the magistrate, Mr Curtis Bennett, charged with 'circulating a handbill likely to cause a breach of the peace'. After a brief hearing the case was adjourned for a week, during which time legal-minded Christabel demanded their cases be heard by a jury, which was refused. She called Herbert Gladstone, the home secretary, and David Lloyd George, the chancellor of the exchequer, as witnesses in the suffragettes' defence. Both men had been present on the occasion and Lloyd George had brought his six-year-old daughter, Megan, to watch. The women were released on bail and addressed a meeting the following evening in St James's Hall in Great Portland Street, where a thousand WSPU members wore purple, white and green. When the leaders walked on to the platform the audience chanted 'votes for women' and Maggie Symons pronounced: 'Friends, I'll do it again.' By the end of the evening £430 had been pledged.[41]

When Ada Flatman was charged with obstructing the police on 13 October she was sent to Holloway for one month. She told the magistrate: 'I did not obstruct the police, they obstructed me from doing my duty.' In Holloway she was ordered to bathe in 'a very dirty old-fashioned bath' but Ada refused to get in and just dipped her toes in the water. The wardresses threw prison clothes into the bathroom and she emerged wearing the oddest assortment of ill-fitting clothing and thick heavy boots: 'we looked so quaint in our caps with broad black arrows and on our clothing.'[42]

In 1907, Ada Flatman, in her early thirties when she joined the WSPU, like Jessie Stephenson lived at the Twentieth Century Club in Notting Hill. Ada was a member of the NUWSS but, after hearing Christabel speak, she was smitten by the drama of militancy and joined the WSPU. She was impressed by the sight of Christabel handing out leaflets at the door, and was swept along by her 'fighting speech' on the platform, criticising the suffragists for failing to grab public attention, and insisting that only the militants could break down press hostility. Years later Ada wrote, 'it thrilled me through and through and I knew that I must be one of that valiant band'.[43]

Una Dugdale was twenty-eight when she joined the WSPU after hearing Christabel Pankhurst at Women's Sunday. The Dugdales were well off, and Una's parents supported women's suffrage. Her father, Commander Edward Dugdale, was an early member of the Men's League for Women's Suffrage founded in 1907. Una's sisters Joan and Daisy were also members.[44]

Mary Leigh, who had only just come out of prison after smashing the prime minister's windows, was soon back in the thick of things. On the night of 14 October she flung herself against two mounted policemen, grabbing a bridle in each hand, and was sent back to Holloway to serve three months. During her time in the second division Mary secretly corresponded with 'Dear Rebel', Ada Flatman, on sheets of prison lavatory paper. The women would meet secretly in the lavatory and pass notes to each other. Mary Leigh was one of the awkward squad, talking to suffragette prisoners through the grille in the door as they trooped past her cell, passing letters to Ada to smuggle around the prison and out into the world.[45]

Marion Wallace-Dunlop, doing a month in Holloway, came to the militant movement by way of the Fabian women's group and the moderate London Society for Women's Suffrage. Her widowed mother, Lucy, also joined. Marion was a descendant of the Scottish patriot William Wallace, had studied at the Slade School of Fine Art and exhibited at the Royal Academy.[46]

When twenty-year-old Mabel 'Mab' Capper was arrested on 13 October, it was the first of the six prison sentences experienced in her suffragette career. Mabel Capper and Clara Codd were arrested for 'wilful obstruction'. Meeting at Clement's Inn for their orders earlier in the day, the women had been asked by Emmeline Pethick-Lawrence to work in a pair: 'how you will do this I leave to your own initiative and judgment ... you must find some means of entering the House of Commons by the Clock Tower door and make a demonstration upon the floor of the House.'[47] They skulked in Westminster underground station all day, hiding behind a pile of mailbags, and by eight o'clock they realised that two of them stood no chance of getting past the police. So Mabel suggested, 'I will walk up as if I have just arrived by train, and let the police put me outside the barrier. Five minutes later you come and walk towards the barriers.' At the appointed time Clara Codd walked brazenly through the police cordon around Big Ben and entered the House of Commons, but she got lost and was chivvied out of the place by three housemaids. When she wandered out she was arrested: 'They gave my arms a peculiar twist which almost forced me to walk on my toes ... I was marched to Cannon Street Police Station where I found a number of my compatriots already arrested. They put us all in the billiard-room and there we had to stay until the House rose and Mr Pethick-Lawrence came to bail us out.'[48]

At Bow Street Court the next day Mabel Capper wore a costume in the colours with a sash and waist belt and hat band bearing the words 'Votes for Women'. She had been a 'voluntary soldier' since leaving school in 1907, by-electioneering and taking part in demonstrations outside Parliament. Her mother was a member of the WSPU, her father the honorary secretary of Manchester's Men's League for Women's Suffrage.[49]

Grace Roe had only been a member of the WSPU for a day when she took part in the 'Rush'. Shortly before Women's Sunday she walked into a commotion outside the Derry and Toms department store in Kensington High Street where a pavement was being chalked by a suffragette with details about the rally in Hyde Park. 'Women were drawing their skirts away horrified as if she had smallpox while a very nice burly policeman tried to get the little lady to move on.' Grace Roe was 'most excited. I rushed forward and said: "Are you a suffragette? I'm simply longing to meet a suffragette." '[50] Florence Haig, who was helping the pavement chalker, suggested Grace should walk with the Kensington contingent to Hyde Park, and wear the colours. Grace went with her grandmother and was 'overcome' when she saw Mrs Pankhurst looking 'so queenly and her oratory was simply amazing'. She was at Christabel's platform: 'She was waving her arms from side to side, you couldn't hear a word she said but she was utterly sincere from the top of her head to the tip of her little finger ... The crowds were singing "Put Me On An Island ... but never with a suffering jet", and you wondered if the lorry might be tipped over.' As Grace Roe walked away from the park she said to herself: 'That's the woman I'm going to follow.'[51]

Kitty Marion, born Katerina Schafer in Germany, a 'refined comedienne', was in her late thirties when she had her first militant moment on 13 October 1908. Her first encounter with the WSPU had been as a member of the Actresses' Franchise League contingent which walked with the WSPU from Chelsea to Hyde Park on Women's Sunday. Kitty's friends spotted her potential as a militant: 'We know your views on things ... and from the way you complain about them, you're a suffragette right enough.' As she walked to the park, surrounded by the sound of brass bands and women singing suffragette songs, she imagined herself on stage: 'When I listened to the speakers I heard my own ideas and ideals expressed much better than I could ever express them. I heard of the injustice to women in being deprived of a voice in government to which they were subservient; of having to pay taxes in the expenditure of which they had no voice, the inequality before the law regarding divorce ... the difference between the sexes regarding conditions and payment in the labour market, and the scales fell from my eyes.'[52]

Kitty was a successful music-hall artiste, popular in theatres throughout the country; she had shared the billing with Vesta Tilley in Liverpool in 1898, and with Harry Houdini in Salford in 1904. She had run away from her father in Germany to live with her aunt and uncle in London. She had a good singing voice, and her first engagement was in 1891, in pantomime in *Robinson Crusoe* at Glasgow's Theatre Royal.

Kitty was inching her way up from the chorus line, until in 1893 she was sacked from the tour of *Madcap Mavis* for rejecting the advances of an agent. Being sexually harassed, losing jobs and being broke made Kitty bitter. Not all actresses could afford to take the moral high ground and refuse the advances of lascivious agents such as the man she liked to disparage by calling him 'Mr Dreck'. It took her ten years to get top billing; most winters she was in panto for three months, often as a highly rated principal boy, blessed with 'a shapely figure and limbs to match'. From 1904 to 1911 Kitty worked 'on the halls', morally upright, often naive but never snobbish about the difference between her work in the theatre and the music hall.[53]

Kitty Marion's commitment was total: her suffragette career, which she juggled with difficulty alongside her professional career, was vivid and increasingly dangerous. In seven giddy years, from 1908 to 1914, she would be arrested nine times, serve six prison sentences and would go on hunger strike during five of her terms in prison and endure months of force-feeding. Feisty and provocative, Kitty's first outing as a suffragette in October 1908 was battering and bruising and this was often to be repeated. Her stage career would be ended by her real-life role as 'that malignant suffragette'.[54]

The cases of those arrested at the 'Rush' demonstration were heard at Bow Street Court on 21, 22 and 24 October. Christabel planned to call fifty witnesses in addition to Gladstone and Lloyd George. There was a big demand for the few places in court, for many wanted to be present at what was an historic occasion, to witness Christabel Pankhurst cross-examine the home secretary, Herbert Gladstone, and the chancellor of the exchequer, Lloyd George: 'In no case heard in this country has a lady possessing all the knowledge of a trained lawyer had the opportunity of examining Cabinet Ministers called as witnesses.'[55] Christabel opened her case in a semantic spat with Lloyd George about the meaning of the word 'rush'. She offered definitions: 'an eager demand'; 'urgent pressure'; and 'in a hurry', and asked him: 'Now if you were asked to help the Suffragettes to make an eager demand to the House of Commons that they should give votes to women, would you feel we were calling on you to do an illegal act?' He replied that it was not for him to say and made it clear he would only give evidence on what he saw. Christabel made much of Lloyd George's decision to take his six-year-old to an event which the government were saying was an incitement to violence: 'You thought it quite safe for a child of tender years to be among the crowd that day in spite of the contemplated rush?' The chancellor told her he was happy to do so 'in view of the police arrangements'.

Christabel next cross-examined Herbert Gladstone, whom Mrs Pankhurst described as 'plump, bald and ruddy'.[56] Christabel referred to intelligence she had received from Georgina Brackenbury that at a private function a magistrate of Westminster Police Court had admitted that he had been instructed in his sentencing by 'the authorities', meaning the government. When she asked Gladstone why the suffragettes were not treated as political prisoners, Mr Curtis Bennett abruptly told the minister he did not have to answer the question. By the end of the first day Christabel had established from more than twenty witnesses, including some women accused of disorderly conduct, that the suffragettes had been orderly and there had been no riot. Max Beerbohm, the writer and caricaturist, was in court, and was impressed by Christabel's confidence and composure: 'Miss Pankhurst in her barred pen seemed as comfortable and self-possessed as Mr Curtis Bennett on the bench. As she stood there with her head inclined merrily to one side, trilling her questions to the Chancellor ... she was like nothing so much as a little singing bird born in captivity ... Mr Lloyd George did not seem at all as though he had been born in the witness box. His Celtic fire burned very low.'[57]

On 24 October the court reassembled and magistrate Mr Curtis Bennett pronounced that the court's time was being wasted and he would not allow Christabel to call the fifty witnesses she wanted to cross-examine, and that she, her mother and Mrs Drummond, had to speak in their own defence. Christabel broke down in tears: 'This is a Star Chamber of the twentieth century and it is in order to huddle us into prison without a fair trial that these proceedings have been taken in their present form.'[58] She recovered her composure and concluded her defence with an impressive closing speech. Mrs Pankhurst's was long, passionate and framed with references to her work in Manchester as a Registrar of Births and Deaths, a Poor Law Guardian and an Education Committee member. Her exposure to the realities of the lives of the poorest women had revealed their vulnerability in the English legal system. Women like herself and members of the WSPU were being driven to break man-made laws – in which they had had no say – in order to voice their wish to be law-makers.

We women have presented larger petitions in support of our enfranchisement than were ever presented for any other reform; we have succeeded in holding greater public meetings than men have ever held for any reform ... We have faced hostile mobs at street corners, because we were told that we could not have that representation for our taxes that men have won unless we converted the whole of the country to our side ... We have been misrepresented, we have been ridiculed, and we have had contempt poured upon us and the ignorant mob have been incited to offer us violence, which we faced unarmed and unprotected by the safeguards the Cabinet Ministers enjoy ... Just as it was the duty of your forefathers, it is our duty to make the world a better place for women than it is today.[59]

Flora Drummond, three months pregnant, told Mr Curtis Bennett that the 'agitation would go on' in their absence. Mrs Pankhurst and Flora Drummond were sentenced to three months, and Christabel to ten weeks' imprisonment. The Pethick-Lawrences and Sylvia Pankhurst took over the day-to-day running of the Union, keeping up the pressure on the government, briefing the members and the press as to how their leader and her daughter and 'the General' were coping with life behind bars.[60]

A *Daily Mirror* photographer, Arthur Barrett, was responsible for some extraordinary photographs of a tight-lipped Mrs Pankhurst, a grumpy-looking Flora Drummond, and Christabel, deadly bored, leaning on the dock at Bow Street while they were being sentenced. Using available light, he recorded an exclusive: 'I fitted a small camera inside my top hat and cut a flap to allow the lens to see through ... I hurried to Bow Street to take my position in the press stand. In filed the three prisoners and while the magistrate [Mr Curtis Bennett] was sentencing them I clicked the shutter and coughed at the same time and hurried out of the court.'[61]

The twelve men who were arrested on 13 October were offered the chance to pay a fine and be bound over to keep the peace, or serve between one and two months in Pentonville Prison. Only three were bound over; the rest were sent to prison. There was a large presence of working men in the square that evening. Faced with the sight of defenceless women being knocked about by uniformed and plain-clothes officers, some had sympathy for the women's aims, and it was also a chance to settle a few scores with the police.[62]

Mrs Pankhurst, on her second prison sentence, refused to undress in front of the wardresses and demanded to see the prison governor, Dr Richard Frith Quinton. She insisted that she be allowed to talk to her fellow suffragettes. Dr Quinton allowed the Pankhursts and Drummond to undress in private and he put mother and daughter in cells adjacent to each other, but he would not waive the rule of silence.[63] On the first day of her sentence Flora Drummond was taken ill and was released on 3 November after nine days in Holloway. Her first child, Percival, had died in 1901, and their son Keir Hardie was two years old. Flora Drummond lost the baby but this information was kept private. She went back to Clement's Inn and threw herself into the fray like a true general, organising and deploying her troops.

While suffragettes served their time, they were serenaded by comrades marching round outside the prison singing 'The Marseillaise'. When prisoners were released there were welcoming parties and prisoners' breakfasts, and they were awarded 'Holloway Medals' to honour their sacrifice. On 28 October, when Muriel Matters and Helen Fox of the Women's Freedom League chained themselves to the grille of the Ladies' Gallery in order to harangue the House of Commons, which resulted in the women being removed still attached to the grille, the prime minister was 'harassed' at the opening of a bazaar during 'disorderly scenes'.[64] Despite a large police presence, a dozen suffragettes wearing their political colours were allowed into the bazaar but later 'carried' out and 'ejected' from the meeting as they made their interruptions amid hissing from the diehard Liberal audience. They were shouting 'votes for women' and yelling: 'What about Mrs Pankhurst in Holloway? You are responsible for that you tyrant ... Down with Liberal hypocrites' and 'Call yourself a Liberal'. The women who were thrown out waited for Asquith to emerge so as to harangue him again. The next day Maud Joachim and Katherine Douglas Smith held up traffic in the West End when they left Clement's Inn on horseback with placards hanging from their saddles advertising the WSPU meeting in the Albert Hall that evening, where the Pethick-Lawrences and Mary Gawthorpe were due to speak. As the ladies rode up the Strand 'on their black bay horses there was considerable excitement'.[65]

Lettice Floyd, who had been arrested in October, had joined the WSPU earlier in the year and campaigned at the Haverford

West by-election. In 1907 Lettice and her sister Mary founded Birmingham Women's Suffrage Society, but the Floyd sisters' impatience with the suffragists' moderate pace led to the branch being dissolved and replaced by the WSPU. Before she took part in the 'Rush', Lettice Floyd, in her early forties, was working with Annie Kenney in Bristol when she met Annie Williams, who was spending the 'harvest holiday' from Crantock Public Elementary School, Newquay, where she was headmistress, helping the suffragettes. In April 1909 Annie would resign her post to devote herself to the suffragettes' cause, becoming an organiser in Newcastle upon Tyne. Miss Floyd and Miss Williams lived together for the rest of their long lives.[66]

The Chelmsford by-election, which took place on 1 December, gave the WSPU a timely opportunity for twelve of their members, all of them ex-prisoners, to take part in a new protest – wearing replica Holloway clothing and marching about the streets of the Essex constituency, protesting that suffragettes were not treated as political prisoners. Travelling atop motor omnibuses trundling from central London to Chelmsford, wearing a coarse green prison dress covered with arrows, their hair stuffed into Dutch bonnets, with their prison numbers painted on a leather disc and worn as a badge, theirs was a dramatic gesture and it had shock value.[67]

The reporter from the *Essex News* was bowled over by the suffragettes: 'they are the brightest, sunniest and happiest people that could possibly be met' and had 'won the hearts and minds of the people of Essex' and perhaps his heart too.[68] The *Observer* liked 'the splash of colour' and noticed how much Chelmsford had 'taken the suffragettes to its heart. Expecting a shrieking sisterhood' the town had been 'agreeably surprised to find that the women combine good looks with good strategy and enterprise with culture'.[69] The Conservative candidate, E. G. Pretyman, fought the seat after the outgoing Conservative candidate retired, and retained it, fighting off the Liberal candidate, Mr Alexander Henry Dence, and improved on the Conservatives' tiny majority in the 1906 election, but this result made no difference to the prospects of a women's suffrage bill being passed.[70]

On 5 December, twenty-five-year-old Helen Ogston used a dog-whip on two men who assaulted her at a meeting in the Albert Hall during a gathering of the Women's Liberal Federation chaired by Lady McLaren. David Lloyd George, chancellor of the exchequer, was the main speaker. Helen Ogston was one of a dozen WSPU hecklers determined to interrupt the cabinet minister's speech, and she took a dog-whip with her to protect herself from 'indecent assault' by unruly members of the audience. Sylvia Pankhurst tried to dissuade her from taking it and offered Helen an umbrella instead, but her advice was rejected. 'Surely you do not desire women to submit to that without protest', she said, insisting she would use it on any man 'who dared to mishandle her'. Helen Ogston was in a box, the other hecklers were in the front row and scattered about the room; they tore off their capes when the meeting began and revealed their replica prison clothing. Women were getting criminal records because they wanted the vote. Helen hit a man who had burnt her wrist with his cigar, and whipped another who hit her in her breast. She agreed to leave, refusing to be manhandled out of the building, but 'they all struck at me ... I do not think we should submit to such violence. It is not a question of being thrown out; we are set upon and beaten.' Sylvia Pankhurst remembered: 'They came [to Clement's Inn] in ones and twos, bruised and dishevelled, hatless, hair dragged down and clothing torn; some had their corsets ripped off, false teeth knocked out, faces scratched, eyes swollen, noses bleeding.'[71] Sylvia telephoned journalists and asked them to come and see the battered hecklers and told them, 'This is how our women return from questioning David Lloyd George.' It was an escalation of militancy which made Fred Pethick-Lawrence nervous, wishing he had known about it beforehand.[72]

The fallout was swift: Lloyd George banned women from his meetings, and, rankled by the suffragettes' panache at by-election campaigns, on 21 December the government rushed through the Public Meetings Act, 'an act to prevent the disturbance of public meetings', which decreed that anyone who

> acts in a disorderly manner for the purpose of preventing the transaction of the business for which the meeting was called together shall be guilty of an offence, and if the offence is committed at a political meeting held in any parliamentary constituency between the date of the issue of a writ for the return of a Member of Parliament

for such constituency to the date at which a return to such writ is made, he shall be guilty of an illegal practice under the meaning of the Corrupt and Illegal Practices Act, 1883 and shall be liable to a fine not exceeding five pounds or imprisonment not exceeding one month.

Anyone inciting such behaviour was liable to the same penalties if convicted.[73]

On Saturday 19 December Mrs Pankhurst, Christabel Pankhurst and Mary Leigh were released from prison early, the authorities keen to avoid the welcome party at Holloway and procession back to central London.[74] Two days later the three women were guests of honour at a welcome breakfast at the Inns of Court Hotel, hastily arranged by the Pethick-Lawrences. Mrs Pankhurst announced a new policy which would inform the rest of the campaign and from the spring of 1909 plunge them into a harrowing conflict with the government. Mrs Pankhurst told WSPU members: 'henceforth we should all insist on refusing to abide by ordinary prison rules. We did not propose to break laws and then shirk punishment. We simply mean to assert our right to be recognised as political prisoners.'[75] She reminded her audience that she had come to this decision only after a great deal of careful thought, listening to the experiences of members who had been to prison, and her own recent spell inside. But 'now that we had in the witness box the admission of cabinet Ministers that we are political offenders we should in future demand the treatment given to male political prisoners in all civilised countries ... we are not going to allow the Liberal government to treat us like ordinary criminals.'[76]

Suffragettes who bought tickets for the evening celebration at the Queen's Hall to be chaired by Mrs Pankhurst were asked to come dressed in the new uniform of 'short skirt [just above the ankle] of purple or green, a white jersey golf coat and a simple hat of purple or green'.[77] That evening Christabel announced an escalation of militancy: 'I say to you that any woman who is content to appeal for votes for women instead of demanding and fighting for it is dishonouring herself.' Cabinet ministers were to be targeted and 'met by constant protests against their continual refusal to enfranchise women'.

Deputations to Parliament would continue 'regardless of the danger of arrest and imprisonment'.[78]

In December, sixteen-year-old Cicely Fairfield (later better known as Rebecca West) returned to her home town of Edinburgh to rouse the locals after a summer of canvassing in England. Cicely was at the first meeting of the Votes for Women Club in Edinburgh, 'a sort of secret militant society for men and women', formed to protest outside the hall where Richard Haldane, the secretary of state for war and MP for East Lothian, was due to speak on 5 January 1909.[79]

6

Stalking Liberals and the Bill of Rights Demonstration

The Women's Exhibition 1909

*The two-week-long 'Women's Exhibition and Sale of Works in the Colours'
at the Princes' Skating Rink, Knightsbridge, raised money for the
WSPU's war chest.*

On 14 January 1909, the WSPU presented Mrs Pankhurst with an amethyst, pearl and emerald necklace at the Queen's Hall. Mabel Tuke, who had organised the fund and commissioned the piece, was confident that it would 'satisfy members and friends who feel that nothing is beautiful enough to express the thoughts and feelings they have about the founder of the Union'.[1] Clara Mordan, the most generous donor apart from the Pethick-Lawrences, presented the gift to their leader.

Mary Leigh, who was not present, was also honoured and given a clock: 'in commemoration of the year 1908, when for taking part in public demonstrations of protest against the political subjection of women, she was sentenced three times to terms of imprisonment amounting to more than six months' incarceration in Holloway, she won by her brave spirit and cheerful endurance the admiration and esteem of all her comrades in the Votes for Women agitation.'[2] Mary Leigh sent a message: 'It will always be a pleasure to me. It is something I can hand down with pride. My absence this evening is a grief it would be impossible to exaggerate.'[3]

The WSPU calendar was dictated by Parliament and its procedures. When politicians returned to London after Christmas, the forthcoming business of both Houses was announced in the King's Speech, and MPs who had secured a private members' bill were hotly pursued by vested interests for their slot in the limited debating time allocated by the government of the day. The WSPU buckled on its breastplate to do battle for a private members' bill.

During the afternoon of 25 January 1909, five women were arrested trying to push their way into 10 Downing Street to lobby the Liberal prime minister, Herbert Asquith, who was chairing the first Cabinet of the year. Lucy Norris, who worked at Clement's Inn, and Mrs Pankhurst's sister, Mary Clarke, were told he was not there but they refused to leave, saying, 'It's a lie, we don't believe you.' They were charged with obstruction. Lucy Norris later told the magistrate: 'we did not care what we did.'[4] A triple-strength police cordon was put across the entrance to Downing Street but a couple of hours later Irene Dallas, Katherine Douglas Smith and Frances Bartlett arrived in a taxi and talked their way through the police cordon. They drove up to the prime minister's residence, asked to see him and tried 'to force their way in'. They refused to leave quietly.

Mrs Frances Bartlett, thirty-five, gave the police her maiden name of Satterley to try to avoid her husband losing his job as a postman because he was married to a member of an anti-government organisation. She had married Daniel Bartlett in 1892, when she was seventeen, and by the time she was twenty-one Frances had had three children. 'I was always very keen on what was going on outside my home life, and so I took up church work, then election work in my spare time.'[5] She was elected to the Executive Committee of the Clapham Women's Liberal Association. In the autumn of 1906 she went to a debate between Christabel Pankhurst and a Liberal politician at the National Liberal Club: 'Christabel was quite alone although she put up a good fight.'[6] Frances jumped up in a fury and announced that if that was the way Liberals treated women she would give no more of her time. Christabel asked Frances to visit Clement's Inn the next day. Frances joined the WSPU and resigned from the Liberal Association, to 'give all my time to the militant movement'.[7]

The WSPU badly needed able women to run the growing organisation and could not rely on chance encounters alone. Before a deputation to the House of Commons on 23 February, in *Votes for Women* Mrs Pethick-Lawrence issued an appeal for 'More Officers':

> I say to you young women who have private means or parents who are able and willing to support you while they give you freedom to choose your vocation. Come and give me one year of your life to bring the message of deliverance to thousands of your sisters who

are still living lives of social and economic and mental and moral bondage ... Put yourself through a short course of training under one of our chief organisers, or at headquarters in London ... every would-be organiser has to undergo a training and testing of three months, and during that time a sum to cover board and lodging expenses is paid to her ... If she is fitted to the work she will become one of the staff organisers.[8]

Coupled with smart administration, ingenuity, which had always been a strong point of the suffragettes' campaign, was becoming the order of the day. The day before the deputation to Parliament, Jessie Kenney took Daisy Solomon and Elspeth McClelland to the post office in the Strand, and paid threepence for them to be 'posted' as 'human letters' to Herbert Asquith at 10 Downing Street. Post office regulations stated that an individual could be 'posted' by an express messenger and the women were delivered by a messenger boy. Christabel Pankhurst and Flora Drummond went too. The *Daily Mirror* sent a reporter and photographer and splashed the story on the next day's front page. The lad was allowed inside Number 10 but after ten minutes was told the 'human letters' would not be accepted. When Flora spotted Winston Churchill approaching, she pounced on him: 'We must have the vote this session, if something is not done we will carry on the struggle till the bitter end.' Churchill told her that the suffragettes had done well so far, 'but if you carry on any further you will damage your cause'.[9] Daisy and Elspeth attended the meeting in Caxton Hall that evening to tumultuous applause.

Daisy Dorothea Solomon was the daughter of Saul and Georgiana Solomon. Saul Solomon (1817–92), the owner of the *Cape Argus* newspaper and later governor-general of the Cape Colony,[10] was a feminist sympathiser who owned a first edition of Mary Wollstonecraft's *Vindication of the Rights of Woman*. In 1907 Georgiana Solomon and Daisy were active in the Women's Liberal Association, but by 1908 the Liberal Party's shilly-shallying on votes for women had driven them into the arms of the WSPU.[11] Elspeth McClelland, born in Yorkshire in 1879, was a furniture designer and decorator. The *Lady's Pictorial* reported: 'Miss McClelland is artistic to the core, she has no fetish, and entirely disbelieves in artistic discomfort ... her ideals are essentially those of sanity.'[12]

At the state opening of Parliament on 16 February 1909, the Women's Freedom League reminded the WSPU that they were not the only innovative organisation.

Muriel Matters, who was from Adelaide, where women had been able to vote and stand for Parliament since 1894, hired an airship from Spencer and Sons, balloon-makers of Highbury, to fly her from the Welsh Harp Reservoir at Hendon to hover above the House of Commons.[13] Her pilot Henry Spencer was a sympathiser who painted the airship with the words 'Votes For Women' on one side and 'Women's Freedom League' on the other. Muriel climbed into the wicker gondola and flew 3,000 feet above the ground, arming herself with fifty-six pounds of handbills to shower down on the King and the crowds in Westminster. She remembered: 'I suppose it was a risky venture … I was young and the experience of the suffragettes taught one to be tough.' Henry Spencer clambered out of the gondola to make an adjustment: 'He was rather like a spider walking across its web for the rigging was quite open and there was nothing between him and the earth, and I suddenly realised that if he fell off I hadn't the faintest idea how to manoeuvre the airship.' The eighty-foot airship was blown off course and got nowhere near Westminster, ending up instead in a tree in Coulsdon, Surrey. The Women's Freedom League and the suffrage cause received lots of publicity.[14]

On 24 February, the deputation to Parliament to seek a meeting with the prime minister and secure a private members' bill included Lady Constance Lytton, who was taking part in her first WSPU action. Recruiting an ardent supporter of the militant campaign of such high social rank (and whose brother Victor, the Earl of Lytton, was a bigwig in the Conservative Party) had been a valuable publicity coup. The suffragettes who had volunteered for 'danger duty' sat on the platform at the Women's Parliament in Caxton Hall. Choral singing was accompanied by a brass band, and Mrs Pankhurst reminded the women they were meeting for the purpose of 'Deeds Not Words'.[15]

A resolution calling on the government 'to introduce and carry into law this session a measure giving votes to women on the same terms as to men' was passed. Mrs Pethick-Lawrence then led thirty women through the fog from Caxton Hall to the House of Commons. The suffragettes were not permitted to walk as a large group, so they walked to the House of Commons in twos and threes, and 'were followed by a jeering mob of youths and girls'. Forty constables 'massed in a solid body in front of the doors'. The crowd pushed the women against the policemen so that they were nose-to-nose. Mrs Pethick-Lawrence asked to see a Member of Parliament and after the usual refusal they 'threw themselves against the solid line of constables'. *The Times* sympathised with the police who 'endured patiently the pushing and scratching of the militants and a vigorous but totally ineffective and unimpressive lashing with the tongue of sarcasm and abuse'. Mrs Pethick-Lawrence and Constance Lytton were taken to Canon Row police station.[16]

Meanwhile, in Caxton Hall Mrs Pankhurst was holding forth when the news came of the rejection and ejection. She sent another deputation. Mrs Solomon and her three comrades were ushered away by the police who 'screened them from the horseplay of the mob'.[17] Mrs Pankhurst was told that Herbert Asquith was dining at Brooks' Club. A hundred women in the audience volunteered to go and tell him what had been happening while he was having dinner and walked to St James's Street to be met by policemen barring their way. When the suffragettes tried to squeeze past, the constables 'charged' and the procession was 'broken up and dispersed in all directions'.[18]

By the end of the night twenty-seven women, and Emmeline Pethick-Lawrence's brother-in-law, Thomas Mortimer Budgett, were charged with obstructing the police. The next day at Bow Street Court their cases were heard by Sir Albert de Rutzen. Apart from Emmeline Pethick-Lawrence, who was sentenced to two months, they were charged with obstructing the police and sentenced to four weeks in the second division. For the majority this was their first brush with heavy-handed policing: Constance Lytton, Caprina Fahey, Daisy Solomon, Rose Lamartine Yates and Sarah Carwin were a new set of first-time suffragette prisoners.[19]

Elsa Gye, an experienced suffragette, partnered Constance Lytton on her first outing. Nervously, Constance asked what she had to do, to which Elsa replied: 'Oh, you needn't bother about what you'll do, it will all be done to you. There is only one thing you must remember. You must on no account be turned back. If the police become too violent you can cut matters short and get arrested instantly by creating a breach of the peace.'[20] Elsa suggested Constance could make a speech, and gather a crowd around her.

Constance's weak heart did not enjoy the experience – she felt breathless, could not lift her head and chest and could barely speak. She became separated from Elsa and when she found herself jammed up against a policeman all she could say was: 'I know you are only doing your duty and I am doing mine.' The constable grabbed her with both hands, and 'squeezed the remaining breath out of me and lifting me completely in the air, threw me with all his strength'.[21] She was caught before she hit the ground, thus avoiding being trampled. One of Constance's most vivid memories of the evening were flashes of bright light and muffled explosions which she later realised were the photographers' flashbulbs. With dogged determination she reached the Strangers' Entrance but was arrested and taken away by two policemen, who held her up as they led her to Canon Row police station.[22]

As Constance waited to be taken to Holloway she scribbled a note to her 'Angel Mum', reassuring her how happy and well she was. She hoped her mother could forgive her 'and bear it for my sake. I have nothing else to wish for as regards myself.'[23] Constance's younger brother, Neville, also wrote home. He told his mother how proud the family might be of Constance 'as courage is the rarest and noblest of all human qualities'. Neville was sure his father would have been respectful of her 'as no one knew better than he the value of courage'.[24]

On the morning of the deputation Constance had sat down in the waiting room at King's Cross station and written to her mother, 'I have something to tell you which – with the help of recent presentiments – you, I know, are half expecting to hear … For months I have been planning this letter to you but now that the time has come it is not any easier to write for all that.' Constance was excited but frightened about coming out as a fully fledged suffragette: 'my hope has been that I should be able to take you into my confidence and have the undeserved heaven-like joy of knowing that although you could not share all my views that you would understand why I held them … and that you would understand my action and the great sacrifice which I know it means to you.'[25]

Constance reassured her mother that she would not follow the WSPU's policies blindly: 'There are several things which the

Suffragettes do which I would not and could not do.' Knowing that her heart condition was her mother's concern, she asked her not to worry about a likely prison sentence: 'I am such a muff, what remains of hardship will be wholesome for me – really "reformatory" for me as prison is seldom in others ... I am no hero but the thought of others' much worse privations on that road, will, I believe, fizzle up my flimsy body enough for what is necessary.'[26]

At Bow Street Court the next morning Constance Lytton was quoted in *The Times* declaring that she 'was more proud to be able to stand by her friends than of anything else she had done in her life'. Lady Constance Bulwer-Lytton was the grandest new member of the WSPU. Born in Vienna in 1869, her privileged spinster life was one of stultifying boredom. Constance's father was Robert Bulwer-Lytton, 1st Earl of Lytton, a diplomat and poet, who had been viceroy and governor-general of India; her mother was the Hon. Edith Villiers.[27] In 1825 Constance's great-grandmother, Anna Wheeler, had helped William Thomson write *Appeal of One Half of the Human Race, Women, Against the Pretensions of the Other Half, Men.*[28]

Constance Lytton's sister Betty was married to Gerald Balfour, the Conservative MP for Leeds Central, whose brother Arthur became Conservative prime minister in 1902. Until Constance joined the WSPU her life was dominated by the companionship and demands of the widowed Edith. In 1892 mother and daughter sailed to Cape Town to visit Constance's godmother. Twenty-three-year-old Constance met the charismatic Olive Schreiner, who was impressed by her young visitor. Constance was also awakened to love, writing to her cousin Adela Villiers, 'I am more happy since I have been here, in a light-hearted, gay kind of way, than I ever remember being in my life before. All the men are so much more courteous and sociable than in England, so that instead of dreading their presence, as I generally do, I feel quite dull when they are not there, and can laugh and joke with them from morning to night.'[29]

The friendliest of these chaps was John Ponsonby, the aide-de-camp to her godmother's husband, Henry Loch. His father, Sir Henry Ponsonby, had a distinguished military career, was equerry to Prince Albert and was Queen Victoria's private secretary for twenty years. His son John got a commission in the Coldstream Guards. Constance fell in love with this tall, dark and handsome second lieutenant. Constance thought the understanding was that they would marry when he had been promoted enough to earn a salary to support them.[30]

The Lytton family, however, rejected the idea of John Ponsonby marrying their eldest daughter. If Constance had married the soldier she would have married below her rank, something not to be borne. Constance wondered if John Ponsonby's hare-lip and cleft palate was an issue: 'Every fresh appointment goes to prove that his speech does not matter.' For seven years Constance refused to give up hope, and then only when she was told he had fallen in love with another woman. On 1 January 1900 she told Adela: 'My own aim of life is to live less, think less, feel less and mind less what I feel. Less, less, less … that's what I've always been striving.' The thwarted lovers wrote to each other for many years; sometimes she saw him and they had snatched conversations. (John Ponsonby did eventually marry, but not until 1935 when he was sixty-nine years old.)[31]

Constance met Emmeline Pethick-Lawrence and the Kenney sisters in 1908 while on holiday at the Green Lady Hostel run by the Esperance Girls' Club in Littlehampton, Sussex. She told Adela she had 'got knotted up with Suffragettes at Littlehampton and through them have come into personal first-hand contact with prison abuses'. She liked Mrs Pethick-Lawrence, 'entirely lovable and sympathetic woman of the Olive Schreiner type … she is the only practising philanthropist I have ever met who is sympathetic to me – one feels she does it all for fun, *not* for the good of her soul, and joins in with, and really appreciates the lives of those she befriends rather than to "save" them.'[32]

Before she joined the WSPU, Constance Lytton became more aware of the escalating political campaign: she was at Bow Street Court to see the leaders sentenced, and she went to see the release from Holloway of the women arrested at the 'Rush' ('the moment was thrilling … they simply ran out, rather dazed, and looking like children, some with their arms outstretched'). Constance spoke nervously at a handful of drawing-room meetings and organised a petition of signatures of the great and the good of Edwardian society. She declared, 'I go deeper and deeper in my enthusiasm for the women and even their tactics as I understand more and more – not only what they do, but what had been done *to* them.' On 19 January 1909 Constance Lytton took the step that would inform the rest of her life and joined the WSPU. Her embracing of morris dancing, the Esperance Club and militant suffrage was the logical result of being forbidden to marry John Ponsonby. Instead of having a life, love and a family, Constance fell in love with the militant WSPU, and despite the Lyttons' disapproval she adopted the suffragettes, treating women like Annie Kenney as members of her family.[33]

Constance Lytton's 'family' expanded and diversified the moment she joined the WSPU. Her fellow 'gaolbirds' included Caprina Fahey, a trained masseuse; Sarah Carwin, who ran a home for illegitimate babies; and Rose Lamartine Yates, who was married to a women's suffrage-supporting solicitor. Caprina Fahey was sentenced to a month in Holloway Gaol. She had attended Women's Sunday at the same time that she was petitioning her husband for divorce for desertion and adultery. Daughter of the famous sculptor Alfred Gilbert, the maker of Eros in Piccadilly Circus, Caprina married one of her father's assistants, Alfred Edward Fahey, in 1901; he walked out on her in 1905, six months after the birth of their son. By the end of 1908 she was divorced, and unusually for the time, was granted custody of the child.[34]

Sarah Carwin was a new recruit to the WSPU when she was arrested on the deputation. She had joined the Methodist Sisterhood of the West London Mission in 1890. Many of the young women Sarah Carwin worked with were seasonal workers in the garment trade who were sacked when the fashion season was over. By 1891 Sarah, aged twenty-eight, had started a co-operative dressmaking business in Marylebone to provide such women with regular employment and a steady income. Then she enrolled as a trainee nurse at Great Ormond Street children's hospital, and qualified in 1896. In 1901 she ran a 'Babies' Home' for a dozen illegitimate babies in Caterham. Sarah had 'always been a feminist', influenced by Olive Schreiner's writings, and 'when the suffragette movement began to be known it strongly appealed to her. She had never taken part in politics or interested herself much in them; but here was an adventure, a crusade against injustice, an ideal to be served.'[35]

Rose Lamartine Yates had only been a member of the newly formed Wimbledon WSPU a few weeks when she was charged with obstructing the police on 24 February and sentenced to one month in gaol. At Bow Street the next day, defended by her husband Tom, she told Albert de Rutzen: 'Every woman must have the courage of

her convictions, and not slink back when she has taken her first step.'
Rose told the court she had an eight-month-old son and that she and
her husband had discussed how she might feel if their son asked her
what she had done 'in the days of the women's agitation, to lay the
views of the women before the Prime Minister'. And because Rose
'could not but blush' if she had to say that she had done nothing,
she said that for 'private and public reason I stand before your worship today to bear whatever punishment you may think me deserving
of'. When Rose returned home after serving her sentence, it had been
decorated in purple, white and green.[36]

Rose studied modern languages at Royal Holloway College. In
1900, aged twenty-five, she married Thomas Lamartine Yates, a
widower twenty years older than her who had known Rose since
she was a girl. In the evenings she studied law with Tom so that she
could help him in his work as a solicitor. To her indignation Rose
learned that women were virtually invisible in the eyes of the law,
writing: 'the reason such a state of affairs exists is that by order of
man woman is dumb with regard to all the legislative and national
affairs'. In 1907 she won a seat on the council of the Wimbledon
District Cyclists' Touring Club, its only female member. In her
election speech she insisted she was not a suffragette. However,
within a year she had an epiphany: 'On looking into the matter seriously I find I have never been anything else [but a suffragette] ...
and I came to realise that I was and must remain one at whatever
personal cost.'[37]

Because of her title most of Constance Lytton's month-long sentence was spent in the hospital wing, which greatly annoyed her.
She wanted to serve her sentence like the rest of her suffragette
comrades and decided to take an extreme step – to her the only
logical way of dealing with the prison authorities. On 16 March
Constance Lytton started to self-harm. In her memoir she describes
why she went to such extremes. 'I had decided to write the words
"Votes for Women" on my body, scratching it in my skin with a
needle, beginning over my heart and ending it on my face. I proposed to show the first half of the inscription to the doctors, telling them that as I know how much appearances were respected by
officials, I thought it well to warn them that the last letter and a
full stop would come upon my cheek, and be still quite fresh and

visible on the day of my release.' Constance Lytton set to work using a needle and broken hatpin; she took twenty minutes to cut 'a very fine V just over my heart' but she cut herself deeper than intended and the scratch bled more than she had expected. Afraid of blood poisoning, she asked a wardress for a small piece of lint and plaster. The prison doctors were 'very much put out' by what she had done, but she took delight in her handiwork: 'the V was very clearly and evenly printed' despite her 'rib bone forming an awkward bump'. She was bandaged up and when healed Constance was allowed to spend time in an ordinary cell. She made notes in 'red ink' for the speech she was determined to make when she was released. The 'red ink' was her blood.[38]

When Constance Lytton was released on 24 March her sister Betty ('Bets') met her at the prison gates: 'As soon as I saw her, I realised as I had not done before that she no longer belonged to us. She belonged to her Union, and nothing else really counted.' Constance's sister Emily, who was married to the architect Edwin Lutyens, wrote a forlorn note to their aunt: 'I must write you a line of deepest sympathy ... I know how you must be suffering about Con ... We cannot disguise from ourselves that our old Con has gone for ever ... I think she has ceased to have any private affection. She has become an impersonal being.'[39]

*

During March that same year, Mrs Pankhurst toured the north-west of England, recruiting volunteers to take part in a deputation of Lancashire women to come to London to see the prime minister at the House of Commons, ending the tour with a rally at the Free Trade Hall in Manchester. Emily Davison was at the Free Trade Hall and volunteered to go on the deputation. Dora Marsden, head-mistress of Altrincham Pupil-Teacher Centre, and Rona Robinson, a teacher and the first woman in England to be awarded a first-class degree in chemistry, resigned their posts to take part in the deputation.[40]

In the afternoon of 30 March, Dora Marsden, carrying a tricolour, led a deputation of twenty-nine women to see Herbert Asquith, even though he had already refused to meet them. Accompanied by a brass band and singing 'The Marseillaise', the women reached

St Stephen's Entrance, but Dora Marsden, less than five feet tall, became tangled up with three police horses and the staff of her banner was broken. One suffragette hit a constable on the head with her umbrella, other policemen had their helmets knocked off. The *Daily Mirror* had photographs of Dora on the front page looking tiny next to Superintendent Wells and his men. Wells caught her in his arms as she tried to hit him in the face. Ten women and the journalist William Hutcheson were charged with obstruction and assaulting the police: nine were sentenced to one month, while Patricia Woodlock was sentenced to three months. An MP who watched from the safety of the House of Commons observed: 'The women squeak like rabbits.'[41]

Emily Davison's case was heard first: a constable testified that she was the most persistent in trying to enter the House of Commons, and that she assaulted him. Unusually, de Rutzen commended the women for their courage, but because they had broken the law he had no option but to send them to prison. For Emily Davison, Dora Marsden and Rona Robinson, found guilty of obstruction and assault, this was their first time in gaol; for Davison and Marsden it would not be their last. The next day a group of suffragettes dashed through the open gates at St Stephen's Entrance to lobby the prime minister and were thrown back into the crowd; nine were arrested and charged with obstruction, including Mrs Louise Eates, secretary of the Kensington branch of the WSPU.[42]

At 8 a.m. on Friday 16 April Mrs Pethick-Lawrence was released from Holloway to a warm welcome at the gates and was met by Mrs Pankhurst and Christabel, Annie and Jessie Kenney, Vera Wentworth, Mary Phillips, Minnie Baldock and Mary Gawthorpe. There was a breakfast at the Criterion restaurant in Piccadilly Circus, at which 500 members of the WSPU were present.[43]

The next day several hundred WSPU members walked from Hyde Park to an afternoon meeting at the Aldwych Theatre, lavishly decorated in the colours. Elsie Howey, as Joan of Arc in shining armour on a white horse holding a purple, white and green flag, led the procession, escorting Mrs Pethick-Lawrence in a carriage drawn by four grey horses. According to Evelyn Sharp, Elsie Howey unsurprisingly attracted the most attention: 'I suppose there is no other character in history needs so little explanation as hers ... the majority knew that the girl on the great white horse stood for a battle against prejudice that is as ancient as it is modern.' The timing of the procession was good: the next day Joan of Arc was beatified.[44]

*

Meanwhile, the suffragette arboretum in the field adjoining the Blathwayts' house flourished. On 23 April two conifers were planted by Annie Kenney, one for herself and one for Constance Lytton. Constance enjoyed her time with the Blathwayts and liked their 'splendid zealous daughter' Mary. After her visit she wrote to Annie Kenney expressing her gratitude for 'all the glow you put into me from your glowing living self in these few times we have been together'. She referred to her time in prison: 'I was so down, so smashed, so failure-filled that it was all I could do not to throw up the Bath plan ... Now I feel mended up – quite different to anything that has been since Holloway and I think I shall not go back down again.'[45]

*

On 27 April Theresa Garnett was one of five suffragettes who entered St Stephen's Hall. They arrived quietly, asking to see a Member of Parliament, but hidden in their clothing were leather belts, handcuffs, padlocks and chains which they used to manacle themselves to the bronze statues of four famous parliamentarians: Lords Walpole, Selden, Falkland and Somers. They were protesting at the proposed 'Brawling Bill', intended to criminalise anyone guilty of disorderly conduct in the Palace of Westminster while Parliament was in session. Although the idea had been thrown out a few days earlier, it was too good for the suffragettes to ignore. Theresa Garnett ran about blowing a whistle and before anyone could stop them they were chained up and shouting 'votes for women'. It took the police ten minutes to free the women, who were detained but not arrested.[46]

Frances Theresa Garnett was born in Leeds in 1888. When she was twenty-one days old, her mother died of 'puerperal mania' at the West Riding Pauper Lunatic Asylum near Wakefield. Theresa Garnett was brought up by her paternal grandparents and was working as a pupil-teacher when she heard Adela Pankhurst speak in 1907, and joined the WSPU.[47]

*

On 28 April, Herbert Asquith was photographed being nobbled by two suffragettes as he left a meeting in Whitehall with three senior Liberal politicians: Grey, the foreign secretary; Crewe, secretary of state for the colonies; and Morley, secretary of state for India. They looked on in astonishment as the women held the prime minister's elbows and 'escorted' him to 10 Downing Street. It was a planned operation, and a *Daily Mirror* photographer was there to capture the moment. Olive Fargus and Mrs Frank Corbett appeared in two of its pages: Olive Fargus, who was twenty-nine, was a solicitor's daughter from Twickenham,[48] and Mrs Catherine Corbett, a 'tall dark and handsome lady', had been out of prison a month after serving four weeks for obstruction on the 24 February deputation. Mrs Corbett told the reporter that Mr Asquith was a 'little surprised and reserved but he showed no resentment'. They asked him when he was going to receive their representatives. After a short pause he told the women, 'I think you are very silly.' On the doorstep of 10 Downing Street they had a few final words, Asquith lifted his hat and went in.[49] The 'pestering' of politicians was an effective WSPU strategy in 1909. The aim was not to give Asquith and his cabinet ministers a moment's peace until women had the vote. The strategy drove home the point that the WSPU would not give up, and at the same time their cheeky behaviour attracted useful publicity. Even though the press were mostly unsympathetic to the women's demands it was hard to resist reporting some of the almost slapstick scenes which erupted whenever ministers were going about their business or were off duty at the weekends and on holiday.

Augustine Birrell, the Liberal MP for Bristol North since 1906, and secretary of state for Ireland, was to make a speech at Colston Hall in Bristol on 1 May and the suffragettes were ready for him. Reporting to Annie Kenney, Minnie Baldock travelled from Canning Town to work with Elsie Howey and Vera Holme. Minnie rented a house opposite the Hall. When they heard that women would not be admitted to the meeting they equipped themselves with megaphones. Elsie and Vera went to a concert the night before and hid in the ladies' cloakroom. The night watchman did not find them; when the coast was clear they hid inside the organ. As soon as the organ started playing 'the noise, the wind, the vibration almost knocked the suffragettes off their perch'. Vera and Elsie waited until Birrell launched into his speech and when he reached his 'most telling sentences', a disembodied voice shouted: 'Votes For Women! Give women their political freedom.' The stewards 'scampered here, there and everywhere' while the suffragettes looked down into the hall from their secret eyrie through the slivers of light between the pipes. No one could find them and Birrell carried on. When he started to talk about liberty one of the women shouted 'Why don't you give women liberty?' The stewards then realised the women were in the organ: 'The hall was in an uproar ... they got a ladder but by the time they got the ladder to one place Elsie and Vera had scrambled to the other side' and they continued to make their political points. They were finally dragged from the organ loft, thrown out into the street but not arrested.[50]

Vera Holme, known as 'Jack' to her thespian and lesbian friends, was a male impersonator and a recent recruit to the WSPU. She was a founder member of the Actresses' Franchise League. She was born in Birkenhead in 1881, and Sylvia Pankhurst remembered her as a 'noisy explosive person'.[51]

*

The 'Women's Exhibition and Sale of Work in the Colours' was held at the Princes' Skating Rink in Knightsbridge, London, in May 1909. The Pethick-Lawrences set out to dazzle Londoners with ingenious ways of using purple, white and green to raise vital funds for the war chest. It was a stimulus to shopkeepers and entrepreneurs – some of whom were members of the WSPU – to merchandise the colours, and also the demand of 'Votes for Women'. Sylvia Pankhurst and seven students from the Royal College of Art painted murals on wood panels which could be dismantled and used at other fundraising events. They painted images of women thirteen feet high sowing grain, carrying sheaves of corn, angels playing stringed instruments, glorious beams of sunshine beating down; pelicans represented sacrifice, olive branches and doves were for peace and hope, and broad arrows were the symbol of imprisonment. Sylvia found it 'an exhilarating experience ... the small designs grew and covered huge surfaces. It was a tremendous rush to get finished, from waking to sleeping I scarcely paused.'[52]

The purple, white and green Women's Drum and Fife Band, led by the drum-major, Mary Leigh, marched about London advertising the exhibition and sale. Suffragette waitresses served tea and cakes in suffragette tea sets decorated with Sylvia Pankhurst's angel design, made in Staffordshire. Fifty stalls were loaded with farm produce, sweets, dresses, badges and jewellery, and chic hats donated by the members of Kensington WSPU: £5,664 was raised for the campaign fund. The Elswick Cycle Manufacturing Company advertised a new model bicycle for the WSPU, painted in purple, white and green and decorated with Sylvia Pankhurst's badge – the angel on tiptoes standing at the signpost for freedom.[53]

On the second day the exhibition was opened by Mrs Hertha Ayrton, a noted electrical scientist. Her father, Levi Marks, was a watchmaker and jeweller whose family had settled in England at the end of the nineteenth century to escape pogroms in Russia. In 1884 she met her future husband, Will Ayrton, a widower, when she took the evening class in electricity he taught at Finsbury Technical College. They married in 1885. Will's daughter Edith, married to the writer Israel Zangwill, joined Mrs Fawcett's National Union of Women's Suffrage Societies, but became a militant in 1909. Hertha's own daughter, Barbara, joined the WSPU in 1906, giving up her research in physics and chemistry to work full-time in 1909 as the honorary secretary of the Westminster branch. Hertha Ayrton was the only woman member of the Institute of Electrical Engineers for more than half a century. She was proposed for membership of the Royal Society in 1902 but the Society's lawyers said that because she was a married woman she was not eligible. In 1906 Hertha Ayrton was awarded a Royal Society Hughes Medal for her research. She joined the suffragettes in 1907 after attending a banquet given to welcome the release of WSPU prisoners.[54]

On 14 May Mrs Pankhurst presented Mrs Pethick-Lawrence with a purple, white and green Austin motor car which she then donated to the Union. It was a 'token of the high esteem and love felt towards her by the membership of the WSPU who can never forget her great and unceasing service to the women's cause ... It is hoped that the car will be one of the agents in the fight against the Liberals in many constituencies.' The first driver was Miss Muriel Thompson, who had won the Ladies' Bracelet Handicap at Brooklands race track in July 1908.[55]

One of the high points of the Women's Exhibition was a demonstration by Mrs Edith Garrud of ju-jitsu, the Japanese art of self-defence. The *Daily Mail* reported how Edith threw 'a burly six-feet tall, fifteen stone policeman even though she was an inch under five feet tall'. The poor chap lost 'his dignity, his balance, and his helmet, whereat militant members of the audience shrieked with delight'.[56] At the end of the Women's Exhibition Mrs Pethick-Lawrence announced that 150 women had joined the WSPU in the two weeks, and that the final takings included: £136 from the Marylebone dress stall organised by Elspeth McClelland; £23 from the 'Lucky Tub'; £132 from the lady palmists; £372 from the Lancashire, Midlands and West of England stall-holders; and £109 from the sale of homemade sweets.[57]

Keeping up the pressure on the government the WSPU now planned a Bill of Rights deputation to the House of Commons on 29 June. It was time for the WSPU to 'test the constitutional right of the subject to petition the Prime Minister at the seat of power'. The right to petition was written into the Bill of Rights [of 1689]: 'It is the right of subjects to petition the King and all commitments and prosecutions for such petitions are illegal.' Mrs Pankhurst argued that the power of the King had passed 'almost completely' into the hands of the Parliament, and that the prime minister now 'stood where the King's majesty stood in former times'.[58]

On 2 June 1909 John Burns, President of the Local Government Board, was repeatedly heckled by suffragettes, whom he called 'vulgar creatures from the West End', at an exhibition at the Whitechapel Art Gallery. The suffragettes had hidden in the gallery overnight as the Liberal Party banned all women from political meetings unless they were accompanied by two men. Herbert Asquith's holiday at Clovelly Court in Devon was disrupted by the arrival of Elsie Howey, Jessie Kenney and Vera Wentworth, who followed him everywhere he went and twice tried to interview him. In church Mrs Asquith recognised the women and passed her husband a note. To avoid the suffragettes Asquith tried to leave by a side door before the end of the service 'looking very flustered and nervous', but the three women intercepted him before he could escape and asked if they could interview him; he

refused them and 'urged them to go away'. The women followed him
and kept up a barrage of questions, reminding him that their comrade
Patricia Woodlock was still in prison serving her 'monstrous sentence'
while he was on holiday. The next day Elsie Howey, Jessie Kenney
and Vera Wentworth returned to his holiday house and hid in the
bushes ready to pounce on him when he emerged, but detectives found
them and took them away. The three suffragettes then hid on the golf
links where he was playing and were able to take him by the arm and
repeat their one-sided conversation of the previous day, until police
constables took them away. The suffragettes said they were leaving
Devon but when they were driven to Bideford railway station they
left their luggage there and walked the twelve miles back to Clovelly
Court, arriving in the early hours determined to decorate the gardens
with purple, white and green. One of the women festooned the rho-
dodendrons with tricolour discs reading 'Release Patricia Woodlock'
and 'Receive Our Deputation On June 29'. Copies of *Votes for Women*
were tied to the balustrade in front of the ground-floor windows, and
'banners made from handkerchiefs and painted from a little paint-box
borrowed from an artist in the village' were draped around the garden.
Then Elsie, Jessie and Vera trudged back to Bideford.[59]

Constance Lytton's brother, the Earl of Lytton, was due to make a
speech at a WSPU meeting on 15 June at St James's Theatre about militant methods. The Lyttons' sister, Betty Balfour, made notes of a conversation at a dinner she attended with Winston Churchill, where she
told him that her brother was planning to speak up for Mrs Pankhurst.
Churchill admitted he had only once voted on women's suffrage and
that had been in favour, 'but I don't think I shall do that again. They
have given me no cause to love them.' Betty Balfour admitted she was
not in favour of militant methods but said, 'I am not sure it is not better to have made you angry than indifferent.' Churchill conceded that
the WSPU 'had done good at first, they woke people up but now they
are alienating people every day'. Betty reminded him that the large
sums of money they collected, and the rising numbers of women joining the organisation, suggested otherwise.[60]

At the meeting Mrs Pankhurst introduced the Earl of Lytton. He
expressed the 'pain and distress' he had felt at the recent escalation of
militancy which had been 'brought home to me closely'. Those who
'deplored' militant methods should look back at events of the past

when the issue had been 'ignored and ridiculed for more than a generation'. Now women's suffrage was a matter of 'burning seriousness' and 'the time has come to take one's stand and show one's colours'. He urged everyone to reject indifference: 'if you are in favour of it, fight for it; if you are against it, fight against it. Fight at the polls, fight in Parliament, fight wherever you can, but at least treat the question seriously, and face the issue.'[61]

Although the Blathwayt family were loyal supporters of the WSPU they would not allow Mary to join the Bill of Rights deputation on 29 June. On 8 June Mary Blathwayt and Elsie Howey had arrived in Bristol on a lorry where a large group of children were waiting for them: 'when we drove away Mary Blathwayt was hit with potatoes, stones, turf and dust.' Mary declined Mrs Pankhurst's invitation 'as Father would not like it', and she sent a postal order for a pound 'for the Cause as I have not been to prison'.[62]

On 22 June 1909 Marion Wallace-Dunlop disguised herself as an old lady, and, carrying a brown bag containing indelible ink and a wooden stamp bearing the words 'Women's Deputation, June 29th, It is the right of the subjects to petition the King – and all commitments and prosecutions for such petitioning are illegal', defaced the wall of the Lobby of the House of Commons. A policeman took her to Inspector Scantlebury who confiscated the stamp and let her go. Two days later she returned and defaced the wall again. This time she was charged with 'wilfully and maliciously' damaging the stonework of the House of Commons and sentenced to a month in the third division cells in Holloway Prison.[63]

On 29 June 1909 Vera Holme rode on horseback from the Women's Parliament being held in Caxton Hall ahead of Mrs Pankhurst, who carried the petition to Herbert Asquith. Mrs Pankhurst led eight women including Mrs Saul Solomon, Maud Joachim and Miss Neligan to St Stephen's Entrance. Mounted police cleared the way for the women to be received at the door of the House of Commons by Inspectors Scantlebury and Jarvis, who handed Mrs Pankhurst a letter from the prime minister stating that he refused to meet her. She threw the note on the ground and refused to move. Inside the Commons Keir Hardie urged his fellow MPs to admit the women into the chamber. To ensure Mrs Solomon, sixty-five, and Dorinda Neligan, seventy-six, were not 'buffeted about' by the police or the crowd on their return to Caxton

Hall, Mrs Pankhurst decided to get herself and the others arrested, and so she slapped Inspector Jarvis lightly on the cheek. He said, 'I know why you did that', and Mrs Pankhurst asked, 'Must I do it again?' When he said she must, she 'struck him on the other cheek'. Another lady knocked his hat off and the women were taken to the police station and charged with obstructing the police and assault. For the next couple of hours a steady stream of suffragettes, a dozen at a time, left Caxton Hall, tried to enter the House and were arrested.[64]

At nine o'clock that night, after the mounted police had cleared Parliament Square, groups of six suffragettes dashed out of the thirty offices that Clement's Inn had hired for the day in the Square and 'made determined rushes for the House'. Simultaneously, fourteen women lobbed stones, wrapped in copies of the WSPU petition to the prime minister, at the windows of the Treasury, the Privy Council and the Home Office. The suffragettes who planned this unauthorised protest argued that it was better to break the windows of government property rather than that women's bodies should be broken in the protracted struggle with police. The stone-throwers were charged with wilful damage. One of the women had found the action painful: 'To women of culture and refinement and of sheltered upbringing the deliberate act of throwing a stone, even as a protest, in order to break a window, requires an enormous amount of moral courage. After much tension and hesitation, I threw my stone at the window ... I was at once arrested and marched off by two policemen.'[65] By the end of the evening, 108 women and 14 men had been charged at Canon Row police station with obstruction, assaulting the police and causing malicious damage.[66]

Alice Paul and Lucy Burns, who had 'brilliant red hair and a generous smile',[67] were Americans studying in London when they met for the first time at Canon Row police station. Lucy told Alice that she had come to London from Germany to take part in the deputation. Alice Paul, born in 1885, was a Quaker who came to England with an MA from the University of Pennsylvania. Having completed a thesis on the equality of women, she was now studying economics at Birmingham University, with particular interest in social work and philanthropy. In December 1907 she heard Christabel Pankhurst, who had been invited to make the case for women's suffrage, shouted down by rowdy male students and commented later, 'I never heard of the idea of anybody being opposed to the idea of the suffrage or equality.'[68]

Alice went to Women's Sunday, and was 'thrilled beyond words to hear Emmeline Pethick-Lawrence speak'. In 1908 Alice met Rachel Barrett at the London School of Economics where they were both studying and was easily persuaded to sell copies of the newspaper: 'I was really happy to be part of it', and found Miss Barrett an inspiring new friend: 'I remember how very bold and good she was and how timid and unsuccessful I was standing beside her trying to ask people to buy *Votes for Women*.'[69]

Alice Paul had finished her course at the LSE and had a ticket to sail home in July when she received a letter from Clement's Inn asking her to go on the deputation of 29 June. After much agonising Alice decided to take part: 'at last I got up enough courage to post my letter saying I would go.' She found it 'very exciting' but was afraid that 'the struggle is getting very grim and deadly earnest', and stayed in England although she had promised her mother she would go home. Her letters home did not mention her run-ins with the police, more arrests, two further prison sentences, a hunger strike and being force-fed before the year was out.[70]

Thirty-year-old Lucy Burns, from Brooklyn, arrived in London in 1909. She graduated from Vassar College in 1902, studied at Yale University for a year and then at the University of Berlin from 1906 to 1908. When she attended her first WSPU meeting in London she joined on the spot, impressed with the quality of the speakers and their fiery resolve, volunteering to sell *Votes for Women* and join the deputation on 29 June from which she gained a prison record and a new friend. Alice Paul said of Lucy: 'she was always much more valiant than I was, about a thousand times more valiant by nature. We became very good friends and remained so all our lives.'[71]

Mary Allen was charged with wilful damage for breaking a window at the Home Office and sentenced to a month in Holloway, her second prison sentence that year.[72] In 1907, aged twenty-nine, Mary, who had been excited by Annie Kenney's deeds and words, left her home in Cardiff and joined the WSPU after a row with her father over her passion for the militants. Mary described her conversion after hearing a speech by Annie Kenney 'who converted me as she converted hundreds of other women and girls all over Great Britain'. Mary did not

return home until her father's death in December 1911. She asked Mrs
Pankhurst 'to use me in whatever capacity she thought best'. Mary
was profoundly affected by her leader: 'She was essentially delicate,
feminine to a degree, pretty and well-dressed; yet there flowed from
her lips the most fiery denunciations, the most natural and inspiring
eloquence.'[73] Twenty-five years later in her autobiography Mary was
still moved: 'When I went to her, I had sacrificed much. She asked me
to sacrifice more.' She described how on 29 June 'Men from the idle
crowd that stood about St Stephen's entrance roared with laughter,
yelled ribald and obscene remarks and clawed and pawed at us, and
in the end the police arrested us and took us off as much for our own
safety as because we had broken any law. Most of us were delicately-
bred women, and our horror of such a scene may be imagined.' In
Holloway the suffragettes were put to work making shirts for male
prisoners, during which they embroidered the words 'VOTES FOR
WOMEN' round the tail of each shirt.[74]

The Honourable Evelina Haverfield was charged with obstructing
the police on 29 June and was offered the choice of paying a fine of
£5 or serving a month in the second division. She chose prison. She
described the day of the deputation to her elder sister, saying that
although she expected 'a violent knocking about between the crowd
and the police' the 'whole affair passed off perfectly quietly', except
for 'some hooligans who always take part in these kind of things'.
Evelina told her sister she was 'very intent upon this matter of votes
for women', and was giving up everything – even her hunting on
Exmoor – for that summer, 'nor will I hunt next winter or do anything in the shape of pleasure until this thing is carried through ... I
shall fight harder for right and truth and justice for our sex.'[75]

Evelina Haverfield was born at Inverlochy Castle in 1867. Her
father was William Scarlett, the 3rd Baron Abinger, an enlightened
man who encouraged her to hunt, fish and shoot on their estate. She
played polo and hunted astride, and was a fine horsewoman. Evelina
was married to Henry Tunstall Haverfield, a major in the Royal
Artillery. In 1895 he died, aged forty-eight, leaving two sons, John
Campbell, seven, and Brook Tunstall, six. Evelina married again in
1899: her new husband was John Balguy, a Royal Artillery officer,
later a Metropolitan Police magistrate. On her wedding day she wrote
in her diary: 'I married Major Balguy with no intention of changing

my name or mode of life in any way. He is an old friend of my darling Jack's.'[76]

Evelina Haverfield's long relationship with her friend Vera Holme, with whom she lived in Devon from 1911, sounds much more of a marriage than the one she had with her new husband. In 1912 Vera made a will and left everything she had to Evelina, including a bed with 'E.H. & V.H.' carved on the sides. In 1921, when Evelina Haverfield's own will was challenged by her husband, it was said that their marriage had been 'an unsatisfactory union'.[77]

Grace Roe returned to the fray on 29 June. She had been asked to 'work up' women from Kensington, Hammersmith and Ravenscourt Park to join the deputation and was told by Clement's Inn that the women should expect to be 'knocked about' by the police and that 'it might be a good idea to make ... corsets of cardboard'. When interviewed in the 1960s Grace explained: 'I rigged up one of these in the bath and fitted it to my shape and put in cotton wool to protect my breasts and then put on my hockey outfit and set off for London.'[78] She collected volunteers at Clement's Inn and they went to one of the offices the headquarters had hired in Parliament Square. When the coast was clear Grace and her team were to try to enter the House. When they emerged Grace noticed a gate open at Palace Yard and headed for it: 'It was like a sprint down a hockey field,' she said, but the police closed the gates before they could enter. 'The mounted police came forward but I wasn't afraid of the horses as I had hunted in Ireland and I yelled at the women to stand together.' Grace found herself 'right under the horses' hooves and I have never seen a man so white in my life as that man on the horse'. The mounted officer lifted her off her feet and rescued her, and they were all taken to Rochester Row police station. One constable even asked Grace for her WSPU badge as a souvenir. Lucy Burns told Grace Roe that she had come to London to be arrested, and that it 'was a very grave honour'.[79]

Sarah Carwin and Ada Wright were arrested for breaking government windows and went to Holloway for one month. There they broke every window in their cells as a protest. When they were called before the Prison Board, faced with twenty seated men, Sarah Carwin went on the attack: 'Give me a chair, why should we stand when all these men are sitting down?' Chairs were provided and the women were placed in damp cells in the basement for their insubordination.

They went on hunger strike and after six days both women were released. Later that summer Mrs Pankhurst sent Sarah Carwin and the other suffragette window-breakers a specially designed 'stone-thrower's badge' of gold decorated with a shard of flint. 'This is in memory of the flinty message you sent through the Government windows on 29 June.'[80]

7

Starving Suffragettes

The Struggle for Political Status in Prison 1909

*The poster shows how hunger strikers were fed by force.
It was produced for the general election of January 1910.*

In the nineteenth century men who were sent to prison for obstructing the police in the course of political campaigning were granted political status, winning the right to serve their sentences in first division cells. They were allowed to wear their own clothes, receive books and letters, have food sent in from outside, enjoy freedom of association with their fellow political prisoners and were not required to do prison work. The suffragettes argued that their campaign was political, demanded political status and denied they were common criminals. The Liberal government refused to concede that the suffragettes' actions were political, and with very few exceptions the women were convicted and treated as common criminals and held in second and third division cells.

On 5 July 1909, Marion Wallace-Dunlop, who was serving a month in Holloway for wilful damage, was the first suffragette to use the hunger strike as a political weapon: 'I threw a fried fish, four slices of bread, three bananas and a cup of hot milk out of my window on Tuesday which was the only day I felt hungry. They threatened all the time to pump milk through my nostrils, but never did.' The wardresses spread the table in her cell with food but she would only drink water. After refusing food for ninety-one hours Marion was released amid great jubilation on 8 July.[1] Frederick Pethick-Lawrence wrote to her saying: 'Nothing has moved me so much – stirred me to the depths of my being – as your heroic action … If I needed anything more than this great movement, which I am privileged to assist, to make life worth living it would be found in what you have done.'[2]

Marion wrote to the Reverend Frederick Hankinson, a Unitarian minister, friend of Fred Pethick-Lawrence and member of the Men's League for Women's Suffrage, whom she knew visited suffragettes in Holloway and Aylesbury prisons. She said that she was afraid the stone-throwers might follow her example, which she found worrying. If they were 'young healthy women with normal appetites' they would find starvation 'horrible'; if Hankinson visited suffragettes he should tell them to drink water and 'lie down all the time, to think of other things, and above all to keep their minds on the funny side of it all'.[3]

Florence Spong had been arrested on 29 June, having got tangled up with the police who were trying to arrest a bystander named Frank Albert Scroggs, a warehouseman employed by the civil service. In court the police said that Scroggs had thrown a stone at a policeman, and that when he was arrested Florence grabbed the policeman's coat saying, 'If you take him you must take me.' There were so many arrests that day that Florence Spong and Frank Scroggs did not appear at Bow Street Court until 12 July, when he was found guilty of 'throwing missiles to the common danger' and she of obstructing the police. Frank was offered the choice of paying a four-shilling fine or going to prison (he paid the fine); Florence chose prison. As soon as she arrived in prison with her suffragette colleagues she went on hunger strike in protest at their being placed in second division cells. The women refused to be stripped and searched, medically examined, to perform the usual prison work, hand over their jewellery or wear prison clothes. It was summer and Florence Spong's cell windows were locked shut, so she broke them. She was then placed in 'close confinement' for seven days in the oldest part of the prison, in a cell which was damp and cold, with a wooden plank for a bed, and a block of wood fixed to the wall for a chair. The first meal was a pint of cocoa and a lump of bread and then the hunger strike began. Florence drank only milk and ate no food, had nothing to read other than a hymn book and a Bible and no visitors other than the governor and the prison doctor coming to 'frighten me into taking food'. She was released from Holloway after four days of fasting. Every night the Women's Drum and Fife Band marched to Holloway to serenade the prisoners.[4]

When Lloyd George tried to address a meeting at the Edinburgh Castle, a hall in Limehouse, on 30 July chaos ensued. The police were watching the house the WSPU had rented behind the hall, but the suffragettes prepared to pounce on the chancellor of the exchequer by rushing at him from two side streets: 'The first party on foot were easily frustrated, but the second party who advanced in a trap got within a few feet of the motor-car before the police stopped the horse.' Thirteen suffragettes were arrested in the fracas and one woman was hurt when a police horse trod on her foot.[5]

Lloyd George was in Limehouse ahead of his forthcoming 'People's Budget', which proposed raising taxes from substantial landowners to finance the Liberal government's plan to fund pensions for the aged poor, and to establish a national insurance scheme for sickness and unemployment, which came to fruition in 1911. (The arms race with Germany also had to be paid for from these taxes.) When Lloyd George rose to speak a male suffragette sympathiser climbed up a pillar while a dozen friends acted as bodyguards to stop the Liberal stewards dragging him down. He took out a purple, white and green flag and waved it with gusto but his friends were attacked by the stewards: wrists and a collarbone and a shoulder were fractured, and the men were thrown out of the building. The sympathiser himself was dragged down from the pillar by his ankles. The *Daily Mirror* reported 'a fierce struggle', a bottle being broken over his head and that he was 'covered in blood from head to foot'.[6]

The thirteen women arrested trying to stop Lloyd George's meeting included Jennie Baines, Mary Leigh, Lucy Burns, Alice Paul, Emily Davison and Mabel Capper. With the exception of Lucy Burns, who was charged with assault for hitting Chief Inspector William Fraser in the face, knocking his hat off and 'wrenching his whistle away', the rest were charged with obstruction. The magistrate singled out Lucy Burns for 'setting an extremely bad example to the people of the district'. Sentences ranged from ten days to three months in the second division; Lucy was put in the third division. In court Mary Leigh defiantly told the magistrate that she intended agitating whatever the consequences.[7]

The women sang and shouted all the way to Holloway Gaol, and insisted on seeing the governor, James Scott, who later told Dr Donkin, the Commissioner of Prisons, that the suffragettes had demanded to be placed in the first division cells, to wear their own clothes and have freedom of association during the day. When Governor Scott said he was unable to put them into first division cells they told him they would not go into their cells or obey any regulations. Scott told Donkin they were 'obstinate and mutinous', and sent them to the second division cells. 'Very soon afterwards I was informed they were breaking windows ... I went at once and found them breaking all the windows with the heels of their shoes, cell dustpans etc.' Within fifteen minutes the women had broken 150 panes of glass, whereupon Scott ordered them to be moved to 'special cells' for 'refractory' prisoners. (The governor could not identify them individually because the women refused to give their names.) Scott ordered that they be 'thoroughly searched and put into prison clothing'. The women resisted and Scott said the prison officers did 'not use any more force than was absolutely necessary'.[8]

Jennie Baines, one of the first hunger strikers, was born in Birmingham in 1866. Her parents, Mr and Mrs Hunt, worked in a gun factory and Jennie was employed there at the age of eleven. The Hunt family were active members of the Salvation Army. In 1888 Jennie married George Baines, a shoemaker in Bolton. When Annie Kenney and Christabel Pankhurst were arrested in 1905, Jennie Baines worked for the WSPU unpaid. Annie Kenney remembered Jennie as 'one of the most kind-hearted women one could meet, a born revolutionary'. Her youngest child was six when Jennie went to prison for the third time.[9] In 1908 she served six weeks in Armley Gaol, Leeds, for organising an 'unlawful assembly' outside the Coliseum where the prime minister and Herbert Gladstone were present.[10]

Back in Holloway, only two of the twelve suffragette prisoners promised to refrain from breaking windows, so the rest were detained in the 'special cells' where they continued to be 'very noisy', broke their earthenware vessels and refused all food. One woman lay down on the floor and refused to go to bed. The next day Governor Scott reported to Dr Donkin that they had all refused food and had sung and shouted all night. Three of the women who had been sent to the hospital wing were quiet and taking their food.

A note from Sir Edward Troup, a permanent under-secretary at the Home Office, to the home secretary dated 2 August, suggests that force had actually been used: 'Dr Scott seems to have done his best in the circumstances. After the window-breaking incident, he was fully justified in using force to search the prisoners and make them wear the prison clothing.' He also reported that the governor and Dr Donkin were 'anxious to feed them forcibly, they are quite clear that it is medically justifiable and that it can be done with safety'. Troup suggested that a doctor be called in to advise in each case of force-feeding as to when 'it is necessary and whether it can be done safely'. Herbert Gladstone added to Troup's report that he did not believe that forcible feeding was advisable. 'It would be a new and picturesque grievance which would be a fine advertisement for these people.'[11]

On 2 August, Emily Davison, whose prison file describes her conduct as 'bad', wrote to Gladstone from Holloway describing what had taken place. Both the governor and the matron, Miss Elizabeth White, denied her claims. Emily said she was 'forced' into a cell and broke seventeen panes of glass to let some air into the cell. She was transferred to a cell where the glass was thicker but still managed to break seven panes, also cutting her hand. They stripped her and put her into a prison chemise; when the doctor tried to 'sound' her heart she resisted and was taken to a punishment cell. 'Ours is a bloodless revolution but a determined one,' she wrote to Gladstone. Emily said that she and others were 'ready to suffer, to die if need be, but we demand justice!'[12]

On the same evening as the Limehouse fracas, Elsie Howey, Vera Wentworth and Mary Phillips were in Exeter trying to attend a meeting at which Lord Carrington, the President of the Board of Agriculture and Fisheries, was speaking at a men-only meeting. They were sentenced to seven days in the second division at Exeter Prison for obstructing the police. They went on hunger strike and the prison doctor threatened to have them declared insane and to force-feed them if they did not eat. They were empty threats and the women stayed on hunger strike. Mary Phillips was released 'in a dangerous state' after four days without eating. Elsie and Vera ate nothing for six days of their entire sentence and went to the Blathwayts' home to 'get strong'.[13]

Seven suffragettes including Mary Leigh, Rona Robinson, Bertha Brewster, 'Annie O'Sullivan' (Theresa Garnett) and Georgina Healiss, were arrested in Liverpool on 20 August, and charged with wilful damage after breaking a dozen windows of the Sun Hall. The women had rented the house next door to the hall where Richard Haldane, Liberal MP for Haddingtonshire and secretary of state for war, was due to speak, from whence they got onto the roof of the hall to launch their attack. Mary Leigh, 'a frail little figure of a woman', was identified as the leader hiding behind a chimney-stack on the roof.[14] The local paper, the *Courier*, admired Mary's actions: 'the frail little woman' threw bricks and stones through the windows of the Sun Hall 'with a dexterity which was nothing short of marvellous'. When Haldane got up to speak a cheer went up in the hall, the signal for Mary Leigh to use her megaphone to demand political justice. Haldane remarked that the women's arguments 'did not touch' him or his fellow politicians and only left them 'with feelings of regret for those who are in outer darkness'. After more windows were smashed the police found a window cleaner to get the women down but his ladder was too short and the fire brigade were called. Eventually they managed to winkle Mary Leigh and her six comrades off the roof 'in a perilous descent'.[15]

Five of the women were sentenced to two months in the second division, and Bertha Brewster, from Lewes in Sussex, to one month. On their way to Walton Gaol they sang 'The Marseillaise', broke the windows of the Black Maria and pushed a 'Votes for Women' flag through the ventilator in the roof. The governor of the prison sat alongside the driver, and four policemen rode on the step of the van. The *Liverpool Daily Post* fumed: 'Seven viragos have given a lesson to the country which it will not be slow to profit by, and we trust that the arm of outraged justice administer to them a lesson which they will not soon forget.' All the women went on hunger strike and were released over the next three days 'owing to their emaciated condition'.[16]

In Glasgow on 22 August 1909, Adela Pankhurst, Lucy Burns, Alice Paul and Margaret Smith failed to appear to answer charges for disturbing Lord Crewe's meeting in Glasgow in St Andrew's Hall on Friday 20 August and warrants were issued for their arrest. On 20 August, Adela, Lucy, Alice and Margaret had been huddling on the roof of the hall and 'much difficulty was experienced getting them down from their perilous position'. They had been on the roof since one in the morning and were in 'a very wet condition'.[17]

On Sunday 5 September, Jessie Kenney, Vera Wentworth (disguised as a nurse) and Elsie Howey stalked Herbert Asquith. The Asquiths were the guests of Mrs Asquith's brother, Frank Tennant, who owned Lympne Castle in Kent. The suffragettes intercepted Asquith as he left St Stephen's Church. Jessie Kenney told a *Daily*

Mirror reporter, 'He was slipping through a side door when we caught him. He was wedged in the door and a little struggle ensued in which Mr Asquith lost his hat.'[18] The women grabbed him but he managed to escape without a word being exchanged. When they heard he was due to play golf with the home secretary, Herbert Gladstone, they pounced on him on the links at Littlestone-on-Sea. As Asquith climbed out of his car Elsie Howey grabbed his arm, and he told her he would have her locked up. He tried to run into the clubhouse but the suffragettes followed in hot pursuit.[19] Jessie told *Votes for Women*: 'It was quite a chase ... as he reached the top step Elsie grabbed him again and he tried to push her away but she was too quick for him, and caught hold of his collar.' The prime minister asked the home secretary for help and Gladstone ran to his aid. The two men struggled to push the women down the steps but they were determined to follow him into the building, and several blows were landed on both sides, with Gladstone fighting 'like a pugilist ... Mr Gladstone lunged out and we lunged out'.[20] The prime minister's son, Herbert, remembered the scene: 'the contest was very evenly balanced, and his [Gladstone's] gay and sunny countenance wore an expression of the most comic embarrassment ... the two women outside obviously meant business; they succeeded in prising the doors a short distance apart and while he stood spread-eagled in front of them with a hand on each door, one of them inserted herself in the crevice between and began butting him in the diaphragm with her head.' Herbert Asquith junior got hold of her wrist and she fought with 'a strange demonic frenzy which I had never met and hope never to see again'.[21] Two other golfers came to help the prime minister and his home secretary who abandoned their plans to play and dashed off in their car.

Later on the same day the three women made a 'night attack' on Lympne Castle, where the Asquiths and Gladstone would be having dinner. During the day the women had hired a boat and rowed it along the Military Canal that ran below the castle grounds. They returned in the early evening: 'We had a lot of slips, and scrambles, falls and tumbles, till at last we made our way up the Castle wall which was only a little distance from the windows of the dining room. We helped each other up on to the wall and saw that two of the windows were open, and judged by the sound of rattling crockery

that the party was at dinner … Little did they know we were under
the window and ready to attack.' Vera Wentworth (still dressed as
a nurse) and Jessie Kenney hoisted Elsie Howey up to the window
and she peeped in and saw that 'everything was quite serene inside'.
Vera and Jessie held Elsie while she poked her head through the window, shouting, 'Mr Asquith, we shall go on pestering you until you
give women the vote.' Then the women threw stones against the
windows, calling out, 'This is what the women of England think of
you.'[22] Herbert Asquith junior remembered his father in 'one of his
mellowest moods when suddenly there was a crash of broken glass,
some window panes were smashed to pieces and a large piece of gran-
ite, which had clearly been aimed at him, missed its target and broke
my neighbour's plate, scattered a lady's dress with a copious fountain
of soup, and bounced off the table to the other side of the room'.[23]
The suffragettes scrambled down the castle wall and over the fences
and ditches until they reached their boat –'We pushed off, rowing
as fast as we could down the canal' – and saw the servants searching with their torches. When they reached safety they realised that
they had left a basket behind with items of disguise. When all was
quiet they rowed back to the castle, retrieved their belongings and
returned to their lodgings.[24]

At Batheaston, meanwhile, Colonel and Mrs Blathwayt's unhappiness at the growing pace of militancy came to a head after they read
about the raid on Lympne Castle. They went to a meeting in Bath
in the garden of their friends the Tollemaches, and heard a speech
from Laurence Housman, the playwright and illustrator who, with
his sister Clemence, founded the Suffrage Atelier in London in 1909
to design and make banners, posters and cards for the WSPU and
the Women's Freedom League. Housman warned the audience that
he would not be criticising the WSPU's methods as the women had
been 'driven to it by the non-action of the men'. Emily Blathwayt
wrote in her diary, 'I cannot feel quite the same. We hear terrible
things by the two hooligans we know, Vera and Elsie and there is
a Kenney in it … missiles have been thrown lately through windows during cabinet ministers' meetings which might injure or kill
innocent persons'. On 8 September 1909 Emily Blathwayt withdrew
her name from the membership list of the WSPU, writing: 'When I
signed the membership paper I thoroughly approved of the methods

then used. When asked by acquaintances what I think of these things [stone-throwing] I am unable to say I approve and people of my village who have hitherto been full of admiration for the Suffragettes are now feeling very differently.'[25] Her husband, who had been seen by local people driving Elsie Howey and Vera Wentworth, wrote to Christabel Pankhurst echoing his wife's views. Annie Kenney wrote a diplomatic note to the couple: 'The only thing I can say is, if we all do what we feel to be right, we cannot go wrong.' Christabel replied to the Blathwayts that she thought the methods were right, and hoped that Mrs Blathwayt would re-join the WSPU 'as soon as all this trouble is over'. A week later Vera Wentworth wrote to Colonel Blathwayt hoping that he was not shocked at them 'punching Asquith's head'. Vera's unrepentant letter to Batheaston said that as long as the prime minister refused to meet members of the WSPU they would 'pummel him again', and insisted they did no real harm to him, reminding the colonel that Mr Gladstone had himself given Jessie 'a nasty blow in the chest'.[26]

Herbert Gladstone wrote to Edward Troup asking if 'the time has not come for a special police organisation for countering suffragette violence'. He asked Troup where 'the Lympne gang' had come from, and who had helped them. The first demand for the surveillance of suffragettes thus emerged: 'It is not enough to deal with these people if and when they come. We ought to know what they are up to locally and the more dangerous should be known to the Home Office.'[27]

Gladstone confided there was a likelihood of a general election in January, making law and order a serious headache while the suffragettes 'were allowed to roam the country unhindered and unobserved'. In the aftermath of events at Lympne Gladstone raised the issue that gathering intelligence about future suffragette outrages was essential, that 'a branch should be formed and special officers be sent beforehand to all the places [where] the Prime Minister and Cabinet Ministers are due to speak' and protect them from 'insult, annoyance and violence'.[28] The home secretary was critical of the Manchester police for being outwitted by the suffragettes who disrupted a meeting addressed by Mr Augustine Birrell at the White City in Manchester the day before the prime minister was confronted at Lympne. The police thought they had secured the building but the suffragettes managed to throw missiles through the windows and their calls for votes for women could be heard as Birrell struggled to make his speech in support of the Budget. Sir Melville Macnaghten, the Chief Constable of the Criminal Investigation Department of the Metropolitan Police, agreed that an officer who knew 'as many as possible of the militant ladies by sight' should be dispatched from London to wherever Herbert Asquith and his Cabinet were due to speak, and 'one or two officers of the "Special Branch" should be officially in charge of this business under Quinn [Superintendent Patrick Quinn] so as to form for a short time a special department'. Special Branch was established in 1883 to deal with the threat of the Irish Republican Brotherhood. Headed by Patrick Quinn since 1887 and based at Scotland Yard, now a newly expanded Special Branch would pursue and monitor the activities of the suffragettes and use tactics they had deployed against Irish republicans.[29]

Lucy Burns, Alice Paul and Edith New joined suffragettes in Dundee who were determined to barge into the meeting of Mr Herbert Samuel, the MP for Cleveland and Chancellor of the Duchy of Lancaster, by rushing the entrance of Kinnaird Hall on 13 September 1909. They succeeded only in causing a commotion outside the hall and were arrested. One local woman had even hoped to abseil into the hall in her gym kit through a skylight in the roof, but it was locked and she was caught trying to enter through another window. In court Lucy Burns, Alice Paul and Edith New admitted disorderly conduct and breaking glass at the police station and were sent to prison, Lucy and Alice for ten days each and Edith for seven.[30] They immediately went on hunger strike, refused to do any prison work, broke the cell windows and defaced the walls of one of the cells. All three were released after three days in a state of 'debility from voluntary starvation'. Edith New was described as 'prostrate', her condition causing some concern.[31]

When the prime minister held a meeting about the proposed People's Budget at Bingley Hall in Birmingham on 17 September 1909, extraordinary precautions were taken to prevent suffragette disturbances inside or outside the building. Barricades nine feet high were built all the way from the railway station, along the streets and leading to the hall, giving the city the appearance of being under siege. Some of the windows of the hall were padded. No women were admitted but the suffragettes created a noisy disturbance outside, organised by Gladice Keevil and Elsa Gye. To stop the women hurling missiles from a nearby roof, the glass roof of the hall was covered with a tarpaulin and two ladders were set up at either end of Bingley Hall, where firemen waited to turn their hoses on the women if necessary. Charlie Marsh and Mary Leigh and her team had set up their headquarters on the roof of the factory next door and used axes to remove the slates which they threw down on to the roof of Bingley Hall, where Asquith struggled to make himself heard. Inside twenty male sympathisers heckled the prime minister on the suffragettes' behalf and were promptly beaten up and thrown out. Twelve women were arrested, and Mary Leigh and Charlie Marsh were sentenced to four months and three months respectively, with hard labour; Mabel Capper got one month, Patricia Woodlock was sent to prison for one month with hard labour and Laura Ainsworth got two weeks with hard labour.[32]

Inspired by Mary Leigh's leadership, as soon as the suffragettes arrived at Winson Green they went on hunger strike. On 24 September 1909, after a week in gaol, they were force-fed. Mary led by example and she was the first to be force-fed. Most were fed by nasal tube. As soon as Mrs Pankhurst and Christabel read the announcement about force-feeding in *The Times* they travelled to Birmingham to visit the women accompanied by a solicitor but were refused permission because the women had not asked to see a legal representative. It would take a week for the women who were being force-fed to initiate proceedings for assault.[33]

On arrival at the prison Mary Leigh broke her cell windows and was transferred to a punishment cell with only a plank bed to sleep on. She was 'stripped and handcuffed with the hands behind during the day, except at meal times when the palms were placed together in front of her'.[34] Potatoes, bread and gruel were brought into her cell but she refused to eat. She was then fed by nasal tube and stomach tube at the same time: 'The sensation is most painful – the drums of the ears seem to be bursting, a horrible pain in the throat and the breast. The tube is pushed down twenty inches. I have to lie on the bed pinned down by wardresses, one doctor stands up on a chair holding the funnel at arm's length, so as to have the funnel end above the level and then the other doctor who is behind forces the other end up the nostrils.'[35] The doctor who held the funnel poured in half a pint of milk, sometimes mixed with egg, and when the feeding was over a signal was given and a basin of warm water was put under Mary's chin and the other doctor pulled the tube from her stomach and plunged the end into water. Before and after the procedure they tested Mary's heart. She wrote an account which was printed as a handbill: 'The after-effects are a feeling of faintness, a sense of great pain in the diaphragm or breast bone, in the nose and the ears ... I was very sick on the first occasion after the tube was withdrawn ... I resist and am overcome by the weight of numbers. If the doctor doesn't think the food is going down sufficiently swiftly, he pinches my nose with the tube in it and my throat, causing me increased pain.'[36] On 2 October 1909, Mary jammed her table, bed and chairs against the door. Male warders were ordered to break down the door but she kept them at bay for three hours.

Charlie Marsh was regarded with awe when she was released from Winson Green on 9 December; she was one of the first suffragettes to be fed by stomach tube, a total of 139 times. Even though the prison authorities and the Home Office knew her father was dying, Charlie was not allowed to visit him in Newcastle until the day before he died, by which time he was unconscious. She was pale and thin, twenty-one pounds lighter, her throat and chest were very painful and she had a burning sensation in her head. Her doctor described her as being 'emaciated, as though recovering from a serious illness and that condition may be extremely prejudicial to her health at some future time'.[37]

Captain Green, the prison governor, had no hesitation in ordering the prison medical officer, Dr Ernest Helby, to feed the hunger-striking suffragettes 'artificially'. Laura Ainsworth, a schoolteacher in her twenties, was placed in a chair and held down by four wardresses who tube-fed her twice every day, and at midday forced meat extract through her teeth. 'My mouth was forced open and a tube inserted and pushed down my throat a foot or more. I was gagged by a cork with a hole through which the tube went, liquid was poured down through a funnel, the tongue was pressed down and the tube forced down the gullet. The sensation caused a horrible choking and stunned feeling. When the tube was withdrawn it seemed as if my inside was being pulled out.'[38]

Laura was sent to a nursing home in Birmingham on her release on 5 October 1906. The doctor who examined her noted a weak and husky voice, a congestion and inflammation of the throat, and that she was in a state of 'nervous prostration'. Within two days of her release Clement's Inn instructed Mr George Elliott, a King's Counsel, to summons the home secretary, Herbert Gladstone, Captain Percy Green and Dr Ernest Haslar Helby for assault. Mary Leigh brought the same case (Leigh v. Gladstone) which was decided on 9 December at the King's Bench Division before the Lord Chief Justice where a special jury took only two minutes to decide in favour of the authorities. The defendants' case was that they had a right and duty to feed the women to prevent them starving themselves to death which could be seen as an act of suicide. When Laura's case came to court the charges against the home secretary, Captain Green and Dr Helby were dismissed.[39]

On 26 September Constance Lytton wrote to Arthur Balfour, asking him to meet Christabel Pankhurst: 'I hope you will not think this an impertinent suggestion ... I feel so very deeply the seriousness and urgency of the Women's Franchise question that I let pass no means of trying to further its welfare.' She reminded him of the urgency of the situation: 'We are threatened with a further extension of the male franchise from which it is likely that women will again be excluded.' Constance reminded him of a speech he made in 1892 when he foresaw a time 'when this question will arise again, menacing and ripe for resolution', and suggested that his prophecy was now being fulfilled. Balfour's reply was that he did not approve of the recent spate of militancy and would not meet Christabel Pankhurst.[40]

The national press reported the suffragettes' rooftop protests with a sense of righteous indignation. The WSPU was able to neutralise this by their campaign of releasing detailed information about the force-feeding of women. Keir Hardie wrote to *The Times* on 27 September 1909: 'That there is a difference of opinion concerning the tactics of the militant suffragettes goes without saying, but surely there can be no two opinions concerning the brutality of these proceedings? ... worn and weak by hunger-strike they are seized upon, held down by brute force, gagged and a tube inserted down the throat and food poured or pumped into the stomach. Let British men think over the spectacle!'[41]

The word 'torture' was being used in some of the press coverage. Normally force-feeding was only carried out when lunatics in hospital refused to eat, and this was the first time that sane British prisoners had been fed by force. Taking the position that what was happening at Winson Green was torture, some doctors, particularly Charles Mansell-Moullin, whose wife, Ruth, was a member of the

WSPU, condemned the practice. Citing his thirty years' experience as a senior surgeon at the London Hospital in a letter to *The Times* of 29 September, he protested at the use of the term 'hospital treatment' by Mr Masterman, the Liberal MP for West Ham North. Mansell-Moullin insisted there was 'not a man in the United Kingdom except those gentlemen of the House of Commons who cheered on Mr Masterman who does not feel absolutely sick at the revolting description'.[42]

The eminent psychiatrist Dr Lyttelton Forbes Winslow wrote to *The Times* to say that force-feeding was so risky he had long since abandoned it. On 4 October 1909, 118 medical practitioners (fifty-two of whom were women) signed a 'memorial' to the prime minister 'most urgently protesting against the treatment by artificial feeding of the suffragettes at Winson Green Gaol'. They believed force-feeding was inhumane, and 'earnestly begged' him to end it.[43] Dr Hugh Fenton, Senior Physician at the Chelsea Hospital for Women, wrote: 'it is an absolutely beastly and revolting process and when patients resist force-feeding it becomes positively dangerous'.[44]

Not all the medical profession shared Mansell-Moullin's views. An anonymous doctor added his own provocative remarks to the debate in a letter to *The Times* in which he tried to justify the practice of force-feeding women who were violent and perhaps hell-bent on martyrdom. He brushed aside the criticism as 'indefensible and absurd', insisting that 'oral and nasal feeding is carried out daily by medical practitioners … it entails no risk or particular discomfort'. He conceded that if any kind of 'deliberate resistance was offered and the condition of the patient affords no other channel for the conveyance of adequate nutrition' the procedure had to be carried out with 'such measures of restraint as are necessary'. Claiming to have forty years of hospital and private practice experience, he said he had only known resistance to come from 'insane patients'. The doctor denounced the means by which the women were seeking to avoid serving their full sentence by refusing to eat, and said that any reduction of their sentences was 'unjustifiable sentimentalism'.[45]

The day after Herbert Asquith received the petition from the doctors, *The Times* printed a letter from the radical journalists Henry Brailsford and Henry Nevinson, both of whom wrote for the Liberal *Daily News*. They resigned because their editor, Alfred George

Gardiner, refused to condemn the force-feeding of suffragette prisoners. 'We have resigned our positions as leader-writers … we cannot denounce torture in Russia and support it in England, nor can we advocate democratic principles in the name of a party which confines them to a single sex.'[46]

Henry Woodd Nevinson, born in 1852, studied at Oxford and worked as a missionary at Toynbee Hall in the East End of London. He reported the Boer War on the ground, and reported on India for the *Manchester Guardian*; he also helped found the Men's League for Women's Suffrage, his consciousness raised perhaps by the novelist Evelyn Sharp, with whom he had a long relationship and whom he married when his wife died in 1933. Evelyn Jane Sharp was a member of the NUWSS, before joining the WSPU and speaking at Women's Sunday. In 1909 Henry Nevinson started the Men's Political Union for Women's Enfranchisement.[47]

Henry Brailsford was born in 1873 and married one of his pupils, Jane Esdon Malloch, at Queen Margaret's College, Glasgow, where he was a fellow in mental philosophy. The ladylike methods of the NUWSS did not appeal to Jane Brailsford's headstrong personality. With her husband's resignation ringing in her ears, she travelled to Newcastle on 9 October 1909 to protest against force-feeding at Lloyd George's Budget meeting at the Palace Theatre. Jane hid an axe in her clothing and with it attacked a barricade that had been thrown up round the building, was arrested and sentenced to a month in the second division. Her husband's name meant that she received preferential treatment, which did not please her. No attempt was made to force-feed her and she was released after three days in Newcastle Gaol.[48]

Scores of local suffragettes 'welcomed' Lloyd George and Sir Walter Runciman who were in Newcastle to drum up support for the government's controversial Budget meeting at the Palace Theatre. The WSPU had been preparing for two weeks, holding meetings in the pit villages, at factory gates and around the town. Twelve women from London, including Christabel Pankhurst, Constance Lytton, Jane Brailsford, Lily Asquith (no relation to the prime minister, she was a Manchester dressmaker), Dorothy Shallard, Dorothy Pethick and Kitty Marion volunteered. The night before Lloyd George's meeting Christabel Pankhurst spoke at the Drill Hall, but was interrupted by a gang of male students who shouted her down for twenty-five minutes, rang bells and blew whistles. Undaunted by the barracking, she focused her attention on the front rows where the press were seated. She repeated her assertion that the WSPU's militant tactics would continue in the face of the government's barbarism. After the stormy meeting Christabel met the dozen volunteers in a boarding house in Newcastle to give them their orders, and to make them aware of the likelihood that they would be arrested. She spelled out what they would face in prison, what was involved if any of them elected to go on hunger strike, and what it was like to be fed by force.[49]

The arrival of suffragettes from London had been anticipated and a number of Special Branch detectives were sent from Scotland Yard to identify their lodgings and follow them everywhere. The streets leading to the Palace Theatre were barricaded to keep the suffragettes as far away as possible from the chancellor. The Special Branch officers did not stop Violet Bryant, who had resigned her job as a hospital nurse in disgust at the force-feeding in order to take 'her place in the fighting line' at Newcastle, Ellen Pitfield, a midwife, Lily Asquith and Dorothy Shallard; they smashed three windows of the Liberal Club in Pilgrim Street. Lloyd George was dropped off at the Palace Theatre, and as Runciman was driven to his meeting at St George's Hall, Constance Lytton and Emily Davison tried to throw stones at the car and were arrested by a plain-clothes officer and a uniformed sergeant. Lytton's stone bounced off the radiator and Davison was grabbed before she could 'deliver her message'. Attached to Lady Constance's stone was a label which read: 'To Lloyd George – Rebellion against tyranny is obedience to God. Deeds Not Words.'

No WSPU members managed to get into the meeting but several male sympathisers heckled the chancellor. The first man who called out 'what about the women?' was grabbed by Liberal stewards and 'violently ejected'. Calm was briefly restored before a student yelled out, 'Women object to paying taxes because they don't get representation.' In the circle seats Henry Brailsford called out about the force-feeding of women in Winson Green and was set upon. He hid under his seat but the stewards winkled him out and as he was being removed he hit one of the stewards with the back of his hand and grabbed another around the neck in an arm lock. He was then thrown down the staircase into the foyer and escorted beyond the barricades.[50]

The suffragettes had not finished with Lloyd George or Walter Runciman. Kitty Marion and Mrs Pethick-Lawrence's sister, Dorothy, were directed by Christabel to throw stones at the windows of the Newcastle General Post Office. When the cathedral clock struck seven Newcastle post offices would have their windows broken, and the stone-throwers were to shout 'Votes for women!' Kitty had two stones in her muff and felt 'deadly sick and nervous' as she made her way with Dorothy to the General Post Office. Without acknowledging each other the women went inside to make sure that no one would be showered by broken glass when they lobbed the stones through the windows. Kitty said to Dorothy 'Now for it' and each of them hurled a stone, but Kitty's window did not break, 'so I hurled a second stone with lightning speed and greater force which shattered it just as a detective grabbed my arm'. Dorothy's first stone also missed, and since she had been followed by plain-clothes policemen she was pounced on. Kitty and Dorothy were marched to the police station, to the accompaniment of clapping and cheering crowds, some shouting 'votes for women'. None of the women arrested that day were allowed bail and they spent two nights in 'insanitary' cells until their cases were heard on Monday 11 October.[51]

Charged with wilful damage, Ellen Pitfield, Lily Asquith, Violet Bryant and Dorothy Shallard were sentenced to fourteen days with hard labour. To especially discourage local women from engaging in suffragette violence, the magistrate sentenced Kathleen Brown to a month with hard labour. Ellen Pitfield, who got fourteen days with hard labour, said she had broken the window 'in cold blood, deliberately, and the blow was against the Government, and would not be the last'.[52]

Constance Lytton was charged with assaulting Sir Walter Runciman by throwing a stone at him in the Haymarket, 'maliciously damaging his motor-car' and disorderly behaviour. She told the court, 'My object was not injury; it was to make a protest in public, with violence.' The catalyst for her journey to Newcastle was the treatment of Mary Leigh who was 'being tortured by the Government in Winson Green prison'. Constance Lytton called on the government to treat her the same way as they had treated 'her sister' Mary Leigh. Because of her connections the charge was reduced to disorderly conduct and she chose to go to prison for one month rather than pay a fine.[53]

Jane Brailsford was sent to gaol for a month (although she only served three days) and told the court that the 'violation of women's bodies' at Winson Green Prison had 'filled her with determination' to travel to Newcastle to protest and to go to prison if necessary. The Brailsfords hoped that their reputation in Liberal circles 'will have a unique influence upon public opinion'.[54]

Kitty Marion and Dorothy Pethick were charged with having 'wilfully and maliciously' damaged a plate-glass window at the General Post Office in Nicholson Street. Kitty pleaded guilty: 'I have only practised what Mr Lloyd George preaches. Mr Lloyd George says that "revolt is the only weapon to carry on a cause".' Kitty was sentenced to a month's hard labour, and Dorothy pleaded not guilty to smashing but 'guilty of trying to'. She told the magistrate, 'My action was entirely prompted by the injustice of the present Government, and if it continues in this way we shall do worse things.' She was sent to prison for the first time for two weeks with hard labour.[55]

In solidarity with their comrades in Winson Green, the women went on hunger strike. While waiting for their cases to be heard, they wrote to *Votes for Women* about their intention to starve themselves and risk being fed by force. Their aim was to raise the stakes by offering the government three options: to release them after a few days of starvation; to force-feed them and 'inflict violence upon our bodies' and run the risk of women dying by allowing them to starve to death; or 'the best and only wise' alternative, which was to give women the vote.[56]

Constance Lytton's mother and sister Emily sent her a telegram of support: 'We uphold you. Shall work for you. God bless you.' Constance described the scene in court as a 'sickening assembly of snobs defending snobbish action – everything predetermined'. To her despair she was released after two and a half days of refusing to eat and being 'medically unfit'. Jane Brailsford was released for the same reason and thanks also to her husband's connections.[57]

This was Kitty's Marion's first time in prison. *The Performer*, the trade paper for actors, took a dim view of her behaviour: 'In the interests of the profession and of the gaiety of nations, we trust that Miss Marion will be kept fit during her enforced retirement, whether by compulsory feeding or otherwise.'[58] Kitty was force-fed by both the

Emmeline Pankhurst founded the WSPU in Manchester in 1903. 'The most rebellious spirits grew calm in her presence, the most obstinate grew amenable. They adored her. There is no other word for it.' (Annie Kenney)

Christabel Pankhurst, twenty-six in 1906, had a first-class degree in law from Owen's College (now Manchester University). As a woman she was not allowed to practise as a lawyer.

Sylvia Pankhurst, twenty-four in 1906, studied at the Royal College of Art. Her artwork gave the WSPU a modern and coherent visual identity.

Adela Pankhurst in 1906, aged twenty-one. She was a schoolteacher before becoming a full-time organiser.

Poster girl Annie Kenney, a mill worker from Oldham, took over the running of the WSPU in 1912 when Christabel Pankhurst fled to Paris.

Hannah Mitchell, a dressmaker's assistant before her marriage, joined the WSPU in 1904 and helped recruit working women in the Lancashire mill towns.

Teresa Billington resigned her teaching post to become a WSPU organiser. In 1907 she married, and became a founder member of the Women's Freedom League.

Flora Drummond was thwarted in her wish to become a postmistress by being an inch too short. She was often known as 'General' Drummond.

Elizabeth Wolstenholme Elmy was seventy years old when she joined Mrs Pankhurst's organisation. She had been involved in feminist and suffragist campaigns in the nineteenth century.

Born in Poplar, east London, Minnie Baldock, a shirt machinist, founded the first WSPU branch outside Manchester, in Canning Town in 1906.

Born in Cornwall in 1874, Nellie Martel emigrated to Australia in the 1890s, and campaigned for the vote in New South Wales. She returned to England and joined the WSPU in 1905.

James Keir Hardie, aged fifty in 1906. He was the first working man to become an MP in 1892, and the most loyal supporter of votes for women in the House of Commons.

Emmeline Pethick-Lawrence joined the WSPU in 1906 and co-edited the newspaper *Votes for Women* with her husband Fred. She was a magnificent patron of and fundraiser for the militant campaign.

Frederick Pethick-Lawrence, a barrister, worked as a 'Poor Man's Lawyer' in Canning Town in the 1890s. His legal expertise and great wealth were both invaluable to the militant struggle.

In June 1906 Annie Kenney, Adelaide Knight and Jane Sbarborough were sent to Holloway for six weeks for obstruction, while trying to interview Herbert Asquith at his home in Cavendish Square.

Science tutor Edith How-Martyn was an early member of the WSPU. In 1907 she questioned the leadership style of the Pankhursts and left to co-found the Women's Freedom League.

Schoolteacher Mary Gawthorpe, twenty-seven, was a feisty speaker and roving organiser for the WSPU. She had many fans who avidly collected postcards of her.

Mabel Tuke, divorced and widowed, met the Pethick-Lawrences on a boat returning from South Africa in 1905. Within six months all three were working with the WSPU.

Aged sixty-two, Charlotte Despard's distinctive mantilla and leather sandals made her an impressive presence at suffragette protests. She joined the WSPU in 1906, but left a year later.

Edith Rigby was the leading light of the Preston branch of the WSPU. She recruited many working women and served several prison sentences for the Cause.

In 1906 Rachel Barrett's suffragette activities ended her teaching career in Cardiff. In 1907 she studied at the LSE and became a WSPU organiser.

Born in West Bromwich, Emma Sproson started her working life in 1874 at the age of nine. Emma joined the WSPU in 1906 and went to prison twice in 1907.

Dora Thewlis was working in a woollen mill in Huddersfield when she was arrested, aged sixteen, at a suffragette protest in Westminster in March 1907.

Georgina Brackenbury and her mother, Hilda and sister, Marie were keen supporters of the WSPU. Their Kensington house became a nursing home for suffragettes recovering from being force-fed.

Marie Brackenbury and her sister Georgina studied at the Slade School of Art. They left the moderate NUWSS and joined the militant WSPU in 1907.

'Vera Wentworth' was the alias of Jessie Spinks. In 1908, aged eighteen, she was working in her father's chemist shop when she became a suffragette.

Beatrice Parlby 'roused' the women of Hereford in 1908. In 1901 she was teaching at Burnley Grammar School.

'Women's Sunday', a 'monster meeting' of WSPU members from all over the United Kingdom, was held in Hyde Park on 21 June 1908.

Emmeline Pankhurst, left, and the diminutive Elizabeth Wolstenholme Elmy, centre, at 'Women's Sunday', 1908. A hundred speakers at twenty platforms demanded women's suffrage.

nasal and stomach tube, and described the first of 300 similar ordeals in her suffragette career. 'I struggled and screamed all the time … thinking it was done through the mouth, I clenched my teeth when they had me in position and helpless, and suddenly I felt something penetrate my right nostril which seemed to cause my head to burst and my eyes to bulge. Choking and retching as the tube was forced down to the stomach and the liquid food was poured in, most of which was vomited back when the tube was withdrawn. There are no words to describe the horrible revolting sensation.' Kitty called the doctors 'a lot of dirty cringing doormats to the government' and she hit one of them across the face with the back of her hand before she was bundled back to her cell.[59] Reflecting on the length of her sentence, and her new role, Kitty wondered how she could alert the world to what was going in Newcastle Gaol, and remembered Harry Houdini with whom she had once shared the billing, and how he might have made his escape.

Kitty realised she could burn her mattress stuffed with straw but 'the casing was made of canvas. How could I get the contents out? I had neither knife nor scissors. The only way was to gnaw a hole large enough and draw the contents out, place them against the door, break the glass of the gas light with the leg of a chair and get a flame.' Kitty lay on her bed 'gnawing at the pillow which was more difficult than it sounds'.[60] Eventually she teased out the coconut fibre and 'made a big heap', and tore a page from the Bible to make a spill to take a light from the gas mantle. She struggled with the idea of treating the Bible in this way but reasoned that 'God's words stand for our fight for Freedom and Justice and a replaceable copy could not be used in a better cause' and proceeded to make her 'fiery protest'. She started the fire by the door and soon the cell was filled with smoke. Overcome by it, she was dragged out of her cell by the wardresses 'and left on the stone cold floor in the corridor while they put out the fire … I was in a state of collapse and did not care what happened.' She was transferred to a cell where 'even the floor was padded and there was no furniture'. After a day she was moved to a regular prison cell, closely watched, and visited by the governor, the matron and the prison doctor. She was fed by the matron who was 'most kind and motherly and gave me milk from a feeding-cup which I was too weak to resist. I could not face the feeding tube again.'[61] Every evening one of the wardresses would sit outside Kitty's cell and talk to her, asking her 'if I was the Kitty Marion she had seen at the Manchester Hippodrome? She had admired me very much and little dreamed she would ever meet me like this.'[62] Kitty received a visit from a local magistrate who thought her sentence excessive, but said the suffragettes were 'very cowardly' to take their 'fight into prison and cause so much trouble'.[63]

When Kitty was released on 10 November the newspapers reported that she was 'looking exceedingly well ... and appeared in robust health and high spirit'.[64] This breezy description was at odds with how Kitty actually felt; while she was delighted to be free, she was unwell, out of work and hard up. She had no bookings and was too ill to look for any employment for a while. She stayed in London with one of her 'Ma's' – the name she gave her landladies – and received letters and telegrams, which she treasured for years, from Mrs Pankhurst, Vera Wentworth and the Pethick-Lawrences, congratulating her with 'hearts full of gratitude and appreciation' for her courage.[65]

A month after her release Kitty and all the other suffragettes who had been force-fed in Newcastle Gaol were awarded 'For Valour' medals in a ceremony at the Royal Albert Hall – the suffragettes' Victoria Cross, given to women who went on hunger strike and were force-fed. Mrs Pankhurst presented the medals. Kitty wrote: 'It was a glorious reunion and a great honour and privilege to walk in that file of splendid fighters for Women's Emancipation.'[66]

A week before the first batch of Newcastle women were released in a sorry state, Emily Davison was on the warpath. She went to Manchester to wait for Sir Walter Runciman who was due to speak on the Budget on 20 October. Davison was not a paid organiser but she acted like one: she was never given a salaried post, which rankled and became a source of anger and financial distress. Using Manchester WSPU-headed notepaper she wrote to a member, 'All hail Newcastle! How I wish I was in gaol there!! I am busy once more acting almost as an organiser here waiting for a certain person.'[67]

Outraged by Mary Leigh's force-feeding, Helen Liddle, a fifty-five-year-old music teacher, Hannah Sheppard, a mill worker from Rochdale, and nineteen-year-old Catherine Tolson joined Emily Davison's protest at Radcliffe, near Manchester. Because women were banned from Runciman's meeting, they held their own meeting on a lorry and had to be rescued by the police who dispersed a gang of rowdy youths who were trying to push the lorry down the hill. The gang would have succeeded had not a male sympathiser managed to lock the wheels. The women threw stones with messages to Runciman through the windows of the Radcliffe Liberal Club and the main post office: Tolson, Liddle and Sheppard were sentenced at Bury Police Court to a month with hard labour in Manchester's Strangeways Prison, and because of Davison's previous convictions she was to serve two months with hard labour.

The four women went on hunger strike and were force-fed throughout their sentence. Emily Davison wedged two beds and mattresses, table and stool against the door. After being warned of the consequences if she did not open the door, a ladder appeared at the cell window, the glass was broken and the nozzle of a hosepipe was pushed through. 'Then came the deluge! At first the stream shot over my head. I took hold of the bed boards and sat firm. Then they got the water trained full on me; the stream came at me full force. I had to hold on like grim death.'[68] The hosing lasted for fifteen minutes and its coldness made her gasp for breath. Then the door was smashed down and a wardress pushed her out of the cell telling her she should be horsewhipped for her behaviour. Emily was taken to the hospital wing where the force-feeding resumed and she was released three days later on 28 October, having served only eight days of her two-month sentence. The legal proceedings she launched for assault and damages of £100 against Strangeways Prison, were eventually won in January 1910, although she was only awarded damages of £2.[69]

The day before the Radcliffe protest, Adela Pankhurst, Maud Joachim, Helen Archdale, Laura Evans and Mrs Catherine Corbett had made life as difficult as possible for Winston Churchill at the Kinnaird Hall in Dundee. Two days earlier at Abernethy, near Perth, Adela had led the protest against Winston Churchill, where two suffragettes were pelted with clods of earth 'which they returned with full force'. The women tried to hold a meeting next to the marquee where Churchill was speaking but their car was picked up and carried away with them inside it. A policeman asked the chauffeur who had driven them from Perth to move on but he refused, explaining that he was acting on 'the ladies' orders'. Adela and Mrs Corbett made their way to Dundee and met up with Maud Joachim,

Helen Archdale and Laura Evans and set off in pursuit of Winston Churchill.[70]

The Kinnaird Hall was filled with 3,000 men with not a woman in sight. In a building overlooking the hall, Adela Pankhurst, Laura Evans and two Dundee men, Owen Clark and William Carr, had hidden themselves in an attic and threw stones, bricks and slates at the roof-light of the hall, calling out 'votes for women' which could be clearly heard by Churchill and his audience. Facing them on their roof were Liberal stewards 'using much bad language' and throwing slates through the window of the room where they were hiding. It took the police forty-five minutes to winkle them out of their hiding place – they had boarded up the door of the attic. Meanwhile, Maud Joachim, Helen Archdale and Catherine Corbett arrived by tram, leaping off to create a stir of surprise, and gathering a friendly crowd to storm the barricades thrown up around the hall, leading 'rushes' towards the barricades, waving the colours and shouting 'votes for women'. The police grabbed the suffragettes and locked them in the basement. Catherine Corbett paid tribute to the courage of the Dundonians who had rioted for three hours: 'they would not stop until they got the barricades down, they were glorious.' The arrival of four mounted policemen caused hisses and hoots, and when the horses were hemmed in by a hostile crowd the order was given for the police to clear the streets with their batons. When interviewed for the Dundee newspaper the *Courier*, Winston Churchill called the militants 'a band of silly, neurotic, hysterical women'. Each woman prisoner made a lengthy speech in court and was sentenced to ten days in prison. They went on hunger strike. The charges against the two men were dropped.

Despite being encouraged by the Prison Commissioners in Edinburgh and the Home Office in London to force-feed the women, the governor, James Crowe, consulted with Dr A. W. Stalker, the medical officer of Dundee Gaol, and decided not to do so. The correspondence between Dundee Gaol and the Prison Commissioners for Scotland reveals there had been a willingness to force-feed at least some of the women – but not Mrs Corbett who was 'betraying signs of being older than her years. She has a rapid action of the heart and palpitation on movement.' According to Stalker, Helen Archdale was 'a big overgrown woman ... and excitable. From her

configuration she would be particularly difficult to feed forcibly.'
Adela Pankhurst 'looked outwardly calm and indifferent but the ...
heart's action is violent and laboured. Mentally she is peculiar, mor-
bid and twisted.' 'Owing to local feeling' they were not sure they
could 'obtain the services of one or two trained nurses'. 'General'
Flora Drummond was at the prison gates to greet the women when
they were released.[71]

Mrs Helen Alexander Archdale, who was thirty-three years old,
had joined the WSPU in 1908. She lived in Preston where her husband
Theodore Montgomery Archdale served with the Lancashire Field
Artillery. Their wedding night in 1901 had come as a shock – Helen
had no idea what to expect. The Archdale marriage would not survive
Helen's embracing of militancy.[72]

Accompanied by Emmeline Pethick-Lawrence's sister, Dr Marie
Pethick, Mrs Pankhurst sailed for New York from Liverpool on the
RMS *Oceanic* on 13 October 1909. Her son Harry was paralysed from
the waist down with poliomyelitis. According to Sylvia Pankhurst, 'so
ruthless was the inner call to action, that finding her son thus stricken
she persevered with her intention'. The Pankhursts were always hard
up; any fees Emmeline could earn by lecturing were needed to pay
for Harry's medical bills and to support WSPU's campaign fund, and
newspaper reports of the tour were useful publicity for the cause on
both sides of the Atlantic.[73]

The stories of her leadership style and case studies of members of
the WSPU who were on hunger strike and being force-fed afforded
Mrs Pankhurst emotive material for her lectures. She opened her first
speech at Carnegie Hall, New York, with the words: 'I am what you
call a hooligan' and was greeted by a 'great shout of warm and sympathetic laughter. Then I knew I had found friends in America.' The
Boston Woman's Journal noted that 'whenever she speaks her intense
earnestness kindles the smouldering equal rights sentiments among
her hearers into flames'.[74]

Back in Britain, on 29 October Mary Leigh was released from
Winson Green where she had been fed by nasal tube two or three
times a day since the middle of September. She was taken in a 'weak
and ill' state by a wardress in a cab to the WSPU office in Birmingham
and handed over to Gladice Keevil. In Miss Keevil's opinion Mary had
been released because she was so frail it would have been dangerous to

force-feed her any longer and the authorities did not want to risk her dying in prison.[75]

On 3 November Dr Ernest Helby, who had force-fed Mary, Charlie Marsh and Patricia Woodlock at Winson Green, was stopped in the street in Birmingham by Patricia Woodlock and Laura Ainsworth. They demanded the release of their friend Charlie Marsh who still had six weeks to serve, and warned him they would 'do something desperate' if she was not released within a week. When a colleague of his reported to the police that his windows had been broken by the suffragettes he was told that they wanted it kept quiet. Charlie Marsh was eventually released on 9 December.[76]

Alice Paul and Amelia Brown disguised themselves as charladies on 9 November 1909 in order to make a protest at the Lord Mayor's Banquet in London. Initially, they hid in a room behind a balcony for twelve hours. Lucy Burns, who had travelled to London from Edinburgh, where she was a paid organiser for the WSPU, was dressed in an evening gown and mingled with those who awaited the arrival of Mr and Mrs Asquith. When Winston Churchill and his wife walked towards Lucy, she pounced and waved a banner in his face calling out: 'How can you dine here while women are starving in prison?' and was removed from the building. Then, when Asquith stood up to speak, Amelia Brown smashed a window above the diners with a shoe and shouted 'votes for women' and both she and Alice were arrested.[77]

The next day the magistrate at the Guildhall Police Court admonished the women: 'I do not understand how you hysterical creatures can think you are furthering your political cause in this way ... You are educated and ought to know better', and sentenced them to a month in Holloway with hard labour.[78] They went on hunger strike and refused to wear prison clothing. Not wanting her mother to find out that she had been arrested, Alice Paul had asked her suffragette friends not to tell the newspapers that she was an American, but the story of her suffering in prison was widely reported in the United States.

After two days of starvation the women were force-fed for the rest of their time in prison. Alice told *Votes for Women* how the largest wardress on the prison staff sat on her knees and 'placed her two hands on her chest to keep her from bending forward'. Two other women held her and a towel was placed under her throat. Then one doctor pushed her head back while another forced the tube through her nostrils. Although Amelia Brown suffered badly from gastritis and vomited continuously, they still used a gag to hold her mouth open, 'and her sufferings were terrible'. Alice wrote how blood streamed down Amelia's face after her first force-feeding.[79]

Reporting to Home Secretary Gladstone, and Lord Pentland, the secretary of state for Scotland, the prison authorities in England and Scotland were devising their joint response to the possibility of women dying for the vote and being venerated as martyrs. Their concerns were pragmatic – how to feed the women by force. Three different procedures were discussed at length: the feeding cup method involved forcing the cup between the teeth and pouring the contents into the 'patient's' mouth. This method was 'attended with considerable risk of injury' if the prisoners offered any resistance. The oesophageal catheter or tube required five assistants to ensure 'full control'. The patient should be put into bed with one assistant sitting on the bed 'at the pillow and steadies the patient's body with his or her knees and steadies the patient's head by pressing the head against his or her chest'.[80] Four people would be needed to control each of the limbs. Once the 'patient' was under control, the doctor would insert a gag into the mouth, and hand over the job of keeping the gag in place to another assistant while he 'introduces the catheter, previously smeared with oil or Castile soap into the upper part of the gullet and when the reflex involuntary contractions of the gullet cease carry the end down into the patient's stomach'.[81] The author of the guidance notes pointed out the risk of the catheter entering the windpipe instead of the gullet, but brushed it aside with the words 'but this is an exceedingly rare accident and the effects of the accident can be obviated by observation after the introduction'.[82] Once the doctor was satisfied that the catheter was in the stomach a feeding funnel would be attached to it and thin custard, milk and eggs or broth were poured into the funnel, a process taking two or three minutes, and while it may 'produce discomfort is not painful'.[83] The nasal tube method was carried out in largely the same way although the catheter was narrower; no gag was needed, it took longer to complete the feeding and there was still the risk of liquid accidentally entering the windpipe.[84]

In November 1909 Mary Allen's active service was ended by the damage caused to her digestion as a result of being force-fed in Horfield Gaol. Mary Allen and Vera Wentworth were imprisoned for two weeks for breaking the windows of the offices of the Inland Revenue and the Liberal Club in Bristol on 13 November, protesting at Winston Churchill's refusal to meet a suffragette deputation. At the railway station Theresa Garnett hit Churchill across the face with a horse whip 'and knocked his hat about', and was sent to prison for a month.[85] When Mary Allen was released she was forbidden by her doctors and Mrs Pankhurst from undertaking any activities which could land her in prison. Mary was frustrated at not being able to 'martyrise myself for the cause, and suddenly deprived of this vehement form of activity, I instantly began to plan a new one'.[86]

Mary was asked to take charge of members selling *Votes for Women* in Ramsgate and Margate; by 1912 she was the organiser of the WSPU's campaign in Eastbourne, Bexhill, St Leonards and Hastings.

On 1 December Mrs Pankhurst set sail for England on the SS *Mauretania*, six weeks after her arrival in the United States. The tour had been a great success, the American press showed interest in her speeches and there were plans for American suffragists to come to England to study the WSPU's campaign. When Mrs Pankhurst landed she learned that the appeal that she and Mrs Haverfield had launched against the charges brought against them following the Bill of Rights deputation on 29 June had been dropped. The women had insisted they had been wrongfully arrested, citing their legal right to petition the King. The government refused to give the WSPU any more publicity and the case was dismissed.[87]

While Mrs Pankhurst and Marie Pethick were crossing the Atlantic, Edith Rigby, Grace Alderman, Beth Hesmondhalgh and other Preston members, assisted by Mrs Rosamund Massy and Margaret Hewitt, a young West Country member, were holding meetings in Preston in the days preceding Winston Churchill's visit on the evening of 3 December. The streets around the Preston Public Hall were barricaded where Churchill was due to talk up the People's Budget. No vehicles or pedestrians were allowed after four o'clock in the afternoon unless they had permission from the police. Members of Special Branch were sent from London to assist. All the windows of the hall were boarded up, the roof was covered with a tarpaulin and a hose pipe was readied in case any women did manage to get onto the roof. Residents who lived nearby were warned by the chief constable of the 'awful consequences that would overtake them if they harboured a suffragette'.[88]

At around midnight on the night before Churchill's visit, four Preston suffragettes armed with posters showing a suffragette being held down by a prison official and fed through a nasal tube stuck them onto the walls of the Public Hall, Preston Gaol, the Liberal Club, post offices and pillar boxes. Later that day Rosamund Massy threw a stone through a window of the post office wrapped in paper bearing the words: 'Message to Mr Winston Churchill: This stone through your post office window is to remind you of your broken promises to the Suffragists of Manchester and Dundee.' She pleaded guilty to causing £2 worth of damage and was sentenced to a month in prison.[89]

In the early evening large crowds gathered near the hall which was packed with five to six thousand people, mostly men, and some 'ladies who were only admitted if their credentials were beyond question'.[90] When a group of suffragettes arrived at the door at eight o'clock, Edith Rigby, Beth Hesmondhalgh, Catherine Worthington and Grace Alderman were ordered to leave; they refused and were bundled into a Black Maria and driven off. In court, Beth Hesmondhalgh said that as a working woman she knew the importance of the vote, and chose to go prison for seven days.[91] Edith Rigby and Mrs Worthington were also sentenced to seven days in prison for obstruction, but Edith's father, Dr Rigby, intervened and to her great annoyance paid her fine. *Votes for Women* reported that Edith's father shouted, 'The lady is my daughter and this is the third time she has been placed in this position by hired women, who are making profit and advertisement.' His son, Arthur, pointed to 'a leading London woman suffragist' in the courtroom (this was Margaret Hewitt, wearing lipstick with her hat at a rakish angle) and shouted: 'It's that little painted Jezebel who has led my sister astray.'[92]

Mary Leigh arrived at the Law Courts in London on 9 December to hear the Lord Chief Justice's verdict on the action for damages for assault, which the WSPU had brought against Herbert Gladstone, when she was force-fed at Winson Green. The case was lost, the Lord Chief Justice ruling that prisons had a duty to prevent inmates from committing suicide. It was a defeat that the WSPU used as a new propaganda lever against a so-called liberal government.[93]

In December 1909 Christabel Pankhurst was finalising the WSPU's strategy for the forthcoming general election in January. The People's Budget had been vetoed by the House of Lords on 30 November, triggering the first election since the Liberals' landslide victory in 1906. Christabel wrote to the leader of the Conservative Party, Arthur Balfour, asking for a meeting. She said: 'until we have explained to you what we should like the next government to do for us and until we have heard what you have to tell us in reply, it is not possible for us to complete the arrangements for the General Election'. Balfour declined to meet her, saying women's suffrage was not a party question and that his colleagues were divided on the matter.[94]

*

In the autumn of 1909 suffragette entrepreneurs and commercial businesses offered purple, white and green goods as the ideal Christmas gift. Since the launch of the colour scheme in the summer of 1908, suffragette shops and ordinary department stores, such as the newly opened Selfridges, were offering an increasingly large selection of clothing and fashion accessories in purple, white and green, and tea, cigarettes and chocolate emblazoned with the slogan 'Votes for Women'. Christmas offered the perfect opportunity for WSPU-supporting jewellers like Annie Steen in Birmingham's jewellery district, who made 'hand-wrought gold and silver jewellery set with stones in the colours'. For shoppers with less to spend glass-bead necklaces could be bought, and for the better-off customer Mappin and Webb of Oxford Street and Regent Street sold 'Suffragette Jewellery', gold brooches and pendants set with amethysts, emeralds and pearls. Games also sold well: 'Panko or Votes for Women, The Great Card Game, Suffragists versus Anti-Suffragists' was on sale for the first time in December 1909. Recommended by the editors of Votes for Women as a way of 'popularising the cause and the colours', it was said to be a game which produced 'intense excitement without the slightest taint of bitterness'. Kensington WSPU's shop in Church Street was typical of about a dozen suffragette shops nationwide in selling 'Cabinet Mincemeat', Christmas puddings, suffragette crackers, jams and sweets. On the last day of 1909 Selfridges took a quarter-page advertisement in *Votes for Women*, cheerfully optimistic that women's suffrage was imminent and 'a new order of things WILL succeed – will prosper with judicious fostering, and so we present for those who are interested, Helps For Suffrage Workers'. There was notepaper and envelopes embossed in the colours, engagement diaries and blotting pads, ladies' fine kid gloves, and wrist bags in the colours: 'soft but durable with cords and tassels most handy for shopping'.[95] The WSPU's innovative merchandising would expand until 1912 after which it declined when escalating militancy made the colours harder to wear.

8

Promise and Betrayal

The Conciliation Bill 1910

*The map was to show how the WSPU's message was spreading.
Branches opened and shops sold purple white and green merchandise.*

On 5 January 1910, a month after Mrs Pankhurst returned from the United States, her son Harry died of polio, aged twenty.[1] The next day she registered his death, revisiting her days as a Registrar of Births and Deaths in Manchester. Later Sylvia would write in her memoir: 'Mrs Pankhurst was broken as I had never seen her; huddled without a care for her appearance, she seemed an old, plain, cheerless woman. Her utter dejection moved me more than her vanished charm.'[2]

Polling for the general election was to take place between 15 January and 10 February. The day before Harry's funeral Emmeline Pankhurst wrote to Mary Phillips, organiser of Bradford WSPU: 'I would be grateful if Bradford friends would just behave to me as if no great sorrow had come to me just now. It breaks me down to talk about it although I am most grateful for sympathy. I want to get through my work and I know you will all help me to do it.'[3] Christabel acknowledged the messages of sympathy that flooded in and confided to Ada Flatman that Harry had 'talked during his illness of the women in prison and felt so much for them'.[4] A young suffragette, Helen Craggs, was romantically linked to Harry and visited him in the nursing home until his death.

The Liberal government wanted a majority in its bitter struggle with the House of Lords over Lloyd George's People's Budget. During the January campaign 245 candidates across all parties mentioned women's suffrage in their election speeches, including, surprisingly, Winston Churchill. Naturally Christabel Pankhurst took some credit: 'For the first time in history a political party went to the country with an admission that the votes for women question was a living political issue ... Militancy had floated the Cause. All that remained was to get it into port.'⁵

The Women's Social and Political Union was in good shape for the January election – a golden opportunity to embarrass the government and gain wider support for women's suffrage. Armed with ninety-eight salaried organisers and staff paid for by donations and membership subscriptions, and several hundred volunteers, there were twenty-three branches outside the capital, from London to Dundee, Edinburgh and Glasgow; in Torquay, Bristol, and Nottingham; Newcastle and Bradford. London had twenty branches in places such as Brixton, Greenwich, Kilburn and Battersea. The war chest contained £60,000. The circulation of *Votes for Women* had grown during 1909 from 30,000 to 40,000: the readership was much higher as the paper was passed on. The national headquarters, run from twenty-one rooms at 4 Clement's Inn, the same building as the Pethick-Lawrences' home, was crammed with staff and volunteers.⁶

Parliament had been dissolved on 3 December 1909 and the WSPU targeted forty seats held by Liberal MPs for 'specially hot fire'. Handbills were distributed outside theatres and cinemas, at sporting events, in high streets and at railway stations. Emmeline Pethick-Lawrence reminded women: 'Votes for Women is a matter of fundamental human liberty, and therefore it is the greatest of all national interests. Abraham Lincoln said once, when an attempt was being made to allow slavery in the Southern States of America and forbid it in the North, "You cannot have a State half-slave and half-free".' She continued: 'You cannot have in a country one-half of the people exercising real liberty, whilst liberty is refused to the other half.'⁷ She asked Liberal women to question their loyalty to a party that 'treats women as the Liberal Party has treated them', and Christabel Pankhurst urged 'the greatest service you could at the present time render to your Party would be to deal straightly and frankly with them in this matter'.⁸

As the election results were announced the leaders of the WSPU wrote asking returning and newly elected MPs if they would take part in the ballot for a women's suffrage bill. On 8 February, the newly elected Liberal Member of Parliament for North Somerset, Mr Joseph King, replied that he would not, but Christabel Pankhurst would not leave the matter. When King criticised the Union's 'self-courted martyrdom', Christabel replied, 'martyrdom is always self-courted so that the reproach which you intend to convey has no sting in it'. She reminded King that the WSPU had suspended militancy 'until the attitude of the Government proves to us that such methods are necessary to the attainment of our political end'.[9]

Incensed by the news of the brutal treatment of suffragette prisoners in Liverpool's Walton Gaol, in particular that of Selina Martin, a servant, aged twenty-seven from Lancaster, who was serving her fourth prison sentence for militant activities, Constance Lytton decided to go to Liverpool to make her protest, disguised as a working-class seamstress. She arrived on 10 January to canvass against the government during the general election campaign and was determined to get herself arrested. Before setting off, Constance Lytton tried to reassure her mother that she was well enough to travel, having been medically examined by Dr Marion Gilchrist, the first woman to get a medical degree in Scotland. Doctor Gilchrist noted that Constance had 'a chronic valvular lesion' which was 'acting well in spite of the fact she had just undergone great exertion'.[10] Constance asked the local WSPU organiser, Ada Flatman, to arrange lodgings 'with the humblest of sympathisers rather than with luxury', and reminded Ada she was a vegetarian and always took her own flannel sheets wherever she went.[11]

In Liverpool Constance Lytton used the alias 'Jane Warton'. She cut her hair short and parted it in the middle in a mid-Victorian style, and bought a badly fitting coat, a pair of pince-nez spectacles, a purse and a string bag. Pinned to her collar were badges of Mrs Pankhurst, Christabel and Mrs Pethick-Lawrence. She removed her embroidered initials from her underwear. Five feet eleven inches tall and gaunt, she had a ghostly appearance.[12]

Constance confided in Christabel Pankhurst her plan to get herself arrested and experience hunger-striking and force-feeding as a poor working woman without the privilege of rank. Christabel urged Ada Flatman 'not to tell a soul about our friend … she is willing we know'.[13] Constance decided to make her protest on 14 January, by calling 'upon the crowd to follow me to the Governor's house and insist on the release of the suffrage prisoners'.[14] She wanted to draw attention to Selina Martin, who was being 'horribly tortured' for throwing a stone ginger-beer bottle through the open window of

Asquith's motor car on 20 December. From the start of her militant career in 1908, Selina Martin had solid support at home. Her mother, Elizabeth, said she would gladly have gone to prison in her daughter's place.[15]

Unrecognised by local women with whom she had worked in the autumn, 'Jane Warton' mingled with a crowd 300-strong that gathered to hear speeches by Ada Flatman, Patricia Woodlock and Jennie Baines. Constance Lytton sensed that the people had turned up out of curiosity and was concerned they would not follow her to the Governor's house, so she 'rudely interrupted' Jennie Baines and asked 'the men and women of Liverpool to be the first to wipe out the stain [of force-feeding] that had been tolerated up to now',[16] by going to the Governor's house and asking him to release the suffragette prisoners. 'Jane Warton' was surprised that the crowd followed her and shouted – perhaps her cut-glass accent surprised them – 'No violence, remember, but call for the Governor and refuse to be dispersed till you have secured the release of the prisoners.'[17] She began to run towards Governor John Dillon's home, chased by three plain-clothes policemen, but before they could stop her 'Jane Warton' dropped stones wrapped in handbills over John Dillon's garden wall. She was taken to the police station and charged with urging the crowd to follow her to the Governor's house, refusing to desist when called upon by the police, and throwing a missile. She was sentenced to two weeks in the third division.

When 'Jane Warton' arrived at Walton Gaol on 15 January she refused to wear prison clothes, to do any kind of work, or eat prison food. She was weighed and stripped, and was visited in her cell by a junior medical officer; she refused to answer any medical questions but agreed to a medical inspection. Dr Price, the senior medical officer, saw her on 16 January and when he left she scratched on the walls of her cell with a hairpin 'Votes for Women. No surrender until they are won.' The following day 'Jane Warton' was placed in a punishment cell for three days. On the evening of 18 January, she was weighed, and, after refusing to be tempted with food left in her cell all day, she was force-fed. Dr Price did not listen to her heart or feel her pulse; 'he did not ask to do so, nor did I, directly or indirectly, say anything which could possibly induce him to think that I would refuse to be examined.'[18] She lay down on the plank bed on the floor, 'shut my mouth and clenched my teeth'. The doctor offered her a choice of a wood or steel gag and 'after failing to unlock my teeth with the wooden gag he used the steel and seemed annoyed at my resistance'. After being fed by the stomach tube 'Jane' was 'much overcome' and vomited. The tube seemed 'much too wide and was something like four feet in length. The irritation of the tube was excessive, I choked the moment it touched my throat ... the horror of it was more than I can describe.'[19]

The second time 'Jane' was fed she was 'violently sick over the doctor's clothes' and he left the cell accusing her of doing it on purpose: 'If you do it again tomorrow I shall feed you twice.'[20] Before being fed for the third time – it was either Bovril (although she had told the gaol she was a strict vegetarian) and brandy, or milk and raw eggs, Constance told the doctor that she was a small eater and that he should use smaller quantities of the liquid food, and 'begged that he would not press the tube so far down into my body'. He ignored her request. She had a violent 'shivering fit and my teeth chattered' and the doctor ordered the wardresses to lay her down and called the junior prison medical officer who, 'after a brief and very superficial investigation', pronounced her heart to be 'quite sound and the pulse steady'.[21] That was the only time her heart was listened to, although her pulse was felt several times during her time in prison. After a sixth feeding she asked the doctor to skip a meal and explained politely that she was constipated. Again he ignored her. While she was in prison her hands and feet were stiff with cold and she was allowed two extra blankets. After five days 'Jane Warton' was allowed out into the exercise yard for fresh air but had to return to her cell because of the pain in her side which caused her to double up. On 21 January she complained to the governor that the senior doctor had never tested her heart or felt her pulse before feeding her, and that he had slapped her on the cheek. A prison inspector from London also visited and noted her complaints.[22]

On the morning of 23 January the governor told Constance that she was being released, and that her sister, Lady Emily Lutyens, was waiting to take her home. Constance felt 'stunned with the quite unexpected joy, it was too good to be true'. Making sure that her fine had not been paid by her family, and that she was being set free on medical grounds because of her weight loss – two pounds for every day she was in prison – she asked for news of her fellow suffragette prisoners but was given no information.[23] Emily Lutyens had arrived in the city that morning and took Constance to the Station Hotel in Liverpool. Before her hunger strike Constance Lytton was underweight anyway and, having lost nearly fourteen pounds, she found it painful to sit down. Her voice 'shook' and she could not speak properly. On the journey to her sister's house in Bloomsbury Square, Constance learned how her family had discovered she was in prison. A member of the Press Association had telephoned the Lytton family after hearing a rumour that the Home Office believed 'there is a prisoner at Walton Gaol whom they have for some days suspected of being other than her declaration'.[24] When the prison authorities learned how high-born she was, they released her early but in Liverpool they had 'not been able to find out who her people were'.[25]

Constance spent the first few days of freedom in bed writing an account of her experiences for *The Times* on 26 January and the 28 January issue of *Votes for Women*, and was visited by Mrs Pethick-Lawrence, Mrs Pankhurst and Christabel Pankhurst. Emily Lutyens wrote to their sister 'Bets' that her body looked 'just like the pictures of famine people in India'.[26] Constance's mother expressed her sense of disgrace at what Constance had done, the hurt she had caused her by this dangerous protest. She replied: 'Your letter is most precious to me. It is so truthful and open ... I know how I make you suffer, what a blight I have put on your happiness, and that I can never bring within your reach an explanation of what I do, and why I do it.'[27] Constance promised her mother that she would do no more campaigning for the next six weeks (she was in no fit state to do so) and offered to forward any letters she received from her comrades, 'so that you may know not everyone sees your Con in the light of a liar and hooligan'.[28]

On 23 January Mrs Pethick-Lawrence wrote to the Earl of Lytton expressing 'a deep and passionate admiration' for his sister, and expressing the WSPU's 'greatest sympathy' for her family: 'we too feel intensely this personal grief but with it are other strong emotions of unutterable reverence for this heroic woman and true saint'. Although Christabel Pankhurst had known of Constance's plan, Mrs Pethick-Lawrence said, 'your sister was not led to take this action by any influence of ours. Such an idea never entered our imagination ...

it was entirely her own thought and idea and carried out secretly and evidently with great effort.' She asked Lord Lytton to convey to his mother that on the morning of her trial she was apparently 'serene and happy and well ... she felt satisfied that all that had happened just as she planned'.[29]

Eighteen days after her release, Anders Ryman, a Swedish doctor, attended Constance. He reported that, although her heart had returned to its normal size, her condition was 'too critical for any but the very mildest form of treatment', and insisted she stayed in bed and kept 'absolutely quiet' and forbade her from having any visitors or letters. Dr Ryman was 'alarmed at the great fluctuations between the heart beat when still and when I moved and spoke', and advised her that if she needed to get upstairs she should climb them backwards.[30]

Despite the cessation of militancy to allow the Conciliation Bill to be debated in a peaceful atmosphere, the suffragettes pursued their 'Keep the Liberals Out' policy during the general election campaign. This strategy meant they were still at risk of being roughed up by Liberal stewards. While electioneering on polling day in Southport on 24 January, Mary Gawthorpe, Mabel Capper and Dora Marsden were attacked and had their tricolour flag broken. Dr Arthur Limont, a Liberal town councillor, took their flag from the car, broke the pole and threw it into the crowd. As soon as the women got out of the car Mary and Mabel were set on by three men and Mabel was 'lifted bodily over the head of Miss Gawthorpe and put back into the car head-first'. The women started legal proceedings against Dr Limont and three other men, but in spite of plenty of evidence the magistrates dismissed the case.[31]

The Liberals lost eighteen of the forty constituency seats targeted by the suffragettes. The WSPU leadership boasted that 'the exposure of the repressive measures adopted by the Government against women' decided the result in another thirty to forty constituencies where the Liberals were returned with reduced majorities.[32] When the final results were announced the Liberal landslide of 1906 had fallen away: the Liberals lost their majority of 84, losing more than a hundred seats, while the Conservatives had gained about a hundred seats. The Liberal government needed support from the Irish Nationalists and the Labour Party. In the new parliament the Liberals had 274 seats, the Conservatives 272, the Labour Party increased their MPs from 29 to 40 and the Irish Nationalists had 82 seats. The consensus was that another general election would be needed before the end of the year.[33]

Lord Lytton took up his sister's cause and wrote to the home secretary about her treatment in Walton Gaol, and objected to the suggestion in the press that she had lied to the prison authorities. 'My sister has stated in public [at a WSPU meeting at the Queen's Hall on 31 January] how she was treated in Liverpool prison and her statement has greatly shocked all who have read it. You have publicly announced that there is not a word of truth in her statement and that the acts that have aroused so much indignation never took place.'[34] Lord Lytton pointed out that Constance was too ill to defend herself, which was why he was undertaking the task of 'vindicating her sanity and her veracity'. Constance Lytton's charges were: she had been force-fed without any medical examination; she was fed seven times even though her 'heart was being injured by the process'; the way she was fed would not have been 'tolerated in any well-regulated infirmary'; and that the doctor had slapped her face in an 'insulting manner'.[35] Lord Lytton politely dismantled Gladstone's response, underlining the central point: 'It was not to be supposed that the doctor would really admit to the truth of the complaints, which, if proved, would lead to his own dismissal, nor was it likely that he would be given away by the wardresses in his own prison.' Lord Lytton asked 'in no cantankerous spirit but merely in the interest of justice' for Gladstone to appoint 'a special commissioner' who could hear 'all the evidence of the person making the charges' and then examine 'separately and minutely the other witnesses, and finally report to the Home Office'.[36]

The next day Herbert Gladstone dashed off a handwritten note 'regretting the circumstances which have brought us into this sharp collision. It has most certainly not been of my making.' Gladstone took exception to the inference that he had authorised Constance Lytton's early release because of her family connections, insisting that her health had been his prime concern, and was affronted that 'Lady Constance and her friends made it a public charge against me that I had discharged her from prison for no other reason than she was "a peer's sister"'.[37] Gladstone wrote that he 'had no suspicion of her identity', and ended by saying that he 'would not pursue this matter further'.[38] On 15 February Herbert Gladstone left the Home Office to become governor-general of South Africa, and Winston Churchill was appointed home secretary.[39]

The new parliament met on 15 February. When the King's Speech was read six days later there was no mention of a women's suffrage bill, nor did any of the suffrage campaigners' allies win a place in the ballot for a private members' bill. All hopes had been pinned on the bill that would be drafted by the Conciliation Committee, formed in the middle of January by Henry Brailsford as its secretary, and chaired by Constance Lytton's brother, the Earl of Lytton. On 18 January Brailsford had written to the moderate Mrs Fawcett, apprehensive about how the Pankhursts would react to the idea of a compromise bill, and proposed forming a 'Conciliation Committee for Woman's Suffrage' of men and women to include representatives of all women's suffrage societies, but not their 'more prominent leaders', to secure a bill which would get through Parliament. However, the Conciliation Committee was all-male: of the 54 MPs, 25 were Liberals, 17 were Conservatives, 6 were Irish Nationalists and 6 Labour members completed the tally.[40]

Henry Brailsford wanted the Committee's style to be discreet, not propagandist and not tread on the toes of the suffragists, the suffragettes or the Men's League for Women's Suffrage. 'It should persuade politicians that a solution is possible on non-party lines.' The need to grant at least some women the vote was overdue and 'above all to end the degradation involved in the repression which the militant campaign has been met with'.[41] Brailsford wrote: 'it is intolerable that this [militancy and force-feeding] should be allowed to recommence.' The prime minister's plan of proceeding by amendment to a Reform Bill 'would end in Manhood Suffrage, and so postpone the emancipation of women for a decade or a generation'. Even though some MPs had mentioned women's suffrage in their general election speeches, progress was likely to be problematic as neither the Liberal nor the Conservative parties had made women's suffrage central to their political landscape. The Conciliation Committee drafted a bill and collected signatures from 'prominent men in all walks of life', and lobbied MPs who were pro-women's suffrage 'to obtain facilities for the Bill' if and when it passed its second reading.[42]

Although Mrs Pankhurst was suspicious of Asquith's true intentions, at a WSPU meeting at the Queen's Hall, London, on 31 January she announced that the Union was calling a truce and suspending its five-year militant campaign to help build support for the bill alongside the peaceful efforts of the National Union of Women's Suffrage Societies, and the Women's Freedom League. Christabel Pankhurst had shaped the WSPU's response to the Conciliation Committee. Writing her memoir *Unshackled* forty years later she reflected, 'My own strongest but unspoken reason for welcoming the Conciliation movement was that it might avert the need for stronger militancy and would at least postpone the use thereof.'[43] She conceded that 'mild militancy was more or less played out'. As noisy, creative and 'shocking' as the WSPU had been the government had ignored them and the union had been warned by 'neutral onlookers' that 'their milder acts would by their monotony grow futile, because they would cease to impress anybody' and would no longer annoy the government. For Christabel, the pause in militancy was opportune: 'it would give time for familiarity to fade, so that the methods could be used again with freshness and effect.' She was the impresario of their protests and her theory was that 'Much depended on militancy ... upon timing and placing, upon the dramatic arrangement and sequence of acts and events.' If the Conciliation Bill failed because of government interference the WSPU's ceasefire would at least have given them the time to devise a protest 'which could in effect be different from the same kind of protest made before'. Christabel Pankhurst revealed that members were incensed by the violence to which they were subjected while trying to see the prime minister and that their thoughts were turning to attacking property rather than being 'thrown about and hurt'.[44]

On 15 March, seeming to embrace the concept of conciliation, one of Winston Churchill's first acts as home secretary was to introduce a new prison regulation, Rule 243a. 'In the case of any offender of the second or third division whose previous character is good, and who has been convicted of, or committed to prison for an offence not involving dishonesty, cruelty, indecency, or serious violence, the Prison Commissioners may allow such ameliorations of the conditions prescribed in the foregoing rules as the Secretary of State may approve in respect of the wearing of prison clothing, bathing, haircutting, cleaning of cells, employment, exercise, books, and otherwise.' Under this new regulation conditions for suffragette prisoners would improve considerably and Christabel Pankhurst conceded that they were a 'step in the right direction' and a sign that Churchill was 'not bound down by the wooden ideas of his predecessor'.[45]

However, the new home secretary refused to concede any ground to Lord Lytton about his sister. Churchill's attitude to Constance Lytton's protest had hardened by the middle of March and he instructed the first assistant secretary, Ernley Blackwell, to write to Lord Lytton to draw a line under the matter. Churchill's position was that Constance Lytton had gone to prison 'with the express purpose of entrapping the Medical Officers into action which might be interpreted as a dereliction of their duty'. In order to do so she had used a false name and 'concealed from them the medical history of her case'. Also, her refusal to be examined on arrival and withholding information about her condition 'deprived them of assistance to which they were entitled, and which would have enabled them to arrive at a correct diagnosis'. Ernley Blackwell said that his master would not be authorising 'any further inquiry' into her case as it would 'justly be regarded as a concession to Lady Constance Lytton's social position which Mr Churchill is confident you would be the first to deprecate'.[46]

While militant acts like pestering and stalking and throwing tiles from roofs were suspended, Katherine Douglas Smith created a delightful stunt to advertise a WSPU fundraising meeting at the Royal Albert Hall on 18 March. She hired a fire engine, and, with six suffragettes dressed in firemen's uniforms in shining helmets and brass-buttoned coats, she took the reins. The fire engine was festooned in purple, white and green: as the horses galloped along Oxford Street, a suffragette hammered on a gong and fooled the police into thinking they were on their way to a fire. The traffic was stopped to let the suffragette 'firemen' through. It was a larky protest but the *Daily Express* sourly condemned the 'shameless exhibition' by its 'hysterical crew'.[47] At the Albert Hall meeting Constance Lytton, Edith Rigby, Beth Hesmondhalgh, Elsie Howey, Selina Martin and Theresa Garnett were presented with 'For Valour' medals. Those women who had already been awarded medals were presented with silver bars engraved with the dates of their latest force-feeding to be added to their medal ribbons.[48]

In early 1910 Adela Pankhurst replaced Helen Archdale as the WSPU's organiser in Sheffield when Helen became unwell. Adela lived with Helen and was also a part-time governess to her children.

Helen had not fully recovered from her ordeal in Dundee Gaol in 1909. The weeks she spent in Dundee before her arrest shook her from her middle-class moorings. One night, standing next to a suffragette speaker addressing a crowd, Helen was 'startled by the sound of people spitting at her'. Another time Helen was hit in the face by a handful of earth and grass, and when she and a comrade addressed a street-corner meeting they were pelted with 'something soft, wet and warm … [that] smelt dreadful … I grabbed it (quite the bravest deed of my life) and flung it back into the crowd'. Helen experienced an epiphany when she met Emmeline Pankhurst at Clement's Inn in 1908: 'I saw a woman standing in the window with her back to us. After some talk she turned round … it was the figure that in the photograph [of Mrs Pankhurst being arrested] had stirred my spark to a blaze. Hardly could I do the ordinary courtesies of handshaking and a few words. It was too soon to be talking to an inspiration.'[49]

On Easter Monday, 28 March, the WSPU's colours flashed round Brooklands race-track. The Reverend Percy Bischoff, a Clapham curate and a suffragette sympathiser, entered his Triumph motorcycle as 'The Suffragette', tied purple, white and green streamers to the handlebars and wore a tricolour sash over his right shoulder. He got off to a poor start but at the end of the race he put a brave face on it and insisted 'a surprisingly large number of spectators expressed sympathy with the suffrage movement'. He may have been drawn to women's suffrage by his fiancée Beatrice Langston, the first woman to compete in a race at Brooklands. After the First World War Percy gave up the church to become a motorcycle salesman, saying he would make the church his hobby instead.[50]

Although the truce was still in place it was flouted by Emily Davison, the loosest cannon in WSPU's arsenal of protest. She decided to confront the prime minister in Parliament and ask him why he would not give the vote to women tax-payers, and why, before he attempted to reform the Lords, he did not 'set his own house in order'. On Saturday 2 April she entered the building, slipped past two policemen and hid in a hot-air shaft in which were ladders which she climbed 'with difficulty, as the place was narrow and reached the first platform' twenty feet above the ground. Emily sat on two planks placed across the rafters in the 'overpowering heat'.[51] She had two bananas and some chocolate but was thirsty and tired and afraid to fall asleep in case she fell into the void below. When Emily felt it was safe to move she climbed down the ladder to get water from the fountain in the vestibule. In so doing she left a trail of water which the night watchman followed and, twenty-eight hours after she had first entered the House of Commons, she was discovered in her hiding place. The authorities decided to let her go: had they pressed charges Emily could not have been prosecuted in a police court, but would have been summoned to the House of Commons, which would have given the WSPU valuable publicity.[52]

The Conciliation Bill was published as a private members' bill in April and was to be presented to the House of Commons by David Shackleton, the Labour MP for Clitheroe, Lancashire, on 14 June.[53]

On 26 April Christabel Pankhurst expressed her 'urgent wish' to Arthur Balfour that he and the Conservative MPs would vote for the bill at the second reading due on 11 and 12 July, and gave him the WSPU's analysis. She was 'certain' of a majority for the bill, but suspected that the government would not offer facilities for the Conciliation Bill until 1913, which, if true, Christabel was sure meant that 'they are scheming to prevent us getting the vote in this Parliament in spite of their pledge to the contrary. We must get the Bill through this session ... There is nothing we would not do to get this through.' Christabel asked Balfour to speak in favour of the principle of the bill, but to say that the prime minister's pledge to grant facilities for the bill ought to be fulfilled in 1910. Christabel felt sure that an intervention by the previous prime minister would mean that the government could not refuse. 'Even if they did, they would put themselves completely in the wrong and our case would be strengthened enormously.' Christabel tried flattery but, despite her entreaties, Balfour did not do as she asked.[54]

On 6 May, King Edward VII died suddenly of pneumonia and heart failure, with the result that the procession organised by the Women's Social and Political Union and the Women's Freedom League to win public support for the second reading of the Conciliation Bill had to be postponed. The new date for the procession was 18 June, four days after the Conciliation Bill was to be introduced by David Shackleton to the House of Commons. On 29 May Emmeline Pethick-Lawrence wrote an optimistic note to Constance Lytton: 'Suddenly the centre has shifted, and upon you and your brother and upon Mr Brailsford, so much rests. I am very pleased about the Bill.' But if 'the scheme miscarries', she described what would be needed: 'the great artificer has need of the furnace again and the smelting trough and the anvil, and we shall be ready with glad hearts.'[55] On the same day Edith How-Martyn of the Women's Freedom League paid an unexpected call on Henry Brailsford at his home in Hampstead. Brailsford said the chancellor's tactics were to 'keep silly women quiet', and urged How-Martyn: 'Please be stiff and critical, but not yet absolutely hostile.' He promised to raise 'the whole question' in a debate in the House in a matter of days, and hoped 'to extract a more satisfactory statement'.[56]

Christabel Pankhurst's editorial in *Votes for Women* on 3 June was cautiously optimistic – 'the prospects of the new suffrage bill are very bright' – but she understood the pivotal role of the prime minister: 'In view of the fact that the Bill is receiving this great and growing measure of support … it becomes more and more obvious that its fate depends, not upon the support of the country and of Parliament – for that support is already assured – but upon the Government's answer to the request that time shall be provided for the discussion of the measure.'[57] She explained that women householders who occupied a house or any part of a house, provided they had full control of that part, would be able to vote – and there was no minimum rental value necessary to secure this vote. Women who occupied business premises or farms would be granted the vote if their rent was at least £10 a year. However, married women whose husbands had the vote were not eligible to vote as occupiers of their residence, thus advantaging unmarried women and widows to the detriment of wives.[58]

On 4 June, Lord Lytton, Chairman of the Conciliation Committee, wrote a letter marked 'private' to Herbert Asquith, 'making an earnest appeal' for the time for the Conciliation Bill to become law in the current session. Lytton reminded Asquith that 'for many years past successive parliaments had passed very large majorities' at the second reading of bills in support of women's suffrage but they had failed to become law. He further reminded him that there had been no acts of violence in the past five months, which had created 'an exceptionally favourable' atmosphere, and that 'an extraordinary spirit of unanimity and hopefulness had been aroused. For the moment all sections of suffragist opinion are willing to unite in its support.' Lord Lytton warned that the current circumstances were 'altogether unique' and that if the momentum was 'allowed to stop they will never recur again'.[59] Lytton appealed to Asquith's integrity: 'I know that you are not in favour of the principle of women's suffrage but I do not imagine that your decision … will be influenced by that consideration.'[60] Asquith responded five days later, instructing Vaughan Nash, his principal parliamentary secretary, to meet Lord Lytton to clarify a few points of detail.[61]

Despite her family's misgivings, in June Constance Lytton insisted she was strong enough to work for the WSPU once again. She was appointed as an organiser on a salary of £2 a week and expenses, back-dated to January, allowing Constance the financial independence to rent a flat in a working-class district near the Euston Road.[62] She relished her tasks of 'working up the respectables' and organising the musicians' contingent of the procession coordinated by the WSPU on 18 June: 'I have had a week of unmitigated rush, assaulting the portals of the great in shabby clothes, asking those who say they are keen, to do some tiny little nominal service, whereupon their keenness melts into thin air.' Constance was turning her back on her own tribe: 'Oh, how I *hate* the respectable world! They are all like a flock of sheep – never take a stand on their own version of what is right, but must all wait to see how someone else moves first.'[63] Constance was proud of the role her brother was playing: 'what rapture I felt when he said in the Albert Hall that "the little he had been able to do to help this Bill had given him more satisfaction than anything he had done in public life".' The three weeks' work before the procession wore Constance out: 'every morning when I woke my body and brain were both on strike and absolutely refused to go on', but somehow she managed.[64]

On 11 June Winston Churchill sent a handwritten letter marked 'private' to Lord Lytton alerting him to the difficulties that lay ahead for the Conciliation Bill. He had sounded out his Cabinet colleagues and warned that he had 'apprehended quite unfavourable feelings about it … I cannot think it possible that this question can be settled in the present Parliament', and said it was likely that the bill would be open to 'many objections on the score of being partial and undemocratic', before signing his letter 'always your friend Winston'.[65]

Two days before the bill was introduced on 14 June, Lord Lytton wrote a terse letter to Asquith's principal private secretary, Vaughan Nash, complaining at Nash's failure to respond. Lytton advised Nash that the women's suffrage campaigners would not be fobbed off with empty promises about facilities for the bill in 1911. Even the moderate suffragists were likely to react badly: 'Mrs Fawcett writes to me in despair and says she will no longer be able to control the members of her society. The utmost consternation and the bitterest disappointment prevails, and matters have now passed beyond my control.' Lytton reminded Nash how hard the Conciliation Committee had worked to keep the truce in place by persuading the women's suffrage activists that the bill was viable in the present session. Lord Lytton told Nash that there was no point in any further communication between himself and the prime minister 'as nothing short of facilities for the passage of the Bill now or in the autumn is worth considering'.[66]

The twenty-four hours leading up to the introduction of the Conciliation Bill in the House of Commons by David Shackleton were tense and bitter. Lytton warned the home secretary that 'all hope of prolonging the truce or settling the question on non-party lines is now at end', and that he had 'done all he could and must now accept the failure with the best grace I can'. Fear of an imminent return to suffragette militancy suffused every word he wrote to Churchill – 'I dread the future more than I can say' – and he firmly placed the blame for 'the storm of indignation which will be aroused with those who steadily refuse to consider the justice of a cause apart from its party interests' on Churchill and his allies in the Cabinet who were 'trifling with a body of opinion, the force of which they were seriously underestimating'.[67] Constance wrote to him the day before the introduction of the bill, 'Beloved Vic … it is unspeakably exciting to think of tomorrow', adding that the New Zealand women had sent 'a splendid protest to Asquith against the imprisonment and treatment of women'.[68]

Victor Lytton did not begrudge the trouble his chairmanship of the Conciliation Committee had heaped on him, but he found dealing with his fragile sister rather harder. On 14 June in the hours before the introduction of the bill he told her of his frustration about the gap between them in their 'suffrage talks' and described their conversations as a 'cross-examination from a hostile counsel'.

He laid bare his feelings about their relationship: 'When I am talking to you on this subject I never feel that you are hearing me and I expect that you feel the same with me', and suggested they pursue their own routes towards women getting the vote. To avoid further conflict Lytton suggested that if she wanted to ask him a question it might be better if she sent him a postcard. He did not want Constance to 'fret about my non-sympathy over some things as time will efface all disagreements. We are fighting in different parts of the field but it is the same battle.'[69]

The Conciliation Bill was not as broad in scope as the WSPU had wanted. It had been narrowly framed to secure Conservative support: under its terms a million women would have been enfranchised – rather than all women over the age of twenty-one which was the age at which men could vote. Politically pragmatic, Mrs Pankhurst had reluctantly accepted the terms and was 'prepared to share in this united and peaceful action'. 'The new Bill does not give us all we want, but we are for it, others are also for it.'[70] Sylvia Pankhurst pointed out that, while one million women might vote, that meant only one woman in thirteen would get the vote. 'While marriage was not to be actually a disqualification it was expressly stated that husbands and wives could not vote from the same property, although two men might qualify as joint householders or occupiers under the existing male suffrage.'[71] Few working-class women would be enfranchised and spinsters and elderly widows would be the main beneficiaries of the new bill, which pleased the Conservatives on the Conciliation Committee and in the wider party – but not Liberals like Lloyd George and Winston Churchill – and Labour counterparts, who were instinctively against women having the vote, and when faced with the prospect wanted married women to be included, fearful that spinsters and elderly widows were probable Conservative voters. Sylvia Pankhurst told her mother she opposed the bill because 'it was too narrow for justice', and that its narrowness 'would not avert, but rather contribute to its failure'. It gave those who paid lip service to supporting women's suffrage a specious excuse to oppose it.[72]

On 14 June the Conciliation Bill won a great deal of support in the House of Commons and hopes were high for its second reading. Four days later, on 18 June, the WSPU's six-mile-long 'Prison to Citizenship' procession of 10,000 suffragists walking from the Embankment to the Albert Hall brought London to a standstill. Its aim was to 'fill with enthusiastic determination those MPs who are favourable to Woman Suffrage, and show those who are hostile the futility of further opposition'.[73] Thirty different contingents from all women's suffrage organisations took part, in their own colours and carrying their own banners. The entire cross-section of WSPU members and sympathisers took part: 'Women of money and leisure walking side by side with the manual workers, women great in the intellectual world, scientists, doctors, teachers, university graduates, painters, musicians, actresses, writers. Women who take part in the busy toil of the city, women in the simple, sweet uniform of nurses ... and women who believe in strictly constitutional action.'[74]

In an article in *Votes for Women* called 'Hints For The Procession', participants were recommended to 'wear white if possible; wear the colours ... and ... march eyes front like a soldier in the ranks'. The women were told not to wear 'gowns that have to be held up'; not to wear enormous hats; to wave white handkerchiefs, and not to think of themselves but of the Union.[75]

The Actresses' Franchise League wore their colours of pink, white and green; the Women Writers' Suffrage League walked behind their gold and black velvet banner. Led by Mrs Hanna Sheehy-Skeffington, the Irish Women's Franchise League were there. The women civil servants, stenographers and typists walked behind a 'beautiful silk banner' demanding 'Fair Play, Fair Pay! For all who Serve the State', and a 'Women Clerks Demand The Vote' banner with an image of a winged pen was carried by the contingent organised by Charlie Marsh. The *British Journal of Nursing* appealed to 'every nurse in sympathy with the women's movement' to contact Nurses Pine and Townend, who were the honorary secretaries of the nursing contingent, to wear their indoor uniform and walk behind their own banner. There were Foreign and Colonial contingents: New Zealand women were led by Lady Stout, Mrs Saul Solomon headed the South African group and representatives from Canada, America and Norway, Sweden and Denmark followed.[76]

Six hundred and seventeen women who had been to prison were represented, all of whom, including proxies who stood in for them, carried broad arrows on sticks covered with silver paper. The procession was led by 'General' Flora Drummond in full regalia riding a large horse, as were her chief marshal, Jessie Kenney, and marshals Vera 'Jack' Holme and Evelina Haverfield. In 'bright heliotrope purple, snowy white and emerald green livery' Mary Leigh led her Drum and Fife Band.[77] A thousand graduates wore their academic robes, and forty brass bands played stirring tunes. A new banner in purple, white and green linen made its debut; bearing the embroidered autographs of eighty women who had gone on hunger strike, it was a roll call of those who had 'faced death without flinching'.[78]

Kitty Marion, who was clinging to a theatrical career that was shrinking as a result of her enthusiastic embracing of her role as a suffragette, marched in the procession with other members of the chorus. It was tricky trying to dovetail the career of a music-hall artiste with the thrilling demands of being a suffragette, and the 'prominent part' she was taking in her 'strenuous propaganda work' for the WSPU. So far that year her engagements had consisted of performing as a comedienne at the King's Theatre in Southsea, and singing a couple of songs at picture palaces – the new cinemas – in London, Reading, Hastings, Blackburn and Wellingborough, where her strong singing voice was mentioned in reviews.[79]

All the women's suffrage campaigners were hopeful that Herbert Asquith would give enough time in the current parliamentary session for the Conciliation Bill's second reading. Lady Carlisle, leader of the Women's Liberal Federation, and Mrs Fawcett of the NUWSS, took a deputation of their members to see Asquith on 21 June to ask him for an early date for the bill's second reading, but he refused to give his own views, saying that some of his cabinet ministers supported the bill while others were very much opposed to it, and that he would leave it to the Cabinet to make a decision as to whether they would allow further time for the second reading of the bill. The prime minister had also agreed to see a deputation of anti-suffragists on the same day: the Women's Anti-Suffrage League and the Men's League for Opposing Woman Suffrage.[80]

When Lady Jersey, President of the Women's Anti-Suffrage League, Mrs Humphrey Ward, Mrs Toynbee, widow of the social reformer Arnold Toynbee, and the Duchess of Montrose put their case against the bill, Lady Jersey persisted that the evidence her organisation had gathered in the past two years showed that women did not really want the vote, and that 'time could better be spent on other social concerns … There is a large field for women in social improvements, in the care of the schools, and in municipal affairs.' Lord Haversham of the Men's League for Opposing Woman Suffrage was most exercised by the fact that, if women were given the vote, they could not be denied the right to be elected as MPs. If this dangerous step was allowed to be taken, female politicians and female voters would be allowed to decide on questions relating to the army, the navy and the police, all services that they could not take part in. John St Loe Strachey, proprietor of *The Spectator*, Professor Albert Dicey, a professor of law and fellow of All Souls, Oxford, John Massie, Liberal MP for the Cricklade division in Wiltshire, and the quintessential British imperialist Sir Alfred Comyn Lyall, were also there to represent the law, the Empire and the press. Asquith told Lady Jersey and her fellow antis they were preaching to the converted.[81]

On 23 June it was announced that the second reading of the Conciliation Bill would take place on 11 and 12 July, but that there would be no possibility of any facilities for it to become law during the current session. The WSPU's truce was shattered by Emily Davison. Furious at Asquith, she broke two windows in the Crown Office at the Houses of Parliament with two lumps of chalk around which messages to the prime minister were tied with string. The notes demanded that Asquith 'give full facilities for the new bill for woman's suffrage', and warned him that 'indignant womanhood will [not] accept this insult'. She urged the prime minister, 'be wise and true for we will not be trifled with'.[82] Emily then gave herself up to the nearest constable who took her to Canon Row police station. To her fury an unnamed woman paid her fine of £5, plus seven shillings and sixpence for the cost of the broken glass. She had wanted to go to prison and had 'stamped her foot in fury in the Bow Street court and refused to budge, but was removed while being told by the magistrate, "You are not wanted here and must go." '[83] When the *Daily Mirror* interviewed Christabel Pankhurst about this first fracture in the truce she slapped down the uppity Miss Davison, making it clear that she was on her own: 'It is premature to again resort to militant action until all peaceful measures are exhausted, and if Miss Davison had consulted us she would have not taken the course she did.'[84]

The four months of delicate negotiations and government obfuscation had taken their toll on a weary Lord Lytton. On 26 June he wrote to his sister. 'Darling Con, the Government have played a dirty trick ... disappointing everyone's hopes in the most objectionable manner possible ... I feel very hard and bitter and my only consolation is that Asquith has made himself thoroughly ridiculous.' He decided he would withdraw from the fray for a while and 'leave the campaign in other hands'. He took the whole business personally but at least now he knew how the women's suffrage campaigners of all kinds felt after forty years of political chicanery. 'The disappointment is cruel and the method of its infliction is exasperating.'[85]

The Conciliation Bill passed its second reading in the House of Commons on 11 and 12 July by 299 votes to 189, but Members of Parliament voted against referring the bill to a Grand Committee of the whole House by 320 votes to 175, which wiped out any chance of the bill becoming law in 1910. When the WSPU published their analysis of the results of the two votes, revealing the names of those MPs who were for the bill, the MPs who were for the bill but against it being sent to the Grand Committee, and those who had voted against the bill and consequently against it going to the Grand Committee, it became obvious who were their friends and who were their foes. The latter included the usual suspects, the prime minister and his cabal of anti-women's suffrage ministers in the Cabinet: Winston Churchill, David Lloyd George, Lewis 'Loulou' Harcourt, Herbert Samuel and Reginald McKenna.[86]

Having written to Arthur Balfour on 10 July, 'We are told that you will take part in the debate ... and we are overjoyed at the news, your support will immensely increase the chances of the Bill', Christabel Pankhurst would have been dismayed to see that Balfour had voted for the bill but against sending it to the Grand Committee. She warned him that if the prime minister did not reconsider his decision, the WSPU 'shall be obliged if only for self-respect's sake to express our indignation and dissatisfaction by means of militant action. To show patience we would consider to condone the Government's destruction of the Bill.'[87] Emily Davison would have been furious to see that her former employer Sir Francis Layland-Barratt had voted for the bill but against sending it to the Grand Committee.[88]

Lloyd George and Winston Churchill argued that the way the bill was framed was undemocratic. They were convinced that its terms would give more votes to the Conservatives. The bill was being kicked into the long grass. The wives of the prime minister and the home secretary, Margot Asquith, an adamant anti, and Clementine Churchill, a believer in votes for women, were in the House to hear the debate and the results.[89]

The WSPU waged a propaganda war against the government, distributing handbills from all branches and devoting many column inches in *Votes for Women* to criticising the government's refusal to grant facilities. Their position was that the Conciliation Bill ought to be made law because it was democratic, moderate, the women of the country wanted it, every organised women's society supported it, that the men (as evidenced by the number of MPs who voted for it) of the country wanted it and the House of Commons had voted for it by an 'overwhelming majority'. They argued that since men who paid rates and taxes, whether they were owners, occupiers or lodgers, could vote, then women who paid rates and taxes under the same criteria should be given the vote, too. They pointed out that there was a problem with married women: they would be given the vote if they fulfilled those criteria but not if their husband already had the vote. A wife would be given the vote if she was running a business on her own account. By their calculations the Conciliation Bill would add one and a half million new women voters to the seven and a half million enfranchised men in the population.[90]

On 16 July the Men's League for Opposing Woman Suffrage held a meeting in Trafalgar Square, advertised on handbills as 'Votes for Women, NEVER!'. The leaflet warned the British public they were in 'urgent danger'.[91] Before the rally the suffragettes had carried out a mass leafleting of Trafalgar Square and its hinterland, handing out WSPU badges to anyone who was interested in hearing their side of the argument.

The Times estimated that up to 2,000 men and women gathered in Trafalgar Square. Three of the five platforms were set up on the Square's plinths and decorated in the antis' colours of pink, white and black. Members of Parliament opposing women's suffrage took up their positions, and read encouraging messages from some of the big-hitters, such as Lords Cromer and Curzon and Mrs Humphry Ward. The meeting passed the resolution protesting 'against woman suffrage in any shape or form and calls upon the Government to give no further facilities for any Bill enfranchising women without previous reference to the judgment of the electorate'.[92]

Annie Kenney remembered Mrs Pankhurst's calming influence on the movement. Faced with the Liberal government's high-handed treatment of the Conciliation Bill, many militants champed at the bit to resume militancy with a redoubled vigour. 'The truce would never have been kept by the more fiery militants had it not been for extra ordinary powers of gentle persuasion. The most rebellious spirits grew calm in her presence, the most obstinate grew amenable. They adored her.' Emmeline Pankhurst's 'calm, quiet, cultured manner appealed to us all, her gentle voice, which could become so passionate in speech, her understanding of human frailty'.[93] Keen to demonstrate the demand for the vote all over again, Mrs Pethick-Lawrence announced that another procession through London would take place on 23 July, the anniversary of the date on which men campaigning for the vote in 1866 had torn down the railings in Hyde Park in protest at the government's tardy response to the demand for male suffrage.[94]

Lord Lytton addressed a WSPU meeting at the Queen's Hall on 18 July about the recent events, and gave his personal account of the quarrel with the home secretary, much of which had been laid bare in *The Times*. Lytton said Winston Churchill had given him and Henry Brailsford 'encouragement that he wished well to our cause, and that as far as he could, he intended to help us'. But the speech in the House of Commons which Churchill delivered had been against the bill and 'was not the speech even of a friendly critic, it was the speech of a man engaged in destructive work for the mere love of destruction'. He had delivered it 'without one word of regret … and it was that which raised in me such a feeling of indignation and drove me to protest against his conduct'.[95]

Churchill still resented the way he had been treated by the WSPU since Christabel Pankhurst and Annie Kenney's pioneering protest in 1905. His feelings were exposed in a Home Office summary of the feud between himself and Lord Lytton compiled by Churchill's private secretary, Edward Marsh. Headed 'Not For Publication', the document defends the home secretary's position in the face of Lord Lytton's 'scoldings and reproaches'. Marsh described the history of Churchill's relationship with the suffragettes: 'For the last five years these people [the WSPU] have attempted in the course of their agitation to break up every meeting he has addressed in any part of the country. They have opposed him with the whole strength of their organisation at four successive elections.' Mr Churchill had been returned to Parliament three times out of four, 'in spite of the utmost opposition which they could offer ... and who have treated him with the vilest discourtesy and unfairness. They have attacked him repeatedly in the most insulting terms ... and assaulted him physically.'[96]

On 23 July 10,000 women set out in two processions. The one starting at Westminster was led by the colour-bearer Charlie Marsh and followed by Christabel Pankhurst and Emmeline Pethick-Lawrence on foot, while the procession from Holland Park in the west was led by Daisy Dugdale carrying the tricolour followed by Flora Drummond, Evelina Haverfield and Vera Holme, all on horseback. Both processions converged on Hyde Park. Three hundred women volunteered to sell *Votes for Women* along the route and twenty booths sold colours and button badges.[97]

In Hyde Park there were forty platforms, 150 speakers and brass bands. Speeches were made by Mabel Tuke, Mrs Pankhurst and her daughters Christabel and Sylvia, Mary Clarke, Annie Kenney, Flora Drummond, Joan Dugdale, Ada Flatman, Rachel Barrett, Jane Brailsford, Mary Leigh, Constance Lytton, Emily Davison, Victor Duval, Henry Nevinson and Lady Stout from New Zealand. At half past six the WSPU resolution was passed that 'this meeting rejoices that the Woman Suffrage Bill has passed its second reading by 110 votes ... and further calls upon the Government to bow to the will of the people as expressed by their elected representatives in the House of Commons and to provide facilities necessary to enable the Bill to pass into law during the present session of Parliament.'[98]

The photographer Mrs Christina Broom and her daughter Winnie managed to capture splendid close-ups of the day. Mrs Pethick-Lawrence had arrived in Hyde Park at the head of a contingent of women and walking alongside her was Sylvia Pankhurst, carrying an outsize cardboard version of the 'Holloway badge', a portcullis representing Parliament with five arrow-shaped prongs to denote imprisonment, which Sylvia had designed to be presented to all suffragettes who had been to prison. Standing slightly behind Sylvia was Emily Davison in her academic robes and mortar-board, looking serious.

Press reports stressed the spectacle on show that day. London's own newspaper, the *Standard*, was impressed: 'Saturday's demonstration

was something more than a mere parade of women. From early morning crowds of women arrived from all parts of the kingdom, and were
at once conspicuous by their dresses and hats, which combined the
colours of the suffragist movement, green, purple and white ... the
scene was a remarkable one. Probably no less than a quarter of a million people were assembled.' The *Manchester Guardian* noted the
dominance of the Union's colours, and the large numbers who had
gathered in the Park: 'Little pennants of the brightest colours – there
was more purple, white and green than any others – fluttered in the
wind ... You heard the rustle of voices and saw the swaying figures
of the speakers, and got more than a vague impression of the mighty
numbers.'[99]

The prime minister wrote to Lord Lytton on 23 July confirming
that the Conciliation Bill would not be granted any more time during
the current session. At the end of July Parliament was prorogued until
18 November, and the WSPU kept the truce in place, deciding to keep
their powder dry until they heard what the government's intentions
were for the autumn session.[100]

*

A suffragette's work was never done: in August and September
WSPU members on holiday were encouraged to take propaganda
for the Cause. Packs of pamphlets, handbills and picture postcards
of the stars of the movement were published by the Woman's Press.
Minnie Baldock spoke on Wimbledon Common, and in the middle
of August Minnie Turner invited Mrs Baldock to stay at her guest
house in Brighton for a week to assist Mary Clarke's holiday campaign, and paid Minnie's railway fares.[101] Unable to afford a holiday,
Kitty Marion was grateful for an engagement in the comedy sketch
King of Sleepland at the Hippodrome in Colchester. Her notoriety
was such that she performed under the name 'Miss Marie Lea'. At the
end of August Mrs Pankhurst went by train to Scotland on a three-
week speaking tour of the Highlands.[102] Una Dugdale was her tour
manager. Comrades in Scotland were asked to offer hospitality, lend
motor cars and help arrange meetings where Mrs Pankhurst would
speak about the Conciliation Bill.[103]

Even though Constance Lytton had a seizure and was temporarily
paralysed in August, and suffered an attack of shingles which kept her

in bed for a month, she was back at work for the Cause in the first week of September. When planning a visit to Liverpool, Constance told Ada that she did not want to stay in an expensive hotel, that she required 'very little attendance', and would be content as long as she could have 'hot water in moderate quantities for washing and to fill my hot bottles (which I bring)'.[104]

On 17 October Victor Duval, the honorary secretary of the Men's Political Union for Women's Enfranchisement, which he had founded in January 1910, was charged with using threatening and insulting language when Lloyd George arrived at the City Temple to address a meeting of the Liberal Christian League. The police alleged that Duval had rushed from the crowd, and grabbed the chancellor's coat lapels as he got out of his motor car, shouting, 'Traitor! Lloyd George, you're a scoundrel, and a traitor to the women's cause.' A seventy-year-old businessman, George Jacobs, shocked at the police behaviour, came to Duval's assistance and was also arrested. Both men denied that Victor Duval had used the words the police cited in court. Both Duval and Jacobs refused the option of paying a fine and were sent to Pentonville Prison for seven days in the second division cells.[105] Victor Duval's behaviour was typical of the protests that would characterise the Men's Political Union for Women's Enfranchisement, so different from the measured Men's League for Women's Suffrage.

Duval, twenty-five, was a clerk when he pounced on Lloyd George, for the third time, in solidarity with the militant women. Seeing a woman being thrown out of a Liberal meeting in 1907, he resigned his membership of the Clapham League of Young Liberals. In the summer of 1909 Duval was charged with 'aiding and abetting' Marion Wallace-Dunlop in stencilling an advertisement for the suffragettes' Bill of Rights procession on the walls of St Stephen's Hall. Duval paid a £10 fine.

For the Duvals women's suffrage was a family affair: Victor's mother, Emily, set the trend by joining the WSPU in 1906, and left for the Women's Freedom League in 1907, becoming chair of the Battersea branch. By the spring of 1909 Emily Duval had served two prison sentences for her part in WFL protests. In October 1908, Emily and her seventeen-year-old daughter, Barbara, were arrested when Muriel Matters chained herself to the grille in the House of Commons. Emily Duval paid her fine and Barbara was released after promising to refrain from further militancy until she was twenty-one. Mrs Duval was accused in court of being 'a lady agitator who was bringing up her daughter to be a lady agitator'. In February 1909 she served six weeks in Holloway, almost all in the hospital wing suffering from acute neuritis. Elsie Duval, now eighteen, had joined the WSPU in 1907 at the age of sixteen, and helped Victor in the offices of the Men's Political Union for Women's Enfranchisement from 1910 to 1913. She was arrested for the first time in 1911.[106]

In October and November 1910 the WSPU asked members to protest when Parliament opened for the autumn session. On 27 October Mrs Pankhurst sent a letter to all 'Friends' which expressed her pessimism about the chance of the bill becoming law. 'Even though the Conciliation Bill has behind it the majority of the House of Commons, until the Government removed their veto the Bill could make no further progress ... We must take warnings from the Government's past record and at once prepare ourselves for action in case they announce their intention to destroy the Bill. We shall know how to respond to such a declaration of war.'[107] A hundred and fifty women had volunteered to accompany her on a deputation to the House of Commons if the facilities were refused, and she asked for more names. Mrs Pankhurst concluded, 'once we have obtained a foothold in the political world, it will be impossible for women to be left out when constitutional changes are being made ... Our power as women is invincible, if we are united and determined.'[108]

Henry Brailsford sent a long letter to Lord Lytton on 7 November after hearing that Asquith had made known his preference for a Manhood Suffrage Bill – to enfranchise men who did not yet have the vote – to a group of adult suffragists who visited him at the House of Commons. Brailsford was right to anticipate the WSPU's fury at the machinations of Herbert Asquith and Lloyd George ahead of the new parliamentary session, and that the suffragettes would declare 'instant and protracted war' when they heard the news. After discussion with Sir Edward Grey, a sincere supporter of women's suffrage, Brailsford went to Clement's Inn and found Christabel Pankhurst and the Pethick-Lawrences 'in conclave'. 'They were furiously angry and very excited, especially Mrs Lawrence', saying that it was a move against them and that Lloyd George, despite his lip service to the contrary, was a 'determined anti'. When Brailsford tried to placate the

WSPU leadership 'they declared our [Conciliation Bill] no longer interested them, they wanted sex equality and would compromise before a Reform Bill but not after manhood suffrage had been granted'. Brailsford left Clement's Inn knowing that the militants' truce was torn up, and told Lord Lytton that they would revert to their anti-government policy, identifying Lloyd George as the 'arch enemy'. Their goal was to 'bring him to his knees'. Brailsford wrote that he had 'tried all he could but they cut me short eventually by saying that they must write their declaration of policy for the press ... I found them so angry they would hardly listen to me at all.'[109]

Five days later Henry Brailsford was near the end of his patience: 'I tell myself that I don't really mind the behaviour of the WSPU except in so far as it betrays a sort of neurotic mania which may ruin our whole enterprise ... but one feels sore and raw.' He was concerned at the strident tone Christabel was taking, declaring that the Conciliation Bill was now a 'positive danger'. Brailsford doubted it was possible for him or Lord Lytton to appear on the same platform as the WSPU, but believed the Conciliation Committee could still work with other women's suffrage societies. Relations between the WSPU and Brailsford were now so delicate that he asked Lord Lytton if the Conciliation Committeee could communicate with the militant leadership via his sister Constance.[110]

On 10 November the Royal Albert Hall was full of WSPU members. Herbert Asquith had received a deputation of Liberal women from his constituency of East Fife, but all he would say to them was that the Conciliation Bill could not be 'advanced that year'. When they asked him about the following year, he replied patronisingly: 'Wait and see.' Mrs Pankhurst was finding it hard to deflect growing calls for a revival of militancy, and at the Albert Hall meeting she threw down the gauntlet: 'This is the last constitutional effort of the WSPU to secure the passage of the Bill into law.' If the bill was killed by the government the truce would be called off and they would 'take it [the bill] out of your hands since you fail to help us we will resume the direction of the campaign ourselves', and return to militancy. Mrs Pankhurst announced that she would lead a deputation to see Asquith at the House of Commons when Parliament reassembled on 18 November.[111]

Sir Edward Grey let it be known on 12 November that it would not be possible for the House of Commons to give adequate time that year for the passage of a women's suffrage bill. The WSPU regarded Lord Grey's statement as the government's definitive refusal. On 17 November Herbert Asquith sent a handwritten note to Lord Lytton making clear the hopelessness of the prospects for the Conciliation Bill in 1910: 'I can only repeat that the time at the disposal of the Government will not admit of any further progress being made with the Bill this year', and he held out little hope of any in 1911. Instead he shuffled the responsibility of making the decision to his Cabinet colleagues, promising to pass Lord Lytton's letter to them, and 'I hope before very long to be able to make a statement on the subject'.[112]

9

'Black Friday'

The Mood of the WSPU Grows Darker 1910

A suffragette fights with a policeman in Westminster, 18 November 1910.
On that 'Black Friday' 150 women were physically and sexually assaulted by police.

The WSPU's ninth Women's Parliament in Caxton Hall preceded Mrs Pankhurst's deputation to the House of Commons on 18 November 1910. Banners were propped on poles behind the platform and festooned the balconies on both sides of the hall. The needlework and paint proclaimed the slogans: 'Deeds Not Words'; 'The Bill the Whole Bill and Nothing but the Bill'; 'Through Thick and Thin We Ne'er Give In'; 'Arise! Go Forth and Conquer'; 'Women's Will Beats Asquith's Won't'; 'Go On Pestering' and 'Taxed But Voteless'. The platform was crammed with women who had volunteered to go to the House of Commons.

As they took their seats the leaders received a message saying that Herbert 'Wait and See' Asquith had made no reference to the Conciliation Bill and had announced that he was dissolving parliament on 28 November, ahead of another general election in December, to try to get a working majority to pass the People's Budget. The remaining ten days of the session would be devoted solely to government business: the Conciliation Bill was well and truly dead.[1] Annie Kenney remembered, 'there was a great storm-burst. All the clouds that had been gathering for weeks suddenly broke, and the downpour was terrific.' The sense of frustration and betrayal was total. Annie wrote: 'There was not one of us who would not have gone to our death at that moment, had Christabel so willed it.'[2] Mrs Pankhurst and Elizabeth Garrett Anderson were determined to enter the House of Commons to speak to the prime minister, and were prepared for arrest and imprisonment.[3] Dr Anderson was seventy-four years old, a suffragist since the 1860s. In 1908 she left her sister Millicent Fawcett's

NUWSS, the same year she became the first woman to be elected a mayor, and joined the WSPU.[4]

Walking with Mrs Pankhurst and Dr Anderson and her daughter, Louisa, were Hertha Ayrton, the dauntless Mrs Elmy, Mrs Hilda Brackenbury, Mrs Saul Solomon and Princess Sophia Duleep Singh, Indian suffragette and god-daughter to Queen Victoria. The princess lived in a grace and favour house at Hampton Court Palace and joined the WSPU after a meeting at Una Dugdale's home in 1909.[5] Constance Lytton was too frail to take part. Mrs Pankhurst carried a copy of the resolution to present to the prime minister: 'This meeting of women protests against the policy of shuffling and delay with which the Agitation for Women's Enfranchisement has been met by the Government', and called on him to remove the government's veto on the Conciliation Bill.[6] Behind her were 300 women walking in groups of twelve, carrying banners and tricolour pennants on bamboo poles. Mrs Pankhurst's deputation arrived in Parliament Square just after one o'clock and waited near St Stephen's Entrance. When Mrs Pankhurst asked to see the prime minister she was told that he was busy and that his private secretary, Mr Vaughan Nash, would see three members of her deputation. She took Hertha Ayrton and Dr Elizabeth Garrett Anderson with her but ten minutes later the trio returned, their time wasted when Nash told them he had no authority. It was decided that Mrs Pankhurst's deputation, and all the women and men who had accompanied them, should stay in Parliament Square and keep trying to enter the building until the House rose. Kindly MPs brought mats for Mrs Pankhurst and her companions to stand on on the cold, wet cobbles, and cake and sandwiches and teas were brought from Caxton Hall. The hinterland around the Houses of Parliament was filled with a 'turbulent mass of men, women and police'. For the next four hours the 'scolding viragoes' tried to break the police cordon and met with fierce, violent treatment by the police.

Mrs Solomon suffered the worst injuries of the women who clustered round Mrs Pankhurst. She was so traumatised at being assaulted by the police that she was confined to bed for a month before she could write to Winston Churchill, 'laying the facts before him of what she had personally suffered'. Her letter, which was later published in *The Times*, said, 'the methods applied to us were those used by the police to conquer the pugilistic antagonist, to fell the burglar, to maim the hooligan'. She was sexually assaulted, 'gripped by the breasts – by no means an exceptional act – I am informed that younger women, women of an age to be my daughters, were also assaulted in this and other repellent and equally cruel "ways"'. As she tried to leave the scene a policeman 'violently shook me while his helpers twirled round my arms as if to drag them from sockets'. The injuries suffered by many of the women that day motivated them to put their embarrassment to one side and tell the world what they had endured.[7]

*

Jessie Stephenson managed to wriggle her way to the front near to Mrs Pankhurst's group and was manhandled more than once. 'More roughs seized hold of me again. I struggled against them for my freedom and they flung me down bodily on the ground. I immediately sprang up in hot indignation ... they seized me again and flung me down with increased violence.'[8] When the crowd began to surge forward the police moved in to disperse it, and the women carrying banners who had managed to manoeuvre their way towards Mrs Pankhurst found themselves surrounded by a mob which pushed and shoved them backwards and forwards. 'Their banners went down ... snatched by members of the crowd and torn and smashed into shreds and fragments.' The suffragettes noticed that the mood of the people they encountered in Parliament Square was different: 'Instead of the rough, but mostly good-natured crowd, this one was sullen, hostile, violent with an overcurrent of bestiality.'[9] All day the police seemed to have been instructed to 'terrorise the women by forcing them back into the mostly male crowd, while the police on foot seized the women by the shoulders and flung them to the ground, plain clothes men, mingling with the crowd kicked them and added to the anguish by dragging them down the side streets where they suffered indecent assaults ... and indescribable violence.'[10] Pretending to be WSPU sympathisers, many of the attackers wore the pin badges of the Men's League for Women's Suffrage.

One hundred and fifty women were assaulted:

For hours I was beaten about the body, thrown backwards and forwards from one to another until one felt dazed with the horror of it ... I was seized by the coat, dragged out of the crowd, only to be pushed helplessly along in front of one's tormentor into a side street … while he beat one up and down one's spine until cramp seized one's legs when he would then release one with a vicious shove, and with insulting speeches: 'I will teach you a lesson. I will teach you not to come back any more. I will punish you, you —, you —.' Once I was thrown against a lamp-post with such force that two of my front teeth were loosened … What I complain of on behalf of us all is the long-drawn-out agony of the delayed arrest, and the continuous beating and pinching.[11]

Twenty-nine suffragettes were sexually molested. One suffragette described how

several times constables and plain-clothes men who were in the crowd passed their arms round me from the back and clutched hold of my breasts in as public a manner as was possible, and the men in the crowd followed their example. I was also pummeled on the chest and my breast was clutched by one constable from the front … I was very badly treated by PC —. My skirt was lifted up as high as possible, and the constable attempted to lift me off the ground by raising his knee. This he could not do so he threw me into the crowd and incited the men to treat me as they wished.[12]

Despite being in a wheelchair May Billinghurst was not spared the police's heavy-handed tactics, in fact she seems to have been singled out for vindictive treatment: 'At first, the police threw me out of the machine on to the ground in a very brutal manner. Secondly, when in the machine again, they tried to push me along with my arms twisted behind me in a very painful position, with one of my fingers bent right back, which caused me great agony.' Their third assault took place down a side street when they dumped her in the middle of 'a hooligan crowd, first taking all the valves out of the wheels and pocketing them, so that I could not move the machine and left me to the crowd of roughs who, luckily, proved my friends'. Someone came to May's assistance and fitted her tyres with a new set of valves but the police targeted her a fourth time. When they could not remove the new valves – and independent witnesses corroborated her account – the police twisted one of the wheels of her tricyle and told a member of the crowd to slash her tyres with a police knife which the man refused to do. The policeman was only prevented from hitting her again when the man made a note of his number. Mary Billinghurst was so badly bruised she could not leave her bed for several days.[13]

The next day *The Times* emphasised the suffragettes' bad behaviour rather than the police's frankly brutal and sexualised handling of the women, focusing on the number of helmets knocked off, and men's cheeks and hats scratched by the ladies, saying that for the most part the men had 'kept their tempers very well, but their method of shoving back any raiders lacked nothing in vigour'.[14] Sylvia Pankhurst was appalled at what she had seen: 'Two girls with linked arms were being dragged about by two uniformed policemen. One of a group of officers in plain clothes ran up and kicked one of the girls, while the others laughed and jeered at her ... for six hours this continued.'[15] The *Daily Mirror* noticed that the police seemed to enjoy the proceedings.

By the time the House rose at six o'clock, 119 arrests had been made. When the police withdrew from the battlefield the dishevelled women who remained trudged back to Caxton Hall, which had been turned into a field hospital where doctors and nurses dealt with black eyes, bleeding noses, sprains and dislocations. Mrs Pankhurst told the women she would return to Parliament on Monday 21 November, and every day until parliament was dissolved on 28 November. The scale of the violence was such that 18 November 1910 would be always be remembered as 'Black Friday'.[16]

Princess Sophia Duleep Singh volunteered to be a member of Mrs Pankhurst's deputation. It was an offer Mrs Pankhurst could not refuse: what stronger point could be made when someone from such a privileged background was prepared to risk the opprobrium of her royal patrons by deliberately placing herself at the heart of such a protest. The Princess Sophia Duleep Singh was born at Elveden Hall in Suffolk in 1876; her godmother, Queen Victoria, took a close interest in her sometimes chaotic childhood. Sophia was a daughter of the Indian Maharajah Duleep Singh; Sophia and her siblings led an English aristocratic life. In 1893 Sophia was orphaned when her father died and Sophia and her sisters were granted a grace and favour home on Hampton Court Green, where they were allowed to live for the rest of their lives. The princess was very much a 'New Woman', smoking twenty Turkish cigarettes a day, and often appeared in the pages of the cycling magazines on her Columbia 41 Ladies' safety bicycle. Sophia Duleep Singh was also a member of the Women's Tax Resistance League. Members were warned that refusing to pay taxes could mean that their assets would be seized to the value of the tax bill and that persistent offenders would go to prison.[17] Sophia had a diamond ring with seven stones seized for the non-payment of taxes for her servants, dogs and carriage: a friend bought it at auction for £10 and returned it to her.[18]

Henria Williams, a leading light of the Upminster suffragettes, was badly injured on 18 November. The thuggish manhandling of her by the police was widely reported in the press after the publication of the report made by Dr Jessie Murray and Henry Brailsford for the Conciliation Committee about the events of 18, 22 and 23 November. On 18 November 1910 Henria was assaulted by three policemen. After knocking her about for a considerable time, the third constable 'finally took hold of me with his great strong hands like iron just over my heart. He hurt me so much that at first I did not have the voice to tell him what he was doing. But I knew that unless I made a strong effort to do so he would kill me.' Eventually she summoned her strength to tell him to take his hand off her heart. In her evidence Henria Williams said she did not wear corsets, therefore her treatment was more painful than if she had been corseted. She thought she was going to be arrested but they took her to the edge of the crowd and 'without mercy, forced me into the midst of it, and with the crowd pushing in the opposite direction for a few minutes of it' she feared she would lose consciousness. Frank Whitty, a gentleman's outfitter from Sidcup, came to Henria's rescue. Whitty told *Votes for Women* that he saw sights that made him feel ashamed of his country. He failed to persuade Henria to leave the riot and stayed to help her as best he could by 'warding off blows, kicks and insults from her fainting body'. Several times Frank Whitty put his arm around Henria to prevent her from falling under the police horses' hooves, or being trampled by the crowd.[19]

Using the name 'Laura Grey', Lavender Guthrie was arrested for obstruction and released without charge. She joined the Union in 1908 when she was eighteen, but waited until she was twenty-one to become a full-time militant, by which time she no longer needed parental consent. Lavender was frustrated by her comfortable middle-class life in Kensington. She was an intense young woman; her mother pronounced her to be mentally unstable after her study of socialism and the lives of working-class women had led her to Number 4 Clement's Inn. Lavender was a handsome, clever girl who had been well-educated, could read Latin and Greek, and was also a poet. She told her mother that she wanted to 'give her life and her all to her more unfortunate sisters'. Lavender became an actress and adopted the stage name 'Laura Grey'.[20] In 1908 Mrs Guthrie presented her daughter at Court.[21] Lavender's friend Dorothea Rock from Essex was one of the few suffragettes to be named in the *Daily Mirror*'s coverage of 18 November.[22] Lavender's suffragette career flourished but in 1914 her life would take a tragic turn.

Hugh Franklin was one of four men to be arrested on 18 November for obstruction, but was discharged the following day. He was born into a community of Liberal Jewish families linked by birth and marriage, and joined the Independent Labour Party, the Fabian Society and, in 1909, the Men's League for Women's Suffrage. His mother, Caroline Franklin, was active in the Jewish League for Women's Suffrage. In 1910 Hugh Franklin joined the Men's Political Union for Women's Enfranchisement founded by Victor Duval, whose sister Elsie he would marry in 1915. Hugh was the uncle of Rosalind Franklin whose contribution to the discovery and understanding of DNA was only recognised long after her death in 1958.[23]

*

On Saturday 19 November the front page of the *Daily Mirror* printed a photograph of Ada Wright, fifty years old, sprawled face down on the pavement outside the House of Commons. When she made a dash for the Strangers' Entrance a policeman 'struck her with all his force and she fell to the ground'. Ada was taken to Caxton Hall and told a *Daily Mirror* reporter she had been at seven suffragette demonstrations, but had 'never known the police so violent'. One of the policemen who 'pushed me as roughly as he would have done any man said: "I won't give you the satisfaction of arresting you"'. There was a double-page spread of suffragettes wrestling with the police, and being marched off to Canon Row police station. The photograph was so bad for the reputation of the Home Office that the government ordered it to be suppressed and the negative to be destroyed.[24]

Mr Charles Mansell-Moullin, who helped treat the wounded at Caxton Hall on 18 November, expressed his dismay in a letter to the *Daily Mirror* about the use of 'organised bands of well-dressed roughs who charged backwards and forwards through the deputations like a football team without any attempt being made to stop them by the police'. Mansell-Moullin asked who had issued the instructions that the women should be treated with 'such brutality', and who had ordered the 'roughs who suddenly sprang up on all sides' to use the forceful tactics. The belief was that these were plain-clothes policemen, and that Home Secretary Winston Churchill had issued the instructions for that day.[25]

The suffragettes were back in action on Monday, Tuesday and Wednesday of the following week. Emily Davison was happy to have been arrested on 18 November, and furious not to have been sent to prison. She did not consult with the leadership about her intentions for 19 November and threw a hammer between the Chamber of the House of Commons and the Division Lobby, breaking a window. Attached to the hammer were labels warning the prime minister: 'Be wise and promise the further facilities at once the women are demanding' and 'Do justice before the General Election or judgment will surely fall'. Emily was taken to Canon Row police station and appeared in court on 30 November; she was sent to Holloway for one month. A note on file in the Parliamentary Archives tells us of Davison's standing with the Union: 'They do not acknowledge her.'[26]

On Sunday 20 November Helen Craggs went to a concert at the Paragon Theatre, Whitechapel, to reconnoitre the building in preparation for her protest at Lloyd George's meeting the following day. At two o'clock in the morning she returned with two more suffragettes and they broke into the building and climbed on to the roof where, 'only sustained by a few pieces of chocolate they lay through the whole bitter freezing night' until they heard the sound of cheering which told them that Lloyd George was speaking. Helen Craggs rushed down from the roof and dashed into the building and was surrounded by Liberal stewards, but 'armed with a super-human strength she tore herself free' and yelled her remarks at Lloyd George. The scene, reported in *Votes for Women*, was 'absolutely appalling in its brutality. Miss Craggs was practically thrown head foremost down the stone steps.' One man who reminded the chancellor that women paid taxes as well as men, had two teeth knocked out before he was ejected.[27]

On Monday 21 November 1910, Kitty Marion returned, bruised, to Caxton Hall with her comrades and waited to hear what Asquith said in the House of Commons about the fate of the Conciliation Bill. Christabel Pankhurst chaired the meeting. Also on the platform were Mrs Pankhurst, Emmeline Pethick-Lawrence and twelve women who had volunteered to go to the House of Commons to speak to the prime minister. When the meeting received word that Herbert Asquith had said nothing about the bill, Mrs Pankhurst led the deputation to the House. Some took camp-stools, ready for the inevitable wait at St Stephen's Entrance. They were allowed to make their way to the House of Commons unhindered, although it was hard to get through the crowds waiting in Parliament Square who were hoping to see the suffragettes tussle with the police. Mrs Pankhurst spoke to Inspector Scantlebury requesting a meeting with the prime minister, but her request was refused.[28]

Three hundred members of the WSPU were at Caxton Hall on Tuesday 22 November to wait for Herbert Asquith's answer to Keir Hardie's question about his intentions for the bill. When the news came that he had dismissed the question with a non-committal answer, the women decided to confront him in Downing Street. Mrs Pankhurst walked at the head of a hundred women while others walked through St James's Park, or via Whitehall. Mrs Pankhurst and her group took the Whitehall route, finding it easy to break through the thin line of policemen on duty at the end of Downing Street, confident they could have entered Number 10 if police reinforcements had not been rushed there from Whitehall. Herbert Asquith arrived unexpectedly, Mrs Pankhurst remembered: 'Before he could have realised what was happening he found himself surrounded by angry suffragettes. He was well-hooted, and it is said, well-shaken, before he was rescued by the police.' As the prime minister was whisked away from Downing Street in a taxicab a missile was thrown, smashing one of the windows.[29]

Mrs Evelina Haverfield was back in the thick of things on Tuesday 22 November, pushing her way through police lines and barking out orders to the other women, 'Shove along girls.' She hit a policeman in the mouth in Downing Street, and at Bow Street Court the next day was reported to have said: 'That is one for Friday [18 November]. That is not quite hard enough. Next time I come I will bring a revolver and shoot you.' She was happy to confirm that they were indeed her words, and told magistrate Sir Albert de Rutzen that she had previously been wrongfully accused and 'this time I thought I would have a run for my money'. De Rutzen announced that all charges except wilful damage and assaulting the police would be dismissed, and told Mrs Haverfield he was familiar with her previous appearances in court, and that he was putting her case aside for further consideration. With that, he released her on bail. She was eventually sentenced to a month in Holloway which she did not serve as the fine was paid anonymously.[30]

Also on Tuesday 22 November Ethel Haslam threw a stone through the window of the Battersea home of John Burns, the President of the Local Government Board, and was sentenced to two weeks in Holloway. Ethel's parents allowed her to use their Ilford home as the branch headquarters, which she did, filling the house with posters and hosting weekly 'At Homes'. On 23 July Ethel had dressed as Boadicea for the WSPU's procession through London to Hyde Park.[31]

Alice Hawkins broke the windows of the home of the colonial secretary 'Loulou' Harcourt in Berkeley Square, and was sentenced to two weeks in prison. On Tuesday Alice and the Misses Bowker and Pethick were in the thick of 'the Battle of Downing Street' and were arrested again. Alice wrote to her husband Alfred that by the time they reached Downing Street there was a large police presence, 'and I can tell you it was awful. The police were simply horrid, and they banged and fought like a lot of tigers ... they eventually got us out of the street into Whitehall. After about half an hour I was completely done up and decided to do something else.' Alice volunteered to lead twelve women to 'Loulou' Harcourt's house. 'It was easier to break windows than have my body broken.'[32]

Maud Fussell came from Bristol to attend the meeting in Caxton Hall on 22 November. She walked through St James's Park with Kitty Marion, who had been arrested on Friday and released without charge. Maud gave Kitty one of the weights in her pocket to break the windows of Number 10, but Kitty's aim was poor and it bounced off the wall without doing any damage. The police who guarded Number

10 were unprepared, however, and there were few constables on duty. Reinforcements were rushed over and Kitty was caught up in the riot, saying that the street 'raged like a seething cauldron' as she and the other women who tried to get into Number 10 were forced back by the police. Eventually, 'breathless and exhausted', Kitty and Maud were arrested with 150 other suffragettes, but were released without charge. Kitty and Maud Fussell became friends for life.[33]

Despite being 'shockingly maltreated' in Parliament Square on 18 November, Mrs Pankhurst's sister, Mary Clarke, was in Downing Street on Tuesday 22 November,[34] where she was arrested for breaking a window. She was sent to Holloway for one month. When she was released 'it was plain to those who knew her best that her health had suffered seriously from the experience of Black Friday and prison'.[35]

On 22 November 115 women and three men were arrested in 'the Battle of Downing Street'. *The Times* said that the women 'fought much more viciously than on Friday' because so many had wanted to go to prison but had been released without charge. Only those charged with wilful damage, or of assaulting the police, were sent to prison. *The Times* recorded, 'the rioters appeared to have lost all control of themselves. Some shrieked and some laughed hysterically, and all fought with a dogged but aimless pertinacity.' Its reporter noted that some of the suffragettes involved were young women, 'who must have been the victims of hysteria rather than of deep conviction.'[36] Many women carrying placards had them torn out of their hands and some used the bamboo poles 'to belabour the constables'. *The Times*' disparaging coverage clearly demonstrates the Victorian prejudice against women who dared to ask for more than a patriarchal society was prepared to concede.

Florence Spong was arrested for stone-throwing and sentenced to two months in Holloway. When she was released on 27 January 1911 she told *Votes for Women*, 'I have come out of Holloway feeling even more keenly that we must have the vote ... it is the only key to open the door behind which are numberless matters waiting for our united efforts to put right.'[37] Florence likened the prison to a whirlpool which 'drags ruthlessly, remorselessly old women and young girls down into its depths and drags the hearts out of them'.[38]

On Wednesday 23 November, Kitty Marion was one of eighteen women arrested trying to enter the House of Commons via the

Strangers' Entrance. The weather was dreadful, the rain pelted down, 'the police tried their hardest to throw us in the mud', and Kitty remembered clinging 'to a bobby's cape while he called me everything but a lady, and a decent woman, for me to let go of his cape, until in "self-defence" he arrested me'. Kitty was acquitted.[39]

Jessie Stephenson knocked on the door of Herbert Samuel's house and was told by a maid that he was not at home. She wrote a note and rang the bell and told the maid, 'We are the Suffragettes. The Suffragettes do not injure flesh and blood.' An alarm rang inside the house and the police were expected at any moment, and most of the women melted away, leaving Jessie and Edith behind. Jessie's stones bounced off the glass panel in the front door, so Edith took off her shoe 'with a magnificently strong heel' and just as the police arrived Jessie smashed the glass with three blows. At Bow Street Court Jessie Stephenson was sent to prison for a month for breaking a glass panel in the door of Herbert Samuel, the Liberal MP for Cleveland.[40] Jessie went there with half a dozen women, including Edith Kerwood, who had travelled from Bromsgrove. Mrs Kerwood, who was married to a solicitor, had been arrested with Mrs Pankhurst in Westminster in February 1908, and shared a platform with her on 'Women's Sunday'.[41]

Jessie took a picnic basket as she waited at Bow Street Court surrounded by suffragettes, most with their charges dismissed. After her recent experience Jessie was pleasantly surprised to see how well the police treated her and the other women, showing great courtesy, stoking up the fires, getting chairs for them and making them comfortable as they waited. Her case was not heard until the end of the day, by which time she was feeling 'mouldy green all over', and her initial bravado had evaporated during the wait. She felt overwhelmed but when she entered court she felt 'gay and bright again' when she recognised comrades in the public seating area 'all nodding and greeting me. I felt myself burst into smiles, I was myself once more and perfectly happy in that space.' In the witness box she was faced by de Rutzen, an 'elderly old wizard ... who was very antique and fuddled'. With Jessie in the dock was Edith Kerwood whom Jessie called 'the Rock'. The stone and Edith's shoe were solemnly produced as evidence, and Edith told de Rutzen: 'I wore it on my foot, I did not take it with me as a weapon.' Jessie was taken with other suffragette prisoners to Holloway in a 'very creaky, smelly old Black Maria' where she was squeezed into a locked cupboard. She was five feet ten inches tall, and had to crouch on a wooden shelf. As they were 'jolted along hither and thither' on the cobbled streets the suffragettes broke into song.[42]

Hugh Franklin travelled to Bradford on 26 November to admonish Winston Churchill at a meeting of young Liberals at St George's Hall. Franklin interrupted Churchill, called him a 'scoundrel' and was ejected. Alfred Hawkins arrived from Leicester and he in turn interrupted Churchill in full flow, was seized by stewards and 'during the struggle which resulted from attempts to eject him his leg was broken'. It took Alfred a long time to recover: when the Census was taken six months later, he was still unable to work and described as an invalid by the Census Enumerator. This was not the first time Alfred Hawkins had got into trouble for supporting his suffragette wife: in September 1909 they were both charged with causing a breach of the peace and obstructing the police outside the Palace Theatre in Leicester, where Winston Churchill was addressing a meeting. Alfred Hawkins was bound over to keep the peace while his wife served five days in prison.[43]

Hugh Franklin discovered which train Churchill was taking to London and bought tickets to travel with Laura Ainsworth. Although two Special Branch officers were travelling with Churchill, Hugh Franklin 'pulled a whip from his pocket, called out, "Winston Churchill, take that you dirty cur for the treatment of the suffragettes"', but the Special Branch Detective-Sergeant, Joseph Sandercock, grabbed Franklin by the throat and arrested him. When the train arrived at King's Cross, Franklin was taken to Somers Town police station, charged with assaulting the home secretary by attempting to hit him with a whip and was released on bail. Three suffragettes waiting for the train rushed at Churchill as he alighted and 'hissing abusive words at him attempted to strike him in the face, and knocked off his hat'. The women were seized by the police but Churchill ordered them to be released. Hugh Franklin's case was heard at Bow Street Court two days later. Archibald Bodkin prosecuted and Superintendent Quinn of Special Branch represented the police. Franklin insisted on conducting his own defence. Bodkin said that not only was Mr Churchill assaulted, but the high office of state was also attacked. Hugh Franklin was sentenced to six weeks in Pentonville Prison, and went on hunger strike.[44]

The WSPU had now heard from well-placed but anonymous sources (probably Henry Brailsford) that Winston Churchill had ordered that, in addition to uniformed police, constables in plain clothes were to be in the crowds on 18 November, 'to throw the women around from one to the other'. Mrs Pethick-Lawrence learned that the demonstrations had not been policed by the 'A Division' which usually guarded the Houses of Parliament, but that policemen had been drafted in from the East End of London. 'They knew nothing of the suffrage agitation and were accustomed to dealing with drunks and roughs ... Large and well-nourished bullies had been imported into Westminster and may have been police in plain clothes.'[45] Unsurprisingly Churchill was keen to avoid being the target of well-founded fury from the WSPU and wrote to the Commissioner of Police on 22 November: 'I am hearing from every quarter that my strongly expressed wishes conveyed to you on Wednesday evening and repeated on Friday morning that the suffragettes were not to be allowed to exhaust themselves, but were to be arrested forthwith upon any defiance of the law, were not observed by the police ... with the result that very regrettable scenes occurred.' If this was the case Churchill's memo is chilling: 'It was my desire to avoid this ... to arrest large numbers and then subsequently prosecute only where serious grounds were shown and I am sorry that, no doubt, through a misunderstanding, another course has been adopted.'[46] If true, it is difficult to imagine who would have countermanded Churchill's instructions to the Commissioner of Police. Three months later, in March 1911, when Black Friday was discussed in the House of Commons at the time of the publication of the Conciliation Committee's report titled *The Treatment of the Women's Deputations of November 18th, 22nd and 23rd, 1910 By The Police*, Churchill explained it differently, insisting that the police had acted under his predecessor Herbert Gladstone's orders that they should avoid arresting the women solely for 'technical obstruction'.[47]

On the same day that Hugh Franklin tried to whip Churchill, Sir Edward Grey wrote to Lord Lytton giving him an insider's view. As the highest ranking cabinet minister of the Liberal government, he was uniquely placed to know how Asquith and his anti-women's suffrage colleagues would react. He advised Lytton: 'All this violence will put the question back and prejudice the chance of any Bill in the next Parliament. I do not say that it absolves the Government from the pledge already given, for I believe that the violent women are a small minority of the great mass interested in the question: but it does make it impossible for any member of the Government to say anything favourable which could be construed as a concession to gross personal attacks upon himself or his colleagues.' Lord Grey went on to confirm a suspicion long held by the women's suffrage movement that 'the question was never taken seriously until a few years ago, but that now the question of electoral reform had created the situation', nothing could change with regard to enfranchising the men who still did not have the vote without addressing the issue of women's suffrage, and 'giving the House of Commons an effective opportunity of putting Women's Suffrage into it'.[48]

Winston Churchill's wife Clementine attended several trials of WSPU members, and would later say that the years of violence had been necessary 'because the day would not have been won without women with a passion that exceeded constitutional and legal binds'. Despite his wife's support for women's suffrage, Churchill would persist in his opinion that women were not ready for the vote. The Churchills' differing views on women's suffrage was symptomatic of a deeper tension: Clementine was jealous of his friendships with other women, especially the prime minister's daughter Violet Asquith, who was infatuated with her husband.[49]

The violence used against the women on Black Friday and the days that followed had an immediate impact on suffragette militancy. Some women were no longer prepared to take part in deputations to Parliament and run such risks again. Others were prepared to throw stones, break windows or commit other acts which would get them arrested immediately. Deputations to Parliament were abandoned, and window-smashing would come to be the order of the day.

For those women who were serving time for their protest Jessie Stephenson's memoir gives an idea of what it was like to be a suffragette in Holloway. Jessie described being inspected on arrival, how her hair was taken down and searched in case anything had been concealed within its elaborate structure. She had to remove her clothes except for her stockings which happened to be made of fine Italian silk, 'so fascinating to touch ... I always remember the wardress kneeling before me long after she had officially searched them, and went on striking my silken legs up and down, up and down, as she asked questions.'[50] This amused Jessie who found the experience 'quite homely'.

Jessie benefited from Churchill's introduction of Rule 243a which allowed her to wear her own clothes (her opera cloak with fur collar kept her warm). The weekly bath posed a challenge to someone as tall as Jessie: 'I held up my towel the size of a handkerchief and asked the wardress how I was supposed to dry myself on something so small.' Her comrades laughed and the 'embarrassed wardress hastily gave me two more to meet my special case'.[51]

While Jessie was in Holloway the governor received a letter from her barrister employer, and allowed her to read it. It brought news that if she did not get out of Holloway soon – by paying her fine – she would lose her position, making her homeless and unemployed. But Jessie refused to have her fine paid and stayed in Holloway until she was released, two days before Christmas.[52]

Polling stations for the general election were open between 3 and 19 December, and the suffragettes told voters about the duplicitous behaviour of the prime minister and his Cabinet. In the run-up to the election, Winston Churchill, accompanied by Clementine, addressed two meetings in Sheffield. It was rumoured that the entire local constabulary, reinforced by a detachment of London detectives, were needed to police the home secretary's visit. Barricades were erected within a hundred-yard radius of the venues. *Votes for Women* pointed out that the authorities 'awaited with trepidation the terrible suffragette raid which Liberal fears and guilty consciences had imagined'.[53] Security was focused on stopping women from getting into meetings – the only ones admitted were Clementine Churchill, her sister-in-law Lady Gwendoline and Mrs Cornwallis-West (whose son George was Churchill's stepfather) – but as soon as proceedings started a male voice piped up, 'You'll ruin the women if you don't give them the vote.' He was dragged from his seat during 'a great and prolonged ... free fight' and he was chucked out. At least ten men were ejected, including a clergyman, for their impertinent interruptions about votes for women.

On 3 December, the prime minister was pursued to the Drill Hall in Newcastle by members of the Men's Political Union for Women's Enfranchisement, and was asked why he had vetoed the Conciliation Bill. The heckler was held down and gagged while Asquith changed the subject. Another MPUWE member sprang to his feet and waved a purple, white and green flag, and he managed to make a speech, although only fragments could be heard amid the chaos. *Votes for Women* reported that Herbert Asquith hurriedly finished to avoid more questions. On 5 December, Churchill went to Dundee hoping to retain his seat, and spoke at the King's Theatre to a men-only audience. Precautions were taken to make sure that no women entered the building, and four 'slaters' spent the night on the roof; Churchill's visit passed without incident.[54]

Three days later the prime minister was in Burnley, where 'the most absurd precautions against the suffragettes were taken'. A suffragette posse went up to Asquith as he alighted from his train, took him by the arm and asked him why he would not revoke his veto at the House of Commons and give facilities for the Conciliation Bill to proceed. In his flustered efforts to get away 'he collided with some railings and looked very foolish and gave no reply'. His detectives finally caught up with him and seized the suffragettes and 'in the mêlée Mr Asquith caught hold of a Liberal woman who was trying to protect him and pushed her away calling, "Here's another."' The prime minister was driven off with suffragettes shouting: 'You are a disgrace to your country, sir ... the women are ashamed of you ... traitor ... coward!'[55]

Before Dundee voters went to the polls, Winston Churchill returned to give his final speech. A local suffragette, Ethel Moorhead, managed to get a ticket to the meeting, and threw an egg at the home secretary, her first suffragette protest. She was removed from the meeting but not arrested.[56] Churchill retained his seat but with a reduced majority: 2,640 fewer Dundonians voted for him, which the *Daily Mirror* noted was 'a striking drop and one of the most pronounced since the election began'. The Labour candidate Alexander Wilkie had eaten into Churchill's vote.[57]

On 20 December Hebert Asquith, their 'avowed enemy', was returned to power, but only just. There was a hung parliament: the Liberals had a majority of 1, having won 273 seats; the Conservatives had 272, and the Irish Nationalists were the third party with 74 seats. The Labour Party trailed with 42 MPs. Asquith could only remain in power with their support.[58]

Jessie Stephenson was in a group of fifteen suffragettes, including Mary Clarke, to be released from Holloway on 23 December: 'Slowly, by driblets of twos and threes, we were let out of the big Holloway gates into the light of heaven and liberty.' They were greeted by Mrs Pankhurst and Mrs Tuke, and 300 WSPU members with purple, white and green flowers, and a brass band playing 'The Marseillaise'. There was a welcome reception at noon at the Criterion restaurant in Piccadilly. For each of the suffragettes remaining in Holloway over Christmas, hampers decorated in the colours, a Christmas card from Mrs Pankhurst and a signed postcard of Christabel were left at the prison by Mrs Kitty Marshall, recently released from Holloway for throwing a potato at Churchill's front door. Mrs Pankhurst presided at the Criterion, and, referring to the horrors of Black Friday, observed that 'women were prepared to face all kinds of suffering in order to win for themselves and their daughters that freedom which they claimed'.[59]

On her way to the reception Jessie Stephenson read a letter from Christabel offering her a job as a paid organiser. She 'took the letter up and gave it a passionate hug'. She was seated next to Christabel who 'was ever so jolly, laughing merrily at every little joke I told her'. But Jessie was terrified and when it came to her turn to speak all she could say was: 'Mrs Pankhurst, Ladies and Gentlemen', followed by a very long pause. 'I, er, er, I have never been able to speak in public, and I can't speak now.' Mrs Pankhurst quickly stood up and said: 'Thrice a prisoner! What an illustration of our motto – Deeds Not Words!'[60]

Mary Clarke was frail when she was released, and may have overexerted herself when she spoke at the welcome luncheon at the Criterion, before going to Brighton to speak to a welcome party given by local suffragettes. She then insisted on travelling back to London on Christmas Eve to spend Christmas at the home of her brother, Herbert Goulden, in Winchmore Hill, with his family and Emmeline and Christabel Pankhurst. On Christmas Day, she left the table and went to her room where Mrs Pankhurst found her in a coma. She died three hours later of a brain haemorrhage. Mary Clarke's injuries suffered on Black Friday were blamed for her sudden death at the age of forty-eight on Christmas Day. On 27 December Emmeline Pankhurst wrote to C. P. Scott, proprietor and editor of the *Manchester Guardian*: 'We who love her and know the beauty of her selfless life feel it very hard to restrain our human desire for vengeance … Violence has been done to us and

I ... have lost a dear sister in the course of this agitation ... she would have been proud and glad to die for the cause of freedom.' Emmeline wrote of the loss of her son, her mother and her sister in 1910, and asked, 'can you wonder that today I want beyond all other things to end this fight quickly and get some rest'.[61]

'The March of the Women'

'No Votes, No Census' 1911

*Indian suffrage supporters at the Women's Coronation Procession,
17 June 1911, carry wooden elephants, the emblem of their country.*

Constance Lytton went to a talk given by Henry Brailsford and left with the clear impression that he believed the government 'really now intend to enfranchise women, that they have a new spell of power and yet no majority to enable them to pass a more democratic measure'. Brailsford told her that the government had expected to win the election with a bigger majority but had failed, and now faced the new parliamentary session with a majority of one and even greater reliance on the support of the Irish Nationalists. Brailsford pointed out that some members of the Conciliation Committee had lost their seats in the election, and until the new MPs returned in early February it was hard to gauge whose support the Committee could count on. He thought that there were a hundred MPs who were 'genuinely and reliably friendly, but not more', and that Augustine Birrell (despite his recent tangle with the suffragettes in Downing Street) was the Committee's 'most trustworthy friend'. Brailsford pointed out 'the two evils': first, the risk of 'Lloyd George and Co.'s opposition killing a new Bill by making too drastic amendments' at the committee stage; second, the danger of the House becoming 'unfriendly to the women [militants]'; the government could exploit this by giving the bill enough time in order to be rejected 'owing to their [the members'] temporary sulkiness'.[1]

In the early hours of the morning of 2 January 1911, Police Constable Girling, walking his beat past Miss Henria Williams' house, heard the sound of groaning coming from her home. She moaned: 'Fetch the doctor and come through the window, I am dying.' She was dead before the doctor arrived. Local newspapers commented that Miss Williams' protest on Black Friday was 'conduct not at all congenial to one who suffered from a weak heart'.² An inquest found that forty-three-year-old Henria had died of angina. *Votes for Women* published a memoir by her younger brother Llewellyn, with a photograph of Henria standing outside Leyton Town Hall during the Walthamstow by-election in November 1910. Llewellyn wrote, she 'knowingly and willingly shortened her days in rendering services to the woman-hood of the nation'. Henria's obituary described her actions on Black Friday: 'she showed marvellous courage', but was 'terribly knocked about and came back to Caxton Hall gasping for breath, with face and lips blackened by suffocation'.³

*

Sylvia Pankhurst crossed the Atlantic during the first few days of 1911 for a three-month speaking tour of the United States that had been arranged by Harriet Stanton Blatch, President of the American Women's Political Union. Arriving in New York she was met off the boat by Mrs Blatch and 'a flock of Pressmen who kept me busy with interviews for three entire days'.⁴ Her first lecture was on 6 January at the Carnegie Lyceum on Fifth Avenue. Sylvia went to Brooklyn, Albany, Philadelphia, Kansas City, Pittsburg, Chicago, Milwaukeee, Wisconsin, Arkansas and Tennessee. Arriving in Des Moines, Iowa, after an all-night journey, she had almost lost her voice and was met by a group of women's suffrage activists who had arranged for her to speak at noon to the Senate and House of Representatives. A women's suffrage bill was pending in Iowa, 'and in view of this I felt very deeply the responsibility laid upon me'.⁵

*

On 8 January Henry Brailsford wrote to Lord Lytton updating him after a long meeting with Mrs Pankhurst, who was 'terribly upset' by the death of her sister and Henria Williams: 'Her mood is one of still fiercer determination to end the struggle before more deaths occur, but also I am sure that she feels that these risks must not be wantonly incurred.' Brailsford thought he had managed to reassure Mrs Pankhurst, and was confident that 'she will allow us <u>some</u> time at the opening of this session before she resumes militancy but I could not get her to say how long'. Brailsford liked Mrs Pankhurst's suggestion that she should meet the Conciliation Committee before Parliament was recalled; 'she has a way of communicating her determination, and our members need to have their nerves sharpened'.[6]

In Mrs Saul Solomon's letter in *Votes for Women*, describing her distress on Black Friday, and knowing that the Cabinet was meeting to draw up the King's Speech ahead of the opening of Parliament, the WSPU staged a protest in Downing Street on 20 January. They marched up and down carrying banners decorated with the prisoners' arrow, and placards demanding the vote.[7] The *Daily Mirror*'s photographer snapped one of the women having 'a momentarily exciting encounter' with Winston Churchill when she poked the arrow end of her banner, which demanded 'Should Mr Churchill Go To Prison?', through the open window of his taxicab. Despite the pole coming into contact with his silk hat, Churchill emerged 'smiling and unconcerned at the incident' as he alighted from the taxi.[8]

'The March of the Women', the new WSPU battle hymn, by the composer Ethel Smyth, with lyrics by the actress and writer Cicely Hamilton, was first performed on 21 January 1911 at an 'At Home' in the Suffolk Street Galleries, Pall Mall, to celebrate the release of some women who had been sent to prison on Black Friday. Ethel Smyth impressed Cicely Hamilton: 'alternately playing her triumphant march on the piano and reading or chanting verses to us'. The first verse of the suffragettes' song was to ring out with a blast from a cornet:

> Shout, shout up with your song!
> Cry with the wind for the dawn is breaking.
> March, march, swing you along,
> Wide blows our banner and hope is waking.
> Sing with its story, dreams with their glory,
> Lo! They call and glad is their word!
> Forward! Hark how it swells
> Thunder and freedom, the voice of the Lord.

Ethel Mary Smyth was born in London in 1858, the same year as Mrs Pankhurst, on whom she doted. Her musical education started late: her governess, Marie Louise Schultz, who had studied at the Leipzig Conservatory, influenced Ethel's entire life. Ethel was then also determined to study music at the Leipzig Conservatory, and refused to take part in the social round to find a husband. Her father, General John Smyth, finally agreed to let her go to Leipzig in 1877, aged nineteen. Ethel's first opera was well received in 1898 at the court theatre at Weimar. One of her best-known pieces is another opera, *The Wreckers*, performed at Covent Garden in 1910, conducted by Thomas Beecham.[9]

When Ethel Smyth went to a meeting addressed by Mrs Pankhurst she, like so many others, was smitten: 'Mrs Pankhurst came into my life, changing its whole tenor.' She decided to devote herself and her music to votes for women for two years. Until she met Mrs Pankhurst Ethel had not been troubled by women's suffrage, but in 1911 'The March of the Women' launched her suffragette career. Ethel was often photographed at Mrs Pankhurst's side like an unofficial bodyguard.[10]

Cicely Hamill changed her name to Hamilton when she went on the stage. Her autobiography, *Life Errant*, speaks of an unhappy childhood, brought about by her mother's disappearance from the family home in 1882. Her father served in Egypt until 1885 and Cicely and her sister were sent to school in Malvern, then Cicely studied in Germany. She taught in the Midlands for a time and wrote for the sensational press.[11]

For ten years Cecily was an actress, performing comic and melo-dramatic roles. She gave up performing in 1905 and turned her hand to writing plays. She wrote a series of curtain-raisers and then in January 1908 had her first big success, *Diana of Dobsons*, a romantic comedy. She joined the 13 June 1908 procession to Hyde Park and helped carry the banner of the Women Writers' Suffrage League, which she and the novelist Bessie Hatton had recently founded. Cicely Hamilton and Christopher St John's play, *How the Vote Was Won*, was put on at the Royalty Theatre in April 1909. In November Cicely wrote and performed in her *Pageant of Great Women* which was staged by many women's suffrage groups.[12]

On 22 January 1910 Henry Brailsford wrote to Lord Lytton about the difficulties which lay ahead, irritated that Lytton was absent from London. Brailsford's opening sentence sets his tone: 'I am afraid, as I told you it would, that your absence just now would mean utter disaster.' No cabinet minister would agree to meet Brailsford and C. P. Scott of the *Manchester Guardian*. Brailsford despaired of the MPs who had made promises of support doing anything for the bill in 1911, and feared that the prime minister intended to pack parliamentary time with other legislation, including an Irish Home Rule Bill, and a manhood suffrage bill, and there was little chance of getting a name on the ballot for a private members' bill. Lloyd George emerges from this correspondence as slippery as an eel. What was needed in dealing with such mercurial types as Herbert Asquith, Winston Churchill and Lloyd George was 'someone who will simply take them by the throat'. Brailsford's postscript asked Lord Lytton to excuse his 'very frank' letter and begged him to return to London and 'give all your time for a week at least to try and save something before the coming wreck'. Brailsford warned Lytton that the moment one or both of them slackened, 'the militants will break out. I think if we are equally resolute in our optimism and our energy we can hypnotise them into trusting us again.'[13]

Christabel told Henry Brailsford she would have nothing more to do with the Conciliation Bill, and a meeting with her mother was 'the angriest and most painful' he had ever had. Mrs Pankhurst reproached Brailsford and Lytton 'most bitterly' for having invented the Conciliation movement, and declared it had been from first to last a disaster for the WSPU. Nevertheless, Henry Brailsford and Lord Lytton persisted in their work with the Conciliation Committee and Mrs Fawcett and her supporters.[14]

The WSPU told the editor of *The Times* that unless the government made a commitment in the King's Speech on 6 February to give facilities to Mr Shackleton's Conciliation Bill in the coming session of parliament, 'our fireworks will immediately begin'. The leadership said, 'no reliance can be placed on the so-called pledges of the Prime Minister and his colleagues ... We mean to win this time, and in view of what we have heard from private sources, the truce will end on 6 February and hostilities will commence.'[15]

On the morning of 6 February 'battalions' of suffragettes pounced on cabinet ministers as they left their homes to go to Westminster. Among their ranks was Princess Sophia Duleep Singh (in her fur coat) and Mrs Kitty Marshall, just out of prison for throwing that potato at the fanlight of Winston Churchill's door. So well-dressed were they that the policemen on duty did not move them on, but when the prime minister left Number 10 Sophia got past the civil servants and policemen who surrounded Asquith and stood in front of the taxi that was to take him to the House. She pulled out a suffragette banner bearing the words 'Give Women the Vote' from her muff. Princess Sophia Duleep Singh's suffragette moment was described in the papers as 'Princess as Picket', but she and Kitty were frustrated at not getting the headlines they craved, being denied a court appearance and prison sentence.[16]

Sir George Kemp, the Liberal MP for Manchester North-West, won first place in the private members' ballot and was given the date of 5 May for the second reading of the Conciliation Bill. Agreeing to sponsor the Conciliation Bill was consistent with Sir George Kemp's objection to key Liberal policies, including Lloyd George on finance and Home Rule for Ireland. Sir George said after his resignation from Parliament in 1912 that he 'loathed politics' and that it had been 'a source of unmitigated dislike and unhappiness to him'. His sponsorship of the bill may have been merely a gesture rather than a genuine interest in women's suffrage.[17]

On 8 February Kitty Marshall was back in Downing Street helping Marion Wallace-Dunlop stencil 'Votes For Women this Session' on the prime minister's doorstep with what looked like a carpet sweeper. In the middle of February Edith How-Martyn of the Women's Freedom League announced a new strategy: women should boycott the Census due to be taken of every household in the United Kingdom on Sunday 2 April 1911. Since 1909 the League had been the architect of women's refusal to pay taxes, and resisting the Census was a logical step. Edith urged women 'to refuse to supply information to assist a Government which governs without their consent'. By completing the forms which supplied information that could prove the basis for the framing of future legislation they 'made themselves consenting parties to the present political status of womanhood on this country'. She urged suffragist men and women to 'refuse to take part in it as a definite, logical and peaceable protest against the callous indifference that has characterised the Government's treatment of woman suffrage up to the present time'. If women were not even classed as 'persons' under British law, and were to continue to be classed politically with criminals and lunatics, 'then at least they should not consent to be numbered merely for the Government's convenience'.[18]

The painful memories of Black Friday on 18 November 1910 returned when the report of *The Treatment of the Women's Deputations on November 18ᵗʰ, 22ⁿᵈ, and 23ʳᵈ, 1910 By The Police* was published. Compiled by Henry Brailsford with the help of Dr Jessie Murray, the public was reminded of the many examples of police misconduct: at least twenty-nine examples of indecency; the brutal handling of women in their sixties and seventies; constables who used their helmets as weapons; women being kicked as they lay on the ground. The report was clear: 'we cannot resist the conclusion that the police as a whole were under the impression that their duty was not merely to frustrate the attempts to reach the House of Commons, but to terrorise the women in the process.' The violence and indecency led Brailsford to believe the police behaved as if they were 'under unlimited licence to treat the women as they pleased', and to intimidate them from taking part in such a protest again. The Conciliation Committee asked Home Secretary Churchill for a public inquiry into police conduct, which would investigate the Metropolitan Police's perception as to how they should handle WSPU deputations, and determine who had given the orders to the police to behave the way they did.[19]

On 3 March Sir George Kemp released the text of his bill which removed marriage as a disqualification for women voters, 'provided that both husband and wife shall not be registered as voters in the same Parliamentary constituency'.[20] Five days later Hugh Franklin threw a stone wrapped in a letter tied with rubber tubing – the same sort as that used to force-feed suffragette prisoners – at the fanlight above Winston Churchill's door in Eccleston Square. Franklin was charged at Bow Street with throwing a missile 'to the common danger … and threatening behaviour likely to lead to a breach of the peace'.[21] Franklin explained to the magistrate, Mr Curtis Bennett, that he was protesting against the treatment of his friend, Mr Abbey, who was being force-fed while on hunger strike in the second division at Pentonville Prison. He was serving a three-week sentence for trying to climb over the garden wall of 10 Downing Street while a Cabinet meeting was in progress. Franklin refused to be bound over and was sent to Pentonville for one month, went on hunger strike and within a week was being force-fed.[22]

The Women's Freedom League and the Women's Social and Political Union urged their members to refuse to supply their personal details to the Census Enumerators on the evening of 2 April 1911. The WSPU also suggested the various ways their members could resist and sabotage the Census: it is estimated that Mrs Pankhurst and 4,000 suffragists and suffragettes evaded, boycotted or refused to complete the forms and wrote diagonally across the Census form 'No Vote, No Census'.[23] They had also suggested that women add: 'If I am intelligent enough to fill in the Census Form I can surely make an X on a Ballot paper.' Some forms were left empty, some women wrote in the column entitled 'disabilities' the word, 'unenfranchised'. Women were advised to spend the evening away from home to frustrate the Census. (Householders were obliged by law to complete the Census form, and made themselves liable to a fine of £5 or a month in prison if they refused.) On 2 April 1911 suffragettes stayed away from home and had fun: the Skating Rink in Aldwych was packed with women all night, and the non-skaters were entertained by the best actresses and singers of the day. Before Mrs Pankhurst joined them she had been one of hundreds of women who walked around Trafalgar Square until the police cleared the area half an hour after midnight.

Wealthy suffragettes opened their homes to Census resisters, and sympathetic heads of colleges filled their buildings with women who did not want to be at home. Some adventurous women hired gipsy caravans and spent the night out. On Census night Kitty Marion was in Trafalgar Square, then she and her comrades left in three horse-drawn caravans for Wimbledon Common.[24] Although Colonel and Mrs Blathwayt disliked militancy, their daughter Mary took part in the protest and spent the night in a house with twenty-eight women who slept on mattresses. Mary's friends Grace and Aethel Tollemache played the violin and piano, and another member of the WSPU gave a lecture on clairvoyance. Women slipped away throughout the night to thwart detectives who had been posted outside to make a note of how many women were present and who they were.[25]

Jessie Stephenson helped coordinate Manchester WSPU's Census protest. 'Our splendid friend Mrs Hyland' offered one of her empty houses where local suffragettes could spend the evening of Sunday 2 April, an offer Jessie found 'too scrumptious'.[26] The building was large enough to house four to five hundred 'packed in of course ... and a good point was that it had seven entrances. From its various frontages, arrivals could split and not attract attention.' Rose Hyland had known the Pankhurst family for twenty years, was a customer of Mrs Pankhurst's 'artistic' shop Emersons, and made a donation to the Dr Pankhurst Fund when Emmeline was widowed in 1898.[27] Jessie Stephenson borrowed hundreds of chairs and a few tables for a night of dancing, a bridge tournament and speeches by 'General' Flora Drummond. News of Jessie's plans reached the Chief Constable of Manchester, who warned her that if she hosted hundreds of women she would be liable for imprisonment for each Census resister she housed. She would have to serve each sentence consecutively or be liable for the £5 fine for each default. He told Jessie, 'the sentences, in the case of large numbers, might mean the rest of your life in gaol'.[28]

Rose Hyland's gardener filled ticking mattresses with hay, fires were lit to welcome the 'flocks' of women who poured in with suitcases, many of whom 'brought their own grub', while volunteers cooked meals in the kitchens. When Jessie heard that the police were outside she ordered coffee to be made for them, and when she delivered it she learned there were newspaper reporters and invited them inside 'Census Lodge' to look around. The men were taken aback at the sight of Flora Drummond reclining on one of the hay mattresses, and the photographers took 'snap shots by lime-light many of which appeared in the next day's press'. The newsmen were having a whale of a time, and 'thought the whole show extremely good fun and begged in vain to be allowed to remain all night for the revels'. Jessie wrote on her form: 'This house is crowded with women who refuse to fill in the Census form until women are recognised as persons and have the vote.'[29]

Like a pigeon coming home to roost, Emily Davison spent Census night in a cupboard in the Chapel of St Mary Undercroft at the House of Commons. She was discovered by a cleaner. In the morning Emily was taken to Canon Row police station where she was detained for a few hours before being released. In Coram Street, Emily's landlady completed her form, giving her lodger's details as she understood them: guessing that Emily was thirty-eight and her occupation was 'political secretary'.[30]

The widespread evasion of the Census by the women's suffrage campaigners led to the government's decision not to give the women more publicity by bringing any prosecutions. The WSPU was irked by the press boycott of 'all their peaceful constitutional campaigning work' which 'distorts and misrepresents our militant action'. Mrs Pankhurst asked WSPU members to take part in a sales drive to increase the readership of *Votes for Women*, 'to have it read by people in every part of the country'. Members were asked to be *Votes for Women* agents, and suggestions were given as to how to boost sales: getting a poster displayed at the local railway station, going from house to house, and selling their paper on the street, or at country markets.[31]

In April a new WSPU shop opened in Streatham, run by the honorary secretary of the branch, Leonora Tyson, who had also been running Lambeth WSPU. The window in Shrubbery Road was 'tastefully dressed in the colours'. There was an abundance of sweets and cakes for the opening party – some donated by Princess Sophia Duleep Singh – but the cost of renting and decorating the shop had used up all their funds. Leonora Tyson asked members if they could donate any unwanted furniture such as a writing table, paper baskets, a bookcase, a coal-scuttle, doormat and chairs. Like all the WSPU shops, Streatham sold postcards and badges, scarves and muffs, and pamphlets and canvas bags for selling copies of *Votes for Women*.[32]

*

On 22 April Constance Lytton had declined an invitation from Rose Lamartine Yates to speak at a meeting in Wimbledon because her health kept 'giving out'. Her shaky hand suggests she was not exaggerating her frailty; she wanted to preserve her strength 'and was laying herself on the shelf' in order to write her book, *Prisons and Prisoners: Some Personal experiences by Constance Lytton and Jane Warton, spinster*, which was published in 1914 by William Heinemann.[33]

*

The day before the Conciliation Bill was due to be read for a second time the National League for Opposing Woman Suffrage marshalled their views in *The Times*. They met at the Criterion restaurant two days before the bill was due to be read, presided over by Mr St Loe Strachey, who opened the proceedings by saying he was sure that women's suffrage could not be granted without incurring the very real danger of 'a sex conflict'. Mrs Archibald Colquhoun of the Women's National Anti-Suffrage League was adamant that 'no change should be made to the franchise until the matter was an issue in a General Election'.[34]

On 5 May Sir George Kemp's Conciliation Bill was read in the House of Commons for a second time. Kemp said that women should be enfranchised because they outnumbered men in the country and suffered many kinds of 'disabilities' such as 'unfair treatment under the marriage laws, chronically low pay', and women tax-payers paid 'a considerable proportion of the taxes'. Mr Edward 'Paddy' Goulding, Conservative MP for Worcester since 1908, seconded Sir George Kemp's motion and expanded the argument, saying it was 'intolerable that the conditions of the employment of women wage-earners, the numbers of whom were increasing day by day, should be regulated by men'.[35] Goulding, an Irish barrister, told the House that he refused to accept that women did not want the vote, and that if women were enfranchised the House of Commons would 'be keener to promote their interests'. Goulding, who had served on the London County Council from 1895 to 1901, was committed to social reform, supported old-age pensions, workers' compensation, shorter hours for shop workers and the payment of MPs.[36]

In response, Edmund Haviland-Burke, an Irish Nationalist MP, said 'the expedients to which the militants have resorted smacked of charlatanry and vulgarity', and he regretted that the 'older and wiser participants [the NUWSS] had been thrust aside by the impudent cuckoos of Caxton Hall', at which point 'the House laughed heartily'. Two hundred and fifty-five MPs voted for the bill, and eighty-eight against, a thumping majority of 168. Sir George Kemp moved that the bill be sent to a Committee of the Whole House (as in the previous year) and threw down the gauntlet to Herbert Asquith to keep the pledge he had made in the previous session to grant facilities for the bill. The prime minister kept Parliament and the women's suffrage campaigners waiting for twenty-four days before giving his response.[37]

On 12 May Constance Lytton and Annie Kenney had a private meeting with Arthur Balfour. Annie wrote a note in a nervous hand expressing her thanks for his agreeing to meet them and rejoicing at the news of 'the grand majority' the bill had won in the House of Commons a week earlier. She told Balfour she would like to have written 'a lot more but I know how dreadfully busy you must be'.[38] While Lytton and Kenney were lobbying Balfour, Mrs Pankhurst was being photographed at the House of Commons with John J. Farrell, the Lord Mayor of Dublin, in his official robes, 'wearing his gold chain of office and carrying a white wand', who later appeared at the Bar of the House of Commons to present a petition from himself and the aldermen and burgesses of Dublin asking that 'the Bill to confer the Parliamentary franchise on women may be passed through your honourable house during the present session of Parliament'.[39]

On 29 May 1911 Lloyd George said no facilities would be granted, and placed other government bills ahead of women's suffrage. All he offered was that the government would allocate a week for the bill's debate in the next session, in 1912, after it had been through the rigmarole of being read a second time. Surprisingly, Christabel Pankhurst did not immediately declare an end to the truce. She had been advised privately that Sir Edward Grey was working behind the scenes on the women's behalf and she held fire. The Conciliation Committee asked the WSPU to accept the government's promise, as they had decided to do. Christabel Pankhurst said: 'Our great appreciation of their work and … our strong wish to retain their cooperation made us wish to accept their advice and not bring the movement of conciliation to an end while there was any remaining possibility of its success.' However, if the Conciliation Committee failed, the WSPU would have no hesitation in resuming 'the entire and independent conduct of our policy'. Christabel knew there was the real risk of being tricked by 'a worthless political promise', and there was the wish 'to keep with us the understanding and sympathy of the Conciliation Committee, the large House of Commons majority which supported the Bill, and the general public, and the vast numbers of as yet non-militant women'. While she felt that they should have accepted 'nothing less than immediate facilities for the Bill', she did not want to risk being seen as the wrecker of the Conciliation Committee. She argued that if the Committee's work was compromised or wrecked, 'it should be the Government, not we, who break it. If renewed militancy became inevitable, better let the Government make the need for it clear.'[40] On 7 June Christabel announced a surprising departure from their five-year by-election policy: the WSPU would not oppose Liberal candidates if they agreed to support the Conciliation Bill and oppose any widening amendments. The policy was only in place for the next two by-elections after events in the House of Commons caused a return to their strategy to 'Keep The Liberal Out'.[41]

Militants like Emily Davison were itching to enact the slogan 'Deeds Not Words'. Christabel urged members to join the Women's Coronation Procession on 17 June and attend the evening meeting at the Albert Hall, to demonstrate the scale and scope of the demand for votes for women: 'Everything depends on numbers, and if the deputation is sufficiently large, the authorities will be placed in an insurmountable difficulty.' Sir Edward Grey announced that the week allocated for the Conciliation Bill would be 'elastic', and there was hope the bill would be passed. Two weeks later, on 16 June, the prime minister wrote to Lord Lytton that Grey had accurately reflected the government's intentions and that they would not oppose 'proper use of the closure', that if the bill got through the Committee of the House the extra time needed for the third reading 'would not be refused'. Asquith reported that the Cabinet had agreed 'to give effect not only in the letter but in the spirit to the promise in regard to facilities which I made on their behalf before the General Election'.[42]

Forty years later Christabel Pankhurst looked back to the beginning of 1911 and remembered the optimism she felt at the prospect of the coronation of King George V and what that might mean for the Cause. 'Never had a year begun in so much hope. It might be coronation year for the women's cause as well as for the King and Queen.'[43] She explained the significance of the Women's Coronation Procession on 17 June 1911, a week before the coronation of the King: 'We decided to prepare the most imposing peaceful demonstration ... a great women's procession and Pageant of Empire to proceed through London.' The WSPU decided shrewdly that votes for women would be presented in a peaceful and spectacular way.[44]

The day before the Women's Coronation Procession the outlook seemed promising even to the hard-headed Christabel, who wrote 'a hasty note' to Lord Lytton sending 'a thousand thanks'. Christabel's note said 'how much relieved we are by the Prime Minister's message which does really seem to give us an assurance on which we can depend and can make the basis of our work for the coming months'. She thought 'immense progress' had been made; 'we may all be happy I think'.[45] When Christabel Pankhurst met Henry Brailsford the day before the procession she told him that the WSPU would be issuing no threats, 'and militancy if it is required will start gradually'.

Brailsford wrote to Lytton that he was 'still altogether more hopeful. The feeling in the House is all that we could wish.'[46]

Estimates of the number of women who took part in the procession range from 40,000 to 60,000 – representing the whole of the women's suffrage movement. They marched to seventy-five bands. A thousand embroidered and painted banners fluttered. Some of the banners which survive are an elegant mix of the beautiful and the homespun. The exquisitely appliquéd Hammersmith WSPU banner, designed by Sylvia Pankhurst, of velvet and damask, measuring 200 by 96 centimetres, with three panels of hammers, horseshoes and irises bearing the slogan 'Deeds Not Words', and the silver-threaded gold satin and silk banner of the Hampstead Church League for Women's Suffrage, the shield-shaped banner of dark pink velvet with 'Victoria Queen and Mother' in cloth-of-gold letters, are in contrast to the homemade banners recycled from old curtains. Chelsea WSPU's banner of several pieces of cotton sewn together, measuring 100 by 84 centimetres, has a painted scene of two chubby policemen guarding Holloway Prison. Behind them a suffragette is waving a flag proclaiming 'Votes for Women' from one window.

One of the striking photographs of the Women's Coronation Procession is of a suffragette dressed as the WSPU's patron saint, Joan of Arc. Margery Bryce, aged nineteen, led the procession on a white horse and in full armour. Her sister, Rosalind 'Tiny' Bryce, aged sixteen, dressed as a medieval page, led the horse by the bridle. The big guns from Clement's Inn, Emmeline Pankhurst, Christabel Pankhurst in her academic robes, Emmeline Pethick-Lawrence and Mabel Tuke walked behind Marjorie on her white charger. The Bryce sisters' membership of the WSPU was provocative to their father, John Annan Bryce, Liberal MP for the Inverness Burghs, who voted against the second reading of the Conciliation Bill and had anti-women's suffrage letters published in *The Times*.[47]

The 'Famous Women's Pageant' had twenty suffragettes dressed up as notable women from the past, among them Grace Darling, who rescued survivors from a boat wrecked off the Farne Islands in 1838; Mrs Somerville, the science writer and advocate of higher education for women and women's suffrage after whom Somerville College, Oxford, was named; the prison reformer Elizabeth Fry; Charlotte

Brontë; Josephine Butler, who campaigned for the repeal of the Contagious Diseases Acts in 1886, and Florence Nightingale.

The Reverend Evan Douglas of Llandrillo gave a goat to the Welsh contingent who marched alongside the Irish and Scottish women. He asked in the pages of *Votes for Women* for 'some kind friend to meet the goat at Paddington station on 16 June, who will stable it and feed it and lead it in the procession'. The Welsh women were led by a 'bard with a circlet of oak leaves binding his long grey locks', and they were 'much applauded in their picturesque dress with sugar-loaf hats, they marched gallantly along, some of them knitting, and all lilting a Welsh ditty'.[48] Christina and Winnie Broom took close-up photographs of the Irish women's contingent, carrying green flags with a piper in national costume. Organised by Geraldine Lennox, several were dressed in cloaks and shawls, with golden harps, outsize shamrocks and shillelaghs.[49]

The procession to the Albert Hall meeting started from Charing Cross Embankment at 5.30 p.m. The streets were packed with bystanders, curious to see what suffragettes really looked like. There were women who had been involved in hand-to-hand fighting with the police, been locked up, gone on hunger strike and been force-fed. 'There were artists, workers of all classes, including toilers in mill and factory and besides being the largest procession of women ever organised, it was the most dignified.' The cheers of men and women struggled to be heard above the brass bands and 'The March of the Women'. Viewers crammed onto balconies and when the women reached Trafalgar Square 'the dense crowd spread over the monuments and walls'. There were several notables on the long walk to the meeting at the Albert Hall, including Mrs Fisher, who was married to the prime minister of Australia, Mrs McGowan, wife of the premier of New South Wales, and Maud Roosevelt, niece of the ex-president of the United States. Demand for tickets was so high that an overflow meeting was held in the Empress Rooms in Kensington High Street.[50]

Members of the press were almost unanimous in their praise for the suffragette spectacle. London's evening paper, the *Star*, thought it 'the most beautiful demonstration ever seen in the streets of London ... A triumph of organising ability ... It also proves that women are capable of emulating masculine endurance of physical fatigue ... Nothing can prevent the triumph of a cause which behind it has such vast reserves of courage and conviction.' The *Dundee Evening Telegraph* said it was 'the best thing the Suffragettes have done'. The *Sheffield Daily Telegraph* reported that the demonstration was on so grand a scale 'it must have impressed even the most rabid and reactionary "antis" with some idea of the driving force behind suffrage agitation'. The *Aberdeen Journal* pronounced that the demonstration was an indication that votes for women 'seems not very far off'. The *Daily Mirror* reported that the mill workers and weavers were dressed in their working clothes, 'and these brave tired women, who had left their homes to demonstrate for their fellow-toilers, were loudly cheered by the crowd'.[51]

Mary Blathwayt came to London with many Bath supporters. As the Royal Albert Hall filled the 'long line of women seemed to wind itself into a great ball'. The fronts of the boxes were draped with suffragette banners. Christabel Pankhurst moved the resolution 'That this meeting rejoices in the coming triumph of the votes for women cause, and pledges itself to use any and every means necessary to turn to account the Prime Minister's pledge of full and effective facilities for the Women's Enfranchisement Bill.' This was a warning: the WSPU's truce was contingent on parliamentary progress in the current session. The resolution, which was seconded by Mrs Pethick-Lawrence and supported by Annie Besant, was carried amid much 'fervour and enthusiasm'. As treasurer, Mrs Pethick-Lawrence's role that evening was to fill the war chest. More than £100,000 was raised; in addition to women removing their jewellery and placing it on the collection plates that were taken round, 'women moved quietly towards the platform from all parts of the building carrying promissory cards, and the treasurer, speaking at the rate of several hundred pounds a minute, read their contents aloud … there was not time to finish the counting of the promised subscriptions before the end of the meeting'.[52]

In the Lytton Family Papers there is evidence of Constance Lytton's proselytising for women's suffrage in her local community. The results of three years of earnest campaigning in her local village of Knebworth are in a handwritten testimonial dated 30 June addressed to Constance's brother, Lord Lytton. Miss Ellen Avery, the headmistress of the village elementary school for the past ten years, and member of the WSPU, wrote: 'We the Suffrage women of Knebworth and Woolmer Green beg that you will accept our most sincere thanks for the splendid way in which you have laboured for our Cause, and for the Pledge which you have given for the coming year.' On behalf of forty-one other women who signed the document, Miss Avery thanked Lord Lytton for 'his faith in us as Women which has so greatly encouraged us, and we hope and believe that in the years to come the Women of our Race – strong in the Freedom which you have done so much to win – will abundantly justify that faith'. Seventeen women bore the WSPU affiliation next to their names. The signatories included Dora Beedham, née Spong, whom we have already met; Jeanie Wilson, whose husband was a land agent; Edith Williams, a farm manager's wife; Mrs Martha Welland, a hotel proprietor and licensed victualler, and her daughters Lillian and Elsie. Florence Sexton was a teacher and her eighteen-year-old sister Annie was a 'monitoress' in the same school; Eliza Hill, a widow of seventy-three; and Ethel Smith, the cook at Constance Lytton's home, who was the only servant in the Lytton household to sign the testimonial.[53]

Nine of the Knebworth women were members of the NUWSS. Elsie Staines was the wife of the congregational minister; Isabella Wallace was a potato farmer's wife and the mother of six children; Edith Ramsay Plowden was a wood carver and designer; Marion Buchanan was the wife of an East India merchant; Mary Muirhead and two of her eight children, Maggie, thirty-two, and Bessie, thirty, also signed.[54]

Illness forced Minnie Baldock, founder of the WSPU in Canning Town, to abandon her organising career in July 1911. Minnie had had an operation for cancer in the summer of 1911 at the New Hospital for Women in Euston Road. Christabel Pankhurst visited her in hospital: the operation was a success – Minnie lived to the age of ninety and died in Dorset in 1954. She occasionally gave speeches for the WSPU, and in 1912 joined the Church League for Women's Suffrage. It was a worrying year: high unemployment led the Baldocks to leave Canning Town for Liverpool in search of work for her husband and sons Harry and John, all of whom worked in the shipbuilding industry.[55]

During the summer Mrs Pankhurst embarked on a five-month campaign tour promoting the Conciliation Bill in England, Scotland and Wales. Her chauffeur was Aileen Preston. That summer Aileen Preston advertised her services in the classified advertisement columns of the *Morning Post* and *Votes for Women*: 'Lady Chauffeur, RAC certificate, can do running repairs. What offers?' She was hired by Clement's Inn to drive Mrs Pankhurst around in an 'enormous forty-horse-power car for a pound a week'. Aileen Preston was at first apprehensive about the prospect of driving the Wolseley car presented by a generous female donor. She remembered the five months 'swathed in motor-veils and swamped in dust ... it was a hot dry summer'. It was a pioneering journey, like driving through the Wild West: 'there were few tarmac roads and shocking cambers ... the engine got hot and boiled and tyres got roasted and burst.' She quickly learned that 'come what may Mrs Pankhurst must be got to her meeting on time and there were some hair-raising moments. In the event of a puncture I would have to jack Mrs Pankhurst up as well as the car.' The intrepid chauffeur saw a great deal of Mrs Pankhurst's 'remarkable forceful and tremendous personality ... she never gave praise or blame ... and we understood that her life was dedicated to the cause and we gave her our best'. The drive through the Lake District included the Kirkstone Pass where her passenger was nervous about the descents, and Aileen had to be careful not to overuse the brakes in case the tyres – which were close to the petrol tank – caught fire. That leg was 'hazardous'. The journey back to London in the heat of August was challenging; the car had five punctures and in the end they had to abandon it and complete their journey by train.

On 4 October 1911 Mrs Pankhurst sailed for New York on a fundraising tour of the United States. She was in Minneapolis when she heard that on 21 November Lloyd George had 'torpedoed' the Conciliation Bill: 'I was so staggered that I could scarcely command myself sufficiently to fulfil my immediate engagements ... my first wild thought was to cancel all engagements and return to England', but she did fulfil her commitments. By the time Mrs Pankhurst returned to England on 11 January 1912 the WSPU 'had entered upon a new and more vigorous stage of militancy'.[56]

*

On 17 October 1911 Millicent Fawcett's letter to *The Times* alerted its readers to the recent enfranchisement of women in California, joining the states of Wyoming (1869); Colorado (1893); Utah (1895); Idaho (1896) and Washington (1910). She included the enfranchisement of women in New Zealand (1893) and states in Australia: South Australia (1894); Western Australia (1899); New South Wales, (1902); Tasmania (1903); Queensland (1905); Victoria (1908); and also Finland in 1906. The recent experience of California was of 'great political significance, and will be an important encouragement to the cause of women's suffrage all over the world'. On the same page *The Times* reported a WSPU meeting at the London Pavilion, presided over by Christabel Pankhurst, who dismissed Lloyd George's attempts to widen the Conciliation Bill, which would wreck the bill – as he well knew – and continue to delay women getting the vote. 'Our conviction is that Mr Lloyd George is promoting his amendment with the object of destroying the Conciliation Bill.' Whenever his name was mentioned there were hisses, and the consensus was that his 'one object was to prevent women getting the vote on any terms whatever before the next General Election ... and he had yet to convince them that they were mistaken'.[57]

Meanwhile, in America Mrs Pankhurst's tour was going well and *Votes for Women* readers were kept up to date as to her progress. When she spoke at the Brooklyn Academy of Music Mrs Harriet Blatch introduced her as 'the woman who in all the world is doing the most for the suffrage'. The *Brooklyn Eagle* reported how 'the roof rang with applause which lasted for five minutes when Mrs Pankhurst made her appearance'. Her choice of words was 'simple and she spoke plainly and directly'. When she addressed the National American Woman Suffrage Association Convention in Louisville, Kentucky, she explained the role of militancy: 'We began with argument, and when we found that argument was accomplishing nothing we went to the record books of man's enfranchisement and decided to adopt some of the methods some of the men themselves had adopted. We made it politically dangerous for the men to oppose us in our movement.'[58]

On 7 November the prime minister took everyone by surprise by announcing that during the following parliamentary session of 1912 the government would introduce a Manhood Suffrage Bill – to grant votes to the small percentage of men who were as yet unenfranchised – and frame it in such a way that it could include a women's suffrage amendment. The WSPU was incandescent. Recalling that autumn in her memoir, Christabel described the feelings of those close to the struggle: 'The mockery of it was that there had been no real work done to bring about a wider franchise, and the Manhood Suffrage Bill was the fruit of our agitation for votes for women!' Mrs Fawcett said that 'if it had been Mr Asquith's object to enrage every Woman Suffragette to the point of frenzy, he could not have acted with greater perspicacity'. Once their incandescence had evaporated, years later Christabel remembered feeling icily calm: 'We militants were not frenzied, we were firm. We were not moved by an impulse of blind rage but by the determination to act.'[59]

Two days later 'General' Flora Drummond wrote to the secretaries of every branch announcing the resumption of their anti-government policy after months of patient truce. A deputation to Westminster was being organised for Tuesday 21 November, and secretaries and organisers were asked to muster their members to come to London. They were also asked to write to their local Liberal or Labour MPs and say they expected them to vote against the proposed Manhood Suffrage Bill at every stage unless the government acted beforehand to introduce a genuine measure of adult suffrage which gave votes to women as well as to men. Flora Drummond told them to make it clear 'that we absolutely refuse to trust any amendment to the Government's Manhood Suffrage Bill and that we regard the proposal that we should do so as insulting to our intelligence'.[60]

11

Breaking Windows

The Conciliation Bill is 'Torpedoed'
21 November 1911

*Mrs Pankhurst's youngest daughter, Adela, far left, and her friends proudly hold
the frame of a window broken by their comrades in 1912.*

On 9 November 1911 Lord Lytton received the dreaded letter from Christabel withdrawing WSPU support for the Conciliation Bill. She reminded him of the prime minister's shoddy behaviour: 'he has twice broken the spirit of his pledge, twice repeated in letters to yourself', and was 'honour bound to offer some sufficient compensation ... the enfranchisement of women as part of the Government's measure to be introduced next session'. She refused to accept the offer of an amendment to the Manhood Suffrage Bill 'as to obtain votes for women in this way is foredoomed to failure'. Christabel Pankhurst also dismissed any promises Lloyd George made: 'his record where woman suffrage is concerned is not a happy one. He inspires us with the most profound distrust, and we regard him as an opponent of our movement.' Christabel promised the WSPU's 'uncompromising hostility' to the government's policy of women having to depend on the fate of amendments to get the vote. She announced that the Union intended resuming and invigorating their anti-government tactics, launched by a large deputation to Westminster on 21 November, 'to express to the Prime Minister and the Chancellor of the Exchequer their profound indignation at the Government's latest betrayal'.[1]

The suffragettes met at the Pavilion Theatre, Shaftesbury Avenue, on 13 November. Christabel Pankhurst was in full battle mode, calling for a thousand women volunteers to take part in the deputation. With memories of Black Friday still raw she also asked Londoners 'to see that the authorities did not ill-use women as they had done on previous occasions'. The women would fight against any Manhood Suffrage Bill which did not include women because 'the glorification of the male just because he was a male was a plunge into barbarism, the negation of progress and a monstrous proposal which women would fight against with every bit of their strength'. Loud cheers greeted Christabel when she said, 'Lloyd Georgitis seemed to be a disease which afflicted men today and with very few exceptions.' She said that women had seen through Lloyd George and 'they must fight against him here and now'.[2]

The next day Emmeline Pethick-Lawrence explained the symbolism of having a thousand women in Westminster that day in a letter to local activists. Members were urged to 'rouse your women up and send me names of volunteers', and gather as many as possible like 'Garibaldi with his thousand who set a nation free'. The WSPU was told, 'if we have a thousand it will be impossible for the Government to punish any ... I will lay this task most seriously upon you, simply everything depends upon it'.

Mrs Pethick-Lawrence described the 'very grave crisis' they were facing: that if the Manhood Suffrage Bill was passed in 1912 British women would be in a position of 'complete political subjection to men as the ruling caste'; that the government's recent behaviour was 'humbug and an affront to our intelligence'; that 'submission was unthinkable' and called on women to consider it their public duty 'to put aside considerations of health, of private ties of friendship and relationships and of personal business of all kinds' to come to Westminster on 'active service' and 'strike a blow against the enslavement of half the nation'. The deputation would take place whatever announcements were made by the government in the following days.[3]

The day before a deputation of nine women's suffrage societies visited Herbert Asquith and Lloyd George at 10 Downing Street on 17 November, the WSPU held a packed meeting at the Royal Albert Hall which could seat 5,000. Pumped up by Mrs Pethick-Lawrence's rhetoric the suffragettes were in no mood for Asquith's shilly-shallying. Mrs Pankhurst had sent a cable to the Albert Hall from America: 'I share your indignation at the Government's insult to women and am ready to renew the fight.' The meeting urged the government to abandon the Manhood Suffrage Bill and to introduce a bill which would grant equal franchise rights to men and women. Mrs Pethick-Lawrence spoke passionately, warning that if the prime minister refused she would lead a protest against his refusal, that the Conciliation Bill was dead, 'slain not by our hand. Militancy is not dead', and that the government 'had nothing to fear from the women except militancy'. She told the meeting that she would remind Herbert Asquith that the WSPU had pledged to end militancy until 1912 because they wanted the coronation of the King to 'pass without any unpleasantness', and she announced the clear threat, 'I think we have got to do more fighting.'[4]

Annie Kenney was present at the meeting. Of the thirty women's suffrage activists Annie felt the WSPU had been admitted 'on sufferance'. Christabel Pankhurst thought the prime minister looked as if he was in a genial mood, so 'rosy-faced and smiling, he might have been Father Christmas with votes for women in his bag of presents', whereas Lloyd George was 'pale and lowering'. So sham was both men's behaviour that a stranger 'would have taken Mr Asquith for the champion of votes for women and Mr Lloyd George for the hardened and implacable anti-suffragist'.[5] Since Mrs Pankhurst was in America, Emmeline Pethick-Lawrence led the militant suffragettes who included Mabel Tuke, Constance Lytton and the American actress Elizabeth Robins.

Mrs Millicent Fawcett represented the NUWSS; Lady Betty Balfour and Lady Selborne spoke for the Conservative and Unionist Women's Franchise Association. Charlotte Despard and Edith How-Martyn expressed the Women's Freedom League's position. Eva Gore-Booth, of the Women Textile and Other Workers' Representation Committee, and Esther Roper of the National Industrial and Professional Women's Suffrage Society, added the views of the women in the north of England. But the women's words fell on deaf ears and Asquith told them that he intended to pass a Manhood Suffrage Bill in the forthcoming parliamentary session in 1912, refusing to abandon his plan to grant votes to men who had not even asked for them instead of giving equal franchise rights to men and women. Asquith also reiterated the unhelpful opinion that if the women were unhappy with the situation they should try a private members' amendment to the Manhood Suffrage Bill. Christabel Pankhurst could not contain her anger and Asquith responded by patronising her, saying her speech was 'very able' which used 'one or two rather strong expressions' to which he insisted he did not take exception. He expressed disquiet that she 'talked in terms of peace … presenting a pistol in one hand and a dagger in the other at the Government'. He disliked Mrs Pethick-Lawrence suggesting the women had been tricked and betrayed by him and his government. Going back on previous pledges, Asquith threw down the gauntlet: 'I quite understand Miss Pankhurst's position. She says it is our duty ourselves to introduce a Bill conferring the franchise on women on the same terms as men … We have never promised to do anything of the kind. If you ask me why we won't do it, I will tell you once more: I am the head of the Government and I am not going to make myself responsible for the introduction of a measure which I do not conscientiously believe to be in the best interest of the country.'[6]

As they listened to their colleagues lobbying the two most important politicians in the country, Annie Kenney and Constance Lytton found themselves standing by Margot Asquith, an adamant 'anti-suffragist'. It was an uncomfortable experience, and years later Annie Kenney remembered Mrs Asquith's unpleasant and sarcastic presence; she 'seemed highly amused at the earnestness of the speakers'. When the meeting ended Annie approached Herbert Asquith and asked him whether he thought of himself as a statesman. Affronted, he asked her who she was and looked 'angry and nervous'. Annie said: 'I'm a militant, and we all hate and distrust you. Do you call yourself a statesman?' Asquith told Annie he would not discuss 'this question' with her and she warned him that she was determined to 'discuss it with you at every public meeting you choose to hold'. Christabel Pankhurst saw Annie Kenney and the prime minister 'mentally at daggers drawn' and walked over to them, looked at Asquith 'with contempt' and told Annie: 'Don't fret yourself about him, he is not worth it. Our fight will be on public ground.'[7]

Christabel and Emmeline returned to Clement's Inn and wrote a press release titled 'Premier's Reply to Suffragists. WSPU's Attitude – Hostilities Resumed'. They announced they were 'entirely dissatisfied with the attitude of the Government as declared … this morning to the Woman Deputation'. They denounced the prime minister's words as an act of 'direct hostility to the claims of women. The Government's cynical manoeuvrings had undermined and destroyed the possibility of a non-party women's suffrage measure standing any real chance of success in the foreseeable future.'[8]

Annie Kenney went to Bath the next day to brief members about her encounter with the prime minister and the chancellor of the exchequer. She 'gave a splendid speech', and reminded the two most important politicians in the country that it was often said that women did not want the vote because men were their natural protectors. She asked Asquith and Lloyd George why women were not afraid of wild animals but of their 'natural protectors'.

The Tenth Women's Parliament at Caxton Hall preceded the WSPU's indignant march to the House of Commons and Downing Street on 21 November. A chorus gathered on the suffragette stage to protest at Lloyd George's 'torpedoing' of the Conciliation Bill. Two hundred and twenty women and four men would be arrested that evening, most sent to prison for offences ranging from obstructing and assaulting the police, to wilful damage, attacking windows of government buildings in Whitehall, the homes of cabinet ministers and shops in the West End of London.[9]

In Caxton Hall Mrs Pethick-Lawrence said that if the government and the police made any attempt to treat women as they had on Black Friday the consequences 'would be on their own head'. The anniversary of that dark day had taken place three days earlier and the memories were painful: 'We who are on the deputation tonight are already outside our body. We know that our hands, our feet and all that we have are being used by the great Spirit to carry out the great purposes of his Will … We go tonight not only to fight for the freedom of women of our own country, but to carry a message of deliverance to the whole world.' At eight o'clock she led a deputation of about thirty women, planning to force their way through the police cordon across Parliament Square, to enter the House of Commons, and on the floor of the Chamber to protest at 'the great insult that had been done to the women of the country … the time for words had passed, the time for action had come'.[10]

The choreography of the events of 21 November took a familiar trajectory: rousing speeches by the leadership in a banner-festooned Caxton Hall, the passing of a strongly worded resolution in a heady atmosphere, and the march of angry feet towards the police cordons across Parliament Square for the pushing and shoving. In keeping with the order with which WSPU events were stage-managed, the participants were well-briefed by the leadership. In her 'final instructions'

Miss A. B. Hambling, who had been at Clement's Inn since 1907, and had worked closely with Jessie Kenney in the 'pester the politicians' campaign of 1909, reminded volunteers 'not to bring more money than is absolutely necessary, not to wear jewellery, furs, not to carry umbrellas'.[11] If they were arrested and charged they were told not to make a statement as anything the women said to the police could be used in evidence against them. They could expect to be bailed out (by Fred Pethick-Lawrence) and would have to appear at Bow Street or any of the other courts that were tasked with handling the arrested women the next day. Miss Hambling said they should go to the court hearing with a handbag and take 'night things and a change of clothing, brush, comb … also do not forget to come provided with food sufficient to keep you going for the next day as the proceedings may be lengthy'. As for those who ended up in prison, they would be further advised by Mrs Pethick-Lawrence 'you need not worry as everything has been foreseen' and Miss Hambling reminded them that Rule 243a 'regarding prison treatment of suffragists still holds good'.[12]

This was a new stage in the suffragette campaign: scores of women had volunteered to deliberately break the law and risk arrest and imprisonment. This took the WSPU's campaign to a new level of mass militancy. At seven o'clock that evening dozens of women left the Woman's Press, 156 Charing Cross Road, armed with bags of stones and toffee hammers and set off in ones and twos, walking or travelling by motor car and taxi to break government windows in Whitehall – the Home Office, the Local Government Board, the Treasury, the Scottish Office – and commercial premises in the West End. This was a new departure: the buildings targeted in the West End had no obvious links with the Liberal Party or the government. The next morning the superintendents and proprietors of Somerset House, the post office and shops in the Strand, the Midland Railway offices in Great George Street, the London and North Western Railway in Parliament Street and the Westminster Palace Hotel, the Guards' Club, Cunard's offices, Dunn's hat shop, Swan and Edgar's store, and unfriendly newspapers like the *Daily Mail* and the *Daily Express*, were confronted with smashed windows. By the end of November 200 suffragettes would be serving time in Holloway.[13]

Only a dozen women reached the cordon drawn up across the road at St Margaret's church next to Westminster Abbey. Several suffragettes

Suffragettes who had been to prison would dress up in replica prison clothing. Here they are canvassing against the Liberals at the Chelmsford by-election in 1908.

Mrs Flora Drummond, centre, gave Mary Phillips, left, a 'Highland welcome' on her release from Holloway in September 1908.

In Trafalgar Square Flora Drummond urges the crown to 'rush' the House of Commons on 13 October 1908.

THE NEW MRS PARTINGTON (OF THE ANTI SUFFRAGE SOCIETY)
'SOMEHOW THE TIDE KEEPS RISING'!

Ernestine Mills, an artist and WSPU member, lampoons the opponents of women's suffrage.

Charlotte Augusta Leopoldine Marsh, known as Charlie, became a WSPU organiser after qualifying as a sanitary inspector in 1908, aged twenty-one. Riding a white horse she was often the standard-bearer at suffragette processions.

In June 1909 Marion Wallace-Dunlop was imprisoned for stencilling 'It is the right of the subject to petition the King, and all commitments and prosecutions for such petitions are illegal,' on the walls of the House of Commons.

Despite having a weak heart Lady Constance Lytton was an ardent suffragette, serving three prison sentences. In 1912 she had a stroke and had to learn to write with her left hand.

Mary Leigh served nine prison sentences during her suffragette career which included rooftop protests and throwing a hatchet into Prime Minister Asquith's carriage in Dublin.

New Yorker Lucy Burns joined the WSPU in London in 1909 while on holiday. She went to prison three times and returned to the US in 1912.

Alice Paul, born in New Jersey, joined the WSPU in 1908 and went to prison four times. She returned to America in 1910.

Vera Holme, known as 'Jack' to her friends, was an actress and male impersonator, a fine horsewoman, and sometime chauffeuse to Mrs Pankhurst.

Mary Leigh was the drum major of the Women's Drum and Fife Band whose uniform was in the WSPU's colours of purple, white and green.

The Woman's Press office and shop opened at 156 Charing Cross Road in May 1910, selling a large range of suffragist literature and merchandise.

Laura Ainsworth, aged twenty-four, was sent to Winson Green Prison for two weeks for throwing stones outside Prime Minister Asquith's meeting at Bingley Hall in Birmingham.

Gladice Keevil was twenty-three when she joined the WSPU in 1907. She campaigned in the Midlands, Devon and Belfast; in 1908 she served six weeks in Holloway.

Jennie Baines witnessed the first militant protest by Annie Kenney and Christabel Pankhurst at the Free Trade Hall, Manchester, in 1905, and joined the WSPU.

Ada Flatman, right, at a demonstration in 1909. She was the WSPU's organiser in Liverpool from 1909 to 1911.

Charlotte Marsh, tall, in the middle, and Vera Holme, in peaked cap, canvassing at the Cheltenham by-election, April 1911.

This postcard and poster was produced by the Suffrage Atelier in 1912.

The WSPU's policy of 'pestering the politicians' gave valuable publicity to the Cause. Two general elections in 1910 presented hundreds of opportunities to heckle Liberal politicians.

Messages sent on postcards were the tweets of their day. From 1909 the force-feeding of hunger striking suffragettes became a popular subject.

were arrested as they tried to barge and squeeze their way past the solid line of policemen, and were taken to Canon Row police station. Three members of the deputation managed to climb the railings in Parliament Square and run towards the statue of Benjamin Disraeli, where they were arrested before they could enter Parliament. Another woman almost got into the Square by 'hanging like a street-boy on to the back of a taxi-cab'; others chained themselves to the railings of Parliament Square. Only the intrepid May Billinghurst reached St Stephen's Entrance in her invalid tricycle decorated with the slogan 'Votes for Women'. Mindful of the bad press they had received a year ago the police allowed her through their lines and arrested her immediately. The women who had volunteered to be window-smashers were told to wait until Big Ben struck the first stroke of eight before taking any action.[14]

Mrs Pethick-Lawrence was arrested for obstruction and at Bow Street Court Constable 274M testified that when he warned Mrs Pethick-Lawrence to 'Mind what you are doing, please', she had punched him twice in the face with her fist. Under cross-examination, the policeman denied he had grabbed one of the women and that Mrs Pethick-Lawrence had asked him to let her go. Emmeline explained to the magistrate, Mr Marsham, that Constable 274M had his hand round the throat of one of her comrades and in order to make him release her she had struck him twice with the back of her gloved hand. Mrs Pethick-Lawrence reminded the magistrate that the last time the WSPU had protested in Westminster a year ago, several women had been badly injured and one woman eventually died. She was glad to say there had been no repetition of the brutal treatment although some of the scenes had been 'as repugnant to the women as they had been to the magistrate'. They did not want to struggle with the police in the streets and had no wish to damage property; they 'suffered acutely in these demonstrations and undergoing the penalties that were inflicted' upon them. However, the women had been forced to learn that this was 'the only way to secure their freedom, and, cost what it might, they were prepared to pay the price. (Cheers).'[15]

Mr Marsham said she had not committed a serious assault but that as she was the leader of the deputation she would have to serve a month in the second division cells. Fred Pethick-Lawrence was waiting for her when she arrived at the gates of Holloway and she told him to tell WSPU members that she was 'glad and proud' to have led the deputation and was ready to undergo imprisonment because she 'would not allow a comrade to be ill-used', and asked Fred to give them all a message: 'Be Ready.' The horrors of hunger-striking and force-feeding endured by suffragettes in the recent past were not repeated as the prisoners served their time in vastly improved conditions under Rule 243a. Emmeline Pethick-Lawrence remembered the time warmly and with a certain affection: 'We wore our own clothes, exercised together in perfect freedom, played a sort of football in the yard, got ourselves in fancy-dress and behaved as though we were at a house party.'[16]

Rose Lamartine Yates's husband Tom was arrested that night but was not charged. His wholehearted support for Rose's involvement with the suffragettes and his membership of the Men's Political Union for Women's Enfranchisement emerged as an issue years later when accounts of the suffragette campaign were being written up. In the 1920s Rose Lamartine Yates asked Edith How-Martyn that 'no reference should be made to my husband's arrests in the press – he suffered in his business on that account and it would not be fair to draw attention to his contact with the police and thus prejudice them [the firm] on account of their senior partner'.[17]

Kitty Marshall's crime was to shout 'Charge' when she was close to Number 10, which she thought was 'not much to say to get ten days in prison'. One of the Misses Beck was 'hurled against the doorstep of Number 10 and was arrested, which the sisters were pleased about, for they felt they had tried to show that militancy was the only way left for us to get votes for women, all other ways having failed'. Miss Beck's fine was paid as the 'valiant lady was rather too old for prison' but was very glad she had 'tried to help in the struggle'.[18]

Kitty Marshall was blessed with a supportive husband whom she married in 1904. Her life had turned full circle since 1901 when she petitioned her first husband, Hugh Finch, for divorce. Finch was the son of a vicar and a doctor, but the epitome of a cad. Within ten months she was free of the man who, in 1899, 'committed adultery with some woman unknown and thereby contracted a venereal disease and wilfully communicated such a venereal disease to her'.[19] Kitty was familiar with Downing Street. Every Friday she would deliver a copy of *Votes for Women*, hammering with the knocker four times and shouting 'Votes for women' before handing the newspaper to the commissionaire.[20]

Lady Constance Lytton's health did not deter her from going with 'Leslie Lawless', the cheeky alias of Leslie McMurdo, to attack the windows of the post office in Victoria Street with a hammer and stones. Constance's comrade from Liverpool, Dr Alice Ker, stayed with Constance in her flat on the night of the raid. Alice, who had a general practice in Birkenhead, and her seventeen-year-old daughter Margaret, were active members. She came to London wanting to 'come to the fray but she did not wish to get arrested'. Constance revealed that the WSPU's aim was for the women 'not to let ourselves be broken to pieces, but [to inflict] damage of an unmistakable kind'.[21] As soon as Big Ben struck eight Constance smashed the glass of two doors and a window, having reconnoitred the building the day before 'to make sure of my bearings. I studied all the windows where it would be safe to do the work of smashing without hurting anyone inside.' She said to 'Leslie Lawless', 'I can wait no longer' and broke the window in such a way that there could be no mistaking that she was responsible. Leslie smashed the windows to Constance's right. Constance was afraid that she had not been seen but two charming policemen smiled and said, 'I'll take you this way, lady', and walked her slowly to Canon Row police station, disarming her on the way. Miss Lawless followed close behind.[22]

When Constance Lytton arrived the police station was already packed with suffragettes. They were searched by a wardress who told them, 'Oh, you ladies, I'd be with you tomorrow if it weren't for my child. I am a widow with one child. If only these politicians knew what that meant.' Constance felt warmed by the atmosphere and 'all was joy and triumph ... I felt quite an old hand.' Fred Pethick-Lawrence arrived to bail them. Constance remembered being driven down Whitehall in a taxi to her sister's house in Bloomsbury, looking out of the window and seeing Whitehall had 'the mark of the women upon it, with the unmistakable smashing, till it looked, as I passed, as though every window smiled'.[23]

Three days later at Bow Street Court Constance Lytton told the magistrate Mr Marsham that she had used a hammer because she realised that 'it was the only form of protest left for the women to make against the action of the government in refusing to all women the elements of representation'. She and 'Leslie Lawless' chose to go

to prison for two weeks rather than pay a fine. On the morning of
her court appearance Constance had a 'heart collapse', a mild stroke,
and could not speak or lift her head. Without calling for a doctor
Constance made her way to Bow Street where her voice returned and
she made a frail but brave speech.[24]

Mary Leigh, one of the first two suffragettes to break windows in
1908, was sentenced to two months in prison with hard labour for
assaulting a policeman in Parliament Square, a charge she denied,
insisting she had acted to defend another woman. Constance Lytton
was outraged at Mary Leigh's sentence and so she wrote to Home
Secretary Reginald McKenna (he had taken office on 24 October
1911) complaining at the harshness of Mary's sentence, accusing him
of giving herself preferential treatment because she was the sister of
Lord Lytton. Since her roof-top and hunger-striking protest of 1909
Mary Leigh had campaigned at by-elections in Wales and was arrested
on Black Friday, but discharged. Earlier in 1911 Mary was living in
north London when she evaded the Census, and was sent to prison
for refusing to pay her dog tax.[25]

The artist Marion Wallace-Dunlop was arrested for the fifth time
and served her last prison sentence, having broken windows at the
Home Office, and was sent to prison for three weeks. Earlier she had
acted as the suffragettes' quarter master, handing out hammers and
black bags filled with stones which had been sourced by suffragettes
in 'motors driven at dusk to quiet country lanes where flints could be
gathered'. Since her last stay in Holloway in the summer of 1909 –
when she introduced the hunger strike to the WSPU's repertoire
of protest – Marion Wallace-Dunlop had worked with fellow artist
Edith Downing to design some of the most handsome suffragette
processions. When asked about her recreations for her entry in the
Suffrage Annual and Women's Who's Who, she replied: 'No time for
them – till the vote is won.'[26]

Four members of the Duval family went on the deputation to
Parliament: Mrs Emily Duval, two of her daughters, Emily and
Barbara, and son Victor. Emily Duval, who had recently rejoined the
WSPU, ending her four-year membership of the WFL because they
were not militant enough, broke windows at the Local Government
Board and was sent to prison for two weeks. Victor ended up in
Pentonville for five days.[27]

Bertha Brewster broke a window of the National Liberal Club and served three weeks in prison, as did Edith Rigby of Preston, who also smashed windows. Ada Wright, whom we last saw sprawling face down across the pavement on Black Friday, was arrested, for the fifth time in her suffragette career, with Joan Dugdale for breaking cabinet minister 'Loulou' Harcourt's windows in Berkeley Square. Ada was sent to prison for two weeks; she wrote to a friend that the night before taking part in any militant event 'the suspense always tries me terribly'.[28]

Evelina Haverfield served her first prison sentence – fourteen days in the second division cells – for obstructing the police. In the mêlée the journalist Henry Nevinson saw Evelina's close friend Vera Holme make the first suffragette attack. Vera 'dashed straight at a mounted policeman and seized the horse's bridle and tried to turn his head against the cordon to lead it away from the line'. Vera was dragged away by three policemen, and 'after a prolonged struggle she was led away' and was sentenced to five days in Holloway.[29]

Kitty Marion threw two stones at the windows of the Home Office in Whitehall and was sentenced to three weeks in prison. When she was arrested she told the constable cryptically, 'Lloyd George will pay.' At Bow Street the next day she said she had committed the acts as a protest against the government's response to the deputation which she said was 'an insult to the women's cause'. When he suggested, 'Possibly you women may get votes if you behave properly', Kitty replied, 'Men don't always behave properly, and they have the vote.' When Kitty was given the option of paying a fine she shouted at the magistrate, 'If I had a million pounds I wouldn't pay.' When she was released from Holloway on 13 December she went to spend Christmas with a new friend, 'Lilla' Durham, who had also been arrested on 21 November. Kitty stayed in Lilla's cottage in Hartfield, Sussex, helping her sell *Votes for Women*, canvassing with her house-to-house in Tunbridge Wells and East Grinstead, both conservative towns which teemed with diehard antis.[30]

Winifred Monck-Mason, an actress whose stage name was 'Winifred Mayo', and a member of the WSPU since 1907, was arrested on 21 November for breaking windows at the Guards' Club in Pall Mall, and served three weeks in Holloway. 'It occurred to us it would be a good thing to wake up the clubmen ... so on that foggy night in

November we set off to break the windows of various clubs'. Winifred
and two others went out with their pockets full of stones but many
of the windows were too small and 'not worthy of our attack'. She
spotted the large glass swing door of the Guards' Club and she 'took
a stone and hurled it and to my great joy it broke the window ... the
porter rushed out in great indignation and seized me and sent for the
police'. When a policeman arrived she confessed to breaking the glass
and when he asked her if she had any more stones she took one out of
her pocket and broke another window while he was still holding her.[31]

On 24 November 1911, Lloyd George travelled to Bath and
spoke to 6,000 local Liberals about women's suffrage at the town's
skating rink. Because of recent events in London, the meeting was
heavily policed, and barriers prevented militant women from entering the meeting. The windows of the post office were smashed. At
the beginning a male sympathiser interrupted and was thrown out.
Despite Lloyd George's recent torpedoing of the Conciliation Bill,
'he pleaded with deep earnestness the merits of woman suffrage'; and
then 'bitterly attacked the militant agitation' which he insisted was
'deplored by most woman suffragists', accusing them of being anti-
Liberal rather than pro-suffrage. As he tried to speak Annie Kenney
took up her position on the roof of a nearby house, addressing the
crowd with a megaphone. Someone threw a missile: 'unluckily it
lodged in the megaphone and spoilt the effect'. Mabel Capper, who
had travelled from Manchester, was arrested for breaking the post
office window, the first militant act of the suffragette campaign in the
town. The next morning Mary Blathwayt carried Mabel's bags to the
Guildhall where her case was heard. She was sentenced to a month in
prison and fined £5 for the damage she caused.[32]

Mrs Millicent Fawcett's letter to Lloyd George was published in
The Times on 5 December, deploring the 'disgusting scenes' of 21 and
29 November when 'wild scenes' orchestrated by the suffragettes had
forced the prime minister to abandon a speaking engagement at the
City Temple, Holborn, to celebrate the twenty-first anniversary of
the Mansfield House university settlement in Canning Town. She told
Lloyd George that her law-abiding suffrage friends 'are constantly
asking me, "can nothing be done to stop them?" ' and that she had
no hope of being able to make the militant leaders refrain from their
tactics, invigorated by almost two years of truce and a deep sense

of betrayal. Mrs Fawcett urged Lloyd George and his allies in the Cabinet to develop a policy of justice to women and enfranchise them before the next general election as this would be 'backed by the good sense and good feeling of the country and it is even possible that the violent tactics of the Women's Social and Political Union may themselves be affected'. If the government pursued this strategy she suggested that 'the supporters and perpetrators of violence will become more and more isolated ... they will have little or no public opinion behind them'. She had been present at dozens of meetings since Lloyd George had first promised support for women's suffrage and each time when the speakers denounced violence the meeting had expressed its unanimous support; 'the English ... are not naturally a revolutionary people; they only condone revolutionary methods when all other courses seem blocked'. Mrs Fawcett was sure the public would 'laugh at riot and tumult when it is absolutely clear that the reform desired can be obtained by constitutional channels'.[33]

The WSPU leadership paid no heed to Mrs Fawcett's letter and in the weeks leading up to Christmas there was a return to noisy demonstrations outside the buildings where cabinet ministers tried to hold meetings. A nineteen-year-old male sympathiser, Allan Ross McDougall from Dundee, was so indignant at the exclusion of women suffragists from Lloyd George's meeting at the Royal Horticultural Hall in Westminster on 17 December that he threw his heavy briefcase at the chancellor as he drove away. McDougall intended to break the window of the car but the case flew though an open window and hit the chancellor on the side of his face, giving him a black eye and a badly bruised mouth, but caused no serious injury. In court he said that a woman standing nearby had wanted to break the car window but was grabbed by a policeman before she could do so and he did so on her behalf. He was sent to prison to serve two months with hard labour.[34]

On 20 December Emily Davison was released on bail of £1,000 to be tried at the Old Bailey early in the new year. Unusually, Emily had not been present at the WSPU's protest on 21 November – she was earning much-needed money 'engaged in secretarial work' – but reports of what happened that night prompted her to resign her position and accelerate the militant momentum by introducing her own new style of protest, to cause damage that could not be repaired. Her friend

Mary Leigh's tough two-month sentence, compared to Constance Lytton's two-week punishment, 'made my blood boil, the injustice and the snobbery was so great … I took it upon myself to make a protest'; she could do nothing immediately as she was employed, 'but soon I resolved to stake all'.[35] Emily gave notice to leave her employment on 1 December and made her plans. At noon on 8 December she left her office in the Strand and walked to the post office in Fleet Street, stopped in front of the 'big open-mouthed receptacle … and took out of my pocket a packet wrapped in greaseproof paper the same size as an ordinary letter. Inside was cotton soaked in kerosene … I calmly applied a match and held it for a second.' A small boy who was passing by 'stopped short on seeing what I was doing'. When the packet was flaming she dropped it into the pillar box and walked away along Fleet Street and had lunch at the first Lyons' tea room she saw. Her heart was 'beating rapidly' as she sat in the café and after ten minutes she heard 'a long shrill whistle followed by others … and I thought to myself that my object was accomplished and the letter-box was well alight'. Emily finished her lunch, returned to the scene of her crime and saw a police constable talking to a man she thought looked like a plain-clothes detective. When she saw the pillar box again she 'rejoiced greatly' to see that she had succeeded. The next day Emily, a prolific letter-writer to the newspapers, scanned the papers and was disappointed that her protest was not reported.[36]

Three days later Emily Davison returned to the scene of the crime and confessed to a policeman on duty that she had set fire to the pillar box and told him she was surrendering herself to him. He told her he knew nothing about it and could not arrest her: 'I should not think of giving you such an advertisement for your cause. You are qualifying for Colney Hatch' (a lunatic asylum). Emily asked to see the manager of the post office. She was taken to the Lady Superintendent who said she knew nothing of the incident. Frustrated and focused, Miss Davison decided to set fire to another pillar box so that she would be arrested.[37]

On 14 December Emily Davison went to the City to attack pillar boxes. Her first target was in Leadenhall Street where she set fire to a box of matches and dropped it into the box. Then she hurried to Aldgate but decided 'to do nothing as the people were all of the poorer class'. She returned to the City by omnibus and found herself at the pillar box outside the jeweller Mappin and Webb, opposite the Mansion House, the official residence of the Lord Mayor of London. She set fire to a box of matches and threw them into the pillar box. She boarded an omnibus to Hyde Park Corner, walked to the post office near Harrods and telephoned the London News Agency to say that she was the suffragette who had set fire to the pillar box in Fleet Street, and in Leadenhall Street and opposite the Mansion House that morning. Emily asked which would be the best target to attack to ensure she got herself arrested. The man she spoke to at the agency was 'very agitated and said they could not possibly give any advice'. She then went by omnibus to Parliament Street and in Bridge Street she came face-to-face with Detective Inspector Wells, who recognised her. He was with two other police-men, one of whom she knew, Detective Inspector Francis Powell, not in uniform but 'private clothes'. Emily walked past them to the post office in Parliament Street and 'took out of my pockets one of my kerosene packets, struck a match and lit it and put it in the pillar-box'. It did not burn well so she repeated the process and 'more ostentatiously set it alight and tried to post it'. Powell fol-lowed her, rushed towards her 'and grabbed the thing out of my hands, blew it out, seized me violently, breathing and trembling with emotion and said, "I knew you would do this Miss Davison."' They took Emily to Scotland Yard, charging her at Canon Row police station where she confessed to firing two pillar boxes that morning in the City. Later that day when Emily appeared before Sir Albert de Rutzen at Bow Street she was defended by the bar-rister Frank Shewell Cooper. De Rutzen asked Detective Inspector Powell if Miss Davison 'was in her right mind' and the policeman replied that she was.[38]

Emily told de Rutzen that her motive had been to protest 'against the vindictive sentence recently passed on Mary Leigh and to call upon the Government to put women's suffrage in the King's Speech at the opening of Parliament in February 1912'. She justified her actions by saying that women were so moved by the suffrage issue that 'they felt that anything that was necessary must be done regard-less of the consequences'. Sir Albert de Rutzen remanded Emily to Holloway Gaol for a week to be kept under observation. The case was adjourned and Emily was released on bail of £1,000 put up by her friends; her trial was scheduled for January 1912 at the Old Bailey.[39]

On 22 December 1911 Emily went by train to Longhorsley where her mother had a baker's shop in the village, seven miles from Morpeth. She wrote to 'dear comrades' Sarah Carwin, who had been arrested and discharged on Black Friday, and Miss Milligan, a teacher for the London County Council, expressing her delight at how high her bail had been set, 'fancy *my* being worth £1,000!! I am amazed! It is a grand advertisement for the Cause, isn't it?' Emily sounded almost ecstatic at being tried at the Old Bailey; she was sure her action 'has given them a *good* fright'.[40]

12

'The Argument of the Broken Pane'

Windows Smashed in the West End and Whitehall 1912

*Donald McGill, famous for his saucy seaside postcards,
started his career by supplying a market hungry for images
ridiculing the suffragettes.*

The front page of the first issue of *Votes for Women* for 1912 showed Joan of Arc in full armour on horseback, her sword raised high. '1912 was a year of great changes ... mild militancy belonged to the past, extreme militancy would belong to the future,' wrote Annie Kenney. *Votes for Women* announced the news of the death on the last day of December 1911 of Cecilia Haig, a tax-resister, the sister of Florence and Evelyn Haig. The notice said that Cecilia died as a result of being assaulted on Black Friday. The death certificate described her end coming after suffering from kidney cancer for seventeen months.[1]

Emmeline Pankhurst's last lecture on her tour of the USA was at Carnegie Hall, New York, on 5 January. The next day she and Marie Pethick boarded the SS *Oceania* which reached Southampton on 16 January. WSPU members were gearing up for the imminent struggle with the prime minister and his cabinet ministers, and in no mood to be conciliatory towards any new Conciliation Bill. The WSPU refused to believe there was any chance of success unless it was a government-sponsored bill giving equal suffrage rights to women.

In the middle of January two suffragettes interrupted Lord Haldane, the leader of the Liberals in the House of Lords, at a meeting in Fulham. They were ejected. At Llanelli there were ugly scenes when a crowd of 2,000 broke up a suffragette outdoor meeting and 'the ladies had to be escorted home by the police'.[2]

On 9 January 1912 Emily Davison was tried at the Old Bailey for having 'unlawfully, wilfully and maliciously placed in a letter-box in the Post Office, Fleet Street, a parcel saturated with kerosene which was likely to endanger the letter-box and its contents', and

for having placed matches in a letter box in Parliament Street on 14
December 1911. Articulate and impassioned, Emily conducted her
own defence: with the exception of a character witness, she was the
only woman in the court.[3]

The prosecution was led by Alexander Boulton, who had been the
Liberal MP for Ramsey in Huntingdonshire until January 1910. Emily
eagerly cross-examined the witnesses. Despite being reprimanded by
the Recorder, who told her that her words did not concern the jury,
Emily ploughed on: 'Although technically you may find me guilty,
morally I am not. The moral guilt lies upon you citizens of this country who stand aside from the fight for the liberties of this country,
and thereby force the women to make protests how and when they
may ... this country cannot possibly be genuinely democratic until
the women, your mothers and sisters, stand side by side with you.'

Emily's character witness was Mrs Eleanor Penn Gaskell, the suffragette organiser for Kilburn and Willesden. She told the court she
had known the prisoner for six years and that she was 'a woman of the
very highest character and honour' whose 'deeds are simply done to
call the attention of the public to the great cause for which we stand'.
The last evidence before the verdict was from Detective Inspector
Powell who said he had known the prisoner for several years. Powell
said that Emily was 'highly respectable beyond this movement'; but
had 'given the police a great deal of trouble'. Emily was sent to prison
for six months and within a few days she launched an appeal, which
was heard in February.[4]

On 13 January a 'Suffragette Wedding' took place: Una Dugdale
and Victor Duval were married at the Savoy Chapel, off the Strand.
The bride was taken down the aisle by her father, Commander
Dugdale of the Royal Navy. Emmeline and Fred Pethick-Lawrence
and Christabel Pankhurst and Constance Lytton wore purple, white
and green. The bride objected to saying that she would 'obey' her husband; despite the Archbishop of Canterbury saying that he doubted
the marriage would be considered legal if she did not say the word,
Una refused to comply. Photographs appeared in the *Daily Mirror*
under the headline 'Bride Who Would Not Promise To Obey'.[5]

Despite being sorely tried by the government's machinations, and
the recent suffragette attack on windows, Henry Brailsford and Mrs
Fawcett persisted with their efforts with the Conciliation Bill. On 22

January Brailsford wrote a gloomy letter to Mrs Fawcett describing his recent reprimand by Emmeline Pankhurst who said she wished she had 'never looked at the abominable Conciliation Bill'. Emmeline was 'optimistic and even triumphant' that she could destroy the government if they failed to deliver full adult suffrage.[6]

On 2 February 1912 Margaret Davison wrote to her daughter in Holloway. Her letter to her well-educated daughter was cheerful and chatty: 'My dear daughter, I was so glad to get your nice long letter giving an idea how you spend the day ... It will be cheery to meet and talk with the other suffragettes ... Oceans of love from your mother.'[7]

Emily was barely eating and secretly on hunger strike. On the same day that Margaret Davison wrote her letter, the recently knighted Sir Horatio Donkin, Medical Adviser to the Prison Commission, minuted his interview with Emily on 28 January, having been asked to assess her by Holloway's governor, Dr James Scott, and Dr William Sullivan, the medical officer. They were concerned that she was eating and drinking very little, not refusing food, and despite her saying she was ill they did not know if she was genuinely unwell.[8]

Emily Davison's appeal was heard on 5 February by the Lord Chief Justice and was quickly dismissed. Her barrister, Herman Schloesser, argued that Davison should be treated as someone who had not committed a serious crime and that her sentence was too severe. The Lord Chief Justice ruled that 'there was not the slightest ground for saying that the sentence was too severe'.[9]

On the day Emily learned of her failed appeal, she received a letter from the editor of the Athenaeum Press, John Francis, who had sent on her manuscript about the struggle for women's suffrage to the publisher Thomas Fisher Unwin. Francis was hopeful that Unwin would publish it if she 'would submit to a good deal of alteration. What Mr Unwin wants is neither accusations nor special pleadings, but what might be called an historical record.' Francis trod carefully: 'Of course this may mean great changes in your work, but if I were you I would submit to it for the sake of getting such a well-known and respected publisher.'[10]

Thomas Unwin was in his sixties, a woman's suffrage sympathiser and married to Jane Cobden, daughter of the radical Richard Cobden. 'The Jane', as she was known on account of her formidable drive, was the vice-president of the NUWSS in 1906, but also supported the

WSPU's *Votes for Women* from its earliest days. She donated money to the campaign fund, helped organise the Indian women's contingent at the Women's Coronation Procession, and was active in the Women's Tax Resistance League. Nothing came of Emily's attempt to get her manuscript published.[11]

In Holloway time was dragging for Emily: there were hardly any suffragette prisoners left after Mary Leigh had completed her sentence and been released at the end of January. Prisoners were not permitted ink, but Mary had managed to smuggle some in to Emily and on 11 February Emily wrote to her 'dear pal', Miss Dixon, and thanked her for her 'kind messages' and asked her to borrow a watch and get it to her 'by stealth' as she did not have hers with her: 'this would be a <u>real</u> deed of kindness and I will take <u>such</u> care of it. It is so awful not to know the time … it will be so odd to be all alone tomorrow, the wing is so <u>quiet</u>.' Emily signed the letter, 'ever so much love, yours in the Cause'.[12]

On 28 February Sir Bryan Donkin visited Emily to assess whether she could be force-fed after her month-long resolution barely to eat and drink. Before Donkin's visit, Dr Scott wrote to the Home Office asking for guidance after his meeting with her when he found her 'even more surly than usual'. Recently she had only taken a cup of coffee in the morning and tea in the afternoon: 'I am pretty sure that her idea is to weaken herself gradually until she has got to the point where she believes that she could not be fed by force without some risk. She is also, I think, under the impression that feeding will not be resorted to unless she is absolutely refusing all food.' Emily refused to be weighed. He could not tell if she was suffering 'a genuine mental disorder which may increase as time goes on', but he was confident that 'further abstinence from food would be harmful and especially so if her present conduct should ultimately prove to be due to real mental disorder.'[13]

On 29 February Emily Davison was fed twice by nasal tube and on both occasions 'offered violent resistance'. Before Dr Sullivan fed her, she warned him that she had been legally advised that so long as she took any food at all, no matter how little, forcible feeding was illegal. Sullivan told her that he was going to feed her on medical grounds because her condition was such that he 'could not take the responsibility of allowing her to remain without sufficient nourishment'.

For the next eight days Emily's prison records offer an account of a war being waged by the prison authorities against a depressed woman who said she had never refused food, but that she was too ill to eat. Dr Sullivan's notes read like an impatient father fighting a wilful teenager. She had been transferred to the hospital wing where she was force-fed fifteen times until 7 March. The short journey from her cell had not been easy: 'she was carried in a chair for part of the way, but owing to her violence the chair had to be abandoned, and she was carried by four of the hospital staff for the remainder of the way. No unnecessary violence was used.'[14]

The WSPU was summoning members to London for the next militant protest on 4 March. The membership was reminded that the efficacy of the protest lay 'very much in numbers, we want next time absolutely to cripple the machinery at the disposal of the Government'. *Votes for Women* explained the WSPU's strategy for the forthcoming parliamentary session by using a cartoon, 'The Haunted House', showing a ghostly woman hovering over the Houses of Parliament demanding 'Votes for Women'. The suffragettes would haunt Parliament until the vote was won; this image was printed as a poster and made into a belt-buckle sold in the WSPU shops.[15]

During the King's Speech at the opening of Parliament on 14 February, women's suffrage was barely mentioned. Proposals were to be brought forward, but even the most optimistic observers assumed that a Manhood Suffrage Bill would be introduced. So much obfuscation surrounded the government's intentions that the WSPU no longer trusted it at all. The lack of any definite proposals for women's suffrage was reported as far away as New Zealand.[16] A long-standing supporter of women's suffrage, Mr James Agg-Gardner, the Conservative MP for Cheltenham, a member of the Conciliation Committee, drew a third place in the ballot for a private members' bill. He announced he would reintroduce the Conciliation Bill on 19 February; the second reading was timetabled for 22 March. Mrs Pankhurst commented, 'this interested us very slightly, for knowing its prospect of success to have been destroyed, we were done with the Conciliation Bill for ever'.[17] Nevertheless, Mrs Fawcett and the NUWSS kept faith with a proposed amendment to a Manhood Suffrage Bill. At a meeting on 16 February at the Connaught Rooms to welcome released prisoners who had broken windows on 21 November, Mrs Pankhurst made a remark about the 'argument of the broken pane' which became the suffragette battle cry, launching a new phase of militancy that had originated in the actions of Mary Leigh and Edith New in 1908. 'The argument of the broken pane is the most valuable argument in modern politics,' said Mrs Pankhurst, insisting that 'We don't want to use any weapons that are unnecessarily strong. If the argument of the stone, that time-honoured official political argument, is sufficient, then we will never use any stronger argument.' She explained that these methods were being used because they were 'the easiest and the most readily understood'. She reminded her listeners of comrades' suffering and how some had died, and to no avail: 'we have made more progress with less hurt to ourselves by breaking glass than when we allowed them to break our bodies.'[18] Not all members of the WSPU agreed with Mrs Pankhurst. Dr Elizabeth Garrett Anderson, an old friend and member of several deputations to the House of Commons, left the militant campaign in the aftermath of the smashed windows on 21 November. Mrs Pankhurst was in charge of the forthcoming protest: 'Is not a woman's life, is not her health, are not her limbs more valuable than panes of glass? ... We only go as far as we are obliged to go in order to win, and we are going forward with this next protest in full faith that this campaign ... will prove effective.'[19]

A remark made by Charles Hobhouse, Liberal MP for Bristol East, at a meeting of the National League for Opposing Woman Suffrage was used as justification for the escalation of militancy. Hobhouse claimed the suffragette campaign was not a popular uprising like that of the male campaigners for suffrage who set fire to Nottingham Castle in 1832 to protest at the Duke of Nottingham's opposition to parliamentary reform, and the tearing down of Hyde Park railings before the 1867 Reform Act. Bristol suffragettes relayed his remarks to Clement's Inn: 'in the case of the suffrage demand there has not been the kind of popular sentimental uprising which accounted for the arson and violence of earlier suffrage reforms.'[20] The suffragettes rose to this challenge.

On 22 November, Winston Churchill was harried by suffragettes travelling on the same train as him to Glasgow. Frances 'Fanny' Parker, from New Zealand, also known as 'Janet Arthur', and Miss Ellison Gibb stood outside his carriage and refused to budge until he came out and made a statement. Churchill's wife, Clementine, asked the women to go away as her husband was tired and had not slept for two days. Then Churchill himself appeared and told the women, 'the only statement I will give you is to go away'. *Votes for Women* reported that Churchill 'seemed to work himself up into a hysterical condition and poured forth abuse on Miss Gibb for some time'.[21] He called her 'intolerable, disgusting' and asked her if she was 'a low woman'. Ellison Gibb lived in Glasgow and was the secretary of the Glasgow Ladies' Chess Club, founded by her mother in 1905. She had been arrested on Black Friday and released without charge.[22]

The next day in Glasgow, Mrs Greig, also known as 'Annie Rhoda Walker', was waiting for Churchill outside his hotel and struck his car with a rock concealed in her muff, 'completely smashing the window', and was sentenced to seven days in prison. When he arrived back at Euston, Geraldine Lennox, who worked at Clement's Inn, dashed towards Churchill's taxicab calling him 'a coward and a traitor' and was bundled away.[23]

Mary Gawthorpe appeared at Bow Street Court on 22 February charged with breaking a pane of glass at the Home Office. She told the magistrate, de Rutzen, she had not broken the window for the cause of women's suffrage, but as a protest against the cruelty meted out to William Ball, a member of the Men's Political Union for Women's Enfranchisement, who had been forcibly fed in Pentonville Prison. Mary's doctor, Flora Murray, told the court that her patient had been on a special diet for more than a year, and warned that if she was placed on a different diet in prison 'the consequences might be more or less serious'. Mary Gawthorpe was remanded for a week in Holloway where she refused all food and water and was released after thirty-six hours.[24]

William Ball, from Birmingham, a member of the National Transport Workers' Federation, had been in prison since late December 1911, for breaking two panes of glass at the Home Office in protest at what he felt was an unjust sentence given to Alan MacDougall, who was in prison for protesting against the exclusion of women suffragists at Lloyd George's meeting, and about the proposed Manhood Suffrage Bill which was due to be introduced on 17 June, which Ball said 'would bar the passage of a measure for votes for women'. Even though this was Ball's first offence, and he was of good character, he was sent to prison for two months where he insisted he was a political

prisoner and entitled to be held under Rule 243a, but he was denied
the same treatment as the twenty suffragettes who were in Holloway
at that time. Refusing to wear prison clothes and to eat prison food,
Ball went on hunger strike and was force-fed for the first time on
Christmas Day, held down by two warders while 'a tube was thrust up
his nose and down his throat'; this 'disgusting process' was repeated
twice a day for five and a half weeks. Ball was not allowed to see his
wife, Jennie, or write to her. Mrs Ball wrote repeatedly to the governor, Major Owen Davies, but her letters were ignored. Her four children depended on their parents' joint wages so she shrewdly wrote
to the Prison Commission at the Home Office saying she wanted to
insure her husband's life, which meant that the insurance company's
doctor would have to visit William Ball in prison to examine him.
This request was refused. Jennie Ball was told that her husband was
in his 'usual health', and would leave prison on 21 February but nine
days before his release she received a letter from Governor Davies:
'I regret to inform you that it is intended to certify your husband
insane', going on to say that he had been sent to a pauper lunatic asylum. Kitty Marshall's solicitor husband, Arthur, took Jennie Ball to
the Home Office where they were told William Ball was at Colney
Hatch Asylum in Barnet. Jennie went there and found William 'very
seriously ill and in an exceedingly emaciated condition with nose and
throat swollen and inflamed from forcible feeding'. He could only
whisper to her that he had twice been locked in a punishment cell.
Arthur Marshall went to the Lunacy Commissioners who allowed
Jennie to take her husband away to a private nursing home paid for
by their suffragette comrades.

Before his incarceration William Ball had been a fit man, an athlete and a 'championship sprinter' of the Midlands. The WSPU distributed a handbill 'Torture In An English Prison' which reiterated
the point that 'neither he nor his relatives have suffered at any time
from any form of mental illness. His condition now is entirely due to
the atrocious treatment which he has received.' The blame was laid
at Home Secretary Reginald McKenna's door. The WSPU made a
familiar point: 'because a working man, presumably without influential friends, dared to protest against injustice, Mr McKenna had
him inhumanely punished and tortured till his mind, not his principle
and courage, gave way under his sufferings, and then had him hustled

away into a pauper lunatic asylum, without any opportunity being allowed for his wife and friends to come to his assistance.' The hand-bill quoted Mary Leigh's description of being force-fed: 'the drums of the ears seem to be bursting, and there is a horrible pain in the throat and breast.'[25]

*

One summer in the late 1960s the Sussex village of West Hoathly had a jumble sale, where the unsold jumble was gathered into a heap for a bonfire. Dora Arnold, the custodian of the Priest House Museum, spotted a linen handkerchief embroidered with sixty-six suffragettes' signatures and two sets of initials, and plucked it from the flames. This precious object gives us the names of the members of the WSPU who had been on hunger strike and fed by force. Sixty-six of the women who took part in the window-smashing protests on 1 and 4 March 1912 embroidered their signatures and two sewed their initials onto the handkerchief while serving their sentences. One of the signatories is Mary Ann Hilliard, a nurse who is thought to have been the originator of this remarkable relic. Born in Cork in 1860 and known as Minnie, by 1908 she held a senior position at the Alexandra Hospital for Children in Queen Square, Bloomsbury. Breaking windows in March 1912 was Mary Hilliard's only militant moment and she served two months with hard labour. Her signature in blue thread floats alongside the title of the piece: 'Votes for Women Holloway Prison March 1912'. Mary Hilliard kept the handkerchief until she died in 1950. This fragment of suffragette history now hangs at the top of the stairs of the medieval Priest House Museum in West Hoathly.[26]

*

The WSPU's observers at the Albert Hall meeting of Mrs Fawcett's NUWSS on the night of 23 February were not surprised to hear Lloyd George's weasel words. The next day Christabel Pankhurst fired off a letter to all WSPU members accusing Lloyd George of evading the question about how women could ever get the vote unless it was a government measure, and only answering in the 'vaguest of generalities', and stressed the importance of the planned militant protest on 4 March. So angry was the leadership that Mrs Pankhurst announced that on 26 February she would call on the prime minister at the House of Commons, or anywhere he preferred, to ask him to make a definitive statement. She said, 'we are dissatisfied with the Government's intentions as declared by Mr Asquith at Downing Street in November'.[27] The prime minister refused to see Mrs Pankhurst.

Emmeline Pankhurst sent letters to the suffragettes acting as recruiting sergeants, warning them to be 'prepared for militant service in the near future'. They were told to cancel all plans and meet her deputy, Marion Wallace-Dunlop, at Georgina and Marie Brackenbury's studio in Campden Hill Square, at 9 a.m. on 28 February where Miss Wallace-Dunlop would explain the 'plan of our campaign'. The next day, 29 February, amid great secrecy, another letter was sent asking for the volunteers to take part in a surprise militant protest on Monday 1 March, to meet at the Gardenia vegetarian restaurant in Covent Garden, at six o'clock. Those taking part were sent a card; no one would be admitted unless they handed in the card; and they were warned, 'on no account reveal the contents of this letter to anyone or speak of it to anyone, even though you know they may have the same information as yourself'.[28]

At half past five on the evening of 1 March Emmeline Pankhurst, Mabel Tuke and Kitty Marshall, each armed with stones, got out of their taxicab in Downing Street and broke two windows of Number 10. Although Mrs Pankhurst had practised throwing stones at trees on Hook Heath where Ethel Smyth lived, Ethel remembered Mrs Pankhurst was not a good shot. 'I imagine she had not played ball games in her youth, and the first stone flew backwards out of her hand, narrowly missing my dog.'[29] Outside Number 10 Mrs Pankhurst only managed to land her missile in the basement, but Kitty Marshall and Mabel Tuke were more successful: all three women were arrested immediately. The police had been taken by surprise. During the next hour, at fifteen-minute intervals, 150 suffragettes, many of whom were making their first militant protest, using hammers supplied by Clement's Inn, broke the windows of shops and businesses in the Haymarket, Piccadilly, Regent Street, the Strand, Oxford Street and Bond Street. The WSPU justified the upping of the militant tempo by arguing that women and retail shops and offices had interests in common, and as such these businesses should support women's suffrage and put pressure on the government to give women the vote. For Christabel Pankhurst the attacks on government windows in November 1911 'had not sufficiently embarrassed them ... the Government and the public are far too calm in the face of these things. The sufferings of the militant women have not been felt keenly enough. That is why commercial and private property is attacked.'[30] By the end of the day 124 women had been arrested and charged with causing £5,000 worth of wilful damage. Mabel Tuke was sentenced to three weeks and Mrs Pankhurst and Kitty Marshall to two months each.

The *Daily Mail* reported: 'People started as a window shattered at their side; suddenly there was another crash in front of them; on the other side of the street, behind – everywhere. Scared shop assistants came running out to the pavements; traffic stopped; policemen sprang this way and that ... five minutes later the streets were a procession of excited groups, each surrounding a woman wrecker being led in custody to the nearest police station.' The effect on the streets was of a 'sudden twilight'. Shopworkers scrambled to fix their shutters, 'the rattle of iron curtains being drawn from every side', and any unaccompanied woman in sight 'especially if she carried a handbag, became an object of menacing suspicion'.[31] At the same time members of the Men's Political Union for Women's Enfranchisement went to a meeting in the Queen's Hall, Langham Place, to publicise the shocking treatment of William Ball in prison and at Colney Hatch Lunatic Asylum. The speakers were some of the most influential male supporters of women's suffrage: George Lansbury, the Labour MP for Bow and Bromley, Charles Mansell-Moullin and Victor Duval.

This was Kitty Marshall's fourth arrest and her third imprisonment. She describes the chaos in Holloway, how the prison system creaked at having to cope with an influx of more than a hundred women, and a mutiny breaking out when the suffragettes were told that women who had been convicted were not allowed to mix with prisoners being held on remand. As the women on remand milled about outside their cells where Mrs Pankhurst – who had already been convicted – would not be allowed to join them, they were pushed back into their cells and the doors were locked. 'Everyone began banging on their doors and singing *The Marseillaise* to the words of a suffragette song and broke panes of glass in the windows of their cells to let in the fresh air. I believe the row we all made could be heard some miles away.'[32] Kitty broke all forty panes in her cell and had to spend five days in solitary confinement, 'in an underground cell with no hot pipe, an iron bedstead ... there was snow on the ground and it was bitterly cold. I kicked the bedstead and sang *The March of The Women* ... A mattress was thrown in towards evening, which I tried to fold round me.' Kitty was severely depressed and 'cried all the time' and was taken to the hospital wing after five days. She was released from Holloway on 12 April.[33]

Nelly Crocker, Emmeline Pethick-Lawrence's cousin, was arrested for the eighth time in her suffragette career on 1 March 1912 and sentenced to three months with hard labour in Holloway for breaking the windows of the King's Road post office. She told Bow Street Court that her actions were a protest against police brutality, reminding the police and judiciary of the painful shadow of Black Friday, a terrifying memory which she and other victims found difficult to forget. Nelly also denounced the vindictive sentences handed down to brave men like Alan MacDougall and William Ball. An ardent Liberal who had canvassed for the party in the 1906 general election, Nelly became disillusioned in 1907 and 'came out on strike against a Government which persecutes women'. She preferred to leave the party 'rather than be guilty of traitorship to her sex'.[34]

On 1 March the artist Edith Downing, not long out of prison, was sentenced to six months. She resented cabinet ministers' taunts at the suffragettes' methods, and warned the court that women were prepared to die for the Cause. Edith broke the windows of a fine-art dealer, and the tea rooms of Messrs Callard, Stewart and Watt. She went on hunger strike and was force-fed, and was released at the end of June before completing her sentence. Florence Haig, in mourning for the death of her sister Cecilia, attacked the windows of D. H. Evans in Oxford Street and was sent to Holloway for four months. She went on hunger strike in June and was released early from her sentence without being force-fed.[35]

Dora Spong was charged, under her married name of Beedham, with breaking two panes of glass at the Westbourne Grove post office. Dora was carrying a hammer and her comrade, Constance Moore, a student from Croydon, went armed with a poker. Both women were sentenced to two months in Holloway with hard labour. Her sisters Florence and Minnie ran a poultry farm in Felbridge, East Grinstead, regularly advertised in the pages of *Votes for Women*, and ran courses for female students. In the summer of 1910 Irene Spong had married

Norman Parley, a managing clerk of the Spong family firm. She carried on with her singing career under her maiden name. Irene and Annie Spong took part in Greek dramas, including *Lysistrata*, performed at the Royal Court Theatre, gave fundraising concerts for the WSPU and offered lessons in singing and voice production to suffragette speakers.[36]

Sarah Carwin caused £100 worth of damage to the windows of J. C. Vickery, jewellers and dressing-case makers to the King, and was sentenced to serve six months with hard labour in Winson Green Prison. This was her fourth arrest and last militant protest. Sarah Carwin was living in Bloomsbury when the Census Enumerator called but she refused to supply any details about herself and the other woman who lived in the mansion flat. Sarah's health was so precarious after being force-fed in Winson Green, which 'she resisted with her utmost strength', that she was released four months into her sentence. Her biographer Frances Unwin believed Sarah's time in Winson Green left her 'permanently injured, her [suffragette] activities were over before the war began'. Sarah and 'a friend to whom she was devotedly attached, and who had kindred interests and sympathies' eventually left London and went to live in Surrey.[37]

Ada Wright broke the windows of the Great Northern Railway Company in Charing Cross causing £9 worth of damage. Holloway had filled up with suffragettes, and because of Ada's previous convictions – she had been in prison for her protest on 21 November – she was sentenced to six months in Aylesbury Prison. Charlie Marsh was sentenced to six months for breaking nine windows in the Strand; Elsie Howey, four months for breaking two of Liberty's windows in Regent Street; and Violet Bland four months for breaking the windows of the Commercial Cable Company in Northumberland Avenue. They went on secret hunger strike. Ada Wright took no food for a week, somehow managing to dispose of it. She thought their protest had gone unnoticed but late one night she was 'lying on her bed feeling ill and weak for the want of food' and wondering how much longer she would have to starve before her release, when she was startled to hear 'the clang of a cell door in the distance' and feared she was about to be fed by force. Ada, 'trembling from head to foot and weak and dizzy', got out of bed and hid behind the bedstead. The door was flung open and wardresses grabbed her and threw her on the floor. A doctor tried to put the feeding tube up her nose but this proved ineffective and Ada 'clenched her teeth to prevent the tube from being pushed into her mouth'. A steel gag was then used to prise open her jaws 'and the tube was rammed down her throat by clumsy and unskilled fingers'. Ada thought she would suffocate; the tube would not go down, she could not breathe, her head and eyes seemed to burst, and as she became unconscious a feeding cup was used. She was left lying on the floor partly conscious. Twice a day for ten days Ada and the other hunger-striking prisoners were fed by force. Ada remembered the wardresses being very distressed and often in tears having to help the doctor in his 'gruesome task'.[38]

After ten days all the suffragettes who were on hunger strike in Holloway, Winson Green, Aylesbury and Maidstone prisons were urged by Clement's Inn to abandon the hunger strike as the government had conceded that they should be treated as political prisoners and would serve their sentences in the second division. Three months later Ada and the others again went on hunger strike in protest at the length of their sentences and were again force-fed. Ada became very ill, 'her throat swelled up so much she could not breathe and her heart became affected'. She was moved to the prison hospital and released on 6 July after serving four months of the six-month sentence. Ada and her friend Charlie Marsh and two other suffragettes went to Switzerland to convalesce from force-feeding.[39]

Violet Bland ran a guest house in London. She wrote to the editors of *Votes for Women* from Holloway citing her reasons for breaking windows: 'I broke the window which was not a Government window in order to help put "Votes for Women" into the minds of the men of the country because they have stood by looking on as spectators as the women fight for their vote.' Violet also wished to challenge cabinet ministers such as Richard Haldane who had 'taunted them with many pinpricks'. She told the magistrate that when she was being bundled along between two police constables to the police station she was assaulted by a member of the public: 'I venture to think that sort of thing will not be so common when we have our vote.' In July Violet went on hunger strike and was force-fed.[40]

Ethel Haslam was charged with breaking the windows of silversmiths Lambert and Co., Piccadilly, and was sentenced to two months with hard labour in Holloway. (Any prisoner sentenced to hard labour was not entitled to be held under Rule 243a.) Magistrate Mr Curtis Bennett commented on Ethel's 'very heavy hammer' and said hers was 'a bad case'. Ethel had set off from her suburban home with a hammer that had belonged to her great-grandfather hidden in her muff. When she arrived in Piccadilly she was astonished to see policemen standing by while women smashed the windows. She chose her windows, broke them and walked off but was grabbed by one of the shop assistants who marched her back to the shop: 'they were all frantically excited.' She was charged at Vine Street police station and released on bail. When she arrived at Holloway Ethel refused to wear prison clothing or do hard labour. When suffragettes were told they were not allowed to exercise with Mrs Pankhurst in the prison yard, Ethel joined the mutiny and broke twenty-four of her cell windows, after which she spent fourteen days in solitary confinement in a third division cell she likened to a coal cellar: 'awfully cold and damp and my bed was made of iron – very horrible to lay upon'. Ethel went on hunger strike for several days and was force-fed for the first time, and overheard other women being fed: 'they made enough noise to scare me. I imagined they were being massacred, for the howling was horrible.' Then it was Ethel's turn: 'They brought a large chair into my cell; it was the most horrible and ghastly affair I had seen. I resisted as best I could, and four wardresses and the doctor put me in the chair … I entreated them not to be so cruel but to no avail. They tied a sheet round my neck; one wardress held my hands, another my head and another my nose while the doctor poured some food down my throat by means of a feeding cup. I had to swallow a pint of this stuff.' This was the only time Ethel was force-fed, and she was released on 5 May.[41]

Olive Wharry broke windows in Whitehall and Regent Street and was sentenced to six months in Winson Green. Olive, who had been in Holloway for two months for smashing windows the previous November, kept an autograph album in which she wrote rhymes about her comrades. She went on hunger strike and was released in July without serving her full sentence.[42]

When Emily Duval was sentenced to six months in Winson Green Prison for breaking two windows in Regent Street, she told the magistrate she had been 'brutally knocked about and thrown on her back'. Referring to the large numbers of young women who were driven into prostitution by poverty, she addressed the court: 'I should like to say that I shattered the glass because I wish the Government to come to their senses, and money can replace broken glass, but it cannot replace the innocence of girls who are outraged daily ... I am prepared to die for Votes for Women.' Four months into her sentence Emily Duval went on hunger strike and was force-fed over a two-day period.[43]

Emily gave an account of being force-fed in a statement she dictated at Birmingham WSPU office. In the hospital wing the doctor had listened to her heart and begged her to take the feeding cup rather than be fed by the nasal tube, but she told him she would rather have her head cut off than do such a thing. They covered her with towels and held her head back and the tube was pushed up her nose, 'which was most agonising – my nerves seemed to prick all the passages of my nose and some in my throat. I did not know how to breathe, I did not struggle or flinch, just gripped the wardresses' hands very tight'. When they finished feeding her and she got her breath back, she told them, 'Mr McKenna deserves shooting.' The next morning the prison doctor urged her to eat but Emily refused and was force-fed once again. The tube was forced down her throat which was 'agonising, it seemed as though I was being suffocated. I could not breathe it was simply horrible.' Emily was helped back to her cell where her throat bled and she vomited 'all over the place'. She was fed several more times and released on 25 June before her sentence was complete and went away to a nursing home to convalesce.[44]

Helen MacRae and her suffragette sister, Georgiana, initially joined the NUWSS, but Helen soon resigned to join the WSPU, and the East Grinstead Suffrage Society. In 1909 the sisters adopted a two-year-old girl from South Wales whom they named Hilda Maud.

Helen came to London on 1 March and broke a window of Hamley's toy shop in Regent Street, causing £200 worth of damage. She was charged at Bow Street Court on 6 March and bailed by Mrs Chapman, whose husband Cecil was the openly pro-women's suffrage magistrate at Tower Bridge Court. Helen MacRae was sent to Holloway for two months, went on hunger strike and was force-fed. She was awarded the suffragettes' equivalent of the VC – the 'For Valour' medal. Helen's circle of friends included Edith Downing and Emily Davison. This would be Helen MacRae's only militant action.[45]

Another first-time militant was Olive Grace Walton, the honorary organising secretary of the Tunbridge Wells branch of the WSPU. Her women's suffrage campaigning began in 1908 with the NUWSS. Olive was a member of Mrs Pethick-Lawrence's deputation to the House of Commons on 21 November 1911, and served one week in Holloway. On 1 March Olive and Eileen Casey were charged with causing 'malicious damage' when Olive broke a window at Marshall & Snelgrove, Oxford Street, and served two weeks on remand. Olive served four months in Aylesbury Prison and suffered two periods of force-feeding in April and June. Olive Walton's family felt the public disgrace keenly, and when her brother John and sister Rosalind tried to bail her from Holloway she rejected their help. When Olive asked her younger sister Mary to meet her on her release in June, Mary refused to see her.[46]

The diary Olive kept reveals both the terrors of force-feeding and the larkiness of a holiday, the latter because the suffragettes were determined to make their time in prison more bearable. On 10 April Olive was force-fed for the first time, and tolerated the experience better than she imagined she could. On the 12th, she and her comrades rushed to the windows of their cells when they heard a band playing 'The March of the Women' and saw 'flags and motor-cars' and our 'people and our colours and they cheer and bravo us. It has all been grand, but oh! what a longing it gives one to be away from this place.' Four days later the authorities started to feed the hunger strikers three times a day: 'we have fine tussles before they get us tied into the chair!' The next day Home Secretary McKenna allowed them to have their rightful privileges. Olive wrote: 'What a victory! How lovely bread is!'[47]

Olive and her pals started exercising on 18 April and were all 'very thin and shaky on our legs'. Olive's diary describes the various activities the women engaged in to pass the time: running and high-jumping were popular, and there was a 'grand obstacle race, we had to do all sorts of peculiar things'. Charlie Marsh was the master of ceremonies of the obstacle race and she gave 'a grand concert on the comb'. Under Charlie's coaching they practised golf strokes with a stick and a stone, and improvised a way of playing tennis using a low bench as the net and a stone they bashed with a dustpan for a tennis racquet. Olive won second prize in the Donkey Race. By sewing prison aprons and behaving well the women could earn time off for remission: the governor, William Winder, turned a blind eye to the suffragette mottoes they embroidered on the aprons – 'Let's Up and at 'Em'; 'Are We Downhearted? No'; 'Deeds Not Words' and 'Dare to Be Free' – but asked them to unpick the embroidery before being released.[48]

Olive Walton's suffragette career filled a big hole in her life that nothing else had been able to do. Her father, Charles, a retired wine merchant, was in his seventies when Olive was born in Tonbridge in 1886. Her mother was a strict disciplinarian. One of Olive's nieces remembered her aunt thinking of herself as the 'misfit' of the family; her education left her feeling intellectually inferior to her brother and sister. Olive was given cookery and art classes and sent to London to do social work. She felt her life really began in 1908 when she became a suffragist, and then, three years later, a militant suffragette.[49]

Eileen Casey served four months in prison. Her mother, Isabella, was also arrested on 1 March for breaking the window of a barber's shop and served one month in Holloway. Eileen was born in Australia in 1881, the daughter of Philip Forth Casey, a doctor. Her younger sister, who was known as Kitty, was also a suffragette. The Caseys left Australia in 1890 and eventually settled in Kew in 1908. The Casey women were active in the WSPU from 1910. For four and a half years Eileen and her mother sold *Votes for Women* outside Victoria station. One day 'a female passer-by whom we suspected of being a provocateur tore the paper out of my mother's hand but my mother caught her scarf and when she demanded to let go my mother said, "yes when you pay me the price." ' When their neighbours in Kew commiserated with Dr Casey about being alone while his wife and daughter were in prison he said: 'Well, if they want the vote they are right to fight for it.'[50]

Newcomers Kate and Louise Lilley from Clacton-on-Sea (whose father co-owned the Lilley and Skinner boot and shoe manufacturing business, makers of purple, white and green shoes for a suffragette clientele since 1909) broke windows at the War Office on 1 March. Their solicitor asked for leniency as this was their first militancy, but Mr Curtis Bennett brushed the plea aside saying that theirs was a 'bad case', that 'if the missiles which were thrown [flintstones the size of a man's fist] had struck anyone it might have led to a fatal result'. The sisters were sentenced to two months' hard labour in Holloway, went on hunger strike and were force-fed.[51]

When the Lilley sisters were released friends in Clacton gave them 'a hearty reception', 'and hundreds of spectators, including many women wearing the WSPU badge, were waiting for them at the station'. Thomas Lilley, a Justice of the Peace, President of the Harwich Division of the Liberal Association, father of two convicted militant suffragettes, was not in the least bit embarrassed. When they arrived the sisters looked 'very little the worse for their imprisonment and appeared in good spirits'. They told the crowd who met them that their suffering for the cause was 'right and just' and had not 'damped their ardour' and they were more determined than ever.[52]

On 2 March at Bow Street Court Mrs Pankhurst reminded Mr Curtis Bennett of her appearance in the dock in 1908: 'At that time I hoped that what we were doing would be sufficient. Since then the Government have left me and other women no possible doubt as to our position.' Mrs Pankhurst said that recently Charles Hobhouse had challenged them to 'do very much more serious things than we are now charged before you with doing'. When she was sentenced to two months she warned the court that the WSPU's agitation would continue. 'As soon as I come out I shall go further and show that the women must have some voice in the making of the laws which they have to obey.'[53]

In the evening of 3 March, suffering from cancer and with only months to live, Ellen Pitfield walked into King Edward Street post office in the City, filled a waste-paper basket with wood shavings, sloshed paraffin over them and set fire to the contents. She also threw a brick wrapped in 'Votes for Women' literature through the post office window. This protest, which was not authorised by the WSPU leadership, inspired similar actions in the following two years.[54] Ellen told a policeman that she had done 'something which I hope will burn the place down'. The next day she explained to Guildhall Magistrates' Court that she had been unable to rest since the arrest of Mrs Pankhurst and the others. Bail was not offered and because of the gravity of her crime she was committed for trial at the Old Bailey on 19 March. She was carried into court from her prison hospital bed, and eagerly pleaded guilty to 'feloniously setting fire to a basket of shavings and other things', but insisted that 'the guilt rested with the Cabinet'. The court was told that Ellen Pitfield had been injured on Black Friday, suffering 'a blow resulting in cancer which despite two operations was incurable'.[55] Ellen's illness was corroborated by the prison doctor who testified that she was so ill she would never walk again. Because she had been arrested on five previous occasions, Justice Horridge handed down a sentence of six months, explaining the state of her health rather than her political motives had been responsible for her sentence being 'such a light one'.

The *British Journal of Nursing* and the Men's League for Women's Suffrage launched a campaign to have Miss Pitfield released early from prison on compassionate grounds. After spending forty-five days in the hospital wing, she was taken to the nursing home run by nurses Catherine Pine and Catherine Townend in Pembridge Gardens, where she died four months later. She was buried at Kensal Green cemetery in August and suffragettes sang 'The March of the Women' at her graveside as her coffin, draped in the colours, was lowered into the ground.[56]

On the evening of 4 March WSPU members were invited to gather in Parliament Square while MPs debated the Conciliation Bill, and 'to take part in a great protest meeting against the Government's refusal to include women in their Reform Bill'. Mrs Pankhurst promised that 'speeches will be delivered by well-known suffragettes, who want to enlist your sympathy and help in the great battle they are fighting for human liberty'. The WSPU women were outnumbered by 9,000 uniformed and plain-clothes policemen. The leadership had tricked the authorities: there was no 'Great Demonstration' and while there was a suffragette presence in Parliament Square there was little trouble and only a few arrests. With so many police on duty there seemed to be no possibility of anyone getting into the House of Commons, yet two women managed to get into Palace Yard that evening. They strolled up to the two constables guarding the gates, and dropped a purse so that coins rolled out. The 'kindly' policemen bent down to pick them up and 'while they were so engaged the women' quickly slipped past and rushed along Palace Yard shouting 'Votes for Women', and were then arrested.[57]

Passionately loyal to Mrs Pankhurst, Ethel Smyth volunteered to join the window-smashing raids, begging to be allowed to attack the home of the colonial secretary, 'Loulou' Harcourt, in Berkeley Square, because 'of an infuriating remark of his to the effect that if all women were as pretty and as wise as his wife we should have the vote tomorrow'. Ethel went into the Square and asked the policeman the name of the person whose house he was guarding. Before he had a chance to answer she threw a stone through the window and said: 'I say, did my stone hit the window? Thank goodness. But it made such an odd muffled sound.' Ethel was sentenced to two months in Holloway in a cell next to Mrs Pankhurst, but was released early on the recommendation of the deputy medical officer who thought she was 'mentally unstable and … highly hysterical and neurotic'. Before she was released the young conductor Thomas Beecham visited Ethel and saw the suffragette prisoners marching round the exercise yard singing 'The March of the Women' while Ethel conducted them with a toothbrush from an upper cell window. In Ethel's memoir, *Female Pipings in Eden*, she said her time in Holloway was bearable because Mrs Pankhurst 'was in with us'. Putting them in adjoining cells, the 'merciful and kind-hearted matron' ensured that Miss Smyth and Mrs Pankhurst saw more of each other at exercise and in the chapel. They managed to have materials smuggled in and they made placards with defiant slogans with which to decorate the exercise yard before they were torn down. Ethel Smyth cherished her time inside: 'For the first and last time of my life I was in good society … more than a hundred women parked together, old and young, rich and poor, strong and delicate, and all divorced from any thought of self, careless as to consequences, forgetful of everything save the idea for which they had faced imprisonment.'[58]

The strongest WSPU protest on 4 March had taken place at eleven o'clock in the morning when more than a hundred well-dressed women who arrived in Knightsbridge, 'walking singly along the street, demolished nearly every pane of glass they passed'. The police were taken by surprise, and most of the offenders got away. The *Evening News* said that when a mounted policeman came on the scene the suffragettes pulled him off his horse.[59]

For breaking nine windows of the office of Black Rod at the House of Lords Mrs Saul Solomon was sent to Holloway for one month. She gave a defiant performance at Bow Street Court the next day and told Mr Curtis Bennett that her protest was inspired by a 'strong religious sense of duty' and that she was 'an old offender' and was sure she 'deserved very much more than one month'.[60]

The Rock sisters, Dorothea and Madeleine, of Ingatestone, Essex, attacked the kitchen windows of the Mansion House, the Lord Mayor's official residence. Dorothea Rock said that they had been 'encouraged to take that step by the Bristol MP Charles Hobhouse's taunts in a recent speech'. The women targeted the Mansion House because of the Lord Mayor's 'discourteous treatment of some of their women at a meeting the other day'.[61] Lavender Guthrie broke the windows of Garrard the jewellers and was charged under her stage name, 'Laura Grey', and sent to Holloway for six months. She wrote to a friend and said she would miss their walks round the Serpentine and was 'sad to miss the strawberries but nothing really matters for we captives know that we are freer than anyone else in the world'. Lavender went on hunger strike and was force-fed and released two months before her sentence was completed.[62]

Victoria Simmons, who came from Bristol on 4 March with her sister Winnie to take part in her second suffragette protest, was arrested for breaking a window and causing £2 worth of damage at the War Office. Looking innocent, Victoria had walked down Whitehall although it was almost cordoned off. She stood next to a policeman, took a stone from her bag and broke a window. 'He was so astonished and he didn't do anything at first, but another dashed along and caught me by the arm and an inspector on horseback came up and I was escorted to Bow Street by a mounted policeman at the front and a policeman at each side and one at the back.' As Victoria walked along she carefully dropped the eight stones she had in her pocket one by one, but when they reached Bow Street 'the policeman behind me produced the stones and said, "She dropped these on the way."' Victoria's sister Winnie came every evening and they shouted messages to each other through the open cell window. Her memories of close friendship with Annie Kenney, Mary Allen, Vera Wentworth and Elsie Howey were recorded in the interviews she gave until she died at the age of 102 in 1992.[63]

Myra Sadd Brown, who was forty, was sent to Holloway for two months with hard labour for causing three shillings' worth of damage by breaking a window at the War Office. When she married Ernest Brown, a cycle manufacturer, in 1896 they joined their names together. A member of the WSPU since 1907, Myra had been arrested at the protest on 21 November 1911 but released without charge. Her husband was supportive, which made her separation from him and their four children easier to bear.

Her children's governess wrote to Myra enclosing messages written by Ernest, Emily and Jean (her eldest daughter, Myra, was away at school). The governess said they were 'quite well and very good. They speak a lot about you, every night they are wishing you "Good Night" and send you kisses … like them, I wish you would come back, the house seems so sad without you.' Myra's eldest son Ernest signed his letter 'your loving "Bubbles"' and hoped mother 'would soon come back' and sent her 'heeps [sic] of kisses'. Emily wrote: 'Dear Mum, I wish you would come quickly, I am thinking of you all the day long' and sent her 'a lot of kisses', and three-year-old Jean was helped to write, 'your little Jean send [sic] you heaps of kisses. When are you coming back?'[64]

Myra replied to the children on flimsy Holloway lavatory paper which she smuggled out to them. 'Mummy thanks you ever so much for all the kisses in the letter – they were such a joy and I wanted to kiss them all over.' She told them a little about her life in prison: 'I have such a funny little iron bed which I can turn right up to the wall when I don't use it.'[65]

On 20 March, Myra wrote her third letter to Ernest in a fortnight, but since she had received no replies she urged him to contact once again a relative of a remand prisoner and arrange for a note to be smuggled in the hem of a skirt. Myra put a brave face on her separation from the family: 'Apart from you and the children it is not so bad here. I am getting accustomed to the life and do not allow myself to dwell on the disagreeableness. The monotony is the worst part … I think it would send you dotty, but as you know dear thought and imagination can do a great deal – the power of thought is wonderful.'[66]

When Myra was released on 28 April her sister Jessie wrote a letter brimming with pride: 'Welcome back to the world sister mine. Would that I could put my arms around you and try to kiss away some of the pain and loneliness and indignation.' Jessie told Myra that a man she knew who had been against militancy had been converted because of the hunger strike. 'If only Englishmen had just a wee scrap

of imagination to help them realise how hard it is for our women to
do these things knowing the suffering that will follow but they just
shut their eyes and prefer to think of them as criminals who cannot be
too severely dealt with.'[67]

Kitty Marion, a tremendous trooper, volunteered for 'danger duty'
on 4 March. She was given a hammer and told which windows to
break at 'lighting-up time when people had finished shopping and
were peacefully wending their way home'. Kitty arrived five minutes
early at the Silversmiths' Association, in Regent Street, 'feeling awful
and looking around for an encouraging friendly fellow in the fray'.
She pushed her way between two shoppers and 'with my hammer
ready, I hit low as we were asked to do, not to have glass falling from
above ... the sound of breaking glass filled the vicinity and electrified
everybody'. Then she attacked Sainsbury's windows, full of boxes of
chocolates, but her hammer was grabbed by two men who dashed out
of the shop. She was taken to Vine Street police station and on the way
a lady asked her: 'Suffragettes?' and Kitty proudly replied, 'Rather',
and the woman said, 'Bravo, good luck!'[68]

On 26 March Kitty made the most of her time at Bow Street Court
performing her favourite role as the Suffragette Warrior. She electrified her audience. 'What is glass – even plate glass – that we have broken as a political protest, and which can be replaced, compared to the
bodies and souls of women and little girl-children that vicious men
have irretrievably broken and ruined for their own unrestrained lust.'
Kitty got six months with hard labour and was sent with twenty-three
window-smashers to serve their time in Winson Green Prison. She
went on hunger strike and was force-fed for eleven harrowing days.[69]

On the first occasion the doctor asked Kitty if she preferred the
nasal or throat tube. While one doctor held her head, and 'tear-
stained' wardresses who had done twenty 'operations' that day held
her down, Kitty 'felt the tube penetrate my right nostril but when
it reached my throat something went wrong. I was suffocating and
in my involuntary struggle for breath I raised myself to my feet and
gasped, "Take the tube out" in spite of which they poured food down
[the funnel] which mostly came back.' When the feeding tube was
taken out Kitty collapsed into the chair, only able to breathe in 'short,
sharp painful gasps. Trying to take a deep breath caused the most
excruciating agony.' Back in her cell she lay on her plank bed and

'from the waist up I experienced every pain imaginable'. What little food she had taken was coughed and vomited up and she became 'icy cold'. The doctors removed her to the hospital wing where she spent a week slowly recovering.[70]

'Vera Wentworth', real name Jessie Spinks, told the court the suffragettes had been goaded into attacking property by the comments made by the Bristol MP Charles Hobhouse. She told Bow Street Court that as long as the Liberal government persisted in their methods, women would persist in theirs, and declared she would have been more militant but had been restrained by the leadership, and publicly warned that she would do the same again, and more. Because she had been convicted in 1909, 1910 and 1911, Vera was sentenced to six months in Holloway for doing £90 worth of damage to the florist Messrs Brooks and Sons, in Regent Street.[71]

Mrs Winefrede 'Win' Rix, a new face, broke windows in the War Office and served two months with hard labour. She was the wife of a solicitor and the mother of a twelve-year-old daughter. Travelling up from Tonbridge, this was her only militant protest. Win evaded the 1911 Census with her husband's support: when he completed the form he gave only his details, omitting any reference to his wife, his daughter and their female servants. John Rix wrote to his sister Lottie telling her about Win's time in Holloway, gleaned from two letters smuggled out of prison. 'They are allowed a good deal of liberty at exercise, and they play cricket with lumps of wood and a board … Dr Louisa Garrett Anderson is the leading spirit, assisted by Dr Ethel Smyth.' Win Rix had seen the daughter of the first woman doctor in England dance a Highland fling with a prisoner who was a ballet dancer. Win Rix smuggled a letter to her daughter, 'her precious lamb', signing it from 'your hugely loving old mum'. Win revealed she had read a copy of *Votes for Women* which had been smuggled into prison, and was pleased to learn that 'Silvia Pankhurst (the ugly nice youngest one) has had a great welcome in New York … I am so glad.'[72]

A 'batch' of 'Scotch women' who travelled from Glasgow, Edinburgh and Dundee to London were arrested for breaking windows in Kensington, Knightsbridge and the West End. Lilias Mitchell, the suffragettes' organiser in Aberdeen, attacked Barkers windows in Kensington High Street. Lilias hit two windows with her hammer and broke one of them. She ran off but was caught by a commissionaire who marched her through the shop and pushed her into a small room: 'I was trembling with fatigue and the general beastliness of it all.' A policeman who arrived was surprisingly sympathetic: 'Never mind miss, we had to do something just the same before we got the vote.' Lilias and her mother heard Emmeline Pankhurst and Emmeline Pethick-Lawrence speaking publicly in 1907. The effect on her was transformative: 'I shall never forget the blazing warmth of that meeting ... I lived and moved and seemed to have my being in working for votes for women.'[73]

The Dundee artist Ethel Moorhead broke two windows in the West End. When Ethel appeared at Bow Street Court the owner of the windows identified her as the perpetrator, reporting how startled he had been by the noise of breaking glass. Scornfully Ethel replied: 'Lovely! I am a householder and taxpayer without a vote. I came from Scotland at great personal inconvenience to myself to help my comrades.'[74]

Janie Allan, the daughter of Alexander Allan, the owner of the Allan Shipping Line of Glasgow, came from a family with socialist beliefs. She served four months in Holloway for breaking windows on 4 March. Ten and a half thousand Glaswegians signed a petition protesting at the length of her imprisonment. In May 1912 Janie would barricade her cell, go on hunger strike and be force-fed for a week. After serving her full sentence, she was released at the end of June. She later wrote: 'I did not resist at all, but sat quite still as if it were a dentist's chair, and yet the effect on my health was most disastrous – I am a very strong woman and absolutely sound in heart and lungs, but it was not till five months later, that I was able to take any exercise or begin to feel in my usual health again.' Before Janie Allan became involved in the struggle for the vote she had done social work among Glasgow's poor. In 1902 she was on the executive committee of the Glasgow and West of Scotland Association for Woman Suffrage. After hearing Helen Fraser and Teresa Billington-Greig speak about militancy, Janie Allan organised a meeting for the WSPU at St Andrew's Hall in Glasgow in the spring of 1907. Ethel Moorhead described Janie Allan: 'her presence had magic and mystery ... she was tall, beautiful and very quiet.'[75]

Another newcomer to this story is Helen Crawfurd, who was sentenced to one month in Holloway for breaking the windows of the London home of Joseph 'Jack' Pease, the Liberal MP for Rotherham.

Helen Jack was born in Glasgow in 1877; her mother had been a steam-loom weaver before her marriage. The Jacks were strict Presbyterians and Helen was a Sunday School teacher and trainee missionary who believed it was God's plan for her to marry their family friend Alexander Montgomerie Crawfurd, a Minister of the Church of Scotland. In 1898 Helen was twenty-one when she became sixty-seven-year-old Alexander Montgomerie's wife.[76]

*

On 5 March 1912 Mabel Tuke and Mrs Pankhurst, who were serving time in Holloway for their window-breaking in Downing Street, were also charged with 'conspiring to incite certain persons to commit wilful damage to property', an offence which was liable to nine months in prison. On 4 April Mrs Pankhurst and the Pethick-Lawrences were remanded and committed to trial, and released on bail on the undertaking they would 'not take part or incite others to public disorder of any kind until after' the Conspiracy Trial which was announced for 15 May. Before Mr Curtis Bennett gave his decision Mabel Tuke fainted; when she came round he said that she 'had suffered for her previous offence and he was inclined to think that in her weak state of health it would be better to take a lenient view', and dismissed the conspiracy charge against her. Mabel was released from prison that day but her health was poor and in the autumn she sailed to South Africa to recuperate.[77] However, despite their trials and tribulations, and the punishment meted out to these remarkable women, the fight would continue.

13

The Great Conspiracy Trial

The WSPU in the Dock and the Eruption of Militancy in Dublin 1912

In May 1912 the leaders of the Women's Social and Political Union were sentenced to nine months in prison for conspiracy to incite violence.

The attacks on the windows of 270 commercial, government and private residences caused an estimated £6,600 worth of damage. At 10 a.m. on 5 March 1912 Detective Inspector McCarthy and twenty of his colleagues raided the WSPU offices at Clement's Inn to arrest Christabel Pankhurst and Emmeline Pethick-Lawrence, who were out on bail, and Fred Pethick-Lawrence. McCarthy arrested the Pethick-Lawrences as they were leaving and charged them with 'conspiring to incite certain persons to commit malicious damage to property'. Jessie Kenney and Miss Vaughan, an assistant editor of *Votes for Women*, were also arrested. Miss Vaughan retorted that if the government thought they were going to crush the women's suffrage campaign they were mistaken, as the raid 'would arouse intense indignation in the movement' and that it would 'bring out many more volunteers for militant work'.[1]

Just before midnight McCarthy returned to Clement's Inn and the WSPU's warren of offices was searched: 'from the noises which could be heard from the outside it was evident that the examination was of a very exhaustive character. Bundles of papers were being thrown about, desks were being opened and closed.'[2] The landing leading to the offices was two feet deep with papers, which were then taken to Scotland Yard. Some of the papers were letters from Emmeline Pankhurst's late husband, as well as photographs of her children which were never returned.

The next day, Christabel, who had not been present, was told by Evelyn Sharp what had happened. Evelyn was sent by Emmeline Pethick-Lawrence (who had been released on bail) with a cheque for Christabel to countersign in order to divert the WSPU's funds of

£7,000 to Hertha Ayrton's bank account to avoid them being confiscated.[3] Christabel took a cab to Nurse Pine and Nurse Townend in
Pembridge Gardens to spend the night there. Nurse Pine was afraid
the police would find Christabel at the suffragette nursing home, so
she dressed her as a nurse and took her to the flat of a suffragette
friend. 'Not long after I left the nursing home,' wrote Christabel later,
'where my too well-known hat was reduced to ashes in the drawing-
room fire, the police arrived to search for me!' She was awake all night
and decided to flee the country. She knew that political offenders were
not liable to extradition, so she elected to go to France. 'I must get to
Paris, control the movement from there – and from there keep the
fight going, until we win.'[4]

Disguised in a black coat and cloche hat, Christabel travelled with
a friend on the boat train from Victoria station to Folkestone. A lady
in the carriage wrote letters throughout the entire journey, 'but was
not too busy to look at me intently every now and again'. When they
reached Folkestone the woman put her head out of the window and
called for a policeman. 'My heart stood still. She gave him her letters
to post!' Christabel travelled alone to Paris, and asked her companion
to return to London to deliver a letter to Annie Kenney, who would
take over the day-to-day running of the WSPU. Annie was the obvious choice for deputy leader: 'I knew from experience that Annie was
the person to hold the fort at headquarters. She had no personal ties
that would impose upon her a divided duty. Moreover, she had earned
by her own service as a militant pioneer the honour of being first in
command at Clement's Inn.'[5]

In Manchester Annie Kenney saw the newspaper placards reporting 'All Suffragette Leaders Arrested', and travelled to London on
the night train to find a message from her sister Jessie: 'All leaders
in prison except Christabel, who has escaped, no one knows how,
where or why. Do not come to the office until dark. Detectives everywhere.'[6] Annie went to Clement's Inn and immediately understood the challenges they faced: 'I knew my life was once again
changing. I had real responsibility to face and genuine burdens to
bear.' Annie was summoned to Holloway by Emmeline Pankhurst
and the Pethick-Lawrences who gave her two firm instructions:
to campaign for first division treatment for the leaders, which
might then be given to the rest of the suffragette prisoners; and

to find Christabel. After two frantic days there was still no sign of Christabel. The next day a letter arrived from Christabel to 'Beloved Annie' asking her to 'take complete charge of the whole Movement' during her absence and while her mother and the Pethick-Lawrences were in prison. Christabel assured Annie that she knew she was able to resist any WSPU members or cabinet ministers who might try to 'swerve you from the policy laid down ... I trust you implicitly and I give you complete control over the whole Movement until the leaders are released and we are all once again united.'7 She asked Annie to come to see her with a French-speaking friend as soon as possible: 'disguise yourself and watch closely for Scotland Yard men. Let your friend do all the talking as you are so well-known.' Annie swathed herself in black as a widow, and took Miss James, a suffragette friend from Bristol who spoke French, and caught the boat train to Paris.8

Christabel was in hiding in the rue Roy in the eighth arondissement, and when Annie Kenney caught up with her they met at the home of the American Winnaretta Singer, heir to the Singer sewing machine fortune, the widow of Prince Edmond de Polignac. Her salon on Avenue Henri-Martin was frequented by Debussy, Ravel, Stravinsky, Satie and Proust, and she was a generous patron of Ethel Smyth. When Annie was shown into the drawing room she was wide-eyed, remembering it as the biggest room she had ever seen in a private house. 'There were beautiful books everywhere. I picked one up and found it to be a translation of Sappho's poetry, so pretty, so simple, and yet so profound.'9 During Annie's stay she and Christabel discussed the future of the WSPU.

Emmeline Pethick-Lawrence remembered the feverish interest in the whereabouts of Christabel. From the outset Emmeline and Fred were especially fond of Christabel, to whom they behaved like aunt and uncle. The long arms of the law were tied up in knots looking for her, and younger members of the WSPU enjoyed leading the police a merry dance: 'Some of our gay young things took delight in writing postcards to put the sleuths of the law on a false scent. Some dressed themselves to represent her ... and the public was agog with interest.' *The Bystander* magazine devoted a full page to 'St Christabel', putting her in the centre of a stained-glass window, 'making her as popular with the masses as any reigning cinema star'.10

Instructed by Christabel, and with the help of Rachel Barrett, Annie Kenney ruled out any possibility of a committee, the idea of which had always been anathema to the leaders of the Women's Social and Political Union. Annie Kenney was determined: 'The people whose idea it was to have a committee honestly thought it was in the best interests of the work.' But she was sure they were overlooking 'the vital fact, that we were still a revolutionary party'.[11]

Rachel Barrett was promoted to be Annie's deputy. Annie found her to be 'a highly-educated woman ... a devoted worker who had a tremendous admiration for Christabel ... she was learned and I liked her.'[12] Annie and Rachel edited *Votes for Women*, with Annie visiting Paris every week to collect copy from Christabel, leaving London on Friday and returning on Sunday, grim for someone who suffered from seasickness: 'Rachel alone knows what we went through during those first few months ... how I hated being on the water ... I would arrive sick, tired to exhaustion, and yet on Sunday morning I felt refreshed and ready for the labour awaiting me.'[13]

There was a game called 'The Elusive Christabel' which had pictures of her overlaid by a sheet of cut paper which could be moved up and down to make her appear and disappear, as if she was the Scarlet Pimpernel. Schoolgirls like Winifred Starbuck remembered that she and her suffragette school friends followed their heroines' activities closely, standing framed photographs of Mrs Pankhurst, Charlotte Despard, Cicely Hamilton and other leading suffragettes on their desks, decorated with purple, white and green. 'We also pinned up newspaper cuttings about "that damned elusive Christabel" on the noticeboard. Our mistresses said nothing and kept very quiet about their own activities but we knew that some of them had thrown themselves into the movement heart and soul.'[14] In March 1912 the schoolgirls read that one of their mistresses had thrown a brick through a window in Whitehall in full view of a policeman, and was sentenced to a month in prison. The girls were taken aback as she had been 'a quiet and nervous woman and we were all very awed and shocked to think of what it must have cost her to throw the brick'. Winifred and her friends were incensed when they learned that their teacher had gone on hunger strike and was being force-fed, so they 'began to take a small part in the activities of the suffragettes such as attending meetings and distributing

leaflets and we were in a state of excitement which was hardly con-
ducive to study'.[15]

The indignation of some suffragists in the NUWSS, who had been
campaigning for years before the WSPU was formed, was expressed in
The Times on 6 March. Caroline Lyttelton wrote from Eton College
where her husband, the Reverend Edward Lyttelton, was a schoolmaster. She fumed about the damage to windows in Bond Street on 1
March, and hoped that 'the mob women who broke windows ... will
realize before long that they, by their wicked and insensate action, have
done more to put off the granting of the suffrage to even a few of their
sex than could all the anti-suffragists'. She wrote that she had long hoped
for 'duly qualified' women to have the vote, but the crazy violence of the
suffragettes led her, and other women she had spoken to, to 'sorrowfully
acknowledge that my sex are not yet fitted for such grave responsibility'
and that the militants had 'brought disgrace upon us all and turned many
of the supporters of the movement in to bitter opponents'.[16]

From the start of the militant campaign acts of reprisal had been
directed at the suffragettes but in the summer of 1912 the violence
intensified. Medical students smashed the windows of the Woman's
Press bookshop in Charing Cross Road on 4 March. On 9 March two
suffragettes holding a meeting outside Catford Town Hall were pelted
with eggs and had to hurry into a tramcar under the protection of the
police. Two brave souls – a middle-aged lady and a young woman –
escorted by two men tried to hold a meeting in Hyde Park and found
out how 'incensed the public were against the window-smashers' and
were mobbed by a thousand people. The suffragettes only escaped
'with the utmost difficulty' as jeering and booing men closed in on
them from all sides. At Harlesden two WSPU members were mobbed
in the High Street. They had tried to speak from a cart but 'the crowd
hooted and sang and threw eggs, oranges, banana-skins and bags of
flour'. The women gave up and were taken under police escort to the
police station until the crowd dispersed.[17]

*

Almost three months into her sentence Emily Davison's isolation
was altered by the influx of many like-minded comrades who had
been convicted for their part in smashing shop windows. Emily and
several others described their feelings and the collective purpose in

poetic form in *Holloway Jingles,* a collection of poems written by suffragettes in March and April 1912, edited by Nancy John of the Glasgow WSPU, and published later that summer. Emily's poem is 'L'Envoi'. Evoking Longfellow's *The Song of Hiawatha* in its tone, language and repetition, 'fearless' is used twice; 'freedom' is invoked four times; there is a pilgrim in a valley, and a pithy line calling up the experience of being force-fed: 'Tyrants, hunger, horror, brute force.'

Stepping onwards, oh my comrades?
Marching fearless through the darkness,
Marching fearless through the prisons,
With the torch of freedom guiding!

See the face of each is glowing,
Gleaming with the love of freedom;
Gleaming with a selfless triumph,
In the cause of human progress!

Like the pilgrim in the valley,
Enemies may oft assail us,
Enemies may close around us,
Tyrants, hunger, horror, brute force.

But the glorious dawn is breaking,
Freedom's beauty sheds her radiance;
Freedom's clarion call is sounding,
Rousing all the world to wisdom.

On 11 March Mrs Pankhurst, suffering from bronchitis after being in a cold, damp third division cell was moved to Holloway's hospital wing. Ethel Smyth revealed: 'Cockroaches, which according to the Home Secretary, are things never seen or heard of at Holloway, are a commonplace', and were sometimes found floating in the boiled milk. In the hospital ward Mrs Pankhurst found one in her bed and one on the wall and was advised not to let the bedclothes touch the floor.[18]

The next day at Westminster Magistrates' Court, Constance Lytton saw her friend Dr Ker, who had broken windows in Harrods, sentenced to three months in Holloway with hard labour. (She became ill and was released after serving one month.) Constance wrote to

Caxton Hall, 18 November 1910. On the platform are, fifth left, Emmeline Pankhurst, Emmeline Pethick-Lawrence and Christabel Pankhurst, standing.

May Billinghurst, in her invalid tricycle, joined the WSPU in 1907. Paralysed in her legs since the age of five, she was a vigorous campaigner for the vote.

Ethel Moorhead was in her thirties when she joined the campaign in Dundee in 1910. She smashed windows in the West End in March 1912.

Several of Hugh Franklin's female relatives were active in the Jewish League for Woman Suffrage. He abandoned his finals at Cambridge to help organise a WSPU procession in 1910.

Ethel Smyth wrote the music for the WSPU's 'The March of the Women' in 1911, and took two years off from her career as a composer to campaign for the cause.

Cicely Hamilton wrote the lyrics to 'The March of the Women'. She left the moderate NUWSS in 1907 to join the WSPU.

All over the country suffragettes held sleepovers to evade the Census of 1911. Others attended concerts given by actresses and singers who supported the campaign.

MISS D. SMITH. SUFFGTE' SPEAKING FRIENDLY ADVICE
TO THE MERE MAN.
NOV 12 B.B
S CRIBB.

The intrepid Katherine Douglas Smith addressing a vast crowd of men during the Portsmouth by-election in November 1909. She abandoned her music career to fight for the vote.

Dressed as Joan of Arc, Marjorie Annan Bryce led by her sister 'Tiny', the daughters of a Liberal MP who opposed women's suffrage, at the Women's Coronation Procession, 17 June 1911.

Emmeline Pankhurst (left), Emmeline Pethick-Lawrence (centre) and Christabel Pankhurst (right) at the Women's Coronation Procession, 17 June 1911.

German-born Kitty Marion, a music-hall actress and comedienne, joined the WSPU in 1908. During one prison sentence in Holloway she was force-fed 232 times.

Victoria Simmons and her mother and sisters travelled to London from Bristol to break windows in the West End in March 1912.

Lilias Mitchell joined the Edinburgh branch of the WSPU in 1907. She served four prison sentences for her militant activities, went on hunger strike and was force-fed.

Eileen Casey, photographed here in the 1920s, campaigned for the vote with her mother, Bella, and sister, Kitty.

Edith Haslam founded the Ilford branch of the WSPU in 1909. She served two months in Holloway with hard labour for breaking windows on 4 March 1912.

Rose Lamartine Yates and her son Paul, born in 1908. She joined the WSPU's Wimbledon branch in 1909. Her husband Tom, a solicitor, gave Rose his full support.

Published during the WSPU's window-smashing campaigns of 1911 and 1912, John Hassall's cartoon shows a masculine suffragette demanding the vote.

In March 1912 Helen MacRae broke shop windows in Regent Street. She served two months and was force-fed in Holloway. She was awarded this medal 'For Valour' by the WSPU.

Hundreds of windows were smashed in the West End of London in March 1912 by suffragettes summoned by Mrs Pankhurst from all over the United Kingdom.

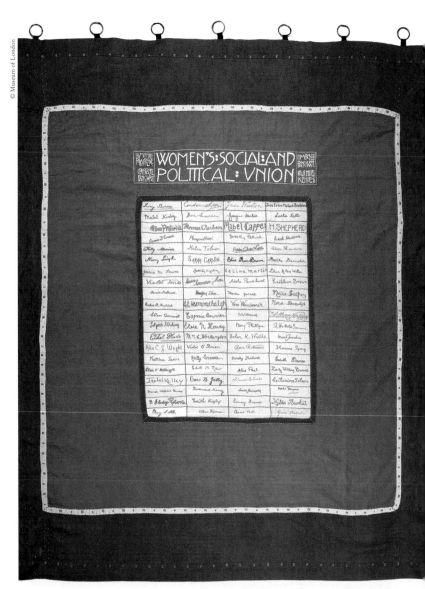

In 1910 a banner was made with the embroidered autographs of eighty suffragettes who had been on hunger strike and were force-fed.

Alice's twenty-year-old daughter, Margaret: 'your mother was absolutely magnificent ... the magistrate was contemptuous and cross, in fact insulting.' Alice Ker had cross-examined the witness, a salesman, as if she had been an expert lawyer. Constance urged Margaret not to be distressed at the sentence of hard labour, 'it is just to satisfy this hysterical moment of public opinion'. She visited the Holloway prison doctor, Dr Sullivan, 'a very kindly official', and she asked if Dr Ker could have the jar of marmalade she had brought 'to keep her in good health'. As a fellow physician, Dr Sullivan had a good opinion of Alice and assured Constance he would do all he could to help.[19]

The most vehement person in the anti movement in 1912 was Sir Almroth Edward Wright, best known for his work at St Mary's Hospital, Paddington, on anti-typhoid vaccine. In 1912 he was becoming notorious for his extreme views on women's suffrage, entering the debate with a shrill letter to *The Times* on 28 March, 'Suffrage Fallacies: Militant Hysteria'. Wright insisted that women were physically, intellectually and morally inferior to men, and to give them the vote would damage the country and the Empire. He explained the rise of the suffragette movement as due to the sexual frustration of the half a million unmarried females in the population: 'that half million which had better long ago have gone out to mate with its complement of men overseas'. Suffragettes and suffragists were 'a class of women who have all their life-long been strangers to joy, women in whom instincts long suppressed have in the end broken into flame. These are the sexually embittered women in whom everything has turned to gall and bitterness of heart and hatred of men.'[20] Their apparent madness was, according to Wright, demonstrated by their demands, including equal pay for equal work, a notion he considered preposterous and impossible.

The WSPU lampooned him in a handbill titled 'The Antediluvian Society for the Propagation of the Principles of Anti-Suffrage', who were to hold a meeting at Stonehenge, chosen because it was 'the best preserved pre-historic relic in England and the one showing least connection with modern times'. A fictitious jamboree was announced by the suffragettes of all the antis where 'Sir Almroth Wrong Will Give a Magical Lantern Entertainment! The series of slides, having been specially prepared by himself, will illustrate clearly and yet modestly, the parallelism between The Real Woman and a Sensitive Plant, The Modern Woman and a Chemical.'[21]

On 28 March the Conciliation Bill was debated in the House of Commons and was narrowly defeated by fourteen votes. The suffragettes' escalation of militancy was perhaps the reason for the result, as many Liberal and Conservative MPs had voted for it in 1910 and 1911. Keen not to jeopardise the Home Rule Bill which Asquith was promoting, John Redmond, the Nationalist MP for Waterford City, urged his forty-one Irish Nationalist Party MPs to vote against the bill, and ten more abstained, although in the previous year thirty-one members of his party had voted for the Conciliation Bill. Sixteen sympathetic Labour MPs who might have voted for the bill were away on constituency business, some of them dealing with strikes in the north of England. Despite the suffragettes' window-smashing campaign, 202 MPs had voted for the bill.[22]

Throughout April the various hearings ahead of the conspiracy trial were used to publicise the defeat of the unsatisfactory Conciliation Bill. Aside from the broken glass and the outrage of insurance companies and businesses, a part of the press was fascinated by the Emmelines, whose looks and dress sense were scrutinised whenever they appeared in court. On 5 April the *Daily Mirror* included photographs of Mrs Pankhurst and Mrs Pethick-Lawrence laughing gaily in the dock at Bow Street and devoted a column to 'Suffragists' Dress'. The article mentioned Mrs Pankhurst's 'fashionable tailor-made costume and a long musquash stole edged with three rows of chinchilla'. Mrs Pethick-Lawrence's large black picture hat was trimmed with a 'profusion of [green] ostrich feathers which are so fashionable this lovely spring'. A WSPU member suggested to the *Daily Mirror* that a fashion offensive was being launched by the leaders: 'the women who desire votes are paying more attention to their appearance ... they are now recognising the fact that for women to appear untidy or weirdly dressed in unfashionable garments damages the cause for which they are working.' The need for the members to maintain a smart and feminine appearance had been emphasised from the earliest days by Mrs Pankhurst, who knew how the press would pick on any garments tinged with any hint of masculinity, and warned the suffragettes to dress in a feminine way at all times.[23]

*

On 6 May 1912 Constance Lytton's charwoman found her in her flat in Euston unable to speak or move, paralysed by a stroke down the right side of her body. She was taken to her sister Emily Lutyens' house in Bloomsbury Square and for several weeks 'she lay between life and death, and finally crawled back to a crippled and invalid existence', returning to Knebworth on 28 July to be cared for by her mother.[24] Constance's closest suffragette friends visited, and left shaken that such a 'noble-hearted woman' had suffered so much. Emmeline Pethick-Lawrence told the Lytton family, 'our reverence for her is as deep as our love ... Every life she has ever touched had been strengthened, purified and ennobled.' Annie Kenney wrote, 'how little we feel, how small-hearted and narrow-minded compared to her! I always think of her as a lamp that throws out its light that those who are stranded can be guided to safety and security.'[25]

Constance was looked after by Nurse Kate Oram for six years until Kate died in 1918. Nurse Oram, who had qualified as a nurse in 1905, cared for Florence Nightingale before her death in 1910.[26] Constance taught herself to write with her left hand and struggled to write her book *Prisons and Prisoners: Some Personal Experiences by Constance Lytton and Jane Warton, spinster*, which would be published in March 1914. After three months Constance was able to take a few steps and could be taken out in her Bath chair. Nurse Oram took her to stay with the Pethick-Lawrences at their country home near Dorking, and to her Aunt 'T' at Cobham, where Ethel Smyth came to sing her 'The March of the Women', which Constance listened to with 'rapture and tears'. Although her active role was over Constance never stopped being a suffragette, deeply frustrated that she could do nothing to help. A year after her stroke she wrote to her cousin Adela, 'my feeling is more of utter lifelessness, and no wish, because so utterly no power, to do anything ... I do sometimes wish tremendously to be near and see my darling suffragettes.'[27] Constance Lytton died in 1923.

*

To maximise the propaganda potential of the conspiracy trial of the leadership in the middle of May, a new image was released by the WSPU to incense public opinion about the 'Torture in English Prisons' in the force-feeding of suffragette prisoners. The poster was captioned 'Forcible Feeding through the Nose of Women Suffragist Prisoners'. It shows a terrified girl being held down as a doctor pushes a rubber tube up her nose, and a harsh-looking prison matron pours liquid into a funnel atop the other end of the rubber tube. Another nurse and a wardress hold the hunger striker down. The *Illustrated London News* and *The Graphic* ran the image, which the WSPU said was 'an indication of the growing public opinion on the subject'.[28]

On 15 May Emmeline Pankhurst and the Pethick-Lawrences were tried at the Central Criminal Court for 'conspiracy to conspire together to unlawfully and maliciously damage and inciting other to unlawfully and maliciously damage certain property, to wit, glass windows, the property of our Lord the King'. The case was presided over by Justice Bernard Coleridge, a Liberal Member of Parliament for Sheffield. Sir Rufus Isaacs, the attorney general, led the prosecution for the Crown. Emmeline Pankhurst and Fred Pethick-Lawrence conducted their own defence; Mrs Pethick-Lawrence was defended by the Irish barrister and MP Tim Healy.[29]

Tim Healy launched into Mrs Pethick-Lawrence's defence with a big statement, his speciality: 'This is a great state trial, it is not the women who are on trial, it is the men. It is the system of our government.'[30] Rufus Isaacs, whom Emmeline Pankhurst described as having a 'clear-cut, hawk-like face, deep eyes, and a somewhat world-worn air', told the jury that the trial was not about politics, 'that all questions of whether a woman is entitled to the Parliamentary franchise, whether she should have the same right of franchise as a man, are questions which are in no sense involved in this trial. Therefore I ask you to discard from your consideration of the matter which will be placed before you any viewpoint you may have on this no doubt very important political issue.'[31] The trial made a deep impression on Mrs Pankhurst: 'The trial is a thing I shall never forget ... the judge impressively bewigged and scarlet-robed, dominating the crowded courtroom, the solicitors at their table, the jury, and looking very far away, the anxious pale faces of our friends who crowded the narrow galleries.'[32]

In addition to the police constables who had witnessed the window-smashing on 21 November 1911 and 1 and 4 March 1912, witnesses were half a dozen detectives from the Criminal Investigation Department at Bow Street and Cannon Row stations, and Special Branch officers at New Scotland Yard. Sergeant Lionel Kirchner of the Special Branch suggested that the leadership of the WSPU had been under surveillance since the middle of 1911. He said he had been present at a WSPU meeting in Kensington Town Hall in November, and on 4 March had been lurking outside Clement's Inn and counted fifty women arrive and leave on foot or in taxis.

Detective Albert Canning of New Scotland Yard produced a file of articles collected from *Votes for Women* from November 1911 to March 1912, which included the transcript of Mrs Pankhurst's speech at the Savoy Theatre on 15 February, inviting men and women to go to Parliament Square on 4 March. Encouraged by Mrs Pankhurst to read the whole speech to the court, Albert read only her inflammatory rallying call: 'We shall secure an Act of Parliament for the abolition of our grievances. The position has got to be carried by storm. The militant woman must create a crisis – a difficulty from which all concerned are eager to escape. Then and then only, will women be politically free.' Inspector Charles Crocker described how the Pethick-Lawrences stood bail for suffragettes while he had been on duty at Canon Row police station: on 21 November 1911, Fred bailed 175 women after they promised him they would not reoffend. On 4 March 1912 he was also present when Emmeline and Fred Pethick-Lawrence bailed forty-seven women.

Jessie Macpherson, a still-room maid at the Gardenia restaurant in Covent Garden, hired by the WSPU on 4 March, told the court she had found two large and a dozen smaller stones in the fireplace of one of the rooms the WSPU had hired. On the larger stones the words 'Votes for Women' had been written in indelible ink. Richard Melhuish, the owner of Melhuish Limited, tool merchants of Fetter Lane, related how he sold three dozen hammers, costing a shilling each, to a lady who visited the shop in the last week of February. Ordinarily, the shop would have been expected to deliver such a heavy order but on this occasion the lady took them with her. Melhuish remembered the 'well-dressed lady of great dignity' whom he had been called on to serve. 'She was so anxious to take them away and so imperious in her manner that he helped his assistant to pack them away and in the hurry one was left behind.'[33]

Other witnesses called by the prosecution included those who had business with the WSPU. When questioned by Mrs Pankhurst, Frank Glenister, manager of the Pavilion Theatre, said that he had been renting his theatre to the suffragettes since the beginning of 1911, and that their meetings had been 'very well attended, and quite orderly'. George Hart, manager of St Clement's Press, printers of *Votes for Women*, revealed that on a couple of occasions he had refused to print certain articles which he feared were inflammatory and those parts of the page had been left blank. Archibald Christy, a chartered surveyor and agent for the owner of the WSPU offices, told the court that Emmeline and Fred Pethick-Lawrence were the signatories on the rental agreements for office space and residential accommodation at Clement's Inn.

In the closing stages of the trial Emmeline Pankhurst called Ethel Smyth as a witness to refute the charge that the leaders' speeches had incited the women to violence. When questioned Ethel told the court, 'I was not incited by anything you said to take the part I subsequently took. I did not wish to take any part in your militant agitation because I was too busy.' However, when she heard reports of Mr Hobhouse's speech at Bristol she felt she had to take part on 4 March. Although she was resting at a sanatorium in Cardiff, Ethel Smyth wrote to Clement's Inn: 'I am coming.' She told the court: 'I did not see how any self-respecting woman could stay at home, I took part in the protest, broke a window, and was sentenced to two months' hard labour, which term I served.'[34]

The all-male jury had been impressed by the five days of evidence the suffragette leaders marshalled in their defence. After many witnesses were heard on both sides the jury found the defendants guilty, although they recommended leniency: 'the jury unanimously desire to express the hope that, taking into consideration the undoubtedly pure motives that underlay the agitation which has led to these troubles, you will be pleased to exercise leniency.' Lord Coleridge ignored their plea and sentenced all three defendants to nine months in the second division, and made Mrs Pankhurst and Fred Pethick-Lawrence liable for the costs of the prosecution.[35]

The verdict was greeted by a noisy hubbub and uproar from the women's suffrage campaigners at the length of their sentences, and the awarding of high costs. The Emmelines were sent to Holloway and Fred to Brixton Prison. All three threatened to go on hunger strike unless they were given political status and first division prison treatment. They won that battle but the privileges were not extended to all suffragettes in other prisons, and a mass hunger-strike would break out on 19 June. After three days Mrs Pankhurst, too weak to be force-fed, and Emmeline Pethick-Lawrence, who was force-fed only once, were released on medical grounds. Mrs Pankhurst heard the violent kerfuffle as her friend was fed nearby and demanded to be allowed to see her. 'There I found my companion in a desperate state. She is a strong woman, and a determined one, and it had required the strength of nine wardresses to overcome her … she resisted so violently that the doctors could not apply the stethoscope, and they had a very difficult time getting the tube down.'[36] Emmeline Pethick-Lawrence fainted and 'for hours afterwards was very ill'. Fred Pethick-Lawrence was force-fed twice a day for more than ten days and was released on 1 July in a state of collapse.

In Dublin in the early hours of 13 June 1912 Hanna Sheehy-Skeffington, Miss Maud Lloyd, Miss Hilda Webb, Miss Marjorie Hasler, the 'Murphy' sisters, 'Maggie' and 'Jane' (Leila and Rosalind Cadiz), Mrs Marguerite Palmer and Miss Kathleen Houston, all members of the Irish Women's Franchise League, were arrested for breaking the windows of government buildings. (Five of these women had been at Black Friday.) Their handbags were full of stones. The Irish Women's Franchise League, founded in 1908, had not long before written to Herbert Asquith reminding him of a recent resolution passed in Ireland asking the government to introduce an amendment to the Home Rule Bill to make the local government register, which included women, the basis for the franchise for the proposed Irish Parliament. Asquith had not replied. Another factor for the IWFL was their disappointment that the Irish MPs at Westminster voted against the Conciliation Bill. The suffragette gang broke windows of the General Post Office, the Custom House, the Local Marine Board, Ship Street Barracks, the War Office and the Land Commission Offices.[37]

Hanna Sheehy-Skeffington broke nineteen panes at the War Office and was sentenced to two months at Mountjoy Prison. At the same time in the House of Commons her father, David Sheehy MP, supported the force-feeding of hunger-striking suffragettes. Hanna went on hunger strike in sympathy with the English prisoners and was released after five days without being force-fed. Hanna's family were long-standing nationalists; her father was a mill owner who had been a Fenian, then the MP for South Galway (1885–1900), becoming MP for County Meath from 1903 until 1918. He had been to prison six times for his opposition to British rule and landlordism. Hanna's husband, Francis Skeffington, was a teetotal, radical socialist, pacifist, feminist and nationalist and member of the Irish Women's Franchise League, who would be shot as a traitor without trial – he had been trying to stop looting – for his role in the Easter Rising of 1916.[38]

The 'Murphy' sisters, Leila and Rosalind Cadiz, were born in India to a Spanish father, a barrister born in Trinidad, and a mother from County Roscommon. The girls were orphaned early and sent to Ireland to be cared for by relations. In 1910 they joined the Irish Women's Franchise League and the Women's Social and Political Union. The sisters witnessed the events of Black Friday and in March 1912, under their *noms de guerre* of Margaret and Jane Murphy, were arrested and sent to Holloway for two months with hard labour for breaking windows. They went on hunger strike and were force-fed and released at the end of their sentence on 15 May. The sisters were not easy comrades. Hanna Sheehy-Skeffington found their high-handed attitude difficult: 'we regard them as crazy, they never speak to anyone now and the others wonder how we could ever have put up with them.'[39]

Kathleen Houston, who had two previous convictions for her protests in London in the aftermath of Black Friday, and for break-ing windows on 21 November 1911, was sent to Mountjoy for six months for breaking the windows of the General Post Office. She served her time as a first-class offender, and was released a month early for good conduct. Between her two prison sentences in Holloway, Kathleen worked as a drapery clerk at Whiteley's department store in Westbourne Grove.[40]

Marjorie Hasler, Kathleen's accomplice, also got six months and was released two months early from her sentence for good conduct. This was her second spell in prison, having served two weeks in Holloway for breaking a window on 21 November 1911. Marjorie saw action on Black Friday; when tussling with the police she hit her head on a wall which left her with headaches. While Marjorie was in Mountjoy she wrote to the *Irish Citizen* newspaper which Francis Sheehy-Skeffington had recently founded, comparing the suffra-gettes' actions with those of the Land League campaigners: 'We don't like smashing windows any more than men like smashing skulls, but in both cases there is, I believe, a strong feeling that something must be done before a wrong can be righted.'[41]

For breaking the windows of the Local Marine Board, Hilda Webb and Maud Lloyd were sent to Mountjoy as first division offenders for six months, and, like their comrades Kathleen Houston and Marjorie Hasler, they were released two months before the end of their sentences. This was Hilda Webb's second time in prison, having served time in Holloway for breaking windows in the days following Black Friday.[42]

During the summer months the window-smashers of March were released from prisons all over England. The backdrop to their welcome parties was the news on 17 June that the Manhood Suffrage Bill, which had replaced the Conciliation Bill, was introduced to the House of Commons. It was revealed that there would be no women's suffrage amendment, which prospect had been dangled by some cabinet ministers. Until early September Lord Haldane, Sir Edward Grey and Lloyd George had encouraged Mrs Fawcett's moderate supporters to think there might yet be a chance for a women's suffrage amendment.[43]

On 24 June Violet Aitken was released from Winson Green, shortly before the completion of her four-month sentence. She had been fed by force twice and returned home to the Cathedral Close, Norwich, to a concerned and chilly reception. Her enthusiastic membership of the WSPU was an embarrassment to her elderly parents who were relieved that Violet's twin sister, Rose, did not share her militancy. Rose took up theosophy, which posed a spiritual conundrum for her father, Canon of Norwich Cathedral, William Aitken. Canon Aitken was bewildered: 'it is all very sad but these are strange days.' His wife, who was 'much exercised' about their wayward suffragette daughter, could 'talk and think of little else'.[44]

Violet Aitken was arrested with Clara Giveen on 1 March 1912, when they broke twelve windows of Jay's, a women's clothing store in Regent Street, causing £100 worth of damage. This was not her first offence: she had been sentenced to a week in Holloway in November 1911 for holding the bridle of a policeman's horse at a WSPU protest.

When Violet wrote to her parents informing them that she would change her role to organiser, this gave them some comfort. She was a journalist on the staff of *The Suffragette*, the militant weekly newspaper, after it was launched in the autumn of 1912. Canon Aitken's feelings about women's suffrage steadied and he was happy to make a speech in support of the moderate women's demands for the vote, 'not concealing my views as to the militants but pointing out that there was more reason for those who disapprove of such tactics to be in earnest for what is after all only an act of justice'.[45]

*

Emily Davison joined the dozens of suffragette prisoners who were officially on hunger strike. In a manuscript prepared for the WSPU she provided a vivid account of the protest made by suffragettes who were being kept in solitary confinement and force-fed in their cells. On 22 June, near the end of her six-month sentence, she threw herself over the handrail and wire netting outside her second-floor cell and landed at the bottom of the steps of the floor below. Earlier in the day she and others had barricaded themselves into their cells, 'a regular siege took place ... on all sides we heard crowbars, blocks, wedges being used, joiners battering on doors with all their might. The barricading was followed by sounds of human struggle, the chair of torture being pushed about, suppressed cries of the victims, groans and other horrible sounds.'[46] The sounds came nearer and nearer, filling Emily with dread. She fought 'like a demon' when her cell door was forced open and she tried to dart out into the passage. Five wardresses grabbed her and tied her into a chair and placed her on her bed. Emily lay like 'a log for some time' and decided that she had to make a 'desperate protest' to end the 'hideous torture'.

Untied from the chair a couple of hours later Emily slipped out of her cell and 'climbed onto the railings threw myself out on to the wire netting below... but it prevented any serious injury'. Four wardresses were needed to peel her off the netting. Emily was taken to the hospital ward and escaped, and for the second time threw herself over the second-floor handrail, and was caught by the netting. As wardresses 'expostulated and called on twenty of my comrades to try and stop me', Emily 'realised there was only one chance left and that was to hurl myself with the greatest force I could summon from the netting onto the staircase ten feet below'. She threw herself forward 'on my head with all my might. I knew nothing except a fearful thud on my head.'[47]

Emily was examined by Dr William Sullivan, who said she did not show any signs of shock or serious injury. On further examination, he found a 'small contused wound of the scalp' at the back of her head, and a 'small bruise over her left hip bone, a trivial bruise on the left elbow and some slight abrasions to the knees'. Emily complained of a painful and stiff neck, and severe pain in her spine, in the 'cervical and lower dorsal regions' when she moved. She said she was in much pain and objected to being force-fed. Dr Sullivan asked Thomas English, the Consulting Surgeon at St George's Hospital, who was also on the surgical staff of the Grosvenor Hospital for Women, to examine her. He stated that Emily had suffered no 'gross injury and there was no reason to abstain from the necessary steps for compelling the prisoner to take nourishment'. Accordingly Emily was fed through a nasal tube the next day 'with satisfactory results'.[48] Discussion of the circumstances surrounding what seemed like a suicide attempt rumbled on for several days: on 24 June Keir Hardie asked the home secretary Reginald McKenna in the House of Commons whether he could give the House any information concerning 'the accident to Miss Davison ... whether she had been forcibly fed and if so how many times before the accident; what was the nature of the injuries sustained; whether she was in hospital and if she was still being forcibly fed'.[49]

On 27 June Drs Maurice Craig and Herbert Smalley examined Emily and found her 'mental condition and intellect' were clear, but were advised by the prison staff that she was 'at times cheerful and at other times sullen'. Emily told Craig that she had jumped over the balustrade because she felt that 'something terrible must be done to bring an end to the present state of affairs', and that she would not have minded if she had killed herself. Craig reported to the Home Office, 'she is evidently a most determined woman and she considers that she is right to do anything for the cause, and is reckless in what she does for the movement.' Emily's health had suffered since her fall and 'continues to suffer'. And yet the prison persisted in force-feeding despite Emily 'working herself up into an excited condition'. Her pulse was low and she needed a hot-water bottle for her feet because 'her extremities were cold'. Emily's tongue was 'coated but moist, her pupils are widely dilated and the body weight is falling rapidly, especially in the last few days' [since the fall]. Dr Craig was concerned that the rapid weight loss 'will tend to increase her tendency to impulsive action'.[50] The Home Office refused to let Mr Charles Mansell-Moullin examine Emily. Ten days before the end of her six-month sentence, on 28 June, Emily Davison was released in a run-down state, two stone lighter, with two scalp wounds. She had been force-fed forty-nine times.

*

On 25 June, George Lansbury, the Labour MP for Bow and Bromley, behaved in what was considered an unparliamentary way towards the prime minister. The *Daily Mirror* headlines shouted: 'Mr Lansbury Storms At Premier', 'Socialist MP's Hysterical Outburst of Insult', 'Member for Bow at Last Persuaded to Leave the House'. After questioning cabinet ministers in the House of Commons about the treatment of suffragette prisoners, Lansbury, 'labouring under immense excitement, stood at the edge of the Treasury bench, shook his fist at the Prime Minister and bawled insult upon insult at him for several minutes'.[51] Lansbury was infuriated by Asquith's disingenuous response to the request by Tim Healy, the Irish MP for North-East Cork, that the remaining women prisoners be released a few days earlier than their full sentences, ending with the remark, 'Why keep up this needless torture?' The prime minister brushed aside Healy's request saying he could not interfere in administrative matters, and that the suffragette prisoners could walk out of the prison any time if they abandoned the militant methods which were landing them in prison in the first place. Lansbury was at 'boiling point', furious that the women were being expected to abandon their principles in such a way, and 'with immense passion the Socialist, purple with passion, fixed his eyes on the Prime Minister, who, with folded arms and highly-coloured cheeks, sat listening' but refused to look at the man who was shouting at him. Lansbury's tirade continued: Asquith should be 'driven out of public life ... You will go down in history as the man who tortured innocent women! It is perfectly disgusting!' It took several urgent demands by the Speaker for George Lansbury to leave the Chamber. 'Purple with rage', he returned to his seat determined to stay, but was persuaded by friends to leave the House of Commons 'amid a cheer of relief'.

George Lansbury lived in Bow with his wife, Bessie, and six children, all active supporters of women's suffrage. In 1884 the Lansburys emigrated to Australia but George failed to find work and they returned to England in 1886. Returning to the squalid East End from the wide-open spaces of Australia opened Lansbury's eyes to the tough conditions in working-class London. He changed his Liberal opinions for socialist politics; from 1892 to 1904 he was a leading figure in the Social Democratic Federation and tried, and failed, twice to become an MP, in 1895 and 1900. George Lansbury inherited his father-in-law's timber business and in 1904 he joined Keir Hardie's Independent Labour Party. Lansbury was a Poor Law Guardian and member of the London County Council. In 1910 he narrowly won the seat of Bow and Bromley from the Liberals. He first became interested in women's suffrage early in 1906 when Sylvia Pankhurst introduced him to Annie Kenney.[52]

*

When Emily Davison was released from prison she convalesced with Minnie Turner in Brighton and by the end of July she felt well enough to go to see her mother in Northumberland. On 1 July, half a dozen 'male and female' suffragettes who were outraged at Emily's treatment in Holloway harassed Dr Thomas English whom they wrongly believed to have force-fed her. They barged into his consulting rooms at 47 Upper Brook Street, Mayfair, threatened to smash windows and burn the house down, and left two signed 'protests'. The police were called and the intruders left. On 5 July an article appeared in *Votes for Women* attacking English for his brutality. A week later Home Secretary McKenna told the beleaguered doctor he found it difficult 'to express in suitable language his reprobation of the conduct of political propagandists who slander a professional man because he has in the course of his professional duties expressed a scientific opinion on a question of fact'.[53]

The Expulsion of the Pethick-Lawrences

Blowing Up Pillar Boxes Summer 1912

A tin toy of 1913 inspired by the WSPU's tactic of planting phosphorous bombs and burning rags in pillar boxes, destroying letters and small parcels.

Only the vigilance of the night watchman at the colonial secretary Lewis 'Loulou' Harcourt's country home on 13 July prevented Nuneham House being torched by Helen Craggs and a friend. Helen's accomplice was thought to be Ethel Smyth but when Ethel was later arrested the failure of the witnesses to identify her, and her solid alibi, led to her being discharged. At one o'clock in the morning the two women had paddled to their destination from Oxford by canoe, with a basket and satchel filled with all the paraphernalia needed for housebreaking and setting fire to the Palladian mansion – bottles of paraffin, matches, twelve firelighters, nine picklocks, a torch, a glasscutter, methylated spirits, cigarettes, chocolate, and a purple, white and green flag. When asked by PC Godden, on duty at the house that evening, what they were doing hiding in the creepers at that time, Helen Craggs said, 'we have come to look round the house, it's a very nice time of night to look round the house'.[1] Helen further explained, 'It's really too hot. We were unable to sleep, we are camping down here.' When Godden asked for a name Helen replied, 'I shall say nothing to incriminate myself.' When PC Godden told her she would have to accompany him as her account was not very satisfactory, she tried to bolt and he grabbed her by the wrist, while her accomplice ran off. When the canoe was searched a change of clothing, books and a song sheet of 'The March of the Women' were found.

Wearing 'a striking costume prominently displaying the suffragist colours' Helen Craggs refused to give her name when she appeared at Bullingdon Petty Sessions the next day. She pleaded guilty to the charge of 'being in the garden ... for an unlawful purpose, to commit a felony, to unlawfully and maliciously set fire to a house and building belonging to Mr Harcourt'. Because of the seriousness of the crime – eight people were asleep in the house – bail was refused. At the Assizes in Oxford on 26 July, Doris Gale, the daughter of Lewis Harcourt's land agent, told the court that, on 11 July, Helen Craggs and her companion had knocked at her father's door at one o'clock in the afternoon asking if 'they could see the pictures' at Nuneham House. Doris told the ladies they could not come into the house and that 'people were not allowed even into the gardens as they did so much harm'.[2]

In Helen's handbag a notebook was found with two telephone numbers, those of Lewis Harcourt and the Oxford Fire Station, and a typewritten statement, signed 'A Suffragette', which was read to the court: 'Sir, it is with a deep sense of my responsibility and a sincere conviction that my action is justifiable that I have taken a serious step in the cause of women's enfranchisement ... I deplore that though during the past six years the demand for political liberty for women has become the greatest agitation of the time, politicians were content to see the supporters violently treated and unjustly imprisoned rather than give them the long-delayed and much-needed measure of justice which they demanded.'[3] After much discussion and undertaking not to commit any unlawful act, Helen Craggs was freed on bail of £1,000 (£100,000 today) half of which was put up by Ethel Smyth. The suffragettes' attempt to burn down Nuneham House may have been foiled but the strategy would be deployed with increasing frequency and devastating consequences during the remainder of the campaign. Charles Hobhouse's speech at Bristol in February was quoted many times at meetings and reproduced in handbills as justification for the WSPU's deliberate escalation of militancy.

Helen Craggs had been arrested for breaking windows in March 1912, held in Holloway on remand and later acquitted and in June she stalked Reginald McKenna while he was accompanying the King and Queen on a visit to Wales, pouncing on him at Llandaff Cathedral, grabbing his arm and berating him for the suffragettes' suffering. She was released without being charged. After her trial for attempted arson she insisted she was 'morally guiltless' of any crime, but was nevertheless sentenced to serve nine months with hard labour in Holloway. She went on hunger strike and was force-fed five times over two days. Her health was delicate and she was released after eleven days, suffering from internal and external bruising. In 1913 she went to Dublin to train as a midwife and a year later married Dr Alexander McCombie, who was working in the East End of London.[4]

Acting on their own initiative, on 16 July 1912 Gladys Evans from London, and 'Lizzie Baker' (real name Jennie Baines) of Stockport, caught the boat from Holyhead to Dublin and took lodgings in Lower Mount Street. Mary Leigh and Mabel Capper arrived two days later. They were in Dublin because Herbert Asquith was to give a speech on Home Rule to 4,000 supporters at the Theatre Royal on 19 July. According to *Votes for Women* the prime minister, his wife Margot and daughter Violet, left Paddington on the morning of 18 July in 'great stealth' for Wolverhampton, crept into a motor car guarded by detectives bound for Holyhead, and were 'safely smuggled' on board a steamer. Asquith was then taken by train from the port of Kingstown to Dublin city centre. Before landing he was 'welcomed' by members of the Irish Women's Franchise League who sailed out in a yacht to greet him with a megaphone demanding he put votes for Irish women into the Home Rule Bill.[5]

That evening Mary Leigh set off to confront Asquith, who had refused to receive any women's suffrage deputations during his stay. A suffragette protest had been feared by the Dublin police, and Augustine Birrell, the chief secretary of Ireland, had intelligence about a plot to assassinate the British prime minister on 19 July: 'The instigators of the plot are the advanced section of the militant Suffragists. The attack is to be made while Mr Asquith is driving through the city from the railway station on his arrival, and will come from a house. In order to guard against failure the horses are to be shot first, and then when the carriage has thus been brought to standstill, several shots are to be fired at Mr Asquith.'[6] Perhaps this was a deliberate smear for there is no evidence to suggest that this was a real threat.

Mary Leigh seized her moment when she spotted Asquith travelling in an open carriage with his family, John Redmond, and the Lord Mayor of Dublin. She hurled a hatchet at him as the open carriage passed the General Post Office taking the Asquiths to their hotel, missing him narrowly but striking John Redmond on one ear, causing a small wound. Mary clung to the back of the carriage, and when the chief marshal of the event, J. J. O'Brien, walking alongside the vehicle, grabbed her 'she beat him in the face for all she was worth'.[7]

In the evening Gladys Evans and Mary Leigh left Lower Mount Street to set fire to the Theatre Royal. As the last stragglers were leaving the theatre Gladys was spotted by Joseph Keogh chucking a burning rag soaked in paraffin into the cinema projection box at the back of the stalls and running away as if she 'expected some explosion'. He asked her if she wanted to burn the theatre down and Gladys told him she would do anything she liked. Sergeant Durban Cooper of the Connaught Rangers, and Colour-Sergeant Shea, from the Royal Welsh Fusiliers, who were stationed at the Curragh Military Camp in Kildare, noticed that the carpet was burning and they put the fire out with their jackets. Then there was an explosion, which Sergeant Cooper described as sounding like 'a report from a cannon', and smoke. Cooper saw Gladys throw a handbag filled with gunpowder and matches into a box next to the stage, and run off. He chased after her: 'I caught hold of her and both of us fell down the stairs but I was not hurt. She warned: "That is only the start of it, there will be more explosions at the second house."'[8] Mary Leigh, who had a smaller role to play, threw a burning chair into the orchestra pit. Gladys was taken away by a policeman, and Mary managed to escape, losing three items of her clothing.

Mary was arrested the next morning at her lodgings. The landlady's daughter had seen her returning and noted she was without her coat, hat and red motor veil. Miss Kelly told the court that Leigh's manner seemed 'peculiar', and that she said she had lost her clothing holding up Mr Asquith's carriage. When Mary asked Miss Kelly to explain what she meant by 'peculiar', she replied: 'You were very shaky as if you had taken a drink' – which was greeted by more laughter in the court – at which Mary asked if Miss Kelly thought she looked as if she had been 'in the hands of a brute who had been knocking me about', with which Miss Kelly agreed.

The day after the hatchet and arson attacks *The Times* reported that Dubliners had been 'moved to the utmost indignation' by the suffraettes' 'outrages' and were in 'a dangerous temper'. Local newspaper headline writers expressed dismay and disgust at the 'Virago and the Hatchet', the suffragettes' 'Reign of Terror' and the 'Dastardly

Outrages'. On 19 July the police arrested 'Lizzie Baker', Mabel Capper and Mary Leigh at their lodgings and jailed them with Gladys Evans at the Central Bridewell prison in the city. The four women were charged with having 'unlawfully conspired with other persons, known, and unknown, to inflict grievous bodily harm and wilful and malicious damage upon property, and to cause an explosion in the Theatre Royal of a nature likely to endanger life or to cause serious injury to property; and that in pursuance of this object they attempted to set fire to the theatre.' Mary Leigh was also charged with having thrown a hatchet which injured Mr Redmond.[9]

On 6 August their barrister Tim Healy conducted a spirited defence of Gladys Evans's actions, saying the suffragettes had been told they would not be taken seriously until they burned down castles. He told the jury it was not his place to justify in any way what had been done but they had 'been provoked by the conduct of those who were now prosecuting them as criminals'. He urged the public that the sooner they made up their minds to 'a settlement of this question the sooner such incidents would become past history'.[10]

Mary Leigh called no witnesses and addressed the jury from the dock in defiant speeches on behalf of all her comrades. She insisted the evidence presented in court had been 'distorted' and there had been no danger to the public in their protest at the theatre and no confusion, and that if they sent her to prison she might not survive the sentence. Mary warned that if convicted she would fight: 'she would put her back against the wall, and nothing, not even the whole army of the Government and officials, would bring her to submission.' The jury returned guilty verdicts on Mary Leigh and Gladys Evans. Mr Justice Madden gave the pair five years each because 'no more terrible catastrophe could occur in a city than a conflagration at a theatre'. 'Lizzie Baker' was sentenced to seven months with hard labour, and Mabel Capper was acquitted for lack of evidence and released.[11]

This was Gladys Evans's first and last militant act. She had joined the WSPU in 1908 and worked at Selfridges when it opened in March 1909, resigning in 1910 to run a WSPU shop. A letter signed by 254 employees at Selfridges praised Gladys's good character: 'We do respectfully urge you that remission of sentence be granted to her. We would plead that the fact that this offence for which the prisoner who was convicted was her first offence against the law, and that her high character, to which we can all testify, are powerful arguments why such remission should be granted.'¹²

To the despair of the prison authorities at Mountjoy, Mary and Gladys went on hunger strike, demanding political status. Dr Bartholomew Hackett, the assistant medical officer, advised the governor they were 'in a very emotional state … and in a highly-strung condition'. Hackett reminded Major Owen-Lewis that Mary told the court she would 'fight the Government in prison with every breath in her body'. Normally the women would have been photographed and fingerprinted but the procedures were abandoned as Dr Hackett was concerned that any attempt to take their fingerprints would 'have resulted in a struggle which might have ended fatally for such patients'.

Mary and Gladys were force-fed for the first time on 20 August after six days of self-starvation. Dr David Flinn, of the General Prisons Board, tried to persuade them to take food. He found them 'absolutely un-moveable and resolute in their determination to continue the hunger-strike'. Flinn found both women 'weaker than at his last visit to the prison'. Mary Leigh resisted 'violently', Gladys Evans was compliant. Mary said she preferred a soft rubber tube (lubricated with glycerine) that was passed up her nose, whereas Gladys chose to hold the tube in place with a finger in her mouth as it was pushed into her stomach. For the first few days the women were fed twice a day, in the morning and afternoon, with a concoction of raw eggs and warmed milk.

On 7 August Mary Leigh weighed ninety-five pounds, and Gladys Evans a hundred and fourteen pounds; both were in good health. Before they were force-fed for the first time, their weight had fallen to ninety and ninety-six pounds respectively. Mary Leigh would bring up almost all the food they had poured into her body, whereas Gladys retained all of hers. On 23 August the prison doctor, Raymond Dowdall, noted that the tube had passed up Mary's nose 'easily, no blood, little discomfort apparently, once she was released from her chair she contrived to vomit' and this material was weighed and found to be six ounces which was 'watery fluid, bile stained, part of the meal had been absorbed'. Gladys Evans, to Dowdall's relief, 'gives little trouble, is fed by oesophageal tube and retains all her food'.¹³

After a week Mary's weight had dropped to eighty-six pounds and Gladys had lost only half a pound. As the tube was fed into Gladys's stomach she 'gave every assistance, placing her own fingers in her mouth to prevent her teeth closing on the tube'. Despite having been fed three times a day, Mary had lost ten pounds in eighteen days.[14]

Dr Flinn offered Mary and Gladys concessions: in addition to the freedom to associate with the other prisoners, and to be able to wear their own clothes, they could receive letters and newspapers if they would end their hunger strike. Both refused. Mary said that she had given him her answer a month ago and that her conditions were 'the Vote or a pledge'. Flinn told her that as a subordinate official it was impossible for him to give any pledge, to which Mary replied: 'I refuse. I'll fight you to the end. There is no need to go over the same ground again. You have my answer.' Gladys Evans also refused to take food.

By 12 September, Mary was losing vitality and her 'extremities were cold'. She told Dowdall that she was feeling unwell, so he washed her stomach out with warm water and thirty grains of bread soda, and noted in her file 'there appears to be a slight change for the worse'. Flinn examined the women and noted that Mary's 'heart action continues normal and sound and her pulse though slower is regular'. She had walked unaided to the room where he watched her being fed: 'There was no trouble or the semblance of resentment on her part, her voice is quite strong and she replied to all questions put to her quite brightly.' Before he left Mary vomited a small amount of food.[15]

In the three days leading up to Mary Leigh's release she refused to allow the doctors to examine her abdomen, would not take exercise and was bringing up all her food. On the day of her release Dr Dowdall reported: 'I find there is a marked loss of vital power and the case has in my opinion become one of urgency. The woman was assisted this morning while walking from her cell, and it was necessary to lift her and place her on the couch before feeding. The pulse is weak, the urine is high coloured.' Sir Christopher Nixon (physician to the Mater Misericordiae Hospital, Dublin) and Sir Thomas Myles (president of the Royal College of Surgeons in Ireland, 1900–1902) were summoned to the prison for their opinion and reported: 'We regard her condition as most serious, one in fact imperilling her life.' Her weight had fallen by twenty pounds in sixty-four days. They also examined Gladys Evans who had been 'most amenable to the treatment and made no complaint', and even though she had been force-fed for thirty-one days they could find no medical grounds to authorise her removal from Mountjoy at that time.[16]

Mary Leigh was released on licence on 20 September 1912, weighing five stone and four pounds. The terms of her licence were that she should 'abstain from any violation of the law', inform the police where she was living, and not leave the country. She was driven away in a state of 'absolute collapse' to a hospital which she refused to enter. It was agreed she could stay in a private home but remain under medical supervision. Gladys Hazel, one of the women who met her at the prison gate, said: 'She looked simply dead, she was absolutely wasted away. One of the few remarks she made was "No Surrender."' One newspaper reported that Mary Leigh was 'dreadfully emaciated, looking wasted and haggard and a shadow of her former self'. On the first night she was free she could not sleep and for the first twenty-four hours she was unable to keep any food down.[17]

Schoolteacher Gladys Hazel was incensed by the poverty suffered by women and children in Birmingham, and joined the WSPU in 1907 after hearing Mrs Pankhurst and Charlotte Despard speak at Birmingham Town Hall. 'It was what I was looking for. It was a society afire with righteous indignation. We called each other by our Christian names ... there was a friendly and unforced intimacy between us.' Gladys's work for the WSPU made trouble in her family, causing distress and anxiety to her parents. A favourite aunt would not have Gladys's name mentioned, and when Gladys's mother died in 1914 her aunt told Gladys she had killed her mother. Before arriving in Dublin Gladys had been on hunger strike in Holloway and was force-fed and became friends with Emily Davison. She was asked by one of the wardresses to dissuade Emily from jumping over the balcony on 22 June, to which Gladys replied, 'Why? She'll be well out of it.' As Gladys turned away she 'heard her fall and saw her lying across the steps as they hustled me into my cell'.[18]

During the summer of 1912 Clement's Inn coordinated a campaign throughout England, Scotland and Wales to demand the release of the women in Dublin and to write letters and send telegrams to King George V and Home Secretary Reginald McKenna, but mostly to Augustine Birrell, expressing anger at the 'spiteful sentences' that had been handed down to Leigh and Evans, and at their harsh treatment in Mountjoy. Writers included disillusioned Liberal male voters and female supporters; the Woolwich Branch of the Women's Labour League; Miss Fedden of St Martha's College of Housecraft in London; the Surbiton, Edinburgh and Glasgow branches of the Independent Labour Party; Willesden Green's branch of the British Socialist Party and the Doncaster branch of the Workers' Union. Several members of the Baptist community in Liverpool told Birrell he was not worthy to be the son of his father Charles Birrell, a Baptist minister.[19]

Gladys Evans was released from Mountjoy on licence on 3 October by the Lord Lieutenant of Ireland on medical grounds, after fifty-eight days of hunger-striking and being fed by stomach tube eighty-eight times. There had been a marked deterioration in her health: from being able to tolerate the feeding, and being amenable to the necessity of it, Gladys seems to have had a crisis exacerbated by lack of sleep. Her heartbeat became irregular and she showed signs of 'great nervous tension and general breakdown'. Two days before her release Gladys 'violently resisted all efforts that were made to feed her and struggled very much'. She refused to be fed and barricaded herself into her cell using her bed, but two nurses managed to get in. Five wardresses were needed to overcome her, and she had to be strapped by the ankles and wrists into the feeding chair. Gladys refused to open her mouth and the tube would not go up her nose owing to 'malformation of both nasal passages' and Dr Dowdall was afraid that if he fed her 'given her present state of health ... it would be attended by serious consequences and possibly by collapse'. Gladys convalesced in the homes of sympathisers and slowly recovered from her ordeal, which left her with kidney problems for the rest of her life.[20]

Several months later all the charges against Mary Leigh and Gladys Evans would be dropped because of prolonged litigation concerning the terms of their licences. Mary and Gladys recovered their health and returned to England in December and were given paid work at WSPU headquarters at twenty-five shillings a week, using the aliases of 'Mrs Brown' and 'Gertrude Bentley'.

On 7 November suffragettes presented a formal declaration to Mrs Pankhurst, 'the Queen of Women', when she spoke in Bath: 'We wish to convey to you our unswerving loyalty to your person, and our grateful appreciation of your leadership of the Militant Campaign in the Women's Movement.' Mrs Pankhurst had been due to stay with the Blathwayts but two weeks earlier Mrs Blathwayt told the Bath organiser, Grace Tollemache, that she was withdrawing her offer of hospitality, 'as she is going about inciting violence. Linley [Blathwayt] always told the Pankhursts how he felt on the subject.' Perhaps the Blathwayts feared they would be the victims of reprisals, although they were happy to pay Mrs Pankhurst's hotel bill and taxi fares. Mary Blathwayt, who was perhaps embarrassed by her parents' refusal to have Mrs Pankhurst to stay, was proud to escort Mrs Pankhurst to her hotel and to the meeting. To her mother's relief, Mary resigned from the WSPU in the summer of 1913, maintaining her close friendships with Annie Kenney and her sisters but preferring to work for the moderate suffragists.[21]

In the summer of 1912 Lucy Burns, who had worked for the WSPU since 1909, left her position as organiser in Edinburgh and after three years returned to America. There she co-founded the National Woman's Party with Alice Paul. They transplanted some of the militant tactics they had learned in England, and adopted a colour scheme of purple, white and gold.[22]

*

In August Sylvia Pankhurst took charge of the WSPU's by-election campaign against the Liberals in Manchester North-West, where militancy had begun seven years earlier. The Liberal incumbent Sir George Kemp stood down from Parliament, and the seat was won by the Conservative industrialist Sir John Scurrah Randles by a majority of 445 votes. Sylvia reinvigorated the WSPU's presence in the East End of London; she would open the new WSPU headquarters in October in an old baker's shop in Bow Road, near the home of her ally George Lansbury. Sylvia wrote, 'the East End was the greatest homogenous working-class area accessible to the House of Commons and popular demonstrations ... the creation of a woman's movement in that great abyss of poverty', she hoped, would be 'a call and rallying-cry to the founding of other such groups in working-class districts throughout the country'. She was helped by the Lansbury family as well as Zelie Emerson, nineteen, whom she had met in Chicago while on a speaking tour; Lady Sybil Smith, who was the treasurer; Elsa Dalglish, the financial secretary; and members who came from Kensington and Chelsea to help. Sylvia put the finishing touches to the bow-fronted eighteenth-century shop by painting 'Votes for Women' in 'early Roman characters in gold leaf'. The shop was a little jewel in the run-down neighbourhood of noxious trades, soap-makers and tanneries, operating cheek-by-jowl with families living in overcrowded, unhealthy conditions. Sylvia could never forget 'the most appalling smells, how my head ached from them'.[23]

Sylvia called Zelie Emerson 'a merry little American', from a Midwest farm, whose love of adventure had brought her to London in May 1912 to join the militant movement, helping for the first time at the Crewe and Manchester by-elections. Lady Sybil Smith was the wife of a merchant banker, Sir Vivian Smith, and the mother of seven children aged between ten and two years old. Sybil had a 'tall and slender figure and flaxen hair' and 'in her long straight gown she looked like a nymph on a Greek vase'. Elsa Noble Dalglish, a Scottish landscape artist, was the daughter of a cotton manufacturer.

It was not easy for Sylvia and her team to campaign for women's suffrage in George Lansbury's constituency. The Bethnal Green branch had to contend with rough crowds, some of whom pelted them with 'fishes' heads and paper soaked in the local public urinal'. Sylvia's ankles were never free from bruises. By the middle of November her artistry was making the East End campaign a distinctive branch of the WSPU brand. A 'very beautiful new banner' was unfurled at West Ham's WSPU shop in Romford Road, measuring 1.2 by 1.7 metres, made of purple, white and green silk, wool and velvet, and bore the appliquéd words 'Courage', 'Constancy' and 'Success', and an angel blowing a clarion, standing at a signpost pointing to Freedom. Sylvia's special relationship with Keir Hardie was behind the creation of the banner: he had been returned as the MP for West Ham South in 1892, becoming the first working man to be elected to Parliament.[24]

In early September there were reports of telegraph wires being cut in Hertfordshire, and literature left at the scene showed that the WSPU was responsible for 'this malicious action' which caused 'great inconvenience'. On 5 September Winston Churchill was harried by suffragettes at Aberdeen, and a few days later at Jarrow. Two suffragettes, one of whom was Lilias Mitchell, replaced the flags at Balmoral golf course with their own tricolour bearing messages, 'Cabinet Ministers! Stop forcibly feeding women!' and 'Votes for Women means peace for Cabinet Ministers'. Herbert Asquith and Reginald McKenna were playing golf in the district and it was an irresistible opportunity. Lilias described it as 'the sort of adventure that is tremendous fun once it is over; the walk there was lengthy and seemed unendingly so when we got within the private grounds'.[25]

Kitty Marion recovered from her prison sentence at the home of Lilla Durham in East Grinstead and made plans to heckle David Lloyd George at the Welsh National Eisteddfod at Wrexham on 5 September. A pavilion was packed with 13,000 'worshippers and admirers', as Kitty called them, and she and two others managed to get tickets near the platform. This was the first time she had set out to interrupt a cabinet minister and 'within ten minutes I experienced all the concentrated essence of coarse brutalities and indecencies of several hours' battle in Westminster'. One man who protested about the way a woman heckler was treated was 'thrown out, badly beaten and had his eyes blackened'. At a pause in the singing Kitty jumped up and shouted, 'how dare you have political prisoners fed by force!' A policeman and a steward bundled her outside where she 'received blows and abuse from every side, my hat being torn off and my hair pulled down. A howling mob almost tore me to pieces. My hair was grabbed and pulled out by the roots.'[26] In *Votes for Women* she gave details of her assault; her clothes were ripped, 'my very undergarments were torn to shreds'. Kitty thought that being thrown to wild beasts was preferable to being thrown to an infuriated mob: 'the former might tear you to pieces but draw the line at indecent assaults, and so do I.' Eventually the police rescued Kitty and her comrades, and sympathetic detectives escorted them to a train to Shrewsbury where Kitty spent the night with WSPU members. Some suffragettes interrupted Lloyd George two weeks later at Llanystumdwy, near Criccieth, his childhood home, and endured a high level of violence. The front page of the *Daily Mirror* was given up to women being surrounded and beaten. Two suffragettes had their skirts ripped off and 'portions cut up and distributed among the crowds as souvenirs'. The police also came under attack from the biting 'mobbers' as they tried to take the women away to safety.[27]

*

During the summer of 1912 Emmeline and Christabel Pankhurst had grown apart from Mr and Mrs Pethick-Lawrence who were unhappy about the militant tempo, and who feared that women would die on hunger strikes. They were also concerned about Christabel's frequent use of the word 'war'. The membership of the WSPU knew that significant changes were in place when they saw the front page of *Votes for Women* for 20 September. Alice in Wonderland is seen bursting through the roof of Clement's Inn and finding herself outside the front door of 'Lincoln's Inn House: The Suffragettes' New Home', in Kingsway. The WSPU's cartoonist, Alfred Pearse, captioned the drawing: 'She went on growing and growing.' Started six years earlier in one room at 4 Clement's Inn, the WSPU had grown to twenty-six rooms, and was renting thirteen more at the Woman's Press in Charing Cross Road. All of the WSPU's departments would now be based at the new premises. There was, however, a less straightforward reason for leaving Clement's Inn.[28]

After the Pethick-Lawrences' release from prison at the end of June they recuperated at their country house in Surrey. In July Fred and Emmeline were en route for a holiday in Switzerland when they were summoned to a meeting with Christabel and Mrs Pankhurst in Boulogne, where the Pankhursts were spending the summer. It soon became clear a deep rift had opened up: the Pethick-Lawrences wanted to build up mass support by publicising the leadership's time in prison, by colourful marches and processions, as in the past. The Pankhursts were determined to continue to escalate the recent attacks on private and public property, 'secretly carried out by suffragettes who would not offer themselves up for arrest, but wherever possible would make good their escape'.[29] Fred and Emmeline feared militancy would alienate the public and risk the safety of the women carrying out such attacks. They asked Christabel to return to London 'and challenge the Government to arrest her', and if they did her trial would be 'the sensation of the day'. If she was tried she would become a figurehead for justice and 'acclaimed by audiences wherever she chose to speak ... and our appeal to the populace would be irresistible'.[30] The Pethick-Lawrences were flabbergasted when she refused to return to England, insisting she would lead the campaign from Paris. The four leaders quarrelled and then made it up, but Emmeline Pethick-Lawrence would later realise that 'a cleavage of the ground had taken place and had left the Pankhursts on one side of the chasm and ourselves on the other'.[31]

After the Pethick-Lawrences returned to England, Mrs Pankhurst wrote to them saying she was unwell and was staying in France until the fundraising meeting at the Albert Hall planned for 17 October. She urged Fred and Emmeline to take a holiday in Canada and the United States in August and September, hoping they would return in good health. Although the Pethick-Lawrences had been shocked by the negative tone of their recent meeting, they took her advice and set off, unaware of what would happen once they were out of the way. That summer they received a letter from Mrs Pankhurst suggesting they stay in Canada and make their home there, and take their assets out of the country, so they could not be confiscated. They declined to take Mrs Pankhurst's advice, writing to her that 'having staked our health and life for the vindication of the principle of human equality, we would not renounce it because of risk to our property'.[32] Eighteen years later Emmeline Pethick-Lawrence recalled that she and Fred had had no idea of what had been going on while they were away, 'until our friend and domestic helper, May Start, met us at the boat in order to break the news of the intrigue that had been hatched during our absence'.[33]

When the Pethick-Lawrences visited Lincoln's Inn House for the first time they learned that no offices had been allocated to them, and Mrs Pankhurst made it clear they were no longer welcome there. Christabel sneaked back from Paris to London in disguise and told them they were no longer needed in the organisation. For daring to question the need for increased militancy the couple were now purged from the WSPU, a betrayal of this most magnanimous couple who had given everything to the organisation: moral and professional support, a great deal of money and countless acts of generosity, taking the Pankhursts and their entourage on holidays to France, Switzerland and Italy. They had, too, to face the painful truth that Christabel, whom they had treated like a daughter, was the instrument of their humiliating expulsion.

Annie Kenney felt torn by the split; the manner of the expulsion revealed Christabel Pankhurst's ruthlessness. 'Once people questioned policy her whole feeling changed towards them.' Annie felt like an adopted daughter of the childless Pethick-Lawrences and she was 'far from happy'. Mrs Pethick-Lawrence had 'sheltered, clothed and loved me like a child', and Fred had taken her to places 'that would have remained day-dreams but for his kindness'. But Annie also admitted she 'worshipped' Christabel, and she knew that Christabel considered Annie her 'first-born militant and mascot'. Annie was proud that in March 1912 Christabel had looked to her 'for help in steering a ship that was to plough turbulent waters'. Annie also felt indebted to Mrs Pankhurst for the sacrifices she herself had made for the struggle for the vote; Emmeline had 'given up homely comforts, an income that meant much to her, who had given her family to the Cause' and who loved Annie 'with a genuine sincerity'.[34]

Annie was 'a little afraid of both sides, both seemed to look to me ... whichever side I took I knew I should bruise and hurt the side I had left'. She chose the Pankhursts; her relationship with the Pethick-Lawrences remained, but it was now strained. At the meeting at Lincoln's Inn House when they were told they were no longer needed, Annie and Mabel Tuke had been too nervous to speak to Fred and Emmeline. Mrs Pethick-Lawrence was livid and wanted to challenge the Pankhursts but Fred did not want to reveal the split to the outside world, telling her, 'We can no longer be creative in the movement, though we can be destructive. If we appeal to the Union we shall split the ranks.'[35]

At the grand meeting at the Albert Hall on 17 October the membership, which had been expecting to see all four leaders, was told that only Mrs Pankhurst would be present. The day before she sent a letter to every WSPU member addressed 'Dear Friend', explaining the split to those who could not be present, and signed the letter 'yours in devotion to the women's cause'. 'History has taught us that divided counsels have been the ruin of more good causes than anything else ... and when such a situation arises separation is inevitable.' At the Albert Hall Mrs Pankhurst said there had been a disagreement about the new militant policy, and that Mr and Mrs Pethick-Lawrence were leaving the WSPU; they would keep control of *Votes for Women*, and that in the interests of the Cause 'rather than make schism in the ranks of the Union', the Pethick-Lawrences had agreed to step down. While the membership was trying to take in the enormity of her announcement, Mrs Pankhurst launched the new, more aggressive militancy: 'I incite this meeting to rebellion. I say to the Government: you dared not take on the leaders of Ulster for their incitement to rebellion – take me if you dare! From henceforward, the First Division or no First Division, the Government will not be able to hold me in prison.'[36] In future

suffragettes would go on hunger strike even if they were given political status.

Laura Ainsworth, who had worked at the Woman's Press shop
in 1910 and been an organiser in Maidstone and Margate in 1911,
left her post at the Newcastle WSPU branch because of the split,
and worked for Votes for Women with the National Political
League. Sensitive and impulsive, Jane Brailsford was very upset
by the Pankhursts' treatment of the Pethick-Lawrences and had
a breakdown. The veteran campaigner Mrs Saul Solomon would
leave the WSPU in 1913 because of the way the Pethick-Lawrences
had been dismissed. Many members would be taking sides, to
choose the Pankhursts' policy of increased militancy or to support
the Pethick-Lawrences' strategy of advancement through greater
use of propaganda. Some members turned on Annie, scornfully
calling her 'Christabel's Blotting Paper', but she took this in her
stride: 'the title neither flattered nor depressed me. I knew that
blotters were useful things, and I had no ambition but to be of use
to the only one I firmly believed who could ever win the vote.'[37]
The Pethick-Lawrences never met Mrs Pankhurst again, and came
to feel that Christabel was a 'stranger' to them. Annie believed that
the movement as a whole lost out: 'two had gone who had been the
creative geniuses of the constructive side of a world-famed fight.'

For the good of the Cause, the Pethick-Lawrences continued to
maintain a dignified silence until Emmeline wrote her memoirs in
1938. *My Part in a Changing World* was published ten years after Mrs
Pankhurst's death, and while both Christabel and Annie were still
alive. The book explained the reason for the WSPU's relocation, their
extraordinary expulsion and the need for a new newspaper called *The
Suffragette*, whose first edition appeared the day after the Albert Hall
meeting of 17 October under the editorship of Christabel Pankhurst.
Fred and Emmeline Pethick-Lawrence would continue to be the
joint editors of *Votes for Women* and lead their own not-so-militant
campaign based at Clement's Inn, calling itself the 'Votes for Women
Fellowship', their logo a bare foot young woman holding a shining
lantern 'To Spread the Light'. Emmeline Pethick-Lawrence explained
their policy in the next edition of *Votes for Women*. The Votes for
Women Fellowship strategy was to support large-scale processions
and meetings advocating women's suffrage. Rather than physically

fighting for the vote, they preferred to proselytise for it. It was also announced at this time that the Pethick-Lawrences would be tried for 'criminal damage to property' and the cost of all the windows broken on 1 and 4 March 1912.

When members wrote to Emmeline Pethick-Lawrence expressing dismay she remained tactful. Receiving such a letter from Myra Sadd Brown she replied: 'I thank you very warmly for your kind letter. Yes, our Cause is greater than any Union or Society and every sacrifice we are called upon to make only makes it the dearer to us. In view of the terrible peril of the present moment we must all devote all the energy and life we have to the emancipation of women.'[38]

As the main protagonist in this dramatic split, Emmeline Pankhurst had surprisingly little to say about it in her autobiography, which she completed in 1914, a few weeks before the outbreak of the First World War. She briskly dismissed the difference of opinion in a single page: 'Since personal dissentions have never been dwelt on in the WSPU, have never been allowed to halt the movement or to interfere for an hour with its progress, I shall not say here any more about this important dissention than I said at our meeting at the Albert Hall on October 17th.'[39] Mrs Pankhurst said the suffragettes had to remember that they were 'fighting in an army, and that unity of purpose and unity of policy are absolutely necessary because without them the army is hopelessly weakened'. She implied their 'old friends and comrades' had left of their own free will, which was not true: 'It is better that those who cannot agree, cannot see eye to eye as to policy, should set themselves free, should part, and should be free to continue their policy as they see it their own way, unfettered by those with whom they can no longer agree.'[40] She ended her brusque summary of events with thanks to the Pethick-Lawrences for the 'incalculable services they have rendered the militant movement for woman suffrage and I firmly believe that the women's movement will be strengthened by their being free to work for woman suffrage in the future as they think best'.[41]

Christabel's memoir, *Unshackled: The Story of How We Won the Vote*, published in 1959, a year after her death, stated baldly that 'this separation on a matter of policy was a cause of deep regret to all concerned'.[42] Written four years after the death of Emmeline Pethick-Lawrence and three before the death of Fred, Christabel described how 'misty' the day was of her visit to London to explain the situation to the Pethick-Lawrences, but revealed nothing of what happened at the meeting. Christabel seemed to blame them for the situation the whole movement found itself in at the meeting on 17 October, at which she was not present: 'To her [Mrs Pankhurst] and the assembled thousands of women this was a grief ... these women knew that Mother had not lightly parted from her who for the past six years had shared the immense moral and material responsibility of the movement ... She knew what ruthless force she was defying for the sake of women, because the alternative to advance was, in her judgment, surrender.'[43]

Interviewed in 1964, Jessie Kenney revealed how grim the split was to the rank and file members. Jessie had been Emmeline Pethick-Lawrence's secretary in the early years of the campaign, the youngest organiser, and had also worked closely with Christabel. Looking back fifty years later, Jessie thought that she and her sister might have remained loyal to the Pethick-Lawrences instead of throwing in their lot with the Pankhursts. Working for the vote might have been more comfortable in the Pethick-Lawrences' well-resourced and better-financed campaign. 'Annie and I could have stayed with the Pethick-Lawrences. It would have been easier.'[44]

While the Pethick-Lawrences were in Canada the bailiffs had taken possession of their country home, The Mascot, near Dorking, to seize goods to be auctioned in lieu of the outstanding costs of the conspiracy trial, £900, and £200 for the expenses of the witnesses, for which Mrs Pankhurst and Fred Pethick-Lawrence were liable. Mrs Pankhurst had no assets, so Fred Pethick-Lawrence was targeted to pay his share first. At the auction on 31 October, family members and friends of the Pethick-Lawrences paid £300 for their furniture and other possessions and returned these to the couple. Even the auctioneer bought something and returned it to them. Emmeline Pethick-Lawrence thanked her friends for stepping in 'to preserve for us those treasures which are associated with the happy memories of our life [and] mean a very great deal'.[45] She explained that the loss of material possessions was not important but now their friends' gesture in returning things meant they 'will be doubly precious'.[46] Fred could have easily afforded to write a cheque for the whole amount; he and his legal advisers noted that although an Act had been passed in 1908 allowing the government to proceed in this way, since 1908, 200 criminals had been prosecuted and had not been liable for Crown and witness costs in such a manner. Fred observed that the war between the women's suffrage movement and the government was now being fought 'on the financial plane'.[47]

*

In Dundee, on 30 October, Frances 'Fanny' Parker, the local WSPU organiser, who had been force-fed while serving four months for breaking windows in March 1912, and Ellison Gibb, from Glasgow, both of whom we last saw in February of 1912 pestering Winston Churchill on a train in Scotland, broke the windows of the Dundee Savings Bank. To deaden the sound of breaking glass they had smeared the windows with treacle and covered them with a sign saying 'Votes for Women'; three hours later they were caught red-handed attacking the windows of the Inland Revenue office with two lumps of iron. In court Ellison Gibb made 'a plucky and dignified stand', but the women were sent to prison for three days and went on hunger strike. They were not force-fed. Earlier that month their colleague Ethel Moorhead (a suffragette with many aliases) was ejected for interrupting a meeting of the attorney general Sir Rufus Isaacs at Edinburgh's Synod Hall, and later marched into the classroom of mathematics teacher Peter Ross, who had assaulted her, and attacked him with a dog-whip. Ethel was convicted of assault and fined £1; it was paid by a friend, which did not please her.[48]

In the middle of November, impatient and disappointed at the government and the Labour Party's response to the demand for the vote, George Lansbury resigned his seat of Bow and Bromley and fought it on the single issue of women's suffrage. At meetings he told audiences that he wanted to return to Parliament with a mandate from the men of Bow and Bromley 'to put the question of "Votes for Women" in the very foremost rank of social reform'.[49] George Lansbury's local Labour Party branch at Poplar would not endorse him, so Lansbury stood as a socialist and suffragist candidate.

Lansbury was supported by an election fund raised by the Pethick-Lawrences. He was helped on the ground by Sylvia Pankhurst and her team of activists and donors. His constituency throbbed to the glamour of a suffragette by-election campaign. Victoria Park in Hackney provided the outdoor rallying ground. At the outset of the campaign Lansbury travelled to France to discuss his strategy with Mrs Pankhurst and Christabel. Mrs Pankhurst chose not to take charge of the campaign, instead holding meetings in Bromley and Bow. Snubbing Sylvia's local contacts, Christabel told Lincoln's Inn House to put Grace Roe in charge of the campaign. Sibling rivalry between Mrs Pankhurst's two eldest daughters seemed to be an obstacle. Sylvia certainly thought so and this feeling has coloured the way November 1912 was described by Sylvia in her memoir, *The Suffragette Movement*.

Sylvia saw the size of the task ahead: she knew that the Liberals would not offer any help to Lansbury, and she knew the attitudes, from indifference to animosity, of the Labour Party leadership towards the question of women's suffrage. The Independent Labour Party's priority was to enfranchise men still without the vote. There was also the deeply held conviction that the first tranche of women voters would not vote for the party of the working man. Looking back, Sylvia observed: 'They objected to Lansbury's championship of the suffragettes, as others had resented their championship by Keir Hardie.'[50] The Labour Party felt affronted by George Lansbury's resignation – and the likely loss of the seat – as an attack upon themselves, and blamed the suffragettes as being unworthy of his action.

Visiting Bow Road four days before polling day *The Times'* reporter saw suffragists resembling an 'army of occupation' holding women-only meetings every afternoon. Mrs Fawcett saluted George Lansbury's 'independence, sincerity and self-sacrifice' in being prepared to give up his £400-a-year MP's salary 'for the sake of those who cannot reward him by their votes'. She asked the male voters of Bromley and Bow to vote for him in order to retain his 'purifying influence' in the House of Commons. George Lansbury lost his seat on 26 November by 751 votes. His opponent was Reginald Blair, a Conservative Unionist accountant from Glasgow who was against women's suffrage.

When the result was declared George said he had been beaten by a 'combination of false friends and open foes ... men who had professed to believe in the principles of democracy had ranged themselves on the side of Toryism and reaction ... which is their business and their disgrace'.[51] From a painful defeat that his Labour colleagues said he had brought upon himself, he pointed out that the 3,291 men who voted for him 'declared that womanhood and motherhood were sacred and joined in for the emancipation of women'. He and his wife Bessie were 'proud and happy in ever such a small way to have been in the fight ... there is no suffering on our side. It is a glory to have been part of this great movement that women are making themselves for their own freedom.'[52] Lansbury's action was a rare gesture of male political solidarity in the struggle for the vote. He would be out of Parliament for the next decade.

Depressed by the defeat and upset by the distress caused to the Lansbury family, Sylvia Pankhurst was further shocked by news from Lincoln's Inn House that their desire was to close the branches and shops she had opened and 'retire from the East End'.[53] Sylvia persuaded her mother it was wrong to let the campaign be wound up in defeat, and she was allowed to work closely with Flora Drummond and organise working women's deputations to the House of Commons. Out of these developments the East London Federation would be born in the early weeks of January 1913 with an expanded role for Sylvia.[54]

On 29 November, using the alias of 'Mary Brown', Emily Davison travelled from Cardiff – where she had been assisting Lettice Floyd and Annie Williams to speak at open-air meetings – to Aberdeen to assault David Lloyd George when he arrived at Aberdeen station. Unfortunately Emily mistook a Baptist minister, the Reverend Forbes Jackson, for the chancellor of the exchequer, and several times she 'struck him across the face with a horse-whip'. Despite the clergyman protesting that he was not Lloyd George, she continued to attack him. Initially she was reported in the press as 'Mary Brown', but before long her true identity and lengthy criminal record were known, and she was sentenced to ten days in prison. In court she cross-examined the Reverend Jackson personally; he told the court he had been offered an apology on her behalf but he refused to accept it, saying the apology was due to Mr Lloyd George. At Craiginches Prison Emily went on hunger strike but was not fed by force and released after five days when her fine was paid by an anonymous well-wisher.[55]

Lloyd George arrived at the Music Hall in Aberdeen unscathed. En route Ethel Moorhead, alias 'Miss Humphreys', had thrown a stone at a car she thought he was travelling in, but broke a window in the wrong vehicle. Hiding in the music hall were three more of Emily's comrades: Fanny Parker, alias 'Janet Arthur', Olive Wharry, alias

'Joyce Locke', and May Pollock Grant, alias 'Marion Pollock', the latter a Dundee clergyman's daughter. They smuggled themselves into the building to interrupt the chancellor of the exchequer's meeting, but were found and their protest was thwarted. They were sentenced to five days in prison for behaving in a disorderly manner and committing a breach of the peace: Fanny Parker went on hunger strike but was not force-fed and was released at the end of her sentence. Ethel Moorhead caused chaos when she refused to leave the court, and Olive Wharry added to the excitement when she threw her shoes at the magistrate and the Procurator-Fiscal. Ethel Moorhead served four days of her ten-day sentence and was released early when her fine was paid. When Olive Wharry was released she told the *Aberdeen Evening Gazette*, using her alias 'Joyce Locke', that she was a 'physical wreck'. Her eyes were 'sunken', her face was pale, her tongue was 'blistered and coated' and she spoke with 'much difficulty and pain'. She had eaten no food and only taken a few drops of water, and felt 'rather nervous, and not in a fit condition to tell you everything'.[56]

Emily Davison spent Christmas with her mother in Longhorsley, Northumberland. On Boxing Day she wrote to an unnamed suffragette, 'My Dear Comrade', thanking for her 'amusing but wicked booklet'. Referring to her recent spell in Holloway, 'As to my little "do", I was very kindly treated by the members when I got "out" and soon pulled round', but since then she had experienced 'a good deal of rheumatism in my head and back'. Emily was disappointed that she had not managed to attack Lloyd George himself: 'Never mind it will no doubt have given him a fright, and he can't always expect to have a double handy.'[57] She was unrepentant at having hit the clergyman, the Reverend Forbes Jackson: 'he was a fool not to accept the apology and did not show up favourably.' She was delighted with her protest: 'We made things hum in Aberdeen!'[58]

The year drew to a close with bangs and bells: letters and packages were damaged or destroyed, and fire alarms were set off in London, Birmingham, Cardiff, Nottingham, Preston, Bradford, Newcastle and Bath. Christabel Pankhurst explained the militants' rationale in *The Suffragette*, whose tone was far more strident than *Votes for Women*, as follows: 'The suffragists who have been burning and otherwise destroying letters have been doing this for a very plain and simple reason. They want to make the electors and the Government so uncomfortable that, in order to put an end to the nuisance, they will give women the vote ... Women will never get the vote except by creating an intolerable situation for all the selfish and apathetic people who stand in their way.'[59] She dismissed the argument that many hundreds of women were being inconvenienced by this form of militancy, saying that such women were at least 'suffering in their own interests and not only in the interests of other people as is so often the case where sacrifices made by women are concerned'.[60]

In December the newspapers carried outraged editorials and letters from readers frustrated that so few culprits were being caught. Most attacks were carried out in the early hours of the morning. Only a handful of women, such as Elsie Howey, were caught red-handed. Elsie, who had not long been out of Aylesbury Gaol, was released in a weak condition from her four-month sentence, during which she was force-fed. Bravely she put herself in trouble again on 10 December when she set off a fire alarm and caused threepence worth of damage to the fire-alarm bell. She was sent again to Holloway, this time for two months, and suffered more than usual from a new bout of force-feeding. In 1928 Elsie's mother wrote to Elsa Gye saying that her daughter had almost lost her voice: 'She almost became dumb for life from the injuries inflicted on her throat ... it took four months' treatment to save her and her beautiful voice was quite ruined.' While Elsie was recovering she had to carry a pencil and paper and write down anything she wanted to say.[61]

Invalid-tricycle-bound May Billinghurst had to hobble and hop into the dock of Greenwich Magistrates' Court on her crutches when she was accused of a 'pillar-box outrage', damaging letters in a pillar box in Blackheath on 17 December. Her case was tried at the Old Bailey on 8 January 1913 and she was convicted of placing a black fluid into pillar boxes. In a written statement May said she wanted to 'wake up the minds of the public to the subject of votes for women'.[62] She made a defiant speech, and was sentenced to eight months in Holloway in the first division; she went on hunger strike and was fed by force 'at a terrible cost to herself', and released ten days into her sentence. During one of the attempts to feed May her teeth were damaged and her face was cut. This was May Billinghurst's second spell in Holloway in 1912; in March she had been sent to prison for a month served with hard labour for breaking windows.[63]

Kitty Marion also spent Christmas in gaol after breaking the glass of a fire-alarm post with a hammer in Wellington Street, Covent Garden, on 17 December, near to Bow Street Court. Five fire engines rushed to the scene. A few hours later at Bow Street Court Kitty proudly reminded the magistrate, Mr Marsham, that three years earlier she had broken windows at the Moss Empire office, to draw attention to the unsavoury conditions under which many actresses worked. Kitty told the court that since 1909 she had been almost boycotted by the profession.

The court heard that the strength of her blow to the glass was such that it broke the hammer, and that she had waited patiently for a police constable to arrest her. As she was taken to the police station she shouted, 'I want to turn the Government out.'[64] Kitty was given the option of paying a £25 fine or going to prison for a month in the second division. She chose the latter. When asked if she had the money to pay the fine she said: 'No; and if I had twenty million pounds I would not pay.'[65] She was taken to Holloway and, after taking breakfast on Christmas Day, Kitty went on hunger strike. The next day two doctors examined her and at tea time she was fed by force: 'I was lying on my bed and turned my face to the wall, but they wheeled the bed into the middle of the cell, and after a violent struggle held me down by sitting on my legs. I was fed through a nasal tube and was so sick and exhausted that a wardress remained with me for some time.'[66] Kitty was fed every day for the rest of her sentence until she was released on 17 January 1913. She put her ability to bear the pain down to her 'robust constitution and excellent health'. She was met at Holloway's gates by her friends who nursed her back to health and when she was fully recovered she stayed with Lilla Durham in her cottage in Sussex.[67]

15

The Arsonists

The WSPU's Response to the Franchise Reform Bill 1913

A refreshment pavilion in Regent's Park burned down by suffragettes on 12 February 1913, the first of many arson attacks on empty buildings.

Members of both the WSPU and the NUWSS gathered in Westminster Abbey for a 'day of prayer' on 2 January 1913. From nine o'clock in the morning until evensong, 'a constant stream' of men and women suffragists and suffragettes 'knelt in constantly changing groups', to 'gather a clearer vision and fuller purpose for the coming days'.[1]

The front page of the first issue of *The Suffragette* for 1913 shows a cartoon of Britannia; trident in one hand, with the other pointing to the Houses of Parliament, she directs a procession of working women. In reality they would be led by Annie Kenney and Flora Drummond, to meet David Lloyd George and Sir Edward Grey on 23 January at the Treasury. The prime minister had announced that during the week of 20 January the amendments to the Manhood Suffrage Bill for women's suffrage would be debated and voted on. Three hundred women were asked to walk from the WSPU's headquarters at Lincoln's Inn House to Downing Street in their working clothes. Alice Hawkins represented the Women's Boot and Shoe Union; Gertrude Townend represented nurses and teachers; shop assistants, fisherwomen from Newhaven, tailoresses, 'pit-brow lasses' who shovelled coal at the mines, laundresses, factory workers and domestic servants also took part.

A 'Private and Confidential' letter from Mrs Pankhurst to members showed what little faith she had in Asquith's latest pledge. She predicted that the 'so-called' pledge would be broken, and the amendments would fail, which made militancy 'more a moral duty and more a political necessity than it has ever been before ... we must prepare beforehand to deal with the situation'. The moral landscape was being reshaped: 'To be militant in some form, or other, is a moral obligation. It is a duty which every woman will owe to her own conscience and self-respect, to women who are less fortunate than she is herself, and to all who are to come after her.' Emmeline asked members to tell her 'that you are ready to take your share in manifesting in a practical manner your indignation at the betrayal of our cause'.²

During January Emily Davison recuperated in Longhorsley from the effects of her four-year career as a militant suffragette. Seven prison sentences, six hunger strikes and many force-feedings had made her tired and gloomy, hard up and angry. A letter from her sister, Letitia, married to a shipbroker and living in France, is evidence that Emily was in a bad way: 'I enclose a postal order that should keep you going for a bit. I hate to think of you without work and feeling as you do. I do think the militants might remember your services and give you something ... what are you doing and how are you living?'³ On 14 January, stuck at her mother's house in snowdrifts, Emily was nervously waiting to hear from an Aberdeen suffragette, Katherine Riddell, who had been trying to sell Emily's prison manuscript. Ten days later the postman brought news. Katherine reported it had 'been examined by a good man ... and he gives it as his opinion that he is <u>sure</u> you would have to publish a book <u>yourself</u>. Failing this, *The People's Friend* might take a few sensational extracts and give them a place ... It seems a shame that this should be the case but of course you will notice that the militant prisoners are now giving their experiences in *The Suffragette* and sad and dreadful experiences they surely are. I trust you are feeling stronger.'⁴ Emily was being crowded out of her own market: suffragettes were copying her attacks on pillar boxes, were being sent to prison, going on hunger strike and being force-fed. She had helped create suffragette copycats who had their own tales to tell, all told free of charge to sympathetic newspapers like the *Daily Herald*.

Given the large hole created by the absence of the Pethick-Lawrences' money, the WSPU was fortunate to have attracted the financial support of Henry Devenish Harben. The Eton and Oxford-educated barrister was a valuable new friend. He had failed twice to become a Liberal MP and, in protest at the Liberals' treatment of the suffragettes, he abandoned a third attempt in 1912, and made regular donations to the WSPU and the NUWSS. Henry and his wife, Agnes, offered their home at Newland Park as a refuge for suffragettes recovering from their time in prison. The left-leaning newspaper the *Daily Herald*, co-owned by Harben, was edited by George Lansbury.[5] Harben supported the East London Federation of the Women's Social and Political Union, pledging, from February 1913, £50 every year for three years, and offering to be their guarantor until Sylvia Pankhurst was able to raise the rest of the money to rent bigger premises. Keen to consolidate her relationship with the Harbens, Mrs Pankhurst invited them to call on her when she was visiting Christabel in Paris in early January. She buttered Harben up: 'it would be so useful to talk over future action with my daughter whose ideas are always helpful. I should so much like to see more of Mrs Harben for one feels attracted to the wife of a man who is doing so much as you are.'[6]

Although not formally inaugurated until May, the East London Federation of the WSPU was already on a firm footing, with branches growing in London's poor neighbourhoods of Bow and Bromley, Poplar, Stepney, Limehouse, Bethnal Green, Hackney and West Ham. Operating from her shop in Bow Road, Sylvia Pankhurst took an increasing role in the suffragette campaign. Attracting women of all classes, from the drawing rooms of Kensington to local women who worked in factories and sweatshops in the East End, 'Our Sylvia' inspired love and loyalty. Leading suffragettes went to the East End to recruit women to go on the working women's deputation to Lloyd George on 23 January. The artist Olive Hockin organised the Poplar contingent from her home at 28 Campden Hill Gardens, Kensington. Zelie Emerson from Michigan, whom Sylvia had met in Chicago, ran the WSPU committee rooms from 393 Bethnal Green Road. Zelie found that 'audiences were quick to grasp the absolute necessity of the vote to the unenfranchised worker, not only for the sake of the women themselves, but for the sake of the men also.'[7] Florence Haig, a founding member of the East London Federation, coordinated efforts to recruit the women of Limehouse from her artist's studio. Eleanor Glidewell ran the Bow and Bromley committee rooms on Roman Road, in what had been George Lansbury's constituency. She knew working-class life: her father worked as a tobacco packer, and five of her siblings had died in childhood. Eleanor left her job in a publisher's office to recruit working women.

All classes of women stood shoulder to shoulder with Sylvia Pankhurst up to and beyond the outbreak of the First World War. Her friends the Pethick-Lawrences were loyal supporters. Emmeline Pethick-Lawrence admired Lady Sybil Smyth, a Sylvia loyalist, and described her as a 'beautiful and gracious woman with a temperament and character as lovely as her person ... Although occupying a commanding position in wealthy society she always kept her heart open to all classes and all human needs.'[8]

Minnie Baldock's campaign for the vote in Canning Town had inspired Marguerite 'Daisy' Parsons to join the burgeoning East London Federation. Daisy was born in Poplar in 1890 and left school at twelve to go into domestic service, earning three shillings and sixpence a week. Her next job was at the Carreras Cigarette Factory in Aldgate, earning threepence for every thousand cigarettes she packed. Most days she earned less than a shilling. The men who worked at the cigarette factory were unionised and had a fixed lunch hour, but the women workers were not unionised and they had to eat their lunch in the lavatory. Daisy Parsons later wrote: 'I left school at twelve years of age and had a delicate father, and a mother who had to work hard at washing and charring. I had very often to help the neighbours do their work for which I was paid sixpence a day and the little food they could give which was not very much, because people in the East End do not have much food to give away.' Daisy made the link between the unequal conditions she had experienced for several years and her votelessness: 'We know that if the men were working under women's conditions, through their trade unions, and through their votes they would say they would not tolerate that sort of thing.'[9]

During the Christmas holiday Annie Kenney had visited Christabel Pankhurst in Boulogne and received instructions about how she should manage the meeting with Lloyd George and Sir Edward Grey. Annie was nervous: 'My position at these deputations was always the most difficult. Mrs Drummond had to interest and amuse the men, I had to fight them.' Christabel explained the minutiae of the parliamentary procedure and what the effect of the government proposal would be: 'then she would explain what they [the deputation] ought to do, following up her arguments with illustrations'. Annie was unsure whether to take the initiative and lay down the WSPU's position, or let Lloyd George start the proceedings. 'If I let [him] have the first say he will commit himself before hearing what our point of view is. This seemed to be unwise. I had heard of his pride ... I had been told he was vain, I thought if these things are true, why let him commit himself before knowing exactly where our party stands on this question?' Annie decided to launch into her argument first, factoring into her decision that Lloyd George 'did not know anything of my make-up, as he had never met me, and I had no political past on which he could form conclusions. My instinct or intuition said, "Give him a chance to listen to your claims."' En route Annie advised Flora Drummond to 'say nothing until the end of the meeting as we shall want all our wits about us to compete with the quick-witted intuitive person we have to meet'.[10]

Alice Hawkins pointed out to Lloyd George the injustice of the fact that two of her sons, who were in the army and the navy, had the vote, but that she, who had brought them into the world, did not. Despite Annie's careful preparation, there was tension between her and Lloyd George. Flora Drummond tried to defuse the situation by cracking a few jokes 'but to little effect'. Lloyd George insisted that the prime minister's pledge would be kept and that there 'was not a scrap of truth' in the rumours that anti-suffrage ministers would resign if the women's suffrage amendments were carried. He repeated that all cabinet ministers were pledged to accept the decision of the House of Commons and went on to say that he would receive the deputation again for 'further consultations' when the amendments had been debated. The deputation left the Treasury in a quietly optimistic mood, with 'compliments and felicitations'.[11]

But, in the days following the deputation, the Speaker of the House of Commons ruled that any women's suffrage amendments to the proposed Franchise Reform Bill would have so changed the character of the bill that it would have to be introduced as a new bill, and all discussion of the proposed amendments was dropped from the forthcoming parliamentary schedule. This was a return to the familiar tactic of postponing any discussion of women's suffrage to the following session as a private members' bill.[12] There was talk of forming another committee, but only the NUWSS had the hope that anything would come of the idea.

The Suffragette's headlines screamed 'A Pair of Traitors', 'Betrayed!!!' Lloyd George and Sir Edward Grey were vilified as men who had posed as 'the champions of women's enfranchisement', but had 'conspired and were conspiring, to wreck that cause'. Despite the pledges made in November 1912 when the Conciliation Bill had been torpedoed, and the government saying it would 'drive women's suffrage into law' in 1913, the government was now withdrawing support.

During the rain-sodden evening of 28 January, some members of the working women's deputation, who were still in London, met at the Horticultural Hall near the House of Commons. Pumped up by strident speeches by Mrs Pankhurst and Sylvia, they set off in the pouring rain with Emmeline Pankhurst's words ringing in their ears: 'We know ... that the whole plot was decided upon long ago ... we know that the Prime Minister knew what was going to be done days before it was done. But what is our answer to this treachery? Militancy.' Flora Drummond and Sylvia Pankhurst took a group of twenty women who were determined to present a letter to Lloyd George. A large police force tried to disperse the women; just beyond Rochester Row police station, Flora Drummond, who by this time had only six women with her, was pounced on by three policemen. Henry Nevinson reported the scene in *Votes for Women*: 'the largest and most brutal seized her by the waist as one "collars" a man in rugby football, lifted her off her feet and dashed her violently upon the stone pavement.' It was a wet day and Flora had to be helped to her feet, 'stunned and almost unconscious', covered in mud and horse manure and minus her hat. Her ankle had been hurt and she was held up by several women including Sylvia Pankhurst. The bedraggled party was allowed through the police cordon as far as St Stephen's Entrance. The senior policeman on duty refused to allow them in and handed them a letter from Lloyd George, refusing to see them. Undaunted by the rebuff, Flora Drummond told Inspector Rogers, 'we are a deputation of twenty or less, and we want to go quietly into the House. If you don't let us there'll be trouble. Enough of this tomfoolery.' There was more rough handling, and Flora and her comrades were taken to Canon Row police station. Flora was 'dragged like a drunken criminal'. There were ugly scenes en route to the station, with gangs of men bawling, 'Duck them in the river' and 'Frog March Them!'[13] When they were taken into the charge room at the station, Sylvia later wrote, 'spurred by an intolerable sense of outrage and disgust, I swept the ink-pot from the recording desk, and in an impulsive gesture, I struck my open hand dripping with ink, into the face of Superintendent Wells not to hurt him but to mark him with my contempt.'[14] The women were charged at Bow Street with obstruction, wilful damage and throwing missiles to the public danger, and were offered the option of paying a fine or being sentenced to a prison term.

Scurrying backwards and forwards to consult with Christabel in France, Annie Kenney was at the heart of the quickening pace of militancy. From 27 January arson would be part of the WSPU's policy: 'Fires everywhere, long prison sentences, hunger-strikes and forcible feeding. We were no longer the happy joking crowd we had been in earlier days.'[15] Annie's visits to Paris were 'no longer a joy but a drag and a dread'.[16] Every time she went abroad she expected to be arrested and every time she returned she expected a police raid on Lincoln's Inn House.

At Bow Street, Flora Drummond gave the magistrate, Sir Albert de Rutzen, a piece of her mind: 'You are the hirelings and we have to fight you all. You have to do your dirty work like the rest of us. Make up your mind that you have got to face a good deal, or else you as well as Lloyd George have got to resign your posts ... Don't you think the whole thing is a farce? Be honest and once and for all say to Mr Lloyd George, "I refuse to do the dirty work for you." '[17] Unmoved by her threats, the magistrate offered her the option of a fine, which she refused, and sent her to prison for two weeks in the second division. She told him she would go on hunger strike unless she was placed in the first division.

Sylvia Pankhurst had applied for an adjournment so she could take legal advice, but she used the time to step up her East End campaign. Back in court she failed to impress Sir Albert, with his 'half-shut eyes which always reminded me of a tortoise', who ordered her to pay a fine or go to prison for two weeks.[18] She was intent on going to prison, where she warned him she would go on a hunger and thirst strike. Sylvia Pankhurst and Flora Drummond's threats came to nothing as the WSPU paid their fines anonymously and all the prisoners were released.

That evening, frustration at Lloyd George's refusal to meet the deputation triggered a spate of window-smashing in Whitehall and the West End, when the windows of the Home Office, the Treasury, the Director of Public Prosecutions, the post office in Dover Street and Liberty's in Regent Street were attacked with hammers, spanners and stones, and thirty women were in custody by the end of the night. Leonora Cohen, who came to London to represent the tailoresses in Leeds, was a newcomer. Frustrated by the politicians' duplicitous behaviour, she went to the Tower of London on 1 February armed with an iron bar wrapped in a piece of paper saying, 'This is my protest against the Government's treachery to the working women of Great Britain.' She called out, and lobbed it over the heads of a group of schoolboys, breaking the glass displaying the regalia of the Order of Merit in the Jewel Room. When the Beefeaters wrestled her to the ground and arrested her she told them: 'I did it intentionally' and was charged with wilful damage. The jury could not agree that she had caused more than £5 worth of damage and she was acquitted.

On 21 November 1911 Leonora Cohen had protested at the House of Commons and was 'thumped on the jaw with the clenched fist of a policeman, and was also knocked down under a mounted policeman's horse'.[19] She then protested against her rough handling by breaking a window in Whitehall and served a week in Holloway. Leonora joined Mrs Pankhurst's bodyguard who were trained to protect all WSPU members 'in danger of arrest and torture'. It was an all-female 'army' and 'makes no appeal to the aid or protection of men'.[20]

Militancy escalated during January and letters and packets were destroyed in pillar boxes in London, Croydon and York. A letter addressed to Lloyd George apparently sprinkled with sulphuric acid burst into flames when it was opened. A shorthand typist, Grace Burbridge from Holloway, was badly burned on the right arm when placing liquid phosphorus in a pillar box in Camden Road. A postman saw that when he emptied the box the postal bag was alight, and a colleague heard Miss Burbridge scream 'with her right arm enveloped in a blue flame'. She was placed on remand and defended by Arthur Marshall, who 'dwelt on her excellent character and the pain and imprisonment she had already suffered' and the fact that her family relied heavily on her salary. The magistrate decided that because of the 'peculiar circumstances' of the case he would bind her over to keep the peace, a situation Grace reluctantly accepted, saying 'most emphatically' it was 'for the sake of her father and sister'.[21]

Writing her memoir eighteen months later Emmeline Pankhurst said that the last day of January 1913 had been the date for the official launch of the WSPU's campaign against the government through attacks on private property, triggered by the meeting of the working women's deputation. For several years WSPU members had made sporadic attacks which were a warning to the prime minister and the cabinet as to what might become their policy. That moment had now arrived, when the Union now 'lighted the torch' convinced that 'no other course was open to us'. Their aim was to force the government to give women the vote by

> making England and every department of English life insecure and unsafe. We had to make English law a failure and the courts into comedy theatres; we had to discredit the Government and Parliament in the eyes the world; we had to spoil English sports, hurt businesses, destroy valuable property, demoralise the world of society, shame the churches, upset the whole orderly conduct of life.[22]

During January 1913 it became clearer to the membership of the Union that they were being led by one woman, Emmeline Pankhurst, helped by Annie Kenney, Flora Drummond and Christabel Pankhurst. The Pethick-Lawrences had been purged. Sylvia Pankhurst was ensconced in Bow and would not be prised from her East End campaign. Jessie Kenney, a keystone at Lincoln's Inn House, was in Switzerland recovering from a lung infection. Mabel 'Pansy' Tuke was convalescing from physical and mental exhaustion at Pine and Townend's nursing home in Pembridge Gardens. Christabel had written to her before Christmas 1912: 'Darling Pansy, when I think of what you have been through ever since March 1912 you have poured out all your nervous and physical strength and its precious vessel has got to get full again.' Christabel suggested Mabel visit her in Paris, and, when well enough, make a visit to South Africa, and urged 'with very much love' that her 'own brave dear' should take care of herself 'because you are very precious to us'. By the end of January Mabel Tuke had set sail for Cape Town, telling the readers of *The Suffragette* that she was embarking on a sea voyage 'in search of renewed health and strength in order that I may return well and strong to work side by side with my tried and trusted comrades in our great Union'.[23]

On 1 February, Winston Churchill wrote to his wife Clemmie from Scotland, urging 'my precious one' to be vigilant:

> Be very careful not to open suspicious parcels arriving by post without precautions. On the other hand do not leave them lying unopened in the house. They should be dealt with carefully and promptly. These harpies are quite capable of trying to burn us out. Telephone to Scotland Yard if you are doubtful about any packet.[24]

Christabel Pankhurst's leadership expressed the Union's feelings of betrayal by the Independent Labour Party, which now had forty-two MPs. On 7 February she wrote in *The Suffragette*:

> The Labour Party have betrayed the cause of working women. They have the power of life and death over the Government, not only because of their actual voting strength in the House of Commons, but because the very fact of their opposition would destroy the Government's prestige. During many divisions in the current session the Labour Party have been solely responsible for saving the Government from defeat.

Christabel's editorial expressed her continued frustration:

> The Labour Members cannot have it both ways ... They cannot be friends of the Government and friends of women too. Because they support the Government, they share the Government's guilt. The Government have betrayed the women, and that means that the Labour Members also have betrayed the women.[25]

Mary Phillips's mother, a member of the WSPU, who had been in poor health, did not send for Mary until she was dying; 'she felt the movement needed her services'. Mrs Phillips died in Cornwall in December 1912, and in the early weeks of 1913 Mary returned to the work she loved, rousing the women of the East End of London. One woman who was inspired by Mary was twenty-nine-year-old Charlotte Drake, a shirt machinist and barmaid, married with four children aged between eight and a few months old, whose husband was a labourer in a chemical manure works. Charlotte became a vigorous member of the WSPU in 1913, and Sylvia Pankhurst made a verbal sketch of her looks and personality: 'a fair Saxon type, bleached by the hardships of an East End mother, clear-eyed in serene tenderness for her children, with a unique bluntness of racy utterance, always decisive.'[26] She noticed the impact Charlotte had on her audiences, telling them about 'incidents, curious and humorous and tragic', and stirring them up 'by their truth … conveyed with her brief, inimitable keenness'.

When Charlotte Drake was interviewed by the BBC in 1968 she recalled: 'If a woman went to work and her husband was out of work, he could come outside the factory, take her money as she earned it, and go and spend it – and she couldn't do anything.' She threw herself into the campaign and once, when her husband accompanied her as she spoke at a meeting in Victoria Park, a man shouted: 'Go home and wash your old man's shirt.' 'My husband got hold of the man's collar and said: "You got a clean shirt on? I have, and my wife's washed it. That's my wife up there. If you don't want to listen to it, get out of it." '[27]

Mrs Drake became a part of Sylvia Pankhurst's inner circle and was one of the WSPU's most effective speakers. Sylvia made funds available to pay for a housekeeper to help Charlotte's husband Bill and look after their children when Charlotte was on active service for the East London Federation. So loyal were the Drakes to the Labour Party that for years a picture of Ramsay Macdonald hung above their bed, and their fifth child, born in 1924, was named Ramsay after the Labour prime minister of the day, James Ramsay Macdonald.[28]

Another young woman from the East End of London took up the suffragette cause in 1913. Annie Barnes was twenty-six when she joined the Federation. Although Italian by birth, she gave no hint of it in her autobiography, *Tough Annie*. When Annie was active in Sylvia's East End campaign she was known as Annie Cappuccio, becoming Annie Barnes when she married Albert Barnes in 1919. Annie's family arrived in Stepney in the 1890s where her father had a fruit, vegetable and sweet shop. Annie recalled her mother's generosity: 'There were a lot of poor people living near us and she did all she could to help them. We always had help in the house and she used to help them too … they were always very poor, quite often they were widows. Mother always believed in treating everyone the same, as equals … That's how I was brought up.'[29]

In July 1909 Annie Cappuccio first became aware of the suffragettes when she walked past the Edinburgh Castle hall in Limehouse and saw crowds of protesters, including Mary Leigh, Mabel Capper and Jennie Baines, locked out of the meeting being held by Lloyd George. Annie saw a 'real to-do' as the women tried to get into the hall and the police tried to stop them. 'A tall posh woman wheeled a woman in a wheelchair [presumably May Billinghurst]. Up and down she went and then she patted the horse. Somehow, she put her hand up under the stirrups, it wasn't clear what she did, and the policeman went headfirst into the horse trough.' Annie and the crowd laughed but the policeman 'took hold of the woman in the wheelchair and put her in a van and took her to the police station'.[30]

Annie and her mother saw four members of the WSPU holding a meeting on a cart, telling the crowd that they wanted to 'do away with sweatshops and all these terrible things that are happening'. Annie saw how the men in the crowd were

> just awful. They wouldn't listen and they just shouted at the women. A city clerk marched to the front and shouted at the women to 'go home and wash your dirty kids. You women are inferior to men anyway.' One of the suffragettes replied, 'I want to ask how an inferior can give birth to a superior.'[31]

Annie thought that a marvellous reply, and her journey to becoming a militant began. Meeting Sylvia Pankhurst in late 1912 she realised that with her domestic responsibilities she would only be able to take part in milder protests as she could not afford to do anything which would land her in prison. The first mission she volunteered for was on 18 April 1913 when she went with two comrades to chuck 'Votes for Women' leaflets off the top of the Monument, the memorial to the Great Fire of London. Before they set off Sylvia told the women to 'Be as quick as possible. Throw them over and get down quickly because the police will be after you.'[32] A photograph shows a huge crowd had quickly gathered to see the women 'take possession of the Monument' in a protest which lasted an hour in Pudding Lane; many in the crowd were unsympathetic Billingsgate fish porters. Two policemen were at the bottom waiting for the culprits but Annie managed to convince them she could not possibly have climbed the 311 steps and had only climbed a few before giving up. Her companions Gertrude Shaw and Ethel Spark unfurled a purple, white and green flag and tied it to the flagpole, and tied a black banner reading 'Death Or Victory' in white letters to the safety railings. They were arrested and later released without charge.[33]

By 9 February Emily Davison was in London and living in lodgings at 133 Clapham Road, Lambeth. Harriet Kerr, the manager of the WSPU's headquarters at Lincoln's Inn House, gave her a letter of introduction to Harry Daniels, the editor of the London office of the *Manchester Guardian* since 1906. Kerr asked Daniels to 'kindly spare a few minutes to Miss Davison' who was 'anxious to get some literary work'.[34] One wonders why Harriet Kerr did not offer the dogged Miss Davison any paid work with the Union.

The first two weeks of February saw an eruption of guerrilla-style militancy throughout the country, with very few culprits caught and punished. On 8 February, two orchid houses at Kew Gardens had been attacked in the early hours of the morning and plants were 'torn from their pots and thrown to the ground, the glasshouse windows were smashed ... and the intruders had wreaked havoc among the rare and beautiful orchids'. A note was left saying that 'orchids could be destroyed but not women's honour'.[35] At a meeting at the Pavilion Theatre on the evening of 10 February, Mrs Pankhurst's defiant words rang round the room, refusing to shy away from taking full responsibility for recent militancy. Provocatively a bunch of orchids was placed on the stage: she said she was entirely indifferent to the outrage which erupted at the smashing-up of the orchid house, the suffragettes' cutting of telegraph wires between London and Glasgow, the breaking of windows of gentlemen's clubs in Pall Mall and the destruction of golfing greens. Mrs Pankhurst explained that the members had not committed such acts 'to win the approval of the people who were attacked'. She said that golfers were especially angry with her and rightly so for she had 'incited other women to bring about those results'.[36]

Surrounded by their members, Sylvia Pankhurst and Zelie Emerson were arrested after a fierce struggle on 14 February, for throwing a stone at the window of the police station in Bow, and were sentenced to six weeks in prison. When Sylvia announced that they would go on hunger and thirst strike, her mother secretly paid their fines. Determined not to be thwarted, on 17 February Sylvia broke the window of a branch of the London County and Westminster Bank in Bow Road, and some of her followers joined in and broke other windows, including that of a local undertaker. Sylvia and Zelie, Annie Lansbury, Mrs Moore and Mrs Watkins, a 'pale and delicate seamstress who struggled to get by doing sweated work', were charged with wilful damage and sent to Holloway.[37] George and Bessie Lansbury's son Willie broke a window of Bromley Public Hall that night and was roughly treated when he was arrested. (Willie Lansbury, who was worried about his wife Jessie's health, had insisted on taking part on her behalf.) Willie was sentenced to serve two months in Brixton Prison with hard labour. Sylvia and Zelie, who were to serve their time with hard labour, went on hunger and thirst strike and were placed in the hospital wing and force-fed. Zelie was kept in prison for seven weeks although she had appendicitis. Mrs Watkins went on hunger strike; she was not force-fed and was released after ten days. Mrs Moore served her sentence but did not go on hunger strike. Sylvia served five weeks before being released on 21 March, in a frail and emotional state. During her sentence she had been force-fed for a month, and also refused to sleep, pacing her cell day and night, hoping to gain an early release. Drs Smalley and Craig were sent to Holloway by the home secretary to examine Sylvia four days before her release. Dr Craig wrote to McKenna:

> I am of the opinion that she is in such a highly nervous state that if force-feeding has to be resorted to she might have a severe mental breakdown. But I wish it to be understood that it is not the actual feeding which is injuring her but the emotional excitement she works herself into before, during and after each feed, together with the strenuous resistance she always offers.[38]

The Refreshment Rooms in Regent's Park were burned down on 12 February. 'Votes for Women' had been scratched on the path, and a ladies' muff had been found in the debris. One park keeper expressed his mistrust of any woman carrying a muff, believing the fashion accessory to be a new type of weapon. On the same evening in foggy Manchester, suffragettes got away with smashing the windows of the Reform Club and the Labour Exchange. In the early morning of 19 February Lloyd George's 'weekend cottage', a new villa near Walton Heath Golf Club, Surrey, was blown up by members of the WSPU. Five rooms in the servants' wing were badly damaged by a bomb, and a second bomb hidden in a cupboard failed to detonate. Because of recent attacks the police were keeping a watch on the house, but they failed to prevent the attack. At six o'clock that morning a loud explosion was heard which rattled the windows of houses within a 300-yard radius. No women's suffrage literature had been left at the scene, but circumstantial evidence told the police it was the work of the WSPU. At a meeting in Cardiff later that evening, a member of the audience asked why the Union had blown up Lloyd George's house. Mrs Pankhurst replied: 'To wake him up.' She told her rapt audience she had 'advised, she had incited, she had conspired, and the authorities need not look for the women who had done what they did, she personally accepted responsibility for it'.[39]

Mrs Pankhurst was arrested five days later on 24 February at her flat in Knightsbridge by Superintendent Quinn and Chief Inspector O'Brien of the Special Branch. She was charged with having

> unlawfully and maliciously counselled and procured certain persons whose names are unknown to feloniously, unlawfully and maliciously place in a certain building … in Walton Heath … certain gunpowder and explosive substances with intent thereby to damage the said building contrary to the Malicious Persons Act, 1861.[40]

She would stand trial at the Old Bailey on 3 April and be sentenced to three years in prison.

Olive Hockin trained at the Slade School of Art, and her paintings and watercolours were regularly exhibited. She joined the WSPU in the summer of 1912 and helped Sylvia Pankhurst make banners for the Bastille Day demonstration in Hyde Park in July. Olive had canvassed for George Lansbury in his campaign for re-election the previous autumn, and since the beginning of 1913 had been busy recruiting in Poplar. Growing outrage at the 'evils' of prostitution drew Olive Hockin to the militant movement. In 1912 she was sharing a flat and studio at 28 Campden Hill Gardens with another artist, Gertude Donnithorne.[41] When the police raided it on 12 March they found a 'suffragette arsenal'. At her trial at the Old Bailey on 1 April 1913, Olive was charged with 'conspiring with others unknown to set fire to the croquet pavilion, the property of Roehampton Golf Club (26 February), to commit damage to an orchid house at Kew Gardens

(8 February) and to cut telephone wires on various dates', and with 'placing certain fluid in a Post Office letter-box in Ladbroke Grove (12 March)'. The first witness was the wife of the caretaker of Olive's studio, who described the to-ing and fro-ing in the early hours of the morning of 25 and 26 February. On 25 February Mrs Hall had seen a motor car arrive with poles strapped to the side of the car, and Olive drove off in the car with a number of ladies. At four o'clock the following morning the caretaker heard the front door bang and was told the next morning – when Olive apologised for the noise – that she would not be requiring Mrs Hall to light her fire. Two pairs of boots were left to be cleaned, only one pair of which belonged to the prisoner. The second pair had mud and grass on them, at the sight of which Mrs Hall remembered reading an article about a fire at the Roehampton Pavilion. Later, Mrs Hall heard Olive being visited by two young women carrying gentleman's 'dressing-cases'. Mrs Hall was shown an array of exhibits and agreed that she had seen objects similar to the exhibits: wood shavings, cotton wool, candles, an electric torch, oil cans, pails, a bag containing flints, bottles containing dark fluid and motor-car number plates.

Olive's solicitor said that her mother had provided her with an alibi for the evening of 26 February, and that she could not have been one of the two women running away from the croquet pavilion at Roehampton. However, the bundle of newspapers left behind bore Olive Hockin's name and address, written by the newsagent for the delivery boy. The two women were disturbed by a club employee, and they ran off. Never identified at the time, we now know that these would-be arsonists were Gertrude Harding and Lilian Lenton.

Before sentencing, Justice Lush formally withdrew the charges relating to the attack on the orchid house, telephone-wire cutting and the pillar-box attack, and made an equivocal summing-up speech for the jury to consider when coming to their verdict, on the charge of conspiracy to set fire to the Roehampton croquet pavilion. Lush said that if he had believed the prisoner had taken an active part in the conspiracy to set fire to the pavilion he would have been obliged to pass a severe sentence. In fact, other than the evidence of her studio being used as a depot to store the paraphernalia which was used to carry out the three protests, there was no evidence that Olive had been present at any of the locations. In his speech Sir Charles

Montague Lush portrayed her as a 'woman who in her zeal had joined in a cause which she thought was a thoroughly good cause, and she might be right in thinking so'.[42] However, by joining 'this union' she had exposed herself to the 'evil teaching of other persons' and she had been induced to break the law which she knew was wrong. Lush explained the mitigating factors: she had no previous convictions, and he was certain she had been swayed by the 'evil teachings' of others. Olive got four months in prison in the second division, and was ordered to pay half the prosecution costs. She told the judge she would continue to break the law until women got the vote. He replied: 'You will be taking a very sorry, foolish and wrong course if you do. That is all I can say.'[43] Arriving at Holloway Olive threatened to go on hunger strike, and she served her sentence in the first division where she was allowed – at her insistence – to carry on her 'professional work' as an artist. Olive was photographed without her knowledge by Special Branch officers as she walked around the exercise yard, and her picture was circulated to all police stations in the country as a 'Known Militant Suffragist'. This would be Olive's first and last prison sentence.[44]

Norah Smyth had helped set fire to Lloyd George's house, and, like Olive Hockin, she got away with it. A painter and sculptor, Norah, who came from a well-heeled family, was Mrs Pankhurst's sometime unofficial chauffeur, putting her car at the Union's disposal. She helped out at Lincoln's Inn House but during 1913 her focus shifted to the East End where she worked with Sylvia Pankhurst, and by 1914 she was the East London Federation's financial secretary, donating much of her inheritance to the Cause.[45]

The day after Lloyd George's house was blown up, 'Joyce Locke' (the alias of Olive Wharry) and Lilian Lenton, also known as 'Ida Inkley' and 'May Dennis', burned to the ground the tea pavilion at Kew Gardens and were charged with arson at Richmond Magistrates' Court. The front page of the *Daily Mirror* of 28 February showed photographs of the accused suffragette arsonists, Wharry and Lenton. Olive Wharry's father was walking behind her as she left court and there is a picture of a policeman holding up the book he had found hidden in Olive's muff. During the hearing, wearing her magnificent muff, trimmed with four fox tails, Olive threw books and papers at the magistrate.[46]

Lilian Lenton was twenty-two when she committed 'the Kew Gardens Outrage'. She was a professional dancer and was keen to join the WSPU after hearing Mrs Pankhurst speak, but she waited until she was twenty-one and 'my own boss' before joining the militants. Interviewed by the BBC half a century later, Lilian recalled: 'In those days I was extremely annoyed at the difference between a boy and a girl. And when I grew up and saw the opportunities that boys had, and those that girls and women had, of course that just increased the feeling. Why should God be male? That was one thing that always struck me.'[47]

In January 1913 Lilian went to Lincoln's Inn House and told them that she did not want to break any more windows, but preferred to burn buildings. She was told that 'a girl named Olive Wharry had just been in saying the same thing, so we two met, and the real serious fires in this country started'.[48] For the remainder of the year Lilian Lenton was unstoppable.

At three o'clock in the morning of 20 February 1913, the tea pavilion at Kew Gardens was set ablaze. Even though security had been increased because of the attack on the orchid house, Olive Wharry and Lilian Lenton managed to set fire to the 'rustic' structure and within an hour it was reduced to ashes, causing £1,000 worth of damage. Two policemen saw Olive and Lilian running away, dropping suitcases as they fled, and they gave chase. When one of the constables grabbed Lilian he asked her what she was doing; she said she had come to see the fire and laughed. When she was told she was being taken to the police station she said: 'All right, don't touch me.' One of the suitcases contained a hammer and a bundle of tow which smelt of paraffin; the other case smelt strongly of pitch. A search of the grounds revealed several cards reading 'Two voteless women', and 'Peace on earth and good will when women get the vote'.

At Richmond Petty Sessions Court Olive Wharry gave the name of 'Joyce Locke', Lilian Lenton that of 'Ida Inkley'. Bail was witheld because of the seriousness of the offence, and their refusal to give their addresses. Later that day when Mrs Drummond was asked by a reporter about the fire she said: 'We are proud of such women, we stand by them.'[49]

Katherine Strange's business had suffered badly from Lenton and Wharry's fiery protest. She and Katherine Potter-Ewens were the proprietors of four teahouses; their premises in Regent's Park had also been attacked by unknown suffragettes on 12 February. So irate was Mrs Strange that she went to Lincoln's Inn House to speak to Mrs Drummond, and to ask that their two other teahouses, in Hyde Park and Kensington Gardens, be spared. Mrs Drummond was not available and Katherine Strange was told by Harriet Kerr that her business was registered in the name of Ewens and Son, and if the Union had known it was owned by two women it would not have been attacked. Mrs Strange told Harriet that between forty and fifty women had been thrown out of work by the two arson attacks, to which Harriet defiantly replied that the women would be glad later on that they had helped women get the vote. Mrs Strange told Miss Kerr: 'You should have seen their faces when they came to work and found there was none, you would have had a contrary opinion.'[50]

The arsonists were taken straight to Holloway and for the remainder of the day Lilian Lenton's conduct was 'very defiant'. She would not allow a medical examination, and 'refused to give any particulars'. The next day she was moved to a special cell after she had 'smashed up everything in the cell she was first placed in', and was kept apart from all the other prisoners, with all privileges suspended.[51] Lilian went on hunger strike immediately and a day later, on 23 February, she was fed by force but she retained very little food; some entered her lungs and made her ill with pneumonia and pleurisy. Her condition was so serious that the prison doctor feared her life was in danger and recommended to Home Secretary McKenna that she be discharged that day. Lilian was carried in a chair to a taxi and taken to stay with friends in Mornington Crescent. The *Daily Mirror* published a photograph of a frail-looking Lilian in bed, supplied to them by the WSPU, a reminder to readers of the sacrifice some women were determined to make.

A letter to *The Times* signed by three doctors, Agnes Savill, Charles Mansell-Moullin and Sir Victor Horsley, gives graphic details of Lilian Lenton's suffering. Her solicitor, Arthur Marshall, had visited her and found her 'absolutely normal and in good spirits and making light of her two-day fast', but within twenty-four hours she was adjudged by the Home Office to be in imminent danger of death. Assisted by another doctor and seven wardresses, Dr Forward, the prison doctor, fed her. 'She was tied into a chair and her head dragged backward across the back of the chair by her hair, the usual method of "restraining" these prisoners.' The tube was forced through her nose twice and no food got through the first time, and when they tried again the food caused 'violent choking'. Lilian's breathing became 'very violent and noisy' and one of the doctors told her to breathe more quietly. The noise of the rattling was so loud that Lilian was afraid it would alarm her fellow prisoners. She 'coughed violently and continuously', so much so that as the food was poured in it 'came back at once and out of the mouth'. When the feeding tube was pulled out she fell against the wall and 'a great pain began extending from the waist upwards and in the front of the chest and the rattling noise in breathing persisted'. Lilian was given hot-water bottles, Bovril, brandy and two injections. The governor of Holloway, Dr James Scott, was called to her cell and authorised her immediate release. Savill, Mansell-Moullin and Horsley challenged the government, saying that Scott had released Lilian because he did not want her to die in his custody and 'compromise the Home Office, and our horrible prison administration, of which they were the instruments'. Before Lilian was taken from Holloway she was given another injection 'for stimulation purposes, saying it was necessary to enable her to stand the journey'.[52]

Fifty years later Lilian Lenton still had harrowing memories of force-feeding:

> They pushed a tube up the nostril which went wriggling down into the stomach, then they poured the food in through the funnel at the end of the tube. But I was determined to stop them if I could. All the time they were trying to push this bally thing down, I kept coughing and coughing incessantly. They kept on trying and after a bit I suppose they thought they had succeeded, because they poured the food in. In almost no time I felt intense pain all round my chest and I could not breathe.

The next day she sent a postcard to her parents in Bristol: 'Out, double pneumonia and pleurisy but quite all right.'[53]

Doctors who worked in asylums added their professional expertise to shore up the Home Office policy. Dr George Roberston, the physician of the Royal Edinburgh Asylum, wrote to *The Times*: 'It has been a source of perplexity and astonishment to all engaged in the treatment of the insane to learn that artificial feeding by means of a tube should be regarded as torture.' He conceded it was 'unpleasant and causes a tendency to retch … but it is certainly not painful in the ordinary sense.' He had performed the operation some 2,000 times on lunatics who would not eat, and blamed the suffragettes' behaviour – their struggling and wriggling – for the pain they suffered rather than the practice itself.[54]

Lilian Lenton was known as 'the Elusive Pimpernel' in suffragette circles. Her ability to elude policemen and detectives was legendary in the campaign. Lilian stood five feet two, had brown eyes and brown hair, a 'tiny china-like figure, but wiry and it must be admitted wily'.[55] While she was in prison she planned her escapes when she was out on licence: after a few days a laundry van called at 34 Harrington Square and the laundry was taken away. The bundle was heavier than normal, but the driver was a female friend in disguise, so no fuss was made about the extra weight. Wrapped in the laundry Lilian was dropped inside the van and driven off, 'leaving a squad of lynx-eyed 'tecs industriously watching an empty nest'.[56] The Elusive Pimpernel lay low until her next mission in Doncaster in June. Using the alias 'May Dennis' she was found inside a burning house near Balby, which she had set fire to with Harry Johnson, a cub reporter for a local newspaper. She escaped, but when she heard that one of the servants who was employed at the house had been arrested and charged with arson, in true Pimpernel fashion Lilian Lenton made a dramatic entrance in court to confess to the arson attack. Harry Johnson was sent to Wakefield Prison for twelve months with hard labour.[57]

Lilian Lenton, alias 'May Dennis', was sent to Armley Gaol, Leeds, for six months for 'entering a house with intent to commit a felony' and went on hunger strike, but was not forcibly fed, and was released after seven days and taken to the home of Frank Rutter and his wife, Thirza. Francis Rutter was the art critic of the *Sunday Times*, a founder member of the Men's League for Women's Suffrage and the Men's Political Union for Women's Enfranchisement. In 1912 he was appointed director of Leeds City Art Gallery, and the Rutter home was offered to suffragettes to recuperate from hunger-striking and force-feeding. Mrs Rutter, Norah Duval and Leonora Cohen helped Lilian Lenton escape from the watching police at the Rutters' home on 20 June. A baker's van drew up outside their house, apparently driven by a man – it was Leonora Cohen in disguise – and the delivery boy was Norah Duval, who was living with the Rutters at that time. Annie Kenney explained the ruse: 'The van-boy walked in with bread, out came the van-boy who was Lilian Lenton, mounted the seat beside the driver and drove away.'[58]

During the summer months Lilian would pass as a boy and criss-cross the United Kingdom, evading the police and Special Branch, and had a series of 'remarkable adventures'. She was spotted in Harrogate, Scarborough, Dundee and Cardiff, always slipping away without being caught. The Elusive Pimpernel left the Welsh capital disguised as an 'old woman with a black shawl over her head, hobbling through the streets' to catch a train to London. She travelled third class to Dover and along the coast where she boarded the yacht of a suffra-gette sympathiser and escaped to France. On 7 October Lilian was arrested while collecting her bicycle from the left-luggage office at Paddington station. She was returned to Holloway and went on hun-ger and thirst strike, and was force-fed and released after eight days on a five-day licence and taken to a house in Putney. The Elusive Pimpernel could not be stopped: 'she changed clothes with a WSPU member and while the "cat" was sauntering down the street, the elu-sive "mouse" strolled up the street, and disappeared.' Lilian remained at liberty until December 1913 when she was arrested for setting fire to a house in Cheltenham.[59]

Lilian Lenton declared she was going to set fire to two buildings every week. 'To say I enjoyed making fires sounds rather awful. But it was really lovely to find that you'd been successful; that the thing really had burned down and that you hadn't got caught. There it was blazing and there we were in the glare of the lights.'[60] Lilian would change her method of fire-raising after she was found in a burning house in Doncaster in June.

> We thought it wasn't such a good idea to start the fire straight away, so that we could be seen in the light of it. We got dark lanterns and directed a trail of cotton wool soaked in paraffin to the lan-tern, wrapping it round the bottom of the candle. Then we put a shade round it in case any light could be seen from any angle, lit the candle and went away. When the candle had burnt down to the cotton wool it presumably – we didn't stop to see it – ran along the cotton wool and set fire to the thing. By then we would very likely be miles away.[61]

Marguerite 'Gretta' Palmer travelled from Dublin to break windows in Westminster on 21 November 1911, and served one week in Holloway.

Accompanied by seven comrades, Hanna Sheehy-Skeffington, a member of the Irish Women's Franchise League, broke the windows of government buildings in Dublin in the early hours of 13 June 1912.

© Museum of London

George Lansbury, who was elected as the Labour MP for Bow and Bromley in 1910, at the family's sawmill in Bow in 1912. He was a keen supporter of women's suffrage.

Elsie Howey, a clergyman's daughter, was twenty-four years old when she became a suffragette. Her vocal cords and singing voice were affected by being force-fed.

Sylvia Pankhurst, known as 'Our Sylvia' in the East End where she lived for twelve years, at the WSPU branch in Bow Road.

Emily Davison added attacks on pillar boxes to the WSPU's repertoire of protest. Her idea was copied throughout the country.

Suffragettes were usually portrayed in postcards as unattractive, unhinged women.

Lilian Lenton and Olive Wharry burned down the tea pavilion in 'the Kew Gardens Outrage' in February 1913.

Lilian Lenton was secretly photographed by Special Branch detectives in Holloway exercise yard.

Olive Wharry photographed in 1913 after long periods of hunger-striking and force-feeding.

Lilian Lenton recovering from pleurisy in 1913. Known as 'the Elusive Pimpernel', she was on the run from the police for several months in 1913 and 1914.

Lady White's house in Surrey was burned out in 1913. She was holidaying on the Riviera and the house was empty at the time.

Charlotte Drake was a sewing machinist married to a factory worker. She joined the WSPU in 1913 to campaign in her Canning Town community to get women the vote.

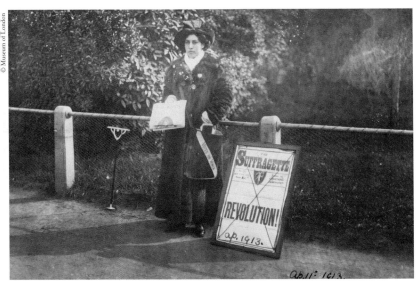

Princess Sophia Duleep Singh, a god-daughter of Queen Victoria, photographed campaigning for the vote in 1913, was an embarrassment to the establishment and to King George V.

Central London came to a standstill on 14 June 1913 as the funeral procession of
Emily Davison made its way to St George's Church, Bloomsbury.

Emily Davison died on 8 June 1913, four days after her protest at the Derby.

Because Lilian was still on the run on 7 March 1913, Olive Wharry stood trial alone at the Old Bailey. She was sent to Holloway for eighteen months for setting fire to the tea pavilion at Kew, and ordered to pay her share of the costs of the trial.[62] In Holloway Olive went on a secret hunger strike which the authorities did not notice for three weeks before they released her unconditionally on 8 April, by which time her weight had dropped by two stone. She was examined by Dr Maurice Craig who reported to the Home Office that the wardresses had looked through the cell inspection slit and seen her 'tie up several small packets and put them in her jersey and when searched these packets were found to contain food'. When challenged about this, Olive told Craig she was taking enough nourishment but refused to allow him to examine her, be weighed, or have her pulse taken. He found her 'a very frail person, with a very defective circulation. Her hands are cold and very blue; her pupils are widely dilated. She will not permit anyone to remain with her during meal times, and says that if she is thus watched, she will go on hunger-strike.'[63]

Olive Wharry's scrapbook of her time in Holloway is proudly illustrated with her own drawings and news cuttings that show defiance about the damage she and Lilian had caused. A photograph of Olive taken on her release after thirty-two days of hunger-striking shows a gaunt woman, too weak to hold her head up to look at the photographer.[64]

Hugh Franklin was committed for trial for endangering the safety of passengers travelling on the Great Central Railway by setting fire to a railway carriage at Harrow station on 25 October 1912. Franklin had caught the train from Marylebone and, as it arrived at Harrow, his carriage was on fire. He was caught by the chief porter, who asked him what his game was. Franklin said that he had lit a cigarette and accidentally dropped the match. Addressing the bench, he accepted that he had committed the act wilfully, but that he would 'not have adopted that form of protest if he thought that it would involve involve danger to human life'.[65] He insisted it was a form of political protest against the treatment of women's suffrage prisoners, and said that if anyone was to be charged with endangering human life it should be the home secretary for his treatment of Miss Lenton.

After his arrest in October, Hugh Franklin had skipped bail and had been on the run for four months. Some of the time he was hiding out at the radical bookshop, Henderson's, known as 'the Bomb Shop' for its anarchist clientele, at 66 Charing Cross Road, and had then been rearrested in February. On 10 March 1913 he was found guilty and ordered to pay the costs of the prosecution, and sent to Wormwood Scrubs for nine months to be served in the second division. He went on hunger strike and was force-fed 114 times – each time requiring two doctors and seven warders to feed him – before being released on 18 April. Franklin was the first suffragist to be freed temporarily on licence under the terms of the Prisoners' (Temporary Discharge for Ill-Health) Act.[66] This act had been rushed through Parliament by Reginald McKenna, to 'provide for the temporary discharge of prisoners whose further detention in prison is undesirable on account of the condition of their health', on 2 April, which came into force on 25 April.[67]

Reginald McKenna had presided over the Home Office since the autumn of 1911, at a time of growing unrest in the labour movement, trouble in Ulster and the increasing militancy of the women's suffrage movement.[68] His 'modest little Bill', as *The Times* described it, 'for dealing with the recalcitrant suffragist prisoners', passed its second reading with a majority of 296 votes in favour and 43 against. Keir Hardie's proposed amendment to the bill was rejected, said *The Times* 'amidst laughter', by the even greater majority of 335 votes to 8 against. *The Times* criticised the Liberal government for its tardy response to the problem: 'the absence of power to show consideration for a prisoner's health without remitting its merited punishment was an inconvenience not very frequently felt until it occurred to the women to manufacture ill-health in order to defy the law.' *The Times* warned that the militant women had 'set a pernicious example which others will not be slow to follow'.[69]

The Act's lightning passage through the House of Commons was the result of shocking accounts of force-feeding, the most recent being the treatment of Lilian Lenton. Under the terms of the Act, suffragettes, or any prisoners who adopted the hunger strike, were allowed to starve themselves and would not be forcibly fed. They were released when their weight dropped enough for it to be considered dangerous. A licence was served on the released prisoners which stated they should remain at their home address, or a pre-agreed address, for a given period of time, where they were liable to be rearrested. If it was found that the women had gained weight they would be returned to prison to continue serving their sentence. The suffragettes likened the regime to a game of cat and mouse, and Frederick Pethick-Lawrence named it the 'Cat and Mouse Act'. In a poster a formidable large cat loomed out of the picture holding a tiny suffragette between its sharp teeth, having drawn blood. The Act was intended to undermine the militants' resolve, expecting that the system of arrest and rearrest would demoralise the women. The Act was a failure: most suffragette prisoners who were released on Cat and Mouse licences disappeared from their homes, recovered their strength in the homes of sympathisers and travelled around the country to commit further militant acts. Very few of the released 'mice' were caught and brought to justice. Eventually the government accepted the Act had backfired and reintroduced force-feeding in the autumn of 1913. Hugh Franklin sent a message to the press that he had torn up his Cat and Mouse licence and went into hiding at the end of April with his suffragette fiancée, Elsie Duval. Hugh, Elsie and her brother, Victor, went to Dresden and then Brussels until the outbreak of the First World War.[70]

On 26 February, Bertha Brewster wrote to the *Daily Telegraph* encapsulating the bitter mood in suffragette circles: 'Sir, Everyone seems to agree on the necessity of putting a stop to suffragist outrages; but no one seems certain how to do so. There are two, and only two, ways in which this can be done. Both will be effectual. 1. Kill every woman in the United Kingdom, and 2. Give women the vote.' On 21 November 1911 she had broken a window of the National Liberal Club and was sent to prison for three weeks.[71]

A letter dated 18 March from a hunger- and thirst-striking Sylvia Pankhurst was smuggled out of Holloway to her mother. She was being tortured by being force-fed while serving two months with hard labour. So powerful were her words that the letter was printed as a handbill. 'Dearest Mother, I am fighting, fighting, fighting. I have four or five wardresses every day and two doctors.' Sylvia was fed by stomach tube twice a day: 'they prise my mouth open with a steel gag, pressing it where there is a gap in my teeth. I resist all the time, my gums are always bleeding.' She had vomited almost all her meals and had been afraid that she would lose her mind: 'I used to feel I should go mad at first … but I have got over that, and my digestion is most likely to suffer now.'[72]

Elsa Myers, 'young, pretty and very vivacious', was charged under the name of 'Marjorie Manners' for breaking a window at the War Office in March 1913. Elsa had already been caught up in several violent clashes but was not arrested until 1913. She had to be careful not to lose her position as a schoolteacher for the London County Council. Elsa was a member of the Jewish League for Woman Suffrage. An opportunity presented itself in March 1913 when the school at which she taught was closed for the holidays. Elsa was sent to Holloway for a month, went on hunger strike, was force-fed and released at eight o'clock on the morning of the day her school reopened. Her colleagues had no idea of what she had done and where she had been.[73]

During the night of 19 March, two women broke into Trevethan, the empty house of Lady White in Egham, Surrey, and set fire to it. Her late husband, Field Marshal Sir George White, was a national hero and a VC.[74] Amelia White was on the Riviera when Trevethan was attacked. The fire burned for seven hours and, despite the best endeavours of the Egham fire brigade, the house was a 'mass of ruins'. The arsonists had used a skeleton key to get in and sprinkled petrol in all twenty rooms, and opened windows to accelerate the fire. In the garden's rockery messages were left: 'Stop torturing our comrades in prison', 'By kind permission of Mr Hobhouse' and 'Votes for Women'. Two women were seen leaving the scene on bicycles. A mile away from the house at one o'clock in the morning, two women cyclists passed PC Alexander 'riding very fast'. They had been seen arriving at Staines railway station with bicycles fitted with baskets. Just before midnight PC William Pickett was overtaken 'at a fairly fast rate' by the women on Staines Bridge. He called out to one of them who had no light and they dismounted. Pickett would later identify 'Phyllis Brady', real name Olive Beamish, as the woman whose light was not working.[75]

On 3 April 1913 Olive Beamish was caught 'behaving suspiciously' with Elsie Duval in Mitcham, carrying paraffin and fire-raising paraphernalia in two suitcases. 'Phyllis Brady' was sentenced to six weeks in Holloway for 'being a suspected person or reputed thief' and 'loitering with intent', and went on hunger strike, was force-fed, and released on 28 April, let out on a Cat and Mouse licence. She slipped away from the address in Regent's Park to which she had been taken, and was on the run, committing more militant acts, until plain-clothes detectives arrested her in Holborn on 17 January 1914. 'Phyllis Brady' was sentenced to eighteen months with hard labour for setting fire to Lady White's house.[76]

Olive Beamish was born in Cork, the daughter of a Protestant gentleman farmer. In 1901 the family was living in Westbury-on-Trym; Olive's parents allowed her to join the WSPU in 1906 and to wear a 'Votes for Women' badge on her school uniform: 'I became an ardent suffragist because in the 1905 election my brothers first became interested in politics and I felt the position keenly, that I would never be equal with them in the political world, and I also realised the inferior position of women everywhere.' Olive studied mathematics and economics at Girton College, Cambridge, in 1912. She worked with the WSPU in the East End, and attacked a pillar box but was not arrested. Prior to her arson attack Olive had been organising in Battersea: the more she immersed herself in the movement, the more her militancy increased.[77]

The last we saw of Elsie Duval was on 21 November 1911 when she was arrested but not charged with obstructing the police. Since then she had been present at the window-smashing protests in March 1912 but avoided arrest. Elsie was sent to Holloway for a month in the summer of 1912 for breaking a window of the Clapham post office in July, was force-fed nine times and released on 3 August. When she was caught with Olive Beamish on 3 April 1913 they had earlier set fire to Sanderstead railway station, for which neither was charged. When Elsie arrived at Holloway in April 1913 to serve a month for 'loitering with intent' with Olive, she went on hunger strike and was force-fed and released on 28 April on a Cat and Mouse licence. In response to questions from the *Daily Mirror* about the disappearance of Elsie Duval, Hugh Franklin and 'Phyllis Brady', a spokeswoman at Lincoln's Inn House said: 'For the moment while the cat is about the mice are away and it will be some little time before they allow themselves to be caught. The fact is, that we shall make the Act as ridiculous as anything the Government has done to frustrate our movement, and we have many things in store of which they little dream.'[78]

On 8 April 1913, the day after Annie Kenney's speech at the London Pavilion at which she declared that the WSPU's policy to attack property 'and property alone' remained in place, she was arrested and charged at Bow Street Court with inciting a riot and released on bail which she and Henry Harben provided, with Annie 'promising to be good'. (This charge would be extended to 'conspiracy to incite damage to property' when Lincoln's Inn House headquarters was raided on 30 April.) While Annie was out on bail she slipped away to France as 'Miss James' to receive her instructions from Christabel Pankhurst, but was arrested at Folkestone when she returned. 'I felt a hand on my shoulder. "Well, Miss James, how are you?" I turned round, knowing who was speaking. So I laughed. "We know you as Miss Kenney. We have a second warrant." '[79]

On 2 April Mrs Pankhurst was tried at the Old Bailey on a two-part indictment: 'feloniously procuring and inciting a person or persons unknown to commit a felony; unlawfully soliciting and inciting persons unknown to commit felony and certain misdemeanours.' The case concerned the attack on Lloyd George's house on 19 February. Standing in the dock, Emmeline Pankhurst was facing Justice Lush. A highly regarded King's Counsel, he was not an intimidating judge. She conducted her own defence, advised by Arthur Marshall. Ranged against her were the Crown's most senior prosecutors, Mr Archibald 'Archie' Bodkin and Mr Travers Humphreys, one of the top criminal advocates of the day, who prosecuted his cases with an eye to detail and had a high success rate.

Mrs Pankhurst pleaded not guilty, but not because she wanted to avoid responsibility for the explosion: 'I had already assumed that responsibility – but because the indictment accused me of having wickedly and maliciously incited women to crime. What I had done was not wicked … but quite the opposite of wicked. I could not therefore truthfully plead guilty.' Archibald Bodkin read out her letter defending militancy which she said was 'a political necessity'. Bodkin said that the letter showed Mrs Pankhurst was the leader of the movement and had great influence over the 'emotional members of the organisation'. Bodkin continued: 'any person, or woman, who wants to indulge in militancy – which is only a picturesque expression for committing crimes against society, has to communicate with her, and with her alone, by word of mouth or by letter.' Bodkin argued that the WSPU's policy was that if they did not get what they wanted the government would be blamed and should be bullied into giving them what they wanted.[80]

The next day the jury found Mrs Pankhurst guilty but made a 'strong recommendation to mercy'. Before her sentence was handed down Emmeline Pankhurst addressed Justice Lush:

Whatever sentence you pass upon me, I shall do what is humanly possible to terminate my sentence at the earliest possible moment. I have no sense of guilt ... I look upon myself as a prisoner of war. I am under no obligation to conform to, or in any way accept, the sentence imposed upon me.

She warned that she would take 'that desperate remedy' and go on hunger strike, that it was obvious the struggle was an unequal one, but she would take it 'as long as she had an ounce of strength left in me, or any life left in me. I shall fight, I shall fight ... I shall resist the doctors if they attempt to feed me.' Mrs Pankhurst said she knew what she was doing and that she had faced it before, and her own daughter Sylvia had just endured it, and that 'there are women still facing that ordeal twice a day. Think of it, my lord, twice a day this fight is gone through ... fights and fights as long as she has strength left; resisting with her tongue, with her teeth, this ordeal.'[81]

When Justice Lush sentenced her to three years in prison, pandemonium broke out. Male supporters joined in the uproar, and women sprang to their feet shouting, 'Shame! Shame!' 'Keep the flag flying!' 'Bravo, three cheers for Mrs Pankhurst.' Despite being threatened with prison if they did not end their demonstration, the women cheered Mrs Pankhurst as she was taken down to the cells and sang 'The Marseillaise' and 'The March of the Women' as they were cleared from the court.[82]

At nine o'clock in the evening of 3 April, Manchester Corporation Art Gallery was about to close when there was a sound of shattering glass in the galleries. Three women were arrested for attacking thirteen paintings by the Pre-Raphaelites John Everett Millais, George Frederick Watts, Edward Burne-Jones, Holman Hunt, Arthur Hacker and Dante Gabriel Rossetti. At the scene Lillian Forrester, who was the organiser of Manchester WSPU, explained that her action was a protest at the 'shameful' sentence passed on Mrs Pankhurst.[83] Lillian, the wife of a cotton merchant, had known Christabel Pankhurst when they were students at Owen's College where Lillian gained a BA in

History. 'Evelyn Manesta' and Annie Briggs were arrested. It has proved impossible to track down 'Evelyn Manesta', who said she was a governess. This was most probably an alias.

A week later at Manchester Assizes Lillian Forrester read out a statement: 'We broke the glass of some of the pictures as a protest, but we did not intend to damage the pictures.' Mr Justice Bankes said that he felt he ought to 'make all possible allowance for the fact that they were acting under strong excitement and a feeling of great resentment operating very likely on highly-strung natures'. 'Evelyn Manesta' was sent to prison for a month, and Lillian Forrester, who had a previous conviction, got three months in the second division cells at Strangeways Prison for malicious damage. Lillian Forrester told the jury that her husband approved of what she did, that her knowledge of history had spurred her to take up the struggle for women's freedom. She told the judge she could not serve the sentence but did not give any reason, and he sent her to prison. Lillian was released early from her sentence because she was pregnant. Her son was born on 28 November.[84]

On 13 April Kitty Marion returned to suffragette action. Kitty was responsible for the arson attack on Levetleigh, the 'finest house in St Leonard's', and until lately the home of Arthur du Cros, the Conservative MP for Hastings. The house was 'completely ruined'; Kitty Marion got away with destroying the house, valued at £10,000.[85] Arthur du Cros was a hardline opponent of women's suffrage, having voted against every women's suffrage bill put before the House of Commons since he became an MP in 1908, and so a target for Kitty's wrath.[86]

The house was empty. The fire started after midnight, and the fire brigade found evidence of fires being started in every room. Kitty Marion left a piece of paper behind on which was written: 'To Stop Militancy Give Votes To Women'. When Kitty was leaving St Leonard's to return to London she chatted to a porter at the station who told her the fire was the work of suffragettes. When Kitty feigned surprise that such women were in St Leonard's, he said: 'Oh, yes, Miss, they're everywhere.' Kitty kept all the newspaper cuttings of the St Leonard's fire, and three other arson attacks she carried out in the summer of 1913, in her scrapbooks which were with her when she died in New York in 1944. This was the first of four raids in which Kitty got away scot-free: in her memoir she wrote, 'the edict went forth "to do all damage possible without being caught"'. All Kitty would admit was 'that after four successful fires and escapes, something went wrong with my fifth'.[87]

In the wake of widespread arson attacks there was a spike in newspaper accounts of stories about public anger against WSPU members and their shops and offices. The day after the attack at St Leonard's, suffragettes outside Holloway Gaol were set upon by a number of women who destroyed their placards and 'harassed the suffragettes until the police arrived to escort them away'. Suffragette shops in Croydon and Newcastle had their windows smashed, and WSPU members who tried to hold a meeting in Hyde Park were pelted with bananas and orange skins and escorted away by the police; one woman had to bang on the door of a house in Park Lane to seek refuge. In Brighton crowds stoned suffragettes holding a meeting on the seafront; they were rescued by the police who bundled the women into a taxicab.[88]

On 13 April five WSPU women were attacked in Regent Street by a crowd of youths. The women jumped on an omnibus but were followed, and when they got off at Oxford Circus they were 'surrounded and roughly handled'. The police came to their rescue but not before one of the women was struck in the face and her hat destroyed. On Wimbledon Common 200 policemen, including several mounted officers, defended a suffragette meeting from rushes by the crowd. On 14 April a bomb was found at the Bank of England. A policeman found a 'scientifically-constructed bomb' in a milk churn, charged with gunpowder, an electric battery, hairpins and a chronometer watch, within the Bank railings, primed to go off at eleven o'clock that evening. It was defective but if it had exploded the *Daily Mirror* declared that passers-by would have been killed or injured by flying metal and stone splinters. No suffragette literature was left at the scene but fingers were quickly pointed at the WSPU when two ladies' hatpins securing the elements of the bomb were found. No arrests were made.

On 15 April the Home Office banned all open-air suffragette meetings but they were held anyway and the police did not enforce the ban, leaving gangs of men and boys and medical students to express their anger freely. The telephones at half a dozen London Underground stations were 'rendered useless', and messages were left behind 'for the worst Government we have ever had' which said 'No Votes, No

Peace', and 'Enough of torture, England is being disgraced'. On 20
April, hearing that suffragettes were due to gather in Hyde Park, a
'huge crowd, distinctly unfriendly in its attitude' was waiting. The
police had removed the suffragettes for their own safety. On 22 April,
at Handsworth Park, Birmingham, five rowing boats and forty-two
pairs of sculls were destroyed by the suffragettes who had tried but
failed to burn down the boathouse. Tunbridge Wells had its cricket
pavilion burned down three days later.

Despite public hostility towards the WSPU their members still
sold copies of *Votes for Women* and *The Suffragette* on the street,
standing in the gutter rather than on the pavement where they ran
the risk of being charged with obstruction. Hastings' local heroine
Elsie Bowerman, who with her mother, Mrs Chibnall, had survived
the sinking of the *Titanic* in 1912, was photographed at the end of
April by the *Hastings and St Leonard's Observer*. She was selling *The
Suffragette* on the seafront. Elsie and her mother were keen WSPU
members. Edith joined in 1908 and founded a branch in St Leonard's
in 1909; her mother ran the WSPU shop in Hastings.[89]

A week after the suffragettes had been escorted out of Hyde Park,
a group of male women's suffrage supporters also held a meeting, but
it turned ugly. The cart on which they spoke was surrounded by a
crowd and dragged away. The police urged the male speakers to leave
the park on foot but they were followed by a mass of hooting and
jeering people. Some of the women suffragists who tried to take the
horse and cart away were chased by the crowd and had to be rescued
by the mounted police. When the women left the park they hailed a
taxi, but not before some of their pursuers pulled off the hood of the
vehicle to attack the women and their male supporters with sticks
and pelted them with 'road refuse' (horse dung).[90] On the same day
Perth Cricket Club pavilion in Scotland was burned to the ground
and two days later the Dundee *Courier* said that the secretary of the
club had received a letter from suffragettes claiming responsibility.
When Fanny Parker, an organiser based in Dundee, held an outdoor
meeting in Perth the day after the fire, a thousand people howled her
and a colleague down and threw missiles at them. The police drew
their batons to protect the suffragettes.[91]

When Superintendent Quinn of Special Branch, the governor of
Holloway and Dr Smalley, the Medical Inspector of Prisons, visited

Mrs Pankhurst on 29 April at Hertha Ayrton's home, intending to re-arrest her, they were greeted with cries of 'Murderer' from a gathering of suffragettes who had picketed the house for several days. 'So threatening was the attitude of the women' that the three men needed the protection of Special Branch detectives to enter the house. Because Mrs Pankhurst was unwell, she was not returned to Holloway to continue serving her sentence. When the men left after ten minutes the suffragettes 'gave vent to their feelings by using the most remarkable language'.

Princess Sophia Duleep Singh took the bold step of selling copies of *The Suffragette* at the front gates of Hampton Court Palace. When the newspaper printed a photograph of Queen Victoria's god-daughter swathed in fur and wearing a *Votes for Women* satchel filled with copies of that week's issue, it attracted the attention of William Carrington, the Keeper of the Privy Purse. He sent a news cutting to the Marquis of Crewe, the secretary of state for India. Sophia's support for the militants and the tax-resistance campaigns had annoyed King George V and he wanted her evicted from Faraday House, her grace and favour lodging, but, because of her closeness to his late grandmother, he felt unable to do so. Perhaps more alarming than the sight of someone so close to the establishment selling an inflammatory newspaper was the placard advertising that week's issue propped against the hedge behind the princess which simply said: 'REVOLUTION!' Princess Duleep Singh's most recent protest had been to refuse to complete her Census Return in 1911, writing across the columns: 'No Vote, No Census. As women do not count, they refuse to be counted, and I have a conscientious objection to filling in this form.'[92]

On 30 April 1913 the police raided the WSPU's office at Lincoln's Inn House where the forthcoming edition of *The Suffragette* was being prepared. Rachel Barrett, in charge of the newspaper's production, Harriet Kerr, the office manager, Mrs Beatrice Sanders, the financial secretary, Geraldine Lennox, the sub-editor, and Agnes Lake, the business manager, were all arrested. At the trial on 17 June they were found guilty of conspiring with Edwy Clayton, an analytical chemist and author of articles on the enfranchisement of women, 'to commit damage to property and inciting others to do so, and to inflict damage on houses, foods and chattels belonging to divers subjects of the King'.[93] The police had raided Annie and Jessie Kenney's flat and found an incriminating letter and a memorandum from Edwy Clayton. Jessie Kenney had left London in a hurry for Switzerland. The memorandum incriminated Edwy Clayton, showing that he was involved in the early stages of a plan to set fire to timber yards, government offices and cotton mills, and that he had carried out work on chemicals for explosive devices.

In 1925 Edwy Clayton wrote to Annie Kenney congratulating her on the publication of her *Memories of a Militant*, and wrote without bitterness of his difficult times in the aftermath of 1913. He praised her book, which 'recalls in a delightfully earnest and simple manner, many phases of the great movement in which we took part'. Clayton also thanked her from his 'innermost heart' for 'the generous references which you have made to myself ... for their extreme kindness ... and also for the reason that they convey a species of what I call the balm of consolation ... and making clear that I was well-meaning and sincere in my efforts to help a great cause'. Edwy Clayton found it hard to understand his treatment at the time and subsequently:

> There can be no doubt that in numerous directions, my actions and motives were both misunderstood – I suppose partly because it was conceived to be unnatural or impossible for a man to assist a women's agitation, without having 'an axe to grind' – and cruelly misrepresented. I have felt this for years. Even now, I am consistently 'boycotted' by certain relations and by some of my most valued and intimate friends. Others thank goodness, by degrees 'have come round!'[94]

Edwy told Annie that he would be writing to her sister, Jessie, a generous gesture since her negligence in failing to destroy his letter had landed him in prison.

Edwy Godwin Clayton, in his mid-fifties, was an active member of the Men's League for Women's Suffrage and the Men's Political Union for Women's Enfranchisement. An expert on the making of matches, he had a business with a laboratory in Holborn. His wife, Clara, and daughter, Hilda, were members of the WSPU: Clara Clayton was the Honorary Secretary of the Richmond and Kew branch from 1909 to 1911, and in May 1912 she founded and ran a local branch of the

Church League for Women's Suffrage. She was also active in the British Women's Temperance Association. This was Edwy Clayton's first offence and he was sentenced to twenty-one months in Wormwood Scrubs, and made liable for a share of the prosecution costs. He went on hunger strike, was released on a Cat and Mouse licence and never rearrested. He was ruined financially by his association with the militant campaign.[95]

On 17 June 1913, on the ninth day of the trial, Justice Phillimore handed down heavy sentences to all the defendants, Edwy Clayton, Annie Kenney and five senior members of the office staff at WSPU headquarters. Conducting her own defence, Annie denied knowledge of the papers which were found at her and her sister's flat. She made an impassioned speech about her working childhood, and said that the injustice of the laws as they affected women had led her to throw in her lot with Mrs Pankhurst. She told the jury that if they could not find a 'not guilty' verdict they should refuse to convict her and the other defendants, who were prepared to face death in order to get this suffrage question settled.

The defendants were mostly of previous 'good character'; two had previous convictions, but otherwise most of them, including Agnes Lake, were unknown to the authorities. Harriet Kerr was told that she was old enough to have known better. A clergyman vouched for Edwy Clayton, stating that he was 'always an upright man'. The jury deliberated for fifty-seven minutes, but, despite their plea for leniency, Sir Walter Phillimore gave lengthy sentences to be served in the third division, and he stated that the prisoners should not under any circumstances be released. When the sentences were announced Annie Kenney told the judge and jury, 'They will have to kill us first', and threatened to go on hunger strike. It took two warders and two wardresses to remove her from the court. Annie enjoyed the trial: 'we never, never, took these trials seriously. They were just part of our propaganda.' In her memoirs, she says that the time she spent in and out of prison, and on the run from the police, was the time of her life. 'Prison! It was not for me. Hunger-strikes! They had no fears for me. Cat and Mouse Act! I could have laughed. Could I not rest and be at peace? A prison cell was quiet – no telephone, no paper, no speeches, no seasickness, no sleepless nights.' It was an enforced holiday which she could enjoy: 'I could lie on my plank bed all day and all night and return once more to my daydreams ... I rather looked forward to these prison days.'⁹⁶

Harriet Kerr was sentenced to twelve months in prison, followed by twelve months of police supervision. She went on hunger strike and eight days later was released on a Cat and Mouse licence. She smuggled out a letter to a friend addressed 'Dearest Puss', telling her the news. Her colleagues had been scattered across the prison system because 'we were such awful criminals ... so many of the wardresses – dear things are friendly and might risk everything and carry news. This letter is being written under difficulties, as every time a step comes, I have to shovel it away and pretend to be writing poetry or something on my slate – the only thing one is allowed for recreation.' In just a few days Harriet had lost weight and was suffering the effects quite badly; she ached all over, her mouth and throat were sore and swollen, 'and worst of all I can't sleep for more than four hours and that is broken up'. In addition to the legal and financial help the WSPU provided to suffragette prisoners, the organisation could call on a network of members and sympathisers who would offer financial and emotional support and hospitality to women when they were released from prison.

When Harriet was released she slipped away to Paris to discuss the summer's fundraising activities with Christabel and dodged rearrest until 1 October, when she and Beatrice Sanders were grabbed by the police after a fierce struggle, headlined in *The Suffragette* as a 'Great Fight In Kingsway', on the doorstep of Lincoln's Inn House. Harriet Kerr was sent back to Holloway, went on hunger and thirst strike and was released five days later on licence, having suffered 'intense blinding continuous headaches, racking rheumatic pains in my back and almost entire sleeplessness'. She was recalled to Holloway after five weeks. Mrs Pankhurst and Christabel agreed that Harriet could give an undertaking not to commit any more militant acts and she was freed and stayed with Janie Terrero in Sussex. By the time the First World War broke out Harriet Kerr was no longer a member of the WSPU.⁹⁷

Beatrice Sanders earned £3 a week as the financial secretary of the Union, and was fortunate to have a supportive husband, William. She was sentenced to fifteen months in Lewes Prison. She went on hunger strike and was released six days later. This was Beatrice Sanders' third time in prison, having served fourteen days for her part in the deputation to the House of Commons after the first Women's Parliament in February 1907, and in November 1910 she was given a month for throwing stones in protest at the treatment of the women on Black Friday.[98]

Thirty-year-old Geraldine Lennox, the sub-editor of *The Suffragette*, was sentenced to six months in Horfield Prison in Bristol, so she went on hunger strike and was released on a Cat and Mouse licence. She was rearrested and returned to prison, went on hunger strike again and was released on another licence. This time Lennox evaded arrest and sold her licence to Henry Harben; she put the money towards opening a WSPU shop in Cork. Geraldine Lennox stayed in hiding in Ireland – the police were looking for her in Dublin – and she worked for the WSPU until the outbreak of the First World War.[99]

Agnes Lake was living in Leytonstone at the time of her arrest. She was sentenced to six months in jail. She was taken to Warwick Gaol and went on a hunger strike. Agnes was released on 21 June on a Cat and Mouse licence and taken to Leamington Hospital. She was released and rearrested several more times, until, in December, she was rearrested on the doorstep of her home in Leytonstone, and was taken back to Warwick after seven weeks on the run.

Rachel Barrett got nine months. She was described by one of the prosecuting barristers at the trial as 'a pretty but misguided young woman'. When she arrived in Holloway she went on hunger strike and was taken to Canterbury Prison and released on a Cat and Mouse licence after starving herself for five days. She spent three weeks at the Brackenburys' house, known as 'Mouse Castle', where suffragettes recovered after being force-fed. Rearrested as soon as she set foot outside the front door, she was returned to prison and went on hunger strike again, was released after four days and returned to Campden Hill Square. Rachel and all the other 'mice' who stayed with the Brackenburys and at the home run by Nurses Pine and Townend in Pembridge Gardens were looked after by Dr Flora Murray. Dr Murray had been a member of the WSPU since 1908, and was an assistant anaesthetist at the Chelsea Hospital for Women.[100]

Despite the presence of Special Branch detectives, Rachel Barrett was smuggled out of 2 Campden Hill Square several times to speak at meetings. She was rearrested on 17 July while leaving a meeting at the Memorial Hall in Farringdon and returned to Holloway where she embarked on a hunger and thirst strike and was released after five days. Rachel escaped to the St John's Wood home of her close friend Ida Wylie. They had met in the autumn of 1912, when Ida was asked to write for *The Suffragette*. Ida was an exuberant Australian novelist and short-story writer, younger than Rachel Barrett, who described Barrett as having 'a fiery disposition'. Ida's home in St John's Wood was used as a bolt-hole for suffragettes on the run. Known as 'the Mouse Hole', it was an excellent hideaway, 'with a back-garden wall six walls removed from that of a secret sympathiser. It was a heaven-appointed refuge for hunger-strikers on ticket-of-leave.' Ida described how ambulances would arrive at her house and detectives would stand across the road with 'their eyes glued to our front door'. As soon as the suffragette fugitives regained their strength, they 'would scramble by night over the intervening walls and slip out of another front door halfway up the street'.

By the summer of 1913 Ida's role was that of a 'sub-reporter and bottle-washer on the editorial staff' at Lincoln's Inn House. At the end of the summer Rachel Barrett and Ida Wylie escaped to Edinburgh where Ida had an aunt, and Rachel underwent an operation. The couple returned to London for Christmas, and Rachel was smuggled into Lincoln's Inn House where she lived in a bedsit, editing *The Suffragette* under the noses of the round-the-clock police surveillance teams until May 1914, when the offices were again raided. By then, Rachel had already left and was visiting Christabel Pankhurst in Paris.

Ida Wylie, 'volatile, funny and erotically daring', had lived an openly lesbian life in Karlsruhe, Germany, for several years before she arrived in London in 1911 and became interested in the suffragette campaign. She was born in Melbourne in 1885; her father, Alexander Wylie, was from Glasgow, became a barrister and had his heart set on a political career but failed to become an MP in the general election of 1880. Alec Wylie's first wife, Emilie, divorced him in 1883 on account of his serial adultery and violence. Emilie won custody of the two children. Alec Wylie sailed to Melbourne and married Ida Ross. Young Ida was born the following year.

Ida Wylie's autobiography, written in America in 1940, where she was a writer whose novels were made into Hollywood feature films, paints a picture of her father as a feckless bully. His mood swings and search for women with money were a large part of Ida's childhood. Ida's schooling was haphazard; she was briefly at Cheltenham Ladies' College, but most of her education took place in Brussels and Germany. She returned to England an 'authoress' in 1911.[101]

While Ida Wylie paints a vivid picture of the dangerous lives lived by suffragettes who were persistent offenders and hunger strikers, behind her larky account of wall-climbing, dressing-up and fooling the police was an escalation of the government's pressure on the Women's Social and Political Union. By making an example of Edwy Clayton, whose wholehearted belief in women's suffrage landed him in prison, the authorities made it clear they would not tolerate the actions of any men who supported the suffragettes with any kind of help or by becoming militants themselves.

16

'That Malignant Suffragette'

The Death of Emily Davison 1913

Emily Davison, forty-one, a governess before becoming a full-time militant suffragette, died on 8 June 1913, four days after her protest at the Derby.

The police now closed in on the printers of *The Suffragette*. Nervous about their clients' editorial, Messrs Speaight had recently ended their contract with the WSPU. The Victoria House Printing Company at Blackfriars, with financial backing from Henry Harben, took over, and were waiting for Christabel Pankhurst's editorial before going to press. The police seized all the copy at the press but the pages were rewritten and printed, with some blank sections. When Edwy Clayton and the five women arrested at Lincoln's Inn were charged at Bow Street Court the day after the raids, the magistrate Archibald Bodkin sent out a fierce warning to any printer who worked for the WSPU, saying that *The Suffragette* 'must be put a stop to, as a continued danger to society ... If there is any printer who can be found after this warning to print and publish the literature of these women associated with the WSPU, he will find himself in a very awkward position as the aider and abetter of these persons.'[1] Bodkin also warned that anyone who spoke in favour of the Union or contributed to its funds would also be 'in a very awkward situation'. The managing director of the Victoria House Printing Company, Sidney Granville Drew, was arrested and charged with conspiracy (along with Annie Kenney, Flora Drummond and five office staff at Lincoln's Inn House). He was released on sureties of £2,000 and agreed not to print *The Suffragette* or any other WSPU literature again. The following week's edition was printed by the National Labour Press of Manchester, whose manager, Edgar Whitely, was similarly charged, found guilty and sentenced to six days in prison before being immediately released.[2]

The government was taking all measures to drive the suffragettes out of existence, and yet they failed. More members of the WSPU emerged or re-emerged to help with the day-to-day running of Lincoln's Inn House. Dorothy Evans, recovered from her time in Aylesbury the previous year, was secretly put in charge of headquarters and was also wanted by the police for her part in the distribution of the edition of *The Suffragette* on 2 May which told the story of the police raid. 'The type was broken up by the police just as we were going to Press and the copy was confiscated.'[3] Grace Roe went to Maud Joachim's flat and they put the abbreviated issue of the paper together which was distributed direct to retailers all over the country and on the streets on 2 May.

Grace Roe had been understudying Annie Kenney as chief organiser in the event of Annie's arrest. When she was interviewed by the BBC in 1968, she recalled that she had visited Christabel Pankhurst and Annie Kenney in Paris, both of whom seemed uncertain as to what the government would do next. When Grace arrived at Lincoln's Inn House on 30 April, 'there was terrific excitement ... the girls said, "We're raided." They had arrested all the departments and didn't realise I was anyone at all. I lost myself with all the office girls – they were so wonderful those girls – no one will ever know.' Grace witnessed rough treatment by the police: 'I heard one of the young office girls clipped right at the top of her ears and flung across the room.' One of the youngest, a girl aged thirteen or fourteen, went up to Grace, 'her eyes sparkling, "Miss Roe, I've got the leading article."' She had been in the editorial room when Rachel Barrett and Geraldine Lennox were arrested and was quick-witted enough to see an article in Christabel Pankhurst's handwriting, 'and the little girl knew it would be our leader seized it and stuffed it into her blouse'. A new printer for the paper was needed and Grace went to her own bank 'to get some money... and told the bank manager, "I want £500 and I want it now ... If I haven't got it I've got bonds to meet it."' The next day, disguised as an old woman, Grace visited Mrs Pankhurst, who was recovering from the effects of her hunger strike at Hertha Ayrton's home, and then travelled to Paris for instructions from Christabel.[4]

Not long afterwards Dorothy Evans also went to Paris in disguise to receive instructions and articles from Christabel. An innocent woman also named Dorothy Evans was arrested by mistake and our

Dorothy slipped back into the country and went on the run for six months, 'moving from place to place leaving evidence as I went for the public to read of our determination to be governed with our consent or not at all'.[5] (This was Dorothy Evans' way of saying she set fire to empty buildings.) During the summer she briefly worked as an organiser in Bristol before being sent to a new WSPU branch in Belfast in September 'to harry Sir Edward Carson, and his "provisional government"'.

In 1913, Sir Edward Carson was the leader of the twenty Irish Unionist Members of Parliament at Westminster, and the MP for Trinity College, Dublin. Since the general elections of January and December 1910, Herbert Asquith had relied on the support of the Irish Nationalist MPs in the House of Commons. The Irish Unionists detested the notion of Home Rule for Ireland and were alarmed that the prospects seemed promising for the Home Rule Bill. Carson led the Unionist opposition. The Liberal government were trying to remove the House of Lords' veto on House of Commons legislation, and once this was achieved the last constitutional barrier to the Irish Home Rule Bill would be dismantled. The price of Irish nationalist support for the Liberals' attack on the House of Lords was a new Home Rule Bill, which Asquith had introduced in April 1912. Edward Carson prepared to confront his biggest challenge, to preserve the union, 'the guiding star of his political life', and defeat Home Rule.[6]

Under the terms of the proposed Home Rule Bill women would not be enfranchised. In September 1913 Carson said that if the Home Rule Bill was passed he would set up a 'provisional government' in Ulster. Also, in a letter to the Ulster Unionist Council, Carson implied that his provisional government would enfranchise women on the Local Government Register. Sir Edward Carson was not known for his women's suffrage sympathies, and, while it was a welcome development, the leadership of the WSPU wanted to hear his position confirmed in public. Under orders from Christabel Pankhurst, Dorothy Evans and her Irish comrades were instructed 'to manoeuvre, and coerce by militancy if necessary' Sir Edward Carson 'by any means they could, to commit himself in public to saying that women in Ulster would be granted the vote'.[7]

While Grace Roe was in Paris a warrant was issued for her arrest on conspiracy charges, and when her train arrived at Southampton the police were looking for her. Grace had suffered from seasickness and was travelling in a first-class carriage with an elderly couple. When a policeman looked into her compartment, they told him to go away as the 'young lady was very ill'.[8] When Grace reached London she went to the home of Arthur Marshall and his wife Kitty, where there were policemen in the street. 'As I got to the house I realised they had retired, the lights were on upstairs and it was dark downstairs. I gave the danger knock, a special knock and Mr Marshall, who was in his dressing-gown, came downstairs very quickly.' He ushered Grace indoors and paid her taxi. Before leaving, Grace raided Kitty's wardrobe. Kitty Marshall was known to wear 'racy outfits', and Grace Roe emerged swathed in a heavy veil and toque hat. Suffragettes on the run were helped by members of the Actresses' Franchise League who loaned them wigs and disguises. Her friend Charlie Marsh would be disguised with a black wig and long silk coat and had to wear 'a type of costume that worn in the day had the wrong sort of man looking at you'.[9]

It is time to introduce Mary Richardson, one of the more unconventional suffragettes. A member of the chorus, Mary always wanted to be a star. Her autobiography, *Laugh a Defiance*, describes someone who was determined to be at the centre of things. While on active service she adopted 'Polly Dick' as her militant moniker. Mary's presence at some of the most dramatic events she describes have proved difficult to corroborate – especially accounts in the (unpublished) second volume of her autobiography. Mary's desire to become a novelist (she made several unsuccessful attempts to be published) may have encouraged her pen to run away with itself.

Mary Richardson was born in Canada in 1883, an only child who was brought up by her mother and her maternal grandparents. In 1900, aged seventeen, she travelled to Europe with friends and when she joined the WSPU she was living above a shop in Bloomsbury. Mary had an allowance, and an inheritance to look forward to, and was desperate for awfully big adventures. She joined the WSPU in 1909 after encountering a persuasive young man on Kingsway – who turned out to be Mrs Pankhurst's son, Harry. He was selling WSPU literature, surrounded by a hostile crowd who were trying to overturn his barrow: 'When I got near I saw what a pale, delicate-looking fellow he was. But he had a very determined expression and he kept waving a pamphlet with "Votes for Women" printed across it.'[10] Mary tells us she helped him by standing between him and 'the threatening crowd', and when he turned the barrow into Clement's Inn, she followed him. The first person she met was Christabel Pankhurst, 'a plump, pretty young woman', who directed her into another room where Flora Drummond, 'a stout little woman with cheery countenance rose at once from a chair and trestle-table, thrust out her hand and clasped mine with warm friendliness. Flora said: "So, you've decided to join us, eh, lassie?" ' Mary writes as if she joined the movement in a daze, not quite sure what she was letting herself in for; she had felt sorry for Harry, and her instinctive dislike of 'injustice and cruelty' drew her further into the campaign.[11] She abandoned her plan of becoming a novelist and threw herself into a new life which would only be halted by the outbreak of the First World War.

Mary worked for the Kilburn branch of the WSPU for six months, reporting to Mrs Eleanor Penn Gaskell, 'a large, full-bosomed lady',[12] and was sent in 1910 to help Helen Craggs at the newly-opened Woman's Press shop in Charing Cross Road. While most of the shop's customers were campaigning for the vote, Mary Richardson would sometimes find herself arguing with 'an irate customer who would buy one of our leaflets and then tear it to pieces in front of us'.[13] Mary also learned from more experienced members how to chair meetings. In 1961 when she was interviewed she recalled being 'showered with vegetables and rotting fruit but what upset me more than anything was the disgusting remarks we were subjected to. Men would come up and whisper in your ear the most obscene remarks and were very nasty.'[14]

Mary Richardson had been sent as an official observer, rather than a participant, to Parliament Square on Black Friday. However, her thirst for excitement led her into one of the many scrimmages. 'Sick at heart, I wandered across the square when it was all over. It was littered with the sticks and stones the ruffians had used on us, with pieces of clothing, hats and the fragments of our literature.'[15] During the final eighteen months of militancy, Mary was arrested nine times, a 'mouse' being pounced on by the government's big black 'cats'. Early in the morning of 11 March 1913, Mary broke a window of the Home Office in protest at the arrest the day before of five suffragettes who tried to throw petitions into the King's carriage en route to Parliament. Although this was Mary's first arrest, she was sent to Holloway for a month in the second division.[16] The rest of her summer was spent released on Cat and Mouse licences, being arrested four times on new charges, returning to prison, going on hunger strike and being released on licence. On 12 July, Mary was released, only to be rearrested six days later, on 18 July, for breaking a Home Office window. When charged at Canon Row police station, she threw an inkpot through the window and was returned to Holloway. By 30 July she was out again and rearrested for obstruction.[17]

Emily Davison went to the 1913 socialist May Day celebration. She marched to Hyde Park, ecstatic to be part of the crowds, singing 'The Marseillaise', 'The Red Flag' and 'The Internationale': 'I felt a revolutionary of the revolutionaries and ready and proud to take part in any great demonstration for the liberties of the people ... We felt ourselves to be the heirs of all the ages and sires of the great, great future.'[18] Emily's exhilaration bubbled in an unpublished article, 'A Militant Mayday', full of fervour. Listening to trade union heroes like Ben Tillett and Will Thorne, Emily got carried away and her conversion took another step in that 'feast of socialism'. Perhaps her genteel but hard-up childhood, ten years of being a governess, a newly independent and frugal life, her radicalisation in prison, and the feeling that she was being ignored by the WSPU leadership were evidenced in a more class-conscious analysis.

On 7 May Emily learned of the failure of Mr W. H. Dickinson's second attempt to introduce women's suffrage as a private members' bill (the first had been in 1907). His 'Representation of the People Bill' had been defeated by forty-seven votes. Sylvia Pankhurst suggested that hopes for success had not been high: there were rumours that despite Asquith promising a 'free vote', the bill, which would have enfranchised women householders and the wives of householders, would not pass its second reading.

Wounded by the rejection of her May Day article by the *Daily Citizen*, and short of money, Emily returned to Longhorsley. She would have enjoyed *The Suffragette*'s call to arms on the front page titled 'A Famous Militant' and showing a bronze statue of Joan of Arc in full armour on horseback. Christabel Pankhurst's caption read: 'Joan of Arc lives on as the glory and inspiration of France. To British women also she has left a great inheritance ... of simplicity, purity, courage, and militancy ... She belongs to the womanhood of the whole world, and the women of our country are one with the men and women of France in adoring her memory.'[19]

The *Daily Sketch* published Emily's last article on 28 May. The language of 'The Price of Liberty' is apocalyptic. 'The perfect Amazon is she who will sacrifice all ... to win the Pearl of Freedom [the vote] for her sex. Some of the bounteous pearls that women sell to obtain freedom ... are the pearls of friendship, love and even life itself.' Emily refers to the 'terrible suffering' she has endured, the loss of 'old friends, recently-made friends, and they all go one by one into the Limbo of the burning fiery furnace, a grim holocaust to liberty'. She argues in favour of making 'the ultimate sacrifice', happy to pay the 'highest price for liberty'. 'The surrender of life itself is the supreme sacrifice ... to lay down life for friends that is glorious, self-less, inspiring!'

On 1 June Robert Field of the *Daily Citizen* started his irascible note to Emily: 'If you had as many preoccupations as I have, you would better understand why I have been such a dilatory letter-writer.' He was cross that she had pestered him about an unsolicited article, and was brutal about a poem she had sent: 'I have worried over it a great deal trying to decide what the author intended. The idea is quite good but the workmanship leaves something to be desired.'[20] For an impecunious would-be poet, desperate to be a journalist, Field's note and an offer of a cup of tea 'one afternoon next week ... not Monday' must have seemed churlish. Two days later Emily received her last letter of rejection. She had applied for a job with the Women's Tax Resistance League, but she was advised they required a junior shorthand typist, not a secretary. Now forty years old, with a first-class honours degree in English, ten years' teaching experience and an impressive suffragette curriculum vitae, Emily could not get a junior post even with a women's campaigning organisation.[21]

Emily had agreed to be a helper at the Suffragette Fair and Festival at the Empress Rooms, Kensington, on Derby Day, but she decided to visit the fair the night before, and discussed with Kitty Marion and others 'the possibility of making a protest on the race course, without apparently coming to any decision'. As the women strolled into the festival, they were faced by a statue of Joan of Arc, bare-headed and holding her sword pointing to heaven. On the plinth were emblazoned Joan's reputed last words: 'Fight On and God Will Give the

Victory.' The event was a fundraiser for the war chest and the mood was sombre. The suffragettes were on a war footing. Emily placed a laurel wreath at the feet of 'the virgin fighter and martyr who uplifts and inspires us all'. Before leaving the fair she gave Kitty Marion 'a tiny green chamois purse containing a sovereign for munitions I might need'.[22] Emily then returned to the Lambeth home of Mrs Alice Green, the friend with whom she was lodging.

The weather on Wednesday 4 June 1913 was forecast to be sultry with thunderstorms. The King's jockey, Bertie Jones, was to ride Anmer in the Derby Stakes at three o'clock. Jones arrived from Newmarket with Richard Marsh, the King's trainer, and half a dozen stable lads. Racegoers caught the last trains from London at midnight and milled about the town in the small hours. Epsom buzzed, cosy Surrey meeting the Wild West. At noon, Bertie Jones and Richard Marsh went to the jockeys' dressing room where Jones dressed in the royal silks, transformed from an eight-stone man-child of thirty-three into an exotic bird with a purple body with gold frogging, black cap and scarlet plumage.

That morning Emily left Alice Green's home at 133 Clapham Road, Lambeth, and walked to Oval to catch a tram to Victoria station, where she bought a return ticket for Epsom Downs. Before she left she told Alice what she was going to do. She pinned a purple, white and green flag inside her jacket and took her latch key, a small leather purse containing three shillings and eight pence and three farthings, eight halfpenny stamps and a notebook. Another suffragette flag was tucked up her sleeve. Emily walked to the racecourse and bought a Dorling's List of Epsom Races.

Emily Davison marked the first three horses past the post on her race card and then came the Derby. It was easy for Emily to identify the object of her journey: the King's horse Anmer was number one, and she had already seen 'Jockey Jones' gallop past in the royal colours. At odds of fifty to one, Anmer was not much fancied that day.

Emily made her way to Tattenham Corner, a tricky place for horse and rider in the gruelling mile and a half race. This was the biggest day out in Edwardian England. Here at three o'clock, the apex of the social pyramid met its base. The King and Queen and their entourage added glamour to an occasion that welcomed both the establishment *and* the working class at play.

Emily squeezed close to the rails. As the race started the sixteen horses and riders ran straight for three furlongs before the course climbed to a gradient of one in fifteen. Anmer made a good start. At seven furlongs the field took the left turn downhill for five furlongs and this is where Anmer fell away to the group at the back. The leading horses pounded towards the spot where Emily was waiting. Tons of horse flesh and men flashed past, spittle, sweat, huge eyes rolling with the effort, the noise of the crowd was bewildering. Everyone was screaming the names of *their* horses for that brief moment, and jumping up and urging them on. The trailing bunch, including Anmer, approached. Emily fiddled with the sleeve of her jacket, bobbed under the white railings, and made history.

Clutching her unfurled tricolour of purple, white and green, Davison dashed out to make her protest at the lack of progress on women's suffrage in general, and the treatment of Mrs Pankhurst in particular. By targeting Anmer she was reminding King George V of his government's callous injustice to women. Emily stood with her arms above her head, and then stepped in front of Bertie Jones and tried to grab the horse's bridle.[23] She was knocked over screaming. 'The horse struck the woman with its chest, knocking her down among the flying hoofs ... and she was desperately injured ... Blood rushed from her mouth and nose. Anmer turned a complete somersault and fell upon his jockey who was seriously injured.'[24] Anmer recovered himself, and Bertie Jones, whose foot was stuck in the stirrup, was dragged for a few yards. Oblivious to what was happening the spectators who stood to the left of Emily turned to follow the race, but those to the right of her were puzzled by what was happening in front of their eyes. There was chaos: the jockeys behind Jones cursed and struggled to pull away from the woman who had invaded the track. Anmer cantered off with a few cuts to his face and body, apparently none the worse for his fall.[25]

Steve Donoghue, one of the top jockeys of the day, was lucky not to be knocked off and wrote later that it was a miracle six more horses had not been brought down. He thought it was an act of 'criminal folly brought on by the freak of a mad woman's brain'.[26] The crowd invaded the course and surrounded the jockey and the suffragette. Emily was unconscious. The police had to hold the crowd back, who were angry with her for spoiling the day and embarrassing the King.

Emily was taken in a motor car to Epsom Cottage Hospital, and was there looked after by the House Surgeon, Dr Peacock. Police Sergeant Frank Bunn filed his report later that evening while the events were still fresh in his memory. [27]

At first Bertie Jones lay unconscious where he fell, the left side of his body badly abraded and bruised. He was attended by a racegoer, Dr Percy Spencer of Tooting, and was taken to the racecourse doctor. Bertie recovered consciousness but was concussed, and his left arm was put in a sling. He tried to shrug off his injuries and refused to go to hospital.

There were film cameras at Epsom that day to satisfy the Empire-wide demand for stories about the royal family and Derby Day. Emily's deathly dash was recorded on film and history was made on twenty feet of silver nitrate. She became the most famous suffragette, a heroine for all women who struggled for equality. Her jerky movements on grey, grainy film have played for a hundred years. Shots of the film were made into stills and distributed to the press ready for the first edition of the next day's newspapers.

At Newmarket they called Emily 'that malignant suffragette'. King George V wrote in his diary:

> A most disastrous Derby ... I ran Anmer, just as the horses were coming round Tattenham Corner, a suffragette (Miss Davison) dashed out and tried to catch Anmer's bridle, of course she was knocked down and seriously injured and poor Herbert Jones and Anmer were sent flying. Jones unconscious, badly cut, broken rib, and slight concussion, a most regrettable and scandalous proceeding ... A most disappointing day.[28]

Queen Mary sent Bertie a note wishing him well after his 'sad accident caused through the abominable conduct of a brutal lunatic woman'.[29] The Home Office and Metropolitan Police revealed that the Director of Public Prosecutions advised: 'If Miss Davison recovers it will be possible to charge her with doing an act to cause grievous bodily harm to the rider of the horse.'[30]

Suffragettes formed a guard of honour around Emily's bed and hung purple, white and green bunting above her. The flag she flourished had traces of her blood and mud and grass stains. The widely held belief is that Emily never regained consciousness, but a letter from Eleanor Penn Gaskell to Emily's friend, Miss Dixon, revealed that she did come round but could not speak. Mrs Penn Gaskell told her:

> Our heroine is now partly conscious, that is to say she shows recognition when addressed by name and can take food but makes no attempt to speak. It is thought she may remain much in this state for about a fortnight but in any case will not be able to be moved for a fortnight. The injury is to the head, the extent will not be ascertained for a fortnight – no bones broken. Her head struck the horse – she suffers no pain. She makes slight favourable progress and I think that is all there is to be said. We must wait patiently … they are most kind at the little hospital and she lacks for <u>nothing</u>.[31]

Mrs Penn Gaskell was proud of Emily's actions: 'What <u>splendid courage</u>. What a wonderful message she has sent through the length and breadth of the land. I am sure the sacrifice will not be in vain. I wish I could give you more definite and better news but it is early days yet and the injury of course was very serious', and signed off the letter, 'Yours in the Cause'.[32]

On 6 June Mr Charles Mansell-Moullin operated to relieve the pressure on Emily's brain but she died, on 8 June. The Coroner recorded a verdict of death by misadventure: the cause 'a fracture to the base of the skull caused by being accidentally knocked down by a horse through wilfully rushing on to the race-course … during the progress of the race'.[33]

A letter from Emily's bewildered mother lay on her bedside table: 'I cannot believe that you could do such a dreadful act. Even for the Cause which I know you have given up your whole heart and soul to, and it has done so little in return for you. Now I can only hope and pray that God will mercifully restore you to life and health and that there may be a better and brighter future for you.' There were cards from well-wishers, a fan letter from a lunatic in Banstead Asylum and two poison-pen letters, one from an 'Englishman' who hoped she suffered 'torture' until she died: 'I consider you are a person unworthy of existence … and I should like the opportunity of starving and beating you to a pulp.'[34]

On 8 June the WSPU's creation of spectacle began. Emily was given a ceremonial funeral for her 'noble sacrifice' and the dues of 'a fallen warrior', 'a brave comrade' and 'crusader'. In *Votes for Women* there were tributes from her closest friends. Mrs Penn Gaskell: 'Emily Davison was one of the most wonderful personalities I have ever known'; Constance Lytton: 'I have known her as the most cheerful companion, the truest upholder of our Great Cause', and Rose Lamartine Yates: 'She had felt the call, she knew that suffering and outraged womanhood looked to her.'[35] In private the WSPU leadership was not pleased with Emily's protest. Before Emily died Christabel Pankhurst distanced the Union, insisting that they knew nothing about it: 'We were as startled as everyone. Not a word had she said of her purpose. Taking counsel with no one, she went to the racecourse, waited her moment and rushed forward.'[36] But Emily's death changed everything: the WSPU had to honour her as their first martyr. A secular saint was about to be sanctified. A year later Mrs Pankhurst wrote: 'The death of Miss Davison was a great shock to me and a very great grief as well and although I was scarcely able to leave my bed, I determined to risk everything to attend her funeral.'[37] However, as Mrs Pankhurst left for Emily's funeral service she was arrested by two detectives waiting outside Hertha Ayrton's house where she was recovering from being on hunger strike. Not all women's suffrage campaigners were uncritical of Emily's protest: Philippa Strachey, Secretary of the London Society for Women's Suffrage, wrote:

> this society is taking no part in ... Miss Davison's funeral. While respecting the fact that Miss Davison's action was done in good faith it is impossible not to realise that she risked the lives of many innocent people, and we deplore her actions. We have to realise that such an occurrence does great harm to our cause by alienating many people who would consider it right to give the vote to women but who do most strongly believe it is wrong to endanger the lives of other people.[38]

On Saturday 14 June 1913, a special guard of honour of Emily's closest friends brought her body from Epsom to Victoria railway station. Six thousand women marched from Buckingham Palace Road to Emily Davison's funeral service at St George's Church, Bloomsbury. Ten brass bands marched behind each section playing funereal marches. The coffin was escorted by Elsie Howey on a white horse dressed as Joan of Arc, and two contingents of hunger strikers walked behind the hearse which was laden with wreaths. Charlie Marsh made her final appearance for the suffragette cause as the standard-bearer at the head of the procession.

Grace Roe, still on the run from the police, organised the funeral. She asked several clergymen to hold the service before the Reverend Charles Baumgarten agreed to hold it in his church. Perhaps he knew Minnie Baldock and the WSPU from its early days in West Ham, when he was the vicar of St Gabriel's church. Grace went in disguise to the funeral. Caprina Fahey, Leonora Tyson, Elsa Myers, Eleanor Glidewell and Dorothea Rock were five of the twenty-two 'group captains' leading sections of the procession.

Banners in purple silk included Joan of Arc's last words: 'Fight On and God Will Give the Victory'. Central London stopped. Some people jeered as the suffragettes walked past. Following the coffin, in the first carriage, were Emily's mother, her sister Lettie, her cousin Jessie, and Miss Morrison, 'Miss Davison's intimate companion'. There were cries of 'Three cheers for Herbert Jones', and a brick hit the coffin. The crowds broke through the police cordon when the suffragette cortège reached the church. Newsreel of the procession showed Mary Leigh saluting Emily's coffin as it left the church. Guarded by suffragettes in white and wearing black armbands, and protected by the police, Emily's body lay in state at King's Cross station, accompanied by a thousand wreaths, before a journey to Morpeth. She was interred in the family grave, alongside her father and his first wife. Emily's posthumous life was about to start with Mary Leigh's plans for the Emily Wilding Davison Club, the Emily Wilding Davison Lodge, and the Emily Wilding Davison Pilgrimage to Morpeth on the anniversary of her death. The possessions found with Emily at Epsom Cottage Hospital were cherished for many years by Rose Lamartine Yates.[39] Gertrude Baillie-Weaver, whose pen name was 'Gertrude Colmore', published *The Life of Emily Davison* before the end of the year.

On the day of the funeral, Canon Aitken and his wife heard that their daughter Violet had reversed her recent decision to leave her job at *The Suffragette* and pursue a literary career. They were unhappy about her determination 'to go on with their wretched paper, she feels it would look like she was deserting the cause to leave them now'.⁴⁰

In private the suffragettes and Emily's family and friends tried to understand her intentions, and a discussion as to whether her protest was an act of suicide persists to the present day. At the time there were plenty who thought that she had deliberately given her life for the Cause. There are several indicators that Emily Davison took her own life. For the last six months of her life, her journalism, mostly unpublished, reads like a suicide note. While the consensus was that she had 'given her life' no one would use the word 'suicide', which was an illegal act until 1961. Perhaps Emily was troubled by the death on 21 February of the clergyman she attacked in Aberdeen six months earlier. The purse she was carrying contained a dog-eared newspaper cutting announcing the Reverend Forbes Jackson's death, leaving a widow and six children. *The Times* was in no doubt that she – although unnamed – was the cause. Emily would not have known he died of pernicious anaemia, caused by a chronic deficiency of the vitamin B12. As she learned more about the man she had whipped – he trained Baptist missionaries for the Congo and had exposed the genocide and amputations practised on the Congolese on the orders of King Leopold of the Belgians – this may have added to her depressed mood suggested in her writings. A good man had died and she was being blamed.⁴¹

People insist that because a return ticket was found in her purse this shows she had not meant to take her own life, but on the day it was cheaper to buy a return than a one-way ticket. Emily knew the risks when she stepped in front of Anmer. She was familiar with horses: in 1900 there were a quarter of a million of them in London, and when she worked as a governess for the Moorhouses in Northamptonshire, the Pytchley Hunt met there. It might be said Emily knew more about horses than most. Bertie Jones suffered from depression after Emily jumped out in front of him; he was 'haunted by that woman's face' as he and Anmer ran her down. His career faltered and ended after the First World War; he suffered from poor health for the rest of his life. Years later, on 17 July 1951, Bertie Jones's son, John, found his father dead in a gas-filled kitchen: the Coroner's verdict 'suicide while the balance of his mind was disturbed'.⁴²

The day before Emily Davison's funeral procession through the streets of London *The Suffragette* depicted Emily on the front page as an angel with large wings; her halo includes the words, 'Love that Overcometh', and the image is captioned: 'In Honour and Loving, Reverent Memory of Emily Wilding Davison. She Died For Women.' Other headlines in the newspaper were: 'Boathouse Burned Down'; 'Mansion Destroyed Near Trowbridge'; 'Station Fired At Glasgow'; 'Attempt To Fire The Royal Academy'; 'Mr Churchill's Stormy Meeting' and 'Grand Stand in Flames'.[43] The battle continued.

Emily Davison was a loose cannon who always pursued her own militant path, inventing a new form of protest – setting fire to pillar boxes, a tactic frequently copied by her comrades. Her cell protests brought militancy into the prisons where she served her sentences, and these methods were also adopted by other suffragette prisoners. While Emily was not disciplined by the WSPU for her wayward behaviour, it was perhaps the reason why her contribution was not rewarded by warmer and closer relations with the leaders and their acolytes, and a senior, paid position. In fact, she was more popular in the WSPU in death than she was in life. Apart from her maverick ways, on a personal level her sometimes overbearing manner grated – perhaps informed by a life of being a poor relation – and meant the obvious promotions did not come her way. When Emily was dead the leaders took notice of her and used her death in their propaganda war. The impact of her sacrifice was immediate: she filled the pages of the national press for days; there was a spike in arson attacks carried out by women who wanted to salute her martyrdom. Politically her actions at the Derby made no difference, but the suffragettes had shown that at least one of their women would give her life for the Cause and raised the possibility there were more waiting in the wings.

17

The Failure of the 'Cat and Mouse' Act

Suffragette Fugitives and Stalkers 1913

*This poster was published in response to the Prisoners'
(Temporary Discharge for Ill-Health) Act of 1913. The establishment
cat chases and pounces on the suffragette mouse.*

Apart from a photograph of Emily Davison in her graduation gown, the only photograph in *The Suffragette* on 13 June was of the damage caused by Emily's friends Kitty Marion and Clara 'Betty' Giveen who had burned down the grandstand at Hurst Park racecourse, near Hampton Court. In honour of Emily, they set fire to it at the dead of night on 8 June, not knowing that she had already died. Kitty and Betty had been tipped off by local WSPU supporters – Eileen Casey and her mother Bella – that the grandstand would be 'a most appropriate beacon, not only as the usual protest but, in honour of our Comrade's daring deed'.[1] They learned that the only way in would be 'to climb a fence the spiked top of which neither of us could reach … about a foot above the spikes were two rows of barbed wire which looked pretty impossible for two long-skirted females to negotiate'.[2] Kitty returned to her lodgings in Kennington and asked her landlady if she had a spare piece of carpet. On Saturday evening 8 June, armed with carpet 'rolled and strapped into a neat looking bit of baggage … and a wicker suitcase with a gallon of oil and fire-lighters',[3] Kitty and Betty went by train and tram to the bridge at Hampton Court Palace. They crossed fields to a cricket pitch and climbed onto the roof of the cricket pitch's tool shed. 'How we got over and back beggars description. We both regretted that there was no movie camera to immortalize the comedy of it.'

They entered the grandstand and soon the place was ablaze. They 'could hardly climb' out of the grounds 'for laughing … we were up against a sheer fence, no foothold anywhere'.[4] They threw the carpet on top of the barbed wire. Betty was fifteen years younger than Kitty, and in 'better athletic trim', and the lighter of the two. Kitty 'could better bear her weight than she mine so I stooped with my hands on my knees as I had done in my childhood days, while Betty climbed up, dragged herself over and then pulled me up and over head first. How she did it I don't know.'⁵ At one o'clock in the morning, when they were walking to the Caseys' house in Kew, they were passed by police motorcyclists and horse-drawn fire engines galloping along to put out their fire. 'We strolled, trying not to look too eager to get away.' Unsure of the way to the Caseys' house they asked a police-man for directions. When the policeman expressed surprise that the two ladies were out at night, Kitty told him, 'Oh, I am a Music Hall artiste and often out late.' He asked them their names and addresses, which they refused to give, but he directed them towards their destin-ation and followed them to the Caseys'. When they arrived at 3 a.m. a policeman was lurking nearby: they had left a copy of *The Suffragette* at the scene of the crime, and the police visited every house within the radius of a few miles known to be occupied by suffragettes. Kitty and Betty were trapped and on the Monday morning the policeman who had followed them arrived with Detective Inspectors Pride and Pike, who arrested and charged them with being 'suspected persons found loitering in certain streets with intent to commit a felony'.⁶ Kitty was too experienced to fall for their bullying tactics: 'When Inspector Pride brought Betty in he barked at me, "What's your name?" Mocking his tone, I barked back. "Kitty Marion!"'⁷ The women were taken to Richmond police station where they denied any involvement in the arson attack; they promised they would do 'nothing militant in the meanwhile', and they were allowed out on bail provided by two wealthy suffragette sympathisers.

On 10 June at Richmond Police Court there was proof of Kitty's involvement in the arson attack – she had dropped her purse 'which must have slipped out of my pocket when I came back over the fence'. The police had already been to her lodgings where they found the same pattern of the carpet as the piece they had used. Kitty and Betty were put into an identity parade with sixteen other women and were picked out by the fireman on duty at Hampton Court Palace who had seen them tottering across the bridge, wearing cloaks and carry-ing two suitcases. They were rearrested for 'maliciously setting fire to Hurst Park Grand Stand'.⁸

Eileen Casey had been active in the struggle earlier in 1913: on 17 March she was charged with malicious damage after pouring a 'noxious or deleterious substance' into a pillar box in Charing Cross and was sentenced, as 'Eleanor Cleary', to two months in prison. Her £10 fine was paid by 'a well-wisher' after she had served just two days in Holloway. Kitty Marion remembered telling their hosts about their caper with the carpet: 'Poor Dr Casey! He was not such a keen suffragist as were his wife and daughter Eileen ... on this Monday morning at his home it was a bit of a shock to him, though he bore it bravely, even seeing the humour of it in the end.'[9]

On 3 July at the Surrey Assizes at Guildford, Kitty Marion and Betty Giveen were found guilty of causing £7,000 worth of damage. Archibald Bodkin was one of the Crown prosecutors. The women were represented by the barrister Ian Stewart McPherson, the Liberal MP for Ross and Cromarty. McPherson contended that the only substantial piece of evidence was the piece of carpet found hanging on the barbed wire, and there was no proof that either of the women had taken it there. At Richmond Police Court Mrs Casey had been cross-examined and great 'astonishment' was expressed that she had entrusted her front-door key to someone she barely knew. She responded: 'She [Giveen] was a suffragette and that was quite good enough for us. We trust anyone who is a suffragette.'[10] Kitty and Betty pleaded not guilty, but the jury found against them and Judge Phillimore sentenced them to three years in prison. Betty Giveen responded: 'I do not think any sentence should be passed upon us, as we have not been tried by our peers. Until women are on the jury – women should not be tried and sentenced. We shall fight and win because there is justice in our cause.'[11] Kitty Marion told the court they had been convicted on 'the flimsiest circumstantial evidence. Had we been men charged with criminal assault on little children or women, we should be set free on a like amount of evidence. I shall go on hunger-strike.'[12] Kitty also gave notice that she would refuse to be released on a Cat and Mouse licence. Suffragette supporters who were in the public gallery sang 'The Marseillaise' and were 'ejected'.

Clara 'Betty' Giveen had been a member of the WSPU since Black Friday, 1910. She served a five-day sentence in Holloway for breaking windows of the Local Government Board on 21 November 1911. In June 1912 she was released early from a four-month sentence in

Aylesbury Gaol for smashing windows with Violet Aitken in Regent Street on 1 March 1912; she had been on hunger strike and was force-fed.[13]

The women were taken to Holloway where Kitty started a hunger and thirst strike and was put in solitary confinement. 'At every meal-time tempting food and drink was placed beside my bed only to be removed untouched.' After four days she was weak; 'normal functioning ceased [constipation] and from the taste in my mouth seemed to have set in. Brushing my teeth and rinsing my mouth, without swallowing a drip of water, was a comfort and luxury to my burning swollen tongue.' Kitty says she slept 'from sheer exhaustion through internal discomfort and pain'.[14] On the fourth and fifth days, 7 and 8 July, she was so dizzy she could not move. Annie Kenney smuggled a note in to her: 'just a line to tell you how much I admire the splendid way you have stuck to your colours. You have been so brave and wonderfully courageous.'[15] Arthur Marshall visited Kitty and inspired her with the news of an arson attack on Sir William H. Lever's summer bungalow at Rivington Pike in the Pennines. 'I gloried in others keeping up the good work.' On 8 July Kitty was released 'in a very weak state of health' and given hot water, brandy and Brand's Essence. When the governor of Holloway presented Kitty with the Cat and Mouse licence she tore it up. Betty Giveen was released in a weakened state on 10 July and disappeared. She went on the run.

Kitty was cared for by Dr Flora Murray at a house which was being used as a suffragette nursing home, and was determined to protest against the Cat and Mouse Act as soon as she felt strong enough 'to crawl to the Home Office and hurl a stone through a window'. She was outraged by reports of the 'Piccadilly Flat Case' of a woman being arrested and sentenced on 10 July to three months in prison for 'keeping a luxurious brothel'.[16] The names of her clients, many of whom were thought to be prominent politicians and society figures, were kept secret. The *Daily Sketch* reported that 'letters had been found signed by men of high positions, revealing an organisation for procuring young girls and little children'.[17] On 12 July Kitty Marion broke a window at the Home Office, was arrested and returned to Holloway for an additional twenty-one days in the second division. She returned to her old cell and after a four-and-a-half-day hunger and thirst strike she was released on a two-day licence feeling 'physically weak, weary and tired'.[18]

On 19 July Kitty wrote a defiant letter to Home Secretary McKenna: 'The sooner we come to an understanding as to whether it is to be <u>votes</u> for women or <u>death</u> for women the better.' She told him she was a German subject but had worked for many years on the English stage and 'I know the ravages the white slave traffic is working in an otherwise English profession. I have seen with horror the conditions of life under which the women have to fight for an existence, and the unnecessary pitfalls and temptations which surround them.' She told McKenna, 'My life is in your hands, you can kill me if you will but you will never make me surrender. Physically I may be as weak as a mouse, spiritually I am as strong as the British Lion and the German Eagle combined.'[19]

Two of Kitty Marion's friends paid a visit to her, 'one like me … but dressed differently to my usual tailor-made style'. Kitty removed her friend's hat and veil and put on her 'the hat and coat in which the detectives had lately seen me'. She reported that Dr Murray gave her a dose of strychnine to 'brace' her up, and then Kitty's double left the house 'leaning heavily on someone else's arm',[20] and entered a taxi which was promptly stopped by two detectives as it drove off towards High Street Kensington. A suffragette on lookout duty in the street gave a signal that it was now safe for Kitty to leave, and, dressed in her friend's clothes, she took a bus to Croydon.

Edith Rigby, the eccentric suffragette whose actions had lifted Kitty's spirits in prison, was back in the limelight in Preston. With five convictions under her belt since joining the WSPU in 1907, Edith returned to the fray in 1913. On Easter Monday she had pelted the Labour MP for Derby, James 'Jimmy' Thomas, with black puddings when he spoke at the Free Trade Hall in Manchester. She was wrongly accused of tarring the statue of Lord Derby in Miller Park, Preston, on 11 May, although years later she admitted arranging for it to be carried out. Mrs Rigby was incensed by reports in the *Lancashire Daily Post* on 7 May of the defeat of Mr Dickinson's 'Representation of the People Bill' by forty-seven votes. She took great exception to the remarks of Sir Joseph Compton-Rickett, the Liberal MP for Osgoldcross, West Yorkshire, that women in Parliament could be of no benefit to the community, so on 5 July she planted a bomb in the basement of the Liverpool Cotton Exchange. A small portman-teau filled with suffragette literature was found nearby with a label addressed 'To Mr McKenna, London: If Sir William Lever [the phil-anthropist and 'Soap King of Port Sunlight'] had been as loyal to us and the Liberal Party as Lancashire is being to its King this would not have happened.'[21] A pair of white kid gloves stained with blood were found, worn by Edith as she broke a window to get in.

In the early hours of 8 July, with help from Albert Yeadon, coffin-maker and member of the Independent Labour Party, Edith burned down the Rivington Pike summer home of Sir William Lever, a Liberal MP until 1909. His large wood-built bungalow was reputed to be filled with valuable paintings, and the damage amounted to £20,000. Edith heard that King George V and Lloyd George were regular visitors. Albert Yeadon stored the paraffin she used to set the place alight, and went with her in her husband's car, driven by their chauffeur. Edith knew the bungalow would be empty on the night of 7 July. Albert helped her to carry the paraffin across the grounds of the house and told him to return to the car: 'I must finish this job myself, I can't have you involved any further in our work.' (Albert was a married man with two children to support.) Edith's niece, Phoebe Hesketh, tells us: 'Very soon my aunt was pushing her way through the thick bushes surrounding the gardens. After walking twice round the place to make sure it was empty, she laid and lit her paraffin trail.' Years later Charles, the chauffeur, told Phoebe: ' "She'd such a smile on 'er face as she climbed into the car, an' she seemed mighty pleased with 'erself. I guessed she'd been up to no good." '[22]

Edith Rigby could have got away with it but she handed herself in to the Liverpool police on 9 July and confessed to causing an explosion and destroying a house, using her appearance before Liverpool Police Court to maximum effect. She took full responsibility: 'I myself did this without any aid. It was my own planning and it was not author-ised.' Edith had placed the explosive at the Cotton Exchange so that everyone would 'realise that when women are driven to these desper-ate measures how comparatively easy it is for women to get explosives and place them in public buildings'. She told the magistrate that her grievance with the Cotton Exchange was that 'the great cotton indus-try in Lancashire is built up, if not entirely, very much on women's labour'. She condemned the merchants for their greed and deplored the fact women were denied the vote even though they paid taxes. Edith linked her protest to the passing of the 'unrighteous law' – the Cat and Mouse Act – and the risk that 'one of the greatest women in the land [Mrs Pankhurst] is going to be done to death'.[23]

Edith Rigby denounced Sir William Lever:

I understand Sir William Lever is an opponent of women's rights. I want to ask him whether his property on Rivington Pike is more valuable as one of his superfluous houses to be occasionally opened to people and used occasionally, or as a beacon lighted for the King and country to see that there were some unsupportable grievances for women.[24]

The magistrate dismissed her remarks as irrelevant and she was remanded in custody at Walton Gaol for a week until she was committed for trial, and was sentenced to nine months with hard labour. At that time suffragettes holding meetings in Preston's market square were sworn at, spat at and pelted with rotten fish. Edith's husband remained her most stalwart supporter, writing to the editor of the *Lancashire Daily Post*:

She has again gone to prison and hunger-striking like a sheep to the slaughter ... I wonder if you are satisfied with women being repeatedly brought to the verge of death, then liberated, afterwards brought back to the same torture? ... It is you and your party who are responsible ... It has been thrown in my teeth that I should have restrained Edith Rigby. How have the powers that be, with all their forces restrained her? By torture.[25]

Between July and December 1913 Edith was released from Walton Gaol and rearrested several times on Cat and Mouse licences. In November Preston suffragettes interrupted the service at the Congregational Church chanting a prayer for Mrs Rigby. After a prayer was offered by the preacher her comrades stood up in the packed gallery and chanted 'God save Edith Rigby and all women who are being tortured for conscience' sake'.[26] The incident caused 'a great sensation' but the women were not ejected; the service continued without further interruption.

Edith's husband begged her not to go on hunger strike, but she persisted. In December, as a released 'mouse', Edith was caught trying to plant a bomb at the Liverpool Cotton Exchange again. Just after Christmas she was released on licence after refusing food and water for four days. Dressed in man's clothes she would escape from her back door on Albert Yeadon's bicycle. She made her way to Galway on the west coast of Ireland, and did not return for several weeks. When one of Edith's school friends wrote a sympathetic letter to Dr Rigby, his reply showed him to be as loving as ever:

> It is a difficult business ... but for me there is only one course and that is to back Edith. I know her perfect sincerity and love of justice; she feels it to be the only course her conscience allows her to follow. She is willing to suffer blows, loss of friends ... and starvation ... she is almost a shadow, scarcely able to stand, with the smile of an angel and the courage of a lion ... I do not have the moral courage to do what she has done, I doubt I could do it for any cause. It makes me so ashamed and I feel so unworthy of her.[27]

On 8 July 1913 Jennie Baines went with her husband, George, and their sixteen-year-old son, Wilfrid, from their home near Manchester to their local railway station to blow up a first-class railway carriage and leave suffragist literature at the scene. When the Baineses were arrested at home the police found a bomb, a loaded revolver, black masks, tools that could be used to cut telephone and telegraph wires and two catapults. They were charged with malicious damage, and after promising not to engage in any outrages while on remand all were released on bail except Jennie who was a 'mouse' on the run from the Metropolitan Police on an expired Cat and Mouse licence. She was returned to Holloway, went on hunger strike and was released.

As Jennie Baines suffered from chorea, a condition causing involuntary spasms, it was impossible to force-feed her. In May 1913 she had been arrested while trying to hold a meeting in Hyde Park and was charged with obstruction and sent to Holloway for one month. She went on hunger strike and was released. The Baines family were due to stand trial in Manchester in November, but Jennie was in hiding in Wales, and at the trial George Baines and his son were acquitted. Travelling under the name of 'Evans' the family left England for

Australia, arriving in Melbourne before Christmas, where Jennie campaigned for women's issues and socialist politics for the rest of her life.[28]

On Saturday 19 July, an attempt had been made to arrest Mrs Pankhurst two days before she was due to speak at a WSPU meeting at the Pavilion Theatre. She was on a Cat and Mouse licence. She had been on a hunger and thirst strike for three days when she was released on 16 June, having refused to take water: 'The body cannot endure loss of moisture. It cries out in protest with every nerve. The muscles waste, the skin becomes shrunken and flabby, the facial appearance alters horribly ... every natural function is suspended and the poisons which are unable to pass out of the body are retained and absorbed.' Mrs Pankhurst also described the 'shivers, the constant headache and nausea, fever' and how her tongue became 'coated and swollen and the voice drops to a whisper'.[29] On her release she was badly jaundiced, and had not fully recovered three months later when she dictated her memoir en route to America for her third lecture tour.

Kitty Marshall described how a 'double' was used to smuggle Mrs Pankhurst out of Ada Wright's flat in Westminster, where she was cared for by Nurse Pine. A female of the same slight build and heavily veiled was pounced on by the police. The last time we saw Ada Wright she was in Aylesbury Gaol serving six months for window-smashing in 1912. The suffragettes who were on picket duty outside the flat screamed, 'They are arresting Mrs Pankhurst' and a free-for-all ensued. The policemen surrounded the 'rocking vehicle', tore 'the veiled figure from the arms of the other women', bundled her into a taxicab and raced off towards Bow Street police station.[30] When the policemen removed her veil and saw they had been tricked, they returned to the flat to find it empty. Mrs Pankhurst spent the weekend at the Marshalls' country home in Essex. Kitty Marshall wrote: 'We had a merry supper party and the next morning Mrs Pankhurst was amused to read in the newspapers, "Mrs Pankhurst Taken Back To Holloway Prison". We had a lovely Sunday, lying out in the garden in deckchairs, but we were rather anxious as to how we should get on at the meeting at the Pavilion.' They went by car, with Mrs Pankhurst wearing her veil: 'We got safely inside ... but the game was up as a number of detectives were inside the hall.' Kitty saw Mrs Pankhurst being grabbed and 'there was a regular scrimmage, friends trying to save her and foes trying to arrest her'. Mrs Pankhurst called out that she was being taken: 'so valiantly did they rush to the rescue that the police had their hands full for nearly an hour before they got me into a taxicab bound for Holloway.'[31]

Kitty Marshall held onto Inspector Riley's tie with one hand, and in the other she was carrying a small suitcase. She was arrested for smacking him in the face, which she denied, and was sent to Holloway for three weeks for assault. Kitty went on hunger strike, but to her regret her fine was paid anonymously. Five other women, including one of the Rock sisters of Ingatestone, Essex, and a Major Fisher were also arrested. The meeting continued when order was restored and the collecting bags were quickly filled with cash and rings and bracelets, to be sold for campaign funds. Two high-profile 'mice', Annie Kenney and Sylvia Pankhurst, also appeared on the platform, surrounded by bodyguards, and made contentious speeches without being arrested.

Mrs Pankhurst was taken to Holloway, but she refused to get out of the cab, so she was lifted and carried into a cell in the hospital wing. Already unwell from her previous incarceration, Mrs Pankhurst refused to undress and would not allow the prison doctor to examine her, refusing food and water. She was released on 24 July. The next day a press bulletin was issued: 'Mrs Pankhurst arrived in a very serious condition. She was immediately seen by several eminent doctors. In view of her extreme weakness it was considered necessary to resort to transfusion.' Nurse Pine reported that 'the patient had received a blood transfusion from one of many volunteers which had been successfully performed'.[32]

*

A letter from Emmeline Pethick-Lawrence to Mrs Saul Solomon, written in the aftermath of Emily Davison's death, reminds us of the generosity and spirit of the Pethick-Lawrences. The couple did not begrudge the many thousands of pounds they had donated to the Cause. Emmeline wrote to Mrs Solomon: 'You know that it is a joy to give to this Movement ... before the window-smashing raid took place we told Mrs Pankhurst exactly what it would mean and we deliberately accepted the consequences. So you must not talk now of debts or obligations ... and you must not think we want any of this money refunded to us by our colleagues in the Suffrage Movement.'[33]

On 26 July Christina and Winifred Broom photographed a group of women's suffrage 'pilgrims', many of whom had set off from Carlisle. Some of the pilgrims, men, women and children, had trudged the whole way since 18 June, their luggage carried in baggage carts which followed behind, while other pilgrims completed stages of the walk. The pilgrimage was the idea of Mrs Katherine Harley, the sister of Charlotte Despard, the President of the Shropshire Society of the NUWSS, and a member of the Church League for Women's Suffrage.

It is some time since the moderate suffragists appeared on the suffrage stage. Their pilgrimage, starting from eight locations, included women from John o' Groats to Land's End, at the very edges of the United Kingdom, and was a deliberate counterpoint to the militancy of the WSPU, which would have been appreciated by the moderate members of the Union who subscribed to the Pethick-Lawrences' *Votes for Women*. The pilgrimage aimed to spread the NUWSS's law-abiding and constitutional message of women's enfranchisement in every town and village through which they passed, and to firmly distance themselves from the shouty and destructive militants. Mrs Fawcett announced that the pilgrimage was

a solemn renewal of the self-dedication to the cause of the freeing of half of humanity from the position of political serfdom ... No men have ever been placed in the position in which women stand of the complete absolute and perpetual exclusion from all share in political power; taxed, legislated for, blundered over as we are, without any power of self-defence by means of representative institutions.[34]

The five-week walk was a vital fundraiser, too: almost £9,000 was collected along the way.

Henry Nevinson witnessed the rally in Hyde Park, reporting that the NUWSS banners were 'all gay ... brilliant with red, white and green'. Nevinson also noted, 'there was no disorder of any kind, no abuse, no filth. The hooligans had not come.' The very few antis present put up their hands when the resolution was put to the crowd of 50,000, 'looking like scattered fish in a net at such a bad haul as ruins the fisherman'.[35]

The NUWSS hoped it was a breakthrough when Prime Minister Herbert Asquith agreed to meet their deputation on 8 August – the

first women's suffrage deputation he had received in two years. The
meeting did not change government policy; it was a symbolic gesture
which served to reinforce the difference between the moderates and
the militants.[36]

Sylvia Pankhurst, who had been released from prison on 14 July
after ten days of hunger- and thirst-striking, was determined to take
the militant voice to Trafalgar Square. On 27 July she addressed a
meeting of between 15,000 and 20,000 working women and men.
The Men's Federation for Women's Suffrage were also permitted
to hold a meeting. Newly founded in 1912, the Federation worked
with Sylvia's East London Federation, and sold the *Daily Herald*
and socialist literature at their meetings. Sylvia wore a wig provided
by Nora Smyth, padded her chest with newspapers for protection
and wore a transparent veil which offered her a disguise and visi-
bility at the same time. She sat on the pedestal of one of Landseer's
lions in the Square: she knew her disguise was working when she
heard Superintendent Wells ask a detective, 'Has Miss Pankhurst
come?', to which he replied that she hadn't. Sylvia and her supporters had been escorted to the meeting by a bodyguard of East End
dockers.[37]

When Sylvia's turn came to speak she was surrounded by her
bodyguard and tore off her wig. She told the crowd: 'We have come
here to hold a council of war, the time for argument is passed. Our
motto is "Deeds Not Words" and we are going to act.' Sylvia held
up a sheaf of papers and said they were 'declarations of independence
signed by the men and women of the East End of London demanding
votes for women this year'.[38] She urged the crowd to follow her to
Downing Street to present a resolution to the prime minister. When
they marched along Whitehall the demonstration turned violent and
Sylvia and twelve women and eleven men were charged with insulting
behaviour, assaulting the police and obstruction.

The *Daily Mirror* headline shouted 'Crowd Fight Police With
Sticks' and described the 'scenes of wild disorder' in Trafalgar Square
and Whitehall. Mounted police allowed Sylvia and a handful of her
supporters through the cordon, and then promptly arrested her, and
'free fights' broke out in all directions. 'Some men and women used
sticks and umbrellas to free her ... the mounted police gave chase and
encounters between the police and the crowd were frequent. One

woman was dragged out of an omnibus in which she was trying to escape.'[39] Six policemen escorted Sylvia to Canon Row police station where she broke a window. Disorder continued outside until she was taken to Holloway where men and women marched up and down singing and whistling 'The Marseillaise'. Sylvia went on hunger, thirst and sleep strike and was released on 1 August after four days on a Cat and Mouse licence: 'I was racked with pain, my legs ached, my feet were swollen burning ... the pain in my back was overwhelming, my throat was parched.'[40]

On 10 August Sylvia broke the terms of her licence and returned to Trafalgar Square to speak at a meeting organised by the Free Speech Defence Committee to protest at the imprisonment of George Lansbury in Pentonville. He had been sentenced to serve three months for making a speech at the Royal Albert Hall on 9 April which seemed to endorse the WSPU's arson campaign.

> There are limits to human endurance ... when you are tricked and deceived, when Parliament betrays its sacred trust, you have a right to rebel. I ask that all of you here will stand shoulder to shoulder with the militant women ... Let them burn and destroy property! Let them do anything they will ... this is a holy war![41]

Lansbury had been on hunger strike and released on a Cat and Mouse licence on 2 August, but would not be rearrested. Sylvia, however, was arrested and returned to gaol. A hunger, thirst and sleep strike followed and she was released again on licence. After a short convalescence, accompanied by Norah Smyth Sylvia fled the country and travelled to Finland to meet women who had been enfranchised in 1906, and gave lectures in several Danish and Norwegian cities en route.[42]

*

The classified advertisement page of *The Suffragette* of 1 August carried a surprising entry in the 'situations wanted' columns. Mary Phillips needed a job as she had lost her place in the WSPU's inner circle. Describing herself as 'EX WSPU ORGANISER 5 years' standing WANTS IMMEDIATE WORK; Secretarial, Literary, Journalistic, or any capacity compatible with loyalty to the Union', Mary also offered to speak for the Cause in the annual Summer Holiday Campaign in return for fares and hospitality.

The story behind this advertisement was a startling one. Mary, who had been campaigning for women's suffrage since 1904, a member of the WSPU since 1907, had served four prison sentences and been a hunger striker, was dismissed by Christabel Pankhurst on 9 July 1913 as the Union's organiser in Plymouth, with four weeks' salary in lieu of notice. On the same day that Mary's advertisement appeared in *The Suffragette*, Christabel Pankhurst wrote a cold letter to her elaborating on why she had been dismissed. She held nothing back: 'I want to say that if we had thought you would make a success of another district we should have asked you to take one.' Christabel insisted she had not wanted to 'hurt' Mary 'needlessly, by saying what has always been felt at headquarters that you are not effective at a district headquarters [despite past letters of praise and an increase in salary]'. Christabel ended her letter with a warning: 'It is not possible that members shall have the impression that you have been unjustly dealt with in spite of your having been a fully competent organiser.'[43] Christabel's cold and high-handed treatment of one of their longest-standing members was a clue to the darkening mood within the leadership. Geographically distant and impatient at the political stalemate, Christabel's dictatorial style would lead to a further fragmentation in the months to come. Mary Phillips remained true to her suffragette beliefs and would take an increasingly visible role as 'Mary Paterson' in Sylvia Pankhurst's East London Federation campaign. She lived in Canning Town and worked closely with Norah Smyth.[44]

Kitty Marion's collection of news cuttings about the burning of the empty Seafield House, a 'Home for Imbeciles', on 23 September, and an attack on Sefton Park Palm House in 14 November, hints that she was involved in both of these 'outrages'. The *Liverpool Express* said Seafield House was 'completely gutted'; the culprits, who had caused £80,000 worth of damage, almost destroying the entire building, were said to be 'mad women in their monstrous campaign', and three women and a man had been seen loitering in a suspicious manner. At Sefton Park a bomb left in the porch had failed to go off. The fuse had been lit but it went out before causing any damage: two postcards left at the scene said, 'Stop torturing God's plants who are fighting for votes for women'; and 'there is a woman at the beginning of all great things'. The bomb was a hot-water bottle filled with explosives.[45]

Letters written by Christabel Pankhurst from Deauville to Annie Kenney and Henry Harben in the first week of August 1913 reveal her firm grip on the militant campaign. A recent visit from George Taylor, a barrister who was interested in Fabianism, to lobby her to form an alliance between 'militant suffragism and militant industrialism', was firmly rebuffed. Her reasons for maintaining the WSPU's women-only membership policy and rejecting any alliance with socialist political groups undermine Sylvia Pankhurst's insistence that Christabel and their mother had abandoned the needs of working-class women to favour the interests of their upper and middle-class contemporaries. This argument, which Sylvia often repeated and committed to print, created an inaccurate impression of the political sympathies of her mother and Christabel with whom she had always had a rivalrous relationship.[46]

Writing to Henry Harben on 7 August, Christabel described George Taylor as a 'person of little importance and ... objectionable' and she dismissed the possibility of any links between the WSPU and the *Daily Herald* League whose readers had organised themselves to influence the direction of the newspaper:

> Ours is a Woman's Movement and the *Herald* League is primarily a Man's Movement, or at any rate a mixed Movement. The great need of this time is for women to learn to stand and to act alone ... No men, even the best of men, ever view the Suffrage question from the same standpoint as women themselves view it. Some day when differences of right and status between men and women are abolished, then the need for a distinct and separate 'Woman's Movement' may disappear. But at the present time the need of it is very urgent indeed.[47]

Christabel told Harben she believed 'the *Herald* people are far from unanimous in their view as to the line to be taken where Suffrage agitation is concerned', and noted the differences between the direction of the WSPU, and that of the *Herald* League. She concluded that while the latter was a class movement, 'ours is not a class movement at all. We take in everybody – the highest and the lowest, the richest and the poorest. The bond is womanhood. After all, why should we recognise class distinction or do anything which might divide us from any one section?' Christabel ended, 'the world is organised according to men's ideas of justice'. Rejecting any alliance with militant industrialism and women's suffrage, she concluded the correspondence, 'The men must paddle their own canoes, and we must paddle ours.'[48]

On 19 August 1913, while out on licence, Annie Kenney escaped to France with her sister Jessie, Mary Richardson and Ida Wylie. In Deauville Christabel Pankhurst was the guest of the American social-ite and women's suffrage campaigner Mrs O. H. P. Belmont. Annie and her party only stayed a week, Annie feeling uncomfortable with the town's smart set and having to 'dress up every day and carry a sun-shade and wear white gloves'. She was used to her freedom, and they instead went to stay at La Guimorais, on the Brittany coast, which was closer to her 'gypsy heart ... with the sweetest and the best of people who loved us like children'. Annie Kenney describes a blissful time, far away from the torments they had all experienced in England. 'We laughed all day and all night. The people at the hotel called me "the laughing one". They little realised that I was a gaol-bird ... and that on my return I should be captured and put into a big London prison.' In the middle of September Annie was smuggled back into England in a large wicker hamper, but was later caught in London by the police and returned to Holloway.[49]

Annie found the hunger strike to be 'child's play' compared to a hunger and thirst strike, but both were 'nothing to being force-fed'. For the first twenty-four hours she felt 'a little hungry'; on the second day, she felt 'a little worse'; on the third day she was a little better; on the fourth day she wanted to cry; on the fifth day she felt 'dazed'; on the sixth day, 'I wanted to cry ... sometimes out of sheer boredom, at other times out of rebellion, and at other times out of weakness'. If her protest lasted longer than six days she would feel 'sleepy, a little feverish and very tired'. In the past Annie had usually been released on the third or fourth day, but this time she realised 'they had no intention of releasing me'. She was examined by the Holloway doc-tors and two Home Office doctors. 'They tried to look at my tongue; they tried to feel my pulse, and they made an attempt to see if my throat was swollen. When they went to one side of the bed I got all the bedclothes round me and turned over on the other side.' When Annie was released she was carried out of Holloway on a stretcher. She was extremely unwell: 'the strange thing was I could not speak, and felt as if I was floating on air ... but I was determined that I would defy Mr Asquith and appear at the next meeting, even if I had to be carried in.' Annie attended a WSPU meeting at the Pavilion Theatre, London, on 6 October, taken there on a stretcher, was 'brutally re-arrested', and because she was so ill was released shortly afterwards. On 7 December 1913 she left for Switzerland for three months to convalesce, and also visited Christabel in Paris. She was back in action by April 1914.[50]

*

On 28 August, while playing golf with his daughter, Violet, Herbert Asquith was involved in a struggle with two suffragettes, Winnie Wallace and Flora Smith, on the links at Lossiemouth, near Elgin. The lurking women rushed up to the prime minister as he was about to play his shot, 'caught him by the coat, shook him violently, and knocked his hat off'.[51] Asquith tried to push them away and Violet rushed at one of the women and after a struggle pulled her away. Two detectives intervened and dragged the suffragettes away from Asquith.

The next day at Elgin Sheriff's Court the women refused to stand up to hear the case against them and were charged with assault; they pleaded not guilty and were released on anonymous bail. The following day Winnie and Flora learned that Asquith and his daughter were due to attend Duffus church and the minister's wife unwittingly allowed them to take a pew opposite Asquith. They stared at him throughout the sermon.

After the service, they waited outside the church, 'directing offensive remarks at Mr Asquith as he left'. They called out, 'You hypocrite', 'You coward, Asquith'. One of the women gleefully reported in *The Suffragette*, 'No one cheered him or molested us at all; they all seemed to be tickled at our knowledge of his movements, and our coolness in continuing to worry him while on bail.'[52] The case against the women was dropped as it would have required the appearance of the prime minister in court.

When Violet Asquith was interviewed by Joan Bakewell for the television in 1968, she recalled being

at the receiving end of the suffragettes. I saw it close up and I was involved physically. I fought them off more than once, I constantly

had to intervene when they made a savage assault on my father ...
I'm rather a weedy athlete and I'm not skilled at wrestling but the
rage gave me a curious sort of strength. I remember playing golf on
the links at Lossiemouth and I suddenly looked up from my putting and saw my father being savaged by two women who looked
quite maniacal and I tore at them. They were trying to tear his
clothes off.[53]

On the evening of 2 September, Eileen Casey of Kew was caught
with her younger sister, Kitty Holtom, hurrying down a side street
in Bradford after they had set fire to a pillar box with phosphorous.
Eileen told the Bradford court that she had committed a political
act, that as 'voteless women they had no power to bring their grievances before the Government and they must make them known to the
general public'. She was sentenced to three months in Armley Gaol,
Leeds, with hard labour.

Eileen's sister Kitty Holtom, who was married to a bank cash-
ier and seven months pregnant, denied all knowledge of the attack
although she was arrested at the scene. She was found not guilty
and discharged. Kitty's daughter, also named Eileen, was born in
November 1913.

At first Eileen Casey's conduct in prison was noted as 'excellent',
but it deteriorated when she was on hunger and thirst strike. After six
days she had lost nine pounds and could only walk with difficulty. She
was released on the sixth day of her sentence on 9 October and taken
to her sister's home in Bradford, on a nine-day Cat and Mouse licence.
When the police went to rearrest Eileen she had disappeared, wearing
men's clothing. She roamed the country for eight months evading the
police and would not be caught until June 1914 in Nottingham, suspected of committing another 'outrage'.[54]

At the end of every year, Votes for Women and The Suffragette
published an audit of that year's campaign. The report of September
1913, produced by The Suffragette, reveals the scale of destruction. A
bomb was found at Cheltenham Town Hall only in the nick of time;
Withernsea Town Hall was gutted; houses were 'fired' at Newcastle,
Finchley, Liverpool, Waltham Cross and Loughton; hay and wheat
ricks were destroyed at Berkhamsted and Oldbury; schools were
burned down in Dulwich, Oldbury, Frensham Hall; a timber yard in

Yarmouth was destroyed; Kenton railway station was burned down; Seafield House, Derby, and Stanstead House, Seaton, were destroyed, and so was the football grandstand at Plumstead.[55]

Mary Richardson and 'Rachel Peace', the alias of Jane Short, were caught in the early hours of the morning of 4 October 1913, a mile from The Elms, an eleven-bedroom house near Bushey Park, Hampton, which they had almost destroyed, causing several thousand pounds worth of damage. A can of paraffin, methylated spirits and a copy of *The Suffragette* were found at the scene. When asked by a policeman why they were out at 3.30 a.m., they said they had missed the last tram and were walking to London. The police refused bail and they were remanded in custody. Mary was on the run from the police on an expired Cat and Mouse licence.

At Teddington Police Court the women refused to give their names, ages and occupations, and, oddly, the magistrate suggested that as they were 'middle-aged' (thirty and thirty-two respectively) they were not to be placed in the dock. Mary Richardson and Jane Short were charged with arson, remanded and went on hunger strike. Because of the seriousness of the offence and the likelihood they would reoffend, it was considered 'unsafe in the public interest' for them to be at large, and Richardson and Short were told they would not be released on licence and warned they would be force-fed if it was felt medically necessary. The *Daily Mirror* reminded its readers of Mary's record this past summer: since July she had received three sentences totalling six months, but had only served fourteen days in prison, four days for the first offence and five days each for the second and third offences.[56]

On 10 October, because Mary Richardson and 'Rachel Peace' would not be released on a Cat and Mouse licence, the houses of eight doctors in Harley Street and Wimpole Street had their windows smashed by suffragettes using bottles and stones wrapped in suffragist literature. A service at St Paul's Cathedral was interrupted by thirty suffragettes chanting 'God save Mary Richardson and Jane Short. They are being forcibly-fed in Holloway Prison. Their enemies torture them. They know their cause is righteous. Hear us when we pray to thee.'[57]

When Rachel Peace – the name by which she was tried – was charged with arson at the Old Bailey on 15 November, there was 'a remarkable manifestation of suffragist violence'. (Mary Richardson was too ill to be tried, and, despite Home Secretary McKenna's announcement that she

would not be released on a licence, she was released from Holloway.)
The judge was Mr Justice Lawrence, and Rachel Peace, who conducted
her own defence, faced the Crown prosecutor Archibald Bodkin. She
refused to go into the witness box, arguing that because she had 'to
endure the horrible torture of forcible-feeding' she was unfit to prepare her defence. Justice Lawrence had barely started his summing-up
when a woman shouted from the back of the court, 'She is not fit to be
tried.' A 'scene of wild uproar' followed and a pane of glass at the back
of the dock was shattered by a hammer wielded by one of Rachel's supporters. A hammer was thrown at the Bench, and Archibald Bodkin's
gown was spattered by a tomato. Justice Lawrence closed the court
and the suffragettes were ejected but not before several more panes of
glass were smashed. The judge told the jury to put any political feelings to one side and only consider the evidence. Without leaving the
room the jury passed a verdict of guilty. Before Justice Lawrence sentenced Rachel Peace to eighteen months with hard labour, he told her
that by committing such crimes she had 'besmirched her ideals', and
said he was sorry to have to sentence her 'because I see you are wrong-
headed; but I must do my duty'.[58]

From prison Rachel Peace smuggled out a statement which ignited
suffragette fury, saying that she was being force-fed three times a day.
'Yesterday they put some thick vegetable soup through the tube and
before it had any opportunity to digest they came and fed me again a
few hours later with the result that I was very sick.' She told the doctor about her problems with indigestion but he took no notice. She
feared for her sanity: 'I am afraid I shall be affected mentally – I feel as
if I should go mad. I have had nervous breakdowns before and I now
have the sensation of an impending crisis. Old distressing symptoms
have re-appeared. I have frightful dreams.'[59]

A month after Rachel Peace began her sentence on 18 December
two loud explosions shattered windows around Holloway Gaol. Two
holes had been made in the west wall of the prison and filled with
gunpowder and ignited by a long fuse. No one was charged with the
attack.[60]

Jane Short, also known as 'Rachel Peace', was an embroideress
and masseuse lodging with a fellow embroideress in Letchworth,
Hertfordshire, when the Census was taken in 1911. She was born in
Lewisham, where her father was a storekeeper for the Metropolitan

Board of Works.[61] Prior to this arson attack, Jane had been convicted three times: in Downing Street in November 1911; she was sent to prison in July 1912 for breaking three windows at Baldock post office; and in February 1913 she got six months in the second division for breaking windows at Messrs Hamptons estate agents in Pall Mall. Jane Short had not long been out of prison when she set off with Mary Richardson on 4 October 1913.[62]

*

On 11 October, while free on an expired Cat and Mouse licence, with the full knowledge of the government (probably keen to have her out of the way) Emmeline Pankhurst sailed to America with the American journalist and women's suffragist Mrs Rheta Dorr (who had published *What Eight Million Women Want*, and who helped Mrs Pankhurst to write her memoir, *My Own Story*). This was Mrs Pankhurst's third fundraising tour of America. On her arrival on 18 October she was refused entry and detained at Ellis Island, New York, for two and a half days as a convicted prisoner and a 'person guilty of moral turpitude'.[63] Mrs Pankhurst threatened to go on hunger strike. Her old friend Harriet Blatch lobbied for her to be set free, and the influential Mrs O. H. P. Belmont sent her lawyer to deal with the matter. Mrs Belmont stood bail for her and only when the US government was convinced that Mrs Pankhurst was not a 'dynamiter, arsonist, seditionist, silly fulminator, nihilistic flouter and mannish Amazon'[64] was she allowed to proceed with the tour without any restrictions, but it had needed the intervention of President Woodrow Wilson.

*

Despite the Prisoners' Temporary Discharge for Ill-Health Act, the force-feeding of suffragettes prisoners had resumed, so Zelie Emerson and two East End WSPU members, Mrs Moore and Mrs Watkins, went to lie in wait for the Holloway doctor, Dr Forward, on 11 October. He lived in prison accommodation nearby in Camden Road. Armed with a sjambok, an African whip made of rhino hide, they arrived early and accosted him: 'Good morning, Dr Forward, you are forcibly feeding our women', and proceeded to give him a thrashing. Sylvia Pankhurst reported that he said: 'You know I cannot help myself.' Zelie Emerson told him he should resign, that he was a disgrace to his profession and had to take the consequences. Zelie 'seized him and beat him till the whip broke', shouting: 'You forcibly fed me for five weeks! You should be forcibly fed yourself!'[65] *The Times* said that although several blows were struck and his hat was knocked off 'no great hurt was done'. Zelie Emerson and her two colleagues were not arrested and a protest meeting outside the prison about the reintroduction of force-feeding was allowed to go ahead, without any arrests being made.[66]

Not long back from Scandinavia, Sylvia Pankhurst, whose Cat and Mouse licence had long expired, went to a meeting at Bow Baths Hall on 13 October in disguise: 'What a triumph it seemed to be back among my people! What rejoicings and cheers! ... Our hopes were high ... we would sweep away poverty and slums.' Mary Leigh and Zelie Emerson made rousing speeches, and Sylvia had been talking for ten minutes about the dangers of force-feeding when detectives rushed in to grab her. The audience shouted, 'Jump, Sylvia! Jump!' with their arms outstretched. Sylvia jumped into the audience, somehow acquiring a hat and coat in the process. Dockers acting as stewards and bodyguards fought hand-to-hand with the police using chairs and benches while the constables and plain-clothes detectives were armed with batons and sticks. Sylvia vanished into the night; the East London Federation's secretary, Mrs Ives, a 'very small delicate woman was held by the coat collar and beaten with a truncheon',[67] and had her collarbone broken. Nurse Pine's colleague, Nurse Townend, had her knee dislocated. Mary Leigh was knocked unconscious in the fracas. She had moved to the front of the platform and 'waved her arms shouting, "Rise up, people" '.[68]

The next day Sylvia was arrested amid a huge police presence while trying to enter Poplar Town Hall. Every woman who entered the building was 'subjected to a searching scrutiny'. As Sylvia placed her foot on the step leading into the hall a detective who had been hiding behind a pillar rushed forward, pulled the veil from her face and yelled her name to his colleagues. During the struggle Sylvia's clothing was 'torn to shreds'. The mounted police had to charge the crowd before she was bundled away in a taxicab to Holloway, leaving behind a riot. Sylvia resumed a hunger and thirst strike for nine days before she was released, and carried on dodging the police, holding meetings protected by her bodyguards, until she was taken back into custody at Shoreditch Town Hall in December.[69]

*

In the United States, meanwhile, Mrs Pankhurst made a keynote speech, 'Why We Are Militant', at Madison Square Garden on 21 October, which was published as a pamphlet by the Woman's Press. Her words emphasised the international sisterly solidarity the WSPU had always cherished and deployed as a propaganda device. She told her audience:

> They sent me to prison, to penal servitude for three years. I came out of prison after nine days. I broke my prison bars. Four times they took me back again; four times I burst open the door again. And I left England openly to come to America with only three or four weeks of the three years' servitude served. Have we not proved that they cannot govern human beings without their consent? We are glad to ... do the fighting for all women all over the world; and all we ask of you is to back us up.

She asked American women 'to show that although, perhaps, you do not mean to fight as we do, that you understand the meaning of our fight; that you realise that we are women fighting for a great idea ... and that we believe betterment is coming through the emancipation and uplifting of women'.[70]

*

In the middle of October Mary Richardson's health was causing such concern that suffragette sympathiser Ellen Newbold La Motte, an American nurse specialising in tuberculosis, wrote to Christabel Pankhurst: 'I think you should know about Mary Richardson's physical condition – I believe she has pulmonary tuberculosis. It evidently is the lighting up of an old lesion which has been caused by the four hunger-strikes to which she has been subjected this past summer.'[71] The Home Office records of Mary's time in prison confirm that she had refused to be examined but had told the doctor on 7 October she had been treated for 'lung trouble' five years ago, and also had a grumbling appendix. In a memorandum Sir Charles Edward Troup was so concerned at the gravity of Mary Richardson and Rachel Peace's offences, and the likelihood that they would disappear and commit 'some fresh outrage', that he advised against them being released on a Cat and Mouse licence. Troup asked the home secretary, if medical opinion agreed 'they could safely be fed', to give his authorisation to the governor of Holloway, and Dr Forward would feed them the next day. The governor telegraphed Troup giving Mary Richardson's pulse, and mentioned that she had the 'odour of malnutrition', said her 'general condition was satisfactory' and there were 'no urgent symptoms' to report. There is a two-week gap in Mary's file until 21 October, when she was 'violently resistive' and 'broke up everything in her cell after being fed' twice that day.[72] Two days earlier there had been another suffragette protest at St Paul's Cathedral when a number of suffragists prayed aloud during the morning service, appealing to the church to make their own protest against the force-feeding of women. Instead of asking the women to leave quietly, which was the usual practice, the vergers 'seized the women with great violence' and pushed them out of the cathedral. Some members of the congregation walked out of the service to show their indignation at the conduct of the vergers. Similar protests in churches, including Westminster Abbey, called for prayers to be heard for Mary Richardson and Rachel Peace who were being tortured in prison.

Telephone messages were left at the Home Office by the governor on 22 October 1913 saying that Mary was fed by the stomach tube, and the following morning a nasal tube was used to feed her; her behaviour was 'violently resistive'. Mary described some of her experiences in a WSPU handbill, 'Tortured Women: What Forcible Feeding means, a Prisoner's Testimony'. 'They forced my mouth open by inserting their fingers and cutting my gums and the lining of my cheeks ... The tubes followed and they pressed my tongue down with their fingers and pinched my nose to weaken the resistance of my throat. My mouth bled and also my throat at times.'[73]

On 25 October, suffering from acute appendicitis, Mary Richardson was temporarily discharged from prison on a Cat and Mouse licence which ended on 5 November, when she was due in court at the Old Bailey to be tried with Rachel Peace 'for the burning down of "The Elms"'. She was taken in an ambulance to 3 Gloucester Walk, Notting Hill. Mary was too ill to stand trial with Rachel Peace, who was sentenced to eighteen months with hard labour. When Mary recovered from the effects of force-feeding and appendicitis, she went on the run using her alias, 'Polly Dick', and vanished altogether until February 1914 when she was reported in *The Times* to have knocked at the door of the Bishop of London with Marion Wallace-Dunlop, demanding a meeting with him. They eventually had a meeting at nine o'clock that evening.[74]

On 23 October three Bristol suffragettes burned down the Sports Pavilion of the Bristol University Athletic Ground at Coombe Dingle, causing £2,000 worth of damage. Suffragist literature was left at the scene, and black-edged notices demanded the release of Mary Richardson, and declared 'Hobhouse Being Responsible Will Pay'. The next day 400 male students wrecked the WSPU's shop in Queen's Road, Bristol: 'a volley of bricks was fired through the plate-glass window of the shop' and the young men smashed up the place, removing the counter, furniture, fittings and books, a roll-top desk and a bicycle and hurling them into the street. When the women ran into the street they were pelted with eggs and other missiles. The police arrived but no arrests were made; a local newspaper reported the students' raid with the words, 'An attack upon a nest of suffragettes is a phase of pest extermination'.[75]

On several occasions the WSPU publicity about politicians being pursued by the suffragettes led to several cases being dropped on the grounds that the cabinet ministers, 'the victims', were too busy to appear in court as witnesses. The prime minister used this tactic several times when it became clear that if the case was prosecuted he risked becoming a laughing stock. On 1 November Asquith's car was flagged down in the village of Bannockburn as he was being driven to unveil a statue of the late Liberal leader Sir Henry Campbell-Bannerman, in Stirling. Two women ran in front of the car, forcing it to stop, a third threw pepper over the prime minister and a fourth tried to attack him with a dog-whip. All four were arrested and taken to Stirling police station where they refused to give their real names, saying instead that they were Margot Tennant (Tennant being Asquith's wife's maiden name); Violet Asquith; the Canadian erotic dancer Maud Allan; and Catherine Douglas. They were charged with assaulting the prime minister and held on remand until their court appearance on 3 November. A large crowd including WSPU members and sympathisers was present, but the Sheriff cleared the room and the case was heard in private. They were released on bail and the charges were dropped as Asquith had no desire to prosecute.[76]

Mrs Pankhurst left New York on 26 November on the SS *Majestic*, her lectures and fundraising events adding £4,500 to the WSPU's war chest. On 4 December, as the ship approached Plymouth, Mrs Pankhurst learned by telegram that she would be arrested on arrival. The *Majestic* anchored two miles out to sea, and was met by the usual tender sent to escort all such vessels into port. Unusually, the tender was flanked by two warships. Pootling past this display of imperial naval power, a fisherman's tug hired by the WSPU – whose members had planned a meeting at the dock gates to welcome her – pulled up alongside the ship, hoping to escort her into port. 'Two women, spray drenched, stood up in the boat as it ploughed swiftly past, the women called out "The Cats are here, Mrs Pankhurst! They're close to you" … Their voices trailed away in the mist and we heard no more.'[77] Scotland Yard sent five men from Special Branch, two constables and a Holloway wardress, who boarded the ship from the tender and rearrested Emmeline under the Cat and Mouse Act. Mrs Pankhurst refused to assist them and was carried off the ship and onto the tender. They took her to the North Devon coast where a car was waiting to take her to Exeter Gaol. She went on hunger strike and was released on licence after four days, before travelling openly to Paris with Dr Flora Murray and Nurse Pine to see Christabel. On her return by boat train she was arrested at Dover. She was taken by the police to Victoria station where a large battalion of police reinforcements were waiting.

Mrs Pankhurst was carried off the train before anyone else could leave and taken to Holloway. 'Around this motor-car were twelve taxi-cabs filled with plain-clothes men, four to each vehicle, and three guarding the outside.' Detectives on motorcycles were also employed at various points to head off any attempt to rescue Mrs Pankhurst from the police convoy. Once in Holloway she refused to be examined by the prison doctor and went on a hunger, thirst and sleep strike and was released after four days. When the prison doctor tried to persuade her to give up her dangerous protest, she told him he was not a doctor, but a 'Government torturer, and all you want to do is to satisfy yourself that I am not quite ready to die'.[78]

The last weeks of 1913 saw the leadership of the WSPU scattered. Christabel was in Paris, living on the Avenue de la Grande Armée, still controlling militant policy and activity. Mrs Pankhurst stayed with her until the end of January 1914. Sylvia was in the East End, frail, but organising her East London Federation's joint 'Suffrage School' with their loyal and well-heeled allies, the Kensington branch of the WSPU in Bow and Kensington. Annie Kenney was convalescing in Switzerland. 'General' Flora Drummond, who had recovered from her two operations that year, had taken charge of the Women's Bodyguard to stop suffragette 'mice' being rearrested by the police 'cats'.[79]

There was at this time a new song doing the rounds in the music halls, which could also be enjoyed by owners of a gramophone. 'PC Forty-nine' was about a rookie policeman who gets tangled up with navvies, burglars, anarchists and suffragettes, while out on the beat:

One night they held a meeting to advance the suffragette.
The sergeant said, 'We need a lot of men they can't upset.'
He looked around the station, then he shouted, you can bet

Chorus: For PC Forty-nine! Anyone can have this little job of mine.

But how those women mauled me, when they caught me by the throat!
They tore the clothes right off my back, to try and get the vote.
For all they left me wearing was the collar of my coat,

Chorus: With PC Forty-nine! Anyone can have this little job of mine.

They ripped my clothes to ribbons, so for help I had to call,
The sergeant looked at me, and said, (as I stood by the wall,)
'I thought it was Maud Allen, but it isn't her at all,'

Chorus: It's PC Forty-nine! Anyone can have this little job of mine.[80]

18

'Slasher Mary'

Mary Richardson Attacks The Rokeby Venus *1914*

On 10 March 1914 'Slasher Mary' Richardson attacked The Rokeby Venus *in the National Gallery in response to the brutal rearrest of Mrs Pankhurst in Glasgow.*

At New Year 1914 Sylvia Pankhurst's Cat and Mouse licence had expired and she was hiding with friends in Old Ford Road in the East End. On 3 January she was walking in Victoria Park, Hackney, with Norah Smyth when plain-clothes officers, who had followed her from the pub opposite her safe house, arrested her. Sylvia might have escaped the 'big, heavy men, not good at running ... but the button came off my shoe and caused me to run lamely. They caught me ... and dragged me back into Hackney. A crowd gathered, sympathetic to me, and menacing towards the two big men dragging me along.'[1] The policemen requisitioned a laundry cart to take Sylvia to Hackney Wick police station. Norah Smyth ran beside it all the way. Sylvia was transferred to Holloway Gaol, went on hunger strike – her sixth since July 1913 – and was released on licence on 10 January.

When Christabel and Mrs Pankhurst summoned Sylvia to Paris, to rail against her close ties with the Labour Party, Sylvia took Norah Smyth, financial secretary of the East London Federation of the WSPU, with her to represent the members. Hidden in a car to Harwich for the boat to the Hook of Holland, weakened and suffering from seasickness, she was glad to land. Sylvia recorded that the meeting with her sister and her mother was perfunctory. Christabel said that the East London Federation of the WSPU must become a separate organisation. She told her sister that *The Suffragette* would announce the news, and that unless Sylvia herself chose a name, a new one would be selected for her organisation. Sylvia's version of this meeting, published twenty years and many family arguments later, describes Christabel as detached and high-handed. Norah Smyth, who knew Mrs Pankhurst well, remained loyal to Sylvia. Christabel suggested that in future they should meet 'not as suffragettes but as sisters', but Sylvia rejected the idea:

> To me the word seemed meaningless; we had no life apart from the movement. I felt bruised ... my mind was thronged with the memories of our childhood, the little heads clustering at the windows in Green Hayes [their home in Manchester]; her pink cheeks and the young green shoots in Russell Square; my father's voice: 'You are the four pillars of my house!'[2]

Heavily disguised, Sylvia returned by a convoluted route through Normandy, and slipped into England unnoticed. When she reported the news to her East End comrades there was an angry response. Sylvia's newly christened East London Federation of Suffragettes (ELFS) added socialist red to the purple, white and green colour scheme. (East End suffragettes had already taken to wearing the 'red caps of liberty'.) Sylvia reports that when her mother returned to England, Mrs Pankhurst 'hastened to the East End to expostulate: 'We are the Suffragettes! and that is the name we are always known by and there will be the same confusion as before!' Sylvia told her mother the members had made the decision and that she would not interfere.[3]

On 7 February 1914 Christabel Pankhurst announced in *The Suffragette* that Sylvia's organisation was no longer connected with the WSPU. She wrote that for 'a long time Miss Sylvia Pankhurst has preferred to work on her own and independently'. Christabel pointed out that the new arrangements should not suggest that there would be any let-up in WSPU militancy.

> The WSPU is a fighting organisation, it must have only one policy, one programme, one command, and the word of command is given by Mrs Pankhurst and myself. From the very beginning of the militant movement this has been the case. Consequently those who wish to give an independent lead, or to carry out either a programme or policy which differs from those laid down by the WSPU, must necessarily have an independent organisation of their own.[4]

Some of the headlines *The Suffragette* used for the first four issues of 1914 made members unhappy about how the campaign would develop: 'Yacht Destroyed at Rosneath Pier'; 'College Ablaze at Cheltenham'; 'Bomb Explosion at Glasgow'; 'Serious Explosion near Cardiff, Suffragettes Suspected'; 'Exciting Scenes at Corner House, Piccadilly'; 'Portsmouth Dockyard Fire'; and 'Scottish Mansion Burnt Down in Lanark'. The fifth issue of 1914 reproduced a force-feeding poster: four hatchet-faced wardresses hold down a suffragette as food is poured from a funnel into a nasal tube, underscored with quotes from doctors who condemned the practice.[5]

On 6 February 1914 the United Suffragists, a new organisation, open to men and women, joined the struggle. This new group included members of the NUWSS, frustrated at the limbo in which their modest tactics had placed them, and some members of the WSPU who could no longer condone the dangerous methods sanctioned by their leaders. The headquarters were in Adam Street, off the Strand. The Pethick-Lawrences, who joined the United Suffragists, reported the doings of the new group in *Votes for Women*. The membership included: Henry and Agnes Harben; George Lansbury and his wife, Bessie; Henry Nevinson; Dr Louisa Garrett Anderson; Evelyn Sharp; Evelina Haverfield and Lena Ashwell. By the time the First World War broke out the United Suffragists had opened offices in London, Edinburgh and Liverpool, and organised three rallies in the capital that summer.[6]

For the remainder of the campaign Sylvia's East London Federation of Suffragettes recruited many members and enjoyed the loyal support of Zelie Emerson, Elsa Dalglish, Myra Sadd Brown and her daughter Myra, Lady Sybil Smith, Charlotte Drake, Daisy Parsons, Norah Smyth, Annie Cappuccio, and WSPU members Mary Leigh, who helped from time to time, and Maud Joachim, who became an organiser. Sylvia's East London Federation of Suffragettes had grown from one paid worker to five, and in a letter to her generous backer, Henry Harben, she hinted: 'work for the coming year should far outdo the past if the necessary funds are forthcoming. The members are in the main working women, who give their time and energy at considerable sacrifice; it is impossible for them to contribute largely to the funds.' Sylvia reminded Harben how much good work local women had done by speaking in 'At Homes' and at concerts in the West End

of London, converting 'many leisured women to the urgent need of
the vote, especially from the working woman's standpoint'.[7]

The Pankhurst family was in crisis at the beginning of 1914. Adela,
Emmeline's youngest daughter, now twenty-nine years old, was travelling in Switzerland and when Annie Kenney caught up with her in
Locarno she told her to go and see her mother and sister in Paris. At
an awkward meeting Adela reluctantly agreed, having suffered from
poor health for two years, to be sent to Australia. Her mother gave her
the fare and £20, some woollen clothing, and a letter of recommendation to the Australian suffragist Vida Goldstein.[8] Helen Archdale saw
her off: 'We went sadly to Tilbury and to see that lonely, little figure
dwindle in the [ship's] tender remains a clear but depressing memory.'[9]

Frail in health since childhood, but a passionate speaker and by-
election campaigner since early 1910, Adela Pankhurst was unhappy
with the militant direction of the WSPU. Christabel considered her
'a very black sheep' and despaired of the intensity of her sister's
socialist views. Adela had collapsed in August 1912 after working on
the North-West Manchester by-election campaign and was forced
to withdraw from campaigning. Her mother enrolled her on an
agricultural course at Studley Hall Horticultural and Agricultural
College for Women in Warwickshire. Adela worked as a head gardener and went to live with Helen Archdale as governess to her
children, while Helen worked at Lincoln's Inn House as a prisoners' secretary.[10] According to Ethel Smyth, who prided herself on
being on close terms with the family, Mrs Pankhurst was unhappy
at the unfocused life Adela was leading, disapproving of her 'travelling about the Continent with a family friend giving desultory
teaching to the children' which Mrs Pankhurst thought 'demoralis-
ing' and beneath her: 'I feel it is high time she settled down to do
real work if ever she is to do any.' Mrs Pankhurst wrote to Ethel:
'Of course now all is settled I have pangs of maternal weakness, but
I harden my heart and I have been busy with domestic cares all the
time, sewing for Adela and Christabel.'[11] Adela died in 1961 without seeing her family again.

*

Sacrifice and suffering were the criteria of stardom in the Women's
Social and Political Union, so Kitty Marion was a big star. On 6

January 1914 she left her hiding place on the Essex coast and travelled to London where she was met by 'Miss Roberts', a prisoners' secretary at WSPU headquarters. Unknown to her, she had been followed by two plain-clothes Special Branch men, Philpott and Kitchener. Kitty was to leave her suitcase in the left-luggage department at Charing Cross station. As Miss Roberts made a telephone call to Lincoln's Inn House, Kitty was identified from her Special Branch surveillance photograph by Ralph Kitchener. He went up to her and said, 'Hullo Katie'. Kitchener had been Kitty's 'own special "shadow"' at Emily Davison's funeral, and on other occasions. 'He insisted I was Kitty Marion which I insisted he must prove before I would accompany him to Holloway. My friend came out of the phone booth and took in the situation at once. While I continued arguing I stealthily passed incriminating evidence to her from my coat pocket.'[12] Kitty was taken to the station master's office while Kitchener telephoned for policemen who could further identify her, stating, 'That's Kitty Marion right enough.'

Kitty refused to go quietly and Kitchener was helped by the police. As she was being lifted into a taxi, feet first, she broke one of the windows. Eight policemen crammed in with her so that she could cause no more damage. She found the constables to be 'quite decent lads and we had a suffrage discussion en route to Holloway'.[13] Kitty was readmitted to Holloway to continue serving her prison sentence and at once went on hunger strike. As a long-time absconder there was to be no Cat and Mouse licence, and she was force-fed immediately by Dr Ahern, who had previously fed her on a ten-day hunger strike in 1912 at Winson Green Prison.

Kitty Marion spent three months in Holloway in 1914 and was force-fed 232 times. She lost thirty-six pounds in weight. Dr Ahern, who did the 'dirty work', recognised 'As fast as they poured the food down it was vomited back up.' At the beginning of her sentence force-feeding did not weaken her, rather, the reverse: 'I became possessed of a most furious rage, like wanting to kill someone.'[14] When Ahern and the wardresses left, she 'smashed every pane of glass in the window and everything else breakable in the cell, the glass over the gas, and the wash-basin and the jug.'[15] Later that afternoon she barricaded her cell to delay the next feed: 'I found blessed relief to my feelings in screaming, exercising my lungs and throat after the frightful sensation of being held in a vice, choking and suffocating. I had to scream or go mad.'[16] The barricade was dismantled and she was fed again. Kitty set fire to the bed but the bed just smouldered and would not burn, and when the smoke was noticed the wardresses rushed in with buckets of water.

When Kitty's weight loss accelerated she was force-fed three times a day:

> Resisting the gag was almost useless but I resisted the tube with my throat, until my mouth was full of coiled tube and when swallowing, which happened involuntarily sooner or later, seemed to go down in lumps, uncoiling as it went ... When in my agony I managed to wrench a hand free from a wardress I would snatch the tube out, which meant a reprimand for her and repeated torture for me.[17]

On the days of a triple feed, the 'vomiting would continue in small quantities for three hours ... the remains of the last meal would come back as soon as the tube touched the back of my throat and I started retching'. Home Office files record that each time Kitty was sick they weighed the vomit (the amounts varied from two ounces to twelve ounces), and reported it daily.[18]

In the latter part of March 1914 Kitty Marion was secretly corresponding in gaol with 'Rachel Peace' (Jane Short) and Mary Richardson, who had just arrived in Holloway to serve a six-month sentence with hard labour. The letters in pencil were written on pale brown prison lavatory paper. Although they survive, the paper is so thin you have to hold them up to the light to read them. They tell of Jane Short's passion for astrology. Based on Kitty's birthday, she made her an astrological chart:

> Mars gives you energy and enables you to be a good fighter – also it gives you your red hair, which by the way I thought was golden – but which ever it is, I know it is gloriously beautiful for that much I have seen of you from the window. I expect you are very pretty really ... I expect you have blue eyes – very bright ones particularly at night! Venus gives a nice complexion and as a rule a nice figure albeit a tendency to plumpness.[19]

Mary Richardson was in awe of Kitty: 'Dear K, I hate to hear them go into you. I cannot tell you how I admire you for holding on so. It is the stuff that has made our Union famous – militant women – a new order of fanatic creation. I know you would rather die than submit, so would I any day.'[20]

Reading these letters today we get a glimpse of the wardresses who helped the doctors to feed Kitty. Kitty said how 'frantic' she had felt when being fed but that 'Miss Chandler was trying to pacify me. Miss R stood in the doorway ... I could have killed her. Miss C was strong enough to hold me otherwise I would have gone for her. I tried hard enough.' Mary Richardson told Kitty how 'Miss Kift got so tired [trying to feed her] they had to fetch her a chair', and 'after it was over I still held onto the tube in my teeth and so the doctor pinched my nose'.[21]

Kitty discovered that the prison authorities were dosing some of the women with bromide to reduce their resistance to feeding and make them more compliant. 'The food was mostly milk and eggs, beef-tea, sometimes cocoa and sometimes something of a peculiar salty taste which I later learned was bromide, though the authorities denied it, since there was a great outcry against giving us sedative drugs.'[22]

Olive Beamish was using her alias of 'Phyllis Brady' when she was rearrested in January 1914 while on the run on an expired Cat and Mouse licence. She was further charged with having set fire to Lady White's house in Egham the previous spring, and sentenced to eighteen months' hard labour. Olive was in Holloway at the same time as Kitty and they were able to talk in the exercise yard. When 'Phyllis Brady' was on remand she went on hunger strike and was released on licence on 11 February to recover so that she could stand trial. The Bishop of London, who had been lobbied by the WSPU to visit Holloway, investigated the force-feeding of suffragette prisoners and came to the bizarre conclusion that they were being fed 'in the kindliest of circumstances' and that he had found 'Rachel Peace' 'somewhat pale'[23] but she showed no sign of emaciation or distress. 'Phyllis Brady' was returned to prison and went on hunger strike again for thirty days and was fed by force. When she was released on 24 March she went to recover at Dr Flora Murray's suffragette nursing home, where a urine test revealed that she had been given bromide, commonly used in lunatic asylums to sedate patients.

On 16 April Kitty was released from Holloway on a six-day Cat and Mouse licence and taken to Mouse Castle in Campden Hill Square. The Home Office had struggled to cope with Kitty and were nervous when she was released. She had no intention of being rearrested and the day before her licence expired she left Mouse Castle accompanied by two friends. The police followed her taxi and at her destination she was helped up the steps looking very weak and wobbly: Kitty's years of experience on the stage were put to good use. The address was under surveillance, but Kitty left by the back door and was taken away by the son of the house in the sidecar of his motorcycle. 'It was my first and only sidecar ride and with the excitement and romance of escaping the police once more, quite enjoyable despite my wretched, weak physical condition and the miraculous avoidance of a collision, by a timely increase of speed, with a car at the corner of a hill up which we were turning.'[24] While Kitty recovered she received letters from many suffragette comrades, including Constance Lytton, writing with her left hand since her stroke: 'My reverence for you is of the greatest, and I feel a love for you which I cannot put on paper. I have thought of you incessantly while you were being force-fed.'[25] Christabel Pankhurst wrote: 'My love and thanks to you for your magnificent fight and heroic endurance ... There is much rejoicing that you are free and out of the clutches of those terribly cruel enemies of our cause.'[26] Mrs Pankhurst sent Kitty a flowering azalea. One of the prisoners' secretaries at Lincoln's Inn House sent Kitty £1 and a pair of shoes and was arranging for Kitty's possessions to be sent to her from Liverpool. She said: 'You can't think how proud I was to be allowed to see you yesterday – you have been just grand.'[27] A Bristol comrade who had been arrested five times and served prison sentences in 1910 and 1911 wrote twice to Kitty using an affectionate nickname, 'Clorf Ears': 'I think dear you are truly marvellous and only wish I had half your pluck'.[28] A friend whom she had served time with in Winson Green in 1912 wrote: 'My dear brave Kitty, I must write a line just to try to tell you how I love and admire you for your long and splendid fight ... I have been fearfully anxious for you for so many weeks.'[29]

On the last day of May Kitty was accompanied to Paris (wearing a dark wig and heavily veiled) by Mary Leigh, Dr Violet Jones and Mrs Alice Green, who had been Emily Davison's landlady. Christabel

Pankhurst could now see for herself how intrepid, loyal, kind-hearted, 'leading comedienne' Kitty Marion had suffered for the cause.[30]

On 10 February Mrs Pankhurst, on the run from the police and staying with the Brackenbury family at Mouse Castle, held an advertised meeting on the balcony of the house. She spoke to a crowd of 600 people, mostly women's suffrage supporters, but also some antis, too, all waiting eagerly for her. Swathed in black and looking frail, Mrs Pankhurst spoke for half an hour in the cold night air:

> We women are fighting not as women, but as human beings, for human rights, and we shall win those human rights ... because nothing on earth can put down this movement ... Let us show the men of the twentieth century that there are things today worth fighting for ... I am here tonight, and not a man is going to protect me, because this is a woman's fight and we shall protect ourselves. I am coming amongst you in a few minutes, and I challenge the Government to re-arrest me.[31]

In an attempt to drown her voice handbells were rung and hostile songs were sung, and a man shouted that she should be 'deported as a mover of sedition'. Mrs Pankhurst turned on him: 'Here is a man whose forefathers were seditious in the past, talking about sedition on the part of women, who are taxed but have no constitutional rights. Yes, my friends, I am seditious, and I shall go on being seditious until I am brought, with other women, within the constitution of my country.'[32]

To prevent Mrs Pankhurst from being rearrested, Florence Smith was dressed in Mrs Pankhurst's clothes by Kitty Marshall, wardrobe lady. At the end of the speech suffragettes and their supporters sang 'The Marseillaise' as 'Mrs Pankhurst' and Kitty Marshall left the house surrounded by her bodyguards, who had been trained in ju-jitsu by Edith Garrud. The bodyguards produced Indian clubs hidden in their clothing when the police – some of whom had been hiding in the bushes – moved forward. Gertrude Harding says: 'Up came the clubs of the bodyguard. Out swung the fists of the police. People stared in shocked silence as the struggling cluster of women and men reached the street, when more plain-clothes police officers surged forward out of the crowd. One policeman yelled, "That's her, I know her" … with his fist he struck her from behind. "Mrs Pankhurst" and Katherine [Kitty Marshall] pushed from all sides fell to the pavement.' Kitty's ribs were badly bruised and 'Mrs Pankhurst' was knocked unconscious in the mêlée. The bodyguards punched and lashed out at the police with their Indian clubs and seven members of the bodyguard and 'Mrs Pankhurst' were arrested and taken to the police station in Ladbroke Grove. After a short time, at Mouse Castle, the real Mrs Pankhurst, accompanied by Gert Harding, who organised her bodyguard, left the house and hailed a taxi to a secret address.[33]

*

On 18 February 1914, Mary Lindsay from London, a new recruit, mistook Liberal politician Lord Weardale, a joint President of the National League for Opposing Woman Suffrage, for the prime minister. She attacked him with a dog-whip on the platform of Euston station. This was her first militant action. It has not been possible to trace 'Mary Ogilvy Lindsay', which suggests this may have been an alias. Mary had mingled with a crowd of 200 wedding guests, of which Weardale was one, on their way to the wedding of Lady Adelaide Spencer of Althorp Park, Northamptonshire. Mary, 'young and pretty' and dressed in black, 'rushed from the crowd and pulled a whip from underneath her coat and struck at Lord Weardale fiercely. So unexpected was the attack, and so energetic was his assailant's rush that Lord Weardale fell headlong onto the platform', and his wife's ear was clipped by the whiplash. Lord Weardale and Mary Lindsay were escorted to Albany Street police station. Later she was charged at Clerkenwell Police Court with assault. When one of the railway policemen described her slashing at Lord Weardale with the whip, Mary Lindsay was reported to have 'laughed softly'. The court heard that as her victim was helped to his feet, Mary said: 'I meant to give him a good thrashing; you don't know what he has done to us.' Before she was taken to gaol, the magistrate remarked that her behaviour 'resembled that of a lunatic'. Mary went on hunger strike for three days and was released on 22 February 'looking very ill' on her own bail of £50. As it was her first offence she was fined forty shillings for whipping Lord Weardale.[34]

On 21 February Kitty Marshall reprised her role as wardrobe mistress to Mrs Pankhurst when she made a speech on the balcony of 63 Glebe Place, the Chelsea home of the suffragette sympathisers Dr Harry and Mrs Gladys Schütze. Twenty members of Mrs Pankhurst's bodyguard 'arrived in various disguises – tradespeople and maids ... they would come singly in order not to attract attention'.[35] The organisers at Lincoln's Inn House issued detailed requests for their leader's stay in Glebe Place:

Mrs Pankhurst will arrive sometime tomorrow afternoon [20 February] soon after lunch. She will rest from tea until dinnertime and go to bed at half-past nine. She will stay in bed during the Saturday morning. You will have lunch at half-past twelve, so that she rests up before she speaks at half-past two. At eleven o'clock Saturday evening, we shall send cars to take her away, so she will need some dinner. And you had better have enough food in the house for her and the bodyguard for over the weekend, just in case anything goes wrong.[36]

Gladys Schütze found the members of the bodyguard charming and easy-going: 'Before bedtime there were ten or so making the best of the floor and easy chairs in my workroom and the drawing-room. I have never come across such cheerful, unfussy young women.'[37] She learned that two were shop assistants, two were teachers, there was a dressmaker, a couple were clerks, one had been a mill worker, there was a children's nurse, three servants, a 'society lady', and the rest were 'middle-class women of no occupation'.[38] The Schützes' cook, Mrs Duckett, was 'a rabid member of the Union'. Hearing that Mrs Pankhurst was coming to stay, Mrs Duckett was 'thrilled to the marrow'.[39]

When the meeting started Glebe Place was 'black with people'. There were dozens of police and more waiting round the corner. In a rerun of the Mouse Castle speech, Mrs Pankhurst addressed the crowd from a first-floor balcony, challenging the government to rearrest her: 'I have served about twenty days of those three years [the sentence handed down in 1912]. They have hauled me back to prison five times ... They may kill me, but they will not make me serve my three years.' She told her audience: 'We are fighting for a time when every little girl born into the world will have an equal chance with her brothers, when we shall put an end to foul outrages upon our sex, when our streets shall be safe for the girlhood of our race, when every man shall look upon every other woman as his own sisters.'[40]

Gertrude Harding arranged for the bodyguards, Indian clubs at the ready, to surround Kitty Marshall and – in the guise of 'Mrs Pankhurst' – Florence White. As soon as the meeting ended two cars drew up and Kitty, 'Mrs Pankhurst' and half of the bodyguards dashed out of the front door and tried to get into the car, but the police were suspicious and stopped Kitty and 'Mrs Pankhurst'. Determined not to be duped again, *The Times* reported: 'A small group of women left the house, and the police, singling out one of whom they imagined to be Pankhurst, deliberately struck her on the head and then knocked her down.'[41] The men lifted her veil and Florence White was taken to the police station, along with two bodyguards. When another group of heavily veiled women left the house, hemmed in by the crowd and plain-clothes policemen, the women drew their Indian clubs from under their clothing and two of them were arrested. Gladys Schütze announced from the front door that the real Mrs Pankhurst had left the house, but no one believed her and the police stayed put. Inside Glebe Place, Gertrude Harding waited with Emmeline to make their escape. On Sunday morning, one of the bodyguards left the house disguised as an elderly maid, prayer book in hand, as if she was going to church, and went to WSPU headquarters for orders. The 'maid' returned to report that the attempt to rescue Mrs Pankhurst would be made later that afternoon. At a given signal at four o'clock the bodyguards rushed out and a fresh contingent of women sprang from two cars that had pulled up.[42] Kitty Marshall remembered how 'the girls attacked the police, there were shouts and shrieks, a scene of great confusion'. At nine o'clock in the evening the bodyguards at 63 Glebe Place again rushed out of the front door. A car was waiting outside the tradesmen's entrance in the back street, and, after a brief scrimmage with a detective, Mrs Pankhurst and three members of her bodyguard escaped. Kitty Marshall's unpublished memoir 'Suffragette Escapes and Adventures' recalled: 'some of us fell on some policemen and detectives. I chose a big man with a large mackintosh cape. I knocked his helmet over his eyes and brandished my club over his head. Out came Mrs Pankhurst and she was driven away by a smart woman driver, hell for leather.'[43] Kitty saw a chief inspector running after the car in order to get the registration number so she ran up to him and knocked off his hat. Mrs Pankhurst was whisked away to Colchester to stay with a colonel and his wife who were sympathisers of the cause. The Schützes went with the women who were arrested to Chelsea police station, and bailed the women out, two of whom were eventually sent to prison for three days.[44]

Mrs Pankhurst's host, Gladys Schütze, whose pen name was 'Henrietta Leslie', was born into a wealthy Jewish family in Mayfair. Gladys's father, Arthur Raphael, a banker, lost a vast amount of the Raphael family wealth, and died when she was seven. Her mother, Marianna Raphael, was an artist. Gladys canvassed for the Liberals in the 1906 election and met Herbert Asquith at a house party – but rejected the party because of her burgeoning views on feminism and women's suffrage. A friend introduced her to the WSPU which she joined in 1908. Although a generous supporter, Gladys was never a militant.

> Although I was in name a suffragette, I fear that during the next year or two I did very little to deserve that title. I subscribed to the paper, and, modestly to the fighting fund, not even Betsy [a relative] could persuade me to take a more active part in the campaign. I was too unhappy in my own life and my sole idea was to forget my unhappiness in leading as gay and crowded a life as possible.[45]

She left her first husband in 1910 and published her first novel, *The Roundabout*, in 1911. In 1913 Gladys married her new love, Dr Harry 'Peter' Schütze, a bacteriologist who worked at the Lister Institute, and who supported his wife's feminist views. Gladys acted as a courier for the Union, carrying documents rolled into her hair, and in the summer of 1914 she was arrested and badly hurt in the WSPU deputation to see the King at Buckingham Palace on 21 May. A kick from a police horse inflamed a childhood injury and Gladys went to convalesce with the MacRae sisters who had opened their home, Comforts Cottage, in Edenbridge, Kent, for all WSPU women who 'needed to be restored by quiet and country air'. Helen MacRae's suffragette sisters were Georgie (Georgiana), who had also been

to prison, and Betty. Henrietta Schütze provides a snapshot of the
MacRae women:

> Miss Georgie, tall and wrinkled, who attended to the animals and
> kitchen-garden, who sawed the wood and pumped the water, who
> pruned the trees and made the hay; Miss Helen, gentle and sweet,
> whose province was darning, embroidering, cooking, bottling,
> jam-making, and Miss Betty... an ex-nurse whose concern was
> the local school-children and who started country dancing in the
> neighbourhood.[46]

Although Annie Kenney had a three-year prison sentence hanging
over her, she slipped back into England from Switzerland in disguise in March 1914. Annie missed the cut and thrust of day-to-day
campaigning, dodging the police and Special Branch. En route from
Switzerland she helped Christabel in Paris. 'Once a Militant, always
a Militant until the vote was won. I knew I was needed at home, so
I returned quite secretly to Mouse Castle, 2 Campden Hill Square.'[47]

In March Mrs Pankhurst wrote to Ethel Smyth from a Scottish
manse where she was being hidden by a clergyman. The 'adventurous' journey from the south of England had not been easy. The car
lights failed and they could not find the house where they were to
stay. The chauffeur and Mrs Pankhurst abandoned the attempt and
slept in the car until dawn. Emmeline slept curled up in the bottom of
the car and was woken by 'an inquisitive farm labourer'. They needed
to hire another car, which was even worse than the first – two tyres
burst and the brakes failed. Mrs Pankhurst told Ethel that she had her
own 'Scotch bodyguard' who were 'eager for the fray'.[48] Whether she
managed to reach Ireland for more meetings, or was arrested, Mrs
Pankhurst was sanguine: 'Whatever happens will hit the Government.
If I get away with it again they will be laughed at, if I am taken the
people will be roused. The fools hurt themselves every time. Everyone
is very kind to me, and I am waited on and coddled far too much.
Bless you, don't worry! Try to rejoice in the sportingness of it all.'[49]

Mrs Pankhurst's advisers knew the police would be out in force and
expected them to rush the platform at the meeting at St. Andrew's Hall,
Glasgow, on 9 March. Smuggled into the building in a laundry basket, she was introduced by Lady Isabel Margesson, whose daughter,

Catherine, was a suffragette. *The Times'* Glasgow correspondent reported how Mrs Pankhurst emerged from the rear of the hall surrounded by her bodyguard, and 'throwing aside her cloak, disclosed herself to the audience, which cheered her to the echo'.[50] She made one of the shortest speeches of her political career to 3,000 people:

> In spite of Her Majesty's Government I am here tonight. Very few people in … this country know how much of the nation's money is being spent to silence the women. But the wit and ingenuity of women is overcoming the power and the money … I propose … equal justice for men and women, equal political justice, equal legal justice, equal industrial justice, and equal social justice. I want … to make it clear to you tonight that if it is justifiable to fight for common ordinary equal justice, then women have ample justification, nay, have greater justification, for revolution and rebellion, than ever men have had in the whole history of the human race.[51]

When she uttered the word 'justice' in her next sentence, a large number of policemen 'burst into the hall and rushed up to the platform, drawing their truncheons'. Led by Scotland Yard detectives they 'surged the platform … but were met with a fusillade of chairs, tables, and other missiles'. The *Daily Mirror* reported: 'In their attempts to keep off the police the women seized flowerpots at the edge of the platform and hurled them at the officers. When this supply of ammunition failed they flung chairs and drenched the attacking force with pails of water.'[52] When the police reached the platform they grabbed the platform railing but found that underneath the decorations and bunting barbed wires had been concealed which 'gave them pause for a moment'. Many had cut hands as a result.

The bodyguards closed in around Mrs Pankhurst and drew batons from their dresses and 'struck fierce heavy blows, while those who were not so armed used broken chairs as clubs. The police drew their truncheons and blows were freely exchanged.'[53] The riot on the platform spilled into the rest of the hall and 'miniature bombs were thrown among the police and more shots were heard … women screamed and fainted and many were hurt in the confusion'.[54] Mrs Pankhurst was found lying on the floor holding her head in her hands and had evidently been struck. The bodyguards surrounded her but despite their best efforts she was 'dragged half-fainting, out of the hall' down the narrow stairs at the back of the hall and 'through a howling mob' and 'pushed violently' into a waiting cab, thrown on the floor: the seats were crammed with constables, some from London, and a matron from Holloway. She was taken to the Central Police Station in St Andrew's Square, where a crowd tried to storm the building but was scattered by mounted police. Mrs Pankhurst spent the night in the police cells and went on hunger, thirst and sleep strike. She refused to leave her cell and was carried on a stretcher to a taxi and taken to Coatbridge station some distance from Glasgow. Knowing that the WSPU would be waiting for the train at Euston, the Scotland Yard detectives took Mrs Pankhurst off the train at South Hampstead. When they arrived at Holloway fifty women were waiting, hoping to liberate her, but they were outnumbered by the police who cleared the way. As the car drove through the prison gates, 'a young woman forced her way through the police ranks and ran towards the car with a dog-whip in her hand'.[55] Intending to strike the detective sitting next to the driver, she was caught by plain-clothes officers. Emmeline Pankhurst spent five days in Holloway and was released on 14 March, 'suffering severely from the hunger- and thirst-strike and the injuries received during her arrest'.[56]

Janie Allan, whom we last saw in action in 1912, being force-fed and barricading her cell while serving four months for breaking windows in London on 4 March, had been on the platform in the Glasgow hall. Looking regal, 'tall and handsome in a black velvet evening gown', she rose from her seat and fired blanks from a revolver in the faces of the advancing policemen. No charges were brought against her, and she waged a six-month campaign to have a public inquiry into police behaviour in St Andrew's Hall that night. 'General' Flora Drummond gave a rousing speech from the platform when Mrs Pankhurst was finally bundled out of the hall, and she toured Scotland making maximum political capital from the riotous conditions under which the WSPU's leader had been arrested.[57]

On 13 March, Mary Richardson joined Kitty Marion in Holloway. Incensed by Mrs Pankhurst's prison treatment and her violent rearrest the day before, she had attacked Velázquez's *The Rokeby Venus*. The press dubbed her 'Slasher Mary'. On 10 March she had gone to the National Gallery in London with an axe hidden in the sleeve of her jacket and taken a few swings at the seventeenth-century painting of a naked Venus reclining on a bed looking at herself in a hand mirror held by Cupid. Venus suffered a gash three to four inches wide on her back. The painting had been bought for the nation in 1906. Mary wanted to draw attention to the public's indifference to 'Mrs Pankhurst's slow destruction and the destruction of some financially valuable object'.[58] In an open letter written after her arrest she said:

> I have tried to destroy the picture of the most beautiful woman in mythological history as a protest against the Government for trying to destroy Mrs Pankhurst who is the most beautiful character in modern history. Justice is an element of beauty as much as colour and outline in canvas. Mrs Pankhurst seeks to secure justice to womanhood and for this she is being slowly murdered by a Government of Iscariot politicians. If there is an outcry against my deed, remember that such an outcry is an hypocrisy as long as they allow the destruction of Mrs Pankhurst and other beautiful women.[59]

Interviewed in 1961, six months before her death, Mary Richardson remembered that she had disliked the depiction of women portrayed as nudes, and loathed the number of men who 'gawped' at the painting.[60]

Mary had been considering this protest for some time and had written to Christabel Pankhurst about it. When she received a message from Paris, 'Carry out your plan', and hearing that Mrs Pankhurst had been violently arrested in Glasgow on 9 March, she decided to act. She spent her 'last few shillings on an axe, the smallest I could get, I wanted one that would fit easily up my sleeve'.[61] Mary left her lodgings in Bloomsbury, telling her landlady that she might be away for two weeks. Mrs Lyon knew of Mary's suffragette career, and addressed her by her suffragette alias as they parted: 'Take care of yourself, Polly Dick.'[62] The axe was 'fixed up the left sleeve of my jacket and held in place by a chain of safety-pins, the last pin only needing a touch to release it'.[63] She saw how thick the glass was on the painting to protect it from suffragette protests. The gallery had been anticipating a 'suffragette outrage' for the past twelve months and had posted plain-clothes detectives and uniformed constables in every room. When one detective guarding the painting left, and the other opened his newspaper and held it in front of his face, Mary seized her moment: 'I dashed up to the painting. My first blow with the axe merely broke the protective glass.' Mary was attacked by two German tourists who hurled their Baedeker guide books at the back of her neck, then the detective grabbed the axe and 'as if out of the walls angry people seemed to appear round me, I was dragged this way and that … in the end all of us rolled in an uncomfortable heap out of the room and down the stairs.'[64] Before Mary was taken to the basement 'to cool off', she told the crowd that had gathered around her: 'Yes, I am a suffragette. You can get another picture, but you cannot get a life, they are killing Mrs Pankhurst.'[65]

At Bow Street Mary Richardson told the magistrate, Mr Muskett, a man who had sent dozens of suffragettes to prison: 'I am not afraid of dying, Mr McKenna [the home secretary] is a coward, he cannot coerce me and he cannot let me serve my sentences.'[66] For the two days she had spent in Holloway before the trial she had been on hunger strike, and when brought into court Mary looked 'weak and ill'. The prosecuting counsel, Mr Travers Humphreys, doubted that anyone in their right mind would have attacked the painting in retaliation at Mrs Pankhurst's rearrest. Mary pleaded guilty and Judge Wallace expressed his disappointment in only being able to sentence her to a maximum term of six months with hard labour. Before Mary was taken to Holloway she said from the dock: 'I care more for justice than I do for art, and I firmly believe when the nation shuts its eyes and prefers to have women who are not only denied justice ill-treated and tortured, then I say that this action of mine should be understandable.'[67]

*

On 13 March 1914 the burgh of Leith police issued a wanted notice in the *Police Gazette* for the arrest of the Scottish suffragette Ethel Moorhead, who was missing from the Edinburgh home of her friend, Dr Grace Cadell, where she was recovering from being force-fed and suffering from double pneumonia. Ethel was due to be rearrested and returned to Calton Gaol to continue serving her sentence but had escaped. Calton Gaol's medical officer, Dr James C. Dunlop, had called at Cadell's house on 12 March 'to ascertain the present condition of Miss Moorhead', and was told by two servants that neither

Dr Cadell nor Miss Moorhead were at home. Grace Cadell had been one of the first students to attend Dr Sophia Jex-Blake's School of Medicine in Edinburgh in 1887. She became a senior consultant at Bruntsfield Hospital, and in 1907 she became the honorary secretary of the WSPU branch at Leith. She joined the Women's Freedom League, refused to pay her taxes and evaded the 1911 Census.[68]

Wearing dark clothing and a large black hat, Ethel Moorhead was driven away in a green motor car with false number plates. The wanted notice issued in the *Police Gazette* described Ethel thus: 'five feet six inches tall, very dark hair, brown eyes, wears pince-nez, oblong face, receding chin, slim build, stooping shoulders'.[69] The police strongly suspected she was responsible for burning down three houses in Comrie, Perthshire, with 'Rhoda Robinson' and others, during the night of 3 to 4 February 1914, and were frustrated at their failure to apprehend her. 'Rhoda Robinson' was the alias of an Englishwoman who had married a Scottish stevedore, Francis McCullogh Craig, in 1899. She was the first woman member of the Independent Labour Party in Dunbartonshire, and became secretary of the WSPU's branch in Dunbarton.

Ethel Moorhead was rearrested on 17 February after being seen acting suspiciously at Traquair House; she went on hunger, thirst and sleep strike and was force-fed. Unlike prisons in England where hunger-striking prisoners had been fed by force since 1909, the 'artificial feeding' of Ethel Moorhead was the first time such action had been sanctioned in a Scottish gaol.[70] On 21 February, she barricaded her cell door but she was fed by Dr James Dunlop, with a stomach tube 'without any serious hitch or difficulty'.[71] The governor of Calton Gaol, Major William Stewart, wrote to the Prison Commissioners that he was present on 21 February when she was fed: 'the prisoner showed no sign of suffering much if any pain. The food given consisted of two eggs and half a pint of milk. It is proposed to repeat the feeding, giving larger amounts of food, later this afternoon. In my opinion this is not only safe but necessary.'[72] Ethel became gravely ill – Dr Cadell was certain it was caused by food entering her lungs while being fed – and Ethel asked to make her will on 23 February. Two days later she was released from Calton and taken to Dr Cadell's home. Dr Dunlop blamed 'Margaret Morrison's [Edith's alias] behaviour' for her pneumonia, which he insisted was 'in no way associated with the feeding'.[73]

On 21 February the prisoner had broken all her cell windows and 'tore at her clothing, thus exposing herself to the danger of a chill'.[74]

The governor discouraged any suggestion that Ethel Moorhead became ill because she had been force-fed:

> We must face the fact that artificial feeding is attended with risks and we must teach them [suffragette prisoners] that while we appreciate the risks we are quite prepared to go on and will not be deterred from detaining people like the prisoner because there is a risk to their health if we take the necessary steps to make sure their detention is effective ... They have the idea that they can frighten us by pointing out the risks to health.[75]

He was adamant the women should remain in detention unless 'some security is given that the property and perhaps the lives of others will not be endangered', and he was also apprehensive: 'I think there is a danger of it [public opinion] insisting on us going too far.'[76]

On Ethel's release the WSPU published a handbill, 'Scotland Dishonoured and Disgraced', about her experiences, which the authorities furiously denied. Here is her description: 'As the tube was being forced down [the nose] I had a curious sensation inside my left ear, as if cold drops or cold wire had touched it and in a minute or two I felt as if a hot iron had been put in, an excruciating pain which made me give a piercing scream.' The next day after she was fed, 'they held me down for an hour after feeding in the same position to prevent sickness, but in spite of this I was sick. My jaw was held firmly to prevent me from turning my head, and the consequence was that when I was sick it all poured down my neck. They refused to give me a basin.'[77]

Ethel would go on the run for the next five months and commit more militant acts. It is thought she was with Frances 'Fanny' Parker, when they were spotted trying to set fire to Robert Burns's cottage at Alloway on 8 July. Ethel managed to escape. Three aliases, 'Margaret Morrison', 'Edith Johnston' and 'Mary Humphreys', had not been used in the suffragette cause since the autumn of 1912, when Ethel whipped a schoolteacher who had chucked her out of a meeting at the Synod Hall in Edinburgh. Since then she had become a dedicated arsonist and hunger striker and a determined fugitive.

On 29 January 1913 Ethel gave her name as 'Margaret Morrison' when she was arrested for throwing pepper in the eyes of George Honeyman, a policeman, at Leven Town Hall, temporarily blinding him. Ethel and two other women had been thwarted from gaining entry to the prime minister's meeting. It took three policemen to get her to the police station, 'struggling and resisting and trying to throw pepper into the eyes of the constables'. At the station she 'kicked out and conducted herself like a demented woman, shook her gloves which were saturated with pepper into the constable's eyes ... she jumped about and had to be forcibly held'.[78] She got some of the pepper in her own eyes and asked for water to bathe them. As soon as PC Honeyman's wife, who was trying to search her, left to get water, 'Miss Morrison' locked herself in the corridor leading to the cells and smashed twelve fanlight windows above the doors. In court next day at Cupar, she treated everyone with 'the utmost contempt' and had to be 'forcibly removed'.[79]

Ethel arrived at Perth Gaol on 4 February 1913 to serve thirty days for two charges of assault, committing a breach of the peace and malicious mischief, and went on hunger strike, refusing to be medically examined. Although the governor at Perth, James Grant, would have force-fed her, it was not carried out as it was deemed too risky to do so without her first being examined. Because she had been hunger-striking while on remand in Dundee, she was only allowed to starve for two days before being released from Perth on a Cat and Mouse licence on 6 February. She was collected by a friend and went on the run.

Ethel wrote a letter from Dundee Gaol to a comrade, Arabella Scott, which was suppressed by the governor, James Crowe, because of its 'indecorous and improper matter', among them allegations about the unsavoury behaviour of one of the Dundee prison doctors. Ethel wrote: 'I want you to warn our people and friends that there is a plot hatching. I was visited today by a bleary-eyed doctor, (I thought smelling of whisky) and with an affectionate manner!' Ethel refused to answer the 'affectionate questions of course but no doubt replies will be manufactured and a sensational report sent in'.[80]

Ethel Moorhead and Dr Elizabeth Dorothea Chalmers Smith appeared in the High Court in Glasgow on 15 October 1913, charged with having broken into a mansion in the city on 23 July to set it on fire. The police found 'Margaret Morrison' in the house, and caught Dr Chalmers Smith, who had refused to give any name, as she tried to escape. In one of the rooms they found firelighters, matches, six flasks of paraffin and a postcard bearing the words 'A protest against Mrs Pankhurst's re-arrest'. The women conducted their own defence. Ethel interrupted Judge Salvesen, 'We do not want to hear any more. We refuse to listen to you. Please sentence us.'[81] They received eight months in Duke Street Prison, Glasgow. When the sentence was passed 'a scene of great excitement followed': apples were thrown at the judge and bundles of suffragist literature were 'hurled into the body of the Court'. Scuffles broke out and three women were arrested. Ethel Moorhead and Dr Chalmers Smith were released after a five-day hunger strike. Ethel went on the run for nearly four months.

Dr Elizabeth Chalmers Smith was the wife of a clergyman and the mother of six children born between 1900 and 1911. One of the first women to graduate in medicine from Glasgow University in 1892, she was a doctor at the Glasgow Samaritan Hospital for Women when she married the Reverend William Chalmers Smith, a minister in Glasgow. When she joined the WSPU in 1912, her enthusiastic embracing of extreme militancy was not welcomed by her husband, who believed adamantly that a woman's place was in the home. Their marriage ended after the First World War when she left him and took her three daughters with her, but she was not allowed to see her three sons again.[82]

In the early hours of the morning of 26 February, Whitekirk Parish Church, twenty-five miles east of Edinburgh, was burned to the ground in retaliation for Ethel Moorhead's force-feeding and general suffering. A red car carrying several women was spotted driving through North Berwick, travelling west. Suffrage literature was found at the scene. Investigations suggested that the suffragette arsonists had sprayed the interior with inflammable material and used explosives, as 'enormous slabs of stones have been shattered'.[83] Slips of paper were left which read 'By torturing the finest and noblest woman in the country you are driving women to rebellion' and 'No surrender'.[84] Even though the police offered a reward of £100 for information leading to the conviction of the women involved, none of the culprits were ever caught.

In June 1914, Janie Allan wrote to the chairman of the Prison Commission saying that Whitekirk had been attacked because of the forcible feeding of Miss Ethel Moorhead in Calton Prison and warned that if Arabella Scott and 'Frances Gordon', the alias of Florence Graves, were force-fed in Perth the imminent royal visit to Scotland would be disrupted. The visit presented 'many opportunities for protests of a memorable and disastrous nature'.[85]

Arabella Scott, born in Argyllshire, had been in and out of prison on Cat and Mouse licences, and was serving nine months for trying to set fire to Kelso racecourse pavilion in 1913; she and 'Frances Gordon', whose real name was Frances Graves, were arrested when found breaking into Springhall House with the intention of setting it on fire on 3 April. On 22 June, Scott was sent to Perth Gaol for a year. As she left the courtroom she shouted: 'Trust in God, constant war and fight on.' Unusually for Scotland, 'Frances Gordon' was fed by force for ten days.[86]

On 16 March, Dr James Devon, a Prison Commissioner for Scotland, was attacked by Miss Jean Lambie, a prominent Edinburgh suffragette, while he was en route to make an unannounced inspection of Duke Street Prison. As he approached the prison he was surrounded by several dozen women, some with 'banners and sashes promenading in front of the prison gate'.[87] Dr Devon was recognised, and as he rang the bell he was struck from behind, 'and a lash coiled over my right cheek, the end striking me half an inch below the eye. I rushed at her and she stood against the wall. I shot out my arm to seize the whip which she was now holding at her breast.' He grabbed her shoulder and 'she collapsed like a sack of potatoes, falling with her head towards the gutter and taking me down in a stooping position'. A man in the crowd punched Devon and another man hit the doctor's attacker. The prison door was opened and Dr Devon was bundled inside; a minute later Jean Lambie was dragged into the prison in a 'very excited and abusive' state. The doctor declined to press charges, ostensibly because he had not been seriously injured, and Lambie accused him of being too afraid to appear in court. He told her he was too busy 'to waste time prosecuting daft women'.[88] Devon noted in his statement to the police that he had not been badly hurt but if the whip had hit him an inch higher he said he might have lost his eye. Jean Lambie, a schoolteacher before becoming a dedicated suffragette, blamed him for the introduction of force-feeding in Scottish prisons.

The imagery on the front page of *The Suffragette*, and Christabel Pankhurst's editorials, show how determined the Union was to

maintain the high militant tempo. Joan of Arc, in full armour on the
front page of *The Suffragette* for 27 February 1914, preceded the publication of Mrs Pankhurst's letter to King George V asking him to meet
a WSPU deputation, 'to protest against the torture of Suffragist prisoners, and to demand votes for women'. In her letter she pointed out:

> Our right as women to be heard and to be aided by your Majesty
> is far stronger than any such right possessed by men, because it is
> based upon our lack of every other constitutional means of secur-
> ing the redress of our grievances. We have no power to vote for
> Members of Parliament, and therefore for us there is no House of
> Commons. We have no voice in the House of Lords. But we have a
> King, and to him we make our appeal.[89]

The date for the deputation to see the King was set for 21 May and 200
women were asked to volunteer to take part.

*

The British Museum was targeted by a woman named as 'Mary Stuart',
a new militant who also used the alias of 'Catherine Wilson', but whose
real name was Clara Mary Lambert, on 9 April. She smashed a display
case in the Asiatic Saloon and broke three Chinese porcelain cups and
a saucer. Dressed in a 'long tweed costume over which she wore a long
coat', Clara appeared to be studying the antiquities when 'she produced
a brand new hatchet from beneath her coat and before the attendants
could seize her, belaboured the cabinet of porcelain'. At Bow Street
Court the next morning Clara, 'in a very excited manner began to shout
and declaim' to the magistrate.[90] She was committed for trial and went
on hunger strike, was force-fed, released on a Cat and Mouse licence
and absconded from her address. On 24 April Scotland Yard circulated
a memorandum to all police stations in the country featuring a Special
Branch surveillance photograph of her, and giving her details: she was
five feet one inch tall, had a sallow complexion, brown hair and grey
eyes. She had been convicted twice for breaking windows and had
recently been found in the House of Commons 'in male attire with a
riding whip in her coat pocket ... for an unlawful purpose'.[91]

Clara Lambert had thrown herself wholeheartedly into the WSPU,
joining soon after it moved to London in 1906. She was arrested on

Black Friday and released without charge. Her hunger-strike medal has three silver bars giving the dates of her force-feeding in 1912, 1913 and 1914. She was employed as a collar-dresser in the family laundry business in Catford.[92]

Mrs Pankhurst was billed to speak at a teachers' conference in Lowestoft on 15 April, but was too ill to attend. She wrote to Ethel Smyth from Mouse Castle on 8 April: 'The police are thick round this house to prevent me going to Lowestoft as advertised ... I have decided my heart is not strong enough.' Annie Kenney, who was recovering with her, volunteered to go instead, and takes up the story: 'At the bottom of Campden Hill Square the detectives were in full force night and day. At the top were men we looked upon with suspicion. What was I to do? How could I escape?' A message reached Annie that a WSPU member had a house whose garden wall was the back-garden wall of Mouse Castle, and the owner of the house agreed that rope ladders should be used to help her.[93]

Annie Kenney's disguise was a 'black bathing costume, black stockings on the arms as well as legs, a black veil with holes for me to see where I was going. I just looked like the Black Cat in the pantomime'. At ten o'clock on the evening of 15 April she was told, '"only 2 tecs but a high moon". I was just ready to go when another message came – "Tecs just arrived in full force", so I had to wait all dressed up until the signal came at about midnight, "All well".'[94] Annie left by the back door. To make as little noise as possible, all the doors had been oiled, greased and sandpapered, and strips of carpet were laid across the back garden. Next to the garden wall was a chair and a rope ladder attached to the top of the wall. Annie climbed and found herself 'sitting alone on the top of the wall. Then I heard a whisper, "It's alright", and there was a ladder being held up for me by two men. How I got down I could never say, but I arrived safely on the ground and I was taken away to a sympathiser's house.'[95] The next morning Annie went with her host's family to church in a taxicab, driving past 2 Campden Hill Square and seeing officers from Scotland Yard looking at Mouse Castle.

Teachers who were WSPU members had booked rooms for Annie and a friend in Lowestoft and provided her with a disguise that 'was very plain, a large fur being the main thing, and no heels to my shoes, so that I looked small. I wore glasses.' Her friend, who was small, was dressed in a sailor suit and carried a school bag full of books playing the part of Annie's niece. The Leighton Assembly Rooms in Lowestoft were packed with teachers, members of the public and detectives.

> Each face seemed to be peered into, but my little sailor-clad 'Niece' did well. She giggled and talked and laughed at the fun she would have when she saw Mrs Pankhurst caught. She chatted and explained loudly what all the school-girls thought of suffragettes. My heart beat rather quickly, but in we marched arm-in-arm, niece and aunt, past the regiment of detectives and I found myself in a few moments inside the dressing-room, changed and ready to speak.[96]

The audience went 'wild with enthusiasm'. Before she left Annie changed into a different disguise by letting her hair down, and looked like a girl. She wore a 'picture-hat' and a scarf round her neck, blackened her eyebrows and rouged her lips and cheeks. She escaped to London without being rearrested, relieved to be back in 'the thick of the fight'.[97]

On 11 April 1914 Hilda Burkitt, alias 'Hilda Byron', and Florence Tunks arrived in Suffolk for two weeks of arson. They took rooms with Alfred Bloxham and his wife in Great Yarmouth, and left a week later. Mrs Bloxham remembered that on 16 April, the day before the Britannia Pavilion was burned down, Hilda told her that she and Florence were going to a meeting in Gorleston, were spending the night with friends and would not return until the next morning. By the time Hilda and Florence returned to their lodgings the pavilion on the pier had been reduced to 'a shapeless mass of twisted girders and charred woodwork'.[98] There had been an explosion at four o'clock in the morning causing damage estimated at £15,000. Mrs Bloxham remembered Hilda buying two postcards of the fire and showing them to her. The owner of the Pavilion received a letter bearing one word, 'Retribution', and a 'Votes for Women' postcard was found on the sands with 'Mr McKenna has nearly killed Mrs Pankhurst. We can show no mercy until women are enfranchised.'[99]

The two suffragettes lodged with the Palmer family in Ipswich from 18 to 25 April. During their stay Mrs Mary Palmer said they went out every day on their bicycles. On 25 April 1914 Burkitt and Tunks took a bedroom and a sitting room at Mayflower Cottage in Felixstowe for three days, the home of Daisy Meadows whose father was a bathing-machine proprietor. Daisy remembered the women arriving with six cases of luggage and a bicycle. Two days later Hilda Burkitt created their alibi, saying they would not be staying the night as they were visiting the theatre in Ipswich that evening and spending time with friends. Daisy told the court: 'I didn't see them go out and didn't see them again until about five minutes to nine next morning … I asked them if they'd had a nice time at the theatre the night before. They both said they'd had a lovely time. They went out again and returned about 1 o'clock. Miss Burkitt asked if I'd heard about the fire. I said I'd been to see it.'[100] Daisy told the women she felt very sorry for the hotel servants who were rumoured to have lost all their possessions in the fire, at which Florence blurted out that no servants had been there. Daisy said that she had heard two guests from the Hotel Felix had been arrested which caused Miss Burkitt 'to look at Miss Tunks and say '"Oh fancy", or "Oh really" and they both smiled.' Hilda remarked that it would 'all be in the papers'.[101]

They did not leave Felixstowe but spent the night in a beach tent they had hired and used it as a base from which to launch their arson attack on the Bath Hotel, the oldest in the town. The alarm was raised by a lookout man on a lightship three miles away who saw the smoke, but by the time the fire brigade arrived 'the whole of the eastern wing was burning furiously'. A Felixstowe police constable was soon on the scene. When he arrived smoke was billowing from the roof and the windows on the top floor. He found labels tied to shrubs, announcing: 'There can be no peace until women get the vote', 'No vote means war' and 'Votes for Women means peace'. The firemen found that the arsonists had gained entry by breaking a window on the ground floor and had put cotton wool on the broken glass to stop them being cut as they undid the latch.[102]

George Meadows was near the Bath Hotel at 7 a.m. when it was blazing fiercely and saw Hilda and Florence at the scene: 'two ladies there who were laughing, one was tall and the other short'.[103] Hilda and Florence were still at their lodgings when Superintendent John Lingley of Woodbridge police arrived after lunch. Lingley arrested them and searched their rooms before taking them into custody. Enraged at his lack of a search warrant Hilda lost her temper when he pulled items from under her bed: 'Do you consider it right to pull women's things about?' Two boxes of matches, four candles, a glazier's diamond, four copies of *The Suffragette* newspaper, a lamp, a hammer and pliers were found.[104]

Richard White, a commander in the Royal Navy, gave evidence that he had been standing outside the Bath Hotel at ten o'clock, just hours before the fire broke out.[105] He saw the two women walking up Bath Hill and was curious to see 'two such people there at that time. I had my suspicions aroused.' Commander White asked the women the time: 'I knew that suffragettes were about. I had it at the back of my mind that probably that's what they might be.'[106] Hilda shouted abuse at him, accusing him of trying to seduce them and threw their shoes at him.

Hilda Evelyn Burkitt worked as a secretary before joining the WSPU in 1907. Before her arson spree in Ipswich and Felixstowe she had been to prison three times, and was force-fed during each sentence, in 1909, 1912 and 1913. She was on an expired Cat and Mouse licence when she was arrested with Florence in Felixstowe.[107] Florence Olivia Tunks was born in Newport, Monmouthshire. She was a bookkeeper in Cardiff in 1911. When Florence and Hilda appeared in court her father Gilbert Tunks told the court he had no knowledge of his daughter's suffragette career: 'She told me she was going to Belfast to assist in an office there, organising.'[108]

On 26 May, Burkitt and Tunks were charged with 'feloniously, unlawfully and maliciously' setting fire to two wheat stacks at Bucklesham Farm, worth £340 on 24 April; destroying a stack, worth £485 on 24 April at Levington; and setting fire to the Bath Hotel in Felixstowe, causing £30,000 worth of damage on 28 April. The women refused to answer any questions in court, sat on a table with their backs to the magistrate, and chatted while the evidence against them was presented. Hilda got two years and Florence nine months. Hilda told the judge to put on his black cap 'and pass sentence of death or not waste his breath'. She said she either wanted liberty or death. In prison she was force-fed over 200 times and was released a month after the outbreak of war.[109]

Rachel Barrett was still in hiding from the police at Lincoln's Inn House in the middle of May. She was smuggled out of the building. Five months of confinement took its toll; she was living in a bedsit at headquarters, where she was responsible for bringing out *The Suffragette*, and the only fresh air to be had was on the roof. In disguise

In April 1914 Hilda Burkitt, a secretary from Birmingham, and Florence Tunks, a bookkeeper in Cardiff, burned down the Bath Hotel in Felixstowe.

On 1 June 1914 the twelfth-century church of St Mary's at Wargrave, near Wokingham, was attacked by suffragette arsonists. The culprits were never caught.

Standard

TUESDAY, JUNE 9.

"LET THEM STARVE"

VIEWS OF PUBLIC MEN

Public opinion hardened against suffragettes who went on hunger strike and were force-fed. On their release many recovered and went on the run, committing more offences, and were rarely caught.

Grace Roe was in charge of the WSPU when she was arrested at Lincoln's Inn House on 23 May 1914 and charged with conspiracy.

Canadian-born Gertrude Harding settled in London in 1912 and joined the WSPU. She got away with her attack on the orchid house at Kew Gardens in 1913.

Grace Marcon, alias 'Freda Graham', was photographed covertly by Special Branch after her arrest for attacking five paintings at the National Gallery on 22 May 1914.

THE DAILY MIRROR, Friday, June 12, 1914.

British Driver Wins the Isle of Man Motor-car Race: Pictures.

The Daily Mirror

LATEST CERTIFIED CIRCULATION MORE THAN 960,000 COPIES PER DAY

No. 3,318.   Registered at the G.P.O. as a Newspaper.   FRIDAY, JUNE 12, 1914.   One Halfpenny.

CORONATION CHAIR DAMAGED BY WILD WOMEN'S BOMB.

CORONER IMPEACHES THE MILITANTS AT THE INQUEST ON LAVENDER GUTHRIE.

Another act of sacrilege was committed by the wild women yesterday, when they placed a bomb under the historic Coronation Chair in Edward the Confessor's Chapel, Westminster Abbey. The white marking shows where it was damaged.—(H. N. King.)

Lavender Guthrie. She was also known as Laura Gray.

Dr. Ingleby Oddie, the well-known coroner.

The W.S.P.U. medal presented to the girl.

Suicide during temporary insanity was the merciful verdict at the inquest on the death of Miss Lavender Guthrie, the militant suffragette who destroyed herself with drugs in her flat in Jermyn-street. It was the verdict the dead woman expected. "Of course, the kindly coroner will call it temporary insanity," she wrote just before the end to her mother. The coroner, Dr. Ingleby Oddie, in his summing up, made a strong indict-ment of the militant suffragette movement. "The militants appeared to have got her thoroughly in their toils," he said, and then, tracing her history, he described it as a story" of drink, drugs, immorality, and finally death by her own hand." "This travesty of a medal," as the coroner described it, was given to the girl by the W.S.P.U. "for valour." The bar across it denotes that she had been a hunger-striker.

Two hundred suffragettes tried to enter Buckingham Palace on 21 May 1914, hoping to present a petition to King George V to grant them the vote.

Women making bullets in 1915. Patriotic duty and high wages motivated working women to make munitions. Almost a million women carried out this dangerous work.

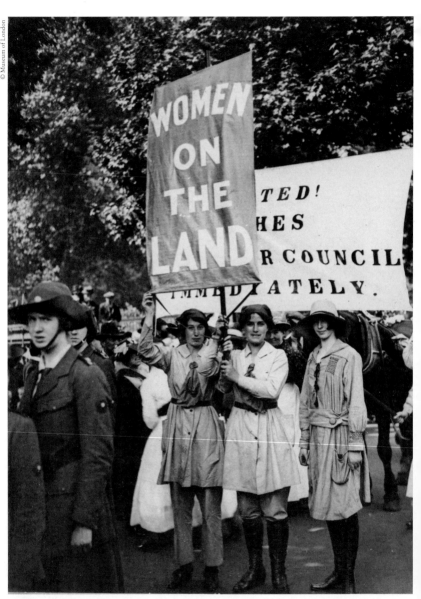

Women working on the land joined the 'Women's Right To Serve' march through London 17 July 1915, which was organised by Mrs Pankhurst.

On 6 February 1918 women over the age of thirty, with certain property qualifications, were given the right to vote.

A month after the Armistice that ended the First World War, 8,400,000 women were enfranchised in the general election of December 1918.

Rachel visited Christabel in Paris. They discussed the authorities' harassment of the printers and it was decided 'we should bring the paper out in Scotland where the law was not the same as in England'. In May the case against the manager of the Victoria House Printing Company, Sidney Drew, was heard at Bow Street Court where he was charged with having published 'matter which was a direct incitement to the commission of crime, especially of damage to public and private property'[110] in the 2 January issue of *The Suffragette*. Drew was later sentenced to two months in prison.

On her return to England in June 1914, Rachel Barrett and her lover Ida Wylie went to stay with Ida's aunt Jane in Edinburgh where Rachel was known as 'Miss Ashworth'. Ida Wylie's aunt did not question her 'inexplicable companion' who only went out at dusk. Ida noticed her aunt inspecting 'Miss Ashworth' with a 'dour distrustful eye but at the worst I'm sure she never guessed that an escaped criminal liable to re-arrest at any moment sat at her decorous Victorian table'.[111] The police had lost Rachel Barrett and she managed to bring out every issue of *The Suffragette* until the last number appeared in the days after war was declared. Every week Rachel was visited by Jessie Kenney bringing copy for the newspaper.[112]

Mrs Fawcett's National Union of Women's Suffrage Societies was still patiently pursuing its own strategy. The NUWSS successfully lobbied Lord Lytton and sympathetic peers to have a private members' bill debated in the House of Lords. It was read for a second time on 5 May, introduced by William Palmer, the Earl of Selborne, whose wife was the President of the Conservative and Unionist Women's Franchise Association. If the bill was successful, one million women who were on the municipal register, and entitled to vote in local elections (since the 1869 Municipal Franchise Act, and Local Government Act of 1894), would have got the parliamentary vote. Lord Selborne opened his speech with a 'vigorous condemnation of the methods of the militant suffragists, which he described as equally criminal and stupid'. He was confident the proposed bill would 'add to the stability of the State'.[113] Eleven members of the House of Lords spoke for the bill and seven against. Mrs Fawcett heard that the House had been 'deeply moved by Lytton's earnestness, transparent sincerity, and closely reasoned argument'.[114] The gossip was that Lord Curzon, the most implacable 'anti', was heard to say when Lytton sat down: 'What a tragedy that such talent should be wasted upon women!'[115] Curzon moved for the bill to be rejected, citing the likelihood that the extended franchise would lead to women becoming Members of Parliament, and members of the cabinet, roles for which he said women were ill suited and 'unfit to discharge the duties of public life'.[116] One hundred and four members of the Lords voted against, and sixty in favour.

The suffragettes were making a deep impression on some teachers and schoolgirls in the summer of 1914. Winifred Starbuck, whom we last saw in 1912, was in the sixth form and taught by teachers and a headmistress with WSPU sympathies. 'A bombshell fell on to our little world. Our headmistress and four other mistresses were given notice to leave, no reason was given for their dismissal. But doubtless it was because of their political activities.'[117] One of the teachers had been sent to prison and lost her job, at which Winifred and the other prefects decided to protest. 'We first canvassed our parents and persuaded them to sign a petition for the reinstatement of the mistresses who had been sacked.'[118] When the petition was ignored Winifred and her friends started 'a term of disorder'. On the first day the girls removed all the registers, 'precious things in those days, almost sacred'. Next they took the bell and the gong, 'so that there was no means of summoning us into school'. An atmosphere of joyous anarchy overtook the school:

> We galloped about the outskirts of the field and couldn't hear the mistresses calling us in and when one of them advanced towards us demanding angrily we come into school we agreed merrily and said, 'Shall we tell the others Miss Jones?' The misguided mistress said yes so we went tearing around telling the others and they told the others but no one came any nearer to the school door.[119]

By the afternoon the teachers had had enough and Winifred and the other sixth formers were suspended until further notice. On the last day of term the schoolgirls forced their way in and Winifred demanded to see the headmistress and 'walked straight through to our old haunts and was able to open side doors and windows to admit the others and we broke up in style'. A few days later

Winifred and some of her friends went 'into the school at night by a window one of the girls had left open for us and wrote slogans all over the walls with india ink. The police were called in but we were not discovered.'[120]

19

The Deputation to See King George V,
21 May 1914

The Drugging of Suffragette Prisoners

A suffragette being dragged off the railings at Buckingham Palace,
21 May 1914, while on a deputation to see the King.

On 4 May Mrs Pankhurst was once again in hiding, resting before leading the deputation to see King George V seventeen days later. She wrote to Ethel Smyth, relishing the secrecy of her hideout (the location was never revealed):

> I am in a country retreat so remote that it seems made for my purpose. You drive in a motor to a wood, which is on both sides of a country road, and there is a gap in the hedge. You get out of the car and then go through the wood ... In a few yards you lose sight of the road, and after following the path for a time you plunge down a slope among the trees and come to a wooden paling ... in which there is a gate padlocked. You unlock the padlock, go along a little path, and there is a house like no other you have ever seen. It commands the most wonderful view of three counties.[1]

The ladies who had built the house were fresh-air fanatics and had designed a shelter under the south gable where Mrs Pankhurst and Annie Kenney lay on camp beds, 'taking an open-air cure'. After a few days Mrs Pankhurst felt 'a different being'. The place was so well concealed that she felt they could 'hold this fortress forever, I am certain they have not the remotest idea where we are'.[2] By the time Ethel received the letter Mrs Pankhurst and Annie Kenney had returned to Nurse Pine and Nurse Townend's place in Pembridge Gardens, London.

On 16 May a letter was sent to WSPU members on Mrs Pankhurst's behalf reminding them of the risks of joining the deputation to see the King. Grace Roe explained the timing: 'The afternoon rather than the evening has been chosen in order that any attempt on the part of the police to repeat the outrages of Black Friday may be more easily detected.' Deputations to Parliament which risked assaults by the police had lately been abandoned. 'It is only a handful of politicians who stand between us and victory.' She called on the members to remember 'the women who at this very moment are being tortured by forcible feeding which is more than enough to rouse us to action'.[3] In fact the battle lines had been drawn since the end of February when the King refused to meet the deputation.

A photograph of Mrs Pankhurst on the front page of the *Daily Mirror* on 22 May showed her trying to present a petition to the King but being arrested at the gates of Buckingham Palace. She is being grabbed around the waist by Chief Inspector Francis Rolfe, losing her hat, her size two feet dangling in mid-air. She was bundled off to Holloway to continue serving her sentence.

One thousand five hundred policemen, and many more on horses, were on duty surrounding the Palace on 21 May 1914. Cordons were thrown round all the entrances and crowds, which started to gather at three o'clock, were mostly dispersed by the police, although gangs of medical students, regulars at suffragette meetings, proved difficult to move on. Traditionally conservative in their views, doctors had fiercely resisted the entry of women into their profession. Elizabeth Garrett Anderson, Britain's first woman doctor, had to overcome years of opposition and obstructionism. The suffragettes' insistent campaign mobilised many trainee doctors into action. A suffragette on horseback reconnoitred the scene and at four o'clock a vanguard of women appeared. *The Times* reported:

> The police had barely time to close their ranks before a shout went up and Mrs Pankhurst, looking very weak, was pushed forward by her supporters right into the arms of the police. She might have been roughly handled had not Chief Inspector Rolfe lifted her into his arms and carried her within the cordon guarding the front gates of the palace. She was helped into a waiting motor car and driven away.[4]

The suffragettes rushed at the police and one woman 'felled an officer with a club'. The first women arrested were 'elderly and all bedraggled' and had to 'run the gauntlet of an unsympathetic crowd as they were marched off'. Only one woman breached the inner cordon in front of the Palace and got to within twenty steps of the main gate but slipped and fell.[5]

This petition to King George V was the last time the suffragettes would go en masse to protest. Nellie Higginson came from Preston where she was running the branch while Edith Rigby was in hiding in Ireland. Nellie was one of the 'wild women' caught up at the Palace gates. All the working-class women who took part were advised to leave their homes spick and span and to cook enough food for their families before going on the deputation. Nellie's friends helped out in her health food shop; one took in her son and daughter for a few days. On the morning many suffragettes waited in a house loaned to them in Grosvenor Place overlooking Buckingham Palace and organised themselves into groups. Just before three o'clock Nellie and her comrades left the house ten abreast, taking the police by surprise. They passed newspaper placards announcing 'Bayonets to meet the Women!' but they marched on. They intended that if one woman was knocked over they would push forward, but this proved impossible: 'The Whitehall police maimed us, they knocked us about the shoulders and we were all of us black and blue the next day,' said Nellie.[6] Sixty-six women and two men were arrested that day. Nellie Higginson slipped away from the riot and went to a safe house. That evening she and others were handed stones and told to break the windows of a public house in Whitehall. Nellie was sentenced to four months in Holloway, went on hunger and thirst strike and was released on a Cat and Mouse licence after being on hunger strike for two weeks. She was rearrested, served three days, and, extremely unwell, was released again on licence; her return to prison was only prevented by the outbreak of war.

Mrs Daisy Parsons took up her position in front of the new statue of Queen Victoria at Buckingham Palace. She noticed many people looking out of the Palace's open windows. There were detectives on the roof and everyone seemed to be waiting for the arrival of the deputation. Between Daisy and the Palace was a long line of policemen and a space – a no woman's land – across which the suffragettes would dash and try to break through the cordon. Daisy saw women darting out, 'the police would catch them and fling them back into the crowd. Then the young men in the crowd would turn on them, beat them, tear their clothes off, pull their hair and shout: "You ought to be burnt!" ' Eventually the mounted police 'came at a gallop and drove the crowd away'.[7] Daisy Parsons was pushed with the suffragettes down Birdcage Walk and saw 'a young woman in the midst of a jeering mob facing her tormentors'. An on-duty soldier pushed her and when she said 'How dare you', he struck her in the face with his fist. Daisy heard an East End male supporter saying, 'What we have to fear is the toffs in silk hats, not the poor people.'[8]

Charlotte Drake from Canning Town, wife of Tom, a labourer, and mother of two girls, aged four and two, volunteered to be on the deputation. Familiar with police handling in the East End, Charlotte was taken aback by their brutal conduct in broad daylight in front of the Palace. She saw lines of policemen charge the women outside Wellington Gate: 'our women were splendid. The policemen got hold of them in dozens and threw them back amongst the crowd ... the women came again, and each time they came back the police took greater liberties with them – twisting their arms, punching them and tearing at their hair.'[9]

Charlotte Drake and May Billinghurst were not arrested. Charlotte remembered May's determination to take her place in her wheeled chair: 'I was beside her. They threw us back but we returned. Two policemen picked up the tricycle with Miss Billinghurst in it, turned it over, and dropped her on the ground.'[10] Charlotte had the strength to pick up May and lift her back in. 'We straightened the machine as much as we could, rested a little to take breath, and struggled on again. The police would knock us about.' Charlotte and May were separated, Charlotte went 'flying one way she another. I tried to find her. It seemed as though the earth had swallowed her.'[11]

Ada Wright accompanied Mrs Pankhurst and her bodyguards and was one of the sixty-two women arrested that day, 'after much buffeting and rough handling'. She spent the night at Canon Row police station and was sentenced to a month in Holloway. To her annoyance her fine had been paid and she was released. Afraid that Ada might die if she was force-fed again, her sister had paid the fine. Ada did not discover what her sister had done for ten years, but at the time she was furious, feeling guilty for betraying the Cause.

Earlier, on 21 May, a flat in Lauderdale Mansions, Maida Vale, had been raided by two Special Branch officers, who found a suffragette 'arsenal'. Nellie Hall, who used the alias 'Nellie Roberts', was a WSPU organiser, her mother Martha (Pattie), father Leonard and younger sister Emmeline, and Julia Jameson and Helen Arnes, were arrested in the possession of half a hundredweight of pebbles that had been brought to London from Southend. Black bags for carrying the stones, three hammers, an axe and suffrage literature were also found.

The Hall family were old Manchester friends of the Pankhursts: Mrs Pattie Hall had joined the WSPU in 1903. In the days following the Black Friday riot she was sent to prison for two weeks for throwing stones and causing wilful damage.[12] The year before, Nellie (then sixteen) had marched around Winson Green Prison singing songs to suffragette prisoners. Nellie worked for two years in the Union's Birmingham branch, and in July 1913 she threw a brick through the window of the prime minister's car during his visit to the city. She was sentenced to three weeks in Winson Green and after being on hunger strike for eight days was released on licence suffering from mumps. She vanished and was working as a prisoners' secretary at WSPU headquarters when she was arrested.

Sylvia Pankhurst provides details about the weapons at Lauderdale Mansions: 'twenty-two pieces of tubing containing gunpowder with fuses attached, a large number of hammers, and seventy-two black calico bags, with strings to tie round the waist, some of them filled with flints.'[13] While the police were carrying out their search, Helen Arnes, a widow from Croydon, had turned up and was found to be carrying a basket of stones covered with lettuce leaves. It was suspected that the flat was the headquarters of a window-smashing raid in protest at the likely arrest of Mrs Pankhurst. The women were charged at Marylebone Police Court with 'conspiracy to commit malicious damage and with injury to property'. In July Miss Jameson and Mrs Arnes were acquitted.

The next morning at Bow Street Court there was pandemonium as the prisoners and their friends filled the court: all the women who had been arrested refused to give their names and were referred to by numbers. Shouts drowned out the voice of the magistrate, Sir John Dickinson, and most of the charges were dropped. A woman addressed as '99' admitted to breaking three panes of glass at the royal storekeeper's premises in Buckingham Palace Road, and said defiantly: 'If the King won't hear voteless women, he must hear broken glass.'[14] Women who refused to walk were dragged into court on their knees, number '3' threw paper missiles and copies of *The Suffragette* at Sir John Dickinson, and 'a little elderly woman wearing a nurse's uniform also struggled into the dock'.[15] One of the women, who had to be held in the dock by four constables, managed to wrench her arms free and tried to climb over the rails. When a bag of flour was thrown from the body of the court the magistrate cleared the place and eight women were arrested in the street outside. Sir John Dickinson even caught the boot thrown at him from the dock by prisoner number '11'. When two women were placed in the dock together they talked non-stop; one of them called the magistrate 'a rusty tool of a corrupt government' and the other a 'wicked old man'. Three women were charged, the rest refused to be bound over and the charges were dropped.[16]

During Nellie Hall's several appearances in court until she was eventually sent to Holloway to serve three months, her behaviour grew ever more defiant. She and her mother were carried into Marylebone Police Court on 29 May in a very weak state, but Nellie still disrupted proceedings by interrupting and shouting that she refused to be tried. On 2 June Nellie and Grace Roe were again in court. Nellie's mother was too ill to attend, and the charges against Mrs Hall were dropped. As Nellie was being carried from court she called out: 'It doesn't matter, we shall go on fighting, fighting, fighting.'[17] On 8 July Nellie and Grace were sent to Holloway for three months, convicted of 'having unlawfully conspired with others to commit damage to windows'. Nellie Hall had been force-fed 137 times while on remand. When asked if she wanted to make any reply to the charge she said that every day they were in prison 'more militancy would take place and more houses would be burnt'.[18] With the outbreak of war on 4 August she was still in prison, and would not be released until the WSPU agreed to end militancy in return for the release of all their prisoners.

Outraged at reports of the riot at the Palace gates, the next day Grace Marcon, alias 'Freda Graham', went to the Venetian Room in the National Gallery and attacked five paintings by Bellini. Despite tight security, two plain-clothes detectives, two attendants and several students in the room could not prevent her from using the hammer hidden in her coat and making a 'promiscuous attack on any picture that she could reach'. In court Grace 'kept up a continual tirade from the prisoners' enclosure and was held fast by two policemen throughout the proceedings'.[19] When she was sentenced as 'Freda Graham' to six months in prison, Grace, referring to the sex industry, said: 'What are five paintings compared with eighty thousand pictures by the greatest artist of all [God] which are being defaced, damaged and degraded by men each night.'[20]

Grace embarked on a secret hunger and thirst strike for fifteen days. She was released on 5 June on a Cat and Mouse licence and taken to Mouse Castle to recover. Grace had become delirious through starvation and dehydration and cut off all her hair, believing that it was growing into her head like 'red hot wires and that if I could cut it off the pain would be somehow reduced. I remembered I had scissors in my case and crawled out of bed to the other side of the cell where the case lay and cut almost all of my hair off. I had not the strength to get back to bed and lay on the floor all night until someone came in the morning and lifted me into bed.'[21]

Sylvia Pankhurst said Grace Marcon was so weak that she was unable to make a statement for three weeks. The nurse who was caring for her told *The Suffragette*: 'I cannot get a statement yet because she talks so very slowly that it would take three or four days, and that if she talks about prison at all she has a wretched night.'[22]

When the police arrived to rearrest Grace on 12 June, the day her licence expired, they found her too ill to be moved. She kept her real name from the press to avoid embarrassing her parents: her father, the Reverend Walter Marcon, the Rector of Edgefield, near Cromer, took over from his father as the vicar of St Peter and St Paul's when he died. Grace's father's love of the village was so great that he moved the church stone by stone from its original location a mile away, where Edgefield had been abandoned when the village was depopulated by the Black Death in the fourteenth century. He raised the money and did much of the physical work himself.[23]

On 29 May 1914 *The Suffragette* escalated the propaganda war against the government and the police in its leading article 'Women Savagely Attacked'. Christabel wrote: 'The savage cruelty to which the deputation members were treated can best be summed up by saying that Black Friday was outdone.'[24] Those who witnessed the events were 'utterly revolted by the appalling attacks upon this peaceful deputation and affirm that they had not before believed such an outrage possible', and descriptions followed of the women being attacked with police truncheons, kicked by police horses and being thrown to the ground. Janie Allan proudly reported: 'Some of the women rushed through the gates [of the Palace] and railings and climbed onto the crossbars, while others attacked the police and tried to force them out of the way. There were a considerable number of police agents present in plain clothes, most of them being men of a very low and brutal type.'[25] According to Janie the police violence continued inside Hyde Park police station. She heard that the police continued to pummel the women and throw them around in 'a savage fashion' and the women responded by breaking windows. The *Daily Mirror* reported that 'the sound of breaking glass from inside the station was almost continuous'.[26] When one of the women tried to leave the room, unsure if she was being arrested or not, a policeman told her: 'I'll have the nose off your face if you move another step.'[27] Gladys Schütze, who was with Mrs Pankhurst on 21 May, made a sworn statement:

> I was standing against the railings of Constitution Hill, a completely passive resister, when one of the constables who was mounted on a grey horse hit me on the head with his baton and deliberately proceeded to back his horse into me with the result that I received a violent kick in the lower abdomen which completely incapacitated me ... I heard one constable advise another to take a woman by the breasts.[28]

On 23 May the police raided Lincoln's Inn House for the second time that year and 'took possession' of the WSPU's headquarters, arresting Grace Roe, who had replaced Annie Kenney as Christabel's deputy. The police found 'bludgeons' similar to those used by the women at Buckingham Palace. While Grace Roe was on remand Arthur Marshall, who was on holiday, arranged to have apomorphine hydrochloride, an emetic drug, smuggled into Holloway in a letter from Arthur Barnett, his firm's managing clerk. The hope was that it would make Grace violently sick when she was force-fed and she would be released early. However, the drug was discovered and when the case was heard in the middle of June Arthur Barnett was let off with a £10 fine and five guineas costs, but only if Hatchett-Jones, Bisgood, Marshall and Thomas, 'a firm of the highest standing', refused to act for the WSPU again.[29]

Dr Flora Murray wrote to editors of the *Glasgow Herald* explaining the difference between bromide and bromine which she classified as hypnotics, and the emetic apomorphine hydrochloride. She said that apomorphine caused vomiting and exhaustion, while bromides reduced muscular resistance and sensitivity in the pharynx and helped prevent vomiting. Apomorphine would depress higher brain function and cause dullness of the brain and helped create a drug habit. Dr Murray released the results of urine tests that had been carried out on Kitty Marion and Olive Beamish, showing high levels of bromide, and said it was unlikely to have been self-administered as it was 'a bulky drug' and difficult to smuggle into prison, and she did not believe it had ever been attempted. A hypnotic drug like bromide or bromine 'could only be harmful' if given to prisoners, whereas in her opinion an emetic 'might be useful'. Murray believed any women being dosed with bromide in prison were being placed at 'considerable risk and it is not surprising that a prisoner should have attempted to have escaped this by procuring an emetic'. She speculated: 'This woman was on remand and had to prepare her defence, she needed to have all her faculties alert, and no doubt tried in this way to counteract the evil effects of the sedative by rejecting it.'[30]

Two new suffragettes went on a mission to the British Museum on 23 May: Nellie Hay, an older Scottish woman, and her accomplice, Annie Wheeler. Even though the women were kept under close observation one of them smashed a glass case containing a mummy. They were charged with malicious damage. Nellie Hay was also charged with obstructing the police and was sentenced to one month in prison. Annie Wheeler was to serve two months and went on hunger and thirst strike and was force-fed and released just a few days before the end of her sentence in July. Two days later the British Museum announced that in future women would only be admitted to the galleries by ticket on condition they produced a 'satisfactory recommendation from a person willing to be responsible for their behaviour'.[31] News of the attack on the mummy case prompted the National Gallery, the Wallace Collection and the Tate Gallery to close their buildings until further notice. The *Standard* described how American women wishing to visit the National Gallery had to be accompanied by one of the American Embassy secretaries. The Tate Gallery and Wallace Collection insisted on a letter of recommendation from public officials such as ambassadors, MPs and judges, accepting 'all responsibility for the acts of the bearer'.[32]

In Hyde Park members of the public vented their anger on suffragettes who tried to address a meeting from a wagon. An elderly male sympathiser who introduced the meeting made a speech and was not molested, but as soon as a woman tried to talk the crowd drowned out her voice by singing and shouting. As the women stepped down the wagon was overturned and smashed to pieces by the crowd. That evening a baying crowd of diners turned on suffragettes at Lyons' Corner House in Piccadilly. When two suffragettes entered and started handing out WSPU leaflets, they were pelted with cutlery, crockery, bread and cake. The women were put in the lift for their own safety but diners and policemen were waiting for them. For fifteen minutes the women were stuck in the lift between floors while cutlery, crockery and glasses were thrown through the metal grilles.[33]

On 24 May 1914 Sylvia Pankhurst's East London Federation of Suffragettes got into a fight with police when they tried to rearrest her as she led a procession to Victoria Park. She was chained to her bodyguard of twenty women and was walking to the park for their 'Women's May Day Rally'. As they approached the park gates a large group of mounted police cut them off and corralled them through the gates which were then locked. 'In the fight which followed the police used their truncheons freely, and the women, who fought desperately with fists and staves to prevent the arrest, were aided by male sympathisers.'[34] The fight continued until the chains were broken and Sylvia was taken to Holloway to continue her sentence, where she immediately went on hunger strike. She was released on 30 May.

Emmeline Pankhurst's letter to Ethel Smyth of 29 May contained details of 21 May. Referring to a story in the Sunday press that said she was dead, Mrs Pankhurst wrote:

I don't think McKenna would have been sorry if that had been the result of the horrible bear's hug that huge policeman [Chief

Inspector Rolfe] gave me when he seized me. Fortunately for me I have 'younger bones' or my ribs would have been fractured. After it I suffered from a form of nausea just like very bad sea-sickness; however, it's all over now and I am getting back my strength slowly but surely ... There has been less waste of tissue [weight loss] than on previous occasions and the blood poisoning was not quite so bad either.[35]

For many of the women arrested on 21 May it had been their first militant protest, and almost all of them went on hunger and thirst strike. Emmeline wrote: 'Think what it means for a first experience of prison to do the whole thing, <u>and be ready to do it again!</u> O my splendid ones.'[36]

The month of June saw another eruption of violence, a frustrated response to the entrenched political position, the force-feeding of women, the reluctance of the church to condemn the way the government was treating suffragette prisoners and the government's strategy to shut down the Union. The WSPU reminded the people of Emily Davison's sacrifice at the Derby. In Epsom, security was tight for the six weeks leading up to the 1914 Derby. Fearing that the course might be attacked by suffragettes, it was guarded day and night, and more than a thousand uniformed and just as many plain-clothes policemen were on duty. There was a 'close cordon' of constables at Tattenham Corner and two more sets of railings were installed.

The Suffragette of 5 June ran Emily Davison's article 'The Price of Liberty' – and on 12 June announced the thrashing of Dr Forward (for the second time) on his way to Holloway by two suffragettes; the destruction of Wargrave Church in Berkshire on 1 June; and the burning of All Saints' Church Breadsall, Derbyshire, on 5 June. While some leading churchmen wrote to *The Times* and other newspapers condemning force-feeding, this did not prevent WSPU members burning down cherished historic churches. It was not official policy but the leadership did not try to stop suffragettes from engaging in perhaps the most shocking form of militant protest. Mrs Pankhurst could have stopped attacks on churches but chose not to.

The cartoonist Will Dyson's drawing of 'Miss Davison' for the *Daily Herald* was shocking: a walking skeleton in a fashionable hat and shoes wearing a sandwich board saying 'Votes for Women', with the Houses of Parliament in the background. On 6 June a memorial service was held at St George's, Bloomsbury. Her friend Mary Leigh started the Emily Wilding Davison Club (which existed until the 1960s) and from 1916 Sarah Benett would take annual pilgrimages to Morpeth for a service at the grave. A letter came from Emily's mother thanking Rose Lamartine Yates for her 'kind sympathy and appreciation of my dear daughter's great sacrifice. It was not made in vain. That I feel and take great comfort in the thought.'[37] It shows Margaret Davison coming to terms with her daughter's protest. She tells Rose that she read a letter Tom Lamartine Yates had published in the *Daily Sketch:* 'I have let several of my neighbours read it and they all say it is most touching and I felt it myself.'[38]

On 7 June worshippers celebrating the noon Mass at the Brompton Oratory ejected more than twenty suffragettes who interrupted the service. At the beginning of the service a woman ran up the aisle towards the altar shouting, 'In the name of Christ stop torturing women' and suffragette supporters sitting in the front two pews, and elsewhere in the church, stood up and chanted: 'O, God, save Emmeline Pankhurst and all our noble prisoners. O rouse this church and its priests to put an end to torture in the name of the blessed Joan of Arc.'[39] Indignant members of the congregation 'promptly rose to expel the invaders' who were labelled 'furies' and 'wild women' in the newspapers the next day, and a 'free fight' lasted ten minutes.[40]

One of the suffragettes had teeth knocked out, and a man who placed his gloved hand over the mouth of the woman chanting at the altar had his fingers bitten. Before one woman was arrested and bundled into a taxi, a female member of the congregation ran after her, pulled her back and hit her in the face. At Westminster Police Court 'Christine Adams' was charged with brawling, and 'Mary Fousten', a married woman from Bayswater, was charged with obstruction and disorderly conduct. At Westminster Cathedral that evening the service was interrupted by a woman entering one of the pulpits, waving her arms and shouting: 'In the presence of the Blessed Sacrament I protest against the forcible feeding of women.'[41] 'Christine Adams' denied she was responsible for any riotous behaviour, blaming the verger and the congregation who 'bashed her face', and she served a month in prison in the second division.[42]

Two Norman churches were burned out on either side of the first anniversary of Emily Davison's protest, Wargrave Parish Church near Wokingham, and All Saints' Church, Breadsall. Although no WSPU members were charged for either attack, three postcards were left at the scene: 'To the Government Hirelings and Women Torturers' on one side and on the reverse, 'A resort to brutality and torture. Let the Church follow its own precepts before it is too late. No surrender'; on another, 'A Reply To Torture'; and on the third, 'Blessed are those that suffer persecution for justice sake, for theirs is the kingdom of heaven.'[43] The destruction of the church at Breadsall with its medieval chained books was mourned. Although no suffragist literature was found in those ruins the police strongly suspected that Eileen Casey was involved, and Hilda Cross, a friend of Kitty Marion. A hatpin was found near a small window through which the arsonists had entered the church. Locals reported hearing a loud explosion but by the time firemen arrived the blaze had taken hold of the building. Eileen Casey, who we last saw with her sister setting fire to a pillar box in Bradford, was arrested in Nottingham on 24 June, the day of the visit of King George V and Queen Mary. When Eileen was searched, a Derbyshire guidebook which included All Saints' Church, was found, suggesting to the police that she was one of the arsonists. Eileen had been travelling the country in disguise for eight months on an expired Cat and Mouse licence.[44] She was spotted in Nottingham the night before with a local militant, Miss Wallis, by Detective Inspector Wright of Leeds, who knew Eileen was on the run from her three-month sentence in Armley Gaol in 1913. The next morning Wright saw her leave the Mansion House Temperance Commercial Hotel with a green dressing-case and a string bag, walking round the market square and inspecting the grandstand that had been installed for the royal visit. She was arrested. Eileen Casey admitted her identity and that she was on the run from Armley Gaol. She did not admit to burning down Breadsall Church but her case contained an arsonist's paraphernalia: firelighters, two torches, a glass cutter, a small bottle of benzene, matches, a road map of Great Britain, pocket knives, scissors, rubber shoes and suffragist literature. In the string bag was chocolate, twenty feet of fuse, a detonator, sixteen ounces of explosive and a notebook with information about other buildings the suffragettes had tried to attack.

In Nottingham Police Court Eileen Casey was charged with 'loitering with intent to commit a felony'. She refused to be tried and did not stop talking throughout the proceedings, twined her arms round the dock rails and repeated incessantly: 'This will go on till women get the vote.' She admonished the magistrate and said she would not keep quiet: 'I am not going to listen and I am not going to let anyone else listen', and warned, 'The next time you will find something more important ... I hope I shall be more dangerous before I finish.'[45] When Eileen was remanded for eight days she fought with five policemen in the dock and Charlie Marsh, the organiser of Nottingham WSPU, and other members cheered and yelled and were carried out of court kicking and screaming. She went on hunger and thirst strike, and because of her low weight was not force-fed at Nottingham Prison, but was taken to London to serve her sentence in Holloway, where she was fed by nasal tube.[46] On 2 July she was returned to Nottingham, remanded for eight days then sent back to London and fed three times a day. If the law's intention was to grind Eileen down so that she would give up the hunger strike it was mistaken. On 8 July she was transferred from Holloway to Winson Green and continued to refuse to eat. For the first time in her suffragette prison career, her time at Winson Green revealed that she suffered from Raynaud's disease (problems with the circulation which cause the fingers and toes to go numb in cold weather) and tuberculosis of the skin. One doctor wrote: 'she is an extremely delicate woman, at present in a very poor state of health, and in an unfit state to stand forcible feeding, I consider she is running a great risk to her life and cannot continue long as matters are at present without great danger.'[47] A doctor who had treated her as an outpatient at the London Hospital reported: 'she has been suffering from lupus erythematosus, affecting the cheeks, ears, and feet. Her circulation is poor, and chilblains have occurred from time to time.'[48] This evidence was disregarded, and on 27 July 1914 Eileen was sentenced at Nottingham to fifteen months with hard labour, for 'feloniously and knowingly having in her possession certain explosives ... under such circumstances as to give reasonable suspicion that she did not have the said explosives with a lawful object'.[49] She only served a week, her long sentence cut short by the First World War.

*

On 8 June, a year to the day that Emily Davison died, 'Laura Grey' (the stage name of the suffragette Lavender Guthrie) was found on the floor of her rooms in Jermyn Street, St James's, dying of an overdose of veronal, her drug of addiction. Despite the best efforts of the police surgeon Dr Percy Edmonds, Lavender died without regaining consciousness. When she was discovered by her char-lady, Mrs Spicer, several empty bottles of veronal tablets – a sleeping draught – were found in the room. The coroner, Dr Ingleby Oddie, and the jury returned a verdict of 'suicide during temporary insanity'.[50]

This was the final chapter in the story of a vulnerable young woman who had gone to the bad, a 'fallen woman'. As the newspapers made the connection between 'Laura Grey' and suffragette Lavender Guthrie who had been arrested five times and convicted four, they blamed her involvement with the militants for her tragic end: 'A Girl's Downfall: From Militancy to Suicide'.[51] A letter from Mabel Tuke with a hunger-strike medal and one silver bar was read out to underline the depth of Lavender's involvement:

> Dear Soldier in the Women's Army, no words can possibly express the feelings of the Committee towards you and the other comrades who have so nobly and with utter disregard of the self, suffered pain of the hunger-strike and horrors of forcible feeding in prison, at the prompting of duty and loyalty to the cause you so passionately love, and which is the dearest of life to us all.[52]

Lavender's chaotic private life was picked over at the inquest. She retired from a four-year career with the WSPU at the end of 1912, after serving a six-month sentence for breaking a window on 4 March, during which time she had been force-fed. On 19 June 1914, Antonia Moser, a suffragette and private detective, described meeting Lavender Guthrie in 1912:

> While she was a member of the Union she led, according to her own statement to me, a perfectly moral and upright life. About eight-een months ago she sought my advice in reference to a certain man who had obtained an improper influence over her. Whilst in prison she had been force-fed and this had apparently a very bad effect

upon her delicate system – and coupled with the man's desertion
had caused her to take drugs.[53]

Lavender Guthrie also drank absinthe, took veronal and became a
prostitute. A photograph taken when she was presented at Court in
1907 appeared on the front page of the *Daily Mirror* under the headline, 'Mysterious Death of Actress-Suffragette'.[54]

The coroner Dr Ingleby Oddie did not spare her mother's feelings when he gave details about Lavender leading 'an immoral life'.
He mentioned the many letters and telegrams addressed to her 'by
men seeking appointments with her'. Oddie thought it was regrettable that, despite her good home and education, she should have
'associated with these law-breakers [the WSPU] … and [it] raises a
very strong presumption as to her mental unsoundness'. He wondered if 'the mental and physical excitement of breaking plate-glass
windows, assaulting policemen, going to prison, being force-fed,
did certainly increase the derangement of a mind that was already
unbalanced'.[55]

During the past eighteen months Lavender Guthrie had frequented
nightclubs. Mrs Baillie Guthrie reported that her daughter had left
home at the end of 1912. The inquest heard that Lavender had written several letters on 28 May which were found on her mantelpiece.
One was to her landlord – 'I am sorry to have to leave the flat in this
way, and to have given you so much trouble' – and enclosed money
for the rent. The last letter Lavender wrote on 5 June was addressed
to her 'dear little mother': 'I am hoping … this foolish epistle … will
not be a great shock to you. I have given you so many… as far as I can
remember I owe no money at all.' Lavender predicted the coroner
would blame her 'temporary insanity' for her act, but 'as a matter of
fact I think this is about the sanest thing I have yet done. I am simply
very, very tired of things in general and cannot see that the world will
progress any the worse for me being out of it.'[56]

Dr Edmonds told the court that Lavender had died of heart failure
and veronal poisoning, and that the postmortem revealed that she had
been 'addicted to alcoholic drinks for some time'. Edmonds kept the
bombshell until last: 'She was expecting to become a mother, and in
a woman of her kind of life he thought she must have known of her
condition.'[57]

The WSPU came out fighting. At a meeting in Knightsbridge on 15 June, the link between Lavender's downfall and militancy was repudiated. A letter to *The Times* was denounced as a 'hypocritical sham'. The writer had blamed militancy as the critical stepping-stone leading to her downfall. At the meeting it was asked why the names of Lavender's 'gentlemen friends' were not 'dragged into the light of day'. The press were called 'vampires' and derided for using Lavender's sad end to try and intimidate women from joining their organisation.[58]

On 9 June, the police raided the temporary headquarters of the WSPU at their Westminster office and shop at 17 Tothill Street. It was a sign of the government's determination to end the militant campaign. Since the raid on Lincoln's Inn House on 23 May, the police had been scouring the offices for names and addresses of subscribers to the funds. The women had learned to be more careful about such sensitive information and the police found nothing of interest at Tothill Street.[59] Now the suffragette campaign was run from Mouse Castle, the home of the Brackenbury family – at least until the police raided them on 12 June. They found Grace Marcon being looked after by two nurses and seized documents but made no arrests. The WSPU announced they would be returning to their office in Tothill Street, where they would remain until the end of July.[60]

The campaign for women's suffrage in the East End of London continued to be dynamic. Despite being arrested and rearrested eight times under her current sentence (and suffering the effects of hunger, thirst and sleep strikes and force-feeding during each imprisonment) Sylvia Pankhurst continued to push the East London Federation of Suffragettes' agenda. She wrote to the prime minister asking him to meet her and a deputation of working women on the evening of 10 June. He refused. She sent a reply reminding Asquith that 'a large proportion of the women of East London are living under terrible conditions ... the women are impatient to take a constitutional part in moulding the conditions under which they have to live'. Sylvia told him she would undoubtedly be rearrested and returned to Holloway to resume her hunger strike, and that when she was released on the usual Cat and Mouse licence she would continue her protest 'at the door of the Strangers' Entrance to the House of Commons and shall not take either food or water until you agree to receive this deputation'. Then she raised the stakes: 'I know very well from what has happened in the past that I am risking my life … because so far you have almost invariably refused the appeals which suffragists have made to you. But I feel it is my duty to take this course, and I shall not give way, although it may end in my death.'[61] Asquith refused.

Looking 'worn and ill', Sylvia left the ELFS headquarters in Bow on the evening of 10 June determined to reach Westminster. After making a short speech she was carried on a bed on the shoulders of six men, preceded by a clergyman. They did not get far before she and her stretcher-bearers were separated and ambushed by the police in a side street. Sylvia was taken to Holloway and a clergyman re-formed the deputation of nine women and three men, and walked through the City, along Fleet Street and Somerset House. They made their way separately to St Stephen's Entrance and asked to see the prime minister, to be told he would not meet them. The deputation 'behaved quite peacefully' and were eventually seen by Sir William Pollard Byles, the Liberal MP for Shipley, and were escorted to an outer lobby by Percy Illingworth, MP for Salford North. Mrs Scurr told Illingworth she thought it very unfair Mr Asquith 'would never receive a deputation of working women', and had to be content with Illingworth repeating the usual mantra that the prime minister could not 'depart from his usual practice'.[62]

In the hungry, thirsty and sleepless eight days and nights leading up to her release on a Cat and Mouse licence on 18 June, Sylvia's time 'crawled by, weary and painful from illness, otherwise calm … My thoughts were occupied with the struggle before me … I had never believed myself so near the limit of my endurance as the doctors in prison, and out, had assured me to be the case'.[63] She was taken by taxi to her home in Old Ford Road by two wardresses and was met by a crowd. True to her threat, as soon as Sylvia arrived in Bow she asked to be taken to the House of Commons where she was determined to lie down outside and make her protest. Shocked by her gaunt appearance, local women cried at the sight of her. Norah Smyth drove Sylvia to Westminster in her car. After much wrangling by Keir Hardie, George Lansbury and Henry Nevinson, they were able to tell her Asquith would receive six members of an East End women's deputation on 20 June.

Sylvia did not go on the deputation but appointed Mrs Scurr to lead the women and prepared a statement for her to read: 'I did not care to go. Let these working women speak for themselves; it was for this

I had struggled.'[64] Julia Scurr had been a Poor Law Guardian in Poplar since 1907 and was closely involved with the running of Poplar workhouse. She was the mother of three children, aged thirteen, eleven and ten. Her husband, John Scurr, was an accountant and trade union activist and a friend of George Lansbury.[65] Two weeks before Julia led the deputation John Scurr stood as a socialist candidate at the Ipswich by-election, his fourth attempt to become a Member of Parliament, and was defeated.

Julia Scurr introduced the prime minister to her comrades and the broad political purpose of their visit: 'We are members of the East London Federation of Suffragettes ... We represent the general popular movement for Votes for Women in East London, which is of tremendous numerical strength and enthusiasm and consists of both men and women.' She asked Asquith to consider the position of women wage-earners and the care and education of children, and housing. Mrs Scurr highlighted the calamitous consequences for women when: 'Our husbands die on the average at a much earlier age than do men of other classes. Modern industrialism kills them off rapidly, both by accident and overwork ... we know by bitter experience the terrible struggle with absolute want that our widowed sisters have to face from no fault of their own.' She ended her speech: 'We are here today to demand a vote for every woman over the age of twenty-one years. Miss Pankhurst is giving her life for the purpose of fighting for this vote.'[66]

The other five women were Daisy Parsons; Mrs Jane Savoy, a sweated homeworker who made brushes; Mrs Jessie Payne, a bootmaker; Mrs Bird, married to a transport worker who earned twenty-five shillings a week to support their family of six children; and Mrs Watkins, the first paid organiser of the East London Federation of the WSPU.[67]

Herbert Asquith's response seemed to imply he was a convert. He told the women:

> You have each given me special illustrations, drawn from your own experience, or from the experience of your leaders, to show that this is not a mere rhetorical statement, but does correspond to the actual facts of East End life ... If the change has to come, we must face it boldly, and make it thoroughgoing and democratic in its basis.[68]

Asquith said he would ask the home secretary to consider the matter of hunger-striking prisoners: 'I am sure there is not the faintest disposition in any quarter to be vindictive.' When Asquith attempted to divide the militant suffragist movement by asking the deputation to repudiate militancy he was disappointed by Julia Scurr's unequivocal response: 'While our organisation has not at present committed arson, we do not want to criticise the other organisations, we know that in the past men have used all sorts of methods.'[69]

Despite 'a general rejoicing' – even Sylvia Pankhurst sensed an 'atmosphere of tremendous hope' at the news of Asquith's positive remarks – events over the following six weeks would prove the prime minister's encouraging words to be hollow. Nothing changed in prisons. The WSPU was reminded that there would be no let-up in the government's attempt to undermine their activities and dismantle their organisation. In the House of Commons on 11 June, before Asquith's meeting with the East End women, Home Secretary Reginald McKenna, informed by the 'unlimited correspondence' he had received on the subject, had debated the four ways of 'dealing with the suffragettes' that had been suggested to him: 'The first was to let them die, the second was to deport them, the third was to treat them as lunatics and the fourth was to give them the franchise.'[70] McKenna declined to pursue any of the options, citing the belief that several women were prepared to die in prison and this would further help their cause. He could not legally send them out of the country, and even if he did send them to the island of St Kilda (the Scilly Isles was also suggested) 'it would have to be turned into a prison' or the authorities faced the risk that 'wealthy supporters of the movement would very quickly fit-out a yacht and take them away', and if a special prison was built the suffragettes would go on hunger strike as they had in every prison in which they were incarcerated. As they were not lunatics, it would have been illegal to treat them as such. (The suggestion of William Pringle, the Liberal MP for North-West Lanarkshire since 1910, that the Home Office invoke the Mental Deficiency Act was greeted with applause.) As for the fourth idea, McKenna brushed off the idea of giving women the vote, saying he was 'not responsible for the state of the franchise'. A letter to *The Times* published four days after the debate suggested St Helena would be a far better destination for the suffragettes: 'St Helena is a dull place, and the prospect of being sent there would be more depressing to the militant temperament than any other form of punishment. Consequently, if some of the militant leaders were transported there no others would wish to follow, and our country would be rid of these mischievous semi-lunatics.'[71]

Reginald McKenna announced on 23 June that the police would prosecute subscribers to the WSPU for any 'crimes and outrages' which were the result of articles in *The Suffragette* inciting women to violence. Also, by hiring out facilities to the Union, the owners of places where 'speeches inciting violence' had taken place were threatened with prosecution. The dedicated arsonists escalated their attacks in the week following his announcement.[72]

In the early hours of the morning of 8 July Fanny Parker and another (thought to be Ethel Moorhead) were caught by a night watchman having planted two bombs at Robert Burns's cottage in Alloway. The women also left canisters of gunpowder and oil. They had travelled there on bicycles. Calling herself 'Janet Arthur', Fanny allowed herself to be caught so that her comrade could escape.[73] 'Janet Arthur' was charged at Ayr Sheriff's Court where she was held on remand until her trial, refusing to take exercise in case 'someone was about who wanted to shoot her'. After four days of hunger and thirst strike she was offered the opportunity of spending her time on remand in a nursing home but she refused and was taken to Perth Prison where suffragette prisoners were being force-fed. Fanny refused to get dressed for the journey and arrived wrapped in blankets and was carried to the motor car. She was force-fed by nasal and stomach tubes, and by the rectum, for three days, and once by the vagina, and was released on a Cat and Mouse licence and taken by her brother, Captain Alfred Parker, to Queen Mary's Home, Chalmers Street, Edinburgh. Captain Parker told the Scottish prison authorities that neither he nor his mother had any sympathy with his sister's views, 'and no very strong hopes of being able to influence her'. He believed 'the suffragist leaders were treating his sister as a cat's paw'.[74]

On arrival in the Edinburgh nursing home, Fanny was found to be suffering extreme pain and injuries to her genital area as a result of torture masquerading as 'feeding'. The matron, Miss Shaw, and the sister, Miss Bennett, examined Fanny. Miss Bennett, who had obstetrical and gynaecological training, told Dr Chalmers Watson that the prisoner's injuries were caused by the 'rough and faulty introduction of instruments', possibly the nozzle of an enema syringe, which had been used on several occasions.

> The prisoner states that in the course of her treatment there was a discharge of thick brown material from the vagina, such a discharge being unusual with her. Local inspection of the front passage revealed distinct swelling of the vulva in its posterior part and also the presence of a raw wound on the mucus membrane of the inner and outer folds on both sides.[75]

On the morning of 18 July, Fanny Parker, having requested a full medical, was given a general anaesthetic and examined by a gynaecologist, and Dr Mabel Jones, a WSPU sympathiser. The headline appeared in *Votes for Women*, 'Inhuman Treatment of an Unconvicted Prisoner in Perth. Rectum Feeding Again Employed'.[76] On 28 July Fanny was missing, having walked 'unobserved by anybody', and vanished into thin air.

Frances Mary 'Fanny' Parker had been a member of the WSPU since 1908. Born in New Zealand, she was the niece of the future Lord Kitchener. He paid for Fanny's education at Newnham College, Cambridge, from 1896 to 1899, but was 'disgusted' by her career as a suffragette. She was arrested in Westminster on a demonstration on 14 February 1908 and served six weeks in Holloway for obstruction. Fanny and Edith Lacheur, a friend from Newnham, ran a 'suffragette dairy' in Sussex to raise money for the suffragettes' war chest. In 1911 she was a delegate at the International Suffrage Convention in Stockholm in 1911. Fanny served four months in Holloway for breaking windows in March 1912 where she met Ethel Moorhead, who liked her 'exquisite <u>madness</u>'. In 1913 Fanny was the WSPU organiser in Dundee and then Edinburgh.[77]

In the first week of July 1914, police finally moved out of Lincoln's Inn House, having caused maximum disruption to the day-to-day running of the WSPU. On 9 July, Mrs Pankhurst was arrested and taken to Holloway, and started her ninth hunger strike. Two days later she was released, extremely weak and nauseous.[78] On the evening of 16 July, Mrs Pankhurst was rearrested while trying to attend the WSPU's fundraising meeting at Holland Park Skating Rink, and was returned to prison, and released two days later.

*

Although she was a 'mouse' out on an expired licence, Annie Kenney was advertised as the main speaker at the morale- and fund-boosting meeting. Elaborate steps were taken to smuggle her out of the flat where she was staying in Maida Vale.

> The disguise decided on was rather unique. I decided to be a fair-haired, gay, flashy East End coster type … My wig was a rich gold with curls over the eyes and ears. I had beads, rings, ear-rings, a feather in my hat, a silk dress, a fancy coat, a feather boa and two inches added to a pair of patent leather shoes. It always took me two or three taxi-cabs to take us to a meeting when in disguise, so that no taxi-cab driver could be traced. News came just before we started for the hall that all detectives, excepting one, were at the main entrance.[79]

When Annie and a friend arrived they went to the side door, 'chatting animatedly all the way which was part of the act. The escort always had to start a voluminous conversation just as I was getting out of the taxi.'[80] They got inside the hall of the skating rink and were taken to a changing room and 'a suffragette, my height, changed into my Cockney clothes, and with profuse apologies was taken back to the seat I had been missed from. This was done so that if any spies were about it would be the one in disguise that would be scented and followed.'[81]

As soon as the meeting started Annie marched boldly on to the platform.

> Storms of cheering took place and enthusiasm was at fever height. Scotland Yard outwitted once more did much to help towards the success of any meeting. We raised about sixteen thousand pounds. Just before the last speaker had finished her speech I left the stage and another disguise awaited me. It was very, very ordinary, the chief features being furs and eye-glasses, and I left with the audience, surrounded by bodyguards. I left by the front entrance and I walked under the noses of the detectives, the fair-haired damsel not far behind me being scrutinised and watched by those who were

waiting to seize me and take me back to Holloway Prison. I arrived home quite safely and we laughed heartily about the scenes and began planning my next move.[82]

*

At midnight on 3 August the ultimatum the British had given to the German government to respect Belgian neutrality and withdraw their troops from Belgian soil was rejected. Britain and Germany were at war. *The Times* reported that when news of the declaration of war was made, 'the crowd [in Downing Street] expressed its feelings in loud cheering ... and gathered in front of the War Office, where patriotic demonstrations continued until the early hours of the morning'.[83] Twenty thousand people gathered around Buckingham Place in a mood of growing excitement, and when the King and Queen went down the Mall 'there was a rush for the royal carriage as it left the Palace gates ... men waved their hats and walking sticks and women fluttered their handkerchiefs'.[84] The crowds stayed until midnight, delighted when the King and Queen and Princess Mary appeared on the balcony during the evening. Hundreds milled about at Downing Street waiting for news. Three thousand men paraded in the West End singing the National Anthem and 'Rule, Britannia'.

On 13 August Mrs Pankhurst wrote to WSPU members:

It has been possible to consider what should be the course adopted by the WSPU in view of the war crisis. It is obvious that the most vigorous militancy is for the time being rendered less effective by contrast with the infinitely greater violence done in the present war not to mere property and economic prosperity alone, but to human life.[85]

She announced that it had been decided to temporarily suspend the campaign for the vote for the duration of the war which would allow the members 'to recuperate after the tremendous strain and suffering of the past two years'. For those who feared the loss of momentum Mrs Pankhurst reassured them that as soon as the conflict ended the 'WSPU will at the first possible moment step forward in to the political arena in order to compel the enactment of a measure giving votes to women on the same terms as men'.[86]

Within ten days of the declaration of war all the suffragette prisoners had been released in an amnesty, having agreed to end all militancy.

The Vote at Last!

Suffragettes and the First World War 1914–18

AT LAST

Punch cartoonist Bernard Partington used Joan of Arc to represent women enfranchised by the Representation of the People Act, which became law on 6 February 1918.

During the first six weeks of the war half a million British men responded to Earl Kitchener, the newly appointed Secretary of State for War's Call to Arms and joined the army. His stern face, moustache and pointing finger loomed out of the most famous poster of the twentieth century as he told British men their country needed them. By Christmas 1914 the men who enlisted numbered 1,186,357, and by July 1915 the figure was 2,008,912.[1]

Working-class women suffered the immediate impact of men's rush to serve their King and country. Many families whose husbands and sons had volunteered faced a sudden drop in income which was not relieved by the War Office's outdated pensions and allowance system. There was widespread female unemployment in dressmaking, millinery and the sweated trades associated with the making of clothing and accessories, as well-off women considered it unpatriotic to buy fashion when the country was at war. Very many domestic servants – the second largest group of female workers – found themselves out of work and with no roof over their heads when their employers adapted to wartime austerity. Some women whose men had been chimney sweeps, bakers, gravediggers and hearse drivers replaced them for the duration of the war, although they did not earn the same wages as the men. A fifth of all coalminers had gone to war by the end of 1914, and, while women were not allowed to work underground, they worked at the surface in other areas of coal production. The shortage of labour meant new opportunities and better pay for working-class women. Women moved into food processing and highly visible occupations in public transport, public utilities and public services. Concerned by the 'dilution' of skilled male labour, trade unions insisted that such work could be done by women only for the duration of the war.[2]

The women's suffrage movement's response to the outbreak of war varied enormously. The moderate suffragists of the NUWSS led by Mrs Fawcett continued to campaign for the vote. They also took up war work and relief work, although some NUWSS members were unhappy about appearing to support the war. On 7 August she wrote in their newspaper, *Common Cause*: 'Let us show ourselves worthy of citizenship, whether our claim to it be recognised or not.'[3] But pacifists within the NUWSS objected to women doing any kind of war work. Others, while admitting the need to continue waging the war, tried to encourage an early peace settlement and worked to alleviate some of the privations suffered by poorer women during the war.[4]

Emmeline and Christabel Pankhurst urged members of the WSPU to halt the campaign for the vote and to wholeheartedly support the government and the nation in a full war effort. In September 1914 Christabel returned to London from Paris, and in October she and Annie Kenney embarked on a six-month tour of America: Christabel's mission was to persuade the United States to join the war, while Annie was instructed to promote militant suffragism. Under Christabel's editorship the pages of *The Suffragette* were filled with increasingly anti-German and patriotic pro-war views, and some suffragettes were known to hand out white feathers, the symbol of cowardice, to young men not in uniform. In 1917 the WSPU changed its name to The Women's Party, and their newspaper was retitled *Britannia*. The party campaigned for the employment of women in munitions factories and condemned pacifism and workers who went on strike.

In 1915 Emmeline and Christabel Pankhurst, Annie Kenney and Flora Drummond toured Britain on an anti-German crusade and organised meeetings criticising trade unions that threatened to go on strike. That same year, helped by Nurse Pine and two of Annie Kenney's sisters, Mrs Pankhurst adopted four 'war babies', orphan girls born out of wedlock. In 1917 Mrs Pankhurst visited Russia and met Alexander Kerensky and advised him to be tougher with the Bolsheviks. In 1918 Mrs Pankhurst toured the United States and Canada.[5]

The arch-loyalist Ethel Smyth disagreed with the Pankhursts' jingoistic stance. She trained as a radiographer and was attached to the

13th Division of the French Army. Mary Leigh, using her maiden name of Brown to escape from her criminal record, drove ambulances for the New Zealand Expeditionary Force Hospital in Surrey, and hearses to military funerals. At the outbreak of war, Mary Allen helped establish the Women's Police Volunteers and was awarded an OBE in 1917 for her services to women's policing. Charlie Marsh's career as a suffragette who dressed up as Joan of Arc and led WSPU processions had a delightful resonance when she became chauffeur to her old enemy Lloyd George.[6]

Sylvia Pankhurst and the East London Federation of Suffragettes, and many other militants, disagreed with WSPU members who followed her mother and sister. During the war, helped by Charlotte Drake, Sylvia continued to campaign for votes for women and spoke on pacifist and socialist platforms. Sylvia and Charlotte also campaigned for better wages and safer conditions for women working in the war industries. In 1915 Sylvia renamed the East London Federation of Suffragettes as the Workers' Suffrage Federation, and provided practical help for the poorest people in the East End of London. Mother and infant welfare clinics and cut-price restaurants were opened, and small factories employing women who had lost their jobs because of the war were funded by Sylvia's organisation. Emmeline and Christabel Pankhurst were furious at Sylvia's left-wing beliefs and her attacks on wartime jingoism: in 1918 Sylvia would visit Russia and meet Lenin, later helping to found the British Communist Party.[7]

Known as 'the Maid of Peace' in Australia, Adela Pankhurst was a fiery anti-war speaker, touring Australia and New Zealand campaigning for peace. Her mother disowned her. Adela was imprisoned several times in 1917 and 1918 for making pacifist speeches.[8]

Emmeline and Fred Pethick-Lawrence were ardent campaigners for peace. Emmeline attended the Women's Peace Congress at The Hague in 1915 and was the treasurer of the International League for Peace and Freedom from 1915 to 1922. Fred was conscripted but refused to serve, appeared before a tribunal, and was sent to work on the land.[9]

Responding to the shortage of munitions on the Western Front, Mrs Pankhurst was proud to be presented with a £2,000 grant by her former bête noire, Lloyd George, the minister of munitions, to organise the 'Women's Right To Serve' procession on 17 July 1915 to recruit women into munitions and all kinds of war work. The procession organised by Grace Roe was reminiscent of the suffragette processions of the recent past: there were 90 brass bands and 125 contingents numbering 60,000 women carrying hundreds of banners urging women to 'drop every mortal thing and send them plenty of munitions'.[10] Children in nurses' uniforms and soldiers' and sailors' uniforms carried child-size banners, calling out 'God Save Our King and Country'. The *Daily Express* said: 'It was impossible for the spectators not to feel touched and stirred and proud of the women of England ... as they trooped through the rain with one fixed aim – the serving of their country in its hour of need ... At points along the route were little tables, the recruiting stations at which women were signing on.'[11]

The first positive government moves towards votes for women were made during the First World War. Millions of men who had volunteered to fight for their country lost the right to vote by default, the law stating that those absent from their home for more than one year relinquished this right, whatever the reason for their absence. This was potentially embarrassing to the government, and so plans were made to re-enfranchise them. It was also an opportunity to tidy up the awkward anomaly that a small percentage of men still did not have the vote. Plans were also made to give a limited measure of women's suffrage to reward women for their war work. The All Party Speaker's Conference of October 1916 to January 1917 made several recommendations which were eventually included in the Representation of the People Act. This, the first Act to give votes to women in Britain, became law on 6 February 1918.

The Speaker of the House of Commons was James W. Lowther, a well-known anti. Despite his views on women's suffrage Mrs Fawcett found Speaker Lowther to be a courteous man with a sense of humour, and able 'to balance contending factions'.[12] The whips in the House of Commons prepared lists from which the Speaker chose thirty-two MPs and peers from all parties to consider the franchise reform, including the re-enfranchisement of serving men who had lost their vote, the granting of votes to some women and other electoral issues. There were twelve Liberals; thirteen Conservatives and Unionists; four Irish Nationalists and three Labour members. Seventeen were women's suffrage supporters, ten were anti-suffragists, and the others undecided or unwilling to express their views whether for or against. The Conference agreed by eighteen votes to four to consider the question of women's suffrage, and by fifteen votes to six that there should be some measure of women's suffrage. The vote to give women the franchise on the same terms as men at the age of twenty-one was lost by ten votes to twelve.[13]

The conference reported at the end of January 1917, after twenty-six meetings. Speaker Lowther kept talk of women's suffrage until the last two weeks of the conference: 'I endeavoured to push off the burning question of women's suffrage as long as I could, and succeeded, for I felt that if we could agree upon other matters ... there might be a greater disposition to come to some satisfactory solution on the women's question.'[14]

Perhaps the most extraordinary moment in the parliamentary debates on the granting of the franchise to women was Herbert Asquith's apparent conversion to the cause of women's suffrage. On 28 March 1917, he was leader of the Liberal Party, but no longer prime minister, having resigned on 5 December 1916 in favour of Lloyd George, the prime minister of the coalition government. The suffragettes' greatest foe said:

> Why and in what sense, the House may ask, have I changed my views? There was in ancient Greece a poet named Stesichorus, who was ill-advised enough, in a fit of perverted [sic] inspiration, to compose a lampoon upon the character and conduct of Helen, the wife of Menelaus ... The result was that Stesichorus was smitten with blindness.

Stesichorus's sight was restored by the timely writing of another poem. Herbert Asquith rejected the notion that his eyes had been clouded on the issue, rather that he had been persuaded by the women's work during the war; 'short of actually bearing arms in the field, there is hardly a service which is contributing to the maintenance of our cause in which women have not been at least as active and efficient as men ... how could we have carried on the war without them?' He noted there had been no return to 'that detestable campaign ... and no one can contend that we are yielding to violence what we refused to concede in argument'.[15] Asquith's apparent conversion was not enduring. When standing in February 1920 for the seat of Paisley – which he won – he remarked: 'There are about fifteen thousand women on the

Electoral Register – a dim, impenetrable lot, for the most part hopelessly ignorant of politics, credulous to the last degree, and flickering
with gusts of sentiment like a candle in the wind.'[16]

When the vote was granted Christabel Pankhurst emphasised concerns about a resumption of suffragette militancy if at least some
women were not given the vote.

> The franchise could not be touched without giving votes to women
> because Mrs Pankhurst and her suffragettes would resume militancy
> as soon as the war was ended, and no Government could arrest and
> imprison women who, in the country's danger, had set aside their
> campaign to help the national cause ... The resumption of militancy
> would have found thousands of new recruits joining the militant
> ranks and even before the war women had proved their power, by
> their unaided exertions, to place any Government that resisted their
> just claim in an impossible position.[17]

Christabel wrote years later that Mrs Pankhurst told Prime Minister
Lloyd George, in March 1917: 'I want to assure you that whatever
you think can be passed, with the least discussion and debate, we are
ready to accept.' Christabel added that she and her mother 'held aloof
from the negotiations, thinking that a certain detachment would give
more effect to the potential post war militancy which was the aim of
political leaders to avert'.[18]

By the end of the war more than a million more women were
employed in the workforce than had been the case in the summer of
1914. Most of them took jobs previously done by the men who were
in the armed forces. Nine hundred thousand young, mostly working-
class, women were working in munitions factories in 1918. Within the
ranks of the munitions workers – often called munitionettes – was
the Leeds suffragette Leonora Cohen, who joined the General and
Municipal Workers' Union and helped organise a three-day strike.[19]

Women from all backgrounds worked as office workers, delivered the post, changed the signals on the railways, were coal heav-
ers, railway porters, land girls, carpenters, mechanics, policewomen
and munition workers. Women's war work gave politicians the excuse
to abandon their anti-suffrage views and vote to give some women
the vote.

Under the Representation of the People Act, a woman over the age of thirty was entitled to vote if she met one of the following criteria as a householder, the wife of a householder, the occupier of property with an annual rent of £5, a graduate of a British university, or similarly qualified but not a graduate. And so 8,400,000 women were entitled to vote in the general election of 1918. Also, women became eligible to stand as Members of Parliament, although none of the suffragists or suffragettes who stood in the general election would be successful.

After campaigning politely and peacefully for forty years and then loudly and violently for a dozen more, women's political demands had forced male politicians to take their ambitions seriously, and in 1918 only the most reactionary men could dismiss the suffragettes.

On 23 January 1918 *Punch* carried a cartoon by the artist Bernard Partridge whose two-word strap line 'At Last!' described the sense of relief and achievement about the granting of the vote. Partridge drew Joan of Arc, bare-headed, planting her boots on the bleak terrain, her uniform tattered by years of battle, her bare hands clenched into a fist, the right hand holding a flag. A strong wind of change is blowing to reveal her victory, bearing the words 'Woman's Franchise'. She stands on rock near a bush which appears to have been torched by war and wind, and there is a burst of light behind her suggesting a new dawn and a new era of women's freedom.[20]

While the news was welcomed by all wings of the women's suffrage movement there was no celebration. Sylvia Pankhurst remembered: 'The pageantry and rejoicing, which in pre-war days would have greeted the victory, were absent when it came. The sorrows of the world conflict precluded jubilations.'[21] Many within the women's suffrage movement were disappointed at the imposition of an age limit. Sylvia Pankhurst thought the age differential absurd but welcomed the fact that 'six times the number of women whose enfranchisement had been attempted in the three Conciliation Bills, for which so much hard effort and painful sacrifice had been given, and to which the opposition was so stubborn and ruthless' now had the vote. If all the women over twenty-one had been enfranchised they would have easily been the majority in the electorate, because of the war dead.[22]

Rewarding women for their war work was certainly a factor, but not the only one in the granting of the limited women's suffrage.

While it would have been difficult for the government to refuse to give women the vote in the light of their contribution, many of the arguments against women's suffrage seemed hollow in the context of the war. After May 1915 the government was a coalition, representative of all the political parties in the House of Commons which included several senior politicians who actively supported the women's suffrage movement. Fears of a revival of suffragette militancy if women were not enfranchised was another significant calculation. Militant Jessie Stephenson was in no doubt about why (some) women were given the vote:

> Governments are not philanthropists – certainly not to non-voters – they seldom give what they are absolutely not forced to, and I say with positive certainty – the Government would not have granted women's suffrage with such a harmless and comparatively poorly-backed demand [of the NUWSS] ... As it was, the Government returning, all tired, to home affairs after the Great War, to a country recently ablaze from end to end with enthusiasm for women's vote, and likely to burst into still more desperate enthusiasm if denied, faced with this threat passed the Electoral Bill in January [1918].

The first instalment of women's suffrage opened the doors to a series of important acts which started to redress some of the many inequalities between men and women. The Sex Disqualification Removal Act of 1919 made it illegal to exclude women from the professions (except the church) because of their sex. This meant that women could now become solicitors, barristers and magistrates. Gradually all of the professions opened their doors to women, if in some cases, like the civil service, slowly and reluctantly.

During the 1920s important improvements were made regarding the position of British women in society. 'Women's Questions' were discussed more seriously in Parliament, helped by the presence of eight women MPs by 1923. Universities were offering more degrees to a growing number of women students. Divorce laws became more favourable to women and for the first time they could divorce their husbands for adultery. The 1920s also saw the beginning of the Equal Pay campaign, although the Equal Pay Act was not passed until 1970. Legislation in the 1920s proved the WSPU's thesis: when the sex barrier in the franchise was breached, laws affecting women's lives in a positive way would make their way onto the statute book.

On the 28 November 1919 the voters of Plymouth returned the first female Member of Parliament to take her seat in the House of Commons.[23] (Constance Markievicz was elected in Dublin in 1918 but refused to take her seat.) Dusted with snow, and chilled by a biting wind, Lady Astor, an American divorcee, rich and stylish, was declared an MP at Plymouth Town Hall. Her husband, Waldorf Astor, was the sitting MP for Plymouth Sutton when his father died on 18 October 1919, and he became the 2nd Viscount Astor with a seat in the House of Lords, so a by-election was called. Electioneering did not daunt Nancy Astor. She had helped her husband win his seat in the 1910 general election, and then retain it in December 1918, and she loved every moment of it: 'I knew Plymouth; I knew its narrow streets and alleys; I knew its mothers and infants ... I made it my business to know the people. I was not a mere passive supporter of my husband.'[24]

'Our Nancy' as she was known to many of her new constituents, polled 51 per cent of the by-election vote with a majority of more than 5,000, pushing the Labour Party candidate, Mr W. T. Gay, into second place.[25] The next day, on her way to Cliveden, her country house on the Thames in Buckinghamshire, Nancy Astor and her husband Viscount Astor and their eldest son, twelve-year-old Bill, changed trains at Paddington. They had tried to keep their travel plans secret, but a big crowd, mostly women, had gathered on the platform to gawp at this unlikely pioneer of women's suffrage, so many keen to shake her hand. Forty-year-old Nancy Astor had never agitated for, or asked for, women to have the vote. A group of suffragettes – their names not known – some of them hunger strikers who had been forcibly fed, pushed to the front to congratulate her. One of them presented Nancy with a badge and said, 'This is the beginning of our era. I am glad to have suffered for this.' The poignancy of the moment was shattered by a man who barked: 'Well, I never voted for you!' Nancy, nimble with a put-down, replied: 'Thanks heavens for that.'[26]

The second instalment of women's suffrage was granted in 1928. In 1924 the Conservative government said it would consider extending the franchise. A bill was introduced in March 1928 and by May it had easily passed all the necessary stages. There was little serious opposition and it was never in danger of being defeated. Emmeline Pankhurst died just before the bill became law on 2 July 1928. All women over the age of twenty-one could vote in elections. It was a time of celebration.[27]

Many decades later, in 1969, the voting age was reduced to eighteen. Despite the fact that men and women have equal voting rights, gender inequality persists in pay in the United Kingdom today.

After-lives of the Suffragettes

The Votes for Women campaign attracted thousands of women from diverse backgrounds and places. However, once the first limited franchise was gained in 1918 the ties which bound them together in the most dramatic single-issue political campaign of the twentieth century dissolved. Many suffragettes put their campaigning skills behind them and retired from the fray. Others took up left-wing and right-wing politics and various feminist campaigns. A number found comfort in theosophy, and some took up the cause of animal welfare. During the campaign many of the suffragettes were at the height of their powers: once the vote was won the future seemed an exciting and uncertain place. We do not know what happened to all of them; some married or emigrated or both, many disappeared perhaps ready to – or needing to – put their tumultuous past behind them and refused to draw attention to their suffragette careers. When asked to write their memories of the campaign a number of women agreed but insisted on writing under their maiden names in case their husbands' careers or businesses suffered. A good number of the women mentioned in these pages have been impossible to find in later life, but here are some whose after-lives we do know which demonstrate the broad variety of women who were attracted to the suffragette movement.

Laura Frances Ainsworth, born in 1885, was active in the Women's Section of the British Legion in the north-east of England in the 1930s. She died in Yorkshire in 1958.

Marian Violet Aitken, born in 1886, died in Hertfordshire in 1987 aged 101.

Grace Muriel Alderman, born in 1885, died in Essex in 1968.

Janie Allan, born in 1868, gave money to Dr Flora Murray and Dr Louisa Garrett Anderson to start the Women's Hospital Corps in September 1914. In 1923 she was the chair of the Women's Watch Committee reporting how public bodies treated women's interests. She was active for twenty years in the Scottish Council for Women's Trades. She died a centenarian in the Highlands in 1968.

Mary Sophia Allen, born in 1878, known to her close friends as 'Robert', helped establish the Women Police Volunteers when war broke out in 1914, and was its commandant from 1918 to 1938. Allen was awarded an OBE in 1917 for her work in women's policing. She stood unsuccessfully as an independent candidate in 1922 for the constituency of Westminster and was also a member of the executive of the Forum Club, the London Centre for members of the Women's Institute. She volunteered to help break the General Strike of 1926. Her enthusiasm for Adolf Hitler (she visited him in 1934) and her work for Oswald Mosley's British Union of Fascists caused great concern.

Gertrude Mary Ansell, born in 1861, was released from prison under the suffragette amnesty on 10 August 1914 having been force-fed 236 times while serving a six-month sentence for attacking a painting in the Royal Academy. She died in Essex in 1932.

Helen Alexander Archdale, born in 1876, worked for the Women's Department of the Ministry of National Service from 1917 to 1918, and was the first editor of *Time and Tide* from 1922 to 1926, published by her friend Viscountess Rhondda, with whom she lived until the early 1930s. Helen was the secretary of the feminist Six Point Group, founded by Rhondda, and a leading advocate of international equal rights feminism and involved with the World Women's Party in the late 1930s. She died in London in December 1949.

Hertha Phoebe Sarah Ayrton, born in 1854, invented a hand-fan device for dispersing poison gas and offered it to the War Office in 1915. Because of opposition, inertia and incompetence it was not given to the troops until a year later in 1916. She helped found the International Federation of University Women in 1919, and the National Union of Scientific Workers in 1920. Ayrton was bitten by an insect and died of blood poisoning in Sussex in 1923.

Sarah Jane 'Jennie' Baines, born in 1866, emigrated to Melbourne, Australia, in 1914. During the war she joined the Women's Peace Army. She was a socialist pacifist and was arrested with Adela Pankhurst in 1917 for protesting against profiteering. In 1918 she served four days of a six-month sentence – after a four-day hunger and thirst strike – after being convicted for flying the red flag in Flinders Park in Melbourne. In 1928 Jennie Baines was appointed a special magistrate in the Children's Court in Port Melbourne, and died there in 1951.

Lucy Minnie Baldock, born in 1864, was living with her husband in Southampton when war broke out. Her active suffragette career was by now over but her pride in having been involved in the militant campaign and fondness of Mrs Pankhurst remained. She carried a purple, white and green banner ahead of Mrs Pankhurst's funeral cortège to Brompton Cemetery in London and witnessed the unveiling of her statue in 1930. Minnie died in Dorset in 1954 aged ninety.

Rachel Barrett, born in 1875, and her lover, Ida Wylie, became friends and literary advisers to Radclyffe Hall and Una Troubridge in the early 1920s, and would later support Radclyffe Hall when she was prosecuted for her 'obscene' publication, the novel *The Well of Loneliness*, in 1928 which was banned in England until 1959. During the First World War Rachel Barrett had taken up Mrs Pankhurst's fierce pro-war stance. In 1919 she set off on a road trip round America with Ida Wylie. A year later they were living in California; Rachel helped raise the money for Mrs Pankhurst's statue. Barrett's relationship with Wylie ended in the 1930s; Ida Wylie stayed in America, and Rachel Barrett relived her suffragette days as an active member of the Suffragette Club, later named the Suffragette

Fellowship, founded by Edith How-Martyn in 1926, 'to perpetuate the memory of the pioneers and outstanding events connected
with women's emancipation and especially the militant campaign of
1905–1914 and keep alive the suffragette spirit'. Rachel Barrett died
in Sussex in 1953.

Olive Bartels, born in 1889, was awarded the OBE in 1920 for her work
with the War Office and the Women's Army Auxiliary Corps. In the
autumn of 1914 she accompanied Christabel Pankhurst on a tour of
America but they fell out over Christabel's views on the war. Bartels
returned to England in 1915. She ran a market garden on Guernsey for
twelve years and became an organiser for the National Union of Women
Teachers in 1934 and joined the Women's Voluntary Service in the
Second World War. Olive Bartels lived for several years in Ireland, her
birthplace, and returned to England in 1960. She died in Kent in 1978.

Frances Clara Bartlett, born in 1873, helped look after the four babies
adopted by Mrs Pankhurst during the First World War. Both her sons
were killed. 'The terrible blow I had at losing my sons made me retire
into seclusion where I have remained ever since.' She died in Kent in
1957.

Olive Agnes Beamish, born in 1890, was a suffrage and socialist organ-
iser in the East End of London during the First World War, based in
Hoxton. She ran her own business, a typewriting bureau in the City,
from 1919 to 1930 and served on the executive of the Association of
Women Clerks and Secretaries, and was a member of the Communist
Party from 1926 to 1929. In 1931 she was the Secretary of the Labour
Party in Chelmsford which she had joined in 1929. She supported the
Republican struggle in the Spanish Civil War. She died in Suffolk in 1978.

Sarah Benett, born in 1850, was active in the Tax Resistance League
until she died in London in 1924, leaving £1,000 to the Elizabeth
Garrett Anderson Hospital.

Rosa May Billinghurst, born in 1875, canvassed for Christabel
Pankhurst when she stood unsuccessfully in the general election of

1918 to be the MP for Smethwick. She joined the Women's Freedom League after the war and gave money to Jill Craigie's Equal Pay Film Fund. She died in 1953 having donated her body to science.

Teresa Billington-Greig, born in 1877, bore a daughter in 1915. Disenchanted with suffrage and Labour Party campaigning she worked for her husband's billiard table business in Glasgow during the First World War, and founded the Women's Billiards Association. In 1937 she rejoined the Women's Freedom League and after the war served as Chairman and Honorary Director for Women for Westminster, which worked to improve women's access to politics. She died in 1964.

Violet Ann Bland, born in 1863, was running her guest house when her sister, a farmer's wife in County Wexford, died in 1915, aged thirty-five, perhaps from childbirth complications. Violet fostered her sister's four youngest children, all under five. In 1917 her home in London was the headquarters of the Hon. Evelina Haverfield and Sergeant-Major Flora Sandes' Fund for Providing Comforts for Serbian Soldiers and Prisoners Fund. Violet died in Tooting in 1940.

The Blathwayt family: Colonel Linley Blathwayt, born in 1839, was survived by his wife Emily and their two children, William and Mary, when he died in 1919. *Mrs Emily Marion Blathwayt* (c. 1852–1940) and *Mary Blathwayt* (1879–1961) died at Eagle House, Batheaston. By that time the suffragette arboretum, known in the family as 'Annie's Arboretum', had been overgrown for years. The house stands today but the garden and surrounding land was built over for a housing estate. Only one suffragette tree, an Austrian pine planted by Rose Lamartine Yates in 1909, and a few plaques, survived the bulldozer.

Elsie Edith Bowerman, born in 1889, worked with the Scottish Women's Hospital Unit in Romania nursing the Serbian and Russian armies in 1916 and she was in St Petersburg at the time of the Revolution in 1917. In 1918 she was Christabel Pankhurst's agent in the general election and co-founded the Women's Guild of Empire with Flora Drummond, to foster greater patriotism among working women, and campaign against strikes and lockouts organised by trade unions. She studied law in 1921 and became one of the first women barristers in 1924. In 1933 she wrote *The Law of Child Protection* and in 1938 co-founded the Women's Voluntary Service with Lady Reading. In the late 1940s she worked at the United Nations in the status of women section. She died in Sussex in 1973.

Dorothy Agnes Bowker, born in 1886, served in the Women's Land Army during the war and travelled around America and Canada in the twenties. She served as a councillor and an alderman in Hampshire from 1938 to the late 1950s. She died in Barnet in 1973.

The Brackenbury family: Mrs Hilda Brackenbury, born 1832, died on All Saints' Day in 1918. When *Georgina Agnes Brackenbury*, born in 1865, and *Marie Venetia Caroline Brackenbury*, born in 1866, died in 1946 and 1949 respectively, their home at 2 Campden Hill Square was left to the 'Over Thirties Association', founded in 1934, which provided clubs and hostel accommodation for women over thirty. The suffragette enameller Ernestine Mills made a magnificent enamel plaque as a tribute to the Brackenbury women which hung in the house, and is now displayed in the Museum of London. A portrait of Mrs Pankhurst, painted by Georgina Brackenbury in 1927, hangs in the National Portrait Gallery, London.

Mrs Jane Esdon Brailsford, born in 1874, parted from her husband Henry Noel Brailsford for the last time in 1921 after years of an unhappy marriage affected by her depression and drinking. She loathed her husband and the institution of marriage, calling it a form of subjugation, and refused to have children. She refused to give Brailsford a divorce, and died of pneumonia and alcoholism in 1937.

Henry Noel Brailsford, born in 1873, failed to become the Labour MP for Montrose burghs in the 1918 general election. In 1922 he was the editor of the weekly ILP newspaper *New Leader*. During the Second World War his regular broadcasts for the BBC Overseas Service were informed by years of travel in Europe and around the world. Legally separated from his wife, Brailsford lived with the artist Clara Leighton, and then married a German refugee in 1944. He died in London in 1958.

Bertha Brewster, born in 1887, was an honorary secretary of the United Suffragists in Birmingham in 1916. The date of her death is unknown.

Myra Eleanor Sadd Brown, born in 1872, supported Sylvia Pankhurst's ELFS, welcoming busloads of working women to her home in Maldon, Essex. After the war she was active in the International Woman Suffrage Alliance and attended conferences with her daughter Myra all over Europe. In 1925 she was a founding member of the British Commonwealth League, a feminist organisation campaigning for women's rights in the Commonwealth. She died in Hong Kong in 1938.

Margaret Vincentia 'Marjorie' Annan Bryce, born in 1891, pursued an acting career, appearing on the London stage and in an early televised play in 1939. Her roles included Nina Zarechnaya in *The Seagull* in 1919, in *The Cloud That Lifted* in 1932, and in 1938 and 1947 she played the Red Queen in *Alice in Wonderland*. She died in London in 1973.

Hilda Evelyn (Evaline) Burkitt, born in 1876, married Leonard Aloysius Mitchener, variously employed as a clerk and tutor and thirteen years younger than Hilda, in the summer of 1916. When Hilda had been fire-raising in Ipswich and Felixstowe in 1914, he had been earning his living as a clerk and tutor in Hove.

Lucy Burns, born in 1879, joined Alice Paul in America in 1912 where both became members of the Congressional Committee for the National American Woman Suffrage Association (NAWSA). They left to form the Congressional Union in 1913, which became the National Woman's Party in 1916 when twenty million women still did not have the vote. Alice Paul was chairman and Lucy Burns was vice-chairman. During the First World War the Woman's Party adopted some of the militant tactics of the suffragettes Burns and Paul learned in England: pavements were chalked, women's suffrage leaflets were scattered over Seattle from a biplane and the White House was picketed by 'Silent Sentinels' carrying banners from January 1917 to June 1919. Their members were arrested and some went on hunger strike. On 18 August 1920 the 19th Amendment was passed granting all women the vote. In 1923 Lucy Burns's youngest sister died in childbirth and Lucy and her sisters brought up their niece. Lucy Burns died in Brooklyn in 1966.

Mabel 'Mabs' Henrietta Capper, born in 1889, was a member of the Voluntary Aid Detachment in the First World War and became interested in pacifism and socialism. From 1919 to 1922 she was on the editorial staff of the *Daily Herald*. In 1921 she married Thomas Cecil Chisholm, a chairman and managing director of Business Publications Limited. She died in Sussex in 1966.

Annie Cappuccio, later Mrs 'Tough Annie' Barnes, born in 1887, joined the Independent Labour Party during the First World War and was secretary of the women's section of Stepney Labour Party. In 1919 she married Albert Barnes, a sawyer. When her father remarried, his new wife had no interest in her stepchildren so Annie and her husband took over the care of her brothers and sisters. In 1929 she founded a branch of the Women's Cooperative Guild in Stepney, and was twice elected as a Stepney councillor on the housing and public health committees, from 1934 to 1937, and from 1941 to 1949. Annie and Albert Barnes lost all their belongings in an air raid in 1944 and lived at Toynbee Hall until 1949, eventually returning to East Ham in the 1950s. Albert died in 1958. In 1980 she said in her autobiography, *Tough Annie*, 'I've had an interesting life. It hasn't all been roses. It was hard when my mother and brother died, I was lucky to have a good husband … I enjoyed all my work for the Party and the Council. I've met so many interesting people. It's not worth being miserable.' Annie died in East London in 1982.

Sarah Carwin, born in 1863, had retired from the campaign in 1910 because of health problems caused by force-feeding. She lived in the country for many years with a woman friend to whom she was 'devotedly attached'. When her friend died Sarah Carwin lived in the South of France and Italy. Her biographer Frances Mabelle Unwin said: 'she spared herself nothing in the pursuit of her ideals ... a few weeks before her death she said that if she could choose any part of her life to live over again she would choose the part she had devoted to the suffrage. It had seemed the most worthwhile.' She died in Kent in 1933.

Eileen Mary Casey, born in 1881, was released from prison when war broke out in 1914. She worked as a land girl and trained as a gardener at Kew Gardens. After the war she worked as the personal assistant to the manager of the Magasin du Louvre which had a shop in London. In 1940 she returned to Australia, where she was born, to work as a translator for the Australian Board of Censors. Eileen kept in touch with Edith How-Martyn and Katherine Gatty, who had already emigrated to Australia. She returned to England in 1951. She was a theosophist. In 1960 she was interviewed by Lady Jessie Street, an Australian suffragette, about her days as a militant. Never wanting to be idle and prizing her financial independence, she sometimes worked as a cleaning lady. Eileen Casey died in Hampshire in 1972.

Edwy Godwin Clayton, born in 1858, died in Berkshire in 1936, his professional career blighted by his prosecution for his involvement with the militant campaign. He earned a small living from writing.

Clara Margaret Codd, born in 1877, gave up the WSPU to commit her life to theosophy in 1909. She worked as a teacher before becoming the librarian of the Theosophical Society in 1911, and travelled to India where she lived for two years at their headquarters at Adyar, reporting directly to Annie Besant, the head of the movement. Clara Codd travelled to America, New Zealand and Australia, and lived in South Africa during the Second World War. She wrote several books on theosophy, and her autobiography, *So Rich a Life*, in 1951. She died in Berkshire in 1971.

Leonora Cohen, born in 1873, became the first woman President of the Yorkshire Federation of Trades Councils in 1923 and was one of the first women to be appointed a magistrate in 1924. She served as a JP for twenty-five years and was awarded an OBE for her services to public life in 1928. In 1974, aged 101, Leonora Cohen appeared on the cover of the *Radio Times* advertising the BBC television series *Shoulder to Shoulder*. She died in 1978 in North Wales, aged 105.

Selina Cooper, born in 1864, had left the WSPU and the ILP in 1907 and joined the NUWSS. When war broke out she and her husband, Robert, opposed it and helped local conscientious objectors. She led a women's peace crusade through Nelson, Lancashire, in 1917. She was outspoken in her views on birth control and socialism, and in 1924 was appointed a magistrate in Nelson. In 1934 Selina Cooper joined a delegation visiting Nazi Germany; her ties with the Communist Party led to her being expelled by the Labour Party in 1940. She died in Lancashire in 1946.

Catherine Isabel Ida Vans Corbett, born in 1869, was widowed in 1912. She died in Surrey in 1950.

Helen Millar Craggs, born in 1888, trained as a pharmacist to help her husband, Dr Duncan Alexander McCombie, whom she married in 1914, and who practised in the East End of London. They had two children; her husband died in 1936. To make ends meet she started a business making jigsaw puzzles. After the Second World War she and her daughter lived in Canada and she returned to London in the early 1950s. She then became the Pethick-Lawrences' private secretary. Emmeline Pethick-Lawrence died in 1954, and Helen married Fred, by now Lord Pethick-Lawrence, in 1957. Baroness Helen Pethick-Lawrence died in Canada in 1969.

Helen Crawfurd, born in 1877, joined the Independent Labour Party in 1914 and in 1915 she co-founded the Glasgow branch of the Women's International League and was involved in the Glasgow rent strikes. She founded the Women's Peace Crusade in 1916. When the war ended Helen Crawfurd was the vice-chairman of the Scottish division council of the ILP. In 1920 she went to Moscow for the Second

Congress of the Third Communist International, and interviewed Lenin, and on her return to Scotland joined the Communist Party of Great Britain. She worked hard to recruit women into the party. She failed to win a seat as a Communist candidate in the 1929 (Bothwell, Lanarkshire) and 1931 (North Aberdeen) general elections. In 1945 she became Dunoon's first woman councillor, where she died in 1954.

Ellen 'Nellie' Crocker, born in 1872, retired from the suffragette campaign when her cousin Emmeline Pethick-Lawrence and her husband were purged from the WSPU. She died in 1962, leaving money in her will to the Suffragette Fellowship.

Louise 'Louie' Cullen, born in 1876, took her husband and children to Australia for health reasons in December 1911, intending to stay for two years, but spent the rest of her life in New South Wales. She kept up with her 'old comrades' via the Australian branch of the Suffragette Fellowship. She died in 1960 having bequeathed her cottage at Lidcombe, Sydney, to the Children's Library and Crafts Movement to be used as a children's centre.

Charlotte Despard, born in 1844, was worried by the effects of the war on the poor and even though her brother, Sir John French, was commander-in-chief of the British Expeditionary Force, she joined the socialist and pacifist movement. In 1918 she stood unsuccessfully as a socialist candidate for Battersea in the general election. In 1921 she moved to Dublin and devoted her time to international socialism; she gave all her wealth to Sinn Fein. She wanted to go to Spain during the civil war to express her support for the republican fight against General Franco but, aged ninety-three, she was too frail. She died penniless in Belfast in 1939.

Edith Elizabeth Downing, born in 1857, designed and helped make toys for Sylvia Pankhurst's toy factory. She died in Surrey in 1931.

Charlotte Drake, born in 1884, worked for the ELFS campaigning for better wages and conditions for women working in the war industries. She attended a peace rally organised by Sylvia Pankhurst in Trafalgar Square in 1916 with her twelve-year-old daughter, Ruby. She was prevented by the government from attending the Women's Peace Conference at The Hague in 1916. She opened a drapery shop in Custom House. She died in Kent in 1970.

'General' Flora McKinnon Drummond, born in 1879, was appointed chief organiser of the Women's Party in 1917. When the war ended she and Elsie Bowerman founded the Women's Guild of Empire, a conservative anti-strike organisation of working-class wives which opposed all state welfare and family allowances. In 1922 she divorced her husband after twenty-four years of marriage, for many of which they were estranged. That year she married a cousin, Alan Simpson, but kept the name of Drummond for her professional work. She presided at the unveiling of the statue of Mrs Pankhurst in Westminster in 1930. In 1944 Alan Simpson, an engineer, was killed in an air raid in London. She died in Argyll in 1949.

Marion Wallace-Dunlop, born in 1864, moved to live in an Elizabethan mansion at Peaslake during the war and adopted a daughter in 1916. She was a pallbearer at Mrs Pankhurst's funeral and looked after Mary, one of Mrs Pankhurst's 'war babies', by then a young woman in her twenties. She died in Surrey in 1942.

Elsie Duval, born in 1892, was on the run from the police with her fiancé Hugh Franklin in Germany when war broke out. They returned to England under the suffragette amnesty and she offered her services to a hospital in France run by Dr Louisa Garrett Anderson. She was not accepted and took part in the 'Women's Right To Serve' procession in July 1915. She married Hugh Franklin later that summer but their marriage was short-lived. She died in London of influenza on 1 January 1919.

Emily Duval, born in 1861, worked with Sylvia Pankhurst's ELFS during the war. She served for three years on Battersea Borough Council from 1918 to 1921. She died in Wandsworth in 1924.

Una Harriet Stratford Duval, born in 1880, bore two daughters, in 1916 and 1920. During the war she ran her husband Victor Duval's export business and played a leading role in the Suffragette Fellowship and the Suffragette Record Room in Cromwell Road. She died in London in 1975.

Victor Diederichs Duval, born in 1885, served with the Royal Engineers in Salonika from 1914 to 1916. He tried and failed three times to become an MP for the Liberal Party. In 1929 he joined the Labour Party; at that time he was the managing director of an export company. He died in Morecambe in 1945.

Louise Mary Eates, born in 1877, was a member of the United Suffragists when the war started. From 1917 to 1923 she was on the Committee of St John's Wood Infant Welfare Centre and Day Nursery. She also lectured for the Workers' Educational Association and was active with the Women's Institute in Kent in the 1920s. She returned to London in 1927, and ran the Citizenship Class and Debating Circle of the Acton branch of the Young Women's Christian Association from 1929 to 1930. Louise Eates died in London in 1944.

Elizabeth Clarke Wolstenholme Elmy, born in 1833, died in Lancashire in March 1918, after fifty years of feminist and suffrage campaigning, and nine months before the general election.

Zelie Emerson, born in 1894, returned to the United States on 6 May 1914. Her skull had been fractured by the police on a demonstration in November 1913 and her health was further undermined by being force-fed while on hunger strike. Charles Mansell-Moullin urged Sylvia Pankhurst to send her home: 'I had the greatest difficulty to induce her to go ... I was grieved to lose her.' The date and place of her death are unknown.

Dorothy Elizabeth Evans, born in 1889, was the honorary secretary of the Ulster branch of the WSPU in 1914 and was on hunger and thirst strike in Tullamore Gaol in Ireland when war broke out. She was released on 8 August 1914 and campaigned for peace during the war, becoming the secretary of the Women's League for Peace and

Freedom. She was also the chairman of the Six Point Group. Her daughter Lyndal was born out of wedlock in West Ham in 1921; the father was Emil Davies, an LCC councillor who did not leave his wife. Dorothy Evans died in 1944.

Gladys Evans, born in 1873, recuperated in Switzerland after being force-fed for several weeks. During the war she drove a lorry in France and worked as a chauffeur based at the Château de Blérancourt, Aisne, for a relief mission funded by American women. After the war she trained as a beautician in New York and lived in Winnipeg in the 1920s with the Ward Skinner family. In the 1930s she worked in a nursing home in Long Island. She died in Los Angeles in 1967.

Charlotte Emily Caprina Fahey, born in 1883, was married again to a Mr Bridge. The date of her death is not known.

Henrietta Olivia Robarts, known as *Olive Fargus*, born in 1880, lived in Westminster during the war. In August 1918 she married Captain Reginald John Durand-Deacon, MC, of the 7th Battalion of the Gloucester Regiment. After leaving the army in 1920 he practised law and died in 1938. She lived at the Langham Hotel until 1942 when she moved into the Onslow Court Hotel in South Kensington. In the summer of 1949 Olive was murdered by the serial killer John Haigh, who lured her to a garage in Crawley on the pretext of discussing a joint business venture. He shot her and put her body in an acid bath. Haigh was hanged at Wandsworth Prison on 10 August 1949.

Susan Ada Flatman, born in 1876, left the WSPU in 1912 and was living in Bristol when war broke out. She worked with the Women's Emergency Corps, founded by Evelina Haverfield. From 1915 to 1917 she lived in America and wrote articles for *The Suffragist*, the newspaper of the Congressional Union for Women's Suffrage. Ada struggled financially. She lived in Canada in the early 1920s before moving to Cape Town before the end of the decade, still campaigning on suffrage matters. She returned to England in the 1930s and was a peace campaigner, enjoyed the comradeship of the Suffragette Fellowship. She died in Sussex in 1952.

Lettice Annie Floyd, born in 1865, lived with her companion Annie Williams, whom she predeceased. Lettice was worn out by her suffrage campaigning, writing to Edith How-Martyn in 1932, 'when war broke out I was very tired and only took part in the making of garments'. One of her sisters served on the War Savings Committee; in 1918 her elder sister, Mary, fifty-eight, poisoned herself, after suffering from 'acute mental depression'. In 1920 Lettice Floyd and Annie Williams helped establish the Women's Institute in Berkswell, near Coventry; Annie was the president from 1926 to 1930 and 1933 to 1934. With the modesty typical of many ex-suffragette campaigners, she told Edith How-Martyn: 'There really is nothing in my life worth writing about … it really does not seem worth writing it down.' In 1932 Lettice Floyd was a member of the National Council of Women and the Women's International League of Peace and Freedom. She told Edith How-Martyn, 'the great thing now seems to me to push on with the peace movement and to improve the status of women'. She died in Birmingham in 1934; Annie Williams died in 1943.

Hugh Arthur Franklin, born in 1889, was in hiding from the British police in Dresden when war broke out. His poor eyesight meant he did not serve in the war but worked as a clerk at Woolwich ordnance factory, marrying suffragette Elsie Duval in 1915 at the West London synagogue. He was disinherited by his father for marrying out of his religion. Elsie died of Spanish flu in January 1919. Having some private means he took up writing. He joined the Labour Party and in 1931 and 1935 he failed to be elected as an MP, but served on a London County Council committee and the Labour Party National Executive. He died in Hampstead in 1962.

Helen Fraser, born in 1881, worked for the Board of Agriculture during the war encouraging women to work on the land. From November 1917 to August 1918 she was in America on a lecture tour to forty states lecturing on Britain's war effort. She stood unsuccessfully three times as the Liberal candidate for Govan (1922), Lanark (1923) and

Hamilton (1924). She married in the 1930s and emigrated to Australia in 1939, where she died in 1979.

Frances Theresa Garnett (also known as Annie O'Sullivan), born in 1887, was uneasy about the escalating militancy of the WSPU and in 1911 was already training as a nurse at the London Hospital. She served on the Western Front with the Civil Hospital Reserve and was commended for her 'gallant and distinguished service in the field'. She joined the Six Point Group and supported various feminist campaigns, enjoying reconnecting with her comrades via the Suffragette Fellowship. She died in London in 1966.

Eleanor Charlotte Penn Gaskell, born in 1860, was one of numerous members of the WSPU who were unhappy at Emmeline and Christabel Pankhurst's abandonment of the campaign for the vote during the war. A close friend of Emily Davison, she worked hard to keep the memory of Emily's protest alive. She died in London in 1937. Her generous and suffragette-supporting husband George Penn Gaskell, a member of the Men's Political League for Women's Enfranchisement, predeceased her in 1934.

Mary Eleanor Gawthorpe, born in 1881, sailed to America on the SS *Adriatic* on 29 December 1915 with her mother, Annie Eliza Gawthorpe. On the passenger list she gave her occupation as an 'organising secretary'. Her mother, sister, brother-in-law and nephew were already settled in New Jersey by 1908. Mary worked for New York State Women Suffrage Party and later the Labour Party in Illinois, and the League of Mutual Aid and Amalgamated Clothing Workers of America. Mary kept in contact with her old comrades via the Suffragette Fellowship and returned to England for a short stay in 1933. In 1962 she published her memoir, *Up Hill to Holloway*. Her husband, John Sanders, died in 1963, and she died in New York in 1973.

Clara Elizabeth known as *Betty Giveen*, born in 1877, married Bertha Brewster's brother, Philip, at Headington on 8 December 1914. Philip Brewster was a conscientious objector. They were living in Gray's Inn

Road when he was conscripted in 1916 and within a month he was convicted for 'disobeying in such a manner as to show wilful defiance of authority and lawful command of his superior officer in the execution of his office'. He was sentenced to two years' hard labour which were served in Wormwood Scrubs and Wandsworth prisons. He was released in January 1919. The couple lived in Peaslake, Surrey, near the Pethick-Lawrences, in the 1920s and 1930s. Betty died in 1967, and Philip, a construction engineer, died in 1973.

Eva Selina Gore-Booth, born in 1870, did welfare work with Esther Roper to help German women and children in England. In 1915 they took part in the Women's Peace Crusade. Eva's sister Constance Markievicz was sentenced to death for treason for her part in the 1916 Easter Rising but was reprieved and served time in Holloway. Until she died in 1926, Eva Gore-Booth worked for peace, and the League for the Abolition of Capital Punishment and anti-vivisection. She died in Hampstead. Her intimate friend Esther Gertrude Roper, who died in 1938, is buried with her.

Barbara Bodichon Ayrton Gould, born in 1886, was active during the war with the United Suffragists which she had helped co-found. In 1945 she succeeded on her fifth attempt to be elected as a Labour MP, in North Hendon. She sat on the executive committee of the Labour Party for twenty years and was the vice-chairman in 1938–9. She also served as a JP in Marylebone. She died in London in 1950.

Elsa Gye, born in 1881, married William Ewart Bullock, the brother of suffragette Daisy Bullock, in Edinburgh in 1911, and had her first child there in 1912. At the time of his marriage Bullock was a medical student in Edinburgh, was awarded a gold medal for his MD thesis in 1913, and embarked on cancer research with the Imperial Cancer Research Fund. During the war he was a pathologist studying wound infection. In July 1919 he changed his name by deed poll to that of his wife. In 1934 William E. Gye was appointed director of the Imperial Cancer Research Fund. Elsa Gye was instrumental in the opening of the Suffragette Record Room in Cromwell Road. She died in Hendon in 1943.

Florence Eliza Haig, born in 1855, abandoned her work for the East London Federation of Suffragettes in 1916 to work with Mrs Pankhurst, Annie Kenney and Mabel Tuke in their patriotic war campaigning. During the twenties she regularly exhibited her paintings in London and joined the Society of Women Artists. She helped carry Mrs Pankhurst's coffin. She died in Wandsworth in 1952.

Nellie Hall, born in 1893, was released from Holloway on 10 August 1914. During the war she was a mail sorter at Birmingham post office and marched in the 'Women's Right To Serve' demonstration in London in July 1915. She was a welfare worker in a munitions factory. In 1920 she married Herbert Stanley Humpherson at King's Norton, Warwickshire and joined their names together. Their two children were born in Liverpool in 1923 and 1926. In 1928 Nellie was the election agent in Mrs Pankhurst's bid to be elected as an MP, but Emmeline Pankhurst died before the general election took place. In 1929 Nellie, her husband, her widowed mother and two sons emigrated to Montreal, Canada. Nellie was on the Board of the Joint Committee for Penal Reform for Women in the state of Ontario. She died in Canada but the date is unknown. Her husband returned to England and died in Warwickshire in 1973.

Cicely Mary Hamilton, born in 1872, was an administrator with the Scottish women's ambulance unit outside Paris, and from 1917 to 1919 was a member of a troop entertainment repertory company directed by Lena Ashwell. In 1919 she worked as a press officer for the International Suffrage Conference in Geneva and wrote for the *Daily Mail*, *Yorkshire Post* and *Manchester Guardian*. In the twenties she was an active member of the Six Point Group campaigning for the rights of children, widows and unmarried mothers; equal guardianship of children; and equal pay in the teaching and civil service professions. She was also an advocate for the birth control movement and the reform of abortion law. Her autobiography *Life Errant* was published in 1935. She died in Chelsea in 1952.

Gertrude Menzies Harding, born in 1889, continued to work on *The Suffragette*, renamed *Britannia*, until 1915. For the remainder of the war she worked to improve the working conditions of the women workers at Gretna munitions factory in Scotland. In 1920 she returned to Canada and in 1921 moved to New Jersey where she worked as a welfare supervisor. She wrote her memoirs in the 1930s and died in New Brunswick in 1977.

Ethel Clarice Haslam was born in 1881. She threw herself into war work with gusto, telling her local newspaper in September 1914 that she knew how to handle a rifle and wanted to join the Civic Guards. She went to first aid classes and helped at flag days raising funds to support local hospitals. In 1915 she collected money for wounded horses and for the ELFS's milk fund for poor children. In 1916 she attended a munitions class at East Ham Technical Schools and loaned her car for wounded soldiers to be taken on outings. Later in 1916 she enrolled as a member of the Voluntary Aid Detachment (VAD), having done two years' training as a nursing sister at Ilford Emergency Hospital. Ethel criticised in the press Sylvia's pacifist demonstrations in 1917: 'peace now would mean throwing away all that our brave soldiers have sacrificed so much to gain.' From 1920 to 1925 she was a Poor Law Guardian with the Romford Board of Guardians. She joined the Theosophical Society in 1922. Ethel died in 1961 in Essex.

The Honourable Evelina 'Eve' Haverfield, born in 1867, helped establish the Women's Emergency Corps as soon as war broke out to provide waged women workers in the country's hour of need. She also established the Women's Volunteer Reserve, becoming its commandant. When her mother died in April 1915 Evelina joined the Scottish Women's Hospitals and served as a hospital administrator for the founder, Dr Elsie Inglis, in Serbia. Her elder son, John Campbell Haverfield, twenty-seven, an officer in the Indian Army, was killed in Mesopotamia while attached to the 35th Sikh Regiment in July 1915, and was buried at Basra. Her younger son, Brook Tunstall Haverfield, emigrated to Canada. She helped nurse the people of Kruševac during a typhus epidemic in 1915 and was taken prisoner by the Germans in October when Serbia was over-run. She was repatriated by the Red Cross in early 1916; in August

1916 she went with Dr Inglis to Russia as the commandant of the Scottish Women's Hospital motor ambulances and transport. Her intimate friend, Vera 'Jack' Holme, was a member of the transport corps – they both served in Serbia and Russia for two years. The situation became too unstable and Evelina returned to England in 1917 and founded 'The Hon. Evelina Haverfield's and Sergt-Major Flora Sandes' Fund for Providing Comforts for Serbian Soldiers and Prisoners'. She returned to Serbia in December 1918 and worked for disabled soldiers and opened orphanages for 'friendless children in the remotest districts'. Her obituary in *The Times* reported her death on March 1920: 'It was in grappling with this difficult task, her strength undermined by the hardships she had faced for so long, that she fell victim to pneumonia.' Her last words were reported to be 'who will look after the children?' Her body was wrapped in a Serbian flag and buried at Bajina Bašta. Her tombstone carried the words: 'A good rider, a good fighter and a most loyal friend.'

Alice Hawkins, born in 1863, remained an active supporter of the Labour Party all her life, helping at the party's headquarters in Leicester in the 1945 general election. Her husband, Alfred, had died in 1928. In the 1920s and 1930s she was also been involved in visiting women who made boots and shoes in their own homes, trying to improve conditions and pay. She died in London in 1946.

Gladys Mary Hazel, born in 1880, looked after her nephew from the age of two when his mother, her sister, died in a canoeing accident in Canada in 1926. His father, who was an astrologer, could not cope and the boy went to live with Gladys in Leicestershire. They moved to Blewbury, near Didcot, where she grew vegetables and kept chickens. In 1920 Gladys had published a book of poems inspired by her time as a suffragette prisoner, describing prison as 'the grey life that fills the cracks where hope had been'. She died in Berkshire in 1959.

Eleanor Beatrice 'Nellie' Higginson, born in 1881, joined Edith Rigby and other members of Preston WSPU in helping on the home front by making jam. After the war Nellie became a local magistrate; during the Second World War she was a representative on Preston council. She was a tutor for the Workers' Education Association. Her husband had died in 1938; in 1954 she left Preston to live with her suffragette comrade Beth Hesmondhalgh in Bognor Regis. She died in Sussex in 1969.

Olive Hockin, born in 1881, was a land girl during the First World War and published *Two Girls on the Land: Wartime on a Dartmoor Farm* in 1918. In 1922 she was married at Haverfordwest to John H. Leared, the owner of a polo pony training school in Cheltenham. They had two sons, in 1926 and 1929. Throughout the twenties she regularly exhibited her paintings. She died in Cheltenham in 1936.

Vera Louise Holme, born in 1881, was in charge of the horses and trucks of the Scottish Women's Hospital in 1915 and 1916. In 1917 she was sent back to England to report to the Foreign Office on the situation on the Romanian front. From 1920 she ran the Haverfield Fund for Serbian Children. She lived in Perthshire and was involved with the Ellen Terry memorial performance in Kent every year; she died in Glasgow in 1969.

Rose Elsie Neville Howey, born in 1884, gave up militant acts after a prolonged period of force-feeding in Aylesbury Gaol in 1912 when several of her teeth were broken. Years later her mother told Elsa Gye that Elsie 'almost became dumb for life from the injuries inflicted on her ... it took four months treatment to save her and her beautiful voice was quite ruined'. She became a theosophist and left most of her estate to the English Theosophical Trust when she died in Worcestershire in 1963.

Maud Amelia Fanny Joachim, born in 1869, in 1914 was living in Cheyne Walk and working with Sylvia Pankhurst's East London Federation of Suffragettes. She and Sylvia Pankhurst returned from Dublin in August 1914 where they had been campaigning. For a while she was the manager of the toy factory started by Sylvia to provide work for East End women who had lost their jobs because of the war. During the 1930s she helped Sylvia agitate against the Italian fascist presence in Ethiopia. She died at Mouse Cottage at Steyning, Sussex, in 1947.

Georgina Gladice Keevil, born in 1884, married Leslie Thomas Richard Rickford in Hendon in the summer of 1913. He was a bank clerk and did not serve in the First World War. Their twin sons were born in 1914 and a third son in 1917. Gladice's husband died in 1956. She died in London in 1959.

Annie Kenney, born in 1879, was secretary of the Women's Party. She raised money for Christabel Pankhurst's failed bid to become the MP for Smethwick in the general election of 1918. When the war ended Annie lived in St Leonards with Grace Roe and while on holiday on the Isle of Arran met James Taylor, a metal worker. Annie gave up politics after the vote was granted in 1918. She married James in 1920, and her son, Warwick Kenney Taylor, was born in 1921. From 1918 Annie devoted herself to theosophy and became an official of the Rosicrucian Order which conducted her funeral in Letchworth in 1953. Annie's ashes were scattered on Saddleworth Moor.

Jessie Kenney, born in 1887, stayed loyal to Mrs Pankhurst and Christabel during the war. In 1917 she visited Russia with Mrs Pankhurst and met Oleg Alexander Kerensky, the prime minister of the Provisional Government before the October Revolution of 1917. She was appointed secretary of the Women's Party, the renamed WSPU, and became a Rosicrucian in 1923. After the war Jessie worked for the American Red Cross in Paris. In the 1930s she worked on cruise liners as a stewardess. Although she had been the first woman to qualify as a ship's radio officer, as a woman she was not allowed to join the profession. In the 1960s she worked as a secretary in a comprehensive school in Battersea. She died in Essex in 1985.

Alice Jane Shannan Ker, born in 1853, took her daughters and left Liverpool for London in 1916. She had been a committed theosophist for several years. She campaigned with the United Suffragists after the outbreak of war. Her daughter, Margaret, had already finished her studies at Liverpool University and worked at the War Office during the war. Daughter Mary studied at Girton College, Cambridge, from 1915 to 1918. In London Alice became more involved with the theosophical movement and lived with her daughters, both of whom were schoolteachers, and their female companions. In the 1920s Dr Ker worked at school clinics and infant welfare centres. She died in London in 1943.

Harriet Roberta Kerr, born in 1859, played no further role in politics when partial female suffrage was granted in 1918 and was reticent about the press showing interest in her suffrage career. She feared the damage to her reputation she had suffered while working for the WSPU would remain with her for the rest of her life. In 1928 she helped collect money to look after Mrs Pankhurst in the final months of her life. Harriet Kerr died in a nursing home in Surrey in 1940.

Edith Kerwood, born in 1858, remained a committed militant until the outbreak of war, writing in 1913: 'I am unshaken in my firm belief that the militancy of women is right. They are showing far more moderation and restraint than men would do under similar circumstances.' Two of Edith's sons were killed in action in France in 1915 and 1916; her third son and only remaining child was discharged from the army as medically unfit. Edith Kerwood died in Devon in 1923.

Eliza Adelaide Knight, born in 1871, left the WSPU in 1907 to work with Dora Montefiore, showing her the homes of sweated homeworkers in Canning Town. In 1910 she was elected a Poor Law Guardian for West Ham; by 1911 Adelaide and her husband, Donald Adolphus, and their three children were living at Abbey Wood where he was the foreman at the Woolwich Arsenal. Adelaide joined the Communist Party of Great Britain. Adelaide died on the Isle of Sheppey in 1949 and Donald in 1950.

Aeta Adelaide Lamb, born in 1886, worked in various war depots during the war. After the war she found it hard to find work and took a course in shorthand and typing, and worked for various women's organisations, but then her health started to fail and severe exhaustion and depression meant she could no longer do office work. Her 'weary and melancholy appearance' made it easy for would-be employers to reject her after interviews. A friend wrote: 'Throughout all these tragic years she never lost her intense enthusiasm and belief in feminism' and described how many of Aeta Lamb's friends, including Mrs Pankhurst, tried to find her a job. She decided to take a cookery course, for which her friends were sure she was ill-suited, borrowing a small sum of money from a relative. Her health collapsed and she died of cancer in the Elizabeth Garrett Anderson Hospital in 1928.

Clara Mary Lambert, born in 1874, was a member of a delegation lobbying for food rationing during the war. In 1915 she joined Mary Allen's Women's Police Service and was sent to do welfare work with women munition workers in South Wales, and there met her lifelong companion Violet Louise Croxford. Violet had been a nurse at the Manor Asylum in Epsom before war broke out. In the 1920s Lambert did rescue work with young girls in London, and in 1926 the couple opened a hostel in Hythe, Kent, for 'unfortunate ladies'. Clara died in Surrey in 1969.

George Lansbury, born in 1859, was editor of the *Daily Herald*, which became a pacifist weekly newspaper during the First World War. In 1919 he was elected the first Labour Mayor of Poplar, and in 1921 he and his son Edgar and daughter-in-law Minnie were Poplar councillors. All three were sent to prison for six weeks during the Poplar rates rebellion which gave rise to the word 'Poplarism'. In 1922 George Lansbury was elected as the MP for Poplar, Bow and Bromley, a seat he held until he died. In 1929 Ramsay Macdonald appointed him First Commissioner of Works; in 1931 he became leader of the Labour Party and resigned the leadership in 1935. Lansbury joined the Peace Pledge Union and visited Hitler and Mussolini. Never moving away from Poplar, he was a charismatic speaker. He died in 1940; his wife Bessie had died in 1933. Of his children who had taken part in the East End women's suffrage campaign, Edgar died in 1935, Willie in 1943, and Daisy married Raymond Postgate in 1918, and died in 1971.

Marie known as *Mary Leigh*, born in 1885. After the war she struggled financially and lived in a caravan near the Thames. Every year until the late 1960s she went on the Emily Wilding Davison Pilgrimage to Morpeth. In 1921, while being arrested for chalking the pavement advertising a meeting for Emily Davison in Hyde Park, she gave a policeman a black eye and went to prison. She attended George Bernard Shaw's funeral in 1950 carrying a purple, white and green tricolour that had been draped on Davison's coffin in 1913, and carried it at the first Aldermaston March in 1958. Mary died in Stockport in 1979.

Laura Geraldine Lennox, born in 1883, worked with a hospital unit in France during the war. Her elder brother, Alfred Edward, was in the 1st Regiment of the South African Infantry when he died in France in October 1916. After the war she ran a secretarial and service bureau and was involved with the Six Point Group's work on women's housing. In 1932 her pamphlet *The Suffragette Spirit* was published. She died in Cork in 1958.

Lilian Ida Lenton, born in 1891, was released from Holloway in August after the outbreak of war. She served with the Scottish Women's Hospital Unit in Serbia under Dr Elsie Inglis. After the war she worked at the British Embassy in Stockholm and went to Russia with the Save the Children Fund. She spoke and organised for the Women's Freedom League and was the financial secretary of the National Union of Women Teachers. When she was interviewed by the BBC in 1955 she said of women getting the vote in 1918: 'I was extremely pleased but very disgusted at the curious terms on which we got it. Men had a vote at 21, all men. Women only had a vote when they were 30, and then only if they were householders or the wives of male householders. Personally I didn't vote for a very long time because I hadn't either a husband or furniture.' She was a member of the Status of Women Committee and the honorary treasurer of the Suffragette Fellowship. She died in Twickenham in 1972.

The Lilley sisters, Kate and Edith Louise, born in 1874 and 1883, lived in the family home in Clacton-on-Sea for the rest of their lives: 'Miss Lou' died in 1943, and Kate died in 1962.

Lady Constance Georgina Bulwer-Lytton, born in 1869, was an invalid from 1912. Despite her frail condition she was determined to hang on to some independence. She refused to live at home with her mother, and instead rented Olive Schreiner's old lodgings in Paddington where she died of heart failure in May 1923.

Edith Ruth Mansell-Moullin, born in 1858, used money raised by the Forward Cymric Suffrage Union which she co-founded in 1912, to help relieve poverty among women and children in Wales during the war. She campaigned for peace and in 1930 wrote an appreciation of her friend Emily Davison. From 1931 she chaired the Society for Cultural Relations with the USSR. She was a helper at St Dunstan's charity for the blind. She died in London in 1941.

Grace Marcon, born in 1889, who used the alias 'Freda Graham', was a masseuse working for the Red Cross during the war. Her obituary says that in 1923 she 'worked her way across the Prairies to British Columbia'. She married the British press photographer Victor Charles Scholey in Duncan, Vancouver Island. Her autograph book from her time at Battenhall, where she was a member of the VAD in the First World War, contains a maple leaf pressed onto the page alongside Victor Scholey's signature in 1917, suggesting that he had served with the Canadian forces and was massaged by Grace. The book also has several saucy rhymes and locks of hair from the men she looked after. Victor Scholey had travelled to Quebec in October 1911, several months after taking the famous photograph of Winston Churchill at the siege of sidney Street on 3 January. A postcard from Mrs Pankhurst to 'Miss Marcon' dated 1926 suggests that news of Grace's marriage had not reached her, and that Grace and her son had already returned to her family home, Edgefield Rectory, within three years of the wedding. Grace died in Oxford 1965 and was buried at her father's old church in Edgefield.

Lady Isabel Augusta Margesson, born in 1863, was a member of the central committee of management of the recently founded Women's Institute in 1917 and later became a JP. Her daughter, Catherine, who had been a WSPU organiser, married Lord Cushenden in 1930, and died in 1939. Lady Margesson died in London in 1946.

Kitty Marion, the stage name of *Katherine Marie Schafer*, born in 1870, as a German national was put under such close surveillance as an 'enemy alien' that she decided to settle in New York in 1915. Her suffragette comrades paid her fare. She spent thirteen years as a worker for Margaret Sanger's birth control movement, and was arrested several times for handing out the *Birth Control Review* magazine outside Macy's department store on Broadway. In the 1920s she wrote her autobiography. She died penniless in the Margaret Sanger Nursing Home in New York in 1944.

Dora Marsden, born in 1882, lived with her mother in the Lake District after the war. In 1935 she had a psychotic breakdown and spent the rest of her life in a mental hospital in Dumfries, where she died in 1960.

Charlotte Augusta Leopoldine Marsh, born in 1887. When the vote was granted in 1918 she worked with the Women's International League for Peace and Freedom, and in San Francisco with the Community Chest Association. She worked for the Public Assistance Board of the London County Council and was also on the executive council of the Six Point Group. She would attend gatherings of the Suffragette Fellowship proudly wearing her prison and hunger-strike medals. The Labour MP Dr Edith Summerskill wrote: 'I marvelled that this handsome, fragile woman could have possessed sufficient physical courage to face her tormentors and that she had such reserves of moral courage to declare her beliefs over the years under circumstances which often called for a solitary effort, unsupported by the warmth and comfort of her comrades.' She died in Wimbledon in 1961.

Emily Katherine 'Kitty' Willoughby Marshall, born in 1870, opened the Pankhurst Testimonial Fund which bought Mrs Pankhurst a house in Devon, although it was rarely used before she left for America. The Marshalls were most loyal and generous friends. Kitty helped carry Mrs Pankhurst's coffin, and organised the unveiling of Mrs Pankhurst's statue in Westminster in 1930. She died in Halstead, Essex, in 1947. Her solicitor husband, Arthur, whose business had suffered as a result of his defending WSPU members, died in 1954.

Ellen 'Nellie' Alma Martel, born in 1855, had resigned from the WSPU by 1910. She attended a dinner given in honour of Dora Montefiore in the 1920s. She died in London in 1940.

Edith How-Martyn, born in 1875, resigned from her senior position in the Women's Freedom League of which she was a co-founder for health reasons in 1912. During the war she worked with Margaret Sanger to spread knowledge about contraception around the world and travelled widely in the twenties and thirties in order to do so. She stood unsuccessfully in the general election in 1918 as an independent candidate for Hendon, but was elected as the first woman councillor in Middlesex County Council in 1919. In 1921 she helped the Malthusian League open one of the first birth control clinics in Britain. She and Lilian Lenton founded the Suffragette Fellowship in 1926 to 'perpetuate the memory of the pioneers and outstanding events connected with women's emancipation and especially the militant campaign 1905–1914, and thus keep alive the suffragette spirit'. During the Second World War she settled in Australia with her husband. She died in Sydney in 1954.

Rosamund Amabel Nora Massy, born in 1870, a close ally of Mrs Pankhurst, helped her in her effort to get elected as the MP for Whitechapel. She died in Sussex in 1947.

Muriel Matters, born in 1877, married William A. Porter, a dentist, in the autumn of 1914 and was known as Mrs Matters-Porter. A leading figure in the Women's Freedom League, she became the organising secretary of the International Council of Women. She travelled to Spain and studied under Maria Montessori, and when she returned helped Sylvia Pankhurst to run her school, which was attached to the Mother's Arms in Bow. In 1916 she went on the Women's Peace Crusade in Glasgow. In the 1920s the Matters-Porters moved to Hastings where she failed to be elected as the Labour MP in the 1924 general election. In 1934 she was on the committee of the Women's Guild of Empire. Her husband died in 1949; she died in Sussex in 1969.

Winifred Mayo, the stage name of *Winifred Alice Monck-Mason*, born in 1869, was a member of the advisory committee of the British

Women's Hospital during the war. She retired from the theatre after the war, and from 1921 to 1926 she was an organising secretary of the Six Point Group, becoming a vice-president in the thirties. She was chairman of the Suffragette Fellowship. Her obituary in *The Times* said: 'her interest in social and political reform and the status of women in society remained unabated. Dainty and dignified, with a clear, carrying voice she appeared in her late eighties with aplomb on the television and though hampered by deafness enjoyed broadcasting her suffrage memories.' She died in Hampshire in 1967.

Elspeth Douglas McClelland, born in 1879, married William Albert Spencer in 1912 and had three children. She died in childbirth in Edgware in 1920.

Hannah Maria Mitchell, born 1871, was a pacifist during the war and worked for the No Conscription Fellowship and the Women's International League. She had left the WSPU after suffering a nervous breakdown and worked with the Women's Freedom League. By 1914 her political emphasis shifted and she devoted more time to her work on the Board of Guardians and the Manchester branch of the ILP. From 1924 to 1935 she served as a councillor on Manchester City Council and she was also a JP, resigning in 1946. She died in Manchester in 1956.

Lilias Mitchell, born in 1884, had been released from Winson Green Prison not long before the outbreak of war, after which she worked as secretary to the Young Women's Christian Association. She died in Edinburgh in 1940.

Dora Frances Barrow Montefiore, born 1851, worked with Charlotte Despard for the Cantines des Dames Anglaises in France during the war. She was a founder member of the Communist Party of Britain in 1920 and served on its first executive. Her autobiography, *From a Victorian to a Modern*, was published in 1927. She died in Hastings in 1933.

Ethel Agnes Mary Moorhead, born in 1869, did relief work with Fanny Parker during the war, settling in France in the 1920s. Fanny

Parker died in 1924 and left Ethel a large legacy which she used to launch *The Quarter*, a literary journal she co-edited with the Irish American poet Ernest Walsh until his death in 1926. Contributors to their magazine included Gertrude Stein, Ernest Hemingway, James Joyce and Ezra Pound. She died in Dublin in 1955.

Clara Evelyn Mordan, born in 1844, died of tuberculosis in January 1915 at Bexhill, Sussex. She left a quarter of her estate to St Hilda's College, Oxford, to assist its building programme.

Eliza known as *Elsa Myers*, born in 1888. Her fiancé was killed in action during the war. In 1920 she became headmistress of Seurat Street Girls' School in London. However, problems with her throat caused by force-feeding made teaching impossible. She qualified as a solicitor, but died in London of tuberculosis in 1926.

Mary Clara Sophia Neal, born in 1860, was a member of the WSPU's London Committee in 1906, but was more active with the Esperance Girls' Club and the revival of folk dancing and singing. She suspended the club during the First World War and worked in pensions admin-istration on the Isle of Dogs. She moved to Littlehampton, Sussex, in 1925 where she was a magistrate for twelve years, working mostly on children's cases. In 1937 she was awarded a CBE for her 'services in connexion with the revival of folk songs and dances'. Mary Neal died in 1944 at the home of the Pethick-Lawrences in Peaslake, Surrey. Mrs Pethick-Lawrence's obituary for her in *The Times* said: 'To the last day of her life she lost none of her worship of rhythm and beauty, nor did she lose her ardent desire to make them the common heritage of the people. Sensitive to every injustice and to every tragedy, she kept a gay and gallant front to life to the very end.'

Edith Bessie New, born in 1877, had ended her militant career by the time she was teaching for the London County Council in Greenwich before 1911, and until the late 1930s. She settled in Cornwall and died in 1951.

Helen Charlotte Elizabeth Douglas Ogston, born in 1883, married twice. When war broke out she had been married to a widowed doctor, Eugene Dunbar Townroe, for two years and had two daughters, Olive, known as 'Bunty', and Helen. Her South African-born husband had been educated in England and qualified as a doctor in London in 1903 after serving in the Boer War, and with the Royal Army Medical Corps from 1914 to 1918. By 1929 the couple had divorced and Helen married Granville Havelock Bullimore, a chartered accountant and the managing director of Curry's, radio and cycle manufacturers. Helen died in 1973 in Malvern.

Adela Constantia Mary Pankhurst, born in 1885, married Tom Walsh, the general secretary of the Seamen's Union, in 1917. By 1926 she had five children and three stepdaughters. The couple were founder members of the Australian Communist Party in 1920. In 1929, disillusioned with unionism, socialism and the Labour Party, her politics moved to the right and she founded the Australian branch of the Women's Guild of Empire, and wrote articles against communism, trade unionism, and in favour of a strong Empire and the importance of family life for the *Empire Gazette*. She later reverted to her pacifist views and denounced the Second World War, favouring cooperation with Japan. Adela and Tom Walsh were guests of honour when they visited Japan in 1940. She was interned in 1941 and released in 1942 after being on hunger strike. Tom Walsh died in 1943, and poor health forced Adela to retire from public life. She died in Sydney in 1961.

Christabel Harriette Pankhurst, born in 1880. In the general election of 1918 she stood as a candidate for the Women's Party at Smethwick but failed to be elected. In 1921 she was a committed Second Adventist, touring America with her mother preaching the second coming of Jesus. In 1936 Christabel was appointed a Dame of the British Empire for her services to women's suffrage. She spent much of her later life in America waiting for the Second Coming of Christ, writing and lecturing on her faith, and kept up a warm correspondence with Annie Kenney. She died in Santa Monica in 1958. Grace Roe was an executor of her will.

Emmeline Pankhurst, born in 1858. After the war she earned money by touring Canada lecturing on social hygiene, and settled in Toronto in 1921. In 1925 she and Christabel helped Mabel Tuke run the English

Teashop of Good Hope at Juan-les-Pins in France. The business failed and Mrs Pankhurst returned to London. In 1926 she joined the Conservative Party and was adopted as a candidate for Whitechapel and St George's in 1927. Mrs Pankhurst died in London in June 1928, two weeks before the second instalment of the vote was granted to all women over twenty-one on 2 July 1928. Ten leading suffragettes carried her coffin. Among the hundreds of mourners was Bertie Jones, the King's jockey, bearing a wreath in the memory of Emily Davison. She was buried in Brompton Cemetery in London.

Estelle Sylvia Pankhurst, born in 1882, was expelled from the British Communist Party in 1921 because of her insistence on freedom of expression. In 1924 she opened a café in London with Silvio Erasmus Corio, a libertarian socialist exile who was concerned at the rise of fascism in Italy, whose views she shared. In 1927 their son, Richard Keir Pethick Pankhurst, was born; Sylvia refused to get married. In the twenties she helped Italian refugees, and in the thirties she spoke out against Italian fascism; she campaigned for peace and took up the cause of Ethiopian independence after the Italian occupation of 1935. When Silvio died in 1954 Sylvia was invited by the Emperor of Ethiopia, Haile Selassie, to take her son and live in Addis Ababa, and settled there in 1956. Selassie awarded her a medal, the Queen of Sheba First Class. When she died in Addis Ababa in 1960 she was given a state funeral attended by Haile Selassie and his family.

Frances Mary 'Fanny' Parker, born in 1875, was on the run from the police when the First World War broke out and was told she would not be tried for her attempt to burn down Robert Burns's cottage. She was asked to lead a new department within the Women's Freedom League, the National Service Organisation, which found suitable war work for women. In 1917 she was appointed the deputy controller of the Women's Army Auxiliary Corps in Boulogne, was twice mentioned in dispatches, and awarded a military OBE in the same year. Fanny was living with Ethel Moorhead near Bordeaux when she died in 1924; apart from a couple of bequests she left all her property to Ethel Moorhead 'in grateful remembrance for her care and love'.

Annie Beatrice Parlby, born in 1872, suffered from delicate mental health and was hospitalised several times at Hereford County Asylum during her life. A nephew's memoir of 'Aunt Bee' paints a gentle picture of an aunt and her younger sister, Florence 'Florrie' Matilda, living with their father in reduced circumstances. Their mother died in the summer of 1918 during one of Beatrice's stays at Hereford Asylum. Her father William Parlby lived until 1932. The sisters were helped by their 'faithful but outspoken' charlady, Miss Dykes. The Parlbys' nephew recalled Beatrice in the 1920s as being 'distinctly eccentric. She walked about at times in an immense golf cape, an Edwardian garment, tartan lined and often concealed the garden shears beneath its folds, possibly for its proper purpose, but not always when the hedge needed trimming.' Beatrice did not change her hairstyle as fashions changed, but kept it in the Edwardian style. She died in Hereford in 1952.

Marguerite 'Daisy' Lena Parsons, born in 1890, was the Honorary Secretary of West Ham ELFS when war broke out and on behalf of the Mayor of West Ham she visited Canning Town to see the plight of the wives and children of soldiers and sailors who had joined up, noting their straitened circumstances. In 1922 she was elected to the borough council, was an alderman in 1935 and the first woman Mayor of West Ham from 1936 to 1937. In 1951 she was awarded an MBE for her public service. She died in West Ham in 1957.

Alice Paul, born in 1885, worked closely with Lucy Burns for the enfranchisement of women in the United States, and was the leader of the National Woman's Party. She was imprisoned three times for picketing the White House. In 1936 she became a member of the Laws Committee of the International Council of Women. She played an important role in getting women protected against discrimination as a group by the Civil Rights Act of 1964. She died in 1977 in New Jersey.

'Rachel Peace' was the alias of *Jane Short*, born in 1882. Nothing is known of her life after her involvement in the suffragette campaign, or when she died.

Emmeline Pethick-Lawrence, born in 1867, was invited to speak at a meeting in Carnegie Hall in New York to found a new women's suffrage organisation in the United States. In 1915 she attended the Women's Peace Congress in The Hague. In the 1918 general election she stood unsuccessfully as the Labour candidate for Rusholme, Manchester. From 1915 she spent many years working for the Women's International League. In 1926 she was president of the Women's Freedom League and was a vice-president of the Six Point Group. She died in Peaslake in 1954.

Frederick Pethick-Lawrence, born in 1871, was liable for conscription in 1918 but refused to serve and appeared before a tribunal and was sent to work on a farm. He stood unsuccessfully as a Labour candidate in 1921. Two years later he defeated Winston Churchill to become MP for West Leicester. In 1929 he was appointed financial secretary to the chancellor of the exchequer. He was awarded a peerage in 1945, becoming 1st Baron Peaslake, and entered the House of Lords, becoming secretary of state for India and Burma and playing a part in the negotiations for Indian independence. In 1957 he married the suffragette Helen Craggs. He died at Peaslake in 1961.

Mary Elizabeth Phillips, born in 1880, was an organiser in London for the United Suffragists from 1915 to 1916. After the war she worked for the Women's International League for Peace and Freedom, and the Save the Children Fund. From 1928 to 1955 she was the editor of a daily news service for the brewing trade and on retirement she worked with the publications department of the national Council of Social Service. She was a member of the Suffragette Fellowship and the Six Point Group, and during her life her left-wing principles never wavered. In 1955 she told an interviewer: 'When we got the vote, it was a sort of an anti-climax actually. It came in such a sneaky way. You couldn't rejoice as you would have done if it had come at a time of militancy. But still it was very good to feel that it was finished and that we had been contributors towards it.' She died in Sussex in 1969.

Catherine Emily Pine, born in 1864, travelled to America with Mrs Pankhurst in 1919 where they were later joined by three of the war babies Mrs Pankhurst had adopted. They settled in Canada the following year. Catherine Pine returned to England in 1923 and joined the state register of nurses, and worked at the Cottage Hospital in Herne Bay. She died in Rochester in 1941.

Mary Raleigh Richardson, born in 1882, published several books during the war. She owned properties and was a somewhat unsuccessful landlady. After the war she adopted a baby boy born to one of her tenants, an unmarried mother, who had died six weeks after his birth. In 1922 she stood unsuccessfully as the Labour candidate for Acton, as an independent socialist in 1924, and as the Labour candidate in Aldershot in 1931. She suggested to Sylvia Pankhurst that they should establish a communist nunnery for social and religious work but nothing came of the idea. In 1932 she joined the New Party founded by Oswald Mosley and became the organising secretary of the women's section of his British Union of Fascists in 1934. She left the BUF in 1935 after a row with Mosley's mother. Her colourful autobiography, *Laugh a Defiance*, was published in 1953. She died in Hastings in 1961.

Edith Rigby, born in 1872, continued to campaign for the vote during the war, contrary to WSPU policy, and joined the Women's Land Army. Her husband retired in 1926 and they started to build a house together at Erdmuth, Caernarvonshire, but he died before it was completed. She became fascinated by vegetarianism, whole foods and Rudolf Steiner's work. In 1939 she sailed to New York to visit the Rudolf Steiner Centre, twenty miles from Manhattan. Edith died at Erdmuth in 1950.

Winefrede Mary Rix, born in 1874, moved in the same circles as Benjamin Britten and his parents in the 1920s and was working as a midwife after the Second World War. She died in London in 1966.

The Rock sisters, Dorothea Edith Meriet and Madeleine Caron Rock, were born in 1882 and 1884 respectively. Dorothea was a member of the International Women's Franchise Club. Madeleine died in London in 1954, Dorothea died in Amersham in 1964.

Eleanor Grace Watney Roe, born in 1885, helped Mrs Pankhurst and Christabel Pankhurst with their pro-war and anti-German work, and was the chief organiser of the 'Women's Right To Serve' procession through London in 1915. After the war she studied theosophy with Annie Kenney and in 1921 went to Canada and the United States with Christabel. They both settled in California. In the thirties Grace was involved in social work and after the Second World War ran a bookshop and a metaphysical library in Santa Barbara. She was with Christabel when she died in 1958 and acted as her literary executor. In 1961 she was the vice-president of the Suffragette Fellowship. She died in Tonbridge, Kent, in 1979.

Jane Sbarborough, born in 1842, died in Wandsworth (as Jane Sbarabara) in 1925.

Gladys Henrietta Schütze, born in 1884, used the pen name 'Henrietta Leslie'. She and her husband suffered during the First World War on two counts, from their German name and their pacifist beliefs. Gladys was forced to leave the Society of Women Journalists and the Literary Club. From 1919 to 1923 she wrote for the *Daily Herald* and was an honorary organiser of the Save the Children Fund from 1924 to 1933. Before the Second World War broke out she looked after Jewish refugees at their house in Glebe Place, Chelsea. Under her pen name she wrote twenty novels and three plays and was a member of the PEN Club. She died in Berne, Switzerland, in 1946.

Arabella Charlotte Scott, born in 1886, had been released from Perth prison after a five-week hunger strike when war broke out. Her married name was Colville-Reeves. She emigrated to Australia where she was active in the Australian Suffragette Fellowship and died in 1980. The *Sydney Morning Herald*'s obituary was titled 'Proud Story of a Woman's Murky Past'.

Isabel Marion Seymour, born in 1882, was working at WSPU headquarters when war broke out. In the 1920s she lived in Canada and returned to England in 1930 and served on Hampshire County

Council. The date and place of her death are not known, but she was alive in 1973 and interviewed by Antonia Raeburn.

Evelyn Jane Sharp, born in 1868, was a tax resister during the war and worked with Barbara Gould and the United Suffragists who helped secure the first instalment of the vote in 1918. She joined the Labour Party, was a pacifist and in 1921 worked for the Society of Friends in Germany. She had a long affair with Henry Woodd Nevinson and they married in 1933, six months after the death of his wife. The Nevinsons moved to the Cotswolds because of the air raids in London; he died in the Cotswolds in 1941, she in Ealing in 1955.

Marguerite Annie Sidley, born in 1886, left the WSPU in 1908 to join the Women's Freedom League. In February 1914 she spent four days in prison for speaking on the steps of the Board of Trade, Whitehall. In the summer of 1914 she married Harold W. Rose in London. She disappeared from the scene until she completed a questionnaire for the Suffragette Fellowship in 1931.

Victoria Simmons, born in 1889, married Alexander Lidiard, MC, of the 5th Manchester Rifles, in 1918. He was a member of the Men's Political Union for Women's Enfranchisement whom she met while selling *Votes for Women* in Bristol. They both worked as opticians; she became one of the first women to qualify in 1927 and the Lidiards had practices in Maidenhead and High Wycombe. She was a vegetarian from the age of ten, campaigned for animal welfare and charities, and for the last ten years of her life she worked for the ordination of women priests. She died in Hove in 1992, aged 103.

Princess Sophia Alexandrovna Duleep Singh, born in 1876, took part in Mrs Pankhurst's 'Women's Right To Serve' procession in London in 1915. In 1930 she was the head of the committee which provided flowers for Mrs Pankhurst's statue and was a lifelong member of the Suffragette Fellowship. In 1934 her entry in *Who's Who* gave her only interest as 'advancement of women'. She died in Buckinghamshire in 1948.

Katherine Douglas Smith, born in 1878, died in London in 1970.

Lady Sybil Mary Smith, born in 1876, contributed generously with time and money to a wide variety of war charities. In 1924 she was the vice-chairman of the Elizabeth Garrett Anderson Extension Committee. She died in Oxford in 1959.

Norah Veronica Lyle-Smyth was born in 1874. The date of her death is not known.

Ethel Smyth, born in 1858, disagreed with Mrs Pankhurst and Christabel's jingoistic pro-war stance. She trained as a radiographer in Paris and was attached to the 13th Division of the French Army. Her first volume of memoirs were published in 1919. In 1922 she was made a Dame of the British Empire. After several rows her friendship with Christabel ended in 1925. She conducted the Metropolitan Police Band at the unveiling of Mrs Pankhurst's statue in Victoria Tower Gardens in 1930. Increasing deafness made conducting a problem but she continued to compose. Often seen in battered trilby hats and tweed suits, accompanied by a large dog, Ethel was energetic, outspoken and kind. She died at Woking in 1944.

Georgiana Margaret Solomon and Daisy Dorothea Solomon, born in 1844 and 1881 respectively, mother and daughter joined the United Suffragists during the war. Georgiana was active in the Ladies' National Society for the Abolition of the State Regulation of Vice and the Association for Moral and Social Hygiene. She remained alert to events in South Africa and in 1919 lobbied against 'the colour bar' which she said 'increased the miseries and perils' of black women. Georgiana Solomon died in Eastbourne in 1933. Daisy attended the International Alliance for Women and Equal Citizenship in Paris in 1923 and was the honorary secretary of the Equal Political Rights Campaign Committee working towards the second instalment of the vote in 1928. She died in Cape Town in 1978.

Annie Eliza Spong, born in 1870, opened the Spong School in Hampstead in 1919, where Spong Rhythmic Dancing was taught and performed. In 1920 it was called Natural Movement Dancing and was heavily influenced by the teachings of the Order of the Cross. From 1920 she began to call herself Annea, and lived with the artist Joseph

Syddall, RA, whom she met at art school. He died in Hampstead in 1942; Annea died in Kensington in 1957.

Dora Spong, born in 1879, married Ralph Beedham before the war, and had two children in 1914 and 1918. Keen vegetarians, they tried their hand at farming in Hertfordshire. Ralph Beedham was a Quaker and refused to serve in the war. They gave up the farm and lived in various houses owned by the Spong family and commonly wore loose-fitting tunics and sandals. Dora died in Surrey in 1969.

Florence Spong, born in 1873, ran a poultry farm in East Grinstead with her sister Minnie. Florence was a weaver and artistic dress-maker. After the First World War she became the housekeeper of the Reverend John Todd Ferrier, the founder of the Order of the Cross, a cult which combined feminism, pacifism and vegetarianism, until he died in 1943. She died in Kensington in 1944.

Irene Osborne Spong, born in 1882, married Norman Ierson Parley, a cricketer and chess player, in 1910 and had two children in 1911 and 1913. He was a Quaker and refused to serve in the war. When Parley went to live in neutral Holland during the war, she and the children stayed with her sister Dora. Irene died in London in 1960.

Minnie Frances Spong, born in 1869, taught in Africa but returned to England in 1911 and took up growing fruit and vegetables on the family farm, selling at East Grinstead Market. Before the Second World War she ran a poultry farm with Florence Spong. She died in Surrey in 1954.

Emma Sproson, born in 1867, left the WSPU in 1908 and joined the Women's Freedom League. Her husband Frank was a postman and secretary of the Wolverhampton branch of the ILP. During the war she worked at a local 'national kitchen' providing food for the needy. She became the first woman councillor in Wolverhampton in 1921 and was re-elected in 1924. When she was elected in 1921 she waved a red flag from the town hall balcony and became known as 'Red Emma'. She served on committees that dealt with homes for unmarried moth-ers and mental health, but in 1922 she was censured by the Labour

Party for exposing financial irregularities in the running of the local fever hospital and thrown off the health committee. Her response was to publish a pamphlet, *Fever Hospital Inquiry – Facts v. Fairy Tales*. She died in Wolverhampton in 1936.

Sara Jessie Stephenson, born in 1873, wrote two volumes of memoir titled 'No Other Way' in 1932. When the vote was granted in 1918 she wrote: 'Woman now has in her hands the key, to get repealed the scandalous laws made against her in the past ... We surviving warriors, battered, mauled and mostly worn out look confidently to her to steadily and surely march towards the greatest reform in the world has ever faced: the Reform, gigantic, colossal, I have dreamt of since my early girlhood, which will, which <u>must</u> come.' She died in Norfolk in 1966.

Janie Terrero, born in 1858, died in Hampstead in 1944.

Dora Thewlis, born in 1890, with her immediate family emigrated to Melbourne, Australia, by 1913. She worked as a weaver before marrying Thomas Dow in 1918. She died in 1976.

Grace and Aethel Tollemache, born in 1872 and 1875, ploughed their own land to help the war effort. Aethel become a pacifist and joined Sylvia Pankhurst's ELFS, and in 1917 she was arrested on pacifist business in east London. She died in Bath in 1955, Grace having died there in 1952.

Margaret Travers-Symons, born in 1873, worked in Egypt during and after the First World War. She returned to England and was living in London from 1945 to 1951. The date and place of her death are not known.

Mabel Kate Tuke, born in 1871, provided the finances to open the English Teashop of Good Hope at Juan-les-Pins in 1925, where Emmeline and Christabel Pankhurst worked for a short time. The business failed and she returned to London, living in St John's Wood for the rest of the twenties and thirties. In 1958, aged eighty-six, she visited Cape Town for the last time. She died in Durham in 1962.

Minnie Sarah Turner, born in 1866, died in 1948 at her Brighton home which had been a suffragette guest house. Her collection of suffragette postcards held by the Museum of London offers a unique insight into her guests and enduring friendships with many WSPU members during the most dangerous time of their lives.

Leonora Helen Tyson, born Wolff in 1883, lived in Streatham with her two sisters for much of her life. She died in London in 1959.

Olive Grace Walton, born in 1886, was one of the first women to enrol in the Women Police Volunteers. In 1920 she was sent to Dublin to work with the Royal Ulster Constabulary. A motorcycle accident ended her career with the police and she was an almoner in a hospital in the East End of London. Olive adopted an orphan, whom she named Christabel, and she supported the miners in the 1920s and voted Labour. She was a vegetarian, and as a dedicated Christian Scientist refused treatment for cancer. She died in Norfolk in 1937.

Vera Wentworth, born in 1890, was the alias of *Jessie Alice Spinks*. She completed her studies at St Andrews University in Scotland in 1914. During the Second World War she was an air raid warden. Jessie Spinks died in London in 1957.

Olive Wharry, born in 1886, was hunger-striking in Holloway at the outbreak of war and released on 10 August. She died in Torquay in 1947.

Adeline Redfern Wilde, born in 1874 in Stoke-on-Trent. She died there in 1924.

Patricia Winifred Woodlock, born in 1873, worked for the WSPU and also spoke at meetings of the Catholic Women's Suffrage Society. The date of her death is not known.

Ada Cecile Granville Wright, born in 1861, volunteered to do her bit for the country in the First World War grooming the Post Office horses, working in canteens and driving hospital ambulances. In the 1920s she did social work, and was a pall-bearer at Mrs Pankhurst's funeral. An active member of the Suffragette Fellowship, she volunteered as an Air Raid Patrol Warden the year before the outbreak of the Second World War. While caring for refugees she died in Finchley in 1939. She was described as 'one of those quiet women whose gentle and calm manner hides a courageous and indomitable nature of unexpected depths'.

Ida Alexa Ross Wylie, born in 1885, ended her relationship with Rachel Barrett in the 1920s. She lived in America for the rest of her life as a successful screenwriter in Hollywood; her novel *The Keeper of the Flame* was made into a film in 1942 starring Spencer Tracy and Katherine Hepburn. She died in New Jersey in 1959.

Rose Emma Lamartine Yates, born in 1875, disliked what she considered Mrs Pankhurst's high-handed suspension of suffrage campaigning in 1914 and in 1916 helped start a new organisation, the 'Suffragettes of the WSPU', which continued to campaign for the vote in a peaceful way during the war. In 1919 she won a seat as an independent on the London County Council representing North Lambeth. She held the seat for three years campaigning for equal pay, increased public housing and the provision of nursery education. Rose died in London in 1954.

SOURCES

Oxford Dictionary of National Biography; Elizabeth Crawford, *The Women's Suffrage Movement: A Reference Guide, 1866–1928*; *The Biographical Dictionary of Scottish Women*, *The Times'* Obituaries; *Australian Dictionary of Biography*; Museum of London Suffragette Collections, Biographical Notes; American National Biography Online; LSE Library Collections; Catalogue Notes, National Library of Australia website; Leah Leneman, '*A Guid Cause': The Women's Suffrage Movement in Scotland*; annesebba.com website; typescript manuscript biography of Eileen Casey by Sarah Laughton; Krista Cowman, *Women of The Right Spirit: Paid Organisers of the Women's Social and Political Union (WSPU) 1904–1918*; www.theaerodrome.com; the ward-skinner family website; Cyril Pearce's database of Conscientious Objectors; Royal College of Physicians Munks Roll Lives of the Fellows website; Pat Heron, *The Life of Ethel Haslam*; Mike Williams's memories of Annie Beatrice Parlby; Godalming Museum (Clara Lambert); Ginny Scholey family archive (Grace Marcon).

On 5 December 1967 some veteran suffragettes and suffragists were photographed by Adrian Flowers to celebrate the fiftieth anniversary of women getting the vote. In the back row are Muriel Perotti, far left, aged 70; Beryl Power, 76; Stella Newsome, 78; Enid Goulden Bach, 67; Grace Roe, 82; and Lady 'Paddy' Winstedt, 81, far right. In the middle row are Lilian Lenton, 77, far left; and below her Mrs Gwen O'Brien, 80; Una Duval, 87; and Jessie Kenney, 80, far right. In the front row are Dame Kathleen Courtney, far left, 90; Lady Stocks, 76; and Dame Margaret Corbett Ashby, 86, far right.

Appendix I

Chronology

Year	WSPU actions	Political situation
1832		Only 'male persons' are enfranchised under the Great Reform Act.
1867		John Stuart Mill presents first women's suffrage petition to Parliament. More men get the vote, but no women.
1869		State of Wyoming gives women the vote.
1884		More men granted the vote in Great Britain but no women.
1893		New Zealand and the state of Colorado enfranchise women.
1897		National Union of Women's Suffrage Societies (NUWSS), a federation of seventeen societies, is founded and led by Millicent Fawcett.
1901		Death of Queen Victoria.
1902		South Australia, Utah, New South Wales and West Australia give women the vote.

Year	WSPU actions	Political situation
1903	Women's Social and Political Union (WSPU) founded in Manchester.	Arthur Balfour is Prime Minister of the Conservative Government.
1904	Mrs Pankhurst holds meeting outside House of Commons when a Women's Suffrage Bill is 'talked out'.	*Daily Mirror* is the first newspaper to make regular use of half-tone photographs.
1905	First militant protest by Christabel Pankhurst and Annie Kenney at the Free Trade Hall, Manchester.	General election called in December 1905.
1906	First WSPU branch opens in Canning Town, east London. WSPU adopts 'Deeds Not Words' as its slogan. WSPU HQ opened at 4 Clement's Inn. WSPU branches opened throughout the UK.	Liberals win landslide election with a majority of eighty-four in January. Henry Campbell-Bannerman is prime minister. The term 'suffragette' is coined by the *Daily Mail.* Women in Finland get the vote.
1907	The First 'Women's Parliament' held at Caxton Hall. Women's Freedom League (WFL) founded. *Votes for Women* newspaper launched.	Mr W. H. Dickinson's Suffrage Bill is 'talked out'.
1908	'Women's Sunday' held in Hyde Park. Purple, white and green colour scheme is announced. First window-smashing raid. Suffragettes 'rush' the House of Commons.	Death of Prime Minister Campbell-Bannerman. He is succeeded by Herbert Asquith, a known 'anti'. Women in Norway get the vote.

Year	WSPU actions	Political situation
	WSPU shops stocking literature and purple, white and green and 'Votes for Women' merchandise are opened throughout the country.	
	'Trojan horse' protest.	
1909	Bill of Rights Demonstration. Marion Wallace-Dunlop becomes first hunger striker.	Government authorises the force-feeding of prisoners.
1910	Conciliation Committee draft Conciliation Bill.	The January general election reduces the Liberal majority to two, leading to a hung parliament.
		Death of King Edward VII in May.
		The MP David Shackleton introduces Conciliation Bill which wins majority, but Asquith refuses to grant facilities for it to progress.
	WSPU protest at government's handling of the Conciliation Bill on Black Friday, 18 November, leads to several days of rioting and police brutality.	The December general election returns a hung parliament. Liberals have no working majority, and rely on support of Irish Nationalist MPs who hold the balance of power in the House of Commons.
		The Conciliation Bill wins a majority in the Commons in May.
1911	No Vote, No Census protest.	Coronation of George V.
	Women's Coronation Procession of 40,000 suffragette marchers carrying 1,000 banners.	Dock strike and two-day railway strike in August.
	Mass window-smashing, 21 November.	Conciliation Bill is 'torpedoed' in November by Asquith's announcement of a Manhood Suffrage Bill.

Year	WSPU actions	Political situation
1912	Windows smashed in Whitehall and West End on 1 and 4 March.	Coal miners' strike. Strike of London dockers.
	WSPU HQ raided, leaders tried at Old Bailey for conspiracy to incite violence and wilful damage.	
	Christabel goes into exile in Paris.	
	English suffragettes target Dublin.	
	Pethick-Lawrences are expelled from the WSPU, and run their own campaign from Clement's Inn.	
	More militant Pankhurst loyalists decamp to new WSPU HQ, Lincoln's Inn House. A more militant newspaper, *The Suffragette*, is launched.	
	Nationwide militancy persists until the outbreak of First World War.	Women in California, Queensland, Victoria, Tasmania, Alaska, Arizona, Oregon and Kansas get the vote.
1913	The Prisoners' (Temporary Discharge for Ill Health) Act, the 'Cat and Mouse' Act is rushed through Parliament. Force-feeding is temporarily halted.	No possibility of women being enfranchised in amendment to the proposed Franchise Reform Bill.
	Mrs Pankhurst sentenced to three years in prison.	
	WSPU HQ at Lincoln's Inn is raided, staff arrested.	
	Emily Davison protests at the Derby. She dies four days later.	House of Lords reject the Home Rule Bill.
	Arson attacks on churches and services interrupted.	
	Sylvia Pankhurst's support of the Labour Party leads to her leaving the WSPU.	

Year	WSPU actions	Political situation
1914	Sylvia forms the East London Federation of Suffragettes.	
	Hunger-striking suffragette prisoners given bromide to reduce resistance to force-feeding.	
	Paintings and museum displays attacked.	
	Deputation to see George V, 21 May. Riot at Buckingham Palace gates.	
	Police raid Lincoln's Inn House and make several arrests.	
	Within a week all suffragette prisoners are released. Mrs Pankhurst suspends militancy and asks WSPU members to support the war.	Outbreak of First World War, 4 August.
1918		The Representation of the People Act gives the vote to all men over twenty-one, and to women aged thirty or over with certain property qualifications.
1928		All women over twenty-one enfranchised.

Appendix II

Money and Value

I chose 1910 as a good year in the middle of the campaign for working out how much various sums would be worth today. I think it is important to appreciate the significant sums the WSPU raised to run the campaign. The Bank of England calculator stops at 2016.

1910	2016
£1	£108
£10	£1,080
£50	£5,404
£100	£10,809
£1,000	£108,093

Notes

ABBREVIATIONS

BL   British Library
Elizabeth Crawford   Elizabeth Crawford, *The Women's Suffrage
                        Movement: A Reference Guide 1866–1928*, UCL
                        Press, 1999
ODNB   *Oxford Dictionary of National Biography*

INTRODUCTION

1. https://www.parliament.uk/about/living-heritage/evolutionofparliament/houseofcommons/reformacts/overview/reformact1832
2. Constance Rover, *Women's Suffrage and Party Politics in Britain, 1866–1914*, p. 3.
3. Hansard, 3s., Col 1,086, vol. 14.
4. A. E. Metcalfe, *Woman's Effort: Chronicle of British Women's Fifty Year Struggle for Citizenship, 1865–1914*, p. 1; Rover, *Women's Suffrage and Party Politics*, p. 3.
5. Christopher Harvie and H. C. G. Matthew, *Nineteenth-Century Britain: A Very Short Introduction*, pp. 38–40.
6. Parliamentary Archives, *Women's Suffrage in Parliament* exhibition catalogue, p. 3.
7. Rover, *Women's Suffrage and Party Politics*, p. 3.
8. *ODNB*: Anne Knight.
9. Lords' Journals, 13 February 1851, p. 23, vol. 83.
10. *Sheffield Independent*, 8 February 1851.
11. *ODNB*: The Langham Place Group.

12. Ibid., The Kensington Society.

13. Ibid., John Stuart Mill; Jack Stillinger (ed.), *J. S. Mill, Autobiography*, p. 179.

14. Elizabeth Crawford, *The Women's Suffrage Movement: A Reference Guide, 1866–1928*, pp. 409–11.

15. http://www.parliament.uk/about/living-heritage/evolutionofparliament/houseofcommons/reformacts/overview/

16. Helen Blackburn (ed.), *Women's Suffrage Calendar for 1899 With Compendium of Dates for the Century*, pp. 10–13.

17. Elizabeth Crawford: Richard Marsden Pankhurst, p. 514; Emmeline Pankhurst, p. 499.

18. Parliamentary Archives, *Women's Suffrage in Parliament*, exhibition catalogue, p. 3.

19. Jill Liddington and Jill Norris, *With One Hand Tied Behind Us: The Rise of the Women's Suffrage Movement*, pp. 20–1; *ODNB*: Selina Jane Cooper.

20. http://www.bbc.co.uk/history/british/pm_and_pol_tl_01.shtml

21. Rover, *Women's Suffrage and Party Politics*, pp. 106–8.

22. Diane Atkinson, 'The Politics of Female Homework: Women's Sweated Labour With Special Reference to Spitalfields, 1880–1909', Ph.D. thesis, 1994, pp. 138–61.

23. http://www.parliament.uk/livingheritage/evolutionofparliament/houseofcommons/reformacts/overview

24. Ibid., pp. 140–1.

25. Harvie and Matthew, *Nineteenth-Century Britain: A Very Short Introduction*, pp. 113–16, 138–9.

1 62 NELSON STREET, MANCHESTER

1. Emmeline Pankhurst, *My Own Story: The Autobiography of Emmeline Pankhurst*, p. 38.

2. Estelle Sylvia Pankhurst, *The Suffragette Movement*, p. 156; Elizabeth Crawford, *The Women's Suffrage Movement: A Reference Guide, 1866–1928*, pp. 499–514.

3. Sylvia Pankhurst describing her mother, Mrs Pankhurst, BBC Sound Archive, 6 February 1953.

4. *ODNB*: Lydia Ernestine Becker, 2005.

5. Letter from Lydia Becker, 7 June 1868, quoted in Crawford, *The Women's Suffrage Movement*, p. 514.

6. Richard Pankhurst, *Sylvia Pankhurst: Artist and Crusader*, p. 15.

7. *ODNB*: Richard Marsden Pankhurst, 2005.

8. Sylvia Pankhurst, *The Suffragette Movement*, p. 116.

9. Emmeline Pankhurst, *My Own Story*, p. 32.

10. Sylvia Pankhurst, *The Suffragette Movement*, p. 165; Paula Bartley, *Emmeline Pankhurst*, p. 60.

11. Sylvia Pankhurst, *The Suffragette Movement*, p. 167.

12. Christabel Harriette Pankhurst, *Unshackled: The Story of How We Won the Vote*, p. 41; Elizabeth Crawford: Esther Roper, p. 607, Eva Gore-Booth, p. 249.

13. Christabel Pankhurst, *Unshackled*, p. 28.

14. Ibid., p. 29.

15. Emmeline Pankhurst, *My Own Story*, pp. 35–6.

16. Christabel Pankhurst, *Unshackled*, p. 43.

17. Lisa Tickner, *The Spectacle of Women: Imagery of the Women's Suffrage Campaign, 1907–1914*, pp. 27–8.

18. Manchester's Radical History Website visited 2012; *ODNB*: Elizabeth Wolstenholme Elmy, 2005; Elizabeth Crawford: Elizabeth Wolstenholme Elmy, pp. 188–206; Census Returns: 1861, Worsley, Lancashire; 1871, Congleton, Cheshire.

19. Constance Rover, *Women's Suffrage and Party Politics in Britain, 1866–1914*, pp. 102–67.

20. *ODNB*: Sir Charles Benjamin Bright McLaren and Laura Elizabeth McLaren, 2005; Emmeline Pankhurst, *My Own Story*, p. 40.

21. Emmeline Pankhurst, *My Own Story*, p. 40.

22. Sylvia Pankhurst, *The Suffragette*, p. 11.

23. Ibid., p. 12.

24. Sylvia Pankhurst, *The Suffragette Movement*, p. 14.

25. Emmeline Pankhurst, *My Own Story*, p. 42.

26. *ODNB*: Nellie Alma Martel; *Australian Dictionary of Biography*, 2005: Nellie Alma Martel; Elizabeth Crawford: Nellie Martel, pp. 385–7.

27. Antonia Raeburn, *The Militant Suffragettes*, pp. 5–6; Sylvia Pankhurst, *The Suffragette*, pp. 14–16.

28. *ODNB*: Robert Peel Glanville Blatchford, 2005; Jill Liddington and Jill Norris, *With One Hand Tied Behind Us: The Rise of the Women's Suffrage Movement*, p. 55.

29. Annie Kenney, *Memories of a Militant*, pp. 23–4.

30. Ibid., pp. 20–1.

31. Ibid., p. 21.

32. Ibid., p. 26.

33. *ODNB*: Annie Kenney; Elizabeth Crawford: Annie Kenney, p. 314.

34. Kenney, *Memories of a Militant*, p. 15.

35. Ibid., pp. 18–19.

36. Ibid., p. 9.

37. Ibid., pp. 27–8.

38. Ibid., p. 28.

39. Kenney Papers, University of East Anglia.

40. Kenney, *Memories of a Militant*, pp. 26–30.

41. *ODNB*: Eleanor Beatrice Higginson, 2005; Census Returns: 1891, Crumpsall; 1901, Preston; Eleanor Higginson interviewed by Antonia Raeburn, BBC Sound Archive, 1968.

42. Emmeline Pankhurst, *My Own Story*, p. 44.

43. Carol McPhee and Ann Fitzgerald (eds), *The Non-Violent Militant: Selected Writings of Teresa Billington-Greig*, pp. 3, 32, 33, 54–5, 89–91; *ODNB*: Teresa Mary Billington-Greig; Elizabeth Crawford: Teresa Billington-Greig, pp. 54–5.

44. Christabel Pankhurst, *Unshackled*, p. 45.

45. *ODNB*: Edith Rigby, 2005; Elizabeth Crawford: Edith Rigby, pp. 598–9.

46. Phoebe Hesketh, *My Aunt Edith*, 1992, pp. 1–13. (This edition cited in all subsequent notes.)

47. Charles Dickens, *Hard Times*, Chapter 5.

48. Hesketh, *My Aunt Edith*, p. 24.

49. Ibid., p. 26.

50. Ibid., pp. 26–9.

51. Ibid., p. 35.

52. Elizabeth Crawford: Flora Drummond, p. 175; *ODNB*: Flora McKinnon Drummond, 2005.

53. Sylvia Pankhurst, *The Suffragette Movement*, p. 191.

54. Birth and death certificates of Percival Drummond.

55. Sylvia Pankhurst, *The Suffragette Movement*, p. 191.

56. Census Returns: 1861 and 1871, Alport, Derbyshire; Hannah Maria Mitchell, *The Hard Way Up: The Autobiography of Hannah Mitchell, Suffragette and Rebel*, p. 39.

57. Mitchell, *The Hard Way Up*, p. 57.

58. Ibid., p. 62.

59. Ibid., p. 64.

60. Ibid., p. 68.

61. Ibid., p. 74.

62. Ibid., pp. 76–81.

63. Marriage certificate of Gibbon Mitchell and Hannah Webster.

64. Mitchell, *The Hard Way Up*, p. 102.

65. Tameside Citizen Website; Census Return: 1901, Ashton-under-Lyne, Lancashire; death certificate of Benjamin Webster.

66. Mitchell, *The Hard Way Up*, p. 122.

67. Ibid., p. 121.

68. Ibid., p. 128.

69. Ibid., p. 126.
70. Ibid., p. 127.
71. Ibid., p. 129.
72. Ibid., p. 128.
73. Sylvia Pankhurst, *The Suffragette*, p. 28.
74. Kenney, *Memories of a Militant*, p. 35.
75. Sylvia Pankhurst, *The Suffragette*, p. 28.
76. Kenney, *Memories of a Militant*, p. 35.
77. Ibid., p. 36.
78. Christabel Pankhurst, *Unshackled*, pp. 51–2.
79. *The Times*, 16 October 1905, p. 4.
80. Ibid.
81. Sylvia Pankhurst, *The Suffragette*, p. 40.
82. Kenney, *Memories of a Militant*, p. 41.
83. Ibid., pp. 37–42.
84. Sylvia Pankhurst, *The Suffragette*, p. 41.
85. Ibid., p. 42.
86. Emmeline Pankhurst, *My Own Story*, p. 51.
87. Letter from Dora Montefiore to Minnie Baldock, 22 December 1905, Museum of London Suffragette Collections.
88. *ODNB*: Dora Frances Barrow Montefiore, 2005; *Australian Dictionary of Biography*, 1986: Dora Frances Barrow Montefiore.
89. Elizabeth Crawford: Dora Montefiore, pp. 418–20; *ODNB*: Francis Fuller; Dora Montefiore, *From a Victorian to a Modern*, 1925, online edition.
90. Elizabeth Crawford: Lucy Minnie Baldock, pp. 26–7.
91. Office for National Statistics, Census for 1901, Table XVI, p. 88, Preliminary Report, England and Wales.
92. Charles Dickens, *Household Words*, vol. XVI, 1857.
93. Montefiore, *From a Victorian to a Modern*.
94. Sylvia Pankhurst, *The Suffragette*, p. 57.
95. Emmeline Pankhurst, *My Own Story*, p. 54.
96. Sylvia Pankhurst, *The Suffragette*, p. 58.
97. Emmeline Pankhurst, *My Own Story*, p. 56.

2 'DEEDS NOT WORDS'

1. *Daily Mail*, 10 January 1906, p. 3.
2. Lynda Mugglestone, OUP blog, blog.oup.com, *Woman – or Suffragette?*, 24 August 2012.
3. *Punch*, 17 January 1906.

4. Annie Kenney, *Memories of a Militant*, p. 71.
5. Emmeline Pethick-Lawrence, *My Part in a Changing World*, p. 147.
6. Ibid., p. 148.
7. Vera Brittain, *Pethick-Lawrence: A Portrait*, pp. 17–18.
8. *ODNB*: Frederick William Pethick-Lawrence, Percy Alden.
9. Brittain, *Pethick-Lawrence*, pp. 20–3; Census Return: 1901, Canning Town.
10. Pethick-Lawrence, *My Part in a Changing World*, pp. 202, 41, 44–5.
11. Ibid., pp. 66, 72–3.
12. Ibid., p. 152.
13. Kenney, *Memories of a Militant*, p. 82.
14. Elizabeth Crawford: Irene Fenwick Miller, pp. 441–5.
15. WSPU First Annual Report, 1906/7, Museum of London Suffragette Collections.
16. Sylvia Pankhurst, *The Suffragette*, pp. 61–3.
17. *ODNB*: Sir Henry Campbell-Bannerman.
18. Sylvia Pankhurst, *The Suffragette*, pp. 61–3.
19. Birth certificate of Keir Hardie Drummond.
20. *ODNB*: James Keir Hardie.
21. *Daily Mirror*, 26 April 1906, p. 3.
22. Sylvia Pankhurst, *The Suffragette*, p. 67.
23. *Daily Mirror*, 26 April 1906, p. 3; 27 April 1906, p. 3.
24. Canning Town Minute Book, Group A, Z6083, Museum of London Suffragette Collections, p. 18.
25. Sylvia Pankhurst, *The Suffragette*, pp. 77–8.
26. *Daily Mirror*, 21 May 1906, p. 3.
27. Ibid., p. 4.
28. Handbills, Museum of London Suffragette Collections; *Daily Mirror*, 16 June 1906, p. 3.
29. *The Times*, 16 June 1906, p. 8.
30. Ibid., 18 June 1906, p. 4.
31. Sylvia Pankhurst, *The Suffragette*, p. 92.
32. Ibid., p. 93.
33. *ODNB*: Herbert Henry Asquith.
34. *Daily Mirror*, 20 June 1906, p. 3.
35. *The Times*, 26 June 1906, p. 3.
36. Elizabeth Crawford: Jane Sbarborough, pp. 617–18.
37. *Berrow's Worcester Journal*, 20 January 1883, p. 2; Mark Stevens, *Broadmoor Revealed: Victorian Crime and the Lunatic Asylum*, pp. 81–2; Census Return: 1901, Sheerness.
38. Elizabeth Crawford: Eliza Adelaide Knight, pp. 325–6.

39. National Archives Exhibition.

40. Canning Town Minute Book, Group A, Z6083, Museum of London Suffragette Collections.

41. *Daily Mirror*, 23 June 1906, p. 5.

42. Canning Town Minute Book, Group A, Z6083, Museum of London Suffragette Collections, p. 30.

43. Ibid., p. 31; *The Times*, 15 August 1906, p. 4.

44. *ODNB*: Charlotte Despard.

45. *The Vote*, 19 March 1910, p. 244; *ODNB*: Edith How-Martyn.

46. Kenney, *Memories of a Militant*, pp. 86–7.

47. Ibid., p. 73.

48. *ODNB*: Clara Evelyn Mordan.

49. WSPU, First Annual Report, 1906/7, Museum of London Suffragette Collections.

50. Kenney, *Memories of a Militant*, pp. 82–3.

51. Elizabeth Crawford: Harriet Roberta Kerr, pp. 323–4.

52. Kenney, *Memories of a Militant*, p. 82.

53. Census Returns: 1891, Chelsea; 1901, Battersea.

54. Biographical Notes: Aeta Lamb, 57.70/3, Museum of London Suffragette Collections; Elizabeth Crawford: Aeta Lamb, pp. 331–2.

55. Christabel Pankhurst, *Unshackled: The Story of How We Won the Vote*, pp. 68–9.

56. Pethick-Lawrence, *My Part in a Changing World*, p. 158.

57. Hannah Mitchell, *The Hard Way Up*, pp. 158–9.

58. Antonia Raeburn, *The Militant Suffragettes*, p. 39.

59. Mitchell, *The Hard Way Up*, pp. 160–1.

60. *The Times*, 25 October 1906, p. 15.

61. Mitchell, *The Hard Way Up*, p. 162.

62. *The Times*, 25 October 1906, p. 15.

63. Ibid.

64. Mary Gawthorpe Autobiographical Notes, 60.15/19, Museum of London Suffragette Collections; Elizabeth Crawford: Mary Eleanor Gawthorpe, pp. 242–4.

65. Pethick-Lawrence, *My Part in a Changing World*, p. 48.

66. Sylvia Pankhurst, *The Suffragette*, p. 124.

67. Dora Montefiore, *From a Victorian to a Modern*, online edition, chapter on Holloway Prison.

68. Ibid.

69. Mitchell, *The Hard Way Up*, p. 164.

70. *Daily Mirror*, 30 November 1906, p. 4.

71. Nellie Martel Biographical Notes, Group A, vol. 2, Museum of London Suffragette Collections.

72. Diane Atkinson, MA dissertation, 'When the Jockey Met the Suffragette', UEA, 2004.

73. *The Times*, 14 December 1906, p. 12.

74. *Daily Mirror*, 21 December 1906, p. 3; 22 December, p. 5.

3 'RISE UP, WOMEN!'

1. Mrs Hesmondhalgh quoted in Phoebe Hesketh, *My Aunt Edith*, p. 35.

2. *Daily Mirror*, 4 January 1907, p. 5; 5 January, p. 5.

3. Ibid., 7 January 1907, p. 5.

4. Ibid., 11 February 1907, pp. 1, 4.

5. Antonia Raeburn, *The Militant Suffragettes*, p. 45.

6. Hesketh, *My Aunt Edith*, pp. 38–9.

7. *Daily Mirror*, 14 February 1907, p. 3

8. Letter from Charlotte Despard to Mrs Fawcett, 7 March 1907 from the LSE Library Collections; *Daily Mirror*, 14 February 1907, p. 3.

9. *Daily Mirror*, 15 February 1907, pp. 3, 5.

10. Ibid., p. 5.

11. *The Times*, 14 February 1907, p. 10.

12. *ODNB*: Emma Sproson; Wolverhampton History website.

13. Elizabeth Crawford: Emma Sproson, pp. 650–51.

14. Sylvia Pankhurst, *The Suffragette Movement*, p. 254.

15. *Daily Mirror*, 18 February 1907, p. 5.

16. Ibid.

17. Letter from Christabel Pankhurst to Dora Montefiore quoted in Dora Montefiore, *From a Victorian to a Modern*, online edition, chapter on Holloway Prison.

18. Hesketh, *My Aunt Edith*, p. 41.

19. Ibid., p. 42.

20. Handbill, 50.82/577, Museum of London Suffragette Collections.

21. Leah Leneman, *'A Guid Cause': The Women's Suffrage Movement in Scotland*, p. 45.

22. Ibid., p. 45.

23. *ODNB*: Helen Miller Fraser; Elizabeth Crawford: Helen Miller Fraser, pp. 230–2; Elizabeth Ewan, Sue Innes and Siân Reynolds (eds.), *The Biographical Dictionary of Scottish Women*, 2007, p. 127; Graham Moffat, *Join Me In Remembering: The Life and Reminiscences of the Author of Bunty Pulls The Strings*, p. 52; Leneman, *'A Guid Cause'*, p. 46.

24. *Daily Mirror*, 9 March 1907, p. 3.

25. Ibid., 20 March 1907, p. 7.
26. Ibid., p. 9.
27. Sylvia Pankhurst, *The Suffragette Movement*, p. 256.
28. *ODNB*: Lady Harberton.
29. *Daily Mirror*, 21 March 1907, p. 3.
30. Ibid.
31. Ibid.
32. Jill Liddington, *Rebel Girls: Their Fight for the Vote*, pp. 112, 122; Census Return: 1901, Huddersfield; *Daily Mirror*, 27 March 1907, p. 4.
33. Ibid., 28 March 1907, p. 3.
34. Ada Wright Biographical Notes, Group C, Vol. II, Museum of London Suffragette Collections; Elizabeth Crawford: Ada Cecile Granville Wright, pp. 759–60.
35. Census Returns: 1901, 1911, Liverpool.
36. Elizabeth Crawford: Patricia Woodlock, pp. 757–8.
37. Elizabeth Crawford: Marguerite Sidley, pp. 637–8; Census Returns: 1901, Hampstead; 1911, Barnet.
38. Marguerite Sidley Biographical Notes, Museum of London Suffragette Collections; Census Returns: 1901, Hampstead; 1911, Barnet.
39. Annie Kenney, *Memories of a Militant*, p. 117.
40. Ibid., p. 118.
41. Canning Town Minute Book, 16 April 1907, Museum of London Suffragette Collections, p. 63.
42. WSPU handbill, 'Why We Oppose the Liberal Candidate', Museum of London Suffragette Collections.
43. *The Times*, 3 May 1907, p. 10.
44. *Daily Mirror*, 6 May 1907, p. 5.
45. Canning Town Minute Book, 15 May 1907, Museum of London Suffragette Collections, p. 67.
46. Elizabeth Crawford: Sara Jessie Stephenson, p. 653; Jessie Stephenson typescript, 'No Other Way', Museum of London Suffragette Collections, vol. 1, p. 63.
47. Stephenson typescript, 'No Other Way', p. 68.
48. Ibid., p. 81.
49. Martin Pugh, *The Pankhursts*, p. 159.
50. Stephenson typescript, 'No Other Way', p. 85.
51. *ODNB*: Peter Francis Curran; Stephenson typescript, 'No Other Way', p. 10.
52. Stephenson typescript, 'No Other Way', p. 10.
53. Ibid., p. 13.

54. Ibid., pp. 8–15.

55. Canning Town Minute Book, 5, 18, 25 June 1907, Museum of London Suffragette Collections, pp. 69–71.

56. Letter to branch secretaries and treasurers, 1907, 57.116/46, Museum of London Suffragette Collections.

57. Ibid., 57.116/47, Rachel Barrett Autobiographical Notes, Museum of London Suffragette Collections, pp. 1–2; Emmeline Pethick-Lawrence, *My Part in a Changing World*, pp. 174–7.

58. *ODNB*: Rachel Barrett; Elizabeth Crawford: Rachel Barrett, pp. 33–4; Census Returns: 1871, 1881, 1891, Carmarthen.

59. Pethick-Lawrence, *My Part in a Changing World*, pp. 174–7.

60. Ibid., p. 176.

61. Ibid., p. 177.

62. Vera Brittain, *Pethick-Lawrence: A Portrait*, p. 51.

63. *Daily Mirror*, 4 September 1907, p. 1; quoted in Antonia Raeburn, *The Militant Suffragettes*, 1974 hardback edition, pp. 40–1.

64. Ibid.

65. Kenney, *Memories of a Militant*, pp. 74–5.

66. *Votes for Women*, October 1907, p. 6.

67. Ibid., October 1907, p. 1.

68. Brittain, *Pethick-Lawrence: A Portrait*, p. 54.

69. By permission of the British Library, The Balfour Papers, Add 49793, ff. 17–18, Correspondence between Christabel Pankhurst and A. J. Balfour, 6 October 1907.

70. Ibid., 23 October, 28 October 1907.

71. Kenney, *Memories of a Militant*, pp. 124–6.

72. B. M. Willmot Dobbie, *A Nest of Suffragettes in Somerset*, p. 13.

73. *ODNB*: Mary Blathwayt; Elizabeth Crawford: Blathwayt Family, pp. 64–6.

74. Canning Town Minute Book, 3 December 1907, Museum of London Suffragette Collections, p. 87.

75. Ibid., 10 December 1907, p. 90.

76. Emmeline Pankhurst, *My Own Story*, p. 90.

77. Ibid., p. 91.

78. Ibid., p. 92.

79. *Votes for Women*, December 1907, p. 28.

4 PURPLE, WHITE AND GREEN

1. Sylvia Pankhurst, *The Suffragette*, p. 191.

2. Ibid.

3. *The Times*, 18 January 1908, p. 12.

4. *Daily Mirror*, 18 January, p. 1; *The Times*, 18 January 1908, p. 12.

5. Census Returns: 1911, Swindon, Greenwich; Elizabeth Crawford: Edith Bessie New, p. 446; Krista Cowman, *Women of the Right Spirit: Paid Organisers of the Women's Social and Political Union 1904–1918*, p. 229.

6. Richard Whitmore, *Alice Hawkins and the Suffragette Movement in Edwardian England*, pp. 25–7; Elizabeth Crawford: Alice Hawkins, p. 282; Census Returns: 1901, 1911, Ratby; Alice Hawkins family website.

7. Richard Pankhurst, *Sylvia Pankhurst: Artist and Crusader*, pp. 94–5; Sylvia Pankhurst, *The Suffrage Movement*, 1977, p. 263. (This edition cited in all subsequent notes.)

8. *Votes for Women,* January 1908, p. 52.

9. WSPU Second Annual Report for the year ending 29 February 1908, Museum of London Suffragette Collections, p. 7.

10. *Votes for Women*, 12 February 1908, p. 3.

11. *Daily Mirror*, 12 February 1908, p. 3.

12. Antonia Raeburn, *The Militant Suffragettes*, p. 64.

13. Phoebe Hesketh, *My Aunt Edith,* p. 45.

14. Ibid.

15. Raeburn, *The Militant Suffragettes*, p. 65.

16. *Votes for Women*, April 1908, p. 99.

17. Hesketh, *My Aunt Edith*, p. 27.

18. Census Returns: 1901, 1911, Preston; Hesketh, *My Aunt Edith*, p. 43.

19. Marie Brackenbury Biographical Notes, Museum of London Suffragette Collections, pp. 77–81; Elizabeth Crawford: The Brackenburys, pp. 75–6.

20. *The Times*, 11 December 1907, p. 11; *Votes for Women*, vol. 1, January 1908, p. 53; February 1908, p. 69.

21. *Daily Mirror*, 20 March 1908, p. 4.

22. Census Returns: 1891, 1901, Westminster; Elizabeth Crawford: Vera Wentworth, pp. 704–5.

23. Fenner Brockway, *Towards Tomorrow: The Autobiography of Fenner Brockway*, pp. 21–2.

24. Sylvia Pankhurst, *The Suffragette Movement*, p. 281.

25. Sylvia Pankhurst, *The Suffragette*, p. 198; Raeburn, *The Militant Suffragettes*, p. 51.

26. *Votes for Women*, vol. 1, March 1908, p. 82; Emmeline Pankhurst, *My Own Story*, pp. 97–9; *Daily Mirror*, 19 February 1908, p. 5.

27. *Votes for Women*, vol. 1, March 1908, p. 82.

28. Annie Kenney, *Memories of a Militant*, p. 139.

29. *Votes for Women*, April 1909, p. 108.

30. Elizabeth Crawford (ed.), *Campaigning for the Vote: Kate Frye's Suffrage Diary*, p. 29.
31. Kenney, *Memories of a Militant*, p. 139.
32. *Daily Mirror*, 23 March 1908, p. 3.
33. Ibid., p. 3.
34. *The Times*, 25 March 1908, p. 6.
35. Census Return: 1901, Hereford; Mike Williams family website.
36. Marion Westbrook, *The Hooks and the Parlbys: A Family History*, privately printed, 1975; Letter from Mrs Pankhurst to Miss Parlby, 22 March 1908, 26 May 1908 and undated letters from Gladice Keevil to Beatrice Parlby, Hereford Archives, BH28/13/1.
37. *The Times*, 4 June 1908, p. 14; Obituary, *The Times*, 23 April 1929, p. 9.
38. *ODNB*: Sir Henry Campbell-Bannerman.
39. *Daily Mirror*, 7 April 1908, p. 3.
40. *The Times*, 23 April 1908, p. 9.
41. *Daily Mirror*, 15 April 1908, p. 3.
42. Elizabeth Crawford: Helen Millar Craggs, pp. 146–7; *Suffrage Annual and Women's Who's Who*, p. 215; *The Times*, 3 May 1928, p. 18; Census Return: 1901, Brighton.
43. Letters from Mary Gawthorpe to Isabel Seymour, Museum of London Suffragette Collections.
44. *Votes for Women*, 14 May 1908, p. 171.
45. *Daily Mirror*, 6 May 1908, p. 1; *Evening Telegram of St John's*, Newfoundland, 15 May 1908, p. 4; *Marlborough Express*, 30 June 1908, p. 3.
46. *Daily Mirror*, 11 May 1908, p. 4.
47. Letter from Mrs Cobb to Mrs Baldock, Museum of London Suffragette Collections; *Votes for Women*, May and June 1908.
48. Sylvia Pankhurst, *The Suffragette Movement*, p. 282.
49. Postcard, private collection.
50. Kenney, *Memories of a Militant*, p. 78; Emmeline Pankhurst, *My Own Story*, p. 112.
51. Diane Atkinson, *Purple, White and Green: The Suffragettes in London, 1906–1914*, p. 15.
52. Kenney, *Memories of a Militant*, p. 76.
53. *Votes for Women*, 18 June 1908, p. 249; 30 June, p. 343.
54. *Daily Mirror*, 13 June, 15 June 1908, p. 4, p. 8; Museum of London, NUWSS handbills.
55. Sylvia Pankhurst, *The Suffragette Movement*, p. 283; *The Times*, 20 June 1908, p. 5.
56. Emmeline Pankhurst, *My Own Story*, pp. 112–13.

57. *Daily Mirror*, 18 June 1908, p. 4.
58. Ibid., p. 4.
59. Museum of London textile collections.
60. *The Times*, 19 June 1908, p. 14.
61. *The Times*, 22 June 1908, p. 9; 11 September 1908, p. 8.
62. *Daily Mirror*, 20 June 1908, p. 3.
63. *Votes for Women*, 18 June 1908, pp. 245–6.
64. Jessie Stephenson typescript, 'No Other Way', Museum of London Suffragette Collections, pp. 116–32.
65. Emmeline Pankhurst, *My Own Story*, p. 114.
66. *Votes for Women*, 25 June 1908, pp. 260–1.
67. Ibid., 30 April 1908, p 133; Census Returns: 1901, Hendon; 1911, Cricklewood; *Votes for Women*, April 1908, p. 129; 7 May, p. 149; 4 June, p. 211; 9 July, p. 295; National Portrait Gallery website; 16 July, p. 317; *ODNB*: Dorothy Adelaide Braddell; *Pall Mall Gazette*, 1 February 1887.
68. Letter from Helen Fraser to Isabel Seymour, 6 July 1908, Museum of London Suffragette Collections.
69. *Votes for Women*, 25 June 1908, p. 265.
70. Ibid.
71. Ibid.

5 WINDOW-SMASHING AND 'RUSHING' PARLIAMENT

1. *The Times,* 1 July 1908, p. 14.
2. Ibid.
3. Elizabeth Crawford: Florence Eliza Haig, p. 257.
4. *Votes for Women*, 25 June 1908, p. 265.
5. *ODNB*: Joseph Joachim.
6. Elizabeth Crawford: Maud Amalia Fanny Joachim, pp. 310–11; *Votes for Women*, 4 October 1908, p. 4.
7. *ODNB*: Mary Phillips; Elizabeth Crawford: Mary Phillips, pp. 544–6; *The Listener*, 8 February 1968, pp. 175–6.
8. *Votes for Women*, 10 September 1908, p. 436; 24 September 1908, pp. 470–1.
9. *The Times*, 1 July 1908, p. 14.
10. Ibid., 2 July 1908, p. 4.
11. *Daily Mirror*, 2 July 1908, pp. 3, 9; Elizabeth Crawford: Mary Leigh, pp. 338–40; *ODNB*: Mary (Marie) Leigh.
12. *The Times*, 2 July 1908, p. 4; Felbridge and District History Group website; Census Return: 1911, Hampstead.
13. *Votes for Women*, 6 May 1910, p. 517.

14. Elizabeth Crawford: Spong Family, p. 650.

15. Felbridge and District History Group website.

16. *ODNB*: Charlotte Augusta Leopoldine Marsh; Elizabeth Crawford: Charlotte Marsh; Marian Lawson (ed.), *Memories of Charlotte Marsh*, Museum of London Suffragette Collections, pp. 7, 13, 16; *The Times*, 24 April 1961, p. 19; Census Return: 1901, Jesmond; private family information.

17. *Daily Mirror*, 28 July 1908, p. 5.

18. Ibid., 31 July 1908, p. 5.

19. Elizabeth Crawford: Rosa May Billinghurst, pp. 53–4; *ODNB*: Rosa May Billinghurst; Billinghurst family website.

20. *The Times*, 22 July 1908, p. 4; *ODNB*: Mary Augusta Ward (Mrs Humphry Ward).

21. *The Times*, 22 July 1908, p. 4.

22. Ibid.

23. *ODNB*: Gertrude Margaret Lowthian Bell; Julia Bush, *Women Against the Vote: Female Anti-Suffragism in Britain*, p. 179.

24. Brian Harrison, *Separate Spheres: The Opposition to Women's Suffrage in Britain*, pp. 118–19; Violet R. Markham, *Return Passage: The Autobiography of Violet R. Markham*, p. 95.

25. *Daily Mirror*, 6 August 1908, p. 5; Lucienne Boyce, *The Bristol Suffragettes*, pp. 16–19.

26. *ODNB*: Clara Margaret Codd; Clara Codd, *So Rich a Life*, p. 46.

27. Codd, *So Rich a Life*, p. 46.

28. Ibid.

29. Ibid., p. 47.

30. Ibid., p. 48.

31. Ibid., p. 51.

32. Churchill Archive, CHAR 1/75/78B, telegram to Winston Churchill, 16 August 1908; *ODNB*: Clementine Ogilvy Hozier.

33. Antonia Raeburn, *The Militant Suffragettes*, pp. 64–7.

34. *Daily Mirror*, 13 October 1908, pp. 1, 3.

35. Emmeline Pethick-Lawrence, *My Part in a Changing World*, p. 196.

36. *Daily Mirror*, 14 October 1908, p. 9.

37. BBC Sound Archive, Una Harriet Ella Stratford Duval interviewed, 1955.

38. *Daily Mirror*, 14 October 1908, p. 3.

39. Ibid.; Elizabeth Crawford: Margaret Travers Symons, pp. 669–70.

40. National Archives, divorce papers of Margaret Travers Symons, J.77/997/279.

41. *The Times*, 15 October 1908, p. 8; *Daily Mirror*, 16 October 1908, p. 4.

42. BBC Sound Archive, Ada Flatman interviewed, 1946.

43. Ada (Susan) Flatman, pp. 221–3; Ada Flatman, 'Reminiscences of a Suffragette', Museum of London Suffragette Collections.

44. Elizabeth Crawford: Una Harriet Ella Stratford Dugdale, pp. 177–9; *Suffrage Annual and Women's Who's Who*, pp. 231–2.

45. Prison letters, SC Box 31, 50.82/1679a, Museum of London Suffragette Collections.

46. *ODNB*: Marion Wallace-Dunlop; Elizabeth Crawford: Marion Wallace-Dunlop; clandunlop website.

47. Codd, *So Rich a Life*, p. 61.

48. Ibid., pp. 63–4.

49. Elizabeth Crawford: Mabel Henrietta Capper, p. 95.

50. *The Listener*, 8 February 1968, p. 175.

51. BBC Sound Archive, Mrs Eleanor Higginson and Grace Roe interview with Antonia Raeburn, 6 February 1968.

52. *ODNB*: Kitty Marion (Katherine Marie Schäfer; Kitty Marion); Diane Atkinson, 'Kitty Marion: From Babes in the Wood to "Black Friday": a "refined comedienne" and militant suffragette', MA Dissertation, UEA, 2003, pp. 1–19.

53. Kitty Marion autobiography, Museum of London Suffragette Collections, vol. I, pp. 5–10, 22–6, 155–62.

54. Pethick-Lawrence, *My Part in a Changing World*, pp. 191–3.

55. *Daily Mirror*, 21 October 1908, p. 4.

56. Emmeline Pankhurst, *My Own Story*, p. 124.

57. Raeburn, *The Militant Suffragettes*, p. 84.

58. *Daily Mirror*, 26 October 1908, p. 5.

59. Emmeline Pankhurst, *My Own Story*, pp. 128–9.

60. *The Times*, 26 October 1908, p. 2.

61. BBC Sound Archive, interview with Arthur Barrett, 1955.

62. *The Times*, 15 October 1898, p. 6.

63. *Daily Mirror*, 17 July 1908, p. 5.

64. *Daily Mirror*, 29 October 1908, pp. 1, 4; *The Times*, 29 October 1908, p. 10.

65. *Daily Mirror*, 30 October 1908, p. 4; 31 October 1908, p. 9.

66. *Suffrage Annual and Women's Who's Who*, pp. 241–2; Elizabeth Crawford: Lettice Annie Floyd; *ODNB*: Lettice Annie Floyd, Census Return: 1901, Steep, Hampshire; Alan Tucker, *Suffragette Partnership: The Lives of Lettice Floyd and Annie Williams, 1860–1943*, pp. 1–7.

67. *Votes for Women*, 26 November 1908, p. 165.

68. Ibid.

69. Ibid.

70. *Daily Mirror*, 2 December 1908, p. 4.

71. Elizabeth Crawford: Helen Charlotte Elizabeth Douglas Ogston, pp. 472–4; Sylvia Pankhurst, *The Suffragette Movement*, pp. 296–7.

72. Sylvia Pankhurst, *The Suffragette Movement*, p. 297.

73. 8 Edw7, CH.66, The Public Meetings Bill, 1908.

74. *Daily Mirror*, 21 December 1908, p. 3.

75. Emmeline Pankhurst, *The Suffragette Movement*, p. 134.

76. Ibid.

77. *Votes for Women*, 17 December 1908, p. 194.

78. Andrew Rosen, *Rise Up, Women!: The Militant Campaign of the Women's Social and Political Union, 1903–1914*, p. 114; WSPU Third Annual Report to end of 1909, Museum of London Suffragette Collections, p. 17; Sylvia Pankhurst, *The Suffragette*, p. 357.

79. Letter from Cicely Isabel Fairfield to Josephine Letitia Denny Fairfield, December 1908, Lilly Library Mss, Indiana University, Bloomington.

6 STALKING LIBERALS AND THE BILL OF RIGHTS DEMONSTRATION

1. *Votes for Women*, 24 December 1908, p. 210; 7 January 1909, p. 242; 14 January 1909, p. 258.

2. Ibid., 21 January 1909, pp. 9, 276–7.

3. Ibid., pp. 276–7.

4. *The Times*, 26 January 1909, p. 10.

5. Elizabeth Crawford: Frances Clara Bartlett, p. 38; Census Return: 1901, Clapham.

6. Frances Clara Bartlett Biographical Notes, Group C, vol. 2, Museum of London Suffragette Collections, pp. 37–9.

7. Ibid., p. 39.

8. *Votes for Women*, 11 February 1909, p. 332.

9. *Daily Mirror*, 25 February 1909, p. 12; *The Times*, 25 February 1909, p. 12.

10. Mark Girouard, *Enthusiasms*, p. 138.

11. Elizabeth Crawford: Mrs Georgiana Margaret Solomon and Daisy Dorothea Solomon, pp. 643–4; *ODNB*: Mrs Georgiana Margaret Solomon.

12. Private collection.

13. Elizabeth Crawford: Muriel Lilah Matters, pp. 392–3.

14. BBC Sound Archive, 1939; Muriel Matters website; Who's Who of Ballooning website.

15. Antonia Raeburn, *The Militant Suffragettes*, pp. 88–9.

16. *The Times*, 25 February 1909, p. 12.

17. Raeburn, *The Militant Suffragettes*, p. 90.

18. *The Times*, 25 February 1909, p. 12.
19. Ibid.
20. Raeburn, *The Militant Suffragettes*, p. 90.
21. Ibid., p. 91.
22. Ibid.
23. Note from Constance Georgina Lytton to her mother, the Dowager Countess Bulwer-Lytton, 25 February 1909, 50.82/1119, Museum of London Suffragette Collections.
24. Letter from Neville Bulwer-Lytton to his mother, Dowager Countess Bulwer-Lytton, 25 February 1909, 50.82/1119, Museum of London Suffragette Collections.
25. Letter from Lady Constance Lytton to her mother, 26 February 1909, 50.82/1119, Museum of London Suffragette Collections.
26. Ibid.
27. Patricia Miles and Jill Williams, *An Uncommon Criminal: The Life of Lady Constance Lytton, Militant Suffragette, 1869–1923*, pp. 1–2; Betty Balfour (ed.), *The Letters of Constance Lytton*, p. 130.
28. Miles and Williams, *An Uncommon Criminal*, p. 3.
29. Letter from Constance Lytton to Adela Villiers, 14 July 1892; Letter from Constance Lytton to Adela Villiers, 23 October 1892, Lytton Family Papers, Courtesy of Knebworth House Archives.
30. Miles and Williams, *An Uncommon Criminal*, p. 7.
31. Letter from Constance Lytton to Adela Villiers, 1 January 1900; Letters from Constance Lytton to Adela Villiers, 24 and 28 August 1900; Letter from John Ponsonby to Lord Lytton, 25 May 1923, Lytton Family Papers, Knebworth House Archives.
32. Balfour (ed.), *The Letters of Constance Lytton*, pp. 135–6.
33. Elizabeth Crawford: Lady Constance Georgina Lytton, pp. 361–2; *ODNB*: Lady Constance Georgina Bulwer-Lytton; Lytton Family Papers, Knebworth House Archives; Miles and Williams, *An Uncommon Criminal*, pp. 1–3; *The Times*, 23 May 1923, p. 13; Balfour (ed.), *The Letters of Constance Lytton*, pp. 141–66.
34. Elizabeth Crawford: Charlotte Emily Caprina Fahey, p. 212; *ODNB*: Sir Alfred Gilbert; Divorce papers, 1908, National Archives, J/8351.
35. Elizabeth Crawford: Sarah Carwin; Census Return: Marylebone; 1901, Caterham, Surrey; Sarah Carwin Biographical Notes, 57.116/35, Museum of London Suffragette Collections; Great Ormond Street Hospital Archives, Nurses' Register.
36. Elizabeth Crawford: Rose Lamartine Yates, pp. 763–4; *ODNB*: Rose Lamartine Yates.

37. Keith Atkinson family history website: William Swindlehurst and the Lamartine Yates; *Votes for Women*, 5 March 1909, p. 407.

38. Constance Lytton, *Prisons and Prisoners: Some Personal Experiences by Constance Lytton and Jane Warton, spinster*, pp. 165–70; *Daily Mirror*, 25 March 1909, p. 4.

39. Balfour (ed.), *The Letters of Constance Lytton*, pp. 158–9; Constance Lytton Papers, 50.82/1119, Museum of London Suffragette Collections.

40. Elizabeth Crawford: Dora Marsden, pp. 379–81; *Votes for Women*, 26 March 1909, p. 479.

41. *Daily Mirror*, 31 March 1909, p. 3; Raeburn, *The Militant Suffragettes*, p. 93.

42. *Votes for Women*, 2 April 1909, pp. 506–7.

43. B. M. Willmott Dobbie, *A Nest of Suffragettes in Somerset*, p. 21.

44. *Votes for Women*, 19 April 1909, p. 551; *Votes for Women*, 23 April 1909, p. 575.

45. Letter from Constance Lytton to Miss Davis, 2 April 1909, 50.82/1119, Museum of London Suffragette Collections.

46. *Daily Mirror*, 28 April 1909, p. 4.

47. *ODNB*: Frances Theresa Garnett; death certificate of Frances Teresa [sic] Garnett; Wakefield Archives, C85/1126; C85/699; C85/3/6/50.

48. *Daily Mirror*, 29 April 1909, p. 5, pp. 8–9.

49. Census Returns: 1891, 1911, Twickenham.

50. Letters from Constance Lytton to Annie Kenney, 4 May, 27 May, 28 May 1909, Kenney Papers, University of East Anglia.

51. *ODNB*: Vera Louise Holme; Elizabeth Crawford: Vera Louise Holme, pp. 288–90; Sylvia Pankhurst, *The Suffragette Movement*, p. 225.

52. Sylvia Pankhurst, *The Suffragette Movement*, p. 305.

53. *Votes for Women*, 14 May 1909, p. 675.

54. Elizabeth Crawford: Hertha Ayrton, pp. 22–3, Barbara Bodichon Ayrton, p. 252; *ODNB*: Sarah Phoebe Hertha Ayrton.

55. *Votes for Women*, 14 May 1909, p. 607.

56. Ibid., 21 May 1909, p. 691.

57. Ibid., 4 June 1909, p. 757.

58. Emmeline Pankhurst, *My Own Story*, pp. 137–8.

59. Annie Kenney, *Memories of a Militant*, pp. 211–12; *The Times*, 3 June 1909, p. 6; *Votes for Women*, 4 June 1909, p. 758.

60. Notes made by Betty Balfour, 3 June 1909, Knebworth House Archives.

61. Ibid.

62. Willmott Dobbie, *A Nest of Suffragettes in Somerset*, pp. 30–1.

63. *The Times*, 25 June 1909, p. 7.

64. Sylvia Pankhurst, *The Suffragette Movement*, p. 308.

65. *The Times*, 30 June 1909, p. 5; Sylvia Pankhurst, *The Suffragette Movement*, p. 308.

66. Sylvia Pankhurst, *The Suffragette Movement*, p. 309.

67. Alice Paul Biographical Notes, 57.116/45, Museum of London Suffragette Collections; Elizabeth Crawford: Alice Paul, pp. 530–1.

68. Alice Paul Biographical Notes, 57.117/45 and 50, Museum of London Suffragette Collections.

69. Ibid, 57.117/50.

70. Amelia R. Fry and Alice Paul, *Conversations with Alice Paul: Woman Suffrage and the Equal Rights Movement: Oral History Transcript and Related Material, 1972–1976*, 1976, pp. 31–48.

71. Elizabeth Crawford: Lucy Burns, pp. 88–9; Fry and Paul, *Conversations with Alice Paul*, p. 25; Mary Walton, A *Woman's Crusade: Alice Paul and the Battle for the Ballot*, pp. 27–8.

72. *Votes for Women*, 13 August 1909, p. 1055.

73. Mary S. Allen, *Lady in Blue: The Autobiography of the First of the Women Police in England*, pp. 13–16; Elizabeth Crawford: Mary Sophia Allen, pp. 8–9.

74. Allen, *Lady in Blue*, p. 18.

75. Boyce Gaddes, *Outward Bound From Inverlochy: A Biography of the Hon. Evelina Haverfield*, pp. 9, 12, 34–5, 52–3.

76. Elizabeth Crawford: Hon. Mrs Evelina Haverfield, pp. 279–80; *ODNB*: Hon. Mrs Evelina Haverfield.

77. Vera Holme's Biographical Notes on Evelina Haverfield, Museum of London Suffragette Collections; Elizabeth Crawford: Vera Louise Holme, pp. 288–90; *The Times*, 8 July 1899, p. 1; death certificate of Henry Wykeham Brook Tunstall Haverfield.

78. BBC Sound Archive, Grace Roe interviewed by Antonia Raeburn, 1968.

79. Ibid.

80. Frances Mabelle Unwin, 'Short Account of Miss Sarah Carwin', 57.116/35, Museum of London Suffragette Collections; Letter from Mrs Pankhurst to Sarah Carwin, 24 September 1909, 57.116/65.

7 STARVING SUFFRAGETTES

1. Antonia Raeburn, *The Militant Suffragettes*, p. 102; *The Times*, 9 July 1909, p. 9.

2. Letter from Frederick Pethick-Lawrence to Marion Wallace-Dunlop, 9 July 1909, 50.82/1117, Museum of London Suffragette Collections.

3. Elizabeth Crawford: Frederick Hankinson, pp. 267–9; letter in private collection.

4. *The Times*, 13 July 1909, pp. 4, 11; *The Times*, 15 July, 1909, p. 12; *Daily Mirror*, 15 July 1909, p. 8.

5. *Daily Mirror*, 31 July 1909, p. 4.

6. Ibid.

7. *Votes for Women*, 13 August 1909, p. 1055.

8. National Archives, HO: Sarah Jane (Jennie) Baines. 144/1040/182086.

9. *Australian Dictionary of Biography*, Baines, vol. 7, 1979, online; Elizabeth Crawford: Sarah Jennie Baines, pp. 24–6; *ODNB*: Sarah Jane (Jennie) Baines.

10. Annie Kenney, *Memories of a Militant*, pp. 143–4.

11. National Archives, HO 144/1040/182086.

12. Ibid.

13. *The Times*, 2 August 1909, p. 8; B. M. Willmott Dobbie, *A Nest of Suffragettes in Somerset*, pp. 32–3.

14. *The Times*, 21 August 1909, p. 2; Elizabeth Crawford: Mary Leigh, p. 338.

15. *Votes for Women*, 27 August 1909, p. 1110.

16. Ibid.

17. *The Times*, 21 August 1909, p. 2.

18. *Daily Mirror*, 7 September 1909, p. 5.

19. *Votes for Women*, 10 September 1909, p. 1157.

20. Ibid., p. 1158.

21. Herbert Asquith, *Moments of Memory: Recollections and Impressions*, p. 156.

22. *Votes for Women*, 10 September 1909, p. 1158; Kenney, *Memories of a Militant*, pp. 215–18.

23. Asquith, *Moments of Memory*, p. 158.

24. *Votes for Women*, 10 September 1909, p. 1158.

25. Willmott Dobbie, *A Nest of Suffragettes in Somerset*, p. 34.

26. Ibid., pp. 34–5.

27. National Archives, HO 144/1431/183461; *ODNB*: Sir Melville Leslie Macnaghten.

28. Ibid.

29. Nigel West, *Dictionary of World War One Intelligence*, p. 296.

30. *The Times*, 15 September 1909, p. 10; Leah Leneman, '*A Guid Cause*': *The Women's Suffrage Movement in Scotland*, pp. 79–80.

31. National Records Scotland, H12/22, Register of Suffragettes Received into Prisons in Scotland, 1900–14, p. 1; HH 16/36.

32. *The Times*, 23 September 1909, p. 10; Raeburn, *The Militant Suffragettes*, p. 115; *The Times*, 25 September 1909, p. 7.

33. Emmeline Pethick-Lawrence, *My Part in a Changing World*, pp. 237–8.
34. WSPU Handbill, 'Fed By Force: How The Government Treats Political Opponents in Prison', 50.82/491, Museum of London Suffragette Collections.
35. Ibid.
36. Ibid.
37. *Votes for Women*, 17 December 1909, p. 181.
38. Ibid., 8 October 1909, p. 20; Elizabeth Crawford: Laura Frances Ainsworth, pp. 5–7.
39. *The Times*, 6 October 1909, p. 12, 7 October 1909, p. 4, 13 October 1909, p. 9.
40. Letter from Constance Lytton to Arthur James Balfour, 26 September 1909, BL MSS Add 49793, ff.144–147; Letter from Constance Lytton to Arthur Balfour, 7 October 1909, BL MSS Add 49793, ff.148–150.
41. *The Times*, 28 September 1909, p. 10.
42. Ibid., 29 September 1909, p. 10.
43. WSPU Handbill, 'The Opinion of Dr Hugh Fenton on The Forcible Feeding of Suffragist Prisoners', Group C, vol. 3, Museum of London Suffragette Collections, pp. 137–8.
44. Ibid.
45. *The Times*, 4 October 1909, p. 5; Ian Lang, 'A Prostitution of the Profession? Forcible Feeding, Prison Doctors, Suffrage and the British State, 1909–1914', *Social History of Medicine*, vol. 26, no. 2, pp. 226, 232–5.
46. Raeburn, *The Militant Suffragettes*, p. 117; *Votes for Women*, 8 October 1909, p. 21.
47. *ODNB*: Henry Woodd Nevinson, Evelyn Jane Sharp; Elizabeth Crawford: Evelyn Sharp, pp. 627–9; *Votes for Women*, 18 June 1908, p. 254.
48. *ODNB*: Henry Noel Brailsford, Jane Esdon Brailsford.
49. *Votes for Women*, 15 October 1909, p. 35.
50. Ibid.
51. Kitty Marion typescript autobiography, 50.82/1123, Museum of London Suffragette Collections, p. 176.
52. *Votes for Women*, 15 October 1909, p. 35.
53. Ibid.
54. Ibid.
55. Ibid., p 36.
56. Ibid.
57. Museum of London, Lady Constance Lytton's family telegrams, 50.82/1119.
58. Kitty Marion Scrapbook, 50.82/1123, Museum of London Suffragette Collections.

59. Kitty Marion typescript autobiography, Museum of London Suffragette Collections, p. 184.

60. Ibid., p. 187.

61. Ibid., pp. 187–9.

62. Ibid., p. 189.

63. Ibid.

64. *Votes for Women*, 12 November 1909, p. 106.

65. Letter from Dorothy Pethick to Kitty Marion, 9 November 1909; Letter from Monica Whateley to Kitty Marion, 10 November 1909, 50.82/1120, Museum of London Suffragette Collections.

66. Kitty Marion autobiography, p. 191; *Votes for Women*, 12 November 1909, p. 106; Letter from Josephine Gonne to Kitty Marion, 2 December 1909, 50.82/1120, Museum of London Suffragette Collections.

67. Letter from Emily Wilding Davison to Mrs Williams, 14 October 1909, Biographical Notes, Group D, vol. 1, Museum of London Suffragette Collections, pp. 88–9.

68. *Votes for Women*, 5 November 1909, p. 85.

69. Elizabeth Crawford: Emily Davison, p. 161.

70. *Daily Mirror*, 18 October 1909, p. 5; *Votes for Women*, 29 October 1909, p. 74.

71. National Records of Scotland, HH. 55/323/162; Leneman, 'A Guid Cause', p. 87; National Records of Scotland, Register of Suffragettes Received into Prison in Scotland, National Records of Scotland, HH. 12/22, pp. 1–2; Scottish Office Prison Correspondence; HH. 55/323/21203, 21219; HH. 16/36; *The Times*, 20 October 1909, p. 6; *Scotsman*, 20 October 1909.

72. Elizabeth Crawford: Helen Alexander Archdale, pp. 15–16; *ODNB*: Helen Alexander Archdale; Deirdre Macpherson, *The Suffragette's Daughter. Betty Archdale: Her Life of Feminism, Cricket, War and Education*, pp. 15–27; Leneman, 'A Guid Cause', pp. 80–1; Scotland's People birth, marriage and death certificates; Amelia R. Fry and Alice Paul, *Conversations with Alice Paul: Woman Suffrage and the Equal Rights Movement: Oral History Transcript and Related Material, 1972–1976*, p. 51; Museum of London.

73. Sylvia Pankhurst, *The Suffragette Movement*, p. 320; *Votes for Women*, 15 October 1909, p. 43.

74. *Votes for Women*, 17 December 1909, p. 188.

75. *The Times*, 1 November 1909, p. 10.

76. Letter from Dr Ernest Helby to the Home Office, 4 November 1909; National Archives, HO 144/1043/183461.

77. Mary Walton, *A Woman's Crusade: Alice Paul and the Battle for the Ballot*, pp. 30–2.

78. *Votes for Women*, 17 December 1909, p. 181.

79. Ibid.

80. National Records Scotland, HH.55/323/112.

81. Ibid.

82. Ibid.

83. Ibid.

84. Ibid.

85. *Votes for Women*, 19 November 1909, p. 116.

86. Mary Allen and Julia Helen Heyneman, *Woman at the Cross Roads*, p. 64; Nina Boyd, *From Suffragette to Fascist: The Many Lives of Mary Allen*, p. 37, p. 42.

87. Sylvia D. Hoffert, *Alva Vanderbilt Belmont: Unlikely Champion of Women's Rights*, pp. 74–5; Emmeline Pankhurst, *My Own Story*, pp. 160–2; Raeburn, *The Militant Suffragettes*, p. 132.

88. *The Times*, 4 December 1909, p. 9; 6 December 1909, p. 6; *Votes for Women*, 10 December 1909, p. 16.

89. Phoebe Hesketh, *My Aunt Edith*, pp. 54–5; Letter from Rosamund Massy to Elsa Gye, 1930, Biographical Notes, Group C, vol. 1, Museum of London Suffragette Collections, p. 108.

90. Hesketh, *My Aunt Edith*, p. 55.

91. *Votes for Women*, 10 December 1909, p. 165.

92. Hesketh, *My Aunt Edith*, pp. 56–7.

93. *Daily Mirror*, 10 December 1909, p. 4; *ODNB*: Mary Leigh.

94. Letter from Christabel Pankhurst to A. J. Balfour, 3 December 1909; BL MSS Add 49793.

95. *Votes for Women*, 1 October 1909, p. 16, 3 December 1909, p. 157, 17 December 1909, p. 183, 3 December 1909, p. 150, 31 December 1909, p. 222; the game of 'Panko', private collection.

8 PROMISE AND BETRAYAL

1. Henry Francis Pankhurst death certificate.

2. Sylvia Pankhurst, *The Suffragette Movement*, p. 324.

3. Antonia Raeburn, *The Militant Suffragettes*, p. 133.

4. Letter from Christabel Pankhurst to Ada Flatman, 7 January 1910, Museum of London Suffragette Collections.

5. Christabel Pankhurst, *Unshackled: The Story of How We Won the Vote*, p. 149.

6. WSPU Fourth Annual Report for the year, 1 January 1909–28 February 1910, Museum of London Suffragette Collections, pp. 2–9.

7. WSPU Handbill, 'A Letter to A Liberal Woman', 1910, 50.82/504, Museum of London Suffragette Collections.

8. Ibid.

9. From the LSE Library Collections, Letter from Christabel Pankhurst to Mr Joseph King, 8 February 1910, Microfiche 184.

10. Betty Balfour (ed.), *The Letters of Constance Lytton*, pp. 188–200; Constance Lytton, *Prisons and Prisoners: Some Personal Experiences by Constance Lytton and Jane Warton, spinster*, p. 233.

11. Constance Lytton Papers, 50.82/1119, Museum of London Suffragette Collections.

12. Lytton, *Prisons and Prisoners*, pp. 239–41.

13. Constance Lytton Papers, 50.82/1119, Museum of London Suffragette Collections.

14. Lytton, *Prisons and Prisoners*, p. 245.

15. Selina Martin blogspot website.

16. Lytton, *Prisons and Prisoners*, p. 244; Lytton Family Papers, Knebworth House Archives.

17. Lytton, *Prisons and Prisoners*, p. 245.

18. Ibid., pp. 261, 264.

19. Ibid., pp. 268–9.

20. Ibid., p. 273.

21. Ibid., p. 274.

22. Ibid., p. 290.

23. Ibid., pp. 293–5.

24. Balfour (ed.), *The Letters of Constance Lytton*, p. 187.

25. Ibid., p. 187.

26. Ibid., p. 189.

27. Ibid., p. 194.

28. Ibid.

29. Letter from Mrs Pethick-Lawrence to the Earl of Lytton, 23 January 1910; Lytton Family Papers, Knebworth House Archives.

30. Lytton, *Prisons and Prisoners*, p. 305.

31. *Votes for Women*, 18 February 1910, p. 321.

32. WSPU Fourth Annual Report for the year ending February 1910, Museum of London Suffragette Collections, p. 9.

33. *Votes for Women*, 4 February 1910, p. 289; Andrew Rosen, *Rise Up, Women!: The Militant Campaign of the Women's Social and Political Union, 1903–1914*, p. 130 (the figures vary between the above sources and modern analysis, with a plus or minus 1 variation).

34. Letter from Lord Lytton to Herbert Gladstone, 14 February 1910, Lytton Family Papers, 41045, Knebworth House Archives.

35. Ibid.

36. Ibid.

37. Letter from Herbert John Gladstone to Lord Lytton, 15 February 1910, Lytton Family Papers, 41964, Knebworth House Archives.

38. Ibid.

39. *The Times*, 15 February 1910, p. 8.

40. Rosen, *Rise Up, Women!*, p. 130.

41. Ibid., p. 131.

42. Letter from Henry Noel Brailsford to Lord Lytton, 14 February 1910, Lytton Family Papers, 42014, Knebworth House Archives.

43. Christabel Pankhurst, *Unshackled*, p. 153.

44. Ibid., p. 154.

45. *Votes for Women*, 18 March 1910, p. 381; Rosen, *Rise Up, Women!*, pp. 133–4.

46. Letter from Ernley Blackwell to Lord Lytton, 16 March 1910, Lytton Family Papers, 41968, Knebworth House Archives.

47. *The Times*, 18 March 1910, p. 12; *Votes for Women*, 18 March 1910, p. 382, 25 March 1910, p. 411.

48. *Votes for Women*, 18 March 1910, p. 411.

49. Deirdre Macpherson, *The Suffragette's Daughter. Betty Archdale: Her Life of Feminism, Cricket, War and Education*, pp. 32–3.

50. *Votes for Women*, 8 April 1910, p. 446; Peter Hartley, *Bikes at Brooklands in the Pioneer Years*, pp. 80–1; *Daily Mirror*, 10 November 1919, p. 8.

51. *Votes for Women*, 8 April 1910, p. 434.

52. Ministry of Works, AD 1143/1; HC/SA/SJ/10/12/26.

53. Raeburn, *The Militant Suffragettes*, p. 143; *ODNB*: David James Shackleton.

54. BL MSS Add 49793, ff.102–107, Letter from Christabel Pankhurst to A. J. Balfour, 26 April 1910.

55. Letter from Emmeline Pethick-Lawrence to Constance Lytton, 29 May 1910, 50.82/1119, Museum of London Suffragette Collections.

56. Letter from Henry Brailsford to Edith How-Martyn, 29 May 1910, Z6073, Museum of London Suffragette Collections.

57. *Votes for Women*, 3 June 1910, p. 581.

58. Ibid.

59. Letter from Lord Lytton to Herbert Asquith, 4 June 1910, Lytton Family Papers, 41974, Knebworth House Archives.

60. Ibid.

61. Letter from Vaughan Nash to Lord Lytton, 9 June 1910, Lytton Family Papers, 41975, Knebworth House Archives.

62. Lytton, *Prisons and Prisoners*, p. 311.

63. Balfour (ed.), *The Letters of Constance Lytton*, p. 206.

64. Ibid., pp. 207–8.

65. Letter from Winston Churchill to Lord Lytton, 11 June 1910, Lytton Family Papers, 42024, Knebworth House Archives.

66. Letter from Lord Lytton to Vaughan Nash, 12 June 1910, Lytton Family Papers, 41976, 41936, Knebworth House Archives.

67. Letter from Lord Lytton to Winston Churchill, 13 June 1910, Lytton Family Papers, 42026, Knebworth House Archives.

68. Letters from Constance Lytton to Lord Lytton, 13, 14 June, Lytton Family Papers, 41940, Knebworth House Archives.

69. Letter from Lord Lytton to Constance Lytton, 14 June 1910, Lytton Family Papers, 41936, Knebworth House Archives.

70. Emmeline Pankhurst, *My Own Story*, p. 169.

71. Sylvia Pankhurst, *The Suffragette Movement*, p. 337.

72. Ibid., p. 338.

73. Raeburn, *The Militant Suffragettes*, p. 144.

74. *Votes for Women*, 3 June 1910, p. 581; Annie Kenney, *Memories of a Militant*, p. 161.

75. *Votes for Women*, 10 June 1910, p. 592.

76. *British Journal of Nursing*, 11 June 1910, p. 480; *Votes for Women*, 17 June 1910, p. 618.

77. *Votes for Women*, 10 June 1910, p. 592.

78. Ibid.

79. Kitty Marion Scrapbook, Museum of London Suffragette Collections; *Votes for Women*, 25 November 1910, p. 121.

80. Raeburn, *The Militant Suffragettes*, p. 146.

81. *The Times*, 22 June 1910, p. 10; *ODNB*: Lady Jersey (Margaret Villiers Child); John Massie; Charlotte Maria Toynbee; Sir George William Goodenough Haversham; John St Loe Stracey; Albert Venn Dicey; Sir Alfred Comyn Lyall.

82. Parliamentary Archives, HC/SA/SJ/10/12 item 27; item 27A.

83. Ibid.

84. *Daily Mirror*, 25 June 1910, p. 4.

85. Letter from Lord Lytton to Constance Lytton, 26 June 1910, Lytton Family Papers, 41937, Knebworth House Archives.

86. *Votes for Women*, 15 July 1910, p. 684; Letter from Christabel Pankhurst to A. J. Balfour, 10 July 1910, BL MSS Add 49793, ff.95–98.

87. *Votes for Women*, 15 July 1910, p. 584.

88. Ibid.

89. Raeburn, *The Militant Suffragettes*, p. 148.

90. WSPU Handbills, 'The Votes for Women Bill', 'Further Facilities for the Woman Suffrage Bill', Museum of London Suffragette Collections.

91. WSPU Handbill, 'Votes for Women, Never!', 50.82/434, Museum of London Suffragette Collections.

92. *The Times*, 18 July 1910, p. 9.

93. Kenney, *Memories of a Militant*, pp. 163–4.

94. *Votes for Women*, 22 July 1910, p. 703.

95. Ibid., p. 711.

96. Edward Marsh to Lord Lytton, 19 July 1910, Lytton Family Papers, 42032, Knebworth House Archives.

97. *Votes for Women*, 22 July 1910, pp. 712–14.

98. WSPU Handbill, 'Hyde Park Demonstration 23 July 1910', 50.82/1117, Museum of London Suffragette Collections.

99. *Votes for Women*, 29 July 1910, p. 726.

100. Rosen, *Rise Up, Women!*, p. 137.

101. *Votes for Women*, 26 August 1910, p. 777.

102. Kitty Marion's Scrapbook, Museum of London Suffragette Collections.

103. *Votes for Women*, 26 August 1910, p. 777.

104. Letters from Constance Lytton to Ada Flatman, 2, 3 September 1910, from the LSE Library Collections, Microfiche, M195.

105. *The Times*, 30 October 1910, p. 9.

106. Elizabeth Crawford: Victor Diederichs Duval, pp. 181–2; Emily Diederichs Duval, pp. 180–81; *The Times*, 26 June 1909, p. 12; *The Times*, 16 November 1909, p. 12; A. V. John and Claire Eustance (eds), *The Men's Share? Masculinities, Male Support and Women's Suffrage in Britain, 1890–1920*, pp. 17–18; Lytton, *Prisons and Prisoners*, pp. 129–30.

107. Letter from Mrs Pankhurst to WSPU members, 27 October 1910, Museum of London Suffragette Collections.

108. Ibid.

109. Letter from Henry Brailsford to Lord Lytton, 7 November 1910, Lytton Family Papers, 42017, Knebworth House Archives.

110. Letter from Henry Brailsford to Lord Lytton, 12 November 1910, Lytton Family Papers, 42016, Knebworth House Archives.

111. Emmeline Pankhurst, *My Own Story*, pp. 177–8.

112. Letter from Herbert Asquith to Lord Lytton, 17 November 1910, Lytton Family Papers, 41920, Knebworth House Archives.

9 'BLACK FRIDAY'

1. Sylvia Pankhurst, *The Suffragette Movement*, p. 342.

2. Annie Kenney, *Memories of a Militant*, pp. 166–7.

3. Ibid., p. 167.

4. Elizabeth Crawford: Elizabeth Garrett Anderson, p. 12.

5. B. M. Willmott Dobbie, *A Nest of Suffragettes in Somerset*, p. 46.

6. Memorial to the Prime Minister, Museum of London Suffragette Collections, p. 35.

7. Quoted in *The Times*, 3 March 1911, p. 10.

8. Jessie Stephenson typescript, 'No Other Way', vol. 2, Museum of London Suffragette Collections, p. 140.

9. Dr Jessie Murray and Henry Brailsford (eds), *The Treatment of the Women's Deputations of 18th, 22nd, and 23rd November 1910 By The Police*, p. 4.

10. Ibid., p. 5.

11. Ibid., p. 6.

12. Ibid., pp. 11–12.

13. Ibid., p. 16.

14. *The Times*, 19 November 1910, p. 10.

15. Sylvia Pankhurst, *The Suffragette Movement*, pp. 343–4.

16. Ibid., p. 343.

17. *ODNB*: Princess Sophia Alexandra Duleep Singh.

18. Anita Anand, *Sophia: Princess, Suffragette, Revolutionary*, pp. 273–4.

19. Upminster history website; Murray and Brailsford (eds), *The Treatment of the Women's Deputations*, pp. 13–14.

20. *Votes for Women*, 25 November 1910, p. 122.

21. *The Times*, 12 June 1914, p. 5; Elizabeth Crawford, woman and her sphere website.

22. *Daily Mirror*, 19 November 1910, p. 4.

23. *ODNB*: Hugh Arthur Franklin; Jennifer Glynn, *My Sister Rosalind Franklin*, pp. 1–11.

24. *Daily Mirror*, 19 November 1910, pp. 1, 4, 10–11; 22 November 1910, p. 7; WSPU Handbill, 'Plain Facts About The Suffragette Deputations'; Ada Wright Biographical Notes, Group C, vol. 2, Museum of London Suffragette Collections.

25. *Daily Mirror*, 22 November 1910, p. 7.

26. Parliamentary Archives, HC/SA/SJ/10/12, items 32, 35.

27. *Votes for Women*, 25 November 1910, p. 131; *The Times*, 22 November 1910, p. 8.

28. *The Times*, 22 November 1910, p. 12.

29. Emmeline Pankhurst, *My Own Story*, pp. 183–4.

30. Elizabeth Crawford: Evelina Haverfield, p. 279; Sylvia Pankhurst, *The Suffragette Movement*, p. 344.

31. Elizabeth Crawford: Ethel Clarice Haslam; Pat Heron, *The Life of Ethel Haslam, an Ilford Suffragette*, pp. 1–12; Ethel Haslam Biographical Notes, Museum of London Suffragette Collections.

32. Richard Whitmore, *Alice Hawkins and the Suffragette Movement in Edwardian Leicester*, pp. 105–8.

33. Kitty Marion autobiography, Museum of London Suffragette Collections, pp. 198–9.

34. Emmeline Pankhurst, *My Own Story*, pp. 185–6; *Votes for Women*, 25 November 1910, p. 121.

35. Ibid., p. 346.

36. *The Times*, 23 November 1910, pp. 8, 12.

37. *Votes for Women*, 27 January 1911, p. 129.

38. Ibid.

39. *Daily Mirror*, 23 November 1910, p. 4; Kitty Marion autobiography, pp. 198–9.

40. Jessie Stephenson typescript, 'No Other Way', vol. 2, Museum of London Suffragette Collections, p. 150.

41. *Votes for Women*, 18 June 1908, p. 251.

42. Stephenson, typescript, 'No Other Way', vol. 2, pp. 164–9.

43. *The Times*, 28 November 1910, pp. 7, 11; *Daily Mirror*, 28 November 1910, p. 5.

44. *The Times*, 29 November 1910, p. 4.

45. Emmeline Pethick-Lawrence, *My Part in a Changing World*, p. 249.

46. Andrew Rosen, *Rise Up, Women!: The Militant Campaign of the Women's Social and Political Union, 1903–1914*, pp. 140–1.

47. Ibid., p. 141.

48. Letter from Sir Edward Grey to Lord Lytton, 26 November 1910, Lytton Family Papers, 42105, Knebworth House Archives.

49. Antonia Raeburn, *The Militant Suffragettes*, p. 158; Sonia Purnell, *The First Lady: The Life and Wars of Clementine Churchill*, pp. 51–2; Letter from Winston Churchill to Lord Lytton, 16 July 1910, Lytton Family Papers, 42031, Knebworth House Archives.

50. Stephenson typescript, 'No Other Way', vol. 2, p. 172.

51. Ibid., p. 178.

52. Ibid., pp. 194–5, 203–5.

53. *Votes for Women*, 9 December 1910, p. 167.
54. Ibid.
55. Ibid., 16 December 1910, p. 200.
56. Ibid.; *ODNB*: Ethel Agnes Mary Moorhead.
57. *Daily Mirror*, 9 December 1910, p. 3.
58. Kenney, *Memories of a Militant*, p. 167.
59. Stephenson typescript, 'No Other Way', vol. 2, Museum of London Suffragette Collections, pp. 214–20.
60. Ibid., pp. 220–5.
61. Paula Bartley, *Emmeline Pankhurst*, pp. 117–18.

10 'THE MARCH OF THE WOMEN'

1. Notes made by Constance Lytton, 3 January 1911, 50.82/ 1119, Museum of London Suffragette Collections.
2. Upminster history website; death certificate; *Votes for Women*, 6 January 1911, p. 205.
3. *Votes for Women*, 20 January 1911, p. 256.
4. Sylvia Pankhurst, *The Suffragette Movement*, p. 347.
5. Ibid., pp. 348–50.
6. Letter from Henry Brailsford to Lord Lytton, 8 January 1911, Lytton Family Papers, 42018, Knebworth House Archives.
7. *The Times*, 21 January 1911, p. 10.
8. *Daily Mirror*, 21 January 1911, p. 3.
9. Elizabeth Crawford: Ethel Mary Smyth, pp. 640–2; *ODNB*: Ethel Mary Smyth.
10. Ethel Smyth, *Female Pipings in Eden*, pp. 190–3.
11. Elizabeth Crawford: Cicely Mary Hamilton, née Hammill; *ODNB*: Cicely Mary Hamilton.
12. Cicely Hamilton, *Life Errant*, pp. ix, 6, 78–80.
13. Letter from Henry Brailsford to Lord Lytton, 22 January and 31 January 1911, Lytton Family Papers, Knebworth House Archives.
14. Letter from Henry Brailsford to Lord Lytton, 2 February 1911, Lytton Family Papers, 41993, Knebworth House Archives.
15. *The Times*, 6 February 1911, p. 12.
16. *Daily Mirror*, 7 February 1911, p. 3; Anita Anand, *Sophia: Princess, Suffragette, Revolutionary*, pp. 266–7; *Votes for Women*, 10 February 1911, p. 310.
17. *Who Was Who*, *The Times*, 26 March 1945, p. 6.
18. Jill Liddington, *Vanishing for the Vote: Suffrage, Citizenship and the Battle for the Census*, pp. 83–4.

19. Dr Jessie Murray and Henry Brailsford (eds), *The Treatment of the Women's Deputations of the 18th, 22nd, and 23rd November 1910 By The Police*, 1911.

20. *The Times*, 3 March 1911, p. 10.

21. Ibid., 10 March 1911, p. 4.

22. Ibid., 14 March 1911, p. 13.

23. Jill Liddington, *Vanishing for the Vote*, pp. 230–1.

24. Kitty Marion Scrapbook, Museum of London Suffragette Collections; *Daily Mirror*, 3 April 1911, p. 1.

25. B. M. Willmott Dobbie, *A Nest of Suffragettes in Somerset*, p. 47.

26. Jessie Stephenson typescript, 'No Other Way', vol. 2, Museum of London Suffragette Collections, p. 253.

27. Liddington, *Vanishing for the Vote*, p. 119.

28. Stephenson typescript, 'No Other Way', vol. 2, Museum of London Suffragette Collections, p. 254.

29. Census Return: 1911, Manchester.

30. Census Returns: 1911, Westminster and Bloomsbury; Parliamentary Archives, HC/SA/SJ/10/12/item 66.

31. *Votes for Women*, 7 April 1911, p. 441.

32. Ibid., p. 451.

33. Letter from Lady Constance Lytton to Rose Lamartine Yates, 22 April 1911, from the LSE Library Collections, Microfiche M195.

34. *The Times*, 4 May 1911, p. 10.

35. Ibid., 6 May 1911, p. 10.

36. *ODNB*: Edward Alfred Goulding, Baron Wargrave.

37. *The Times*, 6 May 1911, p. 10.

38. Balfour Papers, BL MSS Add 49793; Letter from Annie Kenney to A. J. Balfour, 12 May 1911; Christabel Pankhurst, *Unshackled: The Story of How We Won the Vote*, pp. 177–8.

39. *Daily Mirror*, 16 May 1911, p. 13.

40. Christabel Pankhurst, *Unshackled*, p. 183.

41. Andrew Rosen, *Rise Up, Women!: The Militant Campaign of the Women's Social and Political Union, 1903–1914*, p. 150.

42. Letter from Herbert Asquith to Lord Lytton, 16 June 1911, Lytton Family Papers, 41984, Knebworth House Archives.

43. Christabel Pankhurst, *Unshackled*, p. 171.

44. Letters from Henry Brailsford to Lord Lytton, 2 June 1911, Lytton Family Papers, 42006, 42007, 42008, Knebworth House Archives.

45. Letter from Christabel Pankhurst to Lord Lytton, 16 June 1911, Lytton Family Papers, 41932, Knebworth House Archives.

46. Letter from Henry Brailsford to Lord Lytton, 15 June 1911, Lytton Family Papers, 42009, Knebworth House Archives.

47. Margaret V. Annan Bryce Papers, Bodleian Library, University of Oxford, MS Bryce, 506, ff.18; 20; 22; 38; 40; 42; 43; 70–74; 91; 0102; 0104; 0109; 0111; *Votes for Women*, 15 July 1911, p. 684.

48. *Votes for Women*, 9 June 1911, p 598; *The Times*, 19 June 1911, p. 33.

49. Christina Broom Archive, Museum of London.

50. *The Times*, 19 June 1911, p. 33; *Daily Mirror*, 19 June 1911, p. 5.

51. *Votes for Women*, 30 June 1911, p. 64; Diane Atkinson, *The Suffragettes in Pictures*, pp. 112–23.

52. *The Times*, 19 June 1911, p. 33.

53. Testimonial to Lord Lytton, 30 June 1911, Lytton Family Papers, 42012, Knebworth House Archives.

54. Census Return: 1911, Knebworth.

55. Elizabeth Crawford: Minnie Baldock, p. 29.

56. Emmeline Pankhurst, *My Own Story*, pp. 210–12.

57. *The Times*, 17 October 1911, p. 6.

58. *Votes for Women*, 3 November 1911, p. 67.

59. Christabel Pankhurst, *Unshackled*, pp. 186–8.

60. Letter from Flora Drummond to WSPU secretaries, 9 November 1911, Museum of London Suffragette Collections.

11 BREAKING WINDOWS

1. Letter from Christabel Pankhurst to Lord Lytton, 9 November 1911, Lytton Family Papers, Knebworth House Archives.

2. *The Times*, 14 November 1911, p. 8.

3. Letter from Emmeline Pethick-Lawrence to Violet Bland, 14 November 1911, 60.15/8, Museum of London Suffragette Collections, p. 141 and p. 142.

4. Christabel Pankhurst, *Unshackled: The Story of How We Won the Vote*, p. 188.

5. Ibid., pp. 188–9.

6. Ibid., p. 190.

7. Annie Kenney, *Memories of a Militant*, p. 170.

8. WSPU press release, 17 November 1911, Museum of London Suffragette Collections.

9. Antonia Raeburn, *The Militant Suffragettes*, p. 165.

10. *Votes for Women*, 24 November 1911, p. 123.

11. Note from A. B. Hambling, Final instructions to members of demonstration, 21 November 1911, National Library of Scotland, Dep 176/

2/2; Krista Cowman, *Women of the Right Spirit: Paid Organisers of the WSPU 1904–1918*, p. 223.

12. Ibid., NLS, Dep 176/2/2.

13. *The Times*, 22 November 1911, p. 8; *Votes for Women*, 24 November 1911, p. 123.

14. *Votes for Women*, 24 November 1999, p. 123.

15. Emmeline Pethick-Lawrence, *My Part in a Changing World*, pp. 259–60.

16. *The Times*, 24 November 1911, p. 7.

17. Rose Lamartine Yates Biographical Notes, Group C, vol. 3, Museum of London Suffragette Collections.

18. *Votes for Women*, 24 November 1911, p. 123; *Suffrage Annual and Women's Who's Who*, p. 302.

19. National Archives, J/1552.

20. Emily Katherine Willoughby Marshall, 'Suffragette Escapes And Adventures', typescript memoir, Museum of London Suffragette Collections, pp. 57–8.

21. Letter from Constance Lytton to Dr Alice Ker, 20 November 1911, from the LSE Library Collections, Microfiche M195.

22. Constance Lytton, *Prisons and Prisoners: Some Personal Experiences by Constance Lytton and Jane Warton, spinster*, pp. 320–2.

23. Ibid., p. 324.

24. Ibid., pp. 325–6.

25. *ODNB*: Mary Leigh; National Archives, Home Office, 45/2466665.

26. *Suffrage Annual and Women's Who's Who*, p. 386; Sylvia Pankhurst, *The Suffragette Movement*, p. 359.

27. *The Times*, 29 November 1911, p. 6; National Archives, Home Office, 45/246665.

28. Ada Cecile Wright Biographical Notes, Group C, vol. 2, Museum of London Suffragette Collections, p. 66.

29. Boyce Gaddes, *Evelina: Outward Bound from Inverlochy*, p. 59.

30. *Votes for Women*, 31 November 1911, p. 144; Kitty Marion autobiography, pp. 208–9.

31. BBC Sound Archive, 1958; *Suffrage Annual and Women's Who's Who*, p. 306.

32. B. M. Willmott Dobbie, *A Nest of Suffragettes in Somerset*, p. 50.

33. *The Times*, 5 December 1911, p. 7, 30 November 1911, p. 6.

34. Ibid., 18 December 1911, p. 8, 19 December, p. 6.

35. Ibid., 22 December 1911, p. 2.

36. Emily Wilding Davison Papers, from the LSE Library Collections, 'Incendiarism', A4/12, pp. 1–3.

37. Ibid., p. 4.

38. Ibid., pp. 5–10.
39. *The Times*, 22 December 1911, p. 2, p. 7; Old Bailey online, 9 January 1912; t19120109-20.
40. Letter from Emily Davison to Sarah Carwin, 23 December 1911, 57.116/72, Museum of London Suffragette Collections.

12 'THE ARGUMENT OF THE BROKEN PANE'

1. Elizabeth Crawford: Cecilia Wolseley Haig, p. 256; death certificate.
2. *Daily Mirror*, 18 January 1912.
3. Old Bailey online, 9 January 1912, t19120109-20; *The Times*, 11 January 1912, p. 7.
4. *Votes for Women*, 12 January 1912, p. 236.
5. *The Times*, 15 January 1912, p. 11; *Daily Mirror*, 15 January 1912, p. 4.
6. Henry Brailsford letter to Mrs Pankhurst, 22 January 1912, quoted in Andrew Rosen, *Rise Up, Women!: The Militant Campaign of the Women's Social and Political Union, 1903–1914*, pp. 156–7.
7. Letter from Margaret Davison to Emily Davison, 2 February 1912, from the LSE Library Collections, Emily Wilding Davison Papers, A3/5; A2/1.
8. *ODNB*: Sir Horatio Bryan Donkin; National Archives, HO 144/1150/210696.
9. *The Times*, 6 February 1912, p. 3.
10. Letter from Edward Francis to Emily Davison, 6 February 1912, Emily Wilding Davison Papers, from the LSE Library Collections, A4/3.
11. Elizabeth Crawford: Jane Emma Cobden Unwin, pp. 694–5.
12. Letter from Emily Davison to Miss Dixon, 11 February 1912, private collection.
13. National Archives, HO 144/1150/210696.
14. Ibid.
15. Letter from Christabel Pankhurst to Miss M. Kelly, 7 February 1912, Museum of London; *Votes for Women*, 9 February 1912.
16. *Colac Herald, New Zealand,* 16 February 1912, p. 2.
17. Emmeline Pankhurst, *My Own Story*, p. 211.
18. Ibid., pp. 212–13.
19. Ibid., p. 213.
20. *Votes for Women*, 23 February 1912, p. 319; *ODNB:* Sir Charles Edward Henry Hobhouse; WSPU Handbill, 'A Cabinet Minister's Advice', Museum of London Suffragette Collections; Lucienne Boyce, *The Bristol Suffragettes*, p. 45.
21. *Votes for Women*, 16 February 1912, p. 304.

22. http://ilkleychess.blogspot.co.uk/2015/10/suffragette-and-chess-player-ellison.html

23. *The Times*, 17 February 1912; *Votes for Women*, 23 February 1912, p. 304; National Records of Scotland, Register of Suffragettes Received into prison in Scotland 1909–1914, HH12/22.

24. *The Times*, 23 February 1912, p. 7.

25. WSPU Handbill, 'Torture in an English Prison', Museum of London Suffragette Collections; A. V. John and Claire Eustance (eds), *The Men's Share? Masculinities, Male Support and Women's Suffrage in Britain, 1890–1920*, pp. 127–8.

26. Interview with Anthony Smith, Custodian of the Priest House, 28 January 2016; Elaine Beare family history website, Historic Hospital Admission Records project website.

27. Letter from Christabel Pankhurst to WSPU members, 24 February 1912, Museum of London Suffragette Collections.

28. Letter from Emmeline Pankhurst to WSPU members, 29 February 1912, Museum of London Suffragette Collections.

29. *Votes for Women*, 1 March 1912, p. 343; Ethel Smyth, *Female Pipings in Eden*, p. 208.

30. WSPU Handbill, 'Broken Windows', Museum of London Suffragette Collections.

31. Emmeline Pankhurst, *My Own Story*, p. 217.

32. Kitty Marshall, 'Suffragette Escapes and Adventures', 61.218/2, Museum of London Suffragette Collections, pp. 59–61.

33. Ibid., pp. 61–4.

34. Elizabeth Crawford: Ellen Crocker, p. 153; *Votes for Women*, 18 June 1908, p. 253; *Suffrage Annual and Women's Who's Who*, pp. 216–17.

35. *Votes for Women*, 15 March 1912, p. 380.

36. *The Times*, 6 March 1912, p. 6.

37. Elizabeth Crawford: Sarah Carwin, p. 99; Sarah Carwin Biographical Notes, Museum of London Suffragette Collections, pp. 101–3; Jill Liddington, *Vanishing for the Vote: Suffrage, Citizenship and the Battle for the Census*, p. 248.

38. Ada Cecile Wright Biographical Notes, Group C, vol. 2, Museum of London Suffragette Collections.

39. Ibid.

40. Violet Bland Biographical Notes, 50.82/1117, Museum of London Suffragette Collections.

41. Interviews with the *Ilford Recorder* and the *Ilford Guardian*, 10 May 1912, in Pat Heron, *The Life of Ethel Haslam, an Ilford Suffragette*, pp. 21–5.

42. BL Add MS 49976; Elizabeth Crawford: Olive Wharry, p. 707.

43. *The Times*, 4 March 1912, p. 4; *Votes for Women*, 15 March 1912, p. 380.

44. Mrs Emily Duval's Statement, 30 June 1912, private collection.

45. Helen MacRae hunger-strike medal and postcards, private collection; *The Times*, 7 March 1912, p. 7.

46. Elizabeth Crawford: Olive Grace Walton, pp. 699–700; Brian Harrison interview with Mrs Margaret Dunnett, 1976, from the LSE Library Collections, tape 39; *Suffrage Annual and Women's Who's Who*, p. 387.

47. Olive Walton's Prison Diary, 1912, Museum of London Suffragette Collections, pp. 1–4.

48. Ibid., pp. 5–7.

49. Brian Harrison interview with Margaret Dunnett, 1976.

50. C. Sarah Laughton, 'The Woman with the Suitcase', unpublished MS biography of Eileen Casey, 2017, pp. 1, 7, 17, 22, 29. Private family papers.

51. *The Times*, 11 March 1912, p. 7.

52. *East Coast Illustrated News and Clacton Graphic*, 4 May 1912, p. 2; *Illustrated Clacton News, and Visitors' List*, 7 May 1912, p. 6; *Suffrage Annual and Women's Who's Who*, p. 291.

53. BBC Sound Archive, Interview of Ethel Smyth by Vera Brittain, 1937; Christabel Pankhurst, *Unshackled: The Story of How We Won the Vote*, pp. 200–1.

54. Norman Watson, *Suffragettes and the Post*, p. 17; Pitfield family website.

55. The Proceedings of the Old Bailey: t19120319-14; *The Times*, 5 March 1912, p. 6, 20 March 1912, p. 7.

56. *British Journal of Nursing*, 20 April 1912, p. 310.

57. *Votes for Women*, 8 March 1912, p. 354.

58. BBC Sound Archive, Interview of Ethel Smyth by Vera Brittain, 1937; Smyth, *Female Pipings in Eden*, pp. 209–11.

59. Emmeline Pankhurst, *My Own Story*, p. 218; *Votes for Women*, 8 March 1912, p. 354.

60. *The Times*, 5 March 1912, p. 4.

61. Ibid., 6 March 1912, p. 6.

62. Private collection: glenhorowitz.com: the Dobkin Family Collection of Feminism.

63. BBC Sound Archive, Victoria Lidiard née Simmons interview, 1983; *The Times*, 6 March 1912, p. 6; Obituary, *Independent*, 19 October, 1992, p. 6.

64. Myra Sadd Brown Biographical Notes; Letter from Mr Sadd Brown to Myra Sadd Brown enclosing letters from their children, 50.82/1136, Museum of London Suffragette Collections.

65. Ibid., Letter from Myra Sadd Brown to her children, c. 22 March 1912.

66. Ibid., Letters from Myra Sadd Brown to Ernest Sadd Brown, 20 March 1912.

67. Letter from Jessie Girling to Myra Sadd Brown, 28 April 1912, LSE Library Collections.

68. Kitty Marion autobiography, Museum of London Suffragette Collections, pp. 210–11.

69. Ibid., p. 214.

70. Ibid., pp. 216–17.

71. Elizabeth Crawford: Vera Wentworth, pp. 704–5; *The Times*, 11 March 1912, p. 7.

72. Papers of Winefrede Mary Rix, Museum of London Suffragette Collections.

73. Elizabeth Crawford: Lilias Mitchell, pp. 417–18; Leah Leneman, '*A Guid Cause': The Women's Suffrage Movement in Scotland*, pp. 109–15; Lilias Mitchell unpublished memoir 'Suffrage Days', private collection, quoted in Leneman, '*A Guid Cause*', p. 110.

74. Elizabeth Crawford: Ethel Agnes Mary Moorhead, pp. 424–6; *ODNB*: Ethel Agnes Mary Moorhead.

75. Elizabeth Crawford: Janie Allan, pp. 6–8; Leneman, '*A Guid Cause*', pp. 112–13, 253; Elizabeth Ewan (ed.), *The Biographical Dictionary of Scottish Women*, p. 11; Leah Leneman, *The Scottish Suffragettes*, pp. 73–6.

76. Elizabeth Crawford: Helen Crawfurd, pp. 151–2; *ODNB*: Helen Crawfurd; Leneman, '*A Guid Cause*', pp. 111–12, 257–8; marriage and death certificates.

77. *Daily Mirror*, 15 March 1912, p. 6, 29 March 1912, p. 5.

13 THE GREAT CONSPIRACY TRIAL

1. *Daily Mirror*, 6 March 1912, p. 5.

2. *The Times*, 6 March 1912, p. 6.

3. Christabel Pankhurst, *Unshackled: The Story of How We Won the Vote*, pp. 202, 208.

4. Ibid., p. 203.

5. Ibid., pp. 204, 208. Annie Kenney, *Memories of a Militant*, pp. 173–4.

6. Kenney, *Memories of a Militant*, p. 173.

7. Ibid., p. 175.

8. Ibid., pp. 175–6.

9. Ibid., p. 176.

10. Emmeline Pethick-Lawrence, *My Part in a Changing World*, p. 167.

11. Kenney, *Memories of a Militant*, p. 178.

12. Ibid., p. 179.

13. Ibid., p. 182.

14. BBC Sound Archive, Winifred Starbuck interviewed by Marjorie Anderson, 1958. It has proved impossible to locate Winifred Starbuck – which may have been her married name – in the Census Returns or newspapers.

15. Ibid.

16. *The Times*, 6 March 1912, p. 6.

17. *The Times*, 6 March 1912, p. 8; *The Times*, 11 March 1912, p. 7; *Daily Mirror*, 11 March 1912, p. 4.

18. WSPU Handbill, 'Mrs Pankhurst's Treatment in Prison: Statement by Dr Ethel Smyth', 94.97, Museum of London Suffragette Collections.

19. *The Times*, 12 March 1912, p. 6; Letters from Constance Lytton to Margaret Ker, 13, 18, 28 March 1912, LSE Library Collections, Microfiche M196.

20. *The Times*, 28 March 1912, p. 7; *ODNB*: Sir Almroth Edward Wright.

21. WSPU Handbill, 'The Antediluvian Society for the Propagation of the Principles of Anti-Suffrage', 50.82/749, Museum of London Suffragette Collections.

22. Antonia Raeburn, *The Militant Suffragettes*, p. 174; Andrew Rosen, *Rise Up, Women!: The Militant Campaign of the Women's Social and Political Union, 1903–1914*, pp. 162–3; Martin Pugh, *The Pankhursts*, p. 243; *Votes for Women*, 5 April 1912, p. 431.

23. *Daily Mirror*, 6 April 1912, pp. 5, 8–9; *Votes for Women*, 12 April 1912, p. 444.

24. Betty Balfour (ed.), *The Letters of Constance Lytton*, p. 232.

25. Ibid., pp. 232–4.

26. Lyndsey Jenkins, *Lady Constance Lytton: Aristocrat, Suffragette, Martyr*, p. 195.

27. Balfour, *The Letters of Constance Lytton*, pp. 240–1.

28. *Votes for Women*, 10 May 1912, p. 500.

29. Antonia Raeburn, *The Militant Suffragettes*, p. 173.

30. Old Bailey online, 14 May 1912, t19120514-54.

31. Emmeline Pankhurst, *My Own Story*, p. 229.

32. Ibid., p. 230.

33. Old Bailey online, 14 May 1912, t191220514-54.

34. Ibid.

35. Emmeline Pankhurst, *My Own Story*, p. 246.

36. Ibid., p. 255.

37. *The Times*, 14 June 1912, p. 4; 13 July 1912, p. 10.

38. *ODNB*: Johanna Mary [Hanna] Sheehy-Skeffington; *ODNB*: Francis Sheehy-Skeffington; National Archives of Ireland, Prisoners' Record Sheets, Hanna Sheehy-Skeffington; William Murphy, *Political Imprisonment and the Irish, 1912–1921*, pp. 14–19.

39. Sarah-Beth Watkins, *Ireland's Suffragettes: The Women Who Fought for the Vote*, pp. 41–2; National Archives of Ireland Prisoners' Record Sheets, Leila and Rosalind Cadiz.

40. National Archives of Ireland Prisoners' Record Sheets, Kathleen Houston; Watkins, *Ireland's Suffragettes*, pp. 46–7.

41. National Archives of Ireland Prisoners' Record Sheets, Marjorie Hasler; she died of measles in 1913.

42. National Archives of Ireland Prisoners' Record Sheets, Hilda Webb.

43. Raeburn, *The Militant Suffragettes*, pp. 174, 180.

44. *The Times*, 26 June 1912, p. 6; Violet Aitken Biographical Notes, 57.116/43, Museum of London Suffragette Collections; Canon Aitken's Diary for 1912, MC 2165/1/23, 1 September 1912, Norfolk Record Office.

45. Canon Aitken's Diary, 27 November 1912.

46. Emily Wilding Davison's Imprisonment in Holloway, February–June 1912, from the LSE Library Collections, Emily Wilding Davison Papers, A4/4/1, pp. 5–7.

47. Ibid., pp. 7–9.

48. Report by Dr Sullivan to the Home Office, 23 June 1912, National Archives, HO 144/1502/210696.

49. *Votes for Women*, 28 June 1912, p. 650.

50. Letters from Dr Craig and Dr Smalley to the Home Office, 27 June 1912, National Archives, HO 144/1502/210696.

51. *Daily Mirror*, 26 June 1912, p. 3; Hansard, Daily Debates, 25 June 1912.

52. *ODNB*: George Lansbury; Census Return: 1911, Bow; *Votes for Women*, 28 June 1912, p. 635.

53. National Archives, Home Office report, 10 July 1912, HO 144/1502/210696; *Votes for Women*, 12 July 1912, p. 664.

14 THE EXPULSION OF THE PETHICK-LAWRENCES

1. *Daily Mirror*, 15 July 1912, p. 5.

2. *The Times*, 27 July 1912, p. 6.

3. Ibid., p. 6.

4. Elizabeth Crawford: Helen Craggs, pp. 147–8; *Suffrage Annual and Women's Who's Who*, p. 215.

5. *Votes for Women*, 26 July 1912, p. 696.

6. *The Times*, 19 July 1912, p. 6.

7. Ibid., 20 July 1912, p. 10.
8. Ibid.
9. Ibid.; *Daily Mirror*, 22 July 1912, p. 1.
10. *The Times*, 7 August 1912, p. 6.
11. Ibid.
12. Elizabeth Crawford, woman and her sphere blog; Census Return: 1911, Marylebone; Petition re Gladys Evans to Augustine Birrell, General Prisons Board, British Suffragettes, National Archives of Ireland, 7 September 1912.
13. National Archives of Ireland, General Prisons Board, British Suffragettes, Gladys Evans.
14. Ibid.
15. Ibid.
16. National Archives of Ireland, General Prisons Board, British Suffragettes, Mary Leigh; Sir Thomas Myles website.
17. National Archives of Ireland, General Prisons Board, British Suffragettes, Mary Leigh; *Daily Mirror*, 21 September 1912, p. 3.
18. Gladys Hazel Biographical Notes, 57.70/17, Museum of London Suffragette Collections; *Daily Telegraph*, 'I Was Raised By A Suffragette', 21 November 2015, online.
19. Letters to Augustine Birrell, September 1912, National Archives of Ireland, General Prisons Board, British Suffragettes.
20. National Archives of Ireland, General Prisons Board, British Suffragettes, Gladys Evans.
21. Krista Cowman, *Mrs Brown Is a Man and a Brother! Women in Merseyside's Political 1890–1920*, pp. 85–7; Elizabeth Crawford: Susan Ada Flatman, p. 222; Ada Flatman Biographical Notes, Museum of London Suffragette Collections.
22. Elizabeth Crawford: Lucy Burns, pp. 88–9; Leah Leneman, *'A Guid Cause': The Women's Suffrage Movement in Scotland*, p. 256.
23. Sylvia Pankhurst, *The Suffragette Movement*, pp. 416, 417.
24. Passenger Lists, SS *Cymric*, 6 May 1912; Sylvia Pankhurst, *The Suffragette Movement*, p. 419.
25. *Daily Mirror*, 5 September 1912, p. 4; 7 September 1912, p. 11; *Votes for Women*, 13 September 1912, p. 803; Leneman, *'A Guid Cause'*, p. 116.
26. Kitty Marion autobiography, pp. 221–2; Elizabeth Crawford: Kitty Marion, p. 377.
27. *Daily Mirror*, 7 September 1912, p. 11.
28. *Votes for Women*, 20 September 1912, pp. 809–11.

29. Emmeline Pethick-Lawrence, *My Part in a Changing World*, p. 277.
30. Ibid.
31. Ibid., pp. 277–8.
32. Ibid., p. 280.
33. Elizabeth Crawford: Emmeline Pethick-Lawrence, p. 538.
34. Annie Kenney, *Memories of a Militant*, p. 192.
35. Ibid., pp. 194–5.
36. Letter from Mrs Pankhurst to WSPU members, 16 October 1912, Museum of London Suffragette Collections; *The Suffragette*, 18 October 1912, p. 6.
37. Kenney, *Memories of a Militant*, p. 193.
38. Letter from Emmeline Pethick-Lawrence to Myra Sadd Brown, 25 October 1912, LSE Library Collections, Microfiche 191.
39. Emmeline Pankhurst, *My Own Story*, p. 261.
40. Ibid., p. 262.
41. Ibid., p. 263.
42. Christabel Pankhurst, *Unshackled: The Story of How We Won the Vote*, p. 226.
43. Ibid., p. 227.
44. David Mitchell interview with Jessie Kenney, 1964, David Mitchell Papers, Museum of London Suffragette Collections, 73.83/48.
45. Letter from Emmeline Pethick-Lawrence to Mrs Cavendish Bentinck, 6 November 1912, LSE Library Collections, Microfiche 187.
46. Ibid.
47. *Votes for Women*, 25 October 1912, p. 55.
48. National Records of Scotland, HH.16/42; *Evening Telegraph and Post*, 30 October 1912; *Votes for Women*, 8 November 1912, p. 92; Leneman, '*A Guid Cause*', p. 121, p. 123.
49. *ODNB*: George Lansbury; Sylvia Pankhurst, *The Suffragette Movement*, p. 420.
50. Sylvia Pankhurst, *The Suffragette Movement*, p. 422; WSPU Handbill, 'The Unholy Alliance: the Labour Party and the Liberal Government', 50.82/536, Museum of London Suffragette Collections.
51. *Daily Mirror*, 27 November 1912, p. 3; *Votes for Women*, 29 November 1912, p. 132.
52. Sylvia Pankhurst, *The Suffragette Movement*, pp. 426–7.
53. Ibid., p. 427.
54. Ibid., pp. 427–8.
55. *Votes for Women*, 13 December 1912, p. 171.

56. Ibid., p. 17; Leneman, *'A Guid Cause'*, pp. 127–8.

57. Letter from Emily Davison to unnamed recipient, 26 December 1912, private collection.

58. Ibid.

59. *The Suffragette*, 13 December 1912, p. 125.

60. Ibid.

61. *Suffrage Annual and Women's Who's Who*, p. 270; Mrs Howey Biographical Notes, Museum of London Suffragette Collections.

62. Norman Watson, *Suffragettes and the Post*, p. 37; *Daily Mirror*, 19 December 1912, p. 4.

63. Elizabeth Crawford: Rosa May Billinghurst, p. 54.

64. Kitty Marion autobiography, Museum of London Suffragette Collections, p. 225; *The Times*, 18 December 1912, p. 8.

65. *Votes for Women*, 20 December 1912, p. 185.

66. Kitty Marion autobiography, Museum of London Suffragette Collections, p. 226.

67. Ibid., p. 227.

15 THE ARSONISTS

1. *Votes for Women*, 10 January 1913, p. 220.

2. *The Suffragette*, 3 January 1913, p. 200; 24 January 1913, p. 220; 'Private and Confidential' Letter from Mrs Pankhurst to members of the WSPU, 10 January 1913, Museum of London Suffragette Collections.

3. Letter from Madame De Baecker, January 1913, Emily Wilding Davison Papers, from the LSE Library Collections, A3/6/; Diane Atkinson, 'When The Jockey Met The Suffragette', MA Dissertation, 2004, UEA, pp. 27–9.

4. Letter from Katherine Riddell, 24 January 1913, EWD Papers, LSE Library Collections, A3/2.

5. Elizabeth Crawford: Henry Devenish Harben, pp. 269–71; *ODNB*: Henry Devenish Harben.

6. Letter from Emmeline Pankhurst to Henry Harben, 20 December 1912, BL, Harben Papers, Add 58226; Letter from Mrs Pankhurst to Henry Harben 30 January 1913, private collection.

7. Sylvia Pankhurst, *The Suffragette Movement*, p. 395.

8. Emmeline Pethick-Lawrence, *My Part in a Changing World*, p. 297.

9. Elizabeth Crawford: Marguerite [Daisy] Lena Parsons, p. 529; Daisy Parsons, first woman major of West Ham website; Census Returns: 1881, Hackney; 1891, West Ham; 1901, West Ham; 1911, West Ham.

10. Annie Kenney, *Memories of a Militant*, pp. 196, 201, 202, 203.

11. Sylvia Pankhurst, *The Suffragette Movement*, pp. 428–9; Richard Whitmore, *Alice Hawkins and the Suffragette Movement in Edwardian Leicester*, p. 144.

12. Andrew Rosen, *Rise Up, Women!: The Militant Campaign of the Women's Social and Political Union, 1903–1914*, p. 187.

13. *The Times*, 29 January 1913, p. 7.

14. Sylvia Pankhurst, *The Suffragette Movement*, p. 433.

15. Kenney, *Memories of a Militant*, p. 220.

16. Ibid.

17. *The Times*, 30 January 1913, p. 12.

18. Sylvia Pankhurst, *The Suffragette Movement*, p. 434.

19. *Suffrage Annual and Women's Who's Who*, pp. 210–11.

20. Elizabeth Crawford: Leonora Cohen, p. 135.

21. Norman Watson, *Suffragettes and the Post*, p. 38; WSPU Eighth Annual Report, 1914, pp. 19–20.

22. Emmeline Pankhurst, *My Own Story*, p. 280; *Daily Mirror*, 1 February 1913, p. 3.

23. Letter from Christabel Pankhurst to Mabel Tuke, 19 December 1912, Museum of London Suffragette Collections; *The Suffragette*, 24 January 1913, p. 215.

24. Mary Soames (ed.), *Speaking for Themselves: The Personal Letters of Winston and Clementine Churchill*, p. 71.

25. *The Suffragette*, 7 February 1913, p. 259.

26. Sylvia Pankhurst, *The Home Front: Mirror to Life in England During the First World War*, p. 51; Census Returns: 1901, Bromley-by-Bow; 1911, Custom House.

27. *The Listener*, 8 February 1968, pp. 175–6.

28. Interview with Ramsay Drake, son of Charlotte Drake, September, 2013; Correspondence between David Mitchell and Charlotte Drake, 1965, David Mitchell Papers, 73.83/44, Museum of London Suffragette Collections.

29. Annie Barnes, *Tough Annie: From Suffragette to Stepney Councillor*, p. 7; Census Return: 1911, Limehouse.

30. Barnes, *Tough Annie*, p. 11.

31. Ibid., p. 12.

32. Ibid., p. 15.

33. *The Times*, 19 April 1913, p. 10; *Daily Mirror*, 19 April 1913, p. 5.

34. Letter from Harriet Kerr to Harry Daniels, 9 February 1913, Emily Wilding Davison Papers, A.2/2, LSE Library Collections.

35. *The Times*, 10 February 1913, p. 5; *The Times*, 11 February 1913, p. 6.

36. Gretchen Wilson, *With All Her Might: The Life and Times of Gretchen Harding, Militant Suffragette*, p. 104.

37. Sylvia Pankhurst, *The Suffragette Movement*, p. 440.

38. National Archives, HO 144/1558/234191.

39. Emmeline Pankhurst, *My Own Story*, p. 283; Sylvia Pankhurst, *The Suffragette Movement*, p. 43; *Daily Mirror*, 20 February 1913, pp. 1, 3; *The Suffragette*, 21 February 1913, pp. 291–3.

40. *The Times*, 25 February 1913, p. 6.

41. Elizabeth Crawford: Olive Hockin, pp. 287–8.

42. *The Times*, 15 March 1913, p. 10, 21 March 1913, p. 6, 28 March 1913, p. 14, 5 April 1913, p. 4; Old Bailey online, 1 April 1913, t19130401-19.

43. Old Bailey online, 1 April 1913, t19130401-19.

44. Surveillance photograph of Olive Hockin, 53.140/41, Museum of London Suffragette Collections.

45. Sylvia Pankhurst, *The Suffragette Movement*, p. 517.

46. *Daily Mirror*, 28 February 1913, p. 1.

47. *The Listener*, 8 February 1968, p. 175.

48. Ibid., p. 176.

49. *The Times*, 26 February 1913, p. 10.

50. Ibid., 28 February 1913, p. 8.

51. *The Suffragette*, 7 March 1913, p. 324.

52. *The Times*, 18 March 1913, p. 13.

53. *The Listener*, 8 February 1968, p. 176.

54. *The Times*, 28 February 1913, p. 10.

55. Kenney, *Memories of a Militant*, p. 246.

56. Ibid., p. 247.

57. Elizabeth Crawford: Lilian Ida Lenton, p. 341.

58. Elizabeth Crawford: Francis Vane Phipson Rutter, pp. 611–12; *ODNB*: Annie Kenney, p. 248.

59. Sylvia Pankhurst, *The Suffragette Movement*, p. 342; Elizabeth Crawford: Lilian Ida Lenton, p. 341, *Daily Mirror*, 8 October 1913, p. 4.

60. *The Listener*, 8 February 1968, p. 176.

61. Ibid.

62. Elizabeth Crawford: Olive Wharry, p. 707.

63. National Archives, HO144/1255/234788; *ODNB*: Hugh Arthur Franklin; National Archives, HO144/1205/221873.

64. BL MSS Add 49976, ff.64–5.

65. *The Times*, 10 March 1913, p. 6; *ODNB*: Hugh Arthur Franklin.

66. Elizabeth Crawford: Hugh Arthur Franklin, pp. 229–30.

67. Parliamentary Archives, HL/PO/PU/1/1913/3&4G5c4.

68. *ODNB*: Reginald McKenna.

69. *The Times*, 3 April 1913, p. 7.

70. *ODNB*: Hugh Arthur Franklin.

71. *Daily Telegraph*, 26 February 1913, p. 5.

72. Letter from Sylvia Pankhurst to her mother, 18 March 1913, Z6084, Museum of London Suffragette Collections.

73. *Suffrage Annual and Women's Who's Who*, p. 316; Elizabeth Crawford: Elsa Myers, p. 433; Elsa Myers Biographical Notes, Museum of London Suffragette Collections.

74. *ODNB*: Sir Charles Stuart White.

75. *The Times*, 21 March 1913, p. 6; *Bendigo Advertiser*, 22 March 1912.

76. *Daily Mirror*, 14 May 1913, p. 4; *The Times*, 19 January 1914, p. 3.

77. Elizabeth Crawford: Olive Beamish, pp. 40–1; Letter from Olive Agnes Beamish to Edith How-Martyn, 2 February 1931, 57.116/68, Museum of London Suffragette Collections.

78. Elizabeth Crawford: Elsie Duval, pp. 179–80; Women of the West Country website.

79. Kenney, *Memories of a Militant*, pp. 223–4; Antonia Raeburn, *Militant Suffragettes*, p. 208.

80. Old Bailey online, 2 April 1913, t1913-4-1-67.

81. Ibid.

82. *The Times*, 3 April 1913, p. 4.

83. Ibid., 4 April 1913, p. 4.

84. Ibid., 12 April 1913, p. 10.

85. *Daily Mirror*, 16 April 1913, p. 1; *Hastings and St Leonard's Pictorial Advertiser*, 17 April 1913, p. 1.

86. *ODNB*: (Sir) Arthur Philip du Cros.

87. Kitty Marion autobiography, Museum of London Suffragette Collections, pp. 68–9, 229.

88. *Daily Mirror*, 7 April 1913, p. 4, 21 April 1913, p. 5; *The Times*, 28 April 1913, p. 4.

89. Elizabeth Crawford: Elsie Edith Bowerman, pp. 73–4; *ODNB*: Encyclopaedia Titanica, pp. 1–4; http://www.hastingspress.co.uk/history/bowerman.html, pp. 1–7.

90. *Daily Mirror*, 14 April 1913, p. 5, 15 April 1913, p. 3, 21 April 1913, p. 3, 23 April 1913, p. 4, 28 April 1913, p. 3; *The Times*, 30 April 1913, pp. 1, 5.

91. Leah Leneman, *'A Guid Cause': The Women's Suffrage Movement in Scotland*, p. 141.

92. Anita Anand, *Sophia: Princess, Suffragette, Revolutionary*, pp. 286–8.

93. Rosen, *Rise Up, Women!* p. 984; Raeburn, *The Militant Suffragettes*, p. 203.

94. Letter from Edwy Clayton to Annie Kenney, 14 March 1925, Kenney Papers, University of East Anglia.

95. Elizabeth Crawford: Clayton family, pp. 115–16; *Suffrage Annual and Women's Who's Who*, pp. 206–7; Sylvia Pankhurst, *The Suffragette Movement*, p. 462.

96. Kenney, *Memories of a Militant*, pp. 227–9.

97. Copy of letter from Harriet Roberta Kerr to Mary Charlotte Tiltman, 23 June 1913, SC Box 31, 74/440, Museum of London Suffragette Collections; *The Suffragette*, 3 October 1913, p. 881, 17 October 1913, p. 11.

98. Elizabeth Crawford: Beatrice Sanders, p. 614.

99. Ibid., Geraldine Laura Lennox, p. 340.

100. Ibid., Rachel Barrett, p. 36.

101. Ida Alexa Ross Wylie, *My Life with George: An Unconventional Biography*, pp. 165–7, 180–5; Census Return: 1911, St Pancras.

16 'THAT MALIGNANT SUFFRAGETTE'

1. Sylvia Pankhurst, *The Suffragette Movement*, p. 459.

2. Ibid., p. 461.

3. Dorothy Evans Biographical Notes, Museum of London Suffragette Collections.

4. BBC Sound Archive, interview with Grace Roe, February 1968.

5. Dorothy Evans Biographical Notes, Museum of London Suffragette Collections.

6. *ODNB*: Baron Carson, Edward Henry Carson.

7. Dorothy Evans Biographical Notes, Museum of London Suffragette Collections.

8. BBC Sound Archive, interview with Grace Roe, February 1968.

9. Ibid.

10. Mary Raleigh Richardson, *Laugh a Defiance*, p. 1; *ODNB*: Mary Raleigh Richardson; author's interview with Mary Richardson's son, October 2012.

11. Richardson, *Laugh a Defiance*, p. 2.

12. Ibid., p. 3.

13. Ibid., p. 11.

14. BBC Sound Archive, Mary Richardson interviewed by Sorrel Bentinck, 1961.

15. Richardson, *Laugh a Defiance*, p. 9.

16. *The Times*, 12 March 1913, p. 10.

17. Ibid., 18 July 1913, p. 14, 30 July 1914, p. 10.

18. LSE Library Collections, Emily Wilding Davison Papers, A4/4/5, pp. 1–12.

19. *The Suffragette*, 16 May 1913, p. 513.
20. LSE Library Collections, Emily Wilding Davison Papers, A5/ 4/2.
21. Ibid.
22. Kitty Marion autobiography, Museum of London Suffragette Collections, p. 233.
23. Diane Atkinson, 'When The Jockey Met The Suffragette', MA Dissertation, 2004, UEA, pp. 1–4.
24. *Daily Mirror*, 5 June 1913, p. 4.
25. *Sporting Life*, 5 June 1913, p. 5.
26. Steve Donoghue, *Just My Story*, pp. 151–2.
27. Report of PC Bunn, 4 June 1913, Metropolitan Police Museum, New Scotland Yard.
28. Royal Archives Windsor, Diary of King George V.
29. Telegram dated 7 June 1913, private collection.
30. National Archives, MEPO 2/1551; HO144/1150/210696.
31. Letter from Mrs Penn Gaskell to Miss Dixon, 5 June 1913, private collection.
32. Ibid.
33. Emily Davison death certificate.
34. Emily Wilding Davison Papers, LSE Library Collections, A7/ 5-7.
35. *Votes for Women*, 13 June 1913, p. 580.
36. Christabel Pankhurst, *Unshackled: The Story of How We Won the Vote*, p. 254.
37. Emmeline Pankhurst, *My Own Story*, p. 315.
38. Letter from Miss Strachey to Mrs Durrie Mulford, 11 June 1913, LSE Library Collections, Microfiche 189.
39. They are part of the Emily Wilding Davison Papers LSE Library Collections.
40. Diary of Canon Hay Aitken, 2 June, 13 June 1913, Norwich Record Office.
41. Emily Wilding Davison Papers, LSE Library Collections, G2/9; *The Times*, 22 February 1913, p. 9; death certificate.
42. Death certificate of Herbert Ebsworth Jones.
43. *The Suffragette*, 13 June 1913.

17 THE FAILURE OF THE 'CAT AND MOUSE' ACT

1. Kitty Marion autobiography, p. 229.
2. Ibid.
3. Ibid.
4. Ibid., p. 230.

5. Ibid.

6. Ibid., p. 233.

7. Ibid.

8. *The Times*, 12 June 1913, p. 4.

9. Kitty Marion autobiography, p. 232.

10. Ibid., p. 241; *The Times*, 4 July 1913, p. 11.

11. *The Times*, 4 July 1913, p. 11.

12. Kitty Marion autobiography, Museum of London Suffragette Collections, p. 244.

13. *Suffrage Annual and Women's Who's Who*, pp. 251–2.

14. Kitty Marion autobiography, Museum of London Suffragette Collections, p. 246.

15. Kitty Marion Scrapbook, Museum of London Suffragette Collections.

16. Kitty Marion autobiography, Museum of London Suffragette Collections, p. 247.

17. Kitty Marion Scrapbook, Museum of London Suffragette Collections.

18. Kitty Marion autobiography, Museum of London Suffragette Collections, p. 250.

19. Kitty Marion Scrapbook, Museum of London Suffragette Collections.

20. Kitty Marion autobiography, p. 250.

21. Phoebe Hesketh, *My Aunt Edith*, pp. 59–61; *ODNB*: William Hesketh Lever, First Viscount Leverhulme.

22. Hesketh, *My Aunt Edith*, p. 63; *The Times*, 9 July 1913, p. 8.

23. *The Times*, 11 July 1913, p. 11.

24. Ibid.

25. Hesketh, *My Aunt Edith*, p. 65.

26. *The Suffragette*, vol. 2, 7 November 1913, p. 85.

27. Hesketh, *My Aunt Edith*, p. 69.

28. *ODNB*: Sarah Jane Baines; Elizabeth Crawford: Sarah Jennie Baines, p. 25; *Australian Dictionary of Biography*: Sarah Jane (Jennie) Baines, vol. 7, online; *The Times*, 10 July 1913, p. 13, 11 July 1913, p. 11.

29. Emmeline Pankhurst, *My Own Story*, p. 316.

30. *The Suffragette*, 25 July 1913, pp. 699–701.

31. Kitty Marshall, 'Suffragette Escapes and Adventures', Museum of London Suffragette Collections, pp. 70–1.

32. Ibid., p. 71.

33. Letter from Mrs Emmeline Pethick-Lawrence to Mrs Saul Solomon, 18 June 1913, LSE Library Collections, Microfiche 187.

34. *Votes for Women*, 4 July 1913, p. 585.

35. Ibid., 1 August 1913, p. 639.

36. Elizabeth Crawford: Millicent Garrett Fawcett, p. 217.

37. Sylvia Pankhurst, *The Suffragette Movement*, pp. 485–6.

38. Ibid., p. 486.

39. *Daily Mirror*, 28 July 1913, pp. 4, 11.

40. Sylvia Pankhurst, *The Suffragette Movement*, pp. 487–8.

41. Ibid., p. 458.

42. Ibid., pp. 493–5.

43. Elizabeth Crawford: Mary Elizabeth Phillips, p. 545.

44. *The Suffragette*, 1 August 1913, p. 688; *Suffrage Annual and Women's Who's Who*, p. 337.

45. Kitty Marion Scrapbook, Museum of London Suffragette Collections.

46. Letter from Christabel Pankhurst to Annie Kenney, 4 August 1913, BL MSS Add 58226, ff.30–36.

47. Letter from Christabel Pankhurst to Henry Harben, 7 August 1913.

48. Ibid.

49. Annie Kenney, *Memories of a Militant*, pp. 239–41.

50. Ibid., pp. 241–2.

51. *The Times*, 29 August 1913, p. 4; *Daily Mirror*, 29 August, p. 3; BBC Sound Archive, Lady Asquith and Lady Stocks interviewed by Joan Bakewell, 1968; National Records of Scotland, HH 16/45.

52. *The Times*, 30 August 1913, p. 6.

53. BBC Sound Archive, Lady Asquith and Lady Stocks interviewed by Joan Bakewell, 1968.

54. C. Sarah Laughton, 'The Woman with the Suitcase', unpublished MS biography of Eileen Casey, 2017; Private family papers; Eileen Casey Biographical Notes, Group C, vol. 2, Museum of London Suffragette Collections.

55. *The Suffragette*, 26 December 1913, p. 258.

56. *Daily Mirror*, 6 October 1913, pp. 6, 7; *The Times*, 6 October, p. 3.

57. *The Times*, 11 October 1913, pp. 5, 13 October 1913, p. 5.

58. *The Times*, 17 November 1913, p. 3.

59. Statement by Rachel Peace, October 1913, Museum of London Suffragette Collections.

60. *The Times*, 19 December 1913, p. 8.

61. Census Returns: 1901, Lewisham; 1911, Letchworth.

62. Rachel Peace/Jane Short Biographical Notes, 58.87/59, Museum of London Suffragette Collections.

63. Emmeline Pankhurst, *My Own Story*, pp. 324–5 (her account says she arrived on 26 October but the correct date is 18 October); *The Times*, 17 October 1913, p. 6.

64. Sylvia D. Hoffert, *Alva Vanderbilt Belmont: Unlikely Champion of Women's Rights*, p. 89.

65. *The Times*, 13 October 1913, p. 5.

66. Ibid.

67. Sylvia Pankhurst, *The Suffragette Movement*, p. 498; *The Times*, 14 October 1913, p. 5.

68. Sylvia Pankhurst, *The Suffragette Movement*, p. 498; Mary Leigh interviewed by David Mitchell, David Mitchell Papers, 73.83/52, Museum of London Suffragette Collections.

69. Sylvia Pankhurst, *The Suffragette Movement*, p. 499.

70. WSPU pamphlet, 'Why We Are Militant', 1913, pp. 13–14, Museum of London Suffragette Collections.

71. Letter from Ellen La Motte to Christabel Pankhurst in *Votes for Women*, 24 October 1913, p. 51.

72. National Archives, HO 144/1257/235545.

73. Ibid.; WSPU Handbill, 'Tortured Women: What Forcible Feeding Means', 56/176/4, Museum of London Suffragette Collections.

74. *Daily Mirror*, 25 October 1913, p. 4; *Votes for Women*, 24 October 1913, p. 46.

75. Lucienne Boyce, *The Bristol Suffragettes*, pp. 52–5.

76. Leah Leneman, *'A Guid Cause': The Women's Suffrage Movement in Scotland*, pp. 160–1; *The Times*, 3 November 1913, p. 9; *Daily Mirror*, 3 November, p. 5; *The Suffragette*, 7 November, p. 84; Mary Soames (ed.), *Speaking for Themselves: The Personal Letters of Winston and Clementine Churchill*, pp. 81–2.

77. Emmeline Pankhurst, *My Own Story*, p. 326.

78. Ibid., pp. 329–30.

79. *The Suffragette*, 3 December 1913, p. 177, 12 December 1913, p. 202.

80. Song, 'PC Forty-Nine', 1912, http://monologues.co.uk/musichall/Songs-PC-Forty-Nine.htm

18 'SLASHER MARY'

1. Sylvia Pankhurst, *The Suffragette Movement*, p. 515; *Votes for Women*, 9 January 1914, p. 225.

2. Sylvia Pankhurst, *The Suffragette Movement*, p. 518.

3. Ibid., p. 519.

4. Ibid.

5. *The Suffragette*, 2, 9, 16, 23 January, 6 February 1914.

6. Elizabeth Crawford: United Suffragists, p. 694.

7. Letter from Sylvia Pankhurst to Henry Harben, 2 February 1914, BL Harben Papers, Add 58226, ff.96–8.

8. *ODNB*: Adela Constantia Mary Pankhurst.

9. Deirdre Macpherson, *The Suffragette's Daughter. Betty Archdale: Her Life of Feminism, Cricket, War and Education*, pp. 44–6.

10. Elizabeth Crawford: Adela Constantia Mary Pankhurst, pp. 486–7.

11. Ethel Smyth, *Female Pipings in Eden*, pp. 220–1.

12. Kitty Marion autobiography, Museum of London Suffragette Collections, p. 253.

13. Ibid., p. 254.

14. Ibid.

15. Ibid., p. 255.

16. Ibid.

17. Ibid., p. 257.

18. National Archives, HO 144/1721/221874.

19. Prison Letters, 1914, SC Box 31, Museum of London Suffragette Collections.

20. Ibid.

21. Ibid.

22. Kitty Marion autobiography, Museum of London Suffragette Collections, pp. 257–8.

23. Rachel Peace, National Archives, HO 144/1232/229179.

24. Kitty Marion autobiography, Museum of London Suffragette Collections, p. 267.

25. Ibid., p. 264.

26. Ibid.

27. Ibid.

28. Ibid., p. 265.

29. Ibid.

30. Ibid., p. 269.

31. *The Suffragette*, 13 February 1914, p. 397; *The Times*, 11 February 1914, p. 6; *Daily Mirror*, 11 February 1914, p. 4.

32. *The Suffragette*, 13 February 1914, p. 397.

33. *The Times*, 12 February 1914, p. 5; Christabel Pankhurst, *Unshackled: The Story of How We Won the Vote*, p. 265; Gretchen Wilson, *With All Her Might: The Life of Gertrude Harding, Militant Suffragette*, p. 143.

34. *The Times*, 23 February 1914, p. 4; *Daily Mirror*, 19 February, p. 3; *Auckland Star*, 25 February 1914.

35. Henrietta Leslie (Gladys Schütze), *More Ha'pence Than Kicks: Being Some Things Remembered*, p. 103.

36. Ibid., pp. 103–4.
37. Ibid., p. 103.
38. Ibid., pp. 103–4.
39. Ibid., p. 106.
40. *The Suffragette*, 27 February 1914, p. 43.
41. *The Times*, 23 February 1914, p. 4.
42. Henrietta Leslie (Gladys Schütze), *More Ha'pence Than Kicks*, pp. 107–8.
43. Kitty Marshall, 'Suffragette Escapes and Adventures', Museum of London Suffragette Collections, pp. 75–6.
44. Henrietta Leslie (Gladys Schütze), *More Ha'Pence Than Kicks*, p. 109.
45. *ODNB*: Gladys Henrietta Schütze 'Henrietta Leslie', née Raphael, later Mendl, Schütze; Henrietta Leslie (Gladys Schütze), *More Ha'Pence Than Kicks*, p. 78.
46. Henrietta Leslie (Gladys Schütze), *More Ha'Pence Than Kicks*, pp. 111–12.
47. Annie Kenney, *Memories of a Militant*, p. 243.
48. Smyth, *Female Pipings in Eden*, p. 226.
49. Ibid., p. 227.
50. *The Times*, 10 March 1914, p. 6.
51. Emmeline Pankhurst, *My Own Story*, p. 349.
52. *Daily Mirror*, 10 March 1914, p. 4.
53. Ibid.
54. *The Times*, 10 March 1914, p. 6.
55. Ibid., 11 March 1914, p. 5.
56. Emmeline Pankhurst, *My Own Story*, p. 343.
57. Janie Allan Papers, National Library of Scotland, Acc 4498/1.
58. Letter written by Mary Raleigh Richardson, 10 March 1914, Museum of London Suffragette Collections.
59. Ibid.
60. BBC Sound Archive, Mary Richardson interviewed by Sorrel Bentinck, 1961.
61. Mary Raleigh Richardson, *Laugh a Defiance*, p. 166.
62. Ibid., p. 167.
63. Ibid.
64. Ibid., p. 169.
65. Ibid.
66. *The Times*, 11 March 1914, p. 9; *Daily Mirror*, 11 March 1914, p. 4.
67. *Daily Mirror*, 13 March 1914, pp. 4, 9.
68. Elizabeth Ewan, Sue Innes and Siân Reynolds (eds.), *The Biographical Dictionary of Scottish Women*: Grace Cadell, p. 56.

69. Ibid.: Ethel Agnes Mary Moorhead, p. 271; Elizabeth Crawford: Ethel Moorhead, p. 426.

70. *ODNB*: Ethel Moorhead; Leah Leneman, '*A Guid Cause*': *The Women's Suffrage Movement in Scotland*, pp. 266–7.

71. Ethel Moorhead, National Records of Scotland, Police Commission for Scotland, HH 16/40; Register of Suffragettes Received Into Scottish Prisons, 1909–1914, HH 12/22.

72. Ethel Moorhead, Police Commission for Scotland, HH 16/40.

73. Ibid., February 1914.

74. Ibid.

75. Ibid.

76. Ibid.

77. WSPU Handbill, 'Scotland Dishonoured And Disgraced', 50.82/542, Museum of London Suffragette Collections.

78. Ethel Moorhead, National Records of Scotland, Police Commission for Scotland, HH 16/40, January 1913.

79. Ibid.

80. Ibid., February 1913.

81. Ibid., October 1913.

82. Ewan, Innes and Reynolds, *The Biographical Dictionary of Scottish Women*: Dorothea Chalmers Smith, p. 329.

83. *The Times*, 27 February 1914, p. 5.

84. Ibid.

85. Letter from Janie Allan to the Chairman of the Prison Commission, Janie Allan Papers, National Library of Scotland, Acc 4498/2.

86. Leneman, '*A Guid Cause*', pp. 269–70.

87. National Records of Scotland, Police Commission for Scotland, HH 16/40/6.

88. Ibid.

89. Emmeline Pankhurst, *My Own Story*, pp. 337–8.

90. *The Times*, 10 April 1914, p. 6; *Daily Mirror*, 10 April 1914, p. 4.

91. National Portrait Gallery Archive, NPG 136416.

92. *Suffrage Annual and Women's Who's Who*, p. 286; Census Return: 1911, Catford.

93. Smyth, *Female Pipings in Eden*, pp. 229–30.

94. Kenney, *Memories of a Militant*, p. 243.

95. Ibid., p. 244.

96. Ibid., pp. 244–5.

97. Ibid., p. 247.

98. *The Times*, 18 April 1914, p. 9.

99. Ibid.

100. Report of Trial, 50.82/1130, Museum of London Suffragette Collections, p. 7.

101. Ibid., p. 8.

102. *Daily Mirror*, 29 April 1914, p. 1.

103. Report of Trial, 50.82/1130, Museum of London Suffragette Collections, p. 10.

104. Ibid., p. 13.

105. Ibid., p. 9.

106. Ibid.

107. *Suffrage Annual and Women's Who's Who*, p. 195.

108. Report of Trial, p. 8.

109. *The Times*, 30 May 1914, p. 5.

110. Ibid., 14 May 1914, p. 5.

111. Ida Alexa Ross Wylie, *My Life With George: An Unconventional Autobiography*, p. 182.

112. Rachel Barrett autobiography, Museum of London Suffragette Collections, p. 130.

113. *ODNB*: William Waldegrave Palmer; *The Times*, 6 May 1914, p. 8.

114. Millicent Garrett Fawcett, *The Women's Victory and After: Personal Reminiscences, 1911–1918*, pp. 72–3.

115. Ibid.

116. *The Times*, 6 May 1914, p. 8.

117. BBC Sound Archive, Winifred Starbuck interview 1958.

118. Ibid.

119. Ibid.

120. Ibid.

19 THE DEPUTATION TO SEE KING GEORGE V, 21 MAY 1914

1. Ethel Smyth, *Female Pipings in Eden*, p. 231.

2. Ibid., p. 232.

3. Letters from Grace Roe and Emmeline Pankhurst to WSPU members, 6 May and 16 May 1914, Museum of London Suffragette Collections.

4. *The Times*, 22 May 1914, p. 8; *Daily Mirror*, 22 May 1914, pp. 1, 4.

5. Ibid., p. 8.

6. Antonia Raeburn, *The Militant Suffragettes*, p. 231; *ODNB*: Eleanor Beatrice Higginson, née Ellis.

7. *Woman's Dreadnought*, 30 May 1914, quoted on http://freepages.genealogy.rootsweb.ancestry.com/arrow/daisy_parsons.htm

8. Ibid.

9. Sylvia Pankhurst, *The Suffragette Movement*, p. 552.

10. Ibid.

11. Ibid.

12. Elizabeth Crawford: Hall family, pp. 258–9.

13. Sylvia Pankhurst, *The Suffragette Movement*, p. 555.

14. *The Suffragette*, 29 May 1914, p. 122.

15. Ibid.; *The Times*, 23 May 1914, p. 8.

16. *The Suffragette*, 29 May 1914, p. 122.

17. *The Times*, 3 June 1914, p. 3.

18. Ibid., 9 July 1914, p. 4.

19. Ibid., 23 May 1914, p. 8.

20. *The Suffragette*, 5 June 1914, p. 136.

21. Ibid., 3 July 1914, p. 204.

22. Ibid.

23. *The Times*, 20 February 1913, p. 14; private collection.

24. *The Suffragette*, 29 May 1914, pp. 117, 121.

25. Ibid.

26. *Daily Mirror*, 22 May 1914, pp. 3, 8.

27. Ibid., p. 8.

28. *The Suffragette*, 29 May 1914, p. 121.

29. *The Times*, 8 June 1914, p. 48; 10 June 1914, p. 4; 15 June 1914, p. 4.

30. Sylvia Pankhurst, *The Suffragette Movement*, p. 561; Correspondence of Dr Flora Murray, National Library of Scotland, Acc 4498, pp. 83–9; National Archives, Grace Roe, HO 144/1320/252950.

31. *The Times*, 25 May 1914, p. 34; *Daily Mirror*, 25 May 1914, p. 4.

32. Museum of London News Cuttings Book, July 1914.

33. *The Times*, 25 May 1914, p. 34.

34. Sylvia Pankhurst, *The Suffragette Movement*, p. 563; *Votes for Women*, 29 May 1914, p. 576.

35. Smyth, *Female Pipings in Eden*, p. 233.

36. Ibid., p. 234.

37. Letter from Margaret Davison to Rose Lamartine Yates, June 1914, LSE Library Collections, Emily Wilding Davison Papers, 7 EWD, B3/1.

38. *Daily Mirror*, 8 June 1914, p. 4.

39. *The Times*, 8 June 1914, p. 48; *Daily Mirror*, 8 June 1914, p. 4.

40. *Daily Mirror*, 8 June 1914, p. 4.

41. *The Times*, 9 June 1914, p. 9.

42. Ibid.

43. *The Suffragette*, 5 June 1914, pp. 132–3.

44. Elizabeth Crawford: Eileen Casey, p. 100.

45. C. Sarah Laughton, 'The Woman with the Suitcase', unpublished MS biography of Eileen Casey, 2017, p. 41, private family papers.
46. Ibid., pp. 42–3.
47. Ibid., pp. 44–5.
48. Ibid., pp. 45–6.
49. Ibid., p. 46.
50. Lavender Guthrie death certificate; *The Times*, 12 June 1914, p. 5.
51. *The Times*, 12 June 1914, p. 5; *Daily Mirror*, 12 June 1914, p. 3.
52. *The Times*, 12 June 1914, p. 5.
53. *The Suffragette*, 19 June 1914, p. 166.
54. *Daily Mirror*, 13 June 1914, p. 1.
55. *The Times*, 12 June 1914, p. 5.
56. Ibid.
57. Ibid.
58. Ibid., 16 June 1912, p. 12.
59. Ibid., 10 June 1914, p. 8.
60. Ibid., 13 June 1914, p. 9.
61. Sylvia Pankhurst, *The Suffragette Movement*, p. 566.
62. Ibid., pp. 567–8.
63. Ibid., p. 570.
64. Ibid., p. 575.
65. *ODNB*: John Scurr and Julia Scurr.
66. *Votes for Women*, 26 June 1914, p. 594.
67. Sylvia Pankhurst, *The Suffragette Movement*, pp. 573–4.
68. Ibid., p. 575.
69. Ibid., p. 576.
70. *The Times*, 12 June 1914, p. 13; Emmeline Pankhurst, *My Own Story*, p. 355.
71. *The Times*, 15 June 1914, p. 12.
72. Andrew Rosen, *Rise Up, Women!: The Militant Campaign of the Women's Social and Political Union, 1903–1914*, p. 237.
73. *The Times*, 9 July 1914, p. 8.
74. Leah Leneman, *'A Guid Cause': The Women's Suffrage Movement in Scotland*, pp. 206–8; National Records of Scotland: Frances Mary Parker (Janet Arthur) HH 16/43.
75. National Records of Scotland: Frances Mary Parker (Janet Arthur) HH 16/43.
76. Ibid.
77. Elizabeth Crawford: Frances Mary Parker, pp. 525–6.
78. Raeburn, *The Militant Suffragettes*, p. 236.
79. Annie Kenney, *Memories of a Militant*, pp. 251–2.

80. Ibid., p 252.
81. Ibid.
82. Ibid., p. 253.
83. *The Times*, 4 August 1914, p. 3.
84. Ibid., 5 August 1914, p. 6.
85. Letter from Mrs Pankhurst to WSPU members, 13 August 1914, Museum of London Suffragette Collections.
86. Ibid.

20 THE VOTE AT LAST!

1. Peter Simkins, *Kitchener's Army: Raising the New Armies 1914–1916*, p. 78; Keith Grieves, *The Politics of Manpower 1914–1918*, p. 16; War Office, *Statistics of the Military Effort of the British Empire During the Great War*, p. 364.
2. Diana Condell and Jean Liddiard, *Working For Victory! Images of Women in the First World War, 1914–1918*, pp. 7–8, 72–3.
3. Millicent Garrett Fawcett, *The Women's Victory and After: Personal Reminiscences, 1911–1918*, p. 88.
4. Diane Atkinson, *The Suffragettes in Pictures*, pp. 161–5.
5. *ODNB*: Emmeline Pankhurst; Christabel Harriette Pankhurst; Annie Kenney; Flora Drummond.
6. *ODNB*: Ethel Mary Smyth; Mary Sophia Allen; Elizabeth Crawford: Mary Leigh, p. 340.
7. *ODNB*: Estelle Sylvia Pankhurst.
8. *ODNB*: Adela Constantia Mary Pankhurst.
9. *ODNB*: Emmeline Pethick-Lawrence; Frederick William Pethick-Lawrence.
10. Atkinson, *The Suffragettes in Pictures*, p. 173.
11. Ibid., pp. 174–5; Condell and Liddiard, *Working For Victory!*, p. 62.
12. Garrett Fawcett, *The Women's Victory and After*, p. 137.
13. Mari Takayanagi, 'Women and the Vote: the Parliamentary path to Equal Franchise, 1918–1928', to be published in *Parliamentary History*, 2018, pp. 3–8.
14. Andrew Rosen, *Rise Up, Women!: The Militant Campaign of the Women's Social and Political Union, 1903–1914*, p. 261.
15. House of Commons Debates, 28 March 1917, vol. 92, cc 46871.
16. Paula Bartley, *Votes for Women, 1860–1928*, p. 98.
17. Christabel Pankhurst, *Unshackled: The Story of How We Won the Vote*, pp. 292.
18. Ibid., p. 293.

19. Annesebba.com/discovering a new relative, leonora cohen.

20. *Punch*, 23 January 1918.

21. Sylvia Pankhurst, *The Suffragette Movement*, p. 608.

22. Ibid., p. 607.

23. Eva Gore-Booth's sister, Constance Markievicz, was the first woman to be elected as an MP in the general election of 1918. Constance, who had been sentenced to death for her part in the Easter Rising of 1916, had her name put forward as a Sinn Fein candidate and won a seat in Dublin. Her sentence was commuted. When she was released in March 1919 she refused to take her seat in the House of Commons. Elizabeth Vallance, *Women in the House: A Study of Women Members of Parliament*, p. 26.

24. Astor Papers, Museum of Rural Life, University of Reading, draft chapter of autobiography, 1946, p. 5.

25. *ODNB*: Nancy Witcher Astor, Viscountess Astor.

26. John Grigg, *Nancy Astor, Portrait of a Pioneer*, p. 77; Christopher Sykes, *Nancy Astor: The Life of Lady Astor*, p. 230.

27. Atkinson, *The Suffragettes in Pictures*, pp. 166–7.

Bibliography

PRIMARY SOURCES

Archives

Astor Papers, Museum of Rural Life, University of Reading
Balfour and Harben Papers, British Library
British Suffragette Files, General Prisons Board, National Archives of
    Ireland, Dublin
Bryce Papers, Bodleian Library, University of Oxford
Canon William Aitken Diary, Norfolk Record Office
Cicely Fairfield (Rebecca West) Correspondence, Lilley Library, University
    of Indiana, Bloomington
Daily Mirror Archive Online
Emily Wilding Davison Papers, LSE Library Collections
Hansard Debates, Parliamentary Archives, Westminster
Hereford Archives
Home Office and Metropolitan Police Files, National Archives, Kew
Huntington Library, California
Janie Allan Papers, National Library of Scotland
Kenney Papers, University of East Anglia
Lancashire Record Office
Leicestershire Record Office
London Library
Lytton Family Papers, Knebworth House Archives
Museum of London Suffragette Collections
National Records of Scotland
St Bartholomew's Hospital Archive, London
Suffragette Prisoner Files, National Library of Scotland
The Times Digital Archive online
Wakefield Archives

FAMILY PAPERS

Charlotte Drake: Vivienne Cramp and Ramsay Drake Family Papers
Eileen Casey: C. Sarah Laughton Family Papers
Grace Marcon: Ginny Scholey Family Papers
M. V. Goode Suffragette Collection
Mary Richardson: Debby Tyrrell Family Papers

SELECT BIBLIOGRAPHY OF SECONDARY SOURCES

All titles published in London unless stated otherwise.

Allen, Mary S., *Lady in Blue: The Autobiography of the First of the Women Police in England*, Stanley Paul and Co., 1936
—, and Heyneman, Julie Helen, *Woman at the Cross Roads*, The Unicorn Press, 1934
Anand, Anita, *Sophia: Princess, Suffragette, Revolutionary*, Bloomsbury, 2015
Annual Register: A Review of Public Events at Home and Abroad for the Year 1910, Longmans, Green and Co., 1911
Annual Register: A Review of Public Events at Home and Abroad for the Year 1912, Longmans, Green and Co., 1913
Annual Register: A Review of Public Events at Home and Abroad for the Year 1913, Longmans, Green and Co., 1914
Asquith, Herbert, *Moments of Memory: Recollections and Impressions*, Hutchinson and Co., 1937
Atkinson, Diane, *The Suffragettes in Pictures*, Museum of London/Sutton Publishing, Stroud, 1997
Balfour, Betty (ed.), *The Letters of Constance Lytton*, William Heinemann, 1925
Barnes, Annie (in conversation with Kate Harding and Caroline Gibbs), *Tough Annie: From Suffragette to Stepney Councillor*, Stepney Book Publications, 1980
Bartley, Paula, *Votes for Women, 1860–1928*, Hodder & Stoughton, 1998
—, *Emmeline Pankhurst*, Routledge, 2002
Bounds, Joy, *A Song of Their Own: The Fight for Women's Suffrage in Ipswich*, The History Press, 2014
Boyce, Lucienne, *The Bristol Suffragettes*, Silver Wood Books, Bristol, 2013
Boyd, Nina, *From Suffragette to Fascist: The Many Lives of Mary Sophia Allen*, The History Press, Stroud, 2013
Bradley, Katherine, *Friends and Visitors: A History of the Women's Suffrage Movement in Cornwall, 1870–1914*, The Hypatia Trust, Penzance, Cornwall, 2000

Brittain, Vera, *Pethick-Lawrence: A Portrait*, George Allen & Unwin, 1963

Brockway, Fenner Archibald, *Towards Tomorrow: An Autobiography*, Hart-Davis, MacGibbon, 1977

Brookes, Pamela, *Women at Westminster: An Account of Women in the British Parliament 1918–1966*, Peter Davies, 1967

Buckland, Gail, *The Golden Summer: The Edwardian Photographs of Horace W. Nicholls*, Pavilion Books, 1989

Bush, Julia, *Women Against the Vote: Female Anti-Suffragism in Britain*, Oxford University Press, 2007

Cartwright, Colin, *Burning for the Vote: The Women's Suffrage Movement in Central Buckinghamshire, 1904–1914*, The University of Buckingham Press, Buckingham, 2013

Chew, Doris Nield (ed.), *Ada Nield Chew: The Life and Writings of a Working Woman*, Virago Press, 1982

Clifford, Colin, *The Asquiths*, John Murray, 2002

Codd, Clara, *So Rich a Life*, privately published by Caxton Lord, Pretoria, South Africa, 1951

Coleman, Verna, *Adela Pankhurst: The Wayward Suffragette 1885–1961*, Melbourne University Press, Melbourne, 1996

Collis, Maurice, *Nancy Astor, An Informal Biography*, Faber & Faber, 1960

Condell, Diana, and Liddiard, Jean, *Working for Victory? Images of Women in the First World War*, Routledge & Kegan Paul, 1978

Cowman, Krista, *Mrs. Brown Is a Man and a Brother: Women in Merseyside's Political Organisations 1890–1920*, Liverpool University Press, Liverpool, 2004

—, *Women of the Right Spirit: Paid Organisers of the Women's Social and Political Union 1904–1918*, Manchester University Press, 2007

—, *The Militant Suffragette Movement in York*, Borthwick Publications, York, 2007

Crawford, Elizabeth, *The Women's Suffrage Movement: A Reference Guide 1866–1928*, UCL Press, 1999

—, *The Women's Suffrage Movement in Britain and Ireland: A Regional Survey*, Routledge, 2006

— (ed.), *Campaigning for the Vote: Kate Parry Frye's Suffrage Diary*, Francis Boutle Publishers, 2013

Davis, Mark, *West Riding Pauper Lunatic Asylum Through Time*, Amberley Publishing, 2013

Dobbie, B. M. Willmott, *A Nest of Suffragettes in Somerset: Eagle House, Batheaston*, Ralph Allen Press, Bath, 1979

Donoghue, Stephen, *Just My Story*, Hutchinson and Co., 1923

Dove, Iris, *Yours in the Cause: Suffragettes in Lewisham, Greenwich and Woolwich*, Lewisham Library Service and Greenwich Libraries, 1988

Eustance, Claire, Ryan, Joan, and Ugolini, Laura, *Suffrage Reader: Charting Directions in Suffrage History*, Bloomsbury, 2000

Ewan, Elizabeth, Innes, Sue, and Reynolds, Siân (eds), *The Biographical Dictionary of Scottish Women*, Edinburgh University Press, 2007 edition

Fort, Adrian, *Nancy: The Story of Lady Astor*, Jonathan Cape, 2010

Fry, Amelia R., and Paul, Alice, *Conversations with Alice Paul: Woman Suffrage and the Equal Rights Movement: Oral History Transcript and Related Material, 1972–1976*, The Regents of the University of California, 1976

Gaddes, Boyce, *Outward Bound From Inverlochy: A Biography of the Hon. Evelina Haverfield*, Merlin Books, Gloucester, 1995

Gale, Maggie B. B., and Gardner, Vivien (eds), *Auto/Biography and Identity: Women, Theatre and Performance*, Manchester University Press, 2004

Garrett Fawcett, Millicent, *The Women's Victory and After: Personal Reminiscences, 1911–1918*, Sidgwick & Jackson, 1920

Gawthorpe, Mary, *Up Hill to Holloway*, Traversity Press, Maine, 1962

Girouard, Mark, *Enthusiasms*, Frances Lincoln, 2011

Glynn, Jennifer, *My Sister Rosalind Franklin*, Oxford University Press, Oxford, 2012

Grieves, Keith, *The Politics of Manpower: 1914–1918*, Manchester University Press, 1988

Grigg, John, *Nancy Astor: Portrait of a Pioneer*, Sidgwick & Jackson, 1980

Hamilton, Cicely, *Life Errant*, J. M. Dent and Sons, 1935

Harrison, Brian, *Separate Spheres: The Opposition to Women's Suffrage in Great Britain*, Croom Helm, 1978

Hartley, Peter, *Bikes at Brooklands in the Pioneer Years*, Goose Publishing, Norwich, 1973

Heron, Pat, *The Life of Ethel Haslam, an Ilford Suffragette*, Purple, White and Green, Leeds, 2012

Hesketh, Phoebe, *My Aunt Edith*, Peter Davies, 1966, reprinted Lancashire County Books, Preston, 1992

Hoffert, Sylvia D., *Alva Vanderbilt Belmont: Unlikely Champion of Women's Rights*, Indiana University Press, 2012

Holledge, Julie, *Innocent Flowers: Women in the Edwardian Era*, Virago Press, 1981

Hollis, Patricia (ed.), *Pressure from Without in Early Victorian England*, Edward Arnold, 1974

Holton, Sandra Stanley, *Feminism and Democracy: Women's Suffrage and Reform Politics 1900–1918*, Cambridge University Press, Cambridge, 1986

—, *Suffrage Days: Suffrage Stories From the Women's Movement*, Routledge, London and New York, 1996

Howell, Georgina, *Daughter of the Desert: The Remarkable Life of Gertrude Bell*, Macmillan, 2006

Inwood, Stephen, *City of Cities: The Birth of Modern London*, Macmillan, 2005

Jackson, Sarah, and Taylor, Rosemary, *Voices from History: East London Suffragettes*, The History Press, Stroud, 2014

Jenkins, Jess, *The Burning Question: The Struggle for Women's Suffrage in Leicestershire*, Leicestershire County Council, 2007

Jenkins, Lyndsey, *Lady Constance Lytton: Aristocrat, Suffragette, Martyr*, Biteback Publishing, 2015

Joannou, Maroula, and Purvis, June, *The Women's Suffrage Movement: New Feminist Perspectives*, Manchester University Press, Manchester, 1998

John, A. V., and Eustance, Claire (eds), *The Men's Share: Masculinities, Male Support and Women's Suffrage in Britain, 1890–1920*, Routledge, London and New York, 1997

Kean, Hilda, *London Stories: Personal Lives, Public Histories*, Rivers Oram Press, 2004

Kenney, Annie, *Memories of a Militant*, Edward Arnold, 1924

Kent, Susan Kingsley, *Sex and Suffrage in Britain, 1860–1914*, Princeton University Press, New Jersey, 1987

Lawson, Marion (ed.), *Memories of Charlotte Marsh*, The Suffragette Fellowship, 1961

Leneman, Leah, *'A Guid Cause': The Women's Suffrage Movement in Scotland*, Aberdeen University Press, 1991

—, *The Scottish Suffragettes*, National Museum of Scotland Publishing, Edinburgh, 2000

Leslie, Henrietta (Gladys Henrietta Schütze), *More Ha'Pence Than Kicks: Being Some Things Remembered*, MacDonald and Co., 1944

Lewis, Gifford, Gore-Booth, Eva and Roper, Esther, *A Biography*, Pandora, London, Sydney, Wellington, 1988

Liddington, Jill, *The Life and Times of a Respectable Rebel: Selina Cooper 1865–1946*, Virago Press, 1984

—, *Rebel Girls: Their Fight for the Vote*, Virago Press, 2006

—, *Vanishing for the Vote: Suffrage, Citizenship and the Battle for the Census*, Manchester University Press, Manchester and New York, 2014

—, and Norris, Jill, *One Hand Tied Behind Us: The Rise of the Women's Suffrage Movement*, Virago Press, 1978

Lytton, Constance, *Prisons and Prisoners: Some Personal Experiences by Constance Lytton and Jane Warton, spinster*, first published by William Heinemann, 1914, Virago Press edition, 1988

MacKenzie, Midge, *Shoulder to Shoulder: A Documentary by Midge MacKenzie*, Vintage Books edition, 1988

Macpherson, Deirdre, *The Suffragette's Daughter. Betty Archdale: Her Life of Feminism, Cricket and Education*, Rosenberg Publishing, Sydney, 2002

McPhee, Carol, and FitzGerald, Ann (eds), *The Non-Violent Militant: Selected Writings of Teresa Billington-Greig*, Routledge & Kegan Paul, London and New York, 1987

McPherson, Susan, and McPherson, Angela, *Mosley's Old Suffragette: A Biography of Norah Dacre Fox*, lulu.com, 2011

Marcus, Jane, *Suffrage and the Pankhursts*, Routledge, 1987

Markham, Violet R., *Return Passage: The Autobiography of Violet R. Markham*, Oxford University Press, 1953

Marsh, Richard, *A Trainer to Two Kings: Being The Reminiscences of Richard Marsh*, Cassell and Co., 1925

Mayhall, Laura E. Nym, *The Militant Suffrage Movement: Citizenship and Resistance in Britain, 1830–1930*, Oxford University Press, New York, 2003

Metcalfe, A. E., *Woman's Effort: A Chronicle of British Women's Fifty Years' Struggle For Citizenship*, B. H. Blackwell, Oxford, 1917

Miles, Patricia, and Williams, Jill, *An Uncommon Criminal: The Life of Lady Constance Lytton, Militant Suffragette, 1869–1923*, Knebworth House Education and Preservation Trust, 1999

Minney, R. J., *Number 10 Downing Street: A House in History*, Cassell, 1963

Mitchell, David, *The Fighting Pankhursts: A Study in Tenacity*, Jonathan Cape, 1967

—, *Queen Christabel, A Biography of Christabel Pankhurst*, Macdonald and Jane's, 1977

Mitchell, Hannah, *The Hard Way Up: The Autobiography of Hannah Mitchell, Suffragette and Rebel*, Virago Press, 1977

Morrell, Caroline, '*Black Friday': Violence Against Women in the Suffragette Movement*, Women's Research and Resources Centre Publications, 1981

Moss, Alan, and Skinner, Keith, *The Victorian Detective*, Shire Publications, Oxford, 2013

Mugglestone, Lynda, 'Woman or Suffragette?' OUP blog, 2012

Murphy, William, *Political Imprisonment and the Irish, 1912–1921*, Oxford University Press, 2014

Musolf, Karen J., *From Plymouth to Parliament: A Rhetorical History of Nancy Astor's 1919 Campaign*, St Martin's Press, New York, 1999

Otte, T. G., and Readman, Paul (eds), *By-elections in British Politics 1832–1914*, The Boydell Press, Woodbridge, Suffolk, 2013

Owens Cullen, Rosemary, *Smashing Times: A History of the Irish Women's Suffrage Movement 1889–1922*, Attic Press, Dublin, 1984

—, *A Social History of Women in Ireland, 1870–1970*, Gill and Macmillan, Dublin, 2005

Pankhurst, Christabel Harriette *Unshackled: The Story of How We Won the Vote*, Hutchinson, 1959

Pankhurst, Emmeline, *My Own Story: The Autobiography of Emmeline Pankhurst*, Hearst's International Library Co., USA, 1914, reprinted by Virago Press, 1979

Pankhurst, Richard, *Sylvia Pankhurst: Artist and Crusader*, Paddington Press, London and New York, 1979

Pankhurst, Sylvia Estelle, *The Suffragette: The History of the Militant Suffrage Movement 1905–1910*, Sturgis and Walton Co., 1911

—, *The Home Front: A Mirror to Life in England in the First World War*, Hutchinson and Co., 1932

—, *The Suffragette Movement*, Longman Group, 1931, reprinted by Virago Press, 1977

Porter, Bernard, *The Origins of the Vigilant State: The London Metropolitan Police Special Branch before the First World War*, Weidenfeld & Nicolson, 1987

Probert, Laura, *Women of Kent Rally to the Cause: A Study of Women's Suffrage in Kent, 1909–1918*, Millicent Press, Ramsgate, 2008

Pugh, Martin, *Women and the Women's Movement in Britain 1914–1959*, Macmillan, 1992

—, *The March of the Women: A Revisionist Analysis of the Campaign for Women's Suffrage, 1866–1914*, Oxford University Press, Oxford, 2000

—, *The Pankhursts*, Penguin Press, 2001

Purnell, Sonia, *The First Lady: The Life and Wars of Clementine Churchill*, Aurum Press, 2015

Raeburn, Antonia, *The Militant Suffragettes*, Michael Joseph, 1973; 1974 hardback edition

Richardson, Mary Raleigh, *Laugh a Defiance*, Weidenfeld & Nicolson, 1953

Rosen, Andrew, *Rise Up, Women!: The Militant Campaign of the Women's Social and Political Union, 1903–1914*, Routledge & Kegan Paul, London and Boston, 1974

Rover, Constance, *Women's Suffrage and Party Politics in Britain, 1866–1914*, Routledge & Kegan Paul, 1967

Soames, Mary (ed.), *Speaking for Themselves: The Personal Letters of Winston and Clementine Churchill*, Black Swan Books/Doubleday, 1999

Simkins, Peter, *Kitchener's Army: The Raising of the New Armies 1916–1918*, Pen and Sword Publishing, Barnsley, 1988

Smyth, Ethel, *Female Pipings in Eden*, Peter Davies, 1933

Sparham, Anna (ed.), *Soldiers and Suffragettes: The Photography of Christina Broom*, Philip Wilson Publishers, London and New York, 2015

Stevens, Mark, *Broadmoor Revealed: Victorian Crime and the Lunatic Asylum*, Pen and Sword, Barnsley, 2013

Suffrage Annual and Women's Who's Who, Stanley Paul and Co., 1913

Sykes, Christopher, *Nancy Astor: The Life of Nancy Astor*, William Collins, Panther edition, 1972

Tanner, Michael, *The Suffragette Derby*, The Robson Press, 2013

Taylor, Marsali, *Women's Suffrage in Shetland*, Lulu.com, 2010

Taylor, Rosemary, *In Letters of Gold: The Story of Sylvia Pankhurst and the East London Federation of the Suffragettes in Bow*, Stepney Books, 1993

Tickner, Lisa, *The Spectacle of Women: Imagery of the Woman Suffrage Campaign, 1907–14*, Chatto & Windus, 1987

Tucker, Alan, *Suffragette Partnership: The Lives of Lettice Floyd and Annie Williams, 1860–1943*, privately published, Mercian Manuals Ltd., Coventry, 2005

Vallance, Elizabeth, *Women in the House: A Study of Women Members of Parliament*, The Athlone Press, 1979

Van Helmond, Maria, *Votes for Women: The Events on Merseyside 1870–1928*, National Museums and Galleries on Merseyside, Liverpool, 1992

Vellacott, Jo, *From Liberal to Labour with Women's Suffrage: The Story of Catherine Marshall*, McGill-Queen's University Press, Montreal, 1993

Walton, Mary, *A Woman's Crusade: Alice Paul and the Battle for the Ballot*, Palgrave Macmillan, 2010

War Office, *Statistics of the Military Effort of the British Empire During the Great War*, 1922

Waterhouse, Michael, *Edwardian Requiem: The Life of Sir Edward Grey*, Biteback Publishing, 2013

Watkins, Sarah-Beth, *Ireland's Suffragettes: The Women Who Fought for the Vote*, The History Press, Stroud, 2014

Watson, Norman, *Dundee's Suffragettes: Their Remarkable Struggle to Win Votes for Women*, privately published, Perth, 1990

—, *Suffragettes and the Post*, privately published, Forfar, 2010

Weinreb, Benjamin, and Hibbert, Christopher (eds), *The London Encyclopaedia*, Papermac, 1983

West, Nigel, *Dictionary of World War One Intelligence*, Rowman and Littlefield, Maryland, and Plymouth, Devon, 2014

Whitmore, Richard, *Alice Hawkins and the Suffragette Movement in Edwardian Leicester*, Breedon Books, Derby, 2007

Wilson, Gretchen, *With All Her Might: The Life of Gertrude Harding, Militant Suffragette*, Holmes and Meier, New York, 1998

Wilson, Ray, and Adams, Ian, *Special Branch, A History: 1883–2006*, Biteback Publishing, 2015

Wright, Almroth E., *The Unexpurgated Case Against Woman Suffrage*, Constable and Co., 1913

Wright, Maureen, *Elizabeth Wolstenholme Elmy and the Victorian Feminist Movement*, Manchester University Press, Manchester and New York, 2011

Wylie, I. A. R., *My Life with George: An Unconventional Autobiography*, Random House, New York, 1940

ONLINE SOURCES

http://oxforddnb.com
www.ancestry.co.uk
oldbaileyonline
Census Returns
www.mirror.co.uk
www.parliament.uk
Times Digital Archive

Acknowledgements

Every biographer owes a debt of gratitude first to their subjects. My first thanks go to the suffragettes for their courage, and for sacrificing so much so that every woman in Britain over the age of eighteen can now vote for a Member of Parliament. I have been writing about these splendid women for thirty years and when I saw the film *Suffragette* in 2015 I said 'Thank you' out loud when the heroine Maud Watts – a composite character of the many working-class women who fought for the vote (played by Carey Mulligan) – was shown on digitally enhanced archive film joining the real suffragettes going to Emily Davison's funeral in Morpeth in 1913. The film ends with a chronology showing when women around the world got the vote, reminding us of the struggle that women have endured to make their voices heard by their law-makers.

Some women in some places still do not have the vote.

Within the suffragette band of sisters I would like to pay special tribute to the working women who for many years have been overlooked as if they had played no part in the campaign. They were not often snapped by male press photographers, who had an eye for a posh photogenic woman in a pristine white dress and a big hat. But those women were there, and, if unable to take part in processions on a busy day filled with work and childcare, they were in their communities doing what they could: bravely speaking on street corners, encouraging friends and neighbours to join the struggle, canvassing door-to-door, and very often meeting hostility. I looked hard for them and celebrate what they did, and not only what their more privileged sisters achieved.

In 1991 I interviewed Mrs Victoria Lidiard (née Simmons), who was then aged 101 and living independently in her flat in Hove. I spent an afternoon with her, reliving her suffragette days: she was a twenty-three-year-old photographer's assistant who came from Bristol to London in March 1912 and broke a window at the War Office, for which she served two months with hard labour in Holloway Gaol. Victoria Lidiard's eyes sparkled as she relived her suffragette career. The first woman optometrist, she never gave up politics and before she died in 1992 was involved in the campaign for the ordination of women priests.

I thank Alexandra Pringle for commissioning me to write this book, seeing the need for it, and seeing me as the person to do it. Bill Swainson, the editor she gave me, helped a lot to condense these suffragettes' stories into a narrative that commands respect. Angelique Tran Van Sang steered the book beautifully through production. Richard Collins copy-edited it with great care. Catherine Best is the best proofreader. I salute you all.

I am proud to be represented by David Godwin.

At the Museum of London, the home of the Suffragette Fellowship Collection since 1950, Beverley Cook is the epitome of what it means to be a curator: her expertise and helpfulness are unparalleled and exemplary.

Elizabeth Crawford's extraordinary knowledge is distilled in her seminal reference books: *The Women's Suffrage Movement: A Reference Guide 1866–1928*, and *The Women's Suffrage Movement in Britain and Ireland: A Regional Survey*. Anyone writing about the women's suffrage movement is indebted to Elizabeth's dedicated research.

Historians and biographers could not practise their art without archives and their archivists, libraries and their librarians. I thank the librarians at the London Library and the Women's Library. I was helped by Dr Maria Castrillo of the Manuscripts Department of the National Library of Scotland and Jean Crawford at the National Records of Scotland. Mrs Aideen Ireland helped me access the rich suffragette material held by the National Archives of Ireland, Dublin. Bridget Gillies at University of East Anglia made the Kenney Papers available to me.

Clare Fleck, archivist at Knebworth House, helped me to better understand Lady Constance Lytton's suffragette career and her family's response to the challenges her commitment presented. I thank Mari Takayanagi at the Parliamentary Archives for her expertise and speedy response to some big questions, and allowing me to read her paper on 'Women and the Vote: the Parliamentary Path To Equal Franchise 1918–1928', to be published in 2018. Alex Burton, a producer on *Woman's Hour*, helped me get in touch with a number of suffragettes' descendants who had appeared on a programme in 2013.

Susan Grandfield has generously shared memories of her Duval and Dugdale relations. Ginny Scholey let me delve into the papers and memorabilia of her grandmother, Grace Marcon. Sarah Laughton assembled all of her Aunt Eileen Casey's papers, and treated me to warm hospitality. Vivienne Cramp arranged an afternoon with Ramsay Drake: Viv and Ramsay's families shared their memorabilia and their memories of Charlotte Drake. Debby Tyrrell helped me to access a previously unseen manuscript by 'Granny Ricky', Mary Richardson. Peter Barratt shared much information about his great-grandmother Alice Hawkins, and has allowed me to reproduce a photograph of her.

Anthony Smith, curator of the Priest House Museum in West Hoathly, where 'the Suffragette Handkerchief' hangs on the stairs of the medieval house, told me the story of how this unique relic was plucked from a bonfire at the end of a jumble sale. I thank John Harnden at Herefordshire Archive Service for help with my inquiries on Beatrice Parlby. Danielle Mills at the Special Collection, University of Reading, helped me locate their interesting material on Nancy Astor. Dr Jonathan Oates shared a draft of a chapter of a forthcoming book which included the shocking death of Olive Fargus, later Mrs Durand-Deacon. Thanks to Norman Watson of Auchterhouse for his work on the suffragettes' depredations of the British postal service. Mrs Hickey at Lancashire Record Office helped with records relating to Gladice Keevil. Colin Harris directed me to the Bryce Papers at the Bodleian Library, University of Oxford. Megan Dix found material on Theresa Garnett in Wakefield Archives.

Hannah Bedford at Norfolk Record Office showed me Canon Aitken's diary, his despair at his daughter Violet Aitken's suffragette doings coming into it in 1912, 1913 and 1914. David K. Frasier of the Lilley Library, Indiana University, Bloomington, located correspondence between Cicely Fairfield, later known as 'Rebecca West', and her family. Cyril Pearse, the authority on Conscientious Objectors of the First World War, generously shared his data on a number of the husbands of suffragettes who refused to take up arms.

I warmly thank Bryony Evans and Alastair Goode whose late parents assembled a remarkable collection of suffragette ephemera. When they began their collecting in the late 1970s the suffragettes were not popular. If Mr and Mrs Goode had not built up that collection many of these precious things would have been lost. On several occasions the family came to the Museum of London to show me their recent acquisitions. I spent a wonderful day at home with the late Mrs Goode who allowed me unrestricted access to the family collection.

Conversations with friends and colleagues play an important part in the making of a book. Sally Ackerman, Irrum Ahmed, Paula Bartley, Karen Birkin, Ioanna Christoforidou, Krista Cowman, Kelly-Ann Davitt, Katie Elder, Nicola Gooch, Elizabeth Goring, Jayne Grant, Cathy Ingram, Donna Kemp, Eve Kreizman, Zoe Moss, Lif Parker, Kirsty Sellman, Roberta Sergio, Emma Starkings, Pauline Tanner and Lorella Thorp are good friends.

The most forbearing person in my suffragette writing and curating life is my husband, Patrick Hughes. He has made my suffragette friends his suffragette friends, and if we had lived in those times I am sure he would have sacrificed friends and reputation to support the most important political campaign of the twentieth century.

Picture Credits

p.1: © Museum of London
p.11: © Museum of London
p.37: © Museum of London
p.57: © Peter Barratt
p.81: © Museum of London
p.103: © Museum of London
p.129: © Museum of London
p.155: © Museum of London
p.187: © Museum of London
p.219: © Museum of London
p.241: © Museum of London
p.263: © Museum of London
p.281: Private Collection
p.311: Private Collection
p.333: © The March of the Women Collection / Mary Evans Picture Library
p.359: Private Collection
p.401: Private Collection
p.419: © Museum of London
p.449: © Museum of London
p.483: Private Collection
p.511: © Punch Limited
p.566: © Adrian Flowers Archive

Index

JOHN HARVEY

EASY MEAT

arrow books

Reissued by Arrow Books 2008

13

First published in Great Britain in 1996 by William Heinemann
This edition first published in 1996 by Mandarin Paperbacks

Arrow Books
The Random House Group Limited
20 Vauxhall Bridge Road, London SW1V 2SA

www.rbooks.co.uk

Addresses for companies within The Random House Group Limited can be found
at: www.randomhouse.co.uk/offices.htm

The Random House Group Limited Reg. No. 954009

A CIP catalogue record for this book
is available from the British Library

ISBN 9780099421597

The Random House Group Limited supports The Forest Stewardship
Council (FSC), the leading international forest certification organisation.
All our titles that are printed on Greenpeace approved FSC certified paper
carry the FSC logo. Our paper procurement policy can be found at:
www.rbooks.co.uk/environment

Mixed Sources
Product group from well-managed
forests and other controlled sources
www.fsc.org Cert no. TT-COC-2139
© 1996 Forest Stewardship Council

Printed and bound in Great Britain by
CPI Cox & Wyman, Reading, RG1 8EX

The lines from 'Tami Jane Tells Him What Has
Been On Her Mind For a Long Time'
by Albert Baker reprinted here in Chapter Sixteen
are taken from *The Sound of Wings*
(Slow Dancer Press: London, 1995)

1

The last words Norma Snape said to her youngest that Thursday: 'You let me get my hands on you, you little tripeshanks, and I'll wring your miserable neck!' Like so much of Norma's life, their memory would haunt her, words like angry fingers down her throat, again and again until she all but choked. And Nicky – it's doubtful if, between the slam of the door and the ring of his own high-pitched laughter, Nicky heard a thing.

It had started the way it so often did, the four of them tumbling over one another inside the small, flat-fronted terraced house: Nicky's sister, Sheena, out of the bathroom at last and slamming from room to room in search of a clean blouse, her green factory overalls, a right shoe; Nicky, barely fifteen, down the stairs three at a time, chanting along to the Walkman that hung from the belt of his jeans. 'Mum, you seen my blouse?' Sheena called. 'Mum, where's all the toast?' 'Mum, I thought you were going to iron these?' Only the eldest, Shane, fair hair and slate-grey eyes, eight days short of his eighteenth birthday, was still; flush in the centre of the worn settee, eating toast and drinking his third mug of tea while he watched *The Big Breakfast* on TV.

'Mum . . .'

Norma, hair not combed out, still not properly dressed, opened the back door to let out the grey cat, and the dog, which had been scratching at the outside of the door unheeded, scuttled to its empty bowl and began to bark.

'For Christ's sake,' Norma said. 'Don't you start.'

On the enamel drainer alongside the sink, used tea-bags bled orange onto spilt milk; a half-eaten bowl of soggy Coco Pops sat speckled with coffee granules. Shane's best shirt hung drying from the back of a chair; cotton knickers made a patchwork quilt along the radiator top. Norma pulled a can of dog food from the back of the fridge and began to search for the opener.

'Nicky, get out of my bloody way!' Sheena's voice.

'Get out of the way yourself!'

From the other room, Norma heard a punch and a slap and then, above the sound of the TV, Shane's warning shout. Norma stubbed out the smouldering end of the cigarette she had lit earlier and forgotten, and fished another from the packet. Unable to find her lighter, she bent her head and lit the cigarette from the stove.

'Mum, I thought you were going to iron this blouse?' Sheena stood in the doorway, cream blouse in one hand, outline of her ribs visible between her off-white bra and the top of her short black skirt; she still didn't seem to have found her other shoe.

'Will you cover yourself up, for Christ's sake,' Norma said.

'Yeh,' said Nicky, pushing past her into the kitchen, 'nobody wants to see your feeble tits anyway.'

2

'No? Then how come you're always hanging round outside the bathroom every morning?'

''Cause I'm nearly shitting myself, that's why, waiting for you to plaster your spots with Polyfilla.'

Sheena swung out at him with her blouse, flicking it at the kidney-shaped burn mark discolouring the left side of his face. Dancing out of the way, laughing, Nicky collided with the table and then, as he stumbled off-balance, kicked the dog's food all across the floor.

Jesus, Norma thought, when's he ever going to grow up? 'Right!' she shouted. 'That's enough. Nicky, you get down there and clean up that mess. And Sheena, get shifting out of here or you'll miss your bus. A few more times late and you'll be for the sack.'

'Again,' laughed Nicky.

'Shut it!' Norma said.

'I don't suppose,' said Shane, stirring himself during a commercial break, 'there's any more tea in the pot?'

'That's right,' said Norma, 'there's not.'

As Nicky went to move the dog's bowl, the animal nipped at his hand and Nicky hit it smack on the nose with the bowl's edge. Straightening its front legs, the dog showed its teeth and growled but then, thinking better of it, backed off into the corner and whined instead.

'Pick on someone your own size,' said Shane, fetching his brother a kick in the shin.

'Nicky.' Norma pointed from the doorway. 'I want that cleared up by the time I'm back down here. And you can sort out that crap by the sink as well.'

'Why bloody me?'

'Because I told you to, that's why.'

Shane chuckled and went back to watch the TV.

When Norma came back down ten minutes later, wearing an old jumper and sagging stretch pants to do her morning stint of cleaning in the pub, she found Nicky with his hand inside her bag, purse open, the last ten pounds she had about to make their way into his pocket.

'You scuttering little bastard! What d'you think you're doing?'

They both knew the answer to that.

Fear for a moment brightening his eyes, Nicky squeezed around the back of the table and made a dash for the back door. For a big woman, Norma moved fast, faster than Nicky might have thought. He had the door six inches open when with the flat of one hand she slammed it shut and with the other she slapped the side of his face, where the skin wrinkled liverish up from his neck.

'You thieving geck!'

'Here.' Nicky held the two five pound notes towards her, high above his head.

As Norma reached for them, he swivelled fast and left her catching air, the door yanked open wide enough and then pushed shut.

'You let me get my hands on you, you little tripeshanks, and I'll wring your miserable neck!'

She followed his laughter out into the yard, the bins and the empty rabbit hutch, the rusting trolley that had somehow found its way from Kwik Save and never made its way back. Stepping through the gate into the narrow alley that ran between the rows of houses, she started after her son as he ran, not hurrying now, a lazy jinking step between the dog shit and the broken glass. At the alley's end he stopped and waved the stolen money once in triumph, before disappearing from sight into the street.

Norma shivered and turned back towards the house.

'Locking up, that's what he wants.' Sheena was standing with her overall buttoned, ready to leave.

'Here,' Shane said, offering his mother his packet of Silk Cut. 'How much did he get this time?'

Lighting the cigarette, Norma drew in the smoke and slowly exhaled. 'Only all I had.' And then, as she lowered herself onto a chair, 'You'd think somewhere along the line he'd learn his bloody lesson, wouldn't you?' But even the petrol bomb, thrown by an angry neighbour whose house Nicky had burgled twice within the same week, hadn't done that. Oh, yes, when he'd been laid up in the hospital, sure enough, Nicky had confessed the error of his ways; and those evenings when Norma had patiently tended to the burn marks on his arms and legs, blistering across his chest up to his neck and face, then Nicky had promised her, time and again, that he would change.

From his trouser pocket, Shane took a small fold of tens and twenties and pressed one of the twenties into her hand. Norma looked into the grey of his eyes. Don't ask, a voice told her, if you don't want to know. 'Thanks,' she said. 'Thanks, love. Thanks.'

Norma had grown up in Rotherham, the daughter of a steelworker and a mother who, in the lengthening intervals between six children, had worked behind the counter in the local shop. Norma had been the last born, the one who broke her mother's spirit and finally her heart.

By the time she was three years old, her father had thrown in his lot with a wall-eyed girl of seventeen who had come to the house one evening selling lucky heather; Norma knew him only as a memory, an envelope of curling photographs, an edge of bitterness, sharp on the blade of her mother's tongue.

So Norma had spent her early days in a carry-cot beside the jars of sweets and newspapers on the counter, alternately fussed over or ignored. Whenever she cried, she was passed from one customer to another, the recipient of much chin-chucking and baby talk, a great deal of cupboard love and all of it transitory; her mother was ever the last to pick her up, the first to put her down.

'It was you, drove your father away.' The accusation, for years unspoken, had been present only in her mother's eyes until the day, slipping back from the shop unsuspected, she had caught Norma and the ten-year-old Gary Prout, exploring each other behind the living-room settee, Norma's grey skirt inelegantly hiked over her face. 'You, you little slut, it was you!'

Norma was nine and she thought her mother was probably right; after all, two of her brothers had been feeling her up for years.

When Norma was thirteen, the family upped and moved to Huddersfield, a house in Longwood with dark corners and the persistent smell of damp. The two eldest had left home long since, one pregnant and married and miserable, the brother off in the army, drunk in the pubs of Aldershot or Salisbury more nights than not. Norma was filling out fast, almost full-grown; with a little make-up and heels she could pass for sixteen, eighteen even, in pubs and she did. Men nudged one another in the street and stared. Hands going nineteen to the dozen, older lads bumped into her in the corridor at school. One of Norma's biggest thrills, the one she remembered because it involved neither hurt nor harm, was waiting until the lights went up in the interval at the pictures, and then, in the tightest of sweaters, walking slowly, left to right, across in front of the screen. Like a movie star, Norma could feel eyes following her every move.

Of course, as her mother never tired of warning her, there was only one way for it to end. Norma hid the pregnancy successfully for almost seven months, wore her clothes loose, a fat girl getting fatter, nothing more.

When the baby came, three weeks early, it seemed to slip from the folds of her body like a fish, bloodied and wriggling, sliding between the midwife's hands. They let Norma hold it for a minute, wet against her neck and cheek. Too long for what they meant to do.

'Baby's small,' the midwife said. 'Tiny. We'll have to pop him into an incubator, just for now.'

Her mother and the hospital arranged for the adoption: there was no need for Norma, under age, to sign the forms.

'Forget it, lovey,' her married sister told her. 'Plenty more where that came from, you'll see.'

There were but she did not.

Michael. In that brief time that she had held him, she had known his name. Spoken it to him, soft and wondering beneath his cries. Michael. She never saw him again, nor knew where he was. And although now, she supposed, there were ways she could take and means, she had never tried to track him down. Norma liked to think of him happy somewhere, content: a grown man he would be, maybe with a family of his own.

When her mother's man friend, the reason they had

7

moved to Huddersfield, backed Norma up against the cellar wall one night and tried to squeeze her breasts, Norma hit him with the coal scuttle hard below the knees and told him if ever he touched her again, she'd cut off his dick and feed it to the ducks. After that, he could never walk in the local park without his eyes beginning to water. And Norma learned there were things in her life she could control if she tried.

So when she became pregnant again, so stone in love with Patrick Connelly she could no more think of life without him than the air that she breathed, it was a fully thought-out, premeditated act. On Norma's part, at least.

Patrick was part-Irish, part-Scottish, part-wild, at twenty-nine, almost ten years older than Norma herself; he had drifted from Cork to Edinburgh to Glastonbury, a gentle hippy with the most violent of tempers, a musician with a raw and rudimentary guitar technique and the voice of one of Satan's angels – or the lead singer with the Stylistics, at least. Weekends, Patrick would take the train to Manchester or Leeds and busk; midweek, he sang with an uneven eight-piece soul band in the local pubs. One night, eyes closed, when he was singing Al Green's 'Tired of Being Alone', Norma, emboldened by the drink, walked up to the stage and stroked the inside of his thigh.

They lived in two furnished rooms above a shop near the station. Sometimes, Patrick hit her and she hit him back; a big girl – a big woman – growing bigger, Norma was learning to punch her weight. When, one night, blissed out on the after-effects of some good grass, Patrick said that what he wanted most in the world were children, a family, Norma took him at his word.

During her pregnancy, he left her four times, staying

away the Lord knows where for weeks, before moving his few things back in again. He tried to talk her into an abortion and when it was too late for that, pushed her down the stairs of a double-decker bus, travelling between Paddock and Longwood.

Norma took out an injunction against him, but once Shane was born, he began deluging her with flowers stolen from nearby gardens, sang to her from the corridor outside the ward. Five months after they moved back in together, Patrick shook Shane so hard to stop him crying that he cracked three of the baby's ribs.

Norma had a friend in Nottingham, Rosa, who had two kids of her own, but was otherwise living alone. It took Norma no time at all to pack her belongings and the baby onto the bus and travel south. They shared expenses, shared the chores, complained about the social – miserable, conniving bastards, how're we supposed to live on this? – sang in the pub on a Friday night, played bingo, watched TV. This was it, Norma decided: men were shit.

She met Peter at Rosa's sister's wedding; after the reception they went back to the house together, Norma and Peter, Rosa and some bloke none of them had set eyes on before or since. Rosa found a bottle of Drambuie and they drank it from chipped mugs; the man nobody knew passed round a few spliffs. When they paired off, Norma went with Peter. What harm was there in that? A quick shag between friends.

The harm was she fell in love.

Small and gentle was Peter, with delicate fingers that could read her body as if it were Braille, soft dark eyes and lashes, long and curving like a girl's. Whenever Norma rolled on top of him in the night, she was frightened she might crush the breath from out of him.

He played with Shane and rocked him on his knee, even though Shane was slow to laugh and quick to cry. Norma read the look in his eye. Sheena was born when Shane was two, and Nicky no more than eleven months later.

It was you drove your father away.

Nicky screamed whenever Peter touched him, kicked out if ever he picked him up. It got so that he would start to cry whenever Peter walked into the room. The only one who could quieten Nicky was Norma herself; his eyes would follow her from place to place, as soon as he could crawl he would only crawl to her, the only way she could get him to sleep was to take him into her bed.

Peter spent nights on a borrowed mattress laid on the floor, nights on the couch, nights away from home. 'I can't take this,' he told Norma. 'I can't take this any more.'

'It's all right, love,' Norma said. 'Nicky'll come round, you see. You're his dad, after all.'

But Peter stopped coming round himself before the boy had the chance. When Norma arrived back from the shops one afternoon, all of his things had been cleared out of the cupboards, the suit he had worn for best, so strangely like the one her own father wore in one of those old photographs, no longer hung in its place inside the wardrobe.

There was no note. Twice a year, Christmas and birthday, he would send a card to Sheena, always with a different postmark, never with a return address.

Norma told everyone she didn't care: hadn't she and Rosa always said, men were shits. But when Shane sud-

10

denly went off the rails a few years later, she was forced to admit she couldn't cope, not with them all, and Shane went off for the first of his two spells in care. Just to give your mum a break, love, the social worker had explained. He's a good lad, she'd said to Norma, I'm sure he understands. If he did or not, Shane never said. Especially after being released back home the second time, Shane never said much at all.

'You not going into work this morning,' Shane asked, 'or what?'

Norma was sitting at the kitchen table, smoke drifting from her cigarette. 'Yes,' she said. 'Yeh, soon.'

Shane shrugged. 'Suit yourself. I'm off out, right?'

Norma nodded: one more cup of tea, one more cigarette, one more something, she'd pick herself up and get on her way.

2

'I don't want anyone to get too carried away about this,' the Head of Geography said, wriggling out of his anorak as he came into the staff room, 'but there was a rumoured sighting of a lesser spotted Snape earlier this morning.'

'In the general vicinity, is that?' asked one of the Maths staff, glancing up from the crossword. 'Or actually, you know . . .?'

'On the premises, apparently. Somewhere in the vicinity of the toilets. Natural habitat.'

'We ought to put a sign on the notice board, perhaps? Must be quite a few members of staff who've never had the chance to see one at close quarters. After all, I don't suppose he'll be here long.'

'Difficult to predict,' the Head of Geography said, 'the migratory habits of the Snape.'

From her seat across the room, where she was vainly trying to get another set of English folders marked before the bell, Hannah Campbell didn't think it was so funny. The last time Nicky Snape had showed up in her class, a perfectly decent lesson on haiku had been fatally disrupted in less time than it took to count to seventeen. Then again, she knew that if Nicky weren't in school, the chances were he was out getting himself into even more trouble, adding to the list of offences and misdemeanours that, even in this catchment area, was truly impressive. She knew all of that, but even so . . . Hannah sighed as the bell sounded, assigned a mark to the open folder, capped her red uni-ball micro deluxe, and climbed to her feet. Another day.

Nicky was letting a couple of the younger kids examine the label of his black cotton Hugo Boss shirt – not the right size for his skinny frame, but it was difficult to be particular when you picked up clothes the way Nicky did most of his. Today he wore it loose, so that was fine, unbuttoned over a black T-shirt that had been yanked high to hide as much as it could of the burns which spread up from his chest. His black denim jeans turned over at the waist. On his feet were Reebok trainers, scuffed and coming away at one heel; they would have to be replaced.

'Snape, what the fuck are you doing here?' one of the other youths asked, straggling into the building.

'They begged me,' Nicky said. 'All of 'em, down on their hands and knees.'

'Yeh, but you're here anyway.'

'So what about Macbeth and the witches?' Hannah Campbell asked. 'Do you think he believes them or what?'

'Yes, course he does,' said a girl near the front.

'Okay, why?'

''Cause he does.'

'Yes, but why? I mean, would you?'

'Would I what?'

'If you were on your way home across the Forest . . .'

13

'Miss, I don't go home across the Forest.'

'If you were walking across the Forest and just past the Park and Ride you saw these three weird old women . . .'

'Tarts,' shouted somebody.

'Scrubbers.'

'Prostitutes.'

One of the lads at the back jumped up and stood beside his desk, hand extravagantly on hip. 'Hey, Macbeth, duck, lookin' for business.'

'All right, all right.' Hannah smiled and allowed the laughter to subside. 'Let's get back to the question. If you were stopped by three people you didn't know and who looked pretty strange into the bargain, and they told you that something was going to happen in the future, would you believe them?'

'Depend what they said, Miss.'

'All right, Wayne, and why's that?'

'If they said what you wanted to hear, Miss, you'd believe 'em.'

'Yeh, like winning the lottery.'

'Seven million.'

'That bloke, right, shot himself 'cause he never bought the winning number.'

'He couldn't know the winning number, stupid.'

'Yes, he could, 'cause it was the one he picked every week only this week he never did it.'

'Daft sod.'

'Okay,' said Hannah, 'calm down a minute and let's think. Isn't what happens with the witches and Macbeth a bit like what you've just been talking about?'

'There's no lottery in *Macbeth*, Miss.'

'No, but it is about getting what you want most in the

14

world, isn't it? Becoming king. All that glory, all that power. All your dreams come true.'

'Never happens, Miss, does it?' A girl off to the side this time, flicking her hair away from her face with a biro. 'Dreams comin' true an' that.'

'Do you mean in the play or ever? In real life, say?'

'Ever.'

'That bloke,' someone said from near the door, 'the one as worked in the factory. Won all that money and couldn't cope with it, went back to Pakistan.'

'Should've took all his mates.'

'Family.'

'Fazal along with 'em,' Nicky said. It was the first time he had spoken during the lesson, happy fiddling with the Casio Digital Diary he'd pocketed on his last visit to Dixon's.

'I can't go back, clever,' Fazal called back, ''cause I've never bloody been.'

'Right,' Hannah said firmly. 'We'll have no more of that.' And then, taking a few steps towards Nicky, 'What do you think, Nicky? D'you think that's one of the things Shakespeare's trying to get us to think about, what happens when we get what we want most?'

Nicky pushed a few buttons on the keyboard of the diary and the day of the week came up in French. Why didn't she leave him alone and ask somebody else?

'Nicky, do you think he's saying something about ambition in this play?'

'Fuck knows.'

'I'm sorry.'

'I said I don't know.'

'Why don't you know?'

15

Nicky pushed the pocket computer across the desk. 'If he wanted anyone to understand what he was on about, he should've written in normal English, shouldn't he?'

'But he did, the normal English of his day.'

'Yeh, but that's not our day, is it? It's not now. If you expect us to read it, why doesn't someone put it into proper English so's we can all understand?'

'Yeh, Miss,' someone called out. 'Or give it subtitles.'

'Then stick it on Channel Four.'

'How many of you think that Nicky's right?' Hannah asked. 'Shakespeare would be better translated into contemporary language.'

A chorus of shouts suggested that many did.

'All right, but if we did that what would we lose?'

'Nothing.'

'All that lousy spelling.'

'Words you can't understand.'

'Yes,' Hannah said, 'you'd lose the words, you'd lose the language. In fact, it wouldn't really be Shakespeare at all.'

Loud cheers, then: 'Story'd be the same, Miss.'

'I know, Wayne, but don't you think the reason we still bother with Shakespeare after all this time is not so much the stories but the language he told them in? After all, his actual stories weren't so different from anybody else's. In fact, he borrowed most of them from other people anyway.'

'When I did that, Miss, you wouldn't even give me a mark.'

'I don't think, John, Shakespeare copied it out word for word, right down to the spelling mistakes.'

Laughs and jeers.

Hannah glanced at her watch. 'How many of you have seen *Pulp Fiction*?' About half the class, but almost everyone had seen some clips on TV. 'And *Natural Born Killers*?' Two-thirds.

'Right. Two films with quite a lot of violence . . .'

'Not enough, Miss.'

'Bloodshed, violence, criminals and murderers as central characters, quite a lot like *Macbeth*, in fact. But tell me, apart from the basic stories, Quentin Tarantino's *Pulp Fiction* and Oliver Stone's *Natural Born Killers*, what's one of the most obvious differences between them?'

'John Travolta.'

'*Pulp Fiction*'s longer.'

'*Natural Born Killers* is crap.'

Hannah raised a hand for quiet. 'Isn't one of the most important differences in the dialogue, the use of language? Isn't the Oliver Stone film all quick-editing and MTV effects, whereas *Pulp Fiction* is full of scenes with people just talking.'

'Like the bit where they're in the car, going on and on about when you're in France, what d'you call a Big Mac?'

'In *Reservoir Dogs*, Miss, when they're all sitting round that table . . .'

'Yeah, talking 'bout Madonna . . .'

'Right,' Hannah said, 'that's it. Talking. Language. Isn't that what Tarantino loves? If you took all that dialogue out of *Pulp Fiction*, that would change it so much it wouldn't any longer be his film. It certainly wouldn't be as good. And if you took the language out of *Macbeth* . . .'

'It'd be over quicker.'

'. . . it wouldn't be as good either. It certainly wouldn't be Shakespeare.'

17

Before Hannah could say anything else, the bell had sounded for the end of the lesson and everything was lost to a scraping of chairs, the clamour of private chatter, and the movement of thirty-one pairs of feet.

'Nicky,' Hannah tried, 'can I just have a word?'

But Nicky, like the witches, had vanished without trace. As had Hannah's purse, which had been pushed down to the bottom of her bag, between her NUT diary and a Snickers bar she'd been saving for break.

3

Nicky had a grin that left room for him to eat his pizza slice and speak at the same time. 'Roland, you're lucky I bumped into you, right? Just the thing you've been looking for. Exact.'

Roland tipped sugar into his coffee, two sachets and then a third; the last occasion he had bought something from Nicky, a pair of Marantz speakers for thirty quid, he had ended up paying twice that amount to get them repaired after only ten days.

'Here,' Nicky said, sliding what looked at first glance like a glasses case across the table.

'What the fuck's that, man? Polaroids or shit?'

'Look at it, here. Look.'

Roland shook his head. 'You got to be joking, man, wha'do I want with that?'

Nicky couldn't believe it. How could Roland be so thick? 'Business appointments, that's what this is for. Business. You're the one, always telling me how you've got to be this place or that place, meeting someone here, somebody there, doing some deal or other. And sometimes you forget, right? You've told me. Sat there and told me. Well, now if you had this . . .' Experimentally, Nicky fingered a few of the tiny buttons. 'See, this is perfect, right? Neat. What d'you call it? Compact. Slips into your top pocket, inside pocket, anywhere. But everything you want to know, Roland, okay – phone numbers, addresses, appointments – you can store it right in here, yeah? SF-8350. Do anything you want except send a fax or e-mail and there's probably some way you can adapt it to do that. And look, look here, look – how about this? – it can only translate stuff into nine languages. Nine. You believe that? Bet you didn't know there were nine fucking languages.'

Roland picked up the digital organiser and stared at the word *mercredi*, blinking faintly back at him from the top of the oblong screen. 'Fuck, man. Why you fussin' me with this shit?'

'Gonna do you a deal, aren't I?'

Roland laughed and bit into his cherry pie, coming close to burning his tongue. 'Shit! Why's the stuff in these things always so bleedin' hot?'

'Thirty quid,' Nicky said, easing the last piece of mushroom away from his pizza and scraping it onto the side of his paper plate. Never could stand mushrooms, they made him sick. 'Come on, Roland, yeah? Thirty quid.'

Roland pressed a button and the screen went blank. 'Nothing, man. Not interested, okay?'

'Twenty-five.'

Roland shook his head.

'Okay, twenty.'

'Nicky, how many times I got to tell you? Now get this piece of junk out of my face.'

Shit! Nicky dropped the pizza crust onto the table, screwed up the paper plate, snapped the organiser shut and pushed it down into the back pocket of his jeans as he got to his feet. 'See you, Roland.'

'Yeh.'

Fifteen metres short of the door, Nicky spun round on the heels of his Reeboks and hastened back. 'Here,' leaning over Roland from behind. 'Fifteen. You can sell it for twice that.'

'Ten.'

Nicky balanced the machine across Roland's cup. 'Done.'

Roland laughed and laid the note in the palm of Nicky's hand.

Ten, Nicky was thinking as he headed back for the street, ten and the fifty that was in old Campbell's purse, I can get myself something decent for my feet instead of this old crap I'm wearing now.

If Mark Divine noticed the few daffodils that remained unpicked or untrampled on the wedge of green beside the school entrance, he gave no sign. Four hours' sleep was the most he'd caught last night. How many pints of bitter? Six or eight, and then the woman he'd been stalking round from bar to bar had only laughed in his face as she'd climbed into a cab. Two o'clock it must have been before he'd stumbled into bed. No, nearer three. And this morning there'd been Graham Millington, lip curling up beneath his moustache as he delivered a bollocking over some petty bit of paperwork Divine had somehow neglected to get done. 'What are you now?' Millington had asked. 'Twenty-seven, is it? Twenty-eight? Ask yourself, maybe, why it is you're still stuck at DC when there's others, give you three year or four, shooting past like you're standing still?'

It had been on the tip of Divine's tongue to say, 'What about you, Graham? Sergeant since before I bloody joined and about as like to move on as one of them statues stuck round the edge of Slab Square.' But he'd said nothing, had he? Bit his tongue and sulked around the CID room till this call came through, some teacher who'd got her purse nicked from her bag in class. Serve her right, most like, Divine had thought, for taking it in with her in the first place. But it gave him a reason for getting out and about, at least. Hannah Campbell, he could picture her now. Short frizzy hair and flat-chested, blinking at him from behind a pair of those bifocals. Hannah, anyway, what sort of a name was that? Somewhere on the back shelf of his memory, Divine remembered an Aunt Hannah, the kind with whiskers on her chin.

'Can I help you?' The woman in the office looked up from her typewriter and regarded Divine with suspicion.

'DC Divine,' he said, showing her his card. 'CID. It's about the incident this morning. Hannah, er, Campbell. You'll know about it, I reckon.'

'Please take a seat.'

Why was it, Divine wondered, he only had to set foot inside a school, any school, to feel the cold compress of failure shrivelling his balls, packing itself around his heart?

She was waiting for him in a small room on the first floor, the only light coming from a long, high window through which he could see bricks and sky. Two of the walls were lined with shelves, sets of tatty books with fraying covers, some of which didn't seem to have been moved for a long

22

time. Wasn't there supposed to be a shortage of books? Divine thought. Hadn't he heard that somewhere? So what was wrong with all these?

'Miss Campbell?'

'Hannah.'

Divine showed her his identification as he introduced himself and sat down across from her, a narrow table in between.

He could see right off he'd got it wrong. She was younger than he'd imagined, for a start. Middle thirties, maybe; possibly even younger. Scrub the glasses, too. Her hair was longer than he'd pictured, bushing out a little at the sides and back. Light brown. Under a tan jacket she was wearing a lilac top, three buttons to the neck. Lilac or purple, he could never be certain which was which. A black skirt, calf-length, and comfortable shoes on her feet.

'I spoke with two officers already,' Hannah said. 'Explained to them what happened, as best as I know.'

'Uniform, yes. Routine.'

'And you're a detective, isn't that right? CID, that's what it means?'

Divine nodded, resisting the idea that, ever so slightly, she might be sending him up.

'And you'd like me to tell you what happened?'

'Yeh, that's right.'

She looked at him, the natural cockiness of his face offset by the tiredness round his eyes.

'Aren't you going to take notes?' Hannah asked.

Only when Divine had taken out his notebook and pencil did she begin.

*

'So do you think you'll catch him?'

'Nicky Snape?'

'That's who we've been talking about, isn't it?' They were walking along the bottom corridor, Hannah escorting him off the premises, out of school.

'You seem pretty certain it was him,' Divine said.

Hannah shrugged. 'My purse disappeared, Nicky disappeared, both at the same time. Added to which, he does seem to have a penchant for this sort of thing.'

'A what?' Divine wondered again if she were sending him up.

'Stealing. He's been in trouble before.'

The laugh lines crinkled around Divine's mouth. 'Just once or twice.'

'And you didn't catch him then?'

'We caught him right enough, courts bounced him off out again. Can't hold 'em, you see. Not that young. Twelve when he started, thirteen.' Divine looked around them, windows and doors. 'You must know what it's like, mixing with them every day.'

Hannah didn't say anything, carried on walking until they had passed beyond the office and were standing on the shallow steps outside. The building was sending shadows long across the tarmac and there was a bite still in the spring air. Hannah was conscious of Divine looking at her, her neck and breasts.

'You make it all sound pretty much a waste of time,' she said.

'Catch him with any of your property still on him, credit cards, say, someone might actually have the nous to stick him away.'

'And is that likely? Catching him like that, I mean?'

Divine pushed out his chest a little, stood an extra inch taller. 'Best detection figures in the country this year past, you know, Notts.'

'Really?'

'Clear-up rate per officer of fourteen cases a year.'

'That doesn't seem,' Hannah said, 'an awful lot.'

'Better'n anybody else, though, isn't it?'

'Statistics.' Hannah smiled. 'To get a real sense of it, you'd need to set that figure against the one for the amount of crime that took place. You know, to see it in the right perspective.'

'Yes, well,' Divine said, gazing away, 'I can't bring to mind what that was, not exactly.' It was 148 crimes per 1000 of the population, the second highest after Humberside, he knew it by heart. He said, 'I'd better be going, then.'

'All right.' She hesitated a moment longer before turning back into the school.

'Look, I don't suppose . . .' Divine began, a light flush on his cheeks.

'No,' Hannah said. 'I'm sorry, not a chance.'

4

'You'd think,' Skelton said, 'when you get something right, the last thing anyone would want to do is mess about with it and run the risk of losing everything you'd gained.'

From the chair opposite the superintendent's desk, Resnick grunted something which might be taken for agreement.

'You know and I know, Charlie,' Skelton went on, 'most forces in the country would give their eye-teeth for figures like these.'

Nodding, Resnick shifted his weight from left buttock onto right. The idea of a Serious Crimes Unit in the county had been mooted before, but now, with changes in the Police Authority, it looked as though it might actually be going to happen.

Skelton was toying with a pencil, daring to disturb the symmetry of his desk. 'You know what it'll mean, don't you? Two-tier policing, that's what it'll mean. All the high-fliers and bright boys stuck in together where they can polish one another's Ph.Ds and the rest of us left penny-antying about with stolen mountain bikes and traffic offences.'

Resnick wondered if in a way that wasn't happening

already. Helen Siddons, for instance, the bright young DI who had paused at the station long enough to set a seismograph beneath the crumbling structure of Skelton's marriage. She had been made up to inspector at an age when Resnick had still been shy of sergeant; now here he was in his mid-forties, inspector still, and where was she? Holding down a chief inspector's post in Somerset. As Reg Cossall had put it a few nights back in the pub, 'If that self-seeking cow'd had the luck to be black as well as female, she'd've been superintendent by now, never mind fucking chief inspector!'

'No, Reg,' Graham Millington had laughed. 'It were better'n inspector she was fucking, it was our Jolly Jack.'

Looking across at Jack Skelton now, Resnick wondered if that had been true. Oh, Skelton had fancied her, Siddons, clearly enough, and she had turned that to her advantage. But whether it had gone beyond the lingering glances and the barely covert looks, Resnick didn't know. And besides, it hardly mattered: what mattered was what Alice Skelton thought had happened. Adultery in the mind is as hard to shake as love stains on the sheets. The last time Resnick had been round to the Skelton house, it had been like watching bear baiting between barely consenting adults.

'Still, with any luck, Charlie,' Skelton said, 'we'll both be up and gone, the pair of us, before it happens. Put out to grass with a pension and whatever they give you nowadays in place of a gold watch.'

Resnick didn't think so. Skelton, maybe, but as far as he himself was concerned, retirement was something lurking in the last grey hours before morning; one of those beasts like cancer of the prostate that stalked you in your sleep.

'Lynn Kellogg, Charlie.' He had waited until Resnick was almost at the door. 'Okay, is she?'

Resnick was slow to answer, wondering if there were something he should have noticed, something he'd missed. 'Fine. Why d'you ask?'

'Oh, no reason.' Skelton looked at Resnick across the broad arch of his fingers. 'She's started seeing that therapist again, that's all.'

No reason then, Resnick thought, as he headed back along the corridor towards his own office, was not exactly true. As he well knew, there were reasons enough.

Fifteen or so months ago, Lynn had been kidnapped by a man Resnick and his team were tracking down. The man had killed twice before, women whom he had tantalised with the prospect of freedom, before brutally ending their lives; it was a game that he played, and he had played it with Lynn, alternately being kind to her and then threatening her, keeping her cold and in chains. By day he was capable of speaking to her in the soft tones of romance, and at night, in the cramped blackness of the caravan, he would masturbate over her as she feigned sleep.

After a lengthy trial, at which all this was painfully dragged out for everyone to read about in their newspapers and see replayed each night on their TV, the man's pleas of diminished responsibility had been disregarded and he had been sentenced to imprisonment for life. A minimum of twenty-five years.

By the time she herself was little more than fifty –

younger than her own mother was now – Lynn knew he could be walking the same streets, breathing the same air. At the turn of any corner she might meet him, hear him again, clear across the clamour of a crowded bar, asking could he buy her a drink; his fingers tapping at the window the next time her car broke down, face peering in, drizzled out of focus by the rain, the lilt of his voice, that smile . . .

And there were other things that had been stirred into consciousness by the experience, things which Lynn was struggling to forget.

She was at her desk when Resnick entered the CID office, back towards him, a slight hunch of her shoulders as she made notes on her pad while talking on the phone. Kevin Naylor, like Lynn a detective constable in his twenties, was accessing the computer, checking through incidents of arson in connection with a recent fire in which an Asian boy of four had died. Graham Millington, Resnick's sergeant, sat with an elderly black woman, coaxing her through the circumstances of a robbery she had witnessed in a local bookmaker's, three thousand pounds stolen and the manager recovering from serious head injuries in the Queen's Medical Centre. The other desks were empty, officers out and about in the city, asking questions, knocking on doors.

Inside Resnick's office, a partitioned corner of the narrow room, the telephone started to ring. By the time he had entered and closed the door behind him, it had stopped. One glance at the jumble of papers on his desk, and he reached into one of the drawers for a half-empty pack of Lavazze caffé espresso and filled the coffee machine his friend Marian Witczak had given him as a present. 'For you, Charles, to treat yourself well. I know how much you like good coffee.'

The last drops, black and strong, had not finished percolating through before Resnick, unable to distract himself any longer, pushed open the office door and called Lynn Kellogg's name.

'Coffee?'

'No, thanks.'

She kept her hair cut short now, defiantly, brushed forward at the front just like a boy's; the only slight curl, as if to spite her, curved in front of her ears and the plain gold studs that she wore. She had never won back the fullness or the colour of her face. She wore black cotton trousers, a black, round-necked top. No rings.

'Jack Skelton was asking me how you were.'

She hadn't forgotten how to smile, at least with her eyes. 'And you told him?'

'As far as I knew, you were fine.'

'That's okay then.'

Resnick brought the cup towards his mouth, but didn't drink. 'Except, apparently, you're not.'

Lynn looked at him and saw a sad man with sad eyes. When he had been the first to arrive at the caravan where she was being held captive, she had clung to him and thought that she would never let him go. Now that was proving all too true: through therapy and jagged dreams, the memory of him persisted, the bulk of him hard against her, the tears in his eyes.

'The hospital,' Resnick said.

'Dr Carey.'

'You've started seeing her again.'

Lynn sat forward, hands pressed between her thighs. 'So much for confidentiality, then.'

Resnick set the cup back down. 'As far as what's said, whatever passes between you, of course that's true.'

'But if I've gone back into therapy ...'

'We have to be concerned.'

'That I might be cracking up?'

'Concerned for you.'

She laughed. 'Because I might not be able to do the job?'

'Yes.' He looked away and Lynn laughed again.

'What?' Resnick said. 'What?'

'Nothing, it's just ... No, it's okay, I know you're only doing your job, too.'

Resnick shifted again, uncomfortable in his chair. 'It's the nightmares, then? They've started up again. Is that the problem?'

'Yes,' Lynn said. 'Yes, that's right. Same old thing.'

The lie hung between them, tangible as smoke.

'You feel okay, though,' Resnick asked. 'About the job? Carrying on?'

'Yes. Really I'm fine.'

'You'll let me know if there's anything I can do?'

'Of course.' She was on her feet by the door, avoiding his eyes.

'Your case load,' Resnick asked. For whatever reason, he didn't want her to go. 'What's most pressing?'

'That lad, I suppose. The one who absconded from the Secure Unit ...'

'Hodgson?'

'Martin, yes. He could be anywhere, of course. Manchester, London. But I had a call earlier from Vice,

31

thought they might've spotted him, touting for business out on Forest Road.'

Resnick sighed, all too familiar. 'Who are you liaising with?'

'Sharon. Sharon Garnett.'

'Give her my best.'

'Right, yes, I will.'

Just a moment longer Lynn hesitated before going back through the door. Already her phone was ringing again and Graham Millington, having finished with his witness, was waiting to ask her about overtime. Divine was back at his desk with a copy of the *Post* and a brace of Jamaica patties from the baker's on Hartley Road.

In his office, Resnick scanned the response from the Police Authority chairman to claims that the recent Audit Commission survey comparing police forces' efficiency was scarcely worth the paper it had been printed on. He opened an envelope addressed to him in Marian Witczak's precise hand. *Is it true you are never at home any more, Charles, and, if so, who is feeding all of your beautiful cats?* She had enclosed an invitation to a dance at the Polish Club for this coming weekend. Underneath the line, *Dress Informal*, she had added, *But please bring dancing shoes!*

Resnick pushed it out of sight beneath a pile of crime reports, dancing the last of several things occupying his mind. For no clear reason he could discern, unless it were the coffee in the cup that he was holding, the words to an old Bessie Smith blues came filtering to the surface, something about waking up cold in hand.

5

Nicky Snape had been a busy boy. At the back of a pub edging onto the wholesale fruit and veg market he had sold one of Hannah Campbell's two credit cards for twenty pounds; less than thirty minutes later, in the pleasant surroundings of St Mary's Rest Garden, her cheque-book and cheque guarantee card had changed hands for double that. Cutting through the Victoria Centre towards the Mansfield Road, he had chanced to bump into Sally Purdy, who was just leaving the Magistrate's Court, having a few minutes previously been released on her own recognisance on charges of fraud. Purdy sent Nicky back inside to Tesco's to buy a six-pack of Tennents, two of which she shared with him on one of the benches opposite Peachey Street; she then bought the remaining credit card from him for three five-pound notes and an unopened can. 'You give my love to Shane now, will you do that for me? Tell him I was asking after him, make sure that you do.' Nicky could see how that would go down well with his brother, and with a belch and a quick wave of the hand, consigned the idea to oblivion.

He treated himself to a Whopper and fries from Burger King and was finishing them off, window shopping on

Cheapside, when his eyes fell on a pair of purple-and-red Sanmarco walking boots, Gore-Tex lined. No way he could boost them out of there, the boots cost Nicky pretty much all he'd made in the past hour, but what else was money for?

He left his old Reeboks in the shop and was wearing his new boots when he met his mate, Martin Hodgson, in the bowling alley by the Ice Stadium. Martin was not so many months younger than Nicky, but more slightly built; his oversized check shirt hung loose and open over a beige Sweater Shop jumper, black jeans rolled up over high-top trainers. At first glance, it was tempting to dismiss him as soft, but that would have been a mistake.

'Fuck!' Nicky exclaimed. 'Thought you was fucking locked away.'

'Nah. Only that kids' place, weren't it? Not a real fuckin' prison at all.' Martin pushed the fall of dark hair from where it shielded his dark eyes and grinned.

Martin was about the only person Nicky had ever gone on jobs with, breaking and entering in and about the Meadows, which was where Martin lived. Most times, Nicky preferred to stay on his own, a low-profit, low-risk sort of business. Martin, though, was a laugh, which was why Nicky went with him; the only thing was, Martin didn't seem to know what risk meant.

'So what you doing, hanging about here?' Nicky asked.

Martin nodded in the direction of the nearest lane. 'Seeing how many spares I can get in a single game.'

They bowled for the best part of an hour and then, when Martin went to buy more cigarettes, Nicky noticed he was holding what had to be close to a hundred pounds.

'Up on the Forest last night,' Martin explained, offering

34

Nicky a king-size. 'Would've scored more'n this, but the coppers came sniffin' round. Bastards! Had to clear out.'

Nicky stared at him in fascination. 'What d'you have to do?' he asked.

'Easy.' Martin laughed. 'Hang around, just down towards the trees, like, till some punter comes along . . .'

'But how d'you know?'

'You always know. Sometimes they want you to go in their car, I always charge extra for that, mostly you just do it there. Cemetery's a good place.'

'Yeah,' Nicky said, 'but what d'you have to *do*?'

'Jesus! What d'you think? Wank 'em off, that's the easiest. That's a tenner. Sometimes they want to suck you off, that's twenty. Nothin' to it.'

'But you don't let 'em . . .'

'Stick it up me arse? What d'you think I am? Fuckin' mental? Think I want to get AIDS or something?'

'No. No, course not.'

'This bloke once though, dead rich, Mercedes, nearly new. Offered me a hundred if I'd go with him, back to his hotel.' Disgust and dismay mingled on Nicky's face. 'He had a condom,' Martin said, 'so it was okay. Give me these poppers, you know, amyl nitrate, after a bit it never hurt much at all.'

Nicky thought he was going to throw up. He nipped out his cigarette and started to walk quickly away.

'Hold up!' Martin called. 'Where you off to now?'

'Home,' Nicky said. 'Supposed to have been in school, haven't I.'

'Nah,' Martin said, catching him up. 'You don't want to do that. I'm meeting Aasim later. You want to stick around, chill out, we'll have some fun.'

35

Sharon Garnett was wearing a short red skirt over ribbed tights, a dark cotton jacket buttoned over a cream shirt; as if she weren't tall enough already, she was wearing boots.

'Blending in with the scenery?' Lynn asked, the hint of a smile in her eyes.

'Something like that.'

'I got you half of bitter, that all right?'

''S fine.'

They had agreed to meet in the Lincolnshire Poacher, a pub that promised good beer, good food and a courtyard out back which was where they now sat. It was early evening and there was a decided nip in the air, the temperature down below fifty.

'You working?' Lynn asked.

'Yes, later. You?'

Lynn shrugged. 'Depends.'

'Martin Hodgson?'

'Yes.'

Lynn had first arrested the youth when he was thirteen, on the run from a children's home and caught by an alert store detective in Woolworth's with several hundred pounds' worth of computer games stashed inside the Head sports bag he'd stolen just an hour before. Since then, he'd been arrested and charged more than thirty times, running a succession of social workers, short-term foster parents and police officers ragged. Unable to find sufficiently secure local authority accommodation within the county, Martin had finally been sent to a custom-built facility in Northumberland on a temporary basis. When a place became available at the Ambergate Secure Unit, reasonably close to the city, he was brought back and placed there. Eight days later he had escaped and had been living rough ever since.

'Fifteen, isn't he?' Sharon asked.

Lynn shook her head. 'Fourteen.'

'Some future ahead of him.'

Lynn nodded and drank her beer.

By that time, Nicky Snape and Martin Hodgson had met with Martin's friend, Aasim, and they had decided to go off to Derby, where one of Aasim's cousins worked as an attendant at the multiplex cinema and could get them in free. The first car Martin broke into they couldn't get started, but the second, a two-year-old Honda Civic that had been parked on Lenton Road in the shadow of the Castle, that was fine. Aasim had stolen his older brother's licence, so Aasim drove.

'You still applying for CID?' Lynn asked Sharon. They were walking up the Mansfield Road, heading round the block to where Lynn had parked her car.

'Not really,' Sharon said. 'Not since the last time.'

'What did they say?'

Sharon laughed. 'Asked me if I was interested in a place in the Domestic Violence Unit.'

Sharon had begun her police work in London, for her a second career after a spell in community theatre, and domestic violence was where she had quickly become sidelined. Not that it wasn't important, even interesting, but Sharon bridled at the obviousness of the thinking – woman, black woman, area with high ratio of Afro-Caribbean and Asian families, let her deal with them, she speaks the language. But she didn't want to be the token friendly face and she didn't want to be a social worker – she had done her share for her sisters, up and down the motorways of the country, putting on agit-prop plays about incest and wife battering. What she wanted was to be out on the street, solving crime, serious crime, something that would further quicken her wits, sharpen her already sharp reflexes; something to make the adrenalin flow.

And now? Well, most nights, one way or another, she was on the streets at least.

'How d'you feel about Vice?' Lynn asked.

'You mean, am I for it or against it?'

It was Lynn's turn to laugh. 'I meant working it.'

They paused at the corner. Ahead of them, the Victorian headstones of the cemetery on Forest Road East were beginning to stand out, white against the gathering dark. Lower down the hill, the floodlights of a five-a-side soccer pitch were sharpening into focus. The broad expanse of the Recreation Ground eased away to the left, trees shielding the open tarmacked car-park for the daily Park and Ride and, beyond that, the Goose Fair site. It was early yet for many of the prostitutes who worked the area to be on the street, and most of the cars that passed Lynn and Sharon seemed to be heading for other destinations rather than seeking out business. Give it another hour and the kerb crawling would have begun in earnest.

'The girls,' Sharon said. 'I even like them, sort of. The regulars, anyway. Not the little scrubbers who train over on an Away Day, then scuttle back home on their high heels like Cinderella. They're the ones who'll do it without a rubber, some of them, take risks, the stupid tarts.'

'And the boys?' Lynn asked. They were turning the corner into North Sherwood Street, Lynn pleasantly surprised to see her car still there where she'd left it.

Sharon stopped. 'No, it's . . . I don't know, but somehow it's not the same. I can't, I suppose I can't understand – I mean I can *understand* – but I just can't relate to what's going on. And some of them – God, it turns you over – they seem so bloody young.'

'Fourteen.'

'Younger.'

They were walking again, Lynn fishing in her bag for her keys. 'The lad you contacted me about, you think it was him, Hodgson?'

'What I saw from the picture, it could be, yes.'

'I'll meet you, then. Later. If that's okay? Ten o'clock?'

'Better half past.'

They made the final arrangements and Sharon stepped back to watch Lynn make a U-turn and drive away. A nice woman, she thought, straightforward – a little too straight, maybe, uptight even – but no side. Sharon liked that about her. If only she'd take a bit more trouble with herself, she could be nice-looking too.

6

Laden with Pepsis and cartons of popcorn – sweet for
Nicky, salted for Aasim, Martin had mixed – they watched
Dumb and Dumber and then went into one of the other
screens to see *Poetic Justice*, which Aasim insisted on
seeing because one of his mates had told him there were
shots of Janet Jackson naked from the waist up. 'What's
new about that?' Nicky had wanted to know, but they
went anyway. Fifteen minutes into the movie, when they
realised what they were hearing on the soundtrack was
meant to be poetry, they kicked back their seats and left.
'I don't care what her tits are like,' Martin said on their
way through the foyer, 'I'm not listening to no fucking
poetry.'

It was a wonder that Miss Campbell hadn't been there,
Nicky thought, sitting up the back taking notes.

They left the Honda in the Showcase car-park and took
an Escort in its place.

'Wait up,' called Martin, as they were turning past the
Assembly Rooms and in sight of the bus station. 'This is
as good a place as any.'

'What for?' Nicky wanted to know.

'You stay put,' Martin told him. 'Make sure no bastard nicks the fucking car.'

So Nicky popped a Polo in his mouth and lit a cigarette, while Martin and Aasim made their way between the bus stands towards the toilets. Aasim, two years older than Martin, was almost a foot taller, a moustache already thick upon his lip. Martin had met him first in the children's home, Aasim sitting on the top bunk looking at the pictures in *Penthouse* and *Hot Asian Babes* and listening to his Bangra tapes, over and over again.

Twenty minutes and three cigarettes later they were back: Martin had sixty pounds in twenties, fifty in tens and three tatty fives; Aasim had blood drying from a cut alongside his mouth and a graze across his fist.

'Better'n a bank,' Martin said with a grin. 'Now let's get the fuck out of here. This place gives me the runs.'

'Where we going?' Nicky asked.

'What do you care?' Martin said. 'Just wait and see.'

But Nicky was already thinking that wherever it was, it probably wasn't the place he most wanted to be. Sitting around kicking his heels while others were off doing stuff wasn't his idea of a good time.

'I'll tell you what,' Aasim said, 'when we've finished this, let's go to a club.'

This was Chinese takeaway, sweet and sour, chicken and cashew, chicken chow mein; Nicky had ordered two portions of toffee banana as well and now Martin was only reckoning they were for everyone, reaching over into the back of the Vauxhall with his plastic fork.

Oh, yes, another car. As soon as they had reached the ring road, Martin insisted on taking over the wheel and within less than a mile had wrapped the near side of the Escort around a bollard, after which Aasim had made a detour across the grass to the Social Sciences car-park of the University and liberated a Fiesta XR2.

'Fuckin' students, man, got too much money. What's some fucker on a grant doin' with a car like this?'

'Maybe it belongs to some teacher,' Nicky suggested. 'Lecturer, whatever they're called.'

'Don't make me piss myself, man. Whatever sort of teacher drives a fuckin' XR2?'

Nicky finally got tired of fending off Martin's fork and let him have it all, tipping the contents of the container forwards across the seat and into Martin's lap.

'Fuck it, Nicky! Just fuckin' watch it, right?'

But Nicky was rapidly getting to the point where he didn't give a shit.

'Syrup all down my tossin' jeans!'

'Be cool,' Aasim said, 'make you taste sweet.'

Martin laughed and, in disgust, Nicky lowered the window and threw all that remained of the food out onto the street.

'Right,' Aasim said, setting the car in gear. 'We wasted enough time already, right?'

'Where we going?' Martin asked, still brushing away at his clothes.

'Clubbin', I told you.'

'Not me,' Nicky said.

'Come on, you got to. I know this guy, right, works the door at the Black Orchid, yeh? Won't cost us nothin'.'

It was beginning to grate on Nicky more than a little, the way Aasim knew someone who worked *everywhere*, some cousin, uncle, aunt or brother. He'd bet anything you liked, mention somebody doing the most far-out job you could ever think of, personal bodyguard to Madonna, something stupid like that, and Aasim would swear on whatever it was they swore on that he knew the bloke's Siamese twin.

When the XR2 pulled up outside the club, both Nicky and Martin got out but neither of them moved towards the door. 'Suit yourselves,' Aasim said. After he'd parked the car and talked his way inside, the two of them jumped into a cab that had just dropped off four girls with skirts up around their tits and headed into town.

Sitting in the back, Martin did his best to persuade Nicky to work the Forest with him. Martin, he'd get some punter back into the trees and then Nicky could jump him, the two of them would beat the shit out of him and take him for whatever he had. 'They'll never do nothing about it,' Martin assured him. 'Not the coppers nor nothin'. Married, most of 'em, that's why.'

But Nicky wouldn't budge. He left Martin cadging a light from a tart on the corner of Waterloo Road and took off down Southey Street, heading for home.

'Smoke?' Sharon asked.

Lynn shook her head.

'I know, I keep trying to give it up.' Sharon lowered the window on her side of the car a crack before she lit up.

The streets were busier now, small knots of girls in different shapes and sizes, gossiping at corners, blowing into their hands. Others, most often in pairs, walked slow along the pavement's edge, a quick dip of the head towards any car that drew near.

'No lads,' Lynn said.

'Not yet.'

The drill was, park for a while where you have, as far as possible, an unimpeded view of one stretch of the territory; next, drive around the circuit at a steady pace, eyes peeled, letting the ones that knew you were about, casting a careful eye over anyone new on the patch. Look out for trouble, warn persistent punters away. Every now and again, there would be a lot of conspicuous action, rounding the girls up and taking them in. Fines in the coffers, a small knee jerk in the direction of the moral majority. Keeping the trade under wraps.

'You seeing anyone?' Sharon asked, stubbing out her cigarette and resisting the temptation to light another.

'Sorry?'

'A bloke, you know.'

'Oh. No.' In the close proximity of the car, Lynn felt herself beginning to blush and blushed all the more. 'How about you?' she asked.

Sharon smiled, almost a laugh. 'Depends what you mean. Not in the regular sense, no. Friday nights at the pictures, Saturdays a takeaway and a couple of videos from Blockbusters, nothing like that.'

'But?'

To hell with it! Sharon lit up anyway, lowered the window a further half-inch. 'There's this one guy, I don't see him often, just, you know, when we can fix it. When he can.'

'Married, then?'

She did laugh this time. 'Of course he's married.'

Lynn stared out through the window; what she thought were shapes moving was probably nothing more than the wind in the trees. 'He won't leave her. You know that.'

'He'd better not!'

'You know you're just saying that.'

'Like hell I am. Leave her and what'll he expect? Me to dump his washing in the machine last thing at night, collect his suit from the cleaners, cook, be nice to his kids. I've had a bellyful of that once on my own account; I'm not about to fall for it again.'

'What is it then? Why do you keep seeing him?'

Sharon drew in smoke and exhaled slowly through her nose. 'Sex, why d'you think?'

It was quiet inside the car, each woman aware of the other's breathing, the heat of her skin.

'I don't know if I could,' Lynn said. 'Not unless . . .'

Sharon barked out a laugh. 'Unless you loved him?'

'Unless I thought it was leading somewhere.'

In the semi-darkness, Sharon was looking at her. 'You're young, you'll learn.'

'I hope not.'

Sharon lowered the window a little more and tapped ash out into the air. 'Look, me and him, we spend the night together, most of it, once every two or three weeks. He's a nice bloke, a good lover. Treats me with respect. He's never aggressive or over-demanding unless I want him to be, he's got great hands and a lovely cock. And he makes me laugh. You think I should be holding out for what? A co-signee for the mortgage and someone to help me push the trolley round at Safeway?'

For a while Lynn didn't answer. 'Maybe not,' she finally said. 'Only . . .'

'Only what?'

'After you've . . . after you've been to bed and . . .'

'And done the deed.' Sharon laughed.

'Yes, if you like. And he's gone back home to his wife, well, how do you feel?'

Sharon put her hand on Lynn's arm. 'Somewhere between having had a Turkish and a long massage, and being seen to by the Dynorod man.'

The laughter of the two women filled the car and when it faded, Lynn said: 'Look, what's that? Over there.'

'Where?'

'Over there.'

Nicky had walked past the house three times now, a two-storey end-terrace with lace curtains at the window, even those above street level. The kind of house, the kind of street where people put milk bottles out last thing at night, but no one had done that here. Okay, he thought, it was getting late but not that late, most of the other houses had lights showing in their bedroom windows at least. Not here. He turned along the side of the house to where a narrow ginnel ran into the darkness, giving access to the backs.

For as much as five minutes he stood in the centre of the rear yard, letting the darkness gather round him. A few doors along someone was playing their television too loud, someone else was singing, one of those pathetic songs his mum would sing when she was in the kitchen and thought no one else was listening, or when she came back from the pub after last orders and didn't care. There was a gap at the top of the window at least an inch wide and his guess was that whoever lived there had forgotten to close it tight. So simple, Nicky thought, so why was he still standing there when by now he could have been in and out? Another ten minutes and he'd be home. Nicky

46

took a pace towards the window, then another; as far as he was concerned most of the evening had been a wash-out and here was his chance to finish it on an up.

Face close against the glass, he saw, beyond his own reflection, the contours of the neat back room, everything ordered and in its place the way old jossers' homes were. Some of them, anyway. The ones that didn't babble on at you in the street, half-drown in their own dribble, sit in their own piss. Yes, he bet whoever lived here dusted it every morning, moving every sodding ornament on the shelf. Nicky had done places like this before, money hid away in the most stupid places, obvious, inside vases, between the pages of bibles, biscuit tins. Three hundred he'd found once, three hundred almost, pushed up the arse of this donkey, a present from Skegness.

Easing himself silently up onto the tiled sill, Nicky slipped his fingers over the top of the window and began to slide it down.

7

Nicky stood still long enough to let his eyes grow accustomed to the light. Table, chest of drawers, sideboard, mantelpiece, chairs – gradually, the details sharpened into place. Family photographs. He had already turned the key to unlock the back door and slipped back the bolts; he could be out of there in seconds if he had to. But he wasn't going to have to. Wherever they were, the people who lived there – off on one of them geriatric coach trips or boring the balls off their relations – they weren't here. Quiet as the sodding grave.

He would do this room first and then the front. No rush for a change, Nicky, take your time.

Brian Noble had followed the boy down into the trees.

He had driven past him twice, the boy standing in shadow at the edge of the street light's fall, holding his cigarette down by his side, cupped inside his hand. Noble had parked the car on the nearest of the side-streets, careful to push anything which might be stolen beneath the seats. One of the women had called out to him, asked him if he wanted a good time, but that wasn't the kind of good time that interested him. He could get that at home.

The first time he walked on past, just slowing enough to judge the boy's age – fourteen or fifteen, soft flesh still around those hard eyes. On the way back he spoke, stopped and asked him for a light.

'You don't want a light,' the boy said.

'Don't I?'

'Fifteen quid,' the boy said, not looking at the man directly, glancing back and forth along the street.

'What for?'

The boy showed him with an almost elegant gesture of the hand.

'Doesn't that seem rather a lot?' Brian Noble asked.

'Suit yourself.'

Noble was gazing at the boy's face, the dark hair that hung loosely across his forehead, the first beginnings of a moustache darkening along his upper lip. He imagined the pubic hair around the boy's cock and felt himself grow hard.

'Suppose there are things I want to do to you?' Brian Noble asked.

'Cost you.'

'Of course.'

The boy stared at him now. 'Well?'

Across the street a car, an Astra, dark blue, slowed almost to a halt and woman jumped out of the back seat before the car had come to a proper stop. 'Wanker!' She stepped off the pavement, middle finger trust high into the air as the car accelerated away.

'I have a car,' Noble said.

'Fancy that.'

'We could go to it now, it wouldn't take a minute.'

'No.' He didn't know why, but he didn't fancy it. 'No,' the boy said. 'Back here.'

Noble looked at the headlights from Gregory Boulevard, strung in perpetual motion through the trees. 'It doesn't look so very comfortable,' he said.

'Suit yourself.'

The boy ground the nub end of his cigarette beneath his shoe and started to move away. Noble detained him with a hand, restraining yet gentle on the boy's arm. 'All right. Have it your way.'

'The money first.'

'What here? Where everyone can see?'

'The money.'

Noble fingered fifteen pounds away from the fifty he had pushed down into his trouser pocket before leaving the car; his wallet he had locked for safety inside the glove compartment.

'I thought you wanted something more,' the boy said, looking at the money now in his hand.

'Let's just see, shall we? See how we go. I think that's enough to be going on with.'

Without another word, the boy turned and Brian Noble, not without the exhilaration of fear, followed him down towards the trees.

Nicky had upturned every jar and ornament, opened every box and drawer, and all he'd come up with was a few pounds' worth of five-p pieces inside a half-size whisky bottle and a postal order for one pound, forty-two. It went without saying they had neither a stereo nor a VCR, just a poxy plastic radio that wasn't worth taking and a postage stamp TV that was more state of the ark than art.

He would have to try upstairs. See what, aside from the old man's best trousers, they kept under the mattress.

Under the worn tread of the carpet, the stairs squeaked a little and groaned, however lightly Nicky placed his feet.

'Slowly,' Brian Noble said, his voice a hissed whisper. 'Go more slowly. That's it, that's it. There.'

He was leaning back against the rough-hewn stonework of the cemetery wall, its unevenness poking hard against his shoulders, the back of his head, base of his spine.

'That's it, that's lovely. Go on, go on.'

The boy stood close alongside him, always looking away, his elbow pressing into Noble's arm. Noble wanted to dip his head and kiss the V of hair, dark at the back of the boy's neck, but knew that if he did the boy would pull away. Instead, he set his right hand softly against the boy's waist, and when there was no resistance, slid it down over his hip and round until his finger ends were resting on the boy's buttocks. He felt the boy's muscles tense and prepared to pull his hand away but it was all right, there was no need.

Faint, he could see the headlights along Gregory Boulevard, strung like a moving lantern between the trees.

'Christ!' the boy complained. 'How much longer you gonna be?'

'It's okay, okay. Just ... here, here, touch me here as well.' And he caught hold of the boy's other hand and thrust it inside his open trousers, tightening it around his balls.

'Oh, God! Oh, God! Oh, God! Oh, Holy Christ! That's it, that's it!'

Hips thrust forward, back arched, Noble's head

smacked back against the cemetery wall, once, twice, three times as he came between the fingers of the boy's hand. 'Oh, God! Yes!' Eyes closed, he bit down into the flesh of his lower lip and groaned his pleasure and release, even as the boy was squatting low to wipe away the semen from his hand on the rough grass.

When Brian Noble reopened his eyes, the figures were standing silent between the nearest trees.

'We are police officers...' one of them said and the boy was away, leaping for the cemetery wall, both arms hooked over and pulling his legs after, one foot on top and the other swinging round as Lynn caught hold of his ankle tight and dragged him back, the boy kicking now, kicking and swearing, punching out at her with his fists until the other one joined in, the pair of them hauling him back across the grass and twisting him round, arms tight behind his back and close enough to snap the handcuffs shut about his wrists.

'Hello, Martin,' Lynn said, rolling him round onto his side. 'Nice to see you again.'

Martin jerked back his head, but she was ready for him and the mouthful of phlegm sailed harmlessly past.

Brian Noble had sunk down to his knees in front of Sharon Garnett, shaking, tears in his eyes.

'You do not have to say anything,' Sharon was saying. 'But it may harm your defence if you do not mention when questioned something which you later rely on in court. Anything you do say may be given in evidence.'

Through his tears, Noble looked up at her.

'Do you understand that?' Sharon asked.

Noble nodded.

52

'Well, if I were you, I'd zip myself up. Nippy, these squirrels can be, this time of year.'

Eric Netherfield had gone to bed each night for the past dozen years with a length of railing on the floor within reach. He had picked it up one day from a skipful of rubbish where a house was being cleared. 'What on earth've you dragged that back for?' his wife Doris had said, and Eric had given his usual little shrug. 'Come in handy some day, just you see.' Since the burglaries had started in earnest, up and down the street, the last thing Eric had done each night, after dropping his teeth into the glass beside the bed and wishing Doris God bless and good-night, was trail his fingers down towards that piece of iron, as if touching it for good luck.

Up until now, it had done the trick.

Standing back behind the bedroom door and struggling to control the wheezing from his chest, Eric listened as the pressure on the last stair caused it to squeak.

All Nicky saw, a faint bundle off to one side of the high bed, was Doris, one hand clutching at the turn of the sheet. He waited a moment longer, to be certain that she was asleep, then stepped inside the room.

Eric brought the railing down with all the strength he could muster, aiming for the head but striking the top of the shoulder with such force that the weapon was nearly jarred from his hands.

Nicky cried out at the sudden, searing pain and stumbled back across the room, the old man coming at him now, swinging that damned bar towards his face. Why the hell wouldn't he just let him run? The third time the man swung at him, Nicky was in the doorway; he ducked

53

inside the man's arm and came up fast, head-butting him in the face. The iron bar fell past him and bounced haphazardly down the stairs.

Across the room, clothes pulled towards her skinny chest, the old woman was sobbing. Blood trickled from her husband's nose.

Stupid fuckers! Deserve whatever they fucking get! 'Where's your fucking money?' Nicky yelled, driving him back into the room.

Eric made a fist at him and Nicky punched him in the neck, then barged him against the wardrobe hard. Wheezing heavily, Eric sank down to his knees.

'Where's . . . the . . . fucking . . . money?' Nicky shouted in the man's ear, punching him in the head to emphasise each word.

Slowly Eric raised his head. 'Sod off, you little toerag!' he said, spittle on his lips.

Nicky stood back and kicked him in the chest.

'Don't! My dear God, don't! You'll kill him!' Doris cried, and scrambled on all fours across the bed towards them.

Eric had collapsed against the foot of the wardrobe and no longer moved.

'Eric! Oh Eric!'

Nicky pushed Doris back across the bed and raced down the stairs as fast as he could. At the turn, his foot hooked under the length of iron and he tripped and fell headlong.

'Jesus! You bastard! You fucking bastard!'

Winded, aching, Nicky leaned forward, hands on knees. The piece of railing had rolled close to his feet and now he picked it up and with a shout swung it at arm's length, sending every ornament and picture from the mantelpiece flying. His wrist and shoulder where the man had hit him, he thought they might be broken. In the mirror, he caught a glimpse of his reflection, white and scared. Stupid cunt! What'd he have to have a go at him for? Why didn't he let him just run? The mirror was hanging from a chain; he smashed it again. It wasn't enough.

Back upstairs, Doris Netherfield was leaning over Eric, massaging his chest. When Nicky burst back into the room, she cradled herself across her husband to protect him, clinging to him as Nicky raised the bar above his head, then brought it down, time and again until his arms had begun to ache and he had had enough.

Seeing the blood for the first time, Nicky dropped the bar and ran.

8

Resnick's house was a substantial detached property in Mapperley Park, a short distance to the north-east of the city centre. Situated on the curve of a narrow crescent, a white stone wall and a small area of lawn separated it from the road. There was a passage at the side, wide enough to park the car which Resnick seldom used, and beyond that a ragged garden of grass and shrubs, a cherry tree that needed pruning and a shed in sore need of creosote and nails. The cherry tree was already shedding blossoms.

Almost immediately past the hedge at the garden's foot, the land fell steeply away over the allotments of Hungerhill Gardens and the heart of the city was exposed. Between the railway station and Sneinton windmill, the floodlights of the two soccer grounds showed up clearly, perched on either side of the Trent. Terraced houses that had stood in stubby rows since the turn of the century shared the land with curves and courts of new development that was already starting to look careworn and old. Along the canal, warehouses with peeling fronts, home to flocks of greying pigeons if little else, stood beside architect-designed office buildings and the new marina, and a shopping park of superstores encouraging need and envy, good ambition and bad debts. From where he might stand, at an upstairs window or the garden's edge, Resnick could not see the night shelters, the needles discarded below the old railway arch, the benches and shop doorways where the homeless slept, but he knew they were there.

The interior of the house was darker than it would have been, seen with someone else's eyes, the furniture heavy and largely in need of replacement. On the ground floor, at the front, was the living-room, comfortable and large, in which Resnick would sometimes sit late, listening to music, occasionally finding something that interested him on the TV. Past the middle room – a dumping ground for boxes and old magazines, whatever Resnick could not bear to throw away – was the kitchen, large enough to house a scrubbed dining-table, a miscellany of pots and pans, an antiquated stove, a refrigerator stuffed with packages from the deli, cat food and bottled beer.

The stairs, broad, with carved wooden banisters, curved up from the centre of the house towards Resnick's bedroom, the bathroom, other rooms he rarely entered, were less often used. At the top of the house one room had been reduced to bare boards, layers of wallpaper stripped from the walls and not replaced. A man Resnick had been pursuing, a murderer, William Doria, had killed himself there, in front of Rachel Chaplin, a woman whom Resnick had thought, however briefly, he might have loved. Resnick had laboured to remove the stains of blood from his sight, but that was all and not enough; they hung still in that room on the air, floated like feathers, pink-tinged and soft, that brushed his face and stirred his memory, would not let it rest.

Resnick rarely went there, climbed those stairs. He had tried moving once, thought of it many times, but somehow he had stayed. A family house, though he had no immediate family, unless you included the cats and he did not. Cats were cats and people people and Resnick knew the difference, he was clear on that. To all intents and purposes, he lived in just three rooms and let the rest succumb to dust.

When he arrived home that evening on foot, after buying Millington and the CID team a quick round in the pub, the black cat, Dizzy, was waiting for him, as usual, atop the length of wall. Automatically, Resnick reached out a hand to stroke the animal's glossy fur, but Dizzy turned away from his touch and, tail raised, presented Resnick with a fine view of his backside as he ran along the wall and then sprang down towards the door, anxious to be fed. A neat encapsulation, Resnick thought, of man's relationship with cats.

Inside, two of the others, Miles and Pepper, threaded themselves between his legs as he walked towards the kitchen, sifting through the mail he had picked up from the floor. Bud, the fourth and last, eternally young and stupid, lay wedged, for no apparent reason, midway through the cat door, mewing pathetically. Dropping straight into the bin the usual conglomeration of circulars and catalogues, advertisements for a double CD or cassette collection of *Songs that Won the War*, and invitations from his bank to come in and discuss his financial affairs, Resnick bent down and prised open the cat flap and Bud came sprawling through.

Fifteen minutes later, he had fed them, ground coffee

and set the kettle on to boil, improvised a sandwich from scraps of Stilton, a few fading leaves of rocket, a rasher of cold, cooked bacon and the last of a jar of mayonnaise. The *Post* had arrived, offering free tickets to Butlins, free flights to Spain, six hundred pounds' worth of holiday vouchers *and* free beer. Pretty soon, Resnick thought, the entire population of the city would be off sunning itself and singing 'Viva España!' and the crime figures would take care of themselves.

In the front room, he dropped into an easy chair and closed his eyes. When he opened them again the night was gathering close around the windows, the coffee was cold but still drinkable and the sandwich – the sandwich tasted just fine. As he ate it he stared across the room at his recent acquisition, a brand-new CD player to complement his stereo; his nightly project, working through the tracks of the ten-disc Billie Holiday set he had bought himself the Christmas before last.

What would it be this evening?

'Some Other Spring'?

'Sometimes I'm Happy'?

'I Got It Bad (And That Ain't Good)'?

When the call came through, he was listening to 'Body and Soul', the '57 version with Harry Edison taking the bridge. Resnick recognised the slight catch in Kevin Naylor's voice as the younger officer struggled to keep his emotions in check.

'Alive?' Resnick asked, frowning.

'Yes, sir. Last I heard. The old woman, though, got to be touch and go.'

'Anyone gone to the hospital?'

'Mark, sir.'

'Not Lynn?'

'Already out. Something to do with this kid as absconded.'

'Right. Call Graham, tell him to meet me at the house. And you, stay there till I arrive. And for Christ's sake don't let any bugger trample over everything.'

Without waiting to hear Naylor's reply, Resnick set down the receiver and headed for the door. Near enough eleven thirty and it was going to be a long night. He found his car keys on the table in the hall and grabbed a topcoat from the hooks inside the door. Long and likely cold.

Unaware, though she was never really that, Billie Holiday sang on in the empty room.

Graham Millington, burly, hands in pocket, was pacing the pavement inside the area that had been cordoned off, firing an occasional scowl in the direction of those bystanders who were still lingering in the wake of the sirens' call. Naylor stood in the doorway, face paler than usual in the fall of the street light, one of those faces that were for ever young until the day that suddenly they were old.

Resnick parked at the opposite side of the street and strode across.

'Break-in, looks like,' Millington said, falling into step.

'Entry?'

'Round back. Shimmied in through the window.'

'How many?'

'Hard to say as yet. By sight of what's in there, happen half a hundred of 'em.'

Resnick blinked. Something was pulsing away behind his left temple, some premonition of pain.

'I've this minute had a call from Mark,' Naylor said. 'Woman's in the operating theatre, crushed skull. Brain damage, sounds like. Serious.'

'And the husband?'

'Be okay, I think. Cuts and bruises. Shock.'

Resnick turned towards the street, faces indistinct between curtains pulled back. 'Witnesses? Anyone seen running away?'

Naylor fidgeted uneasily on the step. 'None come forward, sir, as yet.'

'Chances are this wasn't the only house broken into. Get yourself about, find out what you can. We'll organise a proper house-to-house first thing.'

'Yes, sir.'

'Think he'll ever break the habit?' Millington asked, watching Naylor in sports jacket and khaki trousers walking towards the next-door house.

'Which habit's that?'

'Calling you sir.'

Resnick didn't bother to reply. He was looking at the turmoil in the small back room, like one of those newspaper photographs showing the spread of damage some distance from the epicentre of an earthquake. A small world turned upside down.

'Something got him in a rare snit,' Millington said.

'Him?'

'Them. Maybe.'

Resnick surveyed the shattered ornaments, broken picture frames, the shards of mirrored glass. In his mind's eye it was the work of one man, one pair of hands, a sudden unleashing of bewildered rage. Which was not to say that others had not been present, looking on.

'It happened up here,' Millington said, close by the foot of the stairs.

Resnick nodded, cast his eyes around one last time before going up. Shielded by the seat of a fallen chair, something caught his eye, shiny and plastic, a library card, computerised. Gloves already on, he bent down and picked it up carefully between forefinger and thumb.

The moment Resnick entered the bedroom it was like stepping back in time. The way the blood seemed to have spun, spiralling around the walls, across the bedspread and the wardrobe face. And the smell of it. The smell he could never clear from his mind.

'Looks like they got trapped somehow,' Millington said, 'between here and the end of the bed.'

'Yes.'

Behind Resnick's temple the same nerve triggered again, a pulse of memory. If he closed his eyes he knew he would hear, along with the cries of those who had been attacked where he now stood, the screams of Rachel Chaplin, jagged and sharp, echoing from the upper bedroom of his own house. Would see the dead man's savagely self-mutilated body lodged between floor and wall.

'Think he was trying to knock it out of 'em, where they were hiding whatever he were after?'

'I don't know, Graham.' Stretching his leg across the perimeter of blood, Resnick moved to the far side of the bed. 'I don't know if whoever did this was being that rational.'

'Makes you wonder, doesn't it? How come she came off so much the worse for wear?'

Resnick was staring at the space, the floor. 'Whatever

damage was done, it was done there. She must have been leaning over him, protecting him in some way. Whatever way she could.'

Naylor called up from below and a few moments later appeared at the door. 'People two doors down, sir, friends of the Netherfields . . .' Netherfield, Resnick thought, up to that moment he had not known their name. '. . . seems the husband, Eric, always kept this piece of iron railing beside the bed. In case of burglars, that's what he always said.'

'Right,' said Resnick, 'find that and I wouldn't mind betting we've found the weapon that did this.'

Sounds from below informed him that the Scene of Crime team had arrived and while they photographed and dusted, employed the proverbial fine-tooth comb, Resnick and Millington could make themselves scarce, make themselves useful elsewhere.

'You'll be wanting to get out to Queen's, I reckon,' Millington said by the front door. 'I'll just hang on and give Kevin a hand here. Get a start on the morning.'

Crossing the street towards his car, Resnick checked his watch: morning had already started.

9

'Why did you run away from the home, Martin?' Lynn asked.

From under the fall of dark hair, Martin Hodgson squinted back at her in disbelief.

'Why, Martin?'

'Why d'you think?'

'I don't know, I'm asking you.'

'If you don't know, you must be thick.'

'And if I were you, I'd watch my mouth.'

Leaning back in his chair, Martin contorted his face and peered downwards. 'All I can see is me top lip.'

She controlled the urge to slap him hard across the face, kick the chair out from under him, cocky little sod, and see him sprawling on the floor. For a moment she wondered whether if someone had done that to him sooner, and hard enough, he would still have turned out the way he had; or was he like he was because that had happened too many times?

'When we brought you in,' Lynn said, 'you had over a hundred pounds in your pockets.'

'So?'

'So where did it come from?'

Martin shook his head; the same expression was back on his face again, sullen and hard. 'Where d'you think?'

'Tell me.'

'You shouldn't be doin' this, interrogating me on me own. You know how old I am, you know the rules.'

Despite herself, Lynn smiled. 'Interrogation? Is that what this is?'

'Yeh. What else d'you call it?'

'It's just a chat.'

'You mean, I could get up and go?'

'No.'

'Then I should have someone here, right?'

'Social services've been informed.'

'Bollocks to that. I want a brief.'

'As soon as one can be found.'

'Then I'm not sayin' another thing till he comes.'

'Just tell me about the money.'

'What about it?'

'Where it came from?'

Martin squinted up his eyes. 'You know where you found me, right?'

'You got it on the Forest?'

'Yeh, grows on trees.'

Caught her! Lynn sat on her hands, staring at the ceiling. Grinning, Martin let his chair rock forward and then slowly folded his arms across the table and lowered his head. Fourteen, Lynn thought, fourteen and he must have been in this situation half a hundred times. She tried to think of the worst thing she might have done, growing up on her parents' poultry farm in Norfolk, by the time she was fourteen. The front of Martin's hair had fallen forward across his wrist and she could see the back of his neck,

65

narrow and exposed. She wondered whereabouts along the line the caring had stopped, the real caring; how long it had been since anyone, any adult, had held him, touched him in anything other than anger or sexual need? From the shift in his breathing she thought he might be asleep.

It was less than ten minutes later that he stirred and opened his eyes. 'Ambergate, you're goin' to send me back there, right?'

Lynn nodded. 'Right.'

Resnick had spoken briefly to the senior registrar in neurosurgery; Doris Netherfield was still in the operating theatre and it was impossible to determine with any certainty which way it would go. Up to the present, Doris was just about holding her own, that was the best she could say. They had contacted her immediate family, who were on their way.

Resnick thanked the registrar and went down to the ward.

Sitting beside Eric Netherfield's bed, Divine was browsing through the pages of yesterday's *Today*.

'Spark out, boss,' Divine said, on his feet and gesturing down.

'Did he say anything?'

'Kept asking about his missus, that were all.'

'Okay, get along home. I'll want you in first thing.'

'You're sure, 'cause I don't mind . . .'

'No, hop it. I'll just hang on here a minute, have a word with the doctor, whoever's on duty.'

Divine didn't need telling a third time.

It was the staff nurse who was in charge, a bright-eyed young woman in a bright-blue uniform, to Resnick's eyes, improbably young. 'We gave him something for the pain,' she said, 'poor old boy. I'm hoping he'll sleep as long as he can.'

'I'll not disturb him,' Resnick said.

There was a bandage round Eric Netherfield's head, light patches around it where the hair had been shaved away. The arm that poked from the end of borrowed pyjamas was shiny and grey. Resnick was thinking about the last time he had seen his own father alive.

'Did you want a cup of tea?' the staff nurse said from behind him.

Resnick took it and sat beside the bed, listening to the old man's halting, stubborn breath. He had sat, virtually alone, in a side ward with his father, thirty-six hours, watching the occasional movement of the older man's mouth, each gasp of air into his damaged lungs like rust scraping against rust. 'Go home,' the sister had said. 'Get some rest. We'll call you if there's any change.' When the phone rang somewhere between four and five, the change had been that his father was dead. It was the hour those calls had come ever since.

Resnick was finishing the tea, about to leave, when Netherfield spoke. 'Doris,' he said, his voice barely audible, little more than a croak.

'She's all right,' Resnick said. 'She's being looked after. She'll be fine.'

'She did it for me,' Eric said. 'She were protecting me.'

'I know.'

The man stretched out the fingers of his hand and Resnick placed his own between them, leaning close over him, smelling his old man's smell.

'The person who did this . . .' Resnick began.

'A lad, nothing but a lad.'

Resnick was about to ask more, but Netherfield's head had slipped a little to one side and his eyes were closed. His fingers, long and bony, were tight around Resnick's hand. As the sound of the old man's breathing steadied down, Resnick continued to sit, arm at an awkward angle, unable to move.

After several minutes the staff nurse came along and freed Resnick's hand, slipping the old man's fingers beneath the edge of the sheet.

'You can go now.' She smiled.

Resnick hesitated, waiting for her to add, we'll call you if there's any change.

The litter of half-smoked cigarettes in the ashtray at Brian Noble's side had grown to the edge of overflowing, though, in truth, he didn't smoke. Rarely, at least. Occasionally, after a meal. He looked at his watch and, again, counted the patches on the opposite wall where the paint had begun to flake away. Shifted awkwardly on the hard seat. Got up, sat down.

'Surely you aren't intending to charge me?' he asked, and Sharon stared back at him, eyebrow raised.

'But whatever with?'

'That's just it,' she said. 'It's difficult. So many possibilities, you know what I mean?' She shrugged. 'Gross indecency, that's the usual, isn't it? That'd be a start.'

'Look, my wife . . .'

'Oh, yes.' Sharon grinned. 'There's usually one of those.'

He demanded to make a phone call and dialled his own number, hanging up at the first ring.

'No one else you want to try?'

'No. Thank you.'

And then they kept him sitting there, looking in from time to time, uniformed officers mainly, once to offer him a hot drink, once a sandwich that was stale, occasionally a head would poke round the door and stare and disappear.

When Sharon came back it was with a lamb kebab inside pitta bread. 'Sorry to have kept you waiting. It's been a busy night.'

Noble said nothing.

Sharon held out the kebab towards him but Noble shook his head.

'Not hungry?'

'I'm a vegetarian.'

She looked at him quizzically. 'You don't like meat?'

'That's right.'

She was still looking at him, a smile at the corners of her mouth. 'You surprise me.' Sharon picked up a cube of lamb with her fingers and lifted it to her mouth.

'Please,' Noble said, 'tell me . . .?'

'What?'

'What you're . . . what you're going to do?'

'With you?'

Noble looked up at her and then away; he couldn't stand the mixture of contempt and mockery in her eyes.

'Did you read,' Sharon asked, 'about that boy? They found him in a wood down near Bristol, a week or so ago? What was left of him. It was on the news, remember? Nine, wasn't he? Nine years old.'

'Look,' Noble said, alarmed, 'I don't know why you're telling me this. That's nothing to do with me. Nothing at all. There's no . . .'

'Comparison?'

69

'No.'

Sharon sat on the corner of the table and crossed her legs, one high above the other. 'You're not a paedophile, is that what you're saying?'

'Of course I'm not!'

'No,' Sharon said. 'You just like sex with young boys.'

Resnick had driven back to the station by way of the Netherfield house. So far, there was no indication that any of the adjacent properties had been broken into. It had been a one-off.

Back in his office, coffee brewing, he was placing a call to the hospital when Lynn Kellogg knocked on his door.

'Not quite ready yet,' Resnick said, indicating the coffee machine.

Lynn smiled, a tired smile, there for a moment and then gone.

'The Hodgson youth,' Resnick said, 'you've got him back in custody.'

She nodded.

'Well done.'

'Earlier this evening, he was hanging out with Aasim Patel and Nicky Snape.'

Resnick's interest quickened. He knew the Snape family well. Shane, the eldest, he'd arrested on a charge of aggravated burglary; the last time he had talked to Norma it had been about Nicky, just a day or two before the lad had been fire-bombed in a vigilante attack.

'Nicky wasn't with him then, up on the Forest?'

'Apparently not. There was some kind of argument by the sound of it. Last he saw of Nicky, he was setting off for home.'

Resnick didn't even need to look at the map. If you drew a straight line from the Forest Recreation Ground to Radford, it would pass right through where the Netherfields lived.

First light was filtering up above the rooftops when Millington and Naylor arrived, Graham Millington, with a broad grin, holding aloft a narrow object secured inside two plastic bags.

'Kevin here found it. Dustbin, two streets off.'

It was the length of iron railing from beside Eric Netherfield's bed.

10

Resnick caught a couple of hours' sleep in his office, chair pushed back, legs forcing a space for themselves amongst the reports and memos that littered his desk. When he woke it was to the sound of Graham Millington clattering the kettle and treating the otherwise empty CID room to a muted rendition of 'Oh, What a Beautiful Morning'.

Resnick had his first mug of tea in his hand before realising that the phone had failed to ring: Doris Netherfield had survived the night.

'What's all this I hear about Serious Crimes?' Millington asked, lighting only his second Lambert and Butler of the day. The expression of unallayed martyrdom that Madeleine assumed if ever he dared to smoke at home was no longer anything he could bear to watch.

'Going on around us, Graham, all the time.'

Millington narrowed his eyes through the spiralling cigarette smoke: what the hell was the boss doing, cracking jokes at this hour of the morning? He presumed it had been meant as a joke.

'You know what I'm on about,' Millington said, 'this new Serious Crimes Unit.'

Resnick sighed. 'Yes, and the answer is, I don't know a whole lot more than you.'

'But if you were to guess?'

'I'd reckon it'll get as far as finance, someone will throw a fit about resourcing new office space, extra personnel, and it'll get lost on its way back to the drawing board.'

Even as the words were being spoken, Resnick wasn't certain how far he believed them; but neither did he want to face the ramifications the establishing of the squad might have for his career. And not solely his own, Millington's as well.

Divine and Naylor arrived within moments of each other, Divine chirpier than the bags beneath his eyes suggested. 'Tea mashed, then, serge?' he said, reaching for his favourite mug, decorated with a fading cartoon about rugby players and odd-shaped balls.

As usual, Naylor was quiet, easy even amongst four people to forget that he was there. It was a characteristic that, in the right circumstances, made him the good detective he could be.

Millington caught Resnick's glance towards his watch. 'Uniform back-up?' he asked.

Resnick shook his head. 'Let's not start World War Three, Graham. It's only one youth, after all.'

A sardonic smile played round the edges of Millington's mouth. 'Well, that's okay then, i'n't it? Piece of piss.'

In his panic to get away from the Netherfields' house, Nicky hadn't even realised the iron railing was still in his hand. Quickly, he had dumped it in the nearest bin and continued to run. Only when he was within sight of his own home did he stop, chest tight, tears stinging his eyes.

Only then did he consider the blood that was splashed across his clothes and staining his face and hands. No way he could go in like that, no way. Backtracking, he climbed into a garden and took two towels from the line, leaned against a wall deep in shadow and rubbed at his skin, his shirt and jeans. It was still likely that if he went home now someone would be up: Sheena, listening to Blur and looking at some stupid magazine; Shane slumped down in front of a video, Jean Claude Van Damme or Bruce Lee; his mum, sewing buttons back on Shane's shirts or lost in a world of her own, reading one of her trashy romances, Mills and sodding Bloom.

Keeping clear of main roads, quick to cross away from any passers-by, Nicky walked and walked, trying not to think about what might happen, what had happened, what he would do if the man or the old woman died.

When he finally turned his key in the front door, legs aching, it was gone two. All of the lights in the house were out. Quick to slip off his boots, Nicky was on his way to the stairs when he heard a muffled groan from the front room: slowly undulating shapes stretched along the settee; his brother was shagging Sara Johnson yet again.

On another occasion, Nicky would have stayed there and watched, but now there were more pressing things. In the bathroom he locked the door before switching on the light.

Jesus Christ!

He might have thought that black wouldn't have shown the stains so clearly, but there was no denying them, thick patches that seemed to have been thrown across his shirt and T-shirt as if he had ridden a mountain bike fast through mud. More across the top of his jeans. And the blood was not only smeared across his skin, it was sticking to his hair. Nicky stripped to his underpants and socks; took off the socks. He thought about rinsing the shirt out in the sink, letting the jeans, perhaps, soak in the bath, but realised there was too little time and anyway, it would never work. He fetched a bin liner from the kitchen and bundled the clothes inside. First thing in the morning, he would get them good and lost. Burn them, that was the thing.

Oh, shit! Footsteps on the stairs. The door handle turned but didn't give.

'Hang on a minute,' Nicky said.

'Nicky?' Shane's voice. 'That you?'

'Yeh, I shan't be long.'

'What the fuck you doin' in there?'

'What d'you think?'

Nicky waited until his brother had walked away before returning to the sink. At least the water was still hot. He found an old scrubbing brush beside the bath and lathered it with soap. He would have to wash his face, clean between his fingers, beneath his nails, shampoo his hair. As he looked into the reddening water, he saw the woman's grey head breaking below him, felt the impact of the blows reverberating back along his arms. Who'd have thought the old girl had as much blood in her as this?

Why didn't he run? Take whatever money was in the house, what he had himself and run. A bus to Manchester, Glasgow, London, anywhere. He could lose himself in London, knew kids who had. Kids who came back with

75

stories of money and crack, of picking up punters on Victoria Station or at Funland in Leicester Square. Doing the kind of stuff Martin Hodgson would have been out doing last night. At the back of his throat, Nicky felt himself beginning to retch. The sensible thing was to stay here. Bugger off and they'll take that as telling them, fair and square, sticking two and two in their hands and saying, right, what's that? No, the thing to do was stay cool, get rid of the clothes, go to school.

Just as his mum was getting up, Nicky fell fast off, sucking at his thumb.

Norma was down in the kitchen when the cars arrived, two of them, Naylor and Divine, hurrying round to the back to cut off any possible escape. If she heard them, taking the carton of milk from the fridge, she gave no sign. Sitting down here with a cigarette, quiet, a fag and a cup of tea was the best part of the day.

First up the path, Resnick stood aside, allowing Millington to ring the bell and knock. The sergeant paused, then rang the bell again.

'Bloody hell! Who's this?' But Norma, padding to the front door in her slippers, knew whoever it was, the news would not be good. Seeing the two men standing there, Resnick, whom she recognised, Norma felt a sudden pain fire, sharp, across her chest.

'Your Nicky,' Millington said. 'Is he in?'

'Of course he's bloody in.' But she was not looking at Millington, but at Resnick, trying to read the expression in his eyes.

'*You can see where it's heading, Norma. Clear as I can myself.*' Resnick's words, the last time he had been to her house.

'What d'you want him for?' Norma asked.

'One or two questions,' Millington told her, 'about what he was up to last night.'

'Last night he was here,' Norma said, 'along of me, all evening.' It was a response as automatic as drawing breath.

'I think we'd best ask him that,' Millington said.

Norma stood her ground, not knowing what to do.

Resnick shifted half a pace towards the doorway. 'Norma, I think maybe you should let us in, don't you?'

Millington wandered off into the front room and then the kitchen, while Resnick stood with Norma near the foot of the stairs.

'He's still in bed, then?'

'Course he bloody is.'

Resnick set his hand upon the banister and she took hold of his wrist. 'You call him, then, Norma. Fetch him down.'

At the edge of his eyeline, Millington had reappeared, slowly shaking his head.

'Norma,' Resnick prompted.

Heavy, she turned and called Nicky's name; set her foot upon the stairs and called again.

In his room, Nicky was instantly awake and throwing back the clothes.

'Nicky, it's the police.'

He grabbed a pair of old jeans and was still pulling them on as he threw up the window and scrambled out onto the sloping roof above what had once been the outside lavatory.

'Nicky!'

First Resnick, and then Millington, elbowed past Norma and took the stairs at a run.

Nicky slithered down the steeply angled roof, dislodging tiles as he went. One of his hands caught at the old iron guttering and it broke. Twisting as best he could, Nicky half-jumped, half-fell and then he was away, jumping the old rabbit hutch and vaulting the gate, straight into Divine's arms where the detective waited behind the wall.

From the upstairs window, Resnick watched as Nicky swore at Divine and struggled, until Naylor had his arms behind him and between them they'd put on the cuffs.

'Kick me again, you little bastard,' Divine said, 'and I'll have your balls for breakfast.'

Resnick, closing the window, didn't hear. Shane was out on the landing, pulling a pair of cords up over his boxer shorts. 'What the fuck's going on?'

'It's okay, nothing to bother you.'

'Well, s'pose I want it to bother me?'

'I'd remind you what the magistrate said, last time you were up in court.'

'Fuck the bastard magistrate!'

'I dare say.' Resnick sighed. 'Now why don't you go downstairs, look to your mum? Make her a cup of tea if nothing else.'

Shane pushed past him and slammed the bathroom door shut behind him.

Norma was in the kitchen, head in her hands.

'I'll take a look round,' Millington said, and Resnick nodded and went to put the kettle on himself. Within five minutes, Millington had found the bin liner full of bloodied clothes stuffed under Nicky's bed.

'Take them in,' Resnick said. 'Let forensic have them, first thing.' He glanced at Norma. 'I'll be along directly.'

He fished out the used tea-bags, tipped the luke-warm tea down the sink and set to making some fresh.

11

Resnick watched her walk across the playground, hair moving lightly in the freshness of the wind. Despite all the forecasts, the temperature had dipped a further five degrees and, in the CID room that day, Millington had been mithering on about having to take his geraniums in again, safe out of the frost.

'Hannah Campbell,' the school secretary had said, 'she's taking a drama group in the main hall. Should be through any time in the next half-hour.'

In no hurry to return to the station, Resnick had elected to wait.

Nicky Snape's interrogation had been careful and slow. For the best part of the first hour, his mother sitting alongside him, a solicitor just behind, Nicky had said nothing; then, after continued questioning, Resnick and Millington alternating, he had admitted to spending the first part of the evening with Martin Hodgson and another friend. Where? Cinema. What did you see? Nicky told them. Had he been near the Netherfield house? No, he had not been near the Netherfield house. Didn't know what they were on about. Didn't know where it was.

'Nicky,' Resnick had said, 'listen to me. We're doing

tests now. They're going on while we're talking here. The blood on the clothes we found underneath your bed, blood around the sink in your bathroom at home, blood on a length of iron railing we found near the house – whose blood, Nicky, do you think that is? Do you think it belongs to that woman lying up at Queen's in intensive care, just about hanging onto her life? Do you think that's what we're going to find?'

Nicky had stared at the table, his hands clenched together. Beside him, with very little noise, Norma had started to cry.

'Whatever you know about this, Nicky,' Resnick had said. 'Anything at all, I think you should tell us now. Let's talk about it now, you and me, while we're here. While we can.'

Norma had turned away, unwilling to look at her son, afraid to, and Resnick had leaned, almost imperceptibly, forward. 'Nicky, this house we're talking about, where all of this happened, were you there?'

Nicky's reply was so quiet it was almost as if he hadn't spoken at all.

'Sorry, Nicky, what did you say? Could you just say that again for us please?'

'I said, yes. Yes.'

Norma hid her face in her hands and began to sob.

'But all I did was break in, right? I never touched nobody, never hit no one. I never even saw nobody, none of that stuff you said. All I did was get in downstairs at the back. I never even went upstairs.'

'All right, Nicky, one thing at a time. We'll get to that later.' And when the solicitor requested a break for his client, Resnick was happy to accede. He had wanted to get out of the station, clear his head, find something else, undemanding, to do. He had come here.

Hannah was wearing a cotton jumper beneath her jacket, pale blue, and she had white-and-blue trainers on her feet. He liked the way she walked, purposefully but not hurrying, a leather bag slung over one shoulder, another, an old briefcase, packed and battered, tight against her side. She slowed to speak to two boys who were engaged in one of those arguments young boys are forever into, a push here, an angry word there, and only when they had shuffled grudgingly away did she carry on towards where her car was parked, a Volkswagen Beetle, painted red.

Resnick got out of his own car and moved to intercept her.

'Hannah Campbell?'

With a slight jump, she turned.

'Sorry, I didn't mean to startle you.'

'That's all right.' She was trying to place him – one of the parents, another teacher she had met somewhere at a conference and forgotten?

'Charlie Resnick. Detective inspector, CID.' He held up his identification for her to see.

'My,' she said, eyes widening. 'I *am* going up in the world. Last time it was only a – what do you call them?'

'Detective constable. DC.'

'An odd sort of a name . . .'

'Divine.'

Hannah smiled. 'He should have gone to ecclesiastical college, become a priest.'

Resnick grinned at the thought and she saw something in his eyes that had not been there before.

He watched her place the briefcase on top of the car and turn back to face him. With the light as it was, he thought he could see traces of red, faint in the brown of her hair.

'Don't tell me you've recovered my purse?'

'Not exactly.'

'Just the money and the credit cards.'

'I wish I could say we had.'

Hannah smiled. It had been a long day and the extra session she'd just had should have left her exhausted but instead it had picked her up, renewed her energy. And here was this shaggy man, hair askew, fawn trousers too baggy, brown jacket unbuttoned or it would have been too tight. She couldn't decide if the top button of his shirt were missing, or if, shielded by the knot of his tie, it were simply undone.

'So what is it?' Hannah asked. She liked the way his eyes stayed focused on her instead of wandering off as so many people's did. It gave the impression he was honest and she wondered if that were true.

Resnick took her library card from his wallet.

'Where did you find that?' she asked.

He told her, light on the details of the injuries the Netherfields had suffered, but making sure she understood the seriousness of what had happened. The skin prickled at the back of her neck when he mentioned Nicky Snape. When he had finished, she stood a while saying nothing, fiddling with a tissue, blowing her nose.

'When you spoke to DC Divine,' Resnick said, 'you said you thought it was Nicky Snape who stole your purse.'

'Yes, that's right.' Somehow, absurdly, Hannah wished that she had not.

'When we brought Nicky in, he had some money on him, though not a lot. As yet it's unclear where he got it from. No sign of your credit cards, I'm afraid.'

'That's okay. It's not exactly important, is it? I mean, not after what's happened.' She looked at him. 'I don't see why you're bothering with this at all.'

'The card, if he did take it from you, if it was in your purse that morning, well, it places him there, in the house.'

'I see.'

'And it would have been in your purse?'

Hannah nodded, yes.

'As it turns out, it likely isn't crucial. There's other evidence enough.'

Hannah looked away from Resnick towards the Boulevard and saw men walking their dogs on the sparse green of the Forest, the slow blur of cars. 'Of course I knew he was always bunking off school, getting into trouble, but this . . .' She turned back to face him. 'It's difficult to believe.'

'Yes,' Resnick said. 'I know what you mean.'

'But you don't?'

He gave a slow shake of the head. 'No, in a way I think I do. It's not the kind of thing I'd've reckoned him for at all.'

'You don't think it could have been somebody else? I mean, with him?'

'That's not what he's saying.'

'I see.'

Below them, home-coming traffic was slowing to a crawl. 'I should be going,' Hannah said.

'Me, too.'

Neither one moved.

'What will happen to him?' Hannah asked. 'Now, I mean?'

'Oh, most likely he'll be taken into local authority care. Secure accommodation somewhere. Until the trial.'

'And then?'

Resnick shook his head and stepped away.

Hannah's keys were in her hand. 'Be seeing you.' It was one of those things you said; it didn't mean anything.

'Yes,' Resnick said.

From the window of her car she watched him, shoulders more hunched than they should be, head a little bowed. She sat a moment longer, wondering without reason if he might turn back, find something more to say. When he didn't, she turned the key in the ignition, backed the car round and headed down to join the traffic. She had one final glimpse of Resnick as he drove off in the opposite direction. That young detective, she thought, so full of himself, the one who had almost asked her out – why was it never the ones to whom you might have said yes?

The investigation went pretty much as Resnick had anticipated; Hannah read the reports in the newspaper the next day, though for legal reasons Nicky's name was omitted. Nicky was remanded into the care of the local authority awaiting trial. Hannah got on with her teaching, poems and book reports, *Break Point, What About It, Sharon?* and *Macbeth*. For Resnick, other things came pressing in, the way things do. A suspected arson attack on a café specialising in Caribbean food; a youth of thirteen who stole a delivery van and drove it into a bus queue, leaving one person dead and four more seriously injured; one doctor who was accused of illegally prescribing drugs, another of procuring an illegal abortion; a gang of teenage girls rampaging through the underpasses around the city centre, mugging two women and a twenty-seven-year-old man. A little shy of six in the morning, a Sunday, Resnick had a call from the social services emergency duty team: Nicky Snape had been found hanging from the shower in the children's home where he was being held.

12

The building was separated from the road by a parade of tightly packed firs. Its brick-and-concrete facia and high barred windows told of decades of institutional use: children's home, assessment centre, now secure accommodation that was less than secure. There were plans to sell it into private hands; a certain amount of modification and a coat or two of paint and it would make a perfect old people's home. Resnick recognised the police surgeon's car at the kerb; the ambulance was parked on the curve of the drive, tight to the front door. He rang the bell. Six thirty: out of the east the sky leaked a stubborn light.

The door was opened by a man in his early thirties, slightly built with thinning hair. 'Paul Matthews, I . . .' He glanced at Resnick's identification and stepped away. 'Mr Jardine's busy with the Director of Social Services, on the phone, er . . . he asked me to show you where . . . where it happened and then he would like to talk to you later. Before you go.'

Resnick stepped onto the worn parquet flooring of the hall. The death of a minor in custody: he thought it would be a long time before he – he and those officers who came after him – would be taking their leave.

'It's the bathroom on the second floor.'

Resnick nodded and followed him towards the stairs. Voices echoed faintly, back and forth along cold corridors; the interior smelled of disinfectant and waste. Several yards short of the bathroom, Matthews stopped and stared at the floor.

In the moment before he went inside, Resnick had an image, clear and defined, of what he would see. For neither the first time nor the last. He turned the rounded handle and went in.

Nicky Snape lay on a sheet of thick polythene, which had been doubled beneath him on the bathroom floor. He was naked to the waist and his soiled pyjamas had been lowered below his buttocks to midway down his thighs. Across the cage of his ribs and taut between his hips, his skin stretched opaque and milky white. The bruising at his neck and underneath his chin had already darkened to a colour that was neither black nor purple. Old burn marks stood out kidney red in the bright overhead light. In death his face was that of a child.

'Charlie.'

Resnick heard the police surgeon's voice, but continued to stare. So small and broken there.

'Asphyxiation, Charlie. Dead, what? Couple of hours, hour and a half.' Parkinson offered Resnick a mint and when the inspector refused, popped one into his own mouth. 'You see the way the lips have turned that shade of blue? And there, the nail beds of the hand.'

Bending, Resnick saw the skin around the fingers chewed raw, nails bitten down to the quick.

'There was a towel by the body, wet and twisted tight. What he used, Charlie, most like.'

Resnick could see it, coiled against the edge of the shower stall, white with a faint blue stripe.

'Your boys'll find fibres a-plenty, like as not.' The mint cracked between the surgeon's teeth.

'You didn't take him down?' Resnick asked.

Parkinson shook his head. 'He was propped up against the wall there, back against the tiles. Staff, I suppose.'

Resnick squatted close to the body, wondering if, when he'd been discovered, Nicky's eyes had already been closed. An illusion he allowed himself for a moment, if he stayed there close the boy would wake.

'What was he, Charlie?' Parkinson asked, fidgeting things back into his case. 'Sixteen?'

'Not that.'

Not ever, Resnick thought. He rose to his feet. Millington would be here soon, roused from his blissful bed, and then Scene of Crime, bemoaning the disruption of their Sunday, even as they counted the overtime. Others, too. Senior social workers in once-good suits engaged on damage limitation, anxious to off-load the blame.

'Nasty burn marks,' Parkinson observed. 'Not above a year old. Caught in a fire or some such, I suppose.'

'Fire bomb,' Resnick said. 'A little surprise as he was walking home. Local vigilantes out to teach him a lesson.'

'Tearaway, then, was he?'

'Fond of what wasn't properly his own.'

'Well,' Parkinson said, snapping the case shut, 'not so different from the rest of us there. But now, if you'll allow me, no excuse for not getting on the green bright and early this morning, at least.'

'No, I suppose not.'

'You don't play, do you, Charlie?' The surgeon voiced it as a matter of regret.

Resnick shook his head.

'Ah, well. I'll give Jack Skelton your regards.'

Paul Matthews was waiting in the corridor. 'Mr Jardine – if you're ready, I'll show you the way to his office.' Resnick looked at him carefully; understood that it was more than tiredness lining his eyes.

'You were the one that found him,' Resnick said.

Matthews flinched and looked away.

'What time was that?'

'Five, it would've been . . . Not long after five.'

'You were the member of staff on duty?'

'Yes.'

'Just you?'

'No, my colleague, Elizabeth, she . . . It was routine, you see, I was just checking the bathroom. Routine.' His words were beginning to collide again, haphazard; at his sides, his hands were never still. 'As soon as I went in there I could see, Nicky, I mean, I could see what had happened, what he'd done. The towel, he'd fastened it around the pipe to the shower. Behind the . . . behind the rose . . . he . . .'

'It's all right, take your time.'

'I could see the way his neck was twisted off to one side . . .'

'Yes.'

'. . . and he'd, you know, messed himself. I mean, I could tell that he was dead, Nicky, dead already. It was too late. There was nothing I could do.'

'You took him down?'

'Not right away. I . . .'

'But you checked for vital signs?'

Matthews's eyes were birds trapped in the space of Resnick's gaze. 'I didn't know what to do. Whether I should touch him or not, I wasn't sure. Elizabeth, she was . . . I said, she was on duty with me. I ran for help.'

Resnick struggled to keep his temper, keep the incredulity out of his voice. 'You left him hanging? Without establishing that he was dead?'

Matthews scratched hard at the side of his face. 'Yes, I mean, no, not for long. Just till . . .' He looked at Resnick imploringly. 'He was already dead. He was.'

'You phoned the emergency services?'

'Yes.'

'You and not your colleague, Elizabeth.'

'I'm not . . . I'm not . . . It might have been Elizabeth, I'm not sure.'

Resnick steadied him with a hand on his arm. 'All right. We'll talk some other time. You can make a statement to one of my officers later. Now let's not keep your Mr Jardine waiting any longer.'

Hand on the banister, Matthews pulled in air gratefully, gathering himself together before leading the way.

The name had been written in black copperplate on white card – DEREK JARDINE – and slipped into the brass frame attached to the oak-finish door, more letters after it than in the name itself. The sound was hollow when Resnick knocked.

'Inspector.' Jardine raised himself from his chair to shake Resnick's hand. 'Please, take a seat.'

Beneath the curtained window and along one wall,

91

shelves stood thick with books on social work and young offenders, bound copies of professional journals and reports. A write-on, wipe-off calendar bearing staff names and duties was fixed to the other side wall; beside it, without apparent pattern, an array of photographs; the youngsters, Resnick assumed, who had passed through Jardine's hands. On top of the grey filing cabinet close by the director's desk, framed by a browning ivy and a spider plant that had known better days, was a photograph of Jardine himself in cap and gown, receiving an academic scroll.

Thirty years on, the face was more fleshy, thin lines had appeared, criss-crossing the nose and cheeks, blue like Roquefort cheese. Dark hair, greying at the temples, was receding; small flakes of dandruff decorated the shoulders of his dark-blue suit.

'Of course, this is terrible,' Jardine was saying and Resnick nodded, waiting for the second 'terrible' to follow, which it predictably did.

'A young boy.'

'Yes.'

'A tragedy.'

He could be, Resnick thought, rehearsing the vicar's empty speech. 'Last night, this morning, when the incident occurred – you weren't on the premises?' He hadn't intended it to sound hostile, but from Jardine's expression he could see that it had.

'I can't be here all of the time, Inspector.'

'No, of course. I didn't mean . . .'

'I left, in fact, quite late. Nine thirty or ten. My staff contacted me at home this morning when the . . . when Nicky's body was discovered.'

'And that was Paul . . . ?'

'Paul Matthews, yes.' Jardine's eyes narrowed and he leaned forward, chest pressing the edge of the desk. 'Inspector, you do appreciate we shall be carrying out a full internal enquiry. I've discussed this already with the Director of Social Services. In the meantime, I must ask you not to question any of my staff unless either myself or a solicitor is present.' He settled back into the curve of his chair. 'I have no doubt whatsoever, the enquiry will establish that, as far as we are concerned, correct procedures were followed.'

If the correct procedures had been followed, Resnick thought, then maybe a boy wouldn't be lying out there dead. He said nothing, but Jardine read the accusation, unmistakable in Resnick's eyes.

'Nicky's mother,' Resnick said, 'she has been informed?'

When Resnick left the building less than ten minutes later, it was with a sense of relief. Graham Millington had arrived moments earlier and met Resnick outside, a few crumbs of toast still caught in his moustache. Easy to imagine Madeleine sitting her husband down at the kitchen table: 'Graham, you're not going off at this hour without something inside you. You know how your stomach plays you up when you do.'

'Straightforward enough, then?' Millington said, apprised of the details.

'Who knows, Graham? The lad's dead, no two ways about that, but how and why . . . ?'

'Topped himself, though, didn't he? I mean, it was suicide?'

Resnick sighed. 'That seems the most likely – at present.'

Millington looked back at him quizzically, eyebrow raised. 'You've no reason to suppose . . .'

'No reason, Graham, to suppose a thing. But there's a social worker in there, Matthews, ready to come apart at the seams. And the director, Jardine, getting the hatches battened down like he was in a time of siege.'

'Or cholera,' Millington said quietly.

'Sorry, Graham?'

'It's a book the wife was reading . . .'

'I dare say, Graham. Anyway, stick around, keep Scene of Crime on their toes. Soon as they're through, you can release the lad's body to the hospital. Oh, and Graham, so you know, Jardine gave me the benefit of a lecture, no talking to the staff without his say-so.'

'And without a social services solicitor to hold their hand.'

'Most likely.'

'Ah, well,' Millington grinned ruefully, 'do what we can, eh?'

'By the book, Graham. If there is anything amiss here, we'll not want to let it slip away.'

Millington nodded and walked towards the entrance. The morning air was cold and the sky was an almost unbroken grey. Whatever had happened to spring, Resnick thought? At the end of the drive, he looked back towards the tall windows and saw the faces staring down.

13

It was still early on Sunday morning. Kevin and Debbie Naylor lay beneath the duvet, Kevin on his back, Debbie curled over on her side; softly, from the adjacent bedroom, the sounds of their daughter holding a long and complicated conversation with one or other of her stuffed animals.

'Kevin?'

'Hmm?'

'What you thinking?'

'Nothing.'

But just by reaching out a hand and touching him, Debbie could tell that he was lying.

'Kevin?'

'What?'

Debbie laughed and slid one leg across his, the laugh stifling against his chest.

'Deb.'

'Mmm?'

'She might come in at any minute.'

'Not if we close the door.' She moved her head again and her mouth found his nipple.

'Ow!'

'Sshh.'

'Is it, you know, all right?'

'Of course it's all right.'

Some months ago Debbie had had a miscarriage; she didn't want to wait too long before giving their only child a little sister or brother.

'Kevin?'

But Kevin was smiling as he rolled off his back towards her, the whole thing easy between them now, easier than it had ever been. Just for a second she tensed when he touched her but then quickly relaxed. His mouth at her neck, her breast, and then her hand around him, guiding him in.

Deftly, Lynn Kellogg fashioned for her mother the story of her Saturday night date; at seven on the dot, her young man, an accountant with a local firm of solicitors, had picked her up at the housing association flat where she lived. They had gone to see the new Alan Bennett play at the Playhouse. Well, not new actually, an old one revived, but with that actor her mum had always liked in *The Likely Lads*. No, not him. The other one. Yes, very good. Funny. And then they'd gone for something to eat at Mama Mia. Yes, tagliatelle. Italian, that's right. Very tasty. And, yes, of course she'd be seeing him again. No, she didn't know exactly when.

She could almost hear her mother, sitting in the kitchen of their Norfolk poultry farm, making calculations, crossing fingers, counting chickens, hatching dreams.

What Lynn had actually done the previous night was read two chapters of a Tom Clancy, walk around the corner for a takeaway chicken korma from the Maharani, pop open a can of Carlsberg and watch Andy Garcia and Meg Ryan drinking their way through *When a Man Loves a Woman* on a rented video.

All those things her mother wanted for her – marriage, babies – Lynn thought she was happy to forgo them all, if that meant she didn't have to go through all of the crap that seemed necessary to get within even spitting distance of them.

'How's Dad?' she asked, breaking across her mother's words.

'Oh, Lynnie, he's fine. Right as rain. Out there with his blessed birds since the Lord knows when. He'll be in soon for his bit of breakfast, you see.'

Almost two years ago, Lynn's father had been diagnosed as having colorectal cancer, cancer of the bowel. He had had an operation, treatment, regained weight, resumed work, almost as if nothing more could happen. It was like sitting on a time bomb, Lynn thought, waiting for the news, imagining what was slowly growing inside him.

'Lynnie, your dad's fine. Honest.'

Her mother who believed in dreams.

For Norma Snape the best Sundays were not present but past. She could remember when she was still with Patrick, waking late in that bed in Huddersfield, sunlight patching across the room and Patrick sitting propped on pillows beside her, building his first joint of the day. Then lying there, getting more and more stoned until finally the munchies overcame them and they raided the refrigerator for leftover pizza and chocolate chip ice-cream. Al Green on the record player all the while: 'Let's Stay Together', 'Here

I Am (Come and Take Me)', 'Call me (Come Back Home)'.

Or later, Sundays with Peter, his hands fluttering at her back like wings, barely touching, never still. Sheena, nine months old, fast asleep close alongside her, thumb in her mouth, hair fair across her eyes. The rise and fall of the child's tiny chest no more than the delicate pressure of Peter's fingers at the base of her spine. The tension within her as she bit into the soft underside of her lip, waiting for his hands to move lower.

Norma stirred and reached for the mug of tea she had fetched earlier and which had long since grown cold. Faint from downstairs she could hear the sound of the television, though she'd swear that she'd heard Shane go out the best part of an hour since. She fidgeted the sheet around her and reached for a magazine. She could hear Sheena now, running herself a bath. But not her Nicky, he wasn't there for certain. Shut up in that place, poor little bastard, shut up in that bastard home. This afternoon she'd get herself up nice, go out and see him, take him some chocolate, cigarettes, something special, something for a treat. No matter what he'd done, when it came down to it he was her son; there was no getting away from that, no getting away from it at all. She'd just stay there ten minutes longer, get up for good then, mash some fresh tea. She lit a cigarette and flicked towards the problem page – anyone else's but her own, they were a cinch.

She was still lying there, half an hour later, when the doorbell rang.

When it became clear that, whoever it was, they weren't

98

going to go away, Norma pulled on her dressing-gown and shuffled to the upstairs window, overlooking the street.

'What the hell . . .?'

She saw Resnick looking up at her and what she saw in his eyes drove into her stomach like a fist.

Downstairs, she could see him silhouetted through the mottled glass panels at the top of the door. Impatient with the bolts, her fingers finally fumbled back the door.

'Norma . . .'

It was still there in his eyes and in the way he stood.

'It's Nicky, isn't it?'

'Yes.'

'Something's happened to Nicky.'

'I'm afraid so, yes.'

Norma's hands were at her sides, clenched; for a moment she closed her eyes.

'Norma, I think we'd best talk inside.'

'Tell me.'

'Norma . . .'

She caught hold of him, the lapel of his coat. 'Fucking tell me!'

Resnick's breath snagged in his throat. 'He was found earlier this morning. Norma, he . . .'

'He's dead.'

Resnick's voice was quiet, each word screaming in her head. 'Yes. Yes, Norma, I'm afraid he's dead.'

She flung back her arm and her hand smashed through the glass of the door. What came from her mouth was more of a hiss than a scream. Resnick caught her and held her close, her breath against his face. Blood ran from her palm and wrist, down past her finger ends onto the floor.

'Norma, come on. Come on now, let's get inside.'

He led her, half-dragging her, along the short hall. Sheena was standing, white-faced, a towel wrapped round her, at the foot of the stairs.

'Help me get your mum into the front room.'

Sheena didn't move.

Over and over again, Norma was saying Nicky's name. Resnick manoeuvred her onto the settee and raised her arm so that her hand was level with her head. Cartoon dinosaurs were doing battle on the TV.

Resnick looked round at Sheena, silent in the doorway. 'Get a clean towel, tea towel, anything as long as it's clean. All right? Now.'

There were slivers of glass visible in the fleshy part of Norma's hand, below the thumb. 'What . . . happened?' she gasped. 'Nicky, what happened?'

'Let's get this mess sorted first . . .'

'No! No. Tell me, I want to know.'

Careful, Resnick eased the longest of the glass shards away; he was holding Norma's arm upright with his hand. Sheena came back carrying a hand towel. She had pulled on a T-shirt and jeans. 'It's all I could find.'

'That's fine. Now phone for an ambulance . . .'

'No.' Norma was sobbing, shaking her head.

'An ambulance, this wants seeing to properly. And get the kettle on, let's have some tea, all right? Sweet tea.'

Gingerly, Resnick fingered out another piece of glass and set it carefully with the first, on the floor by the settee.

'Mr Resnick, please . . .'

He held her other hand as well. 'He was found in one of the bathrooms with a towel around his neck. He was hanging. It looks as if he took his own life.'

She pulled away from him so hard that he was unable to hold her; punched and slapped against him as the cries tore from her throat and didn't stop until he had caught her wrists and pinned them back and by then the front of his shirt and the side of his face were smeared with blood.

'It's okay, Norma,' Resnick said. 'It's okay, it's going to be all right.'

But Norma could only remember Nicky's face as she chased him away, holding her ten pounds aloft and laughing. *You let me get my hands on you, you little tripeshanks, and I'll wring your miserable neck.*

14

When Resnick first worked with him, Jack Skelton had begun his days in track suit and running shoes, jogging a couple of miles down the Derby Road towards the university, one lap round the lake and then back up the hill, forehead glistening with sweat and good intentions. Now, he lit his third or fourth Bensons of the day between the car-park and the rear door of the station, and his breath was audible by the time he reached the second flight of stairs.

Time was, too, when Resnick would have had his work cut out to be at his desk before the superintendent of a morning, but this Monday he had almost finished briefing Millington and the rest of the team before Skelton had arrived.

It had been a weekend like many another. Half a dozen break-ins either side of the Alfreton Road and the same number in the narrow streets at the back of Lenton Boulevard. In one of these, the burglars had made themselves jam and peanut butter sandwiches, opened the mail, then sat around long enough to watch the recording of that Saturday's *Match of the Day*, which had been left in the

VCR. All of this while three lads slept upstairs, out to the world.

A van had been stolen from round the back of a bakery in Radford and driven into the canal behind the Raleigh cycle works. Two men had got into a fight in the early hours which resulted in one biting off the first finger of the other at the tip; the victim had walked into accident and emergency at the Queen's with the finger safe inside a condom he had been keeping providentially in his wallet. And at a little before seven that morning, three girls wearing face masks, one of them in what looked like school uniform, had tried to hold up the petrol station by Abbey Bridge with what proved to be a cucumber inside a plastic bag.

'Another week, eh, Charlie?' Millington had said, stubbing out his cigarette.

'Least we don't have Nicky Snape to fret about,' Divine said, getting to his feet.

Resnick shot him a look that would keep his head down for the rest of the day.

'The Hodgson youth,' Resnick said to Lynn as she walked by, 'safely back at Ambergate?'

Lynn nodded. 'Till the next time.'

'Good work there.'

'Thanks.'

'The man they picked up with him . . .'

'Brian Noble.'

'Vice decide to charge him or what?'

Lynn shook her head. 'More trouble than it was worth in the end. Gave him a warning and kicked him free.' She smiled. 'What's the betting he was in church yesterday with his wife and kids, giving thanks.'

Across the room, Kevin Naylor turned his head from the telephone. 'The hospital, sir, Doris Netherfield...' The skin tightened apprehensively around Resnick's eyes. 'No change, apparently. Still holding her own.'

'Good,' Resnick said, releasing his breath. 'Thank God for that as well.'

Skelton was waiting in his office and listened with barely concealed impatience while Resnick made his report. There were more pressing things on his mind.

'Don't know how you managed it yesterday morning, Charlie, out where that kid was found, but you got a hair stuck up the director's arse of sizeable proportions. I had the ACC on the phone to me last evening, Assistant Director of Social Services had been onto him, asking whatever investigation we carry out, you wouldn't be the officer in charge.'

Resnick grunted in response.

'According to Jardine you questioned staff without his authority.'

'I talked to one, the man who let me in. What was I supposed to do, maintain strict silence?'

'And then, apparently, you all but accused Jardine of culpability in Snape's death.'

'That's nonsense. I accused nobody.'

'All right, then, implied.'

Resnick looked past Skelton's head towards the window; with what seemed unnatural slowness, a plane from East Midlands Airport was making a diagonal pass across a blue-grey sky. 'I'd be tempted to wonder, all this defensiveness, if he hasn't got something to hide.'

'The suicide? You think there's something not kosher?'

Resnick shrugged. 'Not necessarily. But if that is what happened, I'd like to know the reasons why.'

'The way he attacked that old man, kid or not, he might've been facing some heavy time. Maybe it was the thought of being shut away.'

Resnick shook his head. 'I think it would've taken more than that.'

'Bullying, then, some of the other youths, is that what you think?'

'I don't know. Could be a lot of things.'

'Or nothing at all.'

Resnick shifted heavily in his chair. 'Dead fifteen-year-old, that's what there is.'

Hands clenched behind his head, Skelton leaned his chair back onto its rear legs. 'There will be a police enquiry, of course. Routine. The ACC mentioned Bill Aston. What do you think?'

'I thought he'd been put out to pasture long since.'

'Not exactly. They found him an office the size of a shoe box up at headquarters and gave him bits of paper to push around the desk.'

'You make it sound like occupational therapy.'

Skelton unclasped his hands and set his chair level. 'Kinder than kicking him free, a few years short of his pension.'

'And you think he's right for this?'

'Like I say, it's a suggestion.'

Resnick remembered Aston, a tall figure with iron-grey hair and steel-rimmed glasses, ramrod straight. As a uniformed inspector, he would run his morning parades with a fine-tooth comb. Buttons smeared with Brasso, creased jackets, dirty shoes – all enough to earn a reprimand at least. Cleanliness and Godliness and the chief constable sitting up there at the Lord's right hand. Resnick had worked with him after Aston had moved across to CID and found him thorough, painstaking, devoid of imagination. Policing changed and Aston had not. Turning forty, advancement had passed him by. Chief inspector's posts came and went and he had devoted more and more time to his work as a lay preacher and governor of the local primary school; he had been shuffled aside.

'He'll do a careful job,' Skelton said. 'By the numbers, you know that.'

'He'll be polite.'

'You'll have a word with him, make sure he's primed? You know the family pretty well.'

'Yes, I'll tell him what I can.'

'Good.' Skelton was on his feet. 'Jardine's objections aside, you'd not really have fancied this yourself.'

'Probably not.'

'Oh, and Charlie . . .' This when Resnick was almost at the door. '. . . had a call from your mate, Reg Cossall. Setting up an operation in Radford, undercover. Fraud, theft, dealing. Drugs Squad have got their oar in, too. Wants to know if we can spare a body? Three nights or four. Somehow he's scared up some overtime.'

Uncertain, Resnick shook his head. 'We're short-handed as it is, you know that.'

'Charlie, it's only a couple of nights. Divine's kind of thing, this, isn't it?'

Resnick shrugged. 'If it's going to be anyone, better Naylor. Then at least the money might go to good use. Divine'll drink it away and scarce notice the difference.'

'As you say, Charlie, up to you.' Before Resnick had left the office, Skelton was reaching for the phone.

It was ten to one and Resnick was about to take a bite out of his turkey breast and cranberry sandwich when the officer on duty called up from the front desk. There were two visitors to see him, Norma Snape and her son, Shane.

Naturally a big woman, Norma seemed to have suddenly shrunk on her frame. The black dress she wore hung from her shoulders like poorly fitted curtains; her face, previously full, had become gaunt. Darkness around her eyes suggested many tears and little sleep.

Alongside her, Shane was taller than Resnick remembered him, fitter; aside from frequent trips to the betting shop and pool hall, clearly he had been working out. He wore blue loose-fitting jeans and a grey sweat-shirt and his fair hair had been zealously trimmed. Standing alongside his mother at the entrance to the CID room, Shane's eyes fixed on Resnick and dismissed him as so much piss and wind.

'Let's go into my office.' Resnick held open the door and ushered Norma towards a chair. Shane preferred to stand.

'Can I get you anything? Tea, coffee?'

No reply.

Resnick walked around his desk and sat down, Shane's eyes following him all the way. 'Norma, how've you been?'

'How d'you think?' Shane snapped back before his mother could speak.

'And your hand, Norma? How's your hand?'

'Never mind her bloody hand. That's not why we're

107

here.' He stared at Resnick. 'My brother was in your charge and he died, that's why we're here.'

Resnick eased back his chair and sighed. 'Not directly in my charge. The local authority . . .'

'Bollocks to the local authority! You arrested him.' Shane's finger jabbing towards Resnick's face. 'You. You're the one as dragged him out of the house, banged him up in here, got him up in court. And what happened to him, what happened to him, right, that's down to you too. Your fucking fault!'

His fist was now little more than inches from Resnick's face. His voice more than filled the room. Millington knocked on the door and entered without waiting to be asked. 'Everything okay, boss?'

'Thanks, Graham. Everything's fine.' Resnick didn't look at his sergeant, didn't take his eyes off Shane Snape.

'Right, then. If you're sure.' Millington slowly withdrew, leaving the door ajar.

Shane and Resnick were staring at each other and neither would look away.

'Shane . . .' Norma reached up with her bandaged hand and touched her eldest's arm. 'Please.'

With a flex of his muscles, Shane lowered his fist and stepped away. Resnick watched him for ten, fifteen seconds more and then, apparently, dismissed him from his thoughts. 'What is there I can tell you, Norma?'

'My Nicky,' Norma said, leaning closer, 'never mind what happened to him in the past, no matter how bad he got hurt, he'd always bounce back. Always. Even that time those bastards threw that petrol bomb at him. Nicky, he was laughing and joking about it while he was still in hospital. That's why I don't think he would ever have done a thing like that, Mr Resnick, took his own life. It's not the way he . . . not the way he was. Not unless there was good reason, something we don't know about. Something that happened to him while he was there.'

'Norma, there'll be an enquiry . . .' Behind his mother, Shane laughed a short, bitter laugh. '. . . Two. One carried out by social services, and another which we'll conduct ourselves.'

'Bloody whitewash,' said Shane. 'That's what that'll sodding be.'

'You, Mr Resnick,' Norma said, 'you'll be looking into it yourself?'

Resnick shook his head. 'A senior officer will lead the team. Very experienced. You couldn't ask for anyone to be more thorough . . .'

'But you knew Nicky, really knew him. This bloke, whoever he is . . .'

'He's a good man, Norma. I can assure you of that. And I shall be giving him all the help I can.'

A smile showed fleetingly on her face and slipped away. 'Nicky's body, the funeral . . .'

'We'll release it as soon as we can. I'll do my best to find out today and let you know. Okay?'

For a moment, Norma let her head drop forward, eyes closed. Shane started to stay something but Resnick's quick look told him he had already said enough. Resnick got to his feet and started around the desk to help Norma from her chair, but Shane placed himself in his way.

'Come on, Mum, let's get out of here.'

Millington stood alongside Resnick, watching them go. 'Aggravated burglary, wasn't it? What he was up for last?'

Resnick nodded. 'I believe so.'

'Next time, praise God, someone'll send him down for a nice long time.'

Resnick turned aside, went back into his office and closed the door. Untouched, his sandwich waited for him on his desk, but after all the empty words he had offered Norma Snape, his appetite had deserted him. He took hold of the sandwich and dumped it in the bin.

15

Resnick had a call from Bill Aston late that afternoon. For some minutes they exchanged pleasantries, gossiped about the Job. 'Changed a lot since our day, Charlie. Used to be, all you did was put on that uniform, walk into a pub, anywhere in the city, people looked at you with respect. Now they'll as like spit in your face as ask time of day.' Resnick waited for him to get to the point, smarting a little under the implication: as far as he was concerned, this was his day still.

'Thought we might have a jar, Charlie? Once I've got my feet under the table. One or two little things, this Snape youth, background, you could fill me in on.'

'I had the mother here today,' Resnick said. 'Doesn't see Nicky as the suicidal type; not without there was a powerful reason.'

'Only to be expected, given the circumstances. Upset, bound to be. Distraught. Probably shouldn't give her too much credence in the circumstances.'

'She's the lad's mother, Bill, none the less. As a family, I think they were pretty close.'

'If there's anything nasty in the woodshed, Charlie, I'll poke it out.'

'I told her you'd do a good job.'

'Thanks, Charlie. Thanks for that. And our little drink some evening?'

'Ring me, Bill. Any time.'

'I will, Charlie. Thanks again.'

As Resnick rode the escalator upstairs in the Victoria Centre he was thinking about what Aston had said. They were near enough of an age for him to recognise what the older man had described, the shifts and slippages of the last twenty years. And what lay ahead? Promotion into the new Serious Crimes Unit, always supposing that memoranda became reality, or a little room of his own at HQ, a rubber stamp with which he could mark out the end of his days?

He stepped off the escalator and walked towards the market, nodding in the direction of the dozen or so elderly Poles who stood in their grey raincoats and shiny shoes, reminiscing about the good old days fifty years or more before. Resnick's father, had he lived, would have been amongst them, stooped by now and shrunken, an exile from the country of his childhood, the country of his youth.

Resnick entered the market past the corner music stall where the Tremeloes' Greatest Hits were permanently on offer at a special marked-down price. Ahead of him, shoppers hesitated before slabs of local cheddar and Blue Stilton, mushrooms and courgettes, potatoes – reds, whites and the first Jersey Royals – Granny Smiths from France and New Zealand, strawberries from Israel and Spain, thick-stalked cabbages in lustrous green grown no more than a mile or two up the road. Deeper into the market, incongruously, bottles of perfume could be bought, machine-made Nottingham lace, electrical gizmos and Hoover bags by the dozen, kids' shirts and jeans for which Council clothing vouchers were gratefully accepted.

Resnick was heading for the Polish deli, where the cheesecake stared back at him like a government health warning, threatening to push him that extra ten pounds over on the scales. The approximate ideal weight for a male with your bodyframe is . . . Resnick didn't want to know. He made his purchases – several of the salamis sliced thin, a loaf of crusty rye bread with caraway, sour cream – and carried them over to the Italian coffee stall. Someone had left a *Post* on the counter and he skimmed through it while waiting for his espresso. Sea fishing gear had been stolen from a shed, thirty-two prize-winning budgies from a garage; a masked burglar had sat comfortably on a seventy-nine-year-old woman's bed and chatted with her for thirty minutes before making off with her jewellery. He had asked her if she wanted a cup of coffee and when she declined, said he would make her tea instead. It was almost enough to make crime seem cosy, the stuff of Ealing comedies and *Dixon of Dock Green*. Except that Resnick knew what had happened when Nicky Snape had broken into the Netherfield home, and it hadn't been a friendly bedside chat, a pot of tea. Doris Netherfield might be stable and responding to treatment, but her condition was still serious; her husband was nursing his injuries at home, and Nicky Snape had been found hanging from a bathroom shower. That was in the paper, too, front page. ALLEGED AGGRESSOR FOUND DEAD. Resnick's own name was in paragraph three.

Setting down the espresso, the assistant tapped the paper. 'Good riddance, no?'

'No. Not at all.'

The assistant shrugged, uncomprehending, took Resnick's money and turned away to serve an attractive young mother, well-built, bright-eyed, kids fidgeting on stools at either side of her, taking the occasional kick at one another behind her back. 'Cut it out, you two. I'll not tell you again.' Automatically, Resnick's eyes went to her left hand, third finger. No dad at home, presumably, whom she could offer as a threat. A good thing or bad? He wasn't sure.

'Another, Inspector?'

Resnick pushed the empty cup away. 'No thanks, not today.'

He was almost out of the market when he saw her, in the centre row near the exit, buying flowers.

Hannah Campbell had left her VW in the underground car-park and taken the lift to Tesco's, where she had compromised her usual healthy purchases with a Sarah Lee ready-baked Pecan Nut Danish Pastry, an impulse for which she had felt more than a twinge of guilt at the checkout. The two bags of groceries she had locked into the boot of her car, before going up to the market for vegetables, salad stuff and cheese. It was the sign announcing wreaths and floral tributes that stopped her in her tracks.

Of course, what had happened to Nicky – rumours, innuendo, the story imperfectly patched together piece by piece – had been all over the school the entire day. Shock and genuine sympathy in the staff room had been shot

114

through with a malicious righteousness which had made Hannah heave. Smug elegies of the I-told-you-so variety. At least one overheard remark about Nicky's positive contribution to classroom overcrowding.

Floral tributes and wreaths: Hannah asked the aproned woman in charge of the stall about the price of a bouquet. Lilies, those nice carnations, daffs, they're lovely this time of the year. Resnick stood at the end of the aisle, watching her, hair falling across her face as she bent forward towards the flowers; if he went to speak to her, what would he say? Far easier to walk away.

He was downstairs, hesitating outside HMV and considering a quick foray through their meagre jazz section, when Hannah spotted him.

'Inspector Resnick?'

Seeing her reflection in the shop window, he smiled.

'It sounds silly,' Hannah said when he was facing her, 'calling you inspector like that. Like something out of a play. J. B. Priestley. You know, *An Inspector Calls.*'

Vaguely, Resnick thought that he might. 'Charlie, then,' he said.

'That's your name? Charlie?'

He nodded – 'Yes' – and shifted the bag he was carrying from hand to hand.

'Somehow I never think of policemen doing their own shopping.'

'Someone has to.'

'I suppose so.' She smiled. 'I know.'

He looked at the flowers she was carrying; didn't know what more to say. 'Well . . .' A lurch to the left, not really a step away.

'I nearly phoned you,' Hannah said, 'earlier today.'

115

'How come?'

'What happened to Nicky. I just . . .' She pushed a hand up through her hair and stepped back, almost into a push-chair that was being steered past. 'I don't know, I wanted to talk about it, I suppose.'

'To say what exactly?'

She just smiled, just the eyes this time. 'That's it, I don't really know. That's why in the end I didn't phone.'

'There probably isn't a great deal I could tell you . . .'

'No, of course not. I understand.'

'But if . . .'

'Yes?'

For the first time he smiled, his whole face relaxing into it, opening wide.

'You haven't got a few minutes now?' Hannah asked.

Resnick shrugged, glanced towards his watch without registering a thing. 'Why not?'

She led him to the food court where they bought cap-puccinos in waxed paper cups and carried them towards the raised section of seating at the centre. He found it strange to be in the company of this woman he scarcely knew, a good-looking woman, casually but nicely dressed, a large bouquet of flowers in her hand. For no discernible reason, a phrase from 'Roseland Shuffle' sprang into Resnick's head, Lester Young soloing against Basie's sprightly piano.

'Is this okay?' Hannah asked, looking round.

'Fine.'

She set the flowers down carefully on the seat alongside. 'I was going to take them to Nicky's mother,' she said. 'Now I'm not so sure.'

'I didn't realise you knew him that well.'

'I didn't. Not really. To be honest I don't think anyone at the school did, not in the last couple of years anyway. He was scarcely there.' She sipped at her coffee and cradled it in her hands. 'It's awful to say it, but I'd go into my English class, the one Nicky was supposed to be in, and if I saw he wasn't at his desk I'd be relieved. It's not that he was disruptive exactly. Not all the time anyway. Mostly, he'd just sit there and let it wash over him. Never say a word. But occasionally he'd latch onto something, some idea of his own, at a complete tangent from what the rest of the class were doing, and keep on and on about it, question after question, till it was all I could do to get the lesson back on track.'

Hannah stopped and drank a little coffee, looked across into Resnick's patient face, the skin that wrinkled past the corners of his eyes. 'Perhaps I shouldn't have let that matter. The plan for my precious lesson, I mean. Aim, method, conclusion. Perhaps there were more important things.'

'My guess, by the time he got to you, there'd not have been a great deal you could do.'

Hannah gave a wry smile. 'Give me a child until he's seven, isn't that what the Jesuits say? Or is it nine? Either way, they're probably right, don't you think? Or in your book, are criminals born and not made? Nature or nurture, Charlie, which are you?' Even as she said it, she was surprised at the ease with which she used his name.

He had noticed a green fleck in her right eye, close to the iris, and was trying not to stare. 'Some people,' he said, 'they'll engage in criminal behaviour no matter what. Maybe it's psychological, something in their genes, deep in their childhood, who's to say? But average, run-of-the-mill crime, you just have to look at the figures. Unemployment, housing . . .' Resnick gestured with the palm of one hand. '. . . worse those problems are, higher the rate of crime.'

'Tell that to the government,' Hannah said sharply.

Resnick tasted his coffee; despite the paper cup, it was better than he'd thought. 'This last election,' he said, 'local. How many? Sixteen Conservatives kicked out. For Labour almost a clean sweep. Fifty seats on the council now to one Tory, couple of the other lot. I'll be interested to see, by the year's end, how much difference it's made.'

'You don't think that's a little too cynical?'

'How about realistic?'

'And kids like Nicky, you don't think there's anything that can be done? Not with things as they stand?'

He sighed. 'If it can, I'm buggered if I know what it is.'

'Locking them up, though? Prison. Short, sharp shocks. Boot camps, isn't that what they're called? Do you really think that's the answer?'

'I doubt it puts them on the straight and narrow; figures disprove that.'

'But still you carry on, shutting them away.'

Resnick shifted a little awkwardly on his seat. 'No. The courts lock them up. Or they don't, whatever. What we do, what I do, if I can, is arrest those who've broken the law. Not my laws, not my punishment either.'

'But you must agree with them, the courts, what they do, or you wouldn't carry on doing it.'

Resnick pushed back his chair, crossed his legs. 'Are we having a row?'

Hannah smiled. 'No, it's a discussion.'

'That's all right, then.'

118

'But is this your way,' she asked, 'of avoiding the question?'

Resnick grinned and shook his head. 'Youths Nicky's age and younger, persistent offenders, they might get arrested – what? – thirty or forty times in a year. More in some cases. They're too young to be put in prison. Bail, supervision orders, none of that does a scrap of good.'

'You think they should be shut away.'

'I think society needs protecting, yes . . .'

'And Nicky?'

'Look.' Resnick was conscious of his voice being louder than it should, louder than the space allowed. 'I saw that old woman after she'd been beaten about the head, the old man. I'm not saying what happened to Nicky, whatever the reasons, is right, of course I'm not. But he was accused of a serious crime, he had to be kept in custody. Surely you don't think he should have been let back on the streets?'

'If it were a choice between that and him ending up dead, yes, I do. Don't you?'

Resnick glanced around at the people at other tables, just about pretending not to listen to their conversation. The coffee was beginning to grow cold.

'I'm sorry,' Hannah said, 'I'm not trying to make you feel guilty.'

'You're not.' Resnick shook his head. 'I'm sad about what happened. Sad for Nicky's mother. Nicky himself. But what I don't feel is guilt.'

'I do,' Hannah said quietly. 'I do.'

'I don't suppose I can give you a lift anywhere?' she asked.

They were standing in front of the telephones, near the glass doors that opened out onto the Mansfield Road.

'Thanks, no. I'm fine.'

'Okay, 'bye then.' She started to walk away.

'The flowers,' Resnick said, 'shall you be taking them or not?'

'Yes, I think so.'

'Good. I think Norma'll be pleased.' He stood his ground as she walked off in the direction of the lift, plastic bag of shopping swinging lightly from his fist.

When Hannah turned round moments later, before the lift doors closed in front of her, he had gone.

16

A social worker from the Youth Justice Team had called twice and on each occasion the door had been slammed in her face. A reporter from the local BBC radio station had her DAT Walkman hurled back into the street and the crew from Central TV had buckets of water emptied down on them and a spade taken to one side of their van. Shane threw a punch at a stringer for several national tabloids when he came across the man quizzing neighbours in the local pub. 'We'd not said a thing to him, had we, duck?' Hard-eyed, Shane had stared them in the face, smashed an empty bottle against the bar and slammed out: all that rage and nowhere, so far, to bleed it out.

Norma's friend Rosa arrived mid-afternoon with a bottle of white port and a dozen roses, convinced Norma to go into the bathroom and wash her face, put on some make-up and change her clothes. With the afternoon racing from Market Rasen as whispered commentary, the two of them sat on the settee while Rosa plied her friend with glass on glass of port, seizing Norma's wrists in her sudden, flailing fits of anger, holding her tight whenever she gave way to tears. Norma's body shaking inside Rosa's stubborn arms. 'The stupid, stupid geck! Why ever did he want to go and do a think like that?'

Sheena hovered at the edges of the room, watching the two women, riven by the force of her mother's tears which she could not hope to replicate. She went into the kitchen and made tea she never drank, smeared slices of bread with jam she never ate. In her room, she turned her radio up high to drown the sounds of mourning: Lisa I'Anson in the afternoon. Blur. Oasis. Nirvana. Pulp. Take That.

As the racing gave way to *Terrytoons* and *All American Girl*, Norma slept in Rosa's arms, twitching suddenly with the vividness of her dreams. 'Michael. Oh Michael,' she moaned.

'Ssh, now.' Rosa gently stroked her head. And then, as Norma opened her eyes, 'Who's Michael? You kept saying Michael.'

'The baby I lost.'

Rosa squeezed her hand. 'That was Nicky, sweetheart. You're confused, that's all.'

But Norma knew what she had meant. 'No, it was Michael. My little Michael.' And felt again the final thrust and tear, saw him small and bloodied in the midwife's hands.

When Hannah arrived outside the Snape house there were twenty bunches of flowers lining the pavement, others leaning beside the front door. She hesitated, thinking it through, uncertain what she might actually say; she was bending to place her bouquet with the others, turn away, when Sheena came out into the street. Hannah knew her, had taught her in her last year at school, the same school where she had taught Nicky.

'Hello, Sheena, I'm Miss Campbell. I don't know if you remember me.'

She had been a feckless girl, easily led. Left to her own devices she would fidget with her biro, pull at her lank hair, decorate the name of whichever boy friend she aspired to along the edges of her desk, across the front of her notebook, the back of her arm.

'Sheena, I'm sorry about your brother. I really am.' From her reaction, Hannah couldn't tell if the girl remembered her or not, though she supposed she did. 'I brought these flowers for your mum,' Hannah said.

Without speaking, Sheena pushed open the front door and waited for Hannah to step inside.

'Mrs Snape?'

Hannah found them in the kitchen, Norma and Rosa, hunched over the small table, cigarettes and tea.

'Sheena let me in. I'm . . . I was Nicky's teacher, one of Nicky's teachers.' Neither woman looking at her, she stumbled on. 'I wanted to say I was sorry. And to bring you these.' For a few moments longer she held onto the flowers, before laying them down on the table.

'These from the school then?' Rosa asked.

'Yes. I mean, no, not exactly. I brought them myself.'

'So there's nothing from the school?'

'I'm sorry.'

'Bastards, not a sodding word.'

'Look,' Hannah said, 'I think I'd better go. I didn't mean to intrude.'

'Yes,' Rosa said. 'I think you better had.'

She was at the door when she heard Norma's voice. 'You his special teacher, then? Class teacher, whatever it is?'

'No.' Hannah turned back into the kitchen. Norma's eyes were raw and finding it difficult to focus. 'Not really. I was his English teacher, that's all.' Norma blinked and blinked again. 'He was a nice lad, cheerful. I liked him.'

The room expanded to accept the lie, lifted it to the ceiling wreathed in smoke.

'I will go now,' Hannah said.

As she shut the front door behind her, Hannah leaned back against it and closed her eyes. The backs of her legs were shaking, her arms burned cold. *All my pretty ones?* All she could think of were Macduff's words when Malcolm told him that his children had been killed. And what, Hannah, she asked herself, what bloody good is that?

The rain that would saturate the flowers outside Norma's house, mashing the decorated florists' paper against the twisted stems, caught Resnick half a mile from home, no raincoat, plummeting down from a darkening spring sky. Like stair rods, his mother-in-law might have said, back when he had a mother-in-law. By the time he had slipped his key into the front-door lock, his hair was plastered flat against his head, water dripping from his nose and squirrelling past his collar, down his back. As the door clicked open and swung back, Dizzy darted from the shelter of a neighbour's shrub, one touch upon the wall, then in.

Careful, Resnick emptied the contents of his bag, paper-wrapped packages nestling in puddles of water. He took off his coat and hung it over a chair, rubbed a towel briskly through his hair. The meeting with Hannah Campbell kept replaying, sporadically, in his mind.

'Are we having a row?'

124

'No, it's a discussion.'

Automatically, he forked food into the cats' bowls. Is that what it had truly been, a discussion? Academic? Impersonal? Certainly that wasn't the way it had felt. But what did he know? Teachers, perhaps that was what they liked to do, take words and push them back and forth like dominoes, a game to exercise the mind.

He was building a sandwich, waiting for the kettle to boil. Four slices of fresh garlic salami overlapping across rye bread, a pickled cucumber sliced narrowly along its length, goat's cheese that he crumbled between his fingers, a single, thinly cut shallot; finally, the second slice of bread he drizzled with extra virgin olive oil before setting it on top and pressing the sandwich closed, encouraging some of the oil to seep down before he sliced the whole thing in two.

Tinker, tailor, mother-in-law, wife. Slowly, he poured boiling water onto coffee grounds. He had not heard from his ex-wife Elaine since two Christmases ago, not seen her in twice as long. He knew that she had remarried, redivorced, seen the inside of more than one psychiatric ward. When he had seen her it had been like meeting a stranger, someone who had lived for a long time in another country and spoke a language he didn't understand.

'Are we having a row?'

'No, it's a discussion.'

Rather than wait until the lift doors closed across her face, he had walked away.

When the phone ran, it made him jump.

'Charles, I am surprised to find you in.' Marian Witczak's voice, tinged with the accent of a homeland in which she had not been born, which she had not visited until her teens. 'I was wondering, Charles, about the dance. This weekend, you remember? I wonder if you have made up your mind?'

'Marian, I'm not sure.'

He could feel her disappointment as eloquently as words.

'It's difficult, Marian, you know that. To promise. I never know what's going to crop up.'

'All work and no play, Charles, you know what they say?'

'Look, I'll try, that's all I can do.'

'You remember, Charles, that time we persuaded the accordion player to forsake his polkas for "Blue Suede Shoes"? Well, it is the same band again.'

'Marian, I'm sorry, I have to go. I'll be in touch, all right? I'll let you know.'

He ate one half of the sandwich standing near the stove, the other sitting in the front room, listening to Frank Morgan play 'Mood Indigo', the wind curling the rain against the tall panes.

Norma sat up suddenly and opened her eyes. Rosa had been home to sort out the youngest of her own kids and then returned. They had eaten Birds Eye lasagne and chips and drunk two cans of Kestrel, got through the Lord knew how many cigarettes. Norma had slept. 'Nicky's dad!' she shouted, waking. 'Peter. How'm I ever going to get in touch with Nicky's dad?'

Sheena had an address, written on a sheet of torn paper, in pencil that was beginning to smudge and fade.

'How long've you had this? How long?'

'On my birthday,' Sheena said, 'when I was fourteen. It was tucked inside the card.'

Norma rubbed her eyes. Peterborough. 'No saying he's still there now, he could be anywhere.'

'You'll let him know, my dad?'

'Here,' Norma pushed the paper back towards her. 'You let him know. You're the one he give his address to.'

Hannah sat in the chair near the upstairs window, a sweater round her shoulders to foil the draughts. Curtains still open, she could see the rain silvering past the street lights outside, before it was lost against the blackness of the small park facing where she lived. The mug which had held her peppermint tea lay cold in her lap. She was reading a collection of new poems she'd picked up in Mushroom, the soundtrack for *The Piano* playing in the background.

> *As though a man is no more than fear and fire*
> *for a woman to feed and carry like a torch.*
> *As though a woman is no more than light at the*
> *end of a long and hard tunnel. As though my*
> *sweet life needs it. As though ache could be*
> *enough to smooth the edges of a desperate day.*

How different would her life be if she had married, had a child? The same issues, tugging at her beneath the tide of her life. She had her own house, a job – a good job, one most days she valued, and which she thought of as in some small way doing good. Her Visa bill was paid up at the end of each month, her mortgage was manageable, she went abroad three times a year, enjoyed the company of friends. If she saw a new book or CD she fancied she could buy it without too much thought. Aside from those children she taught, the only person she was feeding and caring for was herself.

Her choice.

Why, then, did she feel as empty as the china mug she cradled in her lap, as pale and cold?

Shane walked up to Peter Turvey in the main bar of Turvey's local and head-butted him in the face. 'You, you bastard! You fucking slime!' Blood was running down Turvey's forehead into his eyes, half-blinding him. 'You're paying for what you fucking did.' Shane brought his fist back level with his shoulder and punched Turvey in the face, breaking his nose. Shane's own shirt was ripe with blood and snot. 'Here!' As Turvey sank to the floor, Shane brought his knee up hard and broke his nose a second time. It had been Pete Turvey and his brothers who had hurled a fire bomb from their car into Nicky Snape's path, though it was never proved. Shane caught hold of Turvey's shirt and hauled him off the ground.

'For pity's sake,' called someone, 'leave the poor bastard be. You'll kill him, sure is that what you want?'

Shane let Turvey go and the back of his victim's head collided with the bar; then he walked ten feet away, swivelled back and kicked out at Turvey's chest, burying the toe of his boot in Turvey's gut.

'For Christ's sake,' came the same voice, 'call the law, why don't you?'

Shane slapped two pound coins on the table and ordered a pint of best.

He had it almost finished when the door spun open and Turvey's two brothers arrived. They had others with them:

Gorman, who toured around with the fairs, taking on all comers in the boxing tent; Frankie and Edgar Droy, and Carl Howard, who had served an extra eighteen months in Lincoln for assaulting one of the screws with a bucket, causing him to need twenty-one stitches in his head.

This was what Shane wanted, to be lost in this. They started on him there, inside the bar, beside Pete Turvey moaning over his twice-broken nose and broken ribs. They hauled him off into the urinal, Shane hardly even bothering to fight back now, almost unable to raise his hands. Finally, they dragged him out into the street and left his body slewed across the road, only the sound of police sirens saving Shane from more of a beating.

While a young uniformed officer talked to the landlord, who had seen nothing – maybe a little scuffle, nothing to write down in his little book – Shane was in an ambulance, heading for Queen's. More than an hour later he would be in the cubicle next to Pete Turvey, waiting for the same doctor to examine their injuries.

It was a bad sign, Resnick knew, when he played Monk last thing at night, the pianist's fractured attempts at melody obeying no logic but their own. A big man, as Resnick was big, Monk's fingers stabbed down at single notes, crushed chords into the beauty of an abstract painting, twisted scaffolding seen in a certain light.

Almost an hour ago, certain it would not be there, Resnick had checked through the phone book and found Hannah's number, written it, for want of somewhere else, in biro on the back of his hand. Now he stared at it from moment to moment, sitting near the phone. One of the cats jumped onto his lap and he shooed him off as

'Solitude' came to an end. He pointed the remote control and set it off again.

> As though a woman is no more than light at the
> end of a long and hard tunnel. As though my
> sweet life needs it.

Wetting his thumb, he rubbed the numbers from his skin.

While this was happening, Norma Snape lay in the dark of her room and when she slept she cried and then when she woke she cried some more.

17

Where had Bill Aston read that every pound you put on after age forty takes twice as much effort to get off? And eighteen months sitting behind that desk at Police Headquarters hadn't helped. Fortnightly game of golf aside, for too long the only exercise he had been getting was walking the pair of Jack Russells he and his wife Margaret had bought after their youngest son had left home. Which was why, on the second of January that year, he had instituted his daily swim. There were two pools close to where they lived, Rushcliffe and Portland, and Aston alternated between them pretty much at will. Some days he would stop off on the way to work and put in ten lengths; other times he would call in at home and pick up the dogs, have his swim and then walk them before returning for dinner.

'Should have got a real dog, Dad,' his eldest had said on a brief visit home. 'A labrador or a retriever, something with some size. Chase those two sorry specimens the length of the garden and they're worn out. Expect you to carry them back.'

But Aston was happy enough with his Jack Russells – they would sit in the back of the car if he went for a drive, the pair of them quite content – and as for Margaret . . . well, if Bill had thought they were going to be her new babies, he was wrong, but just as long as they didn't get under her feet . . .

He rustled his paper aside and peered in the direction of the kitchen clock: still time for one more cup of tea. He reached for the pot.

'Bill,' Margaret said, coming back into the room, 'are you sure you want to wear those shoes?'

Aston swung his leg round and glanced down. 'What's wrong with them?'

'I mean with that suit.'

Grey suede with dark blue, why not? 'Yes, love,' he said, 'they're fine.'

Margaret was dressed to go out herself, an early appointment at the hair salon on Trinity Square and then she was meeting her friend, Barbara, for coffee in Jessop's.

'No swim this morning?'

Aston shook his head. 'Evenings all week, I should think. While this lot goes on, anyway.'

Impulsively, she kissed him on the top of his head, behind the ear.

'What was that all about?' Aston asked. Unbidden displays of affection had not been Margaret's style for years, no more than they were his own.

Margaret smiled. 'I'm pleased for you, that's all. Putting you in charge of this enquiry. Something important again. Well, it's no more than you deserve.'

'Thanks, love,' Aston said drily, finding it difficult to respond. 'Right now, though, I'd best be off.'

'You will give me a lift in?'

'Yes, of course.' He swallowed down most of his tea

and tipped the remainder into the sink and started to run the tap.

'Leave that, Bill. Sally's here today, she'll do all of that.'

He looked at her, a dumpy woman with spectacles, wearing a green plaid suit and court shoes, and was surprised by the strength of the conflicting emotions that he felt.

A few minutes later, Margaret beside him, Aston was backing the Volvo out from the drive of the Thirties suburban house they had lived in now for nineteen years. Around him, on either side, neighbours' gardens glowed green from the previous night's rain.

'You remember Charlie Resnick?' Aston said. 'Seems he knew this Snape, the youth in the enquiry. I've got to meet up with him some night this week for a drink. Could well be back a bit late.'

Margaret remembered Resnick well enough, around the same height as her husband but broader – broader still now, most likely. It was years since she'd seen him. But he was a nice enough man, she thought, not foul-mouthed like some of them.

'You ought to invite him round, Bill. Supper. He might appreciate that.'

And he might not, Aston thought, but nodded anyway.

'We used to have people round for dinner all the time.'

Aston grunted. 'We used to do a lot of things.'

Margaret rested her hand on his knee and tried not to notice when he flinched.

Khan was waiting for Aston in reception. Five years in the force, at twenty-seven he had benefited from the aftershock of a well-publicised case in which two Asian officers

133

had taken the police authority to court for racially discriminating against their advancement. Khan had successfully completed his probation, spent his time in a Panda car and out on the beat; now he was in Central Division CID and confidently expecting to be made up to sergeant. The enquiry into Nicky Snape's death would broaden his experience. His tasks were to take notes, facilitate the timetable, keep on top of the documentation and stay alert to any nuances that his superior might miss – and to drive the car.

He greeted Aston with a sir, a handshake and a smile. Five minutes later they were making their way towards the Derby Road, slowed a little by the residue of rush-hour traffic. When they arrived, Derek Jardine greeted both men with brisk enthusiasm and ushered them into his office for coffee and a drab selection of biscuits. There were still twenty minutes before the case conference was due to start.

Phyllis Parmenter, heading up the three-strong team from the Social Services Inspectorate, was already present, balancing cup and saucer on one hand and chatting to the local authority solicitor. Jardine introduced her to Aston and stepped away. Khan snagged the remaining stale bourbon biscuit and examined the photographs on the director's wall.

The conference room had been set out with pads of lined local authority paper, black Bics and sharpened pencils, water glasses, ashtrays and copies of the agenda. The first item was to establish the methods by which the joint investigation should proceed. If we get that far by coffee time, Khan thought, glancing round the table, I shall be well surprised.

134

And he was: they would consider the pathologist's report and then begin interviewing the staff, starting with Paul Matthews and Elizabeth Peck, both of whom had been on duty the night Nicky died, and finishing with Jardine himself. The youth who had shared a room with Nicky would be brought in, along with another of the lads Nicky had apparently befriended. If either the police or social services teams found a need to re-interview separately, that was their prerogative. It was agreed that it was desirable, if possible, for a joint statement to be issued when the enquiry came to an end.

'One point I think I should like to make clear,' Phyllis Parmenter said, 'our aim here is to ascertain all that we can about the circumstances of Nicky Snape's death. It may be, and I have no wish to prejudice the enquiry by saying this, that we discover there are certain procedures which would benefit from overhaul or change. If so, I'm sure we would all agree this can only be beneficial. But what we are not concerned with primarily here is blame; in these sad and unfortunate circumstances, we are not, I think and hope, looking for scapegoats.'

Especially, Khan thought, if they're to be found amongst local authority staff. He edged a sideways look at Aston, who was nodding in thoughtful agreement.

Resnick had tapped Millington on the shoulder as they passed the small café near the fire station and, with a grin, the sergeant had performed a circuit of the roundabout and parked. Resnick had had a lousy night: broken sleep and nightmarish dreams. Finally, at something short of four, he had barefooted downstairs; thirty minutes later he was sitting with rye toast and coffee, Bud and Pepper vying for the prime place in his lap, while he tried to concentrate on a biography of Lester Young. To complicate matters he was listening, not to Prez, but to Monk. *Alone in San Francisco*. Between the notes, the sentences, he was wondering about Norma Snape, alone but not alone in Radford; about his ex-wife, Elaine, hoping that she was not alone anywhere. And Hannah: he was thinking about Hannah. The seriousness that turned down the corners of her eyes when she talked; the way that same seriousness would break suddenly into a smile.

'What's it to be?' Millington asked, as Resnick slumped into a seat near the window.

His face brightened. 'Oh, a bacon sandwich, don't you think, Graham?'

'Is that with the egg or without?'

'Without. But a sausage wouldn't go amiss.'

'Tea?'

'Tea.' The coffee here still had to catch up with the post-powder age.

They ate in near silence, Resnick enjoying the salt, slightly fish-like taste of the smoked bacon, not enquiring too deeply about the occasional gristly blob that the sausage vouchsafed. Later, as Millington relaxed with a Lambert and Butler, Resnick asked about Madeleine's latest forays into amateur dramatics and adult education and received a lecture about the perils of living with a wife who is simultaneously reading Karen Horney and Kate Millett for her course on 'Feminism for Beginners' and rehearsing the part of a frustrated middle-aged wife in an Alan Ayckbourn farce.

'Bit difficult for her, that, Graham. The play, I mean. Well outside her experience, I should reckon.'

Millington drew in smoke and examined Resnick keenly; if that was meant as some kind of joke, he couldn't see the humour. Of late, Millington had taken to eyeing the kitchen knives with suspicion.

Resnick, however, solid food inside him, was beginning to feel better. The day might be salvaged after all. 'All right, Graham,' he said, scraping back his chair. 'Let's not waste any more time.'

Once inside Queen's, they checked on Doris Netherfield, who was still making cautious progress and treated them to a pale smile. Her husband was making slow but significant progress at home. Shane Snape was propped irritably between pillows, fiddling with the headset of his radio. One side of his face showed some deep bruising and a neat line of stitches butterflied its way from behind one ear onto his neck, but those injuries apart he had got off surprisingly lightly. Nothing broken. Another day and he would be discharged.

'Morning, Shane,' Millington said breezily. 'Run into a spot of bother?'

He and Resnick took seats at either side of the bed.

'I've got nothing to say,' said Shane.

'The people who did this,' Resnick said, 'you're not in a position to identify who they were?'

Shane shook his head.

'And the name Turvey,' Millington offered, 'that doesn't ring any bells?'

Shane shook his head again.

'Coincidence, then, Peter Turvey sustaining all those injuries the same time as yourself? Same place?'

'Must've been.'

137

'There's no chance, then,' Resnick said, 'that you'll be making a complaint, pressing charges, anything like that?'

'None.'

'Fine.' Resnick started out of his seat. 'All right, Graham, we might as well go.'

Shane looked surprised they were letting him off so lightly, had just begun to relax back against the pillows when Resnick swivelled on his heels faster than a man of his size might be expected to, something like a dancer. From nowhere he was leaning over the bed, his right hand gripping Shane's shoulder where it was bruised and swollen, finger ends not so far from where the line of stitches finished.

'Understand me. I don't give a toss how you spend your evenings, what flotsam you hang around with, but I do care about your mother. She's had a hard enough time as it is, bringing up the three of you, and now after what's happened to Nicky, you're the last thing she should have to worry about.' Resnick increased the pressure with his hand, enough to force tears to the edges of Shane's eyes no matter how much he fought to deny them. 'So stay out of trouble, right? Or I'll come down on you so fast you'll wish you'd paid attention.' Resnick relinquished his grip and stood tall. 'Okay, Shane. Think you can learn something here?'

Shane stared back at him, humiliated, angry, a single tear making a slow track down his face.

Whistling 'Winchester Cathedral' while they waited for the lift, Millington was still surprised by the force of Resnick's anger.

Sheena had not clocked in at the factory since Nicky had

died. The first day, the Monday, she had phoned in and explained; the second day she had said her mother still needed looking after. Her supervisor had been understanding, had told her to take whatever sick leave she was entitled to and suggested that she make an appointment to see her GP on her own account, have him prescribe a tranquilliser, Valium, that new stuff even – what was it? – Prozac, that's the one.

This morning Sheena had said nothing to her mum, had left home with her uniform ironed and folded in a plastic bag from Tesco, wandered without direction until she ended up in the Old Market Square, watching the gang of youths that sprawled extravagantly on the worn grass near the public lavatories, drinking Strongbow cider and shouting at any passer-by who wore a suit. They were the usual sprinkling of latter-day punks and goths, lads with pink mohicans or hair spiked out around their heads in blue-tipped stars, chains that hung from the pockets and lapels of torn leather jackets, ripped jeans, smaller chains dangling from their ears and the corners of their mouths. Tattoos. Girls younger than Sheena in tight T-shirts and skinny, black-legged jeans, rings through their ears and noses, mouths darkened into little black beaks.

Sheena sat a safe distance away on the low stone wall, wrists trapped between her knees. No way she was about to go near them. The clock above the Council House sounded the quarter-hour.

'Here.'

She turned with a start, almost losing her balance. Janie Cornwall was close behind her, usual superior expression on her face, an open packet of Embassy in her hand.

'Go on, have one.'

139

Sheena blinked up at Janie, her hard young face framed by frizzed-out hair. At the other side of the street, outside Debenham's, Janie's friends stood watching. Lesley Dawson, Irena, Tracey Daniels, Dee-Dee, Diane. Janie shook the packet again and with a breathed 'thank you' Sheena took one and angled back her head as Janie, leaning forward, lit it for her.

Sheena drew in smoke and held it down inside.

After a quick glance back towards her pals, Janie lit a cigarette for herself and sat down. 'Your brother, we're cut up, like, about what happened.'

'Thanks.'

'You must be feeling like shit.'

'Yeh. Yes, I am.'

Janie had been in Sheena's year right through school, they all had, Lesley, Dee-Dee and the rest. Girls whose breasts were obvious sooner, whose periods had started earlier, who were forever bringing scratty little notes to excuse them from games. They would smoke openly on the way to school and light up again the minute they had set foot on the Boulevard. They were the ones who boasted they had done it at thirteen, gone all the way, and Sheena had believed them, jealous, frightened, in awe. When, after school, Janie and the rest had huddled amongst the cars parked on the Forest, laughing with boys who were as old as Shane and older, Sheena had loitered close enough for them to call her over but they never had. Now this. Nicky's death had given her notoriety at second hand, made her acceptable where she had not been before.

One of the girls called out to Janie, who turned her head and gestured for them to go on ahead. 'We're going up Diane's,' she said to Sheena. 'Why'n't you come?'

At the far side of the square, Janie took Sheena's Tesco bag from her and dropped it, uniform and all, into a green council bin.

Diane and Dee-Dee were black. Except for those times when they had briefly fallen out, they told everyone they were sisters, even went out dressed in the same clothes, though it wasn't true. Their families never spoke to one another and would cross the street to avoid contact. Dee-Dee's father was a minister in the Pentecostal church and Diane's was doing fifteen years in Lincoln for shooting another drug dealer in the face at close range. When she fell pregnant just eighteen days short of her fifteenth birthday, Dee-Dee's father prayed for her while her mother took her to the clinic to arrange for an abortion. As soon as Diane heard, she went out and got herself knocked up by a friend of her brother's and miscarried after eight weeks. The next time she was more fortunate. The baby was called Melvin and Diane's elder sister looked after him until Diane had finished school, at which point Diane and the baby's father were given temporary accommodation in a high-rise the council were planning to demolish. The father had left but the flats were still standing.

'Fucking lift!' Diane screamed, kicking at the graffitied doors. 'Never fucking working!'

Diane's neighbour had been looking after Melvin and Diane collected him to show him off to Sheena.

'Gorgeous, i'n't he? I'n't he fuckin' gorgeous?'

Tightly curled black hair, coffee skin, wide brown eyes, Sheena had to admit that he was.

The girls all bundled into Diane's living-room to play

with Melvin and watch TV, pass round the bottle of vodka that Irena had lifted from the corner shop. Seated on the floor by the settee, Lesley carefully rolled a couple of spliffs. An hour or so later, when Janie tipped some pills into Sheena's hand, she didn't think twice, popped them into her mouth and swallowed what was almost the last of the vodka to wash them down.

Peter was waiting when Norma got home from visiting Shane at the hospital, sitting on the uneven paving stones where days before Nicky's flowers had huddled haphazardly against each other. He was leaning back against the wall when Norma saw him, a hand-rolled cigarette between his fingers, his feet bare, shoes neatly placed alongside him, socks rolled into a ball. Something lurched through Norma like a fist and she thought she was going to be sick.

Peter spotted her and stared, then pushed himself slowly to his feet. My God, Norma thought, how he's changed. Most of the hair had gone from his head and what remained was flat against his scalp and dark. His face had never been full, but now the skin seemed to be stretched too tight across his forehead and both cheeks had sunken in. Inside a striped shirt, his chest appeared to have collapsed inwards, though a little pot belly strained awkwardly against the top of his trousers. How long was it since she had seen him? Twelve years? More? She had never imagined he could look so old. He could not have been more than forty-five.

Norma could no more stop the tears than she could stop time.

Peter tossed the nub end of the roll-up towards the kerb and took her in his arms.

'Come away, you great geck! Let's get inside else we'll have neighbours goin' round with a hat.'

In the kitchen she made him tea and toast while he told her how he had hitched three lifts from Peterborough to get there, the last a laundry van on its way in from the RAF base outside Grantham. He asked Norma how she'd been keeping, told her how good she looked in that blue-and-orange dress. Had she lost a bit of weight? Well, it suited her, there was no denying that. He asked her about Sheena and Norma told him she was at work; asked about Shane and looked concerned when she told him about the beating he had received. It was not till Norma had mashed a second pot that he asked about Nicky.

Without crying this time, clear-eyed, Norma told him what she knew.

Peter was silent for a long time and then asked if the inquest had been opened and adjourned.

Norma nodded and Peter, one-handed, rolled another cigarette. 'If you like,' he said, not looking at her, looking at the pile of crockery heaped alongside the sink, 'I could stay for a while. A few days at least. I'd not be in the way.'

Norma didn't reply. She didn't know what Shane, when he got out of hospital, might think. Nor Sheena either for that matter – he was her father, she should be pleased, but after all this time who could tell?

'Just till the funeral, eh? That was what I thought.'

'All right,' Norma said. 'All right.'

He reached a hand to touch her but she pulled away.

At six thirty that evening, Bill Aston plunged into the Portland pool and swam the first of twenty slow, deliberate lengths. After showering and drying himself down, he drove the short distance to the Victoria Embankment and walked the Jack Russells along the north bank of the Trent. All things considered it had not been too bad a day.

Khan's girl-friend was seven years his senior. Light-skinned, lithe-limbed and blonde, Jill was a divorced woman with three kids who were spending the night at her sister's. She had trained as a dancer, worked as a model; now she was a part-time receptionist at Central Television and did a dance class four afternoons a week. Khan liked to imagine he could still smell the sweat on her body.

'What was he like then?' Jill asked. 'This bloke Aston you're working with?'

'After he'd got over the colour of my skin, d'you mean?'

She reached out to stroke his chest. 'What's wrong with your skin? It's beautiful.'

'Yes, well.' Khan grinned. 'You'd not expect Bill Aston to feel the same way about it as you now, would you?'

'Oh, I don't know.' Jill laughed.

'Not him. I doubt he's got the imagination.'

Jill raised her legs and slid her bottom a little further down the bed. 'What's he doing in charge of the enquiry into this kid's death then?'

But by then Khan was in no position to answer.

18

'Old-fashioned Love.' The opening growl from Vic Dickenson's trombone sounds like the fanfare from a fairground barker, but once piano and bass have settled into their gentle stride, he nudges the melody along respectfully enough, just the odd hint of jauntiness to keep sentimentality at bay; then, rolling out from the lower register with that tart huskiness that marks his playing, Edmund Hall takes the tune through a second chorus before the clipped notes of Ruby Braff's trumpet start to lengthen and unwind. Which is as far as Resnick gets, because now the phone is ringing and he reaches awkwardly towards it, fiddling the remote onto pause and then dropping it into his lap where an aggrieved cat wakes with a start and jumps to the floor, one paw tipping the saucer that holds a half-finished cup of coffee growing cold.

'Hello?'

'Charlie. Thought you weren't there.'

Friday night, Resnick thought, where else would I be?

'Wondered how you were placed for this drink we mentioned?'

Resnick angled his wrist around to look at his watch: twenty-five to nine. 'You'll be wanting me to trek out there, I suppose?' He wondered why it had always been difficult to take them seriously, the suburbs south of the Trent.

'No need, I'm in the city. Just tidying up a bit of paperwork.' Aston paused. 'The Partridge, that's your watering hole, isn't it?'

'As good as any.'

'Nine o'clock, then?'

'Best make it quarter past.'

'All right, Charlie. See you there.'

Resnick retrieved his cup and rose to his feet, releasing the pause into the beginning of Sir Charles Thompson's piano solo. Bud's head nudged repeatedly against the backs of his legs as he stood there listening, the cat urging him to sit down so that he could jump onto his lap. Only after the second trumpet solo and Dickenson's closing trombone coda, lazy but exact, did Resnick open the tray and drop the CD back in its case, switch off the stereo, carry cup and saucer into the kitchen to rinse, open the fridge on a well-honed impulse and lift out a slice of ham, wrap it around the last half-inch of Emmenthal cheese, something to nibble while he put on his coat and hesitated in a doorway, patting his pockets for his wallet, money, keys.

For whatever reason, the Partridge failed to attract the Friday night gangs of youths who marauded through the city centre, clad, whatever the weather, in shirt-sleeves or the shortest of skirts, growing noisier and noisier as they moved from pub to pub, more and more obscene. Even so, it was crowded enough for Resnick and Bill

Aston to take refuge in the deep V of the public bar, opposite the door to the Gents.

'Sure that's all you want, Charlie? Not fancy a chaser?'

Resnick glanced at the bottle of Czech Budweiser and shook his head.

'Drop of Scotch, no?'

'Thanks, Bill, I'm fine.'

Aston himself was sitting with a half-pint of mild which Resnick knew from experience he would nurse through the coming half-hour, or however long the conversation took.

Not wanting to shout it out for all and sundry, needing to be heard above the rise and fall of Friday night conversations, Resnick hunched his shoulders forward and leaned in. Aston listened attentively, a nod here and there, while Resnick filled him in on the Snape family background, a relationship that had begun for Resnick when, as detective sergeant, he had questioned Shane about the provenance of two dozen video cassettes that had been in the youth's sports bag when a uniformed officer had stopped him at past two in the morning, crossing Radford Boulevard. Nicky had first come to Resnick's official attention at the age of eleven, when he was caught climbing through the skylight of a neighbour's house. At Norma Snape's request, Resnick had given the boy a royal rollocking; enough to put the fear of God into him, that was how Norma had described it, though it could only be said to have worked in that, as far as anyone knew, Nicky had never since that day set foot inside a church. Other people's houses, that had been a different matter.

'Poor little bastard,' Aston said feelingly. 'Growing up like that, never stood a chance.'

147

Resnick leaned back and lifted his glass. 'She did her best.'

Aston shook his head. 'Never going to be good enough, though, is it, Charlie?' And Resnick drank his beer steadily, while Aston delivered his sermon on the breakdown of the social fabric and the lost virtues of the two-parent family. When it was over, he excused himself and went first to the Gents and then to the bar.

'The enquiry, Bill,' Resnick asked, emptying the second bottle into his glass. 'How's it all going?'

'Oh, shouldn't take long to wrap it up, I'd say. Seems all pretty much above board.'

Resnick regarded him sceptically. 'No funny business, you think? Nothing untoward?'

'No, Charlie, not so far as I can see. Oh, supervision might've been a mite lax the night he died. But if it's reasons you're looking for – ill-treatment, bullying . . .' Aston gave a quick shake of the head. 'Doesn't seem to have been the case.'

'No clear reason, then? For him to do what he did.'

'Not mind readers, Charlie. Not as if he left a note, nothing like that. The other lads, those that knew him, the youth in his room, all swear he never said a word about what he meant to do. Moaned on a bit, like; complained. But then that's just par for the course.' Aston finally supped the last of his mild, froth sliding back down the glass. 'Couldn't face up to being put away. If you ask me, that's what it was. He just couldn't face the thought of going to prison, poor little sod. Terrified. Just a kid, you see. Missed his mam.'

Resnick waited until a sudden splurge of laughter from

148

the table alongside had died down. 'Social services see it the same way?'

Aston nodded. 'Pretty much. Right down the line.'

I bet they do, Resnick thought, stains enough on their copy-book already. He was on his feet, half his beer still untouched. 'At least there's nothing to prevent the body being released. His mother'll be pleased.' He held out his hand. 'Take care, Bill. And give Margaret my best.'

Out on the street, Resnick crossed in the direction of what had once been Bobby Brown's Café and was now another boarded-up testament to free enterprise and the price you eventually had to pay. He thought about picking up a cab from outside the Victoria Stakis, but decided he would walk instead. If Aston had found nothing suspicious then maybe there was nothing to find. Why then did Resnick find that so difficult to believe?

By the time he had reached the Sikh temple he was starting to feel vaguely peckish and began inventorying the contents of his refrigerator; he thought there might be enough left for a decent sandwich before turning in. He could sit up a while longer and listen to those Vic Dickenson sides again: 'Runnin' Wild', 'Keeping Out of Mischief Now'.

'Here, take another one of these prawns while they're still going.'

'No, it's okay . . .'

'Go on. I've had more than my share already.'

'All right, then. Thanks.'

Lynn had two attempts at lifting the king prawn from its chili sauce, before setting down her chopsticks and resorting to a fork.

'Good, aren't they?'

'Great.' Actually, they were too spicy for Lynn's taste, but she wasn't about to say. It had been Sharon's idea, the pair of them having a night out together, and the choice of the restaurant had been Sharon's too. They had met earlier and had a couple of glasses of white wine in one of the wine bars near Lynn's flat in the Lace Market, moving on when the place had begun to get really crowded and the offers of drinks from predatory males had been more than they could shrug off or gracefully turn down.

In the end, Sharon had rounded on one of the more persistent – a good few years younger than herself and certainly no taller – caught hold of him by the lapels of his mid-blue, beautifully tailored Kenzo suit and told him that if he wanted to get sorted in front of his mates by a woman who taught a class in self-defence and close combat, he should just carry on as he was. She could tell from his wilting body language which option he was going to choose. Sharon straightened him out, brushed him down and gave him a quick peck on the cheek; the man blushed deep red and retreated into the huddle of his friends.

'Don't you hate all that?' Lynn asked, once Sharon had perched back on her stool.

'Want to know the truth?' Sharon grinned. 'Actually I enjoy it.'

Now they were at a window table in Ocean City, looking out at four lanes of traffic heading north up Derby Road. They were still attracting more than their fair share of sidelong looks – two youngish women eating alone – one black, one white, and Sharon in a long, loose denim skirt, a denim shirt over a soft grey fitted top, was the focus for most of them. If in some respects that left Lynn relieved, in others it didn't help at all. Just about the last thing you needed, self-image at the low ebb, was playing second fiddle to someone who was not only sure of herself, but looked great into the bargain. And was nice with it.

Lynn could imagine their laughing conversation back in the wine bar, those blokes who'd fancied themselves in with a chance. 'Mine's okay, pal, but I wouldn't go near yours on a dark night with a stick.'

'Here,' Sharon said, tipping the bottle of Australian Chardonnay over Lynn's glass. 'You might as well finish this off, too.'

Lynn laughed. 'I shall be pissed.'

'Not working tomorrow, are you?'

'No, thank God. Nor Sunday, neither. Not unless anything major crops up.'

Sharon raised her glass. 'Lucky you. We're top-handed tomorrow night. Boss wants a bit of a crackdown. Scare the balls off the kerb crawlers, promise to print their names in the paper, send letters home to their wives. Haul in the girls and keep them overnight, pack them off bright and early with a two-hundred-quid fine. All that does, send them back on the streets to earn some more.' With a flourish, she finished her wine. 'Sometimes I think the magistrates do more to keep the trade going than the pimps.'

Lynn nodded and popped the last piece of oyster mushroom into her mouth.

'Right,' Sharon said, looking round for a waiter. 'A couple of banana fritters, coffee, and they can phone a cab for us. Drop you off on the way to mine.' She winked. 'All tucked up before midnight, eh, safe and sound.'

Curtains drawn, only a table lamp at the far side of the room burned its subdued light. Through the speakers, the sound of Steve Jordan's guitar chording evenly above the rhythmic swish of Jo Jones's brushes, while in the easy chair, the smallest of the cats nestling his head beneath his chin, Resnick slept, his breathing a soft counterpoint to the sounds of Sir Charles Thompson, gentling his piano through the tune of 'Russian Lullaby'.

19

While Resnick had slept a house across the city had been torched and now stood gutted, the third instance of serious arson on the Bestwood Estate that month. The incident had taken place at two in the morning, four kids under the age of fourteen asleep upstairs, the youngest of them only escaping serious burns when his mother dropped him from the bedroom window into the arms of neighbours below. Certain in their own minds who had caused the fire, other members of the family had been intercepted on their way across the estate by hastily summoned police. A sawn-off shotgun and a pistol had been found beneath the rear seat of the car they had been driving.

As an excited local radio reporter informed Resnick that morning, an emergency meeting had been called at which the city housing chief and other officials would discuss with police additional ways of constraining an estate which was seemingly in the grip of mob rule. Resnick sighed as he buttered toast. He knew that extra officers had already been drafted in and that during the past few weeks alone there had been around fifty arrests; he also knew that most of those arrested would by now have been released on bail.

Interviewed by the reporter, the city council leader said they were preparing to take legal action against the eight families who were at the heart of the trouble. 'We have no qualms about evicting,' he said. 'The trouble is that we need witnesses – and witnesses can be intimidated.'

Resnick remembered his team going round Radford, door to door, trying to uncover information about the incident in which Nicky Snape had been petrol-bombed. After days of intensive questioning, it had proved impossible to persuade anyone who knew anything to make a statement. If Nicky could be put into hospital, so could they.

The result was a stubborn silence: distrust of the police; fear of reprisals.

Resnick opted for raspberry jam. While the other cats weren't looking, he forked the last of the Whiskas into Bud's bowl before throwing the can away. There was a note from Marian Witczak with the mail, reminding him in her ornate, slightly gothic hand, of the Polish Club dance that evening. Before his second cup of coffee, Resnick phoned the station and got a jubilant-sounding Kevin Naylor, the third of whose nights on observation with Reg Cossall had resulted in five arrests for drugs offences, and three additional charges of passing counterfeit money and attempting to defraud the post office. Resnick could imagine Cossall's obscene expressions of delight.

'Well done,' he said to Naylor. 'Good work. Now get off home and get some sleep. I'll not want you propping your eyes open when you're back on duty.'

Resnick had only that second put the phone down when it rang again. Instantly he recognised Millington's somewhat nasal, bemused tone. In the background he could hear somebody practising scales; after her triumph in the title role of *The Merry Widow*, Madeleine was preparing herself for the amateur operatic season once again.

'Morning, Graham. What can I do for you?'

'I was just wondering,' Millington said. 'You've not heard anything about upping staffing levels? Ours, I mean.'

Resnick hadn't heard a thing.

'Just I caught a whisper things were lightening up; few new bodies transferring in. Thought Jack Skelton might've mentioned something. Only, if it's a case of staking a claim, well, that team of ours has been overstretched for more time'n I care to remember.'

What his sergeant was preferring not to recall was the murder of Dipak Patel, several years before, stabbed in the street when he intervened in a street brawl, his attacker never identified, never apprehended.

'This whisper, Graham, you wouldn't like to be more specific as to the source, I suppose?'

'Rather not, boss.'

Just so, thought Resnick, nobody likes to get caught talking out of turn. 'Okay, Graham, thanks for the tip. I'll give Skelton a ring now, see if there's anything can be done.'

'Right,' said Millington, and then, barely disguising the smirk, 'Off to the match this afternoon, I dare say? Another bit of history in the making.'

Resnick lowered the receiver onto Millington's laugh. After a season in which the club had hired and fired almost as many managers as their strikers had managed goals, today's game was County's last mathematical

155

chance of avoiding relegation. Resnick didn't like to think about it.

He dialled the superintendent's number and was greeted by Alice Skelton's shrewish voice, each syllable like lemon rind squeezed through a grater. 'Jack at home on Saturday morning, Charlie? Be reasonable. Why remain in the bosom of his family when there are stupid little golf balls to be hit about? Or in Jack's case, more like skewed into a bunker.'

'Thank you, Alice,' Resnick said pleasantly, 'perhaps you'll tell him I called.'

He poured his second cup of coffee and drank it black, while reading the Review section of the previous day's *Guardian*; not a natural choice of newspaper for Resnick – hardly the police officer's friend – but recently they'd started a jazz CD review that was half-way decent. Dizzy Gillespie leading a big band that included Clark Terry, now that did sound interesting.

After telling himself he wasn't going to go near the County ground, Resnick turned up with five minutes to spare and found a seat on the same side he had stood in previous seasons, Saturday after alternate Saturday, surrounded by the same loose group of moaners and celebrants with whom he had shared the dubious delights of being a Notts supporter. But now government edicts had been followed and the old place was transformed into a smart all-seater stadium, the price of admission had just about doubled, most of Resnick's friends had drifted away, and after finding all that money for improvements, the club had failed to find a similar amount to improve the team.

On this particular Saturday there seemed to be at least

two players in home team shirts – minimum wage recruits from a youth training scheme, most likely – that Resnick was at odds to recognise and, from the way they began playing, the rest of the side were none the wiser.

Trying to defend their goal, two County defenders collided with each other, jumping for the same ball. For Resnick it was the last straw. Fifteen minutes before the end, head bowed, he turned and headed for the exit, shoulder to shoulder with all those other supporters who had opted to do the same.

After that he knew a night in his own company was not a good idea: he considered phoning Hannah on the off-chance she wasn't already going out, and if that were so she might consider going out with him. But by the time he had reached the main road, he had dismissed the idea from his head. Against all of his previous inclinations, he would go to the Polish Club instead.

He had bought the light-grey suit six years ago or more and in so far as he had a favourite, this was it; there was only one small stain that he could find, a dark patch near the lapel which mostly came away when he scraped at it with a fingernail. He ironed a pale-blue shirt and knotted his dark-blue tie with more than usual care. The bar in the Polish Club divided the large room into two unequal halves, and in the larger of these, the one with a small stage for the band, he found Marian seated at the bar.

'Charles! You are here! Come, come, come over and join us. Oh, you don't know how good it is to see you.' As Marian squeezed his hand and enthusiastically kissed both of his cheeks, Resnick thought he was beginning to get the idea.

157

Wearing a black dress with a discreet white bow, a single strand of pearls at her neck, she was surrounded by several of those married men in late middle age whose fortnightly frisson came from flirting with her out of earshot of their wives. Her hair had been pushed up high on her head and was held in place with a silver barrette; silver earrings accentuated the slenderness of her neck. She was an elegant woman, some would say beautiful; some of those standing by her, Resnick assumed, frequently did. They had stepped back reluctantly to let him through and now continued to stand there, grudgingly, while Marian plied Resnick with questions, offered to buy him the vodka of his choice, smiled into his eyes. Ten minutes more and they had slunk away, back to their wives.

'You're looking happy, Marian.'

'Not beautiful?'

'Of course.'

'Desirable?' She was laughing at him with her eyes.

Why was it, Resnick wondered, and not for the first time, that in all the years he had known her – since, almost, they had been children – he had never entertained about her one sexual thought? Was it that, along with her beauty, she wore her Polishness so obviously on her sleeve? That to think of her as a partner – any kind of serious partner – would be to step back into a life that he had all but rejected. His parents' life, a life in exile. Strangers in a strange land.

He looked around the room at the women in their flared dresses, the men, some of them, in bow ties, the children who skittered between the tables got up like miniature editions of their elders; out on the dance floor, two couples essaying a waltz to the accordion-led band; photographs of fallen generals on the walls.

'Charles, what are you thinking?'

Resnick smiled. 'Oh nothing important.'

'Some dreadful crime?'

He shook his head. 'Marian, I promise you it wasn't that.'

For a moment she rested her hand on his arm. 'You know, Charles, one of the things that would make me most happy? If one evening, like this evening, you would walk in here with a beautiful woman on your arm, someone with whom you are in love.'

Despite himself, Resnick laughed. 'Marian, you're just a dreamer.'

'Oh.' She brought her face close. 'And you are not?'

'I think,' Resnick said, finishing his vodka and turning towards the band, 'it might almost be time for us to have that dance.'

Waltz over, the elderly couples moved slowly back towards their seats, the accordionist tested his fingers with an exploratory flourish and announced the first polka of the evening. Marian slipped out of her high heels into a pair of flat shoes she had brought expressly for the purpose, and took Resnick's arm as they stepped onto the floor.

Forty minutes later, with only two brief intervals, they were still there, perspiring lightly, Resnick's tie loose at his neck, top button of his shirt unfastened.

'You see.' Marian laughed, colliding with his chest as the number came to an unruly end. 'You see what fun you are having? And why you should come here more often?'

Resnick dabbed at his temples and looked longingly towards the bar. 'I think I need a drink.'

She caught at his hands. 'In a little while.' Mischief danced in her eyes. 'I had a talk with my friend the bandleader earlier. I think I know what they are going to play now.'

When Carl Perkins wrote it, it's doubtful if he ever imagined it sounding exactly this way, but Polish rock'n'roll was what it was, 'Blue Suede Shoes' what it is. One of the things Resnick had learned from his uncle, the tailor who had been to America and returned with a love of jazz and the jitterbug, was how to jive; who Marian had learned it from, Resnick had never known. But together, Resnick's unbuttoned jacket performing a dance of its own, while not sensational they were pretty good.

'Roll Over Beethoven.'

'Tutti Frutti.'

'Little Queenie.'

Resnick missed his footing, failed to catch Marian's outstretched hand and came close to trampling a small child underfoot. It was enough. And this time he would brook no argument.

They walked around into the second bar and found two seats; while Marian went to refresh herself in the Ladies, Resnick chatted with the waistcoated barman and came away with two cold beers. I wonder, he thought, whether Hannah can dance like that? Oh, Charles, and you are not a dreamer? He should never have let her into his mind. When Marian returned, he excused himself and went outside to the phone. He had no real expectation that she would be in, but she picked up on the third ring.

'Hello?'

'Hannah?'

'Yes.'

A slight pause, and then, 'I didn't think you'd be there.'

'Who is this?'

When he told her there was a small silence before she said, 'And was that why you phoned, because you thought I wouldn't be here?'

'No.'

He could hear music, faint and distant, something she was listening to, guitars. 'Is it too late,' he asked, 'for you to meet me for a drink?'

20

Hannah had gone to the smaller of the two Broadway cinemas that afternoon and seen a Tunisian film, *The Silences of the Palace*; herself and perhaps half a dozen others watching a woman returning from exile to a newly independent country and slowly coming to terms with the demands of present and past. The woman, a singer, amongst other women for whom silence was the only option. Hannah had sat at the end of one row, close against the wall, trying not to fight against the deliberately slow passing of time, fighting her prejudice against the harsh sounds of Arabic. Gradually, the film had won her over, so that, by the end, she was immersed in its rhythm, and when she left, the voices and the movement in the cafébar next door seemed relentless and loud. She resented the traffic and the crowds out on the streets. Crossing the end of Clumber Street towards the Old Market Square, she thought she spotted Sheena Snape amongst a group of half a dozen or so girls, noisily blocking the pavement outside the bank.

There were young men in the square wearing football shirts with black and white stripes, threatening to push one another into the fountain. Hannah manoeuvred around them and walked up St James Street and past the Tales of Robin Hood, heading uphill towards Lenton, where she lived in a terraced Victorian house overlooking a swathe of grass and a children's playground, a church and a crown bowling green.

The light was blinking twice on her answerphone.

There were people, she supposed, who could take off their coat, change their shoes, put on the kettle, empty the rubbish, do any number of other things before pressing the button marked 'play'. She was not one of them.

The first voice was her father's, calling from the French village to which he had moved three years before. Now his time was taken up in restoring a crumbling barn with the woman for whom he had left Hannah's mother, an architectural student and would-be writer almost ten years younger than Hannah herself.

'She'll leave you, Dad,' Hannah had said, out there to visit last year, the pair of them sitting in the shade while Alexa busied herself inside. 'You know that, don't you?'

He had taken both Hannah's hands in his and kissed the bridge of her nose. 'Of course she will. In time.' He winked. 'Just so long as we get this place finished first, eh? Then at least she'll leave me with a roof over my head to be miserable under.'

On the tape, his voice was robust, happy; happier than she could ever remember him seeming in that commuter town in Kent, in every day on the seven twenty-three, home on the six fifty-four.

Hannah thought the second caller might be her mother, the family symmetry perfect, but it was Joanne, a colleague from work; she had a doubles court booked at the tennis centre at ten tomorrow morning and someone had

163

dropped out, did Hannah want to take their place? Hannah thought that she might; she dialled Joanne's number, but the line was engaged.

She would try later. Now she made the tea and drank it with a slice of coffee-and-almond cake and that day's *Independent*. There was a frozen lasagne she could pop into the microwave, the makings of a salad, two piles of folders on the table waiting to be marked. She had treated herself to the new Marge Piercy and it sat, fat and white, on the arm of her chair in the window, asking to be read. *The Longings of Women*. Ah, yes, Hannah thought, we all know about those.

She was just pouring herself a glass of wine when the phone called her into the other room; certain it would be Joanne, checking about the tennis, she was ill-prepared for her mother's brittle cheeriness, wanting Hannah's advice about holidays – walking in Crete or painting water-colours at Flatford Mill? Hannah understood it was her mother's way of saying, see how well I'm surviving, being positive, still turning your father's desertion into an oasis of opportunity. Go to Crete, Hannah wanted to say, you're more likely to meet a man. Some swarthy shepherd who will adore your trim, well-articulated body and white skin. As if that were all she – her mother – any of them – needed. *The Longings of Women* indeed!

Fifteen minutes later, not unkindly, Hannah told her mother there was marking she had to finish, replaced the receiver and took wine and book upstairs to the bay-windowed room which she used as her study and which looked out over the park. She had arranged a wicker armchair stuffed with cushions close against the window

164

and, curtains open, she liked to sit there in the evenings, reading, glancing out at intervals to watch the light fading through the tops of the trees.

Her father had met Alexa in the same year that she had starting living with Jim, her second attempt at a stable relationship and, she had been certain, the one which would succeed. Jim's predecessor, Andrew, had been a volatile Irishman she had met when he was on a sabbatical from Queen's College, Belfast: a robust, round-faced scholar who wrote long, earnest – and, Hannah now realised, extremely bad – poems about the blackness of peat and the saving grace of the pudendum. Andrew, who on a good day could put an entire bottle of Jameson's away without blinking, and whose idea of good sex was to push her up against a convenient table and hoist her skirt up around her neck. On the first couple of occasions, though she thought it was politically incorrect to admit it, Hannah had found this distinctly exciting; after that, it had been a case of diminishing returns until all she associated Andrew's love-making with were sore thighs and bruised hips.

Jim was different: a peripatetic music teacher whom she had first encountered schooling a nervous thirteen-year-old in national health glasses through the first movement of the Mozart clarinet concerto. Jim had taken Hannah's musical education in hand, too, had got her to realise there was more to Benjamin Britten than his love affair with Peter Pears and that it was possible to see a day of concerts featuring all six Bartók string quartets as more than an endurance test. They had lain in her bed and listened to Schubert, talking about where they would live when they were married, making up names for their

165

children – Béla and Tasmin had been Jim's favourites – and laughing about which reed instruments they would learn to play. A little less than two years later, Hannah still found signs of him around the house, a clarinet reed stuffed down behind the cushions of the sofa, the score of *Billy Budd* amongst the dusty folders in which she kept her old college lecture notes. Peripatetic had proved to be the word.

At the end of another chapter, Hannah closed the book and stood for a while at the window, gazing out. Lights blinked like fireflies from across the park. Downstairs, she called Joanne and said yes to tennis, picked up a folder of work and put it back down, told herself she shouldn't really have another glass of wine and then, after she had poured it, crossed the room to the stereo and rummaged through the piles of CDs which, since Jim's departure, had resumed their previous disorder. Mary Chapin Carpenter, Nanci Griffith, Rosanne Cash? She thought 'Blue Moon with Heartache' might be a little difficult to take. 'Shut up and Kiss Me!' though, that was positive, nothing wrong with that. Maybe she should buy an extra copy and send one to her mum, something to put in her bag for Crete, along with sunblock and a Greek phrase book. Hannah had just set Mary Chapin Carpenter to play when the phone rang again. She nearly decided to ignore it.

'Hello?'

'Hannah?'

'Yes.' She had no idea who it was.

'I didn't think you'd be there.'

Then why on earth did you call, she thought, still trawling through the file of possibilities. Someone on the staff?

A friend of Joanne's? Her partner for tomorrow? 'Who is this?'

'Charlie Resnick, you remember me . . .'

Of course she remembered. She did now, now she recognised the voice. She could even picture him standing there, bulky, telephone to his ear, his mouth. 'And was that why you phoned?' she said, smiling a little. 'Because you thought I wouldn't be here?' She was surprised at how pleased she was that he had.

'No,' he said, and then, 'Is it too late for you to meet me for a drink?'

It was only when she put down the phone that Hannah realised she didn't know exactly where the Polish Club was; she hoped the taxi driver would.

She had changed outfits three times waiting for the cab to arrive, reverting finally to what she had been wearing when Resnick phoned, a soft grey cotton round-neck top over recently washed blue jeans, black shoes, flat and comfortable, on her feet. Front door open, she lifted a stone-coloured linen jacket from the coat rack in the hall.

Resnick was waiting for her when she arrived, moving from the shadows at the top of the steps as her taxi drew away.

'You found it okay?'

'The driver did.'

'You've been here before?'

Hannah shook her head.

The elderly man with white hair brushed back and a blue blazer, buttons shining, looked up at Resnick as he signed Hannah in, Resnick avoiding the questions in his watery blue eyes.

'Look,' Resnick said; he had stopped her in the hallway beyond the desk, hand barely touching her arm. She was vaguely aware of deep red wallpaper, framed photographs, music from another room. 'There are people here I know, I can either introduce you or . . .'

'Or we can hide in a corner.'

He smiled. 'Something like that.'

Hannah smiled back. 'I'm not the hiding type.'

Marian Witczak took Hannah's hand as a doctor might receive a slide on which a rare and potentially dangerous specimen had been prepared. She made the smallest of small talk while Resnick was at the bar and, when he returned, excused herself onto the dance floor. So much for her wanting to see me on the arm of a beautiful woman, Resnick thought.

Hannah accepted the glass of lager and relaxed against the worn leather seat. 'When did that finish?' she asked, looking off in the direction Marian had taken.

'What exactly?'

'Your whatever-you'd-call it. Relationship. Affair.'

'With Marian?'

'Uh-huh.'

Resnick shook his head. 'It never started.'

Setting down her glass, Hannah smiled. 'Well, that explains the welcome, at least.'

They sat and talked for maybe half an hour, respective jobs, contrasting afternoons, Notts County seemingly as foreign to Hannah as Tunisia was to Resnick.

'You never go to the cinema?'

'Not really.'

'I go to Broadway most weeks, I suppose. They show

all kinds of stuff. You know, things you're not likely to see elsewhere, except on Channel Four.'

'Like films from Tunisia.' Resnick smiled.

Hannah nodded. He looked years younger when he did that, the broadening of the mouth, brightening of the eyes.

'You should go,' she said. 'They have some good films. They're not all Tunisian. And besides...' – smiling – '...they serve good food.'

What had it been, she was thinking, the sauce that he had dripped onto his suit and failed to wipe away? Bolognese? Matriciana?

The call for last orders came from behind the bar. They were on their feet when the accordion swayed into the last waltz.

'Should we?' Resnick said, head angled, fingers reaching again for her arm.

'I don't think so,' Hannah said.

But once outside she slipped her arm through his and suggested they walk a little. He asked her where she lived and she him. At the junction of Sherwood Rise and Gregory Boulevard, a black-and-white cab came towards them with its For Hire light shining and Resnick stepped out into the road, arm raised.

'Oh, God,' said Hannah as he held open the door. 'Your place or mine?'

The cab dropped them off at the end of the Promenade. During the short journey they had said little, Resnick aware of Hannah's proximity, the sleeve of her jacket almost resting on his thigh, the sounds, faint, of her breathing, the way her hands rested in a loose cradle above her lap, fingers barely touching.

169

'This is it,' she said, her voice, for that moment unnaturally loud.

Resnick nodded: he had reasons for knowing this street. The houses, tall, to the left as they began to walk along the unmade road, little more than a path; to the right, iron railings and an uneven line of bushes and small trees which separated them from the park.

'I'm at the far end,' Hannah said, 'the terrace.'

These houses they were going past, lights muted by curtains or filtered through lace, were semi-detached; small gardens at the front, squares of grass bordered by shrubs or flowering plants. Indistinct, the sounds of voices, laughter, television, dinner parties winding down. Resnick exchanged automatic greetings with a man out walking his dog. As they passed the house where Mary Sheppard had lived, something in the pit of his stomach knotted and turned.

When Hannah paused to ease back the gate which led to the few terraced houses at the end, she saw Resnick's face, pale in the fall of the overhead light.

'What's the matter? You look as if you've seen a ghost.'

It had been a cold night, far colder than this, and Mary Sheppard had been naked to the waist, next to naked below; Resnick remembered her legs partly raised, arms at extreme angles to the body. The officers who had arrived there before Resnick – Lynn Kellogg and Kevin Naylor had been the first – had covered her with a plastic sheet and then covered that with coats taken from inside the house. Resnick had lifted these back, looked at her with a borrowed torch. Her eyes had been open, gazing up, unseeing, at the moon.

He followed Hannah up the short path towards her

170

front door. When she turned, key in hand, it was almost into his arms.

'You are coming in? Coffee? A drink?'

For a moment he hesitated. 'Maybe better some other time.' Regretful, the slow shake of the head.

'You're sure?' She laid her hand on his, the cold hardness of the key, the sudden warmth of her skin. Resnick didn't move. Hannah was trying to see his face, read the expression in his eyes. After a moment, she turned and slipped the key into the lock, pushed back the door; there was a light burning, warm orange, in the hall. She looked back, then stepped aside as Resnick followed her in.

There was an old fireplace in the living-room, decorated tiles at each side, a vase of dried flowers standing before the matt black grate. Postcards stood on the mantelpiece, a small family photograph in a grey-green frame. A two-seater settee pushed up against one wall, two brightly covered armchairs, cushions on the floor. Not knowing where to sit, Resnick stood.

From upstairs he heard the flushing of the toilet, Hannah's feet upon the stairs.

'What's it to be?' She had taken off her jacket; he noticed, for the first time, two rings, silver with a glint of colour, on the outside fingers of her right hand.

'Coffee, tea? There's a bottle of wine already open. It's not too bad. Actually, it's pretty good.' She was smiling with her eyes.

'Wine sounds fine.'

'Okay.' She flapped a hand in the direction of the settee. 'Why don't you sit down? Put on some music if you'd like. I'll just be a minute.'

Resnick bent over a small pile of CDs beside the stereo in the corner of the room bearing names, mostly female, that he didn't know. He looked at the cover of the case that was standing empty, presumably what Hannah had been playing when he'd called. *Stones in the Road*. Resnick thought he knew some of those.

In the square kitchen, pouring wine, Hannah was amazed at the unsteadiness of her hand. Hannah, what the hell's the matter with you, she asked? And what on earth do you think you're doing?

'Here.'

He was still standing there, too big for the middle of the room. When he took the glass his fingers burned for an instant against the edge of her hand.

'Why don't you let me take your coat?'

'It's okay.' But he put down his glass, shrugged off his suit jacket and Hannah hung it in the hall, beside her own.

'Please, sit down.'

Hesitating, Resnick took the settee. Not quite able to sit beside him, Hannah sat in the easy chair nearest to the stereo.

'You didn't see anything you fancied?' she said, indicating the CDs.

'I didn't know.'

'Not your kind of music, then?'

At last, Resnick smiled. 'I'm a jazz man myself, I'm afraid.'

'Well,' Hannah said, reaching round for the controls, 'nothing ventured . . .'

The sounds of a piano, tentative at first, rolled out across the room. Then a woman's voice, slightly husky, unaccompanied, warm but bare. Why walk, she was singing, when you can fly?

When the other instruments came in behind the vocal, Resnick thought, for a second time that evening, he could hear an accordion. He leaned forward and lifted his glass from the mantelpiece and, without drinking, placed it on the floor beside his feet. Hannah watching him, her lips moving, just faintly, to the words. The space between them seemed a million miles wide, uncrossable. Resnick moved his foot and the glass overturned, spilling wine.

'Oh, shit!'

'It's okay.' Hannah was on her feet, heading for the door. 'Don't worry. Don't worry.' Returning with a tea towel in her hand.

'I'm sorry.' Resnick was still sitting there, legs apart, all but empty glass in his hand.

'It doesn't matter,' Hannah assured him, pressing the cloth hard against the carpet where the wine had spread. 'That's why I bought this colour. Nothing shows.'

'It's my fault for being so clumsy.'

'No, there. See. Nothing. Well,' laughing, 'nothing much.' Straightening, she placed her hand on his leg; as she reached her other hand towards his neck, the darkened towel fell away. His mouth was closed against hers and then it was not. Wine on his tongue. Somewhere inside Hannah's brain she was thinking, I should have waited for 'Shut Up and Kiss Me!', but track six was too far on. Resnick's knees were tight against her side, his hand in her hair.

'Charlie,' she said, some fifteen minutes later. He had swung one of his legs round onto the settee, and she was half-lying across him, trying not to get cramp or notice that her hip was rubbing rather painfully against the settee's sharp edge.

'Mmm?' he mumbled, close against her face. His tie had disappeared and his shirt was mostly undone.

'Come up to bed.'

At the door he stopped her, catching at her hand. 'Look, Hannah, are you sure?'

He was startled by the ferocity of her laugh.

'What is it?'

'Sure?' she said. 'I don't know if I can afford to wait that long.'

The bedroom stretched across the top of the house between two sloping roofs. The floor-boards had been sanded and polished; two chests of drawers and the wardrobe were in stripped pine. There were two rugs, one at either side of the bed, one white, the other blood red. Plants hung in baskets from the ceiling, fronds pushing up towards the light that, even now, showed through the uncovered skylights, one at each side of the room. In the city it was never quite dark. Hannah would lie there some nights, staring up, vainly searching for stars.

Now she lifted herself up onto one arm and was surprised to find that she was still shaking a little; she had not made love to anyone since Jim and that already seemed longer ago than it was. So strange, the first time with anyone new; after the first blind excitement of caressing and undressing, the clumsiness of finding that fit, the almost stubborn awkwardness of it. She remembered in a film she had seen once – Robert De Niro, was it, and Uma Thurman? – charging at it headlong, a mêlée of arms and legs and sheets that ended up with the pair of them, startled and breathless, on the floor. And, of course, in movies there was never that embarrassing non-conversation about the condoms. Which of you, if either, has them and are they within reach? The answer had been on the upper shelf of the bathroom cabinet, behind the mouth ulcer gel and the spare dental floss, down on the second floor.

She noticed Resnick's breathing change and thought he might be asleep again, until, fleetingly at first, he opened his eyes.

'What time is it?'

Hannah narrowed her eyes towards the digital clock on the floor. 'A quarter to four.'

Resnick eased himself up onto his elbow and lay facing her, this woman he scarcely knew who had invited him into her bed. He felt honoured and would have liked to have told her so, but couldn't quite find the words. He kissed a corner of her mouth instead.

'Do you have to go?'

'I ought to, soon.'

'An early start?'

'Responsibilities.' He smiled. 'Cats. And I have to change out of this suit. That suit.' The trousers were somewhere between the bed and the stairs.

'And if you stay the night,' Hannah said, 'it might mean something more.'

He looked at her; in this light her eyes were grey-green, stone polished by water. 'Might it?'

With a swift movement, she was out from beneath the duvet and on her feet. 'We'll see.'

Resnick watched her walk, barefooted, across the floor;

the dark ends of pubic hair visible between her legs before she disappeared behind the door.

In the kitchen they sat and drank tea while the light slowly changed behind the window, Resnick dressed in everything save his suit jacket, Hannah in a T-shirt and chenille dressing-gown, dunking stale dark chocolate biscuits, all she had been able to find. How, Hannah thought, had she ever kept chocolate biscuits long enough to go stale? Her self-control must be better than she'd imagined. Until tonight.

Resnick sat listening for the sound of a car engine; the cab company had told him twenty minutes to half an hour. When he heard it on the road near the rear of the house, he quickly swallowed down the last of his tea.

Slippers on her feet, Hannah walked with him along the narrow alley to where the driver was waiting.

'I'm not much good at one-night stands,' she said.

'Neither am I.' He didn't know if that were true.

She held two of his fingers tight inside her hand. 'Then I'll see you again?'

'Yes. Yes, of course. If that's what you want.'

On the pavement, he kissed her softly on the mouth and she kissed him back; she watched as the car drew away, out onto the Boulevard, indicator blinking orange light. Well, Hannah, she thought as she turned back towards the house, so the earth didn't move, what did you expect? At the gate, she laughed lightly. 'You didn't even see stars.'

The phone was ringing when Resnick entered the house.

'Charlie, where the fuck have you been?'

Taken aback by the ferocity in Skelton's voice, he didn't know how to respond.

'Where the hell was your bleep?'

There on the hall table; he had forgotten to transfer it into the pocket of his suit.

'What's happened?' Resnick finally asked.

'Bill Aston,' Skelton said, his voice like sour milk. 'He's dead. Some bastard's killed him.'

21

You could see the lights of the emergency vehicles once you passed the corner of Meadow Lane and approached the bridge; patches of muted colour bleeding out into the day. Mist hung in low grey rags over the surface of the river. Rain teased the air. A temporary covering had been set up on the flat spread of grass of the Embankment, a tent of ill-fitting orange plastic around which lighting had been quickly rigged. Figures wearing dark-blue overalls were already examining the surrounding ground on hands and knees. At the perimeter of the scene others were gathered in knots of conversation, heads bowed. It was Skelton who turned away from one of these and moved towards the road to meet Resnick, more than tiredness darkening his eyes.

'Jesus Christ, Charlie! Where were you?'

'When was he found?' Resnick asked, scarcely breaking his stride.

'An hour since.'

'What was he doing here?'

'Walking his dogs. They're back there in one of the cars.'

Millington was there, Divine, Reg Cossall, grey-haired,

hands deep in the topcoat he seemed to wear whatever the weather; other officers, in uniform and without. Resnick pushed one of the flaps of plastic aside with an arm and ducked inside. The police surgeon turned his head towards Resnick and then away. Whatever had been used to batter Bill Aston's head and face had been heavy and hard and wielded with frequency and great force. Beneath a coagulation of blood and hair and bone, it seemed as if the top of his skull had been stove in completely. Lower down, more bone, sharp-edged, splintered through the skin. The globe of one eye, iris and retina, lay barely attached, amongst the bloodied pulp of what had been Bill Aston's cheek.

Resnick had to will himself to stay there, bent over, as long as it took. There were mud and grass stains thick on the dead man's clothes, sports jacket and grey trousers, striped shirt. A smear of earth thick on the fleshy palm of his right hand. One of the nails, the finger end, deeply split. One of his shoes was missing, something the vibrant yellow of dog shit, sticking to the heel of his woollen navy sock.

'Time of death?' Resnick asked.

Parkinson removed his spectacles, pinched the bridge of his nose. 'Between four to six hours ago. Around one o'clock.'

Resnick nodded and swung out of the tent to where Skelton stood smoking a cigarette. 'All right,' Resnick said, 'what do we know?'

The superintendent waited until they were up on the road, the houses opposite – mock-Tudor, mock-Gothic, mock-something – at the end of their deep gardens, mostly dark. Skelton lit a fresh cigarette from the nub end of the last.

'This youth found the body around three a.m. He'd been sleeping rough, down by that bandstand, other side of the memorial gardens. Woke up, started to wander, keeping out the cold. That was when he heard the dogs, barking and whining. Followed the sound to the body, so he says.'

'Called it in?'

A shake of Skelton's head. 'Not straight away. Panicked. Ran off. While later – says he's not sure how long, half an hour, maybe more – he went back. Took another look. That was when he phoned.' For a moment, Skelton turned his head, down towards the river, the splash of birds disturbing the water. 'The two lads who arrived first, uniform patrol, they had no idea who he was. It was only after the ambulance had arrived, one of the paramedics found his wallet, kicked it up from the grass. About the only thing left in it, his warrant card. That was when all hell broke loose.'

'The youth who found him . . .'

'At the station now. Being questioned. First reports, seems straight enough.'

'And Aston's wife?'

Again, Skelton shook his head. 'Would you want her to see him first like this?'

Cold air slithered down into Resnick's lungs like a wave; he could already see Margaret Aston's slow-collapsing face, the lance of pain that stripped across her eyes.

'She's not reported him missing? Made enquiries, anything?'

For a second, Skelton's eyes were closed. 'Not as far as

we know.' And then, 'You know her, Charlie, don't you? Socially, I mean.'

'Not well. Not for a long time.'

Skelton nodded; not well was better than not at all. 'There'll be an incident room set up at the station, Charlie. Whoever it was, we'll get him.'

'Yes.' It was almost fully light now to the east. Resnick sighed and began to walk back in the direction of the bridge.

'Charlie?'

'Yes?'

'You talked with him, didn't you? Aston. About the enquiry? That kid Snape's death.'

Resnick nodded. 'Just last night.'

'There wasn't anything he said... Nothing he said about it that might lead you to believe, well, that it had anything to do with this?'

'No. Nothing. But...'

'But?'

Resnick recalled the almost glib ease with which Aston had seemed to be accepting the social services' version of Nicky Snape's death; had there been anything murky going on, Aston didn't seem to have been aware of it – unless something had come to light between his conversation with him in the pub and the attack. 'No,' Resnick said. 'Not as far as I know.'

Skelton released a slow breath of relief. 'Mugging, then. Out on his own, late at night, someone saw their chance.'

'Yes,' Resnick said. 'Likely that's how it was. We'll see.'

Resnick stood with his back half towards the front door as the next-door neighbour eased his BMW out of the

181

drive and onto the road. Birds were making a racket in the trees. The lock clicked open and as the door swung inwards, Resnick turned.

'Bill, I swear you'd forget your head if it wasn't screwed on, never mind our keys ...' Seeing Resnick, only half-recognising him, she faltered into silence.

'Hello, Margaret.' He made a move, unthreatening, towards her.

'Bill, I thought he'd gone out early. With the dogs. To ... to ...' But she had been a policeman's wife long enough to know this moment, to have rehearsed it often enough in the long flat hours before dawn.

'Margaret, why don't you let me come inside?'

Stubby, short, pink dressing-gown tied round her, curlers in her hair, she stood her ground, challenging him for the truth.

'Margaret, I'm sorry ...'

She opened her mouth to scream, drowning out his words.

'... he's dead.'

Resnick caught hold of her and held her close, muffling her screams against his chest. Three minutes, more. When he was able, he shuffled her far enough into the hallway to push the door shut at his back. It smelled of lavender in there, strong, like soap on his fingers, the palms of his hands. His shirt was damp with Margaret Aston's tears.

'Tell ... tell me what happened.'

'Why don't we go and make ...?'

Her voice was shrill and angry. 'I don't want ...! I want to know.'

Resnick took her arm, his hand steady beneath her elbow. 'All right, but let's at least sit down.'

The living-room was at the rear of the house, fussy with tasteful ornaments and family photographs; the curtains, had they been fully drawn, would have revealed french windows and beyond those some eighty feet of flower beds and tidy shrubs, well-groomed lawn. As it was, they sat in facing chairs in the shadowy half-light, Margaret's face angled towards the other armchair, empty by the span of fireside, the one in which, Resnick guessed, her husband would more usually have sat.

He told her such details as were known, restricting the description of Aston's injuries to a minimum. She listened, straining towards him, head angled slightly to one side, her hands in her lap never still.

'Bill,' she said, when Resnick had finished. 'Poor Bill. Whatever has he ever done to deserve this?'

'Nothing, Margaret. Nothing.'

She was on her feet. 'I want to see him.'

'Later, Margaret. Why not let it wait?' Gently, he led her back to the chair. On his feet, he went to the windows and let light into the room.

'When you came to the door,' Resnick asked, 'just now. You thought it was Bill, back from walking the dogs?'

'Yes.'

'But when this happened, as far as we can tell, it was near the middle of the night. One or two.'

He waited while she assimilated this.

'Yes, he ... Sometimes he couldn't sleep. Not right away. So he'd go out again, a walk, anything rather than lie there. He hated that; there was nothing he disliked more. And this past couple of years it had got worse, much worse. That was why we moved, he moved across the hall; separate rooms, you see. That way, if Bill was

183

troubled with his insomnia, he wouldn't feel guilty about waking me.' She plucked at the hem of her dressing-gown, some end of cotton she alone could see. 'Not that I ever minded. Not . . .' And she was lost to tears again, flapping Resnick away when he came near.

He went to find the kitchen and left her there, unembarrassed in her own grief. If Bill Aston had gone out last night after midnight, taking the dogs with him, she would not have thought it unusual; and if she had slept through till morning, possibly gone to look for him in his room and found him not there, she could have imagined him up early, taking a stroll, nothing sinister or alarming there.

The tea was ready in the pot when Margaret, red-eyed, came into the room. 'I do want to see him, now. You must take me to see him.'

On his feet, Resnick tried the beginnings of a smile. 'Let's have a cup of this, why don't we? I'll call the hospital, then drive you over. All right? Margaret, is that okay?'

She stood, staring at him, lost between table and door. How long till it was ever okay again?

22

Eleven forty-four: cigarette smoke hung like a grey-blue cloud from the centre of the windowless room. Enlarged photographs of Aston's body had been tacked to the wall. Colour. Black and white. High, to the right, a picture which had been taken eighteen months before, Bill Aston at the retirement party for a colleague, champagne glass held aloft, dinner-jacket and tie, smiling and alive.

At right angles to these, a blown-up map showed the precise spot on the Embankment where the body had been found; a second map, larger scale, delineated the parameters of the area – the deep southerly curve of the river, forming an almost perfect U between Trent Bridge and the old Wilford viaduct, the Memorial Gardens and flat, open recreation grounds which led up to the predominantly council-owned Meadows residential area in the north; south, the civic blandness of County Hall and then more open ground, playing fields and schools. Further along, a fully detailed map of the city and its surroundings had been marked with Aston's home, the office where he had been based, the local authority accommodation where the Snape enquiry had been carried out. On the far side of the photographs, also attached to the wall, were the two white boards on which the principal lines of enquiry would be followed and marked. A pair of linked video monitors had been set up at the rear; two computers, one of them on line with the national Home Office computer, stood ready to access and disseminate information.

Copies of the pathologist's initial report had been handed out to those present: multiple fractures of the cranial cavity, severe damage to the upper and lower jaw, the mandible and orbit walls, rupturing of the blood vessels to the brain and consequent internal haemorrhaging. Damage to Aston's hands and bruising to the forearms suggested that he had put up a considerable struggle and had made a determined, finally desperate effort to defend himself.

Skelton stood near the front of the room in close conversation with Resnick and the DCI in charge of uniforms. A little to one side, Reg Cossall, thick grey hair brushed back, inevitable cigarette burning from the curve of his hand, spoke in slow undertones to the inspector from the Support Department, emphasising every sentence with a jab of his finger towards the man's chest. Skelton, more alive than Resnick had observed him for months, wearing a double-breasted suit that Resnick had never seen, glanced quickly down at his neatly written notes before slipping them from sight; as soon as this was over he would go directly to the media briefing below. A last word to Resnick and he turned away; two steps forward and the heavy hum and burr of voices around him rose, then died.

Briefly, he introduced Harry Payne, the inspector from the Support Department, fifteen of whose officers would

186

be responsible for the initial close search, and Jane Prescott, the sergeant who would be liaising between the investigation and Force Intelligence. He introduced DC Khan as Bill Aston's assistant on the Snape enquiry, and finally the two civilian computer operators. Everyone else knew everyone else, pretty much.

Skelton cleared his throat. 'I don't need to tell you a fellow officer has been killed. One of us.' Nods of agreement, murmurs of assent and anger from all around. Skelton waited before going on. 'Many of you knew Bill Aston; some of you, like myself, worked with him. He was a good officer. The old school. Decent. Fair. Scrupulous in everything that he did. After all of his years of service, Bill was due to retire at the end of this year. And now this.'

Once again, the litany of voices as though in church. Skelton orchestrating them, call and response.

'We all know what happened in the early hours of this morning. You've all seen the photographs, read the report, some of you were present at the scene where Bill Aston's body was found. This was a callous, brutal attack and I know that you all feel as shocked as I do. And I know that what you all want is to get whoever did this, person or persons, banged up behind bars as soon as possible. We want a result and we want it fast. We want it for Bill Aston's widow ... and before whoever was responsible for this can act again.'

Skelton waited for the volley of sound, fierce and emphatic, to subside. He wanted every face turned towards him, everyone's attention exclusively on what he had to say.

'Before we set to work, I want us to be clear – there

are dangers here. The last thing we can afford to do is rush headlong into this and let feelings, however strong, get the better of judgement. Nobody. None of you is going off at half-cock on this. It's too important.' Skelton's voice clear now, no longer loud, no longer needing to be: silence around him in the room. 'What we can't afford is to bring in the right person, the right people, and then not be able to make it stick. So we're thorough, exact, we work through channels, we check and then we double-check. And then when we've caught the bastard, he stays caught.'

Acclamation. Skelton waited a moment longer before stepping aside. 'Charlie?'

As Resnick began speaking, he moved across until he was positioned in front of the maps of the Trent. 'The most likely scenario so far is that this was a random, unpremeditated attack, carried out for gain. Whatever he had on him at the time. They could have seen Bill as an affluent enough looking bloke, not so young, out on his own with a couple of little dogs. No threat there.' Resnick pointed up at one of the maps. 'Bill parked his car here, opposite the Memorial Gardens and walked, as far as we can tell, in this direction here, along the Embankment towards the bridge. When he couldn't sleep, this was something he did quite a bit, nothing unusual about it at all. We're presuming that whoever it was that attacked him saw him wandering alone, presumably nobody else around, and marked him down as an easy target. He was set upon here, close by these trees, and his wallet was found here, not far from the body, cash and credit cards gone.' Resnick paused and looked around the room. 'Margaret Aston says the most he would have been likely to have had with him was thirty or forty pounds.'

'Bastards!' somebody said, loud and pronounced.

'Thanks, Charlie.' It was Skelton's turn again. 'Right. To specifics. Reg, anything and everything that happened on the Embankment between one and four, anyone who set foot, anything that breathed, that's your bailiwick.' Cossall shuffled a foot and gave the floor a half-smile. 'So, supervision of house-to-house, that's down to you. All those places along Victoria Embankment, they can't all have been tucked up with their Ovaltine, anyone who heard anything, saw anyone, we have to know. And we'll be appealing for anyone who drove along that way after midnight, any late-night fishermen, joggers, whatever, to come forward. Anyone using the pub on his side of the bridge, especially around last orders, or walking back into the city from the TBI. We'll be using local radio, television news, the *Post*. Whatever information we get, once it's been processed, Reg, you and your team, get it prioritised, followed through.

'Charlie, your team, I want you to go in close. Forensics, anything found at the immediate scene, give us as exact a picture as you can of what actually happened. And the twenty-four hours leading up to the attack, we want to know where Bill went, who he spoke to, what he did. Cover ourselves, just in case. If we have to look further afield, that's where we'll start.'

Skelton cleared his throat and wished for a glass of water; he was conscious of speaking for a long time. The troops were getting restless for action and it was time for the last push. 'All right, one of the things we have to be wary of is tunnel vision. The most obvious suspect is not always the one that ends up in the frame. Which is why, even though I don't think there's any connection, I'm

189

going to be talking to Khan here about the enquiry Bill was heading into the apparent suicide of Nicky Snape. There may be no connection, but it has to be checked and eliminated. And there'll be other avenues. Cases Bill worked when he was operational, people he was responsible for getting sent down who've recently been released. Anyone else who might have held a grudge, the Job or personal. Anything out of synch. I don't see Bill as having been a man who made enemies easily, but we'll talk to Margaret, see what she says. Finally, any of you, any ideas you might have, different angles, things that seem to be in danger of being overlooked. Come forward. Talk to me. I want to know.'

Skelton took a step back and inclined his head right, then left. 'Charlie, Reg, anything you want to add?'

Neither did.

'All right, let's be moving. And good luck.'

Less than half an hour later, Resnick was back in his own CID room. Kevin Naylor had just finished mashing tea. Resnick sat on the edge of one of the desks, finishing off a smoked chicken and cranberry sandwich that had been sent across from the deli on the Circus.

'Okay,' he said, taking a mug from Kevin and holding it in both hands, 'let's talk this through.'

Millington was sitting close to Resnick's right, chair angled back onto its rear legs, Divine was down towards the end of the narrow room, chair reversed, legs spread wide; Lynn Kellogg sat with her head resting back against the left-hand wall; Naylor, having handed out the tea, took up a position behind one of the dark-green filing cabinets and leaned forward on both elbows.

'First things first. We already have somebody helping us with our enquiries, this homeless youth who found the body, phoned it in. Graham, I want you and Mark to question him again, push him some more. Let's check out what he knows, make sure he's telling us everything.'

'You think he might've been involved, boss?' Divine asked. 'The attack?' Push him a little, he'd liked the sound of that.

'Wouldn't be the first time, would it?' Millington said. 'Throwing off suspicion, reporting your own crime.'

Resnick nodded and moved on. 'Kevin, Scene of Crime will have details of footprints, boot marks, in the area the body was found – photographs, casts, whatever. Make what sense of them you can. Other things aside, it should help us to pin down how many people were actually involved.'

'We are pretty definite, are we,' Naylor asked, 'we're dealing with more than one person?'

Resnick swallowed a mouthful of tea. 'That's my gut feeling, yes. Two at least, maybe more. Bill had kept himself reasonably fit, he wouldn't have looked such an easy mark to one man on his own. And unless whoever struck the first blow managed to take him completely by surprise, I doubt that a single attacker would have been able to cause as much damage as this.'

He shifted his focus across the room. 'Lynn, we have to build up a detailed picture of Bill Aston's last twenty-four hours; everything he did, everywhere he went, anyone and everyone he spoke to. I'd like you to take care of that. I'll go with you to see Margaret Aston first off, introduce you. Then you're on your own.'

'Right,' Lynn said. 'Thanks.'

'Meantime, I'm going to go over the material from the Nicky Snape enquiry with Khan.' Resnick set both hands on the desk and pushed himself to his feet. 'Before you go off duty tonight, check back with me, let me know what you've got.'

The last drops of water spurted noisily down into the jug of Skelton's coffee machine and, standing close by the side window, looking down, Resnick was aware of his stomach rumbling in sympathy. Past noon and, chicken sandwich aside, the last food that had passed his lips had been at Hannah's house hours before, a couple of chocolate digestives that had seen better days. For a moment he was thinking of her, Hannah, the skin round her hip, along her thigh, smooth and taut against his hand.

'Charlie?'

'Huh?'

'Milk or without?'

'As it comes.'

Skelton took a seat and Resnick did the same. 'Difficult not to think,' Skelton said, 'how close he was to retiring, poor bugger.'

'Yes.' And Margaret, Resnick thought, what kind of life for her? After all that time, that life, how could you hope to adjust? The kids, he supposed, there was always the kids; but then he wondered what kind of an answer that was.

'Press conference at one,' Skelton was saying, 'you're okay about that, fully briefed?'

'I can only say what we know, and up to now that's not too much.'

'Good opportunity, though, ask for information, help.'

Resnick nodded: they would be flooded with calls, extra staff on hand to log them in. Much of the information would prove inconclusive and conflicting; and then there would be the cranks, psychics and back-yard psychiatrists, two or three at least wanting to confess. He set his cup down in its saucer, placed them both on the floor. State-of-the-art coffee maker or not, Skelton's coffee always tasted like instant, and weak instant at that. He got to his feet, thinking that was all, but there was more.

'There's a young DC,' Skelton said, 'looking to transfer up from Leicestershire. Chance he might come here.'

Resnick waited at the back of his chair. 'Is this definite, or just rumour?'

'Definite as these things go.'

'I thought there was a freeze on all recruitment?'

Skelton spread his hands, fingers wide. 'In theory there is, but you know finance, Charlie. Bloody unfathomable.'

'This transfer, does he have a name? You said he.'

'Vincent. Carl Vincent.'

'And he's CID?'

Skelton nodded. 'Five years.'

'Still a DC?'

Nodded again.

There were all kinds of reasons, Resnick knew, why officers applied to transfer. Personality clashes, mostly; sometimes a case goes sour and they're looking for a fresh start. Family reasons for needing to relocate, but this – nothing more than an hour's drive.

'Might be he'll be here in the next couple of days,' Skelton said. 'No bad thing, Charlie. This enquiry, you'll be needing all the bodies you can get. Have him plug a few holes, feel him out. You can afford to give it a while either way, see how it goes. If it turns out he's half the copper young Patel would have been, you'll not be sorry.'

Resnick could still remember the first time he had met Dipak Patel, bright as tomorrow and eager to please. The first from his family to go to university, get a degree. The police force, Patel's father had said, why that? Such waste. Resnick remembered blood drying on the paving stones, the purplish hue around the wound, one single slashing blow that had found the artery by design or chance. A killer never caught. He remembered the father's face, the way it had twisted in; his uncomprehending grief.

Margaret Aston.

Norma Snape.

It went on, without end.

23

Norma had tried not to notice the smell on Sheena's breath when her daughter came in; not tobacco, not quite gin, it was grass, she knew, remembered it distantly but well.

'And where d'you think you got this?' she asked, angling back her head the better to see the black leather jacket, studs around both pockets, zips unfastened along both sleeves.

'I don't *think*,' Sheena said, doing her best to swerve past. 'I know.'

Norma grabbed the back of the jacket with one hand and swung her round. 'So tell me.'

Sheena gazed, not quite steady, not as steady as she would have liked to be, into her mother's accusing eyes. 'Dee-Dee,' she said. 'That's where. My friend, Dee-Dee, she lent it me. Right?'

But before Norma could say anything more, Peter was in the doorway, three cans of Kestrel balanced one above the other on the palm of one hand. 'Let's sit down, eh? Have a drink.' Winking at Norma as he pushed one of the cans into her grudging hands; aiming a kiss at Sheena's cheek which she only partly managed to evade. 'Nice evening, eh, sweetheart? Good time?'

'I don't think,' Sheena said, articulating over-carefully, 'you should call me sweetheart.'

'Oh, and why's that then?'

Sheena thought about it and after some consideration, decided that she didn't know. She sat on the arm of the settee and wobbled just a little.

'For Christ's sake,' Norma said from the armchair beside the TV, 'take that coat off indoors.'

Sheena tried, but her arm got caught up in the sleeve and inexplicably, couldn't get it free. Peter, finally, got up and helped her, Sheena starting again to laugh. Not laughing, really, giggling more like. 'You're not to call . . . you're not to call . . .' Losing her balance, she began to topple backwards, legs kicking high in the air, arms flailing, till all she could do was collapse backwards against her father, Peter not strong enough to hold her, the pair of them sprawling on the carpet, sprawling and rolling until they ended up against the side wall, laughing and crying in each other's arms.

'For the Lord's sake, give over, you pair of great nazzle-heads!' Norma shouted, but soon she was laughing too, despite herself, wiping her sleeve across her eyes before trying to take too much of the lager down at one time, coughing then so bad she couldn't see for the tears and Sheena had to hold her hands while Peter patted her back and whispered in her ear for her to get a grip.

When it was over Sheena wandered off into the kitchen just in case there was any of the ice-cream from Tesco left in the freezer, mint and chocolate.

Peter switched on the TV and switched it back off,

springing onto the settee with arms flung wide. 'Let me call you sweetheart!' he sang at the top of his reedy voice. 'You belong to me!'

'Sit down, you great gillifer,' Norma called, 'before you fall down.'

Which he did, clean over the back of the settee onto his head. And came up singing. Norma and Sheena hauled him to his feet and pushed him down into a chair, Norma plumping herself in his lap, while Sheena sat across the room and spooned with exaggerated care around the tub of ice-cream.

'Sweetheart,' Peter whispered into Norma's bosom and she clipped him none too seriously around the ear and told him to behave and anyway, if that was what he was after, he had another think coming.

Which he did. And when Sheena finally got tired of sitting there, watching the pair of them pretending not to paw at one another, she sashayed out past them, her parting gesture to switch out the light.

'Peter, not here . . .' Norma whispered.

'In that case,' Peter said, 'let's away up to bed.'

Oh, God, Norma thought, how long's it been?

She lay awake, Peter beside her sleeping like a baby, his mouth slightly open close to her breast. Tears that Norma would cry later she had held back for fear of waking him, having to explain what she herself could not understand.

Whatever the deft magic of Peter's hands, he had not lost it all this time away. He would tell her little or nothing about the years between, how he had come to look so downtrodden, so ill, so very thin. There was a curving scar, low on his chest, criss-cross markings, faint, where the stitches had been removed. A bruise, old and yellow, which clung deep to his left thigh.

Soft against her, Peter stirred and she stroked his head, what little remained of his hair; soft it was, like a baby's hair. Don't let me think of Nicky, Norma prayed, don't let me think of him. Nor of Michael, her lovely baby son.

Don't let me think of that.

Not any of that.

She turned, careful, onto her side and ran her other hand along Peter's flank, his skinny buttock, the knobs of spine cresting his curving back. She rested her head towards his and closed her eyes, seeking sleep.

24

The youth eyed the contents of the plate with suspicion. A sausage cob, more than a little mauled in transit, brown sauce sticking it to the skimpy paper napkin in which it had been wrapped.

'What?' Divine said, no more yet than a hint of aggression. Push it, Resnick had said, push him a little.

'What?' the youth said back. He could have been any age between seventeen and twenty-five and already he had admitted to both twenty-one and nineteen. His face was framed by a scrubby haze of beard, a few reddening pustules below his right cheek-bone, whiteheads massing above his nose and across his brow. There was a small gold ring through the upper part of his left ear. He was wearing a combat-type jacket, grey cotton trousers, several T-shirts, one above the other, the uppermost bearing the exhortation, Nuke the Whales!

Alongside Divine, jacket unbuttoned, top button of his shirt unfastened above the knot of his woollen tie, Millington kept his counsel and said nothing.

'That's what you asked for, isn't it?' Divine asked. 'Sausage cob.'

'Not like that.'

'You don't like the sauce or what? Don't like the sauce, scrape it off.'

'It's nothing to do with the sauce, the sauce is fine.'

'What then?'

'Onions.'

'What onions?'

'Exactly.'

Leaning forward, carefully using middle finger and thumb, Divine eased back the top half of the roll. 'No onions.'

'That's what I mean.'

'Do you think,' Millington said, stirred to action, tapping the end of a Lambert and Butler on the surface of the table, 'when all this culinary discussion is through, we could make a start?'

'You going to eat that?' Divine, pointing at the cob. 'Or not?'

The youth shook his head.

Sliding the plate towards him, Divine reopened the roll, picked up the folded sausage, dabbled it around in the wash of brown sauce and, a defiant glint in his eyes, brought it to his mouth. 'Last chance?' Too late, the sausage disappeared into his mouth, two, three bites and it was gone, all save for a nodule of gristle which he delicately extracted from between his teeth and deposited back inside the cob, the whole of which, napkin included, he tipped from the plate into the metal bin beside his chair, where it landed with a soft but satisfying thump.

'This interview,' Millington said, having just switched on the tapes, 'timed at two twenty-three. Present are Detective Sergeant Millington, Detective Constable Divine and Mr St John.'

Out of politeness, Divine stifled a belch.

Millington leaned in a fraction more towards the youth. 'State your full name.'

'You know my name.'

Oh God, Divine thought, he's going to be one of those. Like the onions, all the way through.

'Full name,' Millington said again.

'John Anthony Lawrence St John.'

Divine choked back a snort.

'Address?'

'I have none.'

'Address?'

Just for a moment, light shone in the youth's eyes. 'Wherever I lay my hat is home.'

Smart-arsed bastard, Divine thought.

'Tell us,' Millington said encouragingly, 'about where you laid your hat on Saturday night.'

Reg Cossall and his team were diligently knocking on doors. So far they had been mistaken for Jehovah's Witnesses, Seventh Day Adventists, a succession of distant aunts and uncles, and supervisors from the cable-laying company who'd called to announce one of the workmen had put his spade through the electric again and the power would be off for the best part of an hour. Once problems of identification had been sorted out, they had generally received surprise, sympathy, a great deal of attention but no definite leads.

'There *was* a noise, wasn't there, Geoff? An awful kerfuffle. I remember we switched off the TV, came out to have a look.' A big woman in her fifties, this, Cossall himself the caller, along with a young DC; their house, on the Embankment, backed onto the path near which Aston's body had been found. 'Geoff?' She seemed agitated, her hands in and out of the patch pockets of her red-and-green apron, her mind, maybe, half on whatever she had left simmering on the stove. 'When was that, Geoff? Getting on for eleven o'clock is that when it was? About eleven o'clock?'

Geoff appeared in the hallway, *Telegraph* splaying over his hand, part of it, glasses tripped to the end of his nose.

'Yobs, that's all they are. Plain and simple. It's the same here every Saturday night now; come tipping out the pub, hooting and hollering and carrying on. And the kind of language they use, it beggars belief. But just yobs, nothing more. The sort your lot let have the run of the streets so the rest of us have to stay inside and lock our doors.'

What, instead of boogying off down the disco, Cossall thought, swivelling the old lady's hips around the floor? Couple of cherry brandies and whip her back home for a little of the old adagio on the living-room carpet. He doubted if their carpet had seen more than lemon-scented shampoo and a good hoovering since it had first been laid.

'And the time, sir,' Cossall asked. 'Can you be a bit more precise?'

'Like the wife said, in the region of eleven o'clock. Eleven thirty. You can check your *Radio Times* or whatever, *Match of the Day* that's what was on. That Scottish fellow, Hansen, too much of a know-all for my liking. And you can't understand half of what he says.'

It was the same story all along: there had been a rowdy element fooling about on the Embankment between eleven and eleven thirty, but after that they had gone, made off across the playing fields towards the Meadows, several reports suggested. And good riddance. Two households mentioned a sports car revving its engine loudly at around midnight; one other seemed to recall hearing a motor bike with a faulty silencer. It could have been the same thing.

What this first trawl failed to deliver was anything that tied in with the attack on Bill Aston: but this was only the beginning, Cossall knew that. Once the pubs had been leafleted, the local media had done their work, it would be different, he was certain. A man brutally attacked only a hundred yards from houses, little more than that from a busy main road, someone must have seen or heard something, it stood to reason.

Suddenly it was warm. In Resnick's office, at least. A large blue fly, lazy and fat, had woken from its long sleep and now buzzed the corners of the room, bumped with soft, persistent spats against the glass that looked out over nothing much.

'This is everything? There's nothing more?' Resnick dropped the last stapled sheaf of papers down amongst the rest.

Khan responded to the implicit criticism by tugging at the cuffs of his shirt, sitting straighter in his chair. 'The preliminary interviews, yes. Transcribed from tape.'

'Preliminary? You were planning to interview some of these again?'

'It was a contingency, sir, yes. If necessary.'

'And?'

Khan smoothed the palms of both hands along the tops of his legs; warm in there and he was starting to sweat.

Soon, he thought, he would be able to smell it; how he hated that.

'I'm sorry, sir, I don't fully understand what it is you're asking.'

'What I'm asking,' Resnick trying not to sound irritable, but doing so all the same, 'is were there any definite plans, did Inspector Aston intend to speak again, officially, to any of these people?'

Khan took his time; the fly, which had lain silent for a while, started up again. I shall either have to roll up that copy of the *Post* and kill it, Resnick thought, or prise open the window and let it out.

'No sir,' Khan finally said. 'Not that I was aware.'

'No conclusions here as to why Nicky Snape took his life.'

'No, sir.'

'And no blame.'

'Sir?'

'No culpability attached to any of the staff. No blame.'

'No, sir. That's correct.'

Is it, Resnick wondered? Maybe it is. At the fourth attempt he levered the lower half of the window far enough upwards and used the newspaper to shoo out the fly. 'How do you feel about that? Did you feel everyone was being honest, telling the truth? Nothing to cover up?'

Khan's briefs were beginning to stick uncomfortably to his skin; he had to stop himself from easing his body up from the chair and pulling them free. 'Inspector, I'm not sure . . .'

'What I'm getting at?'

'No, no. I think I understand that. But . . .'

'But Bill Aston was a senior officer and he has just been tragically killed.'

'Yes.'

'You don't want to be thought of as disloyal.'

'That's correct.'

Resnick pushed enough paper aside to make room on the side of his desk and sat looking at the young officer's face; waiting for Khan to look at him.

When he did, Resnick said, 'In your own words, what this represents is the basis of a preliminary report. There's nothing here to say that, had he lived, Inspector Aston would not have taken some of this further. He mentioned to me, for instance, he thought supervision on the night of Nicky's death might have been considered slack. Paul Matthews and Elizabeth Peck, I believe that's right.'

Khan nodded, yes.

'You were present, at their interviews?'

'Yes, sir.'

'And what was your feeling? Did you think they might have had anything to hide?'

'Matthews, he was nervous. Stuttering all the time, you know. Not stuttering exactly, but stumbling more, over his words.'

'And the woman? Peck?'

'Defensive. Yes, that's what I thought. Resentful, as if we shouldn't have been questioning her at all.'

'All right.' Resnick was back on his feet. 'What you do is this. Try and find out when the Social Services Inspectorate are planning to publish their report. Given what happened to Inspector Aston, you might be able to get some idea of which way they're shading, if they think there are any serious causes for concern. Then contact Jardine. Tell him we'll almost certainly need to come back and talk to his people again. Try not to get his back up, get him alarmed. You could always say that there are a few odds and ends need tidying up. In the circumstances, he should buy that. Okay? You can handle all that?'

For the first time Khan felt able to smile. 'Yes, sir. Of course.'

'Good lad.' And, as Khan was opening the door: 'There may be no connection, between the attack on Bill and any of this. Ninety-nine per cent, there is none. None at all. But we have to be sure.'

25

Resnick noticed that Lynn seemed to be wearing more make-up, a dash of colour, blue-green, above the eyes. Lipstick, not heavy, not accentuated, but there. A thin roll-neck top under a light check jacket, comfortable skirt. She took off the jacket once she'd opened the car door and draped it along the rear seat. At the passenger side, Resnick clicked his belt tight. He wondered if she might have started seeing someone again, a man; maybe she was just beginning to feel better about herself. He hoped that was the case. It was no more than she deserved.

A quick adjustment to the mirror and they were pulling out into traffic, heading down towards the city centre, the southbound road out towards the bridge.

'His wife,' Lynn asked, 'Bill Aston's, what's she like?'

Resnick described her: a shortish woman, not especially lively, but a good listener. Those occasions he had met her socially, police functions, she had kept pretty much in her husband's shadow, but whenever he had been to the house, more relaxed, she had been the one who talked, Bill fading into the background, clearing dishes, making sure the drinks were filled.

'A nice woman,' Resnick said. 'Straightforward, sensible.'

'Kids?'

'Two, I think. No, three. Grown up and left home. One somewhere like Canada, Australia.' He seemed to recall that one of them had married, but couldn't remember which. 'You know, I didn't really know him that well. The family. We'd not had a lot of contact these past few years.'

Lynn made a slight nod with her head, concentrating on the driver in front, who couldn't seem to make up his mind which lane he was supposed to be in. Trent Bridge was only a few hundred yards ahead. You could see the spot where Aston's body had been found, still staked out, cordoned off.

'We haven't come up with any kind of weapon?'

'Not as yet.'

There was a lot of water down there, flowing quite fast beneath the bridge.

The young man who came to the door looked enough like his father for Resnick not to wonder who he was. Terry Aston had inherited Bill's facial expression, the colour of his eyes, already the same peaking of the hair; he had enough of his mother's genes to be shorter, stockier, set four-square on the ground. He had travelled up with his wife and eighteen-month-old son from where they lived outside Bedford: Terry, a computer programmer with sidelines in home brewing and ornithology; his wife, Moira, a legal secretary who still temped at ten pounds an hour, those mornings when Steven was with the nanny.

Terry Aston shook hands with Resnick, accepting his condolences, nodded a shade awkwardly at Lynn Kellogg,

208

and led the two officers through the house into the living-room.

'I'll tell Mum you're here.'

Resnick had thought Margaret Aston might have been in bed, resting, somewhere out of the light, alone with her thoughts. But through the french windows, he could see her bending to deadhead one of the early roses, her grand-son behind her, running and falling, arms akimbo, onto the gravelled path. Stifling his squawl of tears, Margaret scooped him into her arms and held him tight against her, ssh-sshhing into his blond hair, until his mother came hurrying and took him from her, hoisting him high into the air and turning tears to laughter. Crushed against Margaret's chest, the white petals of the rose fell aimless to the ground.

'Inspector Resnick?'

The girl who came towards him from the doorway had to be nineteen, possibly twenty, but looked younger, fair hair pulled loosely back, wearing a cream shirt under faded dungarees; the eyes with which she regarded Resnick were alert and half-amused; the hand she offered was smooth and small-boned inside his.

'You don't remember me, do you?'

Resnick looked at her again. 'You're Stephanie?'

'Not a bad try. Actually it's Stella. But I still don't think you really remember.'

Resnick shook his head.

'You came here with Dad. I think I was eleven, some-thing like that. Maybe twelve. I remember pestering you about how you got to be a policewoman. On and on. It's all I wanted to be at the time, all I could think of, and Dad, well, he wouldn't talk about it. Said it was the last thing in the world I should do. No job for a girl, that's what I remember him saying, it's not a job for a girl.' She looked across at Lynn. 'Do you think he was right?'

'It depends.'

'What on?'

Lynn realised she wasn't certain. If there was an easy answer, she couldn't call it to mind. 'I suppose it depends what kind of a woman you are. But then we all have different ideas, don't we? About what work should be.'

'And women,' Stella said.

Lynn looked back at her, saying nothing. There was a clear smile at the sides of Stella's mouth, the corners of her eyes.

'But you do like it?' Stella asked. 'You enjoy what you do?'

'Most of the time, yes.'

'Good. It must be terrible, stuck in some job you can't stand. Boring, nine to five.'

'Well,' Lynn smiled. 'This certainly isn't that.'

'Is it something you're still considering?' Resnick asked. 'Coming on the Job?'

Stella laughed. 'I think all my dad's propaganda must have worked.' Almost apologetically, she looked at Lynn. 'He thought it was man's work, I'm afraid. Men of six foot and over.' She smiled a little wistfully. 'Bit of a traditionalist, Dad, where gender roles are concerned.'

Resnick looked into her face for a sign of what she was feeling, talking about her father as she was; she was forcing herself to do so, he thought, making herself talk that way in order to keep him alive.

'What are you doing?' Lynn asked.

'I'm at agricultural college.'

210

'You're going to be a farmer?'

Stella shook her head. 'Trees. That's what I'd like to do eventually. Get into forestry. Grow trees. Hundreds of them. Thousands.'

Lynn was grinning broadly.

'What?' Stella asked. 'What's the matter?'

'Nothing. I was just wondering where that came on the list of traditional women's jobs. Not very high, I don't suppose.'

'Dad said I'd grow out of it.' Stella laughed again. 'A phase I was going through. Bless him, he didn't really understand. Not that or a lot of other things.'

She was smiling at Lynn as her mother walked into the room. 'All that jollity,' Margaret Aston said, 'I wondered what on earth was going on.'

Stella stepped back, guiltily silent; the smile disappeared. As Resnick moved forward to greet her, Margaret's good intentions evaporated and her brave front collapsed in tears.

'I'm sorry,' she said, again and again, as Resnick hovered, uncertain, awkward, offering her a handkerchief which she refused. 'I kept telling myself I wouldn't do this, create a scene.'

'Mum,' Stella said, 'it's okay to cry.'

Her mother dabbed at her eyes with a wad of damp tissue, blew her nose, pushed automatically at the ends of her hair. 'Time enough for that later. It's not what Charlie's here for, is it, Charlie?' She sniffed. 'I'm sure there are questions to be asked, isn't that right. Work to be done.'

'Mum . . .' Stella started.

'No. It's what your father would have wanted. Eh, Charlie? It's what Bill would have wanted done.'

They had gone out into the garden, the house too cramped for Margaret, too confining, too full of her husband's memory, her grandson's shrill laughter and sudden tears. She had told them all that she could remember, most of what they wanted to know. Bill's early-morning swim, the journeys they had made together to the supermarket and then to the garden centre, later in the day. The letter from Nuneaton, inviting Bill to preach on Sunday fortnight; the phone calls from Stella and from their middle child, the son out in Australia, and the call that Bill had taken in the hall, somebody who'd rung him and he'd phoned them back, talked for quite a while, something else to do with his Church work, she supposed, Bill hadn't said.

Standing now near the bottom hedge, the three of them, Margaret, Resnick and Lynn, they were for that moment a silent tableau, while around them, the electric hum of unseen Flymos rose up and merged with the dulled roar of a passing plane.

'He was angry, Charlie, you can understand that. These last few years. He felt he'd been passed over; he'd given them everything he had and they didn't want any more so they hid him away in that wretched place. Offices with closed doors.' She smiled. 'You knew him, Charlie, better than most. He wanted to be out there, doing things. Real things. Work that mattered. That's what he believed in. He thought that it mattered, what he did. That it made a difference.' She half-turned away, shaking her head. 'That doesn't mean anything though, does it? Not any more. Not now. What you feel. That's old-fashioned. Belief.

212

Values. He was a dinosaur, Bill. That's what he was; he embarrassed them.'

'Margaret, no . . .'

'He embarrassed them and that's why they shut him away and waited for him to die.'

'Margaret . . .'

'And now this . . .'

'Of course, we . . .'

'All this . . .' She was facing him again, eyes raw not with loss but anger. 'All this performance, this great paraphernalia, all of you like headless chickens running around. Who did this? Who did this? Isn't it tragic? Terrible? Of course, it's terrible. He was my husband. But it's what you wanted all along.'

'Margaret, you know that's not true.'

'Isn't it? Not you, maybe. You personally. But the rest of them, all those smart young men – and women – with their smart young attitudes and sociology degrees. They don't care about him, none of them. Not a one.'

'Mrs Aston,' Lynn said, 'we'll catch whoever did this, we will.'

Margaret Aston looked at her long and hard, this young woman who could almost have been her daughter, so earnest, believing what she said. 'And if you do,' Margaret said, 'what difference will that make? What difference will that make now?'

Resnick waited till they were back in the car. 'That call, the one unaccounted for. Have it checked out, the number. Just in case.'

26

It turned out that John Anthony Lawrence St John had walked away from a place on the second year of an undergraduate course in applied mathematics at Bristol University – outside of Oxford and Cambridge, one of the most difficult to get into. His tutor had been convinced John Anthony Lawrence was on his way to a first; one year for his masters and then the Ph.D. A research fellowship for the asking. Before that, he had left his secondary school in Buckinghamshire – a grammar school, that county being just about the only one in which they still had a right to exist – with four high-grade A levels and ten Os. Glory, glory all the way.

'What buggers me,' Divine said, 'he's got all that going for him, all those brains, what's he doing, chucking it all away?'

Divine was in the canteen with Graham Millington, tucking into bacon, double egg and chips and beans, his earlier purloined sausage having sharpened his appetite more than a touch. Opposite him, Millington was slowly forking his way through a meat-and-potato pie that had spent too long in the microwave and whose contents now bore a startling affinity to slurry.

'Fancy it yourself, then, do you?' Millington asked. 'Groves of Academe?'

'Bollocks.'

'Well,' Millington said. 'I suppose that's a point of view.'

Divine dashed a large mouthful of egg and beans down with a quick swill of tea. 'The way I see it, he's so much sodding cleverer than me, he should be out there using it, making a whole lot more money, right? Sight more'n you or me. Instead of which, here am I, bringing in little enough as it is, all those deductions, national insurance, tax, some of which is going to keep him on the dole 'cause he's too fucking lazy to work.'

'His choice,' Millington said.

'Live off you and me? Yeh, thanks a lot!'

Millington pushed his plate aside and reached for a cigarette; one of life's little miracles, he was thinking, no matter how much radiation or whatever you zap those pies with in the microwave, there were always those few bits of gristle left intact, like pearls. 'Only thing need interest us,' he said, 'what he told us about finding Aston, it all holds up. Thank him for his help and kick him free.'

'Aye.' Divine nodded his head. 'More's the sodding pity.'

The river police had two divers working off their launch, searching the Trent either side of the bridge for a possible weapon or weapons. So far they had come up with two stools of the type frequently used by fishermen, several discarded rods, the rusted frame of a Raleigh bicycle, one picnic hamper, four nasty-looking knives, one of which had several triangular sections chipped out of the blade, a child's tricycle, roller skates, assorted pots and pans, a filing cabinet still containing fifty or so manila files, most likely rolled down the slope from County Hall by a disgruntled clerk, and a sawn-off double-barrelled shotgun, which was proving of great interest to the detectives investigating a three-month-old robbery at a bank on Gregory Boulevard. Nothing that might have been used in the attack on Bill Aston.

Forensic had recovered sufficient splintered fragments from the dead man's skull and face to be certain that the weapon involved had been a varnished implement, most likely a baseball bat of some kind. Even in this country where the game was comparatively rarely played, that was more and more the norm.

And blood: quite minute, difficult at first to detect, there were small samples of a second type, mixed in with Aston's. As soon as it was properly isolated, it could be checked against the recently established, steadily growing national DNA bank for comparisons.

Support Department had gone over the ground with a fine-tooth comb. Dog turds, cigarette ends and discarded cigarette packets, fast-food containers, used condoms and the like notwithstanding, they had come up with only two items which held potential interest: a D90 TDK audio cassette tape, unlabelled, which seemed to hold a fairly arbitrary selection of home-taped heavy metal, and a large-sized left-hand leather glove, well-worn, scuffed around the fingers' ends and smooth in the palm. Both of these items were undergoing further tests.

Scene of Crime had presented Naylor with evidence, mostly partial, of twenty-seven sets of footprints within

216

the immediate vicinity of the attack. A chart showing the positioning of these was still in the later stages of completion, but seemed to suggest that of this twenty-seven, nine were strongly present close to where the body had fallen; of that nine, five seemed to have partly circled around it. The impressions of three of these had been made by some kind of running shoe, one by a heavy work boot, the last, most likely, came from a regular, rubber-soled walking shoe.

After being successfully stalled by Phyllis Parmenter's secretary for the best part of a day, Khan had installed himself in the outer offices of the local authority inspectorate, and settled himself down with a copy of Vikram Seth's one-thousand-and-five-hundred-odd-page novel, intent upon a long wait.

The WPC walking away from Cossall had an arse on her like a pregnant duck. Cossall's words, though he kept them to himself and supped his pint; all this questioning – publicans and bar staff – it gave a man a thirst. And besides, where women on the force were concerned, nowadays it paid to keep your mouth closed.

He knew a sergeant at one of the out stations, not so much above a month back, who had chanced to make some innocuous remark about a female officer within her hearing and, within an hour of her lodging an official complaint, the poor sod had been suspended from duty, pending an investigation. A sure sign of the way it was going, Cossall thought, the writing on the menstrual bloody calendar.

Only that morning he had read in the paper, the first

ever woman chief constable had been appointed in Lancashire. A few years shy of fifty and, wouldn't you know it, a graduate from the Open University. And what was her degree in? Psychology. Cossall had read she'd be bringing in over seventy thousand a year salary. Seventy thousand. And a budget of close to a hundred and fifty million to dispose of. How much of that was going to go on setting up crèches, that's what he'd like to know? Counselling sessions? Hiring some poncey interior designer to put in soft furnishings and curtains in the interview rooms, create a more trusting atmosphere.

Still, what had she been quoted as saying? It's never been a man's world, they only think it is. Yes, well, that's where she was wrong: Cossall didn't think, he knew. At least until he chucked it all in, threw in his hand with one of them home security firms, it was his world still.

And if that WPC ever made it to the top they'd have to buy her a specially reinforced chair. Not that, he reflected, he'd say no to charvering it from behind. Nice tits, too, sort of stretch Dunlopillo, wouldn't mind spreading himself over those. He'd thought that when she had first walked in looking for him ten minutes before, Cossall lubricating his tonsils between visiting the pubs along London Road, spaced out between Trent Bridge and the city. Football pubs, most of them; big trade of a Saturday whichever side was at home, Forest or County.

'So what are you telling me, love,' Cossall had asked, 'the landlord won't talk to you, is that it?'

'He'll talk, right enough. Talk the hind legs off that donkey. It's what he won't say bothers me.' No hesitation, coming right back to him, giving as good as she got, Cossall liked her for that. Local, too. That accent. Mansfield, somewhere roundabout. 'Take, for instance, there's a couple of windows broken, right? Stuck together with tape, like he's waiting for them to be properly fixed. Well, that's recent, right? And when I had a shufti round back, there's a couple of chairs there, broken, slung out. But when I tried to ask him about them, any of that, he wasn't having any, just wasn't saying. I thought you might get more out of him.'

Cossall nodded. 'Right, thanks. I'll get right along.' And winked. 'I'd get you a drink, love, only you're on duty.'

She lowered her voice so no one along the bar would hear. 'If I weren't, I'd buy one for myself. But thanks, love, all the same.'

Cossall held back his grin until she had turned away and then watched her all the way to the door, an arse on her like a pregnant duck.

He walked off the street into the main bar of the pub; two men in working clothes were sitting off by the back window, Irish, Cossall could tell without knowing them, something about their complexion, broad, high brows, the natural wave at the front of the hair. An Irish pub, is that what this was?

He eased one of the high stools far enough out from the bar to sit down. Through in the side room, he could see a black youth in white T-shirt and dreadlocks, long baggy shorts and hi-top trainers, playing himself at pool. No, an equal opportunity pub, that's what it was.

'What'll you have?' the landlord asked, appearing at the end of the bar and coming slowly towards him. He was a tall man, rangy, with a flattened face that was more like a child's drawing than the real thing.

Cossall told him and watched the man draw a pint, showing him his warrant card when he set the glass before him. With a generous movement of his hand, the landlord waved Cossall's money away.

'I had one of your lot in here earlier,' the landlord said.

Cossall nodded. 'Tell me about Saturday night.' He could see the windows the officer had spoken of, down towards where the two men were sitting, glass cobwebbed over with brown tape.

'I told her.'

Cossall tasted the beer, grimaced and shook his head. 'If you'd told her, you wouldn't be standing there looking at me. If you don't tell me, tonight you'll be looking at two others like me; and tomorrow there'll be four and so it goes.' He set the glass back down. 'That's not what you want.'

The landlord forced a laugh. 'All this over a pane of broken glass and a few lousy chairs?'

Cossall leaned far enough forward for the man to feel his breath on his face. 'We had an officer killed, not a few hundred yards from here. Saturday night.'

'But that was nothing to do with this.'

'Why don't you,' Cossall said, 'let me be the judge of that?'

The landlord pushed a glass against the optic and gave himself a large Jameson's; sipped at it before, elbow leaning on the bar, he spoke. 'These youths come in sometimes, you know, match days. Skinheads, mostly. Lot of noise, swearing and that, but they spend well so most times I let it go. But this week, one of them gets into an argument with one of the Paddies that use the place all the time. Regulars, like. Well, one thing these lads can't stand, more than the blacks, even, it's the Irish. Just hate them. IRA truce or no truce, it doesn't matter a damn. And this gives them an excuse. One minute these two are squaring up to one another, a bit of pushing and shoving, you know how it goes; next thing, this skinhead's mates start in and before you know it the whole pub's like the last round of a Frank Bruno fight with no holds barred.' He drank a little more of the whisky and wiped the back of his hand across his mouth. 'I doubt if it lasted more than ten minutes at most.'

'You called it in? Called the police?'

'And risk my licence? It's not worth it. That's why I didn't want to say anything before.'

'You've been warned then?'

'Once or twice.'

Cossall nodded. 'These youths, know them well enough to know any names?'

Slowly, the landlord shook his head.

'D'you notice where they went from here?'

'No. But if I was to guess, I'd say on down towards the Trent.'

'And that's all it is, a guess?'

'Afraid so, yes.'

Cossall took a final swallow at his pint and pushed the glass away unfinished. 'Here.' He took a card from his top pocket and set it down on the bar. 'If you do hear a name, or if one comes to mind, give us a call.' He winked. 'It'll count for you, not against. Won't do any harm, someone in your corner, eh?'

The landlord watched Cossall till he was through the door, swallowed down what remained of his whisky and allowed himself another. He'd as soon count on a copper like Cossall, he thought, as back himself to win the lottery without buying a ticket.

27

Resnick was on his way back from the superintendent's office when Lynn intercepted him with her analysis of Bill Aston's movements and contacts during the last twenty-four hours of his life.

'It's pretty much all there,' she said, business-like, not quite looking Resnick in the eye. 'One or two gaps I still have to fill.'

Resnick gave the first sheet a quick glance. 'Anything that looks helpful?'

'Afraid not. Trips to the supermarket and the garden centre, that's about it. The pool. Walking the dogs.'

Resnick nodded, skimming the remainder. A day in the life of a quite ordinary, not especially interesting man. What was interesting about Aston was that he was dead: the manner of his dying.

'Okay, thanks.'

'There's one more thing,' Lynn said. 'You remember you asked me to track down that call Aston made the day of his death? The one that was unaccounted for.'

Resnick looked at her expectantly and she pushed a folded piece of paper into his hand. He opened it, looked thoughtfully at the name, then folded it again before pushing it down into his breast pocket.

'There were two other calls, too. Unanswered, but logged in Aston's office.'

'Right. Good.' And then, as Lynn turned away, 'Are you okay?'

She nodded, still not directly looking at him. 'I'd like to take an hour later, personal time?'

'Fine.'

They continued their separate ways, Resnick along the corridor towards the CID room, Lynn making for the stairs. Whatever else, Resnick was thinking, she's right about one thing – all this stuff that's troubling her, it doesn't seem to be interfering with her work.

The meeting with Skelton had not been encouraging. One of his best hopes had been that the second blood sample taken from Aston's clothes, the blood which wasn't Aston's own, would prove to have come from someone who was known. But Jane Prescott had checked the records available to Intelligence, made comparisons with all known and processed samples. Nothing. No match. Which left the shoe prints, the cassette and – most outside of all outside chances – the bat. After that, they were down to information received, unearthing a witness who had seen or heard more than anyone had so far come forward to say. The media appeals had brought in replies, of course, and these were being processed through the computer and the more promising laboriously checked out. But so far . . .

Sheer accident, Bill Aston's murder? An unfortunate victim who happened to be in the wrong place at the wrong time, or was there a more specific motive? Resnick thought again about the name Lynn had given him and was glad he had already arranged to meet Khan and discuss the Snape enquiry. If there was a connection there, he had to tease it out.

Reg Cossall was waiting for him in his office, using an empty coffee mug as an ashtray. With a degree of show, Resnick unfastened the window catch and lifted the lower frame high, before sitting down and gesturing with a hand to indicate Cossall should do the same.

'This could be nothing, Charlie . . .'

'I doubt that, Reg. If you thought that, you'd not be here.'

Cossall smiled his quick, lop-sided smile and retold the story of his meeting with the publican on London Road, gracing it with not a few embellishments of the scatological kind. A canny copper, Reg, Resnick was thinking, a man content to wear his prejudices on his sleeve, a glint in his eye like steel as if daring rebuke. Someone like Aston – similar age, equal seniority – they had been able virtually to discard, lost in the shuffle. But Cossall was too valuable, his experience too wide and his arrest rate too high.

'I checked back with the chap on the Embankment who'd been moaning on about having his Saturday night soccer disturbed. He's still not positive, but the youths he saw creating a disturbance, they could be the same ones from the pub. Only could, mind. There's a couple of other reports I'm having checked now, might get confirmation.'

Resnick turned it over. A strong possibility, it was true.

'This fight in the pub, fracas, whatever. No way we can place any of them with something like a baseball bat?'

Cossall narrowed his eyes and shook his head. ''Fraid not. But it's got to be a runner, my way of thinking. Specially since we've got Jack-shit else. These blokes, kids, not much more, out on the street, all pumped up from the scene in the pub, tanked up too. Maybe Bill said something to them, you know how he was. Bit high and mighty, holier than thou, could've told them to keep their mouths down, behave. I can see that, see him doing that, can't you?'

Yes. Yes, Resnick could. He'd been in contact with Bill's Sunday school manner more than a few times. He'd had more than a tendency towards sermonising, had Bill. 'You want to chase it down, Reg, or what?'

Cossall leaned back, cigarette spooling up smoke from between the fingers of a crooked hand. 'Like I said, there are a few things I'm checking into. But keeping on top of all that stuff the computer's spewing out doesn't leave a lot of time.'

'I'll have a word with Graham, see if he can help. But this landlord, you think leaning on him some more might loosen his tongue? You think he might know exactly who these youths are?'

'He might. And I'll do what I can.' Cossall winked. 'Within the rules.'

'Divine's got a mate with the Football Intelligence Unit,' Resnick said, as Cossall walked towards the door. 'Might be a contact worth following up. These lads might well be known to them by the sound of it.'

'If they are,' Cossall grinned, 'I doubt they'll be County

226

supporters, eh? Need to be drawing your pension, don't you, 'fore they'll as much as let you in the ground?'

With a sly laugh, Cossall was on his way, leaving Resnick standing beside his desk, picturing the group of young supporters at the last match he had attended. They had been lined up at the back of the stand, Union Jack draped from the wall behind them, raised fists clenched towards the opposition, one of them shielding his face inside a balaclava. He could hear their shrill young voices, lofted in anger. 'No surrender! No surrender!'

It had looked more like news footage from Northern Ireland, a Loyalist rally, than an otherwise tame end-of-season encounter near the foot of the Endsleigh League First Division.

Two of the phones in the CID room were in use as Resnick walked through, late for his meeting with Khan, and when the third phone rang it was Lynn, on her way back in, who picked it up.

'Lynn Kellogg, CID.' Working on auto-pilot, not over-friendly today. And then, as she held the receiver towards Resnick. 'For you.'

He pointed towards his watch and shook his head.

Lynn brought the receiver back towards her and asked who was calling. 'Hannah Campbell,' she said, mouthpiece covered now with her hand.

Surprised at hearing the name, Resnick felt himself beginning to flush. He started towards the desk but stopped short, changed his mind. 'Tell her,' he said, 'I'll call her later.'

'Later this afternoon or . . .?'

'Probably this evening.'

She was looking at him now, interested. 'Shall I get a number?'

'No,' Resnick over his shoulder, departing. 'It's all right. No need.'

Lynn asked anyway, a matter of procedure. Resnick was already descending stairs, two at a time, angry with himself for feeling embarrassed, remembering without pleasure what it had felt like to be twenty-three or -four.

For his meeting with Resnick Khan had worn a blue-black blazer, lightweight wool, tan trousers, highly polished brown shoes. His tie, a deep, dull red, almost rust, was one that Jill had given him a month after their second date and the first time they had slept together.

'What's this all about?' he had asked, amused.

'Call it an anniversary, if you like.'

'Starting off as we mean to carry on, is it?'

'Something like that.'

One month later he had given her a pair of minute white bikini briefs, with tiny bows at the sides, blue, he had said, to match her eyes.

She had punched him, surprisingly hard, on the arm; so hard the bruise didn't fade for days. 'My eyes are brown.'

Khan laughed. 'How should I know? One way or another, they're usually closed.'

This time he had caught the fist inside his palm. They were sitting in Jill's living-room, TV and stereo both switched off so that they could hear any of her kids, if they woke and decided to come downstairs.

Khan was thinking about that now, what had happened next, how it was possible, right down to those last moments, to stay quiet, when he saw Resnick hurrying up the short flight of steps and through the door leading into reception. He had imagined they would talk there, one of the rooms, temporarily spare, at central station, but Resnick insisted that they walk the short distance to the market, Resnick not really wanting to talk until he had downed his first espresso and ordered a second. Khan, not a great drinker of tea or coffee, content to sit and watch, watch and wait, the hubbub of trading all around them.

'Okay,' Resnick finally said, 'how far've we got?'

Khan told him that Phyllis Parmenter had given him a hundred reasons why she could not conceivably reveal the Inspectorate's findings ahead of publication, then hinted quite heavily that in her view there had been no serious lapses in security, nor any reasons other than the balance of his own mind why Nicky Snape had taken his own life.

'And Jardine?'

'Defensive, basically. One minute almost aggressive, the next not able to do enough to help.'

'Then he'd no objections to our re-interviewing the two staff on duty that evening?'

'None, but . . .' Khan smiled, '. . . Paul Matthews is off sick, quite serious, Jardine says, doesn't know how long that might go on, and the woman, Elizabeth, er, Peck, she's on annual leave.'

'Since when?'

'This last weekend apparently.'

Resnick's second espresso gave hot chase to the first. 'Come on,' he said, getting to his feet. 'I think we should pay Mr Jardine a call.'

'D'you want to ring him first? I could . . .'

But Resnick was already on his way. 'Let's make it a surprise.'

Sounds of Blur and Nirvana, identifiable to Khan if not to Resnick, squeezed from beneath a dozen doors. To the accompaniment of swearing and laughter, two youths played pool in one of the larger downstairs rooms, others sitting around watching, waiting their turn. In the television room, on a large-screen monitor, bought from the proceeds of the recent car boot sale and a sponsored run, another few were deep in shabby armchairs with a video recording of the previous season's Forest highlights. Good job it's not County's, Resnick thought, scarcely have time to settle back before you'd be reaching for the remote control, pressing rewind.

Jardine only kept them waiting five minutes and then greeted Resnick with a firm handshake, a surprising show of warmth. 'Afraid we might have got off on the wrong foot last time, Inspector. Put it down to the strain of what had happened, shall we? But now, come in, come in. Please, sit down. Inspector, um, Constable, what can I get you? Tea? Coffee? Mineral water?'

Both Resnick and Khan declined. Khan took his notebook from his inside pocket as he sat down, uncapped his pen. The veins criss-crossing Jardine's face were even more pronounced, Resnick thought, than before. He let his eyes slide again along the rows of photographs on the wall, one at least for each year.

'Well, it looks as if, unofficially as yet of course, but it looks as if the report will put us in the clear. The staff here.' Jardine treated them to his best PR smile, the one more normally saved for the occasional middle-class parent or visiting minor politicians. 'I spoke with Mrs Parmenter only an hour ago. Fortuitous, really. It seems as if she'll be giving us a clean bill of health.' Abruptly, he leaned forward, arms resting on the surface of his desk, serious now, smile set aside. 'Of course, it does nothing to minimise the awfulness of that boy's death.'

If he expected agreement, a sharing of sympathy, congratulations even, he got nothing; Resnick let his weight ease back in the chair a little more and crossed his legs, deep creases in the trousers of his suit.

Nervous under Resnick's gaze, the director flicked at the dandruff on his shoulder, tugged at the lobe of his ear. He looked from Resnick to Khan and back again. 'The, er, officer, DC Khan, explained there would be questions you might wish to put to me . . .'

'Your staff.'

'Sorry?'

'There are questions I need to put to your staff.'

'Of course, if . . .'

'Mr Matthews and Mrs, Miss Peck.'

One of Jardine's hands swotted the air in Khan's direction. 'As I explained to the young man here, unfortunately neither of them is currently available . . .'

'Unfortunately?'

'I'm sorry, I . . .'

'You said, unfortunately.'

'Yes, I . . .'

'Not fortunately?'

Jardine seemed to be suddenly short of breath. 'Inspector, I don't see . . .'

'Miss Peck, she's on holiday?'

'Part of her annual leave, yes.'

231

'Arranged a long time ago?'

Jardine's head swivelled part-way towards the chart attached to the wall behind him, annotations and arrows, neat in coloured inks. 'Usually such things are arranged, you know, at the beginning of the year.'

'So there was nothing sudden about Miss Peck's decision to take her leave now?'

'Oh, no.'

The green lettering denoting her absence looked, to Resnick, remarkably new; he raised an eyebrow in Khan's direction and the DC made a note in his book.

'You've no idea, I suppose where she's decided to take this leave? Abroad, maybe? At home, redecorating the bathroom, something like that?'

Jardine shook his head. 'My staff, their private lives . . .' He shrugged, as though they could be none of his concern.

'And Mr Matthews,' Resnick said, relaxed still, quite relishing this, Jardine's discomfort, relishing it in a way that was unusual for him and perhaps not exactly understanding why. 'I understand he's off sick?'

'I'm afraid so.'

'Tummy bug? Flu? Something more serious?'

Jardine was giving his ear a little more attention; when his hand brushed, inadvertently, against his hair, another little fall of dandruff showered down.

'What is wrong with him, Mr Jardine?'

'I believe the doctor's note mentioned nervous exhaustion.'

'Brought on by what happened here to Nicky Snape?'

'The note gave no indication . . .'

'But that's likely the reason, wouldn't you say?'

'I don't know if it's wise to conjecture . . .'

232

'A member of your staff, you would have realised if he was unduly upset. He found the body, didn't he? That morning I spoke to him, he seemed distressed.'

'Naturally. Paul is a very caring man. Dedicated.' For a moment, Jardine's eyes switched anxiously towards Khan, as if unnerved by the movement of his pen. 'Something like that, he would be bound to be affected.'

Resnick was nodding agreement. 'Then there's nothing else, no other reason that you can think of, no other cause for Mr Matthews to be suffering from – what was the expression? – nervous exhaustion?'

'No.'

'He wasn't apprehensive, for instance, about the results of the enquiry?'

Jardine shook his head. 'He had no need to be. He would have known that. And rightly. As I said, Mrs Parmenter . . .'

'I meant the police enquiry. DC Khan here. Inspector Aston.'

'Certainly not.'

'And Miss Peck, as far as you know, she wasn't unduly concerned about Inspector Aston's findings?'

'If she was, she certainly never expressed these concerns to me. Quite the reverse, in fact. After her interview, as I remember, she said that she thought it had been less of an ordeal than she had feared.' Jardine was feeling secure enough to try a smile again. 'I'm sure in no small way due to your colleague here.'

Resnick nodded. 'I see. You've no idea, then, why she left messages twice at Inspector Aston's office, or why, when she finally did get to speak to him at his home on

233

the day that he died, they apparently talked for almost three-quarters of an hour?'

Jardine's head dipped forward and he closed his eyes. You crafty old bugger, Khan was thinking, looking across at Resnick, you sat on that one well enough.

'Mr Jardine?' Resnick said.

A vein at the side of Jardine's head was beginning to throb. 'I'm sorry, I know nothing about that at all.' He held Resnick's stare for several moments. 'I don't even know if it's true.'

'I'd be obliged,' Resnick said, getting to his feet, 'if you would let DC Khan have home addresses and telephone numbers for both Mr Matthews and Miss Peck. You might as well furnish them for the rest of the staff, while you're about it. I can't be sure how many I might need to speak to and it'll save time later on. Oh, and if you could arrange for a copy of that medical certificate you mentioned?'

Angry but uncertain, Jardine gave it a last try. 'I don't see that you have any right, Inspector . . .'

'Mr Jardine.' Resnick leaning towards him, over him, his own anger taking over. 'Not only has a boy died while in your care, a police officer, the one looking into that death, has been murdered. Just how much right do you think I need?'

28

The first few times Lynn had seen Petra Carey it had been at the hospital, the psychiatric wing, a forlorn section towards the back, close to the kitchens. After that it had been in the large Victorian house the therapist shared with several others; group sessions were held in the lower rooms, individual consultations on the upper floors.

The room in which they met was arranged so that Lynn sat facing a high window, too high to see anything more than the top branches of trees across the broad street, snatches of roofs, the sky. There was a lot of sky. Lynn's chair was comfortable, but not too much so, with polished wooden arms and a back that curved away, a decently cushioned seat. Petra Carey sat to one side, a similar chair placed at right angles, a low square table between them which always held flowers; today they were yellow tulips, already beginning to bend and scoop their swan-like necks. Tulips or not, the room, Lynn thought, smelled of roses just the same. Was it Petra Carey's perfume or something that she sprayed into the air?

Sometimes Lynn would turn her head and look at the therapist when either of them spoke, but more usually she stared ahead, following the slowly shifting kaleidoscope of clouds.

'So, Lynn, how are we today? How have you been since we last met?'

Always the same opening gambit, and always a pause, which seemed to her unnaturally long, before Lynn could bring herself to answer. So aware of the delicate ground on which she might be beginning to tread. 'Fine. I've been fine. At least, I thought so.'

'D'you want to tell me what's happened? What's caused you to change your mind?'

Petra Carey was, Lynn guessed, in her early thirties, not so very much older than Lynn herself, although, without perhaps meaning to, she made Lynn feel young, younger. Lynn was sure the room had something to do with it, that feeling of being summoned there; it reminded her of when she had been at school, the situation more than the room itself. Those occasions when she had been found wanting: you know, Lynn Kellogg, we expected better of you than this.

While Lynn framed her answer, the therapist waited patiently, her only jewellery the broad wedding ring on her left hand.

'The case I've recently started working on,' Lynn said finally. 'The policeman who was just killed. It's that. To do with that.'

Petra nodded. 'Go on.'

Lynn told her about visiting the victim's family with Resnick and Margaret Aston's reactions – her anger, the way even that had seemed controlled. And the daughter, Stella, telling them how she had wanted to join the police when she'd been younger; follow, Lynn supposed, in her father's footsteps. But it had been Resnick whom she had asked. And now she was studying forestry, the daughter, agriculture, pining to go off and do things with trees.

Unusually, Petra Carey smiled.

'What?'

'Nothing, no, go on.'

'But what's so funny?'

'Nothing's funny.'

'Then why are you laughing?'

'I was smiling.'

'What at?'

Touching her ring, forefinger and thumb, Petra Carey turned it around on her hand. 'There's so much there, in that story.'

'Tell me,' Lynn said.

But the therapist shook her head. 'That's not the way it goes.'

And once Lynn had begun to talk, think it through as she spoke, she thought she could see why Petra Carey had been amused. It was all there, much of it, the things that had been worrying her. Niggling away. Undermining her ever since the time she had been held prisoner by that sick bastard; the first time he had spoken to her directly, after leaving the hospital in which her father was being treated for cancer. Her father who she had feared was dying. And here was Bill Aston, near enough her father's age, beaten to a pulp and leaving his wife and family to manage. Wife and daughter. The daughter who wanted to be a policewoman. 'Oh, Lynnie!' Lynn remembered her own mother's disapproving cry. 'No. No, please no.' And, unlike Stella Aston, she had done it anyway, gone ahead and joined. And her father had got sick and now he was in remission. Lynn and her mother waiting, not saying, waiting for the cancer to come back.

'Yes,' Petra Carey said once Lynn had finished speaking, 'of course, you're right. It's no wonder it troubled you, all those similarities, echoes. Your fears about your father's health; that he might die and leave you. The guilt that persists about going against their wishes and joining the police, as if somehow that has contributed to your father's illness.'

They had talked about that before, over and over, around and around – Lynn's sense of guilt. The therapist trying to manoeuvre her into seeing her father's cancer was not her doing, there was no cause and effect. His sickness was not in Lynn's gift, not in her control.

'What else is there?' Petra Carey asked. Faint, from outside, electronic sound, drifting and melodic: one of the other therapists, she had explained, liked to use music with his patients, to have them lie on the couch, eyes closed, and think themselves back into the womb.

'What do you mean,' Lynn asked, 'what else?'

No reply: not quite silently, the clock continued to tick round. Fifty minutes, it wasn't long. At least, for maybe the first half it was; it seemed then as if the hand was hardly moving, as though everything had slowed almost to a halt. And then the final twenty minutes seemed to race. Always. Burdened by the pressure to say something, Lynn sometimes froze.

'What else,' Petra Carey said, 'do these two stories have in common? This man whose death you're investigating and your own. Is there a common factor we haven't talked about?'

'I suppose you mean *him*, don't you? My boss. That's

238

what you're driving at.' Lynn was close to anger now, a pinch of colour in her cheeks.

'Inspector Resnick.'

Lynn looked away.

'The daughter,' Petra Carey asked, 'Stella, I think you said. What's her relationship to Resnick in this story you've told me?'

'I suppose she looked up to him. I mean, he's the one she asked about the police, not her father. Even though her father's a policeman.'

'And why do you think that might have been?'

Shaking her head, Lynn smiled; just a little, around the eyes. 'Because he's her father. She sees him all the time. He's always there. Ordinary.'

'And Charlie Resnick?'

'He's different. He's from outside. More, oh, I don't know, glamorous, I suppose you could say. Not so everyday.'

'But he and her father, they were roughly the same age?'

'Round about.'

'And Stella was how old?'

'Eleven, twelve.'

'You think she could have had a crush on him?'

'Oh, now look.' Alert, Lynn leaned forward in her chair, looking at the therapist directly.

'Yes?'

'I know what you're trying to get me to say.'

'What's that?'

'Listen, I'm not eleven or twelve.'

A small shrug of the therapist's shoulders, a disarming smile.

'And I don't have a crush on my boss. That's so stupid. It's not like that. It's not like that at all.'

'All right,' Petra Carey said encouragingly. 'What is it like?'

'It's not like anything.'

The clock showed there were only two minutes to go; it was one of Petra's rules, she never overran.

'I don't see,' Lynn was saying, 'why it always has to keep coming back to this.'

'It was your story.' The therapist smiled quietly. 'It was what you wanted to talk about today.'

She was on her feet now. The session was over. But Lynn continued to look at her, stubbornly, from her chair. 'It was because of my dad, because I'm afraid of him dying. That's what made me think about it. That's why.'

'I know that. That's clear.'

'Well, then?'

The therapist was standing by the door, looking pointedly at the clock. Anger and distress were clear on Lynn's face and in the way she rose reluctantly from the chair and reached for her bag and coat.

'In your story,' Petra Carey said, 'the daughter, for whatever the reason, might not be able to express her love for her father, all of her love, so she offers it to his friend instead. A man who's like her father, an idealised version of her father. It's part of the normal pattern of growing up. Growing away. Little girls love their fathers. Usually, then, they replace them with other men. Because once you reach a certain age, that love of the father, part of that love, is associated with guilt. Society considers it inappropriate. But if that other man, the man to whom she, the girl, wants to give her love, is too much like her

240

father, she may fall prey to the same taboo. What she ends up feeling is guilt. And guilt is a destructive feeling. It eats away at us from the inside, makes it impossible for us to act.'

There were people moving around on the stairs outside. Lynn walked past the therapist towards the open door.

'I'll see you at the same time next week,' Petra Carey said. 'If you need to get in touch with me beforehand, please ring.'

The music, wherever it had been coming from, had stopped. Part-way down the carpeted stairs, Lynn swung her head. The door to the therapist's room was already closed.

29

Hannah had devised strategies so as not to think about him, this big, bulky man with the sad eyes. That day, at work, it had not been too hard. The demands of thirty adolescents at a time, so often eager for anything but learning, failed to allow her much space for personal day-dreaming. Her attempts to draw Nicky's former classmates into a discussion on gender politics, based around Lady Macbeth's cry of 'unsex me now', had foundered disastrously. But when, discussing with her sixth-form group one of her favourite Jayne Anne Phillips stories, in which a former dancer visits her dying father, she found herself thinking, not about the restraint and control in the writing, but the surprising grace with which Resnick could walk across a room, she knew, restraint or not, she was going to call him the first chance she got. And when what she got was Lynn Kellogg's peremptory voice informing her that the inspector was busy and he would try to call her back later, Hannah thought it no more than she deserved.

Whatever had happened to cool?

Back home, she watered the tubs of flowers and the hanging baskets in the backyard, pulled a few weeds away

242

from around the shrubs which were newly planted along one side of her small front garden and considered cutting the grass; finally she brought out a mug of peppermint tea and the lemon cream biscuits she had bought on the way home, and sat on her front step, sweater round her shoulders, reading Marge Piercy. She found herself feeling so fiercely angry at the efforts the central character was prepared to make to hang onto a husband forever having affairs with younger women, that she forgot to ask herself if anger wasn't precisely what Piercy wanted her to feel.

When the phone called her indoors, a part of her sang with a sweet degree of expectation, but it was only her mother and when the two women had talked long enough for Hannah to realise she was no longer listening, had not really heard anything her mother had said for at least five minutes, she made an excuse and hung up.

She took a ready-to-heat mushroom bake from the freezer and slid it into the microwave. Pouring herself a glass of wine, she began to make a list of all those fiddling little jobs she would do that evening, another of all the friends she should call.

Considering what it had cost, the wine was surprisingly good. The mushroom bake, as usual, was fine. Wanting some bread to go with it, and regretting that she had forgotten to stop for bread on the way home – the biscuits had come from her corner shop, but the bread they stocked was pre-sliced and not worth considering – she found some oatcakes in the back of the cupboard, carefully enough wrapped that they had not lost all their bite.

The first two people she called were seemingly out and Hannah declined their invitation to speak after the tone; the third one was engaged, the fourth had for some reason been disconnected. In the living-room she channel-hopped for all of five minutes before switching off. It was either too late or too early to take a bath. She would do some more reading, listen to the stereo. The way she was behaving was extraordinary: all right, she had slept with the man once but it had not exactly been like Paul on the way to Damascus. No startling revelations, no blinding lights. Just competent, almost comfortable sex. She remembered to switch off the Gregson and Collister CD before it got to 'Last Man Alive', but then realised she had listened three times in succession to 'Baby, Now That I've Found You' – not the old original version by some pop group she vaguely remembered from when she was a child, but this new one, bluegrass, sung by Alison Krauss. Now that I've found you, dum, de-dum, dum, dum, da-dum, gonna build my life around you. Madness, Hannah was certain, that way comes. Time for a slow, hot bath and an early bed.

She was tipping in the peach and honey cream foam when the phone rang again.

'Oh,' Hannah said, flushing, 'it's you.' And, 'Yes, okay.' And, 'You want to come here?' And, 'No, no, half an hour would be fine. Till then, okay, goodbye.'

God, Hannah, she thought, checking the temperature of the water before slipping in, are you a cinch or what?

In the event it was just short of the hour by the time Resnick's cab had dropped him off near the entrance to the recreation ground and he had walked along the shrouded strip of unmade road, once again past the house where Mary Sheppard had died. So many parts of this city from which Resnick now averted his eyes without ever being able to shut the images from his mind.

The front door to Hannah's house was open and his adrenalin immediately began pumping, sensing an intruder, a burglary, something worse. But, no, it was only Hannah, shooing a ginger cat along the narrow hallway, the animal pausing on the front step to look back at her balefully, ears flat to its head.

'Not yours, I take it?'

Hannah made a show of shuddering. 'Can't stand them, I'm afraid. That one especially.' Taking in Resnick while she was talking, the effort he had made to look informal, pale-blue shirt, the top two buttons unfastened, light-grey trousers, a dark tweedy jacket that had seen better days. 'I woke up one night, not so long ago, that wretched animal must have sneaked in somehow and stayed – anyway, I heard this sound, just light, you know, but like someone else in the room, breathing, and there it was, stretched out on the bed next to me, paws right out, fast asleep.'

'Some people,' Resnick said, 'would consider that an honour.' It didn't come out sounding exactly the way it was meant, but like some corny line, the kind he could imagine coming from someone like Divine. 'The cat, I mean,' Resnick said, trying to retrieve the situation, 'it must have felt comfortable, trusted you.'

'Yes, well, when it comes to who's sharing my bed,' Hannah said, 'I like to do the choosing myself.'

Resnick bent towards the animal, which was sitting there cleaning itself, unconcerned. Watching him stroke the cat's head, Hannah imagining him wearing one of those loose linen suits, creased and a little baggy, cream-coloured, or, no, stone; that was it, stone.

She gave a wry smile. 'You obviously don't feel the same way? About cats?'

'There's something easy to like about them. Independence, I think.' The ginger one was now purring quite loudly, a little saliva issuing from its jaw. 'I mean, they'll take any amount of this fuss, all you can give, but as soon as it's over, that's that. It doesn't seem to matter if you never go near them again.'

Not such a bad description, Hannah thought, of men. Some, at least, that she'd known. 'You've got one of your own?'

He did that smiling thing with his eyes. 'Four.'

'Four cats?'

'It was sort of accidental. I didn't intend it to happen.'

Hannah laughed. 'Nobody can have four cats by accident.'

'Well . . .'

'And how many of them get to share your bed?'

'Oh, one or two.'

Then thank God you've come here, she thought. 'Why don't you come in?' was what she said.

The wine was already open. They sat in the small front room, made smaller by his presence, and chatted back and forth. Resnick asked her about her day. He asked her if she'd heard about the policeman who'd been found by the Trent, murdered, and when she said, yes, she had, a little, told her that was what he was working on.

'Is that what you always do? That kind of thing?'

'Murder, you mean?'

Hannah nodded: maybe it explained the look, vaguely haunted, behind his eyes.

246

'Not always,' Resnick was saying. 'Despite what you might read, there aren't so many of them. But yes, I suppose, yes, quite often.'

Hannah edged forward on her seat. 'But doesn't it get to you? I'm sure it must.' Something about Macbeth, so far steeped in blood.

'Sometimes. It depends.' What got to Resnick, what really touched him, was the whole thing: everything he saw. The way people could be with one another, the things they could do: the things they could be made to do in extreme situations – guilt, impotence, poverty, love.

'You become used to it, is that what you mean? Become – what's the word? – inured. Hardened to it, I suppose.'

Resnick wondered whether this was what he wanted to be doing, talking about this. 'To a degree, yes, otherwise you couldn't do the job.' He wanted to go across the room and touch her, but, what had happened the last time notwithstanding, he didn't know how. He wondered if he were guilty of staring too obviously at her mouth. He looked instead at the glass in his hand and drank some more wine.

Hannah was moved by it, the shyness of him. 'A penny for them, Charlie. That's what my dad used to say.'

'Your dad called you Charlie?'

'No.' Laughing. 'You know what I mean.'

Resnick thought that he did. 'So did mine,' he said. 'Except that it was in Polish. But I suspect it was more or less the same.'

'So what were you thinking of?'

He didn't answer.

'Not murder?'

'No.' He shook his head.

247

Hannah set down her glass and got to her feet. 'Just so long as you don't think that whenever you come here, the first thing we do is tumble into bed.'

'No.' Looking at her mouth again, openly this time. 'That's not what I think.'

'Good.' She was holding out her hand.

He was aware of her moving beside him, felt a touch of her shoulder, warm and smooth, as she turned. In the almost dark of the room, he looked at his watch and was surprised that it was only a little after two. He felt as if he had been asleep for hours.

Quietly, Hannah slid her legs from beneath the duvet and sat up. A small gasp as Resnick reached out and touched her back, the knots of spine against the skin. She reached behind and circled her fingers around his wrist.

'Don't stop. That's not to make you stop.'

He kissed the back of her hand, the space between her shoulder blades, her neck; she moved her hand from his and ran it along his chest.

'I was going to the bathroom,' she said. And then, near the door. 'Can I get you anything?'

He looked at her, naked beneath the skylight, unself-conscious now, the dark wedge of hair between her legs that he might cover with his hand. Everything, part of him responded silently, that part to which he usually paid no heed.

'Water, anything?'

'A glass of water would be fine.'

They sat together in the kitchen, dunking biscuits into tea, contentedly not talking, at least not a great deal, Resnick dressed save for his jacket, Hannah wrapped in her dressing-gown, already the beginnings of what seemed like routine.

'What's happening . . .' Resnick began.

She pressed a finger close across his mouth. 'Not now, Charlie. Not now.'

His eyes asked her why.

'If anything's going to happen, there'll be time enough.'

On cue, there was the sound of a cab approaching the rear of the house.

'Maybe next time you'd like to come round to me? I could make a bit of supper, something like that.' He was shrugging on his coat.

Hannah smiled. 'All those cats.'

'They're not always all four there at once.'

'Oh. I suppose that makes it okay.'

At the door she went to kiss him on the cheek and deftly he moved his head so that she kissed him on the mouth instead. At the end of the alley, the taxi driver sounded his horn twice.

'Isn't there supposed to be a law against that?' Hannah smiled.

'Kissing?'

'Using your horn after dark.'

For a moment, he touched her breast beneath the soft fabric of her gown. 'I have to go.'

'Yes.'

Stooping his head, he kissed her where his hand had been.

She watched him walk away towards the light and already those first familiar feelings of pain were swaying inside her.

30

As far as Kevin Naylor was concerned, this was not a good day. It had started when Debbie had walked out of the bathroom that morning, not saying anything, but the expression on her face telling him everything he needed to know. She had got her period. Punctual to the minute.

'Deb . . .'

But she had brushed him away, opening the fridge to stand there, head angled towards it, staring between the flavoured yoghurts, the leftover lemon pie, the lettuce and the film-wrapped cheese at what she could no longer see.

'Deb . . .'

'Leave it, will you! Just leave it.'

And he had, slurping down the last of his tea, grabbing a piece of toast which he ate on the way to the car. The traffic was a bastard as usual that time of the morning, and all the while Debbie's unspoken accusation knifing into him, as if it were all his fault.

'Maybe we should go to the doctor,' she'd ventured once before when they'd been trying. 'See if there's anything, you know, that he can do.'

'I'm not going to see any doctor. Fuck the doctor!' Kevin had replied.

'Okay.' Debbie grinning. 'If you think he'd do a better job.'

'Fuck you too,' Kevin had said, but with a smile. And he had, but it hadn't made a difference, then or now.

'Don't worry,' she had said last night, taking him in her hand. 'You fret too much about it, I reckon that's what it is. I was reading, you know, this article in *Cosmopolitan*, how anxiety, it, you know, it's – what you call it? – inhibiting.'

Sometimes he even wondered if that weren't right; after all, when making a baby had been just about the last thing on their minds, there hadn't been any problem at all. And they'd had their two years of sleepless nights to prove it.

And as if all of that weren't enough, there was this, waiting on his desk for him when he walked in; the analysis of the footmarks around Aston's body. The regular shoe, size eight, had been recently repaired with a rubber stick-on sole and a quarter heel, the kind that were fitted in over twenty instant shoe repair shops in this and any other city. Anonymity guaranteed. The work boot was a Caterpillar, size ten, well-worn. Eight local outlets, God knows how many hundred sold. And the trainer – a Nike indoor sports shoe, badminton or squash, a kidney-shaped zigzag pattern, deeply cut, below the ball of the foot, another, similar, but shaped like an elongated heart, beneath the heel. Relatively new, or, at least, sparingly used. The kind that had a colour flash at the side, a scored section in a contrasting colour just above the heel. *Fabriqué en Thailande.* US size twelve, UK eleven, European size forty-six. One of Nike's more popular lines.

'Jesus wept!' Naylor said, pushing the report to the other side of his desk.

251

'What's up?' Divine asked, squeezing past on his way to the Gents.

'Nothing. Bloody nothing.'

'Suit yourself.'

Naylor sat down, spun a pencil round and round on top of the envelope the report had arrived in, retrieved and reread it, looking at the patterns more carefully this time, and then reached for the phone and began to dial.

Divine stood close up against the stall, grimacing, trying not to notice the burning sensation as he tried to pee. Trying and failing. Even when he wasn't feeling it, which had not been often in the past thirty-six hours, he couldn't seem to shake it out of his mind.

If that little slut he'd picked out round back of the Orchid had given him a dose, he's seek her out and give her a good backhander before she went off to get her penicillin.

Jesus! Ow! Christ allmighty, that hurt.

Almost, but not quite as much as the time he woke up early one morning and stumbled out for his regulation slash and there it was, clear even to his befogged eyes, blood washing around in his piss. That wasn't what had really hurt. It was later, on his back in the clap clinic, this male nurse, chubby little bastard – black, too, that had really been the icing on the sodding cake – telling him, smiling all the while, 'The bad news, you're going to feel this. Nothing we can do about that. But the good news, it'll be over so fast, you won't believe it's happened. Okay. Now just try to relax.' And before Divine could protest he manipulated him a little, before pushing this umbrella-shaped needle down into the end of his penis, down into the opening and scooping it back out. 'There now, all done.' Still grinning, he had patted Divine on the shoulder and for a moment Divine had thought he was going to give him a sweetie for being good, Divine lying there in that narrow cubicle, unable to believe what had just happened to his dick.

Although, he had thought, trousers back up and putting a brave face on it as he walked down the line of men waiting to go and get theirs, it could be a sight worse. Quick dose of NSU, that's all it was. Not like some of these sorry buggers, take a look at 'em, if it wasn't AIDS this time, then likely it would be next. Still, bollocking shirt-lifters, they got what they deserved. Divine shuddered and cupped his gear into his jockeys before zipping up. Anyone who'd get his jollies sticking it up some bloke's arse . . . the thought of it made him want to puke.

Back in the CID room, Millington broke off in the midst of a delicate rendition of 'When I Fall in Love' to remind Divine they needed to be on their way in the next ten minutes or so, a man to go and see about a pub. Though if Reg Cossall hadn't been able to get names or detailed descriptions out of the landlord, Millington was doubtful if they'd have better luck. But it was ground that had to be covered. Good police work, steady and predictable, that's what got results. Well, sometimes . . .

Shane Snape had discharged himself from the hospital and picked up a taxi on the Derby Road, close by the university roundabout. His face still showed signs of bruising and his ribs would have to stay taped up for the next couple of days, but otherwise he was feeling better than perhaps he had a right to, the beating he had taken.

253

Norma greeted him with a kiss and a hug that made him wince, and Peter grinned and reached up from the settee to shake Shane's hand and say welcome home, as though it was his sodding home to welcome him into.

'How much longer's he staying?' Shane asked Norma out in the kitchen, not bothering to lower his voice.

'Come on, love,' Norma said. 'Don't be like that.'

'I'm not being,' Shane said, 'like fucking anything.'

Less than half an hour later he was off out again, ignoring his mother's questions about where he was going and when he might be back. He caught one bus into the city centre and then another out to Ilkeston; it was little more than a ten-minute walk from the bus station to where his mate Gerry Hovenden lived.

Hovenden was one of the blokes Shane hung around with, drank with at weekends: a good mate. When Shane came round the corner, Hovenden was down on his hands and knees by the front path, the exhaust of the motor bike he was repairing laid on an old length of oily blanket near the front door.

'Hey,' Shane said, 'how's it going?'

'Slowly. How about you?'

Shane grinned. 'Slowly, too.'

He stood for a while on the threadbare patch of front garden, feigning interest.

'Not a lot of use asking you to pitch in.' Hovenden grinned. 'Lend a hand.'

'Not a lot.'

'Go on inside if you want, nobody's in. You know where everything is.'

Hovenden lived in the place with his dad, his mum having gone from there to a refuge five years before,

before moving to Birmingham, where she was living with a long-distance lorry driver who hated Gerry's guts. Since she'd left, his dad had taken up with a woman who worked in the local garden centre and spent more time at her house than here. Added to which he worked shifts. So mostly now, it was as if Hovenden lived there on his own.

It was a flat-roofed Fifties house on a spent-up estate, a few of the places owner-occupied, but mainly not. The council, as usual, were behind on maintenance, paint flaked away from around the window frames and once enough water had gathered on the roof, it found a way through.

Shane switched on the TV and wandered off without really looking at it. There were four cans of Strongbow in the fridge and he snapped one open and sat down on the folded piece of foam that served as a settee, someone blabbing away on the TV screen, Shane still not bothering to watch. He pulled a bundle of comics towards him and started to leaf through them; finding a *Judge Dredd* he read it from cover to cover. Shifting it to the bottom of the pile, he found – what was this? – not a comic, some kind of fanzine. A magazine. *The Order.* The cover showed a large white death's head on a black background. One of Gerry's old biker things, Shane guessed, back from when his hair was long and his leather stank of engine oil and never being washed for years on end. But inside, above a picture of a crowd of youths standing outside iron gates, he read: *The Holocaust is a load of bollocks. C18 experts examine the myth.*

As he was starting to read it, Hovenden came into the house, wiping his hands on a piece of rag.

'Oh,' he said, seeing what was in Shane's hands. 'You found that.'

'I didn't know you was into politics,' Shane said.

'Yes.' Gerry Hovenden shrugged. 'Now and again.'

Standing in the queue at the sandwich counter across the street, Resnick pondered on a largely fruitless day. He had driven out with Khan to the house in Colwick where Paul Matthews lived. At first, the place had been so quiet, they'd thought nobody was at home, but then Matthews's mother had come through the side gate that led from the rear of the house. A bird-like woman in a yellow dress. Paul, she informed them, had been terribly upset by what had happened – that poor, poor boy – Resnick had assumed she was referring to Norma's son and not her own, but wasn't sure. The doctor had signed him off work, nervous exhaustion, yes, that was right, signed him off with medication and told Paul to take a rest. Ordered him. He had gone down to stay with a favourite aunt, in Wales, South Wales, Rhossili Bay. Resnick knew it, perhaps? Resnick did not. Ah! Beautiful, still a little wild, you know. And quiet, this time of the year. So restorative, the sea.

'Colour blind,' Khan had said, back in the car.

'Mmm?'

'Colour blind. Every word she said was aimed directly to you. I don't think she knew I was there.'

Elizabeth Peck certainly had not been there either. Her house, one of those new pseudo-Georgian places off Wilford Lane, was locked up tight. Blinds pulled, curtains drawn, burglar alarm armed, not one, but two Banham locks on the front door. The neighbours knew her but not well; knew, at least one of them did, that she had gone away. Holiday. She did not know where. Or when she might return.

Resnick had considered dismissing Khan to the further reaches of the Welsh coast to talk to Matthews, but for now opted to keep that particular powder dry and save on travel expenses to boot. It was Elizabeth Peck whom Bill Aston had spoken to and now Resnick wanted her to speak to him. What he sent Khan off to do was establish whether or not she owned a car; then check with the travel agencies, East Midlands Airport, the railway station, see if he couldn't get a line on where she'd gone, when she might be expected back.

Before Resnick could carry his sandwich into the comparative privacy of his office, Naylor intercepted him, his day looking up at last. 'This shoe stuff, sir, inconclusive's putting it mildly. But I had them look again at the markings and one thing's pretty much agreed. Whoever was wearing the boots, you can tell from the movement, variations in pressure and the like, he was the one did most of the damage, really heavy blows that did for Aston, he was the one.'

'Good work, lad. Well done.'

He was just about to bite into the sandwich, stray mayonnaise already on the cuff of his shirt, when Millington knocked and entered.

'Any luck, Graham?'

'Not a lot, still claiming not to know any names, but he's agreed to go down to Central and look at some photos, may come up with something that way. Did catch a word with one or two regulars who were in there on the Saturday when the fight broke out, though. Confirmed

257

these lads throwing their weight around had been at the match earlier in the day. Regular supporters by the sound of it.'

'Right, Graham. Tell Mark to contact that pal of his in the Football Intelligence Unit, set up a meeting.'

Millington was scarcely out of the door when Lynn Kellogg came in. Resignedly, Resnick pushed the sandwich back in its paper bag and shut the bag in his desk drawer.

'I've been going over that breakdown I did,' Lynn said. 'Aston's last twenty-four hours. And there's one period I'm not clear about. He met you in the Partridge on the Friday evening to talk about Nicky Snape and didn't get back to the house until pretty late, between eleven thirty and midnight Mrs Aston said.'

'And I left him at around half nine, sitting with half an inch of mild.'

Lynn nodded. 'According to Mrs Aston, he said he was there talking to you the whole time. Made a point of it.'

Resnick shrugged. 'She could have been getting confused.'

'She might. Or Aston might have lied.'

Resnick looked at her seriously. 'In which case he'd likely have had good reason.'

'I thought,' Lynn said, 'before taking it any further, I'd pop out there and talk to Mrs Aston again, see if she's still saying the same. If that's okay with you.'

Resnick was already reaching for the phone. 'I'll call her first, then ride out with you. We can ask her together.'

31

Stella Aston met them at the door, wearing jeans and an oversized sweater; her hair hung slightly damp against her shoulders, washed and imperfectly dried. She smiled a greeting and stood back to let Resnick and Lynn enter, but there was a tiredness behind the smile that she couldn't disguise.

'Mum's been lying down,' she said. 'Why don't you come through to the kitchen? She's just getting dressed. I don't suppose she'll be very long.'

Stella made instant coffee, chatting with just a slight awkwardness to Lynn, Resnick off to one side, staring out at the garden. Although he imagined it had not long since been done, the grass would soon be in need of cutting again.

When Stella carried over Resnick's cup, Lynn watched her, without knowing exactly what she was looking for, a change of expression on her face, the way she smiled. *You think she could have had a crush on him*: Petra Carey's words. Well, why not? Others had, Lynn was certain. Fleetingly, Stella's fingers, surely by accident, brushed against the back of Resnick's hand. *Little girls love their fathers. Usually they replace them with other men. But if that other man is too much like her father, what she ends up feeling is guilt.* More of Petra Carey's words.

Petra bloody Carey! What I might do, Lynn thought, is cancel my next appointment, not go back at all.

By the time they had finished their coffee, Margaret Aston had come downstairs and was waiting for them in the living-room, the curtains pulled mostly across. No matter how much powder and foundation she had used, she had not been able to hide the extent to which she had, in these last days, yielded herself up to tears.

'Margaret,' Resnick said gently, 'are you sure you're up to this?'

'Yes, thank you, Charlie. I shall be fine.'

Seated on the carpet close by her chair, Stella reached up and patted her mother's hand.

'Mrs Aston,' Lynn began, 'you remember there was a phone call your husband made, late on the Saturday afternoon?'

'Yes, of course. Someone rang him and he called them back from the hall.'

'Why did he do that?'

Margaret Aston shook her head. 'They hadn't finished their conversation, I suppose.'

'Yes, but, why go out into the hall? Why not ring them back from where he was? The same phone the person had called in on.'

Margaret Aston looked bemused; she transferred her gaze from Lynn to Resnick and slowly back again.

'I mean,' Lynn persevered, 'wouldn't that have been the simplest thing to do?'

'I really haven't given it any thought, but Bill had his reasons, I'm sure.'

'What were you doing, Mum, at the time?' Stella asked, looking round.

'Oh, I don't know, dear. Reading, I suppose. Yes, I was, a book from the library, I can't remember . . .'

'There you are, there's your answer,' Stella said. 'Dad didn't want to disturb Mum's reading, that's what it was. Nothing sinister at all.'

Resnick and Lynn exchanged glances.

'I don't suppose you've been able to remember, Mrs Aston,' Lynn said, 'who it was your husband spoke to? You couldn't when we talked before.'

She shook her head. 'As I told you then, Bill never mentioned who it was. But it'll have been someone from the Church, I'm sure. For years he's been a lay-preacher. Quite famous, isn't he, Charlie, you would know. Famous for it.'

Nodding agreement, Resnick leaned forward lightly in his chair. 'I wonder, Margaret, does the name Elizabeth Peck mean anything to you?'

She gave it several moments' thought. 'No. No, I can't say that it does. But I expect you're about to tell me that's who Bill was speaking to, is that it?'

Resnick nodded. 'It was her number that he called.'

'So who is she?' Stella asked, the beginnings of agitation in her young voice.

'A social worker. She's employed at the place where Nicky Snape died.'

'Well then, of course,' Margaret Aston said, seizing on it quickly, 'that's why she would have wanted to talk to Bill. The enquiry. And why he would have been careful to have spoken to her in private. Confidentially. He was very scrupulous about things like that, Bill, even from me. Charlie, you should know that yourself.'

'The trouble is, Margaret, that only makes it more difficult to understand why he would agree to a long, private conversation with one of his principal witnesses. Especially when it was so clearly off the record.'

'Oh, no, I'm sure he will have made a note at least.'

'I'm afraid not. I've been through all of his papers, notebooks, everything. There's nothing about any such conversation having taken place.'

Margaret Aston sighed; she seemed to have shrunk even deeper into her chair. 'Stella, dear.' Touching her daughter's shoulder. 'I'm feeling very tired. I wonder, would you help me back up to bed. Charlie, you'll excuse me, I know.'

Resnick and Lynn stood as Stella assisted her mother to her feet. Resnick opened the door and as Margaret, leaning on her daughter's arm, passed by him, he asked a further question. 'One thing, Margaret. What time was it Bill got back here on the Friday night?'

She stopped. 'Almost midnight. A quarter, ten to. You should know, Charlie, it was you he was with. I remember him coming in and coming up to my room, I was in bed by then of course. Knocking gently on the door to make sure I was still awake. He sat on the bed for a moment and held my hand, told me what a nice evening he'd had. Charlie, he'd enjoyed talking to you. You could see it, see in his face, some of that old life again. Long time since I've done that, love, he said. Me and Charlie Resnick, closed the bar together. I shall sleep well tonight, he said, and kissed me here, on the top of the head, before saying good-night.'

Unusually, Resnick took the keys and slid behind the wheel. Less than half a mile down the road he signalled right and pulled in outside a small parade of shops. Lynn imagined that he intended to get out, buy a newspaper, or go to the off-licence for beer. But engine idling, he sat there, forearms resting on the wheel.

'You think she's lying?' he said finally. 'Holding something back?'

'No.'

'Telling the truth, then?'

'Yes. As she sees it. All she knows, yes.'

Resnick released a slow breath. 'It would be easier perhaps if she were lying, if she knew there was something going on.'

'And is there?'

As Resnick turned to face her, a middle-aged man coming out of the newsagent stopped and stared at the car, only slowly starting to walk away, *Post* rolled inside his hand. Resnick saw him and wondered what they looked like, himself and Lynn, another mismatched couple, caught in the middle of an affair, one of them married, most likely him.

He had observed couples often enough himself, had leapt, sometimes inappropriately, to the same conclusions. Most usually, though, he had been right: lovers caught in their own cold, sticky web.

'You think it's the woman? Peck?'

'How d'you mean?' Resnick asked.

'Well, you know . . .'

'That he was having an affair? Bill?'

263

'That is what you were thinking, isn't it? The path you're going down.'

'But with Peck?'

'Why not?'

Resnick shook his head, came close to a smile. 'He'd only known her less than a week.'

Lynn's turn to smile. 'Come on,' she said. 'How long does it take?'

Instead of answering, Resnick turned towards the windscreen and stared out. What he was thinking of, what he was seeing, was Hannah that first time, walking across the front of the school towards her slightly battered red VW, pausing to speak to those two kids, firm enough, not without understanding; the way, after they had spoken, she had placed her briefcase on the roof of the car and then turned back to face him, that flash of red, visible in the swirl of her hair. Her smile.

How long does it take?

For a brief period – what was it? Four years ago now, slightly more? – he would have thought of Rachel Chaplin at that moment, after that question. For a long while, before and since, it would have been Elaine.

'Even so,' he said, 'it's doubtful Bill would have had the chance during the enquiry to speak to her alone.'

'The interview?'

Resnick shook his head. 'Khan was there all the time.'

'Then it was to do with the enquiry, maybe something she felt she couldn't say at her interview.'

'Because she was afraid?'

'Possibly, yes. Or maybe it was something she didn't know at the time, that she only learned later.'

264

'Then why on earth did Bill break the habit of a lifetime and not note it down?'

They looked at one another along the front seat of the car. Three kids, one not much more than seven or eight, went past on roller blades, heads bent forward, arms swinging professionally out.

'You think it's something personal, don't you?' Lynn said.

'I don't know. I suppose I do, but I still don't see how that could have worked. Time, access . . .'

'Maybe,' Lynn said, 'it wasn't, you know, an affair. At least, not yet. What if there was just a connection, somehow, between them? Something they were just starting to – I don't know what you'd call it – explore.'

'What? In his own house in the middle of the weekend with his wife in another room.'

'Wouldn't some people find that exciting? The possibility of being found out.'

Resnick gestured with open hands. 'I wouldn't know.'

'And you'd know Bill Aston? Well enough to be sure?'

He shook his head emphatically. 'No.'

'Him and his wife, they've got separate rooms, isn't that right?'

'Yes.'

'Separate beds.'

'Uh-hum.'

'Do you know for how long?'

'Quite a while, I think. I'm not exactly sure. But that in itself doesn't mean anything.'

Lynn smiled. 'Surely it means something.'

Resnick knew: there were times after he had found out Elaine was having an affair that he had lain in their shared bed, unable to sleep, terrified that by accident or habit they might touch, impossible to erase the images his imagination had conjured up so vividly from his mind.

What had happened, Resnick wondered, in the Astons' lives however many years it was ago?

'It is sex, then, isn't it?' Lynn said. 'If it's not to do with the enquiry, it is sex.' She smiled ruefully. 'One way or another, it usually is.' And then, a sudden catch in her voice. 'It nearly got me killed.'

'That was different. He was some kind of psychopath.'

Lynn's head was angled away but he heard her well enough. 'Don't forget, at first I wanted him.'

He drove then without speaking, back towards the centre of town. He would call in at the Partridge, find out if the staff remembered how long Aston had stayed in the bar that night. Lynn sat with her hands clenched, mind churning, overbite of her teeth nervously worrying at the inside of her lip.

'You got business back at the station, or should I drop you near home, it's not far out of my way?'

For the first time since they had moved off, she dared to look into his face. 'Stop here,' she said.

'I can't, not here. I'll just go up to . . .'

'Charlie, stop here!' How long – if ever – since she had called him that?

No mistaking the urgency in her voice, Resnick made a left and a right and came to a halt on one of the narrow cobbled roads that run through the wholesale flower and vegetable market. One glance and he switched off the engine and waited.

Lynn not quite looking at him again, not yet; she was

266

having a little difficulty breathing evenly. 'This isn't – I don't suppose there's ever a right time.'

Not knowing, partly knowing, afraid of what was to come, Resnick's stomach ran cold; for just a moment he closed his eyes.

'You remember,' Lynn said, 'after the kidnapping, the rescue, all of that, something I said to you one day, we were having coffee, I . . .'

'Yes, I think so, go on.' When what he wanted to say was stop.

'I told you I'd been having these – I don't know what you'd call them – nightmares, dreams, fantasies. You, my father, him, the kidnapper. All mixed up together. It was all because of what happened, of course, what might have happened. Would have done if you . . .'

'It wasn't just me.'

'If you hadn't saved me. It sounds melodramatic, I know, but that's what you did.'

'Lynn.' Leaning a shade closer towards her now, though she was still keeping her body, her face angled away. 'It could have been any one of a dozen officers. It just happened to be me.'

She laughed, suddenly and loud.

'What?' Leaning back again, taken by surprise.

'That's what I say to my therapist.'

'And she says?'

'What might have happened doesn't matter. What does is that it was you.'

He looked at her serious, still somewhat round face, though she had never put back the weight she had lost; short brown hair, wide brown eyes.

'I'm glad,' he said quietly. 'Glad that you were safe. Glad that it was me.'

'Yes. Yes, I know.' Her voice so quiet it was almost lost under the noise of cars passing at either end of the street. 'At least, I think I know.'

He had an instinct to take her hand and another which prevented him: instead she took his. 'Charlie, I've got to get this sorted. I mean it's stupid, I can't go on like this. The way I've been lately, walking round you on, I don't know, eggshells; at least that's the way it seems.'

'All right.' Resnick nodded. 'What do you want to do?'

'Nothing. I don't think you understand. I don't want to *do* anything. There's nothing to do.'

'But, then . . .'

She squeezed his hand once, then let go. 'I just needed to say, tell you what's been going on in my mind, not all of it, the stupid details, but that I have been having these thoughts about you . . .'

'That doesn't matter . . .'

'Charlie, I've thought about making love to you, but I know that's not going to happen. Only in my mind.'

'Lynn . . .'

'I don't think I even want it to happen. Not really. I know I don't. But I had to say it, had to tell you. Because if I keep it all inside any longer, it's going to explode.' Slowly, she lowered her face into her hand. 'I'm sorry.'

'There's no need.'

'Isn't there?' Looking at him now.

'No.'

It was hot in the small space of the car, claustrophobic. Resnick could feel the sweat gathering in the palms of his hands and between his legs, dampening the hair at the nape of his neck. A kind of free-floating panic aside, he had no clear idea what he was feeling.

'Well.' Lynn laughed abruptly. 'My therapist will be pleased.'

'Getting it out into the open . . .'

'Yes.'

'Making it all go away.'

She turned towards him in the seat and he thought she was going to take his hand again and he tensed inside, not knowing how he might respond if she did. But she shifted again and leaned forward, face close to the windscreen, staring out.

'Is that what you want?' Resnick heard himself saying. 'To make it all go away?'

She looked round at him, surprised. 'Of course. What good would it do?'

A car went by too fast on the opposite side of the road, music spilling from its open windows.

'None,' Resnick said.

Lynn thought she might get out of the car and walk, not heading anywhere special, just walk. But she continued to sit there, they both did, waiting until the unevenness of their breathing had subsided, until Resnick could trust himself to set the car in gear and drive back into town. 'The Partridge,' he said, 'we could check it out before I drop you off.'

The barman in the Partridge remembered Resnick's friend. He had ordered another half of mild after Resnick had gone, but left it on the table, scarcely bothered, when he left. Fifteen minutes later, twenty tops.

Back home, Resnick fed the cats automatically, made

himself strong coffee and carried it through to the front room where it stayed till morning, cold and untouched. For what seemed a long time he stared at the rows of albums and CDs and saw nothing he wanted to listen to, nothing he wanted to play.

Silent, save for Lynn's words, insinuating themselves into his thoughts no matter how much he tried to keep them out. *I thought about making love to you, but I know it's not going to happen. Only in my mind.*

Resnick crossed the room to the telephone and dialled. 'I was wondering if I could come over and see you,' he said.

'I'm sorry, Charlie.' Hannah's voice sounded distant and tired. 'Not this evening, okay?'

'Of course. It was just an idea. That's fine.'

The Stolichnaya was in the freezer: he wondered how much was in the bottle, how long it would last?

32

The first thing Resnick recognised, warm, soft, and resting close against his ear, was a cat's paw. The second, moments after, close and strangely muted, was the sound of a telephone ringing. And the third, realised with painful accuracy as he lifted Bud cautiously clear and gingerly lowered his own feet towards the floor, was that for the first time in many months he had a hangover of king-sized proportions. He blinked at the clock: six forty-nine. He should have already been up. Louder now, the telephone continued to ring and fearing the worst, without knowing exactly what that worst was, he lifted it towards his ear.

'Yes. Hello.'

'Charlie, is that you?'

'I think so.'

'Did I wake you?'

'Not really, no.'

'Are you okay?'

'Um, why?'

'You sound as if you're at the bottom of the sea.'

'I slept a little heavily, that's all.'

'Look, Charlie, can I see you today? Not for long; lunchtime, maybe. Just for twenty minutes, half an hour. I think we need to talk.'

No reply.

'I could meet you somewhere.'

Resnick wished his head didn't feel like a sack of gently swaying cement. 'Look, let me call you . . . No, I will. This morning. Soon. How long are you around? . . . All right, I'll phone before then. Probably in the next half-hour.'

In the shower, water streaming across the folds and plains of his body, he kept wondering what had prompted Hannah to phone so early, what it was she needed to talk about so urgently, lathering shampoo into his hair now and wincing as he did so, once more fearing the worst.

He hadn't been the only person tying one on last night. The entrance to the police station was crowded with people in various stages of sobriety, many of them adorned with quite spectacular cuts and bruises, most talking at once. Loudly. A uniformed sergeant and two of his minions were patiently trying to sort them out.

Resnick pushed his way through, careful not to slip on the blood. From the corridor to his right came the voice of the custody sergeant, giving one of his overnights a good bollocking for throwing up in his cell. A reedy version of 'Little Brown Jug' from the stairs alerted Resnick to the possibility that Millington was embarking on one of his unbearably jolly days; and sure enough there he was, descending the stairs, smile in place around his moustache, happy to share with the world choice moments of that old Glenn Miller magic. As Divine had announced to the CID room moments before, someone had got his leg over this morning and no chuffin' mistake!

'Boss's been asking for you,' Millington said breezily. 'That new lad in there with him. Least, I reckon that's who it is. Oh, and I've set up a meeting. Eleven. With that feller from soccer unit, all right?'

Resnick continued on his way upstairs. In the men's room he ran the cold tap and sloshed water repeatedly in his face, before heading along the corridor for Skelton's office.

'Charlie, come in, come in.' Skelton exuded neatly suited bonhomie from behind his desk. 'This is DC Vincent.'

Resnick's first impression was of a tallish man in his late twenties, around five eleven, slim, clean-shaven, his dark hair cut quite short; he was wearing a light-coloured suit, creased, but unlike Resnick's, fashionably meant to be that way, an olive-green shirt and black knitted tie.

'This is Detective Inspector Resnick. Day to day, you'll be working to him.'

The two men shook hands, Vincent's grip cool and comfortable, not giving it too much.

'Carl Vincent, sir. Good to know you.'

Resnick nodded and stepped back, Vincent still looking him clear in the eye.

'As you know, Charlie, Carl here's joining us from Leicester. Up a division, eh, Charlie. In a manner of speaking.'

Only if you're a Forest supporter, Resnick thought.

'I've filled him in on the Aston murder, Charlie, basic details. I know you'll want to bring him up to speed.'

'Sir.'

There was a smile in Vincent's eyes now as he watched

him, interested to see how Resnick operated with his superior, sizing him up.

'Anything new there, Charlie? Anything I can pass on to Headquarters? These soccer hooligans in Reg Cossall's report, still the most likely candidates?'

Resnick wondered if he should mention his suspicions surrounding Elizabeth Peck, but opted to wait until he had more evidence, one way or another.

'Seems so, yes. There's a meeting with the Football Intelligence Unit this morning, we'll see if that takes us anywhere closer.'

'You'll let me know?'

'First thing.'

Vincent fell into step beside Resnick in the corridor. 'Found anywhere to stay yet?' Resnick asked.

'Not as yet. Figured I'd travel up from Leicester for a bit, give myself time to look around. Not such a bad journey long as you get the timings right.'

'You might want to have a word with our admin officer, she's usually got her ear to the ground.'

'Right, thanks. I will.'

'Morning briefing any minute. I'll introduce you, find you something to get started.'

'Right,' Vincent said again and then he smiled. 'Never easy are they? Beginnings. First days. Feeling your way.'

'You'll handle it okay.'

'I'll do my best.'

Outside the CID room Vincent hesitated. 'I was wondering, what do I call you? Guv? Sir? Boss?'

'Whatever feels right.'

It fell quiet as they entered the room.

*

Divine settled for a bacon cob, brown sauce, toast, tea with two sugars and a Lion bar for later. Naylor and Lynn Kellogg were already sitting at a table by the window, near the rear of the canteen. The air was thick with tobacco smoke and talk.

'Right,' Divine said, decanting cup and plate onto the table, propping the tray against the leg, from where it fell onto the floor. 'What's going off, that's what I'd like to know?'

'We're talking about last night's *EastEnders*,' Naylor said pleasantly. 'What d'you want to know?'

'Conspiracy of silence then, is it, or what?'

'How d'you mean?'

'You know what I bloody well mean.'

'How's that?'

Divine jerked a hand back round in the direction of the door. 'This bloke. Vincent. Why's nobody said a sodding thing about the fact he's black?'

'He is?' Lynn said innocently.

'Never thought you'd notice, Mark,' Naylor said, amused. 'Reckon that's why.'

'Anyway,' said Lynn, 'he's not really black. More a sort of light chocolatey brown.'

Naylor nodded. 'Milky Way.'

'That's it,' Divine said through a mouthful of bacon roll, 'make a bloody joke out of it.'

'Oh, Mark,' Lynn said, 'come on.'

'Look.' Voice getting louder by the minute. 'If it were anything else, anything else at all, as marked him out of the ordinary . . .'

'Such as?' Naylor asked.

'I don't know, anything. All right, suppose he wasn't a bloke, he was a woman ...'

'Transvestite, you mean?'

'No, you pillock, a proper woman ...'

'Well, that would be out of the ordinary, true enough,' Lynn said, 'Just look around.'

'Right. Exactly. Anything from a club foot to a man with two heads, we'd talk about it, yeh? But, no, not this, this is different. No one's supposed to notice, not a blind thing. So there's the boss, introducing him, welcome to the team. And that's it.'

'Well, what d'you expect?' Naylor asked. 'This is Carl Vincent and in case you haven't noticed, he's black.'

'Why not?'

'Jesus!'

'Because, Mark,' Lynn said, levelling her voice, 'it doesn't matter.'

'Bollocks!'

'What?'

'You heard, bollocks. Of course it bloody matters.'

'Mark,' Lynn said, 'you're so full of crap sometimes.'

'Yeah?' Divine on his feet now, leaning towards her, finger in her face. 'Well, listen up. It matters to him, you can bet your life on that. And I'll tell you something else, it fucking matters to me.'

There was sudden hush around them at the scarcely suppressed anger in Divine's voice, and through it Carl Vincent walked blithely, carrying a cup of coffee and two pieces of buttered toast. 'Mind if I join you?'

'Please,' Lynn said.

'Yes, sure,' said Naylor. 'Pull up a pew.'

Divine had a quick swallow of his tea and grabbed what

276

was left of his bacon roll. Sitting in the vacated chair, Vincent turned his head to watch Divine go.

'There's one in every station,' he said with a slow shake of the head.

'Only one?' Lynn smiled. 'Things must be looking up.'

The Football Intelligence Unit had been at its busiest in the Eighties, when self-styled firms of young men could afford to invest considerable time and money in promoting violence in and around major soccer grounds. Often they would eschew the match itself in order to ambush unsuspecting groups of visiting fans at railway stations before or after the game. Officers went underground, spending months establishing solid cover before infiltrating the more dangerous of the firms – the Chelsea Headhunters, Arsenal, Oxford, Portsmouth, Millwall.

When a move to all-seater stadiums thwarted one of the most popular pastimes – a sudden vicious charge to take the home supporters' 'end' – and with spiralling admission charges ensuring lots of youngsters stayed away, hard-core fans intent upon trouble followed the national flag abroad. And the Unit went with them. Information about known trouble-makers was passed on to other national police forces, and although the violence was to a degree curtailed, it didn't stop. Wrecked bars and cafés, water cannon and baton charges testified to that.

'Here,' Trevor Ulman said, 'take a look at this.'

Resnick and his team watched the monitor as, on somewhat bleached-out video tape, a mob of chanting youths, mostly in shirt-sleeves, Union Jacks to the fore, erupted from a kerbside café and charged across a broad square, despite the attempts of heavily outnumbered uniformed

277

police to stop them. Even mounted officers, swinging their long truncheons, could not deter the English supporters as they raced over cobblestones and tram lines, intent upon catching any local fans with fists or feet or both.

'Now watch this,' Ulman said, as the camera closed in on a group of five young men as they chased, tripped and then proceeded to punch and kick – especially kick – the single youth who had been their quarry. Ulman paused the video a few frames before a boot made contact with the victim's head.

'Here,' he said, pointing. 'The lad with the footwork. Chelsea Headhunter, close links with Combat 18. I'll say a bit more about that in a minute. But look here, this bloke with belly, over to the left – Leicester Baby Squad. And this one here, leaning over to throw a punch – more local, Forest Executive Crew.'

Ulman stubbed out his Silk Cut and lit another, using a slim gold lighter with a dangerously high flame.

'That was two years ago, Rotterdam. But this second clip's more recent. February of this year. Most probably, I don't have to tell you where it's from.'

'Dublin,' Divine said, with an edge of disgust.

'Correct. One friendly international between the Republic and ourselves abandoned thanks to scenes like this.'

The screen, in colour this time, showed a man in the upper tier, his face, save for the eyes, hidden inside a dark balaclava; he stood and turned away from the camera, back towards the crowd, and signalled with his arm. Immediately, the rioting began. Arms were thrust skywards, Union Jacks waved, mouths open with the shouts of 'No surrender! No surrender to the IRA!' and then pieces of guttering were torn away and hurled down upon the unguarded crowd below.

'Combat 18?' Resnick asked.

'Precisely.'

'But you're not saying,' Millington asked, 'that everyone in that upper stand at Dublin, those yobos you showed us running wild in Holland, that they're all political?'

'Well,' Ulman said, 'I doubt they're all fully paid-up members of the British National Party. But that's not the way it works.' Arching back his head a moment, he released an almost perfect smoke ring towards the ceiling. 'Combat 18, no matter how much the BNP might now try to deny it, are enforcers. Write a letter to the *Post* complaining about a Fascist rally, stick an Anti-Nazi League poster in your window, and the lads from C18'll be round to pay you a call.

'Now as far they're concerned, soccer grounds are breeding grounds; they use football as a way of spreading propaganda, gaining converts who'll stay interested just long enough to let them pull off some stunt like Dublin, Rotterdam, Oslo. Then C18 have got maximum publicity and they can rattle on in *The Order* – that's their magazine – about getting a good result.

'The difference is, their racism is real: they believe it. To the rest, most of them, it's unthinking. The kind that'll throw bananas at the visiting team's black players, jump up and down and make monkey noises, but not apparently notice they've got – what? – three or four black players of their own. Most likely they don't think of themselves as racist at all. And when you get down to it, they're probably not a whole lot more so than the rest of us. It's ingrained. Difficult to shake.'

Millington leaned his chair back onto its hind legs. 'This anti-Irish thing, that'd fit in with what the landlord told us, out at this pub we're interested in.'

'It would indeed. Though, I have to say, we've no record of that particular pub being a meeting place for the kind of nice young character we're talking about. However, habits change. It's possible. What I can't do, at least until you can provide me with some kind of visual identification, a name, is tell you whether these youths who were creating a disturbance the night Aston was killed are known to us already.'

'Details about locals who might fit the profile, though,' Resnick began. 'We can go at it that way.'

'Absolutely. No problem.' Ulman took two large envelopes from his case and passed them across to where Resnick was sitting. 'The quality of some of these is a little suspect, they've been blown up from video, but the rest, ones we've taken ourselves, they'll be fine. You've got brief descriptions here too, known associates and addresses, though those do tend to slip out of date pretty fast.'

'And will some of these,' Resnick asked, 'be Combat 18?'

'A few. You want to talk to Special Branch. They'll have this area well sussed.'

Resnick nodded and thanked Ulman for all his help. Making contact with the local office of the Branch was already high on his list. But not until after lunch.

33

The day was sharp and clear, the sky an almost unbroken blue. They walked along the upper path through the cemetery, close by the red brick wall that separated it from the road. Stone angels stared back at them, empty-eyed. *Also Flora, aged four months. Agnes Hilda Jane, wife of the above. Suffer the little children. Gone to a better place.* Below them, amongst a maze of smaller headstones and carefully carved epitaphs, the ground levelled out, before rising again with the trees and shrubs of the Arboretum.

Resnick had brought sandwiches from the deli and slices of rich pecan pie; in her bag Hannah had orange juice, pots of blueberry yoghurt, paper napkins, plastic spoons: the arrangement they had made.

'You know the best places to take a girl, Charlie. I'll say that for you.'

Resnick checked, but she was smiling, that crease that he was getting used to, quite pronounced, at the right side of her mouth.

'Do you want to sit down?'

Hannah looked at her watch. 'Let's walk a little further. Are you okay for time?'

'Fine.'

They went through the gate and across Waverley Street, up between the aviary and the small pond with its low, curved railings, climbing the path that wound towards the bandstand, the borders rich with late spring flowers, purple and gold.

Hannah expressed her approval at the sandwiches, nothing too idiosyncratic, smoked turkey breast with cranberry, egg mayonnaise with cress. Resnick, panicking at the last moment that she might be a vegetarian, had thought this way, at least, they could have one each. But Hannah bit heartily into her half of the turkey sandwich and Resnick contrived, more through luck than judgement, to trap a sudden squish of egg on the back of his hand before it landed on his shirt. He thought he might allow her to take the second yoghurt back for her tea.

'These are good,' Hannah said.

Lower down the slope, three Asian men in shirt-sleeves had spread a newspaper on the grass and were using it as a surface on which to play cards. Mouth full, Resnick nodded agreement.

'D'you always eat this well?'

'If this is well, yes. I suppose so.'

Hannah pushed a straw down into the carton of orange. 'I suppose I think of policemen as eating chips with everything. Or late-night curries, you know, the kind where, no matter what it is, it always tastes the same.'

Recognising the description, Resnick smiled. 'There's a lot of that, too. Sometimes. It depends.'

Swivelling on the bench, she looked at him. 'One thing you don't do, Charlie, is take rejection very well.'

He blinked. 'You mean last night?'

'Uh-huh.'

282

'Who does? Who would? I just wanted to see you, that was all.'

With a slow shake of the head, Hannah said, 'Charlie, you were feeling down. I don't know why . . .'

'I . . .'

'And it doesn't matter, I don't need to know. But there you were, on your own, feeling low, and you picked up the phone. Let's call Hannah, she'll make me feel better, take me out of myself for a few hours. Wasn't that it? Something like that, at least.'

Resnick put the uneaten piece of sandwich back down on the bench, appetite lost in the guilty truth of what she had said. 'I didn't think . . . I mean, is that so wrong?'

Lightly, briefly, she touched his hand, the back of his wrist. 'I'm not a comfort station, Charlie. That's not what I want to be. Waiting around for you to phone so that I can be pressed into service, relieving the stresses and strains of a difficult day.'

'I didn't mean it that way,' he said and she thought he believed it.

'The other evening, the last time I saw you, you asked – I think you were going to ask – what was happening. Between us. And I stopped you; it didn't seem the right time. And I said the one thing I didn't want to happen, that we get into that pattern where all you have to do is call and whenever you came round we ended up in bed.'

'But that's not . . .'

'What's happening?'

'I don't think so, no.'

'Oh, Charlie.' Hannah looked away towards the rose garden on the other side of the hill, the blackened cannons dragged back from the Crimea. Part of Resnick telling

283

him, okay, stop it now, you don't need this, get up and walk away.

'I don't know,' Hannah said, turning back to face him, reading the concern in his eyes, 'if this is going to come to anything. But I've got baggage, Charlie, the same as you.' She smiled, almost a grin. 'Maybe not quite as much. But I'm being careful here. I know it may not always seem so, but I am. Cautious, in my way. And one thing I'm not prepared to do is become a tidy little corner of your life. The place where you go to get rid of a little passion, whatever's extra, whatever you can't somehow soak up in the rest of your day.' She shook her head. 'I don't know if that makes any sense; I don't know if I've made that clear.'

He touched her then, high on her shoulder, his littlest finger resting against her neck; the other fingers then, circling softly against the skin. She had smooth skin.

Hannah waited for him to say something, make some response, but he didn't speak. 'So what do you want to do, Charlie?' she asked.

'You mean now?'

Grinning. 'No, not now.'

'Well, I suppose that depends, you know, on you.'

'God, Charlie!'

'All right, I want to carry on seeing you. I want ... I'd like to find a way, something you feel comfortable with ...'

'You don't want to hide me away?'

'No.'

'Your little bit on the side?'

A shake of the head, emphatic. 'No.'

'Good. Dinner, then. Friday night.'

'All right. Where ...?'

But Hannah was already collecting together her things, brushing crumbs from her lap, getting ready to go. 'You decide. Call me and tell me where you want to meet. Okay?'

'Yes, yes. Of course, that's fine.'

'This yoghurt,' Hannah said, holding it towards him. 'Do you want it or not?'

'Probably not.'

With a small gesture of acceptance she dropped it down in her bag. 'That sandwich, though, you're not leaving that?'

'I'll eat it on the way back.'

'You'll get it all down yourself.'

'Look,' Resnick said, smiling. 'Mothering. That's another habit we could do without. Where I'm concerned, at least.'

Khan was waiting in the CID room when Resnick returned, head stuck into a copy of the *Daily Mail*. Naylor was talking into the telephone, close to the far wall. As soon as he saw Resnick, Khan hastily folded the newspaper and set it aside. 'Elizabeth Peck, sir. Booked herself a holiday through American Express. One of those late-availability deals. Two-city trip to Spain, Barcelona and Madrid.'

'Good. Oughtn't to be too difficult to track her down.'

Khan frowned. 'That's the problem, I'm afraid. The agency were quite good, put me in touch with the hotel, the place she's meant to be saying in Madrid.'

At the 'meant to be', Resnick's heart sank.

'She flew out, right enough, checked in. Signed up for

285

a coach trip the first day, some kind of orientation thing, but after that it seems as if she's disappeared.'

'And the travel company, they've reported this to the local police or whatever?'

Khan shook his head. 'Apparently they're not too concerned. She left a note for the tour guide, saying she had no complaints about what was happening, it simply wasn't what she'd had in mind. She was going to go off, spend the rest of the week on her own.'

'Checked out of the hotel?'

'That afternoon.'

'Which means she could be anywhere.'

'Do you think we should contact the Madrid police, sir? Interpol, perhaps?'

Giving himself room to think, Resnick walked slowly over to where the kettle was standing, lifted it to test the weight, make sure there was water enough, then set it to boil. 'I think what we'll do is send you down to Rhossili Bay after all.' There was a faint ring as, along the room, Naylor set down the phone. 'Kevin can go with you. Dig out Paul Matthews, see what he's got to say about Elizabeth Peck, why she might have wanted to talk so urgently to Aston. Leave now, you can be down there for this evening. Okay?'

'Yes, sir.' Khan had promised he would go with Jill to the Cookie Club, but he would find a way of making it up to her. Besides, they'd been going together long enough now for her to get used to the fact that with a job like his, plans sometimes had to be changed, last minute.

'Kevin,' Resnick said, 'how's your Welsh?'

Divine bounded up the stairs like an oversized Rottweiler

with his eyes on the back of an intruder's bare and fleshy thigh. So intent was he on finding Resnick that he cannoned into a hazy-looking Millington, doing his level best to remember what it was Madeleine had told him not to come home without buying.

'Hey up, youth!' the sergeant exclaimed, spun half around and rubbing his arm. 'What's got up your backside all of a sudden?'

'The boss,' Divine gasped. 'He still around?'

'Off to see DI Woolmer, Special Branch. Only this minute left. Might catch him in car-park if you're sharp.'

Divine didn't need any second urging. Back down the stairs three and four at a time, he was through the front entrance and waving both arms as Resnick indicated right to pull out onto Derby Road.

'Won the lottery, Mark?' Resnick asked, lowering his window.

'It's the cassette, boss. The one as was found on the Embankment, near Aston's body.'

'Music, isn't it? Heavy metal, isn't that what you said?'

Divine was still fighting to get back his breath. 'Aye, well, sent it off to one of our tame boffins just in case. What he's found, recorded over, but none too well, are bits of talking, speech like. This bloke going on about an Englishman's birthright, white power'n crap like that.'

'Well,' Resnick said, a wry smile on his lips, 'I'm glad you think it's all crap, Mark. Here, you'd best jump in.'

Chesney Woolmer was the inspector in charge of the local Special Branch team, two sergeants and a dozen officers under him. Affable, if a little offhand, a portly man with receding hair, he listened to the cleaned-up version of the

287

tape, some fifteen minutes of blinkered ranting which culminated in some ragged cheering and an even more motley version of 'God Save the Queen'.

'Her Majesty,' Woolmer suggested, 'would be shocked and surprised if she knew the amount of odious bollocks that went on in her name.'

Resnick asked him if he recognised the voice.

'Not right off. Besides, the quality leaves a lot to be desired. But if you're happy to leave it with me, I'll get some of my lads to have a listen. Compare it to what we've got.'

'And there's no way of telling where it might have been recorded?'

Woolmer shook his head. 'Some bloke with his own little tape machine, some BNP rally or other. Could be local, but who's to say? Fairly innocuous by their standards, too.'

'We've no way of proving the tape was dropped by the people who attacked Aston, but, all other things being equal, it seems likely. Too much of a coincidence to ignore.'

'Well,' said Woolmer, reaching several perforated sheets of computer print-out from his desk, 'what I can let you have is a list of known right-wing activists in the area. Mansfield, Sutton, Ilkeston, Heanor, they'll likely be your best bets. Any who've got an association with C18, that's shown. Check these against the other names that've been thrown up by the enquiry, you might strike lucky. Failing that, there's the soccer connection.'

Resnick took the list and passed it across to Divine. 'If we decide to move in, knock on a few doors, see what we can turn up that way, you think you might have more than a passing interest in whatever we come across?'

Woolmer smiled. 'Always grateful, Charlie, for any little titbit you care to throw our way.'

'Ah, I was thinking of more active participation than that.'

'Bodies on the ground?'

'Just for a day or two, any you could spare.'

'Give us a bell tomorrow, first thing. If there's anyone I can lose, short of having it checked off as overtime, I'll tell you.' Woolmer grinned broadly. 'Never like to miss a chance to give some of our white supremacist friends a spin.' He walked with Resnick and Divine towards the door. 'Last time we did, we turned up bomb-making equipment and a Russian-made rifle that had made its way to Mansfield Woodhouse by way of Iran and the UDF.'

Gerry Hovenden throttled down and brought the bike through a slow curve that ended outside the house where Frank Miller lived. Couple of years now, him and Frank would spend Saturdays at the match, away games especially, those were the ones they didn't like to miss. Few pints beforehand, more than a few after the final whistle. Blokes to meet. Once in a while it turned heavy and then it was well good, worth the journey – that Frank, didn't know his own strength.

'This is it.' Removing his helmet, Hovenden nodded towards a two-storey brick building, its front door square onto the street; a hand-lettered sign in the frosted door glass, telling callers to go round to the back.

Shane, spare helmet Gerry always lent him in one hand, waited while he lifted the bike onto its stand.

'Frank?' Hovenden pushed at the back door and as usual it swung inwards, unlocked. What cretin'd be fool enough to burgle Frank Miller?

'Frank? 'S Gerry.'

'Through here.' There was music coming from the front of the house, heavily amplified rock.

Hovenden entered, nodding for Shane to follow. The back room was a kitchen, blackened chip pan on the cooker, mugs and plates overflowing the sink. Old newspapers spread across the table, more in piles on the floor. A shelf with books about the SAS and the Falklands, the Second World War.

'Bit of a reader, is he?' Shane asked.

Hovenden didn't reply.

Frank Miller was standing in the middle of the front room, bare to the waist save for tattoos on his back and arms, St George, a Union Jack. He had pushed back to the wall the one piece of furniture in the room, a leather settee one of his bailiff pals had done him a deal on, and had been doing push-ups with alternate hands. There was a television set on the floor, a VCR, a four-section Marantz stereo with speakers mounted high on the ceiling. Right then it was playing Saxon, *Gods of War*.

Miller turned down the volume, but not much. He grinned at Hovenden, nodded abruptly at Shane. 'Beer?' he asked.

'Yeh,' Hovenden said. 'Thanks.'

'Why don't you get a couple of cans, eh, Shane? In the fridge.'

The moment he was out of the room, Miller grabbed

Hovenden between his legs and began to twist. 'What is it with you two, anyway?' Miller hissed. 'In and out one another's pockets, the whole fuckin' time, like a couple of fairies.'

'Christ, Frank, leggo!' Tears in his eyes already. 'It's nothin' like that, honest.'

'It better not fuckin' be.'

'Be what?' Shane asked, leaning against the doorway, three cans of Special Brew balanced on two hands.

'Never you fucking mind.'

Shane stared at him, Miller staring back. You fat bastard, Shane was thinking, you reckon I'm afraid of you like all the rest. And one of these days you're going to have to learn it just ain't true.

'You got a problem,' Miller asked, half a pace towards him.

'Maybe, yeah?'

'What's that then?'

'That,' Shane said, nodding towards the speakers. 'It's a fuckin' row.'

'No.' Miller laughed. 'That's Saxon. They're the best.' But he turned it down some more and Shane tossed him a beer and all three of them drank and started to chat and for now everything was cool.

34

Days into the enquiry, the photographs of Bill Aston's
beaten body had been in danger of becoming little more
than part of the incident room decor, scarcely deserving
a second glance. But now with some concrete information
from Special Branch and the Football Intelligence Unit
to work on, potential suspects to target, the adrenalin was
pumping again, spirits were high, voices boisterous and
loud. Aside from the regular squad assigned to the murder
enquiry, there were six officers from Special Branch, a
further six from the Support Department, a dozen more
drafted in from other duties – amongst these, two out of
Vice, one of them Sharon Garnett.

The map showing a thirty-mile radius out from the city
had been newly marked with pins in three distinct colours:
blue for the Mansfield area to the north, green for Ilkeston
to the west, red for addresses within the city boundary
itself. Along with Lynn Kellogg, Sharon would be working
with Reg Cossall in the green team, Graham Millington
was supervising red; Chesney Woolmer, invited in by
Resnick to assist with the briefing, would be running blue.

'Some of these people we're going to interview,' Woolmer said, 'may surprise you. Some will look like nice law-

abiding insurance salesmen with a wife who works part-time and the regulation two point-whatever kids. Likely not what you're expecting at all. That doesn't mean they haven't got regular subscriptions to a magazine with step-by-step instructions on how to construct a letter bomb and ideas of where to send it. Other times, you'll open the door to three bloody great Alsatians and a bloke with a tattooed beergut hanging over his jeans and you'll think, okay, stupid fat sod, I know where I am here. Don't be fooled. These are people – some of them – capable of running a network of like-minded souls that takes in not just this country, but most of mainland Europe as well. Don't underestimate them. And don't turn your back on the sodding dogs.'

Resnick stepped forward into the ensuing laughter. 'Remember we haven't got warrants here, we're not going barging in. What we're doing is asking questions, establishing links – where were they the night of Aston's murder, where did they go drinking, where were their mates?'

'But if you do get inside,' Woolmer again. 'If you are invited in, be aware, keep your eyes skinned, anything that might be of potential interest to the Branch, I want to know.'

'All right,' said Resnick, 'any more questions?'

There were none: within three minutes the room had cleared. What questions there were snagged in Resnick's mind: he knew much of the circumstantial evidence pointed to a vicious, random attack – the spiralling pattern of footprints, the nature of the blows – and it seemed certain there had been a gang of probably drunken, possibly violent youths in the vicinity at the appropriate time, and yet ... And yet ... he could not let go of the idea that what had happened to Bill Aston had its roots in something more specific, more personal than a random attack in which he was a victim solely by chance and circumstance.

Resnick looked again at the blurred black-and-white images on the wall. Was it only a kind of sentimentality that urged him to see Aston's death as having had reason and purpose, that and nothing more? He looked at his watch: Khan and Naylor should be making contact with Paul Matthews at any time. There were other avenues still open.

Khan and Naylor had spent the night in a B & B in Swansea, close by the old docks, now a smart new marina surrounded by brightly painted rows of flats and a heritage trail. Their landlady had insisted on serving them eggs and bacon accompanied by lava bread. 'It's a delicacy, see. Local.' Whatever it was, Kevin Naylor thought, it wasn't bread. Black and somewhat slimy, it tasted suspiciously of whelks. As soon as they stepped outside the front door into the bright spring day, they could clearly see both hills and sea. Rhossili Bay was little more than fifteen miles along the Gower Peninsula.

Paul Matthews's aunt didn't disappoint. Her cottage was at the end of a rutted lane outside Llangennith, on the north edge of the Rhossili Downs. Two rusted cars lay on their sides, the new year's nettles growing up around them. A van, unlicensed, but apparently still running, sat by the side gate, a black-and-white collie growling at the two detectives through bared teeth.

The aunt walked out into the yard, scattering chickens from around her slippered feet. Face brown and lined beyond her years, hair falling thinly away from a wispy bun, she was wearing an apron with a small floral print and muttering in Welsh.

'It's not lost you are, is it?' she asked, lapsing into English.

When they assured her they were far from lost and explained why they were there, she insisted on sitting them down and making them tea. Paul, she said, had gone off early, down towards the bay most likely; that was what he'd done most days since he'd come.

'Something wrong with that boy,' she told them. 'Not right in the head. Oh, I don't mean he's crazy, mind. Not like that. But troubled.' She smiled at them hopefully. 'Anything you can do now, to ease his mind.'

They found him on a high reach of cliff, gulls riding the currents above his head and wheeling down to where they were nesting on the almost sheer face of rock.

For a fearful moment Naylor thought that he was poised to jump, but he was simply standing, staring out at the dark smudge of a tanker slow-sliding down the horizon, north to south.

'Mr Matthews,' Khan said, speaking quietly, not wishing to startle. 'Paul.'

He didn't seem surprised to see Khan there, simply nodded towards him and Naylor and went back to looking out to sea. The wind was beginning to whip the tops of the waves into crescents of foam. On the horizon, the ship seemed scarcely to have moved.

'Paul? Paul, this is my colleague, Detective Constable Naylor. We need to talk.'

'But we've already . . .'

'We need to talk some more.'

'About Nicky?'

'Yes.'

Matthews looked out beyond the cliff edge towards the pencil-thin line bisecting sea and sky. 'Mr Jardine, does he know?'

'That we're here?'

Matthews nodded.

'No. Anything you say, it's just between us. You have my word.'

'Because he warned me, all of us, we weren't to say anything, anything at all, not without him or a solicitor being there. He . . .'

'But he's not here, Paul,' Khan said reassuringly. 'Look around you. He need never know.'

Mathews took them to a place that stood alone, with white peeling paint, little more than a hut, an owner who had retired there from south-east London, Camberwell, and now sold cans of drink with names neither Naylor nor Khan had ever heard of, and tea from a large and battered silver pot.

They sat outside on rickety bench seats, sheltering from the freshness of the wind.

'I can't stop thinking about him,' Matthews said. 'Seeing him everywhere I look.'

'Nicky, you mean? Nicky Snape.'

'I found him, you see. It was me, I was the one.'

'I know,' Khan nodded.

'I should've took him down. The towel, I should have loosened it from round his neck. Took him down.' His eyes were like the wings of small dark birds, never still. 'I was frightened. Afraid. I don't suppose you can understand.'

'Yes, Paul,' Khan said. 'We can.'

Matthews looked at him and read the lie. 'It doesn't matter, not now.'

'Paul,' Naylor began, 'we wanted to ask you . . .'

'I held him, you see. I did that. I held him. Against me, like this.' He spread his arms from his body and then folded them back carefully through space, enfolding the imaginary boy with tenderness to his chest. 'He was still warm.'

Naylor glanced across at Khan. 'He was still alive?' he asked.

Sobs choked from Matthews's mouth and nose as he shook his head from side to side more and more vigorously, rhythmically, as if dangling from a rope. 'I don't know,' repeating over and over. 'I don't know, I don't know, I don't know.'

Embarrassed, Naylor fished out a pocket-sized pack of Kleenex and gave one to Matthews, then another, Khan inside ordering more tea, sweet this time, three sugars.

Ten minutes later they were walking, Khan alongside Matthews, Naylor several paces behind. This is the sort of place I should come with Debbie, Naylor was thinking, get her mum to baby-sit one weekend; somewhere like this, right away from everything, it'd be different here. Relaxed.

'Elizabeth Peck, she was on duty that evening?' Khan was asking. 'The two of you together, right?'

'Yes, of course. We went through all of this. You know.'

'And she was the one who called emergency services, I think that's what you said?'

Matthews nodded, yes, yes.

They were starting to climb again, the path well-trodden, earth at the field edge almost white.

'You haven't any idea, Paul, have you, why she might have got in touch with Inspector Aston? At home. Privately, you know.'

Matthews had stopped walking and Naylor, still partly day-dreaming, almost bumped into him from behind.

'Elizabeth, you don't know what she would have wanted to talk to him about?'

Matthews seemed dazed, out of focus. Off to the west a group of gulls was noisily baiting a lone crow. 'She did that?'

'Yes. Quite a conversation, apparently. Whatever it was, they found a lot to say. We wondered if you had any idea what she might have talked to him about?'

'I think,' Matthews said, 'I should go back now. I can't walk too far. I'm not well, you understand, I've not been well. The doctor ... that's why I'm here. My aunt ...'

He started to walk, back the way they had just come; Naylor standing there, not hurrying to move aside.

'What did she know, Paul? About what happened to Nicky? Something she hadn't told anyone before, that's what it must have been.'

Matthews shook his head and made an ineffectual attempt to move past, but sharp to his left there was the cliff edge and the other way was Khan, arms folded, smiling.

'Paul?'

'What? I ...'

'You can tell us. Whatever Elizabeth would have talked to Inspector Aston about – tell us now, Paul. What would she have said? What did she know?'

Matthews stepped back, back towards the sea. One foot skidding the coarse grass, arm flailing, he was arching over as Naylor caught him, low about the waist and swinging him inland, snatching him, almost, out of the air, the pair of them falling, bodies awkwardly intertwining across the edge of the path, the first stubby growth of the year.

'Good catch,' Khan said to Naylor, and then, to Matthews, helping him gingerly to his feet, 'You okay? You need to be a bit more careful, narrow paths like these. One foot in the wrong place and then . . .'

There were tears in Matthews's eyes again, clinging there, refusing to fall.

'Come on,' Khan said. 'What d'you say? Why don't we go back down?'

It was, as Reg Cossall would say later over a pint of Shippos, one of those fine spring days when to describe the stink of stale farts and cheap lager breath which greeted them in every doorway would have beggared even the sodding poet laureate's invention.

Exactly so.

Their questions were answered with deviousness, vulgarity, polite lies, numberless requests for them to fuck off out of it and mind their own bleedin' business, and, on one occasion, by a bucket of what startlingly resembled warm piss descending from an upstairs window in a virulent stream.

At least Chaucer could have dealt with that one.

Or Divine.

Divine, who suffered a long harangue from an out-of-work twenty-one-year-old, living with a seventeen-year-old woman and their two kids in a council house in

Kirkby-in-Ashfield. 'You,' he said, jabbing a finger towards Divine's face, 'you ought to be ashamed of yourself, you know that? Goin' round, roustin' blokes just 'cause they show a bit of patriotism, right? Not afraid to stick up for their fuckin' country, right? You know what I'm saying? I mean, you look around you, look around you, okay? Every fuckin' business, who owns it? Pakis, right? Pakis and niggers everywhere you fuckin' look. And the Irish . . . honest to Christ, I hate the fuckin' Irish. Treacherous, murderin' bastards. I mean, look, this country, this country used to be great, right? Look at a map, look at a fuckin' map some time, we used to own half this soddin' world, three-quarters of it and now we're nothing. Less than nothing. And me, blokes like me, we're the only ones standing up, makin' ourselves fuckin' heard. 'Cause we care, right? About this fuckin' country. It's your fuckin' pride, okay? We care and we ain't afraid to let it show and you, you and your mates, as should be standing up with us, side by side, make this country what it once was, what it could be, without all the nignogs and the Pakis and the Jews, all you do is come round hassling us, right? Ought to be fuckin' ashamed!'

Eyes alight, he hawked up a thick gob of spit and unleashed it on the ground some yards wide of Divine's feet. Divine listening, thinking, though he wasn't about to say so, that one way or another, the bloke had a point.

Lynn Kellogg and Sharon Garnett had almost given up trying to rouse anyone from this house, the last but one in the road, what remained of the front lawn blackened with engine oil. Sharon was giving Lynn the thumbs down and turning away, when there were footsteps and a muffled voice from the other side of the front door.

It was a runty little man in a singlet and jeans, scratching himself and yawning, blinking at the light.

'Sorry to wake you,' Sharon said, identifying Lynn and herself. 'We're looking for Gerry Hovenden. That wouldn't be you, by any chance.'

Unaware, possibly, that he was now standing there scratching energetically between his legs, the man shook his head. 'Not by any chance. That's the boy you're wanting and he's away.'

'Away where?'

'Buggered if I know.'

But the sound of a motor bike approaching provided all the answer they needed, Hovenden, moments later, swinging his leg over the rear of the machine, Shane already standing there, helmet in hand, thinking fucking law, what in fuck's name they after now?

It was soon clear.

'Can you tell us, Gerry,' Lynn asked, 'where you were last Saturday evening?'

'Home,' he replied, without hesitation.

'Last Saturday,' his father said dismissively. 'I never saw hide nor hair of you all evening.'

Coloured brightly from his neck, Hovenden shook his head. 'Home round Shane's, that's what I mean. Couple of videos and a curry, eh, Shane?'

'That's right,' Shane said. 'All evening.'

'You're sure about that?' Lynn said, moving a touch closer and fixing him with her best stare.

But Shane was not about to be intimidated. 'I said,

didn't I? Sure.' Those hard, brittle eyes, daring Lynn to call him a liar.

'Well, in that case,' Lynn said, 'we'd best have your name and address, too. You never know when we might want to check.'

'Shane Snape,' Resnick said, 'that's interesting.' Lynn and Sharon had reported back to Reg Cossall initially and then to Resnick direct. The three of them were in his office, the sky through the window slowly darkening towards evening.

'Came up on the back of the bike, large as life,' Lynn said.

'Yes,' Sharon said. 'Gave this Gerry Hovenden his alibi.'

Resnick looked at the two officers, one to another. 'And you didn't believe him?'

Sharon shook her head.

'Not Hovenden, certainly,' Lynn said. 'Lying to his back teeth, if you ask me. Covering up about something, I'd bet on that.'

'And he's on the Branch list? Political?'

Lynn made a face. 'Marginal, really. Not a member of any extremist group, as far as is known. Hangs about with them, that's all. Spotted up a couple of times at rallies. Nothing criminal recorded.'

'Right, let's follow it up. Once we've got some more information in, check Hovenden's contacts with the rest, see if he fits in with anyone else that looks interesting.'

'And Shane Snape?' Lynn asked. 'Do you want us to process him as normal, or . . .'

'I might go round myself,' Resnick said. 'Have a word.'

'Right.' Lynn hesitated at the door after Sharon Garnett

had passed through. 'About the other night,' she said quietly. 'All those things I was saying . . . I know it's difficult, I've probably made it difficult, but it's not going to get in the way . . . I mean, we can work together, it hasn't stopped that?'

'No,' Resnick said, 'of course not, it's fine.'

'You're sure?'

'Sure.'

Resnick's phone rang and as he reached towards it, Lynn slipped out through the door and closed it behind her.

35

It was a little after seven in the morning when Resnick realised he was thinking about Hannah, that he had been doing so for several minutes, ever since hoiking a recalcitrant Dizzy from the centre of the most comfortable armchair and sitting down with his second cup of coffee of the day. He could see her sitting on that bench in the Arboretum, face angled towards him, fixing him with that serious stare as she delivered her lecture on rejection and how not to take it. The schoolteacher in her, he thought; those earnest, serious eyes. And then the phone rang and it was her. Resnick felt uneasy, as if somehow thinking about Hannah had made it happen.

'Charlie, it's not too early . . .?'

'No, no, I've been up a while.'

'Good. Only . . . look, dinner on Friday. You haven't already booked somewhere have you?'

Air sucked cold through Resnick's stomach: she'd changed her mind. 'No, not yet,' he said cautiously.

'Oh, good, because . . .'

'Something else has cropped up.'

'No. Yes. Well, not exactly.'

Resnick fought to keep the disappointment out of his

voice. The last thing he wanted was another lecture on rejection. 'Not to worry, maybe some other time.'

'No,' Hannah said, 'it's not that, Friday's still fine. It's just . . . well, I feel stupid after making such a fuss about you being the one to decide . . .'

'That didn't matter, it's okay, I . . .'

'The thing is, there's this film, at Broadway . . .'

It would be, Resnick thought.

'. . . it's something I really want to see and Friday's the only chance I've got.'

'Look,' Resnick said, the soul of reason, 'that's all right, you go and see your film. We can meet another evening.'

'I was thinking more that you might come with me.'

'Ah.'

'We could get something to eat afterwards; we could eat there even, the food's not bad.' She drew breath, waiting for a response which didn't come. 'What do you think?'

'This isn't,' Resnick asked warily, 'another film from Tunisia about – what was it? – silence?'

Hannah laughed, just a little. 'No, you're quite safe. It's in English. Well, American. *Vanya on 42nd Street.*'

A memory jostled deep inside Resnick's brain. 'That's the Marx Brothers, isn't it?'

Hannah laughed. 'Not exactly.'

'Oh.'

'More Chekhov, I think.' And before he could say anything else, 'If that's okay, why don't we meet there? In the foyer. A quarter past eight.'

'All right.'

'See you then. And Charlie?'

'Mmm?'

'Next time I will let you choose, I promise.'

When he looked back across the room, Dizzy had taken the chance to nip back into the chair and lay there curled, one paw tight across his eyes.

'This carries on, Dizzy, my friend, the way she feels about cats, your days could be numbered.'

When Norma got back from her morning stint of cleaning, there was Sheena, feet up in the kitchen, smoking a cigarette while Peter boiled eggs for his breakfast, his or Sheena's, it was difficult to tell. At least father and daughter were in the same room together and, if not exactly talking, not shouting either.

'That place,' Norma said, shucking off her coat and dropping it onto the back of a chair, 'don't know if the bitter was off last night or what, but the state of that Gents this morning, floor were like a bad night in the scuttering abattoir.'

'Thanks, Mum,' grimaced Sheena, stubbing out her cigarette. 'For sharing that with us.'

'Yes, thanks, love.' Peter grinned. 'Just what I need to give me an appetite for these eggs. P'raps I should have them scrambled after all.'

Sheena leaned over the side of her chair and mimed being sick.

'What I could do with . . .' Norma began, lighting up herself.

'Is a fag and a nice cup of tea.' Peter began it and with Sheena joining in, they finished in unison.

'You two seem perky,' Norma said, filling the kettle at the sink.

'Been getting on all right, haven't we, Sheena?'

'Okay, yeh.'

'Then I'd best not ask you, young lady, why you're not at work, had I? Spoil this grand mood you're in.'

'Leave her be,' Peter urged, bending forward and carefully spooning the first of his eggs from the pan.

'Or where,' Norma went on, 'you got another new jacket from? And don't waste your breath telling me it's borrowed. Or that you bought it from what you've earned, 'cause the number of hours you've been working lately, it's you that'll be owin' them instead of the other way round.'

'Norma, love, leave it.'

''S all right for you, you'll be off out of here soon enough. I'm the one whose pocket'll hurt if she gets her cards.'

'Yeh, well,' said Sheena with a sniff, 'shows what you know, 'cause I already did.'

'What! You soft cow, what's the matter with you? What d'you want to go and do that for?'

'I didn't do it, did I? It were done to me.' Sheena swung her legs round from the seat of the empty chair, revealing a new pair of ankle-length black boots, still bright from their first shine.

'You what? And what about those shoes?'

'What about them?'

'You nicked them, that's what. No two ways about it. You and those fancy new friends of yours. You want to watch out, my girl, else you'll end up inside.'

'Yeah? Well a fucking lot you care.'

Norma coming to stand over her now: 'I've told you before, don't use that language to me.'

'No?' Sheena on her feet, face jutting forward into her

307

mother's. 'I'll use what language I sodding like. You don't own me, you know.'

'Is that right?' Norma swung her arm wildly, and if she hadn't ducked into it instead of away, Sheena would never have got hit. As it was, the heel of her mother's hand caught her hard alongside her mouth and she stumbled away, bleeding from her lip.

'You bitch!' Sheena yelled. 'You bloody bitch!'

Norma let out a sound somewhere between a scream and a howl and weighed into Sheena with both hands, Peter saying, over and over, 'Sheena, Norma, cut it out' and doing his best to drag Norma back; Sheena covering her face with her arms and Norma crying now, Norma and Sheena both crying. 'Sheena, Norma, stop it now.' Peter carrying on till Norma turned on him and pushed him clear across the kitchen. 'Stop whingeing on, you pathetic little shit. You get on my nerves something rotten, you sodding do.'

Sheena seized her moment and ran from the room, up the stairs into the bathroom where she locked the door and sat on the loo seat, arms gripped to her sides, shaking with anger and fear.

She hadn't stolen the boots, Diana had, from Dolcis the other afternoon. And as for the jacket, there they'd been, the whole gang of them, walking down through the city centre by Debenham's, when this girl came down the street in the opposite direction and Janie had reached out and grabbed her by the hair and told her to take off her leather jacket, she was having it, and the girl, of course, she said, no way, so Janie pulled her hair tighter then pushed her hard up against the wall and when she bounced back smacked her in the face with the heel of her shoe and told her to take off the fucking jacket, which now, no problem, the girl did, Janie bowing and laughing and saying, how kind, thank you so very much, and, now that her shoe was back on, giving the girl a good kick before carrying on across the street, not running or nothing, jacket round her shoulders; top of the street, Janie'd stopped and looked at herself in the mirror, crap, she'd said, I look like fucking crap in this, and she'd tossed it over to Sheena, here, you have it, it'd look all right on you, and pranced on across the street in front of the traffic, expecting it to stop for her, which, of course, it did.

Awesome, Sheena had thought. Fucking awesome!

And she still thought the same now, sitting there on the loo, almost able to feel the bruises coming out on her arms and neck.

Khan and Naylor stood respectfully across from Resnick's desk and told him about their conversation with Paul Matthews; told him and then waited patiently for his response. It was interesting, Resnick had thought as he listened, how the pair of them were seemingly alike in some ways, yet different: with Naylor, you felt the deference was natural, in part a product of a lack of confidence, whereas Khan seemed to be reining himself in, not wanting to seem pushy or overbright.

'He reckons he might've saved Nicky Snape's life if he'd acted quicker, that's at the root of it then?'

'Yes, sir,' said Naylor. 'Seems that way.'

'You don't think there's anything more?'

Naylor shook his head, but Resnick was looking at Khan.

'I don't honestly think we could have got anything more

from him that day; he was in a pretty het-up state. But I'm sure he's not told us everything,' Khan said after a moment. 'Not yet.'

'And you think he will?'

Khan nodded. 'I hope so. For his sake as well as ours.' He allowed himself a slight smile. 'Kevin here's not always going to be around to stop him throwing himself off the edge of the cliff.'

'You gave him your number, in case he decides to contact you?'

'Yes, sir.'

'All right. Meantime, let's have a closer look at Jardine. Dig around in his background a little. Previous appointments, whatever you can find. Let's see if there are any other reasons for him wanting to keep this all under wraps. Okay?'

As the two men turned to leave the office, Naylor automatically stood aside to let Khan through the door first.

It was almost an hour later that Resnick met Skelton near the head of the stairs, Skelton just back from a meeting with the Assistant Chief. They were discussing the meeting when Carl Vincent walked along the corridor in front of them, heading towards CID.

'How's he settling in, Charlie?' Skelton asked, voice low.

'Early days yet. But okay, far as I know.'

'No trouble, then? On account of his colour. You know the sort of thing I mean.'

Resnick knew well enough what it would have been like in days not so long past: whispering campaigns, closed ranks in the canteen, loud references to spooks and sooties, nignogs and monkeys, spades and coons. Pakis. And the jokes – What do you call a nigger in a three-bedroom semi? A burglar. Bananas and travel brochures advertising holidays in Africa, the West Indies, all the personal details filled in, those and worse left for black recruits to find. Once, hanging down from the locker-room ceiling, a white sheet with eye holes cut in the manner of the Ku-Klux-Klan. The bad old days.

'I've not heard of anything going off.'

Skelton nodded thoughtfully. 'And you've talked to Vincent himself?'

'Just about to. Off to see Shane Snape, check an alibi he's given for a mate, I thought Vincent could ride along. I'll have a word on the way.'

'What you mean is, Charlie, you thought he could be your driver.'

Resnick grinned. 'That, too.'

There were roadworks south on the Ilkeston Road and an articulated lorry had got itself wedged across the entrance to Garden Street, so they cut left along Kimboulton Avenue, down Ashburnham, past the brightly painted nursery and the recreation ground, swinging out onto the Boulevard and then over the crossroads, through the lights.

'How's it compare, then?' Resnick asked. 'To Leicester?'

Vincent smiled gently, an eloquent shrug of the shoulders.

'Have you been getting any hassle?'

Vincent looked at him, perhaps for longer than he

311

should, considering he was at the wheel. 'You mean on account of being black?'

'That's what I mean, yes.'

'It's cool.'

'You mean there hasn't been any, or there has and you're not bothered? You can handle it.'

'Nobody's spoken out of turn, no – what's the term? – racial epithets.' Quickly this time, he glanced across the front seat. 'Would you expect me to report it if there were?'

'Yes,' Resnick said. 'Yes, I would.'

Vincent nodded, thinking it over. 'Which turning?' he asked. 'Must be pretty soon now. On the left, yes?'

It was Peter who answered the door, a slight figure in a singlet and a pair of old cords, absurd almost with his little belly sticking out from below his concave chest. Resnick identified Vincent and himself and by that time Norma was there, filling out the hall. From inside came the sounds of the two fifteen from Doncaster.

'How's it going, Norma?' Resnick asked, friendly. Norma thinking he had come about Sheena, worried the stupid gillifer had got herself caught in the Broad Marsh Centre, some uptight store detective feeling her collar the minute she set foot outside the shop. But no, not this time.

'Your Shane,' Resnick said. 'He around?'

He was in his usual place when home, stretched out on the settee in front of the TV, can of Carlsberg within reach. Most days, if he didn't come out ahead at the bookie's, he didn't finish up so far behind.

He looked round at Resnick with flat, cold eyes; took in Vincent and dismissed him with a glance. The signs of the beating he had taken at the hands of the Turvey boys were fading but had yet to disappear.

Resnick nodded in the direction of the television and Vincent went round behind the settee and turned the volume down; horse with a white noseband seemed to be winning by seven or eight lengths. 'That pal of yours,' Resnick said. 'Gerry Hovenden.'

'Yeh, what about him?' Shane watching the screen, the last runners fading past the post.

'Last Saturday night, you gave him an alibi.'

'So?'

'I thought now he wasn't here, you might change your mind. Remember things a different way.'

'You're not saying I lied?'

'Loyalty,' Resnick said, 'it's a funny thing.'

'Mum,' Shane said, pushing himself up onto one elbow, raising his voice towards the kitchen, 'where was I Sat'day last?'

'Here,' Norma answering with prompting, walking through. 'Here with that pal of yours. Gerry. Brought back those videos, remember? *Elm Street* and that other one. Horrible bloody things!' And then, looking at Resnick. 'He was here, Mr Resnick. They both was.' Waiting for him to say otherwise.

What Resnick did was move closer to where Shane was sitting, sit down himself, on the arm of the settee. 'You into the same things as him, Shane? Aside from horror movies, I mean. Combat 18 and the like. Extremist stuff. Fascist rallies, racist attacks.'

Shane shifted his glance over towards Vincent, standing easily near the back of the room, and then back again.

''Cause if you were, I'd be surprised. Thought you had more brains than to be taken in by stuff like that.'

Shane made a circling motion with his shoulders before looking back towards the screen and the winning jockey, dismounting in the unsaddling enclosure. After a moment, he reached for the remote and switched the sound back up.

'Take it carefully,' Resnick said, back on his feet. 'Don't get yourself into any trouble you don't need to.'

Shane didn't budge, gave no indication that he heard or heeded Resnick's advice.

Norma walked with the two detectives to the door. 'The old girl,' she said, 'the one, you know, my Nicky . . .'

'Doris. She's getting slowly better, Norma. On the mend. They both are, her and her husband.'

Norma nodded. 'Good. I'm glad for that at least.'

Resnick and Vincent walking away then, back to the car, Vincent unlocking the doors and the pair of them getting in, kids along the street and parents at their windows, watching.

'What in Christ's name,' Norma shrilled at Shane the minute she got back in, 'have you been up to now?'

'Relax,' Shane said. 'First horse of the afternoon just come in, twenty-five to one.'

36

As luck would have it, Stella Aston had answered the phone when Resnick called; yes, of course she'd meet him, how about the Town House? Did he know it? That street off Bridlesmith Gate. Low Pavement, is that what it was called?

It was. Resnick got there early, one of those places he had walked past numberless times in the last three or four years. Slim, pale wooden tables and waitresses who were studying fashion at Trent University; either that, or they were sixth formers from the High School, giving off equal quantities of good breeding and disdain. Inside, casually smart young men, whose designer socks and underwear, Resnick guessed, cost more than he spent on clothes in a year, lolled back in dark glasses and looked cool. An elegant young mother – or was it the au pair? – fed what looked like purple yoghurt to a toddler in a high chair. One elderly woman, grey hair unravelling round her lined face, sat unhappily over the remains of her toasted sandwich, looking as out of place as Resnick felt.

'One, sir?' the waitress asked, friendly enough.

'Er, I'm meeting somebody.'

She gave Resnick a look that seemed to signify 'as if'

and consigned him to a table near the coffee machine, where she promptly forgot about him till Stella walked in. Stella in a bright top, coloured tights and clumpy boots and a skirt so short as to be hardly worthy of the name.

Resnick half-rose to greet her, embarrassed by her youthful attractiveness and conscious of those eyes watching from behind dark glasses, weighing up the nature of their relationship.

'How's your mum holding up?' Resnick asked, once Stella had sat down.

'Oh, you know, pretty well considering. Sometimes I think it still hasn't properly sunk in. Maybe it won't while I'm still around.'

'How long's that likely to be?'

'I ought to go back, oh, the end of the week.'

Resnick ordered a double espresso and Stella a fizzy mineral water and a piece of chocolate cake that came, small and rich, marooned in the middle of a large white plate.

For ten minutes or so they talked about nothing very much, Resnick relaxed enough now to enjoy Stella's company, the way she would throw back her head and laugh aloud at one of her own anecdotes about college. They think I'm her father, he thought, sneaking an hour off work to spend with his daughter, one of her rare visits home from university.

'I don't know what to call you,' Stella said, suddenly. 'I know my dad always used to call you Charlie.'

'Charlie's fine.'

But she shook her head. 'Not serious enough.'

'Is that what I am?'

'Aren't you?' Cake finished, she surprised him by taking

a packet of cigarettes from her bag, signalling to the waitress for an ashtray. 'You see, you're disapproving.'

'Am I?'

'Yes.' Drawing the first lungful of smoke down deep. 'You think, nice young girl, into the environment, ought to be taking care of her body in the same way. Something like that, anyway.'

Resnick supposed she might be right.

'You're not – what's the word? – frivolous, are you, Charlie. You have to do things for a reason.'

Despite himself, almost as if to disprove her, Resnick laughed. 'How do you know, I mean, here you are, the first time I've seen you in years. Certainly the first time we've ever . . .'

'Been alone.'

'Had a proper conversation . . .'

'And I'm analysing you.'

'Yes.'

She smiled. 'Charlie, I don't just know about trees. The reason we're here, for instance, it's not casual. You didn't call me on the spur of the moment. Not that there'd be anything wrong in that, but you just wouldn't do it.' She grinned. 'Even if it occurred to you, you'd hold back. Too many possible complications.'

Uncomfortable, Resnick looked round for the waitress. 'D'you want anything else? I'm going to have another espresso.'

She watched him while he ordered, waited while the waitress cleared their used crockery away. 'Well? I'm right, aren't I?'

Resnick leaned forward. 'I wanted to ask you . . .'

'Yes?'

317

'Your parents, they had separate rooms.'

'Yes, Dad's insomnia . . .'

'And this first happened when?'

'Oh, I don't know. Two or three years ago, maybe. But why do you want to know?'

'You were still living at home then, when they made this decision?'

'Doing A levels, yes.'

'And did they say much, d'you remember, about why they were going to make this change?'

'Yes, like I said, my dad, he couldn't sleep properly, he thought it would be best for my mum, they both thought it would be . . .' Stella broke off abruptly and reached for another cigarette; there were things she didn't want to see forming behind her eyes. 'You think something was going on, don't you? You think he was having an affair? My dad. That's what you were on about the other day, all that fuss about that phone call. God, Charlie! You think he was sleeping around.'

Slowly, Resnick shook his head. 'I don't know.'

Stella shook her head and laughed. 'You didn't know him very well after all. He just wasn't like that. I know that's what you'd expect me to say, but it's true. He just wasn't. Apart from anything else, there was all that religion. His preaching. Even if he'd been tempted, he'd never have let himself.' She held the smoke inside her mouth, releasing it through her nose. 'If it was either of them having an affair, it would have been Mum. Not him.'

It was Resnick's turn to be surprised. For some moments, he tried to imagine Margaret, small, dumpy Margaret . . . 'Why do you say that?' he asked.

'Because she was the one who had nothing else.'

'She had children, you.'

Stella laughed again, brittle and raw. 'I was seventeen, eighteen, my brothers had long left home. I had this boyfriend, older than me. We were sleeping together. Mum and I we never talked about it, but she must have known. It's not so difficult to imagine what that's like, your baby girl out there having sex and enjoying it, night after night, and you . . . I doubt if she and Dad had done it for years.'

Resnick's mind was on overtime. 'What you're saying . . .'

'Do I know it for a fact? No, not at all. I certainly didn't think it at the time. But then I would have been so wrapped up in what was happening to me, I think she could have done it on the kitchen table and I'd hardly have noticed.' She giggled, suddenly young again. 'Well, I think I might have noticed that.'

She stubbed out her half-smoked cigarette. 'About Mum, you won't need to say anything, will you? Ask her, I mean? It probably isn't true, none of it. Just my fertile imagination and besides, even if there was some truth in it, it couldn't have anything to do with what happened to my dad, could it? I mean, how could it?'

Resnick shook his head. 'I don't know. But you're right, it's difficult to see.'

'Then you won't say anything to her, to my mum?'

'I shouldn't think so.'

Stella beamed and ordered a hot chocolate. 'You notice a bit of a theme here?' she asked. 'Hot chocolate, chocolate cake.' And then, 'All those times you used to come round to the house with Dad, I used to hang around, follow you from room to room. I always wanted you to notice me, but you never did.'

'I'm sorry, I . . .'

'I used to think you were lovely. I had this photograph of you, I'd cut it from the paper. I used to keep it in my room, hidden in case anyone saw it. You never even noticed I was there.'

Resnick was blushing. 'God, Stella, you were about twelve.'

Stella laughed, spilling hot chocolate over the table. 'I can't help it, I was advanced for my age.' She was dabbing at the table with her napkin. 'Now I've shocked you.'

'No.'

'Yes, I have. All these steamy revelations about the Aston family women in one afternoon.'

The waitress was weighing in with a cloth, murmuring something about coming back to mop the floor. Stella scraped back her chair, smoothing down her skirt onto royal-blue thighs. 'I think we ought to go, don't you? Before we turn this place into a wreck.'

Resnick thanked the waitress and paid the bill.

On the cobbled street outside, for a moment Stella took his arm. 'So, Charlie – I like calling you that now – how about you, have you got a girl-friend or what?'

It took him a while to answer. 'Yes,' he said. 'At least, I think so.'

'Ooh.' Stella laughed. 'I should make sure, if I were you. You never know, whoever she is, she might not see it that way at all.'

37

He saw her rounding the corner into Broad Street, hurrying a little, but not so much that she didn't pause to check her reflection in the window of an Italian restaurant: a linen jacket over a pale-blue top, dark-blue, wide-cut linen trousers. She looked, Resnick thought, lovely.

'Charlie, I'm sorry I'm late.'

'No, it's me. I was early.'

In a slightly proprietorial way, Hannah touched her lips to his cheek. 'I phoned ahead,' she said, 'and reserved two tickets, just in case.'

Resnick reached for his wallet, but she stopped him, her fingers circling his wrist. 'My treat.'

They took their seats just as the film was about to start. A street scene in what Resnick presumed was New York: the Alfreton Road it certainly was not. Too bright, too brash, too fast-moving – all those garish signs and yellow cabs. But then the camera followed a number of the people into the calmer space of an old theatre, men and women dressed casually, greeting one another as old friends. Actors, Resnick supposed. Hannah had told him – all she had said by way of warning – it was about actors rehearsing a Russian play. Well that, he supposed, was what this was.

A fortyish man complaining to an older woman about how hard he has been having to work, so many jobs, different times of the day. When they sat down, she asked him if he would like a drink, and the man shook his head ruefully and told her he was trying to stop drinking vodka in the middle of the day.

Vodka: Resnick's attention perked up. And as they continued to talk, this couple, their language barely changing, he gradually realised that what he was hearing was the beginning of the play. Without announcement or much preamble, the thing itself had begun. *Uncle Vanya*. They were watching it now.

For close to two hours, Resnick fidgeted a little in his seat – legs too long, body weight not distributed quite right – but his attention rarely wavered from the screen; and when it did, it was only to glance across at Hannah, her close profile, the degree to which she was held rapt. Near the end, the way she pulled a tissue from her bag and dabbed away the tears.

'Well, Charlie, what did you think of that?' They were on their way downstairs, people milling round them in a haze of conversation.

What did he think?

That he had recognised them, these people, quarrelling endlessly about the estate on which they lived and worked, promises not clearly made and never kept, love which remained undeclared until it was too late. The best hopes of their lives had passed them by because they had been afraid to act. To speak. To say what they felt. These people he knew.

'I mean,' they were down at the ground floor now, others spilling round them on all sides, 'did you like it? The film.'

Smiling, Resnick surprised her by taking her arm. 'Yes, I did. Now,' steering her over towards the cafébar, 'did you say something about eating in here?'

It was busy but they found a table close against the back wall and Resnick ate small pieces of chicken steeped in garlic, while Hannah picked at something spicy with red peppers and aubergine and talked about the film. Resnick content for the most part to listen, sneak occasional glances around the room, chip in the odd word or two, sip his wine.

'Come on,' he said, outside, 'let's get a cab. I'll see you home.'

'It's a nice night,' Hannah said. 'We could walk.'

And they did, through the square and up Derby Road, Hannah asking him about his marriage, what had happened, no need for him to talk about it if he didn't want to or if it made him feel uncomfortable, it wasn't any of her business, but talk he did, mapping the slow shifts of his and Elaine's relationship in a way that moved her, as she had been moved earlier, in the cinema. His slow, careful telling of it affecting her with the pain it still rekindled for him, the sense, still there, of loss; the generosity, finally, with which he spoke about Elaine, despite her leaving him, falling in love with another man.

'Do you ever hear from her, Charlie?'

'Not really, no.'

They were crossing at the lights below the Savoy, not so far to go, down past the small hotel and then a left turn onto the path beside the park which led to Hannah's

323

house. Which was where, some fifty yards along, the man stumbled out of the bushes directly in front of them, Hannah jumping back with a stifled scream and Resnick instantly on guard, adrenalin firing in. The man swayed, face a pale blur in the light from the upstairs windows opposite, and then made to hurry past, but when Resnick moved across to block his path, raised a hand to detain him, he cowered back and began to shout.

'It's okay, it's okay,' Resnick said, cautiously moving close, the man not shouting now, but mumbling over and over, words draining into one another, 'Keepbackkeepbackkeepback.'

He made a sudden dart, trying to squeeze past between Resnick and the fence and Resnick caught him by the arm and swung him round and all resistance went out of the man and he cried. There were cuts, Resnick could see now, high on his face, a broad gash above his left eye, a graze all down one cheek.

'It's all right,' Resnick said quietly, and then, to the man, taking another careful step towards him, 'No one's going to hurt you, it's okay.'

'What can we do?' Hannah asked anxiously.

'Nip home. Phone for an ambulance.'

The man began to scream.

'Go on,' Resnick said, Hannah hesitating. 'Do it now.'

'Not the hospital,' the man was moaning. 'Please not.'

'Why don't we take him to my place?' Hannah said. 'He could sit down a minute, calm down. The hospital's only up the road after all.'

Resnick was thinking, thinking about the marks on the man's face, how they might have been caused. 'All right,' he said. 'Maybe that's best.'

324

Hannah moved past him to the man, who flinched when she made as if to touch him, but agreed finally to walk beside her towards the terraced houses at the end, walking slowly as if each step hurt.

He was older than Resnick had first judged, mid-thirties he now would have said, wearing black jeans with patches of dirt down one side and below the knees, a collarless black shirt spotted with blood, white Nike Air trainers with a blue stripe.

'Here.' Hannah coming towards him with a dampened cloth to wipe away some of the blood, the man sitting up to her kitchen table, blinking at the light.

Resnick stopped her with her name, not loud but firm, and she looked across at him, head tilted in a question. 'Gloves,' Resnick said. 'Kitchen gloves, something like that. Use them. Just in case.'

Hannah hesitated on the verge of questioning him, challenging, then did as he said. While she cleaned the man up, Resnick made tea.

'What's your name?' Hannah asked, and when he didn't reply, said, 'I'm Hannah. Hannah Campbell, this is my house.'

'Declan,' he said, so quietly they had to strain to hear. 'Declan Farrell.'

'Would you like to tell us, Declan,' Resnick said, sliding a mug across the table towards him, 'just what happened?'

Farrell stirred sugar slowly into his tea, eyes flicking from one to the other, never still in his seat, forever shifting, forward and back, crossing and re-crossing his legs, tugging at his jeans, not making any attempt to lift the cup to his mouth.

'You were going to tell us,' Resnick said, 'how this happened.'

Farrell started, stopped, started again. 'This man . . . This man . . .' He closed his eyes, began, almost silently, to sob. There was a wedding ring, Resnick noticed, broad and dull, on his hand.

'Go on,' Resnick said gently when the crying had ceased. 'This man . . .'

Farrell sniffed loudly, wincing, rubbing tenderly at his eyes. 'I was in the park,' he began, then stopped a second time.

'Isn't it locked up at night?' Hannah asked. 'The park.'

He nodded, fidgeting again on his seat. 'You can get in, it's easy. Over the fence. People do.'

Resnick nodded, sitting forward; he knew what people did. 'I think you should tell us what happened,' he said.

'I was in the park, walking, cutting across like, you know. On my way home from the pub. I was caught short. Needed to use the Gents.' He paused and looked at the floor. 'I was just coming out when this bloke, he . . . he just come at me with this thing, this – I don't know what it was – bat, I suppose.'

Resnick thinking, remembering: *mud and grass stains on the dead man's clothes, a smear of earth thick on the fleshy palm of his right hand, a varnished implement, a bat of some kind, baseball seemed the more likely.*

Farrell continuing, saying, 'He just started hitting me, here, you can see. I yelled at him, tried to get away but he wouldn't stop. I couldn't run any more, all I could do was lie down on the ground and cover my head until . . . until he stopped.'

'He just stopped, no reason?'

'One minute he was hitting me, shouting, you know, bastard, things like that. Then he ran off. I heard him going, but I was too frightened to look up. Not for ages. And then, when I did, well, that was when I met you.'

'He didn't take your wallet, ask for money, nothing like that?'

Farrell shook his head, not able to look at Resnick for more than moments at a time, squirming on his chair.

Resnick leaned a little towards him and Farrell flinched. 'Would you like a cushion?' Resnick said. 'You don't seem comfortable at all.'

'No, no, no, it's okay. I really ought to – my wife, she'll be worried, you know . . .' Half out of his seat now, the wooden chair on which he had been sitting patched with blood.

Watching Farrell all the while, Resnick beckoned Hannah to the doorway between the two rooms. 'Phone the ambulance,' he said. 'Then the police. Tell them to bleep Graham Millington, have him call Maureen Madden and then contact me here. Tell them assault and suspected rape.'

In the quiet of her house, shock leaped from Hannah's eyes. Resnick touched her hand and held it for a moment, the fingers unnaturally cold. Farrell was sitting with his eyes tight shut, arms clenched across his chest as if it were the only way to hold himself together.

Quietly Hannah rose and went to the telephone and when Declan Farrell started to cry, tears that would never stop, Resnick sat and held him till the ambulance arrived.

38

Maureen Madden was the sergeant who ran the rape suite, an attempt, largely successful, to make rape victims – the ones that came forward – feel more at ease than in the functional brusqueness of the normal police station. Comfortable chairs, subdued lighting, carpet, pictures on the walls; the facilities for medical examination all present. In the three years or so that Maureen had been working there, she had not had one victim to deal with who was male.

And this had begun differently, at the hospital, no time for anything but the most rudimentary counselling before the doctor on duty carried out his examination. Maureen was uncertain whether Declan Farrell would have been relieved to discover the doctor was male, or whether by that stage he even cared; she had no clear idea how he would respond to talking to her rather than to a man about what had happened. It crossed her mind to contact one of the members of the Lesbian and Gay Police Association, but then she had no way of knowing if Farrell himself were gay. A married man, two kids apparently, she wondered if he knew himself. He had pleaded with them, when they informed his wife of where he was, not to give her the details of what had happened.

Now Mrs Farrell was pacing the waiting area, chewing stick after stick of Dentyne, dropping coins into the vending machine for luke-warm cups of tea, and Declan was unburdening himself little by little as Maureen, patient, trained, won his trust.

Millington had rousted out Naylor and Vincent, but found Divine impossible to track down. No surprise. 'Round midnight of a Friday,' as Millington had pointed out, 'state Mark'll be in, likely neither use nor ornament.'

The toilet was in one corner of the recreation ground, close to the gate on the southern edge and in the shadow of the church. They checked the interior, a short stand of unseparated urinals and one cubicle, careful not to disturb anything forensic might turn to good use later. The small, low building was ripe with the stink of stale urine, its walls festooned with barely decipherable graffiti and gouged here and there with slogans: *MUFC Rule! Colleymore Walks On Water* (from which someone had erased the *l* and substituted an *n*) and *Niggers Out!*

Lights were still showing in a good number of the houses in Church Street and Church Grove, as well as along the Promenade, so they began the slow and diligent business of knocking on doors. Uniformed officers, using emergency lighting, made an initial search of the mainly grassed area between the toilet and where Farrell had climbed the fence onto the path where he had been found. At first light, the same process would be gone through more thoroughly, taking in the thick area of shrubs along the church wall.

'Charlie,' Hannah had asked, face still pale, 'how did you know?'

'I didn't at first.' Resnick had shrugged. 'Not for definite. Not till I saw the blood.'

'Oh, Christ! It's horrible.'

'Yes.' Holding her now, hair across his mouth, one hand to his chest. 'Yes, I know.' Except I don't, he thought, not really. I can't. And hope to God I never do.

The doctor was young, Australian, working on a short-term contract he didn't expect to be renewed, though that was due to a lack of funding rather than any fault of his own. The room in which he spoke to Resnick and Maureen Madden was small and white-walled, the overhead lighting so strong it discouraged you from raising your eyes. His voice was occasionally slurred and Resnick might have thought he had been drinking if he were not so obviously tired.

'The cuts to the face were pretty much as you've seen; he took quite a few stitches and he isn't going to be looking in any mirrors for a while, but other than that it's not too serious. There is evidence, though, of quite severe bruising on the neck.'

'Finger marks?' Resnick interrupted to ask.

The doctor shook his head. 'More like some kind of bar, I don't know, something hard, some sort of stick, you know, like a walking stick. Pulled back against the neck below the adam's apple.'

'Forcing back the head?' Resnick asked.

'Yes, quite possibly. We'll know better once the bruises-'ve come out more. But yes, it could be.' He cleared his throat and looked up into the brightness of the light and then at the floor beneath his feet. 'Look, I'm sorry, I seem to be avoiding the issue here.'

'It's all right,' Maureen said, 'take your time.'

Resnick caught himself wondering, would he be so reluctant if this were a woman he'd just seen?

'There was penetration,' Maureen prompted him.

'Yes. Without any doubt. But not . . .' For an instant, he caught Resnick's eye. 'I mean it was sexual, clearly, but I think what was used was some kind of, well, instrument.'

'What, you mean a vibrator?' Maureen asked. 'A dildo, what?'

He shook his head. 'I don't think so. Nothing that appropriate. It probably would have been better for him if it were. No, this was quite large, two to three inches in diameter at the end and solid, probably not tapered towards any kind of a point. Not sharp-edged, though, or the damage would have been even worse than it is. But whatever it was had been used with a lot of force. There's quite a bit of tearing of the sphincter muscles and around the orifice itself, and considerable rupturing of blood vessels along the anal canal.' He shook his head again. 'Poor bastard,' he said.

The story Declan Farrell had told Maureen Madden was this: he had needed to use the toilet on his way home from the pub and shinned over the gate. Easy, he'd done it before. The man was there when he went in; inside the cubicle, so Declan didn't see him. But he had followed Declan out, jumped him from behind. Hit him across the face with some kind of club. Almost knocked him out. Forced him to kneel down on the grass, pulled down his trousers and his pants. Told him he was going to give him what he wanted. His words: this is what you want. And then . . . and then at that point Declan's voice had choked and Maureen had held his hand and said, 'Okay, now. It's all right. Declan, it's okay.'

'I'm going to have to talk to him, Maureen,' Resnick said.

'Tonight?'

'Sooner it's done.'

She nodded. 'I suppose so. You want me with you?'

'Please.'

'Let's take him back to the rape suite, then. Not here.' Resnick agreed.

'And his wife?' Maureen asked.

Resnick looked back at her, unblinking.

'All right,' Maureen said, 'I'll speak to her before we leave.'

Skelton was at the station when they arrived, waistcoat unfastened, no tie; like the reformed non-smoker he was, cigarette never far from his hand.

'So, Charlie, this little effort, we're not thinking there's any kind of link with the attack on Bill Aston?'

'Bit early yet to know what we're saying.'

'But this – nancy boy pick-up gone sour, that's what we're dealing with surely?'

Nicely put, Resnick thought. 'Sexual, certainly,' he said. 'Of a kind. Victim's wallet was still on him, nothing stolen. But to what degree there was ever consent . . .'

'I thought we were talking rape?'

'I mean, whether or not there was anything between them beforehand . . .'

'You show me yours, I'll show you mine, that sort of thing? Bit of hanky-panky up and down the stalls.'

'Something like that, sir, yes.'

'Scarcely matters, does it, one way or another? Bit of flashing in the Gents not that much different from walking into the pub with half your tits hanging out – provocation, not an issue any more where rape's concerned.'

Resnick was far from certain that was true, when it came to juries at least. 'I'm interviewing him, sir, now. I'll bring you up to speed soon as I can.'

'That's it, Charlie.' Skelton winked. 'Get to the bottom of it, eh?'

'Bastard asked for it, didn't he,' Divine said, finally tracked down after one of those rare Friday nights when he had failed to pull. 'No question. Went out looking for a bit of rough and got more than he bargained for. Now he wants us to say there, there and hold his hand. Well, not bloody me and that's a fact. Kev, while you're over there, be a mate will you and fetch us a tea.'

Declan Farrell had refused tea or coffee, didn't want anything to drink at all; he sat there, between Resnick and Maureen, unmoving in the hushed quiet of the room. Numb. Except that's what he wasn't, numb: only what he wished to be.

'The man who attacked you,' Resnick asked for the third time, 'what can you tell us about him?'

Eleven minutes past two.

'His voice, his appearance . . .'

'I didn't see him.'

'You heard his voice. He spoke to you at least once, you said.'

Nervous, Farrell touching the stitches scissoring above his eye, the worst cut and the deepest, fingers going back to it like a tongue unable to stop itself probing a bad tooth. Farrell sitting in hastily borrowed clothes, his own carefully labelled, packaged and shipped off to forensic.

'Semen?' Resnick had asked the doctor.

'Not really. None around the area of penetration. A trace inside his clothing, probably his own.'

His own?

'Why don't you try and concentrate,' Resnick said, 'on the voice?'

As if he could ever forget it, Declan thought. As if there'd ever be a night again when he wouldn't hear it: *This is what you want, you bastard. You fucking cunt!*

'The voice,' Resnick asked, 'was it young or old?'

'Young,' Farrell said, so quietly that both officers had to lean forward to hear him. 'At least, I think ... Oh, God, I don't know, I don't know.'

'An accent? Did he have an accent?'

An age before Farrell answered and then, 'Yes, maybe.'

'Local?'

'Sort of. I mean, around here, yes, but not strong.'

'Is there anything else,' Maureen asked, 'that you can help us with, about the voice?'

Making him play it back, again and again, six seconds on repeat. 'It was rough.'

'Rough?'

'Sort of rasping.'

'As if he had a cold, that sort of sound?'

334

Farrell levelled his gaze and stared. 'As if he was excited,' he said.

Seventeen minutes to three.

'Declan,' Resnick said, 'no one's judging you here, you know that. Maureen and I, we're not passing judgement on what you do. Whatever you've done. That's not what this is about.'

'Then what is it about?' Farrell asked, a sudden unsuspected shout. 'Why can't I just go home? That's what I want.'

'What this is about,' Maureen said, 'part of it, is making sure that whoever it was did this to you won't do it again to somebody else.'

Farrell was leaking tears again; they came and went so frequently now he scarcely bothered wiping them away.

'You're sure you didn't know him, Declan? This man?'

'I told you, I told you I never even saw him. How can I know if I've seen him before?'

'But you have been there before,' Resnick asked. 'Those toilets?'

'Of course I have.'

'I mean, to meet someone. For the purposes of sex?'

'No.'

'Declan . . .'

'No! I've told you, I'm not queer, I'm not gay, not any of the things you think I am.'

'Declan, please . . .'

He was on his feet now and making for the door, Maureen looking quickly across at Resnick, wanting to know should she stop him.

'Declan,' Resnick said, 'I think you had been there

335

before, after closing, around the same time. I think some-times you were lucky, met someone you fancied, sometimes you didn't, gave it up and went on home. I think whoever was shut in the cubicle tonight you thought had gone there for the same reason as you. Now I don't know what you did, whether or not there was some signal between you, whether you showed yourself to him through a hole in the door, hole in the wall. But when you went out onto the Rec I think you thought he would follow you and he did. And Declan, I don't care about any of that, I honestly don't. But what happened next, that's what I care about. This person, whoever it was, viciously assaulted you, assaulted you in the most terrible way imaginable. And as Sergeant Madden said, we want to ensure he doesn't remain free to do this again. To someone else. And because you know what it's like, Declan, you must want that too. So I am asking you, please, to help us as much as you can.'

After several seconds' hesitation, Declan Farrell opened the door and walked out. Maureen looked across at Resnick and slowly shook her head, closed her eyes.

When Carl Vincent came into Resnick's office he was looking a little tired, a man who had been up all night and only snatched a half-hour's sleep, slumped across a table in the canteen. There were a couple of marks on the sleeve of his lightweight suit, picked up during the search and his collar was somewhat awry, but otherwise he didn't look much the worse for wear.

A sight better than Resnick himself. 'Carl, what can I do for you?' he asked.

'This business last night, the talk is you're not making any connection with the Aston murder.'

'That's pretty much right.'

Vincent drew a deep breath. 'Look, sir, maybe I should've said before, but I saw him a year ago, Aston, in a gay club in Leicester.'

For a second, the pulse beating at the side of Resnick's head seemed to stop. 'What are you saying?'

'I'm saying Bill Aston was gay.'

39

Not even minutes, Resnick seemed to have been sitting there for a small eternity.

A year ago ... a club in Leicester ... gay.

It was not only tiredness, but anxiety in Vincent's eyes.

'This club,' Resnick said eventually, 'you were there on duty?'

Fleetingly, the eyes closed and when they looked at Resnick again there was no avoidance, no guile. 'No, sir.'

Resnick breathed through his mouth. He said, 'You'd best sit down.'

Vincent crossed one leg over the other, uncrossed it, sitting with his hands resting just above his knees.

'And Inspector Aston,' Resnick said, 'there's no way he wasn't there on duty either?'

Vincent shook his head.

'You're sure? Positive?'

'He left with somebody,' Vincent said.

Resnick was seeing Aston's wife, her plumpish little body ill-fitting in black, her voice fierce against the afternoon. *You knew him, Charlie, better than most.*

'And you couldn't have been mistaken? Misinterpreted the situation?'

But Vincent was already shaking his head.

'A year ago,' Resnick said.

'The reason I remember, someone pointed him out to me. Someone I knew there, in the Job. He'd seen him at some course, I think. Aston. Knew he was from up here, this force. Said he'd come across him before, you know, in Leicester, once or twice.'

'You didn't speak to him?'

For a moment, Vincent smiled. 'Not my type.'

'But you are gay?'

'It doesn't mean we fancy everyone, you know.'

'I know,' Resnick said. 'But what you're saying is you're gay but you've not gone public about it.'

'That's right.'

Resnick shook his head. 'What's really worrying me is why you didn't tell me about Aston before?'

Vincent didn't respond right away. 'Because I wasn't sure. I mean, I hadn't known his name. And the photograph . . .' Resnick staring at him, waiting for all of the truth. 'No, all right, I thought I recognised him, the connection was made, but then, it seemed to have nothing to do . . . I couldn't see the relevance to what had happened. Gay or not gay, sexuality didn't seem to be an issue.'

'Except for yours.'

'I'm sorry?'

'Except for yours. Your sexuality.'

'Look . . .'

'No, you look.' Resnick leaning forward now, head slightly to one side, fingers beginning to point. 'The reason you didn't come forward with this information sooner was personal. To do with you. Give up Aston and you're giving up yourself. In keeping silent, you were protecting yourself.'

Slightly muffled through the door, the constant, shifting sound of telephones, their call and response. Someone knocked on Resnick's door and receiving no answer, turned away.

'It was an issue for me, yes,' Vincent finally said.

'*The* issue.'

'No, sir. If that was the case I'd never have come forward now. I'd have kept my silence, prayed it didn't matter, or if it did it'd come out some other way. But as soon as I heard, you know, last night, what happened to the guy in the park, there was no way I could keep quiet then.'

'Even though it means exposing yourself like this?'

Vincent shook his head. 'I'm a copper, just like you.'

Not just like me, Resnick thought. 'Carl,' Resnick said, 'I don't care what you do in bed or who you do it with.' Not even sure if that were true. 'The only place it affects me is here, when you let it affect you, how you do your job. And what prevented you from acting as you should, it wasn't the fact of your being gay, it was that you've kept that fact a secret. That's what was wrong.'

Vincent stifled a laugh. 'You think I should come out?'

'That's up to you.'

'But that's what you're saying.'

A shake of Resnick's head. 'What I'm saying, as long as you don't, there'll be other incidents like this, judgement calls you feel you have to make. And they'll be to do with protecting yourself, your secret, and not your job.'

'I'm sorry,' Vincent said, 'I'm finding this a little difficult to take in.'

'That I want you to be honest about yourself? Tell the truth.'

'That here's my senior officer, telling me I have a duty to come out as being gay.'

'I don't think I shall be able to trust you, your judgement, not fully unless you do.'

'And if I did?'

'Your instincts are good, you seem to talk to people well, work hard. You're clearly bright.' He shrugged. 'No reason you shouldn't make a good detective.'

'You'd keep me on your team?'

Resnick thought for longer than probably he should. 'Yes, why not?'

Vincent smiled, pleased like a kid that'd been handed a prize, confused; he touched his hands together and rocked back in his chair. 'I don't know...' Openly, this time he laughed. 'You think it isn't difficult enough, getting on in the Job being black, without having to stand up for being gay as well?'

Skelton had not been having a good twenty-four hours. His daughter had telephoned him in the middle of dinner to tell him she was thinking about dropping out from university to become part of a medical outreach team in Zaire; his wife, whose only recent communication with him had been by means of grunts or notes stuck to the door of the fridge, had launched into a diatribe about setting up a new regime which seemed to be going to start with Skelton laundering his own underpants; and then there had been the call-out on account of that poof who'd been raped on Lenton Rec.

Now this.

'Jesus, Charlie! They're everywhere.'

Resnick offered no comment.

'You can't switch on the television nowadays without there's some clever little bastard smarming on about equal rights for gays. Strikes me, we'll soon be the ones needing extra rights. Blokes on *EastEnders* holding hands and dying from AIDS; lezzies all up and down *Brookside*. And the BBC – the BBC, mind, not Channel 4 – have started this – what is it? *Gaytime TV*. As though it was all a big laugh. Whatever happened to normal, eh, Charlie? Normal blokes with normal families, that's what I'd like to know.'

What happened, Resnick thought, was they turned into Bill and Margaret Aston; or they turned into you.

'And I'd figured him for a decent lad, Vincent,' Skelton said.

'So he is,' Resnick said, earning himself an old-fashioned look.

Skelton fidgeted with papers on his desk, no longer as meticulously ordered as it used to be. 'You really think, Charlie, this radically changes things?'

'I think what it does, maybe, it helps to make more sense of things that up to now never felt quite right. Aston's murder as a mugging. One thing, however drunk you are, if you're looking for an easy victim, why pick someone strongly built, close on six foot? And then there's the degree of force. Way more than necessary, even assuming Bill was fighting back. Those blows to the face and head, that isn't greed, not even ordinary anger, that's rage.'

'Queer-bashing, then? That's where we are.'

Resnick sighed. 'It looks likely, given what we now

know. If Bill wasn't above a bit of occasional cottaging, it might have started off that way. You'd have to say, if he had been that way inclined, he'd have had opportunity galore. All those times he went out last thing with his dogs; little dogs like that you can leave in the car.'

'Come on, Charlie, this is conjecture, nothing more.'

'We know he went to Leicester, socialising, picking up men. Maybe other places, too.' The expression on Skelton's face, listening, was that of someone who has just bitten into a peach to find the inside rotted and sour. 'But closer to home – if he got the urge, where would he go? Not to one of the pubs or clubs here, too great a risk. But somewhere more anonymous, in the dark? He just might. Toilets at Ollerton roundabout, Titchfield Park in Mansfield, Sherwood Library maybe. Where then?'

'Any sodding where nowadays!'

'Closest to where he lives, Gents on the Embankment. Maybe one of them as attacked him saw him there, inside or just hanging about.'

'Even if that were true – and I'm not for one minute agreeing that it is, I don't know what I think about the kite you're flying here – it doesn't prove a link with last night. What happened to Bill, thank Christ, wasn't the same.'

'The anger was,' Resnick said. 'The rage. What happened to them both, it was punitive. Sexuality aside, it was about the same things: power and pain.'

Skelton rose to his feet and half-turned towards the window: the same buildings, same vehicles, same people walking the streets, but underneath the world had turned upside down. 'Once the press get hold of this, Charlie . . .'

'I know.'

'His poor wife and family . . .'

'Yes.'

'Jesus, Charlie! I went to church once when he was preaching, Billy Aston was up there in the pulpit, rabbiting on about the wages of sin.'

And the one about throwing the first stone, Resnick thought, was that one of his favourites as well?

Resnick's briefing was coming to an end: the revelations about Aston had been greeted with shock and loud disbelief. Resnick had let it diminish and moved on. Nothing as good as definite, but some of the boot marks taken from the Rec were at least a partial match with those lifted, more clearly, from the Embankment; and the weapon – it was within the realms of possibility that the implement used, both to strike Farrell and to violate him, was the same baseball bat that had killed Aston.

'Lateral thinking, isn't that what they call it?' Divine muttered, 'making the most of both ends.'

'So we're going to be double-checking back on our files, all reported homophobic incidents, attacks, complaints made and followed up, anything that can be checked against our nationalist friends. Okay? And now, before you disperse, DC Vincent has something he wants to say.'

When Carl Vincent stepped forward, Resnick could see his right hand, trembling at his side. But his voice was level and clear. 'Especially in view of these cases we're investigating, I think it's important that you all know that I am homosexual.' Just for one second, he almost smiled. 'I'm gay.'

40

They sat in the near silence of the cloistered room, curtains once more pulled tightly together, soft patterns in which brown and gold leaves drifted carefully down. From out along the street, muted, came the intermittent rattle of a road drill as workmen dug trenches to lay cable, bringing in a wider world. Margaret Aston sat small in her favourite Parker Knoll chair, bought when real wood and solid craftsmanship were virtues to be praised and admired. Stella – no smile for him today – had left the moment he arrived and Resnick had waited for Margaret to negotiate the stairs, the slow passage – refusing his arm – into what she would always call the lounge.

Abruptly the drilling stopped and all he could sense in the room were loss and regret, the broken reed of her breath. In less than two weeks she had aged ten years.

'Margaret . . .'

When she spoke it was not to him, yet she knew he was there, and whenever he moved, no matter how little, she paused, her fingers plucking at the thread that had come unravelled from the beading on the chair's arm.

'It was after the boys had left home. Stella, she was still here, but . . .' Margaret sighed the first of many sighs.

'. . . she had this boy-friend and she would find reasons for not coming home. Simply excuses, I knew that's what they were; anything so that she could spend the night with him.' Another sigh, pluck and sigh. 'She had discovered sex, my daughter, as we all do, and it was all that she could think of. They used to come round here in the afternoons, when Stella should have been in school, upstairs with the door locked and then running off, giggling and smirking the minute I came home. No shame. Even with a father like Bill, my Stella knows nothing of shame.' She looked up. 'I wonder, Charlie, if that's such a bad thing?'

A pause before she went on. 'I would go sometimes then and stand in her room. Instead of throwing open the window, I would lock it closed. Keep in the smell. Do you know how it makes you feel, Charlie? When the children you nursed and carried are old enough to enjoy sex?'

Curtly, Resnick shook his head.

'No, no, of course, Charlie. You wouldn't. Perhaps you never will. So I'll tell you – it makes you feel old, used up. But it does something else, too. It makes part of you, that part of you, come alive again. Pictures of them wrapped there – am I shocking you, Charlie? – those young girl's legs that had once held tight around this pathetic body of mine, they had been wrapped around him, that feckless youth, there on that bed.'

Resnick looked at the leaves, still trapped mid-fall, the long, tapering slice of light.

'I had a body again, Charlie, my daughter had given me back my body and what was I going to do with it now? Bill and I, we had not had relations for years. Scarcely since after Stella had been born. And during all

346

that time I had lain down next to him every night and never once had I minded. But now . . .' Her fingers moved more nervously at the thread. '. . . I did all the things a woman, even a woman like me, old and fat, is supposed to do. I went to the hair salon, the beauty parlour, I was – what's the word? – made over. I bought new clothes, satin nightdresses and silk underthings in which I felt and looked a fraud. I begged him, Charlie, pleaded with him. I had no dignity. I needed him – needed someone – to make love to me.' The thread that she was twisting snapped in her hand. 'I could see in his eyes the thought of touching me made him feel sick. He told me he was moving across the corridor, into one of the empty rooms. He was having difficulty getting to sleep and he thought if he had his own bed it might be better. For both of us.'

She shrivelled a little more inside her chair.

'It was then that he started going out. Not so frequently at first, and then more and more. Swimming every night. Or so I thought. Twice, sometimes at weekends. He just needs, I thought, to get out of the house, get away from me, what I've been putting him through.' She glanced up at Resnick hastily. 'I was feeling guilty, you see, thought I'd been unfair. Making demands.' She found a new end of thread and worried it with finger and thumb. 'After a while he started going out late at night too, walking the dogs. I did think, it did cross my mind once or twice that he might be having an affair with one of those fine-minded women from the church. And then when you came here asking questions about that woman who called, I thought, yes, yes, it's all right, that's it.'

She looked at him, dull eyes sharpened by deceit.

'But that wasn't it, was it? That wasn't it.'

He thought that she would cry then, but if there were tears there they were still to come. The drilling had started up again outside. She had said what she had to say and now it was done. Resnick sat across from her, trapped in that closed room, willing himself to be patient, trying not to notice that the undersides of his thighs were growing numb.

POLICE MURDER: GAY SEX LINK? the headline suggested. *Startling revelations revealed exclusively to our reporter today* ... There were photographs of Bill Aston in uniform; one, poorly taken, of Margaret's startled face as she turned outwards from her front door. A family portrait, paid for or purloined, of Declan Farrell with his wife and child. *Detective Superintendent Jack Skelton would today neither confirm nor deny that one of the detective constables under his command* ...

Hannah phoned Resnick at home, but of course he was not there; she left a message for him at the police station that he should ring her that evening if he found time. She would be home.

'What amazes me,' Divine said, troughing through pie and double chips in the canteen, 'is any of that lot being queer at all. Thought they were all so busy fostering the old myth, our black brothers, that they're all hung like a fuckin' horse, the last thing any of 'em'd do'd be own up to having a limp wrist.'

'Reckon that's what it is, then, Mark?' said one of the constables, winding him up. 'Big dicks. All a myth?'

'How the bloody hell'd I know?'

'Play your cards right,' the PC said, 'this could be your big chance to find out.'

Sometimes, in Diane's flat, Sheena would sit with the baby, Melvin, for so long she would forget everything else. Times they'd been smoking dope especially. The others, not Sheena, they were popping all those pills too. Sheena was happy to stick to the spliffs Dee-Dee had taught her to roll – one of the skills Dee-Dee's Pentecostal father had never taught her. The stuff, though, it came from Diane's brother – Jamaican. That was what he said and who was she to deny it? Uum, wherever it came from, it was good. Sheena leaning against the sofa, sitting back alongside it, head against the wall. Little Melvin with his thumb stuck in the corner of his mouth, slobbering just a little, eyes closed and Sheena rocking him. That music that was playing, a tape Irena had boosted from one of the stores. Mouldy? No, Moby, that was it. Moby with his funny little pixie face, black eyes staring out of the blue. Orange robes on him like he was one of those Krishnas or something. And water: that's what all that blue was around him. Water. Moby in the middle of it, slowly drowning. Sheena wondered what it would be like, lying there. Drowning. Slowly drowning. A girl's voice singing: *When it's cold I'd like to die.*

'Come on! Get a fuckin' move on!' Sheena could hear Janie's voice, shouting from across the room. Janie in black leggings, DMs, black leather jacket, a bottle of Absolut in her hand.

And Lesley, close alongside her, boots and a black mini-skirt that stopped half-way up her thighs. Irena squatting in a corner, searching for something in the black-and-

349

purple rucksack she always carried, taking everything out and spreading it over the carpet, then stuffing it back. Tracey was still pulling up her jeans as she came out of the loo.

'Diane!' Janie shouted over the sound of the ghetto blaster on the table, the music faster now, more like dance music, *every time you touch me it feels like I need more.* Diane listening, lost in it, starting to shimmy, a dip of her hips and she's shaking it, the other girls starting to laugh and Diane playing up to them, pretending.

'Diane, will you stop that shit? I ain't waitin' too much fuckin' longer!'

Diane just wafting her arms now and smiling, her eyes a little out of it; Dee-Dee finally catching hold of her and pressing her wrists down to her sides, telling her to get it together. Diane nodding, right, girl, right.

Dee-Dee then, going over to where Sheena was sitting, her mouth moving lazily with the music, the girl's reedy voice singing, the joint dead between her fingers. Melvin dribbling onto her skimpy T-shirt, the shadow of her childish breast.

'Sheena, you wake up now. You look after him, right? Melvin. You keep your eye on him. Feed him when he wakes. Girl, you hear what I saying?'

'Yeh, yeh, no problem. Sure.'

'Better not be, that's all.'

Dee-Dee straightening then, pulling down the hem of her denim skirt. With Diane out of it as much as she was, it was just as well she was there to look out for little Melvin, make sure he was going to be okay.

'She all right?' Janie asked, looking over towards Sheena. The other girls were bundling through the door.

'Her?' Dee-Dee said. 'Just asked her, she fine.'

Janie laughed. 'Looks like warmed-over shit to me.' And she slammed the door closed and followed the others down the landing towards the lift that would not be working again.

Norma had picked up a paper on her way home, only glanced at the front page while she fumbled for her keys at the front door.

'Peter? Hey up, Peter, love! Clap your eyes on this.'

But Peter wasn't there, not upstairs or down. His mug and the plate he liked to use for his toast, the one with three concentric yellow rings and cracks, faint, across the centre, had been rinsed under the tap and left to dry.

'Peter?'

He had brought nothing with him so it was no use checking to see if his things had gone.

Norma set the kettle to boil, changed her mind and took one of Shane's cans of Tennents from the fridge. Warm, she opened the back door to the whining of the dog. There were turds in neat, whitening piles near the gate. Norma sat down with her newspaper, lager and a cigarette and began to read.

Supper-time, Peter would be back, she was sure.

What Gerry Hovenden liked to do, work the weights at least an hour each afternoon. Oh, he'd make a change once in a while: rowing machine, one of the bikes; he'd even tried the aerobics once, but felt a fool, jumping around with all those women with their headbands and little water bottles, two-tone leotards disappearing up the cracks in their arse. No, it was the weights, then the steam room, after that a shower, cold and then hot, hot and then cold. Towelling down.

Some days, like this afternoon, he'd persuade Shane to come along. Cost sod all as long as you were on the dole. Shane in a torn T-shirt and a borrowed pair of shorts, sweat pouring off him, stinging his eyes. Shane, he always overdid it, didn't know when to stop.

'Here,' Gerry said, still moving, press and lift. 'You hear about that bloke as got raped on Lenton Rec?'

'Looking for it, wasn't he?' Shane said.

'Prob'ly.'

'Well, then, cunt got what he deserved.'

'Yeh,' Hovenden agreed. 'Most likely.' Watching the way the sweat ran down across the flat of Shane's belly, making the skin glisten, the downward curve of tiny hairs shine gold.

The assistant manager of the audio department assured his would-be customer there was no problem at all: once in a while the machines backed up and it wasn't possible to get immediate clearance from the card company, and she could see why, with an amount that size, close to six hundred pounds for a state-of-the-art, wide screen television receiver, twenty-six-inch screen, well, company policy dictated and so on and so on.

Sally Purdy stood there in an old air force jacket that smelled of port wine and a dress that swept the floor when she walked, hiding old tennis shoes on her feet. Sally, certain that if she could just get a decent TV into the place she was squatting, that'd make all the difference, fuck all this time spent sitting out with a lot of old alkis on benches, she was going to get to grips with herself, start a new life.

Only without a poll-tax form or something similar to verify her address, hire purchase was out of the question; she knew enough people out there on the street who would get her a set cheap, but it wasn't going to be one like this.

Sally saw herself sitting round all summer, watching Wimbledon and Ascot in all their glory, those hats they got themselves up in at Ascot, Ladies' Day, something to dream about. And musicals, she loved musicals, the old ones, not rubbish like *Grease*, but really old: *How to Marry a Millionaire*, *It's Always Fair Weather*. She was sure she'd got the signature right, times she'd practised it, over and bloody over.

'Yes, madam.' Bloke returning now, suit and striped shirt, staff tie, all smiles. 'Please accept my apologies for the delay.' Smarmy bastard, Sally thought. 'Now, if I can explain how to get to our despatch department in the basement, by the time you've collected your car and driven round there, your set will be packed up and ready for you to take.'

Car? What fucking car was this? 'I thought,' Sally said, 'you'd deliver it, right?'

'Certainly, madam. That would be Tuesday or Thursday of next week.'

No way, José! 'How about this,' she said, 'a cab. I'll get a cab, take it home in that. Easy, right?'

'Absolutely.' Smiling his unctuous smile, he gave her the directions to despatch.

The extra time it took Sally Purdy to walk to the nearest rank, meant that by the time she drove up to the door marked despatch, the two uniformed officers were waiting for her inside.

'Sorry, mate,' one of them said to the cab driver, while his oppo was hauling a reluctant Sally to the marked car, 'want to collect on your fare, you'll need to nip over to the station, fill in a voucher.'

When they were booking her, Sally Purdy cursed them all from there to perdition, the custody sergeant downwards.

It was the sergeant, going through Sally's possessions, in particular the small pile of credit cards she'd been carrying in a purse velcroed to the inside of her dress, who had spotted the name and signature of William Aston on one of them.

Lynn Kellogg picked up the call. Inside fifteen minutes she and Kevin Naylor had Sally sitting across from them in an interview room, tapes identified and rolling, stolen credit cards spread out before them like a hand of patience.

'This one, Sally,' Lynn said. 'Aston. Tell us where you got that, we might go easy on you for the rest.'

'How easy?'

'Easier,' Naylor said, 'than you deserve.'

She didn't have to think about it for too long. 'Shane. I got it off've Shane.'

'Shane Snape?' Lynn asked, almost unable to believe her luck.

'No. Alan fucking Ladd, who d'you think?'

41

'This interview,' Resnick stated, 'timed at five twenty-seven.'

They had picked up Shane a couple of streets from his home, winnings that he'd collected from the bookies stuffing out his back pocket. 'One lucky lad, Shane, and no mistake,' the man behind the counter had said, smiling grimly as he counted out the notes. 'One lucky bastard.'

Divine and Naylor had been in the lead car, Millington with Carl Vincent fifty yards behind. Two squad cars were waiting at the house, a couple of uniformed officers in the alley out back. Norma Snape on the front step, cursing them out to the world.

Shane had slammed his bag into Naylor's chest, Naylor staggering back winded against a garden wall, while Divine moved in close, hands outstretched. 'Come on, then, pal. You want to try it? Come on.' Fingers beckoning him, let's go for it. Divine so clearly wanting it: the pair of them about equal height, Divine maybe an inch taller, certainly heavier; Shane probably the fitter, despite another season for Divine in and out of the first fifteen.

'Don't be daft, lad.' Millington from the edge of the kerb. 'Look about you. You'll not get anywhere but hurt.'

A third squad car was arriving fast from the opposite end of the street, siren wailing.

And Shane had stood there, not ever really taking his eyes from Divine, thinking about it, wanting it too, but feeling that first rush of adrenalin start to drain out of him, knowing that he could have taken him, cocky bastard, that someday he would, he'd have him right enough, he was certain of that, but knowing that moment wasn't now.

The instant he had lowered his hands towards his sides, Divine had been in on him fast, spinning him round, cuffs at the ready, propelling him hard towards the side of the nearest car.

'Together, behind your back! Hands together!'

'Fuck you!'

'Now! Do it now!' Divine bending him forward over the car roof, while Naylor, recovered and standing alongside, read Shane his rights.

The metal of the cuffs was biting into Shane's wrists, yet somehow he managed to twist the upper half of his body until his face was inches from Divine's, eyes brittle as ice glaring into his face. 'One of these days, I'll fuckin' kill you!' Spittle lacing Divine's mouth and cheek.

'Mark!' Millington in fast, seizing Divine's shoulder seconds before Divine would have head-butted Shane in the face.

'Mark, leave it. Let it be.'

And Divine, with a final stare, had stepped away. Millington had pushed Shane into the back of the car between Naylor and himself and ordered Vincent to drive off sharpish. Divine could follow on his own.

'I hear,' the solicitor's clerk on call said wearily, 'my

client was subject to physical intimidation in the course of his arrest.'

'Your client,' Millington told him, face close enough for the clerk to smell peppermint fresh on the sergeant's breath, 'came within a virgin's tit of being charged with assaulting a police officer in the course of his duty. Maybe you should suck on that.'

Resnick and Millington would handle the questioning, interview room A. The same scratched table scored with cigarette burns, the same stale smoke lingering in corners, the stickiness of the floor that tugged at the soles of your shoes, the faint crackle of thin cellophane as it slipped reluctantly from around the pair of audio cassettes: the words, the same or similar. 'This interview . . .'

Just over an hour in, the solicitor's clerk leaned forward and asked for a break. 'My client . . .'

'Not now.'

'My client . . .'

'Not yet.' Resnick's voice raised to the edge of irritable, weary of Shane's persistent stone-walling.

'Where did you get the card?'

'I don't know what you're on about, which card?'

'Inspector Aston's credit card. Sally Purdy says she bought it from you in the back room of a pub on the Boulevard.'

'Well, she's mistaken. Either that, or she's lying.'

'Why would she do that?'

'Slag. It's what she does.'

'What?'

'Look at her, the state of her. Pissed out of her brain. Wouldn't know the truth if it crawled out of her arse.'

357

'Not like you, then, Shane, eh?' Millington taking over from Resnick, lighting another Lambert and Butler and leaning towards Shane, almost smiling, a definite twinkle in his eye. 'Expert on the truth.'

Shane looking back at him, defiant. Where were we going now?

'Two Saturdays ago, for instance, you and your pal, Gerry. All cosy at home with your old lady and her fancy man, watching videos and kicking the family cat.'

'What about it?'

'Pack of lies.'

Sneering, Shane turned his face away.

'Lies, Shane, beginning to end.' Millington grinned. 'Pork Farm pies.'

'Bollocks.'

'Exactly.' Millington triumphant.

'Where you were, Shane,' Resnick said forcefully, 'that Saturday, was out drinking with Gerry Hovenden and some of his dubious friends. Doing the pubs between London Road and the bridge, already a bit of excitement on the way, few fists flying, and then on the Embankment, pissed the lot of you, that's where you came across Inspector Aston, out walking his dogs, and you went for him. The pack of you. Stole his wallet, cash, credit cards, *this* credit card, and left him for dead. That's where you were on that Saturday night.'

Unblinking, Shane stared Resnick square in the eye. 'Bollocks,' he said quietly.

'For someone who's not exactly an idiot,' Millington said, 'your conversation tends towards the boring.'

'Then why not stop all this crap and let me go? I don't know nothing about any credit card, nothing about no bloke beaten up on the Embankment, nothing about any of it, right?'

'My client . . .'

'All right.' Resnick quickly to his feet. 'Twenty minutes. No more.'

'Surely he's entitled to a meal?'

'Half an hour.'

'This interview,' Millington said, 'suspended at six thirty-nine.'

'You think he's lying, Charlie?' Skelton was pacing the length of his office between door and desk, conscious of being harassed from above, harassed from below, the local media, national press.

'Sure of it,' Resnick said. 'But I'm not sure about what.'

'Christ, Charlie, don't play games. What the hell's that supposed to mean?'

Resnick was standing also, conscious he had already been sitting too long and likely would do again. 'I put it to him straight, the whole business, Aston, everything. He never as much as blinked. I know he's cool; one of those as can hold it all in tight until something goes and he explodes. But a dead copper, he must know we're not going to mess around. But Shane, he could've been holding a razor blade to his own throat and there'd not have been as much as a nick.'

'Then why's he lying?'

'I don't know.'

'This credit card business, we've enough to charge him?'

Resnick looked doubtful.

'We could stand the woman up in court, sworn statement, her word against his.'

'With Purdy's record they'd not believe the day of the week, even if it was staring at them off the calendar. And Shane knows it.'

'He'll bluff it out, then.'

'He'll try. But I'd like to hang onto him a while longer. If he wasn't there when Aston was killed, likely he knows somebody who was.'

'So he's covering for somebody else?' Skelton was round behind his desk, swivelling his chair so he could lean against the back, hands gripping its sides.

'Could be.'

'This pal of his, then . . . Hovenden?'

Resnick nodded.

'Let's have him in. If we can't budge the one, let's try the other.'

But Resnick was already shaking his head. 'What I'd sooner do, as long as you're agreed, is make sure Hovenden knows we're holding Shane. Let him stew a while. More reason then for him to wonder exactly what his mate Shane has said. If we finesse it right, maybe we can persuade him it's more than it is.'

'No chance of him doing a runner?'

'I doubt it. Must know that'd draw attention to himself quicker than anything else. But we can always keep an eye.'

Skelton levered himself away from the chair. 'Play it your way, then, Charlie. But only for now. Twenty-four hours tops.'

Resnick nodded and moved towards the door. Now that he had some food inside him, Shane might be feeling more amicable: he'd give it another shot.

'She's got something against you, Shane, has she, Sally Purdy? Something personal?'

Shane glanced at Resnick and shook his head.

'Your family, then? Her and Norma, maybe? Argument of some kind, goes back a long while?'

'My mum wouldn't pass wind on her, never mind the time of day.'

'What is it, then? Some kind of death wish?'

'How d'you mean?'

Resnick straightened his back, hands flat near the table's edge. 'I mean, why you? When she gets picked up and she's got to give a name and it's not going to be the truth, wouldn't she have to be stupid pointing at you? I mean, of all the names she could choose. What did she think you were going to do? Next time you see her, slip a fiver into her hand? Thanks for thinking of me when you were talking to the law.' Resnick shook his head in disbelief. 'No, Shane, the only way she'd give you up is if it were true.'

A smile now, wavering about the corners of Shane's eyes, beginning to think, they've got nothing, really nothing, what I can do, relax and enjoy this a bit.

'Mr Resnick,' he said, polite as could be.

'Yes?'

'Prove it.'

They tried. Questions about how Shane put money in his pockets (the horses); where he got the cash from to make his bets (stand in line at the post office and cash me giro cheque like everyone else); about his relationship with Gerry Hovenden (mates, we work out together, down the gym); about Gerry's right-wing connections (politics, no, we never talk about it, what's the point, Labour, Tory, they're all the same); what they were doing the night Bill Aston was killed (round my place watching some videos, how many more times).

Not many.

When the solicitor's clerk asked for a meal break for his client and the chance of a rest, Resnick readily agreed. Lynn Kellogg had phoned in by then: she and Kevin Naylor had spoken to Hovenden and told him the police were holding Shane; nervous, it looked as if Hovenden was about to make some kind of move. All right, Resnick had said, stick close, observe. Anything urgent, you can reach me at home.

When finally they kicked Shane free with a warning they'd be speaking to him again, chance brought Shane and Divine onto the stairs at the same time. Shane walking down with Millington as escort, Divine on his way up to CID.

'Remember,' Shane said softly as they passed, 'me and you, some time soon.'

'Yes,' Divine said. 'In your dreams.'

42

It was late enough for the street lights to be showing clear against the purpling dark of city sky. Khan and Naylor were in the CID room chatting about the relative merits of the city's Indian restaurants when Resnick strode in, nodded in their direction, and went on through into his office.

'The Shand,' Khan said, reaching for the folder on his desk, 'for my money, that's got to be the one.'

Instinctively, he straightened his tie and pushed a hand through his hair before knocking on the inspector's door.

'Jardine, sir. You said to make a check.'

'And?'

'It wasn't easy, getting hold of some of this, I'm afraid it's only sketchy in places. And there are still one or two items I need to double-check. I . . .'

'Khan.'

'Yes, sir?'

'Just get on with it.' All of that waltzing around with Shane Snape had done little to improve Resnick's patience.

'Well . . .' Khan flipped open his folder. '. . . before being appointed to this authority, Jardine worked in Staffordshire and Leicestershire. Regular social work to begin with, but pretty soon he moved into residential care.'

'Staffordshire,' Resnick said, 'that's where there was all that furore about kids being tied to their beds, held in isolation?'

'Yes, sir. Excessive physical restraint. Pindown, that's what it was called. One of the homes Jardine worked in was involved right enough. I've got a copy here of the enquiry report. But compared to some of the other staff, Jardine comes out of it pretty well. The worst that was said about him was that he must have known these practices were being carried out and he did nothing to try and prevent them or to inform his superiors. But there's no suggestion of any direct involvement.

'Not so long after that he moved across to Leicestershire. Promotion. And this might be more interesting. It seems that while he was in acting charge of one of their residential homes for difficult children, there were complaints of sexual abuse . . .'

'By Jardine?'

'No, sir. One of the members of staff.'

'These complaints, were they proved?'

Khan sighed and shook his head. 'Again, it's not really clear. The man concerned claimed that a small group of the boys had a grudge against him and had made up the whole story to get at him. The medical evidence is, well, hazy at best. There was some talk of prosecution, but by then the man had resigned and in the end no charges were brought.'

Resnick sat forward at his desk. 'What did Jardine have to say about all of this?'

Khan smiled. 'Pretty much what you'd expect: the

alleged incidents, which in any case were unsubstantiated, would have taken place before he was appointed; since he'd been in charge, there was a more open regime, staff and boys were encouraged to air their grievances in public.' Khan paused to read from his notes. ' "I give my word that no child under my care need ever have anything to fear." Interview with the *Leicester Mercury*, 1989.'

Resnick rubbed his eyes with the base of his palms. 'Maybe he should've tried telling that to Nicky Snape.'

Khan closed the folder, reversed it, and set it on the desk.

'All right, let's have another go at Matthews. See if he's any more willing to talk. Chances are he's still down in Wales, but best check.'

'Sir, I wonder . . .'

'Yes? What is it?'

'Well, it's just . . . I think if I went back to him too soon, pushed him again, all that would happen, he'd clam up even more. It might even be enough to drive him over the edge.'

'What are you saying, then? That we should leave well alone?'

'No. Just give him some more time. Even if it's only a day or two. If we let him stew in it a little, he might even come to us.'

'To you.'

'Yes.'

Resnick sighed. Not so many hours earlier he had been making a similar request to Skelton, asking a superior officer to trust his judgement.

'Okay, forty-eight hours. Meantime plug the holes in

this report. Let's make sure if we need to use it, it's watertight.'

Gerry Hovenden had found out that Shane had been taken in for questioning, but not that he had been released. After several hours of sitting around worrying himself half-sick, he had decided to seek out Frankie Miller and get some advice. Frank Miller, the kind of man that some people turned to when they were in a fix.

Miller worked security in the clubs, pubs; squeezed himself into a cheap dinner-jacket or a shiny fake-satin jump suit with a matt black headset crammed down onto his head like a crown of thorns and he was in business. Smiling face, raised hand – not now, sunshine, looking like that, no way, try the place down the street, patience, let's have a little patience and an orderly line. Quite often they'd look at Frank – not so tall, more than a little overweight, out of condition, had to be pushing thirty – and think, you fat bastard, you're not going to tell me what to do, where I can go, no way. Frank loved that. Kids giving him some mouth, showing off for the scrawny tarts they'd have up against some back wall later, a quick shag before a late-night curry and the long walk home. He loved the look on their sweaty faces when they finally gave him a push, threw a punch and he didn't give ground. Frank smiling before he started punching back.

Once in a while, he had to admit, things would get a little out of hand; when they did, whoever was in charge – no hard feelings, Frankie, eh? – they'd have to let him go. No sweat. There was always another pub, another door, another Saturday night. And if not ... well, there were other things. Mate of a mate needing a bit of muscle, friend of a friend. He had this arrangement with a bloke who lent out money, you know, when the talking bank wasn't talking no more, council suing for rent arrears and the bailiffs on their way in. Of course the interest was high, what did they think this was? Social fucking security or what? Frank had a way of making sure the debt was paid; or, if not, ensuring folk saw the error of their ways.

Frank Miller? Bit rough, but underneath it all, decent enough. Tell you what, any trouble, he's the one I'd want alongside. Frankie. Good bloke, really, good bloke.

Frank was in his local pub in Heanor, not hurrying his last pint, when Gerry Hovenden came in wearing leathers, helmet in his hand.

'What the fuck's the matter with you?' Miller asked. 'Look like the rats've had your balls for breakfast and now they're startin' on the rest.'

'It's Shane,' Hovenden said, short of breath, near to knocking an empty glass from the table as he sat down.

'What about him?'

'The law, they've got him. Picked him up this afternoon.'

'What the fuck for?'

'I don't know. I don't know. I haven't had a chance to talk to him, have I?'

'Then calm down. May not be anything at all. You know what coppers are like. Shane, he's done time, right? They'll have him in for nothing at all.'

'I know, but . . .'

Frank Miller's hand clamped itself round Hovenden's thigh, squeezing at the muscle behind the knee. 'He won't talk, your mate Shane. And if he does, without dumping himself in the shit, what can he say?'

Hovenden blinked, catching his breath, trying not to

notice the pain in his leg, Miller's thumb weeviling away against the bone.

'Trust him, don't you?'

'Yeh, yes, yeh, of course.'

Miller released his grip and tapped Hovenden on the arm, a couple of times playfully with his fist. 'Nothing to worry about, eh, then?' He lifted his pint. 'I'd get you one in, only they called last orders a while back. 'Sides, drinkin' and driving. Don't want you coming off that bike of yours. Loss to the human race, Gerry, you taking a tumble round Cotmanhey and fetching up in the Erewash Canal.'

Resnick hadn't forgotten Hannah's message: he thought he'd make himself a sandwich first and then give her a call. Indoors long enough to prise Pepper out of the vegetable steamer in which the cat had contrived to get stuck, he reversed the order and she was engaged. Oh, well. Lollo rosso, cucumber, watercress; goat's cheese; a tin of anchovies which he opened, pouring off some of the oil and then mashed the contents into a thick paste with black pepper and some dried basil; the last few pieces of sun-dried tomato fished from the jar and cut into strips. Johnny Hartman drifting through from the other room, Howard McGhee on trumpet. His friend Ben Riley had sent it out of the blue from New York. *Charlie, down here on a visit. Got myself conned into seeing the new Eastwood movie and actually liked it. Well, almost. Anyway, this guy sings all over the soundtrack and I thought you might like him. Always assuming your technology is up to it. Your friend, Ben.* Ben, sounding more acclimatised with every postcard, every year. And now, Resnick's technology was fine.

He cut bread, covered it with lettuce and the other salad things, spread over that the anchovy mixture and sun-dried tomato, finishing up with thin circles of cheese.

While he was waiting for the grill to warm, he went back to the phone: still engaged. At the last minute he dribbled thick, green olive oil across both slices of bread and, licking his fingers clean, opened a bottle of Old Speckled Hen out of the fridge.

Johnny Hartman, deep-voiced: 'They Didn't Believe Me.'

This time when he tried the phone it rang and rang and rang.

Why couldn't he see Shane Snape joining in with a bunch of yobs for whom queer-bashing was a legitimate sport? Trying not to get too much of his supper over the front of his shirt, he broke off a corner of crust, scraped it through the anchovy paste and offered it to a mewing Bud. One of those coincidences: as the track ended, the telephone rang. Hannah, Resnick thought, reaching round for the receiver; Hannah calling him. Or else it could be Lynn.

It was neither. 'Sir?' Carl Vincent's voice, as recognisable to him already as the regular members of the team. 'Sir, I think you'd best come in.'

The man sitting in Resnick's office was forty-two or -three; his hair was medium brown, quite thick, slightly long at the back and in need of a trim, perhaps, where it was beginning to curl around his ears. He had a neat beard, tight to the jaw line; spectacles without rims. He was wearing what seemed to be a good suit, navy blue, one narrow stripe of a darker blue alongside one of grey. The knot of his tie was precise and unfashionably small.

'This is Mr Cheshire,' Vincent said, standing between Resnick and the door.

Resnick nodded and when Cheshire offered his hand, Resnick shook it, observing the slight tremor, the patchiness of sweat.

Resnick moved behind his desk and sat down; motioning for Vincent to close the door and do the same.

'Why don't you tell the inspector,' Vincent said, 'just what you told me?' And then, 'Don't worry, it'll be fine.'

Cheshire's accent was regulation, well-educated, whatever local variation might once have been present was now almost totally submerged. 'Ever since I read the story in the newspaper,' Cheshire said, 'the man who was attacked in the Recreation Ground, I've been considering coming to see you. You see, I couldn't be certain, positive that it was the correct thing to do.'

'If you've got information for us, Mr Cheshire, anything that might help us with what happened...'

'No. No, you see...' A nervous glance round towards Vincent, who nodded encouragingly. 'It isn't about that, at least not directly.'

'Go on.'

'Several months ago, six, six to be exact, six months and seven days, I was attacked by a man on the Promenade alongside the park, the same park.' Cheshire removed his glasses from his face and rested his head forward at an angle into the palm of his hand. 'I was... I was struck to the ground and almost throttled from behind. I was threatened with what would happen to me if I screamed... and then I was forcedly... I was raped,

370

Inspector, that's what happened. Six months, a little more than six months ago.'

It was quiet in the room, just the breathing of three men above the barely audible electric hum.

'This incident,' Resnick said, 'you didn't report it at the time?'

Cheshire shook his head.

'Not your doctor, hospital . . . ?'

'No.'

'Did you tell anyone about this at all?'

'No, I did not.'

'It's okay,' Vincent said reassuringly.

'I feel as if I'm being accused here.'

'No,' Vincent said, glancing across at Resnick.

'No, Mr Cheshire,' Resnick said. 'I assure you, that's not the case at all.'

'Because if I hadn't thought this important, I would never have come forward at all.'

Resnick nodded. 'We understand that.' And then, 'And the reason you've come forward now, you think there might be a comparison between the two attacks . . . ?'

'Well, yes.'

'A possibility they might have been carried out by the same man?'

'Yes, of course. I mean, it has to be likely, doesn't it, after all?'

'There's something I have to ask you, Mr Cheshire,' said Resnick, leaning slightly forward, hands loosely joined. 'When you were in the Recreation Ground that evening, had you gone there with the possibility in mind that you might meet someone, for the purposes of sex?'

'Look, I'm sorry . . .' Cheshire was on his feet and

turned towards the door, Vincent half out of his chair to intercept him.

'Mr Cheshire,' Resnick said. 'Mr Cheshire, please sit down.'

Cheshire took a handkerchief from his suit jacket pocket and wiped at his face, cleared his nose, turning back to face Resnick. 'I'm sorry.' He resumed his seat. 'And yes, your assumption, as to my reasons for being there that night, they are correct.'

'And this wasn't the first or only time you had been there in similar circumstances?'

A slow shake of the head.

'Are you married, Mr Cheshire?'

He glanced towards the third finger of his left hand, the indentation gone now but the skin where the ring had fitted still a touch paler than the rest. 'Not any more.'

'Your job?'

'I work for an investment company, pensions and loans.'

'And this side of your life, no one else knows?'

Avoiding Resnick's eyes. 'That's correct.'

'The person who attacked you,' Resnick asked, 'can you describe him?'

Cheshire shook his head.

'Not in any way at all?'

The silence was long. 'He was strong,' Cheshire finally said. 'Very strong. I thought, of course there is no way to be sure, but I thought he might have been under the influence of drugs.'

'Because?'

'His strength seemed so unnatural, and his anger. I think – I thought – he wanted to kill me. That was what

372

he really wanted to do. And instead he ... he ... he tried to cause me all the pain he could.'

Cheshire's glasses fell from his hand and he cried. Fingers meshed across his face, he cried. After some moments, Vincent went over and stood close beside him, resting a hand across his shoulders. Only when Cheshire had begun to recover himself did Vincent move away to his own chair and sit back down. Resnick fetched a glass of water and Cheshire sipped at it, then gulped, choked a little, thanked him, wiped at his glasses with his damp handkerchief, set them back on, took them off again.

'There's one more thing,' Vincent said quietly, 'I wonder if I could ask you, about what happened.'

Cheshire nodded. 'Go ahead.'

'Penetration, when it took place ...'

'A bottle,' Cheshire said, eyes clenched shut, remembering. 'He used a bottle and then smashed it on the railings when he was through.'

43

If Hannah had woken earlier than usual that morning, and looked out from her upstairs window, she would have seen several men in overalls down on their hands and knees amongst the bushes which grew along the railings separating the Recreation Ground from the Promenade. She would have wondered exactly what, with their reinforced gloves and careful manner, they were looking for.

Up early himself, scarcely able to sleep, Resnick had driven out there and stood, hands in pockets, while the officers were making their search. He was present when one of the men, triumphantly, uncovered one section of bottle, a piece broken away from near its mouth and now wedged full of something dark, excrement or earth or both. Inside a curved oval of glass, there were dried streaks of what was almost certainly blood.

Just to contemplate what had happened, how these things could have come to pass, was enough to make Resnick drive the ends of his fingers hard into the palms of his hands. *He used a bottle and then smashed it on the railings when he was through.* Who, Resnick wondered, did the person who could perform such an act hate most, his victim or himself? Who was suffering the most pain?

He walked down towards the small row of terraced houses nearest to the church. No lights showed on the ground floor of Hannah's house; one only, burning high towards the roof. He thought of knocking, but knew he would be waking her for nothing; there was precious little time for anything approaching conversation and there was nothing he might say at that moment that he could imagine her wanting to hear.

Resnick got back in his car and drove the short distance along Derby Road towards the station. Millington and Carl Vincent were sitting at one side of the CID room, Lynn Kellogg standing close behind them. The latest list Jane Prescott had supplied from Intelligence was on the computer: names of those cautioned for violent behaviour during recent Gay Rights rallies in the city centre. Four charged with various breaches of the peace, 1993, charges dropped before coming to court; six officially warned, three charged, 1994, charges dropped; four warned, two charged, 1995, charges dropped.

'Really got behind these in a big way, didn't we?' Vincent said, sarcasm soft but clear in his voice.

'Evidence,' Millington said, 'not prejudice. Look at the figures for loonie lefties trying to break up right-wing meetings and I'll bet it's just the same.'

Vincent gave the sergeant a wry smile, unconvinced.

'Notice anything interesting here,' Lynn said, pointing at the screen, then scrolling it round. 'Miller, Frank. Three years out of three, a perfect score.'

Resnick had come over to stand with them. 'Miller, that's who Hovenden went to see.'

'Last night,' Lynn said, 'right.'

The door to the office opened and a sleepy-looking Kevin Naylor walked in, followed by Divine, who from somewhere had unearthed a slice of cold pizza and was eating it with gusto.

'Okay,' Resnick said, 'all the names on this list, they'll be matched with the ones we've already had from Special Branch, checked out today. The assumption we've got to go on is that what happened to Farrell and to Cheshire likely weren't isolated cases. It took six months for Cheshire to come forward; there'll be others who never will.'

'And we're still thinking,' Millington said, 'these incidents and Aston's murder, they're linked?'

'Other than the fact,' Lynn said, 'that all the victims are gay?'

Resnick nodded. 'That's what I feel. So what we're going to do is move in fast, follow up on those we know. Snape – Hovenden – Miller, that's the chain and Hovenden, he might be the weak link. Lynn, you and Carl come with me, we'll catch him on the hop if we can. Graham, take Kevin and Mark, see what this Miller's got to say for himself; we still don't have a satisfactory alibi for him at the time Aston was killed.' He looked round the room. 'Questions, comments?'

'Only,' Vincent said, 'in case it was someone in here, I'd like to thank whoever put the condoms and Vaseline in my locker. One small point of sex education though – small but important – Vaseline with condoms isn't really safe, it has a bad effect on the rubber. KY jelly . . .' and he winked at Divine '. . . now that's the thing.'

Kevin Naylor laughed uncertainly; Lynn shook her head in dismay.

'This isn't the time,' Resnick said, 'but any repetition of incidents like that and I'll make it my business to find out who was responsible and have them out of here too fast for their feet to touch the ground.'

Expressionless, Divine dumped what was left of his pizza into the nearest bin.

Resnick was in the back, Lynn driving; fast, north-west out of the city. Vincent was sitting alongside Lynn, half-turned towards the rear of the car.

'Local gay organisations,' Resnick said, 'they'll be informed as a matter of course. Encouraged to ask members to come forward.'

'Problem there is,' Vincent said, swinging further round, 'most of the men likely to have been involved won't be on that scene anyway. And even if they were . . .' He shook his head. 'There's still a lot of distrust.'

'Well,' Resnick said, 'we can step up patrols around toilets and open spaces . . .'

Vincent laughed. 'That should fetch a few of the gay community out on the streets, protesting a violation of their civil rights.'

'What right's that?' Lynn asked sharply. 'The right to go out and put yourself at risk?'

'Hey!' Vincent smiled, backing along the seat. 'Don't get at me. I didn't say that was my point of view.'

Lynn swung wide to overtake a milk float, smoothly changing gear. 'What is your point of view, then, Carl?'

'About cottaging you mean?'

'Uh-hum.'

He shrugged. 'It's not what I would want to do, not for myself. Not doing the job that I do. But I can understand why people feel the need.'

'But not you?'

'Not me, no. Least, not any more.'

None of them spoke again until Lynn signalled left and slowed the car to a halt. 'That's the house, over there.'

Millington glanced down at his watch: it was still shy of seven o'clock. It was quiet in the street. Here and there amongst the lines of dilapidated houses, the odd one had been spruced up with a lick of bright paint, louvred shutters fitted across the upstairs windows, new doors with brass knockers which shone. Not here. He read the notice inviting callers to go round to the back.

'Let's keep it quiet now. No sense waking him till we have to.'

There was a sour-sweet smell seeping across the backyard like blocked drains. Divine, ever hopeful, eased his hand against the rear door and to his surprise it slid open. Eyebrow raised, silently he questioned Millington and the sergeant nodded. Divine pushed the door all the way back and took a step inside. A tap was dripping against the clutter of pots that threatened to overflow the sink. They could hear clearly now, the sound of snoring, harsh and a-rhythmic, from the adjoining room.

Curtains pulled to, Miller had fallen asleep on the settee where he lay, a flotilla of empty cans adrift on the stained carpet, stale tobacco flat and thick in the air. Miller's T-shirt had worked loose from his jeans and was wrinkled up across the hump of his belly, jeans belt unfastened, zip part-way down. He was on his back, one foot touching the floor, one arm thrown back, face to one side close against the cushion, mouth open.

Content they had not disturbed him, Millington pointed to the stairs, back out into the garden to the lean-to shed that was more falling than leaning. After all, the door had been open and Miller hadn't voiced any objections to their looking round.

Late for the early shift, Gerry Hovenden's father had been leaving the house as Resnick and the others approached. 'Inside,' he said brusquely, scarcely slowing to examine Resnick's ID, 'out the bathroom by now, if you're lucky.'

'What the bloody hell's this?' Hovenden emerged into the postage stamp of a hallway, hair wet, an old Forest away shirt hanging over his sagging boxer shorts, bare feet.

'Inspector Resnick, CID. DC Vincent. I believe you know DC Kellogg already.'

Lynn gave him a quick smile, not her best.

'I don't know what you think you're doing,' Hovenden blustered, 'but you can sod off out.'

'Why not pop upstairs,' Vincent said politely, 'put a few more clothes on. Time you're back down, I expect we'll have figured out where the kettle is. Coffee or tea?'

Millington had been standing in the kitchen, idly leafing through Miller's well-thumbed copy of *Above All, Courage*, and wondering what exactly possessed someone to go off and join the SAS, when Naylor beckoned him outside. There in the corner of the shed, soles thick with mud, stood a pair of Caterpillar work boots, size ten.

'Been doing a spot of gardening,' Millington observed.

'Looks like.'

Divine appeared in the doorway behind them. 'Seems as if he might be coming round.'

Millington grinned. 'Let's give him a hand.'

The Saxon CD was still in the machine. Divine turned the volume up to full and pressed play. Miller, startled, tried to push himself up, overbalanced and rolled off the settee to the floor.

'Morning, Frank,' Millington mouthed, waving his warrant card in front of Miller's incredulous face, 'this is your wake-up call.'

Hovenden had pulled on a pair of jeans, wore old trainers, unlaced, on his feet. Carl Vincent had made tea in mugs that Lynn had carefully rinsed under the hot tap.

'Must have a bit of trouble,' Resnick said innocently, nodding towards Hovenden's feet, 'always finding shoes to fit.'

Hovenden sat awkwardly and said nothing.

'Elevens, are they?' Resnick asked.

'What?'

'Size? I said, elevens, twelves?'

'What sodding difference?'

'Just making conversation.'

'Elevens, for fuck's sake! They're elevens, satisfied?'

Resnick smiled.

'You know', Lynn said, 'we've been talking to your friend, Shane?'

'What of it?'

'He had some interesting things to tell us, that's all.'

'Oh, yeh? About me, I suppose?'

Lynn looked at him, her head angled to one side. 'Now what d'you think he could have had to tell us about you?'

'Sod all!'

Lynn nodded. 'Just about that credit card.'

'What credit card's that?'

'Oh, the one he sold to Sally Purdy.'

'Who?'

'Sally Purdy,' Resnick said. 'She was the one who told us she bought it from Shane.'

'What bloody credit card you on about?'

'Inspector Aston's,' Resnick said.

'You know,' said Lynn. 'The police officer who was killed.'

'The night,' Resnick said, 'you seem to be confused about where you were.'

Hovenden pushed himself clumsily back in his chair. 'Which night's this?'

Lynn said, half-smiling: 'You see what we mean?'

'No, look. Look.' Hovenden not looking, not at any of them, not at the table, not at the floor. 'That night, I told you, right? Before. I was home.'

'Is this a different story, Hovenden?' Resnick asked. 'Because if it is . . .'

'Shane's, I was round Shane's. That's what I meant.'

'By home?'

'Yes.'

'Not here?'

Hovenden stared around. 'This shithole?'

'Shane, then,' Vincent asked, leaning close over him, 'he's what? Like your brother?'

'Yes. I s'pose, yeh.'

'Not being very brotherly, then, Shane,' Vincent said. 'Some of the things I hear he was saying yesterday.'

'You're lying.'

'Not exactly brotherly love, dropping you in it the way he did.'

'You're lying!' Hovenden's face was almost white with strain.

'What would you say,' asked Lynn, 'if I told you he claimed he got Inspector Aston's credit card from you?'

Hovenden scrambled to his feet, knocking back his chair, face thrust forward. 'I'd say you were a lying cunt!'

Vincent clicked his tongue against the roof of his mouth twice. 'That's no way to speak to a lady.'

'Fuck you!'

Resnick was standing now, time to move on. 'Had all you want of this tea, Gerry? Or d'you want to finish it before we leave for the station?'

'Turn off,' Frank Miller had shouted, 'that fucking noise!'

'Worried about the neighbours, Frank?' Millington said. 'That's nice. World could do with a few more like you.'

'Saxon, though,' Divine said, flicking open the drawer and removing the CD, 'always did like them. DeMontfort Hall, ooh, must be six or seven years back now. Go down and see them, did you? My ears were ringing for days.'

Miller turned to stare at him: what the fuck was all this about?

'But then that's the way you like 'em, isn't it? In the ears? Fact, I think we might've found a tape of yours a while back. That had quite a bit of Saxon on it, good too.'

'I don't suppose,' Miller said, zipping up his jeans,

382

'there's any way you lot of comedians'd crawl back out the way you crawled in?'

'Course, Frankie,' Millington agreed. 'Just as soon as you're ready.'

Miller snorted and scratched his left armpit energetically. 'Oh, yeh? What is it now?'

'Someone's been putting themselves about amongst our friends in the gay community,' Millington said. 'Looking at your record, you've done a bit of that in your time.'

'Poofs? Yeh, why not? It's what they fuckin' deserve.'

'You don't need a coat,' Millington said, leading the way, 'but if I were you I'd lock this back door. Never know who might come waltzing in.'

44

Khan had woken that morning with Jill's leg hooked over one of his own, her hip pressed against his. It had been light enough in the room to see the inward curve of her spine, the swell of her buttocks when he slipped back the sheet. Fifteen minutes before he had to be getting ready for work, twenty at a push. Experimentally, he tensed himself against her body and felt pressure in return. He knew there were two things he could do and one of them was to bend forward and kiss her lightly between the shoulder blades, slide his leg free and swing out of the bed. He looked at the way she was stretching, legs parted, and knew how warm she would feel if he were to move his hand a little higher along her thigh. She gave a sleepy, satisfied moan when he did this and that was that. Twenty minutes, he thought, would be fine.

In fact, it was closer to fifteen. Khan stood buttoning his pale-blue shirt, fading a shade now, the one his last girl-friend had bought him at Next.

'I swear,' Jill said, sitting up higher in the bed, 'you only wear that to annoy me.'

Reaching for his tie, silver with a blue stripe, Khan laughed. 'Have to get some kind of reaction, don't I?'

She threw a pillow and he ducked low, reaching for the end of the duvet.

'No!' Jill shouted. 'Don't you dare!'

Which was when the phone rang and Khan, chuckling, went to answer it. Paul Matthews's voice was nervous yet unmistakable, a smile broadening across Khan's face as he listened. 'All right,' he said finally, 'give me twenty minutes and I'll be there.'

Back in the bedroom, he kissed Jill languorously on the mouth: five minutes, he was thinking, more than I gave you.

Given the seriousness of the crimes concerned, the weight of evidence, circumstantial at best, had been enough to argue the necessary search warrants. They had twenty-four hours, plus a possible extra twelve, within which either to charge Miller and Hovenden or let them go. Under new regulations, they were allowed to take samples from all suspects in order to establish their DNA; these samples would then be checked against the new national database in Birmingham. Comparisons with the DNA from the blood found on Aston's body would be crucial. But it would not be quick.

'This can't be right,' Frank Miller had said to his solicitor. 'There's no way they can make me agree to this.'

The solicitor was sorry, but under the new law indeed they could.

'And if I won't stand for it?'

'We'll have to find ways,' Divine had grinned hopefully, 'of taking your legs from under you. Nothing to stand on.'

Miller had shaken his head. 'Know what this means, don't you? This DNA business, it's like a fingerprint, right? Once you're in their books, they're gonna come chasin' after you every chance they get.'

'It doesn't work that way,' Naylor said, 'the only times we hang onto the samples is if you're actually convicted, or officially cautioned for a recordable offence. Otherwise, they're destroyed.'

Miller threw back his head and laughed. 'Believe that, you believe the moon's made of fuckin' green cheese!'

'Don't tell me,' Divine said, disappointed, 'that it's not?'

The first thing the search team did at Miller's house was to bag and label carefully the boots in the shed. There was a car ready and waiting to whisk them off for analysis. The house itself, though, proved a disappointment. True, there were back issues of *The Order* and a few other bits of right-wing paraphernalia, but nothing to get Special Branch worked up into a sweat. In a tatty address book, they found a few phone numbers that would ring bells with Trevor Ulman and the Football Intelligence Unit, but again, there were no major surprises. The collection of top-shelf porn devoted to women with abnormally large breasts was well-thumbed, but compared to some of the stuff that was routinely confiscated this was very small beer indeed. And they turned up no likely weapons; nothing resembling a baseball bat.

Once you got beyond the main downstairs rooms, the house Gerry Hovenden shared with his father was indeed a shitheap of the first degree. Hovenden senior was a classic hoarder and the only prerequisite for being an object saved seemed to be that whatever it was, it was covered in dirt. There was a layer of grease along the banister rail, on all the shelves and surfaces, over everything they touched. Engine parts, old clothes, yellowing newspapers, fuse wire, cycle blocks, quarter heels for sticking on shoes, bottles of oil gone rancid, copies of paperback Westerns with the pages bent back, rusty tools. And, in the midst of all of this, the glove – the one that Gerry had hurled there, back amongst the recesses of that upstairs back room, thrown there amongst the cobwebs and the musty boxes, the rat droppings and the silver fish – the leather motor cycle glove which matched the one found on the Embankment near Bill Aston's body. Its identical opposite. Its partner. Its twin.

Paul Matthews's mother sat at her kitchen table, picking crumbs from around a piece of seed-cake and lifting them absent-mindedly to her mouth. 'Be gentle with him, won't you? He's never meant any harm.'

Matthews was upstairs in a bedroom that had scarcely changed in the last fifteen years. Scouting certificates hung on the wall beside a colour photograph of the Forest team from 1981 and a map of South Wales; framed on the window-ledge was a picture of a smiling Paul, new-born lamb in his arms, in the lane alongside his aunt's house.

'How was the rest of the visit?' Khan asked. 'Are you feeling any better?'

Tears at the edges of his eyes, Matthews turned away.

'I'm glad you phoned,' Khan said gently. 'I think it was the right thing.' A pause, then: 'You'll feel better, after you've talked. Got it off your chest.'

'I can't.'

'Yes, it's all right. You can.'

'I can't tell you everything. I don't know . . . Oh, God!'

'It's all right.' Khan put his hand on the base of

387

Matthews's neck and let it rest there. 'Just tell me what you can.'

After some moments, Matthews reached into his pocket for a tissue and Khan moved his hand, sat back and waited. He thought Matthews might break down again and cry, but instead he simply sat there on the side of his bed, telling his story, the one he had told so many times inside his head out walking the cliffs, watching the waves break back upon the shore.

He described how this particular group of youths, the older ones, half a dozen of them, had got up from the television room earlier on the night that Nicky died, and swaggered towards the door. How the biggest of them, at least as big as Matthews himself, if not bigger, had sauntered back over to Paul and fixed him with a grin and told him to stay where he was, carry on watching whatever he was watching – unless he wanted to go up and watch them.

And then they had gone up to Nicky's room, all six of them, and locked the door from the inside. And he hadn't known what to do. He'd been frightened, scared of them, the way they would swagger about the place and smoke and swear and sometimes there were these drugs they got from somewhere, and they would mock him, call him names, make threats, and he knew it was too late to stand up to them, far too late, and when the screams from Nicky's room were so loud they could be heard, even downstairs, all he had done was go over to the TV and turn up the sound.

'You didn't tell anyone?' Khan said after a moment.

'No, not at first. Not then.'

'But later?'

Matthews's eyes were closed. 'I told Mr Jardine.'

Something akin to pleasure lurched deep in Khan's throat. 'You told him what you've just told me?'

Matthews nodded.

'Paul?'

'Yes, yes.'

'And what did Mr Jardine say?'

Matthews opened his eyes. 'He said there was no need to mention it to anyone else, especially at the enquiry. He said it would only muddy the waters. He said anyway it wasn't relevant at all.'

'What about the other staff member on duty? Elizabeth Peck? You didn't say anything to her?'

Matthews pressed the tips of his fingers against his temples so hard that when he finally withdrew them, there were pale ovals clear against the skin. 'She wasn't there. Not all evening. Not until I phoned her and told her she'd best come in.'

'She was ill, sick, what?'

Matthews shook his head. 'She was working at another job.'

Khan got to his feet and went across to the window. On the roof opposite a workman was sitting, a brightly coloured scarf tied round his head, drinking from a Thermos and reading a newspaper.

'These youths,' he said, uncapping his pen. 'What are their names?' And Matthews told him, each name like a nail.

Resnick and Millington had decided to take Hovenden first. The glove they had found in his house? The one matching that discovered at the murder scene? Yes, Hovenden had agreed, it was his, but so what? He'd chucked it up months ago, before Christmas probably, after he lost the other on a ride up through the Peak District. Late November, that would have been. Snow on the tops, he remembered that. Whatever they'd found down by the Trent, no connection, nothing to do with him.

Resnick didn't tell him that forensic were even now checking out the body fibres from inside the glove found near Aston's body, microscopic particles of skin, matching their DNA against Hovenden's own. That could wait till confirmation came through; enough for now to leave him rattled.

'All right, Gerry,' he said, 'play it that way if you like. We'll go and have a chat with your pal, Frank Miller, see if he can't throw a little more light on things.'

Hovenden nervously laughed. 'Frank'd not as much as never cock his leg on one of you lot if you were on fire.'

'Okay, Gerry,' Resnick said pleasantly, getting to his feet. 'Have it your way. For now.'

'Cocky bastard!' Millington said, once they were out in the corridor.

'Bravado,' Resnick said. 'Nothing more. Behind it all, he's one unhappy boy.'

'Thinks his mate Frankie's about to dump him in it, you reckon?'

Outside the second interview room, Resnick grinned. 'Let's see if he isn't right.'

Frank Miller claimed only vague memories of a Saturday night's drinking. Yeh, yeh, this pub and that; a pint with this bloke here, a few more with these pals there. Doner on the way home, curry maybe, fish and chips. Come to think of it, wasn't that the night he never got back at all? Fetched up at his brother-in-law's place in the Meadows, sharing the floor with the pair of Rottweilers his sister was hoping to breed from. Long as they didn't do it, you know, while he was kipping there. Why didn't Resnick send someone round, find out for himself?

Resnick less than well pleased, another alibi depending upon close family more likely to commit any amount of perjury before seeing their nearest and dearest end up in the nick.

'Meantime,' Millington said, 'why don't you try telling us about these?' And with something approaching a flourish, he produced the Caterpillar boots.

'What about 'em?'

'Well, do you recognise them, for a start?'

Miller shrugged. 'Hundreds of pairs like that, must be. Thousands.'

'Are you saying they're not yours?'

'What I'm saying,' a cocky strut to Miller's voice, 'is that I don't know. They could be mine and then again, they could not.'

'Maybe you'd like to try one on?' Millington suggested.

'What is this? Fuckin' *Cinderella*? 'Cause if it is, we got the Ugly Sisters well cast, I can tell you that.'

'These boots were found,' Resnick said, 'in your garden shed. This morning.'

'Really? Amazing, i'n'it, searched for them bastards everywhere.'

'Lost,' Millington mused, 'and then were found.'

Resnick sneaked him a quick sideways look. For a man whose only confessed religious experience seemed to have

391

been Petula Clark singing one of the songs from *Jesus Christ, Superstar*, biblical references were unexpected to say the least.

But Millington was not through. 'Interesting what was found on them, too. That style of boot, you see. All those deep cracks and crevices in the sole, you'd be amazed what gets stuck in them.' He paused, Miller watching him carefully now. 'Or maybe not.'

Miller slouched back in his chair, head round for a moment towards his brief, one eyebrow raised. 'So tell me,' he said.

Millington flipped the cover of his notebook back. 'Mud, for a start . . .'

'Yeh? Surprise, fuckin' surprise,' said Miller, but his heart wasn't in it.

'Earth,' Millington went on, 'consistent with that found on the section of the Embankment where Inspector Aston was murdered. Not only that, we found blood, small traces of blood across the tongue of the left boot, the same blood type as Aston.'

Blood was now in short supply in Miller's face.

'Something else we found,' Resnick said, leaning in, 'a cassette tape with a lot of music by a band called Saxon, a favourite of yours I believe? And that's not all – it seems whoever's tape it was had used it before, recording made at a BNP rally, autumn of last year. Shouldn't be impossible to check if you were there.'

Miller sat there for several moments, arms resting on his knees, staring at the ground. Then he looked up and pursed his mouth into a perfect O. 'Got a cigarette?' he asked. 'I need a fag.'

His solicitor tapped him on the arm. 'You're under no

obligation to talk about this now, not without discussing it with me first.'

'What you can do,' Miller said politely, politely for Miller, 'fuck right off. And poke me in the arm again and I'll break every finger in your fuckin' hand. Understood? I know my rights better'n you.'

It was understood.

A knock on the door fetched Resnick out of the room and the expression on Naylor's face told him the news faster than words.

'Fuck!' Resnick said, not a word he often used, or lightly. It seemed certain that the surplus blood found on Aston's body had come neither from Hovenden nor Miller.

He was on his way back into the interview room when Khan appeared at the end of the corridor, smiling: not all news was bad. After listening he sent Kevin Naylor in to sit with Millington – he wanted to confront Jardine himself.

45

The suit was different, double-breasted with wide lapels, dark with a narrow pinstripe running through, but the amount of dandruff that had fallen from Jardine's greying hair was the same. The veins etched into his nose stood out more prominently, the corners of his eyes were watery, clouded yellow.

He began by offering Resnick his hand and when it was refused, sat back behind his desk and folded his arms across his chest.

'DC Khan and myself have just come from the police station,' Resnick said, each word spoken with especial care, 'where one of your staff, Paul Matthews, has made a statement about the events leading up to the death of Nicky Snape on these premises.'

Jardine flinched and covered his mouth with the opened fingers of one hand.

Resnick nodded towards Khan, who took an envelope containing several sheets of paper from his inside pocket. 'I would like you to read that statement now.'

Jardine hesitated before reaching out and taking the statement from Khan's hand; he still avoided looking either officer in the eye.

'Read it,' Resnick said, 'all of it, carefully, before making any response.'

Jardine's eyes stalled at the end of the first paragraph and then started again. At the end of the second paragraph he glanced sideways towards the wall, the photographs where his career was smeared. By the time he had reached the end and had pushed the sheets away across his desk there were tears in his eyes but not enough.

'What Matthews says is basically correct?'

Jardine nodded: yes.

'He told you those youths had been in Nicky Snape's room the evening he died?'

'Yes.'

'That in his opinion they had been bullying him, at the very least?'

'Yes.'

'And that in his belief that bullying had been of a sexual nature?'

'There is no proof . . .'

'But that was what he said?'

'Yes.'

'The staff member in charge?'

'Yes.'

'And you did nothing.'

Jardine glanced from Khan to Resnick and shook his head.

'You told Matthews to do nothing, say nothing?'

'Yes.'

'Would you mind telling me why that was?'

After a pause, Jardine said: 'It would only disturb the smooth running of the home. I didn't see what good would be served.'

'And why was that?'

Jardine looked at him directly for the first time. 'Nicky Snape was already dead.'

On his feet, Resnick retrieved the statement from the desk. 'Copies of this statement have been sent to the Director of Social Services, to Phyllis Parmenter, the member of the Social Services Inspectorate who chaired the original enquiry, and to the Crown Prosecution Service. Detective Constable Khan will question the youths named in the report as soon as you have arranged for a parent or legal representative to be present. Is that understood?'

Jardine nodded, head once more bowed, and Resnick, after a quick glance towards Khan, left the pair of them in the room. Now that it was done, he couldn't wait to shed himself of the sad, corrupt smell of that room, that man, that institution.

One night on the thin mattress of the police cell had been enough to bring Frank Miller to his senses. Talking his way out of the blood on his boots, the voices on the tape, he knew would be difficult – and why? To save the hides of a pair of queers – he was sure they were, no matter how much they denied it – who just weren't worth saving. Commit perjury for the likes of them! Bugger that for a game of soldiers!

So Miller began banging on the inside of his cell door a little after seven and by nine he was sitting back in the enquiry room with Millington and Naylor and a tape machine. The story he told was this: his brother-in-law, Ian Orston, had had words with some of the Irish who used this pub on London Road and had asked Frank and a few other mates to come and help sort them out. Teach them to pay some respect. Frank had tipped the wink to Gerry Hovenden, who, in turn, had enlisted Shane. But Shane had never showed, not then. And it was Ian who had brought along the baseball bat, a Christmas present to his kids.

They'd done the business in the pub.

Frank couldn't remember whose idea it had been to walk on down to the river, maybe look in at the TBI, but that's what they'd done. After closing, they had all headed back across the bridge, pretty pissed by now and noisy, pushing one another around for the fun of it, because there wasn't anyone else to push. Ian and himself had wandered off in front, aiming for Ian's place in the Meadows and going to take the path across the playing fields, back of the Memorial Gardens. It was somewhere around then, on the other side of the Trent, that the others must've met up with Shane, who was already in an argument with this bloke. The one who turned out to be the copper. Poor bastard!

Anyway, there was so much shouting Frank hadn't been able to hear everything, except he remembered that Shane had accused the bloke of being queer – which was a bit rich, Frank thought, coming from him – and of trying to grab hold of Shane's balls in the Gents. Next thing you knew they were all over him, shouting 'Fucking poof!' and the like, kicking the shit out of him.

Frank and Ian had stood back on the path, watching. Frank fancying a bit of it himself, he didn't mind admitting, but the way they were swarming round the bloke there was sod-all room.

And then Shane had broken away and came at a run

for Ian's bat; gone back in there and smashed the bloke about the face like he wanted to take his head clean off. In the end, Gerry had pulled him away. Tried to give Ian back his baseball bat, but Ian said no way.

'I went over and looked at him,' Frank said. 'Total bloody mess.' He shrugged. 'That must've been when I got his blood on me boots.'

'And at no time while this was going on,' Millington asked, 'did you raise a fist in anger or deliver a blow?'

'Me?' Frank Miller said. 'Not one. You got my solemn word.' And he grinned.

Hovenden denied all of it: every word. The results of the tests on the fibres from the glove had still not returned. 'Give him time chew on it a while.'

'This Ian Orston,' Naylor called from over by the computer, 'he's got some previous. D'you want me to pull him in, see if his account tallies?'

'Yes, get on it now. Take Carl here with you, okay? And stay sharp, the pair of you.'

They were leaving when Resnick returned, sullen and sad-eyed. Millington waited while the kettle boiled and the tea had mashed before filling him in on all the details.

'Right, Graham,' Resnick said, fortified, 'let's get over to the Snape place, you and me, see if we can't lay our hands on Shane. Mark, Lynn, you'd best be along for the ride.'

When Norma opened the door to Resnick, mid-afternoon, she was still wearing what she had slept in, an old dressing-gown pulled loosely round her. One look at Resnick and she turned back into the house. The curtains in the front room were closed and the television on. Norma had one cigarette in her hand, another, forgotten, smouldering alongside cold toast.

'Norma,' Resnick said, 'what's happened? Are you all right?'

She looked at him as if she hadn't properly heard what he had said.

'Norma, it's Shane. Is he here?'

A slow shake of the head.

'We've got a warrant to search the house.'

'What do I care?'

Resnick nodded at Millington and Divine and they moved quickly towards the stairs. He waited until Norma had flopped down into the settee and then he switched down the sound on the TV; outside, in the backyard, the dog was barking frantically to be fed.

'Should I let him in?' Resnick asked.

Norma didn't care about that either.

He motioned for Lynn to stay with Norma while he tipped dog biscuits into a bowl and unlocked the rear door, careful to keep well to one side when the dog tore in. He could hear Millington and Divine moving around, heavy footed, upstairs. Back in the front room, he sat across from Norma, waiting for her eyes to focus on him.

'It's serious, Norma, this time. That alibi you gave him, him and his pal, it doesn't stand up.' Her eyes flickered as if still only half understanding what he was saying. 'Where is he, Norma? Shane. Where is he now?'

Footsteps on the stairs were followed by a slow shake of Millington's head, its expression telling Resnick they'd found nothing. Neither Shane nor any weapon: burned it or hidden it, Resnick thought. He was tempted to see the baseball bat floating off down the Trent, hurled there after Aston's murder and never found – except for what had happened to Declan Farrell, the particular agonies he'd been put through. *A varnished implement, solid, hard.* They had searched along a half-mile stretch of railway line, between overgrown gravestones, in amongst bushes and across fields. Every dustbin, backyard and cranny.

He smashed this bloke about the face like he wanted to take his head clean off.

Resnick pictured Shane standing there, sweat on his lip, breathing hard, hatred and anger bright on his face.

Why?

'Your Shane,' Resnick said, 'when he's not hanging round with this Gerry, are there any other friends he sees? Special, I mean?'

Norma didn't answer.

'Girl-friends?'

'Sara Johnson,' Norma said scornfully. 'Slag.'

'You know where she lives?'

Norma didn't have a clue, couldn't have cared less, but she thought she worked in the Viccy centre, in the Food Court, somewhere like that.

'Make sure the house is watched,' Resnick told Millington when they were back outside. 'Front and back. And keep in touch with the station. Lynn, let's you and me see if we can't find this Sara Johnson.'

At the kerb, he turned back. 'Look sharp, all of you; be on your guard. Think on what he's maybe done. He's young and he's strong, likely he'll not come easy.'

'Just give me the chance,' Divine said, once Resnick had gone. 'Shane Snape, one on one, see how easy he comes then.'

Once in the Food Court, steering his way between the shopping trolleys and the prams, Resnick realised he had seen Sara Johnson before; she had served himself and Hannah with coffee and now she did so for himself and Lynn, strong, small espressos in waxed paper cups. They identified themselves and asked Sara if she wouldn't mind answering a few questions; carried the coffees to one of the nearby tables and sat down, Sara, pretty in her pink uniform, a fine sculptured face and lazy eyes, seventeen.

Self-conscious, she lit a cigarette and wafted the smoke away from her face with her hand.

'I don't know,' she said in answer to Resnick's question. 'I haven't seen Shane for a week or more now.'

'Sara, you do understand this is important?'

The tip of her tongue pressed for a moment against the underside of her upper lip. 'I'm not a liar, you know.'

'I'm sure.'

'I've not seen him. Besides, he wouldn't come round to me, if that's what you're thinking.'

Near them, a man in a shabby overcoat, once someone's best, but a long time ago, was coughing repeatedly into the back of his hand, rough-edged and raw. It was enough to make Resnick's throat sore. 'Why d'you say that?'

'He just wouldn't, that's why.' There was irritation, mixed with amusement, in her eyes. 'For one thing, on account of my old man can't stand him, won't have him inside the house, right? For another, I finished with him. Two weekends ago now.'

Resnick reminded himself not to ignore his espresso.

'Why did you chuck him, Sara?' Lynn asked.

401

Sara tilted back her head and released a thin plume of smoke. Her nails were painted, Resnick noticed, with some kind of varnish that glittered, like the hundreds and thousands kids liked sprinkled over ice-cream. 'We went out, right. The Sat'day. Going to the pictures, that's what I thought, but no, he didn't fancy that, so we went up the Malt House for a drink. After that, I don't know where. The Dog and Bear? Anyway, after that we come back down the Square and Shane, he calls a cab, so I think, oh right, his mum must be out, back to his place, usual thing, as if that's all he's got on his mind. Blokes, you know. Though in Shane's case, you had to sometimes wonder why he bothered. Anyway, I get in the cab and he tells me he's not coming, promised to meet one of his mates. Give the driver a fiver and tells him to take me home. Well, I wasn't having that. I told him if that was how he felt, maybe he should spend all his time with his precious mates and stop wasting it on me.' She looked at Resnick and gave a little shrug. 'That was that.'

'How did he react?' Lynn said. 'When you told him that?'

Sara glanced back over towards the counter where she worked. Watching her, Resnick caught himself wondering if she knew just how pretty she was. 'He didn't care,' she said. 'I don't think he ever did.'

The coughing had been joined by a small child's shrill wailing and Resnick waited for the ensuing shout and slap. Through hidden speakers, a tinkly organ with percussion accompaniment was following 'The Skye Boat Song' with 'How Are Things in Glocca Morra?'

'Look,' Lynn said, lowering her voice, 'I don't want to

pry, but you said, well, you implied, sex with Shane, it wasn't all it might have been.'

Sara grabbed at her packet of Silk Cut and fidgeted back in her chair. 'What d'you want to ask about that for?'

'Sara, I'm sorry, I know it's personal, but believe me, we're not asking for no good reason.'

She took a long drag on her cigarette and momentarily closed her eyes. 'It was like, you know, he always wanted it, just never ... well, not never, but ... Everything was always okay when we, when he ... Look, I can't believe I'm sitting here telling you this, it's like being on that, what d'you call it, Ricki Lake Show. But sometimes, well, let's put it this way, what he was in such a hurry to start, he couldn't always finish. How's that for you?' She stubbed out her cigarette and hurried to her feet, glancing back again at the unattended coffee machine. 'Now I've got to go, I shall get my cards. All right?'

'Yes, of course,' Lynn said, leaning back. 'And Sara, thanks.'

Resnick watched her go, the tight swish of her legs inside her pink uniform. Why was it, since Hannah, he had begun again to notice these things?

'Good,' Resnick said. 'You made a sight better job of that than I would.'

Lynn gave him a quick smile and drained her cup. They found a phone near the Mansfield Road exit and Resnick called the station; so far, there had been no sign of Shane. But twenty minutes previously, the fibres found inside the leather glove had been successfully identified as coming from Gerry Hovenden. Nothing now to stop them charging him with the murder of William Aston.

'Right,' Resnick said, passing on the news to Lynn as they headed for the lift. 'Let's get back sharpish.'

'What you mean is,' Lynn grinned, 'you want me to drive. Again.'

46

Naylor and Vincent relieved Millington and Divine ten minutes short of six o'clock; not that Millington himself was in any hurry – his wife, he knew, was all set for one of her evening classes, and leftover mushroom lasagne, neatly wrapped in environmentally friendly cling film, would be all there was to go home to.

'The daughter,' Millington said, 'Sheena, is it? She came in about an hour ago, left ten, fifteen minutes back. Aside from that, about as quiet as the proverbial.'

Divine and Vincent contrived to change places without exchanging either a look or a glance.

'Nearly forgot,' Millington said, leaning back in through the car window nearest to Naylor. 'How'd it go with Frankie Miller's mate, Orston?'

'Clammed up at first,' Naylor said, 'much as you'd expect. Once he started talking, though, everything he said pretty much agreed with Miller's version of events. Right down to standing there while them others beat Aston senseless. I asked him if he hadn't been tempted to step in, try and put a stop, but he said, no, it weren't none of my affair. Only thing he was sorry about, callous bastard, was that Shane had used his baseball bat to lay into him with.'

'Makes you wonder, doesn't it?' Millington said. 'What it's all coming to, blokes like that.'

'Good bloody thumping,' Divine said, 'that's what he needs. Only thing his sort bloody understand.'

While Naylor and Vincent were on duty outside the Snape house and Millington was watching *The Bill* and washing his microwaved lasagne down with a can of Carlsberg, Divine was mooching around his flat, unable to get interested in either of the videos he'd rented from Block-busters, *The Specialist* and *Highlander III*; the pizza he'd phoned out for sat cold in its cardboard box.

By ten thirty he was so edgy that he'd dialled the number of the staff nurse from the Queen's who'd spent nine months getting him to change his ways and then, when he almost had, had dumped him just the same. At the sound of Divine's voice she set down the phone.

Once in the car, he was on his way along the Radford Boulevard before he was wholly conscious of where he was heading or why.

Naylor was sitting in the unmarked Sierra, seventy yards back along the road, with an unimpeded view of the Snape house.

'Must want something to do,' Naylor remarked, as Divine got into the seat alongside him.

'Reckon so,' Divine said. 'Anything up?'

Naylor shook his head. 'Mrs Snape left. Norma. Some woman friend of hers came round and they went off. Had this small bag with her. Suitcase, like. Asked her where she was going and she said round to this friend's for the night. Made a note of the address just in case.'

'You don't think she could have been sneaking out some clean clothes to her Sonny Jim?'

Naylor laughed. 'Not unless he's into dresses and frilly bras.'

'Never can tell nowadays. Speaking of which, where's our Carl?'

Naylor pointed towards the house. 'Watching the back entry.'

'Who better?' Divine said.

Naylor gave him a look but left it at that. He knew better than to get into an argument with Divine about what was politically correct.

After forty minutes of sporadic conversation, Divine lit another cigarette and said, 'Why don't you get off home, Kev? Keep Debbie company. No point us both sitting here.'

'No, you're okay.'

But when Divine asked him again, twenty minutes later, he agreed. He was getting out of the car when Vincent appeared, out of the alley entrance and walking towards them across the road.

'Seen anything?' Naylor asked hopefully.

Vincent shook his head. 'Only the back of the house with all the lights out. Upstairs curtains drawn. Only sound's from that dog of theirs, carrying on every once in a while to get let out.'

'Mark,' Naylor said, 'if you're serious about hanging on, why don't you go round the back for a spell? Then Carl can take my place here for a change. I'll get off home for a bit. All right?'

Divine didn't like the idea of doing Carl Vincent any kind of a favour, but he agreed all the same. At least round the back he could pace up and down if he'd a mind, better than getting a numb bum in the Ford. And that's what he did: walk, lean, light a cigarette; lean some more, walk.

He was just approaching the house from the further end of the entry, when he saw something move in the yard. A shadow, low against the wall.

Divine waited till his breathing had steadied and then moved on slowly, careful to lift his feet, not to kick a stray stone or stumble. By the time he had got to the gate, he realised it was the dog.

All right. The breath punched out of him with a sigh. Only the sodding dog. And then, instantaneously, his palms began to sweat. The dog: the dog was inside, Carl had said so. Whining inside the house, wanting to be let out. And for him now to be out, someone must have gone in.

He lifted the latch on the gate, and eased it open. Half a dozen paces and he was at the back door. Listening, he heard no sound. He thought the door would have been locked again from the inside, but it had not. At the doorway leading off from the kitchen he paused and listened again, nothing but the pump of his own heart. Sweat was in his hair now, running the length of his neck. Holding his breath he stepped quickly into the front room and waited to let his eyes become more accustomed to the light. Nothing beyond the usual.

Divine turned towards the stairs.

Only once, when he hesitated midway up the stairs, did he ask himself the question he would ask himself a thousand times later, why hadn't he called Vincent for back-up before going in?

Three of the four doors were open, partly at least. Divine's mouth was dry and he ran his tongue across his lips; started counting to three inside his head and on two, turned the handle and pushed the door back as fast as he could. Flicked on the light.

A girl's room, posters of Take That and Keanu Reeves on the walls. Cuddly toys on the bed. The small wardrobe was crammed with clothes, some on hangers, many not.

Maybe, Divine thought, Vincent had been wrong; what he had heard had been the dog in the backyard, yammering to get in.

He could see the shape of a double bed through the doorway to the next room, covers all in a ruck. Norma Snape's room, he supposed. Shoes scattered across the floor, haphazard piles of clothes, pairs of tights hanging from a dressing-table mirror – Jesus! What a mess! He stepped over a discarded pair of jeans and a high-heeled shoe and that was enough; some sense alerted him, so that he swung his head towards a sound felt rather than heard and turned smack into the full curve of a baseball bat, swung with all the force of a young man, fit and in his prime, striving to strike the ball clear out of the park. The crack as Divine's cheek-bone fractured was sharp and clear and as he catapulted back across the room, before he lost all hearing in that ear, he heard Shane say, smiling, 'This what you're looking for?'

Divine bounced forward off the wall and Shane swung the bat again, down onto the top of his shoulder, breaking his collar-bone.

'Didn't I tell you it'd be me and you?'

Without Shane having to do anything more, one of Divine's legs buckled under him and he went sprawling to the floor, crying out as his injured arm fell against the base of the bed.

Shane grabbed him by his other arm, the collar of his coat and shirt and lifted him up, throwing him down again upon the mess of sheets.

Divine wanted to shout, but somehow he couldn't think how. Shane on one knee on the bed beside him, reaching underneath him, feeling for his belt. Oh, Christ!

'Didn't I say I'd have you?'

A wrench and Divine's legs kicked upwards as his trousers were yanked down about his knees, his boxer shorts next, Divine struggling to fight back, use his elbows, arms, the back of his head, anything, but when he did the pain that seared through him was enough to make him cry out and that was before Shane slid one arm around Divine's neck and began to squeeze it back, his other hand feeling between Divine's legs, fingers beginning to push against the clenched sphincter, all the time repeating words Divine could barely hear.

'Slut. Whore. Cunt. This is it, this is what you want, you know it is.'

Shane pulling at the front of his own jeans, freeing himself and then kneeling above Divine, one arm still so tight about his neck that Divine was close to fainting, wishing he could faint, praying for it, rocking his body backwards, trying to throw him off, trying... Oh, God! The pain was sudden like a knife and sharp and then Shane was pushing into him and shouting louder and louder that litany of words again.

'Whore! Cunt! This is what you want, you bastard! You

fucking cunt!' Shane throwing himself across Divine as he came, sinking his teeth into the flesh at the back of his shoulder and puncturing the skin.

The sound of the door slamming downstairs must have registered seconds after it happened. Shane pulling away and clutching at the top of his jeans, trying and failing to cover himself and at the same time reach for the baseball bat that had become jammed between the mattress and the foot of the bed before Carl Vincent burst through the door.

Vincent, diving at Shane headlong, the top of his skull striking Shane's breastbone as the bat flew from Shane's hand and he fell backwards against the wall beneath the window. Vincent punching him once, twice, then slamming the point of his elbow hard into the centre of Shane's face, before seizing his arm and turning him, one knee driving down into the small of his back, Vincent's cuffs in his hand now, one of them fastening about Shane's wrist and the other half locked around the pipe from the radiator.

'You do not have to say anything.' Vincent beginning. 'You do not have to say anything . . .' but stopping, wanting Shane, please, to turn his head and look at him, look at him so that Vincent could hit him again, so that he would have a reason.

Vincent getting up and leaving him cuffed to the radiator, going to where Divine lay sobbing on the bed, sobbing in his embarrassment and pain, and covering him carefully with one of the sheets, as carefully as he had ever done anything in his life.

47

'How is he?' Hannah asked.

They were in her small front garden, overlooking the park. It was two days later. Through the trees, the light angling low across the grass was beginning to fade. A few elderly men stood chatting, pausing on the curve of path as they walked their dogs. The last cries of children rose and fell from the playground at the further side. Some of the cars heading into the city along Derby Road had switched on their lights.

Hannah had been sitting in her doorway when Resnick had arrived, cushions piled beneath her, leaning back against the frame. A pile of folders beside her, pen in hand. A wine glass by her side. When she had heard the gate and seen him approaching along the path, she had smiled. 'Just let me finish this . . .' but he had gestured for her to stay where she was and stepped around her, moving on inside the house. The opened bottle of wine, a semillon chardonnay, was in the door of the fridge and he removed it, letting the door swing closed, and turned to reach a glass down from the shelf.

There was a postcard, propped against a stack of blue and yellow bowls, a reproduction, he supposed, of a painting: a town house in reddish stone, steps that climbed quite high to the front door and a couple standing there, he in a waistcoat, white shirt and tie, she is wearing a blue dress and leaning back against the curve of railing beside the steps. Beyond the house, to the right of the picture, half in shadow, there is a spread of almost impossibly smooth grass and beyond that, rising suddenly, a wall – is it a wall? – and a rich cluster of green trees, the tallest of which is catching the last of the sun. The dull orange glow on the stone, Resnick realised, was caused by the setting sun. Evening, and this couple, they are both looking out towards the light.

Resnick turned over the card to see who the painting was by and before he could do that or put it back he read instead, in purplish ink and lettering that was fussy and none too clear, *nice to see you again*, and *missing you*, and the name. *Jim*. The postmark was unreadable, smudged against the stamp.

'Charlie! Have you got lost or what?'

He picked up the bottle and the glass and carried them out.

'Divine,' Hannah said, after she had sipped her wine. 'How is he?'

'He's a strong lad. Bones'll mend.'

Hannah looked at him, the weariness in his eyes. 'And the rest of him?'

Resnick shook his head. So far Divine had refused to talk about what had happened, not to the doctor who had examined him, not to Maureen Madden, to Resnick, anyone. Shane's statements had so far been only patchily coherent, but what seemed certain was that he had encountered Bill Aston in the public toilets on the

Embankment late on the Friday evening, the day before the murder, and that something had happened between them, something sexual, but exactly what and how mutually consensual, it was difficult to tell. But when Aston had bumped into Shane again, presumably by accident, back on the Embankment the following night and had approached him, Shane had reacted with anger, called over his mates and encouraged them to set upon him, bloody poof, beat him to a pulp. A bit of fun.

Along with Gerry Hovenden, Shane had been charged with the murder of Bill Aston, and on his own account had been charged with two cases of indecent assault and one of causing grievous bodily harm; they were holding back on the charge of rape.

Listening, Hannah reached up and squeezed Resnick's hand.

During the time that Resnick and the team had been preoccupied with Shane, Khan had continued to be busy. The youths who had terrorised Nicky Snape had given conflicting accounts of what had happened leading up to Nicky's death. It was uncertain how far their threatening sexual by-play had gone on that occasion, but what was clear almost beyond dispute was that if they had not forced Nicky to take part in oral or anal sex there and then they had made it clear that the next time he wouldn't be given any choice. Khan also established that, while in care, at least two of the boys had gone out at night for the purposes of engaging in prostitution.

And when he had checked again with Elizabeth Peck's neighbours, several claimed to have seen her, one or two of them, leaving the house in uniform, usually in the evenings, nurse's uniform and arriving home early, between six and seven. Not regular, but quite a few times just the same. Khan checked with the hospitals, the nursing agencies in town. He was waiting for her when her car arrived back from East Midlands Airport, parked across the street with a copy of Nancy Friday he'd borrowed from Jill's bedside. *Women on Top.* He'd given up on Vikram Seth.

When Elizabeth Peck swung into the drive of the neo-Georgian house, on which she was still three mortgage payments in arrears, he walked across and offered to help her with her bags.

At first, she was dismissive, haughty, insistent on standing by rights she didn't have; later, in the living-room with its stone fireplace and fake leaded windows, she was penitent, sniffing back the tears. Khan gave her several clean tissues and waited for the snivelling to stop. Weighed down by debt, unable to sell the house, even had she wanted to, its current market price so far below what she had paid for it, she had been working as an agency nurse at the City Hospital, most often nights, when the pay was better and there was the greatest need. If her shifts at the local authority accommodation clashed, Paul Matthews covered for her, signed her in and out. On the night that Nicky Snape had hanged himself, she had been doing her second job out at the hospital and Matthews had been there alone.

'I don't feel,' she told Khan, 'any real guilt. I mean, whatever he did, he would have done whether I'd been there or not. Well, he would, wouldn't he?'

At the station, Resnick went out of his way to compliment Khan on the way he had handled his side of the enquiry and assured him he would pass that on to Jack Skelton. Khan had tried to disguise his pleasure, without ever quite succeeding.

By then the story of what had happened to Divine, rumour and counter-rumour, had ricocheted around the station and Resnick and Millington had been chipping away at Shane's belligerent stonewalling the best part of fourteen hours.

Off-duty, Carl Vincent had driven out to visit Divine in his side ward at the Queen's and Divine had turned his back and closed his eyes and stayed like that even after Vincent had gone.

Then, on the second morning, when Resnick entered the interview room, Shane, as the result of a long discussion with his solicitor, began to tell them about what had happened to him when he had been taken into care as a boy. About the deputy head of the first children's home he'd been in, who had given Shane cigarettes if he let him slip his hand up inside Shane's short trousers, and a crisp new five-pound note if he would let him pull the trousers down.

'It wasn't the same man?' Hannah asked.

'The same . . .'

'In charge. Of the place where Shane was abused. The same as the place where Nicky died?'

Resnick shook his head. 'I'm afraid that would be too neat,' he said, and gave her a wry smile. 'That sort of thing only happens in books. Not real life.'

What happened in real life was that those who had power all too frequently abused those who did not; and that those who were abused, abused others in turn. What happened was that many of those who grew up, for whatever reason, confused about their sexuality, often succeeded in damaging themselves and others, trying to live up to what they thought of as the norm. What happened in real life, Resnick thought, was all too often a helpless, bloody mess.

They were facing one another in Hannah's bed, features just visible in the opaque light from the ceiling window. 'Just so long as you stay till morning,' Hannah had said. 'Six, at least.'

Now she said, 'How do you deal with it? All of this awfulness.'

He sighed. 'How do I? I went to see Norma Snape this afternoon, before I came round here. She had a friend with her and she'd been drinking, both of which were probably just as well. What else can she do?' He touched Hannah's shoulder lightly with the back of his hand. 'Seems Nicky's dad – the one who came back out of the blue – he's gone off again without a by-your-leave. She doesn't know what's hit her. Likely never will.' He kissed Hannah's fingers when she brought them close against his face. 'First Nicky and then Shane. How can she ever hope to understand?'

'All my pretty ones,' Hannah said.

'Mmm?'

'Nothing. A line from a play.' And then, 'Do you? Do you understand?'

'Only that there's nothing people won't do to one another, if the circumstances are right. No dreadful thing.'

'Or wrong,' Hannah said. 'Surely, if the circumstances are wrong?'

'Yes.' He reached his arm behind her, hand open across the curve of her back, and she eased herself towards him, face close to his face. 'Yes, I suppose that's what I mean.'

After a while she said, 'If they're right, if things are right, do you think, what we do to one another, it can be good?'

'Yes,' Resnick said, kissing her. 'I do think that. I want to.' Hannah brushed her lips again against his mouth. 'It's what,' he said, 'I want to believe.'

Before Peter had left he had written a letter to Sheena and left it on the pillow in her room; there had been nothing, not a message, a blind word for Norma herself. Tears so strong she had not clearly been able to see, Norma had ripped the letter again and again until all that had been left were little pieces, unreadable save for the odd word. 'Love' and 'home'. Norma had scooped the fragments up into her hands and carried them to the sink and burned them. Ashes by now.

Sheena had gone home when she'd heard about Shane, but she hadn't stayed. Her mum bawling and scraighting and wanting to grab hold of her all the time, she couldn't cope with it. It was too much. And besides, Rosa was there for her mum and she was her best friend, after all. She'd look after her, make sure it was all right.

Back at Diane's, Dee-Dee had got some acid, ten quid for a small strip and Sheena was just in time for her share; the others were well away, with the baby crawling between them, nappy filled and nobody paying attention until he started to cry and then Diane pushed him at Sheena and told her to get him into the bathroom and sort him out and Sheena had giggled and done as she was told.

'And get a fuckin' move on,' Dee-Dee had called. 'We're already late as it is.'

They were meeting Janie in town, near the bowling alley. Janie on speed or something when they got there, had to be, she was really manic the way she was carrying on and screaming. Sheena watched as she pushed her way past this bloke, not much older than her but wearing some uniform like he worked there, wasting his breath telling Janie she had to leave. But Janie had laughed in his face and then felt between his legs, just for the hell of it, to see what he'd do.

The bloke saying how if they didn't leave he'd call the police and Janie grabbing hold of him and pointing at Sheena, saying, see her, her brother he just killed a fucking copper, so just you fucking watch out. And then leaving anyway, 'cause he'd run off into the office, probably pissed his pants.

Diane shouting from the burger bar, 'Wait! Hang on a fuckin' minute. I 'in't got my chips yet.'

But Janie didn't care and they pushed their way outside and went off down the street, arms linked, blocking the pavement, singing this stupid song at the tops of their voices.

Then there was this guy, just this old guy, Sheena saw him first, weaving across the road towards them, drunk, right up to Janie, big smile all over his face, singing along even though his was a completely different bloody song. 'Come on, sweetheart! You and me, eh? You and me.'

And this drunken old bastard, must have been forty or fifty years old, pulls up his shirt and starts rubbing his chest all up against Janie. 'Come on, sweetheart, you an' me.' Which is when Janie pulls out this screwdriver she's got inside her jacket, just a screwdriver, broken off half-way down the blade and sharpened to a sort of point, and she sticks it in this drunk's disgusting fat belly, right above the buckle of his belt, and he falls there, down on his knees, this thing sticking out of him, almost to the hilt, and Janie, she's laughing, pointing, and the rest of the girls, most of them, are running.

Diane is standing there outside the bowling alley, chips falling between her fingers, watching Dee-Dee trying to pull Sheena away. 'Come on, for Christ sake, girl! You mad? Let's get out of here.'

Sheena staring at the blood beginning to swell up around the man's white belly, fascinated, and Janie, out of her head beside him, laughing.

'Come on, girl! Move it!'

Running then, leaving Janie to face the music, the first sounds of a police car approaching at speed along Canal Street and Sheena, as she allowed herself to be dragged away, turning now and stumbling, looking back and thinking, awesome, truly awesome. I mean, absolutely fucking brilliant! Brilliant, right?

Ash and Bone

John Harvey

When the take down of a violent criminal goes badly wrong, something doesn't feel right to Detective Sergeant Maddy Birch. And her uneasiness is compounded by her belief that someone is following her home . . .

Retired Detective Inspector Frank Elder's daughter, Katherine, is running wild. Elder's fears for his daughter are underscored by his guilt – it was his involvement in a case that led directly to the abduction and rape which has so unbalanced Katherine's life.

Persuaded out of retirement, Elder reopens a cold case which could have devastating repercussions for the crime squad itself. Elder's investigations take place against the backdrop of his increasing concern for his daughter. he must battle his own demons before he can uncover the truth.

'Harvey once again gets everything right, jangling the nerves and plucking the heart-strings . . . another marvellous read'
Reginald Hill

'Immaculately engineered thriller . . . Harvey's book is fast, fluent and exciting, with a pace and assurance that never lets up'
Literary Review

arrow books

Flesh and Blood

John Harvey

Fifteen years ago Susan Blacklock disappeared. Although Detective Inspector Frank Elder has taken early retirement, the case still plagues his mind. Prime suspects, Shane Donald and Alan McKeirnan, were convicted a year later of the brutal rape and murder of a young girl, and now that Shane has been granted parole, Elder feels compelled to revisit the past.

Then Shane disappears and another young girl is murdered. Elder's involvement is now crucial. Taunted by postcards from the killer, an increasingly desperate Elder battles to keep his estranged family from being drawn into the very heart of the crime.

'John Harvey is lights out one of the best and with this book the word is going to spread far and wide'
Michael Connelly

'A gripping and powerful thriller'
Mark Billingham

'A sinister thriller . . . one of Britain's leading masters of atmosphere'
Guardian

arrow books